Twentieth-
Century
Literary
Movements
DICTIONARY

Twentieth-
Century
Literary
Movements
DICTIONARY

*A Compendium to More Than 500 Literary, Critical,
and Theatrical Movements, Schools, and Groups
from More Than 80 Nations, Covering the Novelists,
Poets, Short-Story Writers, Dramatists, Essayists,
Theorists, and Works, Genres, Techniques, and
Terms Associated with Each Movement*

Helene Henderson and Jay P. Pederson
Editors

Omnigraphics, Inc.

Penobscot Building • Detroit, Michigan 48226

Helene Henderson and Jay P. Pederson, *Editors*

Kelly Howes, Roger Matuz, Norma Merry, Pam Shelton, and Linda Shin, *Sketch Writers*

Amy Marcaccio Keyzer, *Copyeditor*

Fiona Kelleghan and Joan Margeson, *Bibliographic Researchers*

Mark Detlor, Megan Jenkins, and W. Stetson Steele, *Research Assistants*

Library of Congress Cataloging-in-Publication Data

Twentieth-century literary movements dictionary : a compendium to more than 500 literary, critical, and theatrical movements, schools, and groups from more than 80 nations, covering the novelists, poets, short-story writers, dramatists, essayists, theorists, and works, genres, techniques, and terms associated with each movement / Helene Henderson and Jay P. Pederson, editors.

    p.   cm. –

    Includes bibliographical references and indexes.

    ISBN 1-55888-426-2 (lib. bdg. : alk. paper)

    1. Literary movements — History — 20th century Dictionaries. 2. Literature, Modern — 20th century — Terminology Dictionaries. 3. Criticism — History — 20th century Dictionaries. 4. Theater — History — 20th century Dictionaries. 5. Criticism — Terminology Dictionaries. 6. Literary form Dictionaries. I. Henderson, Helene, 1963- . II. Pederson, Jay P. III. Title: 20th-century literary movements dictionary.

PN597.T94 1999

809'.91'090403 — dc21

99-41091

CIP

Omnigraphics, Inc.

* * *

Peter E. Ruffner, *Senior Vice President*

Matt Barbour, *Vice President, Operations*

Laurie Lanzen Harris, *Vice President, Editorial Director*

Jane Steele, *Marketing Coordinator*

Thomas J. Murphy, *Vice President, Finance*

* * *

Frederick G. Ruffner, Jr., *Publisher*

Contents

Movements

ix

Appendices

Indexes

Periods and Movements in Literary History[1]

E very book of literary history is subdivided into periods or movements and uses terms designating specific periods freely and frequently. Nevertheless, only a very few writers of literary history indicate the principles which underlie the formation of periods in literary history. I cannot find an express discussion of our problem in English, though many historians make, of course, incidental remarks and reflect on the nature of specific periods such as "Romanticism." I have found, however, three German papers devoted to a theoretical discussion of our problem: one by Richard Moritz Meyer, dating from 1901, which is a defense of his division of German literature of the nineteenth century according to decades, and two more recent by Herbert Cysarz and Benno von Wiese, which approach the problem in a highly metaphysical manner. Cysarz wants us even to conceive of a period as an almost metaphysical entity, whose nature we have to intuit.[2]

It will be best to start with the opposite point of view. One frequently hears that the term "period" (I leave the discussion of "movement" for a moment) is nothing given or discoverable in reality, but merely a linguistic label for any section of time which we want to consider in isolation for the practical purpose of analysis and description. If this were so, I might as well declare the question closed. The extreme "nominalist"

1. [Eds. This paper, revised in 1941, has been reprinted with the permission of Mr. Wellek.]

2. R. M. Meyer, "Prinzipien der wissenschaftlichen Periodenbildung," *Euphorion,* VIII (1901), 1 ff.; Herbert Cysarz, "Das Periodenprinzip in der Literaturwissenschaft" in *Philosophie der Literaturwissenschaft* (ed. by Emil Ermatinger, Berlin, 1930); Benno von Wiese, "Zur Kritik des geistesgeschichtlichen Epochenbegriffes," *Deutsche Vierteljahrschrift für Literaturwissenschaft und Geistesgeschichte,* XI (1933), 130 ff. As my article was passing through the press, my attention was called to Max Foerster's "The Psychological Basis of Literary Periods," in *Studies for William H. Read,* 1940, pp. 254 ff. This is an attempt, similar to Cazamian's, to establish a "law of polar reaction" (p. 261) in the mental development of mankind.

point of view which assumes that "period" is merely an arbitrary superimposition on a material which in reality is a continuous, directionless flux, leaves us with a chaos of concrete events on the one hand and purely subjective labels on the other. It must lead to barren skepticism, to an abandonment of the whole problem, which is precisely that of discovering crests and troughs in the undulatory stream of literature.

"Period" is a term which cannot be discussed in isolation: a single period, though we may elect to study it to the exclusion of others, is a period only within a series of periods which together make up the development of literature. Our conception of a period is thus inextricably bound up with our conception of the whole process of literature. If we conceive of this development as a directionless flux, then obviously it does not matter where we put a cross-section through a reality which is essentially uniform in its manifold variety. If we hold this view (and it is held consciously and unconsciously by many) it is of no importance what scheme of periods, however arbitrary and mechanical, we adopt. We can write literary history by calendar centuries, by decades, or year by year in an annalistic fashion. We might even adopt such a criterion as Arthur Symons did in his book on the *Romantic Movement in English Poetry* (1909). He discusses only authors born before 1800 and only those who died after 1800. Period is then merely a convenient label: a necessity for subdividing a book or choosing a topic. This view underlies, though frequently unconsciously, the practice of literally hundreds of books which respect the date lines between centuries religiously or which set to a topic exact limitations of date (for example, 1710-1730, 1700-1775) which are not justified by any other reason except the purely practical consideration that their authors have to begin somewhere and stop somewhere else. Of course, such a respect for calendar dates is perfectly legitimate in purely bibliographical compilations, where it serves for orientation as the Dewey decimal system helps us to arrange a library. But it seems to me that one should not pretend that such periodical divisions have anything to do with literary history proper.

If we ignore the worshippers of calendar dates, I think we have to come to the conclusion that most histories of literature divide their periods in accordance with political changes and thus conceive of literature as completely determined by the political or social revolutions of a nation. The problem of determining periods is thus nicely shifted to the shoulders of the political and social historians: their divisions and periods are usually taken over without question. If we look into older histories of English literature, we shall find that they are either written according to number divisions or according to one simple political criterion — the reigns of the English sovereigns. I do not think we need to show how misleading the cutting up of the course of English literature is, if we follow the chance dates of the deaths of the English rulers: nobody thinks seriously of distinguishing in early nineteenth-century literature between the reigns of George III, George IV, and William IV, but the equally artificial distinction between the reigns of

Elizabeth, James I, and Charles I still survive, though scarcely anybody would ascribe any value to them.

Rather, if we look into more recent histories of English literature, we find that the old divisions by calendar centuries or reigns of kings have disappeared almost completely and have been replaced by a series of periods whose names, at least, are derived from the most divers activities of the human mind. We still use the terms "Elizabethan" and "Victorian," which are survivals of the old distinctions between reigns: but they have assumed a new meaning inside a scheme of intellectual history. We keep them because we feel that the two queens seem to symbolize the character of their times. We no longer cling to a rigid chronological framework actually determined by the ascent to the throne and the deaths of these monarchs. We use the term "Elizabethan" to include writers before the closing of the theaters, almost forty years after the death of the queen, and, on the other hand, we rarely speak of a man like Oscar Wilde as a Victorian, though his life falls well within the chronological limits of the reign of Queen Victoria. The terms, originally of political origin, have thus assumed a definite meaning in intellectual and even in literary history. But still the motley derivation of our current labels is somewhat disconcerting. "Reformation" comes from ecclesiastical history; "humanism," mainly from the history of scholarship; "Renaissance" from art history; "Commonwealth" and "Restoration" refer to definite political events. The term "eighteenth century" is an old numerical term which has assumed some of the functions of literary terms such as "Augustan" and "neoclassic." "Pre-romanticism" and "romanticism" are primarily literary terms, while Victorian, Edwardian, and Georgian are derived from the reigns of the sovereigns. The same bewildering picture is presented by almost any other literature: for example, the "colonial period" in American literature is a political term, "romanticism" and "realism" are literary, and so forth.

In defense of this mixture of terms it may, of course, be urged that this apparent confusion was caused by history itself. We, as literary historians, have first of all to pay heed to the ideas and conceptions, the programs and names of the writers themselves, and thus we have to be content with accepting their own divisions. I would not want to minimize the value of the evidence supplied by consciously formulated programs, factions, and self-interpretations in the history of literature. I think the term "movement" might well be reserved for such self-conscious and self-critical activities, which we must, of course, describe as we would any other historical sequence of events and pronouncements. But, I think, they are merely materials for our study of a period, just as much as the whole history of criticism will be a running commentary to any history of literature. They may give us suggestions and hints, but they should not prescribe our own methods and divisions, not because our views are necessarily more penetrating than theirs, but because we have the benefit of seeing the past in the light of the future.

Besides, it must be pointed out, it is simply not true that this welter of terms of different origin was established in their own time. In English the term "humanism" occurs first in 1832; "Renaissance" in 1840; "Elizabethan" in 1817; "Augustan" in 1819; and "Romanticism" in 1844. These dates, which I derive from the *Oxford Dictionary*, are probably not quite reliable, for I have found the term "Augustan" applied to English literature by Leonard Welsted as early as 1724;[3] but they indicate the time lag between the labels and the periods which they designate. We all know that the Romanticists did not call themselves Romanticists, at least in England. So far as I know, the German scholar Alois Brandl, in his book on Coleridge (1887), first connected Coleridge and Wordsworth definitely with the Romantic movement and grouped them with Shelley, Keats, and Byron. In her *Literary History of England between the End of the Eighteenth and the Beginning of the Nineteenth Century* (1882) Mrs. Oliphant never uses the term, nor does she conceive of the "Lake" poets, the "Cockney" school, and the "Satanic" Byron as one movement. There is thus no historical justification for the present usually accepted periods of English literature. One cannot escape the conclusion that it is a motley collection of political, literary, or artistic labels picked up here and there without much rhyme or reason.

I would, however, go further. Even if we had a series of periods neatly following any one periodical division of any cultural activity of man — politics, philosophy, the other arts, and so forth — literary history should not be content to accept a scheme arrived at on the basis of various materials with different aims in mind. This, of course, is a topic far beyond the confines of a short paper: it would require a solution of the whole question of the relation to literature to all the other cultural activities of man. I can only state somewhat dogmatically that literature is not merely the passive reflection or copy of the political, social, or even intellectual development of mankind. It is, no doubt, in constant interrelation with all the other activities. It is influenced by them profoundly, and (what is frequently forgotten) it influences them. But literature has its own autonomous development irreducible to any other activity or even to a sum of all these activities. Otherwise it would cease to be literature and would lose its *raison d'être*. As to politics, it is easy to show that the courses of literature and of political fortune do not run parallel. It suffices to cite as an example Germany during the Napoleonic epoch, when a period of political impotence coincided with the greatest flowering of literature. The arts of painting and music developed differently from literature for the simple reason that neither painting nor music had the support or dead weight of a tradition of classical antiquity. Technical philosophy does not necessarily run parallel with the ideology embodied or implied in the poetry of its time, as witness the rule of Scottish

✤•✦

3. *Epistles, Odes* . . . (1724), p. 45, in "An Epistle to the Duke of Chandos."

Commonsense philosophy and of Utilitarianism during the English Romantic period. Thus I would merely argue that the usual affirmative answer to the question whether political, social, philosophical, or artistic periods coincide with literary periods is too hastily given. I would not deny that there is such a problem as that of the "time spirit," but it seems to me that this unity has to be established with much more careful arguments than are usually given in the German *Geistesgeschichte*. The practical examples one has seen, for instance, Paul Meissner's *Englisches Literaturbarock* (1934), indulge in extravagant speculations which frequently do not amount to more than the construction of an ingenious, but arbitrary, pattern of antithetical concepts.[4] The supposed similarities between the arts are frequently based on little more than elaborate equivocations or extended metaphors, and most of the work seems as far away from the actual process of literature as anything in the more humble studies of social or intellectual historians. I do not, of course, deny the problem of a general history of mankind and its spiritual evolution. I would only plead that this problem is distinct from our aim: the establishment of the development of literature.

This, I think, should be done first by purely literary criteria. If our results should coincide with those of political, social, artistic, and intellectual historians, well and good. But our starting point must be the development of literature as literature. There seem to be great difficulties with this concept. In his stimulating book on *English Poetry and the English Language* (1934) F. W. Bateson comes to the conclusion that a "flux is unintelligible except in reference to something outside itself."[5] As he rejects the usual view of literature as dependent on social evolution, he adopts another equally one-sided causal explanation, that is, linguistic evolution. But the very fact that we can conceive of a universal history of literature (which would be also a history of literary forms and genres) cutting across all linguistic boundaries shows that literature is not a simple reflex of linguistic evolution. We must try to envisage an autonomous development of literature, distinct from its reflection of social change or change of intellectual atmosphere. Few would doubt the possibility of such a history of painting or music. It suffices to walk through any art gallery arranged in chronological order or in accordance with "schools" to see that there is a history of the art of painting which is quite distinct from either the lives of painters or an appreciation of individual pictures. It suffices to listen to a concert in which compositions are arranged in chronological order to realize that there is a history of music which has scarcely anything to do with the biographies of composers, the social conditions under which the works were produced, or the appreciation of individual pieces. Literary history is confronted with the analo-

➹•➷

4. See the criticism by R. S. Crane in the *Philological Quarterly,* XIV (1935), 152-54.

5. Page 7.

gous problem of tracing the history of literature in comparative isolation from its social history, the biographies of its authors, or the appreciation of individual works.

There are, however, scholars who simply deny that literature has a history. W. P. Ker argued that we do not need literary history, since the materials on which the history is based are always present, are "eternal," and therefore have no proper history at all.[6] "Art," one could quote Schopenhauer, "has always reached its goal." It never improves; it cannot be superceded or repeated. In art we need not find out "what it was that actually happened" — as Ranke puts the aim of historiography — because we can experience directly how things are. So literary history is, it has been argued, no proper history, as it is merely the knowledge of the present, the omnipresent, the eternally present. According to this theory, advocated, for instance, by Herbert Cysarz, periods are merely abstract types, not time sections in a historical process. We can therefore speak of Greek romanticism or medieval classicism, as we mean only that this or another work of art shows certain characteristics which we traditionally have come to call "classical" or "romantic" or "realistic."

I think one cannot deny that there is some real difference between political history and the history of art. There is a distinction between that which is historical and past and that which is historical and still somehow present. The battle of Waterloo is definitely past, though its effects may be felt even today and though its course may be reconstructed accurately; but the *Iliad,* the Parthenon, and a mass by Palestrina are still somehow present. Granting this, I think this distinction by no means refutes the fact that there is real history in the constant changes which literary tradition undergoes. It could be shown that even an individual work of art does not remain unchanged in the course of history. Besides, there is constant development of literature, if we contemplate it as a whole fluctuating, growing process. Genres, stylistic types, motifs, linguistic traditions, and periods grow, flower, and decay. It is not a uniform progress toward one aim; it is a patchy development of this art form, of that ideology, of this system of critical values, or of that national talent.

But the concept of development of a series of works of art seems an extraordinarily difficult one. In a sense, at first sight each work of art is a structure or system of signs discontinuous with each neighboring work of art. One could argue that there is no development from one individuality to another. Homer does not change into Shakespeare, nor does Marlowe. One meets even with the objection that there is no history of literature, but only of men writing. According to the same argument we should have to give up writing a history of language, as there are only men uttering words, and a his-

✦●✦

6. *Thomas Warton,* Oxford, 1910, p. 6; also in *Essays,* I, 92.

tory of philosophy, since there are only men thinking. Such extreme "personalism" must lead to anarchy, to a complete isolation of every individual work of art which in practice would mean that it would be both incommunicable and incomprehensible. We must conceive rather of literature as a whole system of works which is, with the accretion of new ones, constantly changing its relationships and growing as a changing whole.

The mere fact, however, that the literary situation of one decade or century differs from that of the preceding decade or century is still insufficient to establish a process of actual historical evolution, as the concept of change applies to any series of natural phenomena. It merely means repeated reshufflings of a kaleidoscope, which are "meaningless" and "incomprehensible." Thus the study of change, as recommended by F. J. Teggart in his *Theory of History* (1925), would lead merely to the abolishment of all differences between historical and natural processes and would leave the historian helplessly thrown back upon borrowings from natural science. If changes recurred with absolute regularity, we should arrive at the concept of law in the physicist's sense of the word. But such predictable changes have never been discovered in any historical process, in spite of the brilliant speculations of Spengler and Toynbee. Those literary historians who have hunted this chimera of literary law have arrived only at a few psychological uniformities (as the supposed "law" of action and reaction or of convention and revolt), which cannot tell us anything significant about the individual historical process. It would lead me into too much detail to show that the one ambitious attempt to arrive at such a law of English literature, Cazamian's "accelerated oscillation of the rhythm of the English national mind," is merely an ingenious construction which at every point does violence to the actual evolution of English literature.[7]

Thus development means something else and something more than change — even regular, predictable change. It seems obvious that the term should be used in the sense elaborated by biology. In biology, if we look closely, there are two very different concepts of evolution.[8] First, the process exemplified by the growth of a hen from an egg or a butterfly from a caterpillar; second, the change exemplified by the evolution of the brain of a fish to that of a man. In the latter case no series of brains ever develops, but rather some conceptual abstraction, the brain, which can be defined only by its function. The individual stages of development are conceived as different approximations to

7. L. Cazamian, *L'Évolution psychologique de la littérature en Angleterre,* Paris, 1920, and the *History of English Literature* (together with E. Legouis), English translation, London, 1929.

8. See Hans Driesch, *Studien über Entwicklung,* Sitzungsberichte der Heidelberger Akademie, Philosophisch-Historische Klasse, 1918, No. 3, p. 60.

an ideal, derived from the human brain. In what sense can one speak of evolution with either of these two meanings in literature? Ferdinand Brunetière and, in England, John Addington Symonds assumed that we can speak in both senses of the evolution of literature.[9] Brunetière and Symonds considered literary genres as analogous to species in nature. According to Brunetière, as soon as a literary genre reaches a certain degree of perfection it must wither, languish, and finally disappear. A genre grows, reaches perfection, declines, and dies, just as the life cycle of an individual; also genres become transformed into higher and more differentiated genres, just as species in the Darwinian conception of evolution. I hardly need to show that the use of the term "evolution" in the first sense is little more than a fanciful metaphor. According to Brunetière, for example, French tragedy was born, grew, declined, and died. But the *tertium comparationis* for the birth of tragedy is merely the fact that there were no tragedies written in French before Jodelle. Tragedy died only in the sense that no important tragedies conforming to a certain ideal pattern were written after Voltaire. But there is always the possibility that such a tragedy will be written in French in the future. According to Brunetière, Racine's *Phèdre* stands at the beginning of the decline of tragedy, somewhere near its old age, but it strikes us as young and fresh compared to the learned and dull Renaissance tragedies which according to this theory represent the "youth" of French tragedy. Even less defensible is the idea that genres become transformed into other genres. French pulpit oratory of the seventeenth and eighteenth centuries was, according to Brunetière, transformed into the lyrical poetry of the romantic movement. Actually no real "transmutation" has, however, taken place: all one can say is that the same or similar emotions were expressed once in oratory and later in lyrical poetry and that possibly the same or similar social purposes were served.

While we must reject the biological analogy between the development of literature and the closed evolutionary process from birth to death, the concept of evolution in the second sense seems to me much nearer to the real concept of historical evolution. It recognizes that a mere series of changes does not suffice, and that a direction of this series must be postulated. The different parts of the series must be the necessary conditions for the achievement of the aim. The concept of evolution toward a specific goal (for instance, the human brain) makes a series of changes into a real concatenation with a beginning and an end. Still there is an important distinction between this second meaning of biological evolution and historical evolution in the proper sense. In

❖•❖

9. See especially Brunetière's *L'Évolution des genres dans l'histoire de la littérature,* I (Paris, 1890), 18 and 277-78, and John Addington Symonds: *Shakespeare's Predecessors in the English Drama* (1884) and "On the Application of Evolutionary Principles to Art and Literature," in *Essays Speculative and Suggestive,* London, 1890, I, 42-84.

order to grasp historical evolution as distinct from evolution in biology we must somehow succeed in preserving the individuality of the historical event, while the historical process must not be left as a collection of sequent but unrelated events.

The solution lies in the attempt to relate the historical process to a scheme of values or norms. Only then can the apparently meaningless series of events be split into its essential and unessential elements. Only then can we speak of historical evolution which still leaves the individuality of the single event unimpaired. In relating an individual event to a general value we do not consider the individual as a mere specimen of a general concept, but we give significance to the individual. The point of view here advocated implies that history does not simply exemplify general values (nor is it, of course, a discontinuous meaningless flux), but that the historical process will produce ever new forms of value, hitherto unknown and unpredictable. The relativity of the individual work of art to a scale of values is thus nothing else than the necessary correlative of its individuality. The series of developments will be constructed in reference to a scheme of values or norms, but these values themselves emerge only from the contemplation of this process. There is, one has to admit, a logical circle in this fact that the historical process has to be judged by values, while the scale of values is itself derived from history. But this seems unavoidable, because otherwise we must either resign ourselves to the idea of a meaningless flux of change or apply some extra-literary set of standards: some absolute derived from religion, ethics, philosophy, or even politics, which is extraneous to the process of literature. Such a judgement by nonliterary absolutes may very well be one of the tasks of criticism which need not be strictly literary, but it scarcely could be called literary history.

All this seems to have led us far afield. But only apparently, because in solving the problem of development (or at least bringing it nearer to a solution) we have solved the problem of periods. A period is after all only a sub-section of the universal development. History can be written with reference to a variable scheme of values, and this scheme of values has to be abstracted from history itself. Such a scheme of values dominates a period. We can, of course, conceive of other historical schemes of values: genres, ideals of versifications, and so forth. A period, therefore, is no metaphysical entity nor an arbitrary cross-section, but rather a time section dominated by a system of literary norms, whose introduction, spread, diversification, integration, and disappearance can be traced. This does not, of course, mean that we have to accept this system of norms as binding for ourselves. We must extract it from history itself: we have to discover it there in reality. For instance, "romanticism" is not a unitary quality which spreads like an infection or a plague (nor is it, of course, merely a verbal label), but a historical category or, if one prefers this Kantian term, a "regulative idea" (or rather a whole system of ideas) with the help of which we interpret the historical process. But we have found this scheme of ideas in the process itself. This concept of the term "period" differs thus from one in frequent use: its expansion into a psychological type which can be taken out of its historical context and transferred anywhere else. I would not necessarily condemn the use even of established historical terms as names for such psychological or artistic types. But it seems to me that such a typology of literature is something very different from the matter we are discussing: it does not belong to literary history in the narrow sense.

Thus a period is not a type or a class, but a time section defined by a system of norms embedded in the historical process, irremovable from its temporal place. If it were merely a general concept, it could be defined exhaustively. But the many futile attempts to define "romanticism" show that a period is not a concept similar to a class in logic. If it were, all individual works could be subsumed under it. But this is manifestly impossible. An individual work of art is not an instance in a class, but a part which, together with all the other works, makes up the concept of the period. It thus itself modifies the concept of the whole. The discrimination of different "romanticisms" or multiple definitions, however valuable they are as indications of the complexity of the scheme to which they refer, seems to me mistaken on theoretical grounds. It should be, I think, frankly realized that a period is not an ideal type or an abstract pattern or a series of class concepts, but a time section, dominated by a whole system of norms, which no work of art will ever realize in its entirety. The history of a period will consist in the tracing of the changes from one system of norms to another. While a period is thus a section of time to which some sort of unity is ascribed, it is obvious that this unity can be only relative. It means merely that during this period a certain scheme of norms has been realized most fully. If the unity of any one period were absolute, the periods would lie next to each other like blocks of stone. There would be no continuity of development. Thus the survival of a preceding scheme of norms and also anticipations of a following scheme are inevitable, as a period is historical only if every event is considered as a result of the whole preceding past and if its effects can be traced into the whole future. One could elaborate on this conception in some detail, but possibly this outline is sufficient here.

Let me sum up some of the results of my reflections:

1. A period is comprehensible only as a section inside the process of development. Thus we have to consider the question of development first. "Movement" is a term which should perhaps be reserved for a self-conscious, collective striving, a series of events and pronouncements, the description of which does not offer particular problems. With a slightly different meaning "movement" is used for the one dominant scheme of values in any one period.

2. The development of literature should be conceived as autonomous. This means merely that the development of literature is not simply a passive reflection or a copy of the political, social, intellectual, or linguistic evolution of mankind. This does not, of course, imply that literature does not have vital relationships with all the other activities of humanity; its course will be, in fact, the resultant of social forces modifying an internal evolution.

3. This development should not, of course, be conceived as a uniform progress toward one model, nor should it be interpreted as analogous to the life cycle of an individual or a species. It is rather a process of continuous evolution toward different and divers specific aims which it is best to conceive as so many systems of norms or values. These have to be discovered in the literary process itself and, as to the future, are still unknown and quite unpredictable.

4. A "period" is a time section in which such a system of norms is dominant. Every individual work of art can be understood as an approximation to one of these systems. Thus "period" is a dynamic "regulative" concept and is not either a metaphysical essence or a purely verbal label.

5. If we take our second point seriously, we must try to derive our system of norms, our "regulative ideas," from the art of literature, not merely from the norms of some related activity. Only then can we have a series of periods which would divide the stream of literary development by literary categories. Thus a series of literary periods can alone make up, as parts of a whole, the continuous process of literature, which is, after all, the central topic in the study of literary history.

6. Only after we have arrived at a series of literary periods does the further question arise how far these periods coincide with those determined by political, sociological, philosophical, linguistic, and other criteria. I am not answering this question, as I am convinced that the answers cannot be merely in the negative or in the affirmative. We must, I think, weigh the pros and cons in every individual instance. But this is a highly speculative topic — one which should be left to historians of the whole spiritual development of humanity. Literary history has not yet achieved its immediate ideal: the description in literary terms of a series of periods.[10]

— René Wellek

⤖•⬅

10. Part of this paper is a revision of my "Theory of Literary History," in the *Travaux du Cercle Linguistique de Prague,* VI (Prague, 1936), 173 ff.

Introduction

Twentieth-Century Literary Movements Dictionary provides entries on more than 500 major and minor literary movements and schools associated with twentieth-century world literature, as well as the novelists, poets, dramatists, short-story writers, theorists, essayists, genres, techniques, and terms identified with those movements. In addition, the most important and representative works of literature associated with the literary schools are included. International in scope, the volume documents these trends as they emerged in every corner of the world.

We have also chosen to include such major nineteenth-century movements as Symbolism, Naturalism, and Realism, which, although they began in nineteenth-century Europe, exerted a great influence on twentieth-century letters and gave rise to similar movements throughout the world in the early decades of the century. For example, American Realism and Naturalism continued well into the twentieth century, whereas their European counterparts had run their course by 1900. The original movements have also been included to assist the student in understanding the scope and precepts of the original school, which are so important to its dissemination to other lands.

Literary criticism, which has had an extraordinary effect on literature in the twentieth century, is also represented in the inclusion of the most significant schools, e.g., New Criticism, Structuralism, and Feminist Criticism. Entries on a number of individuals whose disciplines fall outside the study of literature but whose influence on twentieth-century literature has been enormous, notably Henri Bergson, Sigmund Freud, Carl Jung, Karl Marx, and Friedrich Nietzsche have also been included.

Major theater groups of the twentieth century associated with a particular school or movement, such as the Freie Bühne and the Théâtre Libre, both associated with furthering the aims and influence of such Naturalists as Gerhart Hauptmann and Émile Zola, are included, as is the Abbey Theater, which produced the works of such noted members of the Irish Renaissance as William Butler Yeats and Sean O'Casey.

The Plan of the Work

The volume is arranged alphabetically, and the length of each entry is intended to reflect the importance of the individual movement. A bold-faced heading prefaces each entry, providing the name of the movement and the country and years of its greatest influence. If a commonly accepted English translation for a non-English language movement is available, the English form of the name appears in the heading, followed by the name in the original language. For each of these non-English language movements, a cross-reference appears alphabetically within the text, under the foreign language name, leading the reader to the discussion under the English form.

The essay covering each movement details its philosophical and artistic tenets, the historical and cultural settings out of which it grew, the writers and works of literature with which it is associated, the key era and area of the movement's influence, the way in which it influenced later movements and works of literature, and the literary techniques associated with it. Throughout the essays, the works of authors who write in a language other than English appear first in the language of the original publication, followed by the title and publication date of the English translation, if available. In the cases of large, exceptionally influential movements, the essays are followed by separate sections on the individual authors and works of greatest import to the movement. Words and names set in small capital letters indicate authors and works featured at the end of the essay. Words and names set in regular capital letters indicate separate entries elsewhere in the volume. In some cases, an entry on an author appears without an entry on a corresponding work by that author; in these cases, the editors decided that rather than highlight one of several works relevant to the movement, an overview of the author's oeuvre appropriate to the movement would appear in the author's entry. A list of further reading concludes the entries, leading students to the best known and respected books and articles on the movement available in English.

The entries were prepared using the following standard reference sources:

Benet's Reader's Encyclopedia. 4th edition. New York: HarperCollins, 1996.

The Cambridge Guide to Literature in English. 2nd edition. Edited by Ian Ousby. Cambridge, England: Cambridge University Press, 1994.

Caribbean Writers: A Bio-Bibliographical-Critical Encyclopedia. Edited by Donald E. Herdeck. Washington, D.C.: Three Continents Press, 1979.

Cassell's Encyclopedia of World Literature. Edited by J. Buchanan-Brown. London: Cassell, 1973.

Columbia Dictionary of Modern European Literature. 2nd edition. Edited by Jean-Albert Bédé and William B. Edgerton. New York: Columbia University Press, 1980.

A Companion to Twentieth-Century German Literature. Edited by Raymond Furness and Malcolm Humble. London; New York: Routledge, 1991.

Concise Encyclopedia of Modern World Literature. 2nd edition. Edited by Geoffrey Grigson. New York: Hawthorne Books, 1963.

Dictionary of Literary Terms. Revised edition. By J. A. Cuddon. London: Andre Deutsch Ltd., 1979.

Dictionary of Oriental Literatures. Edited by Jaroslav Průšek. New York: Basic Books, 1974.

Encyclopedia of World Literature in the Twentieth Century. 3rd edition. Edited by Steven Serafin. Chicago: St. James Press, 1998.

Handbook of Russian Literature. By Victor Terras. New Haven: Yale University Press, 1985.

Handbook to Literature. 7th edition. Edited by William Harmon. New York: Prentice-Hall, 1995.

Harper Dictionary of Modern Thought. Revised edition. Edited by Alan Bullock and Stephen Trombley. New York: Harper & Row, 1988.

Longman Companion to Twentieth-Century Literature. Revised edition. By A. C. Ward. London: Longman, 1981.

McGraw-Hill Encyclopedia of World Drama. 2nd edition. Edited by Stanley Hochman. New York: McGraw-Hill, 1984.

Merriam-Webster's Encyclopedia of Literature. Springfield, Mass.: Merriam-Webster, 1995.

New Oxford Companion to French Literature. Edited by Peter France. Oxford: Clarendon Press, 1995.

New Princeton Encyclopedia of Poetry and Poetics. 3rd edition. Edited by Alex Preminger. Princeton, N.J.: Princeton University Press, 1993.

Oxford Companion to American Literature. 6th edition. Edited by James D. Hart. Oxford: Oxford University Press, 1995.

Oxford Companion to American Theatre. 2nd edition. Edited by Gerald Bordman. Oxford: Oxford University Press, 1992.

Oxford Companion to Canadian Literature. 2nd edition. Edited by Eugene Benson and William Toye. Oxford: Oxford University Press, 1998.

Oxford Companion to English Literature. Revised edition. Edited by Margaret Drabble. Oxford: Oxford University Press, 1998.

Oxford Companion to German Literature. Revised edition. Edited by Mary Garland. Oxford: Oxford University Press, 1997.

Oxford Companion to Spanish Literature. Edited by Philip Ward. Oxford: Oxford University Press, 1978.

Oxford Companion to the Theatre. 4th edition. Edited by Phyllis Hartnoll. Oxford: Oxford University Press, 1983.

Penguin Companion to American Literature. Edited by Malcolm Bradbury, Eric Mottram, and Jean Franco. New York: McGraw-Hill, 1971.

Penguin Companion to Classical, Oriental, and African Literature. Edited by D. M. Lang and D. R. Dudley. New York: McGraw-Hill, 1969.

Penguin Companion to English Literature. Edited by David Daiches. New York: McGraw-Hill, 1971.

Penguin Companion to European Literature. Edited by Anthony Thorlby. New York: McGraw-Hill, 1971.

Reader's Companion to World Literature. 2nd edition. Edited by Lillian Herlands Hornstein. New York: Mentor Books, 1973.

Reader's Encyclopedia of Eastern European Literature. Edited by Robert B. Pynsent and S. I. Kanikova. New York: HarperCollins, 1993.

Appendices

1. A Timeline of Literary Movements — Gives a chronological listing of movements by decade, from the 1800s through the 1900s.

2. Chronology by Country — Lists movements in chronological order by country.

3. Journals Cited — Lists journals cited in this volume.

4. Web Sites — Lists general literary sites maintained by such organizations as the Modern Language Association and the Academy of American Poets, dealing with large, multinational movements and writers associated with them, and sites that provide electronic texts.

Indexes

1. Movements Index — Lists movements by foreign and alternate names and by English translations. Movement entries are indicated by bold-faced type.

2. Author Index — Lists novelists, short-story writers, poets, essayists, dramatists, and theorists who are discussed in the volume. Featured authors are indicated in bold-faced type as are the page numbers on which the features appear.

3. **Title Index** — Lists journals, books, stories, poems, plays, and essays discussed in the volume. Foreign-language works that have been translated into English are indexed under the foreign title, with cross-references provided under the English translations. Featured works are indicated in bold-faced type as are the page numbers on which the features appear.

4. **Country and Nationality Index** — Lists movements in alphabetical order by country and nationality.

Audience

Twentieth-Century Literary Movements Dictionary is directed to students in late high school and early college who are examining literature from the perspective of literary movements which chart the development of the literary history of the modern era.

Acknowledgments

The editors wish to thank our Advisory Board, representing public, school, and university libraries, who evaluated *Twentieth-Century Literary Movements Dictionary* in its early stages. We hope their comments and suggestions have helped us to provide a comprehensive and useful guide. We wish to thank Amy Marcaccio Keyzer for lending her editorial expertise, Joan Margeson and Barry Puckett for exercising their keen research skills, Mary Ann Stavros for employing her superb design and typesetting abilities, and Jenifer Swanson for her assistance in compiling the listing of literary web sites. We are grateful to René Wellek who wrote the preface and who, before passing away late in 1995, kindly granted us permission to reprint it here. Fond thanks must also go to Laurence Goldstein, professor of English, University of Michigan, Ann Arbor, for bringing the Spectra hoax to our attention.

I would like to express my gratitude for Gloria Richardson, whose encouragement and guidance made all the difference. I would also like to offer thanks for the support of Jerry Clark.

— Helene Henderson

A

ABBAYE GROUP (Groupe de L'Abbaye)
France, 1906-1908

In 1906 L'Abbaye, a residence at Creteil near Paris, became the temporary home for a few enthusiastic young French intellectuals who formed a literary and artistic commune for creative activity. They supported themselves by sharing food and by printing and selling small-press books. What they had in common was the general sharing of material needs as well as aesthetic values; their premise, although not in written manifesto, was that the sharing of ideas about literature and the arts made for a kind of unity out of which the best creative work would arise. The project lasted for a short time and was abandoned for economic reasons. What is important is that the movement known as UNANIMISME became the end result of the venture. Members of the group included René Arcos (1881-1948), Georges DUHAMEL, Luc Durtain (1881-1959), Pierre-Jean Jouve (1887-1976), the painter Albert Gleizes (1881-1953), Jules ROMAINS, and Charles VILDRAC.

✥•✥

Further Reading

Boak, Denis. *Jules Romains*. New York: Twayne, 1974.
Callander, Margaret. *The Poetry of Pierre Jean Jouve*. Manchester, England: Manchester University Press, 1965.
Colford, Elizabeth E. *Themes of Love and Death in the Poetry of Pierre Jean Jouve*. Thesis, Duke University, 1973.
Duhamel, Georges. *Light on My Days: An Autobiography*. Translated by Basil Collier. London: J. M. Dent, 1948.
Edebiri, Unionmwan. "Georges Duhamel, Individualiste." *Asemka: A Literary Journal of the University of Cape Coast, Ghana* 5 (1979): 83-96.
Keating, L. Clark. *Critic of Civilization: Georges Duhamel and His Writings*. Lexington, Ky.: University of Kentucky Press, 1965.

Knapp, Bettina L. *Georges Duhamel.* New York: Twayne, 1972.

Lemaster Mauzey, Elaine. "Men of Good Will." *Northwest Missouri State College Studies* 11, 1 (1947): 39-61.

Norrish, Peter. *Drama of the Group; A Study of Unanimism in the Plays of Jules Romains.* Cambridge, England: Cambridge University Press, 1958.

O'Neil, Mary Ann. "Pierre Jean Jouve as Meditative Poet: An Analysis of 'La Vierge de Paris'." *Romanic Review* 77, 4 (November 1986): 391-403.

Rivas, Daniel Eusebio. *Jouve's Mnemosyne: An Alchemical View.* Iowa City, Iowa: L'Esprit Createur, 1978. Reprinted from *L'Esprit Createur* 17, 2 (summer 1978): 51-61.

———. "Pierre Jean Jouve's Dark Night of the Soul." *Comparative Literature Studies* 17 (1980): 325-33.

Scott, Joan Wallach. "Popular Theater and Socialism in Late-Nineteenth-Century France." In *Political Symbolism in Modern Europe: Essays in Honor of George L. Mosse.* Edited by Seymour Drescher, David Sabean, and Allan Sharlin. New Brunswick, N.J.: Transaction, 1982.

Starobinski, Jean, Jean Blot, and Pierre Silvain. "In Memoriam: Pierre Jean Jouve." *Nouvelle Revue Française* 281 (1976): 37-60.

Stribling, Jane K. *Plenitude Restored or Trompe L'Oeil: The Problematic of Fragmentation and Integration in the Prose Works of Pierre Jean Jouve and Michael Tournier.* New York: Peter Lang, 1995.

Wakerley, Veronique. "Paris as Unanimist Hero in the Work of Jules Romains." *Romance Studies* 23 (spring 1994): 105-17.

ABBEY THEATER
Ireland, 1904-1930s

The Abbey Theater was born of a combination of phenomena which had begun with the IRISH RENAISSANCE, a late-nineteenth-century movement in Ireland with the purpose of reviving the ancient Celtic and Gaelic culture, folklore, and language which had been displaced centuries before by the English occupation. As a specifically literary movement, it took root in England in 1891, when William Butler YEATS was joined by other London writers of Irish birth in an effort to give "opportunity to a new generation of critics and writers to denounce the propagandist verse and prose . . . [in the] name of Irish Literature and to substitute for it . . . certain neglected [Irish] writers." In 1899 Yeats along with Lady Augusta Gregory (1852-1932), a writer and promoter of cultural literature, playwright-directors Edward Martyn (1859-1923) and George Moore (1852-1933), and actors William (1872-1947) and Frank (1870-1931) Fay all formed the Irish Literary Theatre. These few conceived a general format for Irish theater: that it be devoted to productions of nationalistic literature, that it be politically independent, and that it be beyond the control of what made up only profitable productions. Soon this group attracted other Irish dramatists, actors, and producers of similar mind and enthusiasm such as George W. Russell (pseud. Æ, 1867-1935), Douglas Hyde (1860-1949), John Millington SYNGE, and Padraic Colum (1881-1972).

Some of the initial productions were of Yeats's *Cathleen Ní Houlihan* (1899), *A Pot of Broth* (1902), and *On Baile's Strand* (1903); a collaboration by Yeats and Moore, *Diarmuid and Grania* (1904); Lady Gregory's *Twenty-Five* (1903); and Synge's *Riders to the Sea* (1904). These plays were given wherever an available stage could be found, in Dublin's Camden Street or Molesworth Halls. The dramas reintroduced Irish audiences to a "knowledge of Irish peasantry and its folklore," audiences which had prior to then seen only the productions of English dramatic touring companies. Both Yeats and Lady Gregory had agreed that the poetic and lyrical language of the rural Irish peasantry and their working-class compatriots presented the best of the Irish imaginative mind and that the plays should emphasize that milieu.

On a short but successful London tour in 1903, the group attracted the attention of Miss A. E. F. Horniman (1860-1937), who as an early admirer of Yeats had helped to finance production of his play *The Land of Heart's Desire* (1894) in England. New enthusiasm caused her to find a site for a theater in Dublin, and to provide the group with its own rent-free home. The company could now combine both dramatic and set-design workshops, rehearsals, production, in short, everything an independent theatrical organization needed for a working, living theater. The Abbey Theater would begin its singular contribution to twentieth-century Irish drama.

Productions between 1904 and 1912 featured the works of Yeats, Lady Gregory, Synge, and other Irish playwrights, along with Richard Sheridan's (1751-1816) *St. Patrick's Day, or, The Scheming Lieutenant* (1775) and translations of works by Jean-Baptiste Molière (1622-1673). Having had successful runs of his *Riders to the Sea* (1904) and *The Wells of Saints* (1905), Synge added THE PLAYBOY OF THE WESTERN WORLD to the repertoire in 1907, and its opening caused a public protest. Known today as one of Ireland's outstanding examples of its tradition and culture, the play caused initial audiences to become angry at what one critic has called "imagined" degradation of Irish peasantry and character, but audiences outside of Ireland acclaimed Synge's work with few exceptions. Yeats's poem "On Those That Hate *The Playboy of the Western World*" was a defense of Synge's work.

The following decades brought the Abbey Theater group a mixture of success and failure; a rival theater group, The Theater of Ireland, was formed, causing the defection of some of the Abbey's best-known actors, and Miss Horniman withdrew her support. But in 1917, Yeats's second play in his series depicting the CUCHULAIN legend, *At the Hawk's Well*, was enthusiastically received as an innovative introduction to Japanese Nō (*see* MODERN NŌ) dramatic form, for it incorporated Yeats's interest in mysticism. Moreover, Sean O'CASEY's three plays, *The Shadow of a Gunman* (1923), *Juno and*

3

the Paycock (1924), and *The Plough and the Stars* (1926), aroused new interest in the group. However, in 1928, angered by Yeats's rejection of his new play, *The Silver Tassie*, O'Casey broke with the Abbey and Yeats and permanently exiled himself in England. Despite this, the group continued to produce many of his early and later plays. Noteworthy among numerous productions until 1951 were plays by Eugene O'NEILL (*see* EXPRESSIONISM, United States and PROVINCETOWN PLAYERS), George Bernard SHAW (*see* EDWARDIAN LITERATURE), Oscar Wilde (1864-1900), Oliver Goldsmith (1730-1774), and Yeats's final play, *The Death of Cuchulain* (1939). Audiences were also introduced to dramatic REALISM in works by Henrik IBSEN (*see* REALISM, Norway) and Luigi PIRANDELLO (*see* MODERNISM, Italy), and added to this format was a series of Gaelic plays performed by bilingual actors. Ballets were also included in the repertoire, set to music by Bach, Beethoven, Chopin, and Tchaikovsky, to name a few.

With the deaths of Lady Gregory in 1932 and of Yeats in 1939, World War II and its aftermath found the Abbey Theater and the impact of the Irish dramatic revival in a state of change. Important new playwrights were Michael Molloy (1914-1994) and Brendan Behan (1923-1964), and each one's revaluation of Irish literary tradition had an impact. Molloy's sympathetic but regretful concept that the old ways could no longer sustain the new social and political needs in Ireland is depicted in *The Visiting House* (1956) and *The King of Friday's Men* (1948). Brendan Behan was considered by many to be the most promising of the new dramatists, as his plays show a marked break from the nostalgic and nationalistic Realism which had influenced literary Ireland for decades. His plays *The Quare Fellow* (1954) and *The Hostage* (1958) contain bitter, prophetic, and didactic depictions of the impact of the conflict between Ireland and England; one critic asserts that these are "two of the best plays in modern English."

In 1951 the Abbey Theater burned down and removed to the Peacock Theater until its new home was built in 1966. While it was not to recapture the spirit of its earlier, imaginative, and innovative revival of ancient Irish ideology and tradition, it had paved the way for later and excellent Irish dramaturgy when the Dublin Gate Theater Studio opened at the Abbey's Peacock Theater. There the repertoire has included the best of works by modern Irish playwrights as well as works by writers from around the world, and has attracted actors of note, as well.

O'Casey, Sean (1884-1964), Irish dramatist.

The times in which O'Casey lived provided him with the elements—the Irish political, literary, and nationalistic movements—for sharing through his creative impulse those ideas which meant the most to him. Moreover, his people and their ancient, Celtic background gave him both focus and ample material for his finest work. An ardent nationalist in his youth, O'Casey by midlife was disillusioned with socialism and Irish republicanism and felt that Marxist theories of economic and class liberation should formulate Ireland's primary goals. He deplored the Easter rebellion as a tragic and misguided waste of both Irish blood and mind. *The Plough and the Stars,* one of his best-known plays, is an indictment, often comic as well as bitterly ironic, of what O'Casey saw as a time of emotional chaos in the country he loved.

The Plough and the Stars (1926).

Set in Dublin during the 1916 Easter rebellion, the play is one of continuous discord as it sets characters against one another at every level of interaction, and between characters of both genders. There are fervent, patriotic characters whose desire it is to let blood or to die for the "cause," pitted against those who argue for peace and rational thinking. Themes of alienation and broken relationships underlie almost all of the action. These are introduced when characters Nora and Jack Clitheroe are at odds; her struggle is for their family life and their unborn child, but he sees the struggle for Ireland's independence from England as most important. In the end, he dies for country while she miscarries the child and goes mad. Other characters, in a patriotic fervor which they often do not understand, suffer a comic ambivalence as they decry the war but happily loot the Dublin shops as the battle is being fought in the streets. But there are good characters, mostly female, who are quick to help Nora in her tragic hour and try to protect her from harm and the knowledge of her husband's death. They symbolize O'Casey's belief that attitudes of love and charity are of a higher order than fanatic patriotism, war, and bloodshed. Throughout the work, O'Casey's mastery of the rich cadences of the Irish language shows his ability to represent "a variety of moods and attitudes," at times almost larger than life, which make up the essence of his view of the Irish mind set. The underlying message of his play is that, as he defined it, the egomaniacal patriotism based in warrior lust of the Irish provided only disorder and chaos and shows the futility of misdirected nationalism.

✦•✦

Synge, John Millington (1871-1909), Irish dramatist.

Discovered by Yeats in a Paris boarding house, Synge was convinced by the poet to return to his Irish homeland and write. Earlier, having taken a degree from Trinity College, Dublin, he had spent his time wandering in Europe, unable to successfully focus his talent. Upon his return to Ireland, he became fascinated for the first time by his country and its history. Synge's play *The Playboy of the Western World* had an inauspicious opening at the Abbey, but was later acclaimed as his greatest achievement. In its preface, Synge announced his desire to depict "both reality and joy . . . [that which is] superb and wild." At his tragic and early death, he was acclaimed as the foremost dramatist of the Irish Renaissance. He left behind four other plays, *In the Shadow of the Glen* (1903), *Riders to the Sea* (1904), *The Well of the Saints* (1905), *The Tinker's Wedding* (1907), and the incomplete *Deirdre of the Sorrows* (1910).

The Playboy of the Western World (1907).

The ancient myths of parricide, rites of passage, and reconciliation between father and son are concurrent themes in this play, which is set in rural Ireland. That Charlie, weakling son of the tyrannical Old Mahon, mistakenly thinks that he has murdered his father provides for tragicomic drama; that Charlie is proclaimed a hero for the act by his new, Irish peasant friends compounds the dramatic impact. His lionization provides him with new self-reality, and he plays his role with bravura. Thus when Old Mahon resurfaces to further intimidate him, Charlie strikes again — this time in view of his friends — and Old Mahon appears to die again. But now the villagers become a mob; the tale of the parricide had provided them with the mythic thrill of excitement, but the experiential reality revives the frightening aspect of sin, and they prepare to hang him. However, Old Mahon, like Lazarus, rises again and, overcome with joy that he has at last spawned a man of courage like himself, he sees Charlie in a new light and father and son are reconciled. They leave the rustics behind to grieve their hero who had, for a time, given new dimension to their lives and now have left only the "dreams of battle and love." Synge's combination of poetic reality and restructured myth, set against the despair and decadence of the Irish struggle, provides a masterful tour de force which places him in the forefront of MODERNISM. A fascination with his compatriots and the desire to represent them as both comic and desperate is implicit in *Playboy* and in all of his work; Synge would characterize the Irish as "angels inhabiting the bodies of beasts."

❧•❦

Yeats, William Butler (1865-1939)
English poet, dramatist, essayist, editor, and statesman.

More well known for his poetry than his plays, Yeats was given recognition near the end of his life as a poetic giant of the twentieth century. He received the Nobel Prize for literature in 1923, and in 1928, what most critics agreed to be his finest work, *The Tower Poems,* substantiated his reputation. His career was influenced by an early and passionate interest in mysticism and the supernatural; in his mature work he constantly sought to combine elements of fantasy with metaphysical "abstract speculation [in order to explore] the human situation." His dual vision of the personality and its conflicting attitudes of good and evil, dreams and responsibility, and his admiration for a life to be lived with a noble stance and a pride in the beauty of existence give both his drama and poetry a visionary quality which continues to appeal to the sensitive and introspective reader. An early epic poem, "The Wanderings of Oisin" (1889), points directly to such dramatic works as the Cuchulain cycle, in which he depicts certain of the ancient, Celtic figures in all of their heroic proportion.

The Cuchulain Plays (1903-39).

Among the many plays that Yeats wrote for production at the Abbey Theater, three of his most famous are based on the ancient and legendary folk hero Cuchulain, a character who fascinated Yeats for all of his life. The first play, *On Baile's Strand* (1903), contains Yeats's inversion of ancient Greek myth, as Cuchulain unknowingly murders his son, Conchubar. The work also introduces the characters of blind men and fools who will be present in the plays which complete the cycle. These represent counterparts of the protagonists in their detached, ironic observations of both crises and turning points in dramatic denouement. In *At the Hawk's Well* (1917), Yeats's interest in Japanese Nō plays of mysticism, dance, gesture, and mask are combined in his attempt to adapt these elements into works for European audiences and his own countrymen. The familiar Cuchulain is presented symbolically, as a hero who meets an old man at the well of immortality. But each is prevented from drinking by a mysterious woman and her strange and unfamiliar dance; the waters disappear and the message is that to seek after immortality can only end in futility. *The Death of Cuchulain* (1939) was written just before Yeats died, and has been said by some to be a final poetic gesture, made as the poet faced his own demise. In the play, Cuchulain is lured to his death through the betrayal of his mistress, Eithne, goddess of war. Realizing that his ultimate adversary is death, and not an army in battle, Cuchulain meets his final hour heroically, even though he is blinded and killed by a fool. Yeats's poetic statement that heroism is, in the end, blind and ends in defeat was a sublime effort to demonstrate his lifelong desire as poet and dramatist to "cast experience into symbol."

➹•❦

Further Reading

Armstrong, William A. "Sean O'Casey." In *British Writers*. Vol. 7. New York: Scribner's Sons, 1984.

Bloom, Harold. *Yeats*. New York: Oxford University Press, 1970.

Clark, David R. *W. B. Yeats and the Theatre of Desolate Reality*. Washington, D.C.: Catholic University of America Press, 1993.

Flannery, James W., ed. *Yeats and the Theater: Yeats International Theatre Festival.* Ann Arbor, Mich.: University of Michigan Press, 1992.

Fraser, G. S. "William Butler Yeats." In *British Writers.* Vol. 4. New York: Scribner's Sons, 1983.

Frazier, Adrian Woods. *Behind the Scenes: Yeats, Horniman, and the Struggle for the Abbey Theatre.* Berkeley, Calif.: University of California Press, 1990.

Gerstenberger, Donna Lorine. *John Millington Synge.* Boston: Twayne Publishers, 1990.

Gooddie, Sheila. *Annie Horniman: A Pioneer in the Theatre.* London: Methuen, 1990; distributed in the U.S. by HEB.

Kiely, Benedict. *Yeats' Ireland: An Enchanted Vision.* New York: C. N. Potter, 1989.

Kiely, David M. *John Millington Synge: A Biography.* Dublin: Gill & Macmillan, 1994.

Kilroy, James. *The Playboy Riots.* Dublin: Dolmen Press, 1971.

Laurence, Dan H., and Nicholas Grene, eds. *Shaw, Lady Gregory, and the Abbey: A Correspondence and a Record.* Gerrards Cross, Buckinghamshire, England: Colin Smythe, 1993.

Macrae, Alasdair D. F. *W. B. Yeats: A Literary Life.* New York: St. Martin's Press, 1995.

Mikhail, E. H., ed. *The Abbey Theatre: Interviews and Recollections.* Totowa, N.J.: Barnes & Noble, 1988.

Murray, Christopher. *Twentieth-Century Irish Drama: Mirror up to the Nation.* Manchester, England: Manchester University Press, 1997; distributed in the U.S. by St. Martin's Press.

Nathan, Leonard E. *The Tragic Drama of William Butler Yeats.* New York: Columbia University Press, 1965.

O'Farrell, Padraic. *Green and Chaste and Foolish: Irish Literary and Theatrical Anecdotes.* Dublin: Gill & Macmillan, 1994.

Robinson, Lennox. *The Abbey Theatre: A History.* London: Sidgwick & Jackson, 1951.

Schrank, Bernice. *Sean O'Casey: A Research and Production Sourcebook.* Westport, Conn.: Greenwood Press, 1996.

Schrank, Bernice, and William W. Demastes, eds. *Irish Playwrights, 1880-1995: A Research and Production Sourcebook.* Westport, Conn.: Greenwood Press, 1996.

Skelton, Robin. *J. M. Synge and His World.* New York: Viking; London: Thames and Hudson, 1971.

Watanabe, Nancy Ann. *Beloved Image: The Drama of W. B. Yeats, 1865-1939.* Lanham, Md.: University Press of America, 1995.

Watson, George J. *Irish Identity and the Literary Revival: Synge, Yeats, Joyce, and O'Casey.* 2nd ed. Washington, D.C.: Catholic University of America Press, 1994.

Watt, Stephen. *Joyce, O'Casey, and the Irish Popular Theater.* Syracuse, N.Y.: Syracuse University Press, 1991.

Yeats, W. B. *Synge and the Ireland of His Time.* Dundrum, Ireland: Cuala Press, 1911; Shannon, Ireland: Irish University Press, 1970.

ABSTRACT MOVEMENT. *See* **SECOND NEW**

ACMEISM
Russia, 1910-1917

Acmeism was a movement in early twentieth-century Russian poetry that began as a reaction against the mystical, vague, and allusive qualities of SYMBOLISM. The most notable poets who participated in the movement were Anna AKHMATOVA, Osip MANDEL-STAM, and Nikolay GUMILYOV. Gumilyov, considered the Acmeists' chief theoretician, was the formative influence behind the group's Guild of Poets, founded in 1911, as well as its journal, *Apollon*, which was published from 1909 to 1917. Gumilyov and Akhmatova had been students of the famous Russian poet Innokenty Annensky (1856-1909), whose verse was considered a model by the early Acmeists and who is regarded as a central influence on the movement. *Apollon* had initially been the voice of the Russian Symbolists under the editorship of Sergeí Makóvsky (1877-1962).

The new tenets of the Acmeists were voiced as early as 1910 in an article by the poet Mikhail Kuzmin (1875-1935) that praised clarity in poetry. Two manifestos, written by Gumilyov and Sergey Gorodetsky (1884-1967) and published in *Apollon* in 1913, out-lined their ideals. The poets wished to create verse that was precise in shape and expression and characterized by concise diction, concrete imagery, clarity, and a vivid, sensory response to the physical world. As Gorodetsky said: "For the Acmeists, the rose has again become beautiful in itself, because of its petals, fragrance, and color, and not because of its conceivable likeness to mystical love." In opposition to the aesthetics of the Symbolists who then dominated European and Russian poetry, they saw the poet as a craftsman rather than a visionary. Neoclassical in intent, the Acmeists favored a return to the form and content of a more traditional poetry.

Spanning the years 1910 to 1917, the movement was short-lived, for the Acmeists were judged to be uncommitted to political and social concerns and thus met with condem-nation in post-revolutionary Russia. Each of the major members of the group suffered at the hands of the new regime: Gumilyov was killed in 1921 for his alleged complicity in a counter-revolutionary plot; Akhmatova, who had been married to Gumilyov from 1910 to 1918, lived into the 1960s, but her work was banned during the Stalin era and her son by Gumilyov was repeatedly arrested and imprisoned; Mandelstam, too, was sent to prison, where he died during the Stalinist purges of the 1930s.

Acmeism was one of several literary movements (including FUTURISM) that formed in Russia in opposition to the dominance of Symbolism in the early twentieth century. Along with Akhmatova, Mandelstam, and Gumilyov, such early Acmeists as Georgy Ivanov (1894-1958), Mikhail Lozinsky (1886-1955), and Georgy Adamovich (1894-

1972) forged a poetry whose lasting legacy to Russian poetry lies in its emphasis on the abandonment of the diffuse, mystical tendencies of Symbolism and its insistence on a more rigorous concern for clarity, balance, and direct poetic expression.

❧•❦

Akhmatova, Anna (1886-1966), Russian poet.

A major poet of twentieth-century Russia, Akhmatova began her career as a member of the Acmeist movement in Russian literature. She was married to the movement's main theoretician, Nikolay Gumilyov, until 1918, and with Osip Mandelstam the three were the central members of the group's Guild of Poets. As with the other Acmeists, her poetry is noted for its clarity and concision, as evidenced in her first major work, *CHOTKI* (1914; Rosary), a collection of intimate love lyrics. Her later poetry reflects her tragic life under an often hostile Soviet regime. Gumilyov was executed for his complicity in a counter-revolutionary plot in 1921, and her son by Gumilyov was arrested and imprisoned repeatedly during the Stalin era, in an attempt to censor and silence her. Throughout the adversity that characterized her private life, she continued to write verse noted for its somber tone and tempered by her personal anguish. In such works as *Rekviem* (written 1940; pub. 1963; *Requiem*, 1964) and "Poema bez geroya" (finished 1962; "Poem without a Hero," 1971) she parallels her own suffering with those of her fellow Russians in their despair in war and at the hands of Stalin's brutal reign.

Although several of her patriotic poems appearing during the war won her praise, Akhmatova was denounced by Stalin's literary ministers in the 1940s. Expelled from the Soviet Writers' Union, she was not allowed to publish freely until after Stalin's death, and not until the 1960s was she accorded her rightful place as one of the most important Russian poets of the twentieth century.

Chotki (1914; Rosary).

This collection of poetry by Akhmatova was a well-received and widely popular work upon its publication. The volume indicates the influence of Acmeism on her poetry, most notably in the clarity and economy of her poetic language. These compact lyrics, conversational in style, replicate the emotions of everyday existence in verse characterized by concrete imagery and simple diction. The tone is passionate, but controlled, reflecting the Acmeist's rejection of romantic excess. Akhmatova's theme here, as throughout her poetry, is love, expressed in yearning, joyful, or somber intonations. Like Mandelstam, Akhmatova revealed an understanding of history in her poetry, evoked here in her references to Russian folk tradition.

❧•❦

Gumilyov, Nikolay (1886-1921), Russian poet, dramatist, and critic.

One of the founders and the chief theoretician of the Acmeists, Gumilyov is closely linked to Akhmatova and Mandelstam, the other prominent poets connected with the movement. He was responsible for the formation of the group's Guild of Poets and published, with Sergey Gorodetsky, the two manifestos of Acmeists in their journal, *Apollon*. His first major collection was *Chuzhoye nebo* (1912; Foreign Skies), a work that most reflects the influence of Acmeism. In a simple, direct, and lyrical style, he contemplates the struggle within the human heart for the dominance of spirit over flesh, a theme that is revealed in many of his works. Although Gumilyov expounded the Acmeist objectives of clarity and balance, his own verse often tended toward the exotic and romantic, in which he championed heroism, the battlefield, the warrior, and the wanderer, often incorporating exotic settings. After serving in the cavalry during World War I, he returned to Russia, but soon fell out of favor with the authorities. In 1921 he was executed, without trial, for his alleged complicity in an anti-Soviet plot.

Mandelstam, Osip (1891-1938?), Russian poet, novelist, and critic.

Considered one of the most important lyric poets of the modern era, Mandelstam was an early exponent of Acmeism. With Akhmatova and Gumilyov, he formed the central core of the movement's Guild of Poets and is known for his verse, literary criticism, and theoretical tracts in which he outlined the aesthetics of the movement. His first poems appeared in *Apollon* in 1910. This early poetry exhibits his understanding of history and of classical poetic forms. Rejecting the principles of Symbolism, he favored Acmeism's emphasis on clarity, brevity, and detachment, and he focused most often on the subject of art, particularly music, architecture, and classical literature. His theme is often the poet's place in and relationship to history, as revealed in his first work associated with his Acmeist period, *Kamen* (1913; *Stone*, 1973).

The Acmeists were labelled as decadent in the 1920s, and in the post-revolutionary era Mandelstam suffered first as an exile and later as a political prisoner. Yet in his poetry he remained uncompromising in his political and artistic values. He was arrested in 1934 for writing an epigram on Stalin, which resulted in his exile and declining health. Arrested again in 1938, he was sent to a labor camp, where he perished in the late 1930s.

Kamen (1913; *Stone*, 1973).

Kamen is the first collection of poetry by Mandelstam, written under the influence of the Acmeist principles that guided his early work. It is one of the outstanding works associated with the movement and reflects Mandelstam's deeply personal understanding of history and his emulation of classical poetics. Chronologically arranged, it charts the poet's development toward the Acmeist ideal of clarity in poetic expression, conveyed in Mandelstam's characteristically detached, impersonal tone. The poems often center on great works of architecture, and the poetic persona associates himself with the builders of the great medieval cathedrals of Europe, particularly Notre Dame in Paris.

Encompassing the individual artist, the realm of art, and the importance of the artistic vocation, *Kamen* portrays the poet's confrontation with the cosmic loneliness and emptiness that threaten him. Armed with the knowledge that he and his quest represent a certain foil to those forces, he praises the architectural splendor of the world's great cities, relating the way in which stones, like words, allow the craftsman to leave his mark on the earth.

➹•➷

Further Reading

Akhmatova, Anna. *The Complete Poems of Anna Akhmatova.* Translated by Judith Hemsche-
    meyer; edited and introduced by Roberta Reeder. Somerville, Mass.: Zephyr Press, 1990.
Amert, Susan. *In a Shattered Mirror: The Later Poetry of Anna Akhmatova.* Stanford, Calif.:
    Stanford University Press, 1992.
Brown, Clarence. *Mandelstam.* Cambridge, England: Cambridge University Press, 1973.
Cavanagh, Clare. *Osip Mandelstam and the Modernist Creation of Tradition.* Princeton, N.J.:
    Princeton University Press, 1995.
Chukovskaia, Lidiia Korneevna. *The Akhmatova Journals.* Translated from Russian by Milena
    Michalski and Sylva Rubashova; poetry translated by Peter Norman. 1st American ed. New
    York: Farrar, Straus, and Giroux, 1994-.
Davies, Jessie. *Anna of All the Russias: The Life of Anna Akhmatova (1889-1966).* Liverpool,
    England: Lincoln Davies, 1988.
Driver, Sam N. *Anna Akhmatova.* New York: Twayne Publishers, 1972.
Eshelman, Raoul. *Nikolaj Gumilev and Neoclassical Modernism: The Metaphysics of Style.*
    Frankfurt am Main: Peter Lang, 1993.
Gumilev Centenary Symposium (1986: University of Strathclyde). *Nikolaj Gumilev, 1886-*
    1986: Papers from the Gumilev Centenary Symposium Held at Ross Priory, University of
    Strathclyde, 1986. Edited by Sheelagh Duffin Graham. Oakland, Calif.: Berkeley Slavic
    Specialties, 1987.
Haight, Amanda. *Anna Akhmatova: A Poetic Pilgrimage.* New York: Oxford University Press,
    1976.
Hayward, Max, and Leopold Labedz, eds. *Literature and Revolution in Soviet Russia, 1917-*
    1962. Westport, Conn.: Greenwood Press, 1976.
Hingley, Ronald. *Nightingale Fever: Russian Poets in Revolution.* New York: Knopf, 1981.

Kaun, Alexander. *Soviet Poets and Poetry*. Berkeley, Calif.: University of California Press, 1943.

Mickiewicz, Denis. "Toward a Definition of Acmeism." Issued as a supplement to *Russian Language Journal* (spring 1975).

Mirsky, D. S. *A History of Russian Literature*. New York: Knopf, 1949.

Muchnic, Helen. *From Gorky to Pasternak*. New York: Random House, 1961.

Nayman, Anatoly. *Remembering Anna Akhmatova*. Translated by Wendy Rosslyn. New York: Henry Holt, 1991.

Poggioli, Renato. *The Poets of Russia, 1890-1930*. Cambridge, Mass.: Harvard University Press, 1960.

Polivanov, Konstantin, comp. *Anna Akhmatova and Her Circle*. Translated from Russian by Patricia Beriozkina. Fayetteville, Ark.: University of Arkansas Press, 1994.

Reeder, Roberta. *Anna Akhmatova: Poet and Prophet*. 1st ed. New York: St. Martin's Press, 1994.

Rosslyn, Wendy. *The Prince, the Fool, and the Nunnery: The Religious Theme in the Early Poetry of Anna Akhmatova*. Amersham, England: Avebury, 1984.

Rosslyn, Wendy, ed. *The Speech of Unknown Eyes: Akhmatova's Readers on Her Poetry*. 2 vols. Nottingham, England: Astra Press, 1990.

Sampson, Earl D. *Nikolay Gumilev*. Boston: Twayne Publishers, 1979.

Slonim, Marc. *Modern Russian Literature from Chekhov to the Present*. New York: Oxford University Press, 1953.

Strakhovsky, Leonid I. *Craftsmen of the Word: Three Poets of Modern Russia   Gumilyov, Akhmatova, Mandelstam*. Cambridge, Mass.: Harvard University Press, 1949.

ACTORS' STUDIO. *See* GROUP THEATER, United States

ADAMISM. *See* ACMEISM

AESTHETICISM/DECADENCE
England, 1880s-1900

A child of Victorian England, Aestheticism — or Decadence as it is also referred to — was a reaction to the brash optimism born of lucrative colonial expansion and the Industrial Revolution's creation of a large middle class, whose prudish morality was viewed as an unnatural restriction on human nature. Within this Victorian complacency several seeds of discontent were planted during mid-century. The utilitarianism of John Stuart Mill (1806-1873), who proclaimed standards of morality based on an act's promotion of the happiness of the majority; the socialist fervor of author and artisan William Morris (1834-1896), who was representative of the Pre-Raphaelite brotherhood and its break with traditional artistic canons; and the Romanticism of writers such as poet John Keats (1795-1821): all would serve as inspiration for Aestheticism. "Beauty is

13

truth, truth beauty — that is all/Ye know on earth, and all ye need to know," Keats would write in his "Ode on a Grecian Urn"(1820). The only role of Beauty, as represented by art, should be to generate a momentary intensity of feeling on the part of the viewer, "aesthetes" maintained. In contrast to more pragmatic, socially conservative Victorian strictures, Aestheticism's adherents maintained that true works of art need serve no useful end, political, economic, morally uplifting, or otherwise.

Proclaiming "Ars gratia artis" — Art for art's sake — as its central tenet, Aestheticism found its major purveyor in Walter Pater (1839-1894), an Oxford don whose central concern lay in reevaluating the role of art within everyday life. Pater's pessimistic, melancholy outlook — inspired by the realization that life is fleeting and one should therefore live each moment intensely — would imbue the works of many of his followers, who included poets Algernon Charles Swinburne (1837-1909) and Arthur Symons (1865-1945). William Butler YEATS (*see* ABBEY THEATER and MODERNISM, England and Ireland) was also attracted to the movement because its liberal attitudes meshed with his own early interests in mysticism. While Aestheticism would gain adherents in both France and the United States, it remained primarily a British phenomenon.

Irish poet, playwright, and novelist Oscar Wilde (1854-1900) can be viewed as the consummate aesthete: his flamboyant nature, his penchant for a clever turn of phrase over a substantive remark characterized much of the aesthetic oeuvre. Likewise, Wilde's widely read *The Picture of Dorian Gray* (1890) remains a classic aesthetic work, with its densely scattered *bon mots*, gothic overtones, and underlying perversity. The verse of Swinburne, whose *Poems and Ballads* (1866) would be condemned by fellow Victorians as morally bankrupt and sexually deviant, also rebelled against the rigid moral and spiritual essence of the age through lush, intricate structures, classical imagery, and emphasis upon form over content.

The Aesthetic movement would gain a broad following through two periodicals: *The Savoy,* which was edited by Symons, and *The Yellow Book.* The latter, with its sensual, sinuous illustrations penned by artist Aubrey Beardsley (1872-1898), published many works by such aesthetes as Wilde, Max Beerbohm (1872-1956), and Ernest Dowson (1867-1900) during its three-year run following 1894.

Increasingly, social censure against Wilde's personal and professional notoriety began to cast a shadow on the aesthetic movement as a whole; William Gilbert (1836-1911) and Arthur Sullivan's (1842-1900) 1881 play *Patience* blatantly mocked the effeminate affectations and excessive sensitivity of British aesthetes. Alfred, Lord Tennyson (1809-1892) also rallied against what he viewed as an unfortunate decline in artistic — and moral — standards, writing sarcastically that, in the aesthetic view, "The filthiest of all paintings painted well/ Is mightier than the purest painted ill." In 1895 the sensational aspects of Wilde's trial, conviction, and imprisonment for engaging in homosexual acts sparked a groundswell of disapprobation of decadent art. While the movement had faded from the literary scene by the turn of the century, its stress on novelty and originality of form over content would greatly influence Modernist writers in their efforts to reevaluate both time-honored areas of exploration and concentration and traditional literary forms.

✦●✦

Further Reading

Beckson, Karl E. *London in the 1890s: A Cultural History*. New York: W. W. Norton, 1992.

Bloom, Harold, ed. *Oscar Wilde*. New York: Chelsea House, 1985.

———. *Walter Pater*. New York: Chelsea House, 1985.

Brake, Laurel. *Walter Pater*. Plymouth, England: Northcote House, 1994.

Erickson, Donald H. *Oscar Wilde*. Boston: Twayne Publishers, 1977.

Fletcher, Ian, ed. *Decadence and the 1890s*. London: Arnold, 1979.

Iser, Wolfgang. *Walter Pater, the Aesthetic Moment*. Translated by David Henry Wilson. Cambridge; New York: Cambridge University Press, 1987.

Kooistra, Lorraine J. *The Artist as Critic: Bitextuality in Fin-de-siècle Illustrated Books*. Aldershot, England: Scolar Press; Brookfield, Vt.: Ashgate Pub., 1995.

Monsman, Gerald C. *Walter Pater*. Boston: Twayne Publishers, 1977.

Pine, Richard. *The Thief of Reason: Oscar Wilde and Modern Ireland*. Dublin: Gill & Macmillan, 1995.

Pittock, Murray. *Spectrum of Decadence: The Literature of the 1890s*. London; New York: Routledge, 1993.

Raby, Peter, ed. *The Cambridge Companion to Oscar Wilde*. Cambridge; New York: Cambridge University Press, 1997.

Sinfield, Alan. *The Wilde Century: Effeminacy, Oscar Wilde and the Queer Moment*. London: Cassell, 1994.

Sturgis, Matthew. *Passionate Attitudes: The English Decadence of the 1890s*. London: Macmillan, 1995.

Symons, Arthur. *A Study of Walter Pater*. London: C. J. Sawyer, 1932.

Weir, David. *Decadence and the Making of Modernism*. Amhert, Mass.: University of Massachusetts Press, 1995.

AFRO-CUBANISM
Cuba, 1920s-1930s

The Afro-Cubanists, inspired in part by the NÉGRITUDE writers in Paris and coeval with the HARLEM RENAISSANCE movement in the United States, drove perhaps the most important cultural-literary movement in Cuba before the 1959 revolution. The movement began during the 1920s as a few white Latin American intellectuals, such as

15

Puerto Rican poet Luis Palés Matos (1898-1959) and Cubans Emilio Ballagas (1910-1954) and José Zacarías Tallet (1893-?), began to explore African contributions to Caribbean culture.

Not unlike the CUBISTS in Europe, these early Afro-Cubanists sought to revitalize an increasingly urban and industrial Latin America with African narrative and musical forms and themes. They also wished to create national identities. Alejo Carpentier (1904-1980) spent eleven years in Paris, where he was acquainted with André BRETON and others in the French SURREALIST group. There he presented a cantata, *La passion noire*, in 1932. Cuban ethnologist Fernando Ortiz (1881-1969) provided an important source for some Afro-Cubanists with his two-part study of African cultures in the Caribbean, *Hampa Afrocubana: los negros brujos* (1906; Afro-Cuban Underworld: The Black Witch Doctors) and *Hampa Afrocubana: los negros esclavos* (1916; Afro-Cuban Underworld: Black Slaves). Early proponents attempted to convey spirituality, anti-rationalism, spontaneity, and musicality in literature, particularly poetry, by mimicking formal elements in African songs, dances, and narratives. Carpentier's first novel, *!Écue-Yamba-Ó!* (1933; God Be Praised), written in Ñañigo, is an example.

Before long, some African Caribbean writers, responding in part to the oppressed conditions of blacks in the Caribbean, enriched the trend—most notably, Nicolás Guillén (1902-1989) from Cuba, whose poetry was marked by political awareness and social conscience and influenced by African dances, as well as by various MODERNIST tendencies. Critics often note Guillén's collections of poetry, *Songoro Cosongo* (1931) and *West Indies Ltd.* (1934), as most significant to the movement. Other writers associated with Afro-Cubanism include Ramón Guirao (1908-1949), Amadea Roldán (1900-), José Antonio Fernández de Castro (1897-1951), Juan Marinello (1898-1977), and Uruguayan Ildefonso Pereda Valdés (1899-?).

❖•❖

Further Reading

Adams, Sara Katherine. "Color, Gender, and National Identity: The Body as Metaphor in Nicolas Guillen." Master's thesis, University of Minnesota, 1993.

Boulware-Miller, Patricia Kay. "Nature in Three Negrista Poets: Nicolas Guillen, Emilio Ballagas and Luis Pales Matos." Ph.D. diss., University of California, Berkeley, 1978.

Brotherston, G. "The Genesis of America: Alejo Carpentier." In *The Emergence of the Latin American Novel*. Cambridge, England: Cambridge University Press, 1977.

Callaloo 10, 2 (spring 1987). Special Nicolás Guillén issue.

Cudjoe, S. R. "Back into History and Mankind." In *Resistance and Caribbean Literature*. Athens, Ohio: Ohio University Press, 1980.

Franco, Jean. "Back to the Roots: II. The Indian, the Negro, the Land." In *The Modern Culture of Latin America: Society and the Artist*. New York: Praeger, 1967.

González Echevarría, Roberto. *Alejo Carpentier, the Pilgrim at Home.* Austin, Tex.: University of Texas Press, 1990.

González-Pérez, Aníbal. "Luis Palés Matos." In *Latin American Writers.* Edited by C. A. Solé. Vol. 2. New York: Scribner, 1989.

Harss, Luis, and Barbara Dohmann. "Alejo Carpentier, or the Eternal Return." In *Into the Mainstream: Conversations with Latin-American Writers.* New York: Harper & Row, 1967.

Harvey, Sally. *Carpentier's Proustian Fiction: The Influence of Marcel Proust on Alejo Carpentier.* London: Tamesis, 1994.

Irish, J. A. George. *Nicolas Guillen: Growth of a Revolutionary Consciousness.* New York: Caribbean Research Center, Medgar Evers College, City University of New York, 1990.

Kubayanda, Josaphat Bekunuru. *The Poet's Africa: Africanness in the Poetry of Nicolas Guillen and Aime Cesaire.* New York: Greenwood Press, 1990.

Moore, Robin Dale. "Nationalizing Blackness: Afrocubanismo and Artistic Revolution in Havana." Ph.D. diss., University of Texas at Austin, 1995.

Scott, Daniel Marcellus. "To Dream a New World: 'Race,' Reality and Surreality in Cesaire, Carpentier and Harris." Ph.D. diss., University of Illinois at Urbana-Champaign, 1992.

Smart, Ian. *Nicolas Guillen, Popular Poet of the Caribbean.* Columbia, Mo.: University of Missouri Press, 1990.

Webb, Barbara J. *Myth and History in Caribbean Fiction: Alejo Carpentier, Wilson Harris, and Edouard Glissant.* Amherst, Mass.: University of Massachusetts Press, 1992.

White, Clement A. *Decoding the Word: Nicolas Guillen as Maker and Debunker of Myth.* Miami: Ediciones Universal, 1993.

Williams, Lorna V. *Self and Society in the Poetry of Nicolas Guillen.* Ann Arbor, Mich.: UMI Books on Demand, 1994.

AGITPROP THEATER
United States, 1930s

Founded on the watchwords of *agit*ation and *prop*aganda, Agitprop Theater first emerged in New York City in 1930 under the auspices of the Prolet-Bühne, a German-speaking labor group. Agitprop dramas, consequently, are distinguished by their strident documentation of the growing labor movement, a cause to which many left-wing dramatists devoted themselves at the expense of the purely literary aspects of playwriting. The most notable exception to this is Clifford ODETS's drama *WAITING FOR LEFTY*, produced by the American GROUP THEATER in 1935.

See also PROLETARIAN LITERATURE.

❖•❖

Further Reading

Bodek, Richard. *Proletarian Performance in Weimar Berlin: Agitprop, Chorus, and Brecht.* Columbia, S.C.: Camden House, 1997.

Brown, Lorraine, ed. *Liberty Deferred and Other Living Newspapers of the 1930s Federal Theatre Project.* Fairfax, Va.: George Mason University Press, 1989.

Bull, John. *New British Political Dramatists.* New York: Grove Press, 1984.

Dietz, Robert J. *The Operatic Style of Marc Blitzstein in the American "agit-prop" Era.* Ph.D. diss., University of Iowa, 1970.

Goorney, Howard, and Ewan MacColl, eds. *Agit-Prop to Theatre Workshop: Political Playscripts, 1930-50.* Manchester, England: Manchester University Press, 1986.

Gurganus, Albert E. *The Art of Revolution: Kurt Eisner's Agitprop.* Columbia, S.C.: Camden House, 1986.

Tehranchian, Hassan. *Agitprop Theatre: Germany and the Soviet Union.* Ph.D. diss., New York University, 1982.

Trumbull, Eric Winship. *Musicals of the American Workers' Theatre Movement, 1928-1941: Propaganda and Ritual in Documents of a Social Movement.* Ph.D. diss., University of Maryland at College Park, 1991.

25th Street Theatre. *Paper Wheat: The Book.* Saskatoon, Canada: Western Producer Prairie Books, 1982.

AGRARIANS, THE. *See* FUGITIVES/AGRARIANS

ALIANZA POPULAR REVOLUCIONARIA AMERICANA (APRA). *See* APRISMO

ALL-CHINA ANTI-AGGRESSION FEDERATION OF WRITERS AND ARTISTS (Chung-hua Ch'üan-kuo Wen-i-Chieh K'ang-ti Hsie-hui) China, 1938-1945

The All-China Anti-Aggression Federation of Writers and Artists was officially launched in 1938, shortly after the outbreak of the Sino-Japanese War. LAO SHÊ, an immensely popular and theretofore apolitical writer, was unanimously elected president by the Communist and leftist groups who conceived the Federation. By so doing, these groups ensured the immediate success of their patriotic coalition, for Lao Shê enjoyed good relations with virtually all the major literary circles. Ever since the dissolution of the LEAGUE OF LEFT-WING WRITERS, the Communist Party had advocated literary unity and a widespread call to national defense literature; the Anti-Aggression Federation was the fruition of this impulse and thrived until the end of the Sino-Japanese War in 1945.

Nearly all notable Chinese writers, regardless of political orientation, rallied in support of the Federation. The original group of forty-five executive members included KUO MO-JO (*see* CREATION SOCIETY), MAO TUN (*see* LITERARY RESEARCH ASSOCIATION), Feng Hsüeh-feng (1903-1976), Ting Ling (1904-1986), and Hsia Yen (1900-1995).

"Let writers serve the armed forces" and "let writers go to the villages" became the Federation's ubiquitous slogans, and swift production of propagandistic literature became the norm. Lao Shê typified this wartime phenomenon by abandoning realistic fiction — the foundation upon which his reputation rested — and adopting traditional verse and dramatic forms to sustain the didactic message of common unity against the enemy. Virtually none of the works of Lao Shê or others which stemmed from this period can be considered anything more than ephemeral exercises in political folk writing. The one outstanding exception is Lao Shê's Lo-t'o Hsiang-tzu (1936-37; *Rickshaw Boy*, 1945; also translated as both *Rickshaw: The Novel Lo-t'o Hsiang Tzu*, 1979, and *Camel Xiangzi*, 1981). Although composed and serialized immediately before the war, this work was not published in book form until 1939. Like the majority of works conceived under the auspices of the Anti-Aggression Federation, *Lo-t'o Hsiang-tzu* signals the futility of individual, and the necessity of collective, action; yet, it remains free of the idealistic dogmatism of its counterparts.

Ironically, the Federation's resounding success was due not to Lao Shê's continuation of the high achievement of *Lo-t'o Hsiang-tzu* — for he wrote only one, forgettable patriotic novel during the war years — but to his resolute leadership and implementation of Communist literary policy. His presidency of the Federation and eventual, party-line retraction of *Lo-t'o Hsiang-tzu*'s dark message remain striking examples of the immense impact politics exerted on the course that Chinese literature took during the middle decades of the twentieth century.

❧•❦

Lao Shê (1899-1966), Chinese novelist, short-story writer, and dramatist.

Lao Shê's writing career commenced when he left China in 1924 to teach Mandarin in London, England. There he acquainted himself with the novels of Charles DICKENS (*see* REALISM, England), whose methods of characterization he attempted to emulate in his first work of fiction, *Lao Chang-ti che-hsüeh* (1926; Lao Chang's Philosophy), regarded as the first comic novel to arise from the MAY FOURTH MOVEMENT. Before returning to China in 1930, Lao Shê completed two more novels, *Chao Tzu-yüeh* (1927; Chao Tzu-yüeh) and *Erh Ma* (1929; *Ma and Son*, 1980). All of these works were serialized in the LITERARY RESEARCH ASSOCIATION's *Hsiao-shuo yüeh-pao*; thus his reputation as a fine comic novelist preceded him. Although Lao Shê continued to publish humorous novels during the early 1930s, his concern for the individual's struggle against societal injustices eventually dominated his fiction, culminating in his masterpiece, *Lo-t'o Hsiang-tzu*. Although he never equalled the power and richness of this work, Lao Shê became one of the most prolific Chinese writers of the twentieth century. His life ended abruptly and inexplicably during the Cultural Revolution when, after enduring seemingly unwarranted harrassment by Red Guards, he committed suicide in 1966.

Lo-t'o Hsiang-tzu (1936-37; *Rickshaw Boy*, 1945; also translated as both *Rickshaw: The Novel Lo-t'o Hsiang Tzu*, 1979, and *Camel Xiangzi*, 1981).

Set in Peking during the mid-1930s, *Lo-t'o Hsiang-tzu* is the story of Hsiang-tzu, an ambitious village orphan who believes that individual striving and the opportunities offered by the city will bring him happiness and financial success. After working for three years as an agency rickshaw puller, he saves enough money to purchase his own carriage. Numerous setbacks arise, gradually defeating Hsiang-tzu's optimism and destroying his moral code of conduct. The novel closes on a solemn note with the protagonist's abject demise. However, Lao Shê's indirect advocacy of collective effort to eradicate the social and economic evils which engulfed Hsiang-tzu provides a poignant, meliorative outlook to the work, one which has helped earn *Lo-t'o Hsiang-tzu* a place among the most important serious works of modern Chinese fiction. As translator Jean M. James has written, Lao Shê "wrote the novel the left wing so conspicuously failed to produce, a novel concerned with a worker and his life and the society in which he lived, worked, suffered, failed, and, finally, died."

➔•◄

Further Reading

Akiyama, Yōko. *Ting Ling: Purged Feminist*. Translated by Yōko Akiyama and Larry Taub. Tokyo: Femintern Press, 1974.

Chen, Rose Jui Chang. *Realism and Allegory in the Early Fiction of Mao Tun*. Bloomington, Ind.: Indiana University Press, 1986.

Feuerwerker, Yi-tai Mei. *Ding Ling's Fiction: Ideology and Narrative in Modern Chinese Literature*. Cambridge, Mass.: Harvard University Press, 1982.

Gálik, Marián. *Mao Tun and Modern Chinese Literary Criticism*. Wiesbaden, Germany: F. Steiner, 1969.

Great Modern Chinese Writers: Lu Xun, Guo Moruo, Mao Dun and Ba Jin. Beijing: Foreign Languages Press, 1988.

Hsia, C. T. "Lao Shê." In his *A History of Modern Chinese Fiction*. 2nd ed. New Haven, Conn.: Yale University Press, 1971.

Kao, George, ed. *Two Writers and the Cultural Revolution: Lao Shê and Chen Jo-hsi*. Hong Kong: Chinese University Press, 1980.

Lao Shê. *Lao Shê*. 3 vols. Nanjing, Jiangsu, China: Yilin Press, 1992.

———. "How I Came to Write the Novel *Camel Hsiang-tzu*." *Chinese Literature* 11 (1978): 59-64.

Ling, Ting. *I Myself Am a Woman: Selected Writings of Ding Ling*. Tani E. Barlow and Gary J. Bjorge, eds. Boston: Beacon Press, 1989.

Munro, S. R. *The Function of Satire in the Works of Lao Shê*. Singapore: Chinese Language Center, Nanyang University, 1977.

Průšek, Jaroslav. *Three Sketches of Chinese Literature*. Prague: Oriental Institute in Academia, 1969.

Roy, David Tod. *Kuo Mo-jo: The Early Years*. Cambridge, Mass.: Harvard University Press, 1971.

Słupski, Zbigniew. *The Evolution of a Modern Chinese Writer: An Analysis of Lao Shê's Fiction, with Biographical and Bibliographical Appendices*. Prague: Oriental Institute in Academia, 1966.

Towery, Britt. *Lao Shê, Master Storyteller: China's People's Artist*. Waco, Tex.: Tao Foundation, 1994.

Vohra, Ranbir. *Lao Shê and the Chinese Revolution*. Harvard East Asian Monographs, No. 55. Cambridge, Mass.: East Asian Research Center, Harvard University, 1974.

Wang, Te-wei. *Fictional Realism in Twentieth-Century China: Mao Dun, Lao She, Shen Congwen*. New York: Columbia University Press, 1992.

AMERICAN DECONSTRUCTION. *See* YALE SCHOOL

ANDALUSIAN LEAGUE (al-'Usba al-Andalusiyya)
Brazil, 1932-c. 1940s

The poets of both the Andalusian League and the SOCIETY OF THE PEN are often referred to as the *al-Mahjar* (also rendered *Mahgar*; emigré) *al-Amriki* poets, because members of both groups emigrated from Lebanon to the Americas, where they flourished. However, as many scholars point out, the works and visions of these two groups of writers are nearly as different as their respective adopted countries. As might be expected, the poetry of both groups involve themes of homesickness and alienation. But while the Society of the Pen was formed in New York under the leadership of Khalīl Gibrān (1883-1931), the Andalusian League was centered in São Paulo, Brazil. The Andalusian League was less revolutionary in poetic innovation and cosmopolitan experimentation than the North American poets, while more concerned with supporting Arabic literature and nationalism in Latin America. The name of the group itself — reminiscent of medieval Moorish settlements in Spain — suggests its traditional leanings.

The chief proponents of the Andalusian League were Ilyās Farhāt (1893-?), Shafīq al-Ma'lūf (1905-), his brother, Fawzī al-Ma'lūf (1889-1930), and Rashīd Salīm Khūrī (1887-?), also known as al-Sha'ir al-Qarawī. All had emigrated to Brazil from Lebanon in the 1910s and 1920s and together founded the league in order to strengthen their efforts toward producing Arabic poetry in an alien, though not so inhospitable, culture. As indicated by the above dates, Fawzī's contribution to the group was considerable, but posthumous. His was the most progressive poetry in the group, incorporating romantic elements with bleak, imaginary, and often macabre imagery and detail, as in his best-known poem, "'Ala bisāt al-rīh" (On the Carpet of the Wind; first published in 1929 in the journal *al-Muqtataf*). Farhāt is often considered the most staunchly political and traditional of the League poets, but his work gradually shifted to a more directly personal and romantic poetry.

The Andalusian League poets were influenced by the romanticism of the *DIWAN* SCHOOL OF POETS in Egypt, but conflated this romanticism with the classical Arabic literary tradition. Most of their work displays varying degrees of innovation and conservatism in form and diction, as well as content, in which feelings of homesickness and nostalgia are often confounded by awareness of the reality of the French occupation of Lebanon. The work of Gibrān too had a strong impact on Farhāt and the al-Ma'lūfs, but to a large extent they renounced the New York poets' attempt at universalization of theme, experience, and form, and neglect of Arabic tradition.

⇛•⇚

Further Reading

Badawi, Muhammad M. *A Critical Introduction to Modern Arabic Poetry.* Cambridge, England: Cambridge University Press, 1975.
Jayyusi, Salma Khadra. *Trends and Movements in Modern Arabic Poetry.* Vol. I. Leiden, Netherlands: E. J. Brill, 1977.

ANGLO-IRISH LITERARY MOVEMENT. *See* ABBEY THEATER; IRISH RENAISSANCE

ANGRY PENGUINS. *See* ERN MALLEY HOAX

ANGRY YOUNG MEN
England, 1950-1960

The "Angry Young Men" was a collective term used to describe a group of young writers in England whose work mirrors their disenchantment with their country and its political, social, and economic circumstances immediately after World War II. Members included Kingsley AMIS, John Braine (1922-), John OSBORNE, Alan Sillitoe (1928-), John WAIN, Arnold Wesker (1932-), and Colin Wilson (1932-). While they had no formal manifesto, their work is imbued with what one critic describes as "the sound of human voices in despair." Most had earlier enjoyed the advantages provided by a post-World War I socialistic system which had made them a part of a new and well-educated middle class, but at the end of a second and devastating war they found themselves, in the 1950s, to be on the fringes of a society in which political and intellectual power still remained embedded in the cultural mores of the upper classes. Their works represent for the most part the tragicomic irony of their situation and disillusion with a social system which seemed a mockery of what it claimed to be. These writers sought to change—or at least to attempt to represent—that system in their literature, drama, and poetry.

The literature of the times had been gradually changing since before the turn of the century, and in the early years of the twentieth century, innovational creativity in both arts and letters was holding firm; Virginia WOOLF and James JOYCE (*see* MODERNISM, England and Ireland) had changed the form and structure of the novel, T. S. ELIOT (*see* MODERNISM, England and Ireland), the IMAGISTS, and other poets had developed new ways to create and to criticize poetry, and George Bernard SHAW (*see* EDWARDIAN LITERATURE) had developed a new literature of the drama which was designed to be read as well as performed, and which made strong, satiric social comment. Encouraged by the precedent set by older and more established writers, the writers of the fifties were continuing to work for change from outworn literary and social traditions. Literature, drama, and poetry with symbolic and psychological references and often with ironic and comic overtone provided mechanism for the depiction of an England that these writers felt was politically and intellectually bankrupt.

The theme of alienation, while not new in creative work, was given new emphasis. The plays and novels of these writers depict characters in desperate attempts to establish identity in a disordered and impersonal world; they are antiheroes, "inarticulate . . . in an otherwise articulate world." Combined with themes of frustration and despair are often aspects of the comic, as characters laugh or make light of the absurdity of situations without resolution. While it is the view of some critics that the work of the Angry Young Men gives more emphasis than is necessary to negative values, tends to be weak in character and situation development, and lacks the quality of writing of the more established writers, the best of these works have clearly presented the attitudes of the fifties and have a vitality and an energy which cannot be disclaimed.

By the sixties the times were quickly changing and new critical and creative views were shaping the work of British writers. Cultural, social, and political mores were being affected by a technology that provided a more efficient global communication system which gave rise to investigation of varied value systems. A state of Cold War between major political systems precipitated the threat of nuclear war. To anger was added uncertainty, and this was to lead writers into other channels of creativity for representation of what the poet W. H. Auden (1907-1973) called "the age of anxiety."

❖•❖

Amis, Kingsley (1922-1995), English novelist and poet.

Amis's first success was with the novel *LUCKY JIM* (1954), a comic work about the trials of Jim Dixon, a middle-class university instructor. Amis continued to present the satiric aspects of society in his novels *That Uncertain Feeling* (1955) and *Take a Girl Like You* (1960), which are exposures of what he called a redoubtable and "phony aesthetic cant." Known for his remarkable versatility and humor, Amis also has written supernatural, religious, mystery, and espionage fiction. However, his early and comic prose was to become more conservative and shows in his later work and criticism. Amis was also associated with a group of writers who called themselves members of THE MOVEMENT and were noted for their anthology of poetry, *New Lines* (1956).

Lucky Jim (1954).

The novel follows the misadventures of history lecturer Jim Dixon. Jim's antiestablishment stance and his humorous intellectual perambulations within the bureaucratic bumblings of an academic world he grew to despise depict the reality of a mediocre education system designed for the masses. The bitter but comic overtones of the novel expose what Amis defines as the "academic racket."

❖•❖

Osborne, John (1929-1994), English dramatist.

In younger years, Osborne worked as a journalist, then as an actor, after which he began writing plays. He became well known with *LOOK BACK IN ANGER* (1957), which popularized the Angry Young Men. Another notable work is *Luther* (1961), Osborne's historical drama about Martin Luther and his break with Roman Catholicism and his new religion of protest against it. Along with *Look Back in Anger*, it uses anger as an instrument of conflict, out of which a better life may be constructed. Other plays are *The Entertainer* (1957), a depiction of a music hall entertainer, and *Epitaph for George Dillon* (1958), about a sorry young man in a sorry marriage. His autobiography, *A Better Class of Person*, was published in 1981.

Look Back in Anger (1957).

Osborne's landmark play represents the life of an "angry" character, Jimmy Porter, whose reaction against his working-class background makes him bitter toward his upper-class wife, Alison. A clash of values destroys the ability to communicate, despite strong sexual attraction between them. They become estranged until Alison, unable to understand Jimmy's anger and frustration until her own attitudes about herself are finally broken down, finally identifies with his pain and desolation and brings about reconciliation.

❧•❧

Wain, John (1925-), English critic, novelist, and poet.

From 1945 to 1947 Wain coedited *Mandrake*, a magazine that served as a forum for the Angry Young Men. In 1953 he presented a radio series, "First Reading," that brought more recognition to the movement. His works include *The Contender* (1958), *A Traveling Woman* (1959), and a collection of short stories entitled *Nuncle and Other Stories* (1960), but he is best known for his early novel *HURRY ON DOWN* (1953). Wain has also to his credit a collection of verses in *Poems— 1949-1979* (1981), and, with Amis, was connected to The Movement.

Hurry on Down (1953).

This, Wain's first novel, depicts the character Charles Lumley who, in rejection of the failed expectations of his own middle class and, in an attempt to identify with the working class, becomes a menial laborer. In the end, ironically, his goal is to detach himself from both classes, to avoid responsibility entirely and to find his own social "neutrality."

❧•❧

Further Reading

Allsop, Kenneth. *The Angry Decade: A Survey of the Cultural Revolt of the Nineteen-Fifties*. London: P. Owen, 1958. (2nd ed.: Wendover, England: J. Goodchild, 1985)

Amis, Kingsley. *Memoirs*. New York: Summit Books; London: Hutchinson, 1991.

Anderson, Michael John. *Anger and Detachment: A Study of Arden, Osborne, and Pinter*. London: Pitman, 1976.

Banham, Martin. *Osborne*. Edinburgh, Scotland: Oliver & Boyd, 1969.

Bendau, Clifford P. *Colin Wilson: The Outsider and Beyond*. San Bernardino, Calif.: Borgo Press, 1979.

Bradford, Richard. *Kingsley Amis*. London; New York: E. Arnold, 1989.

Carter, Alan. *John Osborne*. 2nd ed. New York: Barnes & Noble, 1973.

Denison, Patricia D., ed. *John Osborne, a Casebook*. New York: Garland, 1996.

Feldman, Gene, and Max Gartenberg, eds. *The Beat Generation and the Angry Young Men*. New York: Citadel Press, 1958.

Ferrar, Harold. *John Osborne*. New York: Columbia University Press, 1973.

Fussell, Paul. *The Anti-Egotist: Kingsley Amis, Man of Letters*. New York; Oxford, England: Oxford University Press, 1994.

Gardner, Philip. *Kingsley Amis*. Boston: Twayne, 1981.

Gohn, Jack Benoit. *Kingsley Amis, a Checklist*. Kent, Ohio: Kent State University Press, 1976.

Goldstone, Herbert. *Coping with Vulnerability: The Achievement of John Osborne*. Washington, D.C.: University Press of America, 1982.

Hayman, Ronald. *John Osborne*. New York: Ungar, 1972.

Hinchliffe, [sic] Arnold P. *John Osborne*. Boston: Twayne, 1984.

Jacobs, Eric. *Kingsley Amis, a Biography*. London: Hodder and Stoughton, 1995.

McDermott, John. *Kingsley Amis, an English Moralist*. New York: St. Martin's Press, 1989.

Moseley, Merritt. *Understanding Kingsley Amis*. Columbia, S.C.: University of South Carolina Press, 1993.

Northouse, Cameron, and Thomas P. Walsh. *John Osborne, a Reference Guide*. Boston: G. K. Hall, 1974.

O'Connor, William Van. *The New University Wits and the End of Modernism*. Carbondale, Ill.: Southern Illinois University Press, 1963.

Rabinovitz, Rubin. *The Reaction Against Experiment in the English Novel, 1950-60*. New York: Columbia University Press, 1967.

Salwak, Dale. *John Wain*. Boston: Twayne, 1981.

————. *Kingsley Amis, a Reference Guide*. Boston: G. K. Hall, 1978.

————. *Kingsley Amis, Modern Novelist*. Lanham, Md.: Barnes & Noble, 1992.

Salwak, Dale, ed. *Kingsley Amis in Life and Letters*. Houndmills, Basingstoke, Hampshire, England: Macmillan, 1990.

Simons, Judy. "The 'Angry Young Men'." In *Dictionary of Literary Biography*. Vol. 15, *British Novelists, 1930-1959*. Edited by Bernard Oldsey. Detroit: Gale Research, 1983.

Skovmand, Michael, and Steffen Skovmand, eds. *The Angry Young Men: Osborne, Sillitoe, Wain, Braine, Amis*. Copenhagen: Akademisk Forlag, 1975.

Taylor, John Russell. *John Osborne, "Look Back in Anger," a Casebook*. London: Macmillan, 1975.

Trussler, Simon. *John Osborne*. Harlow, England: Longmans for the British Council and the National Book League, 1969.

————. *The Plays of John Osborne, an Assessment*. London: Gollancz, 1969.

ANTA GROUP. *See* MODERNISMO

ANTI-AGGRESSION FEDERATION. *See* ALL-CHINA ANTI-AGGRESSION FEDERATION OF WRITERS AND ARTISTS

ANTIEVASION GROUP (Anti-Evasão)
Cape Verde, 1960s-c. 1975

The Antievasion Group consisted of activist Cape Verdean writers dissatisfied with the subdued tenor of the competing *CLARIDADE* literary movement. Antievasion writing, a form of militant poetry directed at the Portuguese dictatorship which controlled Cape Verde, had its origins in the politico-literary exhortations of Amílcar Cabral (1924-1973) during the 1950s. Eventually, with Ovidio Martins's (1928-) poem "Anti-Evasão" (1962), the new movement gained prominence and contributed to the creation of verse openly defiant of colonial rule. Cape Verde's attainment of independence in 1975 signalled the end of the Antievasion Group as it was originally conceived.

⤖•⤛

Further Reading

Chabal, Patrick. *Amílcar Cabral: Revolutionary Leadership and People's War.* Cambridge, England: Cambridge University Press, 1983.

Chilcote, Ronald H. *Amílcar Cabral's Revolutionary Theory and Practice: A Critical Guide.* Boulder, Colo.: L. Rienner, 1991.

McCulloch, Jock. *In the Twilight of the Revolution: The Political Theory of Amílcar Cabral.* London: Routledge & Kegan Paul, 1983.

ANTI-HERO. *See* **ANGRY YOUNG MEN, EXISTENTIALISM, MODERNISM, NATURALISM, NEW NOVEL, REALISM**

ANTI-JAPANESE FICTION. *See* **ALL-CHINA ANTI-AGGRESSION FEDERATION OF WRITERS AND ARTISTS**

ANTROPOFAGIA GROUP
Brazil, 1930s

The MODERNIST manifesto for Brazilian writers was made public in February of 1922 during a weeklong festival of the arts called A Semana de Arte Moderna (Modern Art Week). Its doctrine was to incorporate the new creative literary movements which had taken hold in Europe since the turn of the century, while at the same time to concentrate upon things Brazilian for content, i.e., its language and dialects, and its native rituals, ethics, and mores. The major literary exponent of the concept of poetic Antropofagia was Oswald de ANDRADE, who was joined by Mario de Andrade (1893-1945; no relation to Oswald) and Raul Bopp (1898-1994). These men were early to embrace the Modernist movement and were among its most ardent enthusiasts. Along with other things Brazilian, they were fascinated by the rituals of jungle cannibalism as practiced by many native tribes in South America. The name Antropofagia (cannibalism) was given to the group of writers who often incorporated the subject in their work. The concept helped to perpetuate the earlier tenets of the new manifesto. Bopp is best known for his long poem *Cobra Norato* (1931; Norato the Snake), which poetically expresses the mystery, terror, and excitement of Brazilian jungle life. Oswald de Andrade is said to be among the first and most influential of the Brazilian Modernists.

⭑•⭒

Andrade, Oswald de (1890-1954)
Brazilian poet, novelist, dramatist, and critic.

An early rebel against the traditional, Andrade visited pre-World War I Europe and became intellectually excited by the new movements in arts and letters which were underway there. When he returned to Brazil, he became involved in the Semana de Arte Moderna and began an enthusiastic campaign among Brazilian writers to adopt some of the new tenets of Modernism. One of his major works, *Pau Brasil* (1925; Brazil Wood), presents his innovative ideas about what he termed "primitive" poetry, which is free of earlier poetic form and which contains new verse, metric, and rhyme schemes. In an essay for the journal *Revista de antropofagia,* begun in 1928, Andrade exalted cannibalism as a metaphorical device to be used by his fellow poets, when he enjoined them to "devour" European literary Modernism and then to disgorge it as literary product. Other work includes *Memorias sentimentais de Jodo Miramar* (1924), a prose fiction work which departs from traditional narrative line and has been compared to fiction by James JOYCE (*see* MODERNISM, England and Ireland); his play *O rei da vela* (1937), cited as a "vanguard work of Brazilian theater"; and a volume of collected poems, *Poesias reunidas* (1945). His work is inventive and innovative, speaks to his country and his heritage with merit and distinction, and has enjoyed recent revaluation by world literary scholars.

✦•✦

Further Reading

Bandeira, Manuel. *A Brief History of Brazilian Literature.* Washington, D.C.: Pan American Union, 1958.

Bishop, Elizabeth, and Emanuel Brasil, eds. *An Anthology of Twentieth-Century Brazilian Poetry.* Middletown, Conn.: Wesleyan University Press, 1972.

Martins, Wilson. *The Modernist Idea: A Critical Survey of Brazilian Writing in the Twentieth Century.* New York: New York University Press, 1970.

Nist, John A. *The Modernist Movement in Brazil: A Literary Study.* Austin, Tex.: University of Texas Press, 1967.

APOLLO SCHOOL OF POETS
Egypt, 1930s

The aim of the Apollos was to introduce a "new [and modern] sensibility" to Egyptian readers which was, in fact, based on an earlier critical perspective. Their journal, *Apollo,* was published by Ahmad Zakī Abū Shādī (1892-1955); they called themselves romantics and their poetry demonstrates a neo-romantic mode. The two best known of the group were Ibrāhīm Nājī (1893-1953) and 'Ali Mahmūd Tāhā (1902-1949).

A variety of poetic agenda influenced the Egyptian poetry of the early twentieth century. There remained still the retention of a long and forceful Arabic heritage, but there had also developed a vital curiosity about modern concepts which had come out of the

United States and Europe. Moreover, many Egyptian writers were absorbing the ideas of writers from other parts of the Middle East, namely Syrians who had fled their homeland because of civil unrest and who now made up a large part of Egyptian culture. These circumstances made for the growth and prevalence of specifically Arabic modern literature; this included elements of the classical, the traditional, and the current techniques — depending on individual point of view. It is of interest, however, that a conservative neoclassicism remained alive, indeed prevalent, and writers of this persuasion remained resistant to change until well into the twentieth century. This last is the mindset which the Apollos rejected; their work shows more the influence of Khalīl Mutrān (1872-1945) and the *DIWAN* SCHOOL of the twenties, whose admonition was that poets should be free to choose whatever strategies were most successful in the expression of experience and their sentiments, much like the British romanticists of the nineteenth century, and not remain stultified by ancient and outmoded tradition. The desire of the Apollos was, for the most part, to keep these earlier poetic notions alive while adding to their own work the later concepts of twentieth-century MODERNISM, thus giving new dimension to the poetry of their time. As the century drew to a close, Egyptian writers had suffered the restriction of war and political upheaval. While there has been some experimentation with new form shown in the poetry, it does not show as much innovation as do the works of drama and of fiction.

⇒•⇐

Further Reading

Badawi, M. M. *A Critical Introduction to Modern Arabic Poetry*. Cambridge, England: Cambridge University Press, 1975.

Jayyusi, S. *Trends and Movements in Modern Arabic Poetry*. Leiden, Netherlands: Brill, 1977.

Ostle, R. C., ed. *Studies in Modern Arabic Literature*. Warminster, England: Aris & Phillips, 1975.

Semah, D. *Four Egyptian Literary Critics*. Leiden, Netherlands: Brill, 1974.

APRISMO
Latin America and Peru, 1930s

The Aprismo (Alianza Popular Revolucionaria Americana — APRA) movement advocated the political and economic emancipation of Latin America from the United States. Politician Victor Raúl Haya de la Torre (1895-1979) founded APRA in 1923 while exiled in Mexico from his native Peru. His manifesto, *Por la emancipación de América Latina*, appeared in 1927 and called for Latin American governments to relinquish land to native Latin Americans and to vitalize Latin American industries through

29

national, rather than international, ownership and control. Though a political movement, Aprismo found many supporters among writers and other members of the Latin American intelligentsia, such as Ciro Alegría (1909-1967) of Peru, whose epic novel *El mundo es ancho y ajeno* (1941; *Broad and Alien Is the World,* 1941) reflects his active membership in APRA. It depicts conflicts between Indian communality and exploitative landowners. José Carlos Mariátegui (1895-1930), a journalist who later founded his own socialist movement as well as the journal *Amauta*, was another early adherent. Haya de la Torre and Mariátegui were both influenced by Manuel González Prada (1848-1918), and became associated with the Peruvian journal *Claridade*. APRA held influence with non-ruling classes in Peru, and eventually came to occupy seats in Peru's cabinet and senate, until Manuel Odría's coup in 1948. Under Augusto B. Leguía's (1863-1932) dictatorship, suspected or actual members of APRA were often imprisoned or exiled.

✤•✦

Further Reading

Franco, Jean. "Back to the Roots: I. Cultural Nationalism." In *The Modern Culture of Latin America: Society and the Artist*. New York: Praeger, 1967.

Herring, Hubert. "Twentieth-Century Peru." In *A History of Latin America: From the Beginnings to the Present*. New York: Knopf, 1968.

Higgins, James. "The Birth of a Literature (c.1915-c.1941)." In *A History of Peruvian Literature*. London: F. Cairns, 1987.

ARBETARDIKTARE. *See* PROLETARIAN WRITERS

ARBUJAD. *See* SOOTHSAYERS MOVEMENT

ARPAS CUBANAS GROUP
Cuba, 1900s

Members of the Arpas Cubanas Group included poet Dulce María Borrero (1883-1945), who published one volume of poetry, *Horas de mi vida* (1912), and the literary/cultural critical works *La poesia a traves del color* (1912) and *El matrimonio en Cuba* (1912); critic and poet José Manuel Carbonell (1880-?), now best known for a literary history, *Evolución de la cultura cubana* (1928); poet Enrique Hernández Miyares (1859-1915), who was interested in MODERNISMO and associated with Julián del Casal (1863-1893); and poet Francisco Díaz Silveira (1871-1924). The group is named after a collection of their poetry published in 1904.

❖•❖
Further Reading

"Borrero, Dulce María." In *Dictionary of Twentieth-Century Cuban Literature*. Edited by Julio A. Martínez. New York: Greenwood Press, 1990.

Jones, Willis Knapp. "Enrique Hernández Miyares." In *Spanish-American Literature in Translation: A Selection of Poetry, Fiction, and Drama Since 1888*. New York: Ungar, 1963.

"Navarro Luna, Manuel." In *Dictionary of Twentieth-Century Cuban Literature*. Edited by Julio A. Martínez. New York: Greenwood Press, 1990.

Parker, William Belmont. "José Manuel Carbonell." In his *Cubans of Today*. New York: Putnam's Sons, 1919.

ASAS '50. *See* GENERATION OF THE 1950s

ASSEMBLY OF THE MEN OF GOOD TASTE
Pakistan, 1939-1940s

The Assembly of the Men of Good Taste was a small Pakistani movement that began in 1939, some eight years before the southeast Asian country was first declared a dominion and later a republic of the British Commonwealth. It existed as an open forum for Pakistani writers of every sort. The well-known poet Miraji (1912-1949), though not an original founder, became the Assembly's primary leader.

❖•❖
Further Reading

Patel, Geeta. "Miraji: Poetry in Motion." Ph.D. dissertation, Columbia University, 1996.

Sadiq, Mohammed. *Twentieth Century Urdu Literature: A Review*. Baroda, India: Padmaja Publications, 1947.

ASSOCIATION FOR REAL ART. *See* OBERIU

ASSOCIATION OF ANGOLA'S NATIVE SONS
Angola, 1950s

A multiracial, anticolonial group of writers, the Association of Angola's Native Sons was founded in 1950 and represented the first serious literary movement in Angolan literature. Through its journals, *Mensagem* and *Cultura*, the Association decried Portuguese rule and called for the self-determination of Angola by its native population. Several of the writers associated with the movement risked exile by joining the activist political group Movement of the Liberation of Angola, such as Viriato da Cruz (1928-1973), António Jacinto (1924-), and António Agostinho Neto (1922-1979).

✦•✦

Further Reading

"Angola's New Boss Antonio Neto, the Poet President." *Drum* (June 1976): 20-21.

Burness, Donald. "Angolan Writing: An Arm of Liberation." In *Critical Perspectives on Lusophone Literature from Africa*. Edited and with an introduction by Donald Burness. Washington, D.C.: Three Continents Press, 1981.

Enekwe, Ossie Onuora. "The Legacy of Antonio Agostinho Neto." *Okike: An African Journal of New Writing* 18 (June 1981): 1-6.

Khazanov, A. M. *Agostinho Neto*. Translated from the Russian by Cynthia Carlile. Moscow: Progress Publishers, 1986.

SWAPO, Information and Publicity Dept. *Comrade Dr. Agostinho Neto, Namibia Mourns You*. Luanda, Angola: The Dept., 1979?

ATHENEUM OF YOUTH
Mexico, 1910-1930s

The revolution of 1910 and the overthrow of dictator Portfirio Diaz (1830-1915) combined to bring change in Mexico; there occurred a reinterpretation of Mexican economic, political, and social standings and a desire among literary intellectuals for release from the rational positivist influence of Auguste Comte (1798-1857), the French philosopher whose theories had dominated Mexican thought for over half a century. The Atheneum of Youth was a group of young writers whose specific aims were to present, in their works, a realistic view of their people and their culture, a return to traditional spiritual values, and a new experimentation in the form of both their fiction and their poetry.

Major writers in the group were Antonio Caso (1883-1946) and Enrique González Martínez (1871-1952); Alfonso Reyes (1889-1959) and José Vasconcelos (1882-1959) were two of the most prolific writers. Having helped to form the group, Reyes returned to Spain after receiving a law degree to absorb what he could of Spanish culture and aesthetics. There he developed into the "brilliant humanist and stylist" which gave him reputation upon his return to Mexico in 1926. He is most remembered for *Vision de Anahuac, 1579* (1917), a reevaluation of ancient Aztec culture in Mexico; a long, dramatic poem, *Ifigenia cruel* (1924); and *Letras de la Nueva Espana* (1948). Vasconcelos was an ardent exponent of political and social reform, and worked arduously for mass education and for stabilization of the Mexican economy under the new regime of President Alvaro Obregon (1880-1928). When he became frustrated by the political system in 1929, he exiled himself for ten years. During this time he wrote the philosophical tracts *Etica* (1932) and *Estética* (1936) and his five-volume autobiography: *Ulises criollo* (1935), *La tormenta* (1936), *El desastre* (1938), *El preconsulado* (1939), and *La flama* (1959). These works express his passionate preoccupation with Latin American people and their Hispanic roots, his disillusion with a Mexican political system patterned after that of the United States, and his hope for a rebirth of Latin American political and aesthetic spirit.

❧•❧

Further Reading

González Peña, Carlos. *History of Mexican Literature,* 3rd ed. Translated by Gusta Barfield Nance and Florence Johnson Dunstan. Dallas: Southern Methodist University Press, 1968.

Henríquez Ureña, Pedro. *Literary Currents in Hispanic America*. Cambridge, Mass.: Harvard University Press, 1945.

Larson, Ross. *Fantasy and Imagination in the Mexican Narrative*. Tempe, Ariz.: Center for Latin American Studies, Arizona State University, 1977.

Martínez, José Luis. *The Modern Mexican Essay*. Translated by H. W. Hilborn. Toronto: University of Toronto Press, 1965.

AUTHENTICISM
Poland, 1930s

Polish literary "authenticism" developed in reaction to such earlier literary movements in that country as the SKAMANDER GROUP and the loosely incorporated CRACOW AVANT-GARDE, both of which had made up the residuals of the YOUNG POLAND group and which had marked the links between early nineteenth-century romanticism and the beginning of MODERNIST trends in central Europe. Skamander poets celebrated Polish life with traditional form, in ordinary language which was relatively free of political implication. Authenticists, on the other hand, wished to express in their work more emphasis on contemporary political and social problems as they then related to the common, working people of their country. The events which led to World War II caused the Authenticists and later literary Modernists to take a "catastrophic" philosophical view of the world and of the coming Holocaust. The major exponents of the movement were Stanisław Czernik (1899-1969) and the poet and essayist Jan Bolesław Ożóg (1913-1991).

❧•❧

Further Reading

Carpenter, Bogdana. *The Poetic Avant-Garde in Poland, 1918-1939*. Seattle: University of Washington Press, 1983.

Kridl, Manfred. *A Survey of Polish Literature and Culture*. Rev. ed. New York: Columbia University Press, 1965.

Miłosz, Czesław. *A History of Polish Literature*. New York: Macmillan, 1969.
Peterkiewicz, Jerzy, and Burns Singer, eds. *Five Centuries of Polish Poetry, 1450-1970*. 2nd ed.
    London: Oxford University Press, 1970.

AUTOMATIC WRITING. *See* **SURREALISM, France**

B

BEAT GENERATION
United States, 1950s-1960s

Founded in the early 1950s by such avant-garde writers as Jack KEROUAC, Allen GINS-
BERG, and William S. BURROUGHS, the Beat Generation arose initially as an artistic protest against conventional mores and established literary theory and technique. As the
movement grew and flourished for nearly two decades, its tenets melded with those of a
burgeoning counterculture who championed free love, mystical self-awareness, musical innovation, drug experimentation, and outspoken opposition to affluent living,
political repression, and authoritarian control. Kerouac, the movement's principal novelist and spokesperson, seized upon the word "beat" in 1948 in an effort to define a
nascent generation of writers and thinkers who, disillusioned, peripatetic, and rebellious, were in many ways affined with the LOST GENERATION of the 1920s. The term
connoted concepts of the beatific as well as the beaten down and impoverished, for the
Beats laid claim to both personal spirituality and a brotherly concern for the common
individual.

Although two first novels, Kerouac's *The Town & the City* (1950) and John Clellon
Holmes's (1926-) *Go* (1952; republished as *The Beat Boys*, 1959), represent the earliest
works documenting the Beat scene, it was not until Kerouac and other writers had
shifted from New York's Greenwich Village to San Francisco's North Beach that the
movement gained national attention. There Ginsberg, with the aid of Michael McClure
(1932-), Gary Snyder (1930-), Philip Whalen (1923-), Philip Lamantia (1927-), and
Kenneth Rexroth (1905-1982), organized a widely celebrated poetry reading in 1955.
Ginsberg's spellbinding performance of "Howl" ignited a host of new writers eager to
break with literary convention. The ensuing publication of *HOWL AND OTHER POEMS*
(1956) and Kerouac's novel *ON THE ROAD* (1957) served to identify the Beats as controversial intellectuals in direct conflict with reigning literary tastes. Burroughs's devastat-

35

ing depiction of modern civilization's depravity in *NAKED LUNCH* (1959) further isolated the Beat movement from mainstream literature. In retaliation, Beat writers across the country developed over the next decades literally hundreds of small circulation magazines — including such eventually successful commercial ventures as *The Village Voice* — to create ample outlets for visually and verbally experimental or controversial expression.

Despite the absence of any overt, detailed manifesto to guide them, the Beats shared a vociferous repudiation of American materialism and moral hypocrisy; an immense thirst for experience; a belief that true artistic expression is synonymous with the spontaneous outpouring of the mind; and a profound aversion of the types of literature fostered by NEW CRITICISM as well as longstanding European literary models. Their distrust of the sociopolitical atmosphere engendered by the Cold War was so considerable that many critics aligned the Beats with the ANGRY YOUNG MEN of postwar England.

Bold stylistic and structural experimentation typifies the best works of the movement. Kerouac, influenced in part by the technique of AUTOMATIC WRITING (*see* SURREALISM, France), flaunted conventions of careful composition and wrote what he termed "spontaneous prose." In his "Essentials of Spontaneous Prose" (1959), he negated the practices of procuring the proper word, selecting and organizing the essential details, and revising and refining. Exemplifying his method, he summarized, "the best writing is always the most painful personal wrung-out tossed from cradle warm protective mind." Ginsberg, employing this technique in his poetry, subsumed a variety of free-verse forms while attempting to reproduce the natural rhythms of informal speech. Burroughs, in turn, emulated the techniques of collage painters through his "cut-up" method to produce fractured prose which suggested the STREAM-OF-CONSCIOUSNESS (*see* MODERNISM, England and Ireland) processes of the human mind.

Literary predecessors of the Beat Generation include William Blake (1757-1827), Walt Whitman (1819-1892), Guillaume APOLLINAIRE (*see* CUBISM), Federico García Lorca (1898-1936), Arthur RIMBAUD (*see* SYMBOLISM, France), Vladimir MAYAKOVSKY (*see* CUBO-FUTURISM), Henry MILLER (*see* LOST GENERATION), and William Carlos Williams (1883-1963). Nonliterary influences are perhaps even more wide-ranging and include hipster argot, the improvisational jazz of Lester Young (1909-1959) and Charlie Parker (1920-1955), Oriental watercolor painting, the action painting techniques of Jackson Pollock (1912-1956), and the beliefs and rituals of Zen Buddhists and Indian peyote cults.

The recipients of Beat influence are equally extensive; both the NEW YORK SCHOOL and the BLACK MOUNTAIN POETS owe a considerable debt to the groundbreaking advances of Beat poetry. In addition, the Beat Generation exerted an enormous impact on such writers as Norman Mailer (1923-) and Ken Kesey (1935-), on such musicians as Bob Dylan (1941-), The Beatles, and The Rolling Stones, and on such public causes as the international peace and social protest movements. Given the continued production of works by Ginsberg and Burroughs, as well as that from lesser-known Beat writers who helped comprise the SAN FRANCISCO SCHOOL, including Snyder, Lawrence Ferlinghetti (1919-), Gregory Corso (1930-), and Diane DiPrima (1934-), the movement has far from exhausted itself. For many years scorned as inept and superfluous by the most powerful literary critics, the Beat writers are now accorded a vital, revolutionary position in American literary history.

⇒•⇐

Burroughs, William S. (1914-1997)
American novelist, short-story writer, nonfiction writer, essayist, scriptwriter, and editor.

Burroughs is best known for his early mentorship of Ginsberg and Kerouac, and for his authorship of *Naked Lunch* (1959). In contrast to nearly all the Beat writers, Burroughs adopted a highly impersonal, violent, and tragic style to undergird his sustained vision of a hopelessly decadent and enslaved society. One of the most experimental writers of the twentieth century, Burroughs abandons a consistent point of view in favor of fragmented narration that relies on a series of "cut ups" and "fold ins" to extend theme and meaning in his surreal, quasi-science fiction.

Naked Lunch (1962; first published in Paris as *The Naked Lunch*, 1959).

A nightmarish satire of American life, *Naked Lunch* is Burroughs's most acclaimed work. On a literal level the novel recounts, through the persona of William Lee, Burroughs's fourteen-year addiction to morphine. On a higher level, however, the protagonist's story of addiction — "necessarily brutal, obscene, and disgusting," according to Burroughs — functions as a dark metaphor for the plight of all humanity, irrevocably controlled by illusory pleasures and institutional power. Like other seminal works of the Beat Generation, *Naked Lunch* marked a radical departure from literary tradition in both form and style. Drawing upon a wide variety of genres, including the Gothic tale, early science fiction, the detective novel, and pornography, Burroughs composed his narrative through a "cut-up" technique which permitted the arbitrary juxtaposition of "routines." These routines consisted of surreal episodes, scene descriptions, dialogues, and pastiches of imagery which, when joined, resembled the collages of close friend and iconoclastic painter Brion Gysin (1916-1986). Despite the novel's excessive profanity, brutality, and concern with psychosexual disorder, *Naked Lunch* survived an early obscenity trial and thus greatly extended the bounds of fictional experimentation for coming generations of writers.

37

❖•❖

Ginsberg, Allen (1926-1997), American poet, memoirist, and essayist.

A leading member of the Beat Generation, Ginsberg is among the most prominent and celebrated poets in contemporary America. Through countless public readings of his poems, beginning with "Howl" in 1955, he greatly advanced poetry as a popular, oral medium as well as a vehicle for social protest. More importantly to literary circles, he exploded traditional genre strictures through shocking language, haunting imagery, elongated thoughts and rhythms, and an explicit exploration of society's most heavily guarded subjects. Ginsberg's reception of the National Book Award for *The Fall of America* in 1974 heralded the commencement of official recognition of the Beat writers by the literary establishment.

Howl and Other Poems (1956).

Ginsberg's first and most successful collection of poetry, *Howl* is the foremost work among the Beat poets. Ginsberg dedicated the title poem — a blistering jeremiad on the evils of an obsessively commercial and military Cold War society — to Walt Whitman (1819-1892) and to the three principal contemporary influences on his writing: Kerouac, Burroughs, and Neal Cassady (1926-1968). The poem is divided into three sections. The first confesses the sins and exonerates the souls of "angelheaded hipsters," a young generation of the lost, disenchanted, drug-addicted, and depraved. The second attributes to Moloch, an ancient, insatiable Phoenician god whom Ginsberg equates with mindless technology and bureaucracy, the source of the stagnation, disease, and death that pervades the hipster's culture. The third symbolically sanctifies Carl Solomon (1928-), a fellow writer who convinced Ginsberg in 1949, when they shared time as psychiatric patients, that the necessary role of the poet was that of social outcast and visionary prophet. Hailing the possibility of redemption for Ginsberg's fallen America, the brief "Footnote to Howl," inspired by readings in Zen Buddhism, asserts the holiness of all that exists. Immediately following publication by fellow Beat Lawrence Ferlinghetti, the enormously influential owner of City Lights Books, *Howl and Other Poems* was officially seized and banned for obscenity. Following a long court battle, the work was released to the public and has since become one of the most popular works of poetry in American literary history.

❖•❖

Kerouac, Jack (1922-1969), American novelist and poet.

The central figure of the Beat Generation, Kerouac led through most of his career a rambling, bohemian lifestyle that informs nearly all his work. Although numerous literary friends appear under guise in his largely autobiographical, experimental fiction,

Neal Cassady is considered the most influential personality within Kerouac's circle. From Cassady's indomitable spontaneity and anarchic individualism, Kerouac derived not only the character Dean Moriarty but the structure and style of his best-known novel, *On the Road* (1957), as well. While *On the Road* circulated in manuscript as an underground classic from 1951 to 1957, Kerouac completed a dozen novels in which he perfected his technique of loosely structured, spontaneous writing first theorized by Cassady in an unrecovered, 23,000-word letter. The best of these works include *The Dharma Bums* (1958), *The Subterraneans* (1958), and *Visions of Cody* (1973). Kerouac shared with other Beat writers an erotic, lyrical style and a dominant interest in drug-altered consciousness, bop music, Zen Buddhism, antimaterialism, and personal freedom.

On the Road (1957).

Considered the manifesto of the Beat Generation, *On the Road* is Jack Kerouac's best-known, though probably not his greatest, fictional work. Completed in 1951, the novel remained unpublished for several years due to Kerouac's refusal to alter his feverishly executed, intentionally unrevised manuscript. Because of Kerouac's eventual acquiescence, the work—though startlingly innovative—exhibits only a fraction of the spontaneous writing technique Kerouac utilized in his other novels. Episodic in structure, *On the Road* focuses on the transcontinental odysseys and deteriorating relationship of the narrator, Sal Paradise (Kerouac), and a self-educated former hustler, Dean Moriarty (Neal Cassady). Unable to establish roots for any period of time, Moriarty remains faithful only to himself and his continual search for IT!, a beatific, timeless experience which he occasionally glimpses through improvisational solos of jazz musicians, sexual release, drug-induced hallucination, and the faces and voices of those he meets on the road. Through a lyrical style and unrestricted inclusion of thoughts and images as they presented themselves, Kerouac championed the Beats' social veneration of uninhibited experience and literary admiration of organic, unstructured thought.

❖•❖

Further Reading

Bartlett, Jeffrey. *One Vast Page: Essays on the Beat Writers, Their Books, and My Life, 1950-1980*. Berkeley, Calif.: J. Bartlett, 1991.

Bartlett, Lee, ed. *The Beats: Essays in Criticism*. Jefferson, N.C.: McFarland, 1981.

Cassady, Carolyn. *Off the Road: My Years with Cassady, Kerouac, and Ginsberg*. New York: Penguin Books, 1991.

Charters, Ann. *Scenes Along the Road: Photographs of the Desolation Angels, 1944-1960*. Jefferson, N.C.: McFarland, 1970.

Charters, Ann, ed. *Dictionary of Literary Biography*. Vol. 16, *The Beats: Literary Bohemians in Postwar America*. Detroit: Gale Research Co., 1983.

Christopher, Tom. *Neal Cassady: A Biography*. Vashon, Wash.: T. Christopher, 1995.

Cook, Bruce. *The Beat Generation*. New York: Portents/Gotham Book Mart, 1971.

Di Prima, Diane. *Memoirs of a Beatnik*. New York: Traveller's Companion, 1969.

Donaldson, Scott, ed. *"On the Road": Text and Criticism*. New York: Penguin, 1979.

Dorfner, John J. *Kerouac: Visions of Rocky Mount*. Raleigh, N.C.: Cooper Street Publications, 1991.

Feldman, Gene, and Max Gartenberg, eds. *The Beat Generation and the Angry Young Men*. New York: Citadel Press, 1958.

Foster, Edward Halsey. *Understanding the Beats*. Columbia, S.C.: University of South Carolina Press, 1992.

Gifford, Barry, and Lawrence Lee. *Jack's Book: An Oral Biography of Jack Kerouac*. New York: St. Martin's Press, 1994.

Ginsberg, Allen. *Howl* (anniversary edition), *Original Draft Facsimile, Transcript & Variant Versions, Fully Annotated by Author, With Contemporaneous Correspondence, Account of First Public Reading, Legal Skirmishes, Precursor Texts & Bibliography*. Edited by Barry Miles. New York: Harper & Row, 1986.

Gysin, Brion, and William S. Burroughs. *Oeuvre Croissée*. 1976. Republished as *The Third Mind*. New York: Viking, 1978.

Hickey, Morgen. [sic] *The Bohemian Register: An Annotated Bibliography of the Beat Literary Movement*. Metuchen, N.J.: Scarecrow Press, 1990.

Hipkiss, Robert A. *Jack Kerouac: Prophet of the New Romanticism*. Lawrence, Kans.: Regents Press of Kansas, 1976.

Hunt, Tim. *Kerouac's Crooked Road: Development of a Fiction*. Hamden, Conn.: Archon Books, 1981.

Jarvis, Charles E. *Visions of Kerouac*. 3rd ed. Lowell, Mass.: Ithaca Press, 1994.

Jones, James T. *A Map of Mexico City Blues: Jack Kerouac as Poet*. Carbondale, Ill.: Southern Illinois University Press, 1992.

Knight, Arthur, and Kit Knight. *The Beat Diary*. California, Pa.: A. and K. Knight, 1977.

Kramer, Jane. *Allen Ginsberg in America*. New York: Random House, 1969.

Lee, A. Robert, ed. *The Beat Generation Writers*. London: Pluto Press, 1996.

McDarrah, Fred W. *Beat Generation: Glory Days in Greenwich Village*. New York: Schirmer Books, 1996.

McNally, Dennis. *Desolate Angel: Jack Kerouac, the Beat Generation, and America*. New York: Random House, 1979.

Maynard, John Arthur. *Venice West: The Beat Generation in Southern California*. New Brunswick, N.J.: Rutgers University Press, 1991.

Merrill, Thomas F. *Allen Ginsberg*. New York: Twayne, 1969.

Mottram, Eric. *Allen Ginsberg in the 60's*. Brighton, England: Unicorn Bookshop, 1972.

———. *William Burroughs: The Algebra of Need*. London: M. Boyars, 1977.

Nicosia, Gerald. *Memory Babe: A Critical Biography of Jack Kerouac*. Berkeley, Calif.: University of California Press, 1983.

Odier, Daniel. *The Job: Interviews with William Burroughs*. New York: Grove Press, 1974.

Parkinson, Thomas, ed. *A Casebook on the Beat*. New York: Crowell, 1961.

Perry, Paul. *On the Bus: The Complete Guide to the Legendary Trip of Ken Kesey and the Merry Pranksters and the Birth of the Counterculture*. Forewords by Hunter S. Thompson and Jerry Garcia. Edited by Michael Schwartz and Neil Ortenberg. 1st ed. New York: Thunder's Mouth Press, 1990.

Phillips, Lisa. *Beat Culture and the New America, 1950-1965*. New York and Paris: Whitney Museum of American Art in association with Flammarion, 1995.

Rigney, Francis J., and L. Douglas Smith. *The Real Bohemia: A Sociological and Psychological Study of the Beats*. New York: Basic Books, 1961.

Stephenson, Gregory. *The Daybreak Boys: Essays on the Literature of the Beat Generation*. Carbondale, Ill.: Southern Illinois University Press, 1990.

Sterritt, David. *Mad to Be Saved: The Beats, the '50s, and Film*. Carbondale, Ill.: Southern Illinois University Press, 1998.

Tonkinson, Carole, ed. *Big Sky Mind: Buddhism and the Beat Generation*. New York: Riverhead Books, 1995.

Tytell, John. *Naked Angels: Kerouac, Ginsberg, Burroughs*. New York: Grove Press, 1991.

———. *Naked Angels: The Lives and the Literature of the Beat Generation*. New York: McGraw-Hill, 1976.

Watson, Steven. *The Birth of the Beat Generation: Visionaries, Rebels, and Hipsters, 1944-1960*. 1st ed. New York: Pantheon Books, 1995.

Wilcox, Fred. *Chasing Shadows*. Sag Harbor, N.Y.: Permanent Press, 1996.

BEHESTS. *See* **ZAVETY SCHOOL**

BERGSON, Henri Louis (1859-1941)
French philosopher

Best known as the originator of "process philosophy," which focuses on motion and change, rather than stasis, Henri Louis Bergson was born into a Polish Jewish family and educated first at the Lycée Condorcet, Paris, then at the École Normale Supérieure in preparation for an academic career. He married a cousin of Marcel PROUST's (*see* MODERNISM, France), Louise Neuburger, in 1891. Until 1921 he taught at the Collège de France. Though his health was worsening, he served from 1921 to 1926 as president of the Commission for Intellectual Cooperation of the League of Nations. Bergson won the Nobel Prize for literature in 1927. On a personal level, his reflections led him to Catholicism, which he saw as the fulfillment of Judaism; he wrote "I would have become a convert, had I not foreseen for years a formidable wave of anti-Semitism about to break upon the world. I wanted to remain among those who tomorrow were to be persecuted." When the Nazis, occupying France, required Jews to register in 1940, Bergson, though offered an exemption, left his sickbed and did so.

In opposition to the criticism of Immanuel Kant (1724-1804), the positivism of Auguste Comte (1798-1857), and the philosophies of history of Georg Hegel (1770-1831) and Herbert Spencer (1820-1903), Bergson challenged the contemporary philosophical status quo — as well as literary NATURALISM's tenets — by expounding a doctrine of dynamism, which takes into account both natural laws and human free will, rather than mechanism, which depends only on natural laws. Man was a spiritual being guided by two ways of knowing: the scientific and analytical which enables him to understand and manipulate the material environment, and the intuitive, which transcends the material world and enables him to create art and experience the mystical.

Most significant was Bergson's work on time and the human conscious experience of time — duration — laid out in *MATIÈRE ET MÉMOIRE: ESSAI SUR LA RELATION DU CORPS À L'ESPRIT* (1896; *Matter and Memory*, 1911). In *L'Evolution créatrice* (1907; *Creative Evolution*, 1911), Bergson expounds on the *élan vital*, the vital impulse, a creating God. Other works include his doctoral dissertation *Essai sur les données immédiates de la conscience* (1889; *Time and Free Will: An Essay on the Immediate Data of Consciousness*, 1910), *Le Rire: Essai sur la significance du comique* (1900; *Laughter: An Essay on the Meaning of the Comic*, 1911), *Introduction à la metaphysique* (1903; *An Introduction to Metaphysics*, 1913), *Les Deux Sources de la morale et de la religion* (1932; *The Two Sources of Morality and Religion*, 1935), and *La Pensée et le mouvant* (1934; *The Creative Mind*, 1946).

By the turn of the century Bergson's ideas had led to vigorously debated controversy throughout Europe and the United States. His influence was great on twentieth-century thought in metaphysics, psychology, and epistemology. Among those indebted to his work are: in philosophy, Alfred North Whitehead (1861-1947); in religion, the leaders of the Roman Catholic revival of the early twentieth century; and in literature, Proust, Henry JAMES (*see* REALISM, United States), Joseph CONRAD (*see* MODERNISM, England and Ireland), William FAULKNER (*see* MODERNISM, United States), Samuel BECKETT (*see* THEATER OF THE ABSURD), Harold PINTER (*see* COMEDY OF MENACE), and the EXISTENTIALISTS.

✦•✦

Matière et mémoire: Essai sur la relation du corps à l'esprit (1896; *Matter and Memory*, 1911).

Bergson's most influential work has had lasting literary impact in its discussion of duration. As opposed to the scientific definition of time, Bergson postulated that the human perception of memory and time passing was an active, rather than passive, function of the human mind, and that "real" time is that which we subjectively experience. Dealing with the nature of human perception of time and memory, Bergson

42

employed the most recent scientific and medical findings to bolster his arguments, though these contemporary source data were usually later superseded. The work also explores the relationship between the body and the mind, previously thought to be working in conjunction with each other on every level. Through an examination of aphasia, for example, a language impairment caused by brain lesions, Bergson concluded that man possesses a mind that operates independently of the body.

⇛•⇚

Further Reading

Antliff, Mark. *Inventing Bergson: Cultural Politics and the Parisian Avant-Garde*. Princeton, N.J.: Princeton University Press, 1993.

Burwick, Frederick, and Paul Douglass, eds. *The Crisis in Modernism: Bergson and the Vitalist Controversy*. Cambridge, England; New York: Cambridge University Press, 1992.

Chevalier, Jacques. *Henri Bergson*. New York: The Macmillan Company, 1928.

Deleuze, Gilles. *Bergsonism*. Translated by Hugh Tomlinson and Barbara Habberjam. New York: Zone Books, 1988.

————. "Movement-Image: Commentaries on Bergson." In *Writing in a Modern Temper: Essays on French Literature and Thought in Honor of Henri Peyre*. Edited by Mary Ann Caws. Saratoga, Calif.: Anma Libri, 1984.

Dodson, George Rowland. *Bergson and the Modern Spirit; an Essay in Constructive Thought*. London: The Lindsay Press, 1914.

Douglass, Paul. *Bergson, Eliot, and American Literature*. Lexington, Ky.: University Press of Kentucky, 1986.

Gallagher, Idella J. *Morality in Evolution: The Moral Philosophy of Henri Bergson*. The Hague: Nijhoff, 1970.

Gillies, Mary Ann. *Henri Bergson and British Modernism*. Montreal: McGill-Queen's University Press, 1996.

Grogin, R. C. *The Bergsonian Controversy in France, 1900-1914*. Calgary, Canada: University of Calgary Press, 1988.

Gunter, Pete A. Y. "Henri Bergson." In *Founders of Constructive Postmodern Philosophy*. Edited by David Ray Griffin, John B. Cobb, Jr., Marcus P. Ford, Pete A. Y. Gunter, and Peter Ochs. Albany, N.Y.: State University of New York Press, 1993.

Hanna, Thomas, ed. *The Bergsonian Heritage*. New York: Columbia University Press, 1962.

Kolakowski, Leszek. *Bergson*. Oxford, England; New York: Oxford University Press, 1985.

Kumar, Shiv Kumar. *Bergson and the Stream of Consciousness Novel*. London: Blackie, 1962.

Lacey, A. R. *Bergson*. London; New York: Routledge, 1989.

MacWilliam, John. *Criticism of the Philosophy of Bergson*. Edinburgh: T. & T. Clark, 1928.

Maurois, André. "Henri Bergson." In his *From Proust to Camus: Profiles of Modern French Writers*. Translated by Carl Morse and Renaud Bruce. Garden City, N.Y.: Doubleday & Company, 1966.

Moore, F. T. C. *Bergson: Thinking Backwards*. Cambridge, England; New York: Cambridge University Press, 1996.

Pilkington, Anthony Edward. *Bergson and His Influence: A Reassessment*. Cambridge, England; New York: Cambridge University Press, 1976.

Russell, Bertrand. *The Philosophy of Bergson*. Cambridge, England: Published for "The Heretics" by Bowes and Bowes, 1914. Reprint, Folcroft, Pa.: Folcroft Library Editions, 1971.

Santayana, George. *Winds of Doctrine: Studies in Contemporary Opinion*. New York: C. Scribner's Sons, 1912. Reprint, 1926.

BERLIN ENSEMBLE (Berliner Ensemble)
Germany, 1949-1950s

A theatrical company, Berlin Ensemble was started by Bertolt BRECHT (*see* EPIC THEATER) and his contemporaries in East Berlin in 1949, when Brecht accepted an offer there to be production director; he had returned to his homeland after a long and self-imposed exile from Germany during the Nazi regime. The purpose of the Berlin Ensemble was to continue and to further develop a concept of theatrical production and audience response which Brecht had helped to formulate during the 1920s with the Epic Theater, in which the primary thrust was the rejection of traditional presentation and a search for MODERNIST interpretation of dramatic value. At that time Brecht had developed a manifesto for the group which included his belief that plays were to be presented in such a way that the spectator would be involved intellectually, but would remain emotionally detached so that *reason* rather than *empathy* might be stimulated; the philosophical theory that thought determines reality must be reassessed to comply with Brecht's notion that it is the social reality, instead, which determines the thought which then provides inspiration for political action toward social change.

Brecht's conversion to Marxist socialism remained a critical part of his own philosophy that the drama could, and should, be a vehicle to mold social attitudes. His disenchantment with a post-World War II German theater which still retained elements of the principles of Johann Wolfgang von Goethe (1749-1832) and Freidrich von Schiller (1759-1805) heightened his determination to reintroduce the precepts of Epic Theater; mere catharsis would not serve the day. For example, a production might contain rotting corpses as parts of stage material which would suddenly rise up and interrupt the action of the play, or perhaps the unexpected addition of discordant music would be used as "contrapuntal critical commentary to the action." Brecht's term for the technique was *Verfremdungseffekt* (strange making), and provided the rationale for the canon of much of his later work. It is generally agreed that what developed was a striking kind of theater which would change the thinking about traditional drama, add a new dimension to modern theatrical experience, and would mark him as one of the most significant and influential dramatists of the century. The common term for this dramatic innovation which followed would be "the theater of alienation." The Berlin Ensemble included earlier associates Erwin Piscator (1893-1966), stage designer Caspar Neher (1897-1962), Erich Engle (1891-1966), and Paul Dessau (1894-1979). Later collaborators were Benno Besson (1922-), Hans (Hanns) Eisler (1898-1962), Peter Hacks (1928-), Peter Palitzsch (1918-), Manfred Wekwerth (1929-), and Brecht's wife Helene Weigel (1900-1971), who replaced him as director after his death. The Berlin Ensemble was highly influential through the 1950s and continued as an active part of theater in Germany through the second half of the twentieth century.

❖•❖

Further Reading

Benjamin, Walter. *Understanding Brecht*. Translated by Anna Bostock. London: NLB, 1973.

Bentley, Eric. *In Search of Theater*. New York: Knopf, 1953.

———. *The Playwright as Thinker: A Study of Drama in Modern Times*. New York: Reynal and Hitchcock, 1946.

Brustein, Robert. *The Theatre of Revolt*. Boston: Little, Brown, 1964.

Esslin, Martin. *Bertolt Brecht*. New York: Columbia University Press, 1969.

———. *Brecht—A Choice of Evils*. London: Eyre & Spottiswoode, 1959.

———. *Brecht: The Man and His Work*. Garden City, N.Y.: Doubleday, 1960.

Gray, Ronald. *Bertolt Brecht*. New York: Grove Press, 1961.

———. *Brecht the Dramatist*. Cambridge, England: Cambridge University Press, 1976.

Grimm, Reinhold. *Bertolt Brecht*. Stuttgart, Germany: Metzler Edition 3, 1971.

Haas, Willy. *Bertolt Brecht*. Translated by Max Knight and Joseph Fabry. New York: Ungar, 1970.

Hill, Claude. *Bertolt Brecht*. Boston: Twayne, 1975.

Mews, Siegfried, and Herbert Kunst, eds. *Essays on Brecht: Theater and Politics*. Chapel Hill, N.C.: University of North Carolina Press, 1974.

Munk, Erika, ed. *Brecht: A Selection of Critical Pieces from the Dramatic Review*. New York: Bantam Books, 1972.

Probst, Gerhard F. *Erwin Piscator and the American Theatre*. New York: P. Lang, 1991.

Rulicke-Weiler, Kathe. "Brecht and Weigel at the Berliner Ensemble." *New Theatre Quarterly* 7, 25 (February 1991): 3-19.

Sartiliot, Claudette. *Citation and Modernity: Derrida, Joyce, and Brecht*. Norman, Okla.: University of Oklahoma Press, 1993.

Schoeps, Karl H. *Bertolt Brecht*. New York: Ungar, 1977.

Thomson, Peter, and Glendyr Sacks, eds. *The Cambridge Companion to Brecht*. Cambridge, England: Cambridge University Press, 1994.

Volker, Klaus. *Brecht: A Biography*. Translated by John Nowell. New York: Seabury Press, 1978.

Willett, John, ed. *Brecht on Theatre: The Development of an Aesthetic*. New York: Hill and Wang, 1964.

Williams, Raymond. *Drama from Ibsen to Brecht*. London: Chatto & Windus, 1965.

————. *Modern Tragedy*. London: Chatto & Windus; Stanford, Calif.: Stanford University Press, 1966.

Witt, Hubert, ed. *Brecht: As They Knew Him*. New York: International Publishers, 1974.

BES HECECILER. *See* SYLLABISTS

BEWEGING, DE. *See* THE MOVEMENT

BEWEGING VAN TACHTIG. *See* MOVEMENT OF THE EIGHTIES

BITTERFELD MOVEMENT (Bitterfelder Weg)
East Germany, 1960s

A late outgrowth of SOCIALIST REALISM in the German Democratic Republic, the Bitterfeld Movement was conceived at a 1959 writers' conference in an attempt to direct fiction toward the accurate documentation of factory and agricultural life by workers who would be encouraged to become authors, and vice versa. Erwin Strittmatter (1912-), a major practitioner of Socialist Realism, was part of the movement, as was Christa Wolf (1929-) who, through her controversial introduction of themes of disillusionment and self-analysis, helped redirect the course of East German fiction and hasten the demise of Socialist Realism during the next several decades.

❖•❖

Further Reading

Buehler, George. *The Death of Socialist Realism in the Novels of Christa Wolf*. Frankfurt and New York: P. Lang, 1984.

Herrmann, Anne. *The Dialogic and Difference: An/Other Woman in Virginia Woolf and Christa Wolf*. New York: Columbia University Press, 1989.

BLACK CONSCIOUSNESS MOVEMENT
South Africa, 1970s

The Black Consciousness Movement was an important part of the protest literature tradition in South Africa. In the late 1960s, the South African government's apartheid policies prompted a group of black writers, many forming the South African Students' Organization in 1971, to depict the harsh realities of township life in emotionally arresting free-verse poems. Initially nonmilitant in ideology, the Black Consciousness Movement employed increasingly aggressive vernacular in following decades and greatly distanced itself from more traditional strains of poetry in South Africa. Writers associated with the movement include Oswald Mbuyiseni Mtshali (1940-) and his important volume *Sounds of the Cowhide Drum* (1971), Mongane Wally Serote (1944-) and his poetry collection *Yakhal'inkomo* (1972) and his novel examining the movement, *To Every Birth Its Blood* (1981), Sydney Sipho Sepamla (1932-) who edited the journal *New Classic* (formerly *The Classic*), and Mafika Pascal Gwala (1946-). Periodicals such as *The Bloody Horse, Ophir, Donga*, and the powerfully revolutionary *Staffrider* (1978-) circulated work by the movement's writers.

➜●❦

Further Reading

Abrahams, Cecil. "The South African Writer in a Changing Society." *Matatu: Journal for African Culture and Society* 2, 3-4 (1988): 32-43.

Barnett, Ursula A. *A Vision of Order: A Study of Black South African Literature in English (1914-1980)*. London: Sinclair Browne; Amherst, Mass.: University of Massachusetts Press, 1983.

Brown, Duncan. "Interview with Mongane Wally Serote." *Theoria: A Journal of Studies in the Arts, Humanities and Social Sciences* 80 (October 1992): 143-49.

Calder, Angus. "Yakhalinkomo: Poems by Mongane Wally Serote." *Joliso: East African Journal of Literature and Society* 2, 2 (1974): 108-11.

"Censor's Report on *A Ride on the Whirlwind.*" *Index on Censorship* 12, 3 (June 1983). 12.

Dale, Leigh. "Changing Places: The Problem of Identity in the Poetry of Lionel Fogerty and Mongane Serote." *SPAN: Journal of the South Pacific Association for Commonwealth Literature and Language Studies* 24 (April 1987): 81-95.

Daymond, M. J., J. U. Jacobs, and Margaret Lenta, eds. *Momentum: On Recent South African Writing*. Pietermaritzburg, South Africa: University of Natal Press, 1984.

Ezenwa-Ohaeto. [sic] "Black Consciousness in East and South African Poetry: Unity and Divergence in the Poetry of Taban Lo Liyong and Sipho Sepamla." *Presence Africaine: Revue Culturelle du Monde Noir/Cultural Review of the Negro World* 140 (1986): 10-24.

February, Vernie. "Sipho Sepamla, *The Soweto I Love.*" *African Literature Today* 10 (1979): 256-58.

Finn, Stephen M. "Poets of Suffering and Revolt: Tschernichowsky and Serote." *Unisa English Studies: Journal of the Department of English* 26, 1 (April 1988): 26-32.

Gardner, Colin. "Jo'burg City: Questions in the Smoke: Approaches to a Poem." *Bloody Horse* 5 (1981): 38-45.

―――――. "Catharsis: From Aristotle to Mafika Gwala." *Theoria: A Journal of Studies in the Arts, Humanities and Social Sciences* 64 (May 1985): 29-41.

―――――. "Negotiating Poetry: A New Poetry for a New South Africa." *Theoria: A Journal of Studies in the Arts, Humanities and Social Sciences* 77 (May 1991): 1-14.

Gray, Stephen. "Sipho Sepamla: Spirit Which Refuses to Die." *Index on Censorship* 7, 1 (1978): 3-5.

―――――. "Stephen Gray Interviews Sipho Sepamla." *Pacific Quarterly* 6, 3-4 (July-October 1981): 257-62.

Gwala, Mafika Pascal. "Tracing the Steps." *Matatu: Journal for African Culture and Society* 2, 3-4 (1988): 76-95.

Livingstone, Douglas. "The Poetry of Mtshali, Serote, Sepamla and Others in English: Notes Towards a Critical Evaluation." *New Classic* 3 (1976): 48-63.

McCord, Andrew. "Black Man's Burden: A Conversation with Mongane Wally Serote." *Transition: An International Review* 61 (1993): 180-87.

Povey, John. "The Poetry of Mafika Gwala." *Commonwealth Essays and Studies* 8, 2 (spring 1986): 84-93.

Ralph-Bowman, Mark. "The Price of Being a Writer." *Index on Censorship* 11, 4 (August 1982): 15-16.

Sepamla, Sydney Sipho. *Selected Poems*. Edited and with an introduction by Mbulelo Vizikhungo Mzamane. Craighall, South Africa: Ad. Donker, 1984.

Serote, Jaki. "Poet in Exile: An Interview." *Staffrider* 4, 1 (April-May 1981): 30-32.

Sole, Kelwyn. *"But Then, Where Is Home?": Time, Disorder and Social Collectives in Serote's* To Every Birth Its Blood. Cape Town, South Africa: Centre for African Studies, University of Cape Town, [1989?].

————. "The Days of Power: Depictions of Politics and Community in Four Recent South African Novels." *Research in African Literatures* 19, 1 (spring 1988): 65-88.

Wilkinson, Jane. *Orpheus in Africa: Fragmentation and Renewal in the Work of Four African Writers*. Rome: Bulzoni Editore, 1990.

BLACK MOUNTAIN POETS
United States, 1950s-1960s

The Black Mountain Poets, one of the major American Postmodernist poetry groups, emerged in the 1950s at Black Mountain College in western North Carolina. The teachers, students, and associates of the college who comprised the movement derived both their moral and aesthetic philosophies from leader Charles OLSON and his widely hailed, anti-formalist manifesto "PROJECTIVE VERSE" (1950). Heir to the poetic traditions of Ezra POUND (*see* MODERNISM, England and Ireland) and William Carlos Williams (1883-1963), Olson constructed an artistic theory that repudiated NEW CRITICISM's constraints of meter, rhythm, logic, locale, and time. Both Alfred North Whitehead's (1861-1947) process philosophy and Carl JUNG's conception of "projection" as a dynamic, twofold expression of the self's creative and repressive psyches markedly shaped Olson's organic conception of his own poetry, which in turn significantly influenced the work of a large segment of younger American poets who launched their careers during the postwar decades.

The enormous depth of Olson's poetic vision may be found in his magnum opus, *THE MAXIMUS POEMS* (1953-75). Yet, most scholars submit that Olson's greatest legacy resides not in his writings but in his vigorous, often brilliant, encouragement and exhortation of his fellow poets. The most notable among this group were Robert Creeley

(1926-), Robert Duncan (1919-1988), and Denise Levertov (1923-); together with a number of other writers, Olson and these poets challenged the foundations of Western thought and literature while successfully evolving a new poetic morality, one genuinely aligned with the insights, rhythms, and spontaneity of consciousness itself. The result has been a poetic contribution equal in magnitude and innovation to that of the other major reactionary groups of the Postmodern age: the BEAT GENERATION, the SAN FRANCISCO SCHOOL, the CONFESSIONAL POETS, and the NEW YORK SCHOOL of John Ashbery (1927-), Kenneth Koch (1925-), and Frank O'Hara (1926-1966).

The *Black Mountain Review*, which Creeley edited, served as the primary medium for the movement's redirection of modern American poetry, a goal largely met by the dawn of the 1960s through a labyrinth of influences and associations between and among the avant-garde circles. It is generally agreed that Olson, perhaps no less than Allen GINSBERG, was at the heart of this sweeping poetic revival, which, despite its obvious sources, remains one of the most original and extended literary impulses in all American literature.

➻•❖

Olson, Charles (1910-1970), American poet, essayist, and editor.

An enormously charismatic and polymathic figure, Olson is remembered not simply as a writer but as an accomplished teacher, lecturer, historian, philosopher, anthropologist, philologist, and mythologist. Following a brief political career during the early 1940s Olson turned decisively toward the vocations of writing and academic scholarship in 1946. Serving as rector of Black Mountain College from 1951 until 1956, when the school closed, Olson oversaw virtually all facets of the improvisational and impromptu learning and creative expression which took place on campus. In later years Olson continued to teach while remaining a vital presence in contemporary American poetry. Following the posthumous publication in 1975 of *The Maximus Poems, Volume Three*, Olson's reputations as a seminal theorist of composition and one of the few great writers of the long poem have continued to grow. In addition to his major work, Olson is also remembered for his first publication, a study of Herman Melville (1819-1891) entitled *Call Me Ishmael* (1947); the poem collection *In Cold Hell, In Thicket* (1953), which contains the early revolutionary poem "The Kingfishers" (1950); and *The Distances* (1961), a compilation of some of his best lyric and confessional work.

The Maximus Poems (1953-75).

A long sequential work loosely modeled on Williams's *Paterson* (1946-58) and Pound's *CANTOS* (1917-70), *The Maximus Poems* are a mythical evocation of Olson's life as it relates historically not only to his native Gloucester, Massachusetts, but to the larger

49

histories of civilization and the cosmos. Olson's approach to his material, however, is ahistorical, for like Pound he perceived history spatially rather than temporally. The predominant theme is that of the modern individual's alienation from himself and his world, his detachment from the dignity and mystery of a completely meaningful life. Although fettered with a difficult, allusive structure, *The Maximus Poems* have won wide acclaim for their underlying organic unity, their moral and philosophical weight, and their exemplary display of the possibilities of "open field" composition.

"Projective Verse" (1950).

First published in *Poetry New York*, "Projective Verse" represents Olson's first articulation of "open field" composition. In the tradition of Walt Whitman (1819-1892), Olson viewed the creation of poetry as a profoundly human act, that is, one tied to all the manifestations of consciousness: rational, irrational, emotional, spiritual, psychological, and physiological. Further, he understood the poem to be not a comment upon but a participation in the chosen subject. In order to implement his theories, Olson introduced the concept of the open field, in which language and meter were free to follow the natural breathing and natural flow of thought of the poet. The result, in the hands of Olson and the Black Mountain Poets, was a spontaneous, intuitive mosaic of ideas, images, and sensations, which when viewed together suggested the creative work as well as the creative artist as living process. Projective verse of this kind has survived the Black Mountain Poets and related movements and continues to inform the poetry of numerous important American writers.

❧•❧

Further Reading

Athanor. Issue no. 4. 1973. Special issue devoted to Robert Creeley.

Berke, Roberta. "'The Will to Change': The Black Mountain Poets." In her *Bounds Out of Bounds: A Compass for Recent American and British Poetry*. New York: Oxford University Press, 1981.

Boer, Charles. *Charles Olson in Connecticut*. Rocky Mount, N.C.: North Carolina Wesleyan College Press, 1991.

Bollobas, Eniko. *Charles Olson*. New York: Twayne Publishers; Toronto: Maxwell Macmillan Canada, 1992.

Butterick, George F. *A Guide to the Maximus Poems of Charles Olson*. Berkeley, Calif.: University of California Press, 1978.

Butterick, George F., ed. *Charles Olson and Robert Creeley: The Complete Correspondence*. Santa Barbara, Calif.: Black Sparrow Press, 1980-.

Byrd, Don. *Charles Olson's Maximus*. Urbana, Ill.: University of Illinois Press, 1980.

Christensen, Paul. *Charles Olson: Call Him Ishmael*. Austin, Tex.: University of Texas Press, 1975.

Clark, Tom. *Charles Olson: The Allegory of a Poet's Life*. New York: Norton, 1991.

————. *Robert Creeley and the Genius of the American Common Place: Together with the Poet's Own Autobiography.* New York: New Directions, 1993.

Creeley, Robert. *Tales Out of School: Selected Interviews.* Ann Arbor, Mich.: University of Michigan Press, 1993.

Duberman, Martin. *Black Mountain: An Exploration in Community.* New York: Dutton, 1972.

Edelberg, Cynthia Dubin. *Robert Creeley's Poetry: A Critical Introduction.* Albuquerque, N.Mex.: University of New Mexico Press, 1978.

Faas, Ekbert. *Towards a New American Poetics: Essays and Interviews (Charles Olson, Robert Duncan, Gary Snyder, Robert Creeley, Robert Bly, Allen Ginsberg).* Santa Barbara, Calif.: Black Sparrow Press, 1979.

Ford, Arthur L. *Robert Creeley.* Boston: Twayne, 1978.

Foster, Edward Halsey. *Understanding the Black Mountain Poets.* Columbia, S.C.: University of South Carolina Press, 1995.

Fox, Willard. *Robert Creeley, Edward Dorn, and Robert Duncan: A Reference Guide.* Boston: G. K. Hall, 1989.

Fredman, Stephen. *The Grounding of American Poetry: Charles Olson and the Emersonian Tradition.* Cambridge, England; New York: Cambridge University Press, 1993.

————. *Poet's Prose: The Crisis in American Verse.* 2nd ed. Cambridge, England; New York: Cambridge University Press, 1990.

Gelpi, Albert, ed. *Denise Levertov: Selected Criticism.* Ann Arbor, Mich.: University of Michigan Press, 1993.

Halden-Sullivan, Judith. *The Topology of Being: The Poetics of Charles Olson.* New York: Peter Lang, 1991.

Layton, Irving. *Irving Layton and Robert Creeley: The Complete Correspondence, 1953-1978.* Montreal; Buffalo, N.Y.: McGill Queen's University Press, 1990.

McPheron, William, ed. *Charles Olson, the Critical Reception, 1941-1983: A Bibliographic Guide.* New York: Garland, 1986.

Maud, Ralph. *Charles Olson's Reading: A Biography.* Carbondale, Ill.: Southern Illinois University Press, 1996.

Merrill, Thomas F. *The Poetry of Charles Olson: A Primer.* Newark, Del.: University of Delaware Press, 1982.

Olson, Charles. *Mayan Letters.* Edited by Robert Creeley. London: Cape, 1968.

Paul, Sherman. *Olson's Push: Origin, Black Mountain, and Recent American Poetry.* Baton Rouge, La.: Louisiana State University Press, 1978.

Riddel, Joseph N. *The Turning Word: American Literary Modernism and Continental Theory.* Philadelphia: University of Pennsylvania Press, 1996.

Rodgers, Audrey T. *Denise Levertov: The Poetry of Engagement.* Rutherford, N.J.: Fairleigh Dickinson University Press; London: Associated University Press, 1993.

Rumaker, Michael. *Robert Duncan in San Francisco.* San Francisco: Grey Fox Press, 1996.

Stein, Charles. *The Secret of the Black Chrysanthemum: The Poetic Cosmology of Charles Olson & His Use of the Writings of C. G. Jung.* Barrytown, N.Y.: Station Hill Press, 1987; distributed by Talman Co.

51

Von Hallberg, Robert. *American Poetry and Culture, 1945-1980*. Cambridge, Mass.: Harvard University Press, 1985.

————. *Charles Olson: The Scholar's Art*. Cambridge, Mass.: Harvard University Press, 1979.

————. "Olson's Relation to Pound and Williams." *Contemporary Literature* 15, 1 (winter 1974): 15-48.

Wagner-Martin, Linda. *Denise Levertov*. New York: Twayne, 1967.

Wilson, John, ed. *Robert Creeley's Life and Work: A Sense of Increment*. Ann Arbor, Mich.: University of Michigan Press, 1987.

BLAST. See **VORTICISM**

BLOOMSBURY GROUP
England, 1910s-1940s

Bloomsbury was not so much a literary school in itself, but rather a coterie of intellectuals that fit firmly into the larger movement known as MODERNISM. Through the works of their most important member, Virginia WOOLF, the group exerted a significant influence on modern European literature, especially in the 1920s and 1930s, representing a rejection of Victorian mores and literary conventions. The group had its beginnings at Cambridge University at the end of the nineteenth century when Clive Bell (1881-1964), Thoby Stephen (1880-1906), Lytton Strachey (1880-1932), and Leonard Woolf (1880-1969) began a discussion group which they named the Midnight Society. Drawn together by a youthful and keen intellectuality, their after-hours discourses about art, literature, and the state of the British realm soon gained them notoriety among their more conventional classmates. Further, they — and such later adherents as E. M. Forster (1879-1970) and Bertrand Russell (1872-1970) — were all fervently devoted to the ideas of the elder academic G. E. Moore (1873-1958) and his philosophical work *Principia Ethica* (1903). This tract espoused a passionate search, through dialogue, for the meanings of Good and Beauty, but only as these concepts had bases in Truth. Thus, all known assumptions and premises must be put to eternal question. As Leon Edel (1907-1997) notes, "Even God [would be] demolished in the name of Truth."

When university life ended, the Midnight Society continued to flourish in the Bloomsbury section of London, now having added to its number the young economist John Maynard Keynes (1883-1946) and Desmond MacCarthy (1877-1952). These two were also fascinated by Moore and his work and had been while at Cambridge members of the prestigious Apostles, as had Woolf and Strachey. Perhaps the most prominent additions to the group were the young sisters of Thoby Stephen, Virginia (later Virginia Woolf) and Vanessa (later Vanessa Bell; 1879-1961). The young women had found new freedom, in London residence with their brothers Thoby and Adrian after the death of their father, Leslie, and their home at 46 Garden Square, Bloomsbury, became a sort of headquarters for the group. They had left behind their father's Victorian house and his matching value system, and were now happy to enjoy a new consortium of the mind, eager to embrace Moore's philosophy that "the pleasures of human intercourse and the enjoyment of beautiful objects" were the goals to pursue in life. Disparate in their early creative activities, what the group had most in common was an almost ferocious rejection of the traditional historical, political and social value systems which were prevalent in England and which would lead them into two world wars.

By 1907, the Bloomsbury group was attracting the attention of the London intelligentsia for its blatant negation of conventional moral and sexual behavior and for its "active mood and a determinedly artistic attitude to life." It was often criticized, and considered by its more conservative precedents to be elitist, impolitic, and of questionable behavior. Writers such as Henry JAMES (*see* REALISM, United States) and F. R. Leavis (1895-1978) deplored the group, but the artist Roger Fry (1866-1934) was soon to join it. In 1910, he and Desmond MacCarthy gained more controversial recognition from London art circles, when they were responsible for the mounting of an art show of French Post Impressionists (Fry's term), at a private London gallery. In Paris, Fry had selected the paintings, with MacCarthy acting as secretary of the venture; in London, viewers were introduced to pictures by Gauguin, Matisse, Picasso, Roualt, Vlaminck, and others. The pictures sold well, and their show was a success. Fry would repeat this action again in 1912, this time with Leonard Woolf as secretary. Bloomsbury's "artistic attitude" had made its mark, as critic Kenneth Clark now named Fry the "champion of Modernism."

Between 1906 and 1912, there were changes in the group, but none which affected its cohesiveness nor its impact. Thoby Stephen died, Vanessa married Clive Bell and had a child; Virginia married Leonard Woolf. But all members continued to work in fields of art, literature, and politics, and the original enthusiasm and group camaraderie were not diminished. The advent of World War I found them all to be of pacifist persuasion, but willing to serve England in other capacities in the long wait for peace.

Maynard Keynes, who had done wartime service with the British Treasury, emerged after the war as a brilliant and eccentric economist. His financial acumen took him, in 1919, to the Paris Peace Conference. There, disillusioned by events which he felt would precipitate a second war, he resigned from the conference to write his pithy, accurate, and humanist tract, *The Economic Consequences of the Peace* (1919). This is an indictment of the vengeful and militarist postwar world view and earned Keynes both fame and blame for his opinions. But his theories of world finance and economics would influence both England and America and his humanist views have been credited by some to have come from his exchange of ideas with other members of the Bloomsbury group.

Lytton Strachey, after many failed attempts at publication, finally achieved success with his biography *Eminent Victorians* in 1918. Taking, as did Keynes, a humanistic world view, his essays on Cardinal Manning, Florence Nightingale, Thomas Arnold, and General Charles Gordon, all of whom represented his book title, he pointed out both the integrity and the foibles of each individual, and his work provided fascinating divergence from previous biographies which had merely idealized prominent figures of the age. In the opinion of critic Malcolm Bradbury, Strachey's book had signalled the end of the Victorian era.

Leonard Woolf had begun his serious writing in about 1912, and continued to be published until his death in 1969. His works were varied and included fiction in addition to essays about economics, imperialism, the political scene, and pacifism. In 1917, the Woolfs had bought a small hand-press and had started their own firm, Hogarth Press. This was primarily for the publication of Virginia's work, but other printings included works by T. S. ELIOT (*see* Modernism, England and Ireland), Katherine Mansfield (1888-1923), and Sigmund FREUD.

Vanessa and Clive Bell continued their proselytization of Modernist art. His first book, *Art*, was published in 1914 and was well received. They both continued to paint and she maintained strong relationships with Roger Fry and with Duncan Grant (1885-1978; whom Clive compared to Gainsborough in stature). The subject of graphic art, her own painting, and her children all had become the primary foci of her life. Her close ties to the other members of the Bloomsbury group provided her a most important role as its mainstay, with her tenacity to keep it and its values alive.

The most famous literary figure associated with the movement is Virginia Woolf. Her first major novel was published in 1919 and from then until her suicide in 1941 she continued to write innovative fiction and literary and social criticism. Her prose fiction style developed, over time, from her early notions that life is a "luminous halo," a changing kaleidoscopic view formed by both internal and external impressions and perceptions. The novelist, she was convinced, must present all of life's variation of sensibility as inclusively and as carefully as possible. Her use of internal monologue to create dramatic tension in character and situation, and her poetic, impressionistic vision of reality are found in such works as *Jacob's Room* (1922).

The close of World War II marked the diminishing of the Bloomsbury group and its immediate impact on artistic and literary circles. Lytton Strachey, Roger Fry, and Virginia Woolf were dead, and Maynard Keynes died in 1946. The others continued to work, and with the death of Duncan Grant in 1978, all members were gone.

※•※

Further Reading

Bell, Clive. "Duncan Grant." In *Since Cezanne*. New York: Harcourt, 1922.

Bell, Quentin. *Bloomsbury Recalled*. New York: Columbia University Press, 1995.

———. *Virginia Woolf: A Biography*. New York: Harcourt Brace Jovanovich, 1972.

Bishop, Edward L., ed. *Dictionary of Literary Biography*. Vol. 10, *The Bloomsbury Group*. Detroit: Gale Research, 1992.

Bradbury, Malcolm. *Modern World: Ten Great Writers*. New York: Viking, 1989.

Caws, Mary Ann. *Women of Bloomsbury: Virginia, Vanessa, and Carrington*. New York: Routledge, 1990.

D'Aquila, Ulysses L. *Bloomsbury and Modernism*. New York: P. Lang, 1989.

Dowling, David. *Bloomsbury Aesthetics and the Novels of Forster and Woolf*. New York: St. Martin's Press, 1985.

Edel, Leon. *Bloomsbury: A House of Lions*. Philadelphia: Lippincott, 1979.

Garnett, Angelica. *Deceived with Kindness: A Bloomsbury Childhood*. Oxford, England: Oxford University Press, 1985.

Johnstone, J. K. *The Bloomsbury Group: A Study of E. M. Forster, Lytton Strachey, Virginia Woolf and Their Circle*. New York: Octagon Books, 1978.

MacWeeney, Alen, and Sue Allison. *Bloomsbury Reflections*. New York: Norton, 1990.

Marcus, Jane, ed. *Virginia Woolf and Bloomsbury: A Centenary Celebration*. Bloomington, Ind.: Indiana University Press, 1987.

Markert, Lawrence W. *The Bloomsbury Group: A Reference Guide*. Boston: G. K. Hall, 1990.

Marsh, Jan. *Bloomsbury Women: Distinct Figures in Life and Art*. London: Pavilion Books, 1995.

Palmer, Alan, and Veronica Palmer. *Who's Who in Bloomsbury*. New York: St. Martin's Press, 1987.

Robbins, Rae Gallant. *The Bloomsbury Group: A Selective Bibliography*. 1st ed. Kenmore, Wash.: Price Guide Publishers, 1978.

Rosenbaum, S. P. *The Early Literary History of the Bloomsbury Group*. 2 vols. New York: St. Martin's Press, 1987, 1994.

Rosenbaum, S. P., ed. *The Bloomsbury Group: A Collection of Memoirs, Commentary, and Criticism*. Toronto: University of Toronto Press, 1976.

———. *A Bloomsbury Group Reader*. Oxford, England: B. Blackwell, 1993.

Shone, Richard. *Bloomsbury Portraits: Vanessa Bell, Duncan Grant, and Their Circle*. Oxford, England: Phaidon; New York: E. P. Dutton, 1976.

Stansky, Peter. *On or About December 1910: Early Bloomsbury and Its Intimate World*. Cambridge, Mass.: Harvard University Press, 1996.

BLUE HORNS GROUP
Georgia, 1910s

Reacting against REALISM in Georgian literature, the Blue Horns formed during World War I and produced poetry influenced by French SYMBOLISM. The two central figures of the Blue Horns were Grigol Robakidse (1884-1962) and Galaktion Tabidze (1892-

1959). Other members included Paolo Iashvili (1895-1937), Giorgi Leonidze (1899-1966), and Titsian Tabidze (1895-1937).

❖•❖
Further Reading

Magarotto, Luigi. "Andrey Bely in Georgia: Seven Letters from A. Bely to T. Tabidze." *The Slavonic and East European Review* 63, 3 (July 1985): 388-416.

―――. "Georgian and Russian Poets: Letters from T. Tábidze to A. Belyi." *The Slavonic and East European Review* 67, 4 (October 1989): 581-95.

Ozerov, Lev. "Half a Century Later." *Soviet Literature* 9 (474) (1987): 153-54.

Rayfield, Donald. *The Literature of Georgia: A History*. Oxford, England: Clarendon Press, 1994.

―――. "The Killing of Paolo Iashvili." *Index on Censorship* 19, 6 (June-July 1990): 9-14.

―――. "The Death of Paolo Iashvili." *The Slavonic and East European Review* 68, 4 (October 1990): 631-64.

―――. "Unicorns and Gazelles: Pasternak, Rilke, and the Georgian Poets." *Forum for Modern Language Studies* 26, 4 (October 1990): 370-81.

BLUE STARS SOCIETY
Taiwan, 1950s

A Taiwanese movement of the 1950s, the Blue Stars Society was important to the development of modern vernacular poetry. The most notable figure of the movement was Yü Kuang-chung (1928-).

❖•❖
Further Reading

Hegel, Robert E. "The Search for Identity in Fiction from Taiwan." In *Expressions of Self in Chinese Literature*. Edited by Robert E. Hegel and Richard C. Hessney. New York: Columbia University Press, 1985.

BOEDO GROUP
Argentina, 1920s

The Boedo Group is named for a street in Buenos Aires in a lower-class area in which many Creole immigrant residents lived. Members were greatly influenced by the Russian Revolution and socialist ideals and writers such as Leo TOLSTOY, Anton CHEKHOV, and Fyodor DOSTOEVSKY (see REALISM, Russia). Some, like Roberto Arlt (1900-1942), were actively involved in Communist movements in Argentina. Arlt is noted for his harsh portrayals of lower-class urban life in novels such as *Los siete locos*

(1929; The Seven Madmen) and its sequel, *Los lanzallamas* (1931; The Flame-throwers). Other members of the Boedo Group included Santiago Ganduglia (1904-), Enrique Amorim (1900-1960), Leónidas Barletta (1902-), Elías Castelnuovo (1893-?), Raul González Tuñón (1905-), Roberto Mariani (1893-1946), Nicolás Olivari (1900-), Gustavo Riccio (1900-1927), César Tiempo (pseud. for Israel Zeitlin, 1906-), and Álvaro Yunque (pseud. for Arístides Gandolfi Herrero, 1893-?). Some of the group were Jewish writers associated with the journal *Los Pensadores*, in which much of the Boedos' writing appeared. The Boedo writers were outspokenly antagonistic to the literary values of the FLORIDA GROUP, which favored eclectic cosmopolitanism over SOCIALIST REALISM. By the time of the revolution in 1930, both groups had dissolved. Leonídas Barletta has discussed the two groups in *Boedo y Florida: una versión distinta* (1967).

❖ • ❖

Further Reading

Anderson Imbert, Enrique. *Spanish-American Literature: A History*. Detroit: Wayne State University Press, 1963.

Foster, D. W. "Roberto Arlt and the Neurotic Rationale." In *Currents in the Contemporary Argentine Novel*. Columbia, Mo.: University of Missouri Press, 1975.

Franco, Jean. *The Modern Culture of Latin America: Society and the Artist*. New York: Praeger, 1967.

BRETON MOVEMENT
France, 1890-1950

Breton writers today are a relatively small group which fits into MODERNISM because of an independent and energetic adaptation of their ancient linguistic roots into work which conceptualizes contemporary literary thinking.

Early Breton literature was concentrated upon the ancient folklore of their forebears — the Celts, the Cornish and the Welsh — many of whom had immigrated to the northwestern coast of France, now Brittany, during the Saxon invasion of England in the sixth and seventh centuries. Until the late nineteenth century, the literature was often romantic, artificial, pedestrian, and perpetuated a particular kind of nationalism. Along with this, there had been, over time, a continuing effort on the part of many Breton writers to remove elements of the French language from their work and to retain a tongue which is specifically their own. This last has proven to be difficult; there are a number of dialects, and while all Bretons can speak the language, until very recently few could write it so as to be clearly comprehended. The major Breton writers have worked long and hard for a standardization which would be flexible enough to attract a wider audience and recognition in the field of modern letters. In 1985, the language received official recognition from the French government, and equal status was given to both the Breton and French languages.

Early in the twentieth century, Breton poets and writers of other genres began to form groups of their own, mainly around such journals as *Dihunamb*, *Gwarlarn*, and *Al liamn*. Today, much of the literary work is both interesting and innovational, and retains all of the vitality which it embodied between the two world wars. There has been new experimentation with metrical form in the poetry, including free verse, and a vigorous attempt to establish new forms of literature which is not limited only to the Breton culture. The most important modern Breton writers are Yann Ber Kalloc'h (1888-1917), Tanguy Malmanche (1875-1953), Jakez Rion (1899-1937), Youenn Drezen (1899-?), Roparz HEMON, Ronan Huon (1922-), and Pierre Hélias (1914-1995).

❖•❖

Hemon, Roparz (1900-), French novelist and poet.

Founder of the most influential literary journal, *Gwalarn* (Northwest), Roparz published translations of major European and British writers (many of the works of W. B. YEATS [*see* ABBEY THEATER and MODERNISM, England and Ireland] and John Millington SYNGE [*see* ABBEY THEATER]), in an effort to introduce them to his audiences and to the writers of his day. His strong interest in Celtic folklore and his desire to give the Breton language "new flexibility" have made him the most distinguished writer of the Breton modernist movement. His works include satiric novels about life in the town of Brest; his poetry often depicts the ancient Celtic as well as modern Irish themes.

❖•❖

Further Reading

McDonald, Maryon. *"We Are Not French!" Language, Culture, and Identity in Brittany*. London: Routledge, 1989.

BUCHAREST GROUP
Romania, 1940s

The end of World War II brought with it an increased awareness of the MODERNIST movement to Romania, along with the social and political changes which were occurring and bringing inevitable change to all of Europe. A new freedom of expression, for a brief time, generated a variety of literary, critical views as well as information about the new directions which creative writers were taking. The mid-forties saw the emergence of two poetic groups—the Bucharest Group and the SIBIU GROUP. The Bucharest Group included the writers Ion Caraion (1923-), Geo Dumitrescu (1920-), Constant Tonegaru (1919-1952), and Dimitrie Stelaru (1917-1971). All were excited by the new literary experimentation but the feeling was tempered by a profound irony and pessimism in the aftermath of the war. There existed also within the Group a state of intellectual rebellion against a tradition of literature they now viewed as a stultification of the creative impulse. They wanted a new freedom for poetic expression and an end to any influence which would hamper their enthusiasm for a life of adventure and experimentation. Their work is marked by the use of devices of irony, insult, and a gross, earthy REALISM.

Caraion, a major representative of the Group, wrote much of his work as a response to his political imprisonment between 1949 and 1963 and to his country's experiences of war and political inhibition. *Cintece negro* (1947; Black Songs) and *Dimineaja nimaniu* (1967; Nobody's Dawn) are counted among his darkest works. His poetry, collected in English translation in *Ion Caraion, Poems* (1981), depicts cruelty, gloom, and an overriding pessimism. It is, on one hand, defiant and insulting and, on the other, pervaded by his hopelessness and despair about the human condition in his perception of an impossibly desolate world.

✦•✦

Further Reading

Catanoy, Nicholas. *Modern Romanian Poetry*. Oakville, Canada: Mosaic Press, 1977.

BUFFALO SCHOOL. *See* **READER-RESPONSE CRITICISM AND RECEPTION THEORY**

BURAI-HA. *See* **DECADENTS**

C

CAMBRIDGE GROUP
England, 1930s

The group, also known as the Cambridge Critics, originated at Cambridge University and was formed in rejection of a prior literary tradition which had examined creative work from a historical and/or biographical position in its evaluation. These poets propagated, instead, an intensely more careful examination of text. This is defined as the scrupulous attention to a close and analytical reading of a piece of work itself; "any verbal nuance which [allowed] for 'alternative reaction' to text became the primary force in critical assessment and the evaluation of creative impulse." The major writers of the group were William EMPSON, Charles Madge (1912-1996), and Kathleen Raine (1908-).

It does not surprise that the Cambridge poets would be responsive to the analytical mode of inquiry. They were the inheritors of a philosophical tradition which had preceded them, scholastically, by at least two decades and which called for the logical integration of the elements of science and philosophy into all intellectuality. This mode had been engendered by such respected scholars as Bertrand Russell (1872-1970), Ludwig Wittgenstein (1889-1951) and Jacob Bronowski (1908-1974), and the political economist John Maynard Keynes (1883-1946); the approach had been adapted in fields of language and literature as well, by I. A. Richards (1893-1979) and F. R. Leavis (1895-1978). Moreover, T. S. ELIOT (see MODERNISM, England and Ireland) and his poetry of the twenties was of great influence, since he had also rejected the earlier literary convention as inadequate to express the "felt experience" of modernism. His criticism and his creative work aimed at providing both reader and critic with new perceptions of poetry and a sharper critical awareness.

To combine analytical argumentation as well as imagery drawn from modern science and its world, while at the same time to recognize the ambiguity of that world, became the creative and the critical order of the day. The rhythm of language as applied to subject matter which is often commonplace, ugly, shocking, or beautiful provided an exciting concept then and is one which continues to influence the writing of poetry today.

❧•❦

Empson, William (1906-1984), English poet and critic.

Empson's initial critical effort, *THE SEVEN TYPES OF AMBIGUITY* (1930), defends the complexity of language and its difficulties as the best way to express the Modernist idiom. His poems, like Eliot's, are disparate, incongruous, and often so ambiguous as to be difficult to understand. A "contrived handling of contradictions" shows, however, a well-intellectualized preparation for his writing of a work. His volume of poems, *The Gathering Storm* (1940), was written in reaction to the fear and uncertainty of the coming Second World War and the poetry reflects the fear and uncertainty of expected catastrophe. An example of his craft is found in "Manchouli": "I find it normal . . ./that the nations seem real; that their ambitions seem sane; I find it normal, so too to extract false comfort from that word." These lines are juxtaposed (see ellipses) with images and concepts which widen the reader's perceptions of the time and the moment. Other critical works include *Some Versions of Pastoral* (1935) and *The Structure of Complex Words* (1951). He held the chair of English literature at the University of Sheffield until 1971, when he retired.

The Seven Types of Ambiguity (1930; rev. 1953).

Empson describes seven, progressively more complicated types of literary ambiguity in this work which is counted among the most influential of the twentieth century. He defines ambiguity as "any verbal nuance, however slight, which gives room for alternative reactions to the same piece of language," and readers bring to a piece of literature their own individual social contexts and histories; in addition, "which [of the seven types to which] any particular poem belongs depends on your own mental habits and critical opinions."

❧•❦

Further Reading

Day, Frank. *Sir William Empson, an Annotated Bibliography*. New York: Garland, 1984.

Fry, Paul H. *William Empson, Prophet Against Sacrifice*. London: Routledge, 1991.

Gardner, Philip. *The God Approached: A Commentary on the Poems of William Empson*. Totowa, N.J.: Rowman and Littlefield, 1978.

Gill, Roma. *William Empson, the Man and His Work*. London: Routledge & Kegan Paul, 1974.

Lehman, John. *New Writing in Europe*. Harmondsworth, England: A Lane; Penguin Books, 1940.

Madge, Charles. *The Disappearing Castle*. London: Faber and Faber, 1937.

61

Norris, Christopher. *William Empson and the Philosophy of Literary Criticism*. London: Athlone Press, 1978.

Norris, Christopher, and Nigel Mapp. *William Empson, the Critical Achievement*. Cambridge, England: Cambridge University Press, 1993.

Roughton, Roger, ed. *Contemporary Poetry and Prose*. London: R. Roughton, 1936-37.

Sale, Roger. *Modern Heroism: Essays on D. H. Lawrence, William Empson, & J. R. R. Tolkien*. Berkeley, Calif.: University of California Press, 1973.

Symons, Julian. *The Thirties: A Dream Revolved*. London: Cresset Press, 1960.

Tolley, A. T. *The Poetry of the Thirties*. London: Gollancz, 1975.

CAROLINA PLAYMAKERS
United States, 1918-1970s

The Carolina Playmakers, a large group of student and academic writers, actors, and directors, was one of the greatest forces behind the growth of American regional theater and folk drama in the decades following World War I. Founded at the University of North Carolina in 1918 by Professor Frederick Henry Koch (1877-1944), the Playmakers thrived as a company devoted to original writing and communal production. It was not until the late 1970s that they abandoned their emphasis on native drama and renamed themselves the Playmakers Repertory Company.

Koch's inspiration for the Playmakers first arose in 1910, when he launched a similar troupe while teaching at the University of North Dakota. His interest in modern dramaturgy itself, however, stemmed from his study under Harvard Professor George Pierce Baker (1866-1935), who founded the renowned 47 WORKSHOP shortly after Koch graduated. Although literally thousands of drama-lovers shared in the Playmakers' phenomenal success, both as an early educational and public theater, Paul Green (1894-1981) and Thomas Wolfe (1900-1938) are the writers most often mentioned in conjunction with the group. Wolfe's one-act tragedy *The Return of Buck Gavin* (1919), in which he assumed the lead role, formed part of the initial production bill. Wolfe composed several more dramas for the Playmakers before advancing to Baker's Workshop and, ultimately, turning to novel writing, a form which brought him lasting fame. Green, conversely, found drama the genre most suited to his talents. In 1927 he won the Pulitzer Prize for *In Abraham's Bosom* and in 1931, another of his best-known works, *The House of Connelly*, was chosen as the New York GROUP THEATER's inaugural production. For much of his remaining, prolific career, Green paralleled the Playmakers' interest in outdoor theater, writing what he termed "symphonic dramas" which blended music, dance, poetry, and dialogue in order to capture the full pageantry of American life.

⇒•⇐
Further Reading

Adams, Agatha Boyd. *Paul Green of Chapel Hill*. Chapel Hill, N.C.: University of North Carolina Press, 1951.

Clark, Barrett Harper. *Paul Green*. New York: R. M. McBride, 1928.

Devany, Ed. "Paul Green: Documentarian." *North Carolina Literary Review* 2, 1 (spring 1994): 47-55.

Fearing, Bertie E. "Weymouth: A Writers Place — From Thomas Wolfe to Tom Wolfe." *North Carolina Literary Review* 2, 1 (spring 1994): 57-60.

Hagan, John P. "Frederick H. Koch and North Dakota: Theatre in the Wilderness." *North Dakota Quarterly* 38, 1 (1970): 75-87.

Henderson, Archibald, ed. *Pioneering a People's Theatre*. Chapel Hill, N.C.: University of North Carolina Press, 1945.

Kenny, Vincent. *Paul Green*. New York: Twayne, 1971.

Kimball, Sue Laslie, and Lynn Veach Sadler, eds. *Paul Green's Celebration of Man, with a Bibliography*. Fayetteville, N.C.: Human Technology Interface, 1994.

Lazenby, Walter S., Jr. *Paul Green*. Austin, Tex.: Steck-Vaughn, 1970.

Rice, Jerry L. "Thomas Wolfe and the Carolina Playmakers." *Thomas Wolfe Review* 5, 1 (spring 1981): 7-17.

Saunders, Frances W. "'A New Playwright of Tragic Power and Poetic Impulse': Paul Eliot Green at UNC-Chapel Hill in the 1920s." *North Carolina Historical Review* 72, 3 (July 1995): 277-300.

Selden, Samuel, and Mary Tom Sphangos. *Frederick Henry Koch, Pioneer Playmaker: A Brief Biography*. Chapel Hill, N.C.: University of North Carolina Press, 1954.

Spearman, Walter S., with the assistance of Samuel Selden. *The Carolina Playmakers: The First Fifty Years*. Chapel Hill, N.C.: University of North Carolina Press, 1970.

Zug, Charles G., III. "Folklore and the Drama: The Carolina Playmakers and Their 'Folk Play'." *Southern Folklore Quarterly* 32 (1968): 279-94.

CARTEL
France, 1920s-1930s

Also known as the Cartel des Quartre (Group of Four), this group of four theatrical actor-managers began their association in the 1920s in France. They were Gaston Baty (1885-1952), Charles Dullin (1885-1949), Louis Jouvet (1887-1951), and Georges Pitoëff (1884-1939).

The Cartel was responding against André Antoine's THÉÂTRE LIBRE and against the overpowering dominance Jacques COPEAU (*see* THÉÂTRE DU VIEUX-COLOMBIER) held on French theater. Characterized by dynamic dramatizations, but an avoidance of commercialism, they sought to reinvigorate French theater through applying the dramatists' and directors' respective visions of a performance, innovative set designs, and physical movement by actors. They held to the imperative of inspiring the audience.

Baty founded the Théâtre Montparnasse in 1930; notable performances include *Martine* (1922) by Jean-Jacques Bernard (1888-1972) and an adaptation of Fyodor DOSTOEVSKY's (*see* REALISM, Russia) *Prestupleniye i nakazaniye* (1866; *Crime and Punishment*, 1886). Dullin, a former collaborator of Copeau, led a company at the Théâtre de L'Atelier from 1920 to 1940. Jouvet also began his career with Copeau; he set up shop at the Athénée in 1934, which produced, among others, *Dr. Knock, ou le triomphe de la médicine* (1923; *Dr. Knock*, 1925) by Jules ROMAINS (*see* UNANIMISME). The Russian-born Pitoëff also previously worked with Copeau; his company at the Théâtre Mathurins was founded in 1934.

In 1936 they became members of Comédie Française together, an established French theatrical company. Though their impact was dominant during the 1930s, their work went on to influence Jean-Louis Barrault (1910-1994) and Jean Vilar (1912-1971) as well as many experimental theaters.

✥•✥

Further Reading

Inskip, Donald Percival. *Jean Giraudoux, the Making of a Dramatist*. London; New York: Oxford University Press, 1958.

Knapp, Bettina L. *Louis Jouvet, Man of the Theatre*. New York: Columbia University Press, 1957.

CATASTROPHISM. *See ŻAGARY* GROUP

CELTIC RENAISSANCE/CELTIC REVIVAL/CELTIC TWILIGHT.
See ABBEY THEATER; IRISH RENAISSANCE

CENÁCULO GROUP
Cuba, 1911-1913

The Cenáculo Group was cohesive in Cuba for a short time during the second decade of the twentieth century. Influenced by the MODERNISMO movement, principal literary figures involved were José Manuel Poveda y Calderón (1888-1926), Fernando Torralva Navarro (1885-1913), Enrique Gay Calbó (1889-?), Ángel Alberto Giraudy (1886-?), Juan Jerez Villarreal (1889-?), and Luis Vásquez de Cuberos (1889-1924). A volume of essays discussing their aesthetics, *Proemios de cenáculo*, by Povedo, was published posthumously in 1948 with an introduction by Rafael Esténger (1899-?).

⇻•⇺
Further Reading

Herdeck, Donald E., ed. "Essay on the Literature of Cuba." In *Caribbean Writers: A Bio-Bibliographical-Critical Encyclopedia*. Washington, D.C.: Three Continents Press, 1979.

CENTRIFUGE (Tsentrifuga)
Russia, 1910s

One of several Russian FUTURIST groups, Centrifuge was active during the few years before the Revolution. Sergei Bobrov (1889-1971) led the group which included such poets as Boris Pasternak (1890-1960), who also aligned himself with the more radical CUBO-FUTURISTS Nikolay Aseyev (1889-1963) and Ivan Aksyonov (n.d.). Though it had no clear manifesto, the Centrifuge poets and critics initially showed the influence of SYMBOLISM, then became aligned with the EGO-FUTURISTS. Bobrov's *Liricheskaya tema* (1914; The Lyric Theme) discusses the aethestic tenets of the group.

Aksyonov's *Neuvazhitel'yne osnovaniya* (1915; Invalid Foundations) is considered the most avant-garde of the Centrifugists' output. Through its publishing activities, Centrifuge issued two collections of its members' work: *Rukonog* (1914; Brachiopod) and *Vtoroi sbornik Tsenttrifugi* (1916; Second Centrifuge Miscellany).

⇻•⇺
Further Reading

Lawton, Anna. "Centrifuge." In *Handbook of Russian Literature*. Edited by Victor Terras. New Haven, Conn., and London: Yale University Press, 1985.
Markov, Vladimir. *Russian Futurism: A History*. Berkeley, Calif.: University of California Press, 1968.

CHĀYĀVĀDA. *See* ROMANTICIST MOVEMENT

CHICAGO CRITICS
United States, 1950s

This group was associated with the University of Chicago and proposed a critical theory which was in opposition to the school of NEW CRITICISM, which had been extant for two decades in both England and the United States and had had considerable influence in universities and among scholars. The New Critics saw the literary work as an "object" important only in and of itself, as it has a language of its own which remains dissociated from that of other disciplines, and must be carefully analyzed and examined in the light of what is called "close reading." The Chicago Critics disagreed. Their concept of the critic's role in literary analysis is that there is not, nor should there be, one universal criterion which determines what a poem should be nor what criticism "ought" to consist of. No critical application should be "too narrowly concerned with the verbal medium" to the exclusion of the many other aspects which might precipitate a literary work. They advocated a pluralistic critical approach which takes into account the various issues which arise in explication of literary subject and were agreed that the work itself is but one part of the critical experience; it is necessarily influenced by its historical and social milieux, its relationships to other genres, and any valid and tacit "assumptions concerning the nature of literature" which are or have been proven reliable. Moreover, they concluded that the singular and limited approach of the New Critics would strongly inhibit the degree to which a literary piece might be evaluated.

In addition, the Chicago Critics also became known as "Neo-Aristotelians," when they called for a revival of the ancient guidelines found in the *Poetics*, in which Aristotle delineated the differences between comic and tragic modes of epic poetry and the different strategies to be employed in their presentation. He gave the poet, as maker, specific guidelines for achievement of desired denouement of the work of art. Aristotle's treatise was the first to be concerned with literary criticism and its basic tenets remain — that the questions any critic asks of a text should be in accordance with the needs of the author and the aim of the work. The Chicago Critics felt that the ancient theory had for too long been disregarded, and that its premise of the importance of "the differential way . . . pointed the way to further inquiries in other literary arts still unrealized at the time in which [Aristotle] wrote."

The Chicago Critics' manifesto emphasized refutation of any imposition of critical value systems which cannot be logically proven, and upheld the right of the critic to inquire into the "philosophical" aspects of literary criticism. An innovator of the group, Elder Olson (1909-1992), noted that "Criticism in our time is a sort of [methodological] Tower of Babel, yet diversity is good and it is in the examination of diversity that some valid assumption can be made about literary criticism." One of his concerns was that any extension of critical knowledge cannot come about if a critic is not "fully aware of what has been accomplished, or what consequences follow from such accomplishments." Another early member was Wayne C. Booth (1921-), whose best-known work, *The Rhetoric of Fiction* (1961), includes his attack on the "ambiguity of modern literature," his insistence upon reliable narration on the part of the novelist, and his "rescue" of novelist criticism from "more rigid confines" of an earlier and symbolist aesthetic. Other group members were R. S. Crane (1886-1967), Norman Friedman (1925-), Walter J. Hipple, Jr. (1921-), William R. Keast (1914-1998), Richard McKeon (1900-1985), C. A. McLaughlin (n.d.), Norman Maclean (1902-1990), Robert H. Marsh (1926-), Bernard Weinberg (1909-1973), and Austin McGiffert Wright (1922-).

⇒•⇐
Further Reading

Antczak, Frederick J., ed. *Rhetoric and Pluralism: Legacies of Wayne Booth*. Columbus, Ohio: Ohio State University Press, 1995.

Booth, Wayne C. *The Company We Keep*. Berkeley, Calif.: University of California Press, 1988.

———. *Modern Dogma and the Rhetoric of Assent*. Notre Dame, Ind.: University of Notre Dame Press, 1974.

———. *The Rhetoric of Irony*. Chicago: University of Chicago Press, 1974.

Bradbury, Malcolm, and David Palmer. *Contemporary Criticism*. New York: St. Martin's Press, 1970.

Cox, C. B., and A. E. Dyson, eds. *The Twentieth-Century Mind: History, Ideas and Literature in Britain*. London: Oxford University Press, 1972.

Crane, Ronald Salmon. *Critics and Criticism, Ancient and Modern*. Chicago: University of Chicago Press, 1952.

Grenander, M. E. "Evolution of an Article: The Chicago Aristotelians." *Hypotheses: Neo-Aristotelian Analysis* 8 (winter 1994): 2-12.

Hipple, Walter John. *The Beautiful, the Sublime, and the Picturesque in Eighteenth-Century British Aesthetic Theory*. Carbondale, Ill.: Southern Illinois University Press, 1957.

Kaplan, Charles. *The Overwrought Urn: A Potpourri of Parodies of Critics Who Triumphantly Present the Real Meaning of Authors from Jane Austen to J. D. Salinger*. 2nd ed. New York: Pegasus, 1969.

Keast, William. *Province of Prose*. 2nd ed. New York: Harper, 1959.

McElroy, George. "Norman MacLean: Teacher and Chicago Aristotelian." *Hypotheses: Neo-Aristotelian Analysis* 8 (winter 1994): 13-18.

CHICAGO LITERARY RENAISSANCE
United States, 1910s-1920s

The Chicago Literary Renaissance helped initiate distinctly modern forms of American literature. During the World War I era, Chicago was a place where many notable poets, fiction writers, and journalists came to hone their craft. Chicago became a center for promoting international literary trends, a cosmopolitan literary environment, and the democratization of American literature, as writers encouraged each other in their efforts to present common social concerns in the vernacular of the American Midwest. In its broadest usage, the movement encompasses poetry, fiction, and journalism. The Chicago Renaissance is associated with two major developments in poetry — free verse, as practiced by Carl SANDBURG, Vachel LINDSAY, and Edgar Lee MASTERS, and IMAGISM, which was introduced to American readers and heavily promoted by Ezra POUND (*see* MODERNISM, England and Ireland) in the pages of Chicago-based *Poetry: A Magazine of Verse*. Several novelists associated with NATURALISM, most notably Theodore DREISER, worked in Chicago. The city was also a hotbed for literary journalism. Ben Hecht (1894-1964), for example, began his career as a Chicago beat writer, and his first novel, *Erik Dorn* (1921), is based on his experiences as Berlin correspondent for the *Chicago News*. However, in a stricter and more appropriate sense, the Chicago Literary Renaissance centers on *Poetry,* founded by Harriet Monroe (1860-1936) in 1912.

Poetry magazine immediately became a source for American writers and readers to share in changing literary values, and it helped launch the careers of three great Illinois poets — Lindsay, Sandburg, and Masters. Monroe founded *Poetry* to champion modernization of the language, forms, and subject matter of verse, with the plain dictum that poetry ought to be about contemporary life. *Poetry* showcased innovations in verse: the rhythmic and oddly structured poems of Lindsay and Sandburg; the international developments of Imagism and free verse forms; distinctly modern idioms as opposed to more traditional and formal poetic language; and the expansion of subject matter to consider the variety of urban experience and images.

The first issue of *Poetry* featured an inaugural statement, "The Motive of the Magazine," in which Monroe asserted that poetry had been shamefully neglected and, indeed, had an important place in American culture. This issue contained two poems by Ezra Pound, who began regular contributions to the magazine as an expatriate in Europe. Pound used *Poetry* as a forum for introducing American readers to the works of T. S. ELIOT (*see* MODERNISM, England and Ireland), W. B. YEATS (*see* ABBEY THEATER and MODERNISM, England and Ireland), H[ILDA] D[OOLITTLE] (*see* IMAGISM), and other innovative Modernist poets and to promote the tenets and verse of Imagism. This accounts for the international flavor of the Chicago Literary Renaissance. Meanwhile, Lindsay's vibrant poetry, meant to be read aloud or sung, was represented in the magazine as early as 1912, the beginning of his period of renown. In fact, Lindsay's greatest poem, "GENERAL WILLIAM BOOTH ENTERS INTO HEAVEN," made its first appearance in *Poetry*. Likewise, the first appearance of Sandburg's famous "CHICAGO" poem was in *Poetry* in 1915, bringing serious attention to his work, which would become among the most popular and recognizable in twentieth-century American verse. Sandburg was encouraged to publish his verse by Masters; several of Masters's lyrical epitaphs also appeared in the magazine and were later included in his highly lauded *SPOON RIVER ANTHOLOGY,* published in 1915.

Poetry magazine continued as an important source for new poetry and poetics throughout the twentieth century, but the Chicago Literary Renaissance, as it is commonly defined, began to wane by the 1920s. Masters's *Spoon River* was his one great poetic triumph, and he soon moved to New York; Lindsay became a popular troubadour traveling around the country, but he experienced increasing bouts of illness, later diagnosed as a form of epilepsy, and took his own life in 1931; Sandburg became "America's poet," expanding his subjects and recreation of idioms to increasingly wider areas, culminating in *The People, Yes* (1936), essentially a large poem about the United States.

A renaissance environment did indeed occur in Chicago during the World War I years, but the diversity of the writers' styles and achievements are underestimated if confined to an all-encompassing, Chicago-based movement. Instead, like the railroads that reached all parts of the United States from roundhouses in Chicago, writers shared a common Chicago base from which they contributed to several innovative literary movements at home and abroad. Nevertheless, as a renaissance environment for variety and innovations in literature, as the home-base of *Poetry*, which achieved Monroe's goal for promoting the serious study, enjoyment, and cultural importance of verse, and as the place where three great American poets found their voices, Chicago's Literary Renaissance had a lasting influence on the course of modern American literature.

Lindsay, Vachel (1879-1931), American poet.

Lindsay was an American troubadour who wrote poems meant to be sung or recited, celebrating common life or paying tribute to such heroes as Abraham Lincoln (1809-1865) and Johnny Appleseed. Through frequent use of alliteration, rhyme, and musical rhythms, Lindsay wrote about familiar events and people but developed an intensity and fervor that often produced mystical effects. He was considered among the finest American poets of the World War I era.

Lindsay was born in Springfield, Illinois; his father was a doctor and his mother taught mathematics and art. Lindsay pursued a career in art, moving to New York for a short period, but focused much of his attention on writing verse, which he often sang, recited, or distributed on street corners. He undertook two long walking tours—from Illinois to Florida in 1906, and from Illinois to California in 1912—reciting his verse along the way and observing American life in its varied and common day-to-day affairs. In California he wrote a visionary, mystical poem, "General William Booth Enters into Heaven," a tribute to the recently deceased founder of the Salvation Army. This poem appeared in *Poetry* magazine and was then published in *General William Booth Enters into Heaven, and Other Poems* (1913). This volume and *The Congo, and Other Poems* (1914) established Lindsay as a popular poet who gave spirited, well-attended recitals across the United States. He became best known as a showman and performer, and his verse continues to be most highly regarded for lyrical verve, rhythm, and mysticism—not qualities as easily appreciated on the pages of anthologies.

Lindsay's reputation, in fact, rests as a troubadour — as one who wrote rhymes to be traded for bread, as the title of one of his earliest self-published pamphlets proclaims.

During the 1920s, Lindsay continued to write and recite heavily symbolic and resonant verses and toured as a self-styled Christian-Democrat poet, but he met with less public success. The strain of performing for audiences that preferred to hear him, rather than to read him, and intermittent problems with mental health, which became more acute in the mid-1920s and may have been related to epilepsy, contributed to his suicide in 1931.

"General William Booth Enters into Heaven" (1913).

Written to be sung to the tune of the hymn "The Blood of the Lamb," and including instructions on which instruments should be used, this poem, one of Lindsay's most famous, imagines the founder of the Salvation Army leading a parade of poor people and criminals into heaven. Lindsay had occasion to stay in Salvation Army quarters at times and admired Booth's administration of the Army.

❖•❖

Masters, Edgar Lee (1869-1950), American poet, biographer, and novelist.

Masters's reputation rests with *The Spoon River Anthology* (1915), a collection of 244 lyrical epitaphs voiced in the first-person by individuals of a small town based on those in the Sangamon Valley of Illinois, where Masters was raised. While studying law at Knox College, he wrote verse as a hobby and had several pseudonymous poems published in Chicago newspapers. Masters moved to Chicago in 1892 and focused on law for the next twenty-five years, including eight as a partner of Clarence Darrow (1857-1938), the famous attorney. He continued contributing verses to periodicals, particularly the St. Louis *Mirror,* whose editor and publisher, William Reedy, introduced Masters to translations of Greek epigrams. Masters, who easily mastered a variety of poetic forms during his career, began writing the free-verse epitaphs that eventually formed *The Spoon River Anthology*.

The Spoon River Anthology (1915).

The 244 dramatic monologues in *The Spoon River Anthology* represent individuals from all levels of small-town society. Many of the epitaphs reflect a sense of frustration and confinement among the speakers. Masters patterned the sequence of poems on Dante's *Divine Comedy,* moving from lost souls to enlightened individuals. In their free-verse forms that accentuate the rhythms of common speech and in their representation of common people, the *Spoon River* pieces helped expand American poetry, matching literary forms and language with the changing social environment of twentieth-century America.

⇛•⇚

Sandburg, Carl (1878-1967)
American poet, historian, journalist, and children's writer.

Sandburg was one of the most popular and honored American writers of the twentieth century. Born in Galesburg, Illinois, to Swedish immigrant parents, he left school at age 13 to help support his family, working numerous odd jobs. He traveled on the railways as a hobo in his late teens and served in the Spanish-American War in 1898. Sandburg was active in politics in Wisconsin from 1908 to 1912, helping elect Milwaukee's socialist mayor and serving as the mayor's secretary. Sandburg returned to Chicago with his wife, Lilian, who was also active in socialist causes, to work as a journalist and continue writing poetry, having had several short-run chapbooks already to his credit. The variety of his work experience, his travels in the Midwest, and his concern for social reform are all hallmarks of his verse.

Sandburg burst onto the literary scene in 1916 with the publication of *Chicago Poems,* which contained oddly structured, free-verse poems startling in their appearance, focus on urban life, and use of common language. In their prosaic, free-verse form and unpolished but rhythmic language, they challenged conventional definitions of poetry and initiated what would become a career-long debate over the quality of Sandburg's verse. Detractors find many Sandburg poems overly sentimental and formless. Yet the poems capture the rhythm of ordinary language and the concerns of common people, attributes in all of Sandburg's verse. He expanded his subjects from Chicago to the Midwest in *Cornhuskers* (1918), and to the entire United States in *Good Morning, America* (1928) and *The People, Yes* (1936).

Sandburg became a beloved literary figure, as a poet who championed the lives of common people, as a biographer of Abraham Lincoln, as a traveling troubadour playing guitar and singing folk songs, as a writer of children's tales, and as a journalist who covered social problems, from poor working and living conditions to racial tensions. He won Pulitzer Prizes for *Abraham Lincoln: The War Years* (1939) and for *Collected Poems* (1950), which includes an Introduction where he discusses his career: "I still favor several simple poems published long ago which continue to have an appeal for simple people." Following his death, Sandburg was given a special funeral service at the Lincoln Memorial.

"Chicago" (1914).

This title poem, published first in *Poetry* in 1914, then in his first important collection *Chicago Poems* (1916), epitomizes Sandburg's boisterous and lusty linguistic style as well as his socialist concerns. Here, he treats a city he loves in Whitmanesque free verse, using colloquial midwestern language. The unusual opening stanza lists nicknames for Chicago according to its industries and Sandburg's anthropomorphizing of them: "Hog Butcher for the World, / Tool Maker, Stacker of Wheat, / Player with Railroads and the Nation's Freight Handler; / Stormy, husky, brawling, / City of the Big Shoulders." In 1913, Sandburg describes the city in a letter to a friend that "it is so good a place for a healthy man who wants to watch the biggest, most intense, brutal and complicated game in the world — the game by which the world gets fed and clothed — the method of control — the economics and waste."

✦•✦

Further Reading

Allen, Gay Wilson. *Carl Sandburg*. Minneapolis: University of Minnesota Press, 1972.

Boynton, Percy H. "The Voice of Chicago: Edgar Lee Masters and Carl Sandburg." *English Journal* XI (December 1972): 610-20.

Cahill, Daniel J. *Harriet Monroe*. New York: Twayne, 1973.

Callahan, North. *Carl Sandburg, Lincoln of Our Literature: A Biography*. New York: New York University Press, 1970.

Crowder, Richard. *Carl Sandburg*. New York: Twayne, 1964.

Duffey, Bernard. *The Chicago Renaissance in American Letters: A Critical History*. East Lansing, Mich.: Michigan State College Press, 1954.

Durnell, Hazel. *The America of Carl Sandburg*. Washington, D.C.: University Press of Washington D.C., 1965.

Flanagan, John T. *Edgar Lee Masters: The 'Spoon River' Poet and His Critics*. Metuchen, N.J.: Scarecrow Press, 1974.

Gregory, Horace, and Marya Zaturenska. "Harriet Monroe and the 'Poetic Renaissance'." In their *A History of American Poetry, 1900-1940*. New York: Harcourt Brace, 1946.

Hallwas, John E., and Dennis J. Reader, eds. *The Vision of This Land: Studies of Vachel Lindsay, Edgar Lee Masters, and Carl Sandburg*. Macomb, Ill.: Western Illinois University, 1976.

Hansen, Harry. *Midwest Portraits: A Book of Memories and Friendships*. New York: Harcourt Brace, 1923.

Hartley, Lois. *Spoon River Revisited*. Muncie, Ind.: Ball State Teachers College, 1963.

Johnson, Abby Arthur. "A Free Foot in the Wilderness: Harriet Monroe and 'Poetry, 1912 to 1936'." *Illinois Quarterly* 37, 4 (summer 1975): 28-43.

Kramer, Dale. "Harriet Monroe: Poetry's Muse." In his *Chicago Renaissance: The Literary Life in the Midwest, 1900-1930*. New York: Appleton-Century, 1966.

Master, Edgar Lee. *Vachel Lindsay: A Poet in America*. New York: Scribner's Sons, 1935.

Monroe, Harriet. *A Poet's Life: Seventy Years in a Changing World*. New York: Macmillan, 1938.

Poetry LXIX, 3 (December 1936). Special dedicatory issue to Monroe and the Chicago poets.

Primeau, Ronald. *Beyond 'Spoon River': The Legacy of Edgar Lee Masters*. Austin, Tex.: University of Texas, 1981.

Smith, Alson. *Chicago's Left Bank*. Chicago: H. Regnery, 1953.

Starrett, Vincent. *Born in a Bookshop: Chapters from the Chicago Renaissance*. Norman, Okla.: University of Oklahoma Press, 1965.

Untermeyer, Louis. "Vachel Lindsay." In his *Modern American Poetry*. New York: Harcourt Brace, 1936.

CH'UANG-TSAO SHE. *See* CREATION SOCIETY

CHUNG-HUA CH'ÜAN-KUO WEN-I-CHIEH K'ANG-TI HSIE-HUI. *See* ALL-CHINA ANTI-AGGRESSION FEDERATION OF WRITERS AND ARTISTS

CLARIDADE MOVEMENT
Cape Verde, 1936-1960

The *Claridade* Movement, the foundation of native Cape Verdean literature, began in 1936 with the first issue of *Claridade*, a cultural journal whose primary audience was the educated bourgeoisie. Writers Jorge Barbosa (1901-1971) and Baltasar Lopes da Silva (1907-) were typical of the movement in their melancholy outlook toward their socially and politically troubled homeland. *Claridade,* which sustained itself until the expiration of the journal in 1960, remains especially important to contemporary Cape Verdean writers for its elevation of the Portuguese-based Creole language spoken by the common people.

✦●✦

Further Reading

Silva, Carlos Alberto Gomes da. "An Introduction to Capeverdean Poetry of Portuguese Expression." In *Emerging Literatures*. Edited by Reingard Nethersole. Bern, Switzerland: P. Lang, 1990.

CLARTÉ
Sweden, 1919-1930s

Clarté was the name for a Marxist-pacifist group that achieved notoriety during and following World War I. French neo-NATURALIST and PROLETARIAN writer Henri Barbusse (1873-1935) founded the group in 1919 with his emblematic novel *Clarté* (1919; *Light,* 1919). Two years earlier Barbusse had won the Prix Goncourt and a large following of sympathizers with his sober antiwar novel *Le feu: Journal d'une escouade* (1916; *Under Fire: The Story of a Squad,* 1917). International in character, *Clarté* provided through its periodicals a forum in which writers, artists, and intellectuals could discuss their respective roles in relationship to the current political climate in Europe. In addition to Barbusse, Swedish MODERNIST Karin Boye (1900-1941) is remembered as one of the group's guiding forces. Her experimental poetic style and interest in the theories of Sigmund FREUD helped expand the literary appeal of *Clarté*, though the movement as a whole remained fundamentally propagandistic and political.

❦•❦

Further Reading

Field, Frank. "Henri Barbusse and Communism." In his *Three French Writers and the Great War: Studies in the Rise of Communism and Fascism*. Cambridge, England; New York: Cambridge University Press, 1975.

Gustafson, Alrík. *A History of Swedish Literature*. Minneapolis: University of Minnesota Press for the American-Scandinavian Foundation, 1961.

Racine, Nicole. "The Clarté Movement in France, 1919-21." In *Literature and Politics in the Twentieth Century*. Edited by Walter Laquer and George L. Mosse. New York: Harper & Row, 1967.

COBRA
Belgium, Denmark, and Holland, 1950s

The name of this group is an acronym formed by the names of the capital cities of the participants from Copenhagen, Brussels, and Amsterdam. Without a specific manifesto, these writers and graphic artists attempted to combine literary sensibility with aspects of modern painting — specifically as embodied in the abstract expressionism movement which is often violently colorful and grotesque in content. The Dutch painter Karel Appel (1921-), a member of COBRA, is said to have reacted to the "austerity" of earlier abstract expressionists in part, as his work contains more uninhibited brushstrokes and boldly violent color.

Pierre Olechensky (1927-), Hugo Claus (1929-), Asger Jorn (1914-1973), and Constant Nieuwenhuys (1930-) were initial members of the group; Claus has been the most critically acclaimed. His association with COBRA solidified his reputation as a writer of incredible skill and artistic virtuosity. His poetry, collected in *Selected Poems, 1953-1973* (1986), shows rejection of traditional form and style and incorporates "oddly-matched images . . . and musical effect." Exemplary of the poetry is the early *Registreren* collection (1948), in which his role is that of poet as "inventor and in search of self."

It is noted that the post-World War II Dutch poets have thus far failed to form cohesive groups or movements; their poetry is direct, straightforward, and "loosely styled." The aim seems to be less experimental than earlier, but remains, however, "completely new and distinct."

74

⇒•⇐
Further Reading

Meijer, R. P. *Literature of the Low Countries: A Short History of Dutch Literature in the Netherlands and Belgium*. New York: Twayne; Assen, Netherlands: Van Gorcum, 1971.
Snapper, J. P. *Post War Dutch Literature: A Harp Full of Nails*. Amsterdam: Delta, 1971.
Stokvis, Willemijn. *Cobra: An International Movement in Art After the Second World War*. New York: Rizzoli, 1988.

COLOGNE SCHOOL OF NEW REALISM (Kölner Schule des neuen Realismus)
Germany, 1960s

The Cologne School of New Realism was founded in the 1960s by Dieter Wellershoff (1925-) in response to the rise of the French NEW NOVEL. Like the New Novelists, the New Realists wished to develop an intensely self-conscious form of fiction to express their alienation in the technological age. In this, they were aided by the anthropological philosophy of Arnold Gehlen (1904-). Original members of the group included Günter Herburger (1932-), U. Chr. Fischer (n.d.), Ludwig Harig (n.d.), Robert Wolfgang Schnell (n.d.), Rolf Dieter Brinkmann (1940-1975), and Günter Seuren (n.d.). Among German poets of the same era, Nicolas Born (1937-) —especially such collections of his as *Marktlage* (1967) and *Wo mir der Kopf steht* (1970) —along with Brinkmann and Herburger, helped advance the New Realist cause. An anthology of their work was published in 1962, *Ein Tag in der Stadt. Sechs Autoren variieren ein Thema*.

⇒•⇐
Further Reading

Demetz, Peter. *After the Fires: Recent Writing in the Germanies, Austria, and Switzerland*. San Diego: Harcourt Brace Jovanovich, 1986.
Durzak, Manfred. "German Literature." In *World Literature Since 1945: Critical Surveys of the Contemporary Literatures of Europe and the Americas*. Edited by Ivar Ivask and Gero von Wilpert. New York: Ungar, 1973.

COLÓNIDA MOVEMENT
Peru, 1916

Poet, fiction writer, journalist, dramatist, and essayist Abraham Valdelomar (1888-1919) founded the literary journal *Colónida* in 1916, around which a group of Peruvian writers gathered. As one critic put it, they "rebelled against the conservatism of the *NOUECENTISTAS*," even as they employed some of the same techniques. Writers

75

associated with *Colónida* included poet César Vallejo (1892-1938), poet Federico More (1889-1954), dramatist Percy Gibson (1908-), Augusto Aguirre Morales (1890-?), novelist Enrique Carillo (1877-1938), poet Enrique Bustamante y Ballivián (1884-1936), poet and theorist Alberto Hidalgo (1897-1967), and Antonio Garland (n.d.). In its pages, they were preoccupied with aesthetic, rather than purely political, issues and admired MODERNISMO writers Rubén DARÍO and Juan Ramón JIMÉNEZ, as well as Julio Herrera y Reissig (1875-1910), Edgar Allan Poe (1809-1849), Oscar Wilde (1854-1900), and Maurice MAETERLINCK (*see* SYMBOLISM, Belgium). Symbolist Peruvian poet José María Eguren (1874-1942) was largely promoted by Valdelomar in the pages of *Colónida*.

Valdelomar was concerned with locating a cultural identity via literature. His prose works are regionalistic, set in coastal villages, such as his own childhood home, and evocative of the Incan past. The posthumously published collection of stories, *Los hijos del sol* (1921; Children of the Sun), is a good example. His social consciousness became evident by 1918; he was spending time speaking to village people in those coastal provinces about modernist art, patriotism, and the importance of building schools. The next year, his last, he was elected a representative to the Central Regional Congress. *Colónida* was discontinued after only four issues.

❖•❖

Further Reading

Aldrich, E. M. *The Modern Short Story in Peru*. Madison, Wis.: University of Wisconsin Press, 1966.

Franco, Jean. *César Vallejo: The Dialectics of Poetry and Silence*. Cambridge, England: Cambridge University Press, 1976.

Henríquez-Ureña, P. "Problems of Today 1920-1940." In his *Literary Currents in Hispanic America*. Cambridge, Mass.: Harvard University Press, 1963.

Higgins, James. *A History of Peruvian Literature*. London: F. Cairns, 1987.

Rodríguez-Peralta, P. "Abraham Valdelomar, a Transitional Modernist." *Hispania* 52 (1969): 26-32.

COMEDY OF MENACE
England, 1950s

This name is given to a dramatic genre in which the characters of a play appear to be in situations where they are menaced by some underlying, often mysterious, and indefinable terror, but find themselves unable to articulate their fears. When they resort, then, to a kind of trivial dialogue which has no obvious relationship to the problem, plot and character denouement are frequently reduced to comedic and absurd interludes, and one critic observes that the plays become "difficult for audiences to understand." The dramatic strategy is also used in the THEATER OF CRUELTY and the THEATER OF THE ABSURD which were popular in France and middle Europe between the thirties and the sixties, for representation of renunciation of the classical dramatic tradition of Greek tragedy. Dramatic elements of menace, cruelty, and absurdity are contemporary manifestations of the concept that modern society has disclaimed religion, ritual, and any need for a "sense of the heroic." David Compton (1924-) and Harold PINTER (1930-) are best known for their comedy of menace.

✦•✦

Pinter, Harold (1930-), English dramatist.

Pinter is best known for his marked, avid interest in modern language and its failure to properly communicate the problems of the vulnerability of humankind; he presents dramatic character as psychically defenseless against the menacing atmosphere of our present sociopolitical environment. Early plays provide examples: a character is placed in a room, alone, and is aware that danger from an outside invader is present, but attempts between the two to come to grips with the problem break down in ambiguous dialogue which allows no resolution and reinforces the ongoing atmosphere of menace and disorientation. Noel Annan marks Pinter's perfection of the "game of vocabulary flashing and cultural reference" so prevalent in British writing today, but James P. Hollis admires Pinter's amazing ability to demonstrate, through use of everyday language, "the outer manifestation of the anxieties and uncertainties which lie within."

Pinter's first three plays are often considered those most representative of Comedy of Menace drama: *The Room* (1957), *THE BIRTHDAY PARTY* (1958), and *The Dumb Waiter* (1960). He has adapted many of his own works to the screen, some of which are *The Caretaker* (1963), released as *The Guest*; *The Birthday Party* (1969); and *The Homecoming* (1973). He has also adapted the work of numerous writers to the screen, and some of these appear in *Five Screenplays* (1971). Other works are *The Hothouse* (1980), *A Slight Ache and Other Plays*, *A Night Out,* and *The Dwarfs* (all 1961), *The Collection and the Lover* (1963), *Dialogue for Three* (1963), *The Compartment* (1963), *Eight Review Sketches* (1965), *Tea Party* (1964), *The Basement* (1966), *Poems* (1968), *Mac* (1968), *Night School* (1968), *Landscape and Silence with Night* (1970), *Monologue* (1973), *No Man's Land* (1975), *Poems and Prose 1949-1977* (1978), *Betrayal* (1978), and *Family Voices* (1981). It is generally agreed that his innovative dramatic style, his prolific output, and his linguistic creativity make him one of the most important and transitional dramatists in the history of English drama.

The Birthday Party (1958).

Produced in 1957 at the Arts Theatre in Cambridge, England, *The Birthday Party* was Pinter's second play, but the first to gain him recognition as a playwright. The birthday party the title refers to is Stanley's, for some time a boarder at a boarding house run by a couple. Two new men have come on as boarders. They attend the party and menace Stanley with a game of blind man's bluff. The following day, they take Stanley to some unknown location. As in his later plays, characters' speeches, and what happens or does not happen as a result, tend to point out the futility of verbal communication as well as the difficulty in truly knowing reality.

❧•❦

Further Reading

Adler, Thomas P. "The Embrace of Silence: Pinter, Miller, and the Response to Power." *Pinter Review* (1991): 4-9.

Blau, Herbert. *The Impossible Theatre: A Manifesto*. New York: Macmillan, 1965.

Brook, Peter. *the empty space*. New York: Atheneum, 1968.

Burkman, Katherine H., and John L. Kundert-Gibbs, eds. *Pinter at Sixty*. Bloomington, Ind.: Indiana University Press, 1993.

Cox, C. B., and A. E. Dyson, eds. *The Twentieth-Century Mind: History, Ideas and Literature in Britain*. London: Oxford University Press, 1972.

Esslin, Martin. *The Peopled Wound: The Work of Harold Pinter*. Garden City, N.Y.: Doubleday, 1970.

Ghose, Meeta. "Harold Pinter's *The Birthday Party* as a Comedy of Menace." *Panjab University Research Bulletin* 18, 1 (April 1987): 59-67.

Hollis, James R. *Harold Pinter: The Poetics of Silence*. Carbondale, Ill.: Southern Illinois University Press, 1970.

Taylor, John Russell. *Anger and After*. London: Methuen, 1969.

————. *The Second Wave: British Drama for the Seventies*. London: Methuen; New York: Hill and Wang, 1971.

CONCRETE POETRY
Austria, Belgium, Brazil, England, Germany, Norway, Sweden, Switzerland, and United States, 1950s-1960s

The Concrete Poetry movement appeared in the early 1950s, and initially consisted of a writer in Switzerland, Bolivian-born Eugen GOMRINGER, and a few writers in Brazil— Haroldo and Augusto de CAMPOS, and Décio PIGNATARI—who simultaneously and independently experimented with poetry incorporating graphic and spatial elements. The unification of this small group of writers and other artists calling for, and creating, a poetry in which form equals content was strong and internationally influential into the 1960s.

Gomringer in 1953 called his poems "constellations" until he became acquainted with Pignatari in 1955 at the Hochschule für Gestaltung at Ulm. Pignatari and the de Campos referred to their work as "concrete poetry," a designation Gomringer, after meeting with the Brazilians, agreed to adopt. The movement officially asserted itself as such at the National Exhibition of Concrete Art at São Paulo in 1956. They announced their aesthetic principles in manifestos: Gomringer's "from line to constellation" (1954), "concrete poetry" (1956) and "the poem as a functional object" (1960), and the Brazilians' "pilot plan for concrete poetry" (1958). The three Brazilians were soon joined by ad man Ronaldo Azeredo (1937-), lawyer and journalist José Lino Grüne-wald (1931-), lawyer, critic, and literature professor Pedro Xisto (1901-), and physician Edgard Braga (1898-?). The Brazilians, adopting the name *Noigandres,* published a literary journal of the same name from 1952 to 1958, by which time the group had grown larger and begun the journal *Invenção* (1962-67).

Within a few years, poets throughout Latin America, North America, eastern and western Europe, and Japan were experimenting with the techniques popularized by the founders, sharing aesthetic ideas and principles with each other, and exhibiting and publishing their works.all over the world. In Austria, Friedrich Achleitner (1930-), Ernst Jandl (1925-), and others formed the VIENNA GROUP. Max Bense (1910-), Jean-François Bory (1938-), Claus Bremer (1924-), Henri Chopin (1922-), Ian Hamilton Finlay (1925-), John Furnival (1933-), Pierre (1928-) and Ilse Garnier (n.d.), Václav Havel (1936-), Dom Sylvester Houédard (1924-), Kitazono Katsue (1902-), Hansjörg Mayer (1943-), Franz Mon (1926-), Edwin Morgan (1920-), Diter Rot (1930-), Seiichi Niikuni (1925-), Mary Ellen Solt (1920-), Emmett Williams (1925-), and Jonathan Williams (1929-) have been, or are, among the most prominent practitioners of the Concretist tendency throughout the world.

Concrete, or visual, poetry is nothing new, as shown in Kenneth B. Newell's book on the history of "pattern poetry." In their manifestos, the mid-twentieth-century Concretists named Guillaume APOLLINAIRE (*see* CUBISM), Stéphane MALLARMÉ (*see* SYMBOL-ISM, France), e. e. CUMMINGS (*see* LOST GENERATION), Ezra POUND (*see* MOD-ERNISM, England and Ireland; the Brazilians took their name "Noigandres" from one of Pound's *CANTOS*), and James JOYCE (*see* MODERNISM, England and Ireland) as artistic precursors. A Brazilian-born Swedish writer, Öyvind Fahlström (1928-), published a manifesto for concrete poetry in 1953. Moreover, Carlo Belloli (1922-), just a decade earlier, working under the influence of Filippo Tommaso MARINETTI and the FUTURISTS, had been producing similar work in Italy. The mood in which the Concretists worked can be seen as a post-World War II extension of the sentiment expressed in the *DE STIJL* manifesto of 1920. Those post-World War I poets pronounced the Word dead, characterized their time as "an exhausted era," and called for a revital-ization of poetry by incorporating sound into idea and by uniting form and content. Similarly, the Concretists insisted on the reciprocal equation of form and content, as well as claimed the music of Anton Webern (1833-1945), Karlheinz Stockhausen (1928-), and Pierre Boulez (1925-) as influences for their creations. The Concretists also included in their repertoire attacks against western commercialism (see Pigna-tari's "bebe coca cola" [drink coca cola]), attempts toward international linguistic uni-fication by blending characters and words from various languages in individual poems (for a simple example, see Pignatari's "life" poem; the penultimate figure in the sequence is the Chinese character for the sun), and efforts to incorporate the visual arts, including typography and pop art, into their poetry (see Augusto de Campos's "ôlho por ôlho" [an eye for an eye] and Gomringer's "silencio" [silence]). Toward the Concretists' goal of rejuvenating poetry for their age, they drew upon elements of space, color, music, typography, the commercial and visual arts, and sculpture to create poems which could be seen, read, pronounced, heard, and experienced in new ways; or, as Gomringer put it, poetry to be "understood as signs in airports and traffic signs."

The bonds of the movement proper had weakened by 1964, when the original members began diversifying their efforts and working in separate directions. Augusto de Campos began experimenting with "popcrete" poems, while his brother Haroldo worked with experimental prose. Also in 1964, Pignatari and Azeredo joined Luis Angelo Pinto (n.d.) to found a semiotic poetry movement. In fact, the work of the original Concretists was most recently reconsidered in relation to post-STRUCTURALIST theories, including SEMIOTICS and DECONSTRUCTION. Poets throughout the world continue to produce what many call concrete poetry, though some rigorously avoid the appellation.

⇒•⇐

Campos, Augusto de (1931-), Brazilian poet, critic, and essayist.

One of the founders, along with his brother Haroldo de Campos and Décio Pignatari, of the *Noigandres* group which produced concrete poetry during the 1950s and 1960s. Augusto's *Poetamenos* (1953; Color Poems), influenced by Webern's "Klangfarben-melodie" (Tone Color Melodies), are perhaps the earliest concrete poems in Brazil. He coauthored the Brazilian "pilot plan for concrete poetry," published in their journal *Noigandres* in 1958. Augusto's concrete poems can be characterized by their socio-political commentary, as well as experimentation with form, color, typography, and pop art. His fold-out poem, "luxo-lixo" (luxury-garbage), is an example whose statement on western materialism is inextricably blended with the formal requirement of physi-cally unfolding the page in order to kinetically and temporally create an impression in characters, which are represented on the page by an excessively ornate typeface.

Augusto has translated works of Pound, cummings, and Joyce. In 1968 he and his brother were visiting lecturers at the University of Wisconsin, the University of Texas, and the University of Indiana. In addition to having contributed to *Noigandres,* its succeeding journal, *Invenção,* and others, Augusto has also written *O Rei Menos O Reino* (1951; The King Minus the Kingdom), *Poesia, antipoesia, antropofagia* (1978), *Poesia 1949-1979* (1979; Poems 1949-1979), and coauthored with his brother and Pignatari *Teoria da Poesia Concreta* (1965; Theory of Concrete Poetry).

Campos, Haroldo de (1929-)
Brazilian poet, critic, essayist, and professor of literary theory.

Haroldo cofounded *Noigandres* with his brother Augusto de Campos and Décio Pignatari in the early 1950s. He played a major role in spreading the concrete poetry movement throughout the world; for instance, after corresponding with Kitazono Katsue in 1957, Katsue responded with the first Japanese concrete poem. Haroldo's poem "fala prata cala ouro" (silver speech golden silence) is representative of the ideogrammatic conceptualization, line redefinition, and semantic play at work in concrete poetry.

Haroldo's knowledge of world literature is punctuated by his translations, or corroboration in translations, of works in Japanese, Chinese, French, German, Italian, Russian, and others. In addition to contributing to *Noigandres* and *Invenção,* Haroldo has written *Auto do Possesso* (1950; Auto of the Possessed), *Servidão de Passagem* (1962; Transient Servitude), *Alea I—Semantic Variations* (1964), *Versuchsbuch Galaxien* (1966), and *Metalinguagem: ensaios de teoria e crítica literária* (1967), and coauthored with his brother and Pignatari *Teoria da Poesia Concreta* (1965; Theory of Concrete Poetry).

Gomringer, Eugen (1924-), Bolivian-born Swiss poet, critic, and essayist.

Working in Switzerland under the influence of concrete artists such as Max Bill (1908-), Gomringer published his first *Konstellations* (a term borrowed from Mallarmé) in 1953, poems within similar aesthetic lines as those being produced in Brazil by the *Noigandres* poets. In 1955 at the Hochschule für Gestaltung, where he worked as a secretary to Bill, Gomringer met Décio Pignatari. Within a year Gomringer and Pignatari were planning an anthology of concrete poetry (which was never published) for which Gomringer had written the introduction/manifesto "concrete poetry" (1956), and Gomringer had decided to enter into an aesthetic corroboration with Pignatari and Haroldo and Augusto de Campos, renaming his constellations concrete poetry.

His "silencio" (1954; silence), printed in the sans serif typeface favored by many Concretists, is an early poignant piece utilizing space, form, and repetition, creating an impression of silence as visual and physical, as well as auditory. Among Gomringer's published works are *33 konstellationen (1960)*, *5 mal 1 konstellationen* (1960), *das studenbuch* (1965; *The Book of Hours and Constellations*, 1968), *manifeste und dartstellungen der konkreten poesie 1954-1966* (1966), and *Josef Albers; His Work as Contribution to Visual Articulation in the Twentieth Century* (1968).

❖•❖

Pignatari, Décio (1927-), Brazilian poet, essayist, graphic artist, and professor of information theory.

Pignatari, with Augusto and Haroldo de Campos, cofounded *Noigandres*, and coauthored the "pilot plan for concrete poetry," the movement's primary manifesto. His meeting with Eugen Gomringer at Ulm in 1955 resulted in the international concrete poetry movement. Later, he edited the journal *Invenção* (1962-67) and coedited *Através* (1977-). Pignatari's poem "bebe coca cola" (1957) composes a caustic statement against advertisement, utilizing color, juxtaposition, and significant plays on the Portuguese words for glue, cocaine, shard, drool, and cesspool. His "life" (1958) poem typifies the Concretist effort to unify world languages by incorporating the Chinese character for sun in a sequential, typographic manipulation of the Roman characters.

Pignatari has written *Comunicação Poética* (1978), and coauthored *Teoria da Poesia Concreta* (1965; Theory of Concrete Poetry) with Augusto and Haroldo de Campos.

❖•❖

Further Reading

Bann, Stephen, ed. *Concrete Poetry: An International Anthology.* London: London Magazine Editions, 1967.

Bory, Jean-François. *Once Again.* Translated by Lee Hildreth. New York: New Directions, 1968.

Brasil, Emanuel, and William Jay Smith, eds. *Brazilian Poetry (1950-1980).* Middletown, Conn.: Wesleyan University Press, 1983.

Espinosa, Cesar, ed. *Corrosive Signs: Essays on Experimental Poetry (Visual, Concrete, Alternative).* Washington, D.C.: Maisonneuve, 1990.

Fernández Moreno, César, ed. *Latin America in Its Literature.* New York and London: Holmes & Meier Publishers, 1980.

Gomringer, Eugen. *The Book of Hours and Constellations.* Translated by Jerome Rothenberg. New York: Something Else Press, 1968.

Kostelanetz, Richard, ed. *The Avant-Garde Tradition in Literature.* Buffalo, N.Y.: Prometheus Books, 1982.

———. *Visual Literature Criticism: A New Collection.* Carbondale and Edwardsville, Ill.: Southern Illinois University Press, 1979.

McCullough, Kathleen. *Concrete Poetry: An Annotated International Bibliography with an Index of Poets and Poems.* Troy, N.Y.: The Whitston Publishing Co., 1989.

Newell, Kenneth B. *Pattern Poetry: A Historical Critique from the Alexandrian Greeks to Dylan Thomas.* Boston: Marlborough House, 1976.

Perrone, Charles A. "The Imperative of Invention: Brazilian Concrete Poetry and Intersemiotic Creation." *Harvard Library Bulletin* 3, 2 (summer 1992): 44-53.

Pignatari, Décio, and Jon Tolman. "Concrete Poetry: A Brief Structural-Historical Guideline." *Poetics Today* 3 (summer 1982): 189-95.

Saper, Craig J. "Instant Theory: Making Thinking Popular." *Visible Language* 22, 4 (autumn 1988): 371-98.

Schmidt, Siegfried J. "Perspectives on the Development of Post-Concrete Poetry." *Poetics Today* 3, 3 (summer 1982): 101-36.

Scobie, Stephen. *Earthquakes and Explorations: Language and Painting from Cubism to Concrete Poetry.* Toronto: University of Toronto Press, 1997.

Seaman, David W. *Concrete Poetry in France.* Ann Arbor, Mich.: UMI Research Press, 1981.

Solt, Mary Ellen, ed. *Concrete Poetry: A World View.* Bloomington, Ind.: Indiana University Press, 1968.

Steiner, Wendy. *The Colors of Rhetoric: Problems in the Relation Between Modern Literature and Painting.* Chicago: University of Chicago Press, 1982.

————. "*Res Poetica*: The Problematics of the Concrete Poem." *New Literary History* 12, 3 (spring 1981): 529-45.

Weaver, Mike. "Concrete Poetry." *The Lugano Review* 1 (summer 1966): 100-25. Includes reprint of the De Stijl manifesto of 1920.

Williams, Emmett, ed. *An Anthology of Concrete Poetry.* New York: Something Else Press, 1967.

CONDEMNED GENERATION POETS
Poland, 1940s

A Polish movement of the 1940s, the Condemned Generation were so named for their almost inevitable deaths either as soldiers or concentration camp victims due to their participation in the Polish Underground Army during World War II. The most important of these wartime poets were Krzysztof K. Baczyński (1921-1944), Tadeusz Borowski (1922-1951), Tadeusz Gajcy (1922-1944), Zdzissław Stroiński (1920-1943), and Andrzej Trzebiński (1922-1943).

❧•❦

Further Reading

Bross, Addison, trans. and ed. "Five Poems by Tadeuz Borowski." *The Polish Review* 28, 3 (1983): 43-49.

Kuhiwczak, Piotr. [sic] "Beyond Self: A Lesson from the Concentration Camps." *Canadian Review of Comparative Literature* 19, 3 (September 1992): 395-405.

83

Levine, Madeline G. "History's Victims: The Poetry of Tadeusz Gajcy and Krzysztof Kamil Baczynski." *The Polish Review* 23, 3 (1978): 30-46.

Miłosz, Czesław. "World War II; First Twenty Years of People's Poland." In his *The History of Polish Literature*. London: Macmillan, 1969. Rev. ed., Berkeley, Calif.: University of California Press, 1983.

Walc, Jan. "When the Earth Is No Longer a Dream and Cannot Be Dreamed Through to the End." *The Polish Review* 32, 2 (1987): 181-94.

Wirth, Andrzej. "A Discovery of Tragedy (The Incomplete Account of Tadeusz Borowski)." *The Polish Review* 12, 3 (1967): 43-52.

CONFEDERATION POETS
Canada, 1880s-1920s

Led by Charles G. D. Roberts (1860-1943), the Confederation Poets were the first group of writers to earn widespread renown in Canada after the country's formation as a dominion. In their attempt to develop a distinctive native poetry the four major Confederation writers — Roberts, his first cousin Bliss Carman (1861-1929), Archibald Lampman (1861-1899), and Duncan Campbell Scott (1862-1947) — focused on the rural landscapes of New Brunswick and Ontario, the provinces from which they hailed. Heavily influenced by Romantic and Victorian poetry, their works, beginning with Roberts's *Orion and Other Poems* (1880), represent the Golden Age of Canadian poetry, an era in which attention to classical forms and subjects merged with realistic description, tentative technical experimentation, and a philosophical exploration of the individual's dual relationship to modern civilization and the natural world.

Roberts, recognized during his lifetime as the father of Canadian poetry, was one of the most prolific and multitalented writers in Canadian literature. His career spanned over sixty years and left distinctive marks first in poetry, then in a number of animal stories, boys' stories, and historical and contemporary romances, and, finally, in a considerable body of nonfiction work on Canadian biography, history, and language. After a long hiatus from poetry, Roberts began publishing verse again in 1927. By the early 1930s he had assimilated many MODERNIST techniques and themes, thereby surpassing a newer generation of Confederation-influenced poets who had become the target of progressive writers within the MONTREAL MOVEMENT. At his death, Roberts was the most honored writer in the literary history of Canada. His best works include *Songs of the Common Day* (1893), *The Heart of the Ancient Wood* (1900), and *Canada Speaks of Britain* (1941).

Of the group, Lampman, who was greatly influenced by Roberts's *Orion* as well as the works of John Keats (1795-1821) and Alfred, Lord Tennyson (1809-1892), is most often regarded as the finest poet. Lampman's close friend, Duncan Campbell Scott, was largely responsible for calling posthumous attention through memorial editions to the brilliance of Lampman's nature lyrics. Scott distinguished himself, above all, through his numerous realistic and sympathetic poems of Canadian Indians. Carman, possibly the most modern of the group, pioneered the exploration of psychological states in his work. Both Carman and Roberts, distantly related to Ralph Waldo Emerson (1803-1882), displayed an affinity for the theories of Transcendentalism in their work. All four, despite occasional lapses into cliche and a strong dependency on such established forms as the sonnet, were preeminent in their time. Their legacy of REALISM, Romanticism, and nationalism was so powerful that it lasted well into the first decades of the twentieth century, beyond when much of their best work had been published. Other members of the movement included George Frederick Cameron (1854-1885), (William) Wilfred Campbell (1858-1918), and Isabella Valancy Crawford (1850-1887).

❧•❦

Further Reading

Adams, John Coldwell. *Sir Charles God Damn: The Life of Sir Charles G. D. Roberts.* Toronto: University of Toronto Press, 1986.

Brown, E. K. *On Canadian Poetry.* Toronto: Ryerson, 1943.

Cappon, James. *Bliss Carman and the Literary Currents and Influences of His Time.* Toronto: Ryerson Press; New York: L. Carrier & A. Isles, 1930.

―――. *Charles G. D. Roberts and the Influences of His Time.* 1905. Reprint, Ottawa, Canada: Techumseh Press, 1975.

Compton, Anne. "The Poet-Impressionist: Some Landscapes by Archibald Lampman." *Canadian Poetry* 34 (spring-summer 1994): 33-56.

Davies, Barrie. *At the Mermaid Inn: Wilfred Campbell, Archibald Lampman, Duncan Campbell Scott in "The Globe" 1892-93.* Toronto: University of Toronto Press, 1979.

Doyle, James. "The Confederation Poets and American Publishers." *Canadian Poetry* 17 (fall-winter 1985): 59-67.

Early, L. R. *Archibald Lampman.* Boston: Twayne, 1986.

―――. "Archibald Lampman (1861-99)." In *ECW's Biographical Guide to Canadian Poets.* Edited by Robert Lecker and Jack David. Toronto: ECW, 1993.

Herbert, Karen. "'There Was One Thing He Could Not See': William Morris in the Writing of Archibald Lampman and Francis Sherman." *Canadian Poetry* 37 (winter 1995): 79-99.

Klinckl, Carl Frederick. *Wilfrid Campbell, a Study in Late Provincial Victorianism.* Toronto: Ryerson, 1942.

McMullen, Lorraine, ed. *The Lampman Symposium.* Ottawa, Canada: University of Ottawa Press, 1976.

Pomeroy, Elsie M. *Sir Charles G. D. Roberts, a Biography.* Toronto: Ryerson, 1943.

Ross, Malcolm, ed. *Poets of the Confederation.* Toronto: McClelland & Stewart, 1960.

Stephens, Donald. *Bliss Carman.* New York: Twayne, 1966.

Stich, K. P., ed. *The Duncan Campbell Scott Symposium.* Ottawa, Canada: University of Ottawa Press, 1980.

Ware, Tracy, ed. "Letters to Carman, 1890-92, from Campbell, Lampman, and Scott." *Canadian Poetry* 27 (fall-winter 1990): 46-66.

Wicken, George. "William Wilfred Campbell (1858-1918)." In *ECW's Biographical Guide to Canadian Poets*. Edited by Robert Lecker and Jack David. Toronto: ECW, 1993.

CONFESSIONAL POETS
United States, 1950s-1960s

Although the label "confessional" has been used to describe a wide range of classical and contemporary poetry, it is most consistently employed when discussing the work of a small, loose circle of markedly autobiographical American poets who achieved renown in the decades following World War II. Chief among this circle was Robert Low-ELL, a prominent academic who had studied before the war under several of the FUGI-TIVES, particularly Allen Tate (1899-1979). Lowell succeeded in shedding this formalistic background during the 1950s, while teaching at Boston University. Drawing upon the free-verse style of William Carlos Williams (1883-1963), as well as the work of a former student, W. D. Snodgrass (1926-), Lowell began lecturing about and publishing poetry — often syntactically and metrically jarring — that expressed both the private and public angst of himself and his generation. Two of Lowell's students, Sylvia PLATH and Anne SEXTON, developed their own Confessional modes and, along with Lowell, established themselves as among the most artistically and emotionally demanding of modern poets.

Scholar Robert Phillips suggests that the Confessional tradition is a longstanding, albeit disjointed, one. He notes that since the time of Sappho (c. 612 B.C.) and Catullus (c. 84-c. 54 B.C.) — perhaps the two earliest Confessionalists — a distinguished procession of writers, including St. Augustine (354-430), Jean Jacques Rousseau (1712-1778), William Wordsworth (1770-1850), Charles BAUDELAIRE (*see* SYMBOLISM, France), Rainer Maria Rilke (1875-1926), and Walt Whitman (1819-1892), fused self-disclosure with the highest literary art. In addition to these figures, more immediate predecessors of the movement include MODERNISTS Ezra POUND, D. H. LAWRENCE, Delmore Schwartz (1913-1966), Randall Jarrell (1914-1965), Elizabeth Bishop (1911-1979), John Berryman (1914-1972), and, especially, Theodore Roethke (1908-1963). Yet, what distinguished the modern Confessional movement from these figures, or from such counterpart movements as the BEAT GENERATION and the BLACK MOUNTAIN POETS, was a restless urge to address the uncharted, murky, and painful subjects at the root of a nationwide postmodern malaise. These included ambivalent parent-child relationships, marital discord, ambiguous religious faith, the expiation of guilt, abnormal sexuality, drug addiction, social alienation, and debilitating mental illness. Although three early collections, Lowell's *LIFE STUDIES* (1959), Plath's *ARIEL* (1965), and Sexton's *LIVE OR DIE* (1966), represent the greatest hallmarks of the movement, Confessional poetry thrived for nearly two decades, until the death of Lowell in 1977. Its list of practitioners was forever expanding and, in addition to those mentioned, came to include Maxine Kumin (1925-), Stanley Kunitz (1905-), Denise Levertov (1923-), and Adrienne Rich (1925-). The decline of the form coincided with the facile and unbridled rendering of emotions, in the work of Beat writer Allen GINSBERG and others, that varied greatly from the powerfully understated, ironic, and structurally refined work characteristic of the original Confessionalists. Although some critics question the value of the narcissism and histrionics that occasionally color even the best Confessional poems, most contend that in no other form can so staggering and vivid a portrayal of the enigmas, tortures, and archetypes of contemporary life be revealed and understood.

❧•❦

Lowell, Robert (1917-1977)
American poet, dramatist, editor, and translator.

Grandnephew of James Russell Lowell (1819-1891) and distant cousin of IMAGIST Amy LOWELL, Robert Lowell inherited a strong sense of family as well as New England literary tradition. His childhood in Boston, for a variety of reasons, was an emotionally turbulent one and the family relationships that evolved inform a significant portion of his work. Lowell began to publish poetry shortly after his conversion to Roman Catholicism (which proved to be temporary) in 1940. His first book, *Land of Unlikeness*, contains religious poems as well as those of more general and immediate experience. Eventually, Lowell abandoned the specifically religious in his work but maintained an acute sense of the moral shortcomings of the modern world. It was the effective expression of this latter concern in his next collection, *Lord Weary's Castle* (1946), that earned him a Pulitzer Prize and brought him wide recognition. Following an unsuccessful exploration of the dramatic monologue in *The Mills of the Kavanaughs* (1951), Lowell labored for several years before producing his next and greatest work, *Life Studies*, which won the National Book Award in 1960. During the last two decades of his life, Lowell, through his writing and through his teaching posts at Harvard, Oxford, and elsewhere, influenced an entire generation of younger poets. At the end of the twentieth century he was ranked as the greatest American poet of the mid-century.

Life Studies (1959).

Life Studies consists of four parts. The first contains four poems similar in composition to Lowell's previous work. The second, which functions as the work's core, is a prose memoir entitled "91 Revere Street." The third contains tributary poems for Ford Madox FORD (*see* EDWARDIAN LITERATURE), George Santayana (1863-1952), Delmore

Schwartz (1913-1966), and Hart Crane (1899-1932). The fourth, titled "Life Studies," contains fifteen decidedly Confessional poems about Lowell's advancement from childhood to middle age. This final section, which has been called a fragmentary novel in verse, is closely tied to the sardonic picture of Lowell's family that emerges from "91 Revere Street." With increasing candor, Lowell turns inward in these last poems and analyzes his mental illness, troubled marriage, and behavioral faults. The poem "Skunk Hour" closes the volume obliquely, contrasting the desperate, lonely voice of Lowell— "I myself am hell; nobody's here" —with the insouciant, swaggering attitude toward life of a mother skunk and her kittens, parading outside.

Plath, Sylvia (1932-1963), American poet, novelist, and short-story writer.
A more artistically consistent and thematically mature poet than Sexton—a significant early influence—Plath ranks as one of the greatest figures in modern American poetry. She began her career in the 1950s while still an undergraduate, sporadically publishing poems and short stories as well as serving as editorial intern for *Mademoiselle*. In 1953 Plath suffered her first nervous breakdown and attempted suicide. This experience resulted directly in her authorship of the best-selling novel *The Bell Jar* (1963). Two years later, upon winning a Fulbright Fellowship to study at Cambridge University, she commenced an alternately rapturous and emotionally exhausting life of writing and child-rearing overseas. Her conflicting moods were inextricably tied to her mental illness as well as her ill-fated relationship with poet Ted Hughes (1930-1998), whom she married shortly after her arrival in England. Although only one volume of her poetry, *The Colossus and Other Poems* (1960), was published before she committed suicide in early 1963, Plath's reputation has risen steadily with the appearance of several posthumous volumes. Her most admired collection is *Ariel*, which contains poems written during an exceptionally prolific and tumultuous period near the end of her life, from early 1960 until late 1962. In 1981, *The Collected Poems of Plath* won a Pulitzer Prize, a rare distinction for a posthumous collection of work.

Ariel (1965).

Ariel embodies virtually all the major themes that Plath addressed in her work: the role of women in modern society, male dominance, family relationships, estrangement, death, and the mystery of the eternal. One of her most powerful and controversial poems, "Daddy," invokes the imagery of the Nazi Holocaust to exorcise Plath's perhaps greatest personal demon, the betrayal of men in her life, particularly that of her father, who died when she was eight. This poem and "Lady Lazarus," with their tersely controlled content of bitterness and anger, are among the best "hate" poems ever written. Plath's real achievement, however, is the creation of a mythic persona in the *Ariel* poems, who heroically counters weakness and despair with a striving, initially, toward vengeance and, finally, toward freedom.

✦•✦

Sexton, Anne (1928-1974)
American poet, short-story writer, dramatist, and author of children's books.

Considered the most daring of the Confessional poets in both subject matter and language, Sexton continually defied conventional tastes with poems about masturbation, menstruation, female anatomy, adultery, and incest. Following a suicide attempt on her twenty-eighth birthday, Sexton, upon the advice of her psychiatrist, began writing poetry. She published her first volume of poems, *To Bedlam and Part Way Back*, four years later. Despite several physical and emotional setbacks, including continual psychiatric care and two more failed suicide attempts, Sexton became a highly visible and admired poet and lecturer. Friendships with Kumin and Plath contributed to her literary development, but her best work was wrought from her own vision of womanhood and the many details of her disruptive life. Her greatest critical success came in 1966 when she received the Pulitzer Prize for her third poetry collection, *Live or Die*. After *Love Poems* (1969) and *Transformations* (1971) Sexton's work showed signs of deteriorating discipline. In 1974, Sexton took her life by carbon monoxide poisoning.

Live or Die (1966).

Live or Die contains two of Sexton's best-known poems, "Flee on Your Donkey" and "Wanting to Die." Like the collection as a whole, these poems explore what Sexton viewed as the major dichotomies of life: childhood vs. motherhood, spirit vs. body, escape vs. survival, death vs. life. Despite a preponderance of death-oriented poems, including an homage to Plath entitled "Sylvia's Death," Sexton's collection closes, with "Live," on a note of resolve to find value in earthly life, no matter how persistent the anguish of existence. In her next collection, *Love Poems*, Sexton largely transcended the scenes of madness and the asylum that characterize *Live or Die*, but it is generally agreed that the earlier work, a consistently ordered and haunting recreation of the world of inner chaos, represents one of the highest achievements in all Confessional poetry.

✦•✦

Further Reading

Alexander, Paul, ed. *Ariel Ascending, Writings About Sylvia Plath*. New York: Harper & Row, 1984.
George, Diana Hume. *Oedipus Anne: The Poetry of Anne Sexton*. Urbana, Ill.: University of Illinois Press, 1987.

Hall, Caroline King Barnard. *Sylvia Plath*. Boston: Twayne, 1978.

Hughes, Ted. "Foreword." In *The Journals of Sylvia Plath, 1950-62*. Edited by Ted Hughes. New York: Dial Press, 1982.

Jones, A. R. "Necessity and Freedom: The Poetry of Robert Lowell, Sylvia Plath, and Anne Sexton." *Critical Quarterly* 7 (spring 1965): 11-31.

Kumin, Maxine. "How It Was: Maxine Kumin on Anne Sexton." In *The Complete Poems* by Anne Sexton. Boston: Houghton Mifflin, 1981.

Lane, Gary, ed. *Sylvia Plath: New Views on the Poetry*. Baltimore: Johns Hopkins University, 1979.

London, Michael, and Robert Boyers, eds. *Robert Lowell: A Portrait of the Artist in His Time*. New York: D. Lewis, 1970.

McClatchy, J. D., ed. *Anne Sexton: The Artist and Her Critics*. Bloomington, Ind.: Indiana University Press, 1978.

Markey, Janice. *A New Tradition? The Poetry of Sylvia Plath, Anne Sexton, and Adrienne Rich, a Study of Feminism and Poetry*. Frankfurt am Main; New York: P. Lang, 1985.

Melander, Ingrid. *The Poetry of Sylvia Plath: A Study of Themes*. Stockholm: Almquist & Wiksell, 1972.

Molesworth, Charles. "'With Your Own Face On': The Origins and Consequences of Confessional Poetry." *Twentieth Century Literature* 22 (May 1976): 163-78.

Newman, Charles, ed. *The Art of Sylvia Plath, a Symposium*. Bloomington, Ind.: Indiana University Press, 1970.

Northouse, Cameron, and Thomas P. Walsh, eds. *Sylvia Plath and Anne Sexton: A Reference Guide*. Boston: G. K. Hall, 1974.

Parkinson, Thomas, ed. *Robert Lowell: A Collection of Critical Essays*. Englewood Cliffs, N.J.: Prentice-Hall, 1968.

Phillips, Robert. *The Confessional Poets*. Carbondale, Ill.: Southern Illinois University Press, 1973.

Rosenblatt, Jon. *Sylvia Plath: The Poetry of Initiation*. Chapel Hill, N.C.: University of North Carolina Press, 1979.

Rosenthal, M. L. "Robert Lowell and the Poetry of Confession." In his *The New Poets: American and British Poetry since World War II*. New York: Oxford University Press, 1967.

Sexton, Anne. *Anne Sexton: A Self-Portrait in Letters*. Boston: Houghton Mifflin, 1977.

Simpson, Louis. *A Revolution in Taste: Studies of Dylan Thomas, Allen Ginsberg, Sylvia Plath, and Robert Lowell*. New York: Macmillan, 1978.

Steiner, Nancy Hunter. *A Closer Look at Ariel: A Memory of Sylvia Plath*. New York: Harper's Magazine Press, 1973.

Uroff, Margaret Dickie. *Sylvia Plath and Ted Hughes*. Urbana, Ill.: University of Illinois Press, 1979.

Wagner-Martin, Linda W., ed. *Critical Essays on Sylvia Plath*. Boston: G. K. Hall, 1984.

———. *Sylvia Plath: A Biography*. New York: Simon & Schuster, 1987.

CONSTRUCTIVISM
Russia, 1920s

In Russia during the 1920s artists Naum Gabo (1890-1977), his brother Anton Pevsner (1886-1962), Vladimir Tatlin (1885-1953), El Lissitzky (1890-1941), Alexander Rodchencko (1891-1956), and Ivan Poughny (1894-1956) developed the Constructivist aesthetic for the visual and architectural arts. This geometric and abstract visual arts movement was influenced by Pablo Picasso's (1881-1973) reliefs and CUBISM as well as FUTURISM. The Constructivists focused on industrial and other utilitarian design after the Revolution. One effect of the Revolution on the Constructivists was to imbue the idea that a new society can be created, constructed. As artists, they sought to construct symbols of the new society. They issued "The Realistic Manifesto" in 1920. The visual art and architectural aspect of constructivism had international influence, spreading to Germany, Hungary, and Britain. The group had been moving along a parallel course with such movements as *DE STIJL, MERZ,* and TODAY after Gabo and Pevsner exiled themselves to France. CONCRETE POETRY developed in part from these tendencies, and Constructivism retained influence in the latter years of the twentieth century.

To these visual artists, "Space and time are re-born to us today. Space and time are the only forms on which life is built and hence art must be constructed. . . . we construct our work as the universe constructs its own, as the engineer constructs his bridges, as the mathematician his formula of the orbits" (Gabo's "The Realistic Manifesto," 1920). They renounced color, for example, as only superficial, having nothing to do with an object's essence. That art needs to represent the kinetic rhythms of life was another major tenet.

Seminal events in the spread of Constructivist ideas occurred in December of 1921, when on two separate occasions Varvara Stepanova (1894-1958) and Tatlin gave talks on Constructivism at the Moscow Institute of Artistic Culture. Exhibits that had taken place earlier in the year also had an impact. The next year Alexei Gan (n.d.) wrote *Konstruktivizm*, a book that further developed Constructivist ideology. Soon other arts followed their lead.

Theater director and designer Vsevolod Emilyevich Meyerhold (1874-1940?) brought Constructivist techniques to the stage with biomechanics — utilizing machines, ramps, and platforms built on the stage — and sociomechanics, the idea that the stage can be made into a mechanism for communicating proper social ideas to the audience. He had worked with the MOSCOW ART THEATER since its founding in 1898. The 1924 production of *The Forest* by Aleksandr Ostorovsky (1823-1886) used Constructivist stage designs, but perhaps best known was Lyubov Popova's (n.d.) design for the 1922 production of *The Magnificent Cuckold* by Fernand Crommelynck (1885-1970). What is known about Meyerhold's fate is that in 1938 his work was branded as "formalist," the Meyerhold Theater was closed by the Soviet government, and he was arrested, along with his wife.

In 1922 a contingent of film Constructivists emerged and published a journal called *Kino-Phot*, to which Gan contributed, all leading to the flowering of documentary film-making in the Soviet Union.

A literary subgroup of Constructivism was formed in 1924—the Literaturnyi tsentr konstruktivistov (LTsK; Literary Center of Constructivists)—which included poet Eduard Bagritsky (pseudonym of E. Dzyubin, 1895-1934), poet Vera Mikhaylovna Inber (1893-1972), Vladimir A. Lugovskoi (1901-1957), Ilya Lvovich Selvinsky (1899-1968), Boris Agapov (n.d.), D. Tumanny (n.d.), I. A. Aksyonov (n.d.), and Korneliy L. Zelinski (1896-?). The Constructivists published an Official Literary Plan—*Gosplan lite-ratury*—in 1924. Signed by Zelinski, Selvinsky, Inber, and others, it proclaimed literary Constructivism to be "motivated art," "a reflection of the organizational onrush of the working class." Every part of a work of literature should be "motivated" by the theme and operate in a system that exploits the theme to the utmost. Zelinski's *Poeziya kak smysl* (1929; Poetry as Sense) defined poetry as "a machine of sense."

According to *Gosplan literatury*, Constructivism is "heightened attention to technological and organizational problems" in an effort to bring the proletariat to cultural technological advancement. In literature, this led to the introduction of prose techniques into the writing of poetry: "The principle of loading, when applied to poetry, comes to mean the demand for the construction of verse in the sphere of local semantics, i.e., the evolution of the whole fabric of verse from the basic semantic content of the theme." The literary Constructivists comprise "an organized society of people united by the common aims of Communist construction. It has set as its aim—by means of the combined, practical study of the formal, technical, and theoretical aspects of constructivism—to give literature, in particular poetry, an active meaning within the conditions of contemporary culture."

Their main theorist was Zelinski, who developed the techniques of *gruzofikatsiya* or "loadification of the word" and *lokal'nyi priem* or "local method." The former was derived from the spatial arts wing of the movement. According to the manifesto: "the so-called principle of loading, i.e., the increased load of demand per unit of material" served to make literature functional, intelligible, and efficient. The local color method, like the later U.S. and Canadian LOCAL COLOR SCHOOLS, employed local scenery, vernacular, etc. The lyric poems of Bagritsky during this period, especially *Duma pro Opanasa* (1926; The Tale of Opanas), are examples of the Constructivists' local method.

The Constructivists were contemporaries of the LEFT FRONT OF THE ARTS movement and found affinities between them. Both groups sought to do battle with groups that "obscure the meaning of our epoch . . . [and] disorganize the cultural class effort of the proletariat" while justifying the imperative of artistic freedom. The RUSSIAN FORMAL-ISTS, also contemporaries of the Constructivists, were intrigued by the idea of setting out to construct works of literature, which complemented their own program of analyzing literary works as constructions.

The Literary Center of Constructivists disbanded in 1930. But some of its principles were integrated into the developing SOCIALIST REALISM movement, especially as drawn in the pages of the journal *New Lef* (1927-1930).

❖•❖

Further Reading

Bann, Stephen, ed. *The Tradition of Constructivism*. New York: The Viking Press, 1974.

Ermolaev, Herman. *Soviet Literary Theories, 1917-1934*. Berkeley, Calif.: University of California Press, 1963.

Holthusen, Johannes. *Twentieth-Century Russian Literature: A Critical Study*. New York: Ungar, 1972.

Struve, Gleb. *Russian Literature under Lenin and Stalin, 1917-1953*. Norman, Okla.: University of Oklahoma Press, 1971.

CONTEMPORÁNEOS (Contemporaries)
Mexico, 1928-1931

Contemporáneos was a journal around which a group of friends gathered for a few years. It was edited by poet Bernardo Ortiz de Montellano (1899-1949). Members included poet, dramatist, and novelist Xavier Villaurrutia (1903-1950); poet, essayist, and short-story writer Jaime Torres Bodet (1902-1974); Jorge Cuesta (1903-1942); poet José Gorostiza (1901-1973); poet Gilberto Owen (1905-1952); poet Salvador Novo Lopez (1904-1974); poet Enrique González Rojo (1899-1939); poet Octavio G. Barreda (1897-1964); and Bernardo J. Gastelúm (n.d.), who helped support and finance the journal through his political position as head of the Department of Health and proximity to the president. Poet Carlos Pellicer (1899-1977) and poet and physician Elías Nandino (1903-) were peripherally associated with the group. An earlier journal, *Ulises* (May 1927-February 1928), was edited by Villaurrutia and Novo Lopez, and may well have attracted some of the members of the new group. A concurrent development, headed by Villaurrutia, Novo Lopez, Owen, and others, was a theater group, Teatro Ulises. It failed within two years, but was followed by other experimental theatrical group efforts, mainly through the determination of Villaurrutia.

Enrique González Martínez (1871-1952; *see also* ATHENEUM OF YOUTH) was an important influence for the *Contemporáneos* writers, as were José Juan Tablada (1871-1945) and Ramón López Velarde (1888-1921) and various European writers, such as T. S. ELIOT (*see* MODERNISM, England and Ireland) and the SURREALISTS. Some of the most remarkable works from the *Contemporáneos* include Gorostiza's poem *Muerte sin fin* (1939; *Death without End,* 1969) and Villaurrutia's poem *Nostalgia de la muerte* (1938; Nostalgia of Death). In an essay, Torres Bodet describes his philosophy: "From being a form of expression, [the novel] becomes a form of exploration. In poetry, style is a frontier; in the novel, it is a highway." He also argues for Art—"the essential element," rather than subject matter or plot—"the episodic element." His novel *Margarita de Niebla* (1927) is cited for its hazily defined characters and a representation of reality as ephemeral.

Contemporáneos sought to bridge "European achievement and American promise," privileging an emphasis on the subjective, the metaphysical, and the avant garde, rather than militantly social or political considerations—except where they can be represented as universal, of the human condition. The group was frequently criticized as xenomanic, elitist, and homosexual by literary and cultural figures in Mexico at the time who disagreed with their cosmopolitan, art for art's sake tenets. While the *Contemporáneos* writers were not radically nationalistic, they did, however, direct attention toward Mexican artists, writers, musicians, etc.

➔•◀

Further Reading

Anderson Imbert, Enrique. *Spanish-American Literature: A History*. Detroit: Wayne State University Press, 1963.

Avrett, R. "Enrique González Martínez—Philosopher and Mystic." *Hispania* 14, 3 (May 1931): 183-92.

Brushwood, J. S. "Contemporáneos and the Limits of Art." *Romance Notes* 5 (spring 1964): 128-32.

———. "The Artists' Intent (1925-1930)." In *Mexico in Its Novel: A Nation's Search for Identity*. Austin, Tex.: University of Texas Press, 1966.

———. "Revolution and Vanguardism: 1910-1934." In *Narrative Innovation and Political Change in Mexico*. New York: P. Lang, 1989.

Camp, R. *Intellectuals and the State in Twentieth-Century Mexico*. Austin, Tex.: University of Texas Press, 1985.

Dauster, Frank. *Xavier Villaurrutia*. New York: Twayne, 1971.

Forster, Merlin H. "The 'Contemporáneos': A Major Group in Mexican Vanguardism." *Texas Studies in Language and Literature* 3, 4 (winter 1962): 425-38.

Franco, Jean. *Introduction to Spanish-American Literature*. London: Cambridge University Press, 1969.

————. *Modern Culture of Latin America: Society and the Artist*. New York: Praeger, 1967.

González Peña, C. *History of Mexican Literature*. Dallas: Southern Methodist University Press, 1968.

Martínez, José L., ed. *The Modern Mexican Essay*. Toronto: University of Toronto Press, 1965.

Moreno, A. "Xavier Villaurrutia: The Development of His Theater." *Hispania* XLIII, 4 (December 1960): 508-14.

Pérez Firmat, Gustavo. *Idle Fictions*. Durham, N.C.: Duke University Press, 1982.

Usigli, R. *Mexico in the Theater*. University, Miss.: Romance Monographs, 1976.

CONTINENTS GROUP. *See KONTYNENTY* GROUP

COSTUMBRISMO. *See* REALISM, Spain

COUNCIL OF BRILLIANT KNOWLEDGE
Uruguay, 1900s

The Council of Brilliant Knowledge was the first MODERNISMO group in Uruguay. Founded at the turn of the century by Horacio Quiroga (1878-1937) — best known for his affiliation with the GENERATION OF 1900 and for his later contributions to REALISM in Latin American fiction — the Council was relatively short-lived and undistinguished in its publication of Modernista-style poetry.

⇒•⇐

Further Reading

Brushwood, John S. "The Spanish American Story from Quiroga to Borges." In *The Latin American Story: A Critical History*. Edited by Margaret Sayers Peden. Boston: Twayne, 1983.

Coons, Dix Scott. "Horacio Quiroga, the Master Storyteller: A Study of the Creative Process." *Dissertation Abstracts* 25 (1965): 2978-79.

Holland, Norman S. "'Doctoring' in Quiroga." *Confluencia: Revista Hispanica de Cultura y Literatura* 9, 2 (spring 1994): 64-72.

Lindstrom, Naomi. "The Spanish American Short Story from Echeverria to Quiroga." In *The Latin American Story: A Critical History*. Edited by Margaret Sayers Peden. Boston: Twayne, 1983.

Param, Charles. "Horacio Quiroga and His Exceptional Protagonists." *Hispania* 55 (1972): 428-35.

Pearson, Lon. "Horacio Quiroga's Obsessions with Abnormal Psychology and Medicine as Reflected in *La Gallina Degollada*." *Literature and Psychology* 32, 3 (1986): 32-46.

Peden, Margaret Sayers, and Leland H. Chambers. "Horacio Quiroga on the Short Story." *University of Denver Quarterly* 12, 3 (1977): 45-53.

Peden, William. "Some Notes on Quiroga's Stories." *Review* 19 (1976): 41-43.

Rosser, Harry L. "Quiroga and Cortazar's Dream Crossings." *Revista/Review Interamericana* 13, 1-4 (1983): 120-25.

Scroggins, Daniel C. "Vengeance with a Stickpin: Barreta, Quiroga, and Garcia Calderon." *Romance Notes* 15 (1973): 47-51.

CRACOW AVANT-GARDE
Poland, 1920s-1930s

A radical Polish poetry movement of the 1920s and 1930s, the Cracow Avant-Garde was opposed to the traditionalism and domesticity of the *SKAMANDER* GROUP and espoused instead a belief in the interrelationship of art to modern cities and technology and had affinities with CONSTRUCTIVISM. Founder Tadeusz Peiper (1891-1969) delineated the complex theories of the Avant-Garde in a number of essays, articles, and poetry collections; foremost among his ideas was the cultivation of a rigorous and precise poetic medium, linking the dynamism of FUTURIST writing with the French concept of *le mot juste* (the proper word). Beginning in 1931, under the new guidance of Julian Przyboś (1901-1970), the movement began placing a greater emphasis on imagery and other technical effects. Other members were Czesław Miłosz (1911-), Jalu Kurek (1904-), Konstanty Gałzyński (1905-1953), and Jan Brzękowski (1903-). The group published a journal, *Zwrotnica* (1922-23, 1926-27; The Switch), in which many of Peiper's articles appeared, and manifestos in *Nowe usta* (1925; New Month) and *Tedy* (1930; This Way).

✦•✦

Further Reading

Carpenter, Bogdana. *The Poetic Avant-Garde in Poland, 1918-1939.* Seattle: University of Washington Press, 1983.

Czarnecka, Ewa, and Aleksander Fiut. [sic] *Conversations with Czesław Miłosz.* Translated by Richard Lourie. San Diego: Harcourt Brace Jovanovich, 1987.

"Czesław Miłosz: A Special Issue." *Ironwood* 18 (1981).

"Czesław Miłosz: Counterpoint of Truth and Rapture." *World Literature Today* 52, 3 (summer 1978): 357-526.

Davie, Donald. *Czesław Miłosz and the Insufficiency of Lyric.* Knoxville, Tenn.: University of Tennessee Press, 1986.

Dompkowski, Judith Ann. *"Down a Spiral Staircase, Never-Ending": Motion as Design in the Writing of Czesław Miłosz.* New York: Peter Lang, 1990.

Fiut, Aleksander. *The Eternal Moment: The Poetry of Czesław Miłosz.* Translated by Theodosia S. Robertson. Berkeley, Calif.: University of California Press, 1990.

Heaney, Seamus. "Laureate in the Time of Catastrophe." *The Irish Times* (December 17, 1988): 9.

Krzyzanowski, Julian. "Neo-Realism in the Inter-war Years." In his *A History of Polish Literature.* Warsaw: PWN-Polish Scientific Publishers, 1978.

Malinoswka, Barbara. *Dynamics of Being, Space, and Time in the Poetry of Czesław Miłosz and John Ashbery.* New York: Peter Lang, 1997.

Miłosz, Czesław. *Beginning With My Streets: Baltic Reflections.* Translated by Madeline G. Levine. New York: Farrar, Straus, Giroux, 1991; London: Tauris, 1992.

————. "Independent Poland: 1918-1939 — Poetry." In his *The History of Polish Literature.* London: Macmillan, 1969. Rev. ed., Berkeley, Calif.: University of California Press, 1983.

Mozejko, Edward, ed. *Between Anxiety and Hope: The Poetry and Writing of Czesław Miłosz.* Edmonton, Canada: University of Alberta Press, 1988.

Nathan, Leonard, and Arthur Quinn. *The Poet's Work: An Introduction to Czesław Miłosz.* Cambridge, Mass.: Harvard University Press, 1991.

Sadkowski, Wacław. "Galczynski and Tuwim on the 25th Anniversary of Their Deaths." *New Polish Publications, a Monthly Review of Polish Books* 26, 8-9 (August-September 1978): 6-9.

CREATIONISM (Creaciónismo)
Chile and Spain, 1916-1918

The Chilean poet Vicente Huidobro (1893-1948) was the founder and primary theorist of Creationism. Some of his early influences were the European SYMBOLISTS and Rubén DARÍO and the MODERNISMO writers. He associated with Guillaume APOLLI-NAIRE *(see* CUBISM) and Pierre (Jacques) Reverdy (1889-1960) in Paris, during which time they founded the journal *Nord-Sun*. In 1918 he went to Madrid, where he helped launch ULTRAISM, through his involvement in the journal *Ultra* (1921-22).

Huidobro's 1914 prose manifesto, *Non serviam* (I shall not be a slave), asserts that the creation of poetry should imitate the creative acts of nature, without imitating nature's products; to "make a poem like nature makes a tree": "I shall not be your slave, Mother Nature; I shall be your master . . . I shall have my trees, and they will not be like yours . . . We have never created our own realities . . . We have accepted, without further reflection, the fact that no other reality exists other than the one around us, and have not thought that we too can create realities in a world of our own, in a world that awaits its own fauna and its own flora." His developed doctrine of Creationism is concerned with twentieth-century humans' conditions in the world, as well as with experimentation with poetic forms and techniques. According to Huidobro's theory, the word is the primary basis for new and striking associations in poetic creation, for metaphor by which new worlds can be created. Also characteristic of Creationism is the importance of visuality, with its affinities with CONCRETE POETRY and employment of calligrammatic techniques. Huidobro wrote in French and Spanish, believing that a particular language per se was not as important as the images created from that language.

Huidobro's *Manifestes* were published in 1925 and included the essay "La creación pura," in which he describes the theory and process of Creationism. His collections of poems, *Adán* (1916; Adam), *El espejo de agua* (1916; The Mirror of Water) and *Horizon carré* (1917), are considered some of the most representative products of his theory of Creationism.

In Spain, poets Gerardo Diego (1896-1987) and Juan Larrea (1895-1982) were major proponents of Creationism *(see also* GENERATION OF 1927). In Chile, other poets who associated themselves with Huidobro and Creationism were Chilean Humberto Díaz Casanueva (1905-1992), and Mexican-born poets Juvencio Valle (1907-) and Rosamel del Valle (1900-).

❖•❖

Further Reading

Admussen, Richard L., and René de Costa. "Huidobro, Reverdy, and the *editio princeps* of *El espejo de agua.*" *Comparative Literature* 24, 2 (spring 1972): 163-75.

Costa, René de. *Vincente Huidobro: The Careers of a Poet.* Oxford, England: Clarendon Press; New York: Oxford University Press, 1984.

Holmes, Henry A. *Vincent Huidobro and Creationism.* New York: Columbia University Press, 1934.

Huidobro, Vicente. *The Selected Poetry of Vicente Huidobro.* Edited with an introduction by David M. Guss. Translated by David M. Guss, et al. New York: New Directions, 1981.

Nicholson, Ana Maria. *Vicente Huidobro and Creationism.* Ann Arbor, Mich.: University Microfilms, 1971.

————. "Vicente Huidobro and Creationism." Ph.D. diss., University of California at San Diego, 1967.

Wood, C. G. *The Creacionismo of Vicente Huidobro.* Fredericton, Canada: York Press, 1978.

CREATION SOCIETY (Ch'uang-tsao She)
China, 1920s

One of the predominant forces in the development of modern Chinese literature, the Creation Society emerged as a result of the MAY FOURTH MOVEMENT, a political and cultural revolution waged against the Peking government in 1919. The small group of writers who formed the offshoot movement did so with the express intent of counteracting REALISM and "art for life's sake," the aesthetic platform of the LITERARY RESEARCH ASSOCIATION, which, like the Creation Society, vigorously attempted to shape the direction of Chinese literature throughout the 1920s.

During the May Fourth Era, study in Japan, a nation which had for some decades benefited from Westernizing influences, was popular among Chinese students. Five such students — Kuo Mo-jo, Yü Tafu, Ch'eng Fang-wu (n.d.), Chang Tzu-p'ing (1893-1947?), and T'ien Han (1898-1968) — banded together in 1921, affirmed their mutual belief in purely creative literature or "art for art's sake," and labeled themselves the Creation Society. This same year a Shanghai publisher issued two works — a volume of poetry and a translation of Johann Wolfgang von Goethe's (1749-1832) *The Sorrows of Young Werther* (1774) — by Kuo, and a collection of three stories by Yü. Although Kuo's works greatly fueled interest in European Romanticism and the problems of the individual, it was Yü's forthright and essentially modern portrayals of post-revolution-

98

ary life in his fiction that the intelligentsia applauded. Yü's selection of the short story form served as an indication of fiction's rapid rise to prominence among Chinese genres, a rise generally credited to the impact of a single work, LU HSÜN's "AH Q CHENG-CHUAN" (1921; "The True Story of Ah Q," 1926; *see* May Fourth Movement). In addition, his collection *Chenlun* (1921; Sinking) gave instant credibility to the Creation Society, one of the few movements at the time in China which hesitated to affirm Realism. Although Yü's technique owed as much to the DECADENTS as Romanticism, his underlying concern was the place of the individual in modern society, a theme with which all May Fourth writers could identify.

The Society extended its influence through a series of successive journals that included *Ch'uang-tsao chi-k'an* (Creation Quarterly), *Ch'uang-tsao chou-pao* (Creation Weekly), and *Ch'uang-tsao jih* (Creation Daily). By 1923 the Society, primarily due to Kuo's mounting activism, changed its focus radically and soon became a conspicuous disseminator of Marxist thought. This commitment to revolutionary ideals as well as revolutionary literature accelerated following the May Thirtieth Movement of 1925. As the Society attracted younger students returning from Japan its renown grew. Despite prohibition of its existence by the conservative Kuomintang government in 1929, the Society continued to exist in the minds of leftist writers as a major force behind the development of modern Chinese literature.

✤•✤

Kuo Mo-jo (1892-1978), Chinese poet, dramatist, and essayist.

Considered the chief theoretician of the Creation Society, Kuo maintained throughout his career an active interest in social and political reform. In 1926 he joined the Northern Expedition, a cooperative revolution between the Kuomintang and the Chinese Communist Party, to help unite his splintered nation. Chiang Kai-shek's coup the following year drove numerous Communists into hiding, including Kuo, who left for Japan in early 1928. While there he studied ancient Chinese history, of which he later became a distinguished scholar. Kuo returned to China in 1937 to participate in the war against Japanese aggression and thereafter assumed a number of governmental posts, including Chairman of the ALL-CHINA ANTI-AGGRESSION FEDERATION OF WRITERS AND ARTISTS. As a writer, Kuo is best known for his early poetry, particularly *NÜ-SHEN* (1921; *Selected Poems from The Goddesses*, 1958), and for such later dramatic works as *Ch'ü Yüan* (1942; *Ch'ü Yüan*, 1955), a historically based play which served nationalistic ends.

Nü-shen (1921; *Selected Poems from The Goddesses*, 1958).

Nü-shen was a pioneering Chinese work of Western-influenced free verse. Kuo's poems, reminiscent of Walt Whitman's (1819-1892) and directed chiefly at young intellectuals,

99

typically contain a mixture of exuberant Romanticism and strident affirmation of individual freedoms. Kuo perceived the resounding impact of the May Fourth Movement as equivalent to the dawning of a new age and, thus, in his verse, ordered mythical and symbolic elements to underscore his conviction. Chief among these is the sun, whose ubiquitous power of light and rebirth Kuo repeatedly praised.

✤•✦

Yü Tafu (1896-1945)
Chinese short-story writer, essayist, travel writer, and diarist.

An essentially apolitical writer, Yü concentrated on examining the moral and psychological plights of his main characters. The highly subjective points of view and self-revealing quality of these characters has led many scholars to posit that much, if not all, of Yü's fiction is autobiographical in the manner of the Japanese I-NOVEL. However, some have recognized Yü's ironic authorial stance, a device which allowed him to construct convincing, indirectly objective portraits of the complex and troubled modern individual. Yü, who was never a dedicated Marxist, severed ties with the Creation Society in 1928 to become coeditor of a magazine with Lu Hsün. He also joined Lu in 1930 as one of the founding members of the LEAGUE OF LEFT-WING WRITERS. A master of the short story form, Yü was among the first Chinese writers to successfully fuse European literary traditions, such as Decadence and Romanticism, with work that was contemporaneous both in psychological insight and social relevancy.

"Ch'en-lun" (1921; Sinking).

A bellwether for young, dissatisfied Chinese intellectuals of the May Fourth Era, "Ch'en-lun" describes the alienation, self-contempt, and purposelessness one student feels while studying in Japan. His melancholic view of his beleaguered homeland parallels the hopeless impression he harbors of his own life. Yü's focus on his protagonist's tortured psyche—his paranoia, bitterness, masturbatory urges, and ultimate suicide—was considered a revolutionary breakthrough in subject matter and character development. Indebted to Goethe's *Young Werther,* various other Romantic works, and the I-Novel, "Ch'en-lun" nonetheless ranks as one of the most strikingly original Chinese stories of the 1920s.

✤•✦

Further Reading

Cheng Ching-mao. "The Impact of Japanese Literary Trends on Modern Chinese Writers." In *Modern Chinese Literature in the May Fourth Era*. Edited by Merle Goldman. Cambridge, Mass.: Harvard University Press, 1977.

Doležalová, Anna. *Yü Ta-fu: Specific Traits of His Literary Creation*. Bratislava, Slovakia: Publishing House of the Slovak Academy of Sciences, 1971.

Egan, Michael. "Yü Dafu and the Transition to Modern Chinese Literature." In *Modern Chinese Literature in the May Fourth Era*. Edited by Merle Goldman. Cambridge, Mass.: Harvard University Press, 1977.

Gálik, Marián. "Kuo Mo-jo's *The Goddesses*: Creative Confrontation with Tagore, Whitman, and Goethe." In his *Milestones of Sino-Western Literary Confrontation (1898-1979)*. Wiesbaden, Germany: Harrassowitz, 1986.

Hsia, C. T. *A History of Modern Chinese Fiction*. New Haven, Conn.: Yale University Press, 1971.

Ming Lai. *A History of Chinese Literature*. New York: John Day Co., 1964.

Průšek, Jaroslav. "Yü Ta-fu," "Kuo Mo-jo." In his *Three Sketches of Chinese Literature*. Prague: Oriental Institute in Academia, 1969.

Roy, David T. *Kuo Mo-jo: The Early Years*. Cambridge, Mass.: Harvard University Press, 1971.

Wu-Chi Liu. "Prose Fiction." Supplement on the Modern Period in Herbert A. Giles. *A History of Chinese Literature*. New York: Ungar, 1967.

Yi Ting. "Kuo Mo-jo and Other Writers Before and After the May 4 Movement." In his *A Short History of Modern Chinese Literature*. Peking: Foreign Languages Press, 1959.

CREPUSCOLARISMO
Italy, 1900s-1910s

The Crepuscolari poets may best be described as one of several transitional waves between the centuries-old Italian lyric poetic tradition — which many poets in the opening years of the twentieth century viewed as staid, confining, and out of touch with modern experience, and which inculcates the poet's world-weary view of life as symbolized by the daily modulation of morning light into the lengthy and somber shadows of the twilight — and the more significant Modernist movements, such as FUTURISM and HERMETICISM. The Crepuscolari poets were among the first to rebel against traditional grandiosity and sentimentality in favor of simplified language and themes and an emphasis on description rather than declamation. They found particular inspiration in the impressionistic work of such French SYMBOLISTS as Paul VERLAINE, whose poetry is characterized by its delicate grace and evocativeness, and Jules Laforgue (1860-1887), who is considered the inventor of free verse.

The term "crepuscolari" (twilight), which was coined by critic Giuseppe Borgese (1882-1952), initially referred to the point in history at which the poets were working — that is, at the sunset of a glorious era. It later came to denote the typical content of Crepuscolari poetry, which was often gently nostalgic or ironic and delineated such themes as the boredom and loneliness of provincial life in humble, colorless language.

Themes of the work are sometimes simple and concentrate on the rustic life of the peasant; the language is solemn, but often musical. This poetry was produced in reaction to that of earlier writers Giosue Carducci (1835-1907) and Gabriele D'Annunzio

(1863-1938), both of whose work expresses the classical mode, an extreme nationalism, and an optimism about the state of humanity. The intensity with which the Crepuscolarismo writers explore the mystery of life and the "beauty" of death, often from an almost trance-like state, produced poetry in which devices of onomatopoeia combined with new forms of diction, rhyme, and structure and would, in its antitraditional view, lead some of its writers into the later Futurist movement. Perhaps its most talented member was Guido Gozzano (1883-1916), whose poems were composed in a narrative style that successfully blended humor, tenderness, description, dialogue, and both ordinary and literary language. Examples of "twilight poetry" were produced between the 1900s and the 1910s and can be found in the work of Corrado Govoni (1884-1965) in *Armonia in grigio et in silenzio; poema* (1903; Harmonies in Grey and Silence), and in *La via del rifugio* (1907; Road of the Shelter) by Gozzano.

Other members include Fausto Maria Martini (1886-1931), Sergio Corazzini (1887-1907), Marino Moretti (1885-1979), Aldo Palazzeschi (1885-1974), Sem Benelli (1875-1949), Dino Campana (1855-1932), Carlo Cheaves (1883-1919), Cesare Vico Lodovici (1885-1968), Eugenio MONTALE, Ercole Luigi Morselli (1882-1921), Giovanni Pascoli (1855-1912), Clemente Rebora (1885-1957), Umberto Saba (1883-1957), and Camillo Sbarbaro (1888-1967). Montale and Campana would later be connected to the Hermeticist movement.

The Crepuscolari movement was finally overshadowed by Futurism, which debuted in 1909 with the publication of the Futurist Manifesto by its founder, Filippo Tommaso MARINETTI. The Futurist poets made an even bolder, more strident break with the past than had those of the Crepuscolari movement.

❖•❖

Further Reading

Blanchard, H. H. *Prose and Poetry of the Continental Renaissance in Translation*. New York: Longmans, Green, 1949.

Golino, Carlo Luigi, ed. *Contemporary Italian Poetry: An Anthology*. Berkeley, Calif.: University of California Press, 1962.

Kay, George, ed. *The Penguin Book of Italian Verse*. Harmondsworth, England: Penguin, 1958.

Lind, L. R. *Twentieth-Century Italian Poetry: A Bilingual Anthology*. Indianapolis, Ind.: Bobbs-Merrill, 1974.

Molinaro, Julius A., ed. *A Guide to Contemporary Italian Literature: From Futurism to Neorealism*. Carbondale, Ill.: Southern Illinois University Press, 1962.

———. *Petrarch to Pirandello: Studies in Italian Literature in Honour of Beatrice Corrigan*. Toronto: University of Toronto Press, 1973.

Williamson, E. "Contemporary Italian Poetry." *Poetry* 79 (December 1951): 159-81.

CRESCENT SOCIETY (Hsin Yüeh She)
China, 1928-1930s

Formed in 1928 by Hsü Chih-mo (also rendered Xu Zhimo, 1896-1931), Wen I-to (1889-1946), and HU Shih (*see* MAY FOURTH MOVEMENT), the Crescent Society was a movement dedicated to counteracting the development of REALISM in Chinese vernacular (*pai-hua*) poetry. Their manifesto proposed a synthesis of the fine arts so that classical diction and form, the beauty of stylized order, might be maintained over personalized and politicized free-verse expression. The movement, which ended with Hsü's death, was heavily attacked by revolutionary writers, particularly LU HSÜN and other members of the LEAGUE OF LEFT-WING WRITERS.

⇸•⇷

Further Reading

Goldman, Merle, ed. *Modern Chinese Literature in the May Fourth Era*. Cambridge, Mass.: Harvard University Press, 1977.
Liu Wu-chi. "The Modern Period: Poetry." In *A History of Chinese Literature* by Herbert A. Giles. New York: Frederick Ungar Publishing Company, 1967.

CRIOLLISMO
Argentina, Chile, and Venezuela, 1890s-1900s

During the early years of the twentieth century, Caribbean countries faced increasing political and economic hegemony from the United States, which had interests in maintaining its banana republics. The Criollismo movement was led by artists, critics, and other intellectuals in attempts to assert cultural identity and independence. Chilean critic Francisco Contreras (1877-1933) wrote about *mundonovismo*, or "new world-ism," in his *Les ecrivains contemporains de l'Amérique espagnole* (1920), while Federico García Godoy (1857-1924) espoused "literary americanism" in his collection of essays, *Americanismo literario* (1917), believing that cultural autonomy was as important to Latin America as economic independence. Uruguayan José Enrique Rodó (1871-1917), during and after the Spanish-American War of 1898, wrote *Ariel* (1900). *Ariel*, named for Shakespeare's sprite in *The Tempest*, made an enormous impact throughout Latin America, with its call for independence from North American utilitarian influences and interests. (*See also* MODERNISMO.)

Many felt that if a native Latin American culture were to be nourished, its origins and essence must first be found. The places to find such originality were rural areas, inhabited mostly by mestizo or indigenous workers and farmers, who had been uninfluenced or far less influenced by European and Euro-American culture than intellectuals living in the cities. Some Criollists—particularly those with urban, upper-class backgrounds—then, faced the dilemma of bridging the social, cultural and economic gap between themselves and those rural masses whom, they believed, must nourish Latin American identity and culture.

Writers involved in Criollismo included: Venezuelans Rufino Blanco Fombona (1874-1944), Vicente Romero García (1865-1917), and José Rafael Pocaterra (1889-1955); Chileans Eduardo Barrios (1884-1963), Joaquín Edwards Bello (1887-1968), Luis Durand (1895-1954), Mariano Latorre (1886-1955), and Baldomero Lillo (1867-1923); and Argentines Ricardo Güiraldes (1886-1927), Carlos Alberto Erro (1899-1968), and novelist Roberto J. Payró (1867-1928).

Texts representative of various aspects of the Criollist movement include Barrio's novels *Un perdido* (1917; A Lost One) and *Gran señor y rajadioblos* (1948; Great Lord and Hellion), Erro's essay *Historia de una pasión argentina* (1937; History of an Argentine Passion), and Güiraldes's masterpiece *Don Segundo Sombra* (1926; *Don Segundo Sombra,* 1948).

❧•❧

Further Reading

Franco, Jean. *The Modern Culture of Latin America: Society and the Artist.* New York: Praeger, 1967.

Previtali, Giovanni. *Ricardo Güiraldes and* Don Segundo Sombra: *Life and Works.* New York: Hispanic Institute in the United States, 1963.

Rodó, José Enrique. *Ariel.* 1900. Reprint, translated by Margaret Sayers Peden. Austin, Tex.: University of Texas Press, 1988.

CRITICA, LA
Italy, 1903-1944

In Italian letters, a sustained, interdisciplinary reevaluation of philosophy, aesthetics, history, ethics, and literature took place through the pages of Benedetto Croce's (1866-1952) *La Critica.* Regarded as the most influential periodical of Italian intellectuals during its forty-year reign, *La Critica* strove to address and resolve such questions as the nature of history, history's relationship to art, art's relationship to philosophy, and the individual's relationship to each. Implicit in all was the purpose and value of criticism and scholarship. Giovanni Gentile's (1875-1944) articles, which led to his three-volume *Le origini della filosofia contemporanea in Italia* (1917-23; The Origins of Contemporary Philosophy in Italy), were important in this regard. However, it was Croce who dominated the discussion in a number of works, including *Esterica come scienza dell'espressione e linguistica generale* (1902; *Aesthetic as Science of Ex-*

pression and General Linguistic, 1909; revised ed., 1922) and *La poesia: Introduzione alla critica e storia della poesia e della letteratura* (1936; *Poetry and Literature,* 1981). Croce's guiding thesis, inspired in part by the thought of Giambattista Vico (1668-1744), is that the essence of reality is evoked not through dead history or "chronicle," but through "the knowledge of the individual," through the union of art and philosophy. *La Critica* was closely linked to several late-nineteenth-century movements as well as to the development of MODERNISM in Italy.

❧•❧

Further Reading

Croce, Benedetto. *Poetry, Philosophy, History: An Anthology of Essays by Benedetto Croce.* London; New York: Oxford University Press, 1966.
De Genarro, Angelo. *The Philosophy of Benedetto Croce.* New York: Citadel Press, 1961.
Orsini, Gian. *Benedetto Croce, Philosopher of Art and Literary Critic.* Carbondale, Ill.: Southern Illinois University Press, 1961.
Sprigge, Cecil. *Benedetto Croce.* London: Bowes and Bowes, 1952.

CRITICAL REALISM, Germany. *See* NEW OBJECTIVITY

CRITICAL REALISM, Russia. *See* REALISM, Russia

CUBISM
France, 1910s

A term which simultaneously served both the graphic and the literary arts, Cubism is one of the many creative phenomena which flourished in Paris early in the twentieth century. While some movements were short-lived and only served as springboards to others of more substance and longevity, all of them engendered a spirit of exciting experimentation among the creative personae of the day who were in search of new techniques which could be used to protest against the old tenets. Artists such as Georges Braque (1882-1963) and Pablo Picasso (1881-1973) were electing to ignore the traditional and painterly perspectives of form and matter found in representational art, and were reducing the depiction of objects to simple, geometric planes. The works are distorted—fragmented and often bizarre—but the method was designed to give new freedom to the painter and allow a more personal response to an intellectual and social environment in which old value systems were being questioned in a new century.

The poet Guillaume APOLLINAIRE was central to the Cubist movement and was intrigued enough by the paintings to adapt the artists' concepts to his experimental poetry. As artistic spokesperson of the time, he had been quick to encourage the combined efforts of artists and writers in all mediums for a revitalization of earlier perceptions of reality and to convey in their work an inner, rather than an outer, sense of it. His prose work, *The Cubist Painters* (1913), outlines his theory and confirmed him as leader of the "scandalous" and irreverent Cubist literary movement. He was joined by the poets Max Jacob (1876-1944), Jacques Reverdy (1889-1960), and André Salmon (1881-1969) in the propagation of the new manifesto in their essays, pamphlets, and poetry, all done in what they called "l'esprit nouveau." Specifically, Apollinaire's return to the "most primitive source of lyricism" in his poetry was inspired by his fascination with the African primitivistic canvases of Paul Cézanne (1839-1906). Similarly, the poet Blaise Cendrars (1887-1961) developed what was called "snap-shot" imagery in his verses, *Dixneul Poems elastiques* (1919), in the adoption of a Cubist perspective.

The writer Jean Cocteau (1889-1963), a quintessential MODERNIST with a prolific output in all the arts, was an early Cubist enthusiast. Although best known as a writer, his collaborations with Picasso, Igor Stravinsky (1882-1971), and Sergey Diaghilev (1872-1929) in the texts and sets for such ballets as *Parade* (1917), *La Boeuf sue le toit* (1920) and *Les Maries de la tour Eiffel* (1921) are clear evidence of his advocacy of Apollinaire's notion of the importance of the freedom of the artist to experiment, in order to stimulate new creative authority. Another addition to the group was the American poet, novelist, and critic Gertrude STEIN (*see* MODERNISM, United States), who was strongly influenced by the movement because of her long association with Picasso and her acute interest in both the visual and the literary arts. Her prose style, a "deliberate counterpart" to Cubist art, and her rejection of conventional grammar, spelling, and syntactical construction are meant to represent the fragmentation of felt experience. Her work includes poems, plays, essays, an opera, a ballet, and two autobiographies, *Everybody's Autobiography* (1937) and the still-famous contrivance, *The Autobiography of Alice B. Toklas* (1933), a description of her life with her long-time companion. While her work has been dismissed by some as inconsequential and confusing and by others as that of a genius, her experimentation with AUTOMATIC WRITING (*see* SURREALISM, France) in the investigation of aspects of the viability of what lies in the unconscious workings of the mind aligns her with Cubist exploration and discovery. Other members of the group were Alexander Archipenko (1881-1964), Sonia Delaunay (1885-1979), Leon-Paul Fargue (1876?-1947), Albert Gleizes (1881-1953), Juan Gris (1887-1927), Henri Laurens (1885-1954), Fernand Léger (1881-1955), Jacques Lipchitz (1891-1973), Jean Metzinger (1883-1956), and Jean Paulhan (1884-1968).

One critical observation is that Cubism began as part of a "farcical festive air" which predominated at the time and nurtured new directions in poetry. This has been obviated by the SURREALIST movement which followed Cubism; since the Cubist intent was to capture both visual and intellectual imagination and inculcate the imperative of a new and enlightened artistic perspective, it quite aptly served the mood and the time in its own and singular revelation.

❖•❖

Apollinaire, Guillaume (1880-1918), French poet, critic, and journalist.
Born Wilhelm Apollinaire Kostrowsky in Rome, he settled in Paris at the age of eighteen and soon became a leading figure in the creative arts. As an innovator of the new and experimental, he was dedicated to Modernism as the tool which would free the artist to explore all aspects of poetic imagination and fancy for the revelation of reality. Thus his work was not constrained by the traditional poetic devices of punctuation and syntax and led to experimentation with a typography which provided pictorial impact along with the message. An example is his poem, "Il Pleut," in which the words on the page are positioned to represent the image of falling rain. He would later be associated with the Surrealist movement, which he named first as "super-realism," and its lengthy literary impact. His theory that the "poetic art is the creative act in its fullest capacity" gave him the utmost opportunity to explore any avenue which would give the incomprehensible the poetic language of explication of the ordinary and the commonplace. He has been called the innovative prophet of poetic techniques which would establish the accepted new forms of modern poetry. Noteworthy works are *Alcools* (1913; *Alcohols*, 1964); the surrealistic drama, *Les mamelles de Tirésias* (1917; *The Breasts of Tiresias*, 1961); novels *Le Poete assassine* (1916; *The Poet Assassinated*, 1923) and *L'hérésiarque et cie* (1910; *The Heresiarch and Co.*, 1965); a verse drama, *Couleur du Temps* (1918; *Color of Time*, 1980); and his posthumously published poems, *Ombre de mon Amour* (1948) and *Tendre comme le souvenir* (1952). Apollinaire was killed in France in World War I.

❖•❖

Further Reading

Alden, Douglas W., and Richard A. Brooks, eds. *The Twentieth Century*. Vol. 6, *A Critical Bibliography of French Literature*. Syracuse, N.Y.: Syracuse University Press, 1947-.

Cooper, Douglas. *The Cubist Epoch*. New York: Phaidon, 1971.

———. *The Essential Cubism, 1907-1920: Braque, Picasso and Their Friends*. London: Tate Gallery, 1983.

Dijkstra, Bram. *The Hieroglyphics of a New Speech: Cubism, Steiglitz, and the Early Poetry of Wm. Carlos Williams*. Princeton, N.J.: Princeton University Press, 1969.

Dubnick, Randa K. *The Structure of Obscenity: Gertrude Stein, Language and Cubism*. Urbana, Ill.: University of Illinois Press, 1984.

Golding, John. *Cubism: A History and Analysis, 1907-1914*. New York: G. Wittenborn, 1959. 3rd ed., Cambridge, Mass.: Belknap Press, 1988.

Gombrich, E. H. *The Story of Art*. London: Phaidon Press, 1950.

107

Gray, Christopher. *Cubist Aesthetic Theories*. Baltimore: Johns Hopkins Press, 1953.

Hannay, Howard. "Cezanne, Cubism and Modern Art." In *Roger Fry and Other Essays*. London: G. Allen & Unwin, 1937.

Komber, Gerald. *Max Jacob and the Poetics of Cubism*. Baltimore: Johns Hopkins Press, 1971.

LeMaitre Georges Edouard. *From Cubism to Surrealism in French Literature*. Cambridge, Mass.: Harvard University Press, 1941.

Mackworth, Cecily. *Guillaume Apollinaire and the Cubist Life*. London: Murray, 1961.

Roskill, Mark W. *The Interpretation of Cubism*. Philadelphia: Art Alliance Press, 1985.

Scobie, Stephen. *Earthquakes and Explorations: Language and Painting from Cubism to Concrete Poetry*. Toronto: University of Toronto Press, 1997.

Steegmuller, Francis. *Apollinaire, Poet Among the Painters*. 1936. Reprint, Freeport, N.Y.: Books for Libraries Press, 1971.

Stein, Gertrude. *Tender Buttons: Objects, Food, Rooms*. New York: Claire Marie, 1914.

Sypher, Wylie. *Rococo to Cubism in Art and Literature*. New York: Random House, 1960.

CUBO-FUTURISM
Russia, 1912-1930

Cubo-Futurism (known as Hylaea in its early days) was the most important of the Russian Futurist movements, which also included EGO-FUTURISM, the MEZZANINE OF POETRY, and CENTRIFUGE. Encompassing art and literature, it was based in Moscow and exerted its strongest influence during the years 1912 to 1918. Inspired in part by the Italian FUTURISTS, the group championed its claims in a manifesto, *Poshchochina obshchestvennomu vkusu* (1912; A Slap in the Face of Public Taste), declaring: "Throw Pushkin, Dostoevsky, Tolstoy . . . overboard from the steamship of modernity." Like the Italian Futurists, the Cubo-Futurists rejected the thematic and artistic tenets of nineteenth-century literature, and they saw themselves in revolt against sentimentalism, SYMBOLISM, and the grammatical rules that they felt restricted their writing. Like them, they were also given to outrageous public spectacle. Yet the Cubo-Futurists disassociated themselves from the Italian movement, whose emphasis on war they rejected, and it is acknowledged that their literary legacy of poetic innovation is much greater than that of their Italian counterparts.

Influenced by the CUBIST and Rayonist movements in painting, several members of the original Cubo-Futurists were artists as well as poets, and the Cubist influence is reflected in their tendencies toward nonrealistic representation and fragmentation in poetry. Demanding thematic as well as stylistic innovation, they abandoned the themes of romantic love traditional to poetry and stressed instead its verbal textures and sonorous nature. The most notable writers associated with the movement are Velemir KHLEBNIKOV, Vladimir MAYAKOVSKY, David Burlyuk (1882-1967), Aleksey Kruchonykh (1886-1968), and Yelena Guro (1877-1913), all of whose work is characterized by stylistic innovation, wordplay, and the importance of form over content and sound over sense. Several of these writers published pieces in the first Futurist collection to appear in Russia, *Sadok Sudey* (1910; A Trap for Judges). Khlebnikov's "ZAKLYATIYE SMEKHOM" (1910; Incantation by Laughter), considered one of the most important and representative works of Cubo-Futurism, reflects the theory of *zaum*, or trans-sense language. A development of Khlebnikov and Kruchonykh, the technique called for the arbitrary arrangement of words to effect a pattern without regard for sense, allowing the word to become free of meaning and to exist of and for itself. In the hands of Kruchonykh, *zaum* was used to create poetry that was merely a series of sounds strung together for their euphonious effect, but in Khlebnikov the technique resulted in poetry of profound scope and feeling.

Mayakovsky, a brilliant poet given to provocative, propagandist display, at first embraced the Bolshevik Revolutionary cause and considered it a positive force, but he and his fellow Cubo-Futurists tried without success to gain acceptance within the new Soviet regime in the 1920s. Indeed, despite their efforts as propagandists for the Revolution, the Cubo-Futurists failed to win favor with the authorities, and by the mid-1920s the movement had dissipated.

❖•❖

Khlebnikov, Velemir (1885-1922), Russian poet and dramatist.

One of the most important of the Cubo-Futurists, Khlebnikov created one of its most distinguished works with his short poem, "Zaklyatiye Smekhom." Characteristic of his style is his use of neologisms and his incorporation of elements drawn from folklore and myth. He was a theoretician of the movement, and he coined the term "self-oriented word," announced in the manifesto of 1912, which signalled the importance of wordplay used to discover the unexpected connotation of words. With Kruchonykh, Khlebnikov created the theory of *zaum*, through which the poets hoped to find and replicate a word's original meaning. He was an eccentric individual, never given to the public, propagandist displays of his fellow Futurists, and he worked throughout his brief life on a theory of history based on mathematics. Anti-Western in his orientation, he saw Russia's links to Asia as more fundamental. He was a celebrant of the ancient, pagan world, and the primitivism that captured the imaginations of the Cubo-Futurists inspired him as well, and under its influence he wrote several notable Slavic idylls. He is remembered for the complexity and variety of his work and for the linguistic innovation that distinguished his work and provided inspiration to a generation of Russian poets.

"Zaklyatiye Smekhom" (1910; Incantation by Laughter).

One of the most significant works associated with the Cubo-Futurist movement, this poem is based on derivations from a single root: the word for laughter. In his typically innovative style, Khlebnikov experiments with a variety of prefixes and suffixes to explore and determine the true, original meaning of the word, to find the essence that has been deformed by time and reactionary poetics, and to restore to the word its original vitality and power. The poem thus displays Khlebnikov's theory of *zaum*.

❖•❖

Mayakovsky, Vladimir (1893-1930), Russian poet and dramatist.

A prominent Cubo-Futurist, Mayakovsky is the most honored of all twentieth-century Russian poets. He was an early supporter of the Bolsheviks and joined the party in 1909. Arrested and imprisoned in that year, he began to write. After his release, he met other poets and painters at the Moscow Institute and contributed to the first Futurist collection, *Poshchochina obshchestvennomu vkasu* (1912; A Slap in the Face of Public Taste) and signed their first manifesto. Boisterous, provocative, and anti-sentimental, his was a poetry of the streets. In his verse he ridiculed traditional poetics, and like his fellow Futurists, he stressed the importance of verbal experiment and the creation of a new vocabulary for poetry. He incorporated freer rhythms and innovative rhyme schemes into his poetry, and his diction is characterized by neologisms, particularly the use of unusual prefixes and suffixes. Thematically his poetry centers on the themes of unhappy love and the fate of the poet. This aspect of his work marks its autobiographical connotations, for he was in love with Lili Brik, the wife of his friend Osip Brik (1888-1945), and his treatment of the theme of love frequently expresses unrequited passion.

Mayakovsky founded the LEFT FRONT OF THE ARTS (LEF) and headed its journal, *LEF*, which was published from 1923 to 1925, and later *Novy LEF*, which appeared from 1927 to 1928. Although he initially embraced the Revolution and devoted himself to propagandist purposes, by the mid-1920s he believed that very little had changed in his country. His new views, coupled with his radical approach to his art, left him out of favor with the conservative, increasingly conventional tastes of the Soviet authorities. Despite the fame of one of his best-known works, a poem on the death of Lenin, his work was rejected and ignored, and during his lifetime he was never accorded a place of honor within the Russian literary establishment. He committed suicide in 1930. Twenty-three years after his death, Lili Brik approached Stalin on his behalf, convincing him of Mayakovsky's exemplary role as a revolutionary poet, after which Stalin decreed Mayakovsky an official poet of the Soviet state.

"Oblako v shtanakh" (1914-1915; "A Cloud in Trousers," 1945).

This long poem by Mayakovsky is an exemplary work of Cubo-Futurism. As he did so often in his work, here Mayakovsky explores the themes of love's frustration, social revolution, and the plight of the poetic genius, who is doomed to be misunderstood and unwanted. The tone is at once tender and raucous, revealing the tension in his poetry and in his life between his lyrical and political inclinations. Mayakovsky was a poet who celebrated street life, and here the streets of the city, with its unwashed, unwanted people, provides his inspiration and affords him the unsentimental vision he strived for.

✥•✥

Further Reading

Banjanin, Milica. "Between Symbolism and Futurism: Impressions by Day and Night in Elena Guro's City Series." *Slavic and East European Journal* 37, 1 (spring 1993): 67-84.

Baran, Henryk. "Pushkin in Khlebnikov: Some Thematic Links." In *Cultural Mythologies of Russian Modernism: From the Golden Age to the Silver Age.* Edited by Robert P. Hughes, Irina Paperno, and Boris Gasparov. Berkeley, Calif.: University of California Press, 1992.

Barooshian, Vahan D. *Russian Cubo-Futurism 1910-1930.* The Hague: Mouton, 1975.

Barron, Stephanie, and Maurice Tuchman, eds. *The Avant-Garde in Russia: New Perspectives.* Los Angeles: Los Angeles County Museum of Art, 1980.

Brown, Edward J. *Mayakovsky: A Poet in the Revolution.* Princeton, N.J.: Princeton University Press, 1973.

———. *Russian Literature Since the Revolution.* Rev. and enl. ed. Cambridge, Mass.: Harvard University Press, 1982.

Hyde, G. M. "Mayakovsky in English Translation." *Translation and Literature* 1 (1992): 84-93.

Ljunggren, Anna, and Nina Gourianova, eds. *Elena Guro: Selected Writings from the Archives.* Stockholm: Almqvist and Wiksell, 1995.

Markov, Vladimir. *Russian Futurism: A History.* Berkeley, Calif.: University of California Press, 1968.

Poggioli, Renato. *The Poets of Russia, 1890-1930.* Cambridge, Mass.: Harvard University Press, 1960.

Struve, Gleb. *Russian Literature Under Lenin and Stalin, 1917-1953.* Norman, Okla.: University of Oklahoma Press, 1971.

CYBERPUNK
United States, 1980s-1990s

The term Cyberpunk is an amalgam of cybernetics, the science of communication and control theory, and "punk," an aggressive, anarchic style of music and writing that emerged in the 1970s. Cyberpunk refers to a science fiction literary movement of the 1980s that projected repressive near-future societies radically changed by information technology and biomedical engineering. Bruce Bethke, whose short story "Cyberpunk" (officially published in 1983) circulated among aficionados of science fiction early in the 1980s, is generally credited with having originated the term. In a 1984 article published in the *Washington Post*, critic Gardner Dozois used "Cyberpunk" to characterize an increasing number of speculative works where streetwise antiheroes struggle against repressive systems that control vast information networks. The publication in 1984 of the most popular and acclaimed work associated with the movement, the novel *Neuromancer*, by William Gibson (1948-), brought the trend to general attention; reviewers in various media began commonly using Cyberpunk in references to *Neuromancer* and works by Greg Bear (1951-), John Shirley (1953-), Rudy Rucker (1946-), and Bruce Sterling (1954-). Sterling did much to promote the trend by collecting the stories published in *Mirrorshades: The Cyberpunk Anthology* (1986), to which he contributed a manifesto-like introduction to Cyberpunk.

Sterling characterizes Cyberpunk fiction as the "overlapping of worlds that were formerly separate: the realm of high tech, and the modern pop underground." Dense with technical information and gadgetry, Cyberpunk clearly falls within the domain of traditional science fiction, but its spare narratives emphasize bleakly surreal urban landscapes, extensive cross-cutting between scenes, and phantasmagoric presentations — an exciting, refreshing approach that helped stimulate science fiction and attract fans of video games, pop counterculture, computer technology, and MTV. Many Cyberpunk works feature hallucinatory adventures in virtual reality — a technologically generated scenario humans can experience sensually. Other distinguishing elements of Cyberpunk include grim characters stripped of idealistic illusions but still struggling for freedom; biological engineering, particularly as it is capable of augmenting the human mind and body with more powerful attributes; and cyberspace — a term coined by Gibson — in which a human consciousness and nervous system connects into an electronic global information network. "Cyberspace" has since found its way into general parlance to refer to information networks of the Internet.

Cyberpunk writers acknowledge the influence of science fiction's New Wave authors — Harlan Ellison (1934-), Norman Spinrad (1940-), and Samuel R. Delaney (1942-) — and their fiction bears stylistic similarities to postmodern works of William S. BURROUGHS (*see* BEAT GENERATION) and Thomas Pynchon (1937-). Cyberpunk elements are clearly evident in such films as Ridley Scott's *Blade Runner* (1982), with its bleak, high-tech, impoverished Los Angeles setting that has distinctive Japanese cultural influences, and David Cronenberg's (1943-) *Videodrome* (1983), which emphasizes bodily metamorphosis, media overload, and destructive sexual relations. Critics have viewed Cyberpunk as an extension of post-modernism and as a continuation of the 1960s hippie counterculture. Norman Spinrad places it within the tradition of questers attempting to save a declining world. The pun-plenty title of *Neuromancer* (new romance, neuro romance, necro-romance) reflects this point.

In terms of popularity and reinvigorating science fiction, Cyberpunk fiction definitely had an impact, and its melding of high-tech and pop culture brought to literature a fusion of styles that the punk, new wave, and techno-pop trends brought to rock 'n' roll music. As a literary movement, its heyday was the 1980s when the fiction projected a wild, frontier spirit similar to the disordered Internet, with antiheroes struggling against order imposed by industrial and political blocs. Cyberpunk brought a youthful counterculture sensibility to science fiction, from the cool and wearied tones of Gibson's and Sterling's characters and narratives to the techno-romance quests in works by Bear, Gibson, and Sterling. The movement reflects the convergence of several writers addressing similar themes in a similar manner. Amid the frequently changing styles of pop culture, Cyberpunk writers risked becoming formulaic and constrained, and by the 1990s most of the movement's authors had moved on to larger themes and more composed narrative styles.

✥•✥

Further Reading

Angulo, Michael Marty. *Random Access Memories: Mechanism and Metaphor in the Fiction of William Gibson*. Doctoral thesis, University of Illinois at Urbana-Champaign, 1993.

Brande, David. *Technologies of Postmodernity: Ideology and Desire in Literature and Science*. Doctoral thesis, University of Washington, 1995.

Cadora, Karen. "Feminist Cyberpunk." *Science-Fiction Studies* 22 (November 1995): 357-72.

Davidson, Cynthia. "*Riviera's Golem, Haraway's Cyborg: Reading* Neuromancer *as Baudrillard's Simulation of Crisis*." *Science-Fiction Studies* 23, 2 (July 1996): 188-99.

Foster, Thomas. "Meat Puppets or Robopaths? Cyberpunk and the Question of Embodiment." *Genders* 18 (winter 1993): 11-31.

Harper, Mary Catherine. "Incurably Alien Other: A Case for Feminist Cyborg Writers." *Science-Fiction Studies* 22 (November 1995): 399-420.

Hassler, Donald M., and Clyde Wilcox, eds. *Political Science Fiction*. Columbia, S.C.: University of South Carolina Press, 1996.

Hicks, Heather J. "'Whatever It Is That She's Since Become': Writing Bodies of Text and Bodies of Women in James Tiptree, Jr.'s 'The Girl Who Was Plugged In' and William Gibson's 'The Winter Market'." *Contemporary Literature* 37, 1 (spring 1996): 62-91.

Howarth, David A. *The Technoculture of Cyberpunk Science Fiction and Its Publics: A Grounded Theory Analysis*. Master's thesis, University of Delaware, 1995.

Killheffer, Robert K. J. "William Gibson: The King of Cyberpunk Adds Another Novel to the Genre That He's Helped to Invent." *Publishers Weekly* 240, 36 (September 6, 1993): 70-71.

Lindberg, Kathryne V. "Prosthetic Mnemonics and Prophylactic Politics: William Gibson Among the Subjectivity Mechanisms." *Boundary 2* 23, 2 (summer 1996): 47-83.

McCaffery, Larry. *Across the Wounded Galaxies: Interviews with Contemporary American Science Fiction Writers*. Urbana, Ill.: University of Illinois Press, 1990.

McCaffery, Larry, ed. *Storming the Reality Studio: A Casebook of Cyberpunk and Postmodern Science Fiction*. Durham, N.C.: Duke University Press, 1992.

Markley, Robert, ed. *Virtual Realities and Their Discontents*. Baltimore: Johns Hopkins University Press, 1996.

Moore, John. "Shifting Frontiers: Mapping Cyberpunk and the American South." *Foundation* (spring 1996): 59-68.

Olsen, Lance. *William Gibson*. San Bernardino, Calif.: Borgo Press, 1992.

Slusser, George, and Tom Shippey, eds. *Fiction 2000: Cyberpunk and the Future of Narrative*. Athens, Ga.: University of Georgia Press, 1992.

Spinrad, Norman. "The Neuromantic Cyberpunks." 1986. In his *Science Fiction in the Real World*. Carbondale, Ill.: Southern Illinois University Press, 1990.

Sponsler, Claire. "Beyond the Ruins: The Geopolitics of Urban Decay and Cybernetic Play." *Science-Fiction Studies* 20 (July 1993): 251-65.

Sterling, Bruce. Preface to *Mirrorshades: The Cyberpunk Anthology*. New York: Arbor House, 1986.

Stockton, Sharon. "'The Self Regained': Cyberpunk's Retreat to the Imperium." *Contemporary Literature* 36, 4 (winter 1995): 588-612.

Tabbi, Joseph. *Postmodern Sublime: Technology and American Writing from Mailer to Cyberpunk*. Ithaca, N.Y.: Cornell University Press, 1995.

Wood, Brent. "William S. Burroughs and the Language of Cyberpunk." *Science-Fiction Studies* 23, 68 (March 1996): 11-26.

CZARTAK GROUP
Poland, 1922-1928

Like *ZDROJ, Czartak* was a Polish EXPRESSIONIST group and journal active during the 1920s. Emil Zegadłowicz (1888-1941), the most celebrated figure of the movement, helped alter the course of modern Polish poetry through a heightened emphasis on regionalism, native religion, and folklore in his popular ballads.

❖•❖

Further Reading

Krzyzanowski, Julian. "Neo-Realism in the Inter-war Years." In his *A History of Polish Literature*. Warsaw: PWN-Polish Scientific Publishers, 1978.

D

DADA
France, Germany, Switzerland, and United States, 1916-1923

A nihilistic reaction on the part of Europe's avant-garde to the moral bankruptcy that they saw as a central cause of the Great War, Dada had its beginnings in Zurich. By 1915 artists from throughout the war-torn continent had gathered in this cultural center to protest — and avoid — World War I (Switzerland would remain an island of political neutrality throughout the war). Although founded by pacifists, Dada reflected the radical anarchic temperament of the era in its violent abhorrence of any attempt to impose structure upon society or human creativity. Mocking both social pretenses and the "pretty" visual artworks being produced amid the political, social, and economic devastation wrought by World War I, the movement directly and irreverently attacked cultural arrogance. Its aim was a total destruction of both bourgeois values and modern artistic standards — including logic, visual composition, and grammar. Dada got its name from the Romanian poet Tristan Tzara (1896-1963), who haphazardly chose the word *dada*—a French word meaning "hobby horse"—from a dictionary while socializing with his comrades at Hugo Ball's (1886-1927) Cabaret Voltaire in Zurich in 1916. The works of artists Jean Arp (1887-1966), Francis Picabia (1879-1953), Man Ray (1890-1976), and Marcel Duchamp (1887-1968) are telling visual reminders of the explosive spirit of this brief artistic movement.

Dada's influence extended beyond the world of visual art, however, entering the literature of the period through the works of such writers as Tzara and SURREALISTS André BRETON and Paul ÉLUARD. Dadaesque writing emphasized and exploited bizarre and accidental cause and effect relationships, creating dreamlike imagery through the sequential depiction of chance events. It aggressively challenged conventional morality and the established literary canon by rejecting them. Dada texts include Tzara's *La Première aventure céleste de Monsieur Antipyrine* (1916) and *Sept Manifests Dada*

(1924); a literary form also characteristic of Dada was the "simultaneous poem," which consisted of a recitation in several languages in unison. Celtic revivalist James JOYCE (*see* MODERNISM, England and Ireland) was strongly influenced by Dada's precepts during his tenure in Paris during the interwar years; his novel *Finnegans Wake* (1939) exhibits much of the discontinuity that was a hallmark of the movement.

Taking its name from photographer Alfred Stieglitz's New York City gallery, a gathering place for U.S. adherents to the movement, the Dada journal *291* circulated throughout New York, Paris, Barcelona, and Zurich between 1917 and 1924. Linking several of the movement's main loci, *291* helped make Dada a quasi-unified international phenomenon, although each of the movement's main centers of activity focused its discontent in a distinct area. While Dada would become highly politicized in Berlin under the leadership of Raoul Hausmann (1886-1971), its focus remained primarily literary in France under the supremacy of Tzara, Breton, and Éluard. In the United States the term "Dada" remained, for the most part, synonymous with visual works of art; its spirit has since resurfaced in the pop art of Andy Warhol (1928-1987) and others.

While the movement lasted less than a decade, Dada's aesthetic worldview — its overt depiction of madness, discontinuity, and perpetual nightmare — would be adopted by French Surrealists, with their postwar emphasis on the subconscious mind and irrationality. Further influenced by the psychoanalytic theories of Sigmund FREUD and the brutality of modern warfare, the Surrealist vision of a disordered world shaped by random events was represented in the works of numerous writers, including Breton, whose journal, *Littérature* (1919), would link Dada with the later movement. Dada's visual legacy can be seen in the works of Surrealist painter Salvador Dalí (1904-1989) and filmmaker Luis Buñuel (1900-1983). As an artistic movement in its own right, Dada is notable in that it did not fade quietly into the background with the rise of Surrealism; after a series of heated debates, Breton's *Manifeste du Surréalisme* (1924) would officially sound Dada's passing.

❖•❖

Further Reading

Browning, Gordon Frederick. *Tristan Tzara: The Genesis of the Dada Poem or from Dada to Aa*. Stuttgart, Germany: Akademischer Verlag Heinz, 1979.

Caws, Mary Ann. *The Poetry of Dada and Surrealism: Aragon, Breton, Tzara, Eluard, and Desnos*. Princeton, N.J.: Princeton University Press, 1970.

Dachy, Marc. *The Dada Movement, 1915-1923*. Geneva: Skira; New York: Rizzoli, 1990. Translation of *Journal du mouvement Dada*.

Freeman, Judi. *The Dada and Surrealist Word-Image*. Los Angeles; Cambridge, Mass.: Los Angeles County Museum of Art and MIT Press, 1989.

Peterson, Elmer. *Tristan Tzara: Dada and Surrational Theorist.* New Brunswick, N.J.: Rutgers University Press, 1971.

Richter, Hans. *Dada, Art and Anti-Art.* Translated by David Britt. New York: Thames and Hudson, 1997.

Rubin, William S. *Dada and Surrealist Art.* London: Thames and Hudson, 1969.

Verkauf, Willy, ed. *Dada: Monograph of a Movement.* London: Tiranti, 1957.

DAGDRIVARNA. *See* LOAFERS

DAV GROUP
Czechoslovakia, 1924-1937

A small Marxist movement in Slovakian literature, the *DAV* Group and journal was active from 1924 until 1937. The leading figures of *DAV* were novelist Peter Jilemnický (1901-1949) and poet Ladislav Novomeský (1904-1976).

❖•❖

Further Reading

Petro, Peter. "Slovak Literature: Loyal, Dissident, and Émigre." In *Czechoslovakia 1918-88: Seventy Years from Independence.* Edited by H. Gordon Skilling. New York: St. Martin's Press, 1991.

DAWN GROUP (Grupo Saker Ti)
Guatemala, 1940s

Grupo Saker Ti, or Dawn Group, was founded in 1947 by Huberto Alvarado (1925-). Members included Melvin René Barahona (n.d.), Olga Martínez Torres (n.d.), Werner Ovalle López (1928-), Oscar Arturo Palencia (n.d.), Oscar Edmundo Palma (n.d.), and Rafael Sosa (1932-). Like the GRUPO *ACENTO* writers, those in Grupo Saker Ti were influenced by the European and Latin American MODERNISTS, but the Grupo Saker Ti augmented their study with writers such as Karl MARX, Friedrich Engels (1820-1895), Louis ARAGÓN (*see* SURREALISM, France), and AFRO-CUBANIST Nicolás Guillén (1902-1989). They wrote socially committed literature, and eventually their ranks grew with former members of Grupo *Acento*.

❖•❖

Further Reading

Foster, David William. "Guatemala." In his *Handbook of Latin American Literature.* New York: Garland, 1987.

DAWN OF THE FUTURE (*Fecr-i Âti*)
Turkey, 1909-1912

The Dawn of the Future group arose after the Young Turk revolution of 1908 weakened the conservative government of Sultan Abdulhamid II (1842-1918) and ushered in a more liberal atmosphere. The group revived the journal *Servet-i Fünun*, the forum of the defunct NEW LITERATURE GROUP (Edebiyat-i Cedide), and renamed it *Fecr-i Âti*. The most prominent figures were Egyptian-born novelist Yakup Kadri Karaosmanoğlu (1889-1974), symbolist Ahmet Haşim (1885-1933), and literary historian Fuad Köprülü (1890-1966). The group published a manifesto in 1910, asserting their affinity with the New Literature Group, and their intentions to employ aspects of Western literature in their work. Many consider Karaosmanoğlu's later and well-known novel, *Yaban* (1932; The Outlander), one of the first VILLAGE FICTION novels written in Turkey, realistically depicting as it does harsh village conditions. But early in his career, he with other members of the Dawn of the Future group generally followed the tenets of New Literature. They experimented with literary innovations springing from French SYMBOLISM and advocated the "art for art's sake" ideology while endeavoring to incorporate these Western aesthetics into the Turkish literary heritage which was fed largely by Arabic and Persian conventions. Dawn of the Future broke up in 1912 but contributed, during its short duration, to the Europeanization of Turkish literature.

❖•❖

Further Reading

Karpat, Kemal H. "Social Themes in Contemporary Turkish Literature, Part I." *The Middle East Journal* 14, 1-2 (winter 1960): 29-44. "Part II" in (spring 1960): 153-68.
Stone, Frank A. *The Rub of Cultures in Modern Turkey: Literary Views of Education.* Bloomington, Ind.: Indiana University, 1973.

DECADENCE. *See* AESTHETICISM/DECADENCE

DECADENTS (Burai-ha)
Japan, 1940s

Considered one of the most notable literary schools of post-World War II Japan, the Decadents were not so much bound by theory and technique as they were by action and outlook. Their lives and works, characterized by sardonic or violent expressions of EXISTENTIAL despair, won a wide, if sometimes critical, readership similarly disillusioned with the social and political upheaval of the period.

Although several writers have been associated with the group, only three — DAZAI Osamu, Sakaguchi Ango (1906-1955), and Oda Sakunosuke (1913-1947) — were conclusively members. Each of these writers began their literary careers before the war but did not attain major literary status until 1945 or later. The Decadents were first termed the New Gesaku writers for their tendency, largely pre-war, to criticize society with a mixture of humor and farce as the Gesaku writers of the Tokugawa period had done. Generally, the farcical element in their works, often resulting from their reformulations of Japanese fairy tales and pre-Meiji stories, diminished during the 1940s and was replaced by self-revealing fiction, explorations of their encounters with drug addiction, mental instability, depravity, and ostracism, which were tinged with ironic and fantastical elements.

The autobiographical nature of much of their work was made necessary by their simultaneous sense of futility with but sensitivity to their massive Japanese heritage and disoriented, ineffectual position in modern society. Yet, their adulation of imaginative Gesaku fiction, particularly that of Ihara Saikaku (1642-1693), prevented them from the selfsame exposure practiced by the I-NOVELists. Despite privileged upbringings, the Decadents regarded themselves, unlike their naturalistic predecessors, as complete social outcasts. Consequently, they regularly sought the company of derelicts and geishas, whose dissipated lives became entwined with theirs and whose open rejection of societal conventions informed their varied fictional worlds.

The works of the Decadents — especially Dazai's *Shayō* (1947; *The Setting Sun*, 1956) and *NINGEN SHIKKAKU* (1948; *No Longer Human*, 1958) — rank not only among the best of modern Japanese literature but of world literature as well. The artistic control, comparative independence from Western literary models, and depth of insight into the human condition present in their works stand as some of the most significant achievements in twentieth-century Japanese literature.

✦•✦

Dazai Osamu (1909-1948)
Japanese novelist, short-story writer, and essayist.

The most celebrated of the Decadents, Dazai led a severely troubled life, attempting suicide several times before finally drowning himself with a young war widow in 1948. Intensively concerned with literary fame, he published his first collection of stories, *Bannen* (Declining Years), in 1936 and gained entrance to several emerging literary circles. Following hospitalization for narcotic addiction, Dazai married in 1939 and during wartime issued several important, comparatively buoyant works. After Japan's defeat he published novels which expressed his mounting social disenchantment and his many professional and private struggles. In so doing, he became the preeminent nihilistic voice of his age. His two greatest works, *Shayō* and *Ningen Shikkaku,* were completed during this brief, generally brilliant period.

Ningen Shikkaku (1948; *No Longer Human*, 1958).

The capstone of Dazai's professional career and torturous life, *Ningen Shikkaku* is the story of Ōba Yōzō's progressive alienation from society. Yōzō, Dazai's alter ego, functions as narrator, recording in a series of notebooks his countless social and moral transgressions with unflinching honesty. The intended effect is to repel the reader while powerfully evoking the world of fear and loneliness which Yōzō inhabits. Although strongly autobiographical in nature, the novel transcends typical I-Novels through its detached, ironic stance. Dazai's inclusion of an epilogue, in which a witness of Yōzō's downfall declares of him, "He was an angel," overturns the reader's preconceptions of the protagonist and, like the best of modern fiction, points to a reality, a human truth, beyond words.

✦•✦

Further Reading

Keene, Donald. "Translator's Introduction." In *No Longer Human* by Dazai Osamu. Tokyo: C. E. Tuttle, 1958.

————. "Dazai Osamu and the Burai-ha." In his *Dawn to the West: Japanese Literature in the Modern Era*. Vol. 1. New York: Holt, Rinehart & Winston, 1984.

Lyons, Phyllis I. *The Saga of Dazai Osamu: A Critical Study with Translations*. Stanford, Calif.: Stanford University Press, 1985.

O'Brien, James A. *Dazai Osamu*. New York: Twayne, 1975.

Rimer, J. Thomas. "Dazai Osamu: The Death of the Past." In his *Modern Japanese Fiction and Its Traditions: An Introduction*. Princeton, N.J.: Princeton University Press, 1978.

Ueda, Makoto. "Dazai Osamu." In his *Modern Japanese Writers and the Nature of Literature*. Stanford, Calif.: Stanford University Press, 1976.

DECONSTRUCTION
France and United States, 1960s

The most controversial and, for several years, the most influential of the Post-STRUCTURALIST critical movements, Deconstruction is a philosophy of language and interpretation that radically elevates the role of the reader in determining multiple meanings of a given text. As such, it affines itself with SEMIOTICS, the NEW NOVEL, READER-RESPONSE CRITICISM AND RECEPTION THEORY, the GENEVA SCHOOL, and such multidisciplinary movements as Phenomenology and EXISTENTIALISM. However, despite several points of accord between these schools and that founded by French scholar Jacques DERRIDA. Deconstruction is unique in that it completely negates the longstanding concepts of authorial intent and inherent meaning. Texts, in Derrida's view, become linguistic structures which can be proven to subvert themselves and their ostensible meaning through an infinite array of contradictions, deceptions, omissions, and unconscious betrayals. The critic's task thus becomes the implementation of a Deconstruction strategy to expose as many of these counter-meanings as possible. Although Derridean criticism—necessarily both difficult in style and import—has been deemed accessible only to the few, Derrida's all-embracing philosophy and strategy have had an enormous impact in recent decades not only on critical theory but on fields throughout the humanities.

Deconstruction emerged suddenly in 1966 during an American conference on Structuralism at Johns Hopkins University. There Derrida, a graduate of the Sorbonne in Paris, delivered a lecture entitled "Structure, Sign and Play in the Discourse of the Human Sciences." Now considered a landmark essay, Derrida's speech questioned the fundamental tenets of Swiss linguist Ferdinand de Saussure (1857-1913), French anthropologist Claude Lévi-Strauss (1908-), and, indirectly, French theoretician Roland Barthes (1915-1980), the three fountainheads of Structuralist theory. His purpose was to extend the boundaries of Structuralism's key position: that the literary text, composed of phonemic and morphemic differences which serve as signs, need not reflect a preexistent, outside reality. Employing the neologism "différance," Derrida outlined a linguistic theory that emphasized the changeability of structures, for "différance" denotes both the differing grammatical properties of texts and the continual deferring of meaning, the infinite "free play" of alternate meanings that texts can support.

Since that time, considerable criticism has been levied against Derrida and his followers, particularly for their seemingly unstinting formalism, their complete devotion to grammatical structures and properties at the expense of the historical, social, and political exigencies of a text. However, the bulk of Derrida's theories, which were devised in part to support tolerant rather than elitist cultural attitudes, are founded upon many of the precepts of the most revolutionary writers and thinkers in modern history; in addition to Phenomenologist Edmund Husserl (1859-1938), Derrida has drawn upon and reacted to the work of G. W. F. Hegel (1770-1831), Friedrich NIETZSCHE, Karl MARX, Sigmund FREUD, Stéphane MALLARMÉ (*see* SYMBOLISM, France), Martin Heidegger (1889-1976), Jacques LACAN (*see* FREUDIAN CRITICISM), Michel Foucault (1926-1984), and fellow *TEL QUEL* associate Alain ROBBE-GRILLET (*see* NEW NOVEL). To varying degrees, their theories and creative writings share a distrust of metaphysical certitude and a consequent grounding in dialectics and ambiguity.

Notwithstanding the objections of the critical mainstream, Deconstruction, in various forms, surfaced in several countries during the 1970s; the most important strain was that of the YALE SCHOOL in the United States. Through the work of Paul DE MAN and others, Deconstruction, and such closely related forms of critical inquiry as FEMINIST CRITICISM, superseded such long-prevalent interpretive theories as NEW CRITICISM. Although it is generally agreed that the merits of Deconstruction cannot yet be fully determined, it is nonetheless true that scarcely any other movement in modern history has had so profound an impact on the study of the relationships between literature, literary structures, and literary criticism.

✥●✦

Derrida, Jacques (1930-)
French essayist, philosopher, critic, and academician.

Derrida began his career as a major twentieth-century writer and thinker with a French translation of and critical introduction to German philosopher Edmund Husserl's *Origin of Geometry* (1900-1; French, 1962; English, 1978). By this time, his initial sympathy for Husserl's Phenomonology, an ahistorical, anti-empirical philosophy of consciousness, had advanced towards an intense distrust of all systems of knowledge and a consequently skeptical reevaluation of the Western philosophic tradition, particularly as it pertained to the uses of language. Such resultant works as *La voix et le phénomène: Introduction au problème du signe dans la phénoménologie de Husserl* (1967; *"Speech and Phenomena," and Other Essays on Husserl's Theory of Signs*, 1973), *L'écriture et la différence* (1967; *Writing and Difference*, 1978), and DE LA GRAMMATOLOGIE (1967; *Of Grammatology*, 1976) are considered excellent examples of his unorthodox approach to determining linguistic meaning, without benefit of existing philosophies and interpretive reasoning. In these, as well as such later, highly idiosyncratic, and provocative works as *Glas* (1974; *Glas*, 1986) and *La carte postale: De Socrate à Freud et au-delà* (1980; *The Post Card: From Socrates to Freud and Beyond*, 1987), Derrida reiterates through cunning and erudite wordplay his one fundamental principle: that there is nothing, no irreducible "presence" that contains meaning, outside the text itself. Although Derrida's influence has extended into the 1990s, most scholars hesitate to assess his final position in literary history. Nonetheless, for his ability to spark debate of some of the most fundamental problems of the relationship between literature and meaning, he is undoubtedly one of the most prominent philosophers to have emerged in the latter half of the twentieth century.

De la Grammatologie (1967; *Of Grammatology*, 1976).

Considered one of Derrida's most challenging and ingenious works, *De la Grammatologie* is a convincing philosophical attack on the logocentric tradition, the belief, since the time of Aristotle, that speech, rather than writing, is the fundamental basis of meaningful, referential communication. Through his refutation of the notion of "presence," Derrida places doubt on the absolute authority of language as a conveyor of singular meaning and upholds "graphocentrism," or the self-referential quality of writing, as the preeminent form of communication. For Derrida, communication through language, then, becomes an endless dialectical enterprise: textual meanings occur, subvert themselves, and suggest others within an infinite play of language and signification. Like much of Derrida's later work, *De la Grammatologie* remains especially interesting to literary critics for its several Deconstructive meditations on classic literary and philosophical texts. Furthermore, Derrida's methodology in this and other works serves the additional purpose of reinvigorating criticism itself, to the degree that the distinction between critical and creative writing, in the hands of Derrida and his followers, becomes startlingly blurred.

➜•➜

Further Reading

Baker, Peter. *Deconstruction and the Ethical Turn.* Gainesville, Fla.: University Press of Florida, 1995.

Caruth, Cathy, and Deborah Esch, eds. *Critical Encounters: Reference and Responsibility in Deconstructive Writing.* New Brunswick, N.J.: Rutgers University Press, 1994.

Culler, Jonathan. *On Deconstruction: Theory and Criticism After Structuralism.* Ithaca, N.Y.: Cornell University Press, 1982.

Dews, Peter. *Logics of Disintegration: Post-Structuralist Thought and the Claims of Critical Theory.* London: Verso, 1987.

Gasche, Rodolphe. *The Tain of the Mirror: Derrida and the Philosophy of Difference.* Cambridge, Mass.: Harvard University Press, 1986.

Harland, Richard. *Superstructuralism: The Philosophy and Post-Structuralism.* London: Methuen, 1987.

Hartmann, Geoffrey H. *Saving the Text: Literature/Derrida/Philosophy.* Baltimore: Johns Hopkins University Press, 1981.

Harvey, Irene E. *Derrida and the Economy of Difference.* Bloomington, Ind.: Indiana University Press, 1986.

Krupniak, Mark, ed. *Displacement: Derrida and After.* Bloomington, Ind.: Indiana University Press, 1983.

Magliola, Robert. *Derrida on the Mend.* West Lafayette, Ind.: Purdue University Press, 1984.

Martin, Bill. *Humanism and Its Aftermath: The Shared Fate of Deconstruction and Politics.* Atlantic Highlands, N.J.: Humanities, 1995.

Muller, John P., and William J. Richardson. *The Purloined Poe: Lacan, Derrida & Psychoanalytic Reading.* Baltimore: Johns Hopkins University Press, 1988.

Nordquist, Joan, ed. *Jacques Derrida: A Bibliography.* Santa Cruz, Calif.: Reference and Research Services, 1986.

Norris, Christopher. *The Contest of Faculties: Deconstruction, Philosophy, and Theory After Deconstruction.* London: Methuen, 1985.

Rapaport, Herman. *Heidegger & Derrida: Reflections on Time & Language.* Lincoln, Nebr.: University of Nebraska, 1989.

Royle, Nicholas. *After Derrida*. Manchester, England: Manchester University Press, 1995.

Sallis, John, ed. *Deconstruction & Philosophy: The Texts of Jacques Derrida*. Chicago: University of Chicago Press, 1987.

Salusinszky, Imre. *Criticism in Society: Interviews with Jacques Derrida, Northrop Frye, Harold Bloom, Geoffrey Hartman, Frank Kermode, Edward Said, Barbara Johnson, Frank Lentricchia and J. Hillis Miller*. New York: Methuen, 1987.

Silverman, Hugh J., ed. *Derrida and Deconstruction*. New York: Routledge, 1989.

Smith, Joseph H., and William Kerrigan, eds. *Taking Chances: Derrida, Psychoanalysis, and Literature*. Baltimore: Johns Hopkins University Press, 1984.

Staten, Henry. *Wittgenstein and Derrida*. Lincoln, Nebr.: University of Nebraska Press, 1984.

Sturrock, John, ed. *Structuralism and Since: From Levi-Strauss to Derrida*. Oxford, England: Oxford University Press, 1979.

Taylor, Mark C., ed. *Deconstruction in Context: Literature and Philosophy*. Chicago: University of Chicago Press, 1986.

Wihl, Gary. *The Contingency of Theory: Pragmatism, Expressivism, and Deconstruction*. New Haven, Conn.: Yale University Press, 1994.

Williams, Jeffrey. "The Death of Deconstruction, the End of Theory, and Other Ominous Rumors." *Narrative* 4, 1 (January 1996): 17-35.

DERTIGERS
South Africa, 1930s

A South African group of poets prominent during the 1930s, the Dertigers helped elevate Afrikaans poetry to a high aesthetic level while displaying a strong awareness of political, social, and technological developments. The chief figure of the Dertigers was Nicholaas Petrus van Wyck Louw (1906-1970). Other members included Elisabeth Eybers (1915-), Ernst van Heerden (1916-1997), Uys Krige (1910-), W. E. G. Louw (1913-), and D. J. Opperman (1914-).

✦•✦

Further Reading

Butler, Guy. *Soldier Heroes in Corrupt Societies: A Comparison of N. P. van Wyck Louw's Germanicus and Shakespeare's Coriolanus*. Johannesburg: Randse Afrikaanse Universiteit, 1976.

Campbell, Roy. "Uys Krige, a Portrait." Wynberg, Cape Province, South Africa: Specialty Press Ltd., 1935. From *The Critic* 3, 2 (January 1935): 61-67.

Goosen, Petro. *Ernst van Heerden, a List of His Writings and Criticisms of Them, 1936-1962*. Johannesburg: University of Witwatersrand, Dept. of Librarianship, 1963.

Maskew, Margaret. *A Portrait of Uys Krige*. Wynberg, Cape Province, South Africa: Chelsea Gallery, 1985.

Van Heyningen, Christina. *Uys Krige, with a Biographical Study in Four Chapters by Jacques Berthoud*. New York: Twayne, 1966.

DEUTSCHES THEATER
Germany, 1880s-1960s

Founded in 1883 by Adolf L'Arronge (1838-1908), the Deutsches Theater a decade later became, under the direction of Otto Brahm (1856-1912), the successor to the FREIE BÜHNE as the center for NATURALISTIC productions. In 1905, Max Reinhardt (1873-1943) launched a sustained program of Naturalistic, SYMBOLIST, and revitalized works of Shakespeare and the German classics for the theater, showcasing in particular the work of Swedish dramatist August STRINDBERG (*see* EXPRESSIONISM, Germany). He quickly became known as a great innovator, not simply through his origination of the revolving stage but through his entire synthetic approach to the demands of direction, design, and staging. Bertolt BRECHT (*see* EPIC THEATER) was among the most notable figures of drama associated with the Deutsches Theater. Others included directors Heinz Hilpert (1890-1967), Wolfgang Langhoff (1901-1966), and Benno Besson (1922-); actors Josef Kainz (1858-1910) and Agnes Sorma (1865-1927); and dramatists Gerhart HAUPTMANN (*see* Freie Bühne), Arthur Schnitzler (1862-1931), Hermann Sudermann (1857-1928), and Carl Zuckmayer (1896-1977). Although the theater suffered a turbulent history during the years surrounding World War II (Reinhardt was forced to surrender management to the Nazi state in 1933), it eventually became the National Theatre of East Berlin; Reinhardt's personal stamp, however, had long since been erased.

✥•✥
Further Reading

Carter, Huntly. *Theatre of Max Reinhardt.* London: F. & C. Palmer, 1914.
Reinhardt, Gottfried. *The Genius: A Memoir of Max Reinhardt.* New York: Knopf, 1979.
Sayler, Oliver M., ed. *Max Reinhardt and His Theatre.* Translated by Mariele S. Gudernatsch, et al. New York: Brentano's, 1968.
Styan, J. L. *Max Reinhardt.* Cambridge, England: Cambridge University Press, 1982.

DEVĚTSIL. *See* NINE POWERS GROUP

DIEPALISMO
Puerto Rico, 1921

Diepalismo was a short-lived connection between the poets Luis Palés Matos (1899-1959)—later a major figure in AFRO-CUBANISM—and José I. de Diego Padró (1899-1974). Palés Matos coined the term, an anagram of his and Diego Padró's names, and it indicates the aesthetic importance Palés Matos attached to onomatopoeia. Thus Diepalismo poetry aimed at a musicality and play with words. They collaborated on a manifesto and a poem, "Orquestació diepálica" (diepalic orchestration).

⇒•⇐

Further Reading

González-Pérez, Aníbal. "Luis Palés Matos." In *Latin American Writers*. Edited by Carlos A. Solé. Vol. 3. New York: Scribner, 1989.

DIWAN SCHOOL OF POETS
Egypt, c. 1912-1919

The *Diwan* group was formed by 'Abbās Mahmūd al-Aqqād (1889-1964), Ibrāhīm 'abd al-Qadir al-Māzinī (1890-1949), and 'Abd al-Rahmān Shukrī (1886-1958), after the latter's return to Egypt in 1912 from a three-year study of English literature at Sheffield University in England. The three were heavily influenced by English romantic poetry and theory, particularly that of William Hazlitt (1778-1830), prompting contemporaries to refer to them as "the English school." Though all three wrote and published poetry, most scholars consider their verse creations mediocre at best, hailing instead the profound impact their critical writings had on later generations of Arab poets.

During the first decades of the twentieth century, Cairo was considered the literary capital of the Arab world, the seat of Islamic tradition and Arab culture during a period of classical revivalism, or neoclassicism, in response to the hostile European presence in the region. The *Diwan* group made its impact on Egyptian and Arabic literature by embodying the rise of an educated, particularly a Western-educated, class struggling with the bombardment of Western cultural values and ideas. They called themselves *madrasat al-tajdid* (the school of innovation), but today they are known by the name of their collection of critical writings, *Al-Diwan* (first issued as two pamphlets, 1921), written by al-Aqqād and al-Māzinī. The two also regularly contributed to Egyptian journals and newspapers. By 1921 Shukrī, considered by many scholars the best poet of the three, was no longer a member of the group, as callously evidenced by al-Māzinī's strong personal criticism of him in *Al-Diwan*; in fact, the group had basically ceased to exist as such by 1919. Around 1916-1918, al-Māzinī and Shukrī engaged in a highly public feud in which each accused the other of plagiarizing Western writers; years later, al-Māzinī publically regretted his attacks on Shukrī. Though Shukrī and al-Aqqād continued writing poetry in later years, al-Māzinī eventually became one of the most popular humorous prose writers in the twentieth century.

In *Al-Diwan*, al-Aqqād attacks the most prominent neoclassicist poets of the day, particularly Ahmad Shawqī (1869-1932), for continuing to imitate the classical Arab poets

126

instead of striving for new forms of literary expression by, for example, looking to French, and especially English, literature for inspiration. Al-Aqqād and al-Māzinī advocated incorporating Western subjectivity and individualism into Arabic poetry, and breaking the classical tradition in which the poet evokes "the voice of the tribe," singing of collective emotion and communal experience. Al-Aqqād insisted that a poem should have organic unity and stressed the importance of the poet's personality and emotional experience — values indicative of al-Aqqād's study of Sigmund FREUD, Friedrich NIETZSCHE, and of course Hazlitt, William Wordsworth (1770-1850), Percy Bysshe Shelley (1792-1822), and other English romantic poets. Their own poetry, most critics agree, falls short of illustrating their critical ideas, conveying almost mechanical reworking of poetic diction, rhythm and form, while communicating more affected sentimentality than authentic emotion. Yet their poetic and critical works reflect the despair and alienation of early twentieth-century educated Egyptians, caught between two worlds and spiritually belonging to neither: the Arab world, ineffectively basking in its renowned past; and the West, foreign, hostile, and technological.

Many scholars consider the *Diwan* writers the founders of modern Arabic literary criticism; some, however, disagree, citing the profound influence of some contemporaries, such as the *Majhar* (*see* ANDALUSIAN LEAGUE and SOCIETY OF THE PEN) poets, as well as the Lebanese poet and critic Khalīl Mutrān (1871-1949). Stylistically, Mutrān and the *Diwans* worked in many of the same directions, but al-Aqqād denied the significance of Mutrān's achievements, and generally tended to ignore the literary production of non-Egyptian Arabs, which leads many critics to note the isolationism al-Aqqād's pro-Egyptian stance created in the Arabic literary world, as well as the resentment al-Aqqād personally incurred from many of his contemporaries. Nevertheless, the critical writings of the *Diwan* group were fundamentally instrumental in laying the groundwork for later generations of poets, including the APOLLO SCHOOL, as well as for the Modernist revolution in Arabic poetry during the 1950s and 1960s.

❖•❖

Further Reading

Arberry, Arthur John. *Modern Arabic Poetry: An Anthology with English Verse Translations.* London: Taylor's Foreign Press, 1950.

Badawi, Muhammad M. *A Critical Introduction to Modern Arabic Poetry.* Cambridge, England: Cambridge University Press, 1975.

Brugman, J. *An Introduction to the History of Modern Arabic Literature in Egypt.* Leiden, Netherlands: E. J. Brill, 1984.

Hourani, Albert. *Arabic Thought in the Liberal Age, 1798-1939.* London: Oxford University Press, 1962.

Jayyusi, Salma Khadra. *Trends and Movements in Modern Arabic Poetry.* Vol. 1. Leiden,
    Netherlands: E. J. Brill, 1977.
Moreh, S. *Modern Arabic Poetry, 1800-1970: The Development of Its Forms and Themes
    under the Influence of Western Literature.* Leiden, Netherlands: E. J. Brill, 1976.
Semah, David. "'Abbas Mahmud al-'Aqqad." In *Four Egyptian Literary Critics.* Leiden,
    Netherlands: E. J. Brill, 1974.
al-Zubaidi, A. M. K. "The Diwan School." *Journal of Arabic Literature* 1 (1970): 36-48.

DZVONY (The Bells)
Ukraine, 1930-1939

Dzvony was a western Ukrainian journal published from 1930 until 1939, edited by
Mykola Hnatyshak (1902-1940) and Petro Isaiv (n.d.), in whose pages appeared much
work by LOGOS writers. Most of the journal's contributors were Catholic; poet Bohdan
Ihor Antonych (1909-1937), noted for his lyrical and idealistic verse, was the most
important contributor to *Dzvony*.

❖•❖

Further Reading

Luckyj, George S. N. "Western Ukraine and Emigration, 1919-39." In his *Ukrainian Literature
    in the Twentieth Century: A Reader's Guide.* Toronto: University of Toronto Press for the
    Shevchenko Scientific Society, 1992.
Rubchak, Bohdan. Introduction to *Square of Angels: Selected Poems* by Bohdan Ihor
    Antonych. Ann Arbor, Mich.: Ardis, 1977.

E

EARTH MOVEMENT
Lithuania, 1950s

Launched in 1952, the Earth Movement elevated the fields of poetry and criticism in Lithuanian literature. Writers associated with the movement included Kazys Bradūnas (1917-), Henrikas Nagys (1920-), Antanas Škėma (1911-1961), and Alfonsas Nyka-Niliūnas (1920-). Their works typically combined a Romantic, love-of-nature aestheticism with a somber view of the modern world.

✦●✦

Further Reading

Kaupas, Julius. "Introducing the Poetry of Henrikas Nagys." *Lituanus: Baltic States Quarterly of Arts & Sciences* 9 (1963): 94-101.
Silbajoris, Rimvydas. "The Tragedy of Creative Consciousness: Literary Heritage of Antanas Skema." *Lituanus: Baltic States Quarterly of Arts & Sciences* 12, 4 (1966): 5-25.
————. "Introduction to *The Awakening*." In *Confrontations with Tyranny: Six Baltic Plays*. Edited by Alfreds Straumanis. Prospect Heights, Ill.: Waveland, 1977.
————. "Introduction to *Five Posts in a Market Place*." In *Confrontations with Tyranny: Six Baltic Plays*. Edited by Alfreds Straumanis. Prospect Heights, Ill.: Waveland, 1977.
"Skema Play in New York." *Baltic Forum* 2, 2 (1985): 132-314.

ÉCOLE LITTÉRAIRE DE MONTREAL. *See* LITERARY SCHOOL OF MONTREAL

ÉCOLE ROMANE
France, 1890s-1910s

This movement was founded and given its name by the Greek poet Iannis Papadiamantopoulos (1856-1910) who, in the late 1890s, adopted France as his country and Jean Moréas for his name. He had earlier considered himself a SYMBOLIST, but had become disenchanted with the mode and inspired the École Romane movement in reaction to it. His purpose was to convince his contemporaries of the need for a MODERNIST revival of the "dignity and restraint" of the classical French poetry of the sixteenth and seventeenth centuries. Moréas saw the best poetry as having roots in the ancient Graeco-Roman tradition, and he argued that Romanticism had sullied the purity of French literature. Other members of the group included Raymond de La Tailhède (1867-1938), Charles Maurras (1868-1952), Ernest Raynaud (1864-1936), and Maurice Du Plessys (1864-1924), whose mastery of parody in imitation of the classicists and prodigious volume of work — including *Dedicace a Appolodore* (1891), *Etudes Lyriques* (1896), and *Odes Olympiques* (1912) — contribute to his stature as a major figure in the movement.

For some readers, the poetry of the movement was accepted as an apt invocation of the classical Mediterranean elements in French verse which were nostalgic and familiar. For a time, it provided a look backward and away from the intensity of the self-preoccupation of the Romanticists and the abstraction of the Symbolists. But by mid-century, many of the French literati were concerned with political action and the upheaval which had been caused by World War II. The writer and philosopher Jean-Paul SARTRE (*see* EXISTENTIALISM) called the new creative impulse *la littérature engagée* — creative work which is addressed to immediate circumstance and social reality; thus, the poets of École Romane were criticized, especially Moréas, for an irrational preoccupation with the imitation of archaic poetry and the classics, which had only resulted in mediocre invention.

However, it is noted by one critic that the group of young poets who enthusiastically supported Moréas have contributed to a minor theme in French literature which, surprisingly, has remained, and consists of a return to authoritarianism, monarchy, and the brilliant intellectualism of the Age of Reason. The concept continues to reinforce the earlier reaction to the sentimentality of the Romantic revolution and the aesthetic "anguish of poetic experience."

❧•❦

Further Reading

Boase, Alan Martin, ed. *The Poetry of France*. London: Methuen, 1952.

Brereton, Geoffrey. *An Introduction to the French Poets*. Fair Lawn, N.J.: Essential Books, 1957.

Brereton, Geoffrey, Anthony Hartley, and Brian Woledge, eds. *The Penguin Book of French Verse*. 4 vols. Baltimore: Penguin Books, 1958-61.

Gilman, Margaret. *The Idea of Poetry in France: From Houdar de la Motte to Baudelaire*. Cambridge, Mass.: Harvard University Press, 1958.

Lucas, St. John Welles Lucas, comp. *The Oxford Book of French Verse, XIIIth C.-XXth C.*. Oxford, England: Clarendon Press, 1957.

EDEBEYAT-I CEDIDE. *See* **NEW LITERATURE GROUP**

EDWARDIAN LITERATURE
England and Ireland, c. 1900-1911

Edward VII was monarch of England in the first decade of the twentieth century and was, with the exception of a group of the GEORGIAN POETS who were briefly popular in the following ten years, the last of the royals whose name graced a literary period; since about 1912, most groups have been categorized generally as part of the larger movement known as MODERNISM. The name "Edwardian" is a deceptive one because the period includes writers who had enjoyed repute in the Victorian era, as well as those who would continue to do so when the Edwardian era was over. The nomenclature also includes the Irish writers John Millington SYNGE, William Butler YEATS (*see* ABBEY THEATER and MODERNISM, England and Ireland), and Lady Augusta Gregory (1852-1932), all of whom had been noteworthy participants of the IRISH RENAISSANCE and the Abbey Theater in Dublin. Moreover, Thomas Hardy (1840-1928), W. H. Hudson (1841-1922), and Samuel Butler (1835-1902) had been and still were recognized as major Victorian writers. The list of Edwardians includes James Barrie (1860-1937), Arnold BENNETT, Joseph CONRAD (*see also* Modernism, England and Ireland), Edward Dunsany (1878-1957), Ford Madox FORD, E. M. Forster (1878-1970), John Galsworthy (1867-1933), Harley Granville-Barker (1877-1946), Douglas Hyde (1911-), Henry JAMES (*see* REALISM, United States), James JOYCE (*see* Modernism, England and Ireland), Rudyard KIPLING, John Masefield (1878-1967), Lennox Robinson (1886-1958), Victoria Sackville-West (1892-1962), George Bernard SHAW, James Stephen (1882-1950), and H. G. Wells (1866-1946).

The Edwardians provided a transitional period between the London of the 1890s and the years following World War I. As a part of this diverse interim, they provided a rich mix of artistic talent. In their short span they represented, at once, a departing point from the old and slowly dying Victorian literary tradition and a growing intimation of the irrevocable changes which were to follow. The period has been described as one of elegance, enthusiasm, and the excesses of the ruling class. While writers were beginning to free themselves from the old queen's rigid propriety of manner, some still adhered to a mode of complacency, comfort, and conservatism. But subtle undercurrents of change, indications of the fragmentation of the old tradition, were in the air. These had begun in the 1890s with a group of young artists and writers who called themselves "Aesthetes" and "Decadents" (*see* AESTHETICISM/DECADENCE), and who had insisted that art should be celebrated for its own sake by the artist who, free of social, moral, and political restriction, could depict individual perception of truth and beauty. The concept was known as *ars victrix*, and embodied firm rejection of a value system artists felt to be outmoded. Among these writers was the young Yeats, whose work would begin to mature in the Edwardian era and whose impact on the poetry of the twentieth century continued at its close.

But if the rebels of the nineties had sought to depict the lonely introspection of the artistic spirit, by the turn of the century Edwardians Rudyard Kipling and John Masefield still remained true to the spirit of Victorian empire. Their work idealized the common man, soldier, seaman, and laborer, and his loyalty to king and country. On the other hand, there was, among writers, a desire to write for "popular audience," that new and growing number of fiction readers who were interested in the "best sellers" of the day (a new phenomenon) as well as journalistic essays and reviews. A rise of little literary magazines was allowing aspiring writers the publication of their views and their creative work. Among these were James Joyce and Arnold Bennett. Joyce began his publishing career in the *Fortnightly Review* with his essay "Ibsen's New Drama" (1900) and Bennett took advantage of an opportunity to publish in the journals for the polishing of his craft. The result was that his most vigorous criticism and finest novels appeared during the Edwardian era. His contemporaries H. G. Wells and John Galsworthy also were popular novelists whose works contain interesting and subtle elements of social criticism which had mass appeal. Joseph Conrad and Ford Madox Ford published their most important works after 1900. Conrad ranks as one of the greatest English novelists of this century, and while Ford has been sometimes underestimated as a novelist from time to time, he has lately been more recognized as one of the most promising of the early Modernists. These two collaborated on the novels *The Inheritors* (1901) and *Romance* (1903), and together sought a new form for the novel.

The Irish dramatist George Bernard Shaw was not well received in London until the Edwardian era began. In disfavor in England prior to 1900 for his outspoken criticism of British colonialism, by the turn of the century and with the help of the eminent critic and Shavian Harley Granville-Barker, Shaw was finally accepted in London as an outstanding Edwardian playwright. His anti-Victorian, satiric wit served as one more metaphor for the changing times.

An interesting illumination of the Edwardian mind-set is discussed by critic Samuel Hynes, and has to do with a reaction to the censorship of English drama which had begun under the Tudors and was reinforced in 1830 by giving the Lord Chamberlain absolute licensing power over productions for the London stage. In 1907 two plays about adultery—Edward Garnett's (1868-1937) *The Breaking Point* and Granville-Barker's *Waste*—both became literary cynosures when The Examiner of Plays censored them. In protest, seventy Edwardian authors petitioned the Prime Minister to take action against the licensing of plays. Signatures on the petition included the names of Barker, Barrie, Conrad, Galsworthy, Hardy, Ford, Masefield, Shaw, Synge, Wells, and Yeats, and the result was that an examining committee was appointed to examine stage censorship, but the controversy continued for half a century. In 1967 a parliamentary committee recommended that the 1843 Act for Regulating Theatre be repealed, providing uncensored theater in London "for the first time in four hundred years." This, it seems, is more indication of how Edwardians were at the forefront of a concept of artistic freedom which has become a cornerstone of Modernism.

If Edwardian writers are observed as having moved toward literary reform, it does not surprise. Reform was in the air at all levels of the culture, and brought about by the impact of the works of Sigmund FREUD and Karl MARX, the newly educated masses, and the gathering momentum of movements such as women's suffrage and the trade unions. The new century had brought with it enthusiastic desire for a change in the old order, combined perhaps with some skepticism and uncertainty about what lay ahead. At the end of a century of literature in which Edwardians played an initial role, a look back finds some of their work conservative and outdated, but that they were a part of a new look at literature is a fact. With the death of the king, the era ended in 1910, but the major works of T. S. ELIOT, Joyce, D. H. LAWRENCE, Yeats, Virginia WOOLF, and others like them were soon to come and with them, a clear signal that the Modernist movement was underway.

❖•❖

Bennett, (Enoch) Arnold (1867-1931)
English journalist, editor, and novelist.

Bennett early aspired to a literary career, but his unsuccessful novel, *A Man from the North* (1898), caused him to switch to the field of journalism and nonfiction. His anonymous authorship of the autobiography of editor C. Lewis Hind appeared in 1898. Its title, *The Truth about an Author*, caused a flurry of criticism, for it contained his own views about the writing game—that authors should earn money as well as fame, since they are human beings and should enjoy some of the luxuries afforded to the wealthy. Its tone was offensive to serious writers, as he had intended it to be, but it brought him the reputation he desired in the eyes of popular audience. There followed a series of mediocre, but best-selling novels and by 1900, his early efforts had culminated in the works for which he remains best known: *Anna of the Five Towns* (1902), *The Old Wive's Tale* (1908), and *Clayhanger* (1910). Each of these has for thesis the concept of repressive parents and how they affected their children's lives. Set in industrial towns or rural areas and about ordinary people, Bennett's ability to depict the times and his unique perception about how environment affected his characters make for fascinating reading. His talent lay in an extraordinary ability to portray the lives of working-class people and their responses to prosaic experience with sympathy and accuracy. This talent served him well, for his time, and earned him the reputation and income he felt he deserved. Other of his many works include the comic novel, *A Great Man* (1904); a satire of the art world, *Buried Alive* (1908); short stories in *Tales of the Five Towns* (1912); and in the same year, *Milestones*, a drama in collaboration with Edward Knoblock (1874-1945). *The Old Wive's Tale* has been adapted for presentation on the BBC television network and has been shown in the United States and Canada as a classic example of Edwardian times.

❖•❖

Conrad, Joseph (pseud. of Josef Konrad Korseniowski, 1857-1924) English novelist and short-story writer.

Born in the Ukraine of Polish origin, Conrad became a seaman at the age of seventeen and his experiences on the sea and his love for it are the bases for much of his work. He is known for his innovative use of narrative, multiple points of view, distortion of time within narrative line, and descriptive passages which set a tone of mystery and ambiguity and often cause digression and disruption of plot. Conrad's aim was to present revelation of truth in sometimes momentary impressions of character and situation. His best-known works are *Lord Jim* (1900), *HEART OF DARKNESS* (1902; *see* Modernism, England and Ireland), and *Nostromo* (1904). In each of these are the themes of irony, betrayal, disillusion, and moral tragedy. Keynoted are characters who are alienated and in isolation from human companionship, and who often come to self-knowledge too late for either psychic or physical preservation. It is the journey of the human spirit and the choices between good and evil inherent in Conrad's creative vision which provide the substance of his work. The exploration of the workings of the mind, he said, allowed the artist to "speak to . . . the sense of mystery surrounding our lives, and to our sense of beauty and pain." It was his willingness to experiment with the form of the novel, his compelling depictions of the differences between appearance and reality in life, and his skepticism about the codes which are used for moral judgment which engage the reader's intellect as well as the emotions. The influence of Henry James and the French writers Stendahl (1783-1842) and Gustave FLAUBERT (*see* NATURALISM and REALISM, France) can be seen in Conrad's style and, like their work, his makes for powerful intellectual exercise. Of his many works, others published in the Edwardian era are *Typhoon* (1902), *Youth* (1902), *A Mirror of the Sea* (1906), *The Secret Agent* (1907), *A Set of Six* (1908), and *Under Western Eyes* (1911).

❖•❖

Ford, Ford Madox (also known as Ford Maddox Hueffer; 1873-1979)
English novelist, editor, critic, and poet.

Born in Surrey, Ford came from an artistic family and was related by marriage to Pre-Raphaelite art critic and writer William Rossetti (1829-1919). Gaining prominence as an editor and a critic, Ford was founder of the literary journal, *English Review*, in 1908 and under his watchful eye it became the most brilliant journal to appear in London. Contributors and friends included D. H. Lawrence, Thomas Hardy, H. G. Wells, and Wyndham LEWIS (*see* VORTICISM). Ford's minor early works were *The Brown Owl: A Funny Story* (1892) and other works of fiction, nonfiction, and poetry. His collaboration with Conrad in 1902 and 1903 on three novels brought him the serious critical attention which he had lacked earlier. His best-known novels are *The Good Soldier* (1915) and *Parade's End,* a tetralogy written under separate titles — *Some Do Not . . .* (1924), *No More Parades* (1925), *A Man Could Stand Up* (1926), and *Last Post* (1928) — and republished under the title *Parade's End* in 1961. The latter is noted by one critic to be "the most unique and comprehensive view of the disorder and changes which occurred in England after World War I." The first has an ironic title, for the "good soldier" is the narrator's friend and earlier comrade in arms, but is really his enemy in matters of treachery — sexual intrigue with the narrator's wife. *Parade's End* has for its main character Christopher Tietjens, whose experiences in the war so disillusioned him that he rejected his former life, his family, and his social responsibilities. Like Conrad, Ford had studied the French writers, and while his style is sometimes impressionistic, casual, and loosely organized, close reading shows his remarkable insight about human relationships and how they work. He would, in turn, influence the work of Lawrence and other modern writers. Other of his works include *No Enemy* (1929), *Return to Yesterday* (1931), and *It Was the Nightingale* (1933). In the fifties and sixties in the United States there was a revival of interest in his method and work in literary circles and in university classrooms.

❖•❖

Kipling, Rudyard (1865-1936)
English novelist, poet, and short fiction writer.

One of the most popular writers of his time, Kipling was born in India, educated in England, and he returned to England at the age of seventeen. There he worked as a journalist and first published verses and short stories which had Indian characters and themes. The mid-1880s found him in London where he contributed work to the journal *Pall Mall,* and his books about India earned him success. Early works were a volume of short stories, *Life's Handicap* (1891); the novel *The Light That Failed* (1890), a story of unrequited love set in the Sudan; and *Barrack Room Ballads* (1892), poems written in celebration of British Army life, including the famous "Gunga Din." He lived in the United States between 1892 and 1897, during which time he wrote prolifically and was married. Important among his literary works were the children's books, *The Jungle Book* (1894) and, in the same year, *The Second Jungle Book*, and novels about the sea, *The Seven Seas* (1896) and *Captains Courageous* (1897). Just before the turn of the century, he returned to England. He found that he had not lost his earlier popular audience, and between 1897 and 1914 his literary output was extraordinary. It includes *The Day's Work* (1898), *Stalky and Company* (1899), *Kim* (1901), and *Just So Stories* (1902); these last were popular fiction for and about children which contain his own illustrations. Other works are *The Five Nations* (1903), *Traffics and Discoveries* (1904), *Puck of Pook's Hill, Actions and Reactions* (1909), *A Diversity of Creation* (1917), and *The Irish Guards in the Great War* (1923). His writing activity diminished in the 1920s, but he wrote a memorial to his son who had been killed in the war and, finally, *Something of Myself*, in 1937, his unfinished autobiography. Kipling remained an imperialist until he died; his aim was to glorify the ordinary men who kept the empire strong. He used the various dialects of the land and especially enjoyed that of the Cockney. He exemplified the new enthusiasm for popular audience which was particularly Edwardian and enjoyed the admiration and popularity accorded him by his many readers, both in England and the United States. His adulation of the soldier-at-war, apparent in some of his poems and stories, caused him to be criticized by the intelligentsia, but he adhered to his rejection of the "art for art's sake" credo and to his agreement with John Masefield that "art should [be clearly enough understood] so as to heighten the ordinary reader's sense of life." In 1907 he was awarded the Nobel Prize for literature.

❖•❖

Shaw, George Bernard (1856-1950)
Irish dramatist, journalist, and critic.

One of the most flamboyant and eccentric of the Edwardians, Shaw was not only the twentieth century's most outstanding dramatist in the Western world but a public figure of renown, since he had many convictions about how society should conduct itself. He was an ardent socialist, and other causes which he vehemently defended were the rights of animals and the spelling reform of the English language. His most important literary theory was that drama should be written to be read as literature as well as to be performed. His dramas are still studied in classrooms as literature, much like Shakespeare's, to whom Shaw unhesitatingly and favorably compared himself. They are as popular now for their careful construction as when first written. Shaw's initial works were novels which appeared in periodicals. He then became a journalist and wrote literary and music criticism. His first play was written in 1892 and, while it was not a success, he had now found the genre which he was to love the most. Two major plays were written before 1901. The first, *The Devil's Disciple* (1897), is about the American Revolution and contains his pacifist views about the military life, but more specifically speaks to the human personality and self-revelation. *Caesar and Cleopatra* (1898) is based on the ancient play by Plutarch, and portrays Cleopatra as a young, naive girl who is molded and directed towards her rulership by the aging Caesar. Shaw's best work was done during the Edwardian era and after. The earliest, which appeared in 1905, is *Man and Superman*, and includes the famous debate, "Don Juan in Hell," which has often been excerpted and performed as its own drama. It embodied Shaw's philosophy of creative evolution and rational goal direction. *Major Barbara* (1905) contains his moral and economic views about war and the military establishment, money and its taint, and the problems of the poor. Others of note are *Misalliance* (1912), a "loquacious fantasy"; *Pygmalion* (1913), a modern version of the legend and since popularized as a musical; and *Heartbreak House* (1920), which contains Shaw's views about good, evil, world problems, and the merit of sound reasoning as the antidote for a better world. Other plays were enjoyed by ardent Shavian audiences of the time but are rarely produced today. His masterpiece is said to be *St. Joan* (1923). Written shortly after her canonization, it is about Joan's virtue and her need to place her conscience above the tenets of church and country, both of which she adored. She was burned at the stake for her beliefs and epitomized, in Shaw's view, the classic ironic figure for the radical but virtuous views which led to her death. "G.B.S.," as he loved to be called, has been regarded as the most brilliant craftsman of the drama seen in this century. Conversely, because much of his work provides a forum for his passionate socialistic and iconoclastic views, he has been criticized as ego-oriented, didactic, over-discursive, and even boring. However, one critic observes that his best work shows a talent no less than magnificent. He was recognized for it when he received the Nobel Prize for literature in 1925.

❖•❖

Further Reading

Anderson, Linda. *Bennett, Wells and Conrad*. New York: St. Martin's Press, 1986.

Batchelor, John. *The Edwardian Novelists*. New York: St. Martin's Press, 1982.

Bennett, Arnold. *Books and Persons: Being Comments on a Past Epoch*. New York: George H. Doran, 1917.

Bentley, Eric. *Bernard Shaw: A Reconsideration*. New York: Norton, 1976.

Bloom, Harold. *Joseph Conrad*. New York: Chelsea House, 1986.

———. *Rudyard Kipling*. New York: Chelsea House, 1987.

Boon, John. *Victorians, Edwardians and Georgians*. London: Hutchinson, 1928.

Brown, Douglas. "From *Heart of Darkness* to *Nostromo*: An Approach to Conrad." In *The Pelican Guide to English Literature*. Vol. 7, *The Age of Modernism*. Edited by Boris Ford. Harmondsworth, England: Penguin, 1983.

Camplin, Jamie. *The Rise of the Plutocrats*. London: Constable, 1978.

Clarke, Ian. *Edwardian Drama*. London: Faber, 1989.

Conroy, Mark. *Modernism and Authority: Strategies of Legitimation in Flaubert and Conrad*. Baltimore: Johns Hopkins University Press, 1985.

Crook, Nora. *Kipling's Myths of Love and Death*. New York: St. Martin's Press, 1989.

Goldring, D. *The Last Pre-Raphaelite: A Record of the Life and Writings of Ford Madox Ford*. London: Macdonald, 1948.

Gross, John. *The Rise and Fall of the Man of Letters: A Study of the Idiosyncratic and the Humane in Modern Literature*. New York: Macmillan, 1969.

Hawkins, Hunt. *Conrad Revisited: Essays for the Eighties*. University, Ala.: University of Alabama Press, 1985.

Holt, Lee. *Samuel Butler*. New York: Twayne, 1964. Rev. ed., New York: Twayne, 1989.

Hunter, Jefferson. *Edwardian Fiction*. Cambridge, Mass.: Harvard University Press, 1982.

Hynes, Samuel. *The Author's Craft and Other Critical Writings of Arnold Bennett*. Lincoln, Nebr.: University of Nebraska, 1968.

————. *The Edwardian Turn of Mind*. Princeton, N.J.: Princeton University Press, 1968.

Miller, Jane Eldridge. *Rebel Women: Feminism, Modernism, and the Edwardian Novel*. London: Virago, 1994; Chicago: University of Chicago Press, 1997.

Petrie, Charles. *The Edwardians*. New York: W. W. Norton, 1965.

Priestley, J. B. *The Edwardians*. New York: Harper & Row, 1970.

Rose, Jonathan. *The Edwardian Temperament: 1895-1919*. Athens, Ohio: Ohio University Press, 1986.

Sackville-West, Victoria. *The Edwardians*. Garden City, N.Y.: Doubleday, Doran, 1930.

Squillace, Robert. *Modernism, Modernity, and Arnold Bennett*. Lewisburg, Pa.: Bucknell University Press, 1997.

Stevens, Mary Ann, et al, eds. *The Edwardians and After: The Royal Academy, 1900-1950*. London: Royal Academy of Arts, 1988.

Thompson, Paul. *The Edwardians: The Remaking of British Society*. Bloomington, Ind.: Indiana University Press, 1975. 2nd ed., London: Routledge, 1992.

Trodd, Anthea. *A Reader's Guide to Edwardian Literature*. Calgary, Canada: University of Calgary Press, 1991.

Wickes, George, ed. *Masters of Modern British Fiction*. New York: Macmillan, 1963.

EGO-FUTURISM
Russia, 1910s

One of four Russian FUTURIST groups, Ego-Futurism arose in St. Petersburg in 1911 under the leadership of Igor Severyanin (1887-1942) and Konstantin Olimpov (n.d.). Severyanin's flair for self-revelation, neologisms, and irrational expressions gave the movement a brief vogue; however, Severyanin himself abandoned the movement by 1912 and soon entered the dominant CUBO-FUTURIST circle. Other writers associated with Ego-Futurism—and its sister movement in Moscow, the MEZZANINE OF POETRY—included Ivan Ignatiev (1892-1914), Georgy Ivanov (1894-1958), Ryurik Ivnev (1891-1981), Sergei Tretyakov (1892-1939), and Vadim Shershenevich (1893-1942).

❖•❖

Further Reading

Lauwers, Lenie. *Igor-Severjanin: His Life and Work—the Formal Aspects of His Poetry*. Leuven, Belgium: Uitgeverij Peeters en Departement Orientalistiek, 1993.

Terras, Victor, ed. *Handbook of Russian Literature*. New Haven, Conn.: Yale University Press, 1985.

ENSUEÑISMO GROUP
Puerto Rico, 1950s

Cesáreo Rosa-Nieves (1901-) led this movement in Puerto Rico during the 1950s, which called for avant-garde, "ultramodernist," and nativist expression in poetry. Félix Franco Oppenheimer (1912-), earlier the founder of the TRANSCENDENTALIST GROUP, was a member by 1954, as were José Luis Martin Montes (1921-) and Eugenio Rentas Lucas (1910-). Together they issued and signed a manifesto in 1954.

❖•❖

Further Reading

Babín, María Teresa, and Stan Steiner, eds. *Borinquen: An Anthology of Puerto Rican Literature*. New York: Knopf, 1974.

Foster, David William. "Rosa Nieves, Cesáreo." In his *A Dictionary of Contemporary Latin American Authors*. Tempe, Ariz.: Center for Latin American Studies, Arizona State University, 1975.

———. "Verastegui, Enrique." In his *A Dictionary of Contemporary Latin American Authors*. Tempe, Ariz.: Center for Latin American Studies, Arizona State University, 1975.

Hill, Marnesba D., and Harold B. Schleifer. "Franco Oppenheimer, Felix." In *Puerto Rican Authors: A Biobibliographic Handbook*. Metuchen, N.J.: Scarecrow Press, 1974.

———. "Rentas Lucas, Eugenio." In *Puerto Rican Authors: A Biobibliographic Handbook*. Metuchen, N.J.: Scarecrow Press, 1974.

———. "Rosa Nieves, Cesáreo." In *Puerto Rican Authors: A Biobibliographic Handbook*. Metuchen, N.J.: Scarecrow Press, 1974.

Jones, Willis Knapp. "Cesáreo Rosa-Nieves." In his *Spanish-American Literature in Translation: A Selection of Poetry, Fiction, and Drama Since 1888*. New York: Ungar, 1963-66.

EPIC THEATER (Episches Theater)
Germany, 1920s-1950s

The term "Episches Theater" comes from an expression used in German dramatic circles which embodies a radical approach of playwrights and producers to influence the ways in which audiences experience theater arts. It negates the conventional Aristotelian concept, in which spectator empathy is derived from a self-contained plot into which dramatic theme is woven. Instead, in Epic Theater, dramaturgical emphasis is on the reduction of the emotional involvement of the audience in order to stimulate "aesthetic distance [for] critical scrutiny of reality." Included in presentations also are innovative theatrical devices such as rotating or treadmill stages and the additional use of such artifacts as film and other graphic materials to further enhance what has come to be known as "documentary drama." These techniques would develop into what Bertolt BRECHT would later call "theater of alienation" and "dialectical theater," as they served his purpose in presenting the theater most appropriate to the need for the societal changes which he advocated. While he developed the concept and continued to use it until his death, he had been introduced to the idea in the 1920s through the works of Erwin Piscator (1893-1966), Arnolt Bronnen (1885-1959), and Alfred Paquet (1881-1944). (*See* BERLIN ENSEMBLE). Other dramatists who were involved in Epic Theater were Tankred Dorst (1925-), Friedrich Dürrenmatt (1921-1990), Max Frisch (1911-1991), Peter Hacks (1928-), Wolfgang Hildesheimer (1916-1991), Martin Walser (1927-), and Peter WEISS (*see* THEATER OF FACT).

✥●✥

Brecht, Bertolt (1898-1956), German dramatist, critic, poet, and novelist.

A towering figure in twentieth-century theater, Brecht was born to middle-class parents in Bavaria. He began his university education as a medical student in Munich, but after his service in World War I, he turned more and more to writing and developing his interest in theater. His dramatic career began as a consultant to the DEUTSCHES THEATER in the mid-1920s. Around this time, he also became an ardent socialist, having recently read Karl MARX's *Das Kapital* (1867, vol. 1, and 1885, vol. 2). At the rise of Hitler in 1933, Brecht went into exile to Sweden, Finland, and, for a lengthy period, to Hollywood, California, where, eventually, his socialist commitment caused him to be duly summoned to testify in front of the House Committee on Un-American Activities in 1947. From the United States, Brecht then moved to Switzerland before returning to Germany for his last years, to East Germany specifically, where, with his wife, actress Helene Weigel (1900-1971), he founded the BERLIN ENSEMBLE in 1949.

By the 1930s Brecht was backing away from the NEW OBJECTIVITY trend, in which he briefly dabbled in an objective prose style; as a socialist, he believed that epic theater should be a radical transformation of theater in order to correspond with a socialist transformation of mentality and appeal to spectators' reason, rather than to emotion. He also wanted dramatic performances to deal with the great social issues: class conflict, mass industrialization, war, and disease.

Brecht's development of Epic Theater involved a continual reworking of his theory that spanned decades. Some of his formative essays include *Über die Verwendung der Musik für eine epische Bühne* (1935), the unfinished dialogue *Der Messginkauf,* written between 1937 and 1951, and published in volume five of the seven-volume *Schriften zum Theater* (1963-64), and numerous other essays translated into English in *Brecht on Theatre* (1964). His theory was most fully developed in "Kleines Organon für das Theater" (1949; "Little Organon for the Theatre," 1951).

In the essay "The Modern Theatre Is the Epic Theatre" (1930) Brecht provides a table comparing elements of dramatic theater versus epic theater; for example, where dramatic theater favors plot, epic favors narrative; where dramatic theater "implicates the spectator in a stage situation, wears down his capacity for action, and provides him with sensations," epic theater "turns the spectator into an observer, but arouses his capacity for action," and "forces him to make decisions." Where dramatic theater operates on the dictum that "thought determines being," epic theater, in a nod to Marx, holds that "social being determines thought."

Brecht coined a German translation of RUSSIAN FORMALIST Viktor Shklovsky's (1893-1984) "making strange": "Verfremdungseffekt" or "V-Effekt" — alienation effect. Chinese theater and acting style also influenced him, out of which he developed the acting technique of "gestus," in which the actor focuses on using gesture to communicate and remains distant rather than emotionally identifying with the character as in, for example, STANISLAVSKY's METHOD (*see* GROUP THEATER, United States).

Brecht had an early Epic success with the play *Die Mutter* (1932), an adaptation of Maxim GORKY's seminal SOCIALIST REALIST novel, *MAT* (1907; *Mother*, 1907); other of Brecht's Epic plays include *Mann ist Mann* (1926; *A Man's a Man*, 1961), *Die Dreigroschenoper* (1928; *The Threepenny Opera*, 1955), *Die heilige Johanna des Schlachthöfe* (1932, performed 1959; *Saint Joan of the Stockyards*, 1956), and *Der aufhaltsame Aufstieg des Arturo Ui* (1941; *The Resistable Rise of Arturo Ui*, 1976).

❖•❖

Further Reading

Arnold, Armin. *Friedrich Dürrenmatt*. Translated and revised with new material by the author with Sheila Johnson. New York: Ungar, 1972.

Benjamin, Walter. *Understanding Brecht*. Translated by Anna Bostock. London: NLB, 1973.

141

Butler, Michael. *The Plays of Max Frisch*. New York: St. Martin's Press, 1985.

Chick, Edson M. *Dances of Death: Wedekind, Brecht, Dürrenmatt, and the Satiric Tradition*. Columbia, S.C.: Camden House, 1984.

Cohen, Robert. *Understanding Peter Weiss*. Columbia, S.C.: University of South Carolina Press, 1993.

Connelly, Stacy Jones. "Forgotten Debts: Erwin Piscator and the Epic Theatre." *Dissertation Abstracts International* 52, 9 (March 1992): 3128A.

Ellis, Roger. *Peter Weiss in Exile: A Critical Study of His Works*. Ann Arbor, Mich.: UMI Research Press, 1987.

Esslin, Martin. *Bertolt Brecht*. New York: Columbia University Press, 1969.

————. *Brecht, a Choice of Evils: A Critical Study of the Man, His Work, and His Opinions*. 4th rev. ed. London; New York: Methuen, 1984.

————. *Brecht: The Man and His Work*. New rev. ed. Garden City, N.Y.: Anchor Books, 1971.

Gray, Ronald. *Bertolt Brecht*. New York: Grove Press, 1961.

————. *Brecht the Dramatist*. Cambridge, England: Cambridge University Press, 1976.

Grimm, Reinhold. *Bertolt Brecht*. Stuttgart, Germany: Metzler Edition 3, 1971.

Haas, Willy. *Bertolt Brecht*. Translated by Max Knight and Joseph Fabry. New York: Ungar, 1970.

Hill, Claude. *Bertolt Brecht*. Boston: Twayne, 1975.

Hilton, Ian. *Peter Weiss: A Search for Affinities*. London: Wolff, 1970.

Innes, C. D. *Erwin Piscator's Political Theatre: The Development of Modern German Drama*. Cambridge, England: Cambridge University Press, 1972.

Köpke, Wulf. *Understanding Max Frisch*. Columbia, S.C.: University of South Carolina Press, 1991.

Ley-Piscator, Maria. *The Piscator Experiment: The Political Theatre*. New York: J. H. Heineman, 1967.

Mews, Siegfried, and Herbert Kunst, eds. *Essays on Brecht: Theater and Politics*. Chapel Hill, N.C.: University of North Carolina Press, 1974.

Munk, Erika, ed. *Brecht: A Selection of Critical Pieces from the Dramative Review*. New York: Bantam Books, 1972.

Peppard, Murray B. *Friedrich Dürrenmatt*. New York: Twayne, 1969.

Pilipp, Frank, ed. *New Critical Perspectives on Martin Walser*. Columbia, S.C.: Camden House, 1994.

Schoeps, Karl H. *Bertolt Brecht*. New York: Ungar, 1977.

Stanley, Patricia H. *Wolfgang Hildesheimer and His Critics*. Camden, S.C.: Camden House, 1993.

Thomson, Peter, and Glendyr Sacks, eds. *The Cambridge Companion to Brecht*. Cambridge, England: Cambridge University Press, 1994.

Tiusanen, Timo. *Dürrenmatt: A Study in Plays, Prose, Theory*. Princeton, N.J.: Princeton University Press, 1977.

Volker, Klaus. *Brecht: A Biography*. Translated by John Nowell. New York: Seabury Press, 1978.

Whitton, Kenneth S. *The Theatre of Friedrich Dürrenmatt: A Study in the Possibility of Freedom*. London: O. Wolff; Atlantic Highlands, N.J.: Humanities Press, 1980.

Willett, John. *The Theatre of Bertolt Brecht*. 3rd ed., rev. London: Methuen, 1967.

————. *The Theatre of Erwin Piscator*. New York: Holmes & Meier, 1979.

Willett, John, ed. *Brecht on Theatre: The Development of an Aesthetic*. New York: Hill and Wang, 1964.

Witt, Hubert, ed. *Brecht: As They Knew Him*. New York: International Publishers, 1974.

ERN MALLEY HOAX
Australia, 1943-1955

Poets James McAuley (1917-1976) and Harold Stewart (1916-) perpetrated the Ern Malley Hoax on Max Harris (1921-1995) and the *Angry Penguins* literary journal in Australia in 1943 and 1944. Their motive was to rebel against what one critic calls the "showy but empty forms of modernism" then extant in the literary world. They assembled verse from bits picked up from such sources as Shakespeare, the *Concise Oxford Dictionary*, a book of quotations, and an American report on swamp drainage as well as earlier poetry of McAuley's, invented an author — Ern Malley, recently deceased auto mechanic — and sent them to Harris who gave them high criticism, to his later detriment. Harris in fact devoted a special issue of *Angry Penguins* to the collection, entitled *The Darkening Ecliptic*. Journalist Colin Simpson (1908-1983) publicly exposed the hoax in the *Sydney Sun*. By the time McAuley and Stewart issued a confession in the *Sydney Sunday Sun* magazine, the "Ern Malley" event had garnered attention all over the world and claimed some serious attention from contemporary literary scholars. Herbert Read (1893-1968), John Ashbery (1927-), and Kenneth Koch (1925-) are among those who liked the poems.

Angry Penguins did not last long after the hoax was exposed. In defiance, Harris and others published *Ern Malley's Journal* from 1952 to 1955 as a forum to continue their espousal of the kind of MODERNIST literary effort represented by the poems. Though Harris professionally suffered at the time, the Ern Malley poems continue to be the subject of some serious literary attention. The collection has been reprinted several times, including in anthologies of Australian poetry. Ian Kennedy Williams (n.d.) wrote a novelistic account of it, *Malarky Dry* (1990). As Frank Kermode notes in the *New Republic*, perhaps today "fewer readers would feel so confident that [Harris] was absurdly wrong" to praise the work.

❧•❦

Further Reading

Carver, Robert. "The Ern Malley Affair." *New Statesman & Society* 6, 265 (August 13, 1993): 37.

"The Ern Malley Affair." *New Yorker* 70, 18 (June 20, 1994): 95.

Ferres, John H., and Martin Tucker, eds. *Modern Commonwealth Literature*. New York: Ungar, 1977.

Green, H. M. *A History of Australian Literature, Pure and Applied*. 2 vols. Sydney: Angus & Robertson, 1961.

————. *Modern Australian Poetry*. Carlton, Australia: Melbourne University Press, 1952.

Harris, Max. *Ern Malley's Poems*. Adelaide, Australia: Mary Martin, 1969.

————. "Angry Penguins and After." *Quadrant* 7 (summer 1963): 5-10.

Heyward, Michael. *The Ern Malley Affair*. London: Faber & Faber, 1993.

————. "The Importance of Being Ern." *National Review* 47, 7 (April 17, 1995): 66.

Hope, A. D. *Australian Literature, 1950-1962*. Parkville, Australia: Melbourne University Press, 1963.

Kermode, Frank. "The Ern Malley Affair." *New Republic* 210, 14 (April 4, 1994): 35.

Kershaw, Alistar. *Heydays: Memories and Glimpses of Melbourne's Bohemia, 1937-1947*. North Ryde, New South Wales: Angus & Robertson, 1991.

McAuley, James. "The Ferment of the Forties." In *A Map of Australian Verse*. Melbourne, Australia; New York: Oxford University Press, 1975.

McCredden, Lyn. *James McAuley*. Melbourne, Australia: Oxford University Press, 1992.

Malley, Ern. *Collected Poems*. Commentary by Albert Tucker, et al. London: HarperCollins, 1993.

Moore, T. I. *Six Australian Poets*. Melbourne, Australia: Robertson & Mullens, 1942.

The Poems of Ern Malley, Comprising the Complete Poems. Commentaries by Max Harris and Joanna Murray-Smith. Sydney, Australia; Boston: Allen & Unwin, 1988.

Thompson, John. *Appendix: The Ern Malley Story, an Australian Broadcasting Commission Feature*. In *For the Uncanny Man: Essays, Mainly Literary* by Clement Semmler. Melbourne, Australia: F. W. Cheshire, 1963.

Thompson, John, Kenneth Slissor, and R. G. Haworth, eds. *The Penguin Book of Australian Verse*. Harmondsworth, England: Penguin Books, 1958.

ESTOS 13
Peru, 1970s

Named for a 1973 anthology of poetry produced by thirteen writers, *Estos 13* was a Peruvian group that directly succeeded and sustained the concerns of LOS NUEVOS. Many of the *Estos 13* group were associated with the progressive journal *Hora Cero*. Enrique Verástegui (1950-) is regarded as the most distinguished member of *Estos*.

Further Reading

"Abelardo Sánchez León." In *Peru: The New Poetry*. Edited by David Tipton. New York: Red Dust, 1977.

Higgins, James. *A History of Peruvian Literature*. London: F. Cairns, 1987.

ESTRIDENTISMO
Mexico, 1922-1927

Estridentismo was initiated by Manuel Maples Arce (1898-?) and included German List Arzubide (1898-1998), who wrote its manifesto, *El movimiento estridentista* (1926), Salvador Gallardo (1893-?), Luis Quintanilla (1900-1980), and Arqueles Vela (1899-?). These writers were reacting against the earlier and strong influence of the Central American writer, Rubén DARÍO, who has been called the greatest poet of the Spanish Modernist movement, MODERNISMO. His deep interest in the French SYMBOLIST movement had so motivated his work and that of his followers that they had become known as the "Spanish Symbolists." Their poetry was romantic, exotic, and consisted mostly of each poet's personal system of symbol and metaphor, developed for the presentation of sensory response to a particular feeling or experience. The Estridentismos deplored the romantic ambiguity of Symbolist poetry and its aesthetic elitism. They chose rather to concentrate creative impulse on the energy which was arising out of twentieth-century industrialism and the excitement engendered by its machines and its volatility. They were in accord with the FUTURIST poets who were concurrently active in Italy.

Maples Arce's contributions to the movement are *Adamios interiores* (1922), *Urbe* (1924), and *Poemas interdictos* (1927). When the Estridentismos disbanded, he moved into other areas of interest; his fascination with other cultures led him into public service abroad. Later works include *Memorial de la sangre* (1947) and *Ensayos japonese* (1959).

Estridentismo was short-lived; the advent of the many political changes and economic crises in Europe, and the rapid advancement of a global industrial technology in preparation for another war caused the movement to lose its momentum and its members their interest in what had earlier held fascination.

❖•❖

Further Reading

Craig, G. Dundas, ed. *The Modernist Trend in Spanish American Poetry: A Collection of Representative Poems of the Modernist Movement and the Reaction*. Berkeley, Calif.: University of California Press, 1934.

Fitts, Dudley, ed. *Anthology of Contemporary Latin American Poetry*. Norfolk, Conn.: New Directions, 1942.

Henríquez Ureña, Pedro. *Literary Currents in Hispanic America*. Cambridge, Mass.: Harvard University Press, 1945.

Rosenberg, S. L. Millard, and Ernest H. Templin, eds. *A Brief Anthology of Mexican Verse*. Stanford, Calif.: Stanford University Press, 1925.

EXCELSIOR GROUP. *See UZVYŠŠA* **GROUP**

EXISTENTIALISM
France, Germany, and Spain, 1940s-1960s

A multinational and multidisciplinary movement, Existentialism surfaced in several European countries, particularly Germany, Spain, and France, as a positive, humanistic advancement of the ethical nihilism engendered by such nineteenth-century figures as Karl MARX, Charles Darwin (1809-1882), Friedrich NIETZSCHE, and Søren Kierkegaard (1813-1855). In France, virtually no other twentieth-century movement—save that of MODERNISM, with which it had intimate ties—so galvanized a shift in the values and concerns of intellectuals and the general populace as did Existentialism. A direct philosophical descendant of German Phenomenology, the atheistic strain of French Existentialism (as distinguished from the counter-movement of Christian Existentialism, led in France by Gabriel Marcel [1889-1973]) exploded onto the literary and political spectrum during World War II and steadily gained momentum in the years of displacement, disillusion, and social revolution that followed. In its purest form, French Existentialism developed through the fiction and nonfiction writings of Jean-Paul SARTRE, Simone de BEAUVOIR, Maurice Merleau-Ponty (1908-1961), Albert CAMUS, and a number of other intellectuals associated with the progressive journal *Les temps modernes*. Despite divisiveness within this group, these writers in general promoted the belief that humans must create themselves, their world, and their art without dependence upon some indeterminate transcendent reality. By so doing, a potentially meaningless world is made meaningful through purposeful decision and action. However, for the Existentialist, the dialectic of personal alienation and responsibility frequently breeds an anxiety bordering on despair. It is the faithful expression of this generalized anxiety, or Angst, that typifies the best Existentialist writing and serves as perhaps the most effective mirror of the intellectual climate that the movement reflected as well as helped create.

The fountainhead of Existentialist thought is generally agreed to be Kierkegaard, a Danish theologian who, reacting to the absolute idealism and synthetic worldview of German philosopher Georg W. F. Hegel (1770-1831), asserted the isolation and the importance of the individual in matters of perception, religious faith, and moral action. Kierkegaard's works, not available in French translation until the 1930s, stand as pivotal documents in the course of both Christian and secular thought. In them, particularly *Enten/Eller* (1843; *Either/Or*, 1944) and *Sygdommen til Døden* (1849; *The Sickness unto Death*, 1941), Kierkegaard espoused the unarguable irrationality of religious belief, a concept underpinned by two additional convictions: that truth equals subjectivity and that "leaps of faith" are required for a full spiritual life. Kierkegaard's "existential dialectic," or theory of crisis, as it came to be known, found its major twentieth-century exponents in German theologian Karl Jaspers (1883-1969) and French philosopher Gabriel Marcel. Yet, it was German theorist Martin Heidegger (1889-1976), a student of Edmund Husserl (1859-1938), who most visibly shaped the early ontological thought of Sartre, whose name, in turn, became synonymous with Existentialism during and following the German occupation of France.

At this difficult time in French history, Sartre was concerned with fashioning and testing a new definition of Being, one predicated upon two states of individual consciousness: Being-in-itself and Being-for-itself. Interestingly, Hegel had been the first to discuss these concepts; Sartre, however, transformed them into a new, subtle, and disturbingly paradoxical system through a linear development of Heidegger's preliminary theories in *Sein und Zeit* (1927; *Being and Time*, 1962). The fundamental ontological principle for Sartre was that existence precedes essence. In other words, humans do not possess innate characteristics, which somehow determine behavior and identity; instead, they freely exist in a realm of nothingness and the primary reality of their existence necessitates that being, or essence, arises as a result of their choices and actions. From this followed the argument that all human decisions, even the decision to refrain from action, are not predetermined but freely made. Consequently, being is variable and discontinuous, while existence is invariable and permanent. Sartre's fullest exposition of this complex theory appears in his treatise *L'etre et le néant* (1943; *Being and Nothingness*, 1956). However, the first serious illustration of Sartre's system occurs in his novel *LA NAUSÉE* (1938; *Nausea*; also published as *The Diary of Antoine Roquentin*, 1949). Sartre's later creative and philosophical work, like Camus's and Beauvoir's, not only furthered the broad appeal of such a human-centered worldview but also helped bring the domains of art and science into closer communion with each other.

The literary roots of Existentialism are myriad and extend back to classical times. However, the greatest artistic predecessor of the movement is undoubtedly Fyodor DOSTOEVSKY, who wrote during the age of Russian Nihilism and REALISM. In such works as *Zapiski iz podpolya* (1864; *Notes from the Underground*, 1913, 1918) and *BRAT'YA KARAMAZOVY* (1879-80; *The Brothers Karamazov,* 1912), Dostoevsky plumbed to the experiential core of the individual and, with uncanny psychological insight, exposed the radical range of beliefs, emotions, and behaviors that the human mind is capable of supporting. Although Dostoevsky's discomforting vision of humanity, like Kierkegaard's, was tempered by the saving grace of Christianity, the various writers who adapted his vision to the concerns of the twentieth century typically removed this spiritual palliative altogether. Before the advent of Sartre, Dostoevsky's chief literary descendant was Franz KAFKA (*see* MODERNISM, Austria and Germany), author of such SURREALIST nightmares as *Die Verwandlung* (1915; *The Metamorphosis*, 1936), *DER*

PROZESS (1925; *The Trial*, 1937), and *Das Schloss* (1926; *The Castle*, 1930). Kafka's intense and unrelenting depiction of life's metaphysical absurdities, and his protagonists' doomed searches for purpose, understanding, and salvation, profoundly underscored the social, political, and moral disillusionment that many Europeans felt following World War I. His works, in addition to those of LOST GENERATION writers Ernest HEMINGWAY and John DOS PASSOS, became widely known in France in the 1930s and afforded such writers as Sartre and Beauvoir a suitable style and thematic apparatus within which to fashion their own bleak views of existence, even more the case following the Second World War. Another key strain of influence came from Spain via the writings of Miguel de Unamuno y Jugo (1864-1936; *see* GENERATION OF 1898) and José Ortega y Gasset (1883-1955). Unamuno's part-treatise, part-meditation *Del sentimiento trágico de la vida en los hombres y en los pueblos* (1913; *The Tragic Sense of Life in Men and in Peoples,* 1926) foreshadowed later philosophical and literary works of Existentialism in Europe. Ortega y Gasset carried on many of Unamuno's ideas, particularly during his association with NOUCENTISMO.

Atheistic and activist in outlook, Existentialism, in both its philosophical and literary forms, remained enormously popular for several decades, sprouting or melding with untold numbers of avant-garde and counterculture groups. Existentialism has, furthermore, exerted an almost incalculable influence not only on the outlook and artistry of numerous leading contemporary writers, including Saul Bellow (1915-), John Fowles (1926-), Iris Murdoch (1919-1999), and William Styron (1925-), but also on the development of such movements as STRUCTURALISM, MARXIST CRITICISM, DECONSTRUCTION, the THEATER OF THE ABSURD, and the NEW NOVEL. Although the power of the European Existentialist movement effectively waned with the death of Sartre, its most salient principles have continued to thrive in the domains of philosophy, theology, literature, and art, and wherever else antirationalist, humanistic thought is given voice.

❧•❧

Beauvoir, Simone de (1908-1986)
French novelist, essayist, autobiographer, and dramatist.

Many regard Beauvoir as second only to Sartre in importance to the French Existentialist movement. In fact, the first murmurings of French atheistic Existentialism occurred with Beauvoir in 1929, when she and Sartre sustained lengthy discussions about the Cartesian question of consciousness while both were studying at the École Normale Supérieure. From this point onward, the two developed a close personal relationship which effectively complemented their professional lives: each served as the other's first editor and critic. Despite the fact that her literary reputation is less than that of Sartre or Camus, Beauvoir holds the distinction of being perhaps the most recognized woman writer of the twentieth century as well as one of the most important early FEMINIST theorists. Among her best works are the novels *L'invitée* (1943; *She Came to Stay*, 1949) and *Les Mandarins* (1954; *The Mandarins*, 1956); the essays *Pour une morale de l'ambiguïté* (1947; *The Ethics of Ambiguity*, 1948) and *LE DEUXIÈME SEXE* (1949; *The Second Sex*, 1953); and the autobiographical and biographical writings *La force de l'âge* (1960; *The Prime of Life*, 1962), *La Cérémonie des adieux* (1981; *Adieux: A Farewell to Sartre*, 1984).

↔•↔

Camus, Albert (1913-1960)
Algerian-born French novelist, dramatist, and essayist.

From the time of the initial rise of Existentialism, Camus assayed to disassociate himself from the movement as a whole and many scholars still consider his Existentialist label a misnomer. Like fellow Frenchman André Malraux (1901-1976), with whom he is occasionally compared, Camus espoused a form of atheistic humanism which, contrary to Sartrean Existentialism, denied humans the right to create new moral values as the changing social climate seemed to dictate. Yet, Camus shared with Sartre and the other Existentialists a preoccupation with a number of important, nonpolitical themes, including the absurdity of life, the relevance of death, the difficulty of relating to others, the function of art, and the moral responsibility of the individual. Camus is perhaps best known for a series of philosophical novels beginning with *L'ÉTRANGER* (1942; *The Outsider*, 1946; also published as *The Stranger*, 1946); these include *La Peste* (1947; *The Plague*, 1948), *La Chute* (1956; *The Fall*, 1957), and *L'Exil et le royaume* (1957; *Exile and the Kingdom*, 1958). However, Camus's reputation as an essayist, dramatist, and theatrical director is equally great, and in such works as *Le Mythe de Sisyphe* (1942; *The Myth of Sisyphus*, 1955), *L'Homme révolté* (1951; *The Rebel*, 1953), and *Caligula* (1945; *Caligula*, 1958) he exerted a profound influence on future generations of writers, particularly those of the Theater of the Absurd. Camus was awarded the Nobel Prize for literature in 1957.

L'Étranger (1942; *The Outsider*, 1946; *The Stranger*, 1946).

Published a year prior to Camus's first meeting with Sartre, *L'Étranger* is one of the preeminent metaphysical novels of the twentieth century. The story, told in the first person, is divided into two sections and concerns the moral and philosophical awakening of Mersault, a French-Algerian clerk. In the first, Mersault reveals that his mother has died. However, he shows no grief or emotion and instead confines his future existence to pleasure-seeking and nonconformity. Mersault undergoes a drastic inward change following his defensive murder of an Arab. He finds himself absurdly placed on trial not so much for the murder as for his socially unacceptable behavior, particularly towards the memory of his mother. Before his certain execution, Mersault understands

149

that the real world, shed of all conventions and illusions, is one of indifference and absurdity. He also realizes that it is his courageous battle against this absurdity that gives meaning to the final moments of his life. The novel's technical virtuosity, particularly its employment of ambiguity surrounding the pivotal actions of the anti-hero, has been praised repeatedly by succeeding generations of writers and critics.

❖•❖

Sartre, Jean-Paul (1905-1980)
French essayist, novelist, dramatist, biographer, and critic.

Sartre has been described as perhaps the most pervasively influential writer in French literary history since Voltaire. Throughout his professional life, particularly after his association with Merleau-Ponty on *Les temps modernes*, Sartre served as a highly visible spokesperson for a number of left-wing causes, including the anti-Vietnam War and anti-apartheid movements, and was for several years a champion of Marxist-Communist revolution, a stance which led to Camus's severance of ties with Sartre in the early 1950s. This strong belief in the interrelationship of literary and political action was outlined by Sartre in a number of works, especially *Qu'est-ce que la littérature?* (1947; *What Is Literature?*, 1949). The idea of *la littérature engagée*, Sartre's term for a socially and politically committed literature, proceeded to dominate virtually all of Sartre's personal and professional endeavors. Some have charged that this artistic bias, coupled with the voluminous extent of his oeuvre, has left Sartre in the second ranks as a literary figure. However, those who defend him have been able to point to any number of works, in addition to *La nausée* and *L'etre et le néant*, that stand among the most original and provocative in twentieth-century literature. These include his dramas *Les mouches* (1943; *The Flies*, 1947) and *Huis clos* (1944; *No Exit*, 1947); his fictional trilogy *Les chemins de la liberté* (1945-49; *The Roads to Freedom*, 1947-51); his philosophical and critical essays *L'Existentialisme est un humanisme* (1946; *Existentialism and Humanism*, 1948) and *Critique de la raison dialectique* (1960; *Critique of Dialectical Reason*, 1976); and his biographical studies *Saint Genet, comédien et martyr* (1952; *Saint Genet, Actor and Martyr*, 1963) and *L'Idiot de la famille: Gustave Flaubert*, 3 vols. (1971-72; *The Family Idiot: Gustave Flaubert*, 1981). In 1964 Sartre was awarded the Nobel prize for literature, which he refused for self-effacing reasons.

La nausée (1938; *Nausea*, 1949; also published as *The Diary of Antoine Roquentin*, 1949).

Written in the form of a diary, *La nausée* is a dark and unrelenting documentation of the scholar Antoine Roquentin's revulsion at the behavior, attributes, and beliefs of humans. Roquentin, a loner who supports himself, has settled in the town of Bouville to conduct research on a minor historical figure. Through his contemplation of the past he arrives at the realization that his project is futile: no being can resurrect or justify the existence of another. He realizes, further, that his life, and that of those around him, is also futile and meaningless. Even the book-devouring Self-Taught Man, whom Roquentin encounters at the library, is seen as repugnant for his self-deluding and purposeless activity. In a moment of extreme, poetic revelation, Roquentin sees that the world in which he lives is one of independent, freely existing objects and that to attach any significance to any object is ridiculous. In the conclusion, rather than despairing over the fundamental absurdity of life, Roquentin pledges to find himself in art, through the creation of some piece of literature which bears reference only to itself. In later years, Sartre distanced himself from Roquentin's noncommitted stance, though his phenomenological approach to reality remained essentially the same.

✦●✦

Further Reading

Ascher, Carol. *Simone de Beauvoir: A Life of Freedom*. Boston: Beacon Press, 1981.

Baker, Richard E. *The Dynamics of the Absurd in the Existentialist Novel*. New York: P. Lang, 1993.

Barnes, Hazel E. *The Literature of Possibility*. Lincoln, Nebr.: University of Nebraska Press, 1959.

Beauvoir, Simone de. *Adieux: A Farewell to Sartre*. Translated by Patrick O'Brian. New York: Pantheon Books, 1984.

Blackham, H. J. *Six Existentialist Thinkers*. New York: Macmillan, 1952.

Boschetti, Anna. *The Intellectual Enterprise: Sartre and* Les Temps Modernes. Evanston, Ill.: Northwestern University Press, 1987.

Brée, Germaine. *Camus and Sartre*. New York: Delacorte Press, 1972.

Brée, Germaine, and Margaret Otis Guiton. "Jean-Paul Sartre: The Search for Identity." In their *An Age of Fiction: The French Novel from Gide to Camus*. New Brunswick, N.J.: Rutgers University Press, 1957.

Carruth, Hayden. *After* The Stranger: *Imaginary Dialogues with Camus*. New York: Macmillan, 1965.

Catalano, Joseph S. *A Commentary on Jean-Paul Sartre's* Being and Nothingness. New York: Harper & Row, 1974.

Charlesworth, Max. *The Existentialists and Jean-Paul Sartre*. New York: St. Martin's Press, 1976.

Cohen-Solal, Annie. *Sartre: A Life*. Translated by Anna Cancogni and edited by Norman MacAfee. New York: Pantheon Books, 1987.

Collins, James Daniel. *The Existentialists: A Critical Study*. Chicago: H. Regnery, 1952.

Cooper, David E. *Existentialism: A Reconstruction*. Oxford, England: Blackwell, 1990.

Davies, Howard. *Sartre and* Les Temps Modernes. Cambridge, England: Cambridge University Press, 1987.

Douglas, Kenneth. *A Critical Bibliography of Existentialism (The Paris School)*. Yale French Studies, No. 1. New Haven, Conn.: Yale French Studies, 1950.

Ellis, Robert R. *The Tragic Pursuit of Being: Unamuno and Sartre*. Tuscaloosa, Ala.: University of Alabama Press, 1988.

Ferrater Mora, José. *Ortega y Gasset: An Outline of His Philosophy*. New Haven, Conn.: Yale University Press, 1963.

————. *Unamuno: A Philosophy of Tragedy*. Translated by Philip Silver. Berkeley, Calif.: University of Calif. Press, 1962. Reprint, Westport, Conn.: Greenwood Press, 1981.

Francis, Claude, and Fernande Gontier. *Simone de Beauvoir: A Life, a Love Story*. New York: St. Martin's Press, 1987.

Hayman, Ronald. *Sartre: A Life*. New York: Simon & Schuster, 1987.

Howells, Christina. *Sartre's Theory of Literature*. London: Modern Humanities Research Association, 1979.

Ilie, Paul. *Unamuno: An Existential View of Self and Society*. Madison, Wis.: University of Wisconsin Press, 1967.

Kaelin, Eugene Francis. *An Existentialist Aesthetic: The Theories of Sartre and Merleau-Ponty*. Madison, Wis.: University of Wisconsin Press, 1962.

Kaufmann, Walter. *Existentialism from Dostoevsky to Sartre*. New York: Meridian Books, 1956.

Keefe, Terry. *French Existentialist Fiction: Changing Moral Perspectives*. Totowa, N.J.: Barnes & Noble, 1986.

Kern, Edith G. *Existential Thought and Fictional Techniques: Kierkegaard, Sartre, Beckett*. New Haven, Conn.: Yale University Press, 1970.

Lacy, Allen. *Miguel de Unamuno: The Rhetoric of Existence*. The Hague: Mouton, 1967.

Lottman, Herbert. *Albert Camus: A Biography*. Garden City, N.Y.: Doubleday, 1979.

McBride, William Leon. *Existentialist Literature and Aesthetics*. New York: Garland, 1997.

McCarthy, Patrick. *Camus: A Critical Study of His Life and Work*. New York: Random House, 1982.

McElroy, Davis D. *Existentialism and Modern Literature*. New York: Citadel Press, 1963.

Madsen, Axel. *Hearts and Minds: The Common Journey of Simone de Beauvoir and Jean-Paul Sartre*. New York: Morrow, 1977.

Marks, Elaine, ed. *Critical Essays on Simone de Beauvoir*. Boston: G. K. Hall, 1987.

Murdoch, Iris. *Sartre: Romantic Rationalist*. New Haven, Conn.: Yale University Press, 1953.

Peyre, Henri. "Existentialism and French Literature: Jean-Paul Sartre's Novels." In his *French Novelists of Today*. New York: Oxford University Press, 1967.

Sanchez Villasenor, José. *Ortega y Gasset, Existentialist: A Critical Study of His Thought and His Sources*. 1949.

Sartre, Jean-Paul. *Being and Nothingness: An Essay on Phenomenological Ontology*. New York: Philosophical Library, 1956.

————. *Literature and Existentialism*. Reprint of *What Is Literature?* Secaucus, N.J.: Carol Publishing Group, 1994.

————. *Sartre in the Seventies: Interviews and Essays*. London: A. Deutsch, 1978.

Schilpp, Paul A., ed. *The Philosophy of Jean-Paul Sartre*. La Salle, Ill.: Open Court, 1981.

Schroeder, William Ralph. *Sartre and His Predecessors: The Self and the Other*. London: Routledge and Kegan Paul, 1984.

Schwarzer, Alice. *Simone de Beauvoir Today: Conversations, 1972-1982*. Translated by Marianne Howarth. London: Hogarth Press, 1984.

Silver, Philip W. *Ortega y Gasset as Phenomenologist: The Genesis of "Meditations on Quixote."* New York: Columbia University Press, 1978.

Wilson, Colin. *The Outsider*. Boston: Houghton Mifflin; London: Gollancz, 1956.

Wolin, Richard, ed. *The Heidegger Controversy: A Critical Reader*. New York: Columbia University Press, 1991.

————. *The Terms of Cultural Criticism: The Frankfurt School, Existentialism, Poststructuralism*. New York: Columbia University Press, 1992.

EXPERIMENTALISM (Prayogavādī). *See* NEW POETRY MOVEMENT (Nayī Kavitā)

EXPERIMENTALISTS (Experimentelen)
Netherlands, 1950s

An artistic and literary group of Dutch writers, the Experimentalists were active in the 1950s. Two figures associated with the movement were Asger Jorn (1914-1973) and Hans Lodeizen (1924-1950).

❧•❦

Further Reading

Atkins, Guy. *Asger Jorn*. London: Methuen, 1964.

————. *Asger Jorn, Supplement to the Oeuvre Catalogue of His Paintings from 1930 to 1973*. London: Asger Jorn Foundation in association with Lund Humphries, 1986.

————. *Jorn in Scandinavia 1930-1953*. New York: G. Wittenborn, 1968.

Atkins, Guy, with the help of Troels Andersen. *Asger Jorn, the Crucial Years 1954-1964: A Study of Asger Jorn's Artistic Development from 1954 to 1964 and a Catalogue of His Oil Paintings from That Period*. New York: Wittenborn Art Books; London: Lund Humphries; Copenhagen: Borgens Forlag, 1977.

————. *Asger Jorn, the Final Years, 1965-1973: A Study of Asger Jorn's Artistic Development from 1965 to 1973 and a Catalogue of His Oil Paintings from That Period*. London: Lund Humphries; Copenhagen: Borgens, 1980.

Birtwistle, G. M. *Living Art: Asger Jorn's Comprehensive Theory of Art Between Helhesten and Cobra, 1946-1949*. Utrecht, Netherlands: Reflex, 1986.

EXPERIMENTAL THEATER, THE. *See* PROVINCETOWN PLAYERS

EXPRESSIONISM
Czechoslovakia, 1910s-1920s

The Expressionist movement was never as strong in Czechoslovakia as in Germany, where it dominated poetry and drama before and after World War I, gradually declining in popularity during the twenties until it was banned by the Nazis in 1933. Many Czech writers chose to join the Expressionist circles in Munich, Berlin, or elsewhere, leaving Prague to the SURREALISTS. Such writers included Franz Werfel (1890-1945), who wrote poetry in the grandiose, rhapsodic style of late Expressionism, and Paul Kornfeld (1889-1942), whose play *Die Verfuhrung* (1913; The Seduction) is infused with the rebellious spirit found in many early Expressionist dramas. The director of the famous Expressionist film *Das Kabinet des Dr. Caligari* (1919), Robert Wiene (1881-1938), was also a Czech who found acclaim in Germany. Czech Expressionist writers who did stay in their own country include Otakar Březina (1868-1929), a poet who wrote Whitmanesque verse and who is also associated with the SYMBOLIST movement; and Karel Capek (1890-1938), a dramatist, novelist, and journalist who gained an international reputation with his science-fiction drama *R.U.R.* (1921; *R.U.R.,* 1923). This play full of bizarre symbolism is credited with introducing the word "robot" to the English language; like much of Capek's other work, it features an anti-totalitarian theme.

❦•❦

Further Reading

Novák, Arne. *Czech Literature*. Translated by Peter Kussi. Ann Arbor, Mich.: Published under the auspices of the Joint Committee on Eastern Europe, American Council of Learned Societies by Michigan Slavic Publications, 1976.
Pynsent, Robert. *Czech Prose and Verse*. London: Athlone Press, 1979.
Wellek, Rene. *Essays on Czech Literature*. The Hague: Mouton & Co., 1963.

EXPRESSIONISM
Germany, 1910s-1920s

Partly a reaction against the NATURALISM that had dominated the art and literature of the late nineteenth century, Expressionism arose within the broader context of MODERNISM. Like other Modernist trends, it was a manifestation of dissatisfaction with the prevailing culture rather than a unified movement of aesthetic principle. In general, the Expressionists rebelled against the realistic representation demanded by Naturalism. They sought to create idea-centered, abstract art that focused not on exterior surfaces but on emotion and on individual rather than collective experience. Expressionist literature usually features compressed language; an intentional disregard for conventional grammar and logic; unusual and often symbolic imagery; and a bold, sometimes violent use of exaggeration and distortion. In Germany, where Expressionist drama and poetry found its most accomplished practitioners, the movement reflected the restlessness and sense of doom that dominated that society before World War I, as well as the disillusionment and yearning for peace of the war and postwar periods. Commentators have identified the five or so years leading up to 1920 as the apex of German Expressionism. Although the rise of the Nazis and a general shift in attitude led to the decline of German Expressionism, the new artistic forms and language it introduced permanently influenced the work of modern writers.

The artistic ideas that came to be known as Expressionism first appeared in the work of such late-nineteenth-century painters as Vincent Van Gogh (1853-1890) and Edvard Munch (1863-1944). In fact, Munch's famous painting "The Scream" (1906) would become a symbol within the development of German Expressionist theater, in which the *schrei* (scream) was an important dramatic device. During the first decades of the twentieth century, a group of German painters known as the "Blue Rider" group came to prominence. These artists—including Emil Nolde (1867-1956), Oskar Kokoschka (1886-1980), Wassily Kandinsky (1866-1944), and Franz Marc (1880-1916)—created abstract, inventive, nonrepresentational works that provided inspiration to the authors who were part of the same cultural milieu.

Of course, the Expressionist writers were inspired not only by the painters who shared their orientation but by literary mentors. The emotional, metaphor-laden poetry of French SYMBOLISTS Charles BAUDELAIRE and Arthur RIMBAUD, the dark themes and violent images of Fyodor DOSTOEVSKY (*see* REALISM, Russia), and the work of German philosopher Friedrich NIETZSCHE with its emphasis on the irrational, are often mentioned as influences on the Expressionists. Although some critics cite the early nineteenth-century dramatists Georg Büchner (1813-1837) and Christian Dietrich Grabbe (1801-1836) as influential, most emphasize the later example of Frank Wedekind (1864-1918) as more important. In such plays as *Frühlings Erwachen* (1891; *The Awakening of Spring*, 1909), *Der Erdgeist* (1895; *Earth Spirit*, 1914), and *Die Büchse der Pandora* (1904; *Pandora's Box*, 1914), Wedekind used grotesque imagery and nonrealistic techniques to expose the hypocrisy of middle-class morality and to condemn a staid, life-stifling educational system.

Also critical of his society was Carl Sternheim (1878-1942), author of a series of satirical dramas entitled *Aus dem bürgerlichen Heldenleben* (1922; Scenes from the Heroic Life of the Middle Classes). Sternheim's plays feature deliberately artificial, clipped, or "telegraphic" language, and a thematic focus on the hope that a "New Man" will create a better future. The most significant playwright to influence the Expressionists, howev-

155

er, was the Swedish playwright August STRINDBERG, who led the rebellion against the determinedly realistic plays of the nineteenth century. Strindberg, whose most famous works include the *Till Damaskus* trilogy (1898-1901; *To Damascus,* 1965) and *ETT DRÖMSPEL* (1901; *A Dream Play*, 1965), established the format of the protagonist who passes through several "stations" of life in his search for meaning. The later Expressionists would adopt many of Strindberg's hallmarks, such as a de-emphasis on plot and focus on interior experience, highly dramatic language, interweaving of dream and reality, and the use of distorted scenery and images.

The rise of Expressionism in Germany was closely linked with the nation's social atmosphere in the opening years of the twentieth century. The writers associated with the movement at its earliest stage were rebelling not just against literary strictures but against the stultifying bonds of a rigidly patriarchal family structure and equally oppressive educational and military systems. Perceiving tyranny in the exterior world, these artists turned their focus inward, seeking to give credence to dreams, confront delusion and insanity, and express their simultaneous loss of faith in the old ways and doubts about what would replace them.

These concerns were no doubt inspired and bolstered by developments in science (especially Einstein's Theory of Relativity) and by Sigmund FREUD's explorations into the human psyche. More tangibly, the fledgling Expressionists were nurtured by the founding of several influential journals that would for some decades provide a forum for the movement's artists as well as its writers. These journals included *Der Sturm* (1910-32) edited by Herwarth Walden (1878-1941), Franz Pfemfert's (1879-1954) *Die Aktion* (1911-32), and *Die Weiden Blätter* (1913-20), edited by Franz Blei (1871-1942) and René Schickele (1883-1940). Another early manifestation of Expressionism's vitality were the Neopathetisches Caberets, a series of poetry readings and musical performances organized by a group of students and writers in Berlin from 1910 to 1912.

Early Expressionist literature is distinguished by its rejection of Naturalistic qualities and techniques. In both poetry and drama (the two genres that were always at the forefront of Expressionism), traditional logic and grammar were rejected and language compressed to expose essential meanings. Unconventional images were employed in the service of the visionary statement, which was favored over the simple conveyance of surface reality. Writers poured their efforts into presenting a highly subjective view of life, often portraying an autobiographical protagonist exploring his own identity.

In Expressionist drama, that quest was usually enacted within the framework of an episodic structure featuring the "stations" first employed by Strindberg; realistic scenes were juxtaposed to dream sequences, and abstract, exclamatory dialogue was delivered in a staccato manner. In what is often cited as the earliest of the German Expressionist dramas, Oskar Kokoschka's *Mörder Hoffnung der Frauen* (1907; *Murderer, the Women's Hope*, 1963), a radically unconventional use of lighting created a dreamlike setting for an emotionally charged psychodrama that depicted the violent gulf between the sexes. The play also features one of the most characteristic techniques of Expressionist drama: the use of stereotypical rather than personalized characters.

Another strong example of early Expressionist theater is Reinhard Sorge's (1892-1916) *Der Bettler* (1912; *The Beggar*, 1963), which has as its central theme the power struggle between a domineering father and a rebellious son. Before the advent of World War I and the wider concerns it generated, the father/son conflict was a major preoccupation of the German Expressionists. In *Der Bettler*, the protagonist is a poet seeking spiritual regeneration in opposition to his highly conventional father, whose approach to life is based in sterile science. In the end, the son's quest for identity leads him to murder his parents. With its nightmarish scenes, harsh lighting, and unnamed characters (referred to only as The Son, The Father, etc.), the play is typically Expressionist. Particularly notable were the innovative arrangement of sets and other stage techniques (such as sets designed to create fragmented, distorted lines) to reflect the protagonist's turbulent emotional state. At the forefront of the development of this new stagecraft was the theatrical producer Max Reinhardt (1873-1943), whose contributions to Expressionist theater would later be employed in film.

Also frequently mentioned as an important early Expressionist is Walter Hasenclever (1890-1940), author of *Der Sohn* (1914; The Son). Like *Der Bettler*, Hasenclever's play centers on a struggle between father and son, with the father serving as a symbol of authority, discipline, and order who tries to suppress the passionate son's quest for freedom and experience. And the father fares no better here than in Sorge's play, falling dead from a stroke after the son has threatened him with a gun. Hasenclever retained a traditional, formal dramatic structure but infused his play with intensely expressive language—a blend of dramatic prose and blank verse—and stereotypical characters (the Son, the Father, the Governess, etc.).

The rebellion against authority embraced by the early German Expressionists was most often accompanied not by hope for the future but by a sense of impending doom. The expected apocalypse did arrive, in the form of World War I. The devastating losses and horrific carnage of the war took their toll on Germany's literary milieu both literally—in the deaths in battle or by suicide of many writers—and figuratively, as its effects were manifested on the stage and in poetry. Unified more than ever before by a sense of shared loss, many authors now channeled their energies into exposing the horrors of war and promoting pacifism. They did so in the midst of a restless, even hysterical political climate, for the establishment of the unpopular Weimar Republic (the democratic parliamentary government that ruled Germany from 1919 to 1933), along with rising inflation and unemployment, led to the rise of various extremist factions that fervently called either for violent revenge or for brotherhood and a utopian future.

Perhaps the best example of how postwar disillusionment found its way into the Expressionist theater is provided by Fritz von Unruh (1885-1970), a Prussian officer who went to war in patriotic fervor and returned in shocked despair. His best-known play, *Ein Geschlect* (1916; A Lineage) exposes the costs of war and the dangers of nationalistic passion through their devastating effects on a family with three sons. Each is affected in a different way: one is a war hero killed in battle and mourned by his mother, sister, and youngest brother; the eldest (the protagonist) is driven to violence — including sexual aggression against his own sister — by the war's brutality; and the third son is finally inspired by his mother's heroism to lead an army into rebellion and toward hope for a new society. Despite its rather formal language, the play is marked by the violent imagery and highly charged emotional atmosphere that characterize Expressionist drama. It is particularly notable for its blend of idealism and sadistic violence, a juxtaposition that would continue to mark the Expressionist plays of the postwar period.

Usually cited as Germany's leading Expressionist playwright, Georg KAISER possessed a diverse and prolific talent: between 1917 and 1923, twenty-four of his plays were performed, ranging in type from intensely Expressionist to lighthearted. But it is for his cerebral, idealistic Expressionist dramas that Kaiser is best known, beginning with *Die Bürger von Calais* (1913; performed 1917; The Burgers of Calais), in which the protagonist seeks redemption through antiwar idealism and sacrifice. *VON MORGENS BIS MITTERNACHTS* (1912, performed 1917; *From Morn till Midnight*, 1919), which many critics consider the quintessential German Expressionist play, chronicles a nameless bank clerk's journey toward self-knowledge. Also highly acclaimed is Kaiser's "Gas Trilogy," which comprises *Die Koralle* (1917; *The Coral*, 1929), *Gas I* (1918; *Gas I*, 1924), and *Gas II* (1920; *Gas II*, 1924). The first two plays feature a Millionaire and his rebellious Son; the latter fails to realize his socialist ideals but retains some hope for the future. In the third play, the Millionaire's grandson, who shares his father's goals, is also defeated in a conflagration that dramatizes the self-destructiveness of war. Typically Expressionist in its automaton characters, abstract scenery, and harsh lighting, the Gas Trilogy reflects the prevailing sense of defeat, collapse, and disillusionment of Kaiser's society.

Also recognized as one of Expressionism's most accomplished playwrights, Ernst TOLLER emerged toward the end of the movement's period of dominance. His most famous work, *DIE WANDLUNG* (1919; *Transfiguration*, 1935), reflects its author's own personal history.

Other significant German Expressionist dramatists include Paul Kornfeld (1889-1942; born in Czechoslovakia but part of the German literary milieu), whose play *Die Verführung* (1913; The Seduction) concerns a rebellious young protagonist who murders a man who symbolizes the societal oppression, then mistreats his own father; and painter and writer Ernst Barlach (1870-1938), whose best-known plays are the ghostly *Der tote Tag* (1912; The Dead Day) and the similarly mysterious *Der arme Vetter* (1918; The Poor Cousin). Although the renowned German playwright Bertolt BRECHT (*see* EPIC THEATER) ultimately rejected Expressionism, some of his early works — such as *Baal* (1918; *Baal*, 1963) and *Trommeln in der Nacht* (1918; *Drums in the Night*, 1961) — are notably Expressionist in their criticism of modern society as well as their unconventional stage techniques.

Poetry proved a genre ideal for the projection of violent, turbulent emotion that Expressionism required, and an impressive number of German poets of varying degrees of talent joined the Expressionist movement. The poets were particularly nurtured by the founding of the literary journals already mentioned, especially *Der Sturm* (1910) and *Die Aktion* (1911). The former showcased both writers and artists, including the drawings of painter/dramatist Oskar Kokoschka and contributions by the French poet Guillaume APOLLINAIRE (*see* CUBISM) and the Italian FUTURIST Filippo MARINETTI, while two groundbreaking Expressionist poems first appeared in the latter, Jakob van Hoddis's (1887-1942) apocalyptic poem "Weltende" (1911) and Alfred Lichtenstein's (1889-1914) "Die Dammerung" (1911), which describes the horrors of a dismal urban setting in an ironic voice.

Strongly infused with a sense of the world's disorder, German Expressionist poetry often features juxtapositions or collages of seemingly arbitrary images. Although the poems are usually conventionally structured, their syntax is compressed, their focus is on subjective emotion, and their tone is frequently ecstatic (sometimes to a ludicrous degree). In keeping with the general spirit of the Expressionist movement and its particular moment in German history, many of the Expressionist poets had a strongly developed sense of their own public role.

The early years of the Expressionist movement saw the emergence of two important poets; both would die young and tragically, but both would be remembered as truly talented writers in an age of poetic excess. George Heym (1887-1912) wrote dynamic, even flamboyant poems focusing on such negative aspects of urban life as poverty and mental and physical illness. Heym reveals the influence of such mentors as SYMBOLISTS Arthur Rimbaud, Paul VERLAINE, and Charles Baudelaire through the expressive, colorful imagery of "Der Krieg" (1912; War) and other poems, in which his deep dismay over humanity's doomed plight is evident. Heym died in an ice-skating accident at age 24. George Trakl (1887-1914), whose life ended in suicide, employed dark, forboding, yet highly evocative images in his poems, which blended traditional forms (especially the sonnet) with original metaphors. His work is dreamlike to the point of incoherence, illustrating the Expressionist preference for emoting over communicating. Such poems as "Siebensang des Todes" (1913; The Sevenfold Song of Death) exemplify both Trakl's skillful use of imagery and the lurking sense of evil and decay evident in all of his writing.

The poetry of August Stramm (1874-1915), which features fragmented syntax and a highly abstracted, concentrated use of language that Stramm adapted from the stripped-down, punctuationless writing of the Futurists, was widely mimicked by poets less skilled than Stramm. These imitators attempted — often with ridiculous results — to create the telegraphic effect more successfully achieved by Stramm in such poems as "Trieb" (Urge) and "Schwermut" (Melancholy). Among the casualties of World War I was Ernst Stadler (1883-1914), whose verse comprised long, Whitmanesque lines of connected images. In his most famous poem, "Fahrt über die Kölner Rheinbrücke bei Nacht" (1914; Night Journey Across the Rhine Bridge at Cologne), realism is blended with subjective emotion to achieve an ecstatic vision. The powerful free verse of physician Gottfried Benn (1886-1956), who was also directly influenced by the Italian Futurists, is marked by cynicism and a Nietzschean contempt for humanity.

The dreamy, emotional verses of Else Lasker-Schüler (1869-1945) were often included in Expressionist anthologies of the period, but she is now recognized more as part of the Expressionist milieu than as an artist in her own right. The Czech poet Franz Werfel (1890-1945), active in the German artistic scene rather than in Prague, wrote rhapsodic, sometimes bombastic poems that were much imitated by poets eager to insert as many exclamation points as possible into their work. Werfel's 1916 poem "Lächeln Atmen Schreiten" (Smiling Breathing Striding) is a hymn to humanity that is characteristically laden with grandiose abstractions. The most notable of Werfel's imitators is probably Johannes R. Becher (1891-1958), whose specialty was fervant odes to brotherhood and peace.

One of the most significant results of the Expressionist movement was its strong influence on the then-fledgling film genre. Filmmakers successfully employed several techniques of Expressionist drama, particularly the innovative use of lighting to create dreamlike settings. The typical Expressionist film tended to a macabre, Gothic slant on insanity, murder, and sadism and evidenced the Expressionist distrust of surface reality. The most renowned of these films is undoubtedly *Das Kabinet des Dr. Caligari* (1919), directed by Robert Wiene (1881-1938), which relates the frightening tale of an enigmatic hypnotist who is finally revealed to be the evil director of an insane asylum.

The film focuses on the concept of the split personality that results from society's demands for conformity. Wiene incorporated unusual visual effects as well as heavily made-up actors practicing a stylized acting technique, and *Caligari* became the first film that was deliberately labeled "Expressionist." Shown in London, Paris, and New York in 1921, the film introduced foreign audiences to German Expressionism and influenced such playwrights as Eugene O'NEILL, some of whose early plays comprise notable examples of EXPRESSIONISM in the United States. Other celebrated Expressionist films include F. W. Murnau's (1889-1931) *Nosferatu* (1922) and Fritz Lang's (1890-1976) *Metropolis* (1926).

The sustained prose of the novel form did not lend itself well to the emotional excesses of Expressionism, and there are few novelists who can rightly be considered part of the movement. The two who are most often mentioned as Expressionists (or as employing some Expressionist techniques) are Heinrich Mann (1871-1950), author of *Der Untertan* (1918; *The Patrioteer*, 1921), and Alfred Döblin (1878-1957), whose *Berlin Alexanderplatz* (1929) features theatrical and grotesque elements and a montage effect similar to that found in James JOYCE's *ULYSSES* (*see* MODERNISM, England and Ireland). Although the nightmarish quality of much of Franz KAFKA's (*see* MODERNISM, Austria and Germany) writing is sometimes identified as Expressionist, most commentators do not classify him as a bona fide member of the movement.

The Expressionist movement lost force as the 1920s progressed, brought down by a combination of factors. One such factor was its own excesses — the inaccessibility of its poetic language, its often bombastic rhetoric and highly subjective approach, and the vagueness of its call for brotherhood and a brighter future. German writers began to infuse their work with more intellect and less emotion as a movement known as the Neue Sachlichkeit (*see* NEW OBJECTIVITY), which promoted a dry, clear, economical use of language, came to the fore. The rise of Hitler spelled doom for any remaining Expressionists, for the Nazis could not tolerate such a cerebral, internationally oriented movement that not only involved a large number of Jews but was associated with the postwar peace movement. Many Expressionist artists left Germany during the 1920s and 1930s (several who stayed would later die in the concentration camps), and in 1937 the Nazis staged a "Degenerate Art" exhibition in Munich that harshly ridiculed the Expressionist painters.

Ultimately eclipsed by other Modernist movements (especially DADA, which arose partly as a reaction against it), Expressionism nevertheless left a permanent impression on literature through the formal and stylistic innovations it introduced and its insistence on the preeminence of the subjective viewpoint. Authors influenced (directly or indirectly) by Expressionism include not only later German playwrights like Friedrich

Dürrenmatt (1921-1990) and Max Frisch (1911-1991), but such diverse and celebrated writers as James Joyce, T. S. ELIOT (*see* MODERNISM, England and Ireland), Gertrude STEIN (*see* MODERNISM, United States), Eugene O'Neill, Edward Albee (1928-), Harold PINTER (*see* COMEDY OF MENACE), Allen GINSBURG (*see* BEAT GENERA-TION), and Thomas Pynchon (1937-).

❖•❖

Kaiser, Georg (1878-1945), German dramatist.

Recognized as the most accomplished playwright of the German Expressionist theater, Kaiser was both talented and prolific: between 1917 and 1923, twenty-four of his plays were performed. His best-known works are characterized by their cerebral focus, com-pressed, staccato language, and essential idealism. Like many other Expressionists, Kaiser looked forward to a regeneration of humanity, but he believed that such a change must originate within the individual psyche rather than through social reform. Other Expressionist works include *Die Burger von Calais* (1913, performed 1917; The Burgers of Calais), whose protagonist seeks redemption through idealism and sacrifice, and the "Gas Trilogy," comprised of three plays—*Die Koralle* (1917; *The Coral*, 1924), *Gas I* (1918; *Gas I*, 1924), and *Gas II* (1920; *Gas II*, 1924)—which chronicles three generations of a family, including a Millionaire father and his idealistic son and grand-son. The three plays are centered on the struggle for regeneration that is made more difficult by the cruel opposition of the powerful. This theme is underlined by the notably Expressionist techniques of harsh lighting, abstract settings, and the use of automaton characters.

Von Morgens bis Mitternacht (1912, performed 1917; *From Morn to Midnight*, 1919).

Von Morgens bis Mitternacht is a "station" drama that moves its protagonist, an anonymous bank clerk, from situation to situation in his quest for self-knowledge. Determined to flee his deadening circumstances, the clerk steals 60,000 marks and sets off to find adventure. He abandons himself to sexual promiscuity and enters a punish-ing six-day bicycle race. Eventually he realizes that such pursuits are pointless and, after throwing the money away, shoots himself. Having been corrupted by his crime, the play suggests, the clerk is unable to attain a meaningful life. *Von Morgens bis Mitternacht* is classically Expressionist in its deliberately unreal, distorted atmosphere and its shift in perspective from outer to inner experience. The characters are abstract rather than psychologically rounded, and the play's jerky action mimics the protago-nist's restless quest.

❖•❖

Strindberg, August (1849-1912)
Swedish dramatist, fiction writer, essayist, and poet.

Though he wrote in Swedish, Strindberg had an enormous influence on the German literary scene during the Expressionist heyday and beyond. His mother died when Strindberg was an adolescent, and his father subsequently married a woman Strindberg grew to despise, events critics often point to as contributing to the ambivalence toward women that would permeate his plays, which are highly autobiographical with introspective, psychically tortured characters. Strindberg's early work is considered NATURALIST, though he did not follow Émile ZOLA's brand. In addition to *Till Damaskus, I-III* (1898-1901; *To Damascus, Parts I-III*, 1933-35) and *Ett drömspel* (1901; *A Dream Play*, 1912) — which fascinated the young Expressionists in Germany — Strindberg is also renowned for his Pre-Inferno (referring to the period before the painful breakup of his first marriage and his own emotional deterioration) plays: *Fadren* (1887; *The Father*, 1907), *Fröken Julie* (1888; *Miss Julie*, 1913), *Fordringsägere* (1888; *Creditors*, 1910), *Den starkere* (1889; *The Stronger*, 1964), and *Bandet* (1892; *The Bond*, 1960), as well as one of his post-Inferno plays, *Dödsdansen* (1900; *The Dance of Death*, 1912).

Ett drömspel (1901; *A Dream Play*, 1965).

Until *Till Damaskus, I-III*, Strindberg's preceding work, he had not written for the theater for some years. In the intervening time he studied Eastern philosophy, occultism, Catholicism, and, perhaps most importantly, Emanuel Swedenborg's (1688-1772) mysticism, all of which nourished his most renowned play, which portrays the nature and course of human life to death in the form of a dream, or as Strindberg wrote in the play's preface, "the author has tried to imitate the disconnected but apparently logical form of a dream. Everything can happen; everything is possible and likely. Time and space do not exist. . . . But one consciousness remains . . . the dreamer's." The protagonist of the play is Indra's Daughter, who comes to earth and embarks on a journey to discern whether its inhabitants are justified in having complaint for their mother tongue, as Indra puts it. Along the way, she encounters the Officer, the Lawyer, and the Poet, who each represent various stages and stations of a man's life, and immerses herself in the tales of woe imparted by everyone she meets. She concludes that humans are indeed to be pitied but, as the Poet's example shows, they are also capable of transcending suffering.

❖•❖

Toller, Ernst (1893-1939), German dramatist.

Recognized as one of German Expressionism's most talented practitioners, Toller emerged on the scene at a time when the movement's light was almost spent. Toller's experience as a soldier in World War I led to an emotional and physical breakdown and to his conversion to pacifism, for which stance he was imprisoned. His masterpiece, *Die Wandlung* (1919; *Transfiguration*, 1935), is characteristically Expressionist in its passion and exclamatory phrasing, as well as the protagonist's movement through stations as he seeks self-knowledge. His later plays include *Masse-Mensch* (1921; *Man and the Masses*, 1924), which portrays the difficulties of leading ordinary people toward idealistic goals, and *Hinkemann* (1924; *Brokenbow,* 1926), which features a war hero whose sense of humiliation and despair — a degradation that is, significantly, impervious to the aid of societal reforms — finally leads him to kill himself. *Hoppla, wir leben!* (1927; *Hoppla!*, 1928) is infused with the idea that political activism is futile, and the suicide of the play's protagonist anticipated Toller's death, two years later, by his own hand.

Die Wandlung (1919; *Transfiguration*, 1935).

Produced toward the end of German Expressionism's period of dominance, *Die Wandlung* is considered one of the strongest examples of the movement's fervor and its hope for redemption. Toller's experiences as a soldier in World War I were essential to the play's conception, for he underwent the same kind of emotional and physical collapse suffered by his protagonist. After the war, Toller was imprisoned for his pacifist activities, and he wrote *Die Wandlung* in jail. The play features a protagonist, Friedrich, who seeks freedom by joining the army but gains only a devastating knowledge of pain, mutilation, and death. After the war, he becomes a sculptor and is commissioned to create a statue representing victory, but when he sees some former soldiers crippled in the war he has a breakdown and destroys his sculpture. Eventually Friedrich becomes the leader of a workers' movement, and he leads his followers in a political and spiritual quest for peace, hope, and rebirth. The play's Expressionist qualities include its exclamatory dialogue, anonymous characters (except for the hero), and scenes that blend the real and the symbolic in a dramatic juxtaposition of utopian and nightmarish imagery. *Die Wandlung* provides a strong example of the passionate idealism — doomed though it was to disillusionment — that dominated the last years of the Expressionist movement.

❧•❦

Further Reading

Benson, Renate. *German Expressionist Drama: Ernst Toller and Georg Kaiser*. New York: Grove Press, 1984.

Carlson, Harry Gilbert. *Out of Inferno: Strindberg's Reawakening as an Artist*. Seattle: University of Washington Press, 1996.

Dahlström, C. W. E. L. *Strindberg's Dramatic Expressionism*. Ann Arbor, Mich.: University of Michigan Press, 1930.

Furness, R. S. *Expressionism*. London: Methuen, 1973.

Garten, H. F. "Georg Kaiser Re-examined." In *Essays in German and Dutch Literature*. Edited by W. D. Robson-Scott. London: University of London, Institute of Germanic Studies, 1973.

Kenworthy, Brian J. *Georg Kaiser*. Oxford, England: Blackwell, 1957.

Lamm, Martin. *August Strindberg*. Translated by Harry G. Carlson. Bronx, N.Y.: Benjamin Blom, 1968.

Madsen, Børge Gedsø. *Strindberg's Naturalistic Theatre: Its Relation to French Naturalism*. Seattle: University of Washington Press; Copenhagen: Munksgaard, 1962.

Paulsen, Wolfgang. "Form and Content in German Expressionist Literature." *Massachusetts Review* 21 (spring 1980): 137-56.

Pickar, Gertrud Bauer, and Karl Eugene Webb, eds. *Expressionism Reconsidered: Relationships and Affinities*. Munich: Fink, 1979.

Pittock, Malcolm. *Ernst Toller*. Boston: Twayne, 1979.

Schürer, Ernst. *Georg Kaiser*. New York: Twayne, 1971.

Sokol, W. *The Writer in Extremis: Expressionism in Twentieth-Century Literature*. Stanford, Calif.: Stanford University Press, 1959.

Sprinchorn, Evert. *Strindberg as Dramatist*. New Haven, Conn.: Yale University Press, 1982.

Tornqvist, Egil. *Strindbergian Drama: Themes and Structure*. Stockholm: Almqvist & Wiksell International; Atlantic Highlands, N.J.: Humanities Press, 1982.

Weisstein, Ulrich, ed. *Expressionism as an International Literary Phenomenon*. Paris: Didier, 1973.

Willeke, Androne B. *Georg Kaiser and the Critics: A Profile of Expressionism's Leading Playwright*. Columbia, S.C.: Camden House, 1995.

Willett, John. *Expressionism*. New York: McGraw-Hill, 1970.

EXPRESSIONISM
United States, 1920s

Expressionism is the broad term applied to a literary movement of the late nineteenth and early twentieth centuries, when writers interested in representing subjective experience rather than exterior reality began to veer away from REALIST and NATURALISTIC techniques and to experiment with abstraction, exaggeration, and distortion. Many of the movement's advocates were committed to ideals of social reform, and sought to expose aspects of modern life that they considered destructive to humanity. In the United States, the most acclaimed practitioners of Expressionism were the playwrights Eugene O'NEILL and Elmer RICE; Expressionist elements have also been identified in the later work of Thornton Wilder (1897-1975), Tennessee Williams (1911-1983), and Arthur Miller (1915-).

Although some commentators cite such nineteenth-century dramatists as August STRINDBERG (*see* EXPRESSIONISM, Germany), Frank Wedekind (1864-1918), and Georg Büchner (1813-1837) as precursors to the twentieth-century Expressionists, the movement's origins are usually traced to the German theater during the period between the turn of the century and the mid-1920s. At that time, the prominent German dramatists Georg KAISER, Ernst TOLLER, and Walter Hasenclever (1890-1940) were writing plays that featured highly subjective perspectives presented in non-realistic forms. Their protagonists grappled with issues of individual identity, often surrounded by secondary figures who were exaggerated types rather than conventional characters. Other hallmarks of Expressionist drama include the use of condensed, sometimes poetic language, episodic structures, dreamlike or nightmarish imagery and scenes, and dialogue delivered in a staccato manner. Scenery and makeup are often distorted, and staging and language may be highly stylized or illogical.

The German Expressionist theater was banned in 1933 by the Nazis, who considered the movement decadent, but by then its influence had spread to other parts of the world, including the United States. Although both O'Neill and Rice denied familiarity with the work of Kaiser and his colleagues, commentators have noted striking similarities between several of the Americans' plays and those of the German Expressionists. (For example, the plot and theatrical technique of O'Neill's play *THE GREAT GOD BROWN* [1926] closely resemble those of Kaiser's *Die Koralle* [1917]).

Developments then occurring in the art of cinema also had an effect on American Expressionism. Often cited as particularly influential is the German film *Das Kabinet des Dr. Caligari* (1919; released in the United States in 1921), with its innovative visual distortions reflecting the crazed mind of the protagonist. In fact, O'Neill admitted that he was inspired to write *THE HAIRY APE* (1922), which he adapted from an earlier short story, several months after seeing *Caligari*.

A central tenet of Expressionist drama was a determination to present not the surface reality of life but its true essence, to illuminate the core by rendering exterior forms abstract or distorted. Thus O'Neill employed mask-like makeup to dramatize, in *The Hairy Ape*, how individuals are dehumanized by technology and materialism. In his other significant Expressionist play, *The Great God Brown*, O'Neill used actual masks as well as stereotypical characters and other non-naturalistic devices to explore the concept of divided identity. Though not as celebrated a dramatist as O'Neill, Rice is credited with successfully incorporating Expressionist techniques in his best-known play, *THE ADDING MACHINE* (1923). Through distorted scenery, nightmarish sound effects, and abstracted characters, Rice relates how human beings may become enslaved by the machines they have created.

Part of a very broadly defined movement with no central thesis, the American Expressionist theater flowered briefly and faded from view, as audiences tired of its dominantly artificial language and general inaccessibility. The non-naturalistic devices and techniques associated with Expressionism continued to surface, however, in the works of later dramatists.

❖•❖

O'Neill, Eugene (1888-1953), American dramatist.

Recognized as the foremost American dramatist of the twentieth century, O'Neill had exposure to the stage early in life, traveling with his father, popular actor James O'Neill (1847-1920). He attended Princeton University for a year, then embarked on a series of adventurous jobs, including gold prospecting in Honduras, a merchant seaman in Argentina, acting with his father, writing for a newspaper in Connecticut, and finally, during hospitalization for an emotional breakdown, writing plays. In 1914-15, he was a student of the 47 WORKSHOP, then began working with the PROVINCETOWN PLAYERS, and later, the THEATER GUILD. O'Neill experimented with many dramatic innovations during his career. Among these was Expressionism, elements of which are notable in several of the plays he wrote during the 1920s. Although O'Neill minimized the influence of the German dramatists credited with introducing Expressionism to the stage, he shared their interest in representing the true essence of reality rather than its surface appearance, and in emphasizing individual thought and feelings. And like the German Expressionists, O'Neill chose non-naturalistic techniques as a means to this end in several significant plays, among them *The Hairy Ape* (1922) and *The Great God Brown* (1926). Other important plays include *The Emperor Jones* (1920), *All God's Chillun Got Wings* (1924), *Desire Under the Elms* (1924), *Strange Interlude* (1928), *The Iceman Cometh* (1946), and *Long Day's Journey into Night* (1956). He was awarded the Nobel Prize for literature in 1936.

The Hairy Ape (1922).

Identified by some commentators as America's first Expressionist drama, *The Hairy Ape* opened on Broadway on April 17, 1922. The first of many works in which O'Neill explores the destructive influence of materialism in American society, the play portrays through non-naturalistic devices the failure of an uneducated laborer to rise above his circumstances.

The central character of *The Hairy Ape* is Yank, who resembles in appearance and behavior the beast referred to in the play's title. Yank is consistently associated with the color black, and his speech is pointedly ungrammatical. The play opens in Yank's workplace, the stoke hole (engine room) of a great ship; O'Neill's stage directions call for a graphically arresting set in which oppressive labor is manifested by a heavy-beamed, low ceiling and nightmarish sound effects. Scorned by the always white-draped, super-civilized Mildred (who speaks in an exaggeratedly artificial manner that contrasts strongly with Yank's speech), Yank decides he will try to join her world.

In a notably Expressionistic scene featuring identical, mechanical figures with mask-like faces (described by O'Neill as a "procession of gaudy marionettes"), Yank is ignored by a crowd of churchgoers. Enraged, he attacks them and is arrested. His subsequent attempt to join the International Workers of the World—a labor union whose members, Yank has heard, intend to blow up society—also ends in rejection. Yank grows progressively more frustrated and desperate, finally finding solace only in the arms of a gorilla at the zoo.

***The Great God Brown* (1926).**

First presented on January 23, 1926, *The Great God Brown* goes a step further than O'Neill's earlier Expressionist play *The Hairy Ape* in that it features actual masks that are used to illustrate the fracturing and confusion of identity that result from the dehumanizing demands of modern life.

The play's first two acts concern Dion Anthony, a sensitive painter who is forced to abandon his art in order to support his family. Dion's wife, Margaret, who loves him but lacks his emotional and intellectual depth, gets him a job in the office of his old schoolmate, William A. "Billy" Brown, a successful but shallow architect. Depressed and humiliated, Dion becomes an alcoholic and seeks comfort from a big-busted, gum-chewing prostitute named Cybel, who is often cited as a pointedly stereotypical character. Dion finally drinks himself to death.

In the second half of the play, Billy puts on Dion's mask, assuming with it Dion's artistic sensibility and integrity. Newly endowed with a sense of honesty, Billy denounces his former life and work as false and empty. He abandons his own identity completely and, masked as Dion, runs to Cybel's arms. In an ironic ending that indicates that the artist and the materialist have destroyed each other, Billy-as-Dion is arrested for murdering Billy. Thus Dion and Billy may be seen either as separate characters or as the separate objectifications of one multiple personality—that is, the divided personality of the modern human being.

Although the play was a commercial success at the time of its initial appearance and has been lauded for its bold use of Expressionistic techniques to represent psychological complexities, many critics deem *The Great God Brown* a dramatic failure due to the confusion and ambiguity caused by the complicated exchange of masks.

Rice, Elmer (1892-1967), American dramatist.

Rice was a prolific and versatile dramatist who made significant contributions to the development of the American theater during the 1920s and 1930s. He graduated from the New York Law School in 1912, but by the end of the 1910s, had plays published by a little theater group, the Morningside Players. Praised for his innovative approach to staging and other theatrical devices, Rice also followed the example of his predecessors George Bernard SHAW (*see* EDWARDIAN LITERATURE) and Henrik IBSEN (*see* REALISM, Norway) by introducing social themes into his plays. Both Rice's innovations and his commitment to social reform are evident in his most ambitious work, *The Adding Machine* (1923), which is considered one of the first and best examples of Expressionism in the American theater. Rice won a Pulitzer Prize for his play *Street Scene* (1929); other plays include *On Trial* (performed 1914, published 1919), *Counsellor-at-Law* (1931), *Left Bank* (1931), *We, the People* (1933), and *Dream Girl* (1945).

The Adding Machine (1923).

Considered one of the best examples of the Expressionism that flowered briefly in the United States in the 1920s, *The Adding Machine* is Rice's most accomplished work. It presents a world in which dignity, dreams, and a clear sense of identity have disappeared in the face of twentieth-century drudgery and boredom. Expressionist elements in the play include not only its nontraditional subject matter and techniques but its thematic emphasis on how technology destroys human identity, asserting further that humanity may even become a slave to technology rather than its master. The play portrays the dehumanization of a middle-class victim of an increasingly mechanized society. The protagonist is Mr. Zero, a bookkeeper who loses his job of twenty-five years when he is replaced by an adding machine. He murders his boss, and is tried, executed, and sent to heaven, only to find that he is also superfluous there. Like Eugene O'Neill, Rice denied having been influenced by the German Expressionists, yet *The Adding Machine* features several notably Expressionist techniques. These include visual distortions as well as repetitive, cliché-ridden dialogue that is delivered in a staccato manner. In addition, the protagonist's inner turmoil is externalized; for example, his distress over being fired from his job is represented by a crazily revolving stage and cacophonous sound effects.

✥•✦

Further Reading

Carpenter, Frederic I. *Eugene O'Neill.* New York: Twayne, 1964.
Durham, Frank. *Elmer Rice.* New York: Twayne, 1970.
Furness, R. S. *Expressionism.* London: Methuen, 1973.
Valgamae, Mardi. *Accelerated Grimace: Expressionism in the American Drama of the 1920s.* Carbondale, Ill.: Southern Illinois University Press, 1972.

EXTERIORISMO
Nicaragua, 1950s-1960s

Ernesto Cardenal (1925-), the primary proponent of Exteriorismo, asserts that the movement refers to a political poetic style of Nicaraguan poetry which had been written for much of the century. Recently, he prefers the descriptive "concrete" (*see also* CONCRETE POETRY). Heavily influenced by the aesthetics of Ezra POUND (*see* MODERNISM, England and Ireland), Exteriorismo, in Cardenal's words, "is objective poetry: narrative and anecdotal, made with the elements of real life and with what is concrete, with personal names and precise details, exact occurrences and number, facts and statements." Though pro-revolutionary and anti-imperialist, Exteriorismo is not to be confused with SOCIALIST REALISM, which Cardenal considers "a warmed-over version of nineteenth-century bourgeois 'realism'." José Coronel Utrecho (1906-), formerly associated with a vanguardist literary alliance, collaborated with Cardenal in setting up a press — El Hilo Azul (The Blue Thread) — in 1951, where they published translations of American poets, and where poets as well as members of the Unión Nacional de Acción Popular (National Union of Popular Action) congregated.

Cardenal was ordained as a Catholic priest in 1965 and founded a retreat, Our Lady of Solentiname, which sponsored cultural activities, such as painting and writing poetry, for people living in the area. After the fall of Anastasio Somoza Debayle's (1925-1980) regime in 1979, he was appointed Minister of Culture, under which office he continues programs which support literary and artistic activities, particularly for workers. Cardenal's Exteriorismo has been influential — in a political as well as a literary sense — throughout Latin America.

❧•❧

Further Reading

Cabestrero, Teófilo. *Ministers of God, Ministers of the People: Testimonies of Faith from Nicaragua.* Translated by Robert R. Barr. Maryknoll, N.Y.: Orbis Books; London: Zed Press, 1983.

Cardenal, Ernesto. *Flights of Victory = Vuelos de Victoria.* Edited and translated by Marc Zimmerman. Maryknoll, N.Y.: Orbis Books, 1985.

———. *With Walker in Nicaragua and Other Early Poems (1949-1954).* Selected and translated by Jonathan Cohen. Middletown, Conn.: Wesleyan University Press, 1985.

Johnson, K. *A Nation of Poets.* Los Angeles: West End Press, 1985.

White, Steven F., ed. *Poets of Nicaragua, A Bilingual Anthology, 1918-1979.* Greensboro, N.C.: Unicorn Press, 1982.

F

FANTAISISTES GROUP
France, 1910s

Without a formal manifesto, and brought together by similarity of temperament and worldview, this group of writers included Jean-Marc Bernard (1881-1915), Francis CAR-CO, Blaise Cendrars (1887-1961), Tristan Derème (pseud. of Phillipe Huc, 1889-1942), Tristan Klingsor (1874-1966), Valery Larboud (1881-1951), and Paul Jean Toulet (1867-1920). Carco and Derème were the principal spokesmen. Simply put, the group was reacting in part against the complexity and obscurity of the synaesthetic, metaphoric, "dark and confused unity" of SYMBOLIST poetry, begun in the nineteenth century, but still strongly influential as the twentieth began. Although the new group was not "anti" Symbolism in the true sense of the word — some of Carco's work was strongly influenced by the works of Charles BAUDELAIRE and Paul VERLAINE (*see* Symbolism, France) — their aim was to reintroduce into poetry elements of a blithe irony and, often, the playful, fairy-tale quality of the grotesque and the humorously bizarre.

A new spirit of creative expression had been brought about by the changes in the graphic arts produced by the impressionistic painters of the late nineteenth century; artists such as Pablo Picasso (1881-1973), Georges Braque (1882-1963), and Henri Matisse (1869-1954) rejected realistic, narrative forms of painting and depicted reality with basic geometric forms, often superimposed on one another with monochromatic severity. Their juxtaposition of diverse concepts provided new freedom of expression for the depiction of the societal breakdown and chaos which they saw around them. Simultaneously, the same new spirit was felt in the literary milieu, and there were fresh attempts by the poets to depict human consciousness and the psyche at work. This made for diversity of poetic concept and new linguistic approaches to meter, form, and structure. While the young Fantaisistes entered into "le spirit nouveau" and

171

were excited by it, they now attempted to "restore poetry to what the Symbolists had eliminated from it," and give it a lighter touch.

Jean-Marc Bernard's pastoral, *Sub tegmine fagi: amours, bergeries et jeux* (1913; In the Shade of the Beech Tree: Loves, Pastorals, Games), was, he said, inspired by the fifteenth-century rogue poet François Villon, whose rowdy, carefree life exemplified the attitude of this group of poets. Similarly, Tristan Derème is said to have been amused by writing verse as prose and by stealing verses of others for inclusion in his own. An intrepid writer, Derème was known to blithely invent subject matter for his essays about literary history. He was fascinated by poetry and versification, especially counter-rhyme and counter-assonance, i.e., the retention of rhyme with similar consonants but with variation of vowels. Bright and witty, his joy in poetry and in his own "petits poemes" and his often elegiac style made for enjoyable reading. His best-known collection of verse is *La Verdure doree* (1922).

These poets considered the earlier poet Jules Laforgue (1860-1887) to be their guide and their main influence because of his mastery of ironic satire and his invention of free verse (*vers libre*). They, in turn, are known to have had a positive effect on the work of their contemporary, Guillaume APOLLINAIRE (*see* CUBISM), in one of his best-known works, *Alcools* (1913; *Alcohols*, 1964), in which his poems combine both free verse and classical, traditional form.

⇒•⇐

Carco, Francis (pseud. of François Marie Alexandre Carcopino-Tusoli, 1886-1958), French art critic, novelist, and poet.

Chief spokesman for the Fantaisistes, Carco had been raised in a punitive family and surrounded by an uncertainty which gave him his passion for the sensual combined with the violent, and a love for nature and for physical sensation. An early love of poetry inspired the writing of verse; his strong sensuality drew him into the circle of bohemian life in Montmartre in pre-World War I Paris. He was moved by the prostitutes, pimps, and drug addicts of the Left Bank and by their attempts to rise above their misery in the creation of their art. He was also attracted, politically, by the bohemian rejection of bourgeois values and the developing of a singular code of loyalty which held them together as aliens in a larger society which they could not understand, could not avoid, and in which they were nonparticipants. Carco's strict, moral stance was that man should not be condemned for his faults in a world where fate could not be avoided and must be endured; on the other hand, his own sensuality drew him passionately to the bohemian life in all of its aspects. Among many early works the novels *La Boheme et mon coeur* (1912; Bohemia and My Heart), *Jésus la Caille* (1914), and *Les Innocents* (1916) were in defense of a marginal society; later works included *Perversité*

(1925; *Perversity*, 1928) and *Rue Pigalle* (1927). He was made a member of the Goncourt Society for his sparseness of style, his clarity of structure, and his classical form. To the end of his life he continued to write reminiscences of his life in Montmartre and his association with painters and other artists. They include *De Montmartre au Quartier latin* (1927; *The Last Bohemia*, 1928), *Bohème d'artiste* (1940; An Artist's Bohemia), and *Mémoires d'une vie* (1942; Memories of a Life). Finally, Carco, the poet, was known as "the defender of the *voyon* and the biographer of the prostitute."

➹•◄

Further Reading

Hartley, Anthony. "The Twentieth Century." In *The Penguin Book of French Poetry*. Harmondsworth, England: Penguin, 1974.

Rexroth, Kenneth. *One Hundred Poems from the French*. Cambridge, Mass.: Pym-Randall, 1972.

Weiner, Seymour S. *Francis Carco: The Career of a Literary Bohemian*. New York: Columbia University Press, 1952.

FECR-I ÂTI. See **DAWN OF THE FUTURE**

FÉLIBRIGE MOVEMENT
Provence, France, 1854-1920s

The name is given to a small group of poets who, in 1854, sought to restore the use of the original language of Provence (*langue d'oc*, sometimes Occitan) to their common birthplace. A Romance language derived from Indo-European dialects, langue d'oc had been used in Provence by the troubadours of the Middle Ages, but had been banned in 1591 by Francis I when he made French the official language. The Félibrige movement was begun in 1854 by Joseph Roumanille (1818-1891), Theodore Aubanet (1872-1950), and Frederic Mistral (1830-1914), in a revolt against the old linguistic dictum. Other followers were Joseph d'Arbaud (1872-1950), Jean Brenet (1823-1894), Michel Camelat (1871-1962), Paul Giera (1816-1861), Felix Gras (1884-1901), Remy Marcellin (1832-1908), Anselme Mathieu (1828-1925), and Antonin Perbosc (1861-1944).

The long, twelve-canto poem by Mistral, *Miréio* (1859; *Mireio*, 1867), established him as a major poet of Provence and gave him European recognition as a revivalist of classical tradition. A prolific writer, he is also known for other epic poetry, memoirs, fiction, translations, and philological treatises. He received the Nobel Prize in literature in 1909 for work which had been translated from the langue d'oc; he is an outstanding representative of Félibrige. Roumanille is called "le pere de Félibrige"; he established the group's official journal, *Armana provençau,* and is most famous for his short stories which were popular with both the working people and the educated class for their amusing, moralistic tone. D'Arbaud was considered by Mistral to be superior to others associated with Félibrige and is known for his serious, meditative work which is carefully wrought in the classical tradition. It is erudite, sensitive, and stems almost exclusively from his deep love for Provence and its people. He was editor and coeditor of *Le Feu,* a journal devoted to Mediterranean regionalism, and was honored by the French Academy for *La Provence, types and coutumes* (1939; Provence: Types and Customs), his only work written in French.

By about 1930, the Félibrige movement was no longer active, but it had been strongly influential in stirring enthusiasm for the recognition of langue d'oc, and a move in Provence towards MODERNISM.

❧•❦

Further Reading

Aldington, Richard. *Introduction to Mistral*. London: Heinemann; Carbondale, Ill.: Southern Illinois University Press, 1960.

Downer, Charles Alfred. *Frédéric Mistral, Poet and Leader in Provence*. New York: Columbia University Press, 1901.

Drutel, Marcello. *Jóusè d'Arbaud, 1874-1950*. Paris: La France Latine, 1971.

Edwards, Tudor. *The Lion of Arles: A Portrait of Mistral and His Circle*. New York: Fordham University Press, 1964.

Ford, Harry Egerton. *Modern Provençal Phonology and Morphology Studied in the Language of Frederic Mistral*. New York: Columbia University Press, 1921.

Girdlestone, C[uthbert] M[orton]. *Dreamer and Striver: The Poetry of Frédéric Mistral*. London: Methuen, 1937.

Lyle, Rob. *Mistral*. Cambridge, England: Bowes & Bowes, 1953.

Mistral, Frédéric. *The Memoirs of Frédéric Mistral*. Translated by George Wickes. New York: New Directions, 1986.

Preston, Harriet W. *Troubadours and Trouvères: New and Old*. Boston: Roberts Brothers, 1876.

FEMINIST CRITICISM
England, France, and United States, 1960s-1990s

Feminist literary criticism can be identified with an ongoing feminist movement, by no means a new force, which has called for equal rights for women at all levels of cultural organization — particularly, the political, the economic, and the intellectual. The literary criticism which has grown out of the movement is addressed to the role of gender

174

in the assessment and the reevaluation of a literary history which has for so long been dominated by the males of a patriarchal society. The genre was given its most dynamic identification and formulation at mid-twentieth century, which firmly places it in the MODERNIST movement.

The validity of the presumption that males are the primary readers, writers, and critical representatives of literary studies has, since the 1960s, been brought into question by both male and female writers. Elaine SHOWALTER observes that such investigation shows that "gender is a fundamental character of literary analysis," while K. K. Ruthven (1936-) notes that all serious literary criticism must consider gender as a profound factor in the "production, circulation, and reception of literary texts." Notable among many writers in the movement are Simone de BEAUVOIR (*see also* EXISTENTIALISM), Hélène CIXOUS, Eva Figes (1932-), Sandra GILBERT, Vivian Gornick (1935-), Germaine Greer (1939-), Susan GUBAR, Elizabeth Hardwick (1916-), Luce Irigaray (1932-), Julia Kristeva (1941-), Kate MILLETT, Ellen Moers (1928-1979), Robin Morgan (1941-), and Miriam Schneir (1933-).

Maggie Humm lists a number of critical theories in *The Dictionary of Feminist Theory* (1989), among which three emerge as main currents of thought. One is found in the Anglo-American approach, which disputes the singular authority of male textual voice and seeks to establish the authenticity of female narrative voice, this being accomplished through exposition of the differences between the two. French critical feminists do not ignore textual voice, but concentrate more upon text itself as fundamental to the issue of how sexuality is used to manipulate the written message. Much of the French feminist criticism requires firm knowledge of the fields of linguistics, psychoanalysis, and modern philosophical thought; it tends to rely on the literary concepts of DECONSTRUCTION, STRUCTURALISM, MARXIST CRITICISM, and FREUDIAN CRITICISM in the development of an investigative approach to the gender factor. A third approach is found in the work of such feminist literary historians as Janet Todd (1942-), who calls for a sociohistorical look at text by feminist scholars, and an agenda which will keep feminist literary theory firmly rooted in feminism itself, "where it belongs." For example, consideration of such early works as Mary Wollstonecraft's *A Vindication of the Rights of Women* (1792), John Stuart Mill's *The Subjugation of Women* (1869), and English Modernist Virginia WOOLF's *A Room of One's Own* (1929), all give added perspective to the dynamics of gender and its literary reverberation in the long struggle for sound recognition.

It should further be noted that the movement includes, beyond the theories mentioned, other groups such as the Marxist feminists, the psycho feminists, black feminists, and lesbian feminists — each with its own frame of reference and developmental theories.

What seems clear is that whatever approach is used to revaluate or to dismantle the old and traditional ways of assessing literary texts and a search for new ones, the gender factor and what has come to be known as the "female aesthetic" must now be given full credibility as a powerful, contemporary manifestation of literary energy.

✦•✦

Beavoir, Simone de (1908-1986), French writer, critic, and philosopher.

Born in Paris, de Beavoir was educated and took her final degree in philosophy from the University of Paris. After World War II she became a writer and political activist; she also began a long and close association with the philosopher Jean-Paul SARTRE (*see* Existentialism). *LE DEUXIÈME SEXE* (1949; *The Second Sex,* 1953) is her most exacting and famous feminist work. The first of her autobiographical works, *Mémoires d'une jeune fille rangée (*1958; *Memoirs of a Dutiful Daughter,* 1959) is an account of the subtle restraints imposed on daughters of the Parisian middle class at the beginning of the century and de Beauvoir's reaction to them. While she has been taken to task by later and more radical feminists for what has been called a limited view of the movement, the consistent demands for a woman's right to be free from unwanted pregnancies led to her determined participation, in the 1970s and 1980s, in the pro-choice movement for abortion and in the support of victims of physical abuse and rape. Later works include *La force de l'âge (*1960; *The Prime of Life,* 1962), *La force des choses (*1963; *The Force of Circumstance,* 1965), and *Tout compte fait (*1972; *All Said and Done,* 1975). She is clearly placed in the forefront of the movement.

Le deuxième sexe (1949; The Second Sex, 1953).

In this landmark feminist work, de Beauvoir points out how the traditional sexualization of attitudes towards women in various segments of society — science, education, history — prevents them from having the freedom of self-determination, in that they have been historically led to believe that they are merely adjuncts to males and have a biological need to procreate. Given these conditions, in the work she calls for the end of the "eternal feminine" and for women to live and work independently, ideally within a socialist society, though she later eschewed the view that socialism was a necessary component.

✦•✦

Cixous, Hélène (1937-), French essayist, novelist, and playwright.

Cixous opposes, as do her compatriots Kristeva and Irigaray, the "phallogocentric" concept of Western culture, i.e., masculine domination, its claim to superiority, and the uses of language by males. The repression of self-love, she claims, prohibits women from true expression of self. She calls for a rejection of patriarchal order in her "ecrit-

176

ure feminine" (female writing), and demands that women examine their sexuality with the imagination and creativity of their own language and reject the credibility of the male concept of women as "submissive other." She strongly feels that the language of the woman "will always surpass the discourse that regulates the phallogocentric system." Her works include *La jeune née (*1975; *The Newly Born Woman,* 1986), with Catherine Clément; "Le Rire de la Méduse" (1975; "The Laugh of the Medusa," 1976); and "Reading the Point of Wheat" (1987).

❖•❖

Gilbert, Sandra M. (1936-) and Susan Gubar (1944-) American critics and writers.

Coauthors of essays about women writers, *Shakespeare's Sisters* (1979) and *The Madwoman in the Attic: The Woman Writer and the Nineteenth-Century Literary Imagination* (1979), their work is said to have "permanently altered" the ways in which we view the texts of women writers of the nineteenth century, such as Emily Dickinson (1830-1886) and Charlotte Brontë (1816-1855). Gilbert and Gubar named their approach "the revisionary imperative"; the new look at old texts provides interesting insights into common feelings of repression expressed by women of a century ago. Gilbert argues for a feminist critical view which demystifies our understanding of Western literary culture and a history which has traditionally obscured the relationships between "texticality and sexuality, genre and gender, and psychosexual identity and cultural authority." She calls for feminist critics to actively revise themselves, their texts, and their traditions for a renewal of creative life. Gilbert's poetry includes *In the Fourth World* (1979), *The Summer Kitchen* (1983), and *Emily's Bread* (1988).

❖•❖

Millett, Kate (1934-), American artist, writer, and activist.

Millett holds a distinctive position in the history of feminist criticism as a result of her classic treatment of the history of the oppression and exploitation of women, *SEXUAL POLITICS* (1970). Other works include her autobiographical books, *Flying* (1974), which provides an early history of feminist-lesbian politics, and *Sita* (1977); *The Basement* (1979); and *Going to Iran* (1982), an account of the convention of the Committee to Defend Women's Rights.

Sexual Politics (1970).

This, Millett's major work, adapted from her doctoral dissertation, presents her view (innovative at the time) that sexual distinctions are political distinctions, and provided a threshold from which radical feminism could step toward firmer equal rights for women. Her perceptive and provocative analysis of how patriarchal values are inculcated in the dynamics of sexual violence, class consciousness, education, and economics changed contemporary thinking about the roles women play in society.

Showalter, Elaine (1941-), American writer, critic, and theorist.

Showalter seeks a theoretical framework which defines what is specifically "female" about writing. Important categories of investigation are biological difference, language, and the female psyche, as all are related to female creativity. In addition to such essays as "Towards a Feminist Politics" (1978), other important works include *A Literature of Their Own* (1977), *The Female Malady: Women, Madness and English Culture, 1830-1980* (1985), and her editorship of *The New Feminist Criticism: Essays on Women, Literature and Theory* (1985). She has written numerous essays about feminist critical theory.

"Towards a Feminist Politics" (1978).

In her introduction to *The New Feminist Criticism* (1985), Showalter builds on this earlier essay, in which she had suggested that a study of female writings and female creativity ("gynocritics") provides the most authoritative base for a substantive concept of feminist literary theory. Thorough investigation of such concepts as the style, history, themes, genre, and structure of writings by women are incorporated in gynocritical theory. Her investigation of the differences which exist between the two sexes can be divided into three phases. The first, or "feminine" phase considers works of women of the nineteenth century who were imitating male writers but who were searching for a new sense of selfhood. The second, or "feminist" phase includes women writers of the period 1880-1920 who were somewhat encouraged by the impact of suffrage and new entry into politics and the work force. And in the "female" phase of 1920 and afterward, writers such as Virginia Woolf, Katherine Mansfield (1888-1923), and Dorothy Richardson (1873-1957) made clearer their efforts to portray the social, political, and economic structures which inhibited the creativity of writers of their gender.

Further Reading

Abel, Elizabeth. *Writing and Sexual Difference*. Chicago: University of Chicago Press, 1982.

Barrett, Michèle. *Women's Oppression Today: Problems in Marxist Feminist Analysis*. London: NLB, 1980.

Champagne, Rosaria. "Feminism, Essentialism, and Historical Context." *Women's Studies* 25, 1 (November 1995): 95-108.

Douglas, Ann. *The Feminization of American Culture*. New York: Knopf, 1979.

Eagleton, Terry. *Literary Theory: An Introduction*. Minneapolis: University of Minnesota Press, 1983.

Friedan, Betty. *The Feminine Mystique*. New York: Norton, 1963.

————. *The Second Stage*. New York: Summit Books, 1981.

Grewal, Inderpal, and Caren Kaplan, eds. *Scattered Hegemonies: Postmodernity and Transnational Feminist Practices*. Minneapolis: University of Minnesota Press, 1994.

Humm, Maggie. *Feminist Criticism: Women as Contemporary Critics*. New York: St. Martin's Press, 1986.

Jacobus, Mary. *Reading Woman: Essays in Feminist Criticism*. New York: St. Martin's Press, 1986.

Kristeva, Julia. *Desire in Language: A Semiotic Approach to Literature and Art*. Edited by Leon S. Roudiez. New York: Columbia University Press, 1980.

Moers, Ellen. *Literary Women*. Garden City, N.Y.: Doubleday, 1976.

Moi, Toril. *Sexual/Textual Politics: Feminist Literary Theory*. London: Methuen, 1985.

Todd, Janet. *Feminist Literary History*. New York: Routledge, 1988.

Warhol, Robyn R., and Diane Price Herndl. *Feminisms: An Anthology of Literary Theory and Criticism*. New Brunswick, N.J.: Rutgers University Press, 1997.

Williamson, Marilyn S. "Toward a Feminist Literary History." *Signs* 10 (autumn 1984): 136-47.

Woolf, Janet. *Resident Alien: Feminist Cultural Criticism*. New Haven, Conn.: Yale University Press, 1995.

Woolf, Virginia. *Three Guineas*. New York: Harcourt, Brace, 1938.

FEM UNGA. See **FIVE YOUNG MEN**

FESTA GROUP
Brazil, 1920s

An adjunct of Brazilian MODERNISM, the *Festa* Group of poets and journal was based in Rio de Janeiro and led by Manuel Bandeira (1886-1968). The most accomplished *Festa* poet was Cecília Meireles (1901-1964). Like her colleagues, she merged a conservative philosophical viewpoint with trends of nationalism and realistic Modernism.

⁂

Further Reading

Anderson, Sandra Janette. "From French Symbolism to Brazilian Modernism, with Special Emphasis on the Poetry of Manuel Bandeira." *Dissertation Abstracts International* 44, 11 (May 1984): 3394A.

Garcia, Ruben Victor. "Modernity and Tradition in Cecilia Meireles." *Dissertation Abstracts International* 36 (1976): 6728A.

————. "Symbolism in the Early Works of Cecilia Meireles." *Romance Notes* 21 (1980): 16-22.

Jentsch-Grooms, Lynda. *Exile and the Process of Individuation: A Jungian Analysis of Marine Symbolism in the Poetry of Rafael Alberti, Pablo Neruda, and Cecilia Meireles*. Valencia, Spain: Abatros Ediciones, 1986.

Nist, John. "The Poetry of Cecilia Meireles." *Hispania* 46 (1963): 252-58.

Pontiero, Giovanni. "Manuel Bandeira in the Role of Literary Critic." *Annali Istituto Universitario Orientale* 20 (1978): 203-40.

Ronai, Paulo, Susan Hertelendy Rudge, and Jean R. Longland. "The Character of a Poet: Cecilia Meireles and Her Work." *Literary Review: An International Journal of Contemporary Writing* 21 (1978): 193-204.

Sayers, Raymond. "The Brazilian Woman Poet in the Twentieth Century: Cecilia Meireles." In *Homenaje a Andres Iduarte: Ofrecido por sus amigos y discipulos.* Edited by Jaime Alazraki, Roland Grass, and Russell O. Salmon. Clear Creek, Ind.: American Hispanist, 1976.

Slater, Candace. Introduction to *This Earth, That Sky: Poems by Manuel Bandeira.* Translated by Candace Slater. Berkeley, Calif.: University Press of California, 1989.

FIFTIES POETS (Vijftigers)
Belgium, 1950s

The Belgian Fifties Poets, so named for their era of prominence, were led by Hugo Claus (1929-), known for his experimental and erotic poetry. For their unique artistic responses to life's absurdities, the Fifties Poets are esteemed as an important branch of avant-garde writing in Belgium. A number of other poets have been grouped under this title, including Albert Bontridder (1921-), Gust Gils (1924-), Hugues C. Pernath (1931-1975), and Paul Snoek (1933-).

❖•❖

Further Reading

Dunkelberg, Kendall Alan. "The Collected Poems of Paul Snoek Translated into English." *Dissertation Abstracts International* 55, 6 (December 1994): 1552A.

Jespers, Henri-Floris. "In Memoriam Hugues C. Pernath." *Nieuw Vlaams Tijdschrift* 28 (1975): 655-56.

Jonckheere, Karel. "In Memoriam Hugues C. Pernath." *De Vlaamse Gids* 59, 4 (1975): 4-6.

Kooistra, Remkes. "Hugo Claus's 'Het verdriet van Belgie': Its Reception and Its Themes." *Canadian Journal of Netherlandic Studies* 7, 1-2 (1986): 92-98.

FIFTIES POETS (Vijftigers)
Netherlands, 1950s

Reminiscent of DADA and SURREALISM, the Fifties Poets were a loosely connected group of Dutch poets who came to prominence during the 1950s. Highly individualistic in temperament and technique, the Fifties Poets were perhaps most distinguished for their resolute disengagement from all intellectual and philosophical currents. Chief among the group were Remco Campert (1929-), Gerrit Kouwenaar (1923-), and Lucebert (1924-).

❖•❖
Further Reading

Eijkelboom, J. *Lucebert*. Translated by C. de Dood. Amsterdam: J. M. Meulenhoff, 1964.
Lucebert Edited by Lucebert. Text by Lucebert; translated by James S. Holmes and Hans Van
   Marle. London: Marlborough Fine Art, 1963.

FIFTY-FIVE POETS. *See* **FIFTIES POETS, Belgium**

FIRST POSTWAR WAVE. *See* **MATINÉE POÉTIQUE**

FIRST STATEMENT **GROUP**
Canada, 1942-1945

The periodical *First Statement* was begun in Montreal in 1942 as an attempt to counter
the sophisticated, predominantly British literary influence of its recently formed com-
petitor, *Preview*, with specifically regional, REALISTIC, and consciously American-
influenced literature. The key editors of *First Statement* were John Sutherland (1919-
1956), Louis Dudek (1918-), and Irving Layton (1912-). Before *First Statement*
merged with *Preview* in 1945, forming the immensely successful national monthly
Northern Review headed by Sutherland, Sutherland himself launched the First
Statement Press, which became an important publisher of modern Canadian literature.

❖•❖
Further Reading

Fisher, Neil H. *"First Statement" 1942-1945: An Assessment and an Index*. Ottawa, Canada:
   Golden Dog Press, 1974.
Waddington, Miriam, ed. *John Sutherland: Essays, Controversies, and Poems*. Toronto:
   McClelland & Stewart, 1972.

FIVE SYLLABISTS. *See* **SYLLABISTS**

FIVE YOUNG MEN (*Fem Unga*)
Sweden, 1920s-1930s

The publication of the anthology *Fem Unga* (1929; Five Young Men) is considered one
of the formative events in MODERNIST Swedish poetry. Artur Lundkvist (1906-1991)
and Harry Martinson (1904-1978) were the most notable contributors and the key figures of the Five Young Men.

Following the precepts of the earlier, experimental poet Pär Lagerkvist (1891-1974),
although later rejecting his rigid humanism, the group aimed for new ways to express

the anxiety and melancholy mood of depression in Sweden which was prevalent between the two world wars. Lagerkvist had been inspired by the revolt of the EXPRESSIONIST painters and their forceful, magnetic paintings; his desire was for the kind of poetic language which would evoke similar, objective images in the mind. The young Swedish poets who favored his views looked to the work of the IMAGISTS for inspiration, as well as to all aspects of modern primitivism (the violent, the crude, and the non-intellectual and ritualistic) for creative ideas. A more specific intention was to re-enliven Swedish literature with the "brutal powerful" vitality of the coarse, earthy, and realistic aspects of the modern world. Lundkvist was the most proficient in the group in theoretic poetic concept; his major interests were in SURREALISM and lyrical Modernism, and he is known as one of the first Surrealists in Sweden. Martinson's experiences as a working seaman and his unhappy childhood illuminate his works *Resor utan mål* (1932; Travels without a Destination) and *Kap Farväl* (1933; *Cape Farewell*, 1934). The autobiographical novels *Nässlorna blomma* (1935; *Flowering Nettle*, 1936) and *Vägen ut* (1936; The Way Out) are sensitively drawn and contain the poignancy of elements of both bitterness and resignation. A profound interest in nature and everything connected with it is apparent in all of Martinson's work, but his most well-received work is the long poem *Aniara* (1956; *Aniara: A Review of Man in Time and Space*, 1963), which describes the flight of a space ship which becomes lost as it flees radiation contamination; it is a fictional expression of his philosophic conception about a universe which has become dangerously victimized by runaway technology. Martinson won the Nobel Prize for literature in 1976.

❖•❖

Further Reading

Algulin, Ingemar. *A History of Swedish Literature*. Stockholm: Swedish Institute, 1989.

Allwood, Martin Samuel, ed. *20th Century Scandinavian Poetry*. Mullsjö, Sweden: Marston Hill, 1950.

Gustafson, Alrik. *A History of Swedish Literature*. Minneapolis: University of Minnesota Press, 1961.

Locock, C. D., ed. *A Selection from Modern Swedish Poetry*. New York: Macmillan, 1930.

Schoolfield, G. C. "Tradition and Innovation in the Occidental Lyric of the Last Decade VI. Canals on Mars: The Recent Scandinavian Lyric." *Books Abroad* 36 (winter 1962): 9-19; 36 (spring 1962): 117-24.

FLAME GROUP
Byelorussia, 1920s

The Flame Group emerged during the mid-1920s in Byelorussia as the result of a split in the large MODERNIST/PROLETARIAN group the SAPLINGS (*see also* SOCIALIST REALISM, Byelorussia). Jakub Kołas (1882-1956) and Janka Kupala (1882-1942) were the chief members of the group; both are remembered for their contributions in poetry, criticism, and other genres to the development of modern Byelorussian literature and language.

❖•❖
Further Reading

Barszczewski, Aless. "Romantic Elements in Kolas' Symon-muzyka." *Journal of Byelorussian Studies* 5, 2 (1982): 27-43.

Berezin, Grigori. "Yanka Kupala." *Soviet Literature* 7 (1972): 133-37.

Byelorussian Society for Friendship and Cultural Relations with Foreign Countries. *National Poets of Byelorussia*. Minsk, Belarus, 1973.

———. *National Poets of Byelorussia, Yanka Kupala and Yakub Kolas*. Minsk, Belarus: Vysheishaya Shkola, 1981.

Hanusiak, Michael, gen. ed. *Four Immortals*. Translated by George Sklyar. Original text edited by Lyudmyla Bruy. Kiev, Ukraine: Ukraina Society, 1980.

Kiselyov, Gennadi. "Yakub Kolas: To Mark the 100th Anniversary of the Poet's Birth." *Soviet Literature* 7 (1982): 92-96.

Kolas, Yakub. *On Life's Expanses: Poems and Prose*. Moscow: Progress Publishers, 1982.

Korotkevich, Vladimir. "Yanka Kupala: For the Centenary of the Poet's Birth." *Soviet Literature* 7 (1982): 82-87.

FLORIDA GROUP
Argentina, 1920s

The Florida Group takes its name from an upper-class street in Buenos Aires. Jorge Luis BORGES (*see* MAGIC REALISM) brought the tenets of ULTRAISM from Spain back to Argentina in 1921, where other writers in the area, including Francisco Luis Bernárdez (1900-), Eduardo González Lanuza (1900-), Norah Lange (1906-1972), Leopoldo Marechal (1900-1970), Carlos Mastronardi (1901-), and Ricardo E. Molinari (1898-1996), were attracted to the art for art's sake, avant-garde cosmopolitanism. The short-lived group wrote mostly poetry, which was published in the pages of such journals as *Prisma*, *Proa*, *Inicial*, and *Martin Fierro*. Members of the Florida Group feuded with some of the BOEDO GROUP, who insisted that literature should express social concerns. Leonídas Barletta, who was affiliated with the Boedo Group, has discussed the two groups and their differences in *Boedo y Florida: una versión distinta* (1967). Distinctions between the two groups had broken down by the revolution of 1930.

❖•❖
Further Reading

Anderson Imbert, Enrique. *Spanish-American Literature: A History*. Detroit: Wayne State University Press, 1963.

FORM REVOLUTION
Iceland, 1940s

More of a transitional phase in the development of Icelandic literature than an actual movement, the Form Revolution changed the way poets conceived their work as well as their critical evaluation of what poetry should conceptualize; these changes bridged the gap between the old, traditional literary value system and MODERNIST thinking. For over four centuries Icelandic literature had flourished; during this time its poetry had retained, for the most part, original forms of alliteration, rhyme scheme, and meter and was primarily of narrative mode and discursive content. The "revolution" and its changes, advocated by the brilliant poet Steinn Steinnar (1908-1958), called for more intense focus on individual, experiential reality, fresh experimentation with imagery, and serious concentration on the universals of a troubled century. Other devotees of such change were Gundmandur Bodvarsson (1904-1974), Einar Bragi (1921-), editor of the Modernist journal *Birtingur* (1953-68), Johannes ur Kotlum (1899-1972), Hannes Sigússon (1922-), and Jón úr Vör (1917-).

❧•❧

Further Reading

Jónsson, Erlendur. "Icelandic Literature." In *World Literature Since 1945: Critical Surveys of the Contemporary Literatures of Europe and the Americas*. New York: Ungar, 1973.

47 WORKSHOP
United States, 1905-1933

The 47 Workshop, a Harvard University dramaturgical program, played a significant role in the early development and popularization of American drama. Professor George Pierce Baker (1866-1935) founded the Workshop in 1913 in response to the burgeoning appeal of his English 47 play-writing course, which he had been teaching since 1905. The Workshop combined an emphasis on the essentials of technique and staging with an encouragement of experimentation and thus attracted aspiring playwrights from around the country. Baker's expertise and magnetic personality galvanized his students, who included Edward Sheldon (1886-1946), Sidney Howard (1891-1939), Philip Barry (1896-1949), S. N. Behrmann (1893-1973), Thomas Wolfe (1900-1938), and American EXPRESSIONIST Eugene O'NEILL.

The successful professional production of Sheldon's debut work, *Salvation Nell* (1908), brought fame to Baker's school and heightened interest in the maturation of American REALIST drama. Although other Workshop successes followed, it was not until O'Neill had departed Harvard and produced such plays as *Beyond the Horizon* (1920), *THE*

EMPEROR JONES (1920; *see* PROVINCETOWN PLAYERS), and *Anna Christie* (1921) that the value of Baker's tutelage became fully apparent. Not only did he help refine the apprentice stagecraft of O'Neill and other talented students, he also inspired innovations in design and direction, while contributing enormously to the spread of similar comprehensive theatrical programs across the nation, including Frederick Henry Koch's (1877-1944) influential dramatic school, the CAROLINA PLAYMAKERS. In 1925 Baker transferred the 47 Workshop to Yale University, where it flourished until his retirement in 1933. Among the many commemorative portrayals of Baker by his students is Wolfe's fictional character Professor Hatcher, who appears in the novel *Of Time and the River* (1935).

❖•❖

Further Reading

Clark, Barrett, John Mason Brown, et al. *George Pierce Baker: A Memorial*. New York: Dramatists Play Service, 1939.
Kinne, Wisner Payne. *George Pierce Baker and the American Theatre*. Cambridge, Mass.: Harvard University Press, 1954.

FORUM GROUP
Netherlands, 1930s

Founded in 1931 by Menno ter Braak (1902-1940), *Forum* gathered some of the period's most accomplished Dutch writers. In addition to Braak, who was esteemed for his sharp and insightful criticism, other writers associated with the journal included Charles Edgar du Perron (1899-1940), Maurice Roclants (1895-1966), Jan Jacob Slauerhoff (1898-1936), and Simon Vestdijk (1898-1971), a MODERNIST whose artistic accomplishments, despite his minor international reputation, have been compared to those of James JOYCE (*see* Modernism, England and Ireland) and Franz KAFKA (*see* Modernism, Austria and Germany). Although the *Forum* writers espoused no single platform of activity, they generally shared an acute awareness of Europe's growing social ills.

❖•❖

Further Reading

Beekman, E. M. *The Verbal Empires of Simon Vestdijk and James Joyce*. Amsterdam: Rodopi, 1983.
———. "The Critic and Existence: An Introduction to Menno Ter Braak." *Contemporary Literature* 9 (1968): 377-93.
———. "Gentleman of Sadness: Simon Vestdijk as Poet." *Books Abroad* 49 (1975): 475-79.
———. "History and Myth: Simon Vestdijk's Historical Fiction." *Review of National Literatures* 8 (1977): 108-36.

Bulhof, Francis. "Slauerhoff's Camoes Novel *Het Verboden Rijk.*" *Texas Quarterly* 15, 4 (1972): 39-46.

⸻. "Introduction." In *Country of Origin* by Charles Edgar du Perron. Translated by Elizabeth Daverman and Francis Bulhof. Edited by E. M. Beekman. Amherst, Mass.: University of Massachusetts Press, 1984.

Duytschaever, Joris. "James Joyce's Impact on Simon Vestdijk's Early Fiction." *Dutch Studies* 2 (1976): 48-74.

Michielsen, John. "Coming to Terms with the Past and Searching for an Identity: The Treatment of the Occupied Netherlands in the Fictions of Hermans, Mulisch and Vestdijk." *Canadian Journal of Netherlandic Studies* 7, 1-2 (1986): 62-68.

FOUR HORSEMEN
Canada, 1970s

In somewhat the same innovative tradition of the earlier Liverpool Poets and some of the ideas put forth by the JAZZ POETRY group, the Four Horsemen use their voices as instruments in poetic readings of "sound poetry," stressing more the sound of poetic language itself rather than the meaning of its words. The group members include Rafael Barreto-Rivera (1944-), Paul Dutton (1934-), Steven McCaffery (n.d.), as well as B[arrie] P[hillip] Nichol (1944-), who also used techniques associated with CONCRETE POETRY. Their improvisations are much the same as those of jazz musicians, but the common device is the use of a repetition of words (instead of musical themes or figures), specific, rhythmic vocal inflection, and verbal counterpoint in order to emphasize the physical, tonal qualities of language. This all provides a "celebration of pure vocal sound" which is inventive and which reinforces the desire of these poets to allow readers of poetry the extra dimension of listening to poetic language for itself alone. "Sound poetry" is often abstract and lacking in subject matter; here the concentration is solely upon a lively and aesthetic concern for language as its own medium. The Four Horsemen have made recordings of their work to augment their public performances. These include *CaNADAda* (1973), *Live in the West* (1977), *Schedule for Another Place* (1981) and *The Prose Tattoo* (1982). Each member has also published written work.

❖•❖

Further Reading

Barbour, Douglas. *BpNichol and His Works.* In *Canadian Writers and Their Works.* Edited by Robert Lecker, Jack David, and Ellen Quigley. Toronto: ECW, 1992.

Clark, David L. "Monstrosity, Illegibility, Denegation: De Man, Nichol, and the Resistance to Postmodernism." In *Negation, Critical Theory, and Postmodern Textuality.* Edited by Daniel Fischlin. Dordrecht, Netherlands: Kluwer Academy, 1994.

Harvey, Roderick W. "BpNichol: The Repositioning of Language." *Essays on Canadian Writing* 4 (1976): 19-33.

Henderson, Brian. "New Syntaxes in McCaffery and Nichol: Emptiness, Transformation, Serenity." *Essays on Canadian Writing* 37 (spring 1989): 1-29.

Miki, Roy, ed. *Tracing the Paths: Reading ≠ Writing The Martyrology*. Vancouver, Canada: Talon Books, 1988.

Nichol, B. P. *Doors to Oz & Other Landscapes*. Toronto: Ganglia Press, 1979.

————. *Selected Organs: Parts of an Autobiography*. Windsor, Canada: Black Moss Press, 1988.

Niechoda, Irene. *A Sourcery for Books 1 and 2 of bpNichol's "The Martyrology."* Toronto: ECW, 1992.

Norris, Ken. "Interview with bp Nichol." *Essays on Canadian Writing* 12 (1978): 243-50.

Perloff, Marjorie. "Signs Are Taken for Wonders: On Steve McCaffery's 'Lag'." In *Contemporary Poetry Meets Modern Theory*. Edited by Antony Easthope and John O. Thompson. Toronto: University of Toronto Press, 1991.

Scobie, Stephen. *BP Nichol: What History Teaches*. Vancouver, Canada: Talonbooks, 1984.

FOUR WINDS MOVEMENT (Keturi Vejai)
Lithuania, 1920s

Led by Kazys Binkis (1893-1932), the Four Winds Movement reflected both FUTURIS-TIC and EXPRESSIONISTIC trends in its poetry but is said to have failed due to the simplistic, lyrical quality of Binkis's work. Other writers associated with the movement included Juozas Petrenas-Tarulis (1896-1980) and Teofilis Tilvytis (1904-1969).

✦•✦

Further Reading

Lankutis, Jonas. *Panorama of Soviet Lithuanian Literature*. Vilnius: Vaga, 1975.

Lituanian Literature. Vilnius: Vaga, 1997.

FRANKFURT SCHOOL. *See* MARXIST CRITICISM

FREE ACADEMY OF PROLETARIAN LITERATURE (Vaplite)
Ukraine, 1925-1929

A short-lived Ukrainian movement, the Free Academy of Proletarian Literature was active during the latter half of the 1920s. Under leader Mykola Khvylovy (1893-1933), the Free Academy, despite a proclivity towards nationalism and Communism, stressed the need for writers to incorporate Western literature and ideas into their work. The downfall of the Free Academy coincided with Joseph Stalin's dictatorial rise to power in 1929. Other key figures of the movement include Oles Dosvitny (1891-1934), Mykola

Kulish (1892-1937), Oleska Slisarenka (1891-1937), Yury Smolych (1900-1976), Yury Yanovsky (1902-1954), and Mayk Yohansen (1895-1937).

⤈•⤇

Further Reading

Ferguson, Dolly Mary. "Lyricism in the Early Creative Prose of Mykola Khvylovy." *Dissertation Abstracts International* 39 (1978): 2254A-55A.

Pikulyk, Romana B. "The Expressionist Experiment in 'Berezil': Kurbas and Kulish." *Canadian Slavonic Papers* 14 (1972): 324-44.

Revutsky, Valerian. "Mykola Kulish in the Modern Ukrainian Theatre." *Slavonic and East European Review* 49 (1971): 355-64.

Shkandrij, Myroslav. "Irony in the Works of Mykola Khvylovy." *Journal of Ukrainian Studies* 14, 1-2 (summer-winter 1989): 90-102.

Slavutyc, J. "Kulish, Mykola: Sonata Pathetique." *Canadian Modern Language Review* 33 (1977): 565-66.

Stech, Marko Robert. "The Dramaturgy of Mykola Kulish: The Disintegration of a Dream of a New Life." *Dissertation Abstracts International* 53, 12 (June 1993): 4346A-47A.

Struk, Danylo. "Tupyk or Blind Alley: Valdshnepy of M. Khvylovyi." *Canadian Slavic Studies* 2 (1968): 239-51.

FREE STAGE. *See* **FREIE BÜHNE**

FREE THEATER. *See* **THÉÂTRE LIBRE**

FREIE BÜHNE
Germany, 1889-1894

A combination of factors that included the international rise of NATURALISM in the 1880s, the influence of André Antoine's (1858-1943) work at the THÉÂTRE LIBRE, and an interest in staging censorship-free drama in Germany led to the creation of the Freie Bühne (Free Stage) in 1889 in Berlin. The essential dramatic elements of the plays championed by the Freie Bühne included the reliance on plots revolving around basic family situations, a natural mode of speech that also included dialect, and an aversion to artificial plot devices. Although the Freie Bühne was in existence only five years, its emphasis on a realistic approach to experience helped influence the adherents of Impressionism and EXPRESSIONISM.

Otto Brahm (1856-1912), perhaps Germany's most important drama critic at the time, led a committee of nine that founded the Freie Bühne in 1889. The enterprise was created as a private company whose audience was considered its shareholders. This structure allowed the Freie Bühne to avoid the censorship laws that plagued the public theater companies and offer as its first production the otherwise banned *Gengangere* (1881; *Ghosts,* 1889) by Henrik IBSEN (*see* REALISM, Norway) on September 29, 1889. The choice of this play as the Freie Bühne's premiere was significant. Ibsen's Naturalistic style had a profound influence on both Brahm and Gerhart HAUPTMANN, who would go on to become the major German dramatist of his time and a Nobel Prize winner in 1912. In fact, Hauptmann attended the first German production of *Gengangere* in 1887, when the play sparked such violent reaction among the audience that police had prohibited any further public performances.

The second play performed by the Freie Bühne was Hauptmann's VOR SONNENAUFGANG (1889; *Before Dawn,* 1909), which premiered on October 20, 1889. It was this Realistic depiction of peasant life that began to bring public attention to the theater's principles and brought Hauptmann his first national acclaim. Hauptmann's *Die Weber* (1892; *The Weavers,* 1899) also premiered there. In addition to plays by Hauptmann and Ibsen, other notable Freie Bühne productions included dramas by Leo TOLSTOY (*see* Realism, Russia), August STRINDBERG (*see* Expressionism, Germany), and Émile ZOLA (*see* NATURALISM, France). The success of the Freie Bühne is evidenced by the fact that some 700 subscribers existed by 1890. The theater had also begun publishing its own magazine by this time, *Freie Bühne für modernes Lebe* (Free Theater for Modern Life), which was devoted to promulgating the theater's tenets. In 1894, amidst belief that its productions had led Germany's larger, more mainstream theaters to begin producing Naturalistic plays, the Freie Bühne disbanded. Its influence persisted though, as Brahm went on to join the DEUTSCHES THEATER, where he continued the Freie Bühne's work in establishing a tradition of modern German drama.

❖•❖

Hauptmann, Gerhart (1862-1946)
German playwright, poet, and novelist.

Hauptmann, often considered the father of modern German drama, began his career as a playwright when his first effort, *Vor Sonnenaufgang* (1889; *Before Dawn,* 1909), was produced for the Freie Bühne. Strongly influenced by Ibsen and fellow German playwright Arno Holz (1863-1929), an early proponent of German Naturalism, Hauptmann's early plays helped establish Naturalism as a viable mode of expression on the German stage. By the time the Freie Bühne disbanded, however, Hauptmann had begun to turn away from strictly Naturalist dramas and his later works were often devoid of Naturalistic elements entirely. He was awarded the Nobel Prize for Literature in 1912.

Vor Sonnenaufgang (1889; *Before Dawn,* 1909).

This play, Hauptmann's first, was also the first German-written drama produced by the Freie Bühne. Set in a rural community whose characters are often wracked by alcoholism and hereditary disease, the play concerns the actions of the idealistic reformer Alfred Loth. Loth begins a relationship with Helene, but betrays her when he learns she is "tainted" by the same problems that affect her family. Despite Loth's idealism, he sees no escape from what he perceives to be the inevitable effects of heredity. Although perhaps not as artistically accomplished as Hauptmann's later works, *Vor Sonnenaufgang* is notable for its pioneering use of harsh and jarring elements that disrupted the complacency of European theater during this time.

❖•❖

Further Reading

Claus, Horst. *The Theatre Director Otto Brahm.* Ann Arbor, Mich.: UMI Research Press, 1981.

Heller, Otto. *Studies in Modern German Literature: Sudermann, Hauptmann, Women Writers of the Nineteenth Century.* Boston: Ginn & Company, 1905.

Holl, K. *Gerhart Hauptmann: His Life and His Work, 1862-1912.* 1913. Reprint, Freeport, N.Y.: Books for Libraries Press, 1972.

Klenze, Camillo von. *From Goethe to Hauptmann: Studies in a Changing Culture.* New York: The Viking Press, 1926. Reprint, New York: Biblo and Tannen, 1966.

Lohner, Edgar, and Hunter G. Hannum, eds. *Modern German Drama.* Boston: Houghton Mifflin, 1966.

Newmark, Maxim. *Otto Brahm: The Man and the Critic.* New York: G. E. Stechert & Co., 1938.

FREUD, Sigmund (1856-1939)
Austrian neuropsychologist, essayist, critic, and autobiographer

As the founder of psychoanalysis and one of the earliest theoreticians to convincingly explain the unconscious mind, Freud has had a profound impact on twentieth-century culture. His writings have not only helped to shape the tenets of modern psychology, sociology, and philosophy but have widely inspired, if not imbued, countless works of art, literature, and literary criticism. Consequently, he is often viewed as the most influential intellectual of his age. Many, however, argue that Freud and his followers only popularized, rather than revolutionized, contemporary thinking regarding the mind's processes. Freud himself, who possessed a remarkable familiarity with English, European, and Classical literature, acknowledged the enormous insights into human motivation that creative, non-scientific writers since the time of Sophocles have contributed to society's self-understanding. His best-known works, in fact, feature frequent literary references in order to undergird his practically researched and applied theories. Nonetheless, Freud must be regarded as a seminal figure, one who intensified interest in the psychological novel, the dream states of SURREALISM, and STREAM-OF-CON-SCIOUSNESS (*see* MODERNISM, England and Ireland) writing; one whose deep understanding of the isolated, irreligious individual was concurrent with that found in GEORGIAN and Modernist literature; and one whose own, highly praised writing gave rise to an entire school of criticism which was still prevalent at the end of the twentieth century.

Following a distinguished early career in neuropathology and cerebral anatomy, a period when microscopic research of and physiological explanations for unusual phenomena absorbed him, Freud turned to the clinical treatment of hysteria and various neuroses, an area in which one of his chief mentors, Jean Martin Charcot (1825-1893), had made substantial advances. He established his practice in Vienna with physician and close friend Josef Breuer (1842-1925), who had been incorporating hypnotism into treatment of hysterics. Although the two made significant strides during the 1880s in exposing and counteracting cases of repression that led to hysteria, they eventually realized that hypnosis alone was an insufficient medical solution. Freud's pursuit of the technique of free, conscious, association of thoughts and images by the patient, and his conviction that sexuality lay at the root of most of his patients' cases, led to a break between the two men and the birth of psychoanalysis, a term which Freud coined in 1896.

About this time Freud had become occupied with the study and interpretation of dreams, a previously chartered but only marginally understood branch of psychology. His extensive analyses of both his own and his patients' dreams, supported by the technique of free association, resulted in what he in later years considered his most valuable work, *DIE TRAUMDEUTUNG* (1900; *The Interpretation of Dreams*, 1913). Freud's frank observations on human sexuality and his singular pronouncement that the mind's principal energy source, libido, was a raw, pleasure-seeking force, earmarked this and subsequent works as inherently reprehensible to some and controversial to many. Nonetheless, a number of other psychologists soon gathered around Freud to discuss, test, and expand his monumental theories. Included in the group, which began meeting in 1902 at Freud's home, were Alfred Adler (1870-1937), Otto Rank (1884-1939), Ernest Jones (1879-1958), Sandor Ferenczi (1873-1933), and Carl Gustav JUNG. The decade became an important one for the growth of psychoanalysis: in 1908 the first international congress of the Vienna Psychoanalytic Society was held and, in 1909, Freud and Jung, at the invitation of American psychologist G. Stanley Hall (1844-1924), journeyed to Clark University in Worcester, Massachusetts, to deliver a series of lectures. The success of the trip prompted Freud to publish *Über Psychoanalyse* (1910; *The Origin and Development of Psychoanalysis*, 1949), a collection of his lectures which would make his work intelligible to an even wider public, the following year.

During this time, and throughout his later career, Freud endeavored to construct a complete system of the mind which would have relevance not only to psychiatric professionals and the mentally disturbed but the entire human race. Such works as *Zur Psychopathologie des Alltagslebens* (1904; *The Psychopathology of Everyday Life*, 1914), *Der Witz und Seine Beziehung zum Unbewussten* (1905; *Wit and Its Relation to the Unconscious*, 1916), *Drei Abhandlungen zur Sexualtheorie* (1905; *Three Contributions to the Theory of Sexuality*, 1910), and *Jenseits des Lustprinzips* (1920; *Beyond the Pleasure Principle*, 1922) greatly furthered this ambition. By the early 1920s Freud had refined in a series of revised editions many of his original conceptions regarding sexuality and the unconscious. Ultimately, he postulated the existence of a tripartite human psyche while reaffirming his belief that the early stages of psychosexual development were of utmost importance to adult personality.

It was this, more than any other contention, that resulted a decade earlier in the rupture of relations between him and his two most famous followers, Adler and Jung. Although criticized for its speculative foundation, *Das Ich und das Es* (1923; *The Ego and the Id*, 1927), represented the capstone of Freud's psychological thought. In this work he traced the nonphysiological geography of the mind, discovering a complex interrelationship between the countervailing tendencies of the ego (the conscious, mediative component of behavior), the id (the unconscious reservoir of libido, which seeks to gratify its instinctual impulses), and the superego (the unconscious, morally superior portion of the ego which censors unreasonable demands of the id). This work led to a major division of specialization among psychoanalysts. One, upheld by Freud's daughter Anna (1895-1982) and prominent in the United States, is known as ego-psychology. The other, first defined by Karl Abraham (1877-1925) and popular in Britain, is termed object-relations theory. Perhaps most significant to literary theory, however, is a third school, begun by French psychoanalyst Jacques LACAN (*see* FREUDIAN CRITICISM). Lacanian literary scholars, much like the NEW CRITICS before them, have concentrated on the centrality of language and the importance of textual peculiarities to overall meaning. Although other psychological schools have refuted, dismissed, or undervalued Freud's speculations, the most salient features of his work still ingrain themselves in the public consciousness and the literary imagination.

Freud's impact on literature, certainly, has been the subject of considerable study. This is due to a variety of factors, but perhaps especially to Freud's own fascination with literary subject matter, the concept of creativity, and the psychology of character types. Numbering among the writers whose works he analyzed are Homer (c. 8th cent. B.C.), Sophocles (c. 496-406 B.C.), François Rabelais (c. 1494-1553), Shakespeare (1564-1616), Heinrich Heine (1797-1856), Johan Wolfgang von Goethe (1749-1832), Henrik

IBSEN (*see* REALISM, Norway), and Fyodor DOSTOEVSKY (*see* REALISM, Russia). His admiration of such writers was great, for he saw in them the capacity to delve deeply into the unconscious mind and expose the sublimations and symbols, the hidden mechanisms of personality, which contribute to the unending drama of human life. Despite his sympathetic stance, contemporary reception by writers of Freud's critical and theoretical work was as varied as that of the psychological profession. Some, such as James JOYCE, D. H. LAWRENCE (*see* MODERNISM, England and Ireland), and Franz KAFKA (*see* MODERNISM, Austria and Germany), expressed disapproval of his sovereign pronouncements while borrowing extensively from his vocabulary and insights. Others, including Virginia WOOLF (*see* MODERNISM, England and Ireland), André BRETON (*see* SURREALISM), Italo SVEVO (*see* MODERNISM, Italy), and Eugene O'NEILL (*see* MODERNISM, United States, and PROVINCETOWN PLAYERS), readily assimilated Freudianism, allowing it to shape both the form and content of some of their best work. Still others, such as W. H. Auden (1907-1973) and Thomas MANN (*see* MODERNISM, Austria and Germany), published laudatory assessments of Freud as well as literature that reflected their manifest acquaintance with Freud's thought. To be sure, Freud's influence stretches far beyond the writers mentioned and can be seen, more recently for example, in several works by English novelist D. M. Thomas (1935-).

In addition to the field of creative writing, where sexual symbolism, dream sequences, and patient-analyst encounters have become commonplace, both the fields of criticism and biography have readily accommodated the central features of Freudian psychology. Indeed, Psychoanalytic Criticism — as initiated by Freud, Rank, and Ferenczi, and made practicable by such scholars as Kenneth Burke (1897-1993), William EMPSON (*see* CAMBRIDGE GROUP), and, especially, Lionel Trilling (1905-1975) — has evolved into a vital, versatile critical school, despite tendencies by several to dilute Freud's scientific principles. Trilling, who was instrumental in clarifying Freud's views for literary intellectuals, regarded Freud's writings on society, in addition to his purely psychological works, as singularly relevant for modern times. As he writes in *Beyond Culture* (1966), "In its essence literature is concerned with self; and the particular concern of the literature of the last two centuries has been the self in its standing quarrel with culture. We cannot mention the name of any great writer of the modern period whose work has not in some way, and usually in a passionate and explicit way, insisted on this quarrel, who has not expressed the bitterness of his discontent with civilization, who has not said that the self made greater legitimate demands than any culture can hope to satisfy. This intense conviction of the existence of the self apart from culture is, as culture well knows, its noblest and most generous achievement. At the present moment it must be thought of as a liberating idea without which our developing ideal of community is bound to defeat itself. We can speak no greater praise of Freud than to say that he placed this idea at the very center of his thought." Although Freud's achievement in modern psychology may be in some sense measured, his contribution to the realms of literature and intellectual life in general remain incalculable.

Die Traumdeutung (1900; *The Interpretation of Dreams*, 1913).

Issued in 1899 but given the symbolic date of the new century, Freud's *Die Traumdeutung* is considered a masterpiece of nonfiction writing and a scientific breakthrough which, though it has suffered from pedestrian explanations as well as later, empirically tested theories of the mind, continues to fascinate the professional and lay communities alike. In this work Freud proposed that all adult dreams are composites of symbols disguising latent wishes which generally stem from childhood experiences. Furthermore, dreams readdress unsolved problems of the waking hours and these problems, in many instances, are linked to one's own sexual memory. For example, a woman who dreams of telling her husband that it is not worthwhile to tune their piano discovers through free association that the piano is a disgusting old box with bad tone and that the word "box" in turn refers to her breasts, which, finally, through their similarity in contour, refer to her buttocks and, in a larger, more meaningful sense, her lifelong dissatisfaction with her figure and bodily functions.

Freud often went to extraordinary, occasionally ingenious, lengths to solve the riddles of the dreams he confronted. Although several valid criticisms of his hypotheses and methodology have shed considerable doubt on his interpretations, Freud has nonetheless been admired for his keen attention to the role language, imagery, and myth play, both in dreaming and waking states, in providing clues to an individual's actual fears, motivations, and desires. Consequently, Freud's case histories have provided for writers a wellspring of readily adaptable, psychically rich story material. Furthermore, Freud's landmark discussion of the Oedipus complex—in which he ranges from contemporary instances of father-son hostility to Sophocles' archetypal drama *Oedipus the King* (430 B.C.) to Shakespeare's classic reformulation of the Greek tragedy in *Hamlet* (1601?)—has contributed especially to the field of literary criticism while simultaneously affecting countless aspects of twentieth-century Western culture.

Further Reading

Arlow, Jacob A. *Legacy of Sigmund Freud.* New York: International Universities Press, 1956.
Baum, R. F. *Doctors of Modernity: Darwin, Marx, & Freud.* Peru, Ill.: Sherwood Sugden, 1988.
Bloom, Harold, ed. *Sigmund Freud's "The Interpretation of Dreams."* New York: Chelsea House, 1987.

Bowie, Malcolm. *Freud, Proust and Lacan: Theory as Fiction*. Cambridge, England: Cambridge University Press, 1987.

Brivic, Sheldon. *Joyce Between Freud and Jung*. Port Washington, N.Y.: Kennikat Press, 1980.

Crews, Frederick. *Psychoanalysis and Literary Process*. Cambridge, Mass.: Winthrop Publishers, 1970.

Dolittle, Hilda. *Tribute to Freud*. 2nd ed. New York: New Directions, 1984.

Donn, Linda. *Freud and Jung: Years of Friendship, Years of Loss*. New York: Scribner, 1988.

Fraiberg, Louis. *Psychoanalysis and American Literary Criticism*. Detroit: Wayne State University Press, 1960.

————. "Freud's Writings on Art." *Literature and Psychology* VI (November 1956): 116-30.

Fromm, Erich. *Greatness and Limitations of Freud's Thought*. New York: Harper & Row, 1980.

George, Diana. *Blake and Freud*. Ithaca, N.Y.: Cornell University Press, 1980.

Green, Geoffrey. *Freud and Nabokov*. Lincoln, Nebr.: University of Nebraska Press, 1987.

Gunn, Daniel. *Psychoanalysis and Fiction: An Exploration of Literary and Psychoanalytic Borders*. Cambridge, England: Cambridge University Press, 1988.

Hoffman, Frederick J. *Freudianism and the Literary Mind*. Baton Rouge, La.: Louisiana State University Press, 1945; 2nd ed., 1957.

Jones, Ernest. *The Life and Work of Sigmund Freud*. 3 vols. New York: Basic Books, 1953-57.

Kurzweil, Edith. *The Freudians: A Comparative Perspective*. New Haven, Conn.: Yale University Press, 1989.

Lawrence, D. H. *Psychoanalysis and the Unconscious*. New York: T. Seltzer, 1921.

Levenson, Michael H. "The Private Life of a Public Forum: Freud, Fantasy, and the Novel." In *Critical Reconstructions: The Relationship of Fiction and Life*. Edited by Robert M. Polhemus and Roger B. Henkle. Stanford, Calif.: Stanford University Press, 1994.

Mahony, Patrick J. *Freud as a Writer*. New York: International Universities Press, 1982; expanded ed., New Haven, Conn.: Yale University Press, 1987.

Mann, Thomas. *Freud, Goethe, Wagner*. New York: Knopf, 1937.

Marcus, Steven. *Freud and the Culture of Psychoanalysis: Studies in the Transition from Victorian Humanism to Modernity*. Boston: Allen & Unwin, 1984.

Meisel, Perry, and Walter Kendrick, eds. *Bloomsbury/Freud: The Letters of James and Alix Strachey 1924-1925*. New York: Basic Books, 1985.

Orlando, Francesco. *Toward a Freudian Theory of Literature*. Translated by Lee Charmaine. Baltimore: Johns Hopkins University Press, 1979.

Roazen, Paul. *Freud and His Followers*. New York: Knopf, 1975.

Robinson, Paul A. *Freud and His Critics*. Berkeley, Calif.: University of California Press, 1993.

Smith, Joseph H., ed. *The Literary Freud: Mechanisms of Defense and the Poetic Will*. Psychiatry and the Humanities, vol. 4. New Haven, Conn.: Yale University Press, 1980.

Strachey, James, ed. *The Standard Edition of the Complete Psychological Works of Sigmund Freud*. 24 vols. London: Hogarth Press, 1953-74; reprint, 1986.

Tennenhouse, Leonard, ed. *The Practice of Psychoanalytic Criticism*. Detroit: Wayne State University Press, 1976.

Timpanaro, Sebastiano. *The Freudian Slip: Psychoanalysis and Textual Criticism*. London: NLB, 1976.

Trilling, Lionel. "Freud and Literature." In his *The Liberal Imagination: Essays on Literature and Society.* New York: Viking, 1950.

FREUDIAN CRITICISM
England, France, and United States, 1910s-1990s

Also termed Psychoanalytic Criticism, Freudian Criticism arose outside Sigmund FREUD's native Austria — especially in France and the United States — in part as a response to the proliferation of a new fictional form, the modern psychological novel. A somewhat amorphous term, the psychological novel was pioneered by such writers as Henry JAMES (*see* REALISM, United States), Joseph CONRAD (*see* MODERNISM, England and Ireland), and Fyodor DOSTOEVSKY (*see* REALISM, Russia) during the latter stages of the Realistic era. Yet, it was not until the height of the Modernist era, during the 1920s and 1930s, that both the psychological novel and the accompanying biographical and psychological criticism — highly investigative and speculative — took firm hold in literary circles. *DIE TRAUMDEUTUNG* (1900; *The Interpretation of Dreams*, 1913) and *Das Ich und das Es* (1923; *The Ego and the Id*, 1927), two of Freud's most influential theoretical works, largely inspired the initial directions of the critical movement. However, many would argue that such creative works as Franz KAFKA's (*see* MODERNISM, Austria and Germany) *Die Verwandlung* (1915; *The Metamorphosis*, 1936) and *DER PROZESS* (1925; *The Trial*, 1937); James Joyce's *ULYSSES* (1922); D. H. LAWRENCE's (*see* MODERNISM, England and Ireland) *SONS AND LOVERS* (1913); Marcel PROUST's (*see* MODERNISM, France) *A LA RECHERCHE DU TEMPS PERDU* (7 vols., 1913-27; *Remembrance of Things Past* (1922-32); Sherwood Anderson's (1876-1941) *Winesburg, Ohio* (1919); and much of the work of Conrad Aiken (1889-1973), Virginia WOOLF (*see* MODERNISM, England and Ireland), W. H. Auden (1907-1973), Thomas MANN (*see* MODERNISM, Austria and Germany), William FAULKNER (*see* MODERNISM, United States), and Eugene O'NEILL (*see* EXPRESSIONISM, United States, and PROVINCETOWN PLAYERS) demanded by their very complex, introspective nature a new form of criticism that would have arisen despite Freud's pioneering theories.

Widely varying in the degree to which Freud's actual theories form a part of their discourse, Freudian Criticism has developed along three lines: examination of characters, including their fears, motives, compulsions, and neuroses (i.e., Ernest Jones's [1879-1958] *Hamlet and Oedipus,* 1949, and Leslie Fiedler's [1917-] *Love and Death in the American Novel,* 1959); examination of authors, particularly their familial relations and traumatic formative experiences (i.e., Edmund Wilson's [1895-1972] *The Wound and the Bow,* 1941, and John Middleton Murry's [1899-1957] *Son of Woman: The Story of D. H. Lawrence,* 1931); and examination of readers in relation to texts, the hermeneutical process and its subjective nature (i.e., CAMBRIDGE GROUP figure William EMPSON's *SEVEN TYPES OF AMBIGUITY,* 1930, and a large number of later works among FEMINIST, MARXIST, DECONSTRUCTIONIST, and READER-RESPONSE critics). Although American Lionel Trilling (1905-1975) is often mentioned as Freud's greatest apologist, it is Frenchman Jacques LACAN, a Poststructuralist by temperament, who has most significantly shaped the content of modern psychoanalytic criticism. Other writers often mentioned in conjunction with Freudian or psychoanalytic criticism are biographers Leon Edel (1907-1997) and Frederick C. Crews (1933-) and theorists Harold Bloom (1930-), David Bleich (1940-), Geoffrey H. Hartman (1929-), Norman Holland (1927-), Susan GUBAR (*see* FEMINIST CRITICISM), Sandra GILBERT (*see* FEMINIST CRITICISM), and Juliet Mitchell (1940-). The contributions of these and others has led not only to advancements in linguistic and critical theory but also to recurrent interest in numerous important precursors of modern literature, including William Blake (1757-1827), Charles DICKENS (*see* REALISM, England), Shakespeare, Edgar Allan Poe (1809-1849), Nathaniel Hawthorne (1804-1864), and Herman Melville (1819-1891).

⤞•⤝

Lacan, Jacques (1901-1981), French psychoanalyst and essayist.

A theorist who is often mentioned in conjunction with DECONSTRUCTIONIST Jacques DERRIDA, given the two writers' shared rejection of SEMIOTICS and willfully difficult literary styles, Lacan is distinctive for his fusion of Freudian psychoanalysis and modern linguistics, hence his most important tenet: "the unconscious is structured like a language." Although Lacan was a member of the Freudian psychoanalytic movement for over two decades, his expulsion in 1959, his subsequent founding in 1964 of L'École Freudienne de Paris, and his polemical nature greatly alienated him from the Freudian mainstream. However, among such contemporary French intellectuals as Michel Foucault (1926-1984), Roland Barthes (1915-1980), Julia Kristeva (1941-), and Louis Althusser (1918-1990), Lacan and his theories have enjoyed continuous admiration and debate. Furthermore, Lacan is celebrated among several Feminist Critics for his seminal reinterpretations of Freud's sexual theories, particularly his removal of Freud's male bias. The work for which Lacan is best known is a collection of essays entitled *Écrits* (1966; *Écrits: A Selection*, 1977), including *Fonction et champ de la parole et du langage en psychanalyse* (1956; *The Language of the Self: The Function of Language in Psychoanalysis*, 1968).

See also STRUCTURALISM.

⋙•⋘

Further Reading

Archard, David. *Consciousness and the Unconscious*. La Salle, Ill.: Open Court Pub. Co., 1984.

Atkins, G. Douglas. *Geoffrey Hartman: Criticism as Answerable Style*. London: Routledge, 1990.

Boothby, Richard. *Death and Desire: Psychoanalytic Theory in Lacan's Return to Freud*. New York: Routledge, 1991.

Bowie, Malcolm. *Freud, Proust, and Lacan: Theory as Fiction*. Cambridge, England: Cambridge University Press, 1987.

————. *Psychoanalysis and the Future of Theory*. Oxford, England: Blackwell, 1993.

Boyers, Robert. *Lionel Trilling: Negative Capability and the Wisdom of Avoidance*. Columbia, Mo.: University of Missouri Press, 1977.

Bracher, Mark. *Lacan, Discourse, and Social Change: A Psychoanalytic Cultural Criticism*. Ithaca, N.Y.: Cornell University Press, 1993.

Brivic, Sheldon. *The Veil of Signs: Joyce, Lacan, and Perception*. Urbana, Ill.: University of Illinois Press, 1991.

Brome, Vincent. *Ernest Jones: Freud's Alter Ego*. New York: Norton, 1983.

Byles, Joan Montgomery. "Desire and Mythic Surmise in the Writings of Sigmund Freud." In *Eighth International Conference on Literature and Psychoanalysis*. Edited by Frederico Pereira. Lisbon, Portugal: Inst. Superior de Psicologia Aplicada, 1992.

Cain, William E., ed. *Making Feminist History: The Literary Scholarship of Sandra M. Gilbert and Susan Gubar*. New York: Garland, 1994.

Castronovo, David. *Edmund Wilson*. New York: Ungar, 1984.

Chace, William M. *Lionel Trilling: Criticism and Politics*. Stanford, Calif.: Stanford University Press, 1980.

David-Ménard, Monique. *Hysteria from Freud to Lacan: Body and Language in Psychoanalysis*. Translated by Catherine Porter. Ithaca, N.Y.: Cornell University Press, 1989.

Davis, Robert Con, ed. *The Fictional Father: Lacanian Readings of the Text*. Amherst, Mass.: University of Massachusetts Press, 1981.

De Bolla, Peter. *Harold Bloom: Towards Historical Rhetorics*. London: Routledge, 1988.

Edel, Leon. *The Modern Psychological Novel*. New York: Grove Press, 1955; 2nd ed., Gloucester, Mass.: Peter Smith, 1964.

Felman, Shoshana. *Jacques Lacan and the Adventure of Insight: Psychoanalysis in Contemporary Culture*. Cambridge, Mass.: Harvard University Press, 1987.

Fite, David. *Harold Bloom: The Rhetoric of Romantic Vision*. Amherst, Mass.: University of Massachusetts Press, 1985.

Forrester, John. *The Seductions of Psychoanalysis: Freud, Lacan, and Derrida*. Cambridge, England: Cambridge University Press, 1990.

Fraiberg, Louis. *Psychoanalysis and American Literary Criticism*. Detroit: Wayne State University Press, 1960.

Fry, Paul H. *William Empson: Prophet Against Sacrifice*. London: Routledge, 1991.

Gallop, Jane. *Reading Lacan*. Ithaca, N.Y.: Cornell University Press, 1985.

Gilman, Sander L., et al, eds. *Reading Freud's Reading*. New York: New York University Press, 1994.

Griffin, Ernest G. *John Middleton Murry*. New York: Twayne, 1969.

Groth, Janet. *Edmund Wilson: A Critic for Our Time*. Athens, Ohio: Ohio University Press, 1989.

Gunn, Daniel. *Psychoanalysis and Fiction: An Exploration of Literary and Psychoanalytic Borders*. Cambridge, England: Cambridge University Press, 1988.

Hoffman, Frederick J. *Freudianism and the Literary Mind*. Baton Rouge, La.: Louisiana State University Press, 1945; 2nd ed., 1957.

Hogan, Patrick Colm, and Lalita Pandit, eds. *Criticism and Lacan: Essays and Dialogue on Language, Structure, and the Unconscious*. Athens, Ga.: University of Georgia Press, 1990.

Johnson, Barbara. "The Frame of Reference: Poe, Lacan, Derrida." *Yale French Studies* 55/56 (1977): 457-505.

Lacan, Jacques. *Écrits/A Selection*. New York: Norton, 1977.

————. *Freud's Papers on Technique, 1953-1954*. New York: Norton, 1988.

Lee, Jonathan Scott. *Jacques Lacan*. Boston: Twayne, 1990.

Lemaire, Anika. *Jacques Lacan*. London: Routledge & Kegan Paul, 1977.

Lupton, Julia Reinhard, and Kenneth Reinhard. *After Oedipus: Shakespeare in Psychoanalysis*. Ithaca, N.Y.: Cornell University Press, 1993.

MacCannell, Juliet Flower. *Figuring Lacan: Criticism and the Cultural Unconscious*. Lincoln, Nebr.: University of Nebraska Press, 1986.

Malin, Irving, ed. *Psychoanalysis and American Fiction*. New York: Dutton, 1965.

Mellard, James M. *Using Lacan, Reading Fiction*. Urbana, Ill.: University of Illinois Press, 1991.

Muller, John P., and William J. Richardson. *Lacan and Language: A Reader's Guide to "Écrits."* New York: International Universities Press, 1982.

Muller, John P., and William J. Richardson, eds. *The Purloined Poe: Lacan, Derrida & Psychoanalytic Reading*. Baltimore: Johns Hopkins University Press, 1988.

Norris, Christopher. *William Empson and the Philosophy of Literary Criticism*. London: Athlone Press, 1978.

Norris, Christopher and Nigel Mapp, eds. *William Empson: The Critical Achievement*. Cambridge: Cambridge University Press, 1993.

O'Hara, Daniel T. *Lionel Trilling: The Work of Liberation*. Madison, Wis.: University of Wisconsin Press, 1988.

Orlando, Francesco. *Toward a Freudian Theory of Literature*. Baltimore: Johns Hopkins University Press, 1979.

Porter, Laurence M. "Real Dreams, Literary Dreams, and the Fantastic in Literature." In *The Dream and the Text: Essays on Literature and Language*. Edited by Carol Schreier Rupprecht. Albany, N.Y.: State University of New York Press, 1993.

Powers, Lyall H. *Leon Edel and Literary Art*. Ann Arbor, Mich.: UMI Research Press, 1988.

Ragland-Sullivan, Ellie. *Essays on the Pleasures of Death: From Freud to Lacan*. New York: Routledge, 1995.

Roazen, Paul. *Freud and His Followers*. New York: Knopf, 1975.

Roudinesco, Elisabeth. *Jacques Lacan & Co.: A History of Psychoanalysis in France, 1925-1985*. Translated with a foreword by Jeffrey Mehlman. Chicago: University of Chicago Press, 1990.

Samuels, Robert. *Between Philosophy & Psychoanalysis: Lacan's Reconstruction of Freud*. New York: Routledge, 1993.

Schneiderman, Stuart, ed. *Returning to Freud: Clinical Psychoanalysis in the School of Lacan*. New Haven, Conn.: Yale University Press, 1980.

Shoben, Edward Joseph. *Lionel Trilling*. New York: Ungar, 1981.

Smith, Joseph H. *Arguing with Lacan: Ego Psychology and Language*. New Haven, Conn.: Yale University Press, 1991.

Smith, Joseph H., and William Kerrigan, eds. *Interpreting Lacan*. New Haven, Conn.: Yale University Press, 1983.

Stoltzfus, Ben. *Lacan and Literature: Purloined Pretexts*. Albany, N.Y.: State University of New York Press, 1996.

Tennenhouse, Leonard, ed. *The Practice of Psychoanalytic Criticism*. Detroit: Wayne State University Press, 1976.

Timpanaro, Sebastiano. *The Freudian Slip: Psychoanalysis and Textual Criticism*. London: NLB, 1976.

Trilling, Lionel. "Freud and Literature." In his *The Liberal Imagination*. New York: Viking, 1950.

Wain, John, ed. *Edmund Wilson: The Man and His Work*. New York: New York University Press, 1978.

Walton, Priscilla L. *Patriarchal Desire and Victorian Discourse: A Lacanian Reading of Anthony Trollope's Palliser Novels*. Toronto: University of Toronto Press, 1995.

Winchell, Mark Royden. *Leslie Fiedler*. Boston: Twayne, 1985.

Zizek, Slavoj, ed. *Everything You Always Wanted to Know About Lacan (But Were Afraid to Ask Hitchcock)*. London: Verso, 1992.

FRINGE THEATER
England, Scotland, and United States, 1960s

Inspired by Julian Beck's (1925-1985) LIVING THEATER, Fringe Theater, or Alternative Theater, arose in Edinburgh, London, and New York during the 1960s through the work of numerous small acting companies critical of both commercial theater and of Western society at large. Beginning with Jim Haynes's (1933-) Traverse Theatre Club, the first British company to produce works by THEATER OF PANIC leader Fernando Arrabal (1932-), Fringe Theater grew to encompass dozens of independent drama groups and ideological platforms. Although Fringe Theater is most often linked with left-wing, AGITPROP productions, the movement was virtually limitless in the subjects it addressed, among them the Black power movement, gay rights, women's issues, and the oppression of Jews. Much of the staging of Fringe Theater work, typically minimalist and shock-laden, was inspired by earlier dramatic experiments within EXPRESSIONISM, the THEATER OF CRUELTY, and the THEATER OF THE ABSURD as well as by the general tenor of the ANGRY YOUNG MEN movement of the 1950s. The list of Fringe exponents and practitioners is large and includes Charles Marowitz (1934-), Ed Berman (1941-), John McGrath (1935-), Peter Brook (1925-), Thelma Holt (n.d.), David Halliwell (1936-), Naftali Yavin (1936-1972), Pip Simmons (n.d.), Nancy Meckler (n.d.), Frank Cousins (n.d.), David Hare (1947-), Tony Bicat (1945-), Howard Brenton (1931-), Snoo Wilson (1948-), Malcolm Griffith (n.d.), Trevor Griffiths (1935-), Caryl Churchill (1938-), and Susan Todd (1942-). Among the more notable Fringe groups were McGrath's 7:84 troupe, Marowitz's Open Space, Simmons's Pip Simmons Group, and Bicat and Hare's Portable Theatre. Of incalculable importance to the flourishing of Fringe Theater are the seminal experiments of Jerzy Grotowski (1933-) and his THEATER LABORATORY and Joan Littlewood (1914-) and her THEATER WORKSHOP.

❧•❦

Further Reading

Ansorge, Peter. *Disrupting the Spectacle: Five Years of Experimental and Fringe Theater in Britain*. London: Pitman, 1975.

Bertolini, John A. "Fringe and Alternative Theater in Great Britain." In *Dictionary of Literary Biography*. Vol. 13, *British Dramatists Since World War II*. Detroit: Gale Research, 1982.

Boon, Richard. *Brenton, the Playwright*. London: Methuen Drama, 1991.

Bull, John. *New British Political Dramatists*. New York: Grove Press, 1984.

Chambers, Colin, and Mike Prior. *Playwrights' Progress: Patterns of Postwar British Drama*. Oxford, England: Amber Lane Press, 1987.

Craig, Sandy, ed. *Dreams and Deconstructions: Alternative Theatre in Britain*. Ambergate, Derbyshire, England: Amber Lane Press, 1980.

Dean, Joan Fitzpatrick. *David Hare*. Boston: Twayne, 1990.

Elsom, John. *Post-War British Theatre*. London: Routledge & Kegan Paul, 1976.

Hayman, Ronald. "The Politics of Hatred." In his *British Theatre Since 1955: A Reassessment*. Oxford, England; New York: Oxford University Press, 1979.

Homden, Carol. *The Plays of David Hare*. Cambridge, England: Cambridge University Press, 1995.

Hunt, Albert, and Geoffrey Reeves. *Peter Brook*. Cambridge, England: Cambridge University Press, 1995.

Itzin, Catherine. *Stages in the Revolution: Political Theatre in Britain Since 1968*. London: Eyre Methuen, 1980.

Jones, David Richard. *Great Directors at Work: Stanislavsky, Brecht, Kazan, Brook.* Berkeley, Calif.: University of California Press, 1986.

Keyes, Mary Quealy Antin. *The Influence of Public Taste on the Experimental Theatre as Illustrated at the Traverse Theatre, 1964-1966.* Master's thesis, Tulane University, 1972.

Kritzer, Amelia Howe. *The Plays of Caryl Churchill: Theatre of Empowerment.* New York: St. Martin's Press, 1991.

Lambert, J. W. *Drama in Britain, 1964-1973.* Harlow, England: Longman, 1974.

Marowitz, Charles. *Burnt Bridges: A Souvenir of the Swinging Sixties and Beyond.* London: Hodder & Stoughton, 1990.

Marowitz, Charles, comp. *The Encore Reader: A Chronicle of the New Drama.* Edited by Charles Marowitz, Tom Milne, and Owen Hale. London: Methuen, 1965.

Mitchell, Tony. *File on Brenton.* London: Methuen, 1988.

Pepper, Kaija. "Review of the Vancouver Fringe Theater Festival at Various Sites, Sept. 7-17, 1995." *Dance International* 23, 3 (fall 1995): 36-37.

Phillips, Levi Damon. *Joint Stock Theatre Group Archives.* Davis, Calif.: Dept. of Special Collections, University Library, University of California at Davis, 1993.

Randall, Phyllis R. *Caryl Churchill: A Casebook.* New York: Garland, 1989.

Roberts, Peter. *Theatre in Britain: A Playgoer's Guide.* 2nd ed. London: Pitman, 1975.

Roose-Evans, James. *Experimental Theatre from Stanislavsky to Peter Brook.* New York: Universe Books, 1984.

Wiles, Timothy J. *The Theater Event: Modern Theories of Performance.* Chicago: University of Chicago Press, 1980.

Williams, David. *Peter Brook: A Theatrical Casebook.* London: Methuen, 1988.

Wilson, Ann, ed. *Howard Brenton: A Casebook.* New York: Garland, 1992.

Wynne-Davies, Marion, ed. "Developments in Modern Drama: 1956 and All That." In her *Prentice Hall Guide to English Literature: The New Authority on English Literature.* New York: Prentice Hall, 1990.

Zeifman, Hersh. *David Hare: A Casebook.* New York: Garland, 1994.

FUGITIVES/AGRARIANS
United States, 1920s-1930s

Organized as literary and social movements in the twenties and made up primarily of students and poets at Vanderbilt University, these two closely related groups of Southern writers saw themselves as fugitives in their disapproval of a society dominated by a Northern, urban-industrial complex and its dehumanization of the quality of American life, and as agrarians, in their adherence to the concepts of a passionate love of the land and an environment characterized by a rural domesticity based in the Christian-humanist value system. From 1922 until 1925, the official organ of the first group to be formed, *The Fugitives,* coedited by John Crowe RANSOM and Allen Tate (1899-1979), was devoted exclusively to poetry and criticism which manifested their views. Later publications by Ransom, Tate, Robert Penn Warren (1905-1989), and Donald Davidson (1893-1968), the core founders of the Agrarians—*Fugitive: An Anthology of Verse* (1928), *I'll Take My Stand* (1930), *Culture in the South* (1934), and *Who Owns America?* (1936), as well as the journals *Southern Review* (1935-42) and *Kenyon Review* (1939-70, 1979-)—reiterate their reactionary stance and heighten identification among the reading public with Southern regionalist literature.

The Fugitives were reacting to a socioeconomic system over which they had had little control, for while most other regions of the nation had maintained some economic solvency after the Civil War, the South had never completely recovered from it; thus, by the time of the Great Depression, it was still struggling to retain its cultural values in the face of poverty and social and political unrest. It is interesting, as one critic notes, and more than coincidental that two major novels about Southern life appeared during the peak of Fugitive/Agrarian literary activity—William FAULKNER's *THE SOUND AND THE FURY* (1929; *see* MODERNISM, United States) and Thomas Wolfe's (1900-1938) *Look Homeward, Angel* (1929)—each containing elements of the alienation, fragmentation, and the hopelessness which were the result of loss of generation and of dignity.

Aside from those mentioned, other writers affiliated with the movements—either directly or tacitly through their works—included Sherwood Anderson (1876-1941), John Gould Fletcher (1886-1950), Laura Riding Jackson (1901-1990), Andrew Nelson Lytle (1902-), Ridley Wills (1871-1949), C. W. Pipkin (n.d.), Stark Young (1881-1963), and Merrill Moore (1903-1957), a poet and psychiatrist whose *Poems from the Fugitive* (1936) exemplify the mindset of the group.

Ransom, Tate, and Warren had all been influenced, as young poets, not only by the MODERNIST verse of T. S. ELIOT but also by his early essay "Tradition and the Individual Talent" (1919), in which he discusses the value of the examination of "models, standards, aims, and procedures" from the literary traditions of the past, despite his reputation as one of the greatest Modernists of his time; the mature work of the three Fugitives shows strong evidence of Eliotic criticism and poetic technique. When the Fugitive/Agrarian movement faded, certain of its writers made a particular mark on the later literary scene. Warren's collaboration with NEW CRITIC Cleanth Brooks (1906-1994) in the now classic college texts *Understanding Poetry* (1938) and *Understanding Fiction* (1943) provided students and scholars with a methodology for close attention to the work itself. With this, a new theory of literature was born and later given its name in Ransom's *The New Criticism* (1941), after which time American literature and literary theory took on a radically new dimension, one which would exert a powerful influence on the literary orthodoxy not only in America but abroad for several decades.

❖•❖

Ransom, John Crowe (1888-1974), American critic, editor, and poet.

Ransom was an active supporter of the Southern Agrarians during his long tenure, from 1914 to 1937, at the English department of Vanderbilt University. During the latter half of his teaching career, from 1937 until 1958 at Kenyon College, he founded and edited the prestigious journal the *Kenyon Review*. His profound interest in the work of Eliot, Ezra POUND (*see* MODERNISM, England and Ireland), and those who saw modern English poetry as grounded in the work and views of the seventeenth-century Metaphysical poets put Ransom at the center of a new theory of the construct and the examination of poetry which was developed by the New Critics and whose manifesto insisted upon the careful and close reading of a piece of text as its own entity, to be interpolated without regard for any biographical, cultural, or social agenda as a measure of its integrity. His work as a New Critic placed Ransom in the forefront of one of the most important twentieth-century literary movements developed in the field of literature. Noteworthy essays are *God Without Thunder* (1930); "Criticism as Pure Speculation" in *The Intent of the Critic,* edited by D. A. Stauffer (1941); "The Inorganic Muse" in *Kenyon Review* 5 (1943); "Poetry: The Formal Analysis" and "Poetry: The Final Cause" in *Kenyon Review* 9 (1947); and *Poems and Essays* (1955). Volumes of poetry include *Poems About God* (1919), *Grace After Meat* (1924); *Two Gentlemen in Bonds* (1927); and *Selected Poems* (1945). The moving force in much of his poetry is in his mastery of irony used to present the dilemma of "human limitations" in an environment "torn between reason and imagination, between science and faith." His reputation remains as an outstanding critic and poet whose work is "remarkably integrated and mature."

❖•❖

Further Reading

Bradbury, John M. *The Fugitives*. Chapel Hill, N.C.: University of North Carolina Press, 1958.

Cecil, Lord David, and Allen Tate, eds. *Modern Verse in English, 1900-1950*. New York: Macmillan, 1958.

Conkin, Paul Keith. *The Southern Agrarians*. Knoxville, Tenn.: University of Tennessee Press, 1988.

Connelly, Thomas L., et al. *A Southern Renascence Man: Views of Robert Penn Warren*. Baton Rouge, La.: Louisiana State University Press, 1984.

Cowan, Louise. *The Fugitive Group: A Literary History*. Baton Rouge, La.: Louisiana State University Press, 1959.

Curry, W. C., Donald Davidson, J. C. Ransom, et al. *The Fugitive*. Nashville, Tenn.: The Fugitives, 1922-25.

Cutrer, Thomas W. *Parnassus on the Mississippi: The "Southern Review" and the Baton Rouge Literary Community, 1935-1942*. Baton Rouge, La.: Louisiana State University Press, 1984.

Davidson, Donald. *Southern Writers in the Modern World*. Athens, Ga.: University of Georgia Press, 1958.

————. "The Thankless Muse and Her Fugitive Poets." *Southern Review* 66 (1958).

Eliot, T. S. *Selected Essays, 1917-1932*. New York: Harcourt, Brace, 1950.

Malvasi, Mark G. *The Unregenerate South: The Agrarian Thought of John Crowe Ransom, Allen Tate, and Donald Davidson*. Baton Rouge, La.: Louisiana State University Press, 1997.

Moore, Merrill. *The Fugitive: Clippings and Comment About the Magazine and the Members of the Group That Published It, with a Post-Script by John Crowe Ransom*. Boston: M. Moore, 1939.

Parks, E. W., ed. *Southern Poets*. New York: American Book Company, 1936.

Quinlan, Kieran. *John Crowe Ransom's Secular Faith*. Baton Rouge, La.: Louisiana State University Press, 1989.

Stallman, Robert Wooster. "The New Criticism and the Southern Critics." In *A Southern Vanguard: The John Peale Memorial Volume*. Edited by Allen Tate. New York: Prentice-Hall, 1947.

Stewart, John L. *Burden of Time: The Fugitives and Agrarians*. Princeton, N.J.: Princeton University Press, 1965.

Winchell, Mark Royden, ed. *The Vanderbilt Tradition: Essays in Honor of Thomas Daniel Young*. Baton Rouge, La.: Louisiana State University Press, 1991.

Young, Thomas Daniel. *Gentleman in a Dustcoat: A Biography of John Crowe Ransom*. Baton Rouge, La.: Louisiana State University Press, 1976.

————. *Waking Their Neighbors up: The Nashville Agrarians Rediscovered*. Athens, Ga.: University of Georgia Press, 1982.

FUTURISM
France, 1910s

When the concept of Italian FUTURISM became known to literary circles in France, one of its enthusiastic experimenters was Guillaume APOLLINAIRE (*see* CUBISM). As an advocate of Cubism, DADA, and later the poet who gave SURREALISM its name, he was open to any poetic strategy which freed the writer for creative experimentation. As a major force in the shaping of the MODERNIST sensibility, Apollinaire supported all innovative techniques which allowed for constant rediscovery of the self and the environment which influences it. The poet, in his view, need not present a reasonable view of the world but should rather put into words a personal view of its incomprehensibility. His work, along with that of French poet and artist Sonia Delaunay (1885-1979) and the painter Fernand Léger (1881-1955) — who was also involved in the artistic movement known as Orphism (*see* SIMULTANÉISME) — was influenced by the dynamic, bombastic tenor of the Futurist movement and its brief but stirring impact on much of the modern poetry which was to follow it.

❖•❖

Further Reading

Brereton, Geoffrey. *An Introduction to the French Poets: Villon to the Present Day*. London: Methuen, 1956.

FUTURISM
Georgia, 1920s

During the first decades of the century, writers of all genres in the independent republic of the Caucasus known as Georgia enjoyed a period of literary activity which was unprecedented. A number of new literary journals provided opportunities for creative work in the MODERNIST mode to be presented, discussed, and analyzed with enthusiasm. The works included drama, poetry, and political tracts, but the stimulating intellectual interim ended with the invasion of the Red Army in 1921, when Georgia was forced to become part of the U.S.S.R. Briefly, in 1920, the Italian Futurist movement with its exciting, dynamic tenets, had been taken up by Georgian writers Simone Chicovani (1903-) and Demna Shengalaia (1896-?), whose work was published in the journals H_2SO_4 and *Memartskheneoba*. Later, when these young poets were compelled to join the Union of Soviet Writers and make a creative commitment to Communist dicta, the tenor of their work changed and became, as one critic observes, "more staid."

❖•❖

Further Reading

Beridze, Chalva. "Georgian Poetry." *Asiatic Review* 26 (1930): 529-40, 766-72.

FUTURISM
Italy, 1910s-1920s

Futurism was a movement that first appeared in early twentieth-century Italian art and literature. Its principles were announced by Filippo Tommaso MARINETTI in his "Manifeste du futurisme" ("The Founding and Manifesto of Futurism," 1972) published in 1909 first in Paris in *Le Figaro* and later in *Poesia*, Marinetti's journal and the organ of the Futurist movement. Anti-romantic, anti-SYMBOLIST, and anti-traditionalist, Futurism was a rejection and denunciation of the past. The Futurists wanted to revolutionize all the arts and advocated the destruction of the artifacts of a waning civilization — universities, libraries, and museums — all of which they saw as the reposito-

206

ries of a dead culture. The Futurists perceived the twentieth century as a time of dynamism, and their art championed the supremacy of speed, motion, color, and the machine, as well as the cataclysm of natural disasters, violence, war, and patriotism. They revelled in the danger inherent in the vehicles of the mechanistic age, celebrating the automobile, the train, and the airplane. As stated in the first manifesto, they intended "to exalt aggressive action, a feverish insomnia, the racer's stride, the mortal leap, the punch and the slap."

The historical antecedents of Futurism lie in the works of such philosophers and writers as Friedrich NIETZSCHE, Alfred Jarry (1873-1907), Gabriele D'Annunzio (1863-1938), Giambattista Vico (1668-1744), and Arthur RIMBAUD (*see* SYMBOLISM, France), whose works represented for the Futurist the spirit of revolution, the liberation of poetics, and the cult of the individual. Consequently, the Futurists' poetic technique called for the abolition of rules of punctuation, grammar, and syntax. Promoting Marinetti's concept of the "free word," they incorporated mathematical symbols in their poetry, shunned the use of adjectives and adverbs, and preferred verbs in their infinitive form. Words were juxtaposed to create a new meaning and to express the raw, emotion-charged image, presenting "the analogical synthesis of the world embraced at one glance." This emphasis on spontaneity accentuated the immediate and the physical, and the geometric configurations, broken syntax, and anti-rational stance of the poetry expressed this view. Marinetti was also influential in the field of drama, where he introduced innovative concepts of character, plot, and dramatic language that heavily inspired subsequent twentieth-century theatrical innovation, including the THEATER OF THE ABSURD.

To promote their new movement, Marinetti and his fellow Futurists travelled throughout Europe giving public demonstrations of their work in drama, music, and poetry that often ended in shouting matches between the audience and the performers. Their goal was to disrupt bourgeois complacency through provocation, which they achieved with their brash methods.

The concepts of futurism spread quickly to other countries and influenced an array of early twentieth-century literary movements, including DADA, CUBISM, and SURREALISM in France, VORTICISM in England, and EXPRESSIONISM in Germany. Many young poets of the early century went through a brief futurist phase in their formative years, including the Italian poets Giovanni Papini (1881-1956), Giuseppe Prezzolini (1882-1982), and Aldo Palazzeschi (1885-1974). Its greatest influence was felt in Russia, where the Russian Futurist movement divided after 1912, breaking off into several groups, the most important of which became known as CUBO-FUTURISM.

The movement exerted a strong influence in Italian plastic arts, architecture, and music, as witnessed in the work of the sculptor and painter Umberto Boccioni (1882-1916), the architect Ardengo Soffici (1879-1964), and the composer Luigi Russolo (1885-1947). Other artists associated with the movement include Franceso Ballila Pratella (1880-1955), Gino Severini (1883-1966), Carlo Carrà (1881-1966), and Paolo Buzzi (1874-1956). Subsequent manifestos further refining Futurism's aims were published by Marinetti as well as other artists affiliated with the movement, outlining their attitudes toward film, music, and theater.

In the 1920s, Marinetti and his concept of Futurism were adopted by the Italian Fascists, who shared his glorification of war and nationalism. The excesses and essential juvenility of the movement was perhaps best expressed in their concept of war as the "hygiene of the world," an idea that caused many to reject Futurism after the debacle of World War I. Although a collection of Futurist poetry was published in 1925, featuring the work of Marinetti, Corrado Govoni (1884-1965), and Buzzi, no poet or prose writer of major stature emerged from the movement, and by the mid-1930s, its influence was spent.

Futurism is best remembered today as a movement that proposed a radical way of looking at the world, offering new material, subjects, and styles and challenging the artist to discard the ways of the past and to create a new vision and method. In this, it was one of the more prophetic movements of the early twentieth century.

❖•❖

Marinetti, Filippo Tommaso (1876-1944)
Italian poet, dramatist, novelist, and essayist.

The founder and chief exponent of Futurism in literature, Marinetti outlined its doctrine in his "Manifeste du futurisme" of 1909. It called for a revolutionary approach to all the arts, condemning Romanticism, Symbolism, and the stagnation of the past. Like the Fascists, Marinetti glorified militarism and patriotism, and his attempt to fuse the literary principles of Futurism with social and political philosophies led to his support of Mussolini and the Fascist Party. Marinetti also founded a journal, *Poesia*, published from 1905 to 1909, in which he and his fellow Futurists published their theoretical and artistic texts. Under the aegis of *Poesia*, Marinetti assembled a group known as the "incendiary poets," who formed the core of the emerging movement.

In his poetry, Marinetti eschewed realistic representation and abandoned traditional syntax and diction, exemplifying his concept of "free words," whose principles he outlined in an essay in the journal *Lacerba*, another militant journal of the era founded by two artists sympathetic to Futurism, Soffici and Papini. As represented most prominently in his collection of poetry *Zang Tumb Tuum* (1914), Marinetti's concept of free words has certain links to the AUTOMATIC WRITING technique of the SURREALISTS, for like them he was attempting to capture the sequence of images emanating from the mind, unencumbered by the rules of grammar and logic. In this work he experimented with color and typeface, arranging type to form graphic designs and incorporating mathematical and musical symbols to express a wide range of moods and impressions. In drama he forged a new aesthetic based on a theater in which automatons replaced conventional characterization and plot development was supplanted by random, disconnected action, a development that influenced the work of Luigi PIRANDELLO (*see* MODERNISM, Italy) and other proponents of the Theater of the Absurd.

The movement that Marinetti so passionately believed in never produced a work or writer of distinction, and it is generally considered that his manifestos are of greater importance than his literary works. He is remembered today as the individual who shaped the precepts of one of the most influential movements in early twentieth-century literature.

❧•❦

Further Reading

Apollonio, Umbro, ed. *Futurist Manifestos*. Translated by Robert Brain, et al. New York: Viking, 1973.

Clough, Rosa Trillo. *Futurism: The Story of a Modern Art Movement—A New Appraisal*. New York: Greenwood Press, 1961.

Kirby, Michael. *Futurist Performance*. New York: Dutton, 1971.

Martin, Marianne W. *Futurist Art and Theory, 1909-1915*. Oxford, England: Clarendon Press, 1968.

Pacifici, Sergio. *A Guide to Contemporary Italian Literature: From Futurism to Neorealism*. Carbondale, Ill.: Southern Illinois University Press, 1962.

Rye, Jane. *Futurism*. New York: Dutton, 1972.

Tisdall, Caroline, and Angelo Bozzolla. *Futurism*. London: Thames and Hudson, 1977.

FUTURISM
Poland, 1920s

The Polish poets who were linked to the Futurist movement wished to go farther than their contemporaries of the previous decade, the *SKAMANDER* GROUP, in avant-garde activity. The earlier group had brought elements of MODERNIST thinking and techniques to poetic art but had retained some elements of traditional schematics and form. The Polish Futurists—Tytus Czyżewski (1885-1959), Bruno Jasieński (1901-1939), Stanisław Młodożeniec (1895-1959), Anatol Stern (1899-1968), and Aleksander

Wat (1900-1967) — all preached "complete dismissal" of all traditional poetic language and versification. Their ideas had a somewhat enthusiastic response for a short time, but World War II brought with it occupation by both Soviet and German forces, and it has remained for those writers of the postwar period to carry on the Futurist influence of experimental versification, dissonance of rhyme and meter, and the often surprising thrust of the images and metaphors of Futurism.

❧•❦

Further Reading

Carpenter, Bogdana. *The Poetic Avant-Garde in Poland, 1918-1939*. Seattle: University of Washington Press, 1983.

Miłosz, Czesław. "Independent Poland: 1918-1939." In his *The History of Polish Literature*. London: Macmillan, 1969. Rev. ed., Berkeley, Calif.: University of California Press, 1983.

FUTURISM
Ukraine, 1910s-1920s

This movement brought MODERNISM to the Ukraine, and Mykhaylo Semenko (1892-1939) was its foremost innovator. He was joined by Geo Shkurupy (1904-1934). The work of both poets inculcated elements of the literary revolt which had begun in Italy. The moment was brief, since by the 1930s Modernist writers in the Ukraine, like those in Georgia, had no choice but to produce creative work which was committed to the Soviet political philosophy.

❧•❦

Further Reading

Andrusyshen, C. H., and Watson Kirkconnell, eds. *The Ukrainian Poets, 1189-1962*. Toronto: University of Toronto Press, 1963.

"Literature." In *Ukraine: A Concise Encyclopedia*. Edited by Volodymyr Kubijovyc. Vol. 1. Toronto: University of Toronto Press, 1963.

FÜYÜZAT MOVEMENT
Azerbaijan, 1906-1907

The most prominent poets involved with the journal *Füyüzat* were Mukhamedi Khadi (1879-1920) and Abbas Sikhat (1874-1918). Established in the wake of the unsuccessful Russian revolution of 1905, *Füyüzat* (1906-7) — one of hundreds of journals then flourishing in the Caucasus — was the center of one of the main literary trends in Azerbaijan during the early 1900s, which focused on romanticist tendencies of the nineteenth century, rather than on socio-political commentary, such as the contemporary movement *MOLLA NASREDDIN*. Western ideas, such as Darwinism, provoked conflict in Sikhat's work, which was also informed by the Persian and Turkish Islamic literary heritage.

❖•❖

Further Reading

Hitchins, Keith. "Azerbaijani Literature." In *Encyclopedia of World Literature in the Twentieth Century*. 3rd ed. Edited by Steven R. Serafin. Farmington Hills, Mich.: St. James Press, 1999.
Swietochowski, Tadeusz. "The Politics of a Literary Language and the Rise of National Identity in Russian Azerbaijan before 1920." *Ethnic and Racial Studies* 14, 1 (January 1991): 55-63.

FYRTIOTALISTER. *See* POETS OF THE FORTIES

G

GAELIC REVIVAL. *See* **ABBEY THEATER; IRISH RENAISSANCE**

GANG GROUP (Khalyastre)
Poland, 1922-1925

The Gang were a group of Yiddish poets centered in Warsaw and markedly influenced by EXPRESSIONISM and FUTURISM. They remained active as a group from 1922 until 1925, at the end of which time the three principals — Uri Zvi Greenberg (1894-1981), Peretz Markish (1895-1952), and Meilech Ravitch (1893-1976) — had dispersed, respectively, to Israel, Russia, and Canada.

Further Reading

Arnson, Curtis. "Uri Zvi Greenberg: The Early Years." *Modern Hebrew Literature* 1 (spring 1975).

Ben-Porat, Ziva. "Forms of Intertextuality and the Reading of Poetry: Uri Zvi Greenberg's 'Basha'ar'." *Prooftexts: A Journal of Jewish Literary History* 10, 2 (May 1990): 257-81.

Goodblatt, Chanita. "Walt Whitman and Uri Zvi Greenberg: Voice and Dialogue, Apostrophe and Discourse." *Prooftexts: A Journal of Jewish Literary History* 13, 3 (September 1993): 237-51.

Jewish Community Center of Metropolitan Boston, Soviet Jewry Committee. *The Family Markish: A Case Study in the Struggle of Soviet Jewry*. Boston: The Committee, 1974.

Klein, Snira Lubovsky. "The Poetry of Uri Zvi Greenberg in Hebrew and in Yiddish during the Years 1912-1924." *Dissertation Abstracts International* 45, 1 (July 1984): 180A.

Markish, Esther. *The Long Return*. 1st ed. New York: Ballantine Books, 1978.

Roberts-Burke, Robin J. *The Country of the Mind: Homeland Symbolism in Twentieth Century Hebrew and Irish Poetry*. Doctoral thesis, UCLC, 1987.

Rosenfarb, Chava. *Yiddish Poets in Canada*. Mississauga, Canada: Benben Publications, 1994.

GARIP GROUP. *See* POETIC REALISM

GATE THEATER
England, 1925-1940

The London Gate Theater was established in 1925 under the direction of Peter Godfrey (1899-1970). A small, private organization devoted to new and innovative drama, the Theater was exempt from censorship laws and thus was able to introduce English audiences to controversial plays by several well-known Continental and American writers. Among the featured playwrights were German EXPRESSIONIST Ernst TOLLER, American Expressionist Eugene O'NEILL, and French experimentalist Jean Cocteau (1889-1963). In 1934 Norman Marshall (1901-1980) assumed management of the Theater and began an annual series of highly successful Gate revues to complement a continually expanding repertoire of important works. The Gate closed six years later amid the disorder of World War II and was never reopened.

➹•❦

Further Reading

Marshall, Norman. *The Other Theatre*. London: J. Lehmann, 1947.

GAUCHO LITERATURE
Argentina and Uruguay, 1870s-1920s

The gaucho was the out-rider of the Argentine Pampas, often beyond the law, always an intriguing figure, and a symbol of the Latin American past who can be compared to the North American frontier cowboy. The gaucho appears sometimes as a realistic representative of an emerging nation which is still unsettled and in other instances is idealized as a victim of the social pressures of national expansion — for whatever reason, he has remained a popular figure in all literary genres. The singular example of Gaucho poetry is in the epic by José Hernandez (1834-1936), *Martin Fierro* (1872-79; *The Gaucho Martin Fierro*, 1935), in which the hero defends his way of life against the evils of socialization and his loss of freedom in the name of civilization. Other like examples are *Santos Vegas* (1851) by Hilario Ascasubi (1807-1875) and *Fausto* (1866) by Estanislao del Campo (1834-1880). In another vein, the Gaucho novel epitomizes a regional movement in literature, examples of which are *Don Segundo Sombra* (1926; *Don Segundo Sombra: Shadows on the Pampas,* 1935) by Ricardo Güiraldes (1886-1927) and the realistic depictions of rural Argentine life by Benito Lynch (1888-1951) in *The Englishman of the Bones* (1924) and *The Romance of the Gaucho* (1930). Eduardo Gutierrez (1853-1890) dramatized his novel, *Juan Moreiea* (1880), and thus introduced the gaucho as a popular theatrical figure. Between 1924 and 1927, the jour-

213

nal *Martin Fierro*, named to honor the Hernandez opus, was started by Jorge Luis BORGES (*see* MAGIC REALISM) to showcase traditional values of Argentine art and literature. This publication and its follower, *Sur*, had significant influence on the publication of the best literary work of the region. Uruguayan writers in the movement included Javier de Viana (1868-1926) and Justino Zavola Muñiz (1898-1968); other Argentineans were Eduardo Díaz Acevedo (1851-1921), Juan Godoy (1793-1864), Bartolome Hidalgo (1788-1822), and Domingo Faustino Sarmiento (1811-1888).

While little new Gaucho Literature appeared in South America in the latter part of the twentieth century, the subject remained of interest to students and critics who continued to study and anthologize the early works of the genre in order to preserve a colorful and important part of early Argentine literary history.

➜•❖

Further Reading

Foster, David William, and Virginia Ramos Foster. *Research Guide to Argentine Literature*. Metuchen, N.J.: Scarecrow Press, 1970.

Jones, W. K. *Behind Spanish American Footlights*. Austin, Tex.: University of Texas Press, 1966.

Nichols, Madaline Wallis. *The Gaucho: Cattlehunter, Cavalryman, Ideal of Romance*. Durham, N.C.: Duke University Press, 1942.

Stabb, Martin S. *In Quest of Identity: Patterns in the Spanish American Essay of Ideas, 1890-1960*. Chapel Hill, N.C.: University of North Carolina Press, 1967.

Tinker, E. Larocque. *Life and Literature of the Pampas*. Gainesville, Fla.: University of Florida Press, 1961.

Torres Rioseco, A. *The Epic of Latin-American Literature*. New York: Oxford University Press, 1942; rev. 1946.

GAY THEATER
England and United States, 1960s-1990s

The gay civil rights movement, which began in earnest in the 1960s, has ever since helped to forge a body of gay drama that dispels the stereotypical portrayals of gays prevalent throughout the history of theater and attempted to replace them with a definition of the gay community as interpreted by the community itself. Important modern forerunners of the movement include Mordaunt Shairp's (1887-1939) *The Green Bay Tree* (1933), Lillian Hellman's (1905-1984) *The Children's Hour* (1934), Robert Anderson's (1917-) *Tea and Sympathy* (1953) and Arthur Miller's (1915-) *A View from the Bridge* (1955), all of which dealt to some extent with gay themes. However, these works often reinforced the mainstream heterosexual belief in homosexuality as deviant behavior.

The development of Off-Broadway and Off-Off Broadway theater as venues for alternative drama beginning in the 1950s and the relaxing of puritanical public mores in the 1960s paved the way for gay actors, directors, and playwrights to begin producing works that dealt with their own experience and were geared toward like-minded audiences. At such theaters as the Caffé Cino (1960-1967) in the Greenwich Village section of New York, important gay playwrights, including Doric Wilson (1939-), Robert Patrick (1937-), Lanford Wilson (1937-), and William Hoffman (1939-), saw their first significant exposure. With the premiere of Mart Crowley's (1935-) *The Boys in the Band* (1968) and the Stonewall Riots in 1969, a new impetus was given to Gay Theater. Crowley's drama, despite still reinforcing negative ideas about gay men, became among the first explorations of gay characters and modern culture to find acceptance with the general theater-going public. The trend of confessional-type Gay Theater, often attempting to use gay life as a metaphor for a more universal experience, culminated with a series of one-act plays by Harvey Fierstein (1954-): *The International Stud* (1978), *Fugue in a Nursery* (1979), and *Widows and Children First!* (1979). Performed collectively as *Torch Song Trilogy* (1981), it began Off-Off Broadway but received a Tony award for best play in its Broadway incarnation. Other important works of this time included Martin Sherman's (1938) *Bent* (1979). The AIDS crisis launched a new phase of Gay Theater, focusing on the effect the disease wrought on the homosexual community. Plays such as Hoffman's *As Is* (1984) and Larry Kramer's (1935-) *The Normal Heart* (1985) were early but important examples of this. Drag shows and revue-style productions represent another significant aspect of Gay Theater, albeit one which many gays view as pandering to heterosexual tastes.

The creation of important Gay Theater troupes outside of New York (including the Theatre Rhinoceros of San Francisco) and the crossover success of productions such as Jean Poiret's (1926-) *La Cage aux Folles* (1978), Manuel Puig's (1932-) *El beso de la mujer araña* (1981; *Kiss of the Spider Woman,* 1985), John Guare's (1938-) *Six Degrees of Separation* (1990), Kramer's *The Destiny of Me* (1993), and Tony Kushner's (1956-) Pulitzer prize-winning *Angels in America* (1993) continued to herald the spread of gay-oriented theater through the 1990s. Paralleling the evolution of Gay Theater in the United States is that in England, with the FRINGE THEATER incubating homosexual talent in much the same way as Off- and Off-Off Broadway did in the United States. Both Shairp and Sherman were English, and other major English contributors to Gay Theater include John OSBORNE (*see* ANGRY YOUNG MEN), Joe Orton (1933-1967), Michael Wilcox (1943-), and Hugh Whitemore (1936-). In addition, a growing tradition of specifically lesbian theater has seen significant work produced by playwrights including Jane Chambers (1937-), Holly Hughes (1958-), and Lisa Kron (n.d.).

❖•❖
Further Reading

Clum, John M., ed. *Staging Gay Lives: An Anthology of Contemporary Gay Theater*. Boulder, Colo.: Westview Press, 1996.

De Johngh, Nicholas. *Not in Front of the Audience: The Making of Gay Theatre*. London; New York: Routledge, 1991.

Drukman, Steven. "Summer Camp." *The Advocate* 636 (1993): 60-62.

Gevisser, Mark. "Gay Theater Today." *Theater* 21. Special issue (summer/fall 1990): 46-51.

Green, W. "*Torch Song Trilogy*: A Gay Comedy with a Dying Fall." *Maske und Kothurn* 30 (1984).

Henry, William A. "The Gay White Way." *Time* 141, 20 (May 17, 1993): 62-63.

Library and Museum of the Performing Arts at Lincoln Center. "Caffé Cino and Its Legacy." Exhibition catalogue. 1985.

Miller, T. "Gay Theatre: Is It Still Dangerous?" *Stages* 1 (1984).

Patrick, Robert. "Gay Theater's Relationship with Its Audience." *Christopher Street* 168 (December 23, 1991): 16.

Perry, David. "Stages of Uncertainty for Gay Theater: The 'Purple Circuit' Faces Changing Audiences and Challenging Times." *The Advocate* 572 (March 12, 1991): 66-67.

Vilanch, Bruce. "The Naked Truth." *The Advocate* 682 (May 30, 1995): 69.

GENÇ KALEMLER. See YOUNG PENS

GENERACIÓN DE LA GUERRA. *See* GENERATION OF 1936

GENERATION OF 1898 (Generación del 1898)
Spain, c. 1898-1910s

Consisting of writers born between approximately 1864 and 1880, the Generation of 1898 coincided with the disastrous outcome of the Spanish-American War of the same year. Spain, now bereft of its vast empire, was in a state of crisis and indirection. A revolution of cultural ideology, similar to the revolution of aesthetics within MODERNISMO, was the almost immediate result through the work of a number of writers, including Azorín (José Martínez Ruiz, 1873-1969), Antonio Machado (1875-1939), Jacinto Benavente (1866-1954), Pío Baroja (1872-1956), Ramiro de Maeztu (1874-1936), Ramón Valle-Inclán (1866-1936), Ramón Pérez de Ayala (1881-1962), and Miguel de Unamuno (1864-1936). In general, these writers believed that in the spiritual and intellectual regeneration of the individual Spaniard resided the revitalized health of the whole nation. Opposed to parochial attitudes, these writers championed both the inculcation of international influences as well as the forgotten virtues and beauty of Old Castile and its people. The essay became the foremost vehicle for the necessarily contemplative expressions of the movement. Unamuno, the most outstanding member of the Generation and perhaps the greatest stylist in twentieth-century Spanish literature, produced the movement's hallmark work, *Del sentimiento trágico de la vida en los hombres y en los pueblos* (1913; *The Tragic Sense of Life in Men and in Peoples,* 1926). Greatly influential inside as well as outside Spain, this fusion of philosophical treatise and personal meditation is recognized as a forerunner of later works of the EXISTENTIALIST movement. José Ortega y Gasset (1883-1955), a younger member of the movement, later continued many of its principles, though in a more obviously aesthetic fashion, in his influence on the GENERATION OF 1927.

✦•✦

Further Reading

Basdekis, Demetrios. *Unamuno and Spanish Literature.* Berkeley, Calif.: University of California, 1967.

Bleiberg, Hermán, and E. Inman Fox, eds. *Spanish Thought and Letters in the Twentieth Century.* Nashville, Tenn.: Vanderbilt University Press, 1966.

Chandler, Richard E., and Kessel Schwartz. "The Generation of 1898." In their *A New History of Spanish Literature.* Baton Rouge, La.: Louisiana State University Press, 1961.

Ellis, Robert R. *The Tragic Pursuit of Being: Unamuno and Sartre.* Tuscaloosa, Ala.: University of Alabama Press, 1988.

Ferrater Mora, José. *Unamuno: A Philosophy of Tragedy.* Translated by Philip Silver. Berkeley, Calif.: University of California Press, 1962.

Ilie, Paul. *Unamuno: An Existential View of Self and Society.* Madison, Wis.: University of Wisconsin Press, 1967.

Jurkevich, Gayana. "Defining Castile in Literature and Art: Institucionismo, the Generation of '98, and the Origins of Modern Spanish Landscape." *Revista Hispanica Moderna* 67, 1 (June 1994): 56-71.

Lacy, Allen. *Miguel de Unamuno: The Rhetoric of Existence.* The Hague: Mouton, 1967.

Nozick, Martin. *Miguel de Unamuno.* New York: Twayne, 1971.

Ribbans, Geoffrey. "Some Subversive Thoughts on Modernismo and the Generation of '98." *West Virginia University Philological Papers* 39 (1993): 1-17.

Rudd, Margaret Thomas. *The Lone Heretic: A Biography of Miguel de Unamuno y Jugo.* Austin, Tex.: University of Texas Press, 1963.

Shaw, Donald L. *The Generation of 1898 in Spain.* London: E. Benn; New York: Barnes & Noble, 1975.

Tuttle, Howard N. *The Dawn of Historical Reason: The Historicality of Human Existence in the Thought of Dilthey, Heidegger and Ortega y Gasset.* New York: Peter Lang, 1994.

Valdes, Mario J. *Death in the Literature of Unamuno.* Urbana, Ill.: University of Illinois Press, 1966.

Wyers, Frances. *Miguel de Unamuno: The Contrary Self.* London: Tamesis Books, 1976.

Young, Howard T. *The Victorious Expression: A Study of Four Contemporary Spanish Poets: Miguel de Unamuno, Antonio Machado, Juan Ramón Jiménez, Federico García Lorca.* Madison, Wis.: University of Wisconsin Press, 1966.

GENERATION OF 1900 (Generación del 1900)
Paraguay, 1900s-1910s

The Generation of 1900 refers to poets, journalists, and essayists who wrote about social conditions in Paraguay, which, to some extent, worsened due to the War of the Triple Alliance during the 1860s. They included essayists Cecilio Báez (1862-1941), Juan E. O'Leary (1879-1969), and Manuel Domínguez (1869-1935), Blas Garay (1873-1899), Manuel Gondra (1871-1927), Fulgencio R. Moreno (1872-1935), and poet Alejandro Guanes (1872-1925). Much of Guanes's poetry dealt with philosophical and religious themes; poems include "Las leyendas" (1910; The Legends) and "Recuerdos" (1910; Memories), both of which appear in *De paso por la vida* (1984; Passing through Life), a collection of his work published posthumously.

✦•✦

Further Reading

"Alejandro Guanes." In *Beyond the Rivers.* Edited by Charles Richard Carlisle. Berkeley, Calif.: Thorp Springs Press, 1977.

Foster, David William, comp. "Paraguay." In *Handbook of Latin American Literature.* New York: Garland, 1987.

Jones, Willis Knapp. "Alejandro Guanes." In *Spanish-American Literature in Translation: A Selection of Poetry, Fiction, and Drama Since 1888.* New York: Ungar, 1963.

————. "Juan E. O'Leary." In *Spanish-American Literature in Translation: A Selection of Poetry, Fiction, and Drama Since 1888.* New York: Ungar, 1963.

"Juan E. O'Leary." In *Beyond the Rivers.* Edited by Charles Richard Carlisle. Berkeley, Calif.: Thorp Springs Press, 1977.

"Juan O'Leary." In *Paraguayans of Today.* Edited by William Belmont Parker. London: Hispanic Society of America, 1921.

"Manuel Dominguez." In *Paraguayans of Today.* Edited by William Belmont Parker. London: Hispanic Society of America, 1921.

"Manuel Gondra." In *Paraguayans of Today.* Edited by William Belmont Parker. London: Hispanic Society of America, 1921.

GENERATION OF 1900 (Generación del 1900)
Uruguay, 1890s-1900s

The Generation of 1900 refers more to a group of Uruguayan writers productive around the turn of the century than to a collaborative and cohesive literary group. They had in common the use of REALIST techniques, carrying over into what is known as GAUCHO LITERATURE, as well as the influence of MODERNISM. Writers typically included in this grouping are Eduardo Acevedo Díaz (1851-1921), Horacio Quiroga (1878-1937), Carlos Reyles (1868-1938), and Javier de Viana (1868-1926). Acevedo Díaz wrote epic novels of the liberation period—particularly, the trilogy *Ismael* (1888), *Nativa* (1890), and *Grito de Gloria* (1894; Cry of Glory). He was a leader of the Blanco Party and fought in civil wars. His was a regionalist gauchoesque literature focusing on rural life. *Soledad* (1894; Solitude) is considered his masterpiece, a novel which greatly influenced later generations of writers, including dramatist and fiction writer Justino Zavala Muñiz (1897-?). Quiroga spent much of his life in Argentina, and wrote short stories which are unusual for their animal protagonists. He was also associated with the COUNCIL OF BRILLIANT KNOWLEDGE. Reyles was a novelist writing gauchoesque novels as well as psychological works, such as *Race of Cain* (1900). Viana's short stories were realist examinations of gaucho life.

❖•❖

Further Reading

Anderson Imbert, Enrique. *Spanish-American Literature: A History*. Detroit: Wayne State University Press, 1963.

Franco, Jean. *The Modern Culture of Latin America: Society and the Artist*. New York: Praeger, 1967.

Torres-Ríoseco, A. *The Epic of Latin American Literature*. New York: Oxford University Press, 1942.

GENERATION OF 1905
Norway, 1905-1920

The Norwegian Generation of 1905 was a group of poets who, in general, hymned the beauties of the landscape, seasons, and rural people. However, Olav Bull (1883-1933), the member who achieved the greatest stature, combined his paeans with a serious exploration of weighty philosophical problems. Bull published his last volume of poetry, influenced by the theories of Henri BERGSON, in 1932. Other important Generation members who survived Bull include Alf Larsen (1885-1967), Tore Ørjasœter (1886-1968), and Herman Wildenvey (1886-1959).

❖•❖

Further Reading

Morris, Walter D. "Norwegian Literature." In *Encyclopedia of World Literature in the Twentieth Century*. 3rd ed. Edited by Steven R. Serafin. Farmington Hills, Mich.: St. James Press, 1999.

GENERATION OF 1918 (Generación del 1918)
Venezuela, 1920s

The Venezuelan Generation of 1918 was a group of poets who objected to MODERN-ISMO's preoccupation with formal concerns. Combining revolutionary sentiment, folklore, and examples of EXPRESSIONISM and SURREALISM, the Generation helped advance modern Venezuelan poetry. The key figures of the movement were Antonio Arraiz (1903-1963), Andrés Eloy Blanco (1897-1955), and Luis Fernández Alvarez (1902-1952).

Further Reading

Caracciolo-Trejo, E. *Penguin Book of Latin American Verse*. Harmondsworth, England: Penguin, 1971.

Flores, Angel. *Bibliography of Spanish-American Writers*. New York: Gordian Press, 1975.

————. "Antonio Arraiz." In his *Spanish American Authors: The Twentieth Century*. New York: Wilson, 1992.

————. "Otero Silva, Miguel." In his *Spanish American Authors: The Twentieth Century*. New York: Wilson, 1992.

Foster, David William, comp. "Venezuela." In *Handbook of Latin American Literature*. New York: Garland, 1987.

Lewis, Marvin A. *Ethnicity and Identity in Contemporary Afro-Venezuelan Literature: A Culturalist Approach*. Columbia, Mo.: University of Missouri Press, 1992.

Ruiz del Vizo, Hortensia, ed. *Black Poetry of the Americas*. Miami, Fla.: Ediciones Universal, 1972.

GENERATION OF 1927 (Generation of 1925; Nietos del '98; Generación de la Dictadura; Generación de la *Revista de Occidente*)
Spain, 1920s-1930s

Born between 1892 and 1905, the Generation of 1927 poets led a renewal of Spanish poetry often referred to as the new Spanish Golden Age, after the *Siglo de Oro* of the sixteenth and seventeenth centuries. Friendship, more than any clearly defined agenda, bonded the group which included Federico García Lorca (1898-1936), Jorge Guillén (1893-1984), Vicente Aleixandre (1898-1984), Dámaso Alonso (1898-1990), Luis Cernuda (1902-1963), Rafael Alberti (1902-), Pedro Salinas (1892-1951), Gerardo Diego (1896-1987), Emilio Prados (1899-1962), and Manuel Altolaguirre (1905-1959). Some, such as Prados and Aleixandre, had known each other since childhood, and others met while attending the Residencia de Estudiantes, a prep school in Madrid, but all had become acquainted with each other over the course of the 1920s.

The significance of the year 1927 is that it was the tercentenary anniversary of the death of Luis de Góngora (1561-1627), whose poetry the group admired. (Luis Cernuda, however, preferred "the generation of 1925," since that year represented the halfway point of the publication of members' first books.) These young poets were attracted to, and for a period many emulated, the baroque poet's techniques, in particular, his elaborate Latinate language and use of imagery and metaphor, in a style that has become known as góngorismo or neogóngorismo. Diego's *Fábula de Equis y Zeda* (1932; Fable of X and Z) and *Poemas adrede* (1932; Poems on Purpose) are representative of the góngorist style.

To commemorate the anniversary members of the group organized various activities. Diego edited a collection of the poets' neogóngorist efforts in *Antología poética en honor de Góngora* (1927; Poetic Anthology in Honor of Góngora). Alonso created a prose edition of Góngora's *Soledades* (1927; Solitudes), and a few years later published *La lengua poética de Góngora* (1935; The Poetic Language of Góngora). Lorca wrote the essay *La imagen poética en don Luis de Góngora* (1926; The Poetic Image in Don Luis de Góngora). In addition to these commemorative publications, the group planned other festivities as a tribute with, according to Diego, "all sorts of serious and frivolous youthful manifestations," including dramatic and musical performances and exhibitions. Instead, according to historian of the generation C. B. Morris, on May 23, 1927, at a location Diego refused to disclose, he, Alonso, and Alberti held a mock inquisitorial ceremony during which, the legend goes, they burned effigies of Góngora's enemies. They also "excommunicated" Guillén for not attending. The next day, all held a "solemn requiem mass" for Góngora. Diego recorded the celebrations in "Crónica de Góngora (1627-1927)" in *Lola* (December 1927-January 1928). Years later, Cernuda would disapprovingly recall "that fondness for irresponsible games which characterized the acts and the poems of some young poets between 1920 and 1930."

Guillén remembers in his *Language and Poetry* that "There was no program, there was no manifesto attacking or defending fixed positions. There were dialogues, letters, dinners, walks, and friendship under the bright light of Madrid." The group enjoyed gathering at Altolaguirre's printing shop, Imprenta Sur (Southern Press), decorated to look like a boat, where he published much of their early work. Another favorite gathering place was Aleixandre's home after he married.

Alonso, chief chronicler of the group, wrote that "the first thing to be noted is that this generation does not rise up against anything." In "The Language of the Poem," Guillén adds that "it would be misleading to think that any organized doctrine existed. What did exist, in abundance, were conversations—and monologues—on the general aspects of poetic craft." In the same essay, Guillén reminisces about the Generation's

221

search for "a poetry that would be both art with all of the severity of art and creation with all its genuine *élan*" and remarks that "the major themes of human existence — love, nature, life, death — filled the lyric and dramatic works of this generation."

The Generation of 1927 poets tended to have an expansive interest in many literatures, from their own Spanish tradition to contemporary European trends. In addition to Góngora, the poets admired Francisco Quevedo (1580-1645), Lope de Vega (1562-1635), Garcilaso de Vega (1539-1616), Luis de León (1527?-1591), and Gustavo Adolfo Bécquer (1836-1870). And they were attracted to such MODERNIST influences as SURREALISM, Sigmund FREUD, SYMBOLISM, especially Arthur RIMBAUD and Charles BAUDELAIRE, and ULTRAISM and CREATIONISM (of which latter two Diego was a proponent). MODERNISMO and the work of Rubén DARÍO had a profound impact on such direct mentors as Juan Ramón JIMÉNEZ (*see* MODERNISMO) and GENERATION OF 1898 writers Antonio Machado (1875-1939) and Miguel de Unamuno (1864-1936), all of whom, according to Guillén, they admired "without reserve." Salina's acquaintance with Enrique Díez-Canedo (1879-1944) provided a direct link to the previous generation. Philosopher José Ortega y Gasset (1883-1955) and his *La deshumanización del arte* (1925; *The Dehumanization of Art*, 1948) touched them as well; he also published the influential journal *Revista de Occidente* from 1923 to 1936.

Though some dabbled with the Surrealist technique of AUTOMATIC WRITING, the Generation of 1927 poets paid stricter attention to craftsmanship than did the Surrealists. Still, they sometimes liked to invent words and write about such nontraditional subject matter as the cinema and other new technologies (cars, electric light, etc.), the circus, games, slapstick, and comedians Charlie Chaplin (1889-1977; or "Charlot," as he was known in Spain) and Buster Keaton (1895-1966).

But each member developed his own distinctive individual approach to poetic craft. García Lorca, widely considered one of the Generation's major poets, published some of his most famous work in *Canciones* (1927; Songs) and *Primer romancer gitano* (1928; *Gypsy Ballads*, 1951); after a visit in New York he focused more on the theater. Guillén's most important work is *Cántico*, which he revised and added to several times (1928, 1936, 1945, 1950). *Cántico* contains poems of joy that soberly celebrate life, though some critics have called his poetry difficult, "cold," and "dehumanized," all of which may well have more to do with the careful discipline and precision in his craft than with his poetic demeanor toward his themes. Guillén was especially influenced by the French Symbolists and translated Paul Valéry (1871-1945) and Paul Claudel (1868-1955) into Spanish. Aleixandre's early poetry was erotic and sensual, but later was characterized by themes of despair and paradise lost. His early verse was rigorously formal in a traditional sense, though his later poetry was mainly in free verse. He also

222

experimented with automatic writing and, like Lorca, was influenced by psychoanalytic theories. Alonso was a major literary critic as well as a poet. His poetry's main themes were death, night, love, loneliness, God, and religion. He also translated James JOYCE's *Portrait of the Artist as a Young Man* into Spanish (*see* MODERNISM, England and Ireland). Cernuda's poetry deals with themes of solitude and loneliness; his first volume was *Perfil del aire* (1927; Profile of the Air). Of the Generation, Alberti was perhaps the strongest admirer of Góngora, while Prados was particularly interested in French Symbolist Baudelaire and the Surrealists; Prados's first volume of poetry was *Tiempo* (1925; Time). Salinas is renowned for his moving love poetry. Altolaguirre's favorite poetic themes were love, solitude, death, and nature.

In 1930 Altolaguirre started the magazine *Poesía,* in which he published works by himself and his friends as well as classical poets. Several other literary magazines published the work of the generation: Salinas and others edited *Los Cuatro Vientos*; Prados and Altolaguirre published the literary journal *Litoral* (1927-29).

By the onset of the Spanish Civil War in 1936, Salinas had left Spain to take a position at Wellesley College in Massachusetts, then later at Johns Hopkins. Guillén also left Spain in 1936 to teach in the United States, mainly at Wellesley. Lorca was killed by a Falangist firing squad for his outspoken anti-Fascism. Diego had been living in France, where he had recently married, and returned to Spain in the summer of 1937 and resided there until his death. Cernuda left Spain and lived in England for some years, then the United States and Mexico. Alonso went to teach at the University of Leipzig in 1935-36, then returned to Spain. Prados had to leave Spain because his earlier political activities put his life in danger; he went with his longtime friend Altolaguirre to live in Mexico. Not surprisingly, the survivors' poetry was afterward marked by an occupation with death, war, and, exile. In *Nacimiento último* (1953) Aleixandre wrote: "Todos partieron, todos juntos en un momento, para muy diferentes caminos" (They all left, all together at one moment, on very different paths).

❖•❖

Further Reading

Brown, G. G. *A Literary History of Spain: The Twentieth Century.* New York: Barnes & Noble Inc., 1972.

Chandler, Richard E., and Kessel Schwartz. "The Lorca-Guillén Generation." In their *A New History of Spanish Literature.* Baton Rouge, La.: Louisiana State University Press, 1961.

Cobb, Carl W. *Contemporary Spanish Poetry (1898-1963).* Boston: Twayne, 1976.

———. *Federico García Lorca.* New York: Twayne, 1967.

Crispin, John. *Pedro Salinas.* New York: Twayne, 1974.

Debicki, Andrew P. *Dámaso Alonso.* New York: Twayne, 1970.

Duran, Manuel, ed. *Lorca: A Collection of Critical Essays.* Englewood, N.J.: Prentice-Hall, 1962.

Guillén, Jorge. "The Language of the Poem." In his *Language and Poetry: Some Poets of Spain.* Cambridge, Mass.: Harvard University Press, 1961.

Jiménez-Fajardo, Salvador. *Luis Cernuda.* Boston: Twayne, 1978.

Jiménez-Fajardo, Salvador, ed. *The Word and the Mirror: Critical Essays on the Poetry of Luis Cernuda.* Cranbury, N.J.: Associated University Presses, 1989.

Mayhew, Jonathan. *The Poetics of Self-Consciousness: Twentieth-Century Spanish Poetry.* Cranbury, N.J.: Associated University Presses, 1994.

Morris, C. B. *A Generation of Spanish Poets, 1920-1936.* London: Cambridge University Press, 1969.

Newton, Candelas. *Understanding Federico García Lorca.* Columbia, S.C.: University of South Carolina Press, 1995.

Schwartz, Kessel. *Vicente Aleixandre.* New York: Twayne, 1970.

Young, Howard T. *The Victorious Expression: A Study of Four Contemporary Spanish Poets: Miguel de Unamuno, Antonio Machado, Juan Ramón Jiménez, Federico García Lorca.* Madison, Wis.: University of Wisconsin Press, 1966.

GENERATION OF 1930
Greece, 1930s

Generally speaking, the Generation of 1930 refers to a group of writers in Greece who produced some of their major works during the 1930s; critics provide a range of descriptive characteristics and goals of the group. Kleon Paraschos wrote in 1937 that the goals of the Generation were to develop fictional techniques and break with ethography, while I. M. Panayotopoulos, in *Ta prosopa kai ta keimena* (1943), describes the post-1922 literary scene as striving for rebirth. Thomas Doulis characterizes the Generation of 1930 as a group of prose writers whose works were concerned with depicting "the social, political, and moral realities of Greece in the interwar period," i.e. 1922-1940.

Writers associated with the Generation of 1930 include poet George Seferis (1900-1971), winner of the 1963 Nobel Prize; poet and artist Odysseus Elytis (1911-1996), poet and sailor Dimitrios I. Antoniou (1906-); poet and novelist Melpo Axioti (1905-1975); poet Alexandros Baras (1906-); poet Rita Boumi-Pappas (1907-); her husband, poet Nikos Pappas (1906-); poet and psychoanalyst Andréas Embirikos (1901-1975); poet Nikos Engonopoulos (1910-); poet Nikos Gatsos (1915-1992); poet Alexandros Matsas (1911-1969); poet, novelist, and critic Ionnis M. Panayotopoulos (1901-); novelist Kosmas Politis (1888-1974); poet Yannis Ritsos (1909-1990); poet Giorgos Sarandaris (1908-1941); lawyer, novelist, playwright, and essayist Yorghos Theotakas (1905-1966); and poet Nikiforos Vrettakos (1911-1991).

Most of these writers employed the demotic, or vernacular, language. They criticized the earlier NEW SCHOOL OF ATHENS writers, though some paved the way for demotic usage. Theotakas wrote an essay which would be the manifesto for the Generation of 1930—*Elefthero pnevma* (1929; Free Spirit), which argues that the ethography of the earlier writers could not represent more than surface realities. It calls instead for "a more serious imaginative prose" which questions a cultural tradition of "narrow limitations and clear-cut values." Seferis joined Theotakas and others to help found the prominent journal *Nea Grammata* (New Letters) during the 1930s, which was edited by poet and critic Andreas Karandonis (1910-), and which published the work of many writers associated with the Generation of 1930.

Elytis, an important figure in Greek literature, adapted elements of SURREALISM to his poetry after he heard lectures given by Embirikos in 1935. His major work from the time includes *Prosanatolizmí* (1939; Orientations), *Ílios o prótos, mazí me tis parallayiés páno se mián ahtídha* (1943; Sun the First Together with Variations on a Sunbeam), and *Ázma iroikó ke pénthimo yia ton haméno anthipolohaghó tis Alvanías* (1946; Heroic and Elegiac Song of the Lost Second Lieutenant of the Albanian Campaign). In Paris, during the late 1940s and early 1950s, Elytis associated with Paul ÉLUARD (*see* SURREALISM, France), Tristan Tzara (1896-1963), René Char (1907-1988), André BRETON (*see* SURREALISM, France), Giuseppe UNGARETTI (*see* HERMETICISM), Henri Matisse (1869-1954), and Pablo Picasso (1881-1973). Other notable works dating from the period include Theotakas's novels *Argho* (1936; *Argo*, 1951) and *Leonis* (1940), and Politis's novel, *Eroica* (1938).

❖•❖

Further Reading

Decavalles, A. "Greekness and Exile." *Spirit: A Magazine of Poetry* (September 1968): 111-15.

Dimiroulis, D. "The 'Humble Art' and the Exquisite Rhetoric: Tropes in the Manner of George Seferis." In *The Text and Its Margins: Post-Structuralist Approaches to Twentieth-Century Greek Literature*. Edited by M. Alexiou and V. Lambropoulo. New York: Pella, 1985.

Doulis, T. "The Generation of the 1930s: The Break from the Greek Ethographic Tradition and the Establishment of the Social Novel." In *Disaster and Fiction: Modern Greek Fiction and the Asia Minor Disaster of 1922*. Berkeley, Calif.: University of California Press, 1977.

Friar, Kimon. *Modern Greek Poetry*. New York: Simon and Schuster, 1973.

———. "George Seferis: The Greek Poet Who Won the Nobel Prize." *Saturday Review* 46 (November 30, 1963): 16-20.

Friar, Kimon, ed. *The Sovereign Sun: Selected Poems of Elytis*. Philadelphia: Temple University Press, 1974.

———. "A Critical Mosaic." *Charioteer* 1, 2 (1960): 20-24.

Ivask, I. *Odysseus Elytis: Analogies of Light*. Norman, Okla.: University of Oklahoma Press, 1981.

Kakavoulia, M. "Telling, Speaking, Naming in Melpo Axioti's *Would You Like to Dance, Maria?*" In *The Text and Its Margins: Post-Structuralist Approaches to Twentieth-Century Greek Literature*. Edited by M. Alexiou and V. Lambropoulos. New York: Pella, 1985.

Kapre-Karka, C. *Love and the Symbolic Journey in the Poetry of Cavafy, Eliot and Seferis*. New York: Pella, 1982.

Keeley, Edmund. *Modern Greek Poetry: Voice and Myth*. Princeton, N.J.: Princeton University Press, 1983.

———. "Seferis's Elpenor, 'A Man of Fortune'." *Kenyon Review* 28 (1966): 378-90.

Keeley, Edmund, and P. Bien, eds. *Modern Greek Writers*. Princeton, N.J.: Princeton University Press, 1972.

Keeley, Edmund, and Philip Sherrard, trans. *Six Poets of Modern Greece*. New York: Knopf, 1960.

Panayotopoulos, I. M., A. Karandonis, and A. Sahinis. "George Theotokas: A Critical Mosaic." *Charioteer* 5 (1963): 60-64.

Sherrard, Philip. "George Seferis." In *The Marble Threshing Floor: Studies in Modern Greek Poetry*. London: Valentine, Mitchell, 1956.

———. "George Seferis 1900-1971: The Man and His Poetry." In *The Wound of Greece: Studies in Neo-Hellenism*. New York: St. Martin's Press, 1979.

Six Poems from the Greek of Sikelianos and Seferis. Translated by Lawrence Durrell. Rhodes, Greece: n.p., 1946.

Thaniel, G. "George Seferis's 'Thrush': A Modern Descent." *Canadian Review of Comparative Literature* 4 (1977): 89-102.

Trypanis, C. A. *Medieval and Modern Greek Poetry: An Anthology*. Oxford, England: Clarendon Press, 1951.

Tsatsos, Ioanna Tsatsos. *My Brother George Seferis*. Translated by Jean Demos. St. Paul, Minn.: North Central Pub. Co., 1982.

GENERATION OF 1936 (Generación del 1936; Generación de la Guerra)
Spain, 1930s

Literary disciples of the GENERATION OF 1927, the Spanish Generation of 1936 writers were generally born between the years 1900 and 1920. All were profoundly affected by the political and cultural upheaval of the Spanish Civil War (1936-39). Although the group lacked artistic cohesion, most members began to distinguish themselves from the abstruse, Góngorist poetics of the 1927 Generation and to instead promote prose and poetry that was intimately connected to the lives and social problems of the Spanish people. Dionisio Ridruejo (1912-1975) and Luis Rosales (1910-1992) were key members of the group, as was Camilo José CELA, who during the 1940s popularized TREMENDISMO, a contemporary form of NATURALISTIC fiction. Others included Gabriel Celaya (1911-1991), Vicente Gaos (1919-), José Hierro (1922-), Blas de Otero (1916-1979), and Leopoldo Panero Torbado (1909-1962).

❖•❖

Further Reading

Barrow, Geoffrey R. *The Satiric Vision of Blas de Otero*. Columbia, Mo.: University of Missouri Press, 1988.

Brooks, Zelda Irene. *The Poetry of Gabriel Celaya: A Thematic Study*. Potomac, Md.: Scripta Humanistica, 1986.

Ferran, Jaime, and Daniel P. Testa. *Spanish Writers of 1936: Crisis and Commitment in the Poetry of the Thirties and Forties*. London: Tamesis, 1973.

Foard, Douglas W. "Poet on Ice: Dionisio Ridruejo and Hitler's Russian Adventure." In *Germany and Europe in the Era of the Two World Wars*. Charlottesville, Va.: University of Virginia Press, 1986.

Holdworth, Carole A. *Modern Minstrelsy: Miguel Hernández and Jacques Brel*. Bern; Las Vegas: Peter Lang, 1979.

Mellizo, Carlos, and Louise Salstad, eds. *Blas de Otero: Study of a Poet*. Laramie, Wyo.: University of Wyoming, Dept. of Modern and Classical Languages, 1980.

Nichols, Geraldine Cleary. *Miguel Hernández*. Boston: Twayne, 1978.

Rogers, Douglass. "Death in a New Key: On a Function of Orality in José Hierro's Agenda." In *A Ricardo Gullon: Sus Discipulos*. Edited by Adelaida Lopez de Martinez. Erie, Pa.: Pub. de la Asociacion de Licenciados y Doctores Espanoles en Estados Unidos, 1995.

Ruiz Fornelle, Enrique. *A Concordance to the Poetry of Leopoldo Panero*. University, Ala.: University of Alabama Press, 1978.

Sanchez Oneida, Maria Luisa. "The Family as a Theme in Some Poets of the Generation of 1936." *Dissertation Abstracts International* 46, 2 (August 1985): 439A.

Sherno, Sylvia R. "Blas de Otero, Postmodern Poet." *Anales de la Literatura Espanola Contemporanea* 19, 1-2 (1994): 133-49.

Ugalde, Sharon Keefe. *Gabriel Celaya*. Boston: Twayne, 1978.

Zupanchich, Maria. "Two Moments in the Life and Poetry of Dionisio Ridruejo." *Romance Notes* 10 (1969): 218-25.

GENERATION OF 1938 (Generación del 1938)
Chile, 1930s

The Chilean Generation of 1938 arose following election results that same year which favored liberal, progressive thinking. Led by Juan Godoy (1911-), the Generation focused on creating works of fiction, inspired by MARXISM, that effectively portrayed the hopes and needs of the lower classes. Among Godoy's followers were Carlos Droguett (1915-1996), Fernando Alegría (1918-), and Nicomedes Guzmán (1914-1964).

❖•❖

Further Reading

Alegría, Fernando. *Changing Centuries: Selected Poems of Fernando Alegría*. Translated by Stephen Kessler. Pittsburgh, Pa.: Latin American Literary Review Press, 1984. 2nd ed., 1988.

Columbus, Claudette Kemper. "'Affective' Strategies for Social Change: Alegria's 'The Chilean Spring'." *Mosaic* 22, 1 (winter 1989): 101-11.

Correas de Zapata, Celia. "Talking with Alegria." *Americas* 24 (August 1972): 9-12.

Epple, Juan. "The Inhabitants of Wing Place." *Third Rail: A Review of International Arts & Literature* 9 (1988): 28-31.

Lyon, Thomas E. *Juan Godoy*. New York: Twayne, 1972.

Pearson, Lon. *Nicomedes Guzmán, Proletarian Author in Chile's Literary Generation of 1938*. Columbia, Mo.: University of Missouri Press, 1976.

GENERATION OF 1940, Guatemala. *See* GRUPO *ACENTO*

GENERATION OF 1940 (Generación del 1940) Paraguay, 1950s-1960s

The Generation of 1940 refers to a group of writers who emerged on the literary scene in Paraguay during the 1950s and 1960s. Hérib Campos Cervera (1908-1953) wrote poetry influenced by SURREALIST techniques and is known for his volume *Ceniza redimida* (1950; Ashes Redeemed). Novelist Gabriel Casaccia (1907-) is another writer associated with the Generation of 1940; his *La babosa* (1952; The Driveler) was written and published in Argentina, though it is concerned with Paraguayan society. Josefina Plá (1909-), born in the Canary Islands, moved from Surrealist techniques to her own style in poetry; she also writes plays and is an art historian. One of her most acclaimed works is the collection of poetry *Rostros en el agua* (1963; Faces on the Water). Augusto Roa Bastos (1917-), a poet and leading novelist, uses MAGIC REALIST modes of expression in, for example, what many consider his masterpiece, *Hijo de hombre* (1960; *Son of Man,* 1965). Finally, Elvio Romero (1926-), a later poet, is frequently mentioned as a successor to Campos Cervera.

❖•❖

Further Reading

Collmer, Robert G. "The Displaced Person in the Novels of Gabriel Casaccia." *Artes Liberales* 3, 2 (1970): 37-46.

Foster, David William. *Augusto Roa Bastos*. Boston: Twayne, 1978.

————. *The Myth of Paraguay in the Fiction of Augusto Roa Bastos*. Chapel Hill, N.C.: University of North Carolina Press, 1969.

Gonzalez, Javier M. "An Interview with Augusto Roa Bastos." *Salmagundi* 72 (fall 1986): 22-30.

"The Initiation Archetype in Arguedas, Roa Bastos and Ocampo." *Latin American Literary Review* 11, 21 (fall-winter 1982): 45-55.

King, John. "Augusto Roa Bastos." *Index on Censorship* 12, 4 (August 1983): 15-17.

Robles, Mercedes M. "Syncretism in Roa Bastos' *Hijo de hombre*." *Romance Notes* 35, 2 (winter 1994): 197-204.

Scroggins, Daniel S. "Brotherhood and Fratricide in the Early Fiction of Augusto Roa Bastos." *Hispanic Journal* 6, 2 (spring 1985): 137-47.
Weldt-Basson, Helene Carol. *Augusto Roa Bastos's* I The Supreme: *A Dialogic Perspective*. Columbia, Mo.: University of Missouri Press, 1993.

GENERATION OF 1940 (Generación del 1940)
Puerto Rico, 1940s

The Generation of 1940 was so named by René Marqués (1919-1979), a prominent literary figure in Puerto Rico, who called for those in his generation to lose their docility and strive for cultural and political independence from Spain and the United States. Asserting the goal of cultural independence did not, however, coincide with a unilateral rejection of Western European and American literature and philosophy. Marqués himself studied with Erwin Piscator's workshop at Columbia University, and read and critiqued writers such as Luigi PIRANDELLO (*see* MODERNISM, Italy), George Bernard SHAW (*see* EDWARDIAN LITERATURE), and Eugene O'NEILL (*see* EXPRESSIONISM, United States, and PROVINCETOWN PLAYERS). He sought to influence writers of this generation, such as Emilio Díaz Valcárcel (1929-), Pedro Juan Soto (1928-), Abelardo Díaz Alfaro (1920-), José Luis González (1926-), Edwin Figueroa (1925-), José Luis Vivas (1926-), and Salvador de Jesús (1927-). Many of these younger writers' short stories were included in a collection for which Marqués wrote one of his best-known essays, "El cuento puertoriqueño en la promoción del cuarenta" (1959; The Puerto Rican Short Story of the Forties Generation). As important as his critical and literary influence, Marqués's strongest impact has been in his theatrical work, having founded numerous theater groups in Puerto Rico and written plays such as *La carreta* (1952; *The Oxcart*, 1969) and *La muerteno entrará en palacio* (1959; Death Will Not Enter the Palace).

❖•❖
Further Reading

Anderson Imbert, Enrique. *Spanish-American Literature: A History*. Detroit: Wayne State University Press, 1963.
Matilla Rivas, Alfredo, and Iván Silén, eds. *The Puerto Rican Poets*. Toronto: Bantam Books, 1972.
Reynolds, B. H. "René Marqués." In *Latin American Writers*. Edited by Carlos A. Solé. Vol. II. New York: Scribner, 1989.

GENERATION OF 1945
Brazil, 1940s

A Brazilian group of poets that gained notice as early as 1942, the Generation of 1945 stressed heightened imagery while employing traditonal forms. João Cabral de Melo

Neto (1920-), an early member of the group, later achieved renown as a seminal influence on the Brazilian CONCRETE POETS. Other members of the Generation of 1945 included Geir Campos (1924-), Lêdo Ivo (1924-), Mauro Mota (1912-), Marcos Konder Reis (1922-), and Domingos Carvalho da Silva (1915-).

☙•❧

Further Reading

Cabral de Melo Neto, João. *Selected Poetry, 1937-1990*. Edited by Djelal Kadir. Translated by Elizabeth Bishop, et al. Hanover, N.H.: University Press of New England for Wesleyan University Press, 1994.

Fonseca, Reynaldo, and João Cabral de Melo Neto. *Brazilian Painting and Poetry*. Rio de Janeiro, Brazil: Spala Editora, 1979.

Nunes, Benedito. *João Cabral de Melo Neto*. Petropolis, Brazil: Vozes, 1971.

Pinto, Julio. "Peircean Semiotic and Narrative Time: Ledo Ivo's 'Ninho de Cobras.'" *Romance Notes* 27, 1 (autumn 1986): 3-12.

Rodman, Selden. *Tongues of Fallen Angels*. New York: New Directions, 1974.

————. "The Ugly Duckling Who Became One of the Forty Immortals." *Review* 15 (winter 1972): 42-47.

World Literature Today 66, 4 (autumn 1992). Special issue devoted to João Cabral de Melo Neto.

GENERATION OF '45
Indonesia, 1945-1960s

In 1942, as part of World War II, the Japanese wrested control over Indonesia from the Dutch and occupied the country until 1945. Following the Japanese surrender, the Dutch, who had considered Indonesia to be their colony since the 1600s, sought to reassert their influence. As Indonesians struggled, both against the Dutch and against themselves, to create a free, unified country, the spirit of revolution infused all aspects of Indonesian life. This spirit showed itself in literary form in the writers who came to be known as the Generation of '45 (Angkatan '45). This label generally refers to all those whose artistic efforts began to bear fruit during the fight for independence, but certain unifying themes are evident, especially a shift toward Western forms and influences (but not language) and a belief that creative works could help further the aims of the revolution.

Chief among the Generation of '45 is the poet Chairil Anwar (1922-1949). The small number of his surviving poems, perhaps 70, belies his continuing influence on modern Indonesian literature. Borrowing from Western poets such as Rainer Maria Rilke (1875-1926), T. S. ELIOT (*see* MODERNISM, England and Ireland), Emily Dickinson (1830-1886), and the Indonesian-born Dutch writer Charles Edgar du Perron (1899-1940), Anwar's poetry is driven by a desire to push the envelope of the Indonesian language and his interest in political and patriotic issues, as shown by poems such as "Aku" (1943; "Me," 1970) and "Persetujuan dengan bung Karno" (1948; "Agreement with Friend Suekarno," 1962). Another pervasive thread in Anwar's poetry is an obsession with things sexual, an example of which may be found in the poem "Lagu biasa" (1949; "An Ordinary Song," 1962). The significant novelist of the Generation of '45, Pramudya Ananta Tur (1925-), wrote realistic books such as *Keluarga gerilja* (1950; Guerrilla Family) and *Bukan pasar malam* (1951; *It's Not an All Night Fair*, 1973) that revolve around themes pertaining to the Japanese occupation and the struggle for independence from the Dutch. Other important members of the Generation of '45 include short-story writer Idris (1921-1979); poets W. S. Rendra (1935-), Sitor Situmorang (1923-) and Ajip Rossidhy (1938-); Islamic writer Bahrum Rangkuti (1919-1977); and journalist Mochtar Lubis (1922-).

When a repressive, right-wing government came to power in the 1960s, many of the Generation of '45 turned their writings against what they saw as a betrayal of their ideals. The results were often predictable. Tur, whose earlier novels were written while in Dutch prisons, was incarcerated by his own government from 1965 to 1979, then published upon his freedom a novel—*Bumi manusia* (1980; *This Earth of Mankind*, 1982) —so successful that it was banned in 1981. Lubis was also jailed in the '60s and produced, in *Twilight in Djakarta* (1963), a caustic attack on life under the Indonesian dictator Sukarno (1901-1970). This continued desire for true independence along with the synthesis of Indonesian life and modern Western themes must be considered the strongest legacy of the Generation of '45.

It should be noted that the term Generation of '45 is also used to describe a variety of sociopolitical groups in Indonesia. A political party of the 1950s that helped Sukarno consolidate his power while under the guise of working to complete the revolution used the name; the term was used pejoratively by student activists of the 1960s to describe those who fought for the revolution then sold out its ideals to Sukarno; and some use the term neutrally when discussing all those who fought, in one sense or another, for Indonesian independence in the late 1940s.

⤖•⬻

Further Reading

Aveling, Harry. *A Thematic History of Indonesian Poetry: 1920 to 1974.* [DeKalb] Center for Southeast Asian Studies, Northern Illinois University, 1974; distributed by Cellar Book Shop, Detroit.

Johns, Anthony H. *Cultural Options and the Role of Tradition: A Collection of Essays on Modern Indonesian and Malaysian Literature.* Canberra, Australia: Faculty of Asian Studies in Association with the Australian National University Press, 1979.

Raffel, Burton. *The Development of Modern Indonesian Poetry.* Albany, N.Y.: State University of New York Press, 1967.
Teeuw, A. *Modern Indonesian Literature.* 2nd ed. Vol. 1. The Hague: Martinus Nijhoff, 1979.

GENERATION OF 1945 (Generación del 1945)
Uruguay, 1940s

The Generation of 1945 refers to a group of writers in Montevideo, the Uruguayan capital, during and after World War II, whose fiction evidenced a shift from rural to urban settings. Their work reflected concerns with city life, bureaucracy, hopelessness, and alienation. Some of the literary figures associated with the Generation of 1945 include Mario Benedetti (1920-), novelist Felisberto Hernández (1902-1964), lawyer and prose writer Carlos Martínez Moreno (1917-1986), Juan Carlos Onetti (1909-1994), and Ángel Rama (1926-). Benedetti, who wrote stories, novels, plays, and criticism, is best known for his collection of short stories, *Montevideanos* (1959; People of Montevideo), and the novels *Quíen de nosotros* (1953; Who Among Us?), *La tregua* (1960; The Truce), and *Gracias por el fuego* (1964; Thanks for the Light). Onetti is an exception to the Montevideo connection, since he has spent much time in Argentina. There, however, he lived in Buenos Aires and wrote much of his work with that city as a backdrop. His novels include *El pozo* (1939; The Well), *Tierra de nadie* (1941; No Man's Land), *El astillero* (1961; The Shipyard), and *Juntacadáveres* (1965). Among Onetti's literary influences are Roberto Arlt of the BOEDO GROUP.

❖•❖

Further Reading

Adams, Michael Ian. *Three Authors of Alienation: Bombal, Onetti, Carpentier.* Austin, Tex.: University of Texas Press, 1975.
Brotherston, Gordon. "Survival in the Sullied City: Juan Carlos Onetti." In his *The Emergence of the Latin American Novel.* Cambridge, England: Cambridge University Press, 1977.
Franco, Jean. *The Modern Culture of Latin America: Society and the Artist.* New York: Praeger, 1967.
Graziano, Frank. *The Lust of Seeing: Themes of the Gaze and Sexual Rituals in the Fiction of Felisberto Hernández.* Lewisburg, Pa.: Bucknell University Press, 1996.
————. "An Introduction to Felisberto Hernandez's Poetics." *Indiana Journal of Hispanic Literatures* 2, 2 (spring 1994): 185-201.
Gregory, Stephen W. G. *Humanist Ethics or Realist Aesthetics?: Torture, Interrogation and Psychotherapy in Mario Benedetti.* Bundoora, Australia: La Trobe University Institute of Latin American Studies, 1991.
Harss, Luis. "Felisberto Hernandez." *Review* 20 (1977): 49-59.

Harss, Luis, and Barbara Dohmann. "Juan Carlos Onetti, or the Shadows on the Wall." In their *Into the Mainstream: Conversations with Latin-American Writers*. New York: Harper & Row, 1967.

Jones, Yvonne Perier. *The Formal Expression of Meaning in Juan Carlos Onetti's Narrative Art*. Cuernavaca, Mexico: Centro Intercultural de Documentación, 1971.

Kadir, Djelal. *Juan Carlos Onetti*. Boston: Twayne Publishers, 1977.

Maloof, Judy. *Over Her Dead Body: The Construction of Male Subjectivity in Onetti*. New York: Peter Lang, 1995.

———. "Male Subjectivity and Gender Relations in Juan Carlos Onetti's *El pozo*." *Chasqui* 23, 1 (May 1994): 44-52.

Millington, Mark. *An Analysis of the Short Stories of Juan Carlos Onetti: Fictions of Desire*. Lewiston, N.Y.: E. Mellen Press, 1993.

———. *Reading Onetti: Language, Narrative, and the Subject*. Liverpool, England: F. Cairns, 1985.

Murray, Jack. *The Landscapes of Alienation: Ideological Subversion in Kafka, Celine, and Onetti*. Stanford, Calif.: Stanford University Press, 1991.

Stone, Kenton V. *Utopia Undone: The Fall of Uruguay in the Novels of Carlos Martínez Moreno*. Lewisburg, Pa.: Bucknell University Press; London: Associated University Presses, 1994.

Sullivan, Mary Lee. "Projection as a Narrative Technique in Juan Carlos Onetti's *Goodbyes*." *Studies in Short Fiction* 31, 3 (summer 1994): 441-47.

GENERATION OF 1950 (Generación del 1950)
Chile, 1950s

Unlike the Chilean GENERATION OF 1938, the Generation of 1950 was a markedly apolitical and introspective group of writers. Their primary influences were English MODERNISTS James JOYCE and Virginia WOOLF and EXISTENTIALISTS Jean-Paul SARTRE and Albert CAMUS. Novelist José Donoso (1924-), considered one of the most distinguished Chilean writers, was the Generation's most prominent member. Other writers linked to the movement include Jorge Edwards (1931-), Luis Alberto Heiremans (1928-1964), Enrique Lafourcade (1927-), and Jaime Laso (1926-).

❖•❖

Further Reading

"Boom Writers: The Last Generation—A Conversation with José Donoso." *Torre de Papel* 1, 2 (winter 1991): 42-47.

Castillo-Feliu, Guillermo I., ed. *The Creative Process in the Works of José Donoso*. Rock Hill, S.C.: Winthrop College, 1982.

Christ, Ronald. "An Interview with José Donoso." *Partisan Review* 49, 1 (1982): 23-44.

Fleak, Ken. "Promotion of the Chilean Short Story." *Language Quarterly* 24, 3-4 (spring-summer 1986): 31-32, 37.

Friedman, Mary Lusky. "The Chilean Exile's Return: Donoso Versus Garcia Marquez." *The Americas Review* 18, 3-4 (fall-winter 1990): 211-17.

Gonzalez Mandri, Flora. *José Donoso's House of Fiction: A Dramatic Construction of Time and Place*. Detroit: Wayne State University Press, 1995.

Gutierrez Mouat, Ricardo. "Beginnings and Returns: An Interview with José Donoso." *Review of Contemporary Fiction* 12, 2 (summer 1992): 11-17.

Kadir, Djelal. "Next Door: Writing Elsewhere." *Review of Contemporary Fiction* 12, 2 (summer 1992): 60-69.

Lipski, John M. "Donoso's Obscene Bird: Novel and Anti-Novel." *Latin American Literary Review* 9 (1976): 39-47.

McMurray, George R. *José Donoso*. Boston: Twayne, 1979.

Magnarelli, Sharon. *Understanding José Donoso*. Columbia, S.C.: University of South Carolina Press, 1993.

Moody, Michael. "Jorge Edwards, Chile, and *El museo de cera*." *Chasqui* 14, 2-3 (February-May 1985): 37-42.

Peden, Margaret Sayers. "The Theater of Luis Alberto Heiremans: 1928-1964." In *Dramatists in Revolt: The New Latin American Theater*. Edited by Leon F. Lyday and George W. Woodyard. Austin, Tex.: University of Texas Press, 1976.

Quain, Estelle E. "The Image of the House in the Works of José Donoso." In *Essays in Honor of Jorge Guillen on the Occasion of His 85th Year*. Cambridge, Mass.: Abedul, 1977.

Reid, Alastair. "Meta-Donoso." *Review of Contemporary Fiction* 12, 2 (summer 1992): 47-49.

Stabb, Martin S. "The Erotic Mask: Notes on Donoso and the New Novel." *Symposium* 30 (1976): 170-79.

GENERATION OF 1950
Indonesia, 1950s

The Indonesian Generation of 1950 was largely inspired by Noto Soeroto (1888-1951), a mystical Javanese poet who wrote in Dutch. Other figures connected with the movement include Sitor Situmorang (1923-), W. S. Rendra (1935-), Asrul Sani (1927-), Nugroho Notosusanto (1931-), Chairil Anwar (1922-1949), and Rivai Apin (1927-).

❖•❖

Further Reading

Jansen, Christel. "A Poet and His Plumage." *Index on Censorship* 21, 6 (June 1992): 15.

Oemarjati, Boen Sri. *Chairil Anwar: The Poet and His Language*. The Hague: Martinus Nijhoff, 1972.

Raffel, Burton. "A Note on W. S. Rendra, Poems from W. S. Rendra." *Literature East and West* 12 (1968): 129-40.

Rendra, W. S. *Ballads and Blues: Poems Translated from Indonesian*. Translated by Burton
   Raffel, Harry Aveling, and Derwent May. Kuala Lumpur, Malaysia; New York: Oxford
   University Press, 1974.

GENERATION OF 1954
Algeria, 1950s

The Generation of 1954 (sometimes also called the Generation of 1952 — the year in
which two of these writers' first novels were published) was more a loose band of young
writers in Algeria with age, French education, and a feeling of cultural ambiguity in
common than a solid, collaborating literary front with a particular manifesto. Mohammed Dib (1920-), Mouloud Mammeri (1917-1989), Mouloud Feraoun (1913-1962),
Kateb Yacine (1929-), and Malek Haddad (1927-1978) are the writers generally associated with the Generation of 1954.

Together their works reflect the profound changes that occurred in Algeria when
Algerians — mainly Arabo-Berber Muslims — rose up against the French colonists in
1954 and fought until 1962 for independence, losing at least ten percent of the population. Muslims had gained "legal citizenship" only as late as 1947, and French racism
and administrative injustices were rampant and blatant. The Generation of 1954 writers were part of a relatively small segment of the Algerian populace — French-educat-
ed Muslims, though not all were born into elite families. Generally speaking, critics
often consider their works of the 1950s and 1960s militant, yet expressive of a poignant
ambivalence about being acculturated in the language of the oppressor and a deep,
though not always overt, sense of alienation from both the traditional Arabo-Berber
culture, which is in danger of decline, and the ruling culture that spread its language
and educational facilities but withheld its privileges. Scholars most often cite several
novels among these writers' works as most representative of this era in Algerian history,
as well as most concerned with the attendant issues of the revolution and independence: Dib's trilogy *Algérie* (Algeria) — *La grande maison* (1952; The Big House),
L'incendie (1954; The Fire), and *Le métier a tisser* (1957; The Loom), and *Qui se sou-
vient de la mer* (1962; He Who Remembers the Sea) — all of which reveal the influence of Franz KAFKA (*see* MODERNISM, Austria and Germany), Virginia WOOLF (*see*
MODERNISM, England and Ireland), William FAULKNER (*see* MODERNISM, United
States), and especially Carl JUNG; Mammeri's novels *Le sommeil du juste* (1955; *The
Sleep of the Just*, 1958) and *L'opium et le bâton* (1965; The Opium and the Stick);
Yacine's novel *Nedjma* (1956; *Nedjma*, 1961); Feraoun's novels *Le fils du pauvre*
(1950; The Poor Man's Son) and *Les chemins qui montent* (1957, The Climbing
Roads); and Haddad's volume of poetry *Le malheur en danger* (1956; Wretchedness Is
in Danger). As well as being testimonials to the cultural and political situation through

which these artists lived, these works are stylistically interesting, innovative, and possess enduring literary value.

Feraoun was an inspector of social welfare centers when he was killed by French terrorists in Algeria. Dib settled in Paris in 1959. Mammeri fled to Morocco during the war but returned after independence where he became a professor of ethnology at the University of Algiers. Yacine, after a youth marked by imprisonment for demonstrating in the massacre of 1945 at Sétif and Guelma, also settled in France. And, until his death in 1978 Haddad, in despondency, reportedly took a vow of silence.

➤•◄

Further Reading

Gordon, David C. *The Passing of French Algeria*. London: Oxford University Press, 1966.
Mortimer, Mildred. "Profile: Mouloud Mammeri." *Africa Report* 16, 6 (June 1971): 26-28.
Ortzen, Len, ed. *North African Writing*. London: Heinemann Educational, 1970.
Sellin, Eric. "Algerian Poetry: Poetic Values, Mohammed Dib and Kateb Yacine." *Journal of the New African Literature and the Arts* 9/10 (winter and spring 1971): 44-68.
Von Grunebaum, Gustave E. *French African Literature: Some Cultural Implications*. The Hague: Mouton, 1964.

GENERATION OF 1955
Hungary, 1950s

Launched around the time of the Russian Thaw in SOCIALIST REALISM, the Hungarian Generation of 1955 opened long-closed avenues in Hungarian prose, including humor and psychological realism. György Moldova (1934-), Ferenc Sánta (1927-), István Csurka (1934-), István Szábo (n.d.), and László Karmondy (1928-1972) were among the writers associated with the movement.

➤•◄

Further Reading

Foldes, Anna. "In Quest of a Generation: Plays by Istvan Csurka, Lajos Maroti, Istvan Orkeny." *New Hungarian Quarterly* 75 (1979): 198-206.
Gyorffy, Miklos. "Male Illusions Lost." *New Hungarian Quarterly* 27, 101 (spring 1986): 149-54.
Halasz, Laszlo. "Affective-Structural Effect and the Characters' Perception in Reception of Short Stories: An American-Hungarian Cross-Cultural Study." *Poetics: International Review for the Theory of Literature* 17, 4-5 (October 1988): 417-38.
Koltai, Thomas. "Transylvania, for Instance." *New Hungarian Quarterly* 30, 114 (summer 1989): 215-21.
Tezla, Albert. "Ferenc Santa." *The Hungarian P.E.N.* 25 (1984): 29-34.

GENERATION OF THE 1950s (Asas '50)
Malaysia, 1950s

The Malaysian Generation of the 1950s — Asmal (1924-), Awam-il-Sarkam (1918-), Hamzah Hussein (1927-), Keris Mas (1922-), Mahsuri Salikon (1927-), Suratman Markasan (1930-), Usman Awang (1929-), and Wijaya Mala (1923-) — were a politically liberal group of writers who stressed attention to current social problems in their prose and poetry.

❖•❖

Further Reading

Zaidi, I. "Ang Pow Not Cash But Love From Motherland." *The Malay Mail* 10 (November 1972): 5.

GENERATION OF THE 1960s (Shestydesyatnyky)
Ukraine, 1960s

An important movement in contemporary Ukrainian poetry, the Generation of the 1960s reaffirmed the independence of the literary work and the validity of "art for art's sake" aestheticism. Ivan Drach (1936-), Vitaly Korotych (1936-), Lina Kostenko (1930-), Maxym Rylsky (1895-1964), Vasyl Symonenko (1935-1963), and Mykola Vinhranovsky (1936-) were all associated with the movement, which, after 1964, became the subject of new policies of repression by the Communist Party.

❖•❖

Further Reading

Drach, Ivan. *Orchard Lamps*. Edited and introduced by Stanley Kunitz. Translated by Daniel Halpern, et al. Toronto: Exile Editions, 1989.
Kostenko, Lina Vasylivna. *Selected Poetry: Wanderings of the Heart*. Translated from Ukrainian with an afterword by Michael N. Naydan. New York: Garland, 1990.
Pidhainy, Oleh Semenovych. *Ukrainian Historiography and the Great East-European Revolution: A Propos of Symonenko's Polemics*. Toronto; New York: New Review Books, 1968.

GENEVA SCHOOL
Switzerland, 1950s-1970s

One of the foremost critical movements that drew upon the Phenomenological theories of German philosopher Edmund Husserl (1859-1938), the Geneva School was extremely influential in Europe and America during the decades following World War II. Like Husserl, the Genevists upheld individual consciousness as the ultimate window through which reality might be analyzed and understood. In opposition to the

American NEW CRITICS, who examined the literary work in isolation and provided evaluative judgments, the Geneva School viewed the work as vitally connected to the author's particular set of experiences and, therefore, to history. Interpretation, consequently, did not necessitate or resemble evaluation; rather, it took the form of a parallel text, which attempted to intuit the psychological and experiential nature of the literary creator. Although this EXISTENTIAL "criticism of consciousness" as practiced by Georges POULET and others fell into disfavor by the late 1960s, important traces of it survived first in STRUCTURALISM and, later, in such Poststructuralist movements as DECONSTRUCTION and READER-RESPONSE CRITICISM.

Phenomenology as a philosophical movement began with the publication of Husserl's *Logische Untersuchungen* (1900-1; *Logical Investigations*, 1970). This work attempted to separate the observable, physical world from the hidden, psychical world for epistemological purposes: to discover the fundamental sources and limits of all human knowledge. Husserl arrived at one principle, in particular, which profoundly affected later aesthetic thought. He posited that objects do not exist independently; instead, their existence becomes real when subjects, individual consciousnesses, observe and derive meaning from them. Of the several intellectual successors to Husserl, Martin Heidegger (1889-1976) was most responsible for bridging the gap between philosophy and literature. His *Sein und Zeit* (1927; *Being and Time*, 1962) presented historical, existential time as an ordering concept which gave unity to the Husserlian notions of consciousness and meaning. Phenomenology also appeared in an altered form in the works of French writers Jean-Paul SARTRE and Maurice Merleau-Ponty (1908-1961). Despite their importance to contemporary Existentialist thought, the influence these thinkers had on the exclusively literary investigations of Poulet, principal spokesman for the Geneva School, is little more than incidental. Some critics submit that it was French philosopher Gaston Bachelard (1884-1962) who most significantly shaped the thought and critical methodology of Poulet and his colleagues. An anti-rationalist, Bachelard laid the foundation in *La psychoanalyse du feu* (1937; *The Psychoanalysis of Fire*, 1964) for later definitions of the critical act not as a cold, sequential determination but as an almost mystical symbiosis between the reader, the work, and the author. There is evidence to suggest, however, that Bachelard's later works were more the result of than the source for works written by the Geneva School during their developing stages.

Centered at the University of Geneva, the Geneva School was comprised of Poulet, Marcel Raymond (1897-1956), Albert Béguin (1901-1957), Jean-Pierre Richard (1922-), and Jean Starobinski (1920-). Both Raymond and Béguin preceded Poulet as theoreticians and exerted, successively, the greatest influence upon his initial work. Raymond's *De Baudelaire au surréalisme* (1933; *From Baudelaire to Surrealism*, 1947), a groundbreaking contribution to French literary criticism, served to uniquely humanize both the literary work and the critical process with the assertion that the author's perceptions of existence are what fuses and sustains the literary experience. Both Raymond and his colleague Béguin extracted examples from the visionary, humanistic literature of Romanticism to underpin their commitment to a subjective, existential critical method. Béguin, a follower of Roman Catholicism after 1940, developed an even less traditional critical apparatus than Raymond. Yet, his was always a sympathetic and highly personal method which, together with the work of Raymond, became the prototype for the more systematic investigations of Poulet.

Poulet remains the most distinguished Genevist for his intensive consideration of consciousness as a dual absolute, present within the literary work and also within the reader. His emphasis upon the inescapable connections between these two consciousnesses, however, preserved the internal, experiential quality he associated with all literary expression. In this, he anticipated the concerns of Reader-Response critics, who deny the independence of verbal texts. Both Raymond and Béguin's most important writing stemmed from a concern with the pre-verbal structures of literature, the author's consciousness as it exists before the genetic assembling of words into intelligible structures. To this concern Poulet added contemplations of time and space in the early works *Études sur le temps humain, I* (1949; *Studies in Human Time*, 1956) and *Études sur le temps humain, II: La distance intérieure* (1952; *The Interior Distance*, 1959). Linking these two coordinates to René Descartes's (1596-1650) concept of the *cogito*, the perception and creation of one's own existence, Poulet was able to synthesize his view of the creative-experiential nature of literature. During the 1950s and 1960s, he expanded the dimensions of his theory, which tended to isolate individual identities, so that separate consciousnesses could be first defined and then unified through the sociohistorical characteristics they shared. In a now-classic essay, "PHÉNOMENOLOGIE DE LA CONSCIENCE CRITIQUE" (1968; "Phenomenology of Reading," 1969), he consolidated his views on the creative, expressive, and participatory facets of literature and also delineated differences between himself and his disciples.

Despite Poulet's extensive influence on the younger members of the Geneva School, the criticism of consciousness he championed is now a largely abandoned discipline. Ironically, one of his most devoted disciples helped hasten the end of the Geneva School. J. Hillis Miller (1928-), an American academic, met and became close friends with Poulet while both were teaching at Johns Hopkins University in the 1950s. Miller soon emerged as one of the most forceful proponents of Poulet's ideas and dedicated the study *Charles Dickens: The World of His Novels* (1958) to his mentor. However, Jacques DERRIDA (*see* DECONSTRUCTION) and Paul DE MAN (*see* YALE SCHOOL) later convinced Miller of the untenable nature of Poulet's metaphysics and made pos-

239

sible his conversion to Deconstruction, one of the most controversial and revolutionary theoretical systems in modern literary history. The factor that most contributed to the Genevists' downfall, though, was their own severely limited philosophy, which enabled them to write convincingly only of those authors possessing a similarly introspective viewpoint. Notwithstanding this, the writings of the Geneva School are still valued for their often uncanny grasp of the artist's mental framework and personal vision of existence.

❖•❖

Poulet, Georges (1902-), Belgian essayist and critic.

Frequently linked with French *nouvelle critique* (new criticism), Poulet was at the forefront of the mid-twentieth-century European revolution in literary theory. His criticism, which ignores genre and form, has sometimes been characterized as dense, repetitious, and abstract; yet proponents of his subjective method explain that these potential flaws are mitigated by the deliberate sense of personal communion with other consciousnesses that pervades his readings. Along with such rival schools as Deconstruction, Poulet and the Geneva School, through inventive and illuminating discourse, helped to radically transform criticism into a creative art in its own right.

"Phénoménologie de la conscience critique" (1968; "Phenomenology of Reading," 1969).

One of Poulet's most coherent and useful essays, "The Phenomenology of Reading" underscores the pure empathic response that is fundamental to all interpretive readings by the Geneva School critics. Poulet asserts both the immediacy and depth of the reading event as he states: "At the precise moment that I see, surging out of the object [book] I hold open before me, a quantity of significations which my mind grasps, I realize that what I hold in my hands is no longer just an object, or even simply a living thing. I am aware of a rational being, of a consciousness; the consciousness of another, no different from the one I automatically assume in every human being I encounter, except that in this case the consciousness is open to me, welcomes me, lets me look deep inside itself, and even allows me, with unheard-of license, to think what it thinks and feel what it feels." For these reasons, Poulet maintained in this essay and throughout his work that only in literature can we find the closest and most valuable reflection of human experience.

❖•❖

Further Reading

De Man, Paul. "The Literary Self as Origin: The Work of Georges Poulet." In his *Blindness and Insight*. 2nd ed. Minneapolis: University of Minnesota Press, 1983.

240

Detweiler, Robert. *Story, Sign, and Self: Phenomenology and Structuralism as Literary-Critical Methods*. Philadelphia: Fortress Press, 1978.

Edie, James M. *Edmund Husserl's Phenomenology: A Critical Commentary*. Bloomington, Ind.: Indiana University Press, 1987.

Lawall, Sarah. *Critics of Consciousness: The Existential Structures of Literature*. Cambridge, Mass.: Harvard University Press, 1968.

Miller, J. Hillis. "The Geneva School: The Criticism of Marcel Raymond, Albert Béguin, Georges Poulet, Jean Rousset, Jean-Pierre Richard, and Jean Starobinski." *Critical Quarterly* VIII (winter 1966).

Poulet, Georges. "Phenomenology of Reading." *New Literary History* I (October 1969).

Spanos, W., ed. *Martin Heidegger and the Question of Literature*. Bloomington, Ind.: Indiana University Press, 1976.

Spiegelberg, Herbert. *The Phenomenological Movement*. The Hague: Nijhoff, 1960.

GENTEEL TRADITION
United States, 1880s-1900s

The Genteel Tradition, a term coined in 1911 by philosopher George Santayana (1863-1952) to refer to the works, attitudes, and social institutions of a large, once-dominant group of New England writers and sophisticates, was a phenomenon of post-Civil War, urbane, and idyllic American literature. Conventional methods, tame subject matter, and Gilded Age values were key watchwords of the highly doctrinaire Genteel writers, who tended to emulate their more original and talented predecessors, New England Brahmins James Russell Lowell (1819-1891), Oliver Wendell Holmes (1809-1894), and Henry Wadsworth Longfellow (1807-1882). Conspicuously at odds with such emerging movements as REALISM, NATURALISM, Impressionism, and SYMBOLISM, the refined literature of the Genteel writers was frequently subjected to parody, satire, and polemical attack. Yet, for some four or five decades the machinery of Genteelism — magazines, publishing houses, social clubs, conservatories, and academies — effectively controlled middle-class tastes while simultaneously limiting the readerships of more experimental and, ultimately, more significant writers.

Centered in the twin cultural citadels of Boston and New York, the Genteel writers were united in their nostalgic view of American history, their abhorrence of vulgar or lowly subject matter, and their inability or unwillingness to explore and understand the problems of their rapidly changing society. Many of them wrote idealistic poetry in the Romantic manner and several of them held prestigious positions as literary editors and critics. Few, despite careers that flourished, had any lasting influence on American literature. Some of the more notable Genteelists were Thomas Bailey ALDRICH, Charles Eliot Norton (1827-1908), Edward Roland Sill (1841-1887), Edmund Clarence Stedman

(1833-1908), Richard Henry Stoddard (1825-1903), Bayard Taylor (1825-1878), Henry Van Dyke (1852-1933), and Charles Dudley Warner (1829-1900). Despite some connection with such American Realists as Mark TWAIN and William Dean HOWELLS, these writers remained largely aloof from new literary currents, favoring instead to preserve the polite literature of the past. Their stronghold on mainstream values, obstinately heedless of the groundbreaking theories and techniques that surrounded them, persisted until the rise of such deadly iconoclasts as H. L. Mencken (1880-1956) and Sinclair LEWIS (*see* JAZZ AGE) and the long-delayed recognition awarded such thoroughgoing Naturalists as Theodore DREISER (*see* NATURALISM, United States), perhaps the most visible victim of Genteel-linked censorship and conservativism.

➹•❦

Aldrich, Thomas Bailey (1836-1907)
American novelist, editor, short-story writer, and poet.

One of the most representative of the Genteel writers, Aldrich began his literary career in 1855 as a poet but eventually became known more for his graceful, cleverly plotted short stories and for his conservative editorship during the 1880s, as successor to Howells, of the *Atlantic Monthly*. Since 1865 he numbered among the elite of Boston and is sometimes classified among the Brahmins, with whom he maintained ties. Aldrich is best known for the poem "The Ballad of Babie Bell" (1855), the short story collection *Marjorie Daw and Other People* (1873), the detective novel *The Stillwater Tragedy* (1880), and his most memorable work, THE STORY OF A BAD BOY (1870).

The Story of a Bad Boy (1870; republished as *Tom Bailey's Adventures; Or, The Story of a Bad Boy*, 1877).

A semi-autobiographical novel set in New Hampshire and New Orleans, *The Story of a Bad Boy* recounts the mischievous youth of small-town banker's son Tom Bailey. In actuality, Tom is an engagingly comic character whose development from boyhood to manhood is filled with adventure, mishap, pranks, and minor catastrophes. Despite adroit narration of episodes and a cast of endearing characters, the one overwhelming quality of the novel is that of tender reminiscence. The novel's widespread popularity sparked numerous imitations, most prominent of which were Mark TWAIN's *The Adventures of Tom Sawyer* (1876) and *THE ADVENTURES OF HUCKLEBERRY FINN* (1884), both markedly superior in technique and thematic richness.

➹•❦

Further Reading

Cary, Richard. *The Genteel Circle: Bayard Taylor and His New York Friends*. Ithaca, N.Y.: Cornell University Press, 1952.
Greenslet, Ferris. *The Life of Thomas Bailey Aldrich*. Boston: Houghton Mifflin, 1908.

Samuels, Charles E. *Thomas Bailey Aldrich*. New York: Twayne, 1965.

Wilson, Douglas L., ed. *The Genteel Tradition: Nine Essays by George Santayana*. Cambridge, Mass.: Harvard University Press, 1967.

GEORGIAN POETS
England, 1910-1922

Noted critic and scholar David Perkins (1928-) places the time of the Georgian poets specifically between 1910 and 1922; thus they fit comfortably into a wider timeframe between 1900 and 1938 which includes those political, social, and literary personages who were of what is called "the Georgian mind-set" and named for the then-ruling monarch of England, George V.

These writers were given the name "Georgian Poets" by Edward Marsh (1872-1953), who enjoyed prestige in the literary circles of the day, was a prominent civil servant, and who convinced the publisher Harold Monro (1879-1932) to present five important anthologies of their poetry. Between 1911 and 1922, these works were well received by a widening readership who continued to enjoy romantic, pastoral, and often nostalgic poetry of an earlier and simpler time. Poetry of this kind had been and was still under the sharp criticism of English MODERNISTS T. S. ELIOT, Ezra POUND, and Edith Sitwell (1887-1964), among others of similar sensibility; these critics felt Georgian poetry to be simplistic, overly sentimental, and irrelevant to the contemporary literary mode.

Early Georgians included Rupert BROOKE, Wilfred Gibson (1878-1962), Edward THOMAS, and the war poets Siegfried Sassoon (1886-1967) and Wilfred OWEN. Both Marsh and Monro were convinced that these young poets and others of their persua sion made up a contemporary, yet more traditionally oriented group of writers whose work contained an exciting and worthwhile vibrancy. Moreover, their work would provide imaginative experience for the general reading public which would be clear of message, pleasant to ear and eye, and absent of the ambiguity of the dissolving images and the disconcertion of free verse.

The first publication, *Georgian Poetry — 1911-1912* (1915), was a critical success, through Marsh's efforts, including his many literary connections which influenced marketing procedures and enthusiastic reviews. The initial volume contained work by Brooke, G. K. Chesterton (1874-1936), Walter De la Mare (1873-1956), and others whom Marsh felt deserved attention. Thereafter, four remaining volumes appeared under the same title, but with consecutive dates until 1922.

Generally, the poetry contained a new realism and strength which had been absent in earlier poetry of its genre, but some of it retained familiar elements of the beauty of the bucolic and a heavy concentration upon nature and its particular appeal to the senses.

However, by 1918, the Georgians had been so severely taken to task by such as John Middleton Murry (1889-1957), whose attack was savage, and other Modernists, that the 1922 publication was the final one; thereafter, the Georgians were anthologized singularly, or not at all.

Thus the Georgian poets enjoyed their brief period in the Modernist literary revolution of the twentieth century. It consisted of their specific reaction against a kind of poetry which, to them, celebrated the sordid, in a disconsolate and anxious world. Contemporary enough and realistic enough in their efforts to improve upon the weaknesses of their predecessors, the Victorians and the EDWARDIANS, the Georgians provided poetry which had popular appeal for contented readers. One modern critic insists that they cannot be discredited, since some of their best work was "sinewy and subtle," and worth reading and reflecting upon.

✦•✦

Brooke, Rupert (1887-1915), English poet and essayist.

An early rebel against his own class, Brooke became a Fabian socialist at Cambridge, and later caused a stir with his *Poems* (1911) in which his aim was to present a realism in his work which would expose the negative aspects of the modern age and their alienating impact upon society. He was also, briefly, a member of the BLOOMSBURY GROUP and adopted its literary principles. However, he soon reflected much of his earlier value system, and by 1912 had returned, intellectually, to his earlier and more traditional background. By 1913, the change in his creative activity manifested itself in poetry which clearly depicted his love for the world of the mind as well as the senses; he was described by a friend as being in love with love itself. It should not pass notice that, while Brooke's stature as a war poet did not compare to that of Owen, his work is exemplary for its often brilliant irony and his perceptive, witty, and sensitive worldview; examples are found in the poems "Menelaus and Helen" (1909) and "The Jolly Company" (1908). He enlisted in the Royal Navy at the outbreak of World War I, and it is his final poem, "The Soldier" (1915), for which he has been most remembered, quoted, and anthologized. It epitomizes a love of country which supersedes death in war and away from beloved homeland and remains eternal; the English soldier's body would sanctify a grave on foreign shore as ". . . A dust whome England bore . . ." Brooke became a war casualty in 1915. He was eulogized as a national hero by statesmen and poets alike.

✦•✦

Owen, Wilfred (1893-1918), English poet.

Although known as one of the best of the Georgian poets, Owen was also strongly influenced by the IMAGISTS, who demanded that poetry should rely more for content upon

Classicism than Romanticism. He agreed with the precept that excessive feeling, if not carefully controlled, caused a weakening of the implement of intention (the poem) and restricted its poetic force. His reputation lies in the fact that his war poetry is clear and passionately intense. Horrified by war experiences, he felt that they should not be glorified—war provided for him only an emotion of pity. "The poetry," he wrote, "is in the pity." A superb technique is seen in a tightly controlled use of assonance and alliteration which provides immediate and sudden experiential report; his innovative use of what he called consonant rhyme was imitated by those who came after him, notably W. H. Auden (1907-1973) and Stephen Spender (1909-1995). His untimely death came as a war casualty in 1918, and his celebrated influence on modern poetry was lost.

Thomas, Edward (1878-1917), English poet, biographer, and critic.

At his death in the war in 1917, it was said that Thomas was another of the great losses to English literature. He discovered his poetic ability late. It was the American Robert Frost (1874-1963) who convinced him to turn some of his prose passages into poetry. Although of Romantic sensibility, Thomas's skill lay in his ability to juxtapose, in his poetry, the effect of his traditional temperament with elements of the commonplace—his descriptive passages are the results of an accurate perception of the world around him, as they provide calm, controlled, yet forceful depictions of the countryside and its inhabitants. But his work is by no means simplistic. Perkins notes that "we feel that the poem presents sights or experiences actually had [but] the steps of the mind and feeling in the poem enact a spontaneous search amid experience for its meaning [and] provide a fine actuality." Certain poems, written while Thomas served in the war, can be compared to those found in the work of Brooke. They are that war will maim and kill—will change life—but that the English spirit will remain constant, as it has for centuries.

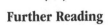

Further Reading

Abrams, M. H., gen. ed. "Rupert Brooke." In *The Norton Anthology of English Literature*. 5th ed. Vol. 2. New York: W. W. Norton & Company, 1986.

Caesar, Adrian. *Taking It Like a Man: Suffering, Sexuality, and the War Poets: Brooke, Sassoon, Owen, Graves*. Manchester, England: Manchester University Press, 1993.

Coombes, H. *Edward Thomas*. London: Chatto & Windus, 1956.

De la Mare, Walter. *Rupert Brooke and the Intellectual Imagination*. New York: Harcourt, Brace and Howe, 1920.

Eliot, T. S. *Selected Essays, 1917-1932*. New York: Harcourt, Brace, 1932.

Farjeon, Eleanor. *Edward Thomas: The Last Four Years*. Oxford, England: Oxford University Press, 1979.

Hibberd, Dominic. *Owen the Poet*. Athens, Ga.: University of Georgia Press, 1986.

────. *Wilfred Owen*. Edited by Ian Scott-Kilvert. Essex, England: Longman Group, 1975.

Kerr, Douglas. *Wilfred Owen's Voices: Language and Community*. Oxford, England: Clarendon Press; New York: Oxford University Press, 1993.

Keynes, Sir Geoffrey. *A Bibliography of Rupert Brooke*. London: R. Hart-Davis, 1954. 3rd rev. ed., 1964.

────. *A Bibliography of Siegfried Sassoon*. London: R. Hart-Davis, 1962.

Kirkham, Michael. *The Imagination of Edward Thomas*. Cambridge, England: Cambridge University Press, 1986.

Lane, Arthur E. *An Adequate Response: The War Poetry of Wilfred Owen & Siegfried Sassoon*. Detroit: Wayne State University Press, 1972.

Laskowski, William E. *Rupert Brooke*. New York: Twayne; Toronto: Maxwell Macmillan Canada, 1994.

Quinn, Patrick J. *The Great War and the Missing Muse: The Early Writings of Robert Graves and Siegfried Sassoon*. Selinsgrove, Pa.: Susquehanna University Press; London: Associated University Presses, 1994.

Scannell, Vernon. *Edward Thomas*. London: Longmans, Green, 1963.

Smith, Stan. *Edward Thomas*. London: Faber and Faber, 1986.

Stallworthy, Jon. *Wilfred Owen*. London: Oxford University Press and Chatto & Windus, 1974.

Sternlicht, Sanford V. *Siegfrid Sassoon*. New York: Twayne; Toronto: Maxwell Macmillan Canada, 1993.

Swinnerton, Frank. *The Georgian Scene: A Literary Panorama*. New York: Farrar & Rinehart, 1934.

Thomas, R. George. *Edward Thomas, a Portrait*. Oxford, England: Clarendon Press, 1985.

Tindell, William York. *Forces in Modern British Literature*. New York: Knopf, 1947.

Welland, Dennis Sydney Reginald. *Wilfred Owen: A Critical Study*. London: Chatto & Windus, 1960.

White, Gertrude M. *Wilfred Owen*. New York: Twayne, 1969.

GÎNDIREA
Romania, 1920s

A Romanian periodical of the interwar years, *Gîndirea* (Thought) attracted a number of both right- and left-wing writers, first under the editorship of Cezar Petrescu (1892-1961), beginning in 1921, and later under that of Nichifor Crainic (1889-?), commencing in 1926. Crainic's devotion to Orthodox Christianity and a national literature focusing on village life gave the journal a distinctly Romanian identity; however, it was the accomplished experimental and EXPRESSIONIST poetry of Tudor Arghezi (1880-1967) and Lucian Blaga (1895-1961) that established *Gîndirea* as especially significant to the country's literary history. The loosely ordered movement surrounding *Gîndirea* continued until 1944 and served to counter the influence of Eugen Lovinescu (1881-1943) and the *SBURĂTORUL* GROUP.

⊰•⊱
Further Reading

Micu, Dumitru. *Tudor Arghezi*. Translated from the Romanian by H. A. Richard and Michael
Impey. Bucharest: Meridiane Pub. House, 1965.
Writer's Union of the S.R. Romania. *Tudor Arghezi: Centenary, 1880-1980*. Bucharest: Cartea
Romaneasca, 1980.

GOLDEN HORN (*Zlatorog* Group)
Bulgaria, 1920s-1944

The center for the best interwar writing in Bulgaria, Golden Horn was noted for its apolitical stance and preoccupation with peasant and native themes. Preeminent among
Golden Horn were poet Elisaveta Bagryana (1893-?), short-story writer Georgi Raychev
(1882-1947), critic Vladimir Vasilev (1883-1963), and novelist, dramatist, and short-
story writer Yordan Yovkov (1880-1963), whom most consider the finest prose writer of
modern Bulgaria. Their forum was the journal *Zlatorog* (1920-44).

⊰•⊱
Further Reading

Bagryana, Elisavota. *Penelope of the Twentieth Century: Selected Poems of Elisavota
Bagryana*. Translated by Brenda Walker with Valentine Borrisov and Belin Tonchev. London:
Forest, 1993.
Elissavota [sic] *Bagryana: Ten Poems, in the Original and in English. Translated by Kevin
Ireland. Her Life and Work in Photographs. Authors and Critics on Bagryana*. Sofia,
Bulgaria: Sofia-Press, 1970.
Mozejko, Edward. *Yordan Yovkov*. Columbus, Ohio: Slavica Publishers, 1984.
Yovkov, Yordan. *The Inn at Antimovo; and, Legends of Stara Planina*. Translated by John
Burnip. Columbus, Ohio: Slavica Publishers, 1990.

GRAND JEU, LE (The Great Game)
France, 1930s

René Daumal (1908-1944) and Roger Gilbert-Lecomte (1907-1943) were innovators of
Le Grand Jeu (The Great Game), a literary review which was published in France in
1928 and 1929, a forum for a small group of writers who were agreeable to its precepts.
Daumal and Roger Vailland (1907-1965) were the coterie's most prominent members.
Others were André Roland de Renéville (1903-1962) and Joseph Sima (1891-1971).
Daumal has been called "heir" to the SYMBOLIST poet Arthur RIMBAUD, since his
work as essayist and poet shows the influence of the experimental mysticism and the
visionary elements embodied in Rimbaud's poetry.

When the SURREALIST movement began in 1924 under the aegis of André BRETON and others, Daumal joined its circle, but when he later rejected Surrealist concepts as "intellectual parlor games," he was in turn rejected by Breton and his group, and began to develop his own theories. He believed that the search for absolute truth could only be found by examination of all the great traditions of religion and intellectualism, of both past and present, and through myriad aspects of spiritual experience. Major works include a collection of poems, *Le Contre ceil (*1936; Against the Heaven), and *La Grande Beuverie (*1938; *A Night of Serious Drinking,* 1979), a satire about the Paris intellectual of the thirties. There are published translations of his many essays, fiction and letters: one critic opines that his essay "Une Expérience fondamentale" (1953; "A Fundamental Experience," 1959) contains the essence of his aesthetic philosophy. Like Daumal, Vailland broke with the Surrealistes after which his membership in the French Resistance during World War II and in the Communist Party influenced his creative output in directions of political action and social justice. Some examples of many works are *Drôle de jeu (*1945; *Playing for Keeps,* 1948); *La Loi (*1957; *The Law,* 1958), for which he won the Prix Goncourt; *Un jeune homme seul (*1951; A Young Man Alone); and *Beau Masque (*1954; A Handsome Mask).

⇢•⇠

Further Reading

Daumal, René. *The Powers of the Word: Selected Essays and Notes, 1927-1943.* Edited and translated with an introduction by Mark Polizzotti. San Francisco: City Lights Books, 1991.
Flower, J. E. *Roger Vailland: The Man and His Masks.* London: Hodder & Stoughton, 1975.
Powrie, Phil. *René Daumal and Roger Gilbert-Lecomte: A Bibliography.* London: Grant & Cutler, 1988.

GREEK PARNASSIANS. *See* NEW SCHOOL OF ATHENS

THE GROUP
England, 1955-1965

Begun as an informal seminar for poets and prose writers, this organization consisted of members who gathered by invitation to give readings of their works, which were then given critical evaluation by peer members. The Group was started by Philip Hobsbaum (1932-), and included Fleur Adcock (1934-), Alan Brownjohn (1931-), Ted Hughes (1930-1998), B. S. Johnson (1933-1973), Edward Lucie-Smith (1933-), George MacBeth (1932-), Peter Porter (1929-), and Peter Redgrove (1932-).

One critic has observed that the post-World War II British poets were less strongly influenced by the innovative work of such writers as T. S. ELIOT and Ezra POUND (*see*

MODERNISM, England and Ireland) than had been the young poets of the twenties and thirties. This was in reaction to the highly allusive ambiguity and inner-personal qualities manifested in the work of the early giants of Modernism. Moreover, the poets of the Second World War were presenting in their poetry a more stoic, less romanticized conception of war than had the war poets of the early twenties. Implicit in much of mid-century war poetry was a concept of the enormity of global warfare, the change it had caused, and the overall effect upon the Empire. This reversal of poetic temperament was newly characterized by a return to a more conventional kind of presentation, with emphasis on simple, understandable language, conventional meter — all combined with a persistent, underlying irony. Beyond this, critic F. B. Millett (1890-1976) notes that the new poetry also led to a new perception of criticism, in which his contemporaries Helen Gardner (1908-) and Graham Hough (1908-1990) called for a revaluation of the dogmaticism and the anti-Romantic tenets of Eliot and Pound and a return to the "lucidity, clarity and the communicativeness of poetry."

While mainly adhering to a revised poetic manifesto, and with some exceptions, the poets of The Group had individual voices and made individual marks. As examples, some of MacBeth's work shows experiments with the violent and the supernatural; Peter Porter's is widely diversified — always sophisticated, sometimes obscure — and incorporates his wide range of interest in classical music and mythology, and has elements of nineteenth-century Romanticism. While Hughes was only briefly connected with The Group, his early work shows evidence of the clarity of message and simple, almost conversational and colloquial language which members of the organization sought. "The pig lay on a barrow dead/It weighed they said, as much as three men/Its eyes closed, pink white eyelashes/Its trotters stick straight out . . . ," from his "View of a Pig" is an example. His great interest in nature, animals, and trees is apparent in much of his work and is always combined with his vision of the sober, often frightening side of life and its ironic twists. His fascination with myths and an inclusion of mythic elements presents an ambiguous, often horrific view of the times and the limitations from time to time of the language which describes them. His volume of poems, *Crows* (1970), in which "Crow Goes Hunting" appears is, as described by Patrick Swindon, "a little gnomic myth about the nature of words" and is reminiscent of T. S. Eliot's primordial prototype, Sweeney, and his frustrating repetition of "But I gotta have words when I talk to you," and the failure to be able to make words work. As these poets all moved in the direction of poetry which is sometimes provincial, concerned with nature and traditional form, they were seeking a responsive audience who would recognize work which speaks to both the stress and the distress of the modern world but for whom poetry is "neither an obstacle nor an occult science."

See also THE MOVEMENT.

❖•❖

Further Reading

Alvarez, Alfred. *The Shaping Spirit: Studies in Modern English and American Poets*. London: Chatto & Windus, 1958.

Bennett, Bruce. *Spirit in Exile: Peter Porter and His Poetry*. South Melbourne, Australia: Oxford University Press, 1991.

Bishop, Nick. *Re-Making Poetry: Ted Hughes and a New Critical Psychology*. New York: St. Martin's Press, 1991.

Brinnin, John Malcolm, and Bill Read, eds. *The Modern Poets*. New York: McGraw-Hill, 1963.

Dickie, Margaret. *Sylvia Plath and Ted Hughes*. Urbana, Ill.: University of Illinois Press, 1979.

Fuller, Roy. *A Lost Season*. London: Hogarth Press, 1944.

Hirschberg, Stuart. *Myth in the Poetry of Ted Hughes: A Guide to the Poems*. Totowa, N.J.: Barnes & Noble, 1981.

Leavis, F. R. *New Bearings in English Poetry: A Study of the Contemporary Situation*. London: Chatto & Windus, 1950.

Lucie-Smith, Edward. *The Burnt Child: An Autobiography*. London: Gollancz, 1975.

Lucie-Smith, Edward, and Philip Hobsbaum, eds. *A Group Anthology*. London: Oxford University Press, 1962.

Lucie-Smith, Edward, and J. E. MacKenzie. *Joan of Arc*. London: Allen Lane, 1976.

Moody, William Vaughn, and Robert M. Lovett. *A History of English Literature*. Edited and revised by F. B. Millett. 8th ed. New York: Scribner, 1964.

Robinson, Craig. *Ted Hughes as Shepherd of Being*. New York: St. Martin's Press, 1989.

Sagar, Keith M. *The Art of Ted Hughes*. 2nd ed. Cambridge, England: Cambridge University Press, 1978.

———. *Ted Hughes*. Edited by Ian Scott-Kilvert. Harlow, England: Longman for the British Council, 1972.

———. *Ted Hughes*. Windsor, England: Profile Books, 1981.

Sagar, Keith M., ed. *The Challenge of Ted Hughes*. Basingstoke, Hampshire, England: Macmillan; New York: St. Martin's Press, 1994.

Scigaj, Leonard M. *The Poetry of Ted Hughes: Form and Imagination*. Iowa City, Iowa: University of Iowa Press, 1986.

———. *Ted Hughes*. Boston: Twayne, 1991.

Scigaj, Leonard M., ed. *Critical Essays on Ted Hughes*. New York: G. K. Hall; Toronto: Maxwell Macmillan Canada, 1992.

Steele, Peter. *Peter Porter*. Melbourne, Australia; New York: Oxford University Press, 1992.

Swinden, Patrick. "English Poetry." In *The Twentieth-Century Mind: 1945-1965*. Edited by C. B. Cox and A. E. Dyson. Vol. III. London; New York: Oxford University Press, 1972.

West, Thomas. *Ted Hughes*. London: Methuen, 1985.

GROUPE DE L'ABBAYE. *See* ABBAYE GROUP

GROUP 42
Czechoslovakia, 1942-c. 1948

Formed in 1942 in Czechoslovakia, Group 42 was a short-lived movement that consisted of poets, largely inspired by Jiří Orten (1919-1941) and František Halas (1901-1949), who wrote of modern city life with a combination of EXISTENTIAL humor and despair. Oldřich Mikulášek (1910-) Jiřina Hauková (1919-), and Josef Kainar (1917-1972) were the group's primary members.

❧•❧

Further Reading

Městan, Antonín. "Czech and Slovak Literature." In *World Literature Since 1945: Criticial Surveys of the Contemporary Literatures of Europe and the Americas*. New York: Ungar, 1973.

Novák, Arne. *Czech Literature*. Translated by Peter Kussi. Ann Arbor, Mich.: Published under the auspices of The Joint Committee on Eastern Europe, American Council of Learned Societies by Michigan Slavic Publications, 1976.

GROUP 47 (Gruppe 47)
Germany, 1947-1967

The brainchild of Hans Werner Richter (1908-), Group 47 was founded shortly after World War II, in 1947, in an attempt to breathe new life into the culture and literature of the recently defeated and directionless German people. Paramount among the group's early concerns was to reclaim the German language from its years of abuse as a result of Nazi propaganda.

Hans Werner Richter had served in the war and ended up in a prisoner of war camp from 1943 to 1946 in Rhode Island. There he met Alfred Andersch (1914-1980), who had served in the army and deserted; the two contributed to a newspaper, *Der Ruh* (1946-47; The Call). Back in Germany after their release in 1947, they continued *Der Ruh* but the publication did not last long due to the objections of American censors; according to Siegfried Mandel, author of a history of the group, it called for "freedom and unity of Germany, a social-humanistic foundation for the new political structure of Germany, a unified socialist Europe, no imposition of the idea of collective guilt upon the German people, and no unnecessary humiliation of Germans." Nonetheless, contributors would gather to read each other's writing, marking the origin of Group 47. Later, the group attempted to start a journal to be called *Skorpian*, but the American military government set prohibitive requirements for a publishing license.

The Group wanted to forge a new literature with the values of democratic socialism and in a language without "'Kalligraphie' (aestheticized style)" but characterized by

Kahlschlag, "bare prose" that emphasized clarity and realism. As early as the November 1946 issue of *Der Ruf*, Gustav René Hocke (1908-) had called for a new realistic, honest prose style for German literature in "Deutsche Kalligraphie oder: Glanz und Elend der moderne Literatur" (German Calligraphy or: The Glory and Misery of Modern Literature). Soon EXPRESSIONIST, EXISTENTIALIST, and REALIST styles dominated as well, along with themes induced by the war. Into the 1950s members read William Faulkner, James JOYCE (*see* MODERNISM, England and Ireland), and Franz KAFKA (*see* MODERNISM, Austria and Germany). These gave way to more avant-garde, as well as political, literature by members in the 1960s.

The work of two members in particular, Günter Grass (1927-) and Heinrich Böll (1917-1985), revitalized literature in Germany. Grass, also a POW, first attended a Group meeting in 1955. During his association with Group 47 Grass's major novels were published and are known as the Danzig trilogy: *Die Blechtrommel* (1959; *The Tin Drum*, 1961), *Katz und Maus* (1961; *Cat and Mouse*, 1963), and *Hundejahre* (1963; *Dog Years*, 1965). Böll joined the Group in 1951. His most acclaimed work during this period was the novel *Billiard um halb zehn* (1959; *Billiards at Half-past Nine*, 1962).

Richter edited the Group's first book, a collection of poems written by German POWs, marked by self-pity and rejection of responsibility or guilt, *Deine Söhne, Europa* (1947; Your Sons, Europe). Contributors included Günter Eich (1907-1972) and Wolfdietrich Schnurre (1920-), who did the first reading at the first meeting of the Group: a poem about the death of God.

Richter's first novels were *Die Geschlagenen* (1949; *The Odds against Us*, 1950) and *Sie fielen aus Gottes Hand* (1951; *They Fell from God's Hand*, 1956). The former was autobiographical in nature, describing his experiences in the war and in prison camp, while the second focuses on the history of one German concentration camp. According to some critics, these novels exhibited a kind of moral equalization (*Gleichmacherei*) of all the characters that avoided any "reconciliation of emotionality and art," and which made them popular with a German public which did not consider German atrocities any worse than atrocities committed by other peoples in other times and places. Critic Hans Egon Holthusen (1913-), in 1960, described the political milieu and historical condition of Group 47: "All of us have to drag with us a political inheritance with which, in all honesty, we cannot appear before the eyes of others. The exhaust gas of a national plunge into hell still poisons the air, oppressive taboos clog the flow of open discussion — a form of self-imposed regulation of speech is not infrequent. How much dishonesty, how much concealed resentment and hidden hysteria on all sides."

Richter called the first meeting in September of 1947, which was attended by many of the contributors to the journal and the anthology. By the next meeting in November, Hans Georg Brenner (1903-1962) had given the group its name. Richter presided over the meetings and instituted certain rules which invitees and members followed if they wished to be invited back. "It was understood that those who were invited — by post-cards — to meetings were anti-Fascists, anti-militarists, politically liberal or leftist-inclined but not toward the extreme of communistic Stalinism. Most of those invited during the early years shared the common experience of war as soldiers of a lowly rank; officers were suspected of having worked too hard for the cause," Mandel writes. And Richter, the model for Simon Dach in Günter Grass's *Das Treffen in Telgte* (1979; *The Meeting at Telgte*, 1981), was a strict moderator at the group's sessions. The chair in which the reader sat was called "the electric chair," and after reading, during comments from the assembled, the reader was not allowed to betray any emotion or speak a word. If during the reading, members didn't want to hear any more, they gave the thumbs-down sign and the reader had to stop. Altogether more than two hundred writers endured this rather ruthless exercise over the years, in large part because the audience tended to be full of publishing and media representatives and critics. Mandel wrote that "Richter admitted that criticism during the early stages was somewhat uncivilized and too blunt; it was a reaction to the repression of all criticism during the Hitler years." According to member Martin Walser (1927-), "Snobs, arrogante Literaten und intellektuelle Zungenkünstler und Wortakrobaten werden nicht mehr eingeladen" (Snobs, arrogant literati and intellectual artists of the tongue and word acrobats are not invited back). Thomas MANN (*see* MODERNISM, Austria and Germany) once referred to Group 47 as "that noisy horde of smart-alecks."

Group 47 was not known for fostering any remarkable amount of literary experimentation, but by the mid-1950s, it counted among its members Germany's most influential critics and publishers. By its last gathering in 1967, nearly every major German literary figure was, or had been, a member. Critics who joined included Walter Jens (1923-), Joachim Kaiser (1928-), Marcel Reich-Ranicki (1920-), Walter Höllerer (1922-), and Hans Mayer (1907-). By this time, too, radio plays were very popular in Germany, radio representatives attended the group's meetings, and many group members wrote them, including Eich, Andersch, Böll, Schnurre, Walser, Wolfgang Weyrauch (1907-1980), fiction writer Ilse Aichinger (1921-), poet and novelist Ingeborg Bachmann (1926-1973), poet Hans Magnus Enzensberger (1929-), and Wolfgang Hildesheimer (1916-1991). Many of Eich's — *Die Mädchen aus Viterbo* (1952; The Girls from Viterbo), *Das Jahr Lazertis* (1953; *The Year Lacertis*, 1968), and *Die Brandung vor Setúbal* (1957; *The Rolling Sea at Setúbal*, 1968) — are considered classics in the genre.

Group 47's membership also included poet Paul Celan (1920-1970), whose volume *Sprachgitter* (1959; *Speech-Grille*, 1971) is widely considered the most important collection of postwar German poetry; poet Erich Fried (1921-1988), whose works include *Reich der Steine* (1963; Realm of Stones) and *Warngedichte* (1964; Poems of Warning); novelist Uwe Johnson (1934-1984), whose major works written during this period include *Mutmassungen über Jakob* (1959; *Speculations about Jakob,* 1963), *Das dritte Buch über Achim* (1961; *The Third Book about Achim,* 1967), and *Zwei Ansichten* (1965; *Two Views,* 1965); poet Helmut Heissenbüttel (1921-); Walter Kolbenhoff (1908-); Siegfried Lenz (1926-); Paul Schallück (1922-1976); and Gabriele Wohmann (1932-).

As the years wore on, most Group members increasingly concerned themselves with enlarging the opportunities for participating in the determination of who is to exercise political power. But the Group came to no consensus on any specific political or aesthetic agenda, or any conclusions about what should be, if any, the relationship between ideology and literature. Radicals, such as Peter Handke (1942-), criticized the Group as being politically impotent. However, some members of the Group occasionally broke out into smaller units with specific political focuses. Hans Jochen Vogel and Gerhard Szczesny formed the Grünwalder Kreis in 1956. Intended as a forum for those on the political left, the Kreis (circle) disbanded two years later. In 1958, the Komitee gegan Atomrüstung (Committee against Nuclear Arms) was formed with Richter at its head until 1961. The Group tried to keep contact alive with East German writers, among whom poet Johannes Bobrowski (1917-1965) was a member of the Group and could attend meetings as the East German government permitted him to visit West Germany. Many members condemned U.S. involvement in Vietnam during the 1960s. Grass became politically active as well and exhorted his fellow group members to engage themselves more concretely.

In 1962, Richter and Walter Mannzen published *Almanach der Gruppe 47, 1947-1962.* Richter's memoirs of the Group 47 years are published in *Im Etablissement der Schmetterlinge* (1986; In the Salon of Butterflies).

The period of the Group's activity witnessed the reemergence of literature in Germany to one of international importance. For more than twenty years Group 47 helped to shape the literary climate and brought together almost all the important writers. The Group 47 prize was one of the most coveted literary awards in Germany. Meetings became media events. When the Group met at Princeton University for a long weekend in the spring of 1966, according to one chronicler, publishers insisted that members fly in separate planes so as to minimize the damage to German literature should one crash.

The Group's heyday was over by 1968, when Russian troops invaded Czechoslovakia, site of their next planned meeting. In response, Richter decided that the Group would not meet until it could safely do so in Czechoslovakia. Richter continued to moderate a literary salon which was made into television and radio programs until 1972. The Group met once more in 1972 at the urging of several of Richter's friends.

❧•❧

Further Reading

Bauke, J. P. "Group 47 at Princeton." *New York Times Book Review* (May 15, 1966): 43-45.

Boulby, Mark. *Uwe Johnson*. New York: Ungar, 1974.

Conrad, Robert C. *Heinrich Böll*. Boston: Twayne, 1981.

Cunliffe, W. Gordon. *Günter Grass*. New York: Twayne Publishers, 1969.

Demetz, Peter. *Postwar German Literature: A Critical Introduction*. New York: Pegasus, 1970.

Diller, Edward. *A Mythic Journey: Günter Grass's "Tin Drum."* Lexington, Ky.: University Press of Kentucky, 1974.

Doane, Heike A. "Hans Werner Richter." In *Dictionary of Literary Biography*. Vol. 69, *Contemporary German Fiction Writers* (First Series). Detroit: Gale Research, 1988.

Fickert, Kurt. *Neither Left nor Right: The Politics of Individualism in Uwe Johnson's Work*. New York: P. Lang, 1987.

Ghurye, Charlotte W. *The Writer in Society: Studies in the Fiction of Günter Grass and Heinrich Böll*. Bern, Switzerland: Herbert Lang, 1976.

Gray, Cleve, ed. *Hans Richter*. New York: Holt, Rinehart and Winston, 1971.

"Group 47: Nation's Conscience." *Newsweek* (May 16, 1966): 67-70.

Heitner, Robert R. *The Contemporary Novel in Germany: A Symposium*. Austin, Tex.: University of Texas Press, 1967.

Hollington, Michael. *Günter Grass: The Writer in a Pluralist Society*. New York: M. Boyars, 1987.

Mandel, Siegfried. *Group 47: The Reflected Intellect*. Carbondale, Ill.: Southern Illinois University Press, 1973.

Moore, Harry T. "Three Group 47 Novelists: Böll, Johnson, Grass." In his *Twentieth-Century German Literature*. New York: Basic Books, 1967.

O'Neill, Patrick, ed. *Critical Essays on Günter Grass*. Boston: G. K. Hall, 1987.

Reddick, John. *The Danzig Trilogy of Günter Grass: A Study of "The Tin Drum," "Cat and Mouse," and "Dog Years."* New York: Harcourt Brace Jovanovich, 1975.

Reid, James H. *Heinrich Böll: A German for His Time*. New York: Berg Publishers, 1988.

GROUP OF GUAYAQUIL (Grupo de Guayaquil) Ecuador, 1930s

The Group of Guayaquil consisted of five writers — Demetrio Aguilera Malta (1909-), José de la Cuadra (1903-1941), Joaquín Gallegos Lara (1911-1947), Enrique Gil Gilbert (1912-), and Alfredo Diezcanseco (1908-) — from the Ecuadorian town of Guayaquil. In 1930 Aguilera Malta, Gallegos Lara, and Gil Gilbert published a collection of their short stories, *Los que se van: cuentos del cholo y montuvio* (Those Who Go: Stories of Cholos and Montuvios), depicting cholos — those of mixed Spanish and Indian heritage — and montuvios — those of mixed African and Indian heritage — in a harshly documentary light, which ran counter to many of the romanticizing visions written before. It is considered the group's manifesto. Gil Gilbert's *Nuestro pan* (1941; Our Bread) may serve as an example of their documentary technique. Aguilera Malta's work evinces a more prominent attention to explicit ideology, while avoiding a reductive SOCIALIST REALISM. His novel, *Don Goyo* (1933), is a good example, representing Don Goyo as an almost shadowy figure who, in death, continues to appear to the living; he enjoyed an economic prosperity and independence, however, which the peasant class he led was denied. Diezcanseco's novels, such as *El muelle* (1933; The Dock) and *Las tres ratas* (1944; The Three Rats), are also concerned with representing social ills caused by economic disparity. Cuadra's novel *Los Sangurimas* (1933; The Sangurima Family), telling the violent story of an interfamily clash, is considered a masterpiece; he is best known, however, as a short-story writer. One critic, Ángel Rojas, summarized the group's philosophy as follows: "La realidad y nada más que la realidad!"; reality and nothing else but reality (*La novela ecuatoriana*, 1948). The Group of Guayaquil writers have been credited with revitalizing Ecuadorian literature and heralding a renaissance of Ecuadorian fiction.

✥•✥

Further Reading

Franco, Jean. "Ecuadorian Realism." In his *Introduction to Spanish-American Literature*. Cambridge, England: Cambridge University Press, 1969.

Sacoto, Antonio. *The Indian in the Ecuadorian Novel*. New York: Las Americas Pub. Co., 1967.

GROUP 61 (Gruppe 61)
Germany, 1960s

A writers'/workers' movement centered in the industrial region around Dortmund, Group 61 was formed in 1961 by coalminer Max von der Grün (1926-), who espoused a REALISTIC and critical approach to the portrayal of the working classes and their attendant social problems. Other members included Fritz Hüser (1908-1979), Wolfgang Körner (1937-), Josef Reding (1929-), and Günter Wallraff (1942-).

✥•✥

Further Reading

Durzak, Manfred. "German Literature." In *World Literature Since 1945: Critical Surveys of the Contemporary Literatures of Europe and the Americas*. Edited by Ivar Ivask and Gero von Wilpert. New York: Ungar, 1973.

Thomas, R. Hinton, and Keith Bullivant. "Literature and the Industrial World." In their *Literature in Upheaval: West German Writers and the Challenge of the 1960s*. Manchester, England: Manchester University Press, 1974.

GROUP 63 (Gruppo 63) and *Officina* Group
Italy, 1950s-1960s

Connected to NEOREALISM in its repudiation of a strictly REALISTIC approach to literature, Group 63 arose in conjunction with the avant-garde literature of the journal *Officina* (1955-59). Pier Paolo Pasolini (1922-1975) and Luciano Anceschi (1911-) were among the first writers to recognize and champion the new generation's work, founded upon the MODERNIST models of James JOYCE, Marcel PROUST, Luigi PIRANDELLO, Italo Svevo (1861-1928), Franz KAFKA, and others. Among the group's loosely affiliated writers were Alberto Arbasino (1930-), Nanni Balestrini (1935-), Renato Barilli (1935-), Piero A. Buttitta (1931-), Furio Colombo (1931-), Oreste Del Buono (1923-), Alfredo Guiliani (1924-), Angelo Guglielmi (1924-), Raffaele La Capria (1922-), Luigi Malerba (1927-), Giorgio Manganelli (1922-), Elio Pagliarini (1927-), Antonio Porto (1935-), Edoardo Sanguineti (1930-), and Umberto Eco (1932-), who in recent decades has distinguished himself as a formidable SEMIOTICIAN and as one of Italy's most important novelists.

❖•❖

Further Reading

Ragusa, Olga. *Narrative and Drama: Essays in Modern Italian Literature from Verga to Pasolini.* The Hague: Mouton, 1976.

GROUP THEATER
England, 1933-1953

Founded by English director-choreographer Rupert Doone (1904-1966) in 1933, the Group Theater was a non-commercial society that typically produced modern plays with minimal sets and props. The majority of the group's productions were staged at the Westminster Theatre. Among the more notable works featured were T. S. ELIOT's (*see* MODERNISM, England and Ireland) *Sweeney Agonistes* (1935), Stephen Spender's (1909-1995) *Trial of a Judge* (1938), and the verse-play collaborations of W. H. Auden (1907-1973) and Christopher Isherwood (1904-1986). During World War II the Group Theater ceased production altogether; however, a revival was sparked in 1950 with the staging of Jean-Paul SARTRE's (*see* EXISTENTIALISM) *Les mouches* (1943; *The Flies*, 1947), and the company continued until about 1953.

❖•❖

Further Reading

Bhattacharyya, B. K. *W. H. Auden and Other Oxford Group of Poets.* New Delhi, India: Bahri Publications, 1989.

Carter, Ronald, ed. *Thirties Poets: "The Auden Group": A Casebook*. London: Macmillan, 1984.

David, Hugh. *Stephen Spender: A Portrait with Background*. London: Heinemann, 1992.

Felperin, Howard. *Dramatic Romance: Plays, Theory, and Criticism*. New York: Harcourt Brace Jovanovich, 1973.

Innes, Christopher D. *Modern British Drama, 1890-1990*. Cambridge, England: Cambridge University Press, 1992.

Jurak, Mirko. *The Group Theatre: Its Development and Significance for the Modern English Theatre*. Ljubljana, Slovenia: University Press, 1969.

Kozlenko, William, ed. *The Best Short Plays of the Social Theatre*. New York: Random House, 1939.

Kulkarni, H. B. *Stephen Spender, Poet in Crisis*. Glasgow, Scotland: Blackie, 1970.

————. *Stephen Spender, Works and Criticism: An Annotated Bibliography*. New York: Garland, 1976.

Medley, Robert. *Drawn from the Life: A Memoir*. London; Boston: Faber and Faber, 1983.

O'Neill, Michael. *Auden, MacNeice, Spender: The Thirties Poetry*. New York: St. Martin's Press, 1992.

Sidnell, Michael J. *Dances of Death: The Group Theatre of London in the Thirties*. London; Boston: Faber and Faber, 1984.

Spender, Stephen. *Stephen Spender: Journals, 1939-1983*. Edited by John Goldsmith. New York: Random House, 1986.

————. *World Within World, the Autobiography of Stephen Spender*. London: H. Hamilton, 1951.

Stanford, Derek. *Stephen Spender, Louis MacNeice, Cecil Day Lewis: A Critical Essay*. Grand Rapids, Mich.: Eerdmans, 1969.

Sternlicht, Sanford V. *Stephen Spender*. New York: Twayne, 1992.

Weatherhead, A. Kingsley. *Stephen Spender and the Thirties*. Lewisburg, Pa.: Bucknell University Press, 1975.

Williams, Raymond. *Drama from Ibsen to Eliot*. New York: Oxford University Press, 1953.

GROUP THEATER
United States, 1931-1941

The Group Theater, an innovative New York collective of actors and directors, exerted a profound influence on the development of twentieth-century American theater. Launched in 1931 as an alternative to what was perceived as the lifeless performances and growing commercialism of the THEATER GUILD, the Group Theater practiced and introduced audiences to the experimental techniques of Konstantin STANISLAVSKY and his MOSCOW ART THEATER and eventually succeeded in producing several original modern plays — a few of lasting fame — which powerfully reflected the social unrest of the times. Among the many important directors, actors, and playwrights associated with the Group were Harold CLURMAN, Cheryl CRAWFORD, Lee STRASBERG, Clifford ODETS, Maxwell Anderson (1888-1959), Elia Kazan (1909-), Stella Adler (1902-1992), Kurt Weill (1900-1950), and Franchot Tone (1905-1968).

The ten-year history of the Group Theater, intimately told by Clurman in *The Fervent Years* (1975), was both exciting and turbulent, marked by extremes for the company of unqualified artistic triumph and petty internal dissent. As early as 1925, two of the Group's principals, Clurman and Strasberg, had met as young actors while working for the New York Theater Guild, a noncommercial venture sustained by memberships and advance subscriptions. A year later, Clurman met Crawford, another young performer within the Guild. Of the three, Strasberg was the first to experiment with Russian acting techniques learned at the recently founded American Laboratory Theater. Strasberg's discussions with Clurman on the suitability of these techniques for the performance of modern drama quickly led to the idea of a permanent, carefully trained acting company. Beginning in late 1930, Crawford, Strasberg, Clurman, and a varying assembly of actors and writers began meeting to discuss such an undertaking. By the spring of 1931 the three directors had chosen an original company of twenty-seven actors (which included Odets) and obtained marginal funding for an opening season. They then gathered as a close-knit community for summer rehearsal at Brookfield Center, Connecticut, where they christened themselves the Group Theater. A partial subsidy for their first production, Paul Green's (1894-1981) *The House of Connelly* (1931), was given by the Guild, which maintained a tenuous relationship with the Group for less than two years.

Despite the overwhelming critical and modest commercial success of *The House of Connelly*, the Group was stricken by financial problems throughout its existence. For many in the Group, however, such problems were secondary to both the intrinsic merits and unexpected difficulties of Strasberg's evolving METHOD, a rigorous approach to acting that involved both mental and physical improvisation. The controlled absence of "stars" within the Group, the near-fanatical approach to rehearsals, and the differing temperaments of the three directors created considerable distress among some of the actors and eventually led to irreparable rifts throughout the company, which, after such successes as Sidney Kingsley's (1906-1995) *Men in White* (1933) — the first of the Group's plays to reach Broadway — and Clifford Odets's successive hits WAITING FOR LEFTY (1935) and *Awake and Sing!* (1935), ceased production in 1941.

An astonishingly bold experiment in dramatic history, the Group Theater is primarily esteemed today as the forerunner of the more widely recognized Actors' Studio, the chief center for Method-training in America. Yet, the Group's influence has been even more pervasive than this suggests. Many of those originally associated with the Group have brought to their own later work — which includes the staging of Tennessee Williams's (1911-1983) *A Streetcar Named Desire* (1947), Arthur Miller's (1915-) *Death of a Salesman* (1949), and Carson McCullers's (1917-1967) *The Member of the Wedding* (1950) — the very ideals and practices that fueled the Group's groundbreaking development during the 1930s. The lofty goal of the original Group, to effect, in Clurman's words, "a spiritual union between those who played . . . and those who saw," has now become the standard of countless theaters around the country.

❧•❧

Clurman, Harold (1901-1980)
American director, historian, critic, essayist, and editor.

Considered the guiding spirit of the Group Theater, Clurman was significantly exposed during his student days at the Sorbonne in Paris to contemporary French drama and the touring Moscow Art Theater. Despite his immense historical and technical knowledge of dramatic production, Clurman refrained from directing any of the Group's plays until 1935. His first production that year, Odets's *Awake and Sing!*, inaugurated his career as a successful director. Following the disbanding of the Group Theater, Clurman continued to direct a number of important new plays by such writers as Eugene O'NEILL (*see* EXPRESSIONISM, United States, and PROVINCETOWN PLAYERS), Jean Anouilh (1910-), McCullers, and Miller. Clurman also distinguished himself as an entertaining and persuasive dramatic critic for the *New Republic*, the *Nation*, and the *London Observer*. His several books on the theater, particularly *The Fervent Years* (1975) and *All People Are Famous (Instead of an Autobiography)* (1974), are valued for their blend of wit, insight, and narrative appeal.

❧•❧

Crawford, Cheryl (1902-1986), American director and autobiographer.

A former actress and casting manager for the Theater Guild, Crawford provided the Group not only with sound directorial skills but the social and business acumen essential to the financial operation of such a venture. Following her departure from the Group, Crawford became a much-admired theatrical producer and one of the chief forces behind the establishment of the American Repertory Theater and the Actors' Studio. Her credits include the Broadway shows *Brigadoon* (1947), *Yentl* (1975), and Tennessee Williams's *The Rose Tattoo* (1951), for which she won a Tony Award in 1951.

❧•❧

The Method.

A highly introspective approach to acting, the Method arose as a reaction to lackluster, stereotyped stage performances. The most salient feature of the Method is the actor's utilization of affective, or emotional, memory to imbue scenes with psychological realism. Embroiled in controversy for many years due to its questionable alteration of the actor's own psyche, the Method is now generally viewed as one of several useful dramatic tools rather than a comprehensive and exclusive model for acting. Among the numerous performers who have been trained in Method-acting are Shelley Winters, Robert DeNiro, Cloris Leachman, Ellen Burstyn, Paul Newman, and Dustin Hoffman.

❖•❖

Odets, Clifford (1906-1963), American dramatist.

As an aspiring stage actor, Odets joined the Group Theater in 1930. After playing minor roles in *The House of Connelly* (1931) and other dramas, Odets dedicated himself to the composition of socially relevant works for the American stage. He maintained close ties to the Group, particularly to Clurman, and eventually succeeded in completing his first drama, *Awake and Sing!* (1935). However, official production of this play, concerning the struggles of a Jewish working-class family, was delayed until after the initial performances of *Waiting for Lefty* (1935). Together, these enormously successful plays quickly established Odets as the central figure of the leftist theater in America. After a brief, introductory stint in Hollywood as a screenwriter and producer, Odets returned to New York with his biggest stage hit, *Golden Boy* (1937). In this work, and in several which followed, Odets moderated the tone of his social commentary but sustained a strong identification with the lives of the downtrodden. As he once wrote: "All of my plays . . . deal with one subject: the struggle not to have life nullified by circumstances, false values, anything."

Waiting for Lefty (1935).

Inspired by the penury and unrest which were rampant during the Great Depression, *Waiting for Lefty* has been labelled the definitive American proletarian drama of the 1930s. Odets centered the one-act play on the New York taxi drivers' strike of 1934. However, the vignette sequences in *Lefty* underscore not simply the taxi union's plight but the social and economic problems of an unlimited number of oppressed groups and classes. The culmination of the play's taut action and dialogue occurs when it is revealed that the conspicuously absent title character has been found shot to death. The union men, who have been contemplating action, unanimously call to "Strike!" Although this exhortatory drama merits little critical attention now, it is nonetheless admired above its AGITPROP counterparts for its forthright artistry and universal social message.

❖•❖

Strasberg, Lee (1901-1982), American director.

The best known of the three Group directors, Strasberg played a crucial role in defining and embellishing the novel Russian acting techniques he first learned at the American Laboratory Theater. Strasberg directed the overwhelming majority of the Group's early plays and through his experience evolved the Method, an approach to stage performance which has in one form or another influenced countless modern-day theater professionals. Following his departure from the Group Theater, Strasberg continued his

261

directorial career, assisting with the development of Elia Kazan's Actors' Studio, the chief center for Method acting, from 1950 until the latter years of his life. In 1974 Strasberg earned an Academy Award nomination for his debut film role in *The Godfather, Part II*.

✦ ● ✦

Further Reading

Adams, C. H. *Lee Strasberg: The Imperfect Genius of the Actors Studio*. Garden City, N.Y.: Doubleday, 1980.

Cantor, Harold. *Clifford Odets, Playwright-Poet*. Metuchen, N.J.: Scarecrow Press, 1978.

Chinoy, Helen K. *Reunion: A Self-Portrait of the Group Theatre*. Washington, D.C.: American Theatre Association, 1976.

Clurman, Harold. *The Fervent Years: The Story of the Group Theatre and the Thirties*. New York: Knopf, 1945.

Crawford, Cheryl. *One Naked Individual: My Fifty Years in the Theatre*. Indianapolis, Ind.: Bobbs-Merrill, 1977.

Gassner, John. "The Group Theatre in Its Tenth Year: A Critical Estimate." *Theatre Arts* 24 (October 1940).

Grismer, Kay L. "Cheryl Crawford Presents . . . A History of Her Broadway Musical Productions, 1936-1949." *Dissertation Abstracts International* 54, 3 (September 1993): 736A.

Hazelton, Nancy J., and Kenneth Krauss, eds. *Maxwell Anderson and the New York Stage*. Monroe, N.Y.: Library Research, 1991.

Mendelsohn, Michael J. *Clifford Odets, Humane Dramatist*. Deland, Fla.: Everett/Edwards, 1969.

Murray, Edward. *Clifford Odets: The Thirties and After*. New York: Ungar, 1968.

Shuman, Robert Baird. *Clifford Odets*. New York: Twayne, 1962.

Strasberg, Lee. *A Dream of Passion: The Development of the Method*. Boston: Little, Brown, 1987.

Weales, Gerald. *Clifford Odets, Playwright*. New York: Pegasus, 1971.

Whitmore, Richard Alan. "The Emerging Ensemble: The Vieux-Colombier and the Group Theatre." *Theatre Survey* 34, 1 (May 1993): 60-70.

Woolf, Michael. "Clifford Odets." In *American Drama*. Edited by Clive Bloom. New York: St. Martin's Press, 1995.

GRUPO *ACENTO*
Guatemala, 1940s

A small group of Guatemalan writers comprised Grupo *Acento* during the early 1940s: Otto Raúl González (1921-), known for *Viento claro* (1953; Clear Wind), *El bosque* (1955; The Forest), and other books of poetry; Raúl Leiva (1916-), whose obscurist style gradually moved to a more populist poetry with the volumes *Angustia* (1942; Anguish), *Oda a Guatemala* (1953; Ode to Guatemala), and *Nunca el olvido* (1959; Never Oblivion); Carlos Illescas (n.d.); and Enrique Juárez Toledo (1919-). They contributed to the journal *Acento* and were interested in experimenting with MODERNIST techniques and reading such writers as Pablo Neruda (1904-1973), James JOYCE (*see*

MODERNISM, England and Ireland), Franz KAFKA (*see* MODERNISM, Austria and Germany), and Federico García Lorca (1898-1936; *see* GENERATION OF 1927 and ULTRAISM). A later Guatemalan literary group, DAWN GROUP, attracted some of the *Acento* writers, and focused on learning from Karl MARX and Marxist literary and social influences as well as the more traditional "art for art's sake" writers.

❖•❖

Further Reading

New Voices of Hispanic America: An Anthology. Edited by Darwin J. Flakoll and Claribell Alegría. Boston: Beacon Press, 1962.

GRUPO ELAN
Ecuador, 1930s

Grupo Elan was a group of writers in Ecuador during the 1930s. Members included Alejandro Carrión (1915-), Alfonso Cuesta y Cuesta (1912-), Jorge Fernández (1912-), Ignacio Lasso (1912-1943), José Alfredo Llerena (1912-), Augusto Sacotto Arias (1907-1979), and Humberto Vacas (n.d.). Carrión wrote poetry and fiction. His lyric poems appear in *Poesía de la soledad y el deseo* (1946; Poetry of Solitude and Desire) and *Agonía del arbol y la sangre* (1948; Agony of Tree and Blood). Prose works include stories of childhood in *La manzana dañada* (1948; The Damaged Apple) and the novel *La espina* (1959; The Thorn). Cuesta y Cuesta also evoked childhood, with juvenile characters in his stories, *Llegada de todos los trenes del mundo* (1932; The Arrival of All the Trains in the World). Fernández began his career as a journalist, then entered a period of novel writing, only to eventually resume a journalistic vocation. He is known for his novels *Agua* (1937; Water), which deals with peasant life, and *Los que viven por sus manos* (1951; Those Who Live by Their Hands), dealing with the urban realm of political and economic corruption. Eugenio Moreno Heredia edited an anthology, *Antología del Grupol "ELAN,"* in 1977.

❖•❖

Further Reading

Ward, Philip, ed. *The Oxford Companion to Spanish Literature*. Oxford, England: Clarendon Press, 1978.

GRUPO *ESPADAÑA*
Spain, 1940s

Victoriano Crémer (1908-) founded the journal *Espadaña* in reaction to literary trends in Spain which, he argued, supported an escapist, neoclassical poetry. *Espadaña* and the group were formed to explore EXISTENTIAL and social concerns through liter-

263

ature. Rafael Múgica Celaya (pseud. Gabriel Celaya, 1911-1991) found the Spanish Civil War and political injustice recurrent themes and social protest a recurrent necessity. He was influenced by the anti-rationality of the SURREALISTS. Collections include *Marea de silencio* (1935), *Tranquilamente hablando* (1947), *Las cartas boca abajo* (1954), and *Lo demás es silencio* (1954). Blas de Otero (1916-1979) was concerned with social and political commitment as well as dealt with religious ideas. He is perhaps best known for *Pido la paz y la palabra* (1955), a work of hope in searching for God and worldly justice. Other members included critic Antonio G. de Lama (n.d.), cofounder of the group; poet and critic Luis de Leopoldo (1918-), known for his *Antología de la poesía social española* (1965); poet and critic Eugenio G. de Nora (1923-), whose three-volume *La novela española contemporánea (1898-1967)* (1970, 1979) is an important critical work; and Salvador Pérez Valiente (1919-).

⇻•⇺

Further Reading

Chandler, Richard E., and Kessel Schwartz. *A New History of Spanish Literature*. Rev. ed. Baton Rouge, La.: Louisiana State University Press, 1991.

GRUPO SAKER TI. *See* DAWN GROUP

GRUPO TZÁNTZICO
Ecuador, 1960s

The small Grupo Tzántzico (Jívaro for "head shrinker") counted among its members playwright Simón Corral (n.d.), poet and short-story writer Ulises Estrella (1940-), Rafael Larrea (n.d.), poet Alfonso Murriagui (1930-), and Antonio Ordóñez (1932-). The group published a literary journal, *Pucuna*, in Quito, which was edited by Estrella. Grupo Tzántzico was responding to what they held to be declining social, cultural, and artistic conditions. They arranged happenings, debates, plays, and poetry readings. Aldo Pellegrini's *Antología de la poesía viva latinoamericana* (1966) includes work by Estrella and Murriagui.

⇻•⇺

Further Reading

Baciu, S. "Beatitude South of the Border: Latin America's Beat Generation." *Hispania* XLIX, 4 (December 1966): 733-39.

GRUPPE 61. *See* GROUP 61

GRUPPO 63. *See* GROUP 63

H

HARD-BOILED SCHOOL
United States, 1920s-1940s

A distinctively American phenomenon in twentieth-century fiction, the Hard-Boiled School arose in part out of the pervasive disillusionment that accompanied the end of World War I as well as the harsh impact of the Great Depression that followed. Artistic influences included dime-novel detective stories, the understated prose of LOST GENERATION writer Ernest HEMINGWAY, and the work of R. Austin Freeman (1862 1943), Freeman Wills Crofts (1879-1957), and other British writers of the crime and mystery Golden Age (1920-55) who were concerned with promoting REALISM in characterization and plot.

The earliest efforts of the Hard-Boiled School writers were laconic and gritty short stories dealing with crime and the often brutal art of detection. One pulp periodical in particular, *The Black Mask* (eventually titled simply *Black Mask*), became the forum for this new style of writing. Launched in the spring of 1920 under the editorship of Henry L. Mencken (1880-1956) and George Jean Nathan (1882-1958), *The Black Mask* originally published a variety of high-adventure stories. During the tenure (1926-36) of editor Joseph T. Shaw, however, the focus of the periodical became increasingly specialized and the quality of the writing decidedly more literary.

Most scholars agree that the original Hard-Boiled detective was Race Williams, a character created by Carroll John Daly (1889-1958) and first introduced to *Black Mask* readers in 1923. Williams, the protagonist of several Daly stories and novels, was as tough as the underworld milieu in which he operated; he carried two .45 automatics (one for each hand) and did not hesitate to use them whenever the situation demanded. Despite Daly's enormous popularity, it was left to another writer of the era, Dashiell HAMMETT, to truly fashion Hard-Boiled fiction into a high art form.

Just a few months following the debut of Race Williams, *Black Mask* published Hammett's first "Continental Op" story, entitled "Arson Plus." The Continental Op was an otherwise unnamed investigator of the San Francisco-based Continental Detective Agency. More refined than his precursor, the Op displayed shrewd intelligence and a singleminded allegiance to his own sense of order and justice.

This character type, a lone, stoic, hero/antihero who operated beyond the fringes of the law and yet adhered to a strict personal moral code, was to become one of the key legacies of the Hard-Boiled School. Hammett's genius was to place his protagonists—first the Op and, later, gun-hating gumshoe Sam Spade—in seamy, frequently dangerous environments and evoke through style and attitude a certain lyrical grandeur and dignity amidst a stream of dark puzzles, filth, madness, and violence. Clearly, he had ventured beyond the mere Realism of the Golden Age. Indeed, "despite the hard-edged vernacular in which the stories are told, and the mean streets in which they take place," according to Robert B. Parker, "Hammett is not writing realistic fiction, he is writing romance. He is writing of heroes who are superior in degree to ordinary men."

In the later 1920s and early 1930s Shaw, recognizing the uniqueness and allure of Hammett's early achievement, attempted to cultivate this type of story not only through Hammett but a number of other authors. These included Raymond Chandler (1888-1959), Paul Cain (1902-1966), Frederick Nebel (1903-1967), Raoul Whitfield (1898-1945), Horace McCoy (1897-1955), George Harmon Coxe (1901-1984), and Erle Stanley Gardner (1889-1970).

Although Gardner achieved singular fame for his creation of lawyer-detective Perry Mason, it was Chandler who most fully assimilated and expanded upon Hammett's lead through, among other things, a mastery of metaphor, simile, and terse dialogue that has ever since spawned countless imitators. Capping the most important decade in Hard-Boiled writing—and firmly establishing the novel as its preeminent form—Chandler published *The Big Sleep* in 1939 featuring Philip Marlowe, the archetypal P.I. by which all later Hard-Boiled detectives would be measured (like Spade, Marlowe was immortalized on film by Humphrey Bogart, in Howard Hawks's 1946 movie).

The only other landmark that came close in significance for the genre was the introduction of Mickey Spillane's (1918-) Mike Hammer eight years later in *I, the Jury* (1947), which sold over six million copies, the most ever for any mystery up until that time. Spillane's Hammer series, more inspired by Daly than either Hammett or Chandler, helped launch the original paperback form in American publishing and a renaissance of Hard-Boiled writing during the 1950s. Around the same time, filmmakers were discovering and bringing to the big screen the works of such Hard-Boiled-style writers as James M. Cain (1892-1977), Cornell Woolrich (1903-1968), and David Goodis (1917-1967), defining *film noir* in the process.

Other writers over the years, including Harry Whittington (1915-1989), Ed Lacy (1911-1968), Charles Williams (1909-), Peter Rabe (1921-1991), Gil Brewer (1922-1983), Lionel White (1905-), John D. MacDonald (1916-1986), Chester Himes (1909-1984), Max Allan Collins (1948-), Andrew Vachss (1942-), Elmore Leonard (1925-), Walter E. Mosley (1952-), James Lee Burke (1936-), Robert B. Parker (1932-), Jim Thompson (1906-1977), Sara Paretsky (1947-), and Sue Grafton (1940-), have helped to broaden and sustain the impetus of Daly, Hammett, and Chandler. Mosley, with his Easy Rawlins series set in post-World War II Los Angeles, ranks among those who have been instrumental in sparking a 1990s renaissance in Hard-Boiled writing. Effectively spanning eight decades, this literary "school" showed no signs of dying out and could even be said to be thriving as a new century approached.

→•←

Hammett, (Samuel) Dashiell (1894-1961)
American novelist, short-story writer, and screenwriter.

According to William L. DeAndrea in his *Encyclopedia Mysteriosa,* Hammett is "the most important hard-boiled writer in the history of the genre" and "ranks with Edgar Allan Poe and Sir Arthur Conan Doyle in terms of his influence on the mystery story." A private detective for the Pinkerton Agency for over a decade, Hammett became a full-time writer in 1922. His professional background proved invaluable to his writing career, particularly in his portraits of detectives, the most famous of which was the now-legendary Sam Spade.

Hammett, along with John Carroll Daly and Erle Stanley Gardner, was one of the most popular of the *Black Mask* writers during the 1920s. With the serialization at the end of the decade of *The Maltese Falcon,* the first Sam Spade novel, Hammett attracted the attention of Hollywood (the labyrinthine mystery was filmed twice before being immortalized in a third adaptation in 1941 under first-time director John Huston, with Humphrey Bogart as Spade). Moving there in 1930, he worked as a screenwriter on a number of projects, notably the first three *Thin Man* movies featuring husband-and-wife detective team Nick and Nora Charles, played by William Powell and Myrna Loy. Hammett's sole novel featuring the Charleses, *The Thin Man* (1934), was his last full-length work and also his most commercially successful.

His other novels consist of *Red Harvest* (1929) and *The Dain Curse* (1929), featuring the Continental Op, and *The Glass Key* (1931), with antihero Ned Beaumont. Collections of his short stories include *The Adventures of Sam Spade and Other Stories* (1944) and *The Continental Op* (1945). Hammett's influence stretched far beyond the subgenre of Hard-Boiled fiction, touching the French EXISTENTIALISTs in particular, and pervading American pop culture even to the present day. Hammett is also remembered for his longtime relationship with playwright Lillian Hellman (1905-1984). Hellman's memoir of their time together, *Pentimento,* was published in 1973.

☙•❧

Further Reading

Breen, Jon L. "Hard-Boiled Mysteries: Introduction." In *The Fine Art of Murder.* Edited by Ed Gorman, Martin H. Greenberg, and Larry Segriff. New York: Carroll and Graf, 1993.

Collins, Max Allan. "The Hard-Boiled Detective." In *Encyclopedia Mysteriosa: A Comprehensive Guide to the Art of Detection in Print, Film, Radio, and Television.* Edited by William L. DeAndrea. New York: Prentice Hall, 1994.

Dooley, Dennis. *Dashiell Hammett.* New York: Ungar, 1983.

Gregory, Sinda. *Private Investigations: The Novels of Dashiell Hammett.* Carbondale, Ill.: Southern Illinois University Press, 1984.

Johnson, Diane. *Dashiell Hammett: A Life.* London: Chatto and Windus, 1984. Published by Random House, 1983, as *The Life of Dashiell Hammett.*

Layman, Richard. *Shadow Man: The Life of Dashiell Hammett.* New York: Harcourt Brace; London: Junction, 1981.

Madden, David, ed. *Tough Guy Writers of the Thirties.* Carbondale and Edwardsville, Ill.: Southern Illinois University Press, 1968.

Marling, William. *The American Roman Noir: Hammett, Cain, and Chandler.* Athens, Ga.: University of Georgia Press, 1994.

————. *Dashiell Hammett.* Boston: Twayne, 1983.

Metress, Christopher. *The Critical Response to Dashiell Hammett.* Westport, Conn.: Greenwood Press, 1994.

Nolan, William F. *Hammett: A Life at the Edge.* New York: Congdon and Weed; London: Barker, 1983.

Parker, Robert B. "Dashiell Hammett." In *St. James Guide to Crime & Mystery Writers.* Edited by Jay P. Pederson. Detroit: St. James Press, 1996.

Shaw, Joseph T. *The Hard-Boiled Omnibus: Early Stories from Black Mask.* New York: Simon and Schuster, 1946.

Symons, Julian. *Dashiell Hammett.* San Diego: Harcourt Brace, 1985.

Wolfe, Peter. *Beams Falling: The Art of Dashiell Hammett.* Bowling Green, Ohio: Popular Press, 1980.

HARLEM RENAISSANCE
United States, 1920s

Between the years immediately following World War I and the Great Depression of the 1930s, black writers made themselves an important and exciting part of the American literary scene. When Langston HUGHES issued an unequivocal declaration that the voices of black Americans would become loud and clear, the Harlem Renaissance began. The end of a war in which many blacks had participated gave rise to a number of black-oriented social and political organizations, among which were the National Association for the Advancement of Colored People (NAACP) and the Urban League. These groups, along with their political attributes, provided black writers with publishing opportunities which had earlier been nonexistent and thus a wider readership which gave new insight into the culture that is integral to the fabric of the American heritage.

The Harlem Renaissance poets were strongly influenced by the MODERNIST tenets and techniques then in vogue both in the United States and Europe, such as IMAGISM, free verse, and experimentation with new form and structure; they began what George E. Kent calls "an attempt to assert . . . a 'dissociation of sensibility' from that which had been enforced by American culture and its institutions." They would also make known the influence as well as the inspiration of jazz and its rhythm and blues syncopation, which had its roots in the music of southern blacks who had migrated north and which contained the exuberant, free-riding style and form found in much of their poetry. A wider dissemination of work by black writers gave authority for a rise in black-consciousness and new voice for the achievements of black writers and their fellow artists, dramatists, actors, and musicians.

A number of early and older members of the movement had already attained status in the intellectual milieu. These included W. E. B. DuBois (1868-1963), editor of the journal of the NAACP, *The Crisis,* and an established international scholar; lecturer Alain Locke (1886-1954), a Rhodes scholar and Harvard graduate; James Weldon Johnson (1871-1938), the novelist, poet, and educator; and Claude McKay (1889-1948), early political activist and poet whose sonnet "If We Must Die" (1919) not only advocated a new black radicalism but showed also "a new ease with poetic form and the ability to bend traditional form to his purpose." Younger members were Langston Hughes, reputedly the voice of the Harlem Renaissance, who provided a manifesto for the group with his essay, "The Negro Artist and the Racial Mountain" (1926), in which he described the attraction of white, middle-class values for blacks who were suppressing their "black selves" in an attempt to identify with white culture. His contemporary Countee Cullen (1903-1946) remained an integral member of the movement, but is called atypical because of his conventional style and dedication to traditional form. A major figure, Jean Toomer (1894-1967), saw the Renaissance as inspiration for his collection of poems and essays in *Cane* (1923). He is, however, quoted as not wanting fame as a "Negro" poet; thus his work did not appear in James Weldon Johnson's famous anthology, *The Book of American Negro Poetry* (1922; reprint 1931). In 1926, Hughes and group members Gwendolyn Bennett (1902-1981), Zora Neale Hurston (1903-1960),

269

and Wallace Thurman (1902-1924) introduced a new periodical called *Fire,* designed to provide publication opportunities for writers who were rejecting, in Hughes's words, "the old, dead, conventional Negro-white ideas of the past." It was an unfortunate endeavor; most black critics found the first issue unsatisfactory, and a second issue did not appear.

Arna Bontemps (1902-1973) has provided an excellent overview of the movement in his essay, "The Awakening: A Memoir," in *The Harlem Renaissance Remembered* (1972; reprint 1984). Here he traces his personal experiences and his participation in a reawakening of black energy and aesthetic spirit, and the "incandescence" of the Harlem Renaissance era. His observations about black writers, artists, and musicians of the movement are noteworthy; he quotes Carl Van Doren's remarks in 1922, as printed in the black journal *Opportunity*: "What American literature needs at the moment is color, music, gusto and free expression of gay or desperate moods. If the Negroes are not in a position to contribute these items, I do not know what Americans are."

The stock market crash and the depression which followed it caused the loss of much of the white patronage which writers of the movement had found useful. But, in the main, they continued to work hard to provide fresh illumination upon black Americans of the new century and a base of creative, black self-definition for which all modern writers owe considerable gratitude.

Other group members included Rudolph Fisher (1897-1934), best known for the novels *The Walls of Jerico* (1928) and *The Conjure Man Dies* (1932) and short stories "High Yaller" and "The City of Refuge"; Wallace Thurman, remembered for the novel *Infants of the Spring* (1932); and Sterling Brown (1901-1959), valued for such folk poems as "Southern Road" (1932). A larger list includes Jessie R. Fauset (1884-1961), Georgia Douglas Camp Johnson (1886-1966), Helene Johnson (1907-1995), Anne Spencer (1882-1975), Waring Cuney (1906-1976), Frank Horne (1899-1977), Nella Larson (1891-1964), George Schuyler (1895-1977), Angelina Weld Grimke (1880-1958), Alice Moore Dunbar-Nelson (1875-1935), Eric Walrond (1898-1966), and Walter White (1893-1955).

✦•✦

Hughes, Langston (1902-1967)
American poet, novelist, essayist, and playwright.

Known for a widely diversified canon of work, Hughes remains a renowned black voice of American letters. His first book of poems, *The Weary Blues* (1926), provides a look at Harlem life, gives the rhythms of black music a new dignity, and contains his hallmark poem, "The Negro Speaks of Rivers," in which he extols his black pride and his aggressive spirit. A second volume, *Fine Clothes to the Jews* (1927), is said to have had mixed reviews—good by white critics but poor by black—because it contained dialect poems and was thought then to defame the race rather than to elevate it. His novel, *Not Without Laughter* (1930), brought good public notice and was translated into eight languages. These initial works were published by Knopf editor Carl Van Vechten (1880-1964), a good friend who was responsible for bringing Hughes's work to a wide public audience. His first published play was *The Gold Piece* (1921). Another, written during the Renaissance but not produced on Broadway until 1935, was called *Mulatto* and marked the beginning of his long-time enthusiasm for drama and his active participation in dramatic theater groups of all kinds. His autobiography, *The Big Sea* (1940), is noted to be indispensable to students of the Harlem Renaissance. Other works include numerous plays, musicals, and his invention of the gospel-song plays which include the melodic rhythms of black religious music. His many translations include work by Nicolás Guillén (1902-1989), Federíco García Lorca (1898-1936), and Gabriella Mistral (1889-1957). *The First Book of Negroes* (1952) and *Famous American Negroes* (1954) were biographies specifically designed for young readers. His character, "Simple," was created for his newspaper column in *The Chicago Defender* and is famous for the personification of the combined simplicity and complexity of black experience. Called the black Everyman, "Simple," in his "not-so-simple as he seems" aspect, provides apt depiction of both the humor and the irony of African-American culture. Hughes's attention to form, his aesthetic integrity, his concern for the troublesome issues that have affected black people, and a zealous desire to communicate with all Americans, creatively, place him among the outstanding writers of the Modernist period. A comprehensive listing of his many publications is found in D. C. Dickenson's *A Bio-Bibliography of Langston Hughes, 1902-1967* (1967).

⇒•⇐

Further Reading

Baker, Houston A., Jr. *Modernism and the Harlem Renaissance*. Chicago: University of Chicago Press, 1987.

————. *Singers at Daybreak: Studies in Black American Literature*. Washington, D.C.: Howard University Press, 1974.

————. "Modernism and the Harlem Renaissance." *American Quarterly* 39 (spring 1987): 84-97.

Bamikunle, Aderemi. "The Harlem Renaissance and White Critical Tradition." *College Language Association Journal* 29 (September 1985): 33-51.

Barksdale, Richard K. *Langston Hughes: The Poet and His Critics*. Chicago: American Library Association, 1977.

Bigsby, C[hristopher] W. E., ed. *The Black American Writer*. Deland, Fla.: Everett/Edwards, 1969.

Bone, Robert. *The Negro Novel in America*. Rev. ed. New Haven, Conn.: Yale University Press, 1965.

Bontemps, Arna. *The Harlem Renaissance Remembered.* New York: Dodd, Mead, 1972, repr. 1984.

Bremer, Sidney. "Home in Harlem, N.Y.: Lessons from the Harlem Renaissance." *Publications of the Modern Language Association* 105 (January 1990): 47-56.

Bronz, Stephen H. *Roots of Negro Racial Consciousness — the 1920s: Three Harlem Renaissance Authors*. New York: Libra, 1964.

Chapman, Abraham. "The Harlem Renaissance in Literary History." *College Language Association Journal* 11 (September 1967): 38-58.

Chauhan, P. S. "Rereading Claude McKay." *College Language Association Journal* 34 (September 1990): 66-80.

Davis, Arthur P. *From the Dark Tower*. Washington, D.C.: Howard University Press, 1974.

De Jongh, James. *Vicious Modernism: Black Harlem and the Literary Imagination*. Cambridge, England; New York: Cambridge University Press, 1990.

Diepeveen, Leonard. "Folktales in the Harlem Renaissance." *American Literature* 58 (March 1986): 64-81.

Ferguson, Blanche E. *Countee Cullen and the Negro Renaissance*. New York: Dodd, Mead, 1966.

Gayle, A., Jr. "The Harlem Renaissance: Toward a Black Aesthetic." *Midcontinent American Studies Journal* 11 (1970).

Gibson, Donald B., ed. *Modern Black Poets: A Collection of Critical Essays*. Englewood Cliffs, N.J.: Prentice-Hall, 1973.

Harris, Trudier, and Thadious M. Davis, eds. *Dictionary of Literary Biography,* Vol. 50. *Afro-American Writers from the Harlem Renaissance to 1940*. Detroit: Gale Research Co., 1987.

Honey, Maureen. "Survival in Song: Women Poets of the Harlem Renaissance." *Womens' Studies* 16, 3-4 (1989): 293-315.

Howard, William. "Failure and the Harlem Renaissance." *The Georgia Review* 42 (fall 1988): 638-43.

Huggins, Nathan Irvin. *Harlem Renaissance*. New York: Oxford University Press, 1971.

Hughes, Langston. "The Twenties: Harlem and Its Negritude." *African Forum* I (spring 1966): 11-20.

Hutchinson, George. *The Harlem Renaissance in Black and White*. Cambridge, Mass.: Harvard University Press, 1995.

Jackson, Blyden, and Louis D. Rubin. *Black Poetry in America*. Baton Rouge, La.: Louisiana State University Press, 1974.

Keller, Francis Richardson. "The Harlem Literary Renaissance." *North American Review* V (May-June 1968): 29-34.

Levy, Eugene. *James Weldon Johnson: Black Leader, Black Voice*. Chicago: University of Chicago Press, 1973.

Lewis, David Levering. *When Harlem Was in Vogue*. New York: Oxford University Press, 1981.

McKay, Claude. *Harlem Shadows*. New York: Harcourt Brace, 1922.

Monroe, John G. "The Harlem Little Theater Movement, 1920-1929." *Journal of American Culture* 6 (winter 1983): 63-70.

O'Daniel, Therman B., ed. *Langston Hughes: Black Genius: A Critical Evaluation*. New York: Morrow, 1971.

Presley, J. "The American Dream of Langston Hughes." *Southwestern Review* XLVIII (1963).

Redding, J. Saunders. *To Make a Poet Black*. Chapel Hill, N.C.: University of North Carolina Press, 1939.

Scott, Freda. "Black Drama and the Harlem Renaissance." *Theatre Journal* 37 (December 1985): 426-39.

Smith, Gary. "Gwendolyn Brooks' 'A Street in Bronzeville': The Harlem Renaissance and Mythologies of Black Women." *Melus* 10 (fall 1983): 33-46.

Turner, Darwin. *In a Minor Chord: Three Afro-American Writers and Their Search for Identity*. Carbondale, Ill.: Southern Illinois University Press, 1971.

Wagner, J. *Black Poets of the United States: From Paul Lawrence Dunbar to Langston Hughes*. Urbana, Ill.: University of Illinois Press, 1973.

HECECILER. *See* SYLLABISTS

HEIMATKUNST
Germany, 1900s-1930s

Growing out of NATURALISM and reacting against the urban novel and cosmopolitanism, Heimatkunst ("art of the homeland") was a regionalist literature, representing a nationalistic endeavor to create an authentically German literature. Major proponents of the movement were Heinrich Sohnrey (1859-1948), Friedrich (Fritz) Lienhard (1865-1929), and Adolf Bartels (1862-1945). Bartels was a literary historian who was openly anti-Semitic. He wrote an early village novel, *Die Dithmarscher* (1898), then later, *Einführung in das deutsche Schrifttum für deutsche Menschen* (1933), a survey of German literature acceptable to the Nazis. Sohnrey glorified simple peasant life and folk customs in his stories in the two-volume collection *Die Leute auf der Lindenhütte* (1886-87) and in the novels *Philipp Dubenkropps Heimkehr* (1888) and *Der Bruderhof* (1897). Literary predecessors include Jeremias Gotthelf (1797-1854) and his novels of Swiss peasant life, REALISTS Adalbert Stifter (1805-1868) and Theodor Storm (1817-1888), Johann Peter Hebel (1760-1826), and Fritz Reuter (1810-1874). Some Heimatkunst writers were also influenced by racist philosophers Julius Langbehn (1851-1907), who was an advocate of the Aryan regeneration of Germany, and Paul Antoine De Lagarde (1827-1891).

Heimatkunst literature appeared in the journals *Der Bote für deutsche Literatur* (1897-1904; after 1900, *Deutsche Heimat*), *Der Türmer* (1898-1943), and *Die Heimat* (1900-). The most notable Heimatkunst fiction includes the early regional work of Hermann Löns (1866-1914), such as *Aus Flur und Forst* (1907; From Field and

273

Forest), *Der letzte Hansbur* (1909; The Last Hansbur), *Da hinten in der Heide* (1910), and *Die Häuser von Ohlendorf* (1917); the rural Naturalist novels of Clara Viebig (1860-1952), especially *Das Weiberdorf* (1900; Village of Women); and Wilhelm von Polenz's (1861-1903) novel *Der Büttnerbauer* (1895).

By region, Alsatian Friedrich Lienhard discussed his literary tenets in *Neue Ideale* (1901) and wrote the novels *Oberlin* (1910) and *Lieder eines Elsässers* (1895); in *Der Spielmann* (1913), he stands out from other Heimatkunst writers in his criticism of nationalism. Bavarian Ludwig Ganghofer (1855-1920) wrote such Volksstücke (folk plays) as *Der Herrgottschnitzer von Ammergau* (1880), and fiction in *Jäger vom Fall* (1883), *Der Klosterjäger* (1892), *Das Schweigen im Walde* (1899), and *Der hohe Schein* (1904). From the Black Forest area, the stories by Heinrich Hansjakob (1837-1916) collected in *Wilde Kirschen* (1888), *Schneeballen* (3 volumes, 1892-94), *Bauernblut* (1896), and *Erzbauern* (1898) are representative. Hamburger Otto Ernst (1862-1926) was known for satirizing the educational system, as in *Flaschmann als Erzieher* (1902). Associated with Holstein are bestselling author Gustav Frenssen (1863-1945), who wrote what many consider the best regional novel, *Jörn Uhl* (1901), and Helene Voight-Diederichs (1875-1961), whose novels on rural life and marriage include *Auf Marienhoff* (1925), *Regine Vosgerau* (1901), *Dreiviertel Stund vor Tag* (1905; Three-Quarters of an Hour before Daybreak), and *Ring um Roderich* (1929; A Ring about Roderich); short stories appear in *Schleswig-Holsteiner Landleute* (1898). Lower Saxony was favored by Fritz Stavenhagen (1876-1906), known for his Volksstücke, and Lulu von Strauss und Torney (1873-1956), who wrote heroic ballads out of the Germanic ballad tradition, collected in *Reif steht die Saat* (1919; Ripe Stands the Grain), as well as peasant stories in *Bauernstolz* (1901; Peasant Pride) and *Judas* (1911; published as *Der Judashof* in 1937). Wilhelm Lobsien (1872-1947) wrote novels of the distinct culture of the people living in the Hallig, North Sea islands off the coast of Germany (as did Zacchi and Storm). Influenced by Frenssen, his other works include the novel *Der Halligpastor* (1914) — considered his best — and Novellen collected in *Wellen und Winde* (1908) and *Friesenblut* (1925). Frisia is prominent in such novels by Ferdinand Zacchi (1884-1966) as *Klaar Kimming* (1922) and *Freygeboren* (1927), and by Wilhelm Jensen (1837-1911), in particular, *Nirvana. Drei Bücher aus der Geschichte Frankreichs* (1877), *Flut und Ebbe* (1877), *Luv und lee* (1897), and *Aus See und Sand* (1897).

German-language writers elsewhere in this region of Europe also wrote Heimatkunst literature. Austrian precursors were Peter Rosegger (1843-1918) and Ludwig Anzengruber (1839-1889). A shepherd-turned-writer, Rosegger's major works include his collection of dialect poetry *Zither und Hackbrett* (1869), short stories in *Allerhand Leute* (1888), and autobiographical prose in *Waldheimat* (1897) and *Mein Weltleben*

(1898). Among his village novels are *Die Schriften des Waldschulmeisters* (1875), *Der Gottsucher* (2 volumes, 1883), *Jakob der Letzte* (1888), *Das ewige Licht* (1897), *Mein Himmelreich* (1901), and *INRI* (1905). Also a forerunner of Naturalism, Anzengruber wrote comedies of village life and was a pioneer in using Naturalistic speech for his characters, modernizing the traditional Volksstücke. His most notable plays include *Der Pfarrer von Kirchfeld* (1870) and *Die Kreuzelschreiber* (1872). *Das vierte Gebot* (1878; The Fourth Commandment) and *Der Doppelselbstmord* (1876; The Double Suicide) were produced by the FREIE BÜHNE. In addition, he wrote the village novels *Der Schandfleck* (1876) and *Der Sternsteinhof* (1883-84). Later Austrian Heimatkunst writers were Rudolf Hans Bartsch (1873-1952), whose novels include *Zwölf aus der Steiermark* (1908) and *Die Haindlkinder* (1908), Emil Ertl (1860-1935), who wrote a regional novelistic tetralogy, *Ein Volk an der Arbeit* (1906-31), and Josef Friedrich Perkonig (1890-1959), a prominent humorist of Blut-und Bodenliteratur, whose novels include *Der Schinderhannes zieht übers Gebirg* (1935), *Nikolaus Tschinderle, Räuberhauptmann* (1936), *Honigraub* (1935), and *Lopud, Insel der Helden* (1934). In the Tyrol, dramatist Karl Schönherr (1867-1943) was influenced by Anzengruber. His dialectic plays set in Tirolese villages include *Sonnwendtag* (1902), *Familie* (1905), *Das Krönigreich* (1908), and *Erde* (1908).

Significant Heimatkunst writers in Switzerland were Jakob Christoph Heer (1859-1925), especially his novels *Der König der Bernina* (1900) and *Joggeli* (1923); Heinrich Federer (1866-1928), a retired Catholic priest whose stories of rural Swiss life appear in *Lachweiler Geschichten* (1911), *Berge und Menschen* (1911), and *Pilatus* (1912); and Ernst Zahn (1867-1952), whose short stories are collected in *Helden des Alltags* (1906; Everyday Heroes); some of his most popular novels dealing with Swiss life are *Albin Indergand* (1901), *Die Clari-Marie* (1904), and *Lukas Hochstrassers Haus* (1907).

In the 1930s Heimatkunst literature was revived and put to the service of Hitler's National Socialist regime. The romanticization of the peasant and the manual laborer of this literature, as well as, of course, its focus on Germanness, appealed to the Nazis who appropriated it as signifying that which is purely German, called it "Blut-und Bodenliteratur," and rallied several of the Heimatkunst writers to its cause. Hans Friedrich Blunck (1888-1961) wrote regional novels in a historical-mythical vein, especially the trilogies *Urväter-Saga* (1928-33), depicting the historical German search for a national god, and *Werdendes Volk* (1934; originally published during the 1920s), which had as a theme the evolution of the German people. Other novels included *Stelling Rotkinnsohn* (1923), *Hein Hoyer* (1919), and *Berend Fock* (1921). Blunck was president of the Reichsschrifttunskammer from 1933 to 1935, an office within Goebbels's Ministry of Propaganda, which monitored cultural production and oversaw the production, publication, and sale of literature to be used as a tool to further Hitler's goals. Wilhelm Schäfer (1868-1952) wrote prose, novels, and short stories about Germany's history: *Theodorich, König des Abendlandes* (1939), *Huldreich Zwingli* (1926), *Winckelmanns Ende* (1925), *Hölderlins Einkehr* (1925), and *Der Hauptmann von Köpenick* (1930), as well as a history of his own family in *Meine Eltern* (1937) and himself in *Mein Leben* (1934) and *Lebensabriss* (1918). One of his favorite themes was traditional German heroism, which made him a Nazi favorite. Schäfer was an original member of the new academy set up by National Socialists in 1933, the National Socialist Akademie der Dichtung, along with Blunck and Friedrich Griese (1890-1975), who wrote such Blut-und Bodenliteratur novels as *Feuer* (1921), *Ur* (1922), *Alte Glocken* (1925), and *Winter* (1927). Notable protesters included Stefan George (1868-1933), who refused the presidency of the Akademie, and Ernst Jünger (1895-1998) and Hans Carossa (1878-1956), who refused membership. Hermann Stehr (1864-1940) wrote novels of German traditional folk in the earlier part of the century. Initially considered a Naturalist, his later writings were more mystical, spiritually searching, such as the short stories in *Auf Leben und Tod* (1898) and the novels *Der begrabene Gott* (1905; The Buried God), *Drei Nächte* (1909; Three Nights), *Der Heiligenhof* (1918; The Court of Saints), and its sequel *Peter Brindeisener* (1924). Stehr took a position in the Reichsschrifttunskammer. Other approved writers included Frenssen, whom the Nazis held up as a prophet of racial purity, and Löns, whose most famous work was a patriotic folk novel popular among the Nazis, *Der Wehrwolf* (1910; *Harm Wulf*, 1931). Löns once wrote: "We Germans make out that we are Christians, but we are nothing of the sort, and never can be. For Christianity and race-consciousness are as incompatible as Socialism and culture are."

✥•✥

Further Reading

Bithell, Jethro. "The Regional Novel." In his *Modern German Literature, 1880-1950*. London: Methuen, 1959.

Eloesser, Arthur. *Modern German Literature*. New York: Alfred A. Knopf, 1933.

Taylor, Ronald. "The Nazi Canon of Literature." In his *Literature and Society in Germany 1918-1945*. Totowa, N.J.: Barnes & Noble Books, 1980.

HERETIKA POETS
Denmark, 1948-1953

This group was formed in connection with the literary journal *Heretika*, which was published by group member Ole Wival (1921-). Ove Abildgaarde (1916-), Thornkild Bjornvig (1918-), Tove Ditlevsen (1922-), Erik Knudsen (1922-), and Ole Sarvig

(1921-1981) were other *Heretika* poets. They were in theoretical opposition to the critical perspectives about literature which were put forth by Danish writers of the two previous decades. During that time there had been a general mood of pessimism, disillusion, and deeply rooted cynicism about the future of Western civilization, and the earlier writers had been looking for new ways to reestablish a diminishing socio-cultural unity in their land. The philosophy called for a sound political and economic system, based in tenets of rationalism and materialism, and these concepts underlaid much of their creative activity. But the Heretikas opposed such a value system; their attitude was that national unity be achieved through the rebirth of Danish spiritual unity which, in turn, could be found through a search for those universal truths which transcend the materialistic and the profane. Their timing was apt, for there had come at the end of the Nazi occupation in 1945 an unexpected surge of vitality and enthusiasm in the country. Freedom from constriction and the Allied victory gave new optimism and excitement at the thought of peace. Concurrently, there was also a resurgence of literary activity and new ideas in connection with it, among which were those of the *Heretika* poets. Their manifesto was based on their determination to revive, in poetry, the medieval concept that love, in its spiritual, mystical, and physical aspects, would provide individual unification of self and would promote healing of both national spirit and homeland.

The early works of Sarvig and Wival show the influence of T. S. ELIOT (*see* MODERNISM, England and Ireland) and his use of Christian symbolism in an effort to speak to twentieth-century problems of human alienation and isolation. Moreover, while remaining in the EXISTENTIALIST tradition, each of the *Heretika* poets managed to find unique and singular voices. Tove Ditlevsen reassessed the value of rhymed "simple, melancholic stanzas" and clearly defined, understandable language in her work. Bjornvig saw the poem itself as of most decisive importance, and his use of love and death as main motifs made each work a vehicle of spiritual reorientation. Knudsen was inclined to political and social comment, and his poems sometimes contain biting satire about ordinary life. Frank Jaeger (1926-1977), on the other hand, depicts the humor, frailty, and irony of the human condition in both playful and mournful poems.

Best known for his lyrical style, Sarvig is considered the most important of the *Heretika* poets; his early work, *Menneske* (1945; *Man*, 1948), is called a major work of Danish lyricism. His interest in abstract art stimulated a concurrent interest in abstract poetry, as it presents the juxtaposition of illusionary, metaphoric, and symbolic devices with the free association of mood, image, and time perception as design for revealing the attempts of humankind to relate to a complex universe. Like T. S. Eliot, and strongly influenced by his work, Sarvig saw redemption in the symbols of religion and saw regeneration and hope as embodied in love of both the religious and earthly kind. His

Gronne digte (1943; Green Poems), *Jeghuset* (1944; The House of Self), and *Menneske*, as well as much of his later work, all see modern man at a "historical turning-point" and in search of answers to the ideological crises of the century. His novels, which contain similar themes of resolution, include *Stenrosen* (1955; The Rose Stone), *Limbo* (1963), *De Rejsende* (1978; The Travelers), and two mysteries, *De Sovende* (1958; The Sleepers) and *Havet under mit Vinder* (1960; The Sea Under My Window). These last two draw parallels between the forces of good overcoming the force of crime (evil) as an example of man in a larger pattern of the search for a "good" existence, as found in spiritual love.

It has been suggested that since the Heretikas were of the SYMBOLIST tradition which preceded them, they were nonetheless clearly moving in the direction of European Modernism in their use of its precepts to depict the sensory experience of existing reality, its excitement, and its grave inevitability. Their willingness to put themselves in step with the creative thrust of Modernists in other Western cultures has provided impetus for new and innovative Danish literary development in the final decade of the century. For example, the experimentation with lyrical Modernism appeared in the sixties and, while some poets still remain traditionalists, others have expressed strong interest in Concretism (*see* CONCRETE POETRY), the literature of social protest, and Neoromanticism, among other literary devices. All of this makes for a Danish literature that is exciting, versatile, and embodies the zest of its many and talented exponents.

❧•❦

Further Reading

Allwood, Martin Samuel, ed. *20th Century Scandinavian Poetry: The Development of Poetry in Iceland, Denmark, Norway, Sweden, Finland, 1900-1950.* Copenhagen: Gyldendal, 1950.

Barfoed, Niels Aage. *Danish Literature, 1962.* Translated by Chris Bojesen. Copenhagen: Litteraturudvalget, Samvirkerådet for Dansk Kulturarbejde, 1963.

Borum, Poul. *Danish Literature, A Short Critical Survey.* Copenhagen: Det Danske Selskab, 1979.

Bredsdorff, Elias. *Danish Literature in English Translation: A Bibliography.* Copenhagen: Munksgaard, 1950.

Claudi, Jorgen. *Contemporary Danish Authors.* Translated by Jorgen Andersen and Aubrey Rush. Copenhagen: Det Danske Selskab, 1952.

Fredericksen, Emil. *Danish Literature 1960-61.* Translated by David S. Thatcher. Copenhagen: Samvirkerådet for Dansk Kulturarbejde, Udlandet, 1962.

Mitchell, P. M. *A History of Danish Literature.* Copenhagen: Gyldendal, 1957. Rev. ed., New York: Kraus-Thomson Organization, 1971.

Mogensen, Knud K., ed. *Modern Danish Poems.* 2nd ed. Copenhagen: Andr. Pred. Host & Son, 1951.

Rossel, Sven H. *A History of Scandinavian Literature—1870-1970*. Translated by Anne C. Ulmer. Minneapolis: University of Minnesota Press, 1982.

————. "Crisis and Redemption: An Introduction to Ole Sarvig." *World Literature Today* 53, 4 (1979): 606-9.

Stangerup, Hakon. *Danish Literature in 1955*. Copenhagen: Litteraturudvalget, Samvirkerådet for Dansk Kulturarbejde I Udlandet, 1956.

————. *Danish Literature in 1956*. Translated by Ingeborg Nixon. Copenhagen: Litteraturudvalget, Samvirkerådet for Dansk Kulturarbejde I Udlandet, 1957.

————. *Danish Literature in 1957*. Copenhagen: Litteraturudvalget, Samvirkerådet for Dansk Kulturarbejde I Udlandet, 1958.

————. *Danish Literature in 1959*. Copenhagen: Litteraturudvalget, Samvirkerådet for Dansk Kulturarbejde I Udlandet, 1960.

Topsoe-Jensen. *Scandinavian Literature from Brandes to Our Day*. New York: American-Scandinavian Foundation; W. W. Norton, 1929.

HERMETICISM
Italy, 1915-1940s

Hermeticism was an early-twentieth-century poetic movement that developed within the broader context of MODERNISM, with its call for cultural reevaluation and renewal. Influenced by several other Modernist movements, such as SYMBOLISM and FUTURISM, Hermetic verse was characterized by unconventional structure and syntax, emotional restraint, and highly subjective, cryptic, involuted language. In fact, it was the introverted nature of this poetry that led one of its commentators, the renowned Italian critic Francesco Flora (1891-1962), to coin the term "Hermeticism," in reference to the occult author Hermes Trismegistos, whose work he described as similarly obscure and abstruse.

Although the roots of Hermeticism could be said to go back as far as the German romantic poet Novalis (1772-1801) and the American short-story writer and poet Edgar Allan Poe (1809-1849), its more immediate antecedents are found in the French Symbolist movement led by such poets as Charles BAUDELAIRE and Paul Valéry (1871-1945), whose groundbreaking work featured an inward focus and an impressionistic writing style. The Hermeticists were also influenced by Futurism, a radical cultural movement founded in 1909 by the Italian novelist and poet Filippo Tommaso MARINETTI, who advocated complete stylistic freedom (including the abolition of syntax).

The historical context in which Hermeticism developed is also significant: in the years immediately following the profoundly disillusioning World War I, Italian poets—like those of other European countries—found their highly constrained, ornate traditional verse inadequate for the expression of twentieth-century concerns and experiences. In addition, the dawn of the Fascist period forced independent-minded Italian writers to find ways to evade the propagandistic rhetoric and censorship of Mussolini's regime. The brevity and obscurity of Hermetic poetry allowed them a covert means to express their dismay and pessimism over the current state of affairs in their country.

The leading poet of the Hermetic movement was Giuseppe UNGARETTI, whose experiences both as a soldier in World War I and as a member of the early-twentieth-century literary scene in Paris profoundly influenced his poetry. In his first volume, *Il porto sepolto* (1916; *The Buried Port*, 1958), Ungaretti purged his verse of traditional rhyme schemes and, in an effort to expose the pure power and suggestiveness of words, pared his language down to the essential. In such later volumes as *Il sentimento del tempo* (1933; *Sentiment of Time*, 1958) and *Il dolore* (1947; *Grief*, 1958), Ungaretti reintroduced some traditional elements, such as classical rhyme patterns and punctuation, but retained his inward focus.

Another important Hermetic poet is Salvatore QUASIMODO. The poems collected in Quasimodo's first volume, *Acque e terre* (1930; Water and Lands), which provide a nostalgic portrait of the poet's Sicilian home, are written in stripped-down, allusive language that conveys a deep sense of anguish and exile. Quasimodo's later works — particularly those written after World War II — evidence his turning away from the introversion of Hermeticism toward social commitment and dialogue.

Also frequently identified as a hermeticist, despite his own refusal to claim membership in any particular movement, is Eugenio MONTALE (*see* MODERNISM, Italy). Written in compressed, highly personal, often difficult language, Montale's verse — especially that collected in his first volume, *Ossi di seppia* (1916; *The Bones of Cuttlefish*, 1983) — does contain some Hermetic elements. Perhaps the most notable of these is Montale's deliberate rejection of the Italian lyric tradition in favor of a cryptic, Symbolist poetic style.

The extreme difficulty and obscurity of Hermetic poetry made it inaccessible to most readers and led to its gradual downfall, as even its most prominent practitioners moved on to different styles; Ungaretti, for instance, began to write more straightforward verse, and Quasimodo's became more socially committed.

❖•❖

Quasimodo, Salvatore (1901-1968), Italian poet, critic, and translator.

Quasimodo's stature as a major literary figure of the twentieth century was confirmed in 1959, when he received the Nobel Prize for Literature. His poetry can be divided into two periods, with World War II the boundary between them. Born in Sicily, Quasimodo moved to Milan in 1929 and became part of the thriving literary scene there. His first volume of verse, *Acque e terre* (1930; Water and Lands), which collects poetry written between 1920 and 1929, is characterized by its distinctly Hermetic qualities. In language that is economical and deceptively simple as well as highly evocative, Quasimodo describes scenes from his Sicilian childhood, casting this remembered past as a lost Eden. Dominated by a deep sense of anguish, *Acque e terre* features an effective use of analogy, allusion, and metaphor.

Despite his roots in Hermeticism, Quasimodo's later poetic development took him in a different direction. The poems collected in *Nuove poesie* (1942; New Poems) evidence a less private focus, and Quasimodo's growing social commitment dominates such succeeding volumes as *Giorno dopo giorno* (1947; Day After Day) and *La vita non è sogno* (1949; Life Is Not a Dream). The poetry in these collections features a notably simpler syntax and vocabulary and focuses on the need to improve humanity's lot. Although Quasimodo retains the melancholy tone and allusiveness of his earlier work, these poems are less introspective—they are presented as a dialogue with the outer world. Quasimodo's acclaimed later works include *La terra imparreggiabile* (1958; *The Incomparable Earth*, 1958) and *Dare e avere* (1966; *To Give and to Have, and Other Poems*, 1969).

✦•✦

Ungaretti, Giuseppe (1888-1970), Italian poet.

One of the most important twentieth-century Italian writers, Ungaretti was a leading practitioner of Hermeticism and probably the most successful in carrying out its principles. Educated at the Sorbonne in Paris, Ungaretti was well acquainted with Modernism's cultural innovators, including the Symbolist poet Paul Valéry, whose work influenced Ungaretti's. Ungaretti was also deeply affected by his participation as a soldier in World War I, an experience that left him with the desire to express an anguish both personal and universal. To that end he sought a poetry purged of traditional rhyme, stripped down and reduced to isolated parts that would enhance the power of each word and increase the overall suggestiveness of the verse.

The poems in Ungaretti's first volume, *Il porto sepolto* (1916; *The Buried Port*, 1958), comprise a kind of diary of the poet's inner life, replete with highly personal, impressionistic images and infused with an awareness of words as symbols and even as sounds, capable of evoking profound emotion.

In a later collection, *Il sentimento del tempo* (1933; *Sentiment of Time*, 1958), Ungaretti reintroduced some traditional elements into his verse, such as a classical rhyme scheme and punctuation, but retained the difficulty that led critic Francesco

Flora to fault Ungaretti and the other Hermeticists for their obscurity. With *Il dolore* (1947; *Grief*, 1958), Ungaretti began to move away from Hermeticism and toward a more accessible, articulate style.

✦•✦

Further Reading

Jones, Frederic J. *Giuseppe Ungaretti*. Edinburgh, Scotland: Edinburgh University Press, 1977.
Molinaro, Julius A., ed. *Petrarch to Pirandello: Studies in Italian Literature in Honour of Beatrice Corrigan*. Toronto: University of Toronto Press, 1973.
Singh, G. *Eugenio Montale: A Critical Study of His Poetry, Prose, and Criticism*. New Haven, Conn.: Yale University Press, 1973.

HET FONTEINTJE (The Little Spring)
Belgium, 1920s-1930s

Also known as *t'Fonteintje*, this group and literary journal were known for their humanistic and humorous proclivities in writing. Novelist, poet, and critic Maurice Roelants (1895-1966) was one of the founders, while poet Raymond Herreman (1896-1971) became the group's best-known spokesman. Intended as a continuation of the *VAN NU EN STRAKS* group's tenets, *Het Fonteintje* was a source of invigoration for Flemish writers, particularly into the 1930s. Other members included novelists Johan Daisne (1912-1978) and Louis-Paul Boon (1912-).

✦•✦

Further Reading

Mallinson, Vernon. *Modern Belgian Literature, 1830-1960*. London: Heinemann, 1966.

HET GETIJ. *See* TIDE

HEXAGONE GROUP
Canada, 1953-1963

Named after the Quebec publishing house Les Édition de l'Hexagone, which its members founded in 1953, the Hexagone Group thoroughly revitalized French-Canadian poetry through a strong emphasis on untried meter and language and a broad appreciation of the creative arts. Paul-Marie Lapointe (1929-), Gaston Miron (1928-), Fernand Ouellete (1930-), and Jean-Guy Pilon (1930-) were among the leading figures of the movement, which greatly influenced the reading public not only through Hexagone publications but also through works and sponsored events of the journal *Liberté*, founded in 1959.

Further Reading

Bayard, Caroline. "Miron, Gaston." In *The Oxford Companion to Canadian Literature*. Edited by William Toye. Toronto; New York: Oxford University Press, 1983.

May, C. R. P. "Poetry in French: 5." In *The Oxford Companion to Canadian Literature*. Edited by William Toye. Toronto; New York: Oxford University Press, 1983.

HID GROUP
Yugoslavia, 1930s

A collection of Hungarian-language writers in 1930s Yugoslavia, the *Hid* Group and journal was — far more so than its counterpart *KALANGYA* — profoundly concerned with how their literature could influence the country's sociopolitical climate. The most important writer in the group was novelist Ervin Sinkó (1898-1967).

Further Reading

Demaitre, Ann. "Yugoslav Literature: Hungarian Literature." In *Encyclopedia of World Literature in the Twentieth Century*. 3rd ed. Edited by Steven R. Serafin. Farmington Hills, Mich.: St. James Press, 1999.

HOTOTOGISU SCHOOL
Japan, 1900s-1920s

The dominant force of the twentieth-century haiku revolution, the Hototogisu School became known, ironically, for its professed adherence to the longstanding traditions of uniform scope and syllabic structure established during previous centuries. Under the direction of Takahama KYOSHI, the Hototogisu poets emphasized precise expression, acute awareness of the natural world, and the singular effectiveness of the three-line verse form to evoke brief impressions rich in both meaning and beauty.

The magazine *Hototogisu* (Cuckoo), from which the movement derived its name, was founded in 1897 as a prominent platform, alongside the newspaper *Nippon,* for Masaoka Shiki's (1867-1902) Nihon-Ha, a movement which had by that time resurrected, dissected, and revitalized the haiku as a major Japanese literary form. Shiki's foremost disciples, Kyoshi and Kawahigashi Hekigotō (1873-1937), largely assumed control of the magazine's content and operation, particularly after 1899, the year in which Shiki founded the NEGISHI TANKA SOCIETY and became almost exclusively involved with the reformation of another classical Japanese verse form. A widening rift between the two younger poets, whose interpretations of Shiki's haiku theories differed radically, became irremediable following Shiki's death in 1902.

Hekigotō, through his new post as column editor for *Nippon*, proceeded to found the NEW TENDENCY SCHOOL, attract a wide following of haiku poets, and institute bold experiments in the genre. By contrast, Kyoshi, for nearly a decade, rarely displayed interest in haiku composition and concentrated instead on fiction, while simultaneously broadening *Hototogisu*'s literary platform to counter the NATURALISTIC currents of the day. In 1912, however, Kyoshi returned his attention to haiku. Unsettled by Hekigotō's increasing disregard for formal constraints and clear, seasonal topics, he reclaimed the historicity of the genre and accepted its limitations as the best, indeed the only, avenues by which one could attain mastery of the difficult art.

Among Kyoshi's numerous followers were Murakami Kijō (1865-1938), Iida Dakotsu (1885-1962), Hara Sekitei (1886-1951), Maeda Fura (1889-1954), Sugita Hisajo (1890-1946), Hino Sōjō (1901-1956), Kawabata Bōsha (1897-1941), Yamaguchi Seishi (1901-1994), and Mizuhara Shūōshi (1892-1981). Several of these writers, after joining *Hototogisu*, established haiku magazines of their own and, in the case of some, such as Shūōshi, directly revolted against the conservative influence of Kyoshi's theories. Nonetheless, Hototogisu-style haiku remained popular until Kyoshi's death, some fifty years after the movement had begun.

⇜•⇝

Kyoshi, Takahama (1874-1959)
Japanese poet, critic, short-story writer, and novelist.

Selected by Shiki to be his literary successor, Kyoshi did not begin to fulfill his obligation until 1912, the year in which he formally announced his renewed devotion to haiku. Kyoshi, like Shiki and Hekigotō, upheld throughout his career the concept of *shasei* — the nonidealized description of the immediately perceptible. Yet, he differed from both poets in his subordination of shasei to the example of tradition, particularly that regarding subject matter. As Kyoshi declared in 1928 to a now zealously supportive league of readers and fellow artists, the domain of haiku could not reasonably be expanded beyond the "singing about flowers and birds," that is, the practiced and objective contemplation of the natural world. Aside from creating a number of widely revered poems, Kyoshi's greatest contribution to twentieth-century Japanese literature was his successful promotion of haiku as a national pastime, a form which anyone might choose to memorably capture the infinite, fleeting moments of reality.

⇜•⇝

Further Reading

Higginson, William J., with Penny Harter. "Modern Japanese Haiku." In their *The Haiku Handbook: How to Write, Share, and Teach Haiku*. New York: McGraw-Hill, 1985.

Keene, Donald. "The Modern Haiku." In his *Dawn to the West: Japanese Literature in the Modern Era*. Vol. 2. New York: Holt, Rinehart & Winston, 1984.

HSIN CH'ING-NIEN. *See* **MAY FOURTH MOVEMENT**

HSIN YÜEH SHE. *See* **CRESCENT SOCIETY**

HU FENG CLIQUE
China, 1940s-1950s

The story of the Hu Feng Clique is the story of a clash between two diametrically opposed literary ideologies. One, that of HU Feng and such like-minded writers as LU Hsün (*see* MAY FOURTH MOVEMENT), HU Shih (*see* MAY FOURTH MOVEMENT), and Lin Yutang (1895-1976), was doomed to triumphant failure. The other, that of CHOU Yang (*see* LEAGUE OF LEFT-WING WRITERS), Mao Tse-tung (1893-1976), and the Communist Party as a whole, was destined for dubious success. The battle, first begun in the 1930s within the League of Left-Wing Writers, extended over some twenty years, before culminating in the arrest of Hu Feng and the complete suppression of his thought. The central issue was nothing less than the integrity and future of modern Chinese literature, a cause to which Hu, as an enormously influential essayist and editor, wholeheartedly dedicated his career.

For Hu, literary creativity was the one unassailable element necessary for fine writing. He allowed neither Marxism nor party politics to alter this view. Consequently, his membership in the League of Left-Wing Writers, an organization which became increasingly authoritarian under the leadership of Chou Yang, was a difficult one. In 1936 Hu launched a debate with Chou concerning the use of stereotypical characters in fiction. Chou, adhering to the party line, stressed the continued importance of depicting two major groups: revolutionary heroes and revolutionary traitors. Hu, contrarily, argued against such enforced narrowness and in favor of a literature embracing the good and exposing the harmful aspects of humanity. The initial triumph Hu enjoyed was short-lived, for Chou, though less adept at analytical argumentation, commanded overwhelming political support due to his unquestioned stature within the party. Like Lu Hsün, Hu became one of the chief targets of party excoriation that same year, when Chou engineered the dissolution of the League and the creation of the Association of Chinese Writers and Artists.

Until 1954 Hu, given his outspokenness, succeeded only in securing nominal posts within the party whose outlook he so desperately hoped to change. Finally, he was appointed representative to the National People's Congress as well as a member of the editorial board of *Jen-min wen-hsüeh* (People's Literature), a leading party periodical. Emboldened by his rise in rank, Hu issued a 300,000-word memorandum—assembled during his nine years of polemical battles—to the Central Committee on the causes of literary stagnation in China. Hu's message was the same as that of Lu Hsün some twenty years earlier: literature should be freed to portray all classes, all characters, and all situations. Hu's position was strengthened by his distinguished reputation and considerable literary following. Included among Hu's disciples were Lü Ying (n.d.), Lu Ling (1921-), Lü Yüan (1922-), A Lung (n.d.), and Chang Chung-hsiao (n.d.), each of whom had played a role in defending Hu against past attacks from Chou and the Maoist orthodoxy. However, Hu's current criticism of party ideology was so sweeping as to make his ostracization imperative and his retaliation a virtual impossibility. The campaign of 1955 against Hu became a national event, a stunning exhibition of the party's firm resolve to identify and punish heterodoxy in all its forms. After nearly a year of public excoriation, Hu was falsely accused of being a counterrevolutionary leader; the campaign ended with his arrest and imprisonment.

Ironically, the year following Hu's incarceration the government greatly loosened its controls on the arts and launched the Hundred Flowers Campaign to heighten public interest through variegated literary production. For a time, Hu's ideals were widely praised by the very critics who had helped to incriminate him. Eventually though, these critics were silenced as well when the Communist hierarchy reasserted its stranglehold on artistic expression.

❖•❖

Hu Feng (1902-1985), Chinese critic, essayist, and poet.

Although he never became a member of the Chinese Communist Party, Hu was a Marxist intellectual who maintained a lifelong interest in the cause of revolutionary writing. In 1925, as a member of the Communist Youth League, he participated in the May Thirtieth Movement. At this time he also began to write poetry. In 1928 he traveled to Japan, where he studied and wrote essays advocating social and political change in China. Following his association with a leftist movement, Hu was expelled from Japan in 1933; a year later he joined the League of Left-Wing Writers in Shanghai and became one of Lu Hsün's chief disciples. His strong advocacy of Realism and individual expression from this time forward has inspired C. T. Hsia to call him "the critic who has done the most to counter the baleful influence of Maoist orthodoxy in the war years and after."

❖•❖

Further Reading

Fokkema, D. W. "War and Postwar Years: Hu Feng," "Feng Hsüeh-feng and Hu Feng." In his *Literary Doctrine in China and Soviet Influence, 1956-1960*. The Hague, Netherlands: Mouton, 1965.
Goldman, Merle. "Hu Feng's Conflict with the Communist Literary Authorities." *Papers on China* 11 (1957). Reprint, *China Quarterly* 12 (1962).

————. "The Hu Feng Campaign of 1955." In her *Literary Dissent in Communist China*.
   Cambridge, Mass.: Harvard University Press, 1967.
Hsia, C. T. "Conformity, Defiance, and Achievement." In his *A History of Modern Chinese
   Fiction, 1917-1957*. New Haven, Conn.: Yale University Press, 1961.
"Hu Feng." In *Biographical Dictionary of Republican China*. Edited by Howard L. Boorman
   and Richard C. Howard. Vol. II. New York: Columbia University Press, 1968.
Yang I-fan. *The Case of Hu Feng*. Hong Kong: Union Research Institute, 1956.

HUMANISME
France, 1900s

In 1902, Fernand Gregh (1873-1960) began this small and short-lived movement and
published its manifesto in the Paris journal *Le figaro*. He was antipathetic to the then
relatively new impact of the SYMBOLISTS, whose wide appeal was yet to be fully realized. Gregh deplored their idiosyncratic and obscure poetic modality and called for a
concentration in poetic art on a love of nature (*see* NATURISM) and classical, humanistic spirituality. Examples of his extensive output as a critic, poet, and essayist include
Le Maison de l'enfance (1897), *La Beaute de vivre* (1900), *Les Clares humaines*
(1904), *La Gloire de coeur* (1932), and *Étude sur Victor Hugo* (1904).

⤙•⤚

Further Reading

Alden, Douglas William, and Richard A. Brooks, eds. *A Critical Biography of French Literature*.
   Vol. VI, *The Twentieth Century*. Syracuse, N.Y.: Syracuse University Press, 1980.
Cruickshank, John. "French Literature Since 1870." In *French Literature from 1660 to the
   Present* by W. D. Howarth, Henri M. Peyre, and John Cruickshank. London: Methuen, 1974.

HYLAEA. See **CUBO-FUTURISM**

I

IKINCI YENI MOVEMENT. *See* **SECOND NEW**

IMAGINISTS
Russia, 1920s

This group was one of the many MODERNIST poetic coteries, some of which were short-lived, which began in the period around World War I and were reacting to the social and political revolution which followed it. Specifically, Russian Imaginism was given its impetus by the poet Vadim Shersenevich (1893-1942) and included others such as Sergei Aleksandrovich ESENIN and Nikolai Klyuev (1887-1937). The Imaginists were in accordance with the poets of the British IMAGIST movement, and also stressed the importance of image in poetry that is strong, direct and clear, and of the depiction of emotion as manifested in carefully wrought metaphor that engages the mind as well as the sensibility. Both Esenin and Klyuev, as poet novitiates, had been associated with the group known as the Peasant Poets, and much of their early work attended to farm workers, was concerned with the melancholy of the lover, or was of religious nature. However, it is generally referenced that as Imaginists, they wrote "shocking and blasphemous pieces, often meagre in content," and became notorious for their outrageous conduct and bohemian ways in a deliberate attempt to bring attention to themselves and to their philosophy.

The Russian Modernists of the twenties were the mid-century result of an aesthetic and spiritual reformation which had begun in the 1890s, in which writers had then demanded a move away from what is now called their inheritance of a "heterogeneous" form of SYMBOLISM. Such groups as the FUTURISTS, the EGO-FUTURISTS, and the CUBO-FUTURISTS were in clear rebellion against past tradition and seeking new avenues for expression of poetic attitude. Thus the Imaginists found themselves in the midst of what is noted as the most fertile and innovative period of literary activity in

Soviet-Russian history; the spirit of revolution and the optimism which it engendered gave rise to new ideas brought about by the freedom to exchange them with writers of other countries. But by the thirties, with Stalin's rise to power, writers were expected to concentrate on the political party-line; SOCIALIST REALIST restrictions diminished earlier, individual enthusiasm and drove many Russian writers into exile.

❧•❦

Esenin, Sergei Aleksandrovich (also rendered Sergey Yesenin, 1895-1925) Russian poet.

At seventeen, Esenin's gift for poetic expression gave him wide acceptance in the literary circles of Moscow and St. Petersburg, and led him into a bohemian environment which was to influence his life, work, and early demise. Disappointed that an American tour with his wife, the dancer Isadora Duncan (1877-1927), did not provide him the recognition he felt due him, Esenin returned to Moscow where he became more popular than ever. His early lyrics are sometimes religious in content and most often describe the Russian rural scene; they are characterized by the simple, joyful — though not always realistic — depiction of the life of the peasant and his folk rituals. Later poems include serene and tender portrayals of the peasantry he had known as a child, but often contain overtones of sadness as he seems to recognize in them the evidence of that same, simple life beginning to disappear, overtaken by the technology of the modern world. His best works are said to be his later ones, the result of his imagistic mode, since they present a more universal and realistic view of life. For example, "Inoma" (1918) depicts a new attitude, brought about by his early and positive response to the revolution; here he exhorts the peasantry to "forsake religion and industrialization" and seek the rewards of materialism under the new regime. However, as he became more aware of the pain and violence that are a part of any revolution, he concentrated once again on his romantic vision of peasant life, and his poems became contrived, artificial, and elaborately overdone. But his lyrical drama, *Pugachyov* (1922), is said to be his most outstanding endeavor and shows his final mastery of the Imaginist technique and his control over his subject matter. A self-destructive bent and severe depression combined with hallucinations caused the breakdown which ended in suicide, after which his fellow poets wrote eulogies of lamentation in his honor and gave him, too late, the accolades he had sought all of his life. Ironically, his lyrics enjoyed a new popularity then, which continued through the end of the twentieth century.

❧•❦

Further Reading

Baring, Maurice. *The Oxford Book of Russian Verse*. 2nd ed. Oxford, England: Clarendon Press, 1948.

Bowra, C. M. *A Book of Russian Verse*. London: Macmillan, 1943.

Davis, J., ed. and trans. *Esenin: A Biography in Memoirs, Letters and Documents*. Ann Arbor, Mich.: Ardis, 1982.

De Graaff, Frances. *Sergej Esenin: A Biographical Sketch*. The Hague: Mouton, 1966.

Deutsch, Babette, and Abraham Yarmolinsky, eds. *Russian Poetry, an Anthology*. New York: International Publishers, 1927.

Gibian, George, and H. W. Tjalsma, eds. *Russian Modernism: Culture and the Avant Garde, 1900-1930*. Ithaca, N.Y.: Cornell University Press, 1976.

Glad, John. Introduction to Nickolay Klyuev in *Poems*. Ann Arbor, Mich.: Iowa Translation Series, University of Iowa, 1977.

Kaun, Alexander S. *Soviet Poets and Poetry*. Berkeley, Calif.: University of California Press, 1943.

Klyuev, Nikolai. *Poems*. Translated by John Glad. Ann Arbor, Mich.: Ardis, 1977.

McVay, Gordon. *Esenin: A Life*. Ann Arbor, Mich.: Ardis, 1976.

————. "Yesenin's Posthumous Fame and the Fate of His Friends." *Modern Language Review* 67 (July 1972): 590-602.

Poggioli, R. *The Poets of Russia: 1890-1930*. Cambridge, Mass.: Harvard University Press, 1960.

Prokushev, Yuri. *Sergei Yesenin: The Man, the Verse, the Age*. Translated by Kathleen Cook. Moscow: Progress Publishers, 1979.

Slonim, Marc. *Soviet Russian Literature: Writers and Problems*. New York: Oxford University Press, 1964.

Trotsky, Leon. *Literature and Revolution*. New York: Russell & Russell, 1957.

Visson, L. *Sergei Esenin: Poet of the Crossroads*. Würzburg, Germany: Jal-Verlag, 1980.

Yarmolinky, A., ed. *An Anthology of Russian Verse: 1812-1960*. Garden City, N.Y.: Doubleday, 1962.

Zavaiashin, Viacheslav. *Early Soviet Writers*. New York: Praeger, 1958.

IMAGISM
England and United States, 1912-1917

Imagism began in England at the turn of the century in reaction to an earlier tradition which seemed to the proponents of Imagism to be steeped in the sentimental contemplation of nature and the mystical, symbolic association of imaginative and idealistic notions. These concepts were viewed by these new poets as inadequate for the presentation of creative work, which they agreed should clearly, even harshly, speak to the issues of the times. By 1909, T. E. Hulme (1883-1917) was insisting that new poetry should begin with strong emotion on the part of the poet, who should then manifest it in the accomplished use of clear imagery and forceful metaphor. Ezra POUND (*see* MODERNISM, England and Ireland) was in agreement, and in 1912 along with H[ILDA] D[OOLITTLE], Richard Aldington (1892-1962), and F. S. Flint (1885-1960), contrived the first, three-principled manifesto for the poetry of the "Imagistes." They believed the poet must provide a "direct" treatment of the concept presented, whether objective or subjective; must use no word which does not contribute to exact presentation; and must combine verse and rhythm as in "the sequence of musical phrase, and not in the sequence of the metronome." Later additions to the formula included the use of common language, the "exact" word or phrase (not the "nearly" exact), and absolute freedom in the choice of subject matter. Finally, Aldington, in the *Egoist* (1914), would produce a singularly influential statement for the movement, stating that poetry must be "hard and clear," and that "concentration [comprise] the very essence of poetry."

In the United States, the poet Amy LOWELL was fascinated by Pound's anthology, *Des Imagistes*, and joined him in London to learn more about his new literary insights. At this point, Pound, who had built a substantial reputation as a critic, editor, and able force in the field of poetry, and was able to help her to crystallize her own poetic vision. Unfortunately, on her return to America, her enthusiasm for the new techniques created the assumption (which she did not hesitate to help propagate) that she had become the "foremost" member of the Imagist group, and compared her work to that of both W. B. YEATS (*see* ABBEY THEATER and MODERNISM, England and Ireland) and Ezra Pound. This caused Pound enough irritation to denounce her as a poor imitator and become her intellectual enemy. However, Lowell continued in America to promote Imagism through her lectures, readings, and publications, despite adverse critcism which appeared in major critical magazines, until 1917. By 1918, the Imagist movement was in competition with other innovational and like literary phenomena which appeared as separate movements, in the desire to create new poetic guidelines. Among these should be mentioned an "invented" movement created to poke fun at the Imagists and other Modernist movements. In 1916, fellow poets Arthur Davison Ficke (1883-1945) and Witter Bynner (1881-1968) published a volume of *SPECTRA* poems and included in it a satiric manifesto of explanation for a "new" poetic form. Instead of causing the comedic stir they expected, they were surprised when the literary establishment took them as seriously as it did the many new and other movements which continued to come into play.

While Imagism as a poetic device was a precursor of exciting change in poetic expression, critic David Perkins observes that it was itself the result of a synthesis of earlier movements which had begun before the turn of the century. In the 1890s, the "decadents" (*see* AESTHETICISM) and the Impressionists had existed in England — these *avant gardistes*, in turn, had been strongly influenced by the French SYMBOLISTS of the mid-nineteenth century and their concentration upon the expression of subjective emotion.

In England, Wyndham Lewis (1882-1951), a novelist, literary and political critic, and painter became interested, with Ezra Pound, in a movement for art and literature called VORTICISM. Together they conceived the literary magazine *Blast* (1914-15). In it, they advocated the concept that the poetic image should be like a vortex, a moving, whirling source of energy, at the heart of all good poetry. They were blatant in their pronouncement that the old literary order must come to an end. In Italy, the cause was taken up by Filippo Tommaso MARINETTI, whose notion of the poet as revolutionary was embodied in FUTURISM, which provided new freedom of poetic expression and the rejection of conventional syntax, among other things. (The English writer D. H. LAWRENCE [*see* MODERNISM, England and Ireland] was so taken with this idea that he began what he called the "modernization" of his work). In Russia, a group called the IMAGINISTS was begun by poets who were in agreement with the English Imagists. The most important of these was Sergei Aleksandrovich ESENIN, whose lyric poetry adhered to the new form. By the thirties, the political connotation of revolution was the rockbed of the Russian system; it is not surprising that a literary revolution against such traditional, REALIST writers as Leo TOLSTOY and Fyodor DOSTOEVSKY was taken up by poets who had been earlier and strongly influenced by Russian CUBO-FUTUR-ISTS Velemir KHLEBNIKOV and Vladimir MAYAKOVSKY, the latter having been named as the best and most exciting of the new Russian poets. His enthusiasm for the idea of poet as revolutionary is shown in his work, which contains new rhythms, excessively strong imagery, an abandoning of metrical structure and a preponderence of rhyming, irregular lines. "Oda revolutzi" (1918; Ode to the Revolution), "Levyi marsh" (1918; Left March,) and "Vladimir Ilyich Lenin" (1924; "Vladimir Ilyich Lenin [A Poem]," 1939), his panegyric to his leader, are examples of his many and varied works.

Hulme and Pound had thus concretized an idea about poetry in their Imagist manifesto which would provide impetus for a definite break with the immediate, poetic past. It exerted uncommon influence on the Modernist movement at the time and would continue through the century. It has been noted that such a break was necessary for a new literature to appear. The movement's impact on the work of Yeats and Eliot has been acknowledged by each of them, and can be seen in later work by Stephen Spender (1909-), W. H. Auden (1907-1973), and countless modern poets. By the 1920s, Imagism, along with other, ongoing concepts, had begun the rejuvenation of the poetic instinct "to imitate . . . [feeling] in harmony and rhythm," as first put down by Aristotle.

✥•✥

D[oolittle], H[ilda] (1886-1961), American poet and prose writer.
Noted by her contemporaries for work made up of "purist" images, H. D. left America in 1911, and remained in Europe until she died. She became closely affiliated with Pound and the Imagists, married Richard Aldington, and was at the forefront of the movement until she, like Pound and others, abandoned it. Her poetic aim was to perfect clear, precise images and to incorporate in her work the concision and spareness of phrase

which was at the heart of the Imagist manifesto. Her early and sustained interest remained in the classics, especially the Greek poets, whom she translated and imitated. Like Lowell she was encouraged by Pound, who promoted publication of her work. Her poems are expressions of what is immediate, actual, and contain an almost physical sense of felt emotion; her short poem "Heat" (1916) exemplifies this strength. Her later work became less lyrical and was often made up of narratives which contained both prose and poetry. Longer, meditative works, such as *The Walls Do Not Fall* (1944) and *Tribute to Angels* (1945), show the influence of psychoanalytic conceptualization and ambiguous and diversified symbolism.

❖•❖

Lowell, Amy (1874-1925), American poet and biographer.

Although she was strongly attracted to the Modernist movement, specifically Imagism, today she is considered one of the lesser writers of the movement and is rarely anthologized. Her reputation has been based more on her controversy with Ezra Pound and her intrepid promotion of the Imagist movement in America than on her creative work. One critic notes that she was a Modernist in only a few aspects of its style and form, but that her sensibility remained that of a romantic. Her long poem, "Patterns" (1916), has been considered an example of a well-drawn and interesting dramatic monologue, but her other works, including a biography of John Keats (1795-1821) which was published in 1925, have received only moderate acclaim. Diverse criticism was a part of her heritage; one critic has called her work "a heap of labored and synthetic decorations," while another, kinder voice maintains that her lifelong determined, energetic devotion to all things poetic was commendable, and that her indomitable spirit will never die.

❖•❖

Further Reading

Cassell, Richard A. *Ford Madox Ford: A Study of His Novels*. Baltimore: Johns Hopkins Press, 1962.

Cassell, Richard A., ed. *Critical Essays on Ford Madox Ford*. Boston: G. K. Hall, 1987.

Coffman, Stanley K. *Imagism: A Chapter for the History of Modern Poetry*. Norman, Okla.: University of Oklahoma Press, 1951.

Csengeri, Karen, ed. *The Collected Writings of T. E. Hulme*. Oxford, England: Oxford University Press, 1994.

Damon, S. Foster. *Amy Lowell, a Chronicle with Extracts from Her Correspondence*. Hamden, Conn.: Archon Books, 1966.

Davie, Donald. *Studies in Ezra Pound*. Manchester, England: Carcanet, 1991.

Davis, Katharine Mordoch. "John Gould Fletcher Remembered." *Delphian Quarterly* 34, 2 (April 1951): 31-32, 38.

De Chasca, Edmund S. *John Gould Fletcher and Imagism*. Columbia, Mo.: University of Missouri Press, 1978.

Des Imagistes: An Anthology. London: Poetry Bookshop; New York: Albert and Charles Boni, 1914.

DiPace Fritz, Angela. *Thought and Vision: A Critical Reading of H. D.'s Poetry*. Washington, D.C.: Catholic University of America Press, 1988.

Doyle, Charles. *Richard Aldington, a Biography*. Carbondale, Ill.: Southern Illinois University Press, 1989.

Doyle, Charles, ed. *Richard Aldington: Reappraisals*. Victoria, Canada: English Literary Studies, University of Victoria, 1990.

DuPlessis, Rachel Blau. *H. D., the Career of that Struggle*. Bloomington, Ind.: Indiana University Press, 1986.

Durant, Alan. *Ezra Pound, Identity in Crisis: A Fundamental Reassessment of the Poet and His Work*. Brighton, England: Harvester Press; Totowa, N.J.: Barnes & Noble, 1981.

Edmunds, Susan. *Out of Line: History, Psychoanalysis and Montage in H. D.'s Long Poems*. Stanford, Calif.: Stanford University Press, 1994.

Flint, F. Cudworth. *Amy Lowell*. Minneapolis: University of Minnesota Press, 1969.

Friedman, Susan Stanford. *Penelope's Web: Gender, Modernity, H. D.'s Fiction*. Cambridge, England: Cambridge University Press, 1990.

———. *Psyche Reborn: The Emergence of H. D.* Bloomington, Ind.: Indiana University Press, 1981.

Friedman, Susan Stanford, and Rachel Blau DuPlessis, eds. *Signets: Reading H. D.* Madison, Wis.: University of Wisconsin Press, 1990.

Froula, Christine. *A Guide to Ezra Pound's Selected Poems*. New York: New Directions, 1983.

Gage, John. *In the Arresting Eye: The Rhetoric of Imagism*. Baton Rouge, La.: Louisiana State University Press, 1981.

Gates, Norman T. *A Checklist of the Letters of Richard Aldington*. Carbondale, Ill.: Southern Illinois University Press, 1977.

———. *The Poetry of Richard Aldington: A Critical Evaluation and an Anthology of Uncollected Poems*. University Park, Pa.: Pennsylvania State University Press, 1975.

Gilkes, Martin. *A Key to Modern English Poetry*. London: Blackie and Son, 1937.

Gould, Jean. *Amy: The World of Amy Lowell and the Imagist Movement*. New York: Dodd, Mead, 1975.

Green, Robert. *Ford Madox Ford: Prose and Politics*. Cambridge, England: Cambridge University Press, 1981.

Guest, Barbara. *Herself Defined: The Poet H. D. and Her World*. New York: Quill, 1985.

Hampson, R. G., and W. A. Davenport, eds. *Ford Madox Ford*. New York: St. Martin's Press, 1991.

Hoffmann, Charles G. *Ford Madox Ford*. Updated ed. Boston: Twayne, 1990.

Hollenberg, Donna Krolik. *H. D., the Poetics of Childbirth and Creativity*. Boston: Northeastern University Press, 1991.

Imagist Anthology, 1930: Poems by Richard Aldington, John Cournos, H. D., John Gould Fletcher, F. S. Flint, Ford Madox Ford, James Joyce, D. H. Lawrence, William Carlos Williams. Foreword by Ford Madox Ford and Glenn Hughes. London: Chatto & Windus, 1930.

The Imagist Revolution, 1908-1918: An Exhibition of Books and Manuscripts by the Imagist Poets. Austin, Tex.: Harry Ransom Humanities Research Center, University of Texas at Austin, 1992.

Jackson, Laura. *Contemporaries and Snobs.* Garden City, N.Y.: Doubleday & Doran; London: J. Cape, 1928.

Johnson, Ben F. *Fierce Solitude: A Life of John Gould Fletcher.* Fayetteville, Ark.: University of Arkansas Press, 1994.

Jones, Alun R. *The Life and Opinions of T. E. Hulme.* Boston: Beacon Press; London: Gollancz, 1960.

Judd, Alan. *Ford Madox Ford.* London: Collins, 1990; Cambridge, Mass.: Harvard University Press, 1991.

Kershaw, Alister, ed. *Richard Aldington: An Intimate Portrait.* Carbondale, Ill.: Southern Illinois University Press, 1965.

King, Michael, ed. *H.D., Woman and Poet.* Orono, Maine: National Poetry Foundation, 1986.

Kreymborg, Alfred, ed. *Others: An Anthology of the New Verse.* New York: Knopf, 1917.

Lowell, Amy. *Tendencies in Modern American Poetry.* New York: Macmillan, 1917.

MacGreevy, Thomas. *Richard Aldington, an Englishman.* London: Chatto & Windus, 1931.

MacShane, Frank, ed. *Ford Madox Ford: The Critical Heritage.* London: Routledge & Kegan Paul, 1972.

Niven, Alastair. *D. H. Lawrence, the Writer and His Work.* Harlow, England: Longman, 1980.

Parrinder, Patrick. *James Joyce.* Cambridge, England: Cambridge University Press, 1984.

Peake, Charles. *James Joyce, the Citizen and the Artist.* Stanford, Calif.: Stanford University Press, 1977.

Perkins, David. *A History of Modern Poetry: From the 1890s to the High Modernist Mode.* Cambridge, Mass.: Harvard University Press, 1976.

Peterson, Richard F. *James Joyce Revisited.* New York: Twayne, 1992.

Pratt, William. *The Imagist Poem: Modern Poetry in Miniature.* New York: Dutton, 1963.

Quinn, Vincent. *Hilda Doolittle (H. D.).* New York: Twayne, 1968.

Roberts, Michael. *T. E. Hulme.* London: Faber and Faber, 1938.

Robinson, Janice S. *H. D., the Life and Work of an American Poet.* Boston: Houghton Mifflin, 1982.

Ruihley, Glenn Richard. *The Thorn of a Rose: Amy Lowell Reconsidered.* Hamden, Conn.: Archon Books, 1975.

Smith, Richard Eugene. *Richard Aldington.* Boston: Twayne, 1977.

Some Imagist Poets, an Anthology. Boston: Houghton Mifflin, 1915-17.

Stang, Sondra J. *Ford Madox Ford.* New York: Ungar, 1977.

Stephens, Edna B. *John Gould Fletcher.* New York: Twayne, 1967.

Swann, Thomas Burnett. *The Classical World of H. D.* Lincoln, Nebr.: University of Nebraska Press, 1962.

Tiffany, Daniel. *Radio Corpse: Imagism and the Cryptaesthetic of Ezra Pound.* Cambridge, Mass.: Harvard University Press, 1995.

Upward, Allen. *Some Personalities.* Boston: Cornhill, 1922.

Wood, Clement. *Amy Lowell.* New York: H. Vinal, 1926.

Woolmer, J. Howard. *A Catalogue of the Imagist Poets.* New York: J. H. Woolmer, 1966.

THE INKLINGS
England, 1940s

Of all the English literary groups active in the twentieth century, the Inklings were probably the most loosely united and the least consciously defined. Nonetheless, the group's central figures — C. S. LEWIS, J. R. R. TOLKIEN, and Charles WILLIAMS — represented in many ways a unique force among writers of the 1930s and 40s. In particular, their profound belief in Christian doctrine, which they regularly incorporated into spiritually edifying fantasies, and their penchant for pre-nineteenth-century poetry set them largely apart from the currents of MODERNISM which then dominated English literature. Yet such contrariety, even toward the pre-Modernist tenets of REALISM, did not prevent the Inklings, especially Lewis, from attracting a wide public following, one interested in the reaffirmation of past values as well as the reinvigoration of twentieth-century life.

Tolkien and Lewis, the primary founders of the Inklings, first met in 1926 at Oxford. Lewis, a recently appointed fellow of English language and literature at Magdalen College, and Tolkien, professor of Anglo-Saxon at Merton College, found that despite fundamental differences in personality they shared an extreme distaste for modern poetry and harbored an accompanying passion for the mythic and allegorical literature of previous centuries. Lewis's preferences were broad and included George MacDonald's (1824-1905) *Phantastes* (1858), John Milton's (1608-1674) *Paradise Lost* (1667), Edmund Spenser's (1552-1599) *The Faerie Queene* (1590-96), and a number of Old English poems. Tolkien's, on the other hand, were narrow, confined in general to such pre-Chaucerian works as *Sir Gawain and the Green Knight* (c. fourteenth century), *Beowulf* (c. eighth century), and a sizeable body of Old Norse sagas and eddic poetry. This last interest, more than any other, united the two scholars and became the basis for perhaps their most important creative principle in subsequent years. The principle, indebted to Owen Barfield's (1898-1997) *Poetic Diction: A Study in Meaning* (1928), stresses that a carefully chosen and detailed mythology may become an indispensible vessel for expressing both doctrinal and spiritual truths, and may become in fact a reality in and of itself.

Tolkien's formation in 1927 of the Kolbitars, a small circle dedicated to the reading and study of the Icelandic collections *Younger Edda* (c. 13th century) and *Elder Edda* (c. 900-1200), represented in a sense the embryo of the Inklings, for Lewis and sometime Inkling Nevill Coghill (1899-1980) numbered among its members. The group as a whole, like the Inklings, emphasized oral reading, scholarship, and debate. In late 1929 a development of singular significance occurred. Tolkien, after having found in Lewis a man whose passion for language and myth equalled his own, submitted to his friend a narrative poem from a work-in-progress, *The Silmarillion* (1917). Lewis responded with both encouragement and well-intended criticism. As the friendship blossomed during the early 1930s, Tolkien continued to share his writing drafts, most notably those which eventually formed *The Hobbit; or There and Back Again* (1937), with Lewis. Tolkien later analyzed the importance of these early encounters in this way: "The unpayable debt that I owe to him was not 'influence' as it is ordinarily understood, but sheer encouragement. He was for long my only audience. Only from him did I ever get the idea that my 'stuff' could be more than a private hobby."

Lewis, to be sure, similarly benefited from discussions with Tolkien, particularly those centering upon theology. A devout Roman Catholic, Tolkien was instrumental in Lewis's conversion to Christianity in 1932. G. K. Chesterton's (1874-1936) *The Everlasting Man* (1925), and a series of intense debates with Barfield, a longtime friend and proponent of Rudolf Steiner's (1861-1925) Anthroposophy, had certainly prepared Lewis, but it was the late-night Oxford talks with Tolkien, and Hugo Dyson (1896-1975), that cemented Lewis's faith. His distinguished career as a lay theologian began immediately thereafter with the publication of *The Pilgrim's Regress, an Allegorical Apology for Christianity, Reason and Romanticism* (1933).

Precisely when the Inklings began meeting regularly is not clear. The first mention appears in a 1938 letter by Tolkien in which he refers to "our literary club of practising poets." However, it is generally assumed that the Inklings, who gathered each Thursday evening at Lewis's Magdalen rooms, had been in existence since at least the middle of the decade. The name Inklings itself was appropriated by Lewis from an undergraduate club which met at University College until about 1933 and with which he and Tolkien were briefly associated. Like its University namesake, Lewis's group was launched so that its members could read from their unpublished writings and receive comments and criticisms. Very often, however, such readings functioned as preludes to lofty and heated theological and artistic debates. Usually present at the meetings were Tolkien, Lewis, his brother Warren (1895-1973), and Dr. R. E. Havard (1901-). Frequent visitors included Dyson, Coghill, Barfield, Charles Wrenn (1895-1969), and Adam Fox (1883-1977). It was not until 1939 and the onset of World War II that Williams, arguably the most dynamic Inkling, became a regular member of the group.

Lewis had been an admirer of Williams since 1936, after having read *The Place of the Lion* (1931) upon the recommendation of Coghill. Remarkably, at this same time Williams, as editor at Oxford University Press in London, was introduced to Lewis through the proofs of *The Allegory of Love, a Study in Medieval Tradition* (1936), which he had been reading enthusiastically. The two soon met and became fast friends. During wartime the O.U.P., and along with it Williams, evacuated to Oxford. Together with Lewis and Tolkien, Williams became one of the chief contributors of new material at the weekly meetings. His sudden death in 1945 seriously dampened the spirit of the group and by 1949 the Thursday gatherings ceased.

From a specifically literary standpoint, the most fundamental link for the Inklings was their high regard for myth and fantasy. Likewise, their most representative works in this genre, Tolkien's *The Lord of the Rings* (1954-55), Lewis's Ransom Trilogy, and Williams's *All Hallows' Eve* (1945), portions of which were read at the weekly gatherings, all display a chilling understanding of evil and an ultimately comforting affirmation of human good that underscores the religious groundings of each writer. Finally, they were all guided, Lewis and Tolkien consciously, Williams intuitively, by the theory of sub-creation. Tolkien, who outlined the theory in talks and letters, held that authors by nature mimic the original processes of the Creator. Further, the works they produce represent sub-creations, creations that possess a separate, but parallel, reality. Most importantly, all of these sub-creations, whether sacred or profane, stem ultimately from God and therefore reflect some form of eternal and undeniable truth.

Although frequently overlooked as a group by literary historians, the Inklings made a sizeable impact on twentieth-century literature. Their most important contributions include the revival of the medieval romance, the critical restoration of Milton, the popularization of fantasy writing, and the strengthening of a religious mythos in the public consciousness. Notwithstanding this, the Inklings are remembered foremost for their works, the best of which uniquely combine superior romance with timeless wisdom.

✦●✦

Lewis, C. S. (1898-1963)
Irish-born English novelist, essayist, critic, autobiographer, and poet.

An amazingly versatile writer, Lewis gained distinction in several fields, including Christian polemics, medieval and Renaissance scholarship, fantasy literature, and literary criticism. In addition to his Christianity, a love for logical debate infused much of his work. His mentor in this regard was W. T. Kirkpatrick (1848-1921), a boyhood teacher whose verbal aggressiveness and emphasis on empirical proof Lewis adopted until his conversion, at which time Lewis acknowledged the existence of truths beyond the realm of reason. After publishing two early and little-noticed volumes of poetry,

Lewis settled upon the novel and the essay as his chief forms of artistic and intellectual expression. From the mid-1930s until his death he enjoyed exceptional popularity for his characteristic blend of wit, imagination, erudition, and compelling argument. His most notable works include *Out of the Silent Planet* (1938), *The Problem of Pain* (1940), *The Screwtape Letters* (1942), *Perelandra* (1943), *Mere Christianity* (1952), and the "Chronicles of Narnia" (1950-56), a series of children's fairytale novels written to encourage interest in the New Testament.

Out of the Silent Planet (1938); *Perelandra* (1943); *That Hideous Strength* (1945).

Of all Lewis's imaginative works, his science-fiction trilogy stands as the most compelling and comprehensive representation of his Christian philosophy and enormous creative powers. The protagonist of Lewis's mythopoeic novels is Dr. Elwin Ransom, a Cambridge philologist who travels to Malacandra (Mars) as the captive of Dr. Weston, a brilliant but demented physicist who plans to unite the universe under his rule. Gradually, Lewis reveals Malacandra, with its population of eldila (angels), to be a sinless planet, one vitally connected to the myths of creation. Thulcandra (Earth), on the other hand, he shows to be the Silent Planet, ruled by the "Bent One." After a brief return to Earth, Ransom journeys to the Edenic world of Perelandra (Venus) at the secret behest of the Oyarsa of Malacandra, the chief eldil of that kingdom. There the philologist encounters the Green Lady, an Eve-like figure susceptible to the temptations of Weston, who soon arrives on the planet. Through his increasingly cunning and sadistic behavior, Weston himself emerges as the Bent One, the Un-Man. But by first mental and then physical battle Ransom vanquishes the Un-Man, thus preventing a terrible fall from grace for the Lady, who in turn emerges as the Queen of Perelandra. In the final volume of the trilogy Ransom resurfaces on Earth as the Fisher King. Aided by the magician Merlin and the Oyarsaas of all the heavenly worlds, he destroys N.I.C.E., a corrupt scientific organization which is plotting to seize control of the world.

Two common criticisms levied against Lewis's trilogy are that its scientific apparatus is, at best, skeletal and that its artistic coherence, from one novel to the next, is severely limited. Rather than defend such criticisms, Lewis proponents suggest that the author was earnestly concerned with the spiritual future of humanity and selected the science-fiction genre not because of any specific trust he placed in the scientific community — in fact, he shunned the notion that all human progress was good — but because he saw an opportunity to engage the modern imagination with the timeless, restorative qualities of religious knowledge. Scholars agree that in *Perelandra* in particular, Lewis met this challenge fully and produced a lasting literary classic.

✥•✦

Tolkien, J[ohn] R[onald] R[euel] (1892-1973)
South African-born English novelist, short-story writer, poet, editor, and critic.

Tolkien first earned fame as a leading philologist. In 1922, while teaching English language at Leeds University, he published *A Middle English Vocabulary*. Three years later, after removing to Oxford where he served initially as professor of Anglo-Saxon and later as professor of English language and literature, he and a colleague issued an edition of *Sir Gawain and the Green Knight* that is still greatly valued. Tolkien's deep appreciation for the composite powers of words and myth led him to the construction of a highly detailed, imaginative cosmology and accompanying body of songs, legends, and stories of tragedy and triumph. Begun as early as 1917 with *The Silmarillion*, Tolkien's masterwork grew to include *The Hobbit*, THE FELLOWSHIP OF THE RING (1954), THE TWO TOWERS (1955), and *THE RETURN OF THE KING* (1955). These classics of fantasy literature have engaged generations of readers, not only with their evocation of a strange enchanting world but with the profusion of details that makes that world real and the marshalling of characters and events that makes it, in addition, eternally meaningful. The enormous popular and critical success of Tolkien's writings has fostered a number of other heroic fantasies by such authors as Ursula K. Le Guin (1929-) and Patricia McKillip (1948-).

The Lord of the Rings: The Fellowship of the Ring (1954); *The Two Towers* (1955); *The Return of the King* (1955).

Set in Middle-earth near the end of the Third Age, *The Lord of the Rings* documents the adventures of Frodo, nephew of Bilbo Baggins, protagonist of *The Hobbit*. Frodo, a reluctant and unassuming hero, accepts the grave task of disposing of the Ring of Power before the evil wizard Sauron, Lord of Darkness, can acquire it. To accomplish this Frodo attends a great council, where a fellowship of dwarves, elves, and men are assigned to assist him and his three hobbit companions, Samwise, Merry, and Pippin. Before long the fellowship is endangered and separated. While Merry and Pippin fight important battles near one tower of evil, Orthanc, Frodo, and Sam journey through Mordor to the other tower, Cirith Ungol, where they will destroy the ring in the volcanic fires of Mount Doom, where it was originally forged. Frodo's apparent death causes Sam to continue the quest alone, but the two are eventually reunited and Frodo succeeds in his mission.

The final battle the hobbits wage after their return to their own land underscores Tolkien's theme that evil is omnipresent and must be countered perpetually. Frodo's function as a Christlike figure, in addition, helps illustrate Tolkien's conception of the

300

ideal Christian: a person who, empowered with the gift of free choice, acts in a courageous, humble, and self-sacrificing manner. Significantly, Tolkien denied that he conceived his trilogy with allegorical intentions and emphasized instead the fundamentally linguistic aspects of the story. In any case, Tolkien's masterpiece is abundant in both detail and significance and has helped elevate fantasy writing to a level of unparalleled importance in literary history.

➹•❦

Williams, Charles Walter Stansby (1886-1945)
English novelist, poet, essayist, dramatist, and critic.

Of the major Inklings, Williams was the most markedly individual in artistic temperament and, consequently perhaps, the least publicly known. An adherent of Anglicanism and onetime student of Rosicrucianism, Williams sought to portray in his novels worlds in which the contemporary combines with the magical, the mythical, and the preternatural. His most important novels, supernatural thrillers in which the forces of good and evil do battle, include *War in Heaven* (1930), *The Place of the Lion* (1931), and *All Hallows' Eve* (1945). Although formally unlettered, Williams's knowledge of English and European poetry, and of Arthurian legend, was vast. His *Taliessin through Logres* (1938) and *The Region of the Summer Stars* (1944), both highly complex and allusive works, are testaments to his passion and erudition, if not his stylistic brilliance. Far less influenced than influential, Williams, through his theology, imaginative work, and magnetic presence, affected not only the literary outlook of Lewis, but of a number of other major writers of his day, including W. H. Auden (1907-1973), Dorothy Sayers (1893-1957), and T. S. ELIOT (*see* MODERNISM, England and Ireland).

All Hallows' Eve (1945).

All Hallows' Eve, portions of which were read before the Inklings, is Williams's last complete novel. Like his previous novels, *All Hallows' Eve* describes two interconnected realities: the present, immediately perceiveable milieu of post-World War II London and the transcendent, superimposed existence of the spiritual City, inhabited by the dead and the supernatural. The plot centers on Lester Furnival, a married woman who has died in a plane crash. Her spiritual growth and reaffirmation of love for her husband become the thematic focalpoint, for Williams intended her to function as a modern-day version of Dante's Beatrice.

Lester's emerging propensity toward pure goodness is balanced by the absolute evil of Simon the Clerk, the leader of a deviant religious sect. She eventually prevails over Father Simon's diabolical intents, insuring her own redemption as well as the love of a young couple whose sanctity and future Father Simon had nearly destroyed.

Crucial to an understanding of the novel's metaphysics is Williams's own theology. As spiritual leader of a semi-mystical following which he termed the Companions of the Co-inherence, Williams developed these four essential beliefs: 1) all human action, good or evil, coinheres, is directly attributable to other human action; 2) the Dantean concept of love forms a useful Romantic Theology through its suggestion that active love places one in closer contact with God; 3) Substitution, the willful acceptance of another's pain, is one of the highest expressions of this love; 4) the Way of Affirmation, a life-embracing, love-empowered manner of living, is the true measure of fully human, fully Christian behavior. These doctrines were, to a large degree, shared by Lewis and Tolkien, but it was Williams who originated and propounded them in his novels with the most startling effects.

⤗•⤙

Further Reading

Bloom, Harold, ed. *Modern Fantasy Writers*. New York: Chelsea House, 1995.

Carpenter, Humphrey. *The Inklings: C. S. Lewis, J. R. R. Tolkien, Charles Williams, and Their Friends*. Boston: Houghton Mifflin, 1979.

———. *J. R. R. Tolkien: A Biography*. London: Allen & Unwin, 1977.

Cavaliero, Glen. *Charles Williams: Poet of Theology*. Grand Rapids, Mich.: Eerdmans, 1983.

Crabbe, Katharyn F. *J. R. R. Tolkien*. New York: Ungar, 1981.

Gibb, Jocelyn, ed. *Light on C. S. Lewis*. New York: Harcourt, Brace & World, 1965.

Giddings, Robert, and Elizabeth Holland. *J. R. R. Tolkien: The Shores of Middle-earth*. Frederick, Md.: Aletheia Books, 1981.

Green, Roger Lancelyn. *C. S. Lewis*. San Diego: Harcourt Brace, 1994.

Hadfield, Alice Mary. *Charles Williams: An Exploration of His Life and Work*. New York: Oxford University Press, 1983.

Hannay, Margaret Patterson. *C. S. Lewis*. New York: Ungar, 1981.

Helms, Randel. *Tolkien's World*. Boston: Houghton Mifflin, 1974.

Hillegas, Mark R., ed. *Shadows of Imagination: The Fantasies of C. S. Lewis, J. R. R. Tolkien and Charles Williams*. Carbondale, Ill.: Southern Illinois University Press, 1969.

Hooper, Walter. *C. S. Lewis: A Companion and Guide*. San Francisco: Harper, 1996.

Howard, Thomas T. *The Achievement of C. S. Lewis: A Reading of His Fiction*. Wheaton, Ill.: H. Shaw, 1980.

———. *The Novels of Charles Williams*. New York: Oxford University Press, 1983.

Isaacs, Neil D., and Rose A. Zimbardo, eds. *Tolkien: New Critical Perspectives*. Lexington, Ky.: University Press of Kentucky, 1981.

Lewis, C. S. *The Pilgrim's Regress: An Allegorical Apology for Christianity, Reason and Romanticism*. London: J. M. Dent, 1933. Rev. ed., Grand Rapids, Mich.: Eerdmans, 1981.

———. *Surprised by Joy: The Shape of My Early Life*. London: G. Bles, 1955.

Lewis, C. S., with A. O. Barfield, W. H. Lewis, Gervase Mathew, Dorothy Sayers, and J. R. R. Tolkien. *Essays Presented to Charles Williams*. London: Oxford University Press, 1947.

Myers, Doris T. *C. S. Lewis in Context*. Kent, Ohio: Kent State University Press, 1994.

Neimark, Anne E. *Myth Maker: J. R. R. Tolkien*. San Diego: Harcourt Brace, 1996.

Pavlac, Diana Lynne. *The Company They Keep: Assessing the Mutual Influence of C. S. Lewis, J. R. R. Tolkien, and Charles Williams*. Ph.D. dissertation, University of Illinois at Chicago, 1993.

Purtill, Richard. *Lord of the Elves and Eldils: Fantasy and Philosophy in C. S. Lewis and J. R. R. Tolkien*. Grand Rapids, Mich.: Zondervan Pub. House, 1974.

Ready, William. *Understanding Tolkien and the Lord of the Rings*. New York: Warner Books, 1969.

Reilly, Robert J. *Romantic Religion: A Study of Barfield, Lewis, Williams and Tolkien*. Athens, Ga.: University of Georgia Press, 1971.

Rosebury, Brian. *Tolkien: A Critical Assessment*. New York: St. Martin's Press, 1992.

Schakel, Peter J., ed. *The Longing for a Form: Essays on the Fiction of C. S. Lewis*. Grand Rapids, Mich.: Baker Book House, 1977.

Shideler, Mary McDermott. *The Theology of Romantic Love: A Study in the Writings of Charles Williams*. New York: Harper, 1962.

Shippey, T. A. *The Road to Middle-earth*. Boston: Houghton Mifflin, 1983.

Sibley, Agnes. *Charles Williams*. Boston: Twayne, 1982.

Stevens, David. *J. R. R. Tolkien—The Art of the Myth-Maker*. San Bernardino, Calif.: Borgo Press, 1993.

Walsh, Chad. *The Literary Legacy of C. S. Lewis*. New York: Harcourt Brace Jovanovich, 1979.

Williams, Charles. *Religion and Love in Dante: The Theology of Romantic Love*. Westminster, England: Dacre Press, 1941.

Wilson, A. N. *C. S. Lewis*. New York: Fawcett Columbine, 1991.

I-NOVEL (Shishōsetsu)
Japan, 1910s-1920s

A literary form with roots in Japanese NATURALISM, the I-Novel is both the most prevalent and longstanding literary phenomenon in twentieth-century Japan. Although there are several variations on the form, the essential I-Novel characteristics are: autobiographical confession in the first or third person; the self-destructive protagonist's (author's) search for a personal ideal, typically antithetical to societal values; and the protagonist's growing alienation from and eventual rejection by society.

The I-Novel attained its height during the Taishō era (1912-26), a period of monumental literary experimentation and Westernization. TAYAMA Katai's *FUTON* (1907; *The Quilt and Other Stories*, 1981) is frequently named as the prototypical work; despite the author's self-exposure, though, this Naturalist novel employs such techniques as authorial distancing and linear progression which preclude its placement among true I-Novels. Perhaps Chikamatsu Shūkō's (1876-1944) *Giwaku* (1913; Suspicions) is the first unequivocal example of the form. Chikamatsu, who considered himself an anti-

Naturalist, favored a far more personal and lyrical approach to fiction. In contrast, his novels feature a primarily plotless, poetic rendering of his life.

Scholars caution that the I-Novel should not be equated with Western autobiography, a literary genre often perceived as peripheral or of secondary importance. Rather, it must be understood within the Japanese tradition of "pure" literature. Stemming from the premodern era, this esteemed form of composition predicated itself on the unfabricated, nonfictionalized representation of the self and the perceived world. Conversely, "popular" literature with its contrived scenes and characters was treated with disdain, being necessarily untruthful and impure.

A further consideration is the audience for which the I-Novel was written. Never large in numbers, readers of the form, in contrast to the general public, were well-educated, less bound by societal conventions, and more inclined toward articulating an ideology of the individual. They thus formed a close alliance with the *bundan* (literary intelligentsia); theirs was the task of evaluating works based upon the author's sincerity and emotive intensity; the author's, in turn, was to forego fictional artifices in an effort to present works of psychological and experiential clarity and Realism.

With very few exceptions, Japanese authors, regardless of sensibility or theoretical affiliation, have at some point written in the I-Novel vein. From the formative attempts by Chikamatsu, Kasai Zenzō (1887-1928), and Kamura Isota (1897-1933) to countless latterday approaches, the I-Novel rightfully occupies a singularly important position in modern Japanese fiction.

➸•⧉

Further Reading

Fowler, Edward. *The Rhetoric of Confession: Shishōsetsu in Early Twentieth-Century Japanese Fiction*. Berkeley, Calif.: University of California Press, 1988.
Keene, Donald. "The I-Novel." In his *Dawn to the West: Japanese Literature of the Modern Era*. New York: Holt, Rinehart & Winston, 1984.

INTELLECTUAL REVOLUTION. *See* **MAY FOURTH MOVEMENT**

INTIMISMO
Italy, 1900s

An ephemeral Italian dramatic movement, Intimismo was analogous to CREPUS-COLARISMO, though it had its origins as early as the 1880s and 1890s, in the dramas of Roberto Bracco (1862-1943) and Giuseppe Giacosa (1847-1906). Bracco's work in particular, which had ties to VERISMO, the REALISM of Henrik IBSEN, and SYM-

304

BOLISM, pioneered a more prevalent Intimist — that is, psychologically suggestive, FREUDIAN-influenced — drama in the 1920s. Works of this period had much in common with the French THEATER OF SILENCE of Jean-Jacques Bernard (1888-1972).

⇒•⇐

Further Reading

Kuitunen, Maddalena. "Ibsen and the Theatre of Roberto Bracco." In *Petrarch to Pirandello: Studies in Italian Literature in Honour of Beatrice Corrigan* by Julius A. Molinaro. Toronto: University of Toronto Press, 1973.

Manganiello, Dominic. "The Italian Sources for Exiles: Giacosa, Praga, Oriani, and Joyce." In *Myth and Reality in Irish Literature* by Joseph Ronsley. Waterloo, Canada: Wilfrid Laurier University Press, 1977.

INTROSPECTIVISTS MOVEMENT (Inzikh)
United States, 1920s-1930s

Opposed to the impressionism of the YOUNG ONES, the Introspectivists were a New York Yiddish group of the 1920s and 1930s who embraced European EXPRESSIONISM. Their poetic platform, however, was amenable to virtually all styles, provided the author somehow encapsule his own thoughts and experiences. The chief writers of the movement were Aaron Glanz-Leyeles (1889-1966), Jacob Glatstein (1896-1971), and Nokhum Borekh Minkoff (1893-1958), all of whom inspired members of the Polish GANG GROUP.

⇒•⇐

Further Reading

Glatstein, Jacob. *I Keep Recalling: The Holocaust Poems of Jacob Glatstein*. Translated by Barnett Zumoff with an introduction by Emanuel S. Goldsmith. Hoboken, N.J.: Ktav, 1993.

———. *The Selected Poems of Jacob Glatstein*. Translated and with an introduction by Ruth Whitman. New York: October House, 1972.

———. *Selected Poems of Yankev Glatshteyn*. Translated, edited, and with an introduction by Richard J. Fein. Philadelphia: Jewish Publication Society, 1987.

Hadda, Janet. *Language Experimentation in the Early Poetry of Yankev Glatshteyn*. New York: Max Weinrich Center for Advanced Jewish Studies of the YIVO Institute for Jewish Research, 1976.

———. *Yankev Glatshteyn*. Boston: Twayne, 1980.

Liptzin, Sol. *A History of Yiddish Literature*. Middle Village, N.Y.: Jonathan David Publishers, 1972.

IRISH LITERARY THEATER. *See* ABBEY THEATER

IRISH RENAISSANCE
Ireland, 1890s-1920s

The Irish Renaissance was part of a multifaceted movement to provide cultural support for an intensifying nationalist spirit in Ireland in response to the British occupation which has existed in one form or another for centuries. This movement began slowly in Ireland in the early nineteenth century with the Gaelic Revival and gathered momentum by the end of the century. Its objective, although never presented in written manifesto, was to revive a national interest in ancient Irish culture, known as the "Celtic Twilight," in its language, its history, and its spirit.

By 1893 a revival of Irish culture and the ancient language of Gaelic was promoted by the newly formed Gaelic League of Ireland, founded, in part, by future president of the Irish Free State, Douglas Hyde (1860-1949). Hyde's 1892 essay, "The Necessity for De-Anglicising Ireland," championed the use of Gaelic over English, the language of the oppressor. In 1898, the Anglo-Irish Literary Movement began, for presentation of Irish plays, poems, and stories in English, but giving full emphasis to that life force that is specifically Irish, in both manner and custom.

There were concentrated efforts to recover lost or displaced manuscripts and to translate them, as well as to search out artifacts and any remnants of the myths and folklore which had begun as Celtic oral tradition. Standish O'Grady's (1846-1928) *History of Ireland: Heroic Period* (1878-80), Hyde's *A Literary History of Ireland* (1899), and W. B. YEATS's (*see* ABBEY THEATER and MODERNISM, England and Ireland) *The Celtic Twilight* (1893) were influential in bringing to light long-forgotten elements of Irish history and lore — such as Cúchulain, the mythological hero of the Ulster cycle, Deirdre, Fergus, and the Finian cycle about Finn mac Cumaill and his son Oisín — which served to encourage the movement and to stimulate a new flush of Irish awareness. Some outstanding examples of literature that was inspired by Irish mythology include Hyde's *Love Songs of Connacht* (1893), Lady Gregory's "Cuchulain of Muirthemne" (1902), and Yeats's poems "The Man Who Dreamed of Faeryland" (1891), "Cuchulain's Fight with the Sea" (1892), "Who Goes with Fergus?" (1892), "Fergus and the Druid" (1892), and "To Ireland in the Coming Times" (1893).

In the forefront of the dramatic movement were Yeats, with his plays *Cathleen Ní Houlihan* (1902) and *The Death of Cuchulain* (1939) and other of his CUCHULAIN PLAYS, Lady Augusta Gregory (1852-1932), John Millington SYNGE, and later, Sean O'CASEY, all of whom wrote material for the Abbey Theater, which actively attracted writers and playgoers until the 1960s. In its early days the Abbey productions included plays performed by bilingual actors who spoke Gaelic as well as English—for further perpetuation of the ancient language.

Other participants in the Irish Renaissance were Æ (George Russell, 1867-1935), Padraic Colum (1881-1972), Oliver St. John Gogarty (1878-1957), Frederick Robert Higgins (1896-1941), James Stephens (1882?-1950), Sean O'Faoláin (1900-1991), Liam O'Flaherty (1896-1984), and Samuel Ferguson (1810-1886), who helped popularize Celtic folk songs in his *Lays of the Western Gael* (1865).

The Irish civil war during the 1920s and its relevant circumstances disrupted the movement as a literary force, but some Irish writers have worked to keep the tradition alive. Noteworthy among these have been James JOYCE (*see* MODERNISM, England and Ireland); Frank O'Connor (1903-1998); Brendan Behan (1923-1964), who wrote poetry and plays in the Gaelic language, as well as in English; and Samuel BECKETT, the Irish-born writer known best for his work in the THEATER OF THE ABSURD.

❧•❧

Further Reading

Boyd, Ernest A. *Ireland's Literary Renaissance*. Rev. ed. New York: Knopf, 1922. Reprint, New York: Barnes & Noble, 1968.

Brugsma, Rebecca Pauline Christine B. *The Beginnings of the Irish Revival*. Groningen, Netherlands; Batavia: P. Noordhoff, 1933.

Clarke, Austin. *The Celtic Twilight and the Nineties*. Dublin: Dolmen Press, 1969; distributed by Dufour Editions.

Edelstein, T. J., ed. *Imagining an Irish Past: The Celtic Revival, 1840-1940*. Chicago: University of Chicago Press, 1992.

Fallis, Richard. *The Irish Renaissance*. Syracuse, N.Y.: Syracuse University Press, 1977.

Flower, Robin. *The Irish Tradition*. Oxford, England: Clarendon Press, 1947.

Foster, John Wilson. *Fictions of the Irish Literary Revival: A Changeling Art*. Syracuse, N.Y.: Syracuse University Press, 1987.

Freyer, Grattan. "The Irish Literary Scene." In *The New Pelican Guide to English Literature: From James to Eliot*. Edited by Boris Ford. Vol. 7. Harmondsworth, England: Penguin Books, 1983.

Kohfeldt, Mary Lou. *Lady Gregory: The Woman Behind the Irish Renaissance*. New York: Atheneum, 1985.

Marcus, Phillip L. *Yeats and the Beginning of the Irish Renaissance*. Ithaca, N.Y.: Cornell University Press, 1970.

Morris, Lloyd R. *The Celtic Dawn: A Survey of the Renascence in Ireland, 1889-1922*. New York: Macmillan, 1924.

Murphy, Maureen O'Rourke, and James MacKillop. *Irish Literature: A Reader*. Syracuse, N.Y.: Syracuse University Press, 1987.

Robinson, Lennox. *Ireland's Abbey Theatre: A History, 1899-1951*. London: Sidgwick and Jackson, 1951.

Schleifer, Ronald, ed. *The Genres of the Irish Literary Revival*. Norman, Okla.: Pilgrim Books, 1980.

Sheehy, Jeanne. *The Rediscovery of Ireland's Past: The Celtic Revival, 1830-1930.* London: Thames and Hudson, 1980.

Skelton, Robin. *J. M. Synge and His World.* New York: Viking, 1971.

Skelton, Robin, and David R. Clark, eds. *Irish Renaissance: A Gathering of Essays, Memoirs, and Letters.* Dublin: Dolmen Press, 1965.

Thompson, William I. *The Imagination of an Insurrection, Dublin, Easter, 1916: A Study of an Ideological Movement.* New York: Oxford University Press, 1967.

Yeats, William Butler. *The Celtic Twilight: Men and Women, Dhouls and Faeries.* London: Lawrence and Bullen, 1893.

J

JAZZ AGE
United States, 1920s

Possibly the most amorphous of American literary movements yet the most identifiable of historical periods, the Jazz Age and the writing borne of it are synonymous with the many attributes, often sharply conflicting, of the Roaring Twenties. Prohibition, women's suffrage, iconoclasm, material excess, Dixieland jazz, flapper fashions, speak easies, stock and real-estate speculation, boosterism, the rise of big business and organized crime, religious fundamentalism, the pursuit of the American Dream, travel abroad, expatriation, the liberation of art, the relaxation of sexual mores, transcontinental flight, the decline of puritanism, a growing preoccupation with the interior life of the individual — all of these helped define one of the most productive and colorful eras in literary history. The two most representative writers of the period were F. Scott FITZGERALD and Sinclair LEWIS, each of whom could lay claim to producing the Great American Novel, one of the foremost ambitions of the reigning literati. Fitzgerald typically chronicled the period from the point of view of one who, despite a strongly moral outlook, lived the age to its fullest; Lewis, of one who, detesting its crassness, vulgarity, and hypocrisy, kept himself at a sharp satirical remove. Besides these two figures, the writers commonly associated with the Jazz Age — here distinguished from American JAZZ POETRY, the overseas work of the LOST GENERATION, or the broader trend of American MODERNISM — include John Peale Bishop (1892-1944), James Branch Cabell (1879-1958), Theodore DREISER (see NATURALISM, United States), James T. FARRELL (see PROLETARIAN LITERATURE, United States), Edna Ferber (1887-1968), Ben Hecht (1894-1964), Joseph Hergesheimer (1880-1954), Ring Lardner (1885-1933), H. L. Mencken (1880-1956), George Jean Nathan (1882-1958), Dorothy Parker (1893-1967), Elizabeth Madox Roberts (1886-1941), Upton Sinclair (1878-1968), Booth Tarkington (1869-1946), Carl Van Vechten (1880-1964), Edmund Wilson (1895-1972), Alexander Woollcott (1887-1943), and Elinor Wylie (1885-1928).

Of this list, the editor-essayist Mencken was probably the most colorful and notorious. Through his association with first the *Smart Set* and later the *American Mercury*, Mencken became one of the most vociferous arbiters of taste throughout the twenties. Although often lacking in critical sophistication, his *Prejudices* (1919-27) decrying the complacency and provincialism of the "booboisie" mirrored the dominant literary trend of hard-hitting social and psychological realism. The revolt from the village which had begun with CHICAGO LITERARY RENAISSANCE writers Carl SANDBURG and Edgar Lee MASTERS and Modernist Sherwood Anderson (1876-1941) was now completed with the commentary of Mencken and the novels of Fitzgerald and Lewis. Already by 1921 the satirization of American shortcomings had become so popular among the cognoscenti that Lewis's *Main Street* (1920) easily outdistanced less volatile works and became the year's top-selling novel. Although some authors, such as Hergesheimer and Tarkington, objected to the method of overstatement inherent in the work of Fitzgerald and Lewis, and so retreated to earlier traditions, most began stretching the boundaries of style, subject matter, and form as they addressed the new views of the interbellum years. The most singularly damning appraisal of the evils of American society came from Dreiser, an aging Naturalistic writer whose career had long suffered from censorship. Unfortunately, Dreiser's *AN AMERICAN TRAGEDY* (1925) was the most overlooked work of the decade. It was not until the height of the Great Depression, when such writers as John STEINBECK and Farrell acquired fame, that severe Social Realism in the form of PROLETARIAN LITERATURE achieved prominence. Even so, Lewis's *BABBITT* (1922) and Fitzgerald's *THE GREAT GATSBY* (1925), the two most critically acclaimed works of the Jazz Age, share much with Dreiser's masterpiece, for each is fundamentally concerned with the corruptive influences of capitalism and conformity. George F. Babbitt and Jay Gatsby — one character comic, the other tragic, both helpless in the face of social and biological forces — stand finally as powerful literary symbols of a dissolute and disillusioned age, the same as that of T. S. ELIOT's *THE WASTE LAND* (*see* MODERNISM, England and Ireland) and Ernest HEMINGWAY's *THE SUN ALSO RISES* (*see* LOST GENERATION).

❧•❦

Fitzgerald, F. Scott (1896-1940)
American novelist, short-story writer, and essayist.

Fitzgerald launched his publicly successful but personally devastating career with an immediate bestseller, *This Side of Paradise* (1920), a markedly modern, if flawed, novel about college life and changing morals which he had first begun writing while attending Princeton. Just as immediate was the Younger Generation's acceptance of Fitzgerald as their artistic spokesperson. His publication of a second novel, *The Beautiful and Damned* (1922), and two collections of stories, *Flappers and Philosophers* (1920) and *Tales of the Jazz Age* (1922), solidified this reputation and led many observers aware of the author's extravagant, fast-paced lifestyle to regard Fitzgerald and his wife, Zelda (1900-1948), as the living embodiments of the new era. Fitzgerald's first undisputed critical success came with *The Great Gatsby* (1925). By employing a detached observer in the manner of Joseph CONRAD (*see* MODERNISM, England and Ireland), in this work, Fitzgerald achieved this time a startling objectivity over his Jazz Age characters which served to balance his romantic and elegiac style. Although Fitzgerald completed a number of exceptional stories during the next ten years, his alcoholism, Zelda's mental illness, the lure of screenwriting for Hollywood, and the pressure to create a novel surpassing *The Great Gatsby*, prevented him from publishing another major work until the middle of the Great Depression. When *TENDER IS THE NIGHT* (*see* LOST GENERATION), a brilliantly evocative novel of expatriate Saturnalia and self-destruction, appeared in 1934, few readers were receptive to his dated subject matter. By the time of his death in 1940, Fitzgerald was largely forgotten by the general public; however, the posthumous publication of *The Last Tycoon* (1941) and a resurgence of interest in his life and career have engendered a favorable reexamination of Fitzgerald's contributions to twentieth-century fiction.

The Great Gatsby (1925).

Set in New York during the early 1920s and concerned predominantly with the lives of the idle rich, *The Great Gatsby* is to the Jazz Age what Ernest Hemingway's *The Sun Also Rises* is to the Lost Generation: a faithful, alternately alluring and repellent portrait of a social set who came to symbolize the moral emancipation and spiritual malaise of the postwar age. The story — a compelling blend of mystery, romance, and ironic tragedy — revolves around narrator Nick Carraway, a transplanted Midwesterner who becomes enmeshed in the meaningless partying and selfish pursuits of his Long Island cousin, Daisy Buchanan, her husband, Tom, and their mutual, enigmatic neighbor, Jay Gatsby. Gatsby's infatuation with Daisy, which began during the war, has propelled him into the racketeering business to make a fortune solely in order to impress Daisy. A surprising climax, involving the death of Gatsby and two minor characters — events for which the Buchanans, insulated from suspicion and completely remorseless, are largely responsible — underscores the novel's theme of the moral vacuousness of the American Dream.

➵•➶

Lewis, Sinclair (1885-1951)
American novelist, short-story writer, and essayist.

Lewis, the first American to win the Nobel Prize in literature, is widely remembered for his satirical novels, the best of which are *Main Street* (1920), *Babbitt* (1922), *Arrow-*

smith (1925), *Elmer Gantry* (1927), and *Dodsworth* (1929). Although Lewis began his writing career around 1908, it was not until 1920 that he was fully capable of rebelling against the ethics and optimism of the small-town, middle-class society in which he was raised. His depiction in *Main Street* of the people of Gopher Prairie, a fictional Midwestern town based on his own Sauk Centre, Minnesota, was at once a scathing and delightful caricature, similar in vein to the best social portraiture of Mark TWAIN (*see* REALISM, United States). Lewis maintained his popularity as an extraordinarily perceptive and iconoclastic writer for most of the decade. His rapid deterioration as an artist following the publication of *Dodsworth* has been cause for considerable speculation. Most likely, Lewis's special satirical bent fell out of favor during the Depression years and he was never again able to find subject matter suitable for his narrative gifts. Today Lewis is remembered most for the characters he created, who with their frequently ambivalent stances toward mainstream American culture reflect the disruption of values that raged throughout the twenties.

Babbitt (1922).

Although slightly less known today than *Main Street*, *Babbitt* is generally regarded as Lewis's greatest novel. George F. Babbitt, the protagonist, lives in the small Midwestern city of Zenith, where he pursues power, respectability, and material wealth through his work as a real-estate broker and Booster Club official. Babbitt rises easily in stature because of his glad-handing, simplicity, and shallowness. However, he loses all sense of purpose when his closest friend suddenly commits murder. Descending into a mire of wild Bohemian behavior and "dangerous" ideas, Babbitt isolates himself from his wife, business circle, and civic responsibilities. The novel concludes with Babbitt's return to his former self; he has, through his ordeal, been forced to confront his life and is thus somehow changed, but outwardly he conforms to his self-image of model businessman and citizen.

Lewis, considered a master at mimicking idiomatic speech and dialogue, was at the height of his powers when he composed *Babbitt*. Babbitt's volubility and vapidity, obvious vehicles for satirizing middle-class small-mindedness and hypocrisy, became so real to the public that the term Babbittry quickly entered into commonplace usage. At once likeable and ludicrous, Babbitt has become one of the most memorable characters in American fiction. The story of his revolt and return, although conceptually simple, possesses an archetypal importance rarely found in modern fiction.

❧•❦

Further Reading

Brooks, Van Wyck. *Days of the Phoenix: The 1920's I Remember*. New York: Dutton, 1957.
Callahan, John F. *The Illusions of a Nation: Myth and History in the Novels of F. Scott Fitzgerald*. Urbana, Ill.: University of Illinois Press, 1972.

Churchill, Allen. *The Literary Decade*. Englewood Cliffs, N.J.: Prentice-Hall, 1971.

Dooley, D. J. *The Art of Sinclair Lewis*. Lincoln, Nebr.: University of Nebraska Press, 1967.

Fahey, William A. *F. Scott Fitzgerald and the American Dream*. New York: Crowell, 1973.

Hoffman, Frederick John. *The Twenties: Writing in the Postwar Decade*. New York: Viking, 1955.

Hoffman, Frederick John, ed. *"The Great Gatsby": A Study*. New York: Scribner, 1962.

Hutchens, John K., ed. *The American Twenties: A Literary Panorama*. Philadelphia: Lippincott, 1952.

Light, Martin, ed. *The Merrill Studies in* Babbitt. Columbus, Ohio: Merrill, 1971.

———. *The Quixotic Vision of Sinclair Lewis*. West Lafayette, Ind.: Purdue University Press, 1975.

Lockridge, Ernest H., ed. *Twentieth Century Interpretations of "The Great Gatsby": A Collection of Critical Essays*. Englewood Cliffs, N.J.: Prentice-Hall, 1968.

Martin, Edward A. *H. L. Mencken and the Debunkers*. Athens, Ga.: University of Georgia Press, 1984.

Mizener, Arthur. *The Far Side of Paradise: A Biography of F. Scott Fitzgerald*. Boston: Houghton Mifflin, 1951.

Parrington, Vernon L. *Sinclair Lewis: Our Own Diogenes*. New York: Haskell House, 1973.

Schorer, Mark. *Sinclair Lewis, an American Life*. New York: McGraw-Hill, 1961.

Wilson, Edmund. *The Shores of Light. A Literary Chronicle of the Twenties and Thirties*. New York: Farrar, Straus and Young, 1952.

JAZZ POETRY
England, 1950s

Defined as the act of reading poetry designed for jazz accompaniment, the Jazz Poetry genre had its origins in the United States with some of the balladic poetry of Vachel LINDSAY (*see* CHICAGO LITERARY RENAISSANCE), and the work of Imamu Amiri Baraka (originally, LeRoi Jones [1934-]) and Langston HUGHES (*see* HARLEM RENAISSANCE), among others, who were drawn to the early and uniquely black American musical rhythms of the South. Later American poets of the BEAT GENERATION are also connected to the phenomenon. The Jazz Poets consisted of a group of young, post-World War II British writers who adapted the earlier mode to their own use. They included Pete Brown (1940-), Michael Dorovitz (1935-), Roy Fisher (1930-), Spike Hawkins (1942-), and Christopher LOGUE. The creation of poetry to be performed to live audiences with a background of jazz provided for innovative presentation for both genres. Later groups used the concept for the proliferation of songs and poetry of social protest against nuclear armament, warfare, and the social alienation so prevalent in the twentieth century.

❖•❖

Logue, Christopher (1926-)
English actor, journalist, playwright, and poet.

Jazz poetry was only one of Logue's many interests. His plays include *The Lily-White Boys* (1960), a satiric musical; *Trials by Logue* (1966); and *Cob and Leach* (1968). Principal poetic works are *Wand and Quadrant* (1953), *Maggot and Son* (1956), *Songs* (1959), and *Songs from* "The Lily-White Boys" (1960). He has been called the "born rebel and self-appointed outcast" by one critic but much of his work, though controversial, is both energetic and passionate as it speaks to the temper of the times.

❖•❖

Further Reading

Blackburn, Thomas. *The Price of an Eye*. New York: Morrow, 1961.

Case, Brian, and Stan Britt, eds. *The Illustrated Encyclopedia of Jazz*. New York: Harmony Books, 1978.

Cox, C. B., and A. E. Dyson, eds. *The Twentieth Century Mind: 1945-1965: History, Ideas and Literature in Britain*. Vol. 3. London: Oxford University Press, 1972.

Murphy, Rosalie, ed. *Contemporary Poets of the English Language*. New York: St. Martin's Press, 1970.

Taylor, John Russell. *Anger and After: A Guide to the New British Drama*. Baltimore: Penguin, 1962.

Thwaite, A. *Contemporary English Poetry*. Philadelphia: Dufour Editions, 1961.

Tomlinson, Charles. "The Middlebrow Muse." *Essays in Criticism* VII, 4 (October 1957): 460-62.

JINDYWOROBAK MOVEMENT
Australia, 1938-1950s

Rex Ingamells (1913-1955) founded the Jindyworobak group in Australia with a manifesto called *Conditional Culture,* coauthored by Ian Tilbrook (n.d.), that appeared in 1938. Ingamells's manifesto was written partly as a response to University of Melbourne English professor G. H. Cowling (1881-1946) and his 1935 article on Australian literature that appeared in the journal *Age*. The term "Jindyworobak" is a native one, meaning to annex or join.

Others associated with the movement were English poet William Hart-Smith (1911-1990), who joined shortly after he moved to Australia; poet Flexmore Hudson (1913-1988); Victor Kennedy (1895-1952), whose essay *Flaunted Banners* (1941) defended the movement; poet Ian Mudie (1911-1976), whose poems "This Land" and "This Is Australia" (1941) are considered strong articulations of Jindyworobak cultural ideology;

and Irish poet Roland Robinson (1912-1992), whose interest in Australia long predated his joining the group and whose poetry is thought among the best of the movement.

The literary tenets of Jindyworobak had affinities with the political agenda of the Australia First movement (which Ingamells joined), a radical nationalist group founded in 1941. The first journal Ingamells edited to propagate the ideas of Jindyworobak was *Venture: An Australian Literary Quarterly* (only one issue appeared, July 1937). *Venture* was eventually replaced with *The Jindyworobak Revue* (1938-1948). Anthologies of Jindyworobak writing were edited and published by its members annually until 1953. All of these provided a forum for Ingamells's demand that Australian history, especially the inclusion of aboriginal influence, should be more widely publicized, and Australian literature should attend to Australia, its land, history, and people. One example is the Jindyworobak appropriation of the concept of "altjira" or native "dream time" which is basic to aboriginal culture. "Environmental values" was another of Ingamell's key concepts, denoting the imperative to create a national culture out of the natural environment, eschewing outside influences. This indicated a sort of isolationism that ran parallel to one of Australia First's main tenets. Much criticism was directed toward the Jindyworobak movement under the assumption that the group meant to incorporate aboriginal culture into Australian culture when in fact the Jindyworobak vision meant to use aboriginal culture as an example of a culture with "environmental values."

Ingamells's work depicts the decimation of native culture because of colonization, his most important piece being the 8000-line narrative poem, *The Great Southland* (1951), which outlines the history of Australia and its origins.

Though the movement had run its course by the mid-1950s, scholars continue to see its influence on such writers as Peter Porter (1929-), Xavier Herbert (1901-1984), and Les Murray (1938-).

❧•❦

Further Reading

Elliott, Brian, ed. *The Jindyworobaks*. St. Lucia, Australia: University of Queensland Press, 1979.
Green, H. M., ed. *A Book of Australian Verse*. London: Oxford University Press, 1956.
Miller, E. M. *Australian Literature: A Bibliography to 1938, Extended to 1950*. Sydney, Australia: Angus & Robertson, 1956.
Thompson, John, Kenneth Slessor, and R. G. Howard, eds. *The Penguin Book of Australian Verse*. Harmondsworth, England: Penguin, 1958.
Wright, Judith, ed. *A Book of Australian Verse*. London: Oxford University Press, 1956.
———. *New Land, New Language*. Melbourne, Australia: Oxford University Press, 1957.

JOURNAL DE POÈTES
Belgium, 1920s-1940s

An important force in Belgian poetry from the 1920s through the 1940s, the *Journal de Poètes*, under the editorship of Arthur Haulot (1913-), lent prominence to such figures as Maurice Carême (1899-1978) and Fernand Verhesen (1913-) not only in Belgium but throughout the French-speaking world.

❖•❖

Further Reading

Bourgeois, Pierre, and Fernand Verhesen, eds. *A Quarter Century of Poetry from Belgium in the Original Text and with the English Translation*. Brussels: A. Manteau, 1970.

JUGENDSTIL
Germany, 1890s-1900s

A German artistic and literary movement that flourished from about 1895 to 1905, Jugendstil (or, Youth Style) paralleled the fin de siècle aesthetics of French Decadence, SYMBOLISM, and Art Nouveau painting. The Munich literary journal *Jugend* (1896-1940), founded by Georg Hirth (1851-1916), was a primary outlet for Jugendstil writing, which typically took the form of critical essays and poetry. The Symbolism of Stefan George (1868-1933) and the Neoromanticism of Richard Beer-Hofmann (1866-1945) and Hugo von Hofmannsthal (1874-1929) helped to partially define the nonetheless nebulous literary characteristics of the Jugendstil writers, a group which also included Max Dauthendey (1867-1918) and Richard von Schaukal (1874-1942).

❖•❖

Further Reading

Bennett, Benjamin. *Hugo von Hofmannsthal: The Theatres of Consciousness.* Cambridge, England: Cambridge University Press, 1988.

Goldsmith, Ulrich K. *Stefan George.* New York: Columbia University Press, 1970.

Gsteiger, Manfred. "Expectation and Resignation: Stefan George's Place in German and in European Symbolist Literature." Translated by Sonja Bahn-Coblans. In *The Symbolist Movement in the Literature of European Languages*. Edited by Anna Balakian. Budapest: Akademiai Kiado, 1982.

Kovach, Thomas A. *Hofmannsthal and Symbolism: Art and Life in the Work of a Modern Poet.* New York: Lang, 1985.

Van Handle, Donna C. "Hugo von Hofmannsthal." *The German Quarterly* 68, 2 (spring 1995): 174-80.

Webb, Karl Eugene. *Rainer Maria Rilke and Jugendstil: Affinities, Influences, Adaptations.* Chapel Hill, N.C.: University of North Carolina Press, 1978.

JUNG, Carl Gustav (1875-1961)
Swiss psychiatrist and essayist

The most distinguished of Sigmund FREUD's disciples — particularly in terms of his influence on the interdisciplinary fields of psychology and literature — was Carl Jung. Jung founded his own school of Analytical Psychology, following his break with Freud in 1912, in order to advance his own theories of the unconscious. Predicated upon his studies in anthropology, alchemy, primitive religions, and comparative mythology, Jung's schematic for the unconscious — first outlined in his groundbreaking work *Wandlungen und Symbole der Libido: Beiträge zur Entwicklungsgeschichte des Denkens* (1912; *Psychology of the Unconscious: A Study of the Transformation and Symbolism of the Libido: A Contribution to the History of the Evolution of Thought,* 1916, see also *Collected Works*) — consists of an approachable, thin layer of repressed memories beneath the conscious mind termed the "personal unconscious" and a larger layer, approachable and understandable only through response to universal symbols, termed the "collective unconscious," or racial memory. Central to this depth psychology is Jung's concept that human archetypes — innate symbols and symbolic structures — recur throughout history and across all cultural boundaries. An important precursory work for this concept, and for much of Jung's later meditations on the relationship between myth, psychology, and religion, was Sir James G. Frazer's (1854-1941) *The Golden Bough* (1890-1915). Equally important to Jung's overall psychological theory is his *Psychologische Typen* (1921; *Psychological Types; or, The Psychology of Individuation,* 1959), in which he introduced the terms "extrovert," "introvert," "individuation," "complex," the "shadow," the "anima" (the feminine ideal), and the "animus" (the masculine ideal). Despite a complex and prolific body of work built upon these two texts, the core of Jung's thought remains relatively simple: given that human personality is composed of the four elements of thinking, feeling, sensation, and intuition, an individual's health depends upon the unity and balance of these aspects. Therapy, in turn, requires the stirring of unconscious racial and recent memories to illuminate basic patterns of behavior and aid one in the universal search for meaning and fulfillment.

Notably absent from Jung's thought is the Freudian preoccupation with sexual urges and sexual neuroses. For Jung, such a limited approach tended to blind the therapist to a host of other contributing factors that might aid in the explanation of a patient's particular illness. Not surprisingly, one of his recommended preparations for the therapist was a solid working knowledge of the classics of literature, to aid in the uncovering of personal archetypes he deemed so important to diagnoses. Although Jungian psychology has met with only limited acceptance among the scientific community, literary scholars, as well as a number of authors, have borrowed extensively from Jung's works. Among the first scholars to apply his theories to the study of literature were members of the CAMBRIDGE GROUP, who played a prominent role in English criticism of the 1930s. Other critics and theorists, working independently, who have benefited from Jung's writings include Maud Bodkin (1875-1967), Leslie Fiedler (1917-), Norman Holland (1927-), Sir Herbert Read (1893-1968), Joseph Campbell (1904-1987), and, especially, Northrop Frye (1912-1991). Among the numerous authors conclusively affected by Jung are Hermann Hesse (1877-1962), Robertson Davies (1913-1995), Charles OLSON (*see* BLACK MOUNTAIN POETS), Robert Bly (1926-), and James Wright (1927-1980).

❖•❖

Further Reading

Barnaby, Karin, and Pellgrino D'Acierno, eds. *C. G. Jung and the Humanities: Toward a Hermeneutics of Culture*. Princeton, N.J.: Princeton University Press, 1990.

Campbell, Joseph. Introduction to *The Portable Jung*. Edited by Joseph Campbell. New York: Viking, 1971.

Donn, Linda L. *Freud and Jung: Years of Friendship, Years of Loss*. New York: Scribner, 1988.

Dry, Avis M. *The Psychology of Jung: A Critical Interpretation*. London: Methuen; New York: Wiley, 1961.

Fordham, Frieda. *An Introduction to Jung's Psychology*. 3rd ed. Harmondsworth, England: Penguin, 1966.

Goldbrunner, Josef. *Individuation: A Study of the Depth Psychology of Carl Gustav Jung*. Notre Dame, Ind.: University of Notre Dame Press, 1964.

Hall, Calvin S., and Vernon J. Nordby. *A Primer of Jungian Psychology*. New York: New American Library, 1973.

Jaffé, Aniela, ed. *C. G. Jung: Word and Image*. Princeton, N.J.: Princeton University Press, 1979.

Jung, Carl Gustav. *The Collected Works of C. G. Jung*. 2nd ed. 20 vols. Edited by Herbert Read, Michael Fordham, and Gerhard Adler. London: Routledge & Kegan Paul, 1953-66; Princeton, N.J.: Princeton University Press, 1966-.

Knapp, Bettina L. *A Jungian Approach to Literature*. Carbondale, Ill.: Southern Illinois University Press, 1984.

Monk, Patricia. *The Smaller Infinity: The Jungian Self in the Novels of Robertson Davies*. Toronto: University of Toronto Press, 1982.

Pauson, Marian L. *Jung the Philosopher: Essays in Jungian Thought*. New York: P. Lang, 1988.

Robertson, Robin. *C. G. Jung and the Archetypes of the Collective Unconscious*. New York: P. Lang, 1987.

Samuels, Andrew. *Jung and the Post-Jungians*. London: Routledge & Kegan Paul, 1985.

Steele, Robert S. *Freud and Jung: Conflicts of Interpretation*. London: Routledge & Kegan Paul, 1982.

Wehr, Demaris S. *Jung and Feminism: Liberating Archetypes*. Boston: Beacon Press, 1987.

Wood, Douglas Kellogg. *Men Against Time: Nicolas Berdyaev, T. S. Eliot, Aldous Huxley, & C. G. Jung*. Lawrence, Kans.: Regents Press of Kansas, 1982.

Yandell, R. James. *The Imitation of Jung: An Exploration of the Meaning of Jungian*. St. Louis, Mo.: Centerpoint Foundation, 1977.

JUNGIAN CRITICISM
Canada, England, and United States, 1930s-1990s

Also termed Myth Criticism or Archetypal Criticism, Jungian Criticism has been a prevalent form of literary interpretation for much of the twentieth century. Its origins are to be found more in Jung's psychological theories than in his own examples of literary criticism, which were, like Freud's, slight. [Jung's most famous example is his essay on Irish MODERNIST James JOYCE's *ULYSSES* (1922), initially written as an introduction to the German edition of Joyce's novel. The essay, alternately condemnatory and congratulating, was refused publication; Jung eventually published his piece in 1932, and expanded and republished it again in 1934.]

The most often cited examples of Jungian or Jungian-influenced criticism are English scholar Maud Bodkin's (1875-1967) *Archetypal Patterns in Poetry* (1934) and *Studies of Type-Images in Poetry, Religion, and Philosophy* (1951) and Canadian critic Northrop Frye's (1912-1991) *Anatomy of Criticism: Four Essays* (1957). Frye's work is especially distinctive in that it brilliantly proposes an independent science of literary criticism based upon Aristotelian theory, Jungian mythology, and Frye's own unique insights. Divided into sections on historical criticism, ethical criticism, archetypal criticism, and rhetorical criticism, Frye's *Anatomy*, for its recognition of the power and recurrence of myth in literature, has reigned as one of the most important critical documents of the post-World War II era. In addition to Frye and Bodkin, other scholars who have been associated with Jungian criticism include G. Wilson Knight (1897-1985), C. Day-Lewis (1904-1972), Leslie Fiedler (1917-), Norman Holland (1927-), Sir Herbert Read (1893-1968), and Joseph Campbell (1904-1987).

✦•✦

Further Reading

Aronson, Alex. *Psyche and Symbol in Shakespeare*. Bloomington, Ind.: Indiana University Press, 1972.

Balfour, Ian. *Northrop Frye*. Boston: Twayne, 1988.

Bodkin, Maud. *Archetypal Patterns in Poetry*. London: Oxford University Press, 1934.

———. *Studies of Type-Images in Poetry, Religion, and Philosophy*. London: Oxford University Press, 1951.

Brivic, Sheldon R. *Joyce Between Freud and Jung*. Port Washington, N.Y.: Kennikat Press, 1980.

Clipstone, Anna. *Archetypes in Action*. New York: Vantage Press, 1987.

Denham, Robert D. *Northrop Frye and Critical Method*. University Park, Pa.: Pennsylvania State University Press, 1978.

Frye, Northrop. *Anatomy of Criticism: Four Essays*. Princeton, N.J.: Princeton University Press, 1957.

Knapp, Bettina L. *A Jungian Approach to Literature*. Carbondale, Ill.: Southern Illinois University Press, 1984.

————. *Music, Archetype, and the Writer: A Jungian View*. University Park, Pa.: Pennsylvania State University Press, 1988.

Krieger, Murray, ed. *Northrop Frye in Modern Criticism*. New York: Columbia University Press, 1966.

Lesser, Simon O. *Fiction and the Unconscious*. Boston: Beacon Press, 1957.

Meurs, Jos van, with John Kidd. *Jungian Literary Criticism, 1920-1980: An Annotated Critical Bibliography of Works in English (with a Selection of Titles After 1980)*. Metuchen, N.J.: Scarecrow Press, 1988.

Olney, James. *The Rhizome and the Flower: The Perennial Philosophy—Yeats and Jung*. Berkeley, Calif.: University of California Press, 1980.

Priestley, J. B. *Literature and Western Man*. New York: Harper, 1960.

Skura, Meredith Anne. *The Literary Uses of the Psychoanalytic Process*. New Haven, Conn.: Yale University Press, 1981.

Snider, Clifton. *The Stuff That Dreams Are Made On: A Jungian Interpretation of Literature*. Wilmette, Ill.: Chiron Publications, 1991.

Wright, Elizabeth. *Psychoanalytic Criticism: Theory in Practice*. London; New York: Methuen, 1984.

JUNGWIEN. *See* YOUNG VIENNA GROUP

K

KALANGYA GROUP
Yugoslavia, 1930s

More conservative in its political emphasis than the *HID* GROUP, *Kalangya* was a group of Hungarian-Yugoslavian writers of the 1930s who concerned themselves primarily with the impact of society on the individual. The two founders of the journal were Zoltán Csuka (1901-) and Kornél Szenteleky (1893-1933). Others associated with the group were Jósef Debreczeni (1905-), Kálmán Dudás (1912-), and János Herceg (1909-).

Further Reading

Demaitre, Ann. "Yugoslav Literature: Hungarian Literature." In *Encyclopedia of World Literature in the Twentieth Century.* 3rd ed. Edited by Steven R. Serafin. Farmington Hills, Mich.: St. James Press, 1999.

KEN'YŪSHA. *See* SOCIETY OF FRIENDS OF THE INKSTONE

KETURI VEJAI. *See* FOUR WINDS MOVEMENT

KHALYASTRE. *See* GANG GROUP

KHITSAM or KHITSAN. *See* TESTING OF THE AGE

KIEV GROUP
Ukraine, 1920s

The Kiev Group of Yiddish Ukrainian writers served during the 1920s as an effective mouthpiece of SOCIALIST REALISM. Ironically, the two leaders of the movement, David

Bergelson (1884-1952) and Der Nister (1884-1950), had made their early reputations through nonpolitical, SYMBOLIST writing. The key followers of Bergelson and Nister were poets David Hofstein (1889-1952), Leib Kvitko (1890-1952), and Peretz Markish (1895-1952). Under Joseph Stalin (1879-1953), all but Nister, who preceded the others in death, were executed in 1952 for alleged crimes against the state.

☙•❧

Further Reading

Bechtel, Delphine. *Der Nister's Work, 1907-1929: A Study of a Yiddish Symbolist*. Berne, Switzerland: P. Lang, 1990.

Bergelson, David. *The Letters of David Bergelson*. Transcribed from manuscripts of the Yivo Institute by Simon Davidson. San Antonio, Tex.: S. Davidson, 1978.

————. *The Stories of David Bergelson: Yiddish Short Fiction from Russia*. Translated and with an introduction by Golda Werman. Syracuse, N.Y.: Syracuse University Press, 1996.

Maggs, Peter B. *The Mandelstam and "Der Nister" Files: An Introduction to Stalin-Era Prison and Labor Camp Records*. Armonk, N.Y.: M. E. Sharpe, 1996.

Mantovan, Daniela. *Der Nister and His Symbolist Short Stories (1913-1929): Patterns of Imagination*. Doctoral thesis, Columbia University, 1993.

Slotnick, Susan A. *The Novel Form in the Works of David Bergelson*. Doctoral thesis, Columbia University, 1978.

KIILA. *See* WEDGE GROUP

KITCHEN SINK DRAMA
England, 1950s

The name, as explicit metaphor, was given to a small group of dramatists — Shelagh Delaney (1939-), John OSBORNE (*see* ANGRY YOUNG MEN), Alun Owen (1926-), Kenneth Tynan (1927-1980), and Arnold Wesker (1932-). Their plays were written to showcase the lives of working, lower-class Britons who were attempting to cope with the residuals of a depressed economy, unemployment, and other social problems caused by England's tedious recovery from a devastating war. The dramas were in deliberate contrast to those written about the middle and upper classes and set in the "polite drawing rooms" of metropolitan society. In 1950, Tynan had published a collection of essays, *He That Plays the King*, which describes the plays designed for the "heroic" acting of Laurence Olivier (1907-1989), John Gielgud (1904-) and Ralph David Richardson (1902-1983), but by the mid-fifties, such groups as Angry Young Men and the Kitchen Sink dramatists in England and the THEATER OF THE ABSURD in France were changing the contemporary theater offerings with the depiction of the ironic, the confusing, and the harsh reality of a conflicted society and its class systems. Representative Kitchen Sink Dramas include Delaney's *A Taste of Honey* (1959) and *The Lion in Love* (1961), Osborne's *LOOK BACK IN ANGER* (1957), and Wesker's *The Kitchen* (1961).

✦•✦

Further Reading

Bentley, Eric. *The Playwright as Thinker*. New York: Meridian Books, 1955.
————. *The Theatre of Commitment*. London: Methuen, 1968.
Blau, Herbert. *The Impossible Theatre*. New York: Macmillan, 1964.
Tynan, Kenneth. *Tynan on Theatre*. Harmondsworth, England: Penguin, 1964.
Williams, Raymond. *Modern Tragedy*. Stanford, Calif.: Stanford University Press, 1966.

KÖLNER SCHULE DES NEUEN REALISMUS. *See* COLOGNE SCHOOL OF NEW REALISM

KOMMA
Belgium, 1965-1969

A highly experimental Belgian movement of the 1960s, the *Komma* group and magazine sought to redefine contemporary Flemish prose through a fusion of literary genres. Rene Gysen (n.d.), Willy Roggeman (1934-), Julien Weverbergh (1930-), and Paul de Wispeleare (1928-) were all members of *Komma*.

✦•✦

Further Reading

Goris, Jean-Albert, and Paul van Aken. "Belgian Literature in Flemish." In *Columbia Dictionary of Modern European Literature*. 2nd ed. Jean-Albert Bédé and William B. Edgerton, gen. eds. New York: Columbia University Press, 1980.

KONTYNENTY GROUP (Continents Group)
Polish emigrés in England, 1960s

The *Kontynenty* Group of Polish emigrés in London published a journal from 1959 until 1964. Their ostensible purpose was to continue the radical poetic programs of the CRACOW AVANT-GARDE and related organizations that had been prominent in Poland during the interwar years. Key members of *Kontynenty* included Andrzej Busza (1938-), Bogdan Czaykowski (1932-), Adam Czerniawski (1934-), Zygmunt Ławrynowicz (1925-), Florian Śmieja (1925-), and Bolesław Taborski (1927-). The Group published an anthology of their poetry in 1965, *Ryby na piasku* (Fish on the Sand).

323

❖•❖
Further Reading

Czerniawski, Adam. *Scenes from a Disturbed Childhood*. London: Serpent's Tail, 1991.
Miłosz, Czesław. "World War II: First Twenty Years of People's Poland — Emigré Literature." In
   his *The History of Polish Literature*. London: Macmillan, 1969. Rev. ed., Berkeley, Calif.:
   University of California Press, 1983.

KŬK YESEL YŎN'GUHOE. *See* **THEATRICAL ARTS RESEARCH SOCIETY**

KUZNITSA. *See* **SMITHY**

KVĚTEN. *See* **MAY GROUP**

L

LANKA. *See* **LINK**

LEAGUE OF LEFT-WING WRITERS (Tso-i Tso-chia Lien-meng) China, 1930s

The League of Left-Wing Writers, the largest Chinese literary organization that emerged in the MAY FOURTH era, represented the culmination of a disunified, often factious, proletarian literary revolution which had begun in the early 1920s. Formed under the auspices of the Chinese Communist Party, the League sought to firmly implant left-wing ideals through whatever means available, including rallies, social projects, propaganda and reportage, recruiting, and a proliferation of literary magazines which led directly to the dominance of proletarian literature during the 1930s. Its overwhelming emphasis on membership size and ideological impact hampered the creation of any lasting literature, though outside the movement significant advances were made in both the novel and essay just as the League reached the height of its influence before the second Sino-Japanese War.

The beginnings of the League were rooted in extremely contentious polemical battles between the revolutionary forces of the CREATION SOCIETY and more purely literary organizations, who wielded greater influence during the 1920s. These included the LITERARY RESEARCH ASSOCIATION, guided by MAO Tun; the CRESCENT SOCIETY, founded by Hsü Chih-mo (1896-1931) and HU Shih (*see* MAY FOURTH MOVEMENT); and the YÜ SSU GROUP, composed of LU Hsün (*see* May Fourth Movement), CHOU Tso-jên (*see* May Fourth Movement), and Lin Yutang (1895-1976). Lu Hsün and Mao Tun, in particular, were the subjects of repeated attacks from the revolutionary camp in the late 1920s, this due to the two writers' longstanding, apparent sympathy for the proletariat yet reluctance to unite with the Communist Party, which proposed a wholesale, propaganda-fueled reconstruction of the literary arts. Increasingly repressive actions by

325

the Nationalist government eventually brought about the capitulation of Mao Tun and Lu Hsün, the two most outstanding figures of the period. Thus legitimized, the League of Left-Wing Writers, some fifty members strong, was launched in Shanghai in early 1930. From its inception, an executive committee governed its operations and that of various satellite organizations, collectively known as the *Tso-i wen-hua tsung t'ung-meng* (Left-Wing Cultural Coalition). Lu Hsün served as the nominal head of the League, and his first-hand instruction and encouragement of younger writers was vital to its success. However, such party members as CH'Ü Ch'iu-pai, CHOU Yang, Hsia Yen (1900-1995), and Feng Hsüeh-feng (1903-1976) masterminded the meetings, propaganda, and task forces which formed the basis of the League's existence.

Ch'ü, a former party chairman who shared with Lu Hsün a keen interest in Russian translation, was initially the most important of these figures, for it was he who spearheaded the League's primary effort to make literature accessible to the workers and peasants. Less dogmatic than many of his colleagues, Ch'ü viewed the League as an opportunity not to promulgate and enforce strict standards of proletarian writing but instead to attract a wide assortment of writers whose works, though independently conceived and executed, would have at heart the interests of the common people. In 1932, by which time the League had effectively minimized the influence of the few remaining societies founded upon creative, rather than political, principles, Ch'ü proclaimed the necessity for a new revolution in language. He contended that *pai-hua*, which emerged as a result of the May Fourth Movement, was a contaminated language serving the needs of a small group of intellectuals rather than the overall populace. His advocacy of *ta-chung hua* (mass language), a new popular language that approximated urban working-class dialect, generated considerable debate and became one of the chief controversies within the League. The issue was resolved in 1934 by excising all the undesirable, elitist elements of pai-hua. The related issue of devising a new phonetic scheme was then addressed but the resulting *Latinxua* (Latinized Chinese) proved to be impracticable.

In a flurry of internecine quarrels, termed the Battle of Slogans, the League dissolved in 1936. At this time, when the problem of mounting Japanese aggression occupied both left and right political strategists, Chou Yang dominated League policymaking. He favored the creation of a new, more comprehensive league, the Association of Chinese Writers and Artists. Lu Hsün, HU Feng (*see* HU FENG CLIQUE), and others refused to join. At stake was both the principle of creative freedom and the integrity of the proletarian movement. Ironically, Chou, with his slogan of "national defense literature," simultaneously affirmed a concessionary attitude toward Nationalist forces and a doctrinaire approach toward literary production. Lu Hsün, Mao Tun, Hu Feng, and Feng Hsüeh-feng were among those who vociferously opposed such a plan; they campaigned instead for "mass literature of national revolutionary war," hoping to counter the common enemy of Japan while avoiding contrived, thematically restricted responses to sociopolitical events.

The Battle of Slogans was resolved shortly before Lu Hsün's death when a declaration proclaiming a united front of all Chinese writers was issued. Yet, Chou's dismantlement signalled the dawn not of a free and cooperative but of a puerile and propagandistic period in Chinese literature, one particularly suited for the acute SOCIALIST REALISM of Mao Tse-tung (1893-1976). Not surprisingly, nearly all the works directly sanctioned by the League have dwindled into critical obscurity. Of all the Communist writers active at the time, only Ting Ling (1904-1986), a later target of Maoist suppression, succeeded in uniting ideology with literary integrity. Perhaps the most telling example of the League's single-minded view of literature is the case of Mao Tun's *TZU-YEH* (1933; *Midnight*, 1957). A work which more than any other lent esteem to the League, *Tzu-yeh* was nonetheless harshly criticized by hardliners for its inordinate focus on the privileged classes, the very targets of Mao Tun's own, proletarian-oriented criticism. Although the League struck a serious blow against literary creativity and the free exchange of ideas, its importation of Soviet writing, particularly of such important Russian authors as Maxim GORKY (*see* SOCIALIST REALISM, Russia) and Nikolay Chernyshevsky (1828-1889), was instrumental to the close alliance between politics and literature in China which lasted well into the 1970s.

☙•❧

Chou Yang (1908-), Chinese essayist, critic, and translator.

Although less esteemed than Ch'ü as an essayist and scholar, Chou is regarded as one of the most important polemicists of Republican China. After studying literature and Marxism during the late 1920s, Chou joined the League of Left-Wing Writers and served as its secretary general from 1931 to 1936. During the 1940s and 1950s Chou, through various official posts, assumed much of the responsibility for reeducating intellectuals, condemning Western literary and cultural influences, and renewing interest in traditional Chinese poetry and drama. The execution of these tasks contributed greatly to Mao's political power and involved Chou in notorious public campaigns against such major writers as Hu Shih, Feng Hsüeh-feng, and Hu Feng.

☙•❧

Ch'ü Ch'iu-pai (1899-1935), Chinese essayist, critic, translator, and poet.

A dedicated Marxist-Leninist writer, Ch'ü was one of the first Chinese observers to visit Russia following the October Revolution. His impressionistic sketches of this journey are collected in *O-hsiang chi-ch'eng* (1922; Journey to the Land of Hunger) and *Ch'ih-tu hsin-shih* (1924; Impressions of the Red Capital). His fluency in Russian, knowledge of contemporary political events, university lectures, and pamphleteer work aided his rapid rise within the Chinese Communist Party ranks. However, due to flawed policies of expansion and fomentation, he was forced to abandon the post in less than a year. From 1928 until mid-1930 Ch'ü lived in Moscow, where he continued to write polemical essays and, most importantly, began to research the feasibility of romanizing the Chinese language. After returning to China and becoming a prominent theoretician for the League of Left-Wing Writers, Ch'ü also resumed an active political role, expressing his views on the relationship between a new literature and a new society in numerous pseudonymously published articles. For his subversive writings and alliance with Mao Tse-tung's Chinese Soviet Republic government, Ch'ü was captured and publicly executed in 1935.

➻•➼

Further Reading

Chou Yang. *China's New Literature and Art: Essays and Addresses*. Peking: Foreign Languages Press, 1954.

Feuerwerker, Yi-tsi M. "The Changing Relationship Between Literature and Life: Aspects of the Writer's Role in Ding Ling." In *Modern Chinese Literature in the May Fourth Era*. Edited by Merle Goldman. Cambridge, Mass.: Harvard University Press, 1977.

Goldman, Merle. *Literary Dissent in Communist China*. Cambridge, Mass.: Harvard University Press, 1967.

Hsia, Chih-Tsing. *A History of Modern Chinese Fiction*. 2nd ed. New Haven, Conn.: Yale University Press, 1971.

Hsia, Tsi-an. "Lu Hsün and the Dissolution of the League of Leftist Writers." In his *The Gate of Darkness: Studies on the Leftist Literary Movement in China*. Seattle: University of Washington Press, 1968.

Lee, Leo Ou-fan. "Literature of the Thirties, 1927-1937," "The League of Left-wing Writers and the Polemics on Literature." In *The Cambridge History of China*. Edited by John K. Fairbank and Albert Feuerwerker. Vol. 13, pt. 2. Cambridge, England; New York: Cambridge University Press, 1978-.

Pickowicz, Paul. *Ch'ü Ch'iu-pai and the Origins of Marxist Literary Criticism in China*. Thesis, University of Washington, 1973.

Ting Yi. "Mao Tun and the Revolutionary Writers of the Period of the League of Left-Wing Writers." In *A Short History of Modern Chinese Literature*. Peking: Foreign Languages Press, 1959.

LEFT FRONT OF THE ARTS ([LEF], Levyi front iskusstva)
Russia, 1920s

The Left Front of the Arts (Levyi front iskusstva) was a group that formed in Moscow in 1922; its members included former CUBO-FUTURIST poets Vladimir MAYAKOVSKY, Osip Brik (1888-1945), Nikolay Aseyev (1889-1963), Sergei Tretyakov (1892-1939), photographer Alexander Rodchenko (1891-1956), and critic Nikolay Chuzhak (1876-1937).

Chuzhak, Brik, Boris Kushner (1888-1937), and Boris Arvatov (1896-1940) were LEF's primary literary theoreticians. Chuzhak thought LEF should be a unifying force for leftist art in order to organize the proletariat psyche for class struggle. This line of thought brought LEF into a temporary alliance with PROLETKULT. Art, Chuzhak postulated, should be in motion, as is real life, and should anticipate what will be, in order to fulfill its mission to build life. Arvatov advocated a blend of Formalism and MARXISM; experiments with words were to be combined with "social command," though LEF interpreted social command not as a Party imperative but as the poet's social responsibility. LEF also encouraged the development of such realistic documentary literature as the novels of Dmitry Furmanov (1891-1926).

The group published a journal, *Left Front of the Arts* (*LEF*), under Mayakovsky's editorship, from 1923 to 1925, and later *Novy LEF*, which appeared from 1927 to 1928. Its office took up the second floor of Osip and Lili Brik's house in Moscow. Brought together in its pages were representatives from the major contemporary movements: Cubo-Futurists, CONSTRUCTIVISTS, RUSSIAN FORMALISTS all found themselves mingling in the pages of *LEF*. Contributors included Boris Pasternak (1890-1960), Vasily Kamensky (1884-1961), Viktor Shklovsky (1893-1984), Boris Eikhenbaum (1886-1959), and Aleksey Kruchonykh (1886-1968). LEF's more direct connection to the Russian Formalists lay in the friendship that both Mayakovsky and Velemir KHLEBNIKOV (*see* CUBO-FUTURISM) shared with leading Formalist theoretician Roman JAKOBSON. Mayakovsky was chief editor of the journal, which mainly served to propagate manifestos and be a print forum for ideas toward the development of literature in the new post-revolutionary society. Though the Cubo-Futurists' manifestos were particularly bombastic, an editorial from *LEF*'s first issue in March is not far behind. It asks: "Whom Is *Lef* Alerting?" and rants instructions to "Comrades," "Futurists," "Constructivists," "Production artists," "Formalists," "Students," "Everyone together," and "Masters and students of LEF," and concludes that:

Lef is on guard.

Lef *is the defender for all inventors.*

Lef is on guard.

Lef *will throw off all the old fuddy-duddies, all the ultra-aesthetes, all the copiers.*

LEF was at ideological odds with the OCTOBER GROUP; where LEF pronounced that art should create, Octobrists argued that it should reflect, life. But the Octobrists' reliance on REALISM was to prove more durable in the Soviet Union than LEF's innovative tendencies. Mayakovsky founded a new group, Ref (Revolyutsionnyi front iskusstva), in 1929, which fell apart the same year under what was becoming a universal mandate to join RAPP (*see* October Group and SOCIALIST REALISM).

⇒•⇐

Further Reading

Brown, Edward J. *Mayakovsky: A Poet in the Revolution*. Princeton, N.J.: Princeton University Press, 1973.

————. *The Proletarian Episode in Russian Literature, 1928-1932*. New York: Octagon Books, 1971.

Maguire, Robert A. *Red Virgin Soil: Soviet Literature in the 1920s*. Princeton, N.J.: Princeton University Press, 1968.

Markov, Vladimir. *Russian Futurism: A History*. Berkeley, Calif.: University of California Press, 1968.

Shklovskii, Viktor. *Maiakovsky and His Circle*. New York: Dodd, Mead, 1972.

Stephan, Halina. *"Lef" and the Left Front of Art*. Munich: Sagner, 1981.

Struve, Gleb. *Russian Literature under Lenin and Stalin 1917-1953*. Norman, Okla.: Oklahoma University Press, 1971.

LEFT-WING CULTURAL COALITION.
See LEAGUE OF LEFT-WING WRITERS

LETTRISM
France, 1940s

This, one of the many French, avant-garde literary trends categorized as "isms," was a minor and short-lived movement whose products resembled those of the CONCRETE POETRY movement that spread during the 1950s and 60s. It is identified with Isidore Isou (pseud. of Jean-Isidore Goldmann, 1925-) and Maurice Lamaitre (1926-). The poetry of the Lettristes depends upon calligraphic exercises, unconventional typography, something known as "picture writing," and the use of the various sign and symbol systems involved in the study of semiology. Lettrism's influence on French poetry was slight, but its purpose was to designate, among other things, a breaking down or "annihilation" of language which is symbolic of a cacophonous universe. It has been called a "fearsome" theory of politics, albeit an intellectual one, and as such is a relatively fitting adjunct to the MODERNIST movement.

⇒•⇐

Further Reading

Curtay, Jean-Paul. *Lettrism and Hypergraphics: The Unknown Avant-Garde 1945-1985*. [s.l.]: F. Furnace, 1985.

Ferrua, Pietro, ed. *Lettrism Collection*. Portland, Ore.: Lewis and Clark College, 1980.

Home, Stewart. *The Assault on Culture: Utopian Currents from Lettrism to Class War*. 2nd ed. Stirling, Scotland: AK Press, 1991.

Makar, Nabil Anis. *Variations in Lettrism: Paintings in Oil and Encaustic*. Master's thesis, George Washington University, 1979.

Morrice, Marjorie Ellen. *Lettrism: Art-Language in the Twentieth Century*. Master's thesis, University of Texas at Dallas, 1985.

LEVYI FRONT ISKUSSTVA. *See* LEFT FRONT OF THE ARTS

LINK (Lanka)
Ukraine, 1920s

A minor Ukrainian group of the 1920s, Link promoted an apolitical approach to literature. Guided by novelist Valeriyan Pidmohylny (1901-1941), the group also included short-story writer Hryhoriy Kosynka (1899-1934) and poet Yevhen Pluzhnyk (1898-1937).

❖•❖

Further Reading

Luckyj, George S. N. "The Failed Revolution, 1917-32." In his *Ukrainian Literature in the Twentieth Century: A Reader's Guide*. Toronto: University of Toronto Press for the Shevchenko Society, 1992.

"Rediscovering Poet Yevhen Pluzhnyk." *News from the Ukraine* 1 (1989).

LIRIKA. *See* CENTRIFUGE

LITERARY NONFICTION. *See* NEW JOURNALISM

LITERARY RESEARCH ASSOCIATION (Wen-hsüeh Yen-chiu Hui)
China, 1920s

The Literary Research Association was the most sizeable and among the most influential of the intellectual and artistic groups that proliferated in China following the MAY FOURTH MOVEMENT. Founded upon the principle of "art for life's sake," the Association promulgated REALISTIC, socially conscientious, Western-influenced literature through a number of periodicals, but especially *Hsiao-shuo yüeh-pao* (Short Story Monthly), the leading organ of serious creative writing during the 1920s.

The idea of a scholarly group dedicated to translating Western literature, appraising traditional literature, and fashioning a new literature for the modern age was conceived in 1920 by twelve intellectuals in Peking. Following the Association's inauguration in January of 1921, and the prompt issuance of a renovated *Hsiao-shuo yüeh-pao,* the group quickly grew to include some 170 members. The manifesto of the Association, drafted by CHOU Tso-jên (*see* May Fourth Movement), heralds writing as one of the noblest of professions and the development of literary excellence as the utmost responsibility of Chinese writers. Chou's assertion that "Literature is a form of labor, and a form of labor very significant for humanity" reiterates a 1918 manifesto he published in *Hsin ch'ing-nien* (New Youth), the chief periodical of the May Fourth Movement. Despite Chou's pioneering pronouncements, his ties to the Association were always tenuous. Of more significance, particularly in terms of creative output, were such other founding members as MAO Tun and YEH Sheng-t'ao. Under Mao's early direction the Association's monthly built a strong reputation not only as a forum for the best story writers but as a showcase of accomplished work in all genres. What most distinguished it, however, from competing periodicals were its regular translations and critical studies of foreign works from a large list of European and Asian nations. In accordance with the Association's humanitarian platform, writers from oppressed nations and writers sympathetic to proletarian causes were commonly featured. Of these, those who figured prominently included Russian REALISTS Leo TOLSTOY and Ivan TURGENEV, SOCIALIST REALIST Maxim GORKY, and French NATURALIST Émile ZOLA.

Yeh was the preeminent short-story writer during the formative years of the Association. As was typical of his colleagues, Yeh catalogued, with minute detail and objective presentation, the social ills of Chinese city and village life and the indomitable human spirit that suffers such ills. The absence of didacticism in his work proved a high standard to which numerous later writers tried to aspire. The Association itself, however, though revolutionary in the literary principles it advocated, was a comparatively apolitical organization, so much so that Mao Tun's editorial position was withdrawn in 1923 due to his overt Communist activities. By 1930, with the formation of the LEAGUE OF LEFT-WING WRITERS, the Association's interest in European literary styles and theories had become somewhat outmoded. In 1932, the Association became a casualty of the Sino-Japanese War, its primary publishing house having been demolished by Japanese bombing.

Although scholars emphasize the loose, almost amorphous, nature of the Literary Research Association, they also assert the unifying function of its most notable journal, which significantly shaped twentieth-century Chinese literature and, as a consequence, helped establish the careers not only of Mao and Yeh, but of LAO Shê (*see* ALL-CHINA ANTI-AGGRESSION FEDERATION OF WRITERS AND ARTISTS), Pa Chin (1904-), and Ting Ling (1904-1986), some of the most recognized names in modern Chinese fiction.

❧•❧

Mao Tun (1896-1981), Chinese novelist, short-story writer, and essayist.

Mao was one of the most prolific and accomplished writers of modern Chinese literature. Although he was well known among literary circles during the early years of the 1920s as an editor of *Hsiao-shuo yüeh pao*, advocate of Realistic fiction, and ardent political activist, it was not until 1928 that he established himself as one of the foremost writers of fiction. During that year he published his first novel, *Huan-mieh* (1928; Disillusion). With the two novels that followed and formed the trilogy *Shih* (1930; Eclipse), Mao carefully scrutinized the rise and fall of Communist idealism in the period surrounding the Kuomintang's seizure of power. Shortly after the demise of the Literary Research Association, he completed his most celebrated work, *Tzu-yeh* (1933; *Midnight*, 1957). Mao is also known for his numerous fine short stories, of which "Ch'un ts'an" (1932; "Spring Silkworms," 1956), considered an outstanding example of proletarian fiction, is the most popular.

Tzu-yeh (1933; *Midnight*,1957).

Tzu-yeh is a panoramic study of political, economic, and cultural conflict in China, specifically the various class and ideological differences found among the people of Shanghai during 1930. A work imbued with the narrative methods and thematic concerns of Zola and Tolstoy, Mao's novel stresses the inevitable defeat of overbearing capitalist power by the proletariat. However, Mao was criticized by some leftists for creating a wealthy industrialist as his protagonist and for focusing his narrative on the controlling, rather than subjugated, classes. In any case, *Tzu-yeh* is recognized as an exemplary Chinese novel of the Realistic-Naturalistic type and an illuminating account of a turbulent era in modern history.

❧•❧

Yeh Sheng-t'ao (1894?-1988)
Chinese short-story writer, novelist, and essayist.

A schoolteacher for many years, Yeh often wrote stories peopled with instructors and students. His themes, however, varied widely and included close examinations of the numerous social and psychological problems associated with the modern scientific age. During his most prolific period, from 1921 to 1937, Yeh published six collections of stories, two volumes of children's fables inspired by those of Hans Christian Andersen (1805-1875), and one novel, *Ni Huan-chih* (1928; *Schoolmaster Ni Huan-chih*, 1958). Notably influenced by Russian Realist Anton CHEKHOV, Yeh's best prose consists of simple, unadorned accounts of life's poignant truths.

Ni Huan-chih (1928; *Schoolmaster Ni Huan-chih*, 1958).

Ni Huan-chih is considered one of the most forceful and representative novels of the period extending from the May Fourth Movement in 1919 to Chiang Kai-shek's coup against the Communist Party in 1927. The protagonist is a teacher in a village elementary school. Burning with idealism and the spirit of reform at the beginning of the novel, Ni Huan-chih gradually loses all hope of successful revolution and begins drinking to assuage his sorrow; he eventually dies of typhoid fever. Although the high level of objectivity Yeh attained in his stories is reduced in the novel, Yeh is nonetheless credited with producing one of the most accomplished pieces of long fiction in the early modern era.

✥•✥

Further Reading

Berninghausen, John. "The Central Contradiction in Mao Dun's Earliest Fiction." In *Modern Chinese Literature in the May Fourth Era*. Edited by Merle Goldman. Cambridge, Mass.: Harvard University Press, 1977.

Chen Yu-shih. *Realism and Allegory in the Early Fiction of Mao Tun*. Bloomington, Ind.: Indiana University Press, 1986.

Chow Tse-tsung. "The Literary Revolution." In his *The May Fourth Movement: Intellectual Revolution in Modern China*. Cambridge, Mass.: Harvard University Press, 1960.

Gálik, Marián. *Mao Tun and Modern Chinese Literary Criticism*. Wiesbaden, Germany: F. Steiner, 1969.

————. "Mao Tun's *Midnight*: Creative Confrontation with Zola, Tolstoy, Wertherism and Nordic Mythology." In his *Milestones in Sino-Western Literary Confrontation (1898-1979)*. Wiesbaden, Germany: Harrassowitz, 1986.

Hsia, C. T. "The Literary Association." In his *A History of Modern Chinese Fiction*. New Haven, Conn.: Yale University Press, 1971.

Liu Wu-chi. "Prose Fiction." Supplement on the Modern Period in *A History of Chinese Literature* by Herbert A. Giles. New York: Ungar, 1967.

Ming Lai. "The Literature of Modern China (I)." In his *A History of Chinese Literature*. New York: John Day, 1964.

LITERARY REVOLUTION. *See* MAY FOURTH MOVEMENT

LITERARY SCHOOL OF MONTREAL (École Littéraire de Montreal) Canada, 1895-1925

Founded in 1895 by Jean Charbonneau (1875-1960), the Literary School of Montreal was a loose-knit poetry society that successfully countered Romanticism while introducing SYMBOLISM and other forms of MODERNIST verse into Quebec literature. The group made an enormous impact on younger generations of writers through its public readings — the most famous of which was that by Émile Nelligan (1879-1941) in 1899 — collective publications, and the literary journal *Le Terroir* (1909-10). In addition to the introduction of Nelligan, considered Canada's first great poet, the Literary School fostered the careers of Louis Fréchette (1839-1908), Charles Gill (1871-1918), Claude-Henri Grignon (1894-1976), Albert Laberge (1871-1960), Jean-Aubert Loranger (1896-1942), Albert Lozeau (1878-1924), and Philippe Panneton (Ringuet; 1895-1960). After a series of destructive rivalries and changes in membership, the Literary School floundered around 1925, though its influence continued to be felt.

❖•❖

Further Reading

Condemine, Odette. *Octave Crémazie, 1827-1879. Emile Nelligan, 1879-1941* by Paul Wyczynski. Ottawa, Canada: National Library of Canada, 1979.

Nelligan, Emile. *The Complete Poems of Emile Nelligan.* Translated and with an introduction by Fred Cogswell. Montreal: Harvest House, 1983.

Skinner, Daniel T. *The Poetic Influence of Victor Hugo on Louis Frechette.* Baltimore: [D.T. Skinner], 1973.

Wyczynski, Paul. *Albert Laberge, 1871-1960. Charles Gill, 1871-1918.* Ottawa, Canada: National Library of Canada, 1971.

LITERATURE AND INDUSTRY
Italy, 1960s

Literature and Industry was an Italian movement in fiction that underscored the isolation of the modern individual in an industrial and technological society. Two novels in particular, Ottiero Ottieri's (1924-) *Tempi stretti* (1957; Hard Times) and Paolo Volponi's (1924-) *Officina Memoriale* (1962; *My Troubles Began*, 1964), exemplified the movement's concern for the worker and distrust of the impersonal world of commerce. Literature and Industry fiction remained prevalent throughout the 1960s in Italy.

❖•❖

Further Reading

Bradley, Dick. "Paolo Volponi." *Forum Italicum* (1992): 316-33.

Capozzi, Rocco. "The Narrator-Protagonist and the Divided Self in Volponi's Corporale." *Forum Italicum* 10 (1976): 203-17.

Fantazzi, Charles. "Ottiero Ottieri: Involvement Italian Style." *Symposium* 25 (fall 1971): 236-48.

Ferreti, Gian Carlo. *Volponi.* Firenze: n.p., 1972.

Lucente, Gregory L. "The Play of Literary Self-Consciousness in Paolo Volponi's Fiction: Violence and the Power of the Symbol." *World Literature Today* 61, 1 (winter 1987): 19-23.

————. "An Interview with Paolo Volponi." *Forum Italicum* 26, 1 (spring 1992): 218-35.
Pedroni, Peter N. "The Quest for Self-Fulfillment in Paolo Volponi's Fiction." *Canadian Journal of Italian Studies* 9, 33 (1986): 156-73.
————. "Volponi and Desired Exile." *Italian Culture* 10 (1992): 195-203.

LITTLE THEATER MOVEMENT
France, Germany, Russia, and United States, 1910s

Under the influence of such European theaters as the MOSCOW ART THEATER in Russia, FREIE BÜHNE in Germany, and THÉÂTRE LIBRE in France, American theatrical directors and producers began establishing small experimental dramatic groups throughout the United States during the 1910s. *See* GROUP THEATER, PROVINCE-TOWN PLAYERS, THEATER GUILD, THÉÂTRE DU VIEUX-COLOMBIER, THÉÂTRE LIBRE, WASHINGTON SQUARE PLAYERS.

LIVING THEATER
United States, 1950s-1960s

Founded in 1948 by Julian Beck (1925-1985) and his wife, Judith Malina (1926-), the Living Theater represents the beginning of the off-off Broadway experimental movement in modern drama. Advocating an anti-REALISTIC and improvisational approach to theatrical production, Beck and Malina produced plays by Gertrude STEIN (*see* MODERNISM, United States), Luigi PIRANDELLO (*see* Modernism, Italy), and Bertolt BRECHT (*see* EPIC THEATER), and also helped launch the careers of several important contemporary dramatists, most notably Jack Gelber (1932-), author of the shocking and widely praised work about heroin addiction entitled *The Connection* (1959). the origins of Living Theater productions may be found in Antonin Artaud's (1896-1948) THEATER OF CRUELTY and works of the THEATER OF THE ABSURD. Other associates of the movement, which united with FRINGE THEATER, were Kenneth Brown (1936-), Joseph Chaiken (1935-), and Jackson MacLow (1922-).

✦•✦

Further Reading

Beck, Julian. *The Life of the Theater*. San Francisco: City Lights, 1972.
Biner, Pierre. *The Living Theatre*. New York: Horizon Press, 1972.
Little, Stuart W. *Off-Broadway: The Prophetic Theater*. New York: Coward, McCann & Geoghegan, 1972.
Malina, Judith. *The Diaries of Judith Malina, 1947-57*. New York: Grove Press, 1984.

LOAFERS (Dagdrivarna)
Finland, 1900s

Made up of members of Finland's Swedish community, which in the early 1920s constituted a majority, these writers worked energetically, proselytizing the attributes of Sweden, its writers, and its language. They are known for prose pieces which contain acute psychological insight and for poetry which appealed to their wide audience of Swedish readers. They were also highly concerned with the political and moral issues of a bicultural country in which all of the writers were richly creative and could serve to enhance the literary milieu of their adopted country. Novelist and dramatist Runar Schildt (1888-1925) and poet Jarl Hemmer (1893-1944) were the best known of the Loafers.

❖•❖

Further Reading

Ahokas, Jaakko. *A History of Finnish Literature*. Bloomington, Ind.: Indiana University
   Research Center for the Language Sciences, 1973.
Schoolfield, George C., comp. *Swedo-Finnish Short Stories*. Translated and with an introduction
   by George C. Schoolfield. New York: Twayne, 1974.
Zuck, Virpi. *Runar Schildt and His Tradition: An Approach Through Genre*. Helsingfors,
   Finland: Avdelningen för Svensk Litteratur, Nordica, Helsingfors Universitet, 1983.

LOCAL COLOR SCHOOL
Canada, 1900s-1920s

LOCAL COLOR writing gained force as a movement in Canada at least a decade after it reached its peak in the United States. Beginning around 1900, such writers as Hiram Cody (1872-1948), Norman Duncan (1871-1916), Ralph CONNOR, Alice Jones (1853-1933), Stephen Leacock (1869-1944), Lucy Maud Montgomery (1874-1942), Gilbert Parker (1862-1932), Charles G. D. Roberts (1860-1943), and Robert Service (1874-1958) fueled the interest of Canadian readers in the landscape, culture, and history of Ontario, Nova Scotia, New Brunswick, Quebec, and other provinces. Much like in the States, the area of greatest interest was perhaps the wildest and most remote: the far Northwest. The fundamental difference between the Canadian and the American Local Colorists was the former's general unwillingness to jeopardize a positive national identity through narration that relied upon pessimism, NATURALISM, or scientific determinism. Instead, the Canadians kept to a Romantic, if geographically and sociologically authentic, point-of-view. The larger-than-life characters they drew and the mythic aura of the wilderness and countryside which they captured soon attracted an international audience. The movement itself remained a powerful influence on Canadian literature well into the 1920s.

❖•❖

Connor, Ralph (pseud. of Charles W. Gordon, 1860-1937)
Canadian novelist, short-story writer, and autobiographer.

Among Connor's most important formative experiences were his Presbyterian upbring-ing in rural Ontario and his pursuit of graduate degrees in both divinity and literature. Following his education, Connor worked as a frontier missionary in Alberta during the early 1890s. His first fictional sketches, collected as *Black Rock: A Tale of the Selkirks* (1898), grew out of his experiences observing miners and lumberjacks amidst the harsh Canadian wilderness. While pursuing a religious career, Connor continued to write extensively. His novel of life in the Rocky Mountains, *The Sky Pilot* (1899), and a series of works set in his boyhood county of Glengarry, helped earn him distinction as the first bestselling author in Canada. Virtually all of Connor's works exhibit his belief in the principles of Christianity, particularly his conviction that "good," which he dra-matized as physical and moral courage, always vanquishes "evil," which he portrayed as dissolute and anarchic behavior.

❖•❖

Further Reading

Connor, Ralph. *Postscript to Adventure: The Autobiography of Ralph Connor*. New York: Farrar & Rinehart, 1938.
McCourt, Edward A. *The Canadian West in Fiction*. Toronto: Ryerson Press, 1949. Rev. ed., 1970.

LOCAL COLOR SCHOOL
United States, 1860s-1900s

The Local Color School arose after the Civil War during what one critic calls "a period of national self-definition, an accounting of the peoples, dialects, folkways, and diverse traditions of the geographic sections of the United States, with much emphasis on the South." Regionalist literature was not new to the States—precursors include James Fenimore Cooper's (1789-1851) treatment of the West, Washington Irving's (1783-1859) of the Hudson River valley, Nathaniel Hawthorne's (1804-1864) New England, and Catharine Maria Sedgwick's (1789-1867) western Massachusetts—but there was a new desire after the war to develop a national literature, to describe regional identities and acquaint Americans with their diversity. The movement is considered to have start-ed in 1865 with the publication of Mark TWAIN's "JIM SMILEY AND HIS JUMPING FROG," while Bret HARTE's "THE LUCK OF ROARING CAMP" (1868) secured its popularity, enter-taining readers with a tale about a mining town in the recently explored and settled West.

The short story was the Local Colorists' genre of choice. The focus was on atmosphere, setting, and locality represented with as much accuracy as possible. Geographic locale and character types took priority over plot and complex psychological characterizations. The Local Colorists nurtured the development of distinctly American tall tales as well as character types: the Yankee peddler, the Southern trickster, and others from various regions. Hamlin Garland (1860-1940) put forth his theory of veritism in which he propounds that Local Color is a form of Realism or Realist technique in *Crumbling Idols* (1894), and advocated Local Color as a means of developing a national literature.

Notable American writers of Local Color include Sarah Orne Jewett (1849-1909), whose penetrating sketches and novels of New England life — *The Country of the Pointed Firs* (1896) being considered her finest — influenced numerous later writers, including Willa Cather (1873-1947). Also writing about New England were Rose Terry Cooke (1827-1892), Mary Wilkins Freeman (1852-1930), and, influencing many, Harriet Beecher Stowe (1811-1896). Joel Chandler Harris (1848-1908) set his Uncle Remus stories in Georgia, George Washington Cable (1844-1925) and Kate Chopin (1851-1904) wrote about life in Louisiana, Francis Hopkinson Smith (1838-1915) focused on New Jersey and Virginia, and Mary Noailles Murfree (1850-1922) wrote stories in *In the Tennessee Mountains* (1884), Thomas Nelson Page (1853-1922), in *In Ole Virginia* (1887), and John Fox (1862?-1919) set stories in Kentucky. New York City was a favored locale of O. Henry (1862-1910), H. C. Bunner (1855-1896), Brander Matthews (1852-1929), and Richard Harding Davis (1864-1916). Moving westward, brothers Edward (1837-1902) and George Cary (1839-1911) Eggleston wrote about life in their home state of Indiana, as did James Whitcomb Riley (1849-1916) in his poems. Zona Gale (1874-1938) is known for her fiction set in Wisconsin. Garland is famous for his works set in the prairielands. Frontier poet Joachin Miller (pseud. of Cincinnatus Hiner [or Heine] Miller, 1837-1913), known as the Byron of Oregon, also wrote novels and plays.

William Dean HOWELLS (*see* REALISM, United States) encouraged many Local Color writers — Twain, Jewett, Harte, Garland — to write about their own locales and people rather than focus on plot or structure. And James Russell Lowell (1819-1891) supported the writers involved in the movement, publishing many Local Color stories under his editorship of *The Atlantic Monthly*. Short stories were at that time particularly marketable for a writer. Magazines in the United States proliferated from 1860, when there were about 200 — e.g. *Harper's New Monthly*, *The Century*, and *Scribner's Monthly* — to more than 1,800 by 1900. According to one chronicler, "from 1887 to 1900 more than a hundred volumes of local-color stories were published."

Mary Wilkins Freeman, in a letter to Hamlin Garland, wrote that she had "a fancy that my characters belong to a present that is rapidly becoming *past* and that a few generations will cause them to disappear."

Local Color writing served, with its frequent admixture of sentimentalism and verisimilitude, as a transition between Romanticism and Realism. Yet it also, through the vigilant editorship and polemicism of Howells, became a vital component of Realism itself as it sought a stronghold in the American consciousness during the Reconstruction era. Though the popularity of Local Color fiction fell off after 1900, its influence remained in early decades of the twentieth century when writers such as Sherwood Anderson (1876-1941) and Sinclair Lewis (1885-1951) incorporated Local Color techniques into their fiction; some of the Local Colorists—notably, Twain and Garland—moved on to more Naturalistic modes of expression.

❧•❧

Harte, (Francis) Bret (1836?-1902)
American short-story writer and journalist.

At eighteen, Harte left his native New York for California and briefly became acquainted with the mining camp life with which he would fascinate the rest of the country. He eventually settled in San Francisco and edited the *Californian*—to which publication his friend Mark Twain contributed—and later, the *Overland Monthly*. As editor of the latter, Harte wrote and published "The Luck of Roaring Camp" in 1868 which created an instant sensation. "The Outcasts of Poker Flat" and "Tennessee's Partner" followed the next year. In 1871 Harte became the highest-paid writer in the United States when *The Atlantic Monthly* offered him $10,000 for twelve stories, though he never submitted more than nine. Collections of some of his Local Color stories include *The Luck of Roaring Camp and Other Sketches* (1870), *Mrs. Skagg's Husbands* (1873), *Tales of the Argonauts* (1875), and *An Heiress of Red Dog, and Other Sketches* (1878).

"The Luck of Roaring Camp" (1868).

Published in the August 1868 issue of *Overland Monthly*, this, one of Harte's best-known stories, exposed Easterners to a description of the characters and life in a western mining town and was a great success, making the Local Color story popular throughout the nation. "The Luck of Roaring Camp" tells of the spiritual, moral, and social regeneration of the men living and working in a mining camp in the Sierra foothills effected through their adoption of a child whose mother died giving birth and whose father is never identified. The sentimentality and romantic allegorical aspects of the tale are tempered by Harte's humorous drawing of these rather coarse characters, their use of a crude vernacular, and the narrator's distance and irony.

❧•❧

Twain, Mark (pseud. of Samuel Langhorne Clemens, 1835-1910)
American novelist, short-story writer, journalist, essayist, and memoirist.

One of America's most popular humorous writers, Twain's renowned career began as a Local Colorist and wrote what is widely considered the first American Local Color story of the mid-nineteenth century, "Jim Smiley and His Jumping Frog," published in 1865. Several of his works in a Local Colorist vein made his reputation: *The Adventures of Tom Sawyer* (1876), *Life on the Mississippi* (1883), and *THE ADVENTURES OF HUCK-LEBERRY FINN* (*see* REALISM, United States).

"Jim Smiley and His Jumping Frog" (1865).

After writing this short story, which launched his writing career, Twain initially termed it "a villainous backwoods sketch." Originally published in the November 18, 1865, issue of the *Saturday Review*, the story was later reprinted in the collection *The Celebrated Jumping Frog of Calaveras County and Other Sketches* (1867). With its use of the vernacular and non-idealization of humanity, the tale has contributed to the development of American Realism. The source for the story of Jim Smiley and his frog is an old folk tale in print at least a decade before Twain wrote his version, a framed story, in which the genteel narrator recounts his interview of a local character in a tavern. Through this latter voice, with vernacular dialect, is told the story of the bet Smiley makes with a stranger that his frog Dan'l Webster can jump higher than any frog the stranger can produce, a bet Smiley loses after the stranger fills Dan'l Webster with quail shot when Smiley turns his back.

❧•❧

Further Reading

Banta, Martha. "Realism and Regionalism," "Women Writers and the New Woman." In *Columbia Literary History of the United States.* Edited by Emory Elliott. New York: Columbia University Press, 1988.

Cady, Edwin H. *The Road to Realism: The Early Years, 1837-1885, of William Dean Howells.* 1956. Reprint, Westport, Conn.: Greenwood Press, 1986.

Campbell, Donna M. *Resisting Regionalism: Gender and Naturalism in American Fiction, 1885-1915.* Athens, Ohio: Ohio University Press, 1997.

Cary, Richard. *Sarah Orne Jewett.* New York: Twayne Publishers, 1962.

Chase, Richard. *The American Novel and Its Tradition.* Garden City, N.Y.: Doubleday Anchor, 1957.

Conn, Peter. *The Divided Mind: Ideology and Imagination in America, 1898-1917.* Cambridge, England: Cambridge University Press, 1983.

Donovan, Josephine. *New England Local Color Literature: A Women's Tradition.* New York: Ungar, 1983.

Duckett, Margaret. *Mark Twain and Bret Harte*. Norman, Okla.: University of Oklahoma Press, 1964.

Elfenbein, Anna Shannon. *Women on the Color Line: Evolving Stereotypes and the Writings of George Washington Cable, Grace King, Kate Chopin*. Charlottesville, Va.: University Press of Virginia, 1989.

Fetterley, Judith, and Marjorie Pryse. *American Women Regionalists 1850-1910*. New York: Norton, 1992.

Foster, Edward. *Mary E. Wilkins Freeman*. New York: Hendricks House, 1956.

Fussell, Edwin. *Frontier: American Literature and the American West*. Princeton, N.J.: Princeton University Press, 1965.

Geismar, Maxwell. *Rebels and Ancestors: The American Novel, 1890-1915*. Boston: Houghton Mifflin, 1953.

Gish, Robert. *Hamlin Garland: The Far West*. Boise, Idaho: Boise State University, 1976.

Hamblen, Abigail Ann. *The New England Art of Mary E. Wilkins Freeman*. Amherst, Mass.: Green Knight Press, 1966.

Hicks, Granville. *The Great Tradition: An Interpretation of American Literature Since the Civil War*. New York: Macmillan, 1993.

Jordan, David, ed. *Regionalism Reconsidered: New Approaches to the Field*. New York: Garland Publishing, 1994.

Kazin, Alfred. *On Native Grounds: An Interpretation of Modern American Prose Literature*. New York: Reynal and Hitchcock, 1942.

McCullough, Joseph B. *Hamlin Garland*. Boston: Twayne Publishers, 1978.

McKay, Janet H. *Narration and Discourse in American Realistic Fiction*. Philadelphia: University of Pennsylvania Press, 1982.

Mathiessen, F. O. *Sarah Orne Jewett*. Boston: Houghton Mifflin Company, 1929.

Mobley, Marilyn Sanders. *Folk Roots and Mythic Wings in Sarah Orne Jewett and Toni Morrison: The Cultural Function of Narrative*. Baton Rouge, La.: Louisiana State University Press, 1991.

Morrow, Patrick. *Bret Harte*. Boise, Idaho: Boise State College, 1972.

Nagel, James, ed. *Critical Essays on Hamlin Garland*. Boston: G. K. Hall, 1982.

Pizer, Donald. *Hamlin Garland's Early Work and Career*. New York: Russell & Russell, 1969.

Reichardt, Mary R. *Mary Wilkins Freeman: A Study of the Short Fiction*. Boston: Twayne Publishers, 1998.

Rhode, Robert. *Setting in the American Short Story of Local Color, 1865-1900*. The Hague; Paris: Mouton, 1975.

Silet, Charles L. P., Robert E. Welch, and Richard Boudreau, eds. *The Critical Reception of Hamlin Garland, 1891-1978*. Troy, N.Y.: Whitson Publishing Company, 1985.

Simpson, Claude M. *The Local Colorists: American Short Stories, 1857-1900*. New York: Harper and Brothers, 1960.

Skaggs, Merrill Maguire. *The Folk of Southern Fiction*. Athens, Ga.: University of Georgia Press, 1972.

Stewart, George R. *Bret Harte, Argonaut and Exile: Being an Account of the Life of the Celebrated American Humorist*. Boston: Houghton Mifflin, 1931. Reprint, New York: AMS Press, 1979.

Warfel, Harry R., and G. Harrison Orians. *American Local-Color Stories*. New York: American Book Company, 1941.

Westbrook, Perry D. *Acres of Flint: Sarah Orne Jewett and Her Contemporaries*. Rev. ed. Metuchen, N.J.: Scarecrow Press, 1981.

————. *Mary Wilkins Freeman*. Rev. ed. Boston: Twayne Publishers, 1988.

LOGOS GROUP (Lohos)
Ukraine, 1930s

One of several western Ukrainian movements active during the 1930s, Logos was composed of novelist Natalena Koroleva (1888-1960) and poet and critic Hryhor Luznytsky (1903-1990). The *DZVONY* Group's journal served as a forum for Logos writers.

⋙•⋘

Further Reading

Luckyj, George S. N. "Western Ukraine and Emigration, 1919-39." In his *Ukrainian Literature in the Twentieth Century: A Reader's Guide*. Toronto: University of Toronto Press for the Shevchenko Scientific Society, 1992.

LOST GENERATION
American writers in France, 1920s

Although neither formally inaugurated nor consciously defined, the Lost Generation surfaced in Paris in the 1920s as an outgrowth of MODERNISM and rapidly became one of the most important and influential literary phenomena of the twentieth century. The American expatriate writers who comprised the movement derived their collective sobriquet from prose experimentalist and reigning salon figure Gertrude STEIN (*see* MODERNISM, United States). Her declaration "You are all a lost generation" formed the epigraph for Ernest HEMINGWAY's *THE SUN ALSO RISES* (1926), an enormously influential novel which powerfully evoked the disillusionment and ethical nihilism indicative of the generation that came of age during and immediately following World War I. Hemingway's development of a highly original prose style — deceptively simple and reliant on such rhetorical effects as repetition, parallelism, and verbal irony — exemplified the Lost Generation's anti-Romantic outlook and accompanying demythologization of human experience. Psychologically astute, politically critical, and spiritually disenchanted, the Lost Generation rendered postwar society in their fiction with a form of detached psychological REALISM that became a model for countless writers for decades to come.

Prior to World War I, the sophistication, intellectual excitement, and estimable literary tradition of Europe had attracted on a small, individual scale such early expatriate writers as Henry JAMES and Edith WHARTON (*see* Realism, United States), Natalie Barney (1876-1972), and Stein. However, Woodrow Wilson's reversal of isolationist policy, the participation of a number of young literati in the war, the favorable exchange of the American dollar, and, finally, the signing of the armistice caused a huge influx of writers to embark on an extended tour of Europe. This formless group consisted, most notably, of Hemingway, John DOS PASSOS, F. Scott FITZGERALD, e. e. CUMMINGS, Djuna BARNES, Margaret Anderson (1886-1973), Stephen Vincent Benét (1898-1943), Kay Boyle (1902-1992), Louis Bromfield (1896-1956), Malcolm Cowley (1898-1989), Robert McAlmon (1896-1956), Archibald MacLeish (1892-1982), Harold Stearns (1891-1943), Thornton Wilder (1897-1975), William Carlos Williams (1883-1963), Katherine Anne Porter (1890-1980), and, near the end of the twenties, Henry MILLER and Anaïs Nin (1903-1977). Claiming Paris's Montparnasse, or Left Bank, district as their literary capital, the majority of these writers settled in France for several years, finding the city's liberal attitudes toward sex and life in general compatible with their own carpe diem philosophy and rebellious literary stance. Through informal discussions and readings — many conducted at Stein's lodgings or Sylvia Beach's (1887-1962) Shakespeare and Company, an avant-garde bookstore and lending library — and contact with many of Europe's most celebrated authors, they expressed their intent of rebuking provincial American society while discovering advances in literary form and style to support their sensed alienation from the past.

They looked first to the complex poetry of established expatriates Ezra POUND and T. S. ELIOT (*see* MODERNISM, England and Ireland) for inspiration. Eliot's *THE WASTE LAND* (1922), in particular, represented a watershed work, a model of erudition, perspicuity, and linguistic power to which, they agreed, all modern literature should strive in some manner to attain. By this time, though, the newer writers were studiously exploring the flowerings in France of DADA as well as the work of a long list of French writers, among them Gustave FLAUBERT (*see* REALISM, France), Marcel PROUST (*see* MODERNISM, France), André GIDE (*see NOUVELLE REVUE FRANÇAISE*), Arthur RIMBAUD, and Stéphane MALLARMÉ (*see* SYMBOLISM, France). From the Dadaists, the Americans extracted their sense of a negative value system and an appreciation for the irrational. From the French as a whole, they gained their devotion to writing as a sacred craft, one for which selecting *le mot juste* (the exact word) represented the writer's foremost responsibility.

Undoubtedly though, what exerted the greatest impact on the course of expatriate fiction during the twenties was James JOYCE's *ULYSSES* (1922; *see* MODERNISM, England

and Ireland). Received with incredulity, incomprehension, or vehement censorship by the majority of editors and reviewers, Joyce's work was widely hailed as a masterpiece by his more forward-thinking contemporaries. The Irish writer's success in recreating the psychological processes of the human mind were of especial import to the Lost Generation, who like Joyce were fascinated by the lately expounded theories of Sigmund FREUD and Carl JUNG. Djuna Barnes—claimed to have said upon completing her reading of *Ulysses,* "I shall never write another line. . . . Who has the nerve to after that?" —was typical in both her envy and admiration of the work. Not surprisingly, virtually every writer of fiction in some way adapted or exploited Joyce's mastery of STREAM-OF-CONSCIOUSNESS (*see* MODERNISM, England and Ireland) passages, the interior monologue, and presentation of nonlinear time. In addition, Joyce's central theme of existential flux as source of both suffering and happiness underscored the sense of "lostness," that is, "modernness," that unified the American expatriates.

Aside from the individual achievements of the Lost Generation writers, which were staggering, another significant outcome during this period of monumental innovation and change was the proliferation of small periodicals devoted to showcasing the talents of the new writers. Some of the most notable journals included *Broom, 1924, This Quarter, Secession, transatlantic review,* and *transition.* The last and largest of these to appear, *transition,* issued a proclamation in 1928 which could well serve as the manifesto for many of the Lost Generation. In it, editor Eugene Jolas (1894-1952) declared his contempt for "the banal word, monotonous syntax, static psychology, descriptive naturalism" and his belief that "narrative is not mere anecdote, but the projection of a metamorphosis of reality."

Although Hemingway, Fitzgerald, Dos Passos, and others certainly differed in the method of their experimentation—they ranged in their styles alone from dispassionate, verbal concision to haunting, self-revelatory lyricism to suprareal, documentary montage—what finally united them was their dedication to a new, vital literature devoid of the idealism and narrative simplicity of the previous century. The list of works, particularly those of fiction, that achieved notoriety during the 1920s is impressive and attests to the vast importance of the Lost Generation to the very society from which it was attempting to rebel. Stein's *THE MAKING OF AMERICANS* (1925), cummings's *THE ENORMOUS ROOM* (1922), Fitzgerald's "Babylon Revisited" (1931) and *TENDER IS THE NIGHT* (1934), Hemingway's *In Our Time* (1925), *The Sun Also Rises* (1926), and *A Moveable Feast* (1964), Dos Passos's *Three Soldiers* (1921) and *U.S.A.* (1938), Barnes's *NIGHTWOOD* (1936), Miller's *TROPIC OF CANCER* (1934), Nin's *The House of Incest* (1936), Wilder's *Our Town* (1938), and Pound's *THE CANTOS* (1917-70) are just some of the many works by the expatriate coterie which continue to be studied and admired today.

❖•❖

Barnes, Djuna (1892-1982)
American novelist, dramatist, short-story writer, and poet.

Barnes began her career as a poet and dramatist, attaining some notoriety with her chapbook *The Book of Repulsive Women* (1915) and the staging of three of her plays by the PROVINCETOWN PLAYERS. Her early influences included *fin de siècle* literature and the drawings of Aubrey Beardsley (1872-1898). Barnes relocated to Paris in the early 1920s and soon came to admire Joyce's many technical innovations within the novel form. She published her first novel, *Ryder*, in 1928. Although neither structurally nor stylistically her best work, *Ryder* is esteemed for its virtuoso display of narrative forms spanning the entire range of literary history. *Ladies Almanack* (1928), a plotless novel concerning a society of lesbians, followed the same year. Each of these works reveals a preoccupation with sexual identity and the unrelieved rootlessness and restlessness of modern life—themes she more fully addressed in her greatest novel, *Nightwood* (1936). Published long after many of the Lost Generation had concluded their expatriation and most important literary experiments, *Nightwood* nonetheless stands as one of the most stunning and sophisticated syntheses of twenties avant-garde writing. Barnes returned to New York in 1940 and published one last major work, *The Antiphon* (1958), a complex blank-verse tragedy. By century's end Barnes was regarded as an undeservedly neglected writer whose impact on modern fiction had yet to be fully assessed.

Nightwood (1936).

Abounding in dark, bestial, and violent images, *Nightwood* is an essentially plotless novel set primarily in 1920s Paris and centered around a young, enigmatic lesbian named Robin Vote. Two men and two women are irresistibly drawn, each for a different reason, to Robin, who functions as an archetypal, paradoxical human: part primordial beast, part modern sophisticate. As the novel progresses through sections arranged in the manner of a Baroque fugue, Barnes's guiding theme of the unreliability of all physical and psychological boundaries becomes increasingly apparent. Like its characters, the novel defies easy classification, for however modern and prevalent its SURREALIST and Symbolist passages are, there are equally numerous passages recalling the Old Testament, the Metaphysical poets, and Elizabethan drama. A tour de force of language, imagery, and poetic vision, *Nightwood* is, next to Joyce's *Ulysses* and *Finnegans Wake*, the most stunningly experimental novel of the Modernist era.

❖•❖

cummings, e. e. (1894-1962), American poet and nonfiction writer.

Like Hemingway and Dos Passos—the latter a close friend since student days at Harvard—cummings enlisted as a volunteer ambulance driver during the war. His association with the Norton-Harjes Corps afforded him his first exposure to French language and customs and to the teeming cosmopolitanism of Paris. Cummings's service was curtailed by a series of events as bizarre and frightening as the war itself, for with his friend W. S. Brown he was arrested, placed in a concentration camp, and repeatedly interrogated about possible sedition against the French government. Brown, apparently, had written letters whose politically critical content had alarmed the French censors; cummings, in turn, refused to defame his friend or, for that matter, the German people. Charges against the two were eventually dropped after laborious negotiations on their behalf by family and friends. The experience led directly to the writing of *The Enormous Room* (1922), a highly entertaining prose work emphasizing individual victory over a corrupt system, a theme cummings would recurrently address in his succeeding volumes of poetry.

His first collection of poems, *Tulips and Chimneys* (1923), established him as a highly controversial poet, a reputation that has persisted. Typographically and syntactically innovative, cummings's poems—typically of love, nature, the persecutors, and the persecuted—are sometimes considered singularly brilliant expressions of an idealistic mind. However, they are just as frequently faulted for their simplistic observations and technical trickery. In any case, cummings has earned a high place in modern literature as both the creator of a new poetic idiom and of one of the most powerful prose accounts of World War I.

The Enormous Room (1922).

The Enormous Room was the first American prose work of the postwar period to completely merit the label "modern," for its transcendence of genre, distinctively individual style, and self-possessed distillation of experience were without any obvious precedent in literary history. The only comparison that has been made with any frequency is that with John Bunyan's (1628-1688) *The Pilgrim's Progress* (1678), for which *The Enormous Room* reigns as a wittily ironic counterpart. Concerned with the author's incarceration, cummings's work is less a straightforward autobiography than it is a poetically charged, occasionally Surrealistic narrative, which, despite its temporal relevance, stands as a timeless meditation on the tragedy and triumph of humanity. Both a summation of and contribution to the Lost Generation's identity, *The Enormous Room* is remembered today for its enduringly fresh insights and for the many indelible portraits of the colorful figures who populated cummings's absurdist nightmare.

❧•❦

Dos Passos, John (1896-1970)
American novelist, short-story writer, historian, and travel writer.

Described by Malcolm Cowley as "the greatest traveler in a generation of ambulant writers," Dos Passos was more an American harshly critical of, rather than an expatriate far removed from, his own country. Dos Passos first gained prestige with *Three Soldiers* (1921), a novel which stemmed from his experiences with the ambulance corps during World War I. His first markedly experimental novel, *Manhattan Transfer* (1925), appeared four years later. The work, with its cinematic style of narration, striking objectivity, and unusual prose-poems, was enthusiastically received, especially in France. Much of its poetic content, in particular, was derived from two important influences, French poets Blaise Cendrars (1887-1961) and Guillaume APOLLINAIRE (*see* CUBISM). Following the publication of a travel book, *Orient Express* (1927); a polemic in defense of alleged anarchists Nicola Sacco and Bartolomeo Vanzetti, *Facing the Chair* (1927); and a few minor plays, Dos Passos turned to his most ambitious undertaking, the three-part novel *U.S.A.* (1938). Perhaps the most transitional of the Lost Generation works, *U.S.A.* blends the bold narrative experimentation indicative of the twenties with the forthright political and economic commentary typical of the thirties. It has often been said that Dos Passos's greatest character was that of American society itself and in this work, especially, he succeeded in capturing this character's multitude of voices and attributes. Dos Passos's leftist views softened in later years, though he maintained a sharp critical eye in his essays, fiction, and journalism. His reputation as a major novelist has dwindled due to his topicality, though not substantially, from the time of the height of his career, when he was hailed by French EXISTENTIALIST Jean-Paul SARTE as "the greatest writer of our time."

U.S.A. (1938).

Consisting of the novels *The 42nd Parallel* (1930), *1919* (1932), and *The Big Money* (1936), *U.S.A.* is an epic recapitulation of the first three decades of the twentieth century, from the conclusion of the Spanish-American War to the onset of the Great Depression. As such, the trilogy constitutes John Dos Passos's greatest fictional achievement and his most sweeping denunciation of the dehumanizing aspects of American capitalism and political corruption, a stance echoing that of economist Thorstein Veblen (1857-1929). Affiliated with other Lost Generation works through its themes of alienation and despair, *U.S.A.* also affines itself with the best expatriate literature through its experimental advances. In addition to straightforward narrative, Dos Passos employed techniques suggested by his exposure to Cubism and collage painting. These include "Camera Eye" sequences, composed of subjective thoughts and memories in the form of prose poems; "Newsreel" sections, consisting of news articles and popular lyrics; and "Biographies" of actual people, including Rudolph Valentino, Thomas Edison, Theodore Roosevelt, and Woodrow Wilson. Despite Dos Passos's later novels and social histories, as well as his denial of the label "expatriate," he remains one of the key literary figures of the 1920s, whose best work stemmed from that era.

❖•❖

Fitzgerald, F. Scott (1896-1940)
American novelist and short-story writer.

With the exception of *Tender Is the Night* (1934) and a few short stories, Fitzgerald, though he regularly visited Paris and closely associated with numerous expatriate writers, particularly Hemingway, remained largely distant from the exile literature of the 1920s. While many Americans in Paris attended to the experiments of Stein, the Cubists, and the Dadaists, Fitzgerald virtually on his own fashioned a distinct, hauntingly romantic style, one which owed most to that of Joseph CONRAD (*see* MODERNISM, England and Ireland). His thematic preoccupations, as well, were primarily those not of the Parisian circle but of mainstream American writers: the rise of the JAZZ AGE, the loss of innocence, and the elusive nature of the American Dream. Following *Tender Is the Night*, Fitzgerald largely abandoned work which treated or incorporated the special themes and qualities of the Lost Generation. Ironically, his most perfect work, *THE GREAT GATSBY*, which had first brought him into close contact with the expatriates, and had allowed him to hasten the early artistic advancement of his friend Hemingway, was also the work which signalled his critical and popular demise. A figure whose genius was thwarted by the pressures of fame, alcoholism, and marital discord, Fitzgerald represents perhaps better than any other writer of the era the twin poles of freedom and chaos that formed the heart of the 1920s cultural milieu.

Tender Is the Night (1934; rev. ed., 1951).

One of F. Scott Fitzgerald's most complex works, *Tender Is the Night* takes place in Paris and on the French Riviera during the postwar decade of the 1920s. Inspired by Fitzgerald's six-year residence in Europe with his wife, Zelda, the story traces the moral and psychological disintegration of Dick Diver, an expatriate American psychiatrist. Fitzgerald makes apparent the tragic irony of Diver's downfall through the concomitant ascendancy of Nicole, a beautiful, schizophrenic heiress whom Diver treats at a Zurich clinic and then later marries. The Divers's life together is essentially one of riotous, extravagant partying tempered by ennui and rootlessness. Thus Fitzgerald's novel, though neither as masterfully structured nor as widely known as *The Great Gatsby* (1925), tellingly depicts the social climate that pervaded the Lost Generation.

❖•❖

Hemingway, Ernest (1899-1961)
American novelist, short-story writer, essayist, memoirist, and poet.

Profoundly affected by his World War I service as a Red Cross ambulance driver, Hemingway became an expatriate in 1921. Settling in the European literary hub of

Paris, he developed and perfected a prose style based partially on his apprenticeship as a journalist and on the early writings of Gertrude Stein. His first notable publication, the short story collection *In Our Time* (1925), challenged traditionally held conceptions regarding tone, character development, and narrative technique. By interspersing tautly written stories of the Midwest and wartime Europe with brief, frequently violent impressionistic vignettes, Hemingway demonstrated his skill of eliciting the maximum emotion and meaning with the fewest possible words. From this early work, he went on to establish a reputation as one of the world's greatest short-story writers with such memorable stories as "The Snows of Kilimanjaro" (1936), "The Short and Happy Life of Francis Macomber" (1936), and "Big Two-Hearted River" (1925).

Upon publishing *The Sun Also Rises* in 1926 he immediately became the most visible spokesperson for the Lost Generation. Although Hemingway, an essentially moral writer, denied the severest connotations of Stein's phrase, he later wrote *A Farewell to Arms* (1929), in which he memorably conveyed the impermanency of life in a war-ravaged world. In his later career, Hemingway is best known for his novella *The Old Man and the Sea* (1952), a parable of a Cuban fisherman that epitomizes the author's long-standing theme of "victory in defeat." The work earned Hemingway the Pulitzer Prize and was instrumental in garnering the Nobel Prize for him in 1954. He is also remembered for *A Moveable Feast* (1964), a posthumously published autobiography centering on his early life in Europe and influential association with the Lost Generation writers.

The Sun Also Rises (1926).

Generally considered Hemingway's best novel, *The Sun Also Rises* captures the pervasive sense of disillusionment and repudiation of traditional values that characterized the Lost Generation. The story begins in Paris's Left Bank but gradually shifts to Pamplona, Spain. There an assortment of friends, including the American newsman Jake Barnes and the thrill-seeking femme fatale Lady Brett Ashley, gather for the dissipation and drunkenness of the San Fermin bullfight festival. An aficionado of the Spanish sport, Jake alone finds meaning and solace in the commingling of grace, integrity, and danger that fills the arena. His ineffectuality, however, is underscored by the emasculation he suffered during the war, an injury which prevents him from fully expressing his love for Brett.

The characters' barren consciences and hedonistic lifestyles became a model for scores of dissatisfied and aimless Americans; similarly, Hemingway's terse prose style and highly effective, clipped dialogue became the prototype for numerous emulators within the HARD-BOILED SCHOOL, including Dashiell HAMMETT, James M. Cain (1892-1977), Raymond Chandler (1888-1959), and John O'Hara (1905-1970).

❧•❧

Miller, Henry (1891-1980), American novelist and essayist.

In 1930, after having spent several frustrating years as a part-time writer in New York City, Miller relocated to Paris and embarked upon a full-time literary career. The French city, bustling with culture, contrariety, and the spirit of life, sparked a rebirth in Miller which was immensely important to his career. His impoverishment, his experience of the seamier avenues of Paris, his anti-materialistic outlook, and his encounter with Surrealist and Dadaist literature, led directly to his first and most famous novel, *Tropic of Cancer* (1934). Like several of his works, the novel, unable to find a publisher for some time, was heavily censored in Britain and America. Upon the novel's appearance under a French imprint, Miller received letters of praise from numerous Modernist writers, including Aldous Huxley (1894-1963), Eliot, Pound, Porter, and Boyle. A circle of younger writers soon gathered around him at Villa Seurat and Miller, with the help of longtime companion Anaïs Nin, launched the Siana Series of books to promote his, Nin's, and their circle's work. Although Miller never equalled the achievement of *Tropic of Cancer*, such works as *Black Spring* (1936), *Tropic of Capricorn* (1939), and *The Colossus of Maroussi* (1941) have been widely admired. Miller's best work was always that which documented his experiences as they occurred. His interest in the writer as protagonist, and the creative work as autobiographical confession, has wielded an enormous influence on twentieth-century writing, particularly that of Lawrence Durrell (1912-1990), Norman Mailer (1923-), and members of the BEAT GENERATION.

Tropic of Cancer (1934).

An unabashedly autobiographical and sexually explicit novel, *Tropic of Cancer* documents Miller's first year in Paris, during which time he was almost always jobless, hungry, and without permanent residence. The tone of the book — at once comic and tragic — is established from the first sentences: "I am living at the Villa Borghese. There is not a crumb of dirt anywhere, nor a chair misplaced. We are all alone here and we are dead. . . . I have no money, no resources, no hopes. I am the happiest man alive. . . . This is not a book, in the ordinary sense of the word. No, this is a prolonged insult, a gob of spit in the face of Art, a kick in the pants to God, Man, Destiny, Time, Love, Beauty . . . what you will." Miller's underlying exposition of chaos as the natural and preferable mode of human existence has been likened to the profound searches for aesthetic and personal freedom that guided the lives of his closest predecessors, Henry David Thoreau (1817-1862) and Walt Whitman (1819-1892). It is this strong note of individuality that has incited such a relentless debate over the novel's artistic merits; Miller's detractors are as numerous as his admirers. Perhaps no one, though, has so succinctly defined the controversial author's achievement as Edmund Wilson, who in his essay "Twilight of the Expatriates" hailed Miller as "the spokesman, par excellence, for the Left Bank" and *Tropic of Cancer* as "the epitaph for the whole generation of American writers and artists that migrated to Paris after the war."

✦•✦

Further Reading

Aldridge, John W. *After the Lost Generation: A Critical Study of the Writers of Two Wars.* New York: McGraw-Hill, 1951.

Benstock, Shari. *Women of the Left Bank: Paris, 1900-1940.* Austin, Tex.: University of Texas Press, 1985.

Bloom, Harold, ed. *F. Scott Fitzgerald.* New York: Chelsea House, 1985.

Burke, Kenneth. "Version, Con-, Per-, and In-: Thoughts on Djuna Barnes' Novel, *Nightwood.*" *Southern Review* 2 (winter 1966): 329-46.

Clark, Michael. *Dos Passos's Early Fiction, 1912-1938.* Selinsgrove, Pa.: Susquehanna University Press, 1987.

Cohen, Milton A. *Poet and Painter: The Aesthetics of E. E. Cummings's Early Work.* Detroit: Wayne State University Press, 1987.

Cowley, Malcolm. *Exile's Return: A Literary Odyssey of the 1920s.* New York: Norton, 1934. Rev. ed., New York: Viking, 1951.

———. *A Second Flowering: Works and Days of the Lost Generation.* New York: Viking, 1973.

Dolan, Marc. *Modern Lives: A Cultural Re-Reading of the "Lost Generation."* West Lafayette, Ind.: Purdue University Press, 1996.

Fitch, Noel Riley. *Sylvia Beach and the Lost Generation: A History of Literary Paris in the Twenties and Thirties.* New York: Norton, 1983.

Friedman, Norman. *E. E. Cummings: The Growth of a Writer.* Carbondale, Ill.: Southern Illinois University Press, 1964.

Gajdusek, Robert E. *Hemingway and Joyce: A Study in Debt and Payment.* Corte Madera, Calif.: Square Circle Press, 1984.

Gordon, William A. *The Mind and Art of Henry Miller.* Baton Rouge, La.: Louisiana State University Press, 1967.

Hook, Andrew, ed. *Dos Passos: A Collection of Critical Essays.* Englewood Cliffs, N.J.: Prentice-Hall, 1974.

Kannenstine, Louis F. *The Art of Djuna Barnes: Duality and Damnation.* New York: New York University Press, 1977.

LaHood, Marvin J., ed. *"Tender Is the Night": Essays in Criticism.* Bloomington, Ind.: Indiana University Press, 1989.

Meyers, Jeffrey. *Hemingway: A Biography.* New York: Harper & Row, 1985.

Meyers, Jeffrey, ed. *Hemingway: The Critical Heritage.* London: Routledge & Kegan Paul, 1982.

Miller, Linda Patterson, ed. *Letters from the Lost Generation: Gerald and Sara Murphy and Friends.* New Brunswick, N.J.: Rutgers University Press, 1991.

Mitchell, Edward B., ed. *Henry Miller: Three Decades of Criticism.* New York: New York University Press, 1971.

Mizener, Arthur. *The Far Side of Paradise: A Biography of F. Scott Fitzgerald.* Boston: Houghton Mifflin, 1949.

Pizer, Donald. *Dos Passos' U.S.A.: A Critical Study.* Charlottesville, Va.: University Press of Virginia, 1988.

Putnam, Samuel. *Paris Was Our Mistress: Memoirs of a Lost and Found Generation.* New York: Viking, 1947.

Reynolds, Michael S. *"The Sun Also Rises": A Novel of the Twenties.* Boston: Twayne, 1988.

Rood, Karen Lane, ed. *Dictionary of Literary Biography.* Vol. 4, *American Writers in Paris, 1920-1939.* Detroit: Gale Research Co., 1980.

Stuhlmann, Gunther, ed. *A Literate Passion: Letters of Anais Nin and Henry Miller, 1932-1953.* San Diego: Harcourt Brace Jovanovich, 1987.

Wagner-Martin, Linda W. *Dos Passos: Artist as American.* Austin, Tex.: University of Texas Press, 1979.

Wegner, Robert E. *The Poetry and Prose of E. E. Cummings.* New York: Harcourt Brace & World, 1969.

Williamson, Alan. "The Divided Image: The Quest for Identity in the Works of Djuna Barnes." *Critique: Studies in Modern Fiction* 7 (spring 1964): 58-74.

Wilson, Edmund. *The Shores of Light: A Literary Chronicle of the Twenties and Thirties.* New York: Farrar Straus & Young, 1952.

M

MA GROUP. *See* **TODAY GROUP**

MAGIC REALISM
Latin America, 1950s-1990s

Magic Realism is neither a literary movement nor group, but a term employed by critics to describe narrative tendencies — particularly in Latin American novels and short fiction — characterized by depicting fantastic events, circumstances, and miracles in otherwise seemingly ordinary surroundings. Not to be confused with the genre of fantasy literature, Magic Realism in fiction depicts the unexpected and the mysterious in everyday reality. Critical and artistic cognizance of such an aesthetic tendency has furthered inquiry into what in fact is meant by "realism" in literature. Gabriel GARCÍA MÁRQUEZ, perhaps the best known Magic Realist writer, has said, in response to those who describe his work as fantastic, "actually I'm a very realistic person and write what I believe is the true socialist realism."

German art critic Franz Roh (1890-1965) is believed to have first used the term in *Nach Expressionismus: Magischen Realismus: Probleme der neusten europäischen Malerei* (1925; After Expressionism: Magic Realism: Problems of the Newest European Painting). Roh's use of the phrase intended to describe the expression of the wonders of ordinary reality in European post-EXPRESSIONIST art, similar to André BRETON's SURREALIST "hyperawareness."

From the late 1940s to the mid 1950s, a few Latin American writers and critics used the same, or similar, terms to indicate the effects created by blending the magical and the realistic. In *Hombres y letras de Venezuela* (1948; Men and Letters of Venezuela), novelist, dramatist, and critic Arturo Uslar Pietri (1906-) called the "discovery of mystery immanent in reality" *realismo mágico*.

Novelist Alejo Carpentier (1904-1980), also associated with AFRO-CUBANISM, wrote about *"lo real maravilloso americano,"* a "marvelous American reality" in the prologue to his novel *El reino de este mundo* (1949; *The Kingdom of This World*, 1957). The novel depicts the revolt of an African slave in the context of French colonialism in Haiti during the rule of Henri Christophe (1767-1820). The nature of history and the efficacy of revolution are complicated as Christophe is driven by images and myths of both French and African histories, as history seems to repeat itself in the present, and as revolutions also repeat themselves and accomplish their ends only by their recurrence. Carpentier portrays the multiplicity of cultural influences at work in the Caribbean — Indian, European, African — as contributory to this "marvelous reality."

Magic Realism, according to Ángel Flores (1900-) in his essay "Magical Realism in Spanish American Fiction," is the "general trend" of contemporary Latin America's "authentic expression." He locates its beginnings in 1935 with the publication of Jorge Luis BORGES's *Historia universal de la infamia*. For Flores, Magic Realism is an "amalgamation of realism and fantasy," bound up in the diverse historical circumstances of Latin America from Columbus to Rubén DARÍO (*see* MODERNISMO). Contemporary Latin American novelists and short-story writers who employ Magic Realism "cling to reality as if to prevent 'literature' from getting in their way, as if to prevent their myth from flying off, as in fairy tales, to supernatural realms," leading, in their narratives, to "a confusion within clarity," a phrase he borrows from Austrian writer Joseph Roth (1894-1939). Another Austrian, Franz KAFKA (*see* MODERNISM, Austria and Germany), is noted as a major influence on Magic Realist writers. And Miguel Ángel Asturias (1899-1974) is often counted among the prominent writers and theorists who concern themselves with Magic Realism. He describes his own narrative style, in, for example, *Hombres de maíz* (1949; *Men of Maize*, 1975), as Magic Realism. The novel explores mythologies and histories of Maya Indians in Guatemala.

Numerous writers around the world have been described as Magical Realists: Demetrio Aguilera Malta (1909-), Jacques-Stéphen Alexis (1922-1961), Massimo Bontempelli (1878-1960), Angela Carter (1940-), Julio Cortázar (1914-1984), Johan Daisne (1912-1978), Carlos Fuentes (1929-), Milan Kundera (1929-), Hubert Lampo (1920-), Juan Rulfo (1918-1986), Salman Rushdie (1947-), Emma Tennant (1937-), and Mario Vargas Llosa (1936-).

While some critics assert that Magic Realism is a distinctly Latin American technique grounded in attempts to create cultural independence from Europe and the United States, others suggest that Latin American Magic Realists, such as Borges, were heavily influenced by European Modernists. Finally, some prefer to recognize Magic Realism as a thematic narrative style which, even if many of its roots are in Latin America, is available to, and has been employed by, writers of many nations.

❖•❖

Borges, Jorge Luis (1899-1986)
Argentine short-story writer, essayist, and poet.

Borges is widely recognized as a monumental figure in twentieth-century literature for his metaphysical searching and narrative innovation. Early in his literary career Borges was associated with the ULTRAISM avant-garde movement in Spain and brought it to Argentina in 1921, where he gathered with the FLORIDA GROUP, fellow-poets on Florida Street in an upper-class neighborhood of Buenos Aires. During the 1920s he was also involved in various literary journals, such as *Prisma, Proa,* and *Martin Fierro.* Poetry was his dominant medium until the 1930s, when he worked increasingly in prose narrative, the fictions for which he would be renowned. Borges read and reread, widely: Robert Louis Stevenson (1850-1894), Rudyard Kipling (1865-1936), the Bible, the *Arabian Nights,* Samuel Johnson (1709-1784), Miguel de Cervantes (1547-1616), Icelandic and Germanic mythology, H. G. Wells (1866-1946), G. K. Chesterton (1874-1936), Emanuel Swedenborg (1688-1772), Arthur Schopenhauer (1788-1860), and Gnostic and Cabalist texts. He was fascinated with the phenomena of time, dreaming and waking, identity, and the human search for meaning — themes which are most brilliantly pronounced in the stories collected in *Ficciones* (1944; *Ficciones,* 1962) and *El Aleph* (1949; *The Aleph, and Other Stories,* 1970).

"Tlön Uqbar, Orbis Tertius" (1941; "Tlön, Uqbar, Orbis Tertius," 1962).

One of Borges's short masterpieces, the narrator relates an account of the discovery and creation of the world of Tlön. The story begins as the narrator's friend, Adolfo Bioy Casares [(1914-1999); Bioy Casares was a friend of Borges's, and the two collaborated on several anthologies of their fiction between 1942 and 1967], presents him with an encyclopedia article on a place called Uqbar, which appears in no other edition of the encyclopedia, insofar as they are able to discover. The literature of Uqbar, the article states, refers exclusively to "the two imaginary regions of Mlejnas and Tlön. . . ." Some time later, the narrator happens upon *A First Encyclopedia of Tlön,* which indicates that Tlön exists on another planet, *Orbis Tertius,* and he describes the inhabitants' scientific, philosophic, psychological, and aesthetic systems — all of which deviate in interesting ways from the tenets of earthlings. On Tlön the world is temporal, not spatial; laws of cause and effect do not operate here; thinkers seek "the astounding," rather than "the truth"; the idea of individual subjecthood is not valid — instead there is only one "indivisible subject" which equals every being in the universe; and "a book which does not contain its counterbook is considered incomplete." The narrator goes on to relate how, a few years later, various objects from Tlön began to surface. By the end of the narrative, Tlön is asserted to be the creation of a secret society on earth, which has gradually infiltrated the earth; a fantastic world which began to intrude into the real world: "reality yielded on more than one account. The truth is that it longed to yield. . . . A scattered dynasty of solitary men has changed the face of the world. Their task continues." In one hundred years, the narrator estimates, "English and French and mere Spanish will disappear from the globe. The world will be Tlön."

⤞•⤝

García Márquez, Gabriel (1928-)
Colombian novelist and short-story writer.

Before García Márquez emerged as a major international literary figure, he studied law and worked as a professional journalist. This latter vocation took him, during the 1950s, to Geneva, Paris, and the former Soviet Union and eastern block, and nourished his concurrent efforts to teach himself the craft of fiction writing, helping him to "maintain contact with reality," as he put it. He continues to write articles which appear most often in papers in Latin America.

García Márquez began publishing short stories during the late 1940s. His first novel, *La hojarasca* (*Leafstorm*, 1972), appeared in 1955. Here is the first extended portrayal of Macondo, the fictional town which figures in much of his fiction and finds its culminating expression in CIEN AÑOS DE SOLEDAD (1967; *One Hundred Years of Solitude*, 1970). He was influenced by the stories his grandparents told him during the first eight years of his life, as well as by MODERNISTS — Franz Kafka and William FAULKNER, in particular. One of the most striking and remarked upon elements of what most critics consider his masterpiece, *Cien años de soledad,* is the narrative voice, which García Márquez links to his grandmother's storytelling style: "She told things that sounded supernatural and fantastic, but she told them with complete naturalness. . . . I discovered that what I had to do was believe in [the stories] myself and write them with the same expression with which my grandmother told them: with a brick face."

Other works include: *El coronel no tiene quien le escriba* (1961; *No One Writes to the Colonel*, 1968), *La mala hora* (1962; *In Evil Hour*, 1979), the collections of stories *Los funerales de la Mamá Grande* (1962; *No One Writes to the Colonel, and Other Stories*, 1968) and *La increíble y triste historia de la cándida Eréndira y su abuela desalmada* (1972; *Innocent Eréndira, and Other Stories*, 1979), and novels *El otoño del patriarca* (1975; *The Autumn of the Patriarch*, 1976), *Crónica de una muerte anunciada* (1981; *Chronicle of a Death Foretold*, 1983), *El amor en los tiempos del cólera* (1985; *Love in the Time of Cholera*, 1988), and *El general en su laberinto* (1989; *The General in His Labyrinth,* 1990). The tremendous international impact of *Cien años de soledad* not only revived the popularity of the concept of Magic Realism, but inaugurated a wide recognition of García Márquez as an important literary artist. He received the Nobel Prize for literature in 1982.

Cien años de soledad (1967; *One Hundred Years of Solitude,* 1970).

This novel recounts the story of the Buendía family of Macondo, a fictional town somewhere in South America. Macondo has been described as a microcosm of the world, with a beginning, an end, and, in between, a space in which the seven generations of the Buendía family make discoveries and love, wars and revolutions, institutions and philosophies. García Márquez's language is at turns dense, exhuberent, rich, and humorous. Critics often point to opening scenes or even the first sentence in the novel — "Many years later, as he faced the firing squad, Colonel Aureliano Buendía was to remember that distant afternoon when his father took him to discover ice" — in attempts to grasp, describe, articulate its multifarious weight. In *Cien años de soledad,* characters return from death to, or never leave, the world of appearance, while events in history are denied, retold, recreated. In the opening chapter, the town is visited by the gypsy Melquíades, who leaves documents which no one can decipher until Aureliano, descendent of Macondo's founder, José Arcadio Buendía, does so at the very end of the novel: *"The first of the line is tied to a tree and the last is being eaten by the ants. . . .* [Aureliano] knew then that his fate was written in Melquíades' parchments. . . . It was the history of the family, written by Melquíades, down to the most trivial details, one hundred years ahead of time."

✤•✦

Further Reading

Agheana, Ion Tudro. *The Prose of Jorge Luis Borges: Existentialism and the Dynamics of Surprise.* New York: P. Lang, 1984.

Aizenberg, Edna, ed. *Borges and His Successors: The Borgesian Impact on Literature and the Arts.* Columbia, Mo.: University of Missouri Press, 1990.

Alazraki, Jaime, ed. *Critical Essays on Jorge Luis Borges.* Boston: G. K. Hall, 1987.

Alifano, Roberto. *Twenty-Four Conversations with Borges, Including a Selection of Poems: Interviews 1981-1983.* Housatonic, Mass.: Lascaux Publishers, 1984.

Angulo, Maria-Elena. *Magic Realism: Social Context and Discourse.* New York: Garland, 1995.

Barnstone, W., ed. *Borges at Eighty: Conversations.* Bloomington, Ind.: Indiana University Press, 1982.

Barrenechea, Ana Maria. *Borges the Labyrinth Maker.* New York: New York University Press, 1965.

Bell-Villada, G. H. *Borges and His Fiction: A Guide to His Mind and Art.* Chapel Hill, N.C.: University of North Carolina Press, 1981.

Bloom, Harold, ed. *Gabriel García Márquez.* New York: Chelsea House, 1989.

——. *Jorge Luis Borges.* New York: Chelsea House, 1986.

Brotherston, Gordon. *The Emergence of the Latin American Novel.* Cambridge, England: Cambridge University Press, 1977.

Brushwood, J. S. *The Spanish-American Novel: A Twentieth Century Survey.* Austin, Tex.: University of Texas Press, 1975.

Ciplijauskaité, B. "Foreshadowing as a Technique and Theme in *One Hundred Years of Solitude*." *Books Abroad* 47, 3 (1973): 479-84.

Cohen, J. M. *Jorge Luis Borges*. New York: Barnes & Noble, 1974.

Cortínez, Carlos, ed. *Borges, the Poet*. Fayetteville, Ark.: University of Arkansas Press, 1986.

————. *Simply a Man of Letters: Panel Discussions and Papers from the Proceedings of a Symposium on Jorge Luis Borges Held at the University of Maine at Orono*. Orono, Maine: University of Maine at Orono Press, 1982.

Cudjoe, Selwyn R. *Resistance and Caribbean Literature*. Athens, Ohio: Ohio University Press, 1980.

Di Giovanni, Norman Thomas, ed. *In Memory of Borges*. London: Constable in association with the Anglo-Argentine Society, 1988.

Dunham, Lowell, and Ivar Ivask, eds. *The Cardinal Points of Borges*. Norman, Okla.: University of Oklahoma Press, 1971.

Faris, Wendy B. *Carlos Fuentes*. New York: Ungar, 1983.

Fernández-Braso, Miguel. *Gabriel García Márquez*. Madrid: Editorial Azur, 1969.

Fishburn, Evelyn, and Psiche Hughes. *A Dictionary of Borges*. London: Duckworth, 1990.

Flores, Ángel. "Magical Realism in Spanish American Fiction." *Hispania* 38, 2 (May 1955): 187-92.

Foster, David William. *Studies in the Contemporary Spanish-American Short Story*. Columbia, Mo.: University of Missouri Press, 1979.

Franco, Jean. "The Limits of Liberal Imagination: *One Hundred Years of Solitude* and *Nostromo*." *Punto de contacto/Point of Contact* 1, 1 (December 1975): 4-16.

Friedman, Mary Lusky. *The Emperor's Kites: A Morphology of Borges' Tales*. Durham, N.C.: Duke University Press, 1987.

Garzilli, Enrico. *Circles without Center*. Cambridge, Mass.: Harvard University Press, 1972.

González Echevarría, R. *Alejo Carpentier, the Pilgrim at Home*. Ithaca, N.Y.: Cornell University Press, 1977.

————. "The Parting of the Waters." *Diacritics* 4 (1974): 8-17.

————. "The Dictatorship of Rhetoric/The Rhetoric of Dictatorship: Carpentier, García Márquez and Roa Bastos." *Latin American Research Review* 15, 3 (1980): 205-28.

Harss, Luis, and Barbara Dohmann. *Into the Mainstream: Conversations with Latin American Writers*. New York: Harper & Row, 1967.

Janes, Regina. *Gabriel García Márquez: Revolutions in Wonderland*. Columbia, Mo.: University of Missouri Press, 1981.

Kadir, Djelal. "The Architectonic Principle of *Cien años de soledad* and the Vichian Theory of History." *Kentucky Romance Quarterly* 24, 3 (1977): 251-61.

Levy, Kurt L. "Planes of Reality in *El otoño del patriarca*." In *Studies in Honor of Gerald E. Wade*. Edited by Sylvia Bowman, et al. Madrid: José Porrúa Turanzas, 1979.

Lindstrom, Naomi. *Jorge Luis Borges: A Study of the Short Fiction*. Boston: Twayne, 1990.

Luchting, Wolfgang A. "Gabriel García Márquez: The Boom and the Whimper." *Books Abroad* 44, 1 (winter 1970): 26-30.

McMurray, George E. *Gabriel García Márquez*. New York: Ungar, 1977.

————. *Jorge Luis Borges*. New York: Ungar, 1980.

Mendoza, Plinio Apuleyo. *The Fragrance of Guava*. Translated by Ann Wright. London: NLB, 1983. (Interviews with Gabriel García Márquez.)

Menton, Seymour. "Magic Realism: An Annotated International Chronology of the Term." In *Essays in Honor of Frank Dauster*. Edited by Kirsten F. Nigro and Sandra M. Cypess. Newark, Del.: Juan de la Cuesta, 1995.

Ortega, Julio, ed. *Gabriel García Márquez and the Powers of Fiction*. Austin, Tex.: University of Texas, 1988.

Rodríguez Monegal, Emir. *Jorge Luis Borges: A Literary Biography*. New York: Dutton, 1978.

————. *"One Hundred Years of Solitude*: The Last Three Pages." *Books Abroad* 47, 3 (1973): 485-89.

Sims, R. L. "Theme, Narrative Bricolage and Myth in García Márquez." *Journal of Spanish Studies: Twentieth Century* 8, 1-2 (spring-fall 1980): 145-59.

Sorrentino, Fernando. *Seven Conversations with Jorge Luis Borges*. Translated by Clark M. Zlotchew. Troy, N.Y.: Whitston, 1982.

Stabb, Martin S. *Borges Revisited*. Boston: Twayne, 1991.

Sturrock, John. *Paper Tigers: The Ideal Fictions of Jorge Luis Borges*. Oxford, England: Clarendon Press, 1977.

Wheelock, Carter. *Mythmaker: A Study of Motif and Symbol in the Short Stories of Jorge Luis Borges*. Austin, Tex.: University of Texas Press, 1969.

Williams, Raymond L. *Gabriel García Márquez*. Boston: Twayne, 1984.

Zamora, Lois Parkinson, and Wendy B. Faris, comps. *Magical Realism: Theory, History, Community*. Durham, N.C.: Duke University Press, 1995.

MAHGAR or *MAHJAR* POETS. *See* ANDALUSIAN LEAGUE and SOCIETY OF THE PEN

MALADNIAK. *See* SAPLINGS

MANZANILLO GROUP
Cuba, 1920s

Manuel Navarro Luna (1897-1966) and Luis Felipe Rodriguez (1888-1947) were the main proponents of the Manzanillo, or Mantanzas, group of writers from the Matanzas Province in Cuba, whose aim during the 1920s was to write subversive, socially committed literature. Navarro Luna's collection of poems, *Surco* (1928; Furrow), is an example. Rodriguez is better known for his short stories, though his novels are also interesting in the context of the group's vanguardist tendencies. His novels, *Cómo opinaba Damián Paredes* (1916; What Damián Paredes Thought) and *Marcos Antilles* (1932), and stories in *La pascua de la terra natal* (1923; Home Town Easter) criticize imperialism and social and economic injustice.

⤙•⤚
Further Reading

Foster, David William, comp. "Cuba." In his *Handbook of Latin American Literature*. New York: Garland, 1987.

González, Manuel Pedro, and Margaret Hudson, eds. *Cuban Short Stories*. New York: Thomas Nelson, 1942.

Minc, Rose S., ed. *Literatures in Transition: The Many Voices of the Caribbean Area, a Symposium*. Gaithersburg, Md.: Hispamérica; Montclair, N.J.: Montclair State College, 1982.

Padilla, H., and L. Suardiaz. "Manuel Navarro." In their *Cuban Poetry, 1959-1966*. Havana: Book Institute, 1967.

"Rodríguez, Luis Felipe." In *Dictionary of Twentieth-Century Cuban Literature*. Edited by Julio A. Martínez. New York: Greenwood Press, 1990.

MARX, Karl (1818-1883)
German philosopher and social activist

Karl Heinrich Marx was born in Trier, Prussia (now Germany) to Jewish parents. His father was a lawyer with the Prussian civil service and encouraged Karl to utilize his university education to prepare to enter the legal profession. Marx, however, spent his early adult years in university writing poetry and studying philosophy: his dissertation was entitled "The Differences between the Natural Philosophy of Democritus and the Natural Philosophy of Epicurus" (1841). The University of Bonn dismissed Marx's mentor, Bruno Bauer, which thwarted Marx's prospects for an academic career and, in 1842, he began editing the *Rheinische Zeitung,* a liberal newspaper in Cologne which became the major organ for the Young Hegelians, a group of philosophers who were concerned with critiquing Hegel's theories.

According to Georg W. Hegel (1770-1831), man is God, and history is the process by which man alienates himself (thus alienating God). Ludwig Feuerbach (1804-1872) inverted that thesis, stating that history is the process by which man realizes himself when he stops projecting himself in God; God, in other words, is man alienated from himself. Man must be liberated from religion in order to commune with others. The effect of Feuerbach's inversion was to bring into sharp focus man's social reality, rather than an otherworldly mysticism. Marx extended Feuerbach's thesis of alienation in religion by bringing it to bear on politics and the alienation in social institutions. The greatest development of this idea appears in Marx's ECONOMIC AND PHILOSOPHIC MANUSCRIPTS OF 1844. His formulations in these manuscripts begin to shape his most profound construct: historical materialism. According to historical materialism, history cannot be described only in terms of man and nature, as in Hegel's idealism. Society — that is, politics and economic conditions — must enter into a philosophic analysis of

361

history. Marx's sharpest critique of Hegel was embodied in his demystification of Hegel's philosophically derived rationale for the political bourgeois status quo. "The political system," Marx wrote, "is the political system of private property." He would proclaim that man could be reunited with man—that is, working men with the wealthier classes—only if systems of private ownership were abolished. But, in order to further this project, another fundamental philosophical tenet must be turned upside down: "It is not the consciousness of men that determines their being, but on the contrary, their social being that determines their consciousness" (*Contribution to the Critique of Political Economy*, 1859). Such an examination of consciousness in the context of social being is a driving construct employed by literary scholars who developed and continue to develop Marxist modes of aesthetic analysis and theory.

When the *Rheinische Zietung* was banned in 1843, Marx went to Paris, where he began editing the *Deutsches-Französische Jahrbücher*, met Heinrich Heine (1797-1856), Pierre-Joseph Proudhon (1809-1865), and Mikhail Aleksandrovich Bakunin (1814-1876), and was reacquainted with Friedrich Engels (1820-1895), with whom he would collaborate until his death. He was ordered to leave France in 1845 for associating with the radical paper *Vorwärts!*, and spent the next few years in Brussels, where he involved himself with labor organizations and wrote, with Engels, *Die heilige Familie* (1845; *The Holy Family*, 1956), *Die deutsche Ideologie* (1845-46; *The German Ideology*, 1933), and the *Manifest der kommunistichen Partei* (1848; *Communist Manifesto*, 1850, 1872). By 1852 he settled in England, where he wrote articles for *The New York Daily Tribune* and founded the International Workingmen's Association (1864). During the 1840s and 1850s, he spent much of his time with the Communist League and other working-class organizations, speaking at meetings and composing manifestos and strategies. His major writings from this time until his death were the *Grundrisse* (1857-58; trans. 1971) and *Das Kapital* (1867, vol. 1 and 1885, vol. 2, compiled by Engels; *Capital*, 1886, 1907-9).

While Marx never elaborated an aesthetic theory per se, much of his work draws on literary and artistic examples from Shakespeare, Johann Wolfgang von Goethe (1749-1832), Friedrich von Schiller (1759-1805), Charles DICKENS (*see* REALISM, England), Honoré de Balzac (1799-1850), and classical Greek art. He made scattered references throughout the body of his work to the position of art and the artist in society, describing "acquired forces of production, material and spiritual, language, literature, technical skills, etc." One of the most explicit statements Marx made on stylistics— "form is of no value unless it is the form of its content" —indicates his stance on an economy and ideology of aesthetic expression. An example of Marx's literary-social analysis appears in his Economic and Philosophic Manuscripts of 1844, in a section on "The Power of Money in Bourgeois Society" (see below). While many MARXIST CRITICS have studied his writings on modes of production in capitalist societies and honed the implications Marx implicitly or explicitly raised for artistic and literary production as well as the production of political ideology in works of literature, others have picked up on Marx's use of literature in his political-economic analyses and have attempted to fill in the gap left by the absence of an aesthetic theory. Critical analyses such as Mikhail Lifshits's *The Philosophy of Art of Karl Marx* (1938), Peter Demetz's *Marx, Engels, and the Poets* (1959), Henri Arvon's *Marxist Esthetics* (1973), Georgy Plekhanov's *Unaddressed Letters: Art and Social Life* (1957), and S. S. Prawar's *Karl Marx and World Literature* (1976) are attempts to construct what such theses by Marx would be, based on how he did write about literature and art in his political treatises.

Theory, in fact, was not Marx's first priority, although at one time he did envision eventual projects focusing on romanticism, religious art, and Balzac. In his "Theses on Feuerbach," he wrote: "The philosophers have only *interpreted* the world, in various ways; the point is to *change* it" — a rigorous challenge as legacy to committed Marxist literary critics.

❖·●·❖

Economic and Philosophic Manuscripts of 1844 (trans. 1959).

The 1844 manuscripts were not published until 1927 in an incomplete Russian translation. Marx never completed what he intended as a book marking out his theory of history and history's goal of proletarian revolution. In places, he suggests how literature is used to enforce the hegemony of the ruling classes. In the section "The Power of Money in Bourgeois Society," Marx employs excerpts from Goethe's *Faust* (Part I — Faust's Study, III) and Shakespeare's *Timon of Athens* (Act 4, Scene 3) to illustrate the figurality of money, arguing that the possession of money transforms both the identity and the value of the possessor and fosters illusions about material reality: "the *divine* power of money — lies in its *character* as men's estranged, alienating and self-disposing *species-nature*. Money is the alienated *ability of mankind*."

The Economic and Philosophic Manuscripts of 1844 do not represent an exception out of the larger body of his work in terms of his use of aesthetics in his formulations; literature was one of his lifelong interests and permeates most of his major philosophical work. Later Marxist-oriented literary critics have drawn on ideas raised in virtually all his works.

❖·●·❖

Further Reading

Arvon, Henri. *Marxist Esthetics.* Translated by Helen R. Lane. Ithaca, N.Y.: Cornell University Press, 1973.

Berlin, Isaiah. *Karl Marx: His Life and Environment.* Rev. ed. London: Fontana, 1959.

363

Evans, Michael. *Karl Marx*. London: Allen & Unwin; Bloomington, Ind.: Indiana University Press, 1975.

Garaudy, Roger. *Karl Marx: The Evolution of His Thought*. New York: International Publishers, 1967.

Lifshits, Mikhail. *The Philosophy of Art of Karl Marx*. Translated by Ralph B. Winn. Edited by Ángel Flores. New York: Critics Group, 1938.

Manuel, Frank E. *A Requiem for Karl Marx*. Cambridge, Mass.: Harvard University Press, 1995.

Marx, Karl, and Friedrich Engels. *Literature and Art: Selections from Their Writings*. New York: International Publishers, 1947.

Mayer, Gustav. *Friedrich Engels: A Biography*. New York: Knopf, 1936.

Mehring, Franz. *Karl Marx: The Story of His Life*. Edited by Ruth and Heinz Norden. New York: Covici, Friede, 1935; London: John Lane, 1936.

Nicolaevsky, Boris, and Otto Maenchen-Helfen. *Karl Marx: Man and Fighter*. Translated by Gwenda David and Eric Mosbacher. Philadelphia: J. B. Lippincott, 1936.

Plekhanov, Georgii. *Unaddressed Letters: Art and Social Life*. Moscow: Foreign Languages Publishing House, 1957.

Prawer, S. S. *Karl Marx and World Literature*. Oxford, England: Clarendon Press, 1976.

Rubel, Maximilien, and Margaret Manale. *Marx without Myth: A Chronological Study of His Life and Work*. New York: Harper & Row, 1975.

Rühle, Otto. *Karl Marx: His Life and Work*. New York: Viking, 1929.

Solomon, Maynard, ed. *Marxism and Art: Essays Classic and Contemporary*. New York: Knopf, 1973.

Tucker, Robert C., ed. *The Marx-Engels Reader*. New York: Norton, 1972.

Williams, Raymond. *Culture & Society: 1750-1950*. New York: Columbia University Press, 1958.

──────. *The Long Revolution*. New York: Columbia University Press, 1961.

──────. *Marxism and Literature*. Oxford, England: Oxford University Press, 1977.

MARXIST CRITICISM
England, Europe, and United States, 1920s-1970s

Practitioners of Marxist criticism have produced a diversity of thought and method in many countries. This movement in literary criticism ranges from the mid-nineteenth century, when Marx himself elaborated much of his work with literary examples, to the present day. The term Marxist criticism implies studies ranging from Marx's statements pertaining to art and literature in lieu of an aesthetic theory he never systematically formulated (for example, Mikhail Lifshits's *The Philosophy of Art of Karl Marx*, 1938) to political-economic readings of literary works (for example, Ian Watt's look at eighteenth-century English novels in *The Rise of the Novel*, 1947). It is generally concerned with understanding literature and writers as products of particular historical circumstances and ideologies. A distinction is made, in addition, between *interpreting* aesthetic events and *explaining* them.

Around the turn of the century, Georgy Valentinovich Plekhanov (1856-1918) and Franz Mehring (1846-1919) emerged as the earliest Marxist aesthetic theorists. Plekhanov's *Unaddressed Letters: Art and Social Life* (1899-1918; collected and published in 1957) asserts the necessity of utilizing a materialist view of history as he attempts to analyze the cultural and aesthetic production in both European and non-European cultures, while Mehring, in *Lessing-Legende* (1893), attempts a sociological analysis of works by Gotthold Lessing (1729-1781).

In Russia, Marxist aesthetics gradually became institutional doctrine, with the emergence of PROLETKULT after the revolution and, eventually, SOCIALIST REALISM. Bolshevik party leaders decided that writers must instill proper party consciousness and ideology through literature; Andrey Zhdanov (1896-1948) was a major proponent of this view. The 1934 Congress of Soviet Writers ushered in an era of such prescribed "proletarian" art. Before Socialist Realism became policy in the Soviet Union, however, writers and activists such as Lenin, Leon Trotsky (1879-1940), Vladimir Pereverzev (1882-1968), Maxim GORKY, and Plekhanov put forth diverse theses about art's role in society.

By the late 1920s and early 1930s, Marxist aestheticism had spread to England and the United States, where writers such as Christopher Caudwell (1907-1937) in *Illusion and Reality* (1937), Ralph Fox (1900-1937) in *The Novel and the People* (1937), Bernard Smith (1906-) in *Forces in American Criticism* (1939), and Granville Hicks (1901-1982) in *The Great Tradition* (1928) endeavored with varying degrees of success to situate literature and literary history as both social product and social instrument. During the 1920s in Germany, Georg LUKÁCS was formulating the body of work which would bring him wide recognition as the most important Marxist critic of his time. Lucien Goldmann (1913-1970) associated with Lukács and was influenced by his early work, *Die Theorie des Romans* (1920; *The Theory of the Novel*, 1971), as were philosophers from the Frankfurt School — Theodor W. Adorno (1903-1969), Walter Benjamin (1892-1940), Max Horkheimer (1895-1973), Herbert Marcuse (1898-1979), Jürgen Habermas (1929-), and Ernst Bloch (1885-1977). In Italy, Antonio Gramsci (1891-1937), Italian Communist Party founder, composed the influential *Quaderni del carcere* (1948-56; *Prison Notebooks*, 1991-) during the last years of his life while imprisoned by the Fascist government. His literary writings appear in *Letteratura e vita nazionale* (1950; Literature and National Life).

Elsewhere on the continent, some of the most notable Marxist treatises were seen a bit later. In *Pour une théorie de la production littéraire* (1966), Pierre Macherey (1938-) argues against Lukács, that the critic must examine a text's transformation of ideology from experience to art. Jean-Paul SARTRE (1905-1980) brings his EXISTENTIALIST ideas to bear on the concerns of Marxist criticism in *Critique of Dialectical Reason*

(1976), *What Is Literature?* (1949) and *Search for a Method* (1963). In *D'un réalisme sans rivages* (1963; Of a Realism without Shores), Roger Garaudy (1913-) calls for an expanding of the strictures of Socialist Realism to allow more creativity. Louis Althusser (1918-1990) explores the relationship between art and ideology, countering the claim that art is ideology. He writes that Marx's theories of history and dialectics indicate a new science, that of the history of "social formations," and describes Marxist practice in terms relating to scientific analysis.

Of recent importance are contributions from the United States and England by Raymond Williams (1921-), Fredric Jameson (1934-), and Terry Eagleton (1943-). Williams, in studies such as *Culture and Society: 1780-1950* (1958) and *Marxism and Literature* (1977), examines "the social experience of culture as others had lived it, and as one was trying to live it oneself" in the context of social literary analysis. Eagleton, a former student of Williams, writes in *Criticism and Ideology* (1976) about problems of Marxist criticism in achieving "a materialist *explanation* of the bases of literary value." Jameson's important *The Political Unconscious* (1981) explores "narrative as a socially symbolic act," in historical context while also situating constructs of the unconscious and desire, drawing on psychoanalytic modes of critique (*see* FREUDIAN and JUNGIAN CRITICISM).

New methods and fields of theory have grown out of Marxist criticism, most notably, new historicism and postcolonial and cultural theory; in many senses these trends overlap both with each other and with what is known as the "traditional" Marxist criticism surveyed above. Where traditional Marxism is concerned with economy and power bases as they operate among realms of social class (ostensibly within one region or nation), postcolonial and cultural theory extends political economy and power, bringing these to bear on international relationships of domination and revolution, colonialism and imperialism. Ways of describing historical processes are imperative to both orientations. It is perhaps too soon to satisfactorily assess these developments, but their current and projected impact warrants mention. Some of the main critics associated with new historicism include Stephen Greenblatt (n.d.), Joel Fineman (n.d.), Elizabeth Fox-Genovese (1941-), and Stanley Fish (1938-) [for an introduction, see H. Aram Veeser's *The New Historicism*, 1989]; with postcolonial and cultural criticism: Edward Said (1935-), Gayatri Chakravorty Spivak (1942-), Omafume F. Onoge (n.d.), Homi K. Bhabha (1949-), and Benedict Anderson (1936-). These critical tendencies may be said to overlap because they are certainly to some extent inspired by the socially cataclysmic events in the postwar world: violent revolutions for independence throughout Asia, Africa, South and Central America, and the Middle East; invigorated attention to social problems around dimensions of ethnicity, class, national origin, and gender (*see also* FEMINIST CRITICISM); and increased travel, emigration, and exile of scholars from these parts of the world to western Europe and the United States, bringing multiple cultural experiences to bear in the academy.

While the body of Marxist aesthetic criticism is seen by some as offering another approach to literary analysis, such as psychoanalytical criticism and SEMIOTICS, strong Marxist scholars insist on an active critical methodology that could lead to social change.

✦•✦

Lukács, Georg (1885-1971)
Hungarian-born German philosopher, political activist, and literary critic.

Lukács's interest in literature predated his activities in politics and coexisted with social and political concerns throughout his life. His early work includes such philosophical-literary analyses as *Die Seele und die Formen* (1911; *Soul and Form,* 1975), *A modern dráma fejlödésének története* (1911; History of the Development of Modern Drama), and *Die Theorie des Romans* (1920; *Theory of the Novel,* 1971). In this last, Lukács describes the history of the novel in terms of the history of the rise of capitalism, paralleling a shift in consciousness from wholeness to fragmentation. His conversion to Marxism led to his writing of GESCHICHTE UND KLASSENBEWUSSTSEIN (1923; *History and Class Consciousness,* 1971). Lukács's later works, such as *Literaturnii teorii xix veka i marxizma* (1937; Marxism and Nineteenth-Century Literary Criticism), *Essays über den Realismus* (1948; *Essays on Realism,* 1980), *A realizmus problémái* (1948; *Studies in European Realism,* 1950), *Der russische Realismus in der Weltliteratur* (1949; Russian Realism in World Literature), and *Der historische Roman* (1955; *The Historical Novel,* 1962), though not without their problems (as raised by Bertolt BRECHT [*see* EPIC THEATER], Eagleton, and others), evidence attempts at synthesizing dialectical materialism, German classical tradition, and aesthetic analysis.

Geschichte und Klassenbewusstsein (1923; *History and Class Consciousness,* 1971).

Lukács wrote this, his major Marxist theoretical work, in exile in Vienna in 1919 after the Communist government in Hungary was overthrown. As a leader of the Hungarian Communist Party, he was closely involved in the political upheavals. Three of the essays first appeared, in different versions, in Max Weber's (1864-1920) *Economy and Society* (1920).

Lukács's major achievement in this work is his elaboration of a theory of reification. Capitalism produces reification—the making of myths from things, transforming that which is concrete into an abstract idea of the concrete thing—which enables the ruling classes to exploit things and people. "Its basis is that a relation between people takes on the character of a thing and thus acquires a 'phantom objectivity,' an autonomy that seems so strictly rational and all-embracing as to conceal every trace of its fundamental nature: the relation between people." As Marx put it, a commodity fetishism infects society. Commodity fetishism produces the alienation of cultural and organic objects, including human beings and, according to Lukács, the fostering in people of passivity and a sense of personal and social fragmentation. Lukács therefore calls for methods to transform the passive subject into an active agent with a critical consciousness. Consciousness must become conscious of itself as consciousness; once workers become conscious of themselves as workers as well as the material conditions which have determined them to be workers, change is possible.

⇝•⇜

Further Reading

Adorno, Theodor. *Prisms*. Translated by Samuel and Shierry Weber. Cambridge, Mass.: MIT Press, 1981.

Althusser, Louis. *Essays in Self-Criticism*. London: NLB; Atlantic Highlands, N.J.: Humanities Press, 1976.

———. *For Marx*. Translated by Ben Brewster. New York: Pantheon Books, 1969.

———. *Lenin and Philosophy*. New York: Monthly Review Press, 1971.

———. *Politics and History: Montesquieu, Rousseau, Hegel and Marx*. Translated by Ben Brewster. London: NLB, 1972.

Anderson, Benedict. *Imagined Communities: Reflections on the Origin and Spread of Nationalism*. London: Verso, 1983. Rev. ed., London: Verso, 1991.

Arato, Andrew, and Paul Breines. *The Young Lukács and the Origins of Western Marxism*. New York: Seabury Press, 1979.

Arvon, Henri. *Marxist Esthetics*. Translated by H. R. Lane. Ithaca, N.Y.: Cornell University Press, 1973.

Bahr, Ehrhard, and Ruth Goldschmidt Kunzer. *Georg Lukács*. New York: Ungar, 1972.

Benjamin, Walter. *Understanding Brecht*. London: NLB, 1973.

Bennett, Tony. *Formalism and Marxism*. London: Methuen, 1979.

Bernstein, J. M. *The Philosophy of the Novel: Lukács, Marxism and the Dialectics of Form*. Minneapolis: University of Minnesota Press, 1984.

Bhabha, Homi K., ed. *Nation and Narration*. London: Routledge, 1990.

Brecht, Bertolt. *On Theater: The Development of an Aesthetic*. Edited and translated by John Willett. New York: Hill and Wang; London: Methuen, 1973.

Brewer, Anthony. *Marxist Theories of Imperialism: A Critical Survey*. London: Routledge & Kegan Paul, 1980. 2nd. ed., London: Routledge, 1990.

Caudwell, Christopher. *See* Sprigg, Christopher St. John

Demetz, Peter. *Marx, Engels, and the Poets: Origins of Marxist Literary Criticism*. Translated by Jeffrey L. Sammons. Chicago: University of Chicago Press, 1959.

Eagleton, Terry. *Criticism and Ideology*. London: NLB; Atlantic Heights, N.J.: Humanities Press, 1976.

————. *Literary Theory: An Introduction*. Minneapolis: University of Minnesota Press, 1983. 2nd. ed. Cambridge, England: Blackwell, 1996.

————. *Marxism and Literary Criticism*. Berkeley, Calif.: University of California Press, 1976.

Eagleton, Terry, and Brian Wicker, eds. *From Culture to Revolution*. London: Sheed and Ward, 1968.

Fox, Ralph. *The Novel and the People*. New York: International Publishers, 1937.

Goldmann, Lucien. *The Hidden God*. New York: Humanities Press, 1964.

Gramsci, Antonio. *Prison Notebooks*. Edited by Joseph Buttigieg. New York: Columbia University Press, 1991-.

Gugelberger, Georg M., ed. *Marxism and African Literature*. London: Longman, 1985.

Horkheimer, Max, and Theodor Adorno. *Dialectic of Enlightenment*. Translated by John Cumming. New York: Herder & Herder, 1972.

Jameson, Fredric. *Marxism and Form: Twentieth-Century Dialectical Theories of Literature*. Princeton, N.J.: Princeton University Press, 1971.

————. *The Political Unconscious*. Ithaca, N.Y.: Cornell University Press, 1981.

Jay, M. *The Dialectical Imagination: A History of the Frankfurt School and the Institute of Social Research, 1923-1950*. Boston: Little, Brown, 1973.

————. *Marxism and Totality*. Berkeley, Calif.: University of California Press, 1984.

Kadarkay, A. *Georg Lukács: Life, Thought, and Politics*. Cambridge, Mass.: Blackwell, 1991.

Lang, Berel, and Forrest Williams, eds. *Marxism and Art: Writings in Aesthetics and Criticism*. New York: McKay, 1972.

Lenin, Vladimir Ilich. *Articles on Tolstoy*. Moscow: Progress Publishers, 1951.

Lifshits, Mikhail. *The Philosophy of Art of Karl Marx*. Edited by Ángel Flores. Translated by Ralph B. Winn. New York: Critics Group, 1938.

Marx, Karl, and Friedrich Engels. *Literature and Art: Selections from Their Writings*. New York: International Publishers, 1947.

Plekhanov, Georgii. *Unaddressed Letters: Art and Social Life*. Translated by A. Fineberg. Moscow: Foreign Languages Publishing House, 1957.

Prawer, S. S. *Karl Marx and World Literature*. Oxford, England: Clarendon Press, 1976.

Resnick, Stephen A., and Richard D. Wolff. *Knowledge and Class: A Marxian Critique of Political Economy*. Chicago: University of Chicago Press, 1987.

Said, Edward W. *Orientalism*. New York: Pantheon Books, 1978.

————. *The World, the Text, and the Critic*. Cambridge, Mass.: Harvard University Press, 1983.

Sánchez Váchez, A. *Art and Society: Essays in Marxist Aesthetics*. Translated by Maro Riofrancos. New York: Monthly Review Press, 1974.

Sartre, Jean-Paul. *Search for a Method*. Translated by Hazel E. Barnes. New York: Knopf, 1963.

————. *What Is Literature?* Translated by Bernard Frechtman. New York: Philosophical Library, 1949.

Solomon, Maynard, ed. *Marxism and Art: Essays Classic & Contemporary*. New York: Knopf, 1973.

Spivak, Gayatri C. *The Post-Colonial Critic: Interviews, Strategies, Dialogues*. New York: Routlędge, 1990.

Sprigg, Christopher St. John. *Illusion and Reality*. London: Macmillan, 1937.

Tar, Zoltán. *The Frankfurt School: The Critical Theories of Max Horkheimer and Theodor W. Adorno*. New York: Wiley, 1977.

Trotsky, Leon. *Literature and Revolution*. Translated by Rose Strunsky. New York: International Publishers; London: Allen & Unwin, 1925.

Veeser, H. Aram, ed. *The New Historicism*. New York: Routledge, 1989.

Watt, Ian. *The Rise of the Novel*. Berkeley, Calif.: University of California Press, 1957.

Williams, Raymond. *Culture & Society: 1750-1950*. New York: Columbia University Press, 1958.

————. *The Long Revolution*. New York: Columbia University Press, 1961.

————. *Marxism and Literature*. Oxford, England: Oxford University Press, 1977.

————. *Problems in Materialism and Culture*. London: Verso, 1980.

MATINÉE POÉTIQUE
Japan, 1940s-1970s

Matinée Poétique, also termed the First Postwar Wave, was a small left-wing Japanese group that rose to prominence following the end of World War II. Far less concerned with politics than their counterparts, the group most distinguished itself by its initial scathing assessments of Japanese culture and literature and its later scholarship of both Japanese and European letters. Formed in 1942 by Katō Shūichi (1919-), Nakamura Shin'ichirō (1918-), and Fukunaga Takehiko (1918-1979), the Matinée Poétique group chose its foreign name, that of a Parisian poetry troupe, in calculated defiance of nationalistic legislation and public patriotism. Their most representative work is the critical manifesto entitled *1946: Bungakuteki* (1977; 1946: Literary Inquiry). In it the three authors commented on a wide cross-section of classical and modern world literature, during the course championing left-wing French writers of the 1930s and excoriating the stylistic simplicity, unimaginativeness, and provincialism of most contemporary Japanese writing. Their purpose was to refute the common perception that Japanese culture and literature represented entirely unique phenomena in contrast to that of other nations and that Japanese writers, therefore, were impervious to the type of criticisms and evaluations issued elsewhere.

In the individual careers that followed upon their mutual pronouncement, Katō, Nakamura, and Fukunaga strove to create works that could be judged by universal standards. Theirs was an attempt to disprove the validity of such popular, and to their minds undemanding, forms as the I-NOVEL and, in their place, create unmistakably modern and original works that reflected their absorption of the techniques and concerns of a variety of literary traditions. Although none succeeded in attaining major status outside their country, the members of Matinée Poétique are regarded as among the most significant spokespersons for integrity and change in postwar Japanese literature.

Further Reading

Keene, Donald. "Postwar Literature." In his *Dawn to the West: Japanese Literature in the Modern Era*. New York: Holt, Rinehart & Winston, 1984.

MAY FOURTH MOVEMENT (Wu-ssu Yün-tung)
China, 1916-1921

The May Fourth Movement's literary arm, also termed the New Culture Movement, the Intellectual Revolution, or the Literary Revolution, arose during the late 1910s in the newly formed Republic of China to depose classical language and instate the vernacular. The May Fourth writers strove, in addition, to supplant Confucianism with secular REALISM and construct a democratic literature accessible to the masses. The success of the movement was virtually instantaneous, the influence on younger writers incomparably profound. Nearly all the literary societies, periodicals, and works published in the tumultuous decade that followed stemmed in some manner from the May Fourth Movement.

An American-educated scholar named HU Shih cautiously began the movement for literary reform in 1917. Recently returned from Columbia University to National Peking University, where a vanguard of liberal intellectuals were teaching, Hu decided to publish "WEN-HSÜEH KAI-LIAN CH'U-I" (1917; A Tentative Proposal for Literary Reform). The essay was enthusiastically welcomed by CH'EN Tu-hsiu, editor of *Hsin ch'ing-nien* (New Youth) and newly appointed dean of the College of Letters at Peking University. The preceding year Hu had proclaimed in a letter to Ch'en that *ku wen* (classical language) had been dead for two thousand years. Now he determined the time was auspicious for *ku wen* to be replaced by *pei hua*, the plain, colloquial language of the common people. As both Hu and Ch'en fortified this proposal with ensuing essays, such prominent literary conservatives as Lin Shu (1852-1924) expressed their outrage, believing that reforms in language would mean the collapse of a dignified national literature. By 1919, however, opposition all but disappeared in the wake of the May Fourth Student Movement, which erupted in response to the Chinese government's pro-Japanese concessions during the Versailles Peace Conference. At this point the student and literary movements naturally merged, united in their belief that Western examples of science and democracy could help correct the cultural and political problems of China, which had been floundering under warlordism since 1911. Although the political wishes of the May Fourth Movement never materialized, the Ministry of Education was persuaded in 1920 to announce that vernacular coursework would be introduced at the elementary level. A further outcome occurred in 1921, when *pei hua* was relabeled *kuo yü* (national language). Consequently, mass education was greatly facilitated and groups that had been discriminated against for generations, particularly women, began to enjoy an increase in social freedoms and opportunities.

The movement to eradicate classical literature fostered new challenges for the May Fourth writers, the two foremost being how to establish new models of artistic excellence and how to redefine the purpose of creative writing. Like their Japanese counterparts, these writers settled upon the values and techniques of European literary movements to establish a foundation for addressing specifically Chinese concerns. The era thus inaugurated became one of heightened interest in the importation and translation of literary models. Although experimentation in the essay, poem, and drama forms helped further the literary revolution, the dominant forum for experimentation was the short story. The first writer to publish Western-influenced, yet accomplished original stories in the vernacular was Lu Hsün. His "K'uang-jen jih-chi" (1918; "The Diary of a Madman," 1941), though patterned after Nikolai Gogol's "Notes of a Madman" (1835), fixed a high standard of psychological Realism, concision, and thematic import. Lu Hsün's later story "Ah Q cheng-chuan" (1921; "The True Story of Ah Q," 1926), with its original style, acute social criticism, and timeless message, confirmed the rapid ascendancy of vernacular fiction in China.

Ironically, given the morass of political events and outcries for reform that governed the late 1910s, the core of the May Fourth group attempted to remain disengaged from active politicizing. This policy was established early in 1918 when Ch'en agreed to share editorship of *Hsin ch'ing-nien* with Hu Shih, Ch'ien Hsuan-t'ung (1887-1939), Li Ta-chao (1888-1927), and Liu Tu (n.d.), all fellow professors at Peking University. Although the cumulative efforts of these academics inspired the appearance of numerous other periodicals and societies devoted to vernacular writing and the introduction and emulation of Western literature, the movement itself was short-lived. This was largely due to mounting public dissatisfaction with the government and the activist temperament of Ch'en, who by the end of 1918 had, with Li Ta-chao, founded a new weekly expressly designed to comment on political policy. In 1920 the movement became decidedly leftist under Ch'en's direction, alienating such moderate supporters as Hu Shih and Chou Tso-jên, Lu Hsün's younger brother. Ch'en's transference of *Hsin ch'ing-nien* from Peking to Shanghai, where the periodical became the organ of the nascent Chinese Communist Party, effectively marked the dissolution of the literary movement as it was originally conceived.

The legacy of the May Fourth Movement — the establishment of a new literary language and the advancement of the short story and essay genres — was inherited during the 1920s by two powerful factions, the CREATION SOCIETY and the LITERARY RESEARCH ASSOCIATION. Through these groups as well as through the continuing activities of Hu Shih, Lu Hsün, and Chou Tso-jên, the May Fourth Movement extended its vitality and ushered in the modern age of Chinese letters.

⤞•⤝

Ch'en Tu-hsiu (1879-1942), Chinese essayist and editor.

The founder of *Hsin ch'ing-nien*, Ch'en was a strong advocate of cultural, educational, and political change in Republican China. His support of Hu Shih's proposals for literary reform — a cause that had garnered his interest since 1904, when he launched his first vernacular newspaper — was instrumental to the rapid success of the May Fourth literary Movement. Ch'en's opposition to Tuan Ch'i-jui's monarchical, pro-Japanese rule precipitated his further involvement in the actual student uprising of 1919. Following a brief imprisonment, Ch'en left for Shanghai and furthered his understanding of and allegiance to Marxist-Leninist thought. He became the primary force behind the formation of the Chinese Communist Party and served as its general secretary until 1927, when he provoked the disfavor of party officials for his efforts at conciliation with the Kuomintang. After promulgating Trotskyism for a time, Ch'en in his last years reaffirmed his belief in the institutions of science and democracy to bring about China's regeneration. In addition to his lifelong work as social critic and political propagandist, Ch'en also distinguished himself in the fields of philology and etymology.

"On Literary Revolution" (1917).

Published one month after Hu Shih's "Wen-hsüeh kai-lian ch'u-i" (1917; A Tentative Proposal for Literary Reform), Ch'en's essay alerted literary conservatives to the militant core of *Hsin ch'ing-nien* while inciting intellectual liberals to adopt ever more progressive, Western-influenced cultural stances. The three basic principles Ch'en enunciated were: "down with ornate toadying aristocratic literature, to build a simple and lyrical national literature"; "down with outdated elaborative classical literature to build up a fresh and sincere realistic literature"; and "down with obscure and obdurate reclusive literature of mountains and forests to build up a clear, popular social literature."

⤞•⤝

Chou Tso-jên (1885-1966?)
Chinese essayist, poet, translator, and historian.

More well-known at the beginning of the May Fourth Movement than Lu Hsün — with whom he participated in a number of editorial ventures — Chou began his career as a translator, but after moving to Peking in 1917 he became attached to the aggregate of writers and intellectuals interested in literary reform. Chou is remembered for his peaceful, Enlightenment outlook and estimable scholarship, reflected in such works as "Jen ti wen-hsueh" (1918; Humane Literature) and *Ou-chou wen-hsueh shih* (1918; History of European Literature). An authority on foreign literature and a master of the social essay, Chou typifies many of the finer features associated with the May Fourth Movement.

"Jen ti wen-hsueh" (1918; Humane Literature).

One of Chou's most important essays, "Jen ti wen-hsueh" posits that humans are both animal and rational beings. The literature of the new age, therefore, must address humanity in its entirety, displaying an awareness of present social and individual problems as well as a view toward their improvement. Chou reaffirmed these convictions in his manifesto for the Literary Research Association, a group which shared his marked interest in foreign scholarship.

✦•✦

Hu Shih (1891-1962)
Chinese essayist, poet, historian, and short-story writer.

Hu Shih was one of the most illustrious literary figures of modern China. As early as 1915, while still completing his doctorate in philosophy at Columbia under John Dewey, he expressed the need for comprehensive reform of language and literature in his country. Less interested in the political ramifications of such reforms, Hu disassociated himself from the May Fourth Movement in 1921. His interest in vernacular literature, however, continued unabated and led to such works as *Pai-hua wen-hsüeh shih* (1928; A History of Vernacular Literature), a study which emphasized the deep-rooted tradition of *pai-hua* in Chinese letters. Hu held several posts of distinction during his lifetime, including that of Chinese ambassador to the United States from 1938 to 1942.

"Wen-hsüeh kai-lian ch'u-i" (1917; A Tentative Proposal for Literary Reform).

The opening salvo in the movement for literary reform, Hu Shih's essay is peculiar in that it is written in a classical, albeit familiar, style. Scholars regard this publishing decision as an indicator of Hu's seriousness and a polite concession to reigning traditionalists who, above all, required a convincing and dignified argument for the necessity of reform. In later essays, Hu adopted a less apologetic stance and switched to the vernacular, having gained the support of a large literary community in Peking with his original proposal.

❧●❧

Lu Hsün (pseud. of Chou Shu-jên, 1881-1936)
Chinese short-story writer and critic.

Lu Hsün is recognized not only as a leader of the May Fourth Movement but as the father of modern Chinese literature. Lu Hsün abandoned a career in medicine in 1905, believing that serious literary endeavor promised a more efficacious solution for his nation's ills. However, it was not until the appearance of "K'uang-jen jih-chi" in 1918 that he firmly established himself as a writer. From then until 1926 he wrote twenty-five stories, collected in *Na Han* (1923; *Call to Arms*, 1981) and *P'ang huang* (1926; *Wandering*, 1981). During this time he also published *Chung-kuo hsiao shuo shih lüeh* (1924; *A Brief History of Chinese Fiction*, 1959), a pioneering work of pre-modern scholarship.

Dedicated to the tasks of supporting younger writers and introducing foreign works to Chinese readers, Lu Hsün helped found a number of small societies, each with its own periodical. His reputation as a cunning sociopolitical satirist and a bold spokesman for human rights eventually brought him into close contact with the Chinese Communist Party, whose leadership prevailed upon him to head the LEAGUE OF LEFT-WING WRITERS, a large organization formed in 1930 and devoted to proletarian literature. Rumors of his planned assassination by the Nationalist Party forced him to seek refuge in Shanghai, where he continued composing his *tsa-wen* (topical essays) until his death. Because of his highly compressed, lyrical, and engaging style, and the wide scope of his literary activities both during and after the May Fourth era, Lu Hsün has become the most revered name in modern Chinese literature.

"Ah Q cheng-chuan" (1921; "The True Story of Ah Q," 1926).

The most representative work of the May Fourth Movement, "The True Story of Ah Q" is a long, politically pointed narrative set in 1911, the time of the Manchu Dynasty's fall and the rise of the Republic of China. Ah Q, an unthinking, pitiful coolie, daydreams of gaining the respect of his fellow villagers but mishandles several opportunities to do so. Because of his overwhelming sense of self-importance, however, each defeat becomes for him a "spiritual victory." When he sees signs of the impending revolution he aspires to join the cause, but is shunned by the local gentry, who have only lately, and spuriously, preceded him. Although an alternately comic and repellent character, Ah Q becomes by the end of the story a tragic figure who, despite his many faults, shines in comparison to his social superiors, who dispassionately execute him for a crime he did not commit.

Lu Hsün presented Ah Q as a critical portrait of the pre-modern national character, committed to Confucianism and the perpetuation of a system rife with injustices. More importantly, however, is Lu Hsün's indirect indictment of post-revolution society, which he perceived as little altered with regard to palpable social changes.

375

❦•❧
Further Reading

Chen Po-ta, et al. *Commemorating Lu Hsün — Our Forerunner in the Cultural Revolution*.
Peking: Foreign Languages Press, 1967.

Ch'en Shou-yi. "The Literary Revolution." In *Chinese Literature: A Historical Introduction*.
New York: Ronald Press Co., 1961.

Chou Min-Chih. *Hu Shih and Intellectual Choice in Modern China*. Ann Arbor, Mich.:
University of Michigan Press, 1984.

Chow Tse-tsung. *The May Fourth Movement: Intellectual Revolution in Modern China*. Ann
Arbor, Mich.: University of Michigan Press, 1960.

Elegant, Robert S. "A Villain and a Hero: Ch'en Tu-Hsiu and Ch'ü Ch'iu-Pai." In *China's Red
Masters: Political Biographies of the Chinese Communist Leaders*. New York: Twayne, 1951.

Grieder, Jerome B. *Hu Shih and the Chinese Renaissance: Liberalism in the Chinese
Revolution, 1917-1937*. Cambridge, Mass.: Harvard University Press, 1970.

Hsu, Raymond S. W. *The Style of Lu Hsün: Vocabulary and Usage*. Hong Kong: Centre of
Asian Studies, University of Hong Kong, 1979.

Huang Sung-K'ang. *Lu Hsün and the New Culture Movement of Modern China*. Westport,
Conn.: Hyperion Press, 1975.

Hu Shih. *The Chinese Renaissance*. Chicago: University of Chicago Press, 1934.

Kuo, Thomas C. *Ch'en Tu-hsiu and the Chinese Communist Movement*. South Orange, N.J.:
Seton Hall University Press, 1975.

Lyell, William A., Jr. *Lu Hsün's Vision of Reality*. Berkeley, Calif.: University of California Press,
1976.

Mills, Harriet C. "Lu Xun: Literature and Revolution — from Mara to Marx." In *Modern
Chinese Literature in the May Fourth Era*. Edited by Merle Goldman. Cambridge, Mass.:
Harvard University Press, 1977.

Pollard, D. E. "Chou Tso-jen and Cultivating One's Garden." *Asia Major* XI, 2 (1965): 180-98.

Semanov, V. I. *Lu Hsün and His Predecessors*. White Plains, N.Y.: M. E. Sharpe, 1980.

Wolff, Ernst. *Chou Tso-jen*. New York: Twayne, 1971.

Yang, Gladys, ed. Introduction to *Silent China: Selected Writings of Lu Xun*. London: Oxford
University Press, 1973.

MAY GROUP (Květen)
Czechoslovakia, 1950s-1960s

A Czechoslovakian movement launched in part by the Russian thaw of 1956, the May
Group concentrated on poetry freed from political ideology. The most notable writers of
the May Group were Miroslav Holub (1923-) and Jiri Šotola (1924-).

❦•❧
Further Reading

Alvarez, A. "Miroslav Holub." In his *Beyond All This Fiddle: Essays 1955-1967*. New York:
Random House, 1969.

French, A. *Czech Writers and Politics, 1945-1969*. Boulder, Colo.: East European Monographs, 1982; distributed by Columbia University Press, New York.

MBARI CLUB
Nigeria, 1960s

The Mbari Club, a West African publishing enclave christened by noted novelist Chinua Achebe (1930-), was founded by Ulli Beier (1922-) in the Nigerian university town of Ibadan. Its purpose was to foster native African literature in English. The group was most active between 1961 and 1964 and spread throughout Nigeria with the assistance of such regional leaders as YORUBA dramatist Duro Ladipo (1931-1978).

❖•❖

Further Reading

Beier, Ulli, ed. Introduction to *African Literature: An Anthology of Critical Writing*. London: Longmans, 1979.
———. *Black Orpheus: An Anthology of African and Afro-American Prose*. Ikeja, Nigeria: Longmans of Nigeria, 1964.
Carroll, David. *Chinua Achebe*. New York: Twayne, 1970.
Champion, Ernest A. *Mr. Baldwin, I Presume: James Baldwin — Chinua Achebe, a Meeting of the Minds*. Lanham, Md.: University Press of America, 1995.
Focus on Duro Lapido: A Nigerian Playwright Views Today's Theater in His Country. North Hollywood, Calif.: Center for Cassette Studies, 1969.
Innes, C. L. *Chinua Achebe*. Cambridge, England: Cambridge University Press, 1990.
Innes, C. L., and Bernth Lindfors. *Critical Perspectives on Chinua Achebe*. Washington, D.C.: Three Continents Press, 1978.
Obafemi, Olu. *Forty Years in African Art and Life: Reflections on Ulli Beier*. Bayreuth, Germany: Iwalewa-Haus, University of Bayreuth, 1993.
Peters, Jonathan. *A Dance of Masks: Senghor, Achebe, Soyinka*. Washington, D.C.: Three Continents Press, 1978.
Ravenscroft, Arthur. *Chinua Achebe*. Harlow, England: Longmans, 1969.
Wren, Robert M. *Achebe's World: The Historical and Cultural Context of the Novels of Chinua Achebe*. Washington, D.C.: Three Continents Press, 1980.

MEHIAN GROUP
Armenians in Turkey, 1910s

Central to the modern revolution in Armenian literature, the *Mehian* Group and journal was formed by Armenian writers in Constantinople in 1914 and led by the celebrated poet Daniel Varoujan (1884-1915). Despite Varoujan's early death during the Turkish massacre of Armenians, the movement continued with the work of Aharon Dadourian (1877-1965), Hagop Oshagan (1883-1948), and Kostan Zaryan (1885-

1969), all of whom favored a broad literature of ideas, unhindered by narrow rules of objectivism.

Further Reading

Margossian, Marzbed. "Armenian Literature." In *Encyclopedia of World Literature in the Twentieth Century*. 3rd ed. Edited by Steven R. Serafin. Farmington Hills, Mich.: St. James Press, 1999.

Tolegian, A. "Daniel Varoujan." *Ararat* 17 (1976): 16-26.

MERCURE DE FRANCE GROUP. *See* SYMBOLISM, France

MERZ
Germany, 1920s

Merz, begun in Hanover, Germany, around 1920, was the brainchild of DADA poet and collage artist Kurt Schwitters (1887-1948). The one-man movement arose as the result of an aesthetic disagreement between Schwitters and the leader of Cologne Dada, Richard Huelsenbeck (1892-1974). Unlike Huelsenbeck, Schwitters advocated art's independence from political theory and political activism. Consequently, he was more closely aligned with Zurich/Paris Dadaists Jean (Hans) Arp (1887-1966), Francis Picabia (1879-1953), Georges Ribemont-Dessaignes (1884-1974), and Tristan Tzara (1896-1963).

The term Merz, possibly a portmanteau word but more likely a fragmentary Germanic syllable, was created by Schwitters to emphasize the uniqueness of his vision. For him, it was an all-encompassing term suggesting both process and product, a term that exploded existing boundaries of literature and art. As he wrote in an explanatory essay published in 1921: "My aim is the Merz composite art work, that embraces all branches of art in an artistic unit." Specifically, Schwitters was intensively interested in the interplay of words, materials, and people. Hence, such works as his poem "Anna Blume" (1919; "Anna Blossom Has Wheels, Merz Poem No. 1," 1981 [in Motherwell, 1981]) assumed collage form. One of Schwitters predominant activities was to glean from his personal environment unrelated objects—the substances, signposts, and detritus of society—and make of them something new and dynamic. Schwitters's work spanned the disciplines of poetry and polemics, architecture and sculpture, painting and graphics, drama and music. From 1923 until 1932, the years during which he published his magazine *Merz*, Schwitters attempted to rekindle the spirit of Dada, with the occasional aid of such figures as Arp, Russian CONSTRUCTIVIST El Lissitzky (1890-1941), and *DE STIJL* founder Theo van Doesburg (1883-1931). Like the major figures of Dada, Schwitters has exerted an incalculable influence on the direction of contemporary experimental art and literature.

❖•❖
Further Reading

Dietrich, Dorothea. *The Collages of Kurt Schwitters: Tradition and Innovation*. Cambridge, England: Cambridge University Press, 1993.

Elderfield, John. *Kurt Schwitters*. New York: Thames & Hudson, 1985.

Fuchs, Rudolf Herman. *Conflicts with Modernism, or, The Absence of Kurt Schwitters*. Bern, Switzerland: Gachnang & Springer, 1991.

Last, Rex W. *German Dadaist Literature: Kurt Schwitters, Hugo Ball, Hans Arp*. New York: Twayne, 1973.

Mac Low, Jackson. *42 Merzgedichte in Memoriam Kurt Schwitters: February 1987-September 1989*. Barrytown, N.Y.: Station Hill, 1994.

Morton, Colin. *The Merzbook: Kurt Schwitter's Poems*. Kingston, Canada: Quarry Press, 1987.

Motherwell, Robert, ed. *The Dada Painters and Poets: An Anthology*. 2nd ed. Boston: G. K. Hall, 1981.

Schmalenbach, Werner. *Kurt Schwitters*. New York: H. N. Abrams, 1970.

Schwitters, Kurt. *Kurt Schwitters: A Retrospective Exhibition*. Dallas, Tex.: Dallas Museum of Fine Arts, 1965.

————. *Merz*. 2nd ed. New York: Marlborough Gallery, 1973.

————. *Merz = Kurt Schwitters*. London: Marlborough Fine Art Museum, 1972.

————. *Poems, Performance Pieces, Proses, Plays, Poetics*. Edited and translated by Jerome Rothenberg and Pierre Joris. Philadelphia: Temple University Press, 1993.

Steinitz, Kate T. *Kurt Schwitters: A Portrait from Life*. Berkeley, Calif.: University of California Press, 1968.

Strauss, Monica J. *Kurt Schwitters, Words and Works: Art and Publications*. "Biographical Chronology" by Hans Bollinger. New York: Helen Serger/La Boetie, 1985.

Themerson, Stefan. *Kurt Schwitters in England*. London: Gaberbocchus, 1958.

Webster, Michael. *Reading Visual Poetry after Futurism: Marinetti, Apollinaire, Schwitters, Cummings*. New York: P. Lang, 1995.

METACRITICISM. *See* READER-RESPONSE CRITICISM AND RECEPTION THEORY

METAREALISM
Israel, 1960s

Metarealism originated in Israel during the 1960s as a Hebrew-language movement dedicated to a metaphysical portrayal of reality much in the manner of Albert CAMUS (*see* EXISTENTIALISM) and Franz KAFKA (*see* MODERNISM, Austria and Germany). Writers associated with the movement, which drew much of its power from prose that grappled with the Holocaust, included Romanian-born Aharon Appelfeld (1932-), Israel Eliraz (1936-), Russian-born Yitzhak Orpaz (1923-), David Shahar (1926-), Russian-born Benyamin Tammuz (1919-1989), and Avraham B. Yehoshua (1936-).

⇒•⇐

Further Reading

Alter, Robert. "Fiction in a State of Siege." In his *Defenses of the Imagination: Jewish Writers and Modern Historical Crisis*. Philadelphia: Jewish Publication Society of America, 1977.

Appelfeld, Aron. *Beyond Despair: Three Lectures and a Conversation with Philip Roth*. Translated by Jeffrey M. Green. New York: Fromm International, 1994.

Barzel, Hillel. *Metarealistic Hebrew Prose*. Tel Aviv: Agudat ha-sofrim ha-'irrim be-Yisra'el le-yad Hotsa' at Masadah, Ramat-Gan, 1974.

Bernstein, Michael André. *Foregone Conclusions: Against Apocalyptic History*. Berkeley, Calif.: University of California Press, 1994.

Ginsburg, Alix E. *Jerusalem Diminished: Aspects of Jerusalem in the Contemporary Hebrew Short Story (in the Works of David Shachar, Aharon Apelfeld, Amos Oz and A.B. Yehoshua)*. Doctoral thesis, Brandeis University, 1984.

Ramraz-Raukh, Gilah. *Aharon Appelfeld, the Holocaust and Beyond*. Bloomington, Ind.: Indiana University Press, 1994.

Shahar, David. *News from Jerusalem: Stories*. Translated by Dalya Bilu and others. Boston: Houghton Mifflin, 1974.

METHOD, THE and METHOD-ACTING. *See* GROUP THEATER, United States

MEZZANINE OF POETRY
Russia, 1910s

The Mezzanine of Poetry, the Moscow branch of EGO-FUTURISM, was formed in 1913 by Vadim Shershenevich (1893-1942) and Lev Zak (1896-?). Of the Russian Futurists, Shershenevich was one of the most strongly affected by Italian FUTURISM; following completion of his treatise *Futurizm bez maski* (1913; Futurism without a Mask), the earliest comprehensive account of the movement in Russia, Shershenevich translated several seminal works by Filippo MARINETTI. Like Marinetti, Shershenevich conceived the Futurist poem as a fluid series of word images. Other writers associated with the Mezzanine included Konstantin Bolshakov (1895-1940) and Ryurik Ivnev (1891-1981). By 1914 Shershenevich had allied himself with the CUBO-FUTURISTS; a few years later he went on to found the IMAGINISTS.

☙•❧
Further Reading

Lawton, Anna. *Vadim Shershenevich: From Futurism to Imaginism*. New Haven, Conn.: Yale University Press, 1981.

Terras, Victor, ed. *Handbook of Russian Literature*. New Haven, Conn.: Yale University Press, 1985.

MILLÎ EDEBIYAT. *See* NATIONAL LITERATURE MOVEMENT

MINSK GROUP
Byelorussia, c. 1925-1937

Active from approximately 1925 to 1937, the Minsk Group took its name from the Byelorussian capital in which it was centered. The Minsk writers, all Yiddish-speaking poets and novelists, were proponents of SOCIALIST REALISM and thus opposed to their SYMBOLIST counterparts in Kiev. Chief among the group were Selig Axelrod (1904-1941), Izzy Charik (1898-1937), Max Erik (1898-1937), and Moshe Kulbak (1896-1940).

☙•❧
Further Reading

Ashes out of Hope: Fiction by Soviet-Yiddish Writers. New York: Schocken Books, 1978.

Liptzin, Sol. "Soviet Yiddish Literature." In his *A History of Yiddish Literature*. Middle Village, N.Y.: Jonathan David Publishers, 1972.

MISUL GROUP
Bulgaria, 1892-1907

A Bulgarian movement of the 1890s and early 1900s, *Misul* transformed the country's intellectual climate through its emphasis on a sweeping Westernization of art and literature. Led by Krustyo Krustev (1866-1919), the writers most closely associated with the movement were Pencho Slaveykov (1866-1912), Petko Todorov (1879-1916), and Peyo Yavorov (1878-1914).

☙•❧
Further Reading

Ivanoff, Albert Manoloff. *German Influences in the Work of Pencho Slaveikov*. Ph.D. dissertation, Boston University, 1940.

Moser, Charles A. "The Age of Modernism and Individualism (1896-1917)." In his *A History of Bulgarian Literature, 865-1944*. The Hague: Mouton, 1972.

MŁODA POLSKA. *See* **YOUNG POLAND**

MODERNA. *See* **MODERNISM, Croatia, Serbia, Slovenia**

MODERNISM: An Overview

At once the most singular and diverse of all multinational movements, Modernism naturally defies simple definitions and classifications. This is especially due to the fact that, more so than any of the large movements which preceded or followed it, Modernism came to represent the sum of a host of movements within an entire cultural/historical period — that between the two world wars — by both anticipating and reflecting monumental ideological changes resulting from a new world order, including those in politics, philosophy, psychology, theology, science, and, above all, the arts. These last changes, which surfaced first in painting and music, signalled a conscious reevaluation of the purpose of art: the artist's role as perceiver, communicator, and intellectual agitator, and the aesthetic potential of the medium when purified of inherited traditions and conventions. Although heirs to the literary traditions of REALISM and NATURALISM, the Modernists took pains to develop a distinctively new emphasis on the rhythms and internal structures of language and on the increasingly complex and disillusioning realities of twentieth-century life; they systematically approached each of the four major genres — poem, novel, short story, and drama — with the intent of radically refashioning them so as to concretize their self-conscious separation, even alienation, from the writers and beliefs of the past.

The originality and integrity of the numerous breakthrough works produced during this extended period were in some sense, however, a reflection of the newer writers' conspicuous admiration for such immediate and reactionary predecessors as Henry JAMES (*see* Realism, United States), Walt Whitman (1819-1892), Fyodor DOSTOEVSKY and Anton CHEKHOV (*see* Realism, Russia), Stéphane MALLARMÉ and Arthur RIMBAUD (*see* SYMBOLISM, France), Henrik IBSEN (*see* Realism, Norway), August STRINDBERG (*see* EXPRESSIONISM, Germany), Thomas Hardy (1840-1928), and George Bernard SHAW (*see* EDWARDIAN LITERATURE). In addition, the recent and controversial success of Decadent (*see* AESTHETICISM/DECADENCE) and Symbolist writing and Impressionist and Postimpressionist painting, all of which followed the dictum "art for art's sake," greatly expanded the modes of technical experimentation and alternate views of reality available to the Modernists. Such influences would suggest that Modernism had its origins in America and Europe at least as early as the 1890s, during the height of the Industrial Revolution but before such inventions as the wireless radio, the Model T, air travel, the incandescent lamp, and motion pictures.

Although no doubt true, it was the ensuing cosmopolitanization of Western society and the heightened exchange of ideas and values among nationalities in the following decade that hailed the true ascendancy of Modernism.

This fruitful exchange appears largely indebted to the expatriation of American writers to Europe, a cultural exodus first begun by James in 1875. James's eventual association in England with a circle who included the Americans Stephen CRANE (*see* Naturalism, United States) and Edith WHARTON (*see* Realism, United States), as well as British subjects H. G. Wells (1866-1946), Ford Madox FORD (*see* Edwardian Literature), and Joseph CONRAD (*see* Modernism, England and Ireland), greatly enhanced the reputation of American literature, for James's experimentation with the psychological novel, shifting points-of-view, and the interior monologue — all signposts of Modernist work — were far in advance of new writing elsewhere in England and on the continent. However, an overriding concern with matters of social propriety in his fiction and an often laborious style prevented James, despite his towering stature among fellow writers, from being more closely identified with the Modernists than this. Instead, the landmark transition from a nineteenth- to an unmistakably twentieth-century prose style and outlook was completed by Conrad, one of James's greatest admirers. In 1902, after having mastered an impressionistic voice that owed much to the work of Gustave FLAUBERT (*see* Realism, France) and Guy de MAUPASSANT (*see* Realism, France) as well as James, Conrad published the novella *HEART OF DARKNESS*. One of the most studied works of modern fiction, this tale of moral and social decay earns its place in the Modernist corpus, above all, for its psychological depth, achieved by a consciously ambiguous method of narration that forces the reader into the active role of determining meaning.

The same year that Conrad published his short masterpiece, an American named Gertrude STEIN (*see* Modernism, United States) arrived in Europe and settled in Paris. Although Modernism's intellectual centers included Moscow, Zurich, Rome, Berlin, London, New York, and Chicago, none could so rightfully be called its epicenter as Paris and no individual could so rightfully be labelled its animator and patron as Stein. A former student of psychologist and philosopher William James (1842-1910) — brother of Henry, founder of Pragmatism, and originator of the term STREAM OF CONSCIOUSNESS (*see* Modernism, England and Ireland) — Stein was intensively concerned in her writing with capturing the continuous present as revealed to the conscious mind. Such works as *Three Lives* (1909) and *THE MAKING OF AMERICANS* (1925), completed in 1904 and 1908 respectively, exemplify this as well as her willingness to eschew existing standards of plot and characterization in order to achieve a more vitalized view of personality and of the meanings of words themselves. Perhaps more important than her fiction, which in the coming decades increasingly undercut conventional notions of coherence and semantics, were Stein's close associations, as sponsor and salon magnet, with the most important artists and writers of her time. Chief among the former were Georges Braque (1882-1963), Pablo Picasso (1881-1973), and Juan Gris (1887-1927), whose CUBIST theories of abstract composition (intended to challenge the viewer's culturally based norms of perception), Stein championed and attempted to emulate in her writing. Among the latter were Sherwood Anderson (1876-1941), who credited Stein's *Tender Buttons* (1914) with directly inspiring his highly influential story collection *Winesburg, Ohio* (1919), and virtually the entire wave of postwar American expatriates, the LOST GENERATION of Ernest HEMINGWAY, F. Scott FITZGERALD, John DOS PASSOS, and numerous others.

If Paris was the epicenter of Modernism, London was its seismic focal point. Here again, an American led the assault on Realism, Romanticism, and all superfluous, value-laden writing. His name was Ezra POUND (*see* MODERNISM, England and Ireland). Far more critical of American hypocrisy and mediocrity than Stein, Pound, upon settling in London in 1911, quickly entered the ferment of literary debate, innovation, and radical pronouncement. His first major coup came the following year with his inauguration of IMAGISM, a poetic school devoted to streamlined, impressionistic renderings of the visual experience. Despite his English residency, Pound's literary allegiances remained with the French. Symbolist Rémy de Gourmont (1858-1915), in particular, who was vociferously devoted to individual and arresting expression, became Pound's model of the aesthetically honest writer. The advent of Imagism coincided with Chicago writer Harriet Monroe's (1860-1936) ambitious publication and editorship of *Poetry: A Magazine of Verse*, one of the earliest and in many ways best of the numerous little magazines which were founded to provide a crucial outlet for emerging Modernist writers. During *Poetry*'s formative years, Pound served as its foreign editor and was instrumental in introducing American readers to the work of William Butler YEATS (*see* ABBEY THEATER and MODERNISM, England and Ireland), fellow expatriate T. S. ELIOT (*see* MODERNISM, England and Ireland), Rabindranath Tagore (1861-1941), and Imagist associates H[ilda] D[oolittle] and Richard Aldington (1892-1962). Monroe, in turn, provided an early forum for the poetry of Robert Frost (1874-1963) and CHICAGO LITERARY RENAISSANCE poets Carl SANDBURG, Vachel LINDSAY, and Edgar Lee MASTERS, who together ushered in the modern era in American poetry by simultaneously capturing the essence of small-town life and exposing its spiritual bankruptcy, an achievement later duplicated in the fiction of Anderson and Sinclair LEWIS (*see* JAZZ AGE). Although Pound, despite his considerable ability to recognize and foster great writing, can hardly be given credit for the overwhelming success of the Chicago Renaissance, his public admonition to "make it new" served as the guiding motto for writers on both sides of the Atlantic.

However indispensable Pound, Stein, Conrad, and James were to the birth of Modernism, their work and that of their younger colleagues would have been unthinkable without the preexistence of Friedrich NIETZSCHE's writings on human capability, Sigmund FREUD's theories of sexual identity and the unconscious, Karl MARX's indictment of capitalism, and Henri BERGSON's speculations on free will and the nature of time. These pivotal figures, despite their differing disciplines and emphases, ultimately focused attention on the complexity and power of the individual, rather than society as a whole, as was common with most thinkers during much of the nineteenth century. Consequently, as their views gained currency in the first decades of the twentieth century, writers were forced to define themselves and their world in a new light. This process of rediscovery was aided by Picasso's grotesque Cubist representation of the human form in *Les Demoiselles d'Avignon* (1907); by Russian composer Igor Stravinsky's fragmentary, polytonal ballet *The Rite of Spring* (1913); by the rise of FUTURISM, VORTICISM, ACMEISM, and EXPRESSIONISM; by the decline of the Edwardian age; and by such major events as BLOOMSBURY member Roger Fry's (1866-1934) exhibition of modern art in 1910 and the equally sensational New York Armory show of 1913. Notwithstanding this swirl of influence, the most decisive factor directing the course of Modernism was the staggering impact of World War I. Until the outbreak of war, Europeans and Americans had been reasonably complacent and trustful of Western society's capacity to weather the exigencies of the moment. The widespread death and destruction of the four-year war rent asunder such notions. The nightmarish war poetry of GEORGIANS Wilfred OWEN and Siegfried Sassoon (1886-1967) and such grim war novels as Dos Passos's *Three Soldiers* (1921) and Hemingway's *A Farewell to Arms* (1929) are just a few examples of the war's imprint on the minds of writers who had recently come of age.

In the period of the aftermath, many intellectuals found truth and meaning in art alone; thus art absorbed the difficult responsibility of both distancing itself from a society gone awry and documenting the disillusion and psychological isolation that haunted its inhabitants. One writer whose reclusivity exemplified this general air of displacement and whose work embodied this reverential attitude toward art was Frenchman Marcel PROUST (*see* MODERNISM, France). Proust began his multivolume masterpiece, *A LA RECHERCHE DU TEMPS PERDU* (7 vols., 1913-27), well before the war but was still expanding it at the time of his death in 1922, the first year in which the English translation *Remembrance of Things Past* began appearing. With his rejection of a unilinear plot and his penetrating analysis of the interconnections among time, memory, and occurrence, Proust inspired much of the psychological fiction written during the twenties and thirties.

More explosive, if less enduring, in impact was DADA, a highly reactionary Modernist movement which emerged in 1916 in Zurich and New York to proclaim a doctrine of nihilism and promote the depiction of the irrational. The Dadaists relocated to Paris in 1920 and gave impetus to the two most significant movements that share the Modernist umbrella: the Lost Generation and SURREALISM. The former, through such works as e. e. CUMMINGS's *THE ENORMOUS ROOM* (1922), Hemingway's *THE SUN ALSO RISES* (1926), Fitzgerald's *THE GREAT GATSBY* (1925) and *TENDER IS THE NIGHT* (1934), and Dos Passos's *U.S.A.* trilogy (1930-36), debunked the myth of the American Dream while evolving a fictional style suggestive of the dispossession and ennui that were a part of the Jazz Age of the twenties. The latter, through such works as Louis ARAGON's *LE PAYSAN DE PARIS* (1926; Paris Peasant), Paul ÉLUARD's *CAPI-TALE DE LA DOULEUR* (1926; *Capital of Pain*, 1973), and André BRETON's *NADJA* (1928; *Nadja*, 1960), paralleled in writing Freud's investigations of dream states and the unconscious by a free-flowing association of unrelated objects and ideas, a technique they termed AUTOMATIC WRITING (*see* SURREALISM). More revolutionary in intent than were the members of the Lost Generation, the Surrealists hoped to change the world by liberating the imagination and freeing the French language from the stagnation of the past.

Independent of these two movements, yet intimately tied to their success and to the character of the entire Modernist era are two archetypal works of twentieth-century literature, both of which, written in English, appeared in 1922 and forever changed the foundation of all serious writing that followed. Not surprisingly, the most ubiquitous presence in English and American Modernism, Pound, helped bring the works — Eliot's long, richly allusive poem *THE WASTE LAND* and James JOYCE's mythologically resonant stream-of-consciousness novel *ULYSSES* — to completion. Pound had met Eliot in 1914 and was instrumental in providing early advice, encouragement, and contacts that led to the publication of Eliot's first major artistic success, "The Love Song of J. Alfred Prufrock" (1915). While working intermittently on his *CANTOS* (1917-70), a vast, highly erudite progression of poems, Pound maintained a close association with Eliot, whom he regarded as a thoroughly self-taught and original Modernist. In 1921, offering both financial assistance and a keen editorial eye, Pound helped Eliot weather a mental collapse brought on by overwork on his masterpiece which, when published in final form in *The Criterion* a year later, benefitted greatly from Pound's several large, scrupulous excisions. Generally indebted to Arthurian legend, the metaphysical thought of F. H. Bradley (1846-1924), and Sir James Frazer's (1854-1941) survey of myth entitled *The Golden Bough* (1890-1915), *The Waste Land* is a work rife with symbolic meaning; its central theme, however, is the spiritual void of contemporary existence, the tragic isolation of the modern individual. Upon its publication the work was widely hailed as the supreme expression of postwar despair; its magnitude and innovation have ever since been emulated, often unsuccessfully, by scores of poets worldwide. Upon locating Joyce in Trieste, Pound persuaded the struggling novelist to return to Paris, promising lodging, sustaining funds, and a publisher for *Ulysses*. He found the latter in Sylvia Beach (1887-1962), an American whose bookshop/library Shakespeare and Company was the literary beacon of Paris' Left Bank. With Pound's assistance, Joyce was finally able to see his masterpiece into print, though it would be banned in both the United States and England on the grounds of obscene content.

Following the appearance of *The Waste Land* and *Ulysses*, a labyrinthine network of influences and counter-influences stretching between nations and across continents served to augment and enrich Modernist experimentation in all literary forms. Although some would argue that certain Modernist notions have been kept alive long after World War II through the rise, for example, of EXISTENTIALISM, the BEAT GENERATION, and CONFESSIONAL POETRY, the movement's distinctive character may be said to have ended with the religio-philosophical volte-face of Eliot; the political shift to the left by numerous writers during the 1930s; the disintegration of artistic vision within the Lost Generation and the Surrealists; the rise of Nazi Germany; and, finally, Joyce's culminative and unduplicated experiment in fiction, *Finnegans Wake* (1939). What remains indisputable is that there are as many quintessential Modernists as there are styles, genres, and nationalities of Modernist writing. In addition to those mentioned, André GIDE (*see NOUVELLE REVUE FRANÇAISE*), Antonin Artaud (1896-1948), Franz KAFKA (*see* Modernism, Austria and Germany), Thomas MANN (*see* Modernism, Austria and Germany), E. M. Forster (1879-1970), Virginia WOOLF (*see* Modernism, England and Ireland), Aldous Huxley (1894-1963), D. H. LAWRENCE (*see* Modernism, England and Ireland), Katherine Mansfield (1888-1923), W. H. Auden (1907-1973), Dorothy Richardson (1873-1957), Wallace STEVENS, William Carlos Williams (1883-1963), Eugene O'NEILL (*see* EXPRESSIONISM, United States, and PROVINCETOWN PLAYERS), William FAULKNER (*see* Modernism, United States), Luigi PIRANDELLO (*see* Modernism, Italy), Konstantin STANISLAVSKY (*see* MOSCOW ART THEATER), and José Ortega y Gasset (1883-1955) are among the legions of now classic writers who contributed to the development of Modernism. Even such incomplete lists as this are astonishing when one considers the enormous variety of works represented, works which have done more to define and shape the intellectual climate of the twentieth century than all those of previous centuries combined.

❖•❖

Modernism: A Timeline

1902 CONRAD publishes *HEART OF DARKNESS*; STEIN settles in Paris.

1904 Stein completes *Three Lives*, which remains unpublished until 1909.

1906 LITTLE THEATER movement is launched in America.

1907 Picasso completes *Les Demoiselles d'Avignon*, the revolutionary painting that spawned Cubism.

1908 FORD begins editing *The English Review*, the first little magazine devoted to Modernist literature; POUND travels to Italy and publishes *A Lume Spento*.

1910 Roger Fry organizes his first exhibition of Postimpressionist painting in London.

1912 *Poetry: A Magazine of Verse* launched by Monroe in Chicago; beginning of the CHICAGO LITERARY RENAISSANCE, which coincides with Pound's founding of IMAGISM.

1913 New York Armory exhibition of modern art; Imagism manifesto published; PROUST publishes *Du côté de chez Swann* (*Swann's Way*, 1922), the first volume of *A LA RECHERCHE DU TEMPS PERDU* (7 vols., 1913-27; *Remembrance of Things Past*, 7 vols., 1922-32), which he commenced writing around 1905 and which occupied him well into the 1920s; FREUD's *DIE TRAUMDEUTUNG* (*The Interpretation of Dreams*) translated into English.

1914 Austrian Archduke Francis Ferdinand assassinated on June 28; Germany declares war on Russia and France in August, thus beginning World War I. JOYCE publishes *Dubliners*; advent of VORTICISM and *Blast*.

1916 Joyce publishes *A Portrait of the Artist as a Young Man*.

1917 The Hogarth Press, founded by Leonard and Virginia WOOLF, publishes its first book, *Two Stories*; Pound publishes his first *CANTOS*; Russian Revolution; United States enters the war.

1919 Eighteenth Amendment (prohibition) is ratified in the United States; Treaty of Versailles is signed.

1920 Nineteenth Amendment (women's suffrage) is passed in the United States.

1921 Irish Free State established.

1922 Joyce publishes *ULYSSES*; Eliot publishes *THE WASTE LAND*; Sinclair LEWIS publishes *BABBITT*.

1924 MANN publishes *DER ZAUBERBERG* (*The Magic Mountain*, 1927).

1925 FITZGERALD publishes *THE GREAT GATSBY*; Stein publishes *THE MAKING OF AMERICANS*; HEMINGWAY publishes *In Our Time*; Woolf publishes *Mrs. Dalloway*.

1926 Hemingway publishes *THE SUN ALSO RISES*.

1927 Lindbergh makes nonstop solo flight across the Atlantic; Sacco and Vanzetti are tried and executed; Woolf publishes *TO THE LIGHTHOUSE*.

1929 New York Stock Exchange crashes in October, ushering in the era of the Great Depression; FAULKNER publishes *THE SOUND AND THE FURY*; the motion picture industry produces the first "talkies."

1933 Prohibition is repealed.

1934 Fitzgerald publishes *TENDER IS THE NIGHT*.

1936 DOS PASSOS publishes *The Big Money*, completing his *U.S.A.* trilogy.

1939 YEATS dies; Joyce publishes *Finnegans Wake*; STEINBECK publishes *The Grapes of Wrath*; Stalin and Hitler sign non-aggression pact.

1960 Unexpurgated text of *Lady Chatterley's Lover* found not obscene in court of law.

MODERNISM
Austria and Germany, 1910s-1930s

Modernist trends in Germany grew out of a reaction against NATURALISM, though Naturalism was constituted in Berlin of such Modernist precursors as the poet Arno Holz (1863-1929) and poet and novelist Hermann Conradi (1862-1890), who with poet Karl Henckell (1864-1929) wrote what may be considered an early manifesto in their anthology *Moderne Dichter Charaktere* (1885; Modern Poetic Characters), ushering in the vogue of the term "modern" and influencing those who later continued working to define it. Modernism in Germany comprised a period of acceptance and excitement about cultural cosmopolitanism that for a time existed uneasily aside a growing new Reich with its racism and rejection of all that was not German and of the Volk (*see* HEIMATKUNST). Modernism was comprised of such movements as DADA, JUGEND-STIL, MERZ, NEW OBJECTIVITY, SURREALISM, DEUTSCHES THEATER, FREIE BÜHNE, EPIC THEATER, and in Austria, the YOUNG VIENNA GROUP. The STORM CIR-CLE group provided two major vehicles for Modernist literature, the journals *Der Sturm* (1910-32), edited by Herwarth Walden (1878-1941), and *Die Aktion* (1911-32), edited by Franz Pfempfert (1879-1954). By the time Modernism came to the fore in England, Germany had exhausted the term and subsequent modern developments were largely centered around EXPRESSIONISM, prominent between 1910 and 1925.

It is necessary as well to mention three German thinkers integral to the development of European Modernism: Sigmund FREUD, whose *DIE TRAUMDEUTUNG* (*The Interpretation of Dreams,* 1913) appeared in 1900, Karl MARX, and Friedrich NIETZSCHE. On the literary front, Franz KAFKA's *DER PROZESS* (begun 1914, published 1925; *The Trial,* 1937) and Thomas MANN's *DER ZAUBERBERG* (1924; *The Magic Mountain,* 1927) are landmark Modernist pieces. Rainer Maria Rilke's (1875-1926) masterpiece *Die Aufzeichnungen des Malte Laurids Brigge* (1910; *The Notebook of Malte Laurids Brigge,* 1959), which centers on a protagonist who is psychologically alienated from the modern world, and Arthur Schnitzler's (1862-1931) novel *Leutnant Gustl* (1901; *None But the Brave,* 1931), which employs interior monologue and STREAM-OF-CONSCIOUSNESS techniques along with psychoanalytic perspective, are important, as are the works of Austrian novelists Robert Musil (1880-1942) and his *Die Verwirrungen des Zöglings Törless* (1906; *Young Törless,* 1955), and Hermann Broch (1886-1951), Expressionists Georg Trakl (1887-1914), George Heym (1887-1912), Ernst Barlach (1870-1938), Gottfried Benn (1886-1956), and Carl Sternheim (1878-1942), German SYMBOLISTS Stefan George (1868-1933) and Hugo von Hofmannsthal (1874-1929), and Belgian Symbolist Maurice MAETERLINCK.

Many of these looked to Henrik IBSEN, who lived in Germany from 1864 to 1891 and whose play *Gengangere* (1881; *Ghosts,* 1889) caused a sensation when produced in Berlin in 1887; other plays of his were often produced by the Freie Bühne (*see* REALISM, Norway). Expressionist August STRINDBERG, who came to Germany in the early 1890s and briefly lived in Berlin and in a rural suburb of Berlin, Friedreichshagen am Müggelsee, was another important influence. Later German Modernists turned inward; instead of the traditional Expressionist conflicts between father and son, they moved inward to struggles of consciousness and complex psychological states, often referred to as *Nervenkunst,* "art of the nerves."

❖•❖

Kafka, Franz (1883-1924), Austrian novelist and short-story writer.

Kafka was born to German-Jewish parents in Prague, when it belonged to the Austro-Hungarian Empire. He studied law and worked as an insurance specialist until poor health due to tuberculosis, as well as several stays in sanitariums, forced him to resign by 1922. He wrote in the evenings after work and managed to produce numerous short stories and three novels—*Amerika* (written 1912-14, published 1927; *America,* 1938), *Der Prozess* (begun 1914, published 1925; *The Trial,* 1937), and *Das Schloss* (begun 1921, published 1926; *The Castle,* 1930)—only the first of which was completed. Variously considered an Expressionist, Surrealist, and Existentialist, Kafka also displays the influence of Symbolism, Naturalism, and Cubism. Though not directly affiliated with Expressionism, or any other movement for that matter, Kafka is a master of its theme of conflict between the authoritarian father and the son, in no small part because of his difficult relationship with his own father. *Die Verwandlung* (1915; *The Metamorphosis,* 1936) illustrates this eloquently: Kafka's father called him an insect, then Kafka wrote this story in which a son turns overnight into a giant insect.

In his work normal causality does not obtain. Time is distorted, or as one critic put it, "paralysed," since its passage, to characters, is meaningless. Kafka's humor is farcical, parodic, grotesque, macabre, and explores the unavoidable contradictions of human existence. His characters function as types; they have no histories and often are portrayed as merely fulfilling, unquestioningly, their appointed role as, for example, lawyer, judge, warder. Kafka has been cited as a precursor of MAGIC REALISM, for his blending of the ordinary and the fantastic; in Kafka, as one critic puts it, the "heroes fight for reality, though without reaching it." Critic Frederick Karl (1927-) wrote that the adjective "Kafkaesque in our century has replaced the now old-fashioned *fate* or *destiny* or even circumstance or happenstance. It has become the representative adjective of our times."

Der Prozess (written 1914-15, published 1925; *The Trial*, 1937).

In this novel Kafka's critique of authoritarianism moves the typical Expressionist confrontation with authority out of the familial and into the public realm as it takes the form of a citizen versus the powers of the state. The reader, as well as the protagonist, is in a world in which the nature of reality is unknown; neither, for instance, ever knows for what charge the former has been arrested and eventually executed. The novel has been interpreted as an allegory for Kafka's struggle with tuberculosis — supported, among other, textual reasons, by the fact that in German, "der Prozess" means "consumption" as well as "lawsuit" or "trial"; Kafka had written most of the text, however, before he was diagnosed with the disease.

✦•✦

Mann, Thomas (1875-1955), German novelist and short-story writer.

Son of a prominent burgher in Lübeck, Thomas Mann worked briefly in an insurance company before beginning university with the goal of becoming a journalist. In the late 1890s he traveled to Italy with his older brother, the novelist Heinrich Mann (1871-1950), worked for the weekly magazine *Simplicissimus*, and began writing and publishing short stories. Influenced by Schopenhauer, NIETSZCHE, and the French REALISTS, especially the GONCOURTS, Mann is known for his subtle craftsmanship and ironic analysis of the human condition, dealing in numerous ways with the contemporary state of the fruits of Western rationality and enlightenment. In addition to

Der Zauberberg (1924; *The Magic Mountain,* 1927), other important works include *Buddenbrooks* (1901; *Buddenbrooks,* 1924), *Tonio Kröger* (1903; *Tonio Kröger,* 1914), *Der Tod in Venedig* (1913; *Death in Venice,* 1925), *Joseph und seine Brüder* (1933-42; *Joseph and His Brothers,* 1934-45), *Doktor Faustus* (1947; *Doctor Faustus,* 1948). He won the Nobel Prize for literature in 1929.

Der Zauberberg (1924; *The Magic Mountain,* 1927).

Often called a Zeitroman — in which the author analyzes the society he or she inhabits — and an anti-Bildungsroman — the reverse of the narrative tradition in which the protagonist, usually a young person, is shown to learn and mature in important ways — *Der Zauberberg* tells the story of Hans Castrop, who goes to a sanitarium to visit a cousin whereupon he also is diagnosed with tuberculosis, remains at the sanitarium—for years, in fact, after the doctor has released him — and becomes increasingly introspective and obsessed with death and positing relationships between health and disease, stupidity and wisdom, life and death.

❖•❖

Further Reading

Apter, T. E. *Thomas Mann: The Devil's Advocate.* London: Macmillan, 1978.

Berman, Russell A. *The Rise of the Modern German Novel: Crisis and Charisma.* Cambridge, Mass.: Harvard University Press, 1986.

Bloom, Harold, ed. *Franz Kafka.* New York: Chelsea House, 1986.

Bradbury, Malcolm, and James McFarlane. *Modernism 1890-1930.* Hassocks, Sussex, England: Harvester Press; Atlantic Highlands, N.J.: Humanities Press, 1978. Reissued with new preface, London: Penguin Books, 1991.

Broadsky, Patricia P. *Rainer Maria Rilke.* Boston: Twayne, 1988.

Dowden, Stephen D. *Sympathy for the Abyss: A Study of the Novel of German Modernism: Kafka, Broch, Musil, and Thomas Mann.* Tübingen, Germany: M. Niemeyer, 1986.

Emrich, Wilhelm. *Franz Kafka: A Critical Study of His Writings.* Translated by Sheema Zeben Buehne. New York: Ungar, 1968.

Flores, Ángel, ed. *The Kafka Debate: New Perspectives for Our Time.* Staten Island, N.Y.: Gordian Press, 1977.

Gray, Ronald. *The German Tradition in Literature, 1871-1945.* Cambridge, England: Cambridge University Press, 1967.

Gray, Ronald, ed. *Kafka: A Collection of Critical Essays.* Englewood Cliffs, N.J.: Prentice-Hall, 1962.

Greenberg, Martin. *The Terror of Art: Kafka and Modern Literature.* New York: Basic Books, 1968.

Hatfield, Henry. *From "The Magic Mountain": Mann's Later Masterpieces.* Ithaca, N.Y.: Cornell University Press, 1979.

————. *Modern German Literature: The Major Figures in Context.* New York: St. Martin's Press, 1967.

Hatfield, Henry, ed. *Thomas Mann: A Collection of Critical Essays*. Englewood Cliffs, N.J.: Prentice-Hall, 1964.

Hibberd, John. *Kafka in Context*. London: Studio Vista, 1975.

Hollingdale, R. J. *Thomas Mann: A Critical Study*. London: Hart-Davis, 1971.

Huyssen, Andreas, and David Bathrick, eds. *Modernity and the Text: Revisions of German Modernism*. New York: Columbia University Press, 1989.

Jephcott, E. F. N. *Proust and Rilke: The Literature of Expanded Consciousness*. London: Chatto and Windus, 1972.

Karl, Frederick R. *Franz Kafka: Representative Man*. New York: Ticknor & Field, 1991.

Pascal, Roy. *The German Novel: Studies*. Toronto: University of Toronto Press, 1956.

————. *Kafka's Narrators: A Study of His Stories and Sketches*. New York: Cambridge University Press, 1982.

Politzer, Heinrich. *Franz Kafka: Parable and Paradox*. Ithaca, N.Y.: Cornell University Press, 1966.

Quinones, Ricardo J. *Mapping Literary Modernism: Time and Development*. Princeton, N.J.: Princeton University Press, 1985.

Rühle, Jürgen. *Literature and Revolution: A Critical Study of the Writer and Communism in the Twentieth Century*. Translated and edited by Jean Steinberg. New York: Frederick A. Praeger, Publishers, 1969.

Ryan, Judith. *The Vanishing Subject: Early Psychology and Literary Modernism*. Chicago: University of Chicago Press, 1991.

Sandbank, Shimon. *After Kafka: The Influence of Kafka's Fiction*. Athens, Ga.: University of Georgia Press, 1989.

Sokel, Walter H. *The Writer in Extremis: Expressionism in Twentieth-Century German Literature*. New York: McGraw-Hill, 1959.

Spann, Meno. *Franz Kafka*. Boston: Twayne, 1976.

Stern, J. P., ed. *The World of Franz Kafka*. New York: Holt, Reinhart and Winston, 1980.

Swales, Martin. *Thomas Mann: A Study*. London: Heinemann; Totowa, N.J.: Rowman and Littlefield, 1980.

Tauber, Herbert. *Franz Kafka: An Interpretation of His Works*. 1948. Reprint, New York: Haskell House, 1967.

Tayler, Ronald. *Literature and Society in Germany, 1918-1945*. Totowa, N.J.: Barnes & Noble Books, 1980.

Webb, Karl E. *Rainer Maria Rilke and Jugendstil: Affinities, Influences, Adaptations*. Chapel Hill, N.C.: University of North Carolina Press, 1978.

Weigand, Hermann J. *Thomas Mann's Novel "Der Zauberberg."* New York: D. Appleton-Century, 1933.

Whitlark, James. *Behind the Great Wall: A Post-Jungian Approach to Kafkaesque Literature*. Rutherford, N.J.: Fairleigh Dickinson University Press; London: Associated University Presses, 1991.

Winston, Richard. *Thomas Mann: The Making of an Artist, 1875-1911*. New York: Knopf, 1981; distributed by Random House.

MODERNISM
Brazil, c. 1922-1940s

Brazilian Modernism, unconnected with MODERNISMO, was a broad artistic and literary revolution that spanned much of the first half of the twentieth century. Influenced by CUBISM, EXPRESSIONISM, and, especially, FUTURISM, the first generation of Brazilian Modernists—who gained wide attention through their attachment to a revolutionary modern art exhibit held in São Paolo in 1922—were noted for their severance of ties with SYMBOLISM, their preference for the Brazilian vernacular language over classical Portuguese, and their radical mixture of avant-gardism, nationalism, and regionalism. The leader of this group was Oswald de ANDRADE (*see* ANTROPOFAGIA), who in his manifesto *Pau Brasil* (1924; Brazil Wood) called for a new native poetry which would rank with the best in world literature.

A number of other important writers, many of whom were connected to specific regions, spinoff movements, or later developments and factions, have also shared credit with Andrade for their important contributions; these include essayist José da Graça Aranha (1868-1931); Mário de Andrade (1893-1945), author of *Paulicéia desvairada* (1922; *Hallucinated City,* 1968) and the epic novel *Macunaíma* (1928; *Macunaíma,* 1984); Modernist forerunner José Monteiro Lobato (1882-1948); poets Manuel Bandeira (1886-1968) and Cecília Meireles (1901-1964), key figures of the Rio de Janeiro group; Cassiano Ricardo (1895-1974), author of the epic poem *Martim Cererê* (1928; Martim Cererê); Carlos Drummond de Andrade (1902-1987); João Cabral de Melo Neto (1920-); critic Ronald de Carvalho (1893-1935); and the writers of the Northeast, Jorge de Lima (1895-1953), Gilberto Freyre (1900-1987), Jorge Amado (1912-), Graciliano Ramos (1892-1953), and José Lins de Rêgo (1901-1957). These and other writers carried the Modernist impetus forward in all branches of literature until the end of World War II.

See also FESTA GROUP and VERDE-AMARELISMO.

❧•❧

Further Reading

Coutinho, Afranio. *An Introduction to Literature in Brazil*. New York: Columbia University Press, 1969.

Craig, George Dundas. *The Modernist Trend in Spanish American Poetry*. Berkeley, Calif.: University of California Press, 1934.

Lowe, Elizabeth. *The City in Brazilian Literature*. Rutherford, N.J.: Fairleigh Dickinson University Press, 1982.

Martins, Wilson. *The Modernist Idea: A Critical Survey of Brazilian Writing in the Twentieth Century*. Translated by Jack E. Tomlins. New York: New York University Press, 1979.

Nist, John. *The Modernist Movement in Brazil.* Austin, Tex.: University of Texas Press, 1967.
Stern, Irwin, ed. *Dictionary of Brazilian Literature.* New York: Greenwood Press, 1988.

MODERNISM (Moderna)
Croatia, Serbia, and Slovenia, 1895-1918

The term Moderna, or Modernism, was borrowed from the Austrian professor and YOUNG VIENNA leader Hermann Bahr (1863-1934) by a group of Croatian expatriate students who were studying in Vienna because of their dissatisfaction with the regime of the Hungarian emperor Franz Josef. Gradually, the term was adopted by literary groups in Serbia and Slovenia, all of whom became enjoined politically when Yugoslavia became a state in 1918. Thus, any discussion of the various Moderna groups must take into account individual nationalistic background and development, although all had in common the desire to reject the Romanticism of the past and become part of the new literary currents which were prevalent prior to the two world wars and directly thereafter.

Of the three national groups which adopted the spirit of Moderna, Croatians made up the majority and had been mainly influenced by concurrent literary movements in France, Italy, Poland, and the Scandinavian countries. Their wish was to propagate in their work a fervid love of the land, but also to use it for critical response to sociopolitical situations; moreover, they were determined to remain united against outworn literary tradition at any cost. Group members included Milan Begović (1876-1948), Ivana Brlić-Mažuranić (1874-1938), Milutin Chihlar-Nehajev (1880-1931). Dragutin Domjanić (1875-1933), Fran Galović (1887-1914), Josip Kosor (1879-1961), Silvije Strahimir Kranjčević (1865-1908), Milan Marjanović (1879-1955), Tomáš Masaryk (1850-1937), Gustav Matoš (1873-1914), Vladimir Nazor (1876-1949), Milan Ogrizović (1877-1923), Dinko Šimunović (1893-1933), Vladimir Vidrić (1875-1909), Branko Vodnik (1879-1926), and Ivo Vojnović (1857-1929). Noteworthy are Begović, Ogrizović, and Galović, the dramatists who introduced a new sophistication into theatrical productions providing a more realistic depiction of human problems as against the earlier Romantic trend toward extreme, idealistic nationalism. Serbian Modernas show the influence of French SYMBOLISM; Modernist in philosophy, contemplative, often melancholy and pessimistic, their work responds to the social ills of the fin de siècle. The three most important poets were Jovan Dučić (1871-1943), Milan Rakić (1876-1938), and Aleksa Šantić (1868-1924), who are said to represent the Moderna character.

Slovenian writers were early portrayers of the movement in their adoption of a more realistic and rational view of their culture than ever before. The most important figure was the poet, dramatist, and essayist Ivan Cankar (1875-1918), whose vision combined biblical zeal with social reform. Others were the poet Oton Župančič (1878-1949), whose mastery of language allowed him to translate the plays of Shakespeare to perfection; and the lyrical poets Josip-Murn Alexandrov (1879-1901) and Dragotin Kette (1876-1899). Izidore Cankar (1889-1957), one of the most astute of the early Slovenian literary critics, was also a member of the group.

✦•✦

Further Reading

Barac, Antun. *A History of Yugoslav Literature*. Translated by Petar Mijušković. [Belgrade] Yugoslavia: Committee for Foreign Cultural Relations of Yugoslavia, 1955.

Kadić, Ante. *Contemporary Serbian Literature*. The Hague: Mouton, 1964.

Herrity, Peter. "Poems of the Slovene *Moderna*." In *Russian and Yugoslav Culture in the Age of Modernism*. Edited by Cynthia Marsh and Wendy Rosslyn. Nottingham, England: Astra Press, 1991.

Lukić, Sveta. *Contemporary Yugoslav Literature: A Sociopolitical Approach*. Edited by Gertrude Joch Robinson. Translated by Pola Triandis. Urbana, Ill.: University of Illinois Press, 1972.

Mihailovich, Vasa D., and Mateja Matejic, eds. *Yugoslavian Literature in English: A Bibliography of Translations and Criticism, 1821-1975*. Cambridge, Mass.: Slavica Publishers, 1976.

Milojkovic-Djuric, Jelena. *Tradition and Avant-Garde: Literature and Art in Serbian Culture, 1900-1918*. Boulder, Colo.: East European Monographs, 1988.

MODERNISM
Czechoslovakia, 1905-1910s

A movement partially indebted to SYMBOLISM that began around 1905 in Czechoslovakia, Slovakian Modernism introduced fiction and poetry intended for the cultural and economic betterment of the common people. The movement lasted for over a decade and firmly established the careers of such writers as Janko Jesenský (1874-1945), Ivan Krasko (1876-1958), Martin Rázus (1888-1937), Vladimír Roy (1885-1935), and František Votruba (1880-1953).

See also MODERNISM, Croatia, Serbia, Slovenia.

✦•✦

Further Reading

Petro, Peter. "Slovak Literature: Loyal, Dissident, and Émigre." In *Czechoslovakia 1918-88: Seventy Years from Independence*. Edited by H. Gordon Skilling. New York: St. Martin's Press, 1991.

MODERNISM
Denmark, 1950s-1960s

MODERNISM, as it had been developing in England, France, and Germany, did not flower in Denmark until the late 1950s. The *HERETIKA* poets of the late 1940s were forerunners, who were influenced in particular by T. S. ELIOT (*see* MODERNISM, England and Ireland), while fictional prose in the 40s and 50s was largely concerned with World War II and tended to reveal the influence of EXISTENTIALISM. Eventually, in the 1960s, writers were steeped in the European Modernists and tended to take up phenomenological concerns. The journal *Vindrosen* (1954-74; The Compass) was a primary vehicle for this younger generation of writers. Prose writer Villy Sørensen (1929-) coedited *Vindrosen* from 1959 to 1963.

Critics often cite Klaus Rifbjerg (1931-) and his volume of poems *Konfrontation* (1960; Confrontation) as the work that most powerfully brought Modernism into Danish literature; it treats confrontations between subjective consciousness and the outside world. Often pessimistic and nihilist, this aesthetic attitude attends to the contradictory nature of reality and the individual's experience of it. Poet Jess Ornsbo (1932-), whose first collection was *Digte* (1960; Poems), uses the confrontation technique; his subject matter includes social consciousness, with regard to working-class themes and urban life. Other poets writing in similar veins include Ivan Malinovski (1926-); other prose experimenters include Svend Åge Madsen (1939-) and Sven Holm (1940-).

Narrative experiments in the French NEW NOVEL had an impact on the new Danish Modernists as well. New experimentation in literature in the early 1950s can be found in such prose works by Peter Seeberg (1925-) as the novels *Bipersonerne* (1956; The Secondary Characters) and *Fugls føde* (1957; Bird's Scrapings) and short story collection *Eftersøgningen* (1962; The Search). He found inspiration in absurdists Samuel BECKETT and Eugene IONESCO (*see* THEATER OF THE ABSURD), while Sørensen, who was mainly influenced by German Modernists Thomas MANN, Franz KAFKA, and Hermann Broch (1886-1951), wrote collections of short stories *Sære historier* (1953; *Tiger in the Kitchen; and Other Strange Stories*, 1969) and *Ufarlige historier* (1955; Safe Stories) that are considered important Danish Modernist works.

→•←

Further Reading

Borum, Poul. *Danish Literature; A Short Critical Survey*. Copenhagen: Det Danske Selskab, 1979.

Gray, C. S. "Klaus Rifbjerg: A Contemporary Danish Writer." *Books Abroad* (January 1975): 25-28.

Mitchell, P. M. *A History of Danish Literature*. 2nd ed. New York: Kraus-Thomson Organization, 1971.

Øhrgaard, Per. *Klaus Rifbjerg*. Copenhagen: Gyldendal, 1977.

Rossel, Sven H. *A History of Scandinavian Literature, 1870-1980*. Translated by Anne C.
Ulmer. Minneapolis: University of Minnesota Press, 1981.

MODERNISM
England and Ireland, 1910s-1930s

Nowhere was the advent of Modernism more disruptive and threatening to literary tradition than in staid Victorian England. However, signs of this transition during the late
Victorian and fin de siècle periods were plentiful. Beginning with the deaths of Charles
DICKENS in 1870 and George ELIOT in 1880 (*see* REALISM, England), Victorian, or,
conventionally moral and reservedly Realistic fiction, began to wane. Curiously, the
emergence of Realists George Meredith (1828-1909) and Thomas Hardy (1840-
1928) — two writers who more resolutely explored the psychological aspects of character as well as the effects of social and biological determinism — only seemed to hasten
this end, for in their hands the novel form itself failed to advance. The necessity for new
means and attitudes of expression was enhanced by such figures as Charles Darwin
(1809-1882), T. H. Huxley (1825-1895), Friedrich NIETZSCHE, and Karl MARX, men
whose scientific and philosophical conclusions challenged the most fundamental institutions of civilized society and, by extension, many of the artistic tenets of the literary
period. The first European novelist to completely accept and incorporate these new
intellectual currents was French NATURALIST Émile ZOLA. Originator of the novel
conducted as scientific experiment, Zola greatly helped to counteract long accepted
barriers of subject matter and character depiction and his influence was felt in Ireland
and England in the fiction of George Moore (1852-1933), George Gissing (1857-1903),
H. G. Wells (1866-1946), and, much later, James JOYCE. Zola's method, if not his material, was much admired as well by Anglo-American Henry JAMES (*see* Realism, United
States). With his subtle studies of character and circumstance in his international novels, James, more than any other novelist, anticipated many of the Modernists' technical
advances. However, James, and Zola, especially, were reluctant to sacrifice a surfeit of
detail, or to juggle chronological time, for potentially greater thematic power. These
developments were carried out by Joseph CONRAD, writing during the turn of the century, whose consummate impressionistic style, juxtaposition of viewpoints, use of time-
shifts, and intended ambiguity inaugurated the modern revolution in literature.

Although fiction became the dominant genre of Modernist writing in England and elsewhere, its metamorphosis of form and purpose closely followed that within poetry. The
success of the anti-Victorian Pre-Raphaelite movement, whose members included art
and social critic John Ruskin (1819-1900), writer-printer William Morris (1834-1896),
and poet-painter Dante Gabriel Rossetti (1828-1882), helped create an atmosphere in

which the purposes and cultural biases of literature and art could be validly questioned and reformulated. Subsequently, the French doctrine of "art for art's sake" gained increasing support in England and became one of the chief maxims of AESTHETI-CISM/DECADENCE, a movement led by Walter Pater (1839-1894). Numbering among this diverse group were Oscar Wilde (1854-1900), illustrator Aubrey Beardsley (1872-1898), poet Algernon Charles Swinburne (1837-1909), and Celtic Revivalist William Butler YEATS (*see also* ABBEY THEATER and IRISH RENAISSANCE). Although each of these figures exerted an impact on the development of modern poetry, it was Yeats who most thoroughly oversaw this revolution. With the aid of American poet Ezra POUND, who had come to London to learn from him, Yeats outstripped his fashionable but limiting Irish concerns of the 1890s and proceeded to brilliantly reform the English poem in such works as "Sailing to Byzantium" (1927) and "Among School Children" (1927).

Seminal, however, was *THE WASTE LAND* (1922), written by one of the so-called "Men of 1914," T. S. ELIOT, who along with Joyce, Pound, and Wyndham LEWIS (*see* VORTI-CISM), were united in their pessimism, unlike Wells and George Bernard SHAW (*see* EDWARDIAN LITERATURE). World War I had an enormous impact, witnessed in part by the war poetry of some of the GEORGIAN POETS, which fostered a feeling of alienation from the past. Virginia WOOLF articulated the sense of the old world ending and a new world beginning in "Mr. Bennett and Mrs. Brown" (1924): "On or about December 1910 human nature changed . . . All human relations shifted — those between masters and servants, husbands and wives, parents and children. And when human relations change there is at the same time a change in religion, conduct, politics, and literature." And D. H. LAWRENCE wrote in *Kangaroo*: "It was in 1915 the old world ended."

Defining techniques and formal characteristics of Modernist poetry and fiction included requiring the reader to construct meaning out of fragments; affinity with the music of Igor Stravinsky (1882-1971); self-consciousness of literature; concern with form rather than imitation, with form creating content; compression of content and expression; use of the image to create more an impressionistic collage than linear narrative, and employing myth as a structural organizer (as in *Ulysses*, *The Waste Land*, and Yeats's Celtic poetry). It has been said that the overarching theme of the Modernist novel is the art of the novel itself, the aesthetic presentation and portrayal of consciousness. A guiding principle for the Modernists was to place greater demands upon the reader so as to lead to greater rewards.

Some of the Modernists' most important periodical forums were *The Egoist* (1914-19) and Lewis's *Blast* (1914). Other notable English Modernists were novelist Dorothy Richardson (1873-1957), who developed STREAM-OF-CONSCIOUSNESS writing, poet Edith Sitwell (1887-1964), and Imagist theorist and poet T. E. Hulme (1883-1917).

Before 1920 London was a magnet for writers from Ireland, the United States, and elsewhere—Conrad, Stephen Crane, Yeats, Pound, H. D., Robert Frost (1874-1963), Eliot, Katherine Mansfield (1888-1923), Wyndham Lewis, Ford Madox Ford—after which many migrated to Paris, including Joyce and Lawrence.

�֍•֎

Conrad, Joseph (pen-name of Józef Teodor Konrad Korseniowski, 1857-1924), Polish-born English novelist and short-story writer.

Born in the Ukraine to Polish parents, who were both deceased by the time he was twelve, Conrad became a seaman at the age of seventeen but eventually turned completely to writing as he continued having no success in obtaining command of a ship. After moving to England, Conrad became friends with Ford Madox FORD (*see* Edwardian Literature), on whose property Conrad lived with his family. The two collaborated on the novels *The Inheritors* (1900) and *Romance* (1903), though afterward their friendship waned. Conrad is known for dealing with themes of the individual's struggle with darkness and humanity's betrayal of humanity, using techniques of multiple points of view and narrative temporal distortion. The influence of Henry James and the French writers Stendahl (1783-1842) and Gustave FLAUBERT ([1821-1880]; *see* Naturalism and Realism) can be seen in Conrad's style. His works include *The Nigger of the 'Narcissus'* (1897), *Lord Jim* (1900), HEART OF DARKNESS (1902), *Typhoon* (1902), *Youth* (1902), *Nostromo* (1904), *A Mirror of the Sea* (1906), *The Secret Agent* (1907), *A Set of Six* (1908), and *Under Western Eyes* (1911). Among the many writers Conrad influenced are T. S. Eliot, F. Scott FITZGERALD (*see* LOST GENERATION), Virginia Woolf, William FAULKNER (*see* Modernism, United States), Jean-Paul SARTRE (*see* EXISTENTIALISM), and Ernest HEMINGWAY (*see* Lost Generation).

Heart of Darkness (1902).

Based on Conrad's experiences piloting a steamboat up the Congo River in 1890, memories that stayed with him for the rest of his life, *Heart of Darkness* employs an ambiguous narrator to give the sort of psychological depth typical of Modernist novels. "Like travelling back to the earliest beginnings of the world," Marlow travels up the Congo to locate Kurtz, another employee of the trading Company, who has disappeared. Marlow serves as a device for an unreliable narrator—he is telling the story to listeners while sitting on a boat on the Thames in England—as well as a character in both this work and in *Lord Jim*. The story he tells, depicting his experiences trying to find Kurtz, and what happens when he does finally encounter the latter, is part critique of the Western European imperialist project and part exploration of man's inhumanity to man to the diminishment of all.

❖•❖

Eliot, T. S. (1888-1965)
American-born English poet, critic, essayist, and dramatist.

Born in St. Louis, Missouri, Eliot spent most of his adult life in England, beginning with his visit to study at Oxford University, where he completed his Ph.D. dissertation for Harvard in 1916; he became a British citizen in 1927. While there, he met Ezra Pound, who would have a tremendous effect on his life. After graduating, Eliot taught school for a brief time, then worked at Lloyd's Bank. He served as an assistant editor of *The Egoist* from 1917 to 1919. In 1925 he became employed by the British publisher Faber and Gwyn (later Faber and Faber) where he worked until his death. Eliot's first important poem, "The Love Song of J. Alfred Prufrock" (1915), appeared in *Poetry* magazine (*see* CHICAGO LITERARY RENAISSANCE), and garnered him much attention. It was published in his first volume, *Prufrock and Other Observations,* in 1917. His second volume of poetry, *Poems* (1919), was published by Leonard and Virginia Woolf's Hogarth Press. In 1922 he founded the literary journal *The Criterion*; *The Waste Land* appeared in its first issue. "The Hollow Men" (1925) inaugurates Eliot's conversion to the Anglican Church and his searches for faith, the nature of time and eternity, and metaphysical revelation that lasted the rest of his life. It was followed by "The Journey of the Magi" (1927), "Ash Wednesday" (1930), and the beautifully visionary *Four Quartets* (1935-42). Though best known for his poetry and criticism, Eliot also wrote a few plays, the most important of which was *Murder in the Cathedral* (1935), based on the murder of Thomas à Becket. Others were *The Rock* (1934), *The Family Reunion* (1939), *The Cocktail Party* (1950), *The Confidential Clerk* (1954), and *The Elder Statesman* (1959). He also wrote a book of verse for children, *Old Possum's Book of Practical Cats* (1939), later adapted into a popular musical stage production, *Cats* (1981).

Eliot's critical concepts — in particular, "dissociation of sensibility" and the "objective correlative" — left indelible marks on subsequent twentieth-century writers. While awareness of his literary and cultural heritage is one of the most prominent features of Eliot's criticism and poetry, he also created the critical perspective that led to the elaborate rhetorical analyses of NEW CRITICISM. His most important critical piece was "Tradition and the Individual Talent" (1919) in *The Sacred Wood* (1920), postulating an anti-Romantic stance in which the poet should be impersonal and cognizant of the mainstream of tradition. He elaborates his concept of the "objective correlative," found in "Hamlet and His Problems" (1919), that emotion should not be stated but embodied in an image or a scene. Eliot's body of work shows the influence of Pound, T. E. Hulme and the IMAGISTS, and the French SYMBOLISTS, especially poets Jules Laforgue (1860-1887), Théophile Gautier (1811-1872), and Charles BAUDELAIRE. His influence on his contemporaries and later writers has been momumental.

The Waste Land (1922).

Considered by many to be the most important poem of the twentieth century, *The Waste Land* is notable for its heavy reliance on literary and classical allusions; Eliot's sources include James Frazer's (1854-1941) *The Golden Bough* (1890-1915), Dante's (1265-1321) *Inferno*, and Richard Wagner's (1813-1883) operas, as well as the Bible, the Buddha's Fire Sermon, and the Upanishads, Hindu scriptures—with many of which even most educated readers of the time would not be familiar. Yet many of Eliot's literary contemporaries felt that the poem spoke for them, their disillusionment after World War I, and their resultant pessimism about the state of Western civilization. Eliot, like the Symbolists, thought poetry should merely evoke or suggest meaning; in addition to its arcane and classical references, *The Waste Land* is striking in its refusal to link images through a narrative authority. Composed in five main sections, the poem jumps from scene to scene, beginning with an image of children sledding in Germany in Part I, "The Burial of the Dead," and concluding with, in "What the Thunder Said," an Upanishad meditative chant. Ezra Pound is rightly credited for much judicial editing of the original manuscript.

⇢●⇠

Joyce, James (1882-1941), Anglo-Irish novelist and short-story writer.

Joyce was born in Dublin, received a Catholic education, then moved to Paris in 1902. He returned to Ireland when his mother died, then headed back to Europe, living and working as an English teacher in, at turns, Trieste, Paris, and Zurich, where he died. At one point, one benefactor, the former Edith Rockefeller, wanted Joyce, a heavy drinker, to undergo psychoanalysis under Carl JUNG, which he refused and which cost him her financial support. He did, however, find other sources of support, in no small part through the efforts of Ezra Pound.

Though he never lived there after moving to the Continent, the setting for all of Joyce's work was Dublin. His first collection of prose, *Dubliners* (1914), included "The Dead," a superb short story in which Joyce aims at portraying artistic neutrality, which he believed necessary to attain genuine awareness. His autobiographical novel, *A Portrait of the Artist as a Young Man* (1916), develops that theme, also utilizing the device of epiphanies, moments of aesthetic and personal revelation. With his next, and final, novels, *Ulysses* (1922) and *Finnegans Wake* (1939), Joyce produced revolutionary structural and linguistic innovations in the form of the novel. Joyce was a great admirer of Henrik IBSEN (*see* Realism, Norway) and learned Norwegian in order to be able to read his work in the original and write to him. His work influenced, among others, ABSURDIST Samuel BECKETT, Existentialist Jean-Paul SARTRE, American Modernist William FAULKNER, and the NEW NOVELISTS.

Ulysses (1922).

The most widely studied and perhaps the greatest novel of the twentieth century, *Ulysses* brought Joyce instant acclaim and criticism upon its publication in 1922. Lauded by the likes of Ezra Pound, who found its publisher for Joyce, others found it unreadable. After enduring censorship from virtually every corner of the mainstream publishing world, Joyce was finally able to see his masterpiece into print within two years, after which, however, it was banned in the United States and in England for obscenity. The ban was lifted in the United States in 1933 and in England shortly after. Pound was among the few early reviewers who, completely dedicated to the ideals of Modernism, recognized Joyce's achievement for what it was: a herculean synthesis of ancient and modern epic, of fable and Realism, of the history of knowledge and perception down through the centuries, all rendered with startlingly new precision and complexity. The novel follows Leopold Bloom and Stephen Dedalus (who first appeared in Joyce's earlier novel, *A Portrait of the Artist as a Young Man*) — who are only in general Ulysses and Telemachus; Stephen is also Hamlet; Bloom/Ulysses is Jesus, Socrates, Shakespeare — over the course of one day, June 16, 1904. The modern-day odyssey of Joyce's protagonist Bloom became the archetype for every intellectual's journey toward sexual, psychological, and spiritual self-discovery.

✦•✦

Lawrence, David Herbert (1885-1930)
English novelist, short-story writer, poet, and essayist.

Lawrence was born into a poor family, and it was largely through his mother's vision and encouragement as well as a scholarship, that he was educated through high school, then found work as a clerk, then a teacher, until he saved enough to attend teacher's college and earn his certificate. He suffered from poor health as a child and later suffered from tuberculosis. One of Lawrence's great themes was vitality, the life force, as he put it, "the supreme impulse" — paritally accounting for his explicit treatment of sex as a rejuvenating natural force. Lawrence hated industrialization, contending that it inhibited humanity's sense of connection with nature, and at one point he tried to organize a utopian community. He lived in England during World War I, where his friends included Ford Madox FORD (*see* Edwardian Literature), Aldous Huxley (1894-1963), Katherine Mansfield (1888-1923), E. M. Forster (1879-1970), and Bertrand Russell (1872-1970).

His poetry volumes include *Look! We Have Come Through!* (1917) and *Birds, Beasts, and Flowers* (1923). His essays on major American nineteenth-century writers in *Studies in Classic American Literature* (1923) are completely original in method. Lawrence is best known, however, for his novels: *The White Peacock* (1911); *The*

Trespasser (1912), *SONS AND LOVERS* (1913), *The Rainbow* (1915), which was banned for obscenity because of its eroticism, *Women in Love* (1921), *Aaron's Rod* (1922), *Kangaroo* (1923), *The Plumed Serpent* (1926), and his last novel *Lady Chatterley's Lover* (1928), which also busied censors, as did his paintings.

Sons and Lovers (1913).

Autobiographical in nature, *Sons and Lovers* was Lawrence's first major novel. It follows the lives of coal miner Walter Morel, his educated and refined wife, and their sons William and Paul. Paul, based on Lawrence himself, struggles with his close attachment to his mother—whose intellectualism and gentility he vastly favors over the easygoing coarseness of his father—particularly when he becomes romantically interested in Miriam. Though early critics recognized an oedipal theme running through the novel, Lawrence had not read FREUD until 1912, well after he had begun the novel.

❖•❖

Pound, Ezra (1885-1972)
American-born English poet and critic.

Born in Idaho to Quaker parents, Pound met H. D. while students at the University of Pennsylvania; later they led the Imagist movement. His academic career in the States ended when he was asked to leave Wabash College in Indiana. In 1908 he went to Europe, where he would live out the rest of his life, first in Italy, then in London. Rather flamboyant in dress and manner, fascist in politics, and acutely skilled at leading the literary world, Pound, more than anyone else, was the consummate marketer of Modernism and its writers. From his home in Paris, he, more than anyone else, even Gertrude STEIN, influenced what works were to be included under the Modernist rubric and fostered their publication, writing in an editorial capacity for such journals as *Poetry*, the *Egoist*, and the *Little Review*. Critics agree that Pound's editorial interventions, for example, did a great service to T. S. Eliot's *The Waste Land*. For these reasons, critic Hugh Kenner (1923-) famously referred to Modernism as "the Pound Era." (Later, Wyndham Lewis would refer to "the Pound Circus.")

Pound's volumes of poetry included *A Lume Spento* (1908), *Personae* (1909), *Canzoni* (1911), *Ripostes* (1912), *Lustra* (1916), *Quia Pauper Amavi* (1919), *Hugh Selwyn Mauberley* (1920), and *The Cantos* (1917-68). His university training in Renaissance Romance literature informed his poetry in numerous ways as did Chinese literature, especially the basic unit of the language, the ideograph; he translated the great Chinese poet Li Po's (701-762) poems in *Cathay* (1915). He put great emphasis on the craft of writing poetry as well as precision in writing and is well known for proclaiming that "the age demands an image" and "make it new."

The Cantos (1917-70).

Pound did not live to complete his most ambitious poetic project. He did finish 109 cantos ("song" in Italian; a poetic division used in Italian poetry) following the example of Dante's *Divine Comedy*, as well as fragments of eight more. In *The Cantos*, Pound employs mythic themes and images from such classical sources as the *Odyssey* and the stories of Roman deities and mythological figures to present a vision of Western and Far Eastern history, its evils and its promises.

⇒•⇐

Stream of Consciousness.

Philosopher and psychologist William James (1842-1910) first used this term in *Principles of Psychology* (1890) in a psychological context to indicate "the flow of inner experiences." Similarly, in a literary context, the phrase denotes the portrayal of a character's "flow of inner experiences"—the verbalization of a character's inner thoughts, perceptions, and feelings. Such prose may or may not be fragmentary in a grammatical sense, but usually is so in a logical, syntactical one. "Interior monologue," representing a character's inner, often disjointed, "conversation" with him or herself, is a common way of effecting the stream-of-consciousness technique in literature. Dorothy Richardson's (1873-1957) *Pilgrimage* (13 vols., 1915-67) was a pioneering stream-of-consciousness novel in English as was Édouard Dujardin's (1861-1949) *Les lauriers sont coupés* (1887; *We'll to the Woods No More*, 1938) in French. James Joyce borrowed the technique from the latter in his masterpiece *Ulysses*. Other notable examples include Virginia Woolf's *To The Lighthouse*, William FAULKNER's *THE SOUND AND THE FURY* (*see* Modernism, United States), Marcel PROUST's (*see* Modernism, France) *A LA RECHERCHE DU TEMPS PERDU* (1913-27), and Arthur Schnitzler's (1862-1931) novella *Leutnant Gustl* (1901; *None But the Brave*, 1931) and parts of his one-act collection *Anatol* (1893).

⇒•⇐

Woolf, Virginia (1882-1941)
English novelist, critic, essayist, short-story writer, diarist, and biographer.

Woolf is often regarded as the most important woman writer, and one of the most important novelists, of the twentieth century. The youngest daughter of Sir Leslie Stephen (1832-1904), Woolf enjoyed a privileged, if somewhat secluded, upbringing. Following the early deaths of her mother and father, she, two of her brothers, and her sister Vanessa Bell (1879-1961) took a house in the Bloomsbury district in London. Gradually, particularly following her marriage to Leonard Woolf (1880-1969) and the inception of their joint publishing venture, the Hogarth Press, she became the central figure of the highly influential BLOOMSBURY GROUP. Yet, like most of the members of this politically progressive, aesthetically minded group, she remained markedly individual and innovative in her own work.

Woolf's first tentative breakthrough as a distinctively modern novelist occurred with *Jacob's Room* (1922), a work in which the central character is viewed through the experimental prisms of interior monologue and recurrent imagery. With her next novel, *Mrs. Dalloway* (1925), Woolf allowed her highly impressionistic and poetic style to dominate and succeeded in creating a rich and memorable stream-of-consciousness narrative that has fared well in critical comparisons with Joyce's similarly constructed but considerably longer novel, *Ulysses*. However, *To the Lighthouse* (1927), her next novel, marked an even greater departure from traditional techniques, particularly the architectonics of plot. She is also esteemed as one of the finest essayists in English literary history, most notably for *A Room of One's Own* (1929), a seminal feminist manifesto, and *Mr. Bennett and Mrs. Brown* (1924), in which she compares how John Galsworthy, Arnold Bennett, and H. G. Wells would depict a character she envisions each sitting opposite to on a train. After having suffered several years from recurrent, incapacitating depression, Woolf committed suicide by drowning herself.

To the Lighthouse (1927).

Although less popular, and readable, than *Mrs. Dalloway*, *To the Lighthouse* is a powerful example of Woolf's Modernist innovations. Using stream-of-consciousness narration and rich poetic imagery, Woolf draws on her memories of her own family's summer home to portray that of the Ramsays and their friends in three sections — "The Window," "Time Passes," and "The Lighthouse." Driving a main theme of the novel are the characters of Mr. and Mrs. Ramsay, who represent extremes in, respectively, masculine and feminine qualities and limitations, while the character of their artist friend, Lily Briscoe, gradually develops throughout the novel as a blending of the two.

➻•➼

Yeats, William Butler (1865-1939)
Irish poet, dramatist, essayist, and novelist.

The single most important figure in modern Irish letters, Yeats began his career during the 1880s as a dramatist and upholder of cultural nationalism, supporting the ABBEY THEATER and propelling the IRISH RENAISSANCE. In his mature work Yeats constantly sought to combine elements of fantasy with the metaphysical, drawing upon occult material of the Rosicrucian society, The Order of the Golden Dawn. His dual vision of the personality and its conflicting attitudes of good and evil, dreams and responsibility, and his admiration for a life to be lived with a noble stance and a pride in the beauty of existence give both his drama and poetry a visionary quality which continues to appeal to the sensitive and introspective reader. An early epic poem, "The Wanderings of Oisin," points directly to such dramatic works as the Cuchulain cycle, based on the ancient and legendary folk hero, Cuchulain, a character who fascinated Yeats for all of his life. But he is most renowned for his later poems, such as "Easter 1916," "The Second Coming," "Among School Children," "Under Ben Bulben," "Sailing to Byzantium," and "The Circus Animals' Desertion." He received the Nobel Prize for literature in 1923, and in 1928, what most critics agreed to be his finest work, "The Tower Poems," substantiated his reputation.

⋙•⋘

Further Reading

Albright, Daniel. *Quantum Poetics: Yeats, Pound, Eliot, and the Science of Modernism.* Cambridge, England: Cambridge University Press, 1997.

Bell, Quentin. *Virginia Woolf: A Biography.* 2 vols. London: Hogarth Press, 1972.

Bender, Todd K., et al. *Modernism in Literature.* New York: Holt, Rinehart and Winston, 1977.

Bornstein, George. *Ezra Pound among the Poets.* Chicago: University of Chicago Press, 1985.

Bradbury, Malcolm. *The Modern World: Ten Great Writers.* New York: Viking, 1989.

Bradbury, Malcolm, and James McFarlane. *Modernism 1890-1930.* Hassocks, Sussex, England: Harvester Press; Atlantic Highlands, N.J.: Humanities Press, 1978. Reissued with new preface, London: Penguin Books, 1991.

Brown, Dennis. *The Modernist Self in Twentieth-Century English Literature: A Study in Self-Fragmentation.* New York: St. Martin's Press, 1989.

Bush, Ronald. *The Genesis of Pound's "Cantos."* Princeton, N.J.: Princeton University Press, 1976.

Chiari, Joseph. *The Aesthetics of Modernism.* London: Vision, 1970.

Connolly, Cyril. *The Modern Movement: One Hundred Key Books from England, France, and America, 1880-1950.* New York: Atheneum, 1966.

Cox, C. B., and Arnold P. Hinchcliffe, eds. *T. S. Eliot: The Waste Land: A Casebook.* London: Macmillan, 1968.

Craig, Randall. *The Tragicomic Novel: Studies in a Fictional Mode from Meredith to Joyce.* Newark, Del.: University of Delaware Press, 1989.

Delany, Paul. *D. H. Lawrence's Nightmare: The Writer and His Circle in the Years of the Great War.* New York: Basic Books, 1979.

Edel, Leon. *The Modern Psychological Novel.* New York: Grove Press, 1955.

Fabricius, Johannes. *The Unconscious and Mr. Eliot.* Copenhagen: Nyt Nordisk Forlag, 1967.

Faulkner, Peter. *Modernism.* London: Methuen, 1977.

Frye, Northrop. *T. S. Eliot: An Introduction.* Chicago: University of Chicago Press, 1981.

Gordon, Lyndall. *Eliot's Early Years.* London: Oxford University Press, 1977.

Gross, John, ed. *The Modern Movement: A TLS Companion.* Chicago: University of Chicago Press, 1992.

Gunter, Bradley, ed. *The Merrill Studies in The Waste Land.* Columbus, Ohio: Merrill, 1971.

Howe, Irving, ed. *The Idea of the Modern in Literature and the Arts*. New York: Horizon Press, 1968.

————, ed. *Literary Modernism*. Greenwich, Conn.: Fawcett, 1967.

James, Henry. "The New Novel, 1914." In his *Notes on Novelists*. 1914. Reprint, New York: Biblio and Tannen, 1969.

Kampf, Louis. *On Modernism*. Cambridge, Mass.: MIT Press, 1967.

Kenner, Hugh. *The Pound Era*. Berkeley, Calif.: University of California Press, 1971.

————. *A Sinking Island: The Modern English Writers*. New York: Knopf, 1988.

Kiely, Robert. *Beyond Egotism: The Fiction of James Joyce, Virginia Woolf, and D. H. Lawrence*. Cambridge, Mass.: Harvard University Press, 1980.

Leavis, F. R. *D. H. Lawrence, Novelist*. London: Chatto & Windus, 1955.

Lee, Hermione. *The Novels of Virginia Woolf*. New York: Holmes & Meier, 1977.

Levenson, Michael H. *A Genealogy of Modernism: A Study of English Literary Doctrine 1908-1922*. Cambridge, England: Cambridge University Press, 1986.

Levin, Harry. *Ezra Pound, T. S. Eliot and the European Horizon*. Oxford, England: Clarendon Press, 1975.

Lucy, Sean. *T. S. Eliot and the Idea of Tradition*. London: Cohen & West, 1960.

Materer, Timothy. *Vortex: Pound, Eliot and Lewis*. Ithaca, N.Y.: Cornell University Press, 1979.

Menand, Louis. *Discovering Modernism: T. S. Eliot and His Context*. New York: Oxford University Press, 1987.

Meyers, Jeffrey, ed. *D. H. Lawrence and Tradition*. Amherst, Mass.: University of Massachusetts Press, 1985.

Moore, Harry Thornton. *The Priest of Love: A Life of D. H. Lawrence*. Rev. ed. New York: Farrar, Straus, Giroux, 1974.

Niven, Alastair. *D. H. Lawrence, the Writer and His Work*. Harlow, England: Longman, 1980.

Norris, Margot, ed. *A Companion to James Joyce's* Ulysses: *Biographical and Historical Contexts, Critical History, and Essays from Five Contemporary Critical Perspectives*. Boston: Bedford Books, 1998; distributed by St. Martin's Press.

Padhi, Bibhu. *D. H. Lawrence: Modes of Fictional Style*. Troy, N.Y.: Whitston, 1988.

Parrinder, Patrick. *James Joyce*. Cambridge, England: Cambridge University Press, 1984.

Peake, Charles. *James Joyce, the Citizen and the Artist*. Stanford, Calif.: Stanford University Press, 1977.

Peterson, Richard F. *James Joyce Revisited*. New York: Twayne, 1992.

Quinones, Ricardo J. *Mapping Literary Modernism: Time and Development*. Princeton, N.J.: Princeton University Press, 1985.

Robinson, Lilian S., and Lise Vogel. "Modernism and History." *New Literary History* 3 (1971): 177-99.

Rosenberg, Beth Carole, and Jeanne Dubino, eds. *Virginia Woolf and the Essay*. New York: St. Martin's Press, 1997.

Schwartz, Sanford. *The Matrix of Modernism: Pound, Eliot, and Early Twentieth-Century Thought*. Princeton, N.J.: Princeton University Press, 1985.

Stead, C. K. *Pound, Yeats, Eliot and the Modernist Movement*. New Brunswick, N.J.: Rutgers University Press, 1986.

Sultan, Stanley. *"Ulysses," "The Waste Land," and Modernism*. Port Washington, N.Y.: Kennikat Press, 1977.

Svarny, Erik. *The Men of 1914: T. S. Eliot and Early Modernism*. Milton Keynes, England: Open University Press, 1988.

Tedlock, Ernest W. *D. H. Lawrence, Artist and Rebel*. Albuquerque, N.Mex.: University of New Mexico Press, 1963.

Woolf, Virginia. *The Diaries of Virginia Woolf, Vols. 1-5*. Edited by Anne Olivier Bell. New York: Harcourt Brace Jovanovich, 1978-85.

MODERNISM
Finland, 1940s-1950s

A poetic movement of the 1940s and 1950s, Finnish Modernism relied upon the example of T. S. ELIOT as well as the ideological currents of the day. Numerous writers associated themselves with the movement; perhaps the most notable was poet, novelist, and dramatist Paavo Haavikko (1931-). Others included Tuomas Anhava (1927-), Lasse Heikkilä (1925-1961), Pentti Holappa (1927-), Helvi Juvonen (1919-1959), Eila Kivikkaho (1921-), Liisa Manner (1921-), Aila Meriluoto (1924-), and Lassi Nummi (1928-).

✦●✦

Further Reading

Ahokas, Jaakko. *A History of Finnish Literature*. Bloomington, Ind.: Indiana University, 1973.

Anhava, Tuomas. *In the Dark, Move Slowly: Poems*. Selected and translated by Anselm Hollo. London: Cape Goliard, 1969.

"Hommage to Paavo Haavikko, Our 1984 Neustadt Laureate." Norman, Okla.: University of Oklahoma Press, 1984. Originally published in *World Literature Today* 58, 4 (autumn 1984): 493-560.

Paavo Haavikko, the Neustadt Prize 1984. Helsinki, Finland: Helsinki University Library, 1984.

MODERNISM
France, 1900s-1930s

The beginnings of Modernism in France and elsewhere can be traced most directly to the SYMBOLIST movement, and eventually manifested in various avant-garde movements: Jean Moréas's (1856-1910) ÉCOLE ROMANE with its neoclassicism that presaged other Modernists' use of classical images (e.g. T. S. ELIOT), CUBISM, SURREALISM, FANTAISISTES, and THÉÂTRE LIBRE. The history of Modernism in France is largely aligned with the history of the *NOUVELLE REVUE FRANÇAISE*, created in 1909 at the instigation of André GIDE and director Jacques COPEAU, who later founded the THÉÂTRE DU VIEUX-COLOMBIER.

409

The way toward the new, toward freedom from the old artistic orders, was paved via various outbreaks of turmoil in other spheres: the rise of the socialist movement, the appearance of anarchists in trade unions in the early years of the century, and the general strikes of 1906 and 1909. Later the devastating impact of World War I most powerfully articulated the fact that Europe was changed forever. After the war, in 1919, Paul Valery (1871-1945) spoke for many: "We civilizations now know we are mortal." But coexisting uneasily alongside a push toward the new was a conservative backlash against Modernist trends constituted by the rise of widespread xenophobia — particularly as the prospect of war with Germany became inevitable in 1911 — the continued dominance of Wagnerism in music, and of Impressionism and Symbolism in art and poetry, and in particular Moréas's École Romane. In the early 1910s the Cubists, considered barbarians by the reactionary contingent, could not get exhibited in any of the city's major galleries. Before 1914, Marcel PROUST, Gide, and Guillaume APOLLINAIRE (*see* Cubism) were relative unknowns. It was not until after the war that the figures known as the leading lights of Parisian Modernism came to be regarded as such in their homeland, with the rise of DADA in Zurich in 1916, its landing in Paris in 1920, and, since the Russian Revolution of 1917, the reinforcement of the socialist movement, culminating, in the artistic world, in the Surrealist manifesto of 1924.

In addition, Paris was the center of the most radical changes in the visual arts represented by Pablo Picasso (1881-1973), Henri Matisse (1869-1954), Georges Braque (1882-1963), and others who migrated there such as Marc Chagall (1887-1985), Paul Klee (1879-1940), Juan Gris (1887-1927), Piet Mondriaan (1872-1944), and in music, with Igor Stravinsky (1882-1971), Claude Debussy (1862-1918), and Maurice Ravel (1875-1937). In art the appearance of Picasso's *Les Demoiselles d'Avignon* (1907) and in music the debut of Stravinsky's *Le Sacre du printemps* in 1913 were landmark cultural events, defining moments in the crystalization of Modernism in Paris. In literature Apollinaire reached beyond the Symbolists with his Cubist-inspired poetry, such as "Zone" in the collection *Alcools* (1913; *Alcohols*, 1964); André Gide contributed another watershed publication with *Les Caves du Vatican* (1914; *Lafcadio's Adventures*, 1928).

Paris also became a cultural magnet for expatriate English and American writers, like Gertrude STEIN (*see* MODERNISM, United States) and members of the LOST GENERATION, T. S. ELIOT and Ezra POUND (*see* MODERNISM, England and Ireland), William Carlos Williams (1883-1963), Edith WHARTON (*see* REALISM, United States), Sylvia Beach (1887-1962), and Djuna BARNES (*see* Lost Generation), as well as the likes of Eugenio MONTALE (*see* HERMETICISM) from Italy, Dadaists from Zurich, Russian emigrants, and Samuel BECKETT and James JOYCE from Ireland. There they basked in the experimental climate and collectively changed the course of Western literature.

❖•❖

Proust, Marcel (1871-1922), French novelist and critic.

Affiliated with none of the Modernist literary movements and, in fact, relatively unrecognized as a peer by his literary contemporaries, Proust is generally considered a paramount French Modernist. He was born in Paris, son of a doctor, and suffered poor health due to asthma throughout his life. He attended the Lycée Condorcet, where his studies of the philosophy of Henri BERGSON in particular would make a profound and lasting impression. He was friends with Fernand Gregh (1873-1960), a proponent of HUMANISME and others with whom he founded a small literary review, *Le Banquet*. Proust's first book was a collection of stories, *Les Plaisirs et les Jours* (1896; Pleasures and Days), but his life's work was the 3000-page novel *A LA RECHERCHE DU TEMPS PERDU* (7 vols., 1913-27; *Remembrance of Things Past*, 7 vols., 1922-32). He is renowned as a stylist, for his dialogue, imagery and metaphor, his comedic talent, and his experiments in structure. A novel Proust wrote during the 1900s, *Jean Santeuil* (1952; *Jean Santeuil*, 1956) was discovered and published after his death.

A la recherche du temps perdu (7 vols., 1913-27; *Remembrance of Things Past*, 7 vols., 1922-32).

Rejected by four publishers, including *Nouvelle Revue Française* (NRF) Proust paid for the first novel to be published by Bernard Grasset, originally in separate volumes under different titles: volume I, *Du côté de chez Swann* (1913; *Swann's Way*, 1922); volume II, *A l'ombre des jeunes filles en fleurs* (1919; *Within a Budding Grove*, 1924), which won the Goncourt Prize and earned Proust fame; volume III, *Les côté de Guermantes I* (1920-21; *The Guermantes' Way*, 1925); volume IV, *Sodome et Gomorrhe* (1921-22; *Cities of the Plain*, 1927); and posthumously, volume V, *La prisonnière* (1923; *The Captive*, 1929); volume VI, *Albertine disparue* (1925; *The Sweet Cheat Gone*, 1930); and volume VII, *Le temps retrouvé* (1927; *Time Regained*, 1931). *NRF* did publish the second volume, *A l'ombre des jeunes filles en fleurs*, for which Proust won the Goncourt Prize, gaining him, finally, serious regard from the French literati.

Widely considered the most innovative French novel of the twentieth century, the novel's primary theme is memory, time, and how its passing is experienced, and the complex, fragmented self, "the multiple ego." The volumes explore how characters are gradually revealed to observers in real life, as opposed to traditional novelistic characterizations. Memories are evoked through stimuli in the present that coincide with stimuli associated with the memory — what Proust called "involuntary memory." *A la recherche du temps perdu* had a profound impact on many later writers, including those associated with the NEW NOVEL, EXISTENTIALISM, and DECONSTRUCTION.

❧●❦
Further Reading

Beckett, Samuel. *Proust*. New York: Grove Press, 1931.

Benstock, Shari. *Women of the Left Bank: Paris, 1900-1940*. Austin, Tex.: University of Texas Press, 1986.

Bloom, Harold, ed. *Marcel Proust*. New York: Chelsea House Publishers, 1987.

Bradbury, Malcolm, and James McFarlane. *Modernism 1890-1930*. Hassocks, Sussex, England: Harvester Press; Atlantic Highlands, N.J.: Humanities Press, 1978. Reissued with new preface, London: Penguin Books, 1991.

Brée, Germaine. *Gide*. New Brunswick, N.J.: Rutgers University Press, 1963.

———. *Marcel Proust and Deliverance from Time*. Translated by C. J. Richards and A. D. Truitt. 2nd ed. New Brunswick, N.J.: Rutgers University Press, 1969.

———. *The World of Marcel Proust*. Boston: Houghton Mifflin, 1966.

Ciholas, Karin Nordenhaug. *Gide's Art of the Fugue: A Thematic Study of "Les Faux-Monnayeurs."* Chapel Hill, N.C.: University of North Carolina, Department of Romance Languages, 1974.

Gide, André. *Journal of "The Counterfeiters."* New York: Knopf, 1951.

Goux, Jean-Joseph. "Mise en Abyme." In *A New History of French Literature*. Edited by Dennis Hollier, et al. Cambridge, Mass.: Harvard University Press, 1989.

Jephcott, E. F. N. *Proust and Rilke: The Literature of Expanded Consciousness*. London: Chatto and Windus, 1972.

Maurois, André. "Marcel Proust." In his *From Proust to Camus: Profiles of Modern French Writers*. Translated by Carl Morse and Renaud Bruce. Garden City, N.Y.: Doubleday & Company, 1966.

Peyre, Henri. *Marcel Proust*. New York: Columbia University Press, 1970.

———. "The Legacy of Proust and Gide." In his *The Contemporary French Novel*. New York: Oxford University Press, 1955.

Pizer, Donald. *American Expatriate Writing and the Paris Moment: Modernism and Place*. Baton Rouge, La.: Louisiana State University Press, 1996.

Poulet, Georges. *Proustian Space*. Translated by Elliott Coleman. Baltimore, Md.: Johns Hopkins University Press, 1977.

Quinones, Ricardo J. *Mapping Literary Modernism: Time and Development*. Princeton, N.J.: Princeton University Press, 1985.

Terdiman, Richard. *Present Past: Modernity and the Memory Crisis*. Ithaca, N.Y.: Cornell University Press, 1993.

Wilson, Edmund. *Axel's Castle: A Study in the Imaginative Literature of 1870-1930*. New York: Charles Scribner's Sons, 1931.

Zurbrugg, Nicholas. *Beckett and Proust*. Gerrards Cross, Buckinghamshire, England: C. Smythe; Totowa, N.J.: Barnes and Noble Books, 1988.

MODERNISM
Iceland, 1940s-1950s

Icelandic Modernism surfaced during the 1940s and 1950s as a direct challenge to the conservative literary traditions still dominant in the country. Typically sympathetic to leftist politics and the issues raised by EXISTENTIALISM, such writers as Einar Bragi (1921-), Jón Óskar (1921-), Hannes Sigússon (1922-), and Thor Vilhjálmsson (1925-) made significant contributions to the creation of a new Icelandic literature.

➔•◄

Further Reading

Three Modern Icelandic Poets: Selected Poems of Steinn Steinarr, Jón úr Vör and Matthías Johannessen. Translated and introduced by Marshall Brement. Reykjavik, Iceland: Iceland Review, 1985.

MODERNISM
Italy, 1900-1950s

The various trends that came collectively to be known as "Modernism" emerged in Italy, as in other countries around the world, in response to circumstances both literary and political. Several centuries of foreign dominance of Italy finally ended in 1870, when the French finally left the country. Nineteenth-century Italian literature was influenced not only by the classicism and romanticism practiced by other European and American writers but by a distinctly Italian form of nationalism called *risorgimento* which led to a heightened interest in history, tradition, and regionalism. Alessandro Manzoni's (1785-1873) great novel *I promessi spozi* (1827; *The Betrothed,* 1898) reflects this focus, chronicling in clear, straightforward prose the story of peasant lovers finding in traditional values and faith the strength to fight oppression.

In the years just before and after the turn of the century, Italy joined the worldwide trend toward REALISM and NATURALISM—which was then being practiced by such European and American authors as Emile ZOLA, Honoré de Balzac (1799-1850), and Stephen CRANE—through the VERISMO movement. Verismo was also a reaction against the extreme romanticism and overblown rhetoric of traditional Italian literature. Led by the acclaimed novelists Giovanni VERGA and Luigi Capuana (1839-1915), the Verists aimed for objective works that conveyed human experience in accurate, impersonal, and simplified language. Verga is particularly credited with blending literary language with local dialect to create a revolutionary new narrative style that came closer to real life while retaining its artistic integrity.

413

During the first quarter of the twentieth century, many writers began to turn their focus inward to explore the mysteries of the human psyche and of subjective experience. In his novel *Una vita* (1893; *A Life*, 1963) as well as later works, Italo SVEVO portrayed the same kind of alienated anti-hero that would later come to dominate much of twentieth-century literature. One of Italy's greatest literary figures, Luigi PIRANDELLO, incorporated psychological insights into his dramatic works and novels, particularly highlighting the conflict between reality and illusion. Another important influence on the artists of this period was the philosopher and historian Benedetto CROCE with his inspiring idealism and belief in the intuitive basis of art.

Perhaps the most significant of several transitional movements between the centuries-old Italian poetic tradition — which many modern poets viewed as staid, confining, and out of touch with their experience — and such Modernist trends as FUTURISM and HERMETICISM were the CREPUSCOLARI poets. They were among the first to rebel against traditional grandiosity and sentimentality in favor of simplified language and themes and an emphasis on description rather than declamation. The Crepuscolari movement was finally overshadowed by Futurism, which debuted in 1909 with the publication of the Futurist Manifesto by its founder, Filippo Tommaso MARINETTI. The Futurist poets made an even bolder, more strident break with the past than had those of the Crepuscolari movement.

Another important movement in the Italian literature produced during the early twentieth century was Hermetic poetry, which developed in response not only to the Modernist call for general cultural reevaluation and renewal but in reaction to the perceived inadequacy of the constrained, ornate verse tradition to express twentieth-century concerns and experiences. In addition, the brevity and obscurity of Hermetic poetry allowed independent-minded Italian writers a covert means to evade the propagandistic rhetoric and censorship of Mussolini's regime. Influenced by several other Modernist movements, such as SYMBOLISM and Futurism, Hermetic verse was characterized by unconventional structure and syntax, emotional restraint, and highly subjective, cryptic, involuted language. The leading poets of the Hermetic movement include Giuseppe UNGARETTI, whose first volume, *Il porto sepolto* (1916; *The Buried Port*, 1958) featured verse purged of traditional rhyme schemes and pared down to the essential; Salvatore QUASIMODO, author of *Acque e terre* (1930; Water and Lands), which paints a nostalgic portrait of the poet's Sicilian home in stripped-down, allusive language that conveys a deep sense of anguish and exile; and (despite his own refusal to claim membership in this or any other movement) Eugenio MONTALE, whose first volume, *Ossi di seppia* (1916; *The Bones of Cuttlefish*, 1983), features verse written in compressed, highly personal, often difficult language.

Although World War I had profound effects on the entire world, Italy suffered particularly devastating economic and psychological damage. Widespread disillusion, discontent, and confusion led to societal fragmentation that contributed to the rise of Benito Mussolini and his Fascist political party. Mussolini seized power in October of 1922, and his regime immediately began to establish a series of "reforms" that were enforced by violent means. Cultural oppression was an integral part of Mussolini's system, and writers were silenced through exile abroad (as in the case of Ignazio SILONE) or to remote Italian villages (Cesare PAVESE and Carlo Levi [1902-1975]); Alberto MORAVIA was prevented from signing his own work and Eugenio Montale lost his job.

Although the Fascist period is generally considered a dark and culturally vacant expanse in the development of modern Italian literature, some glimmers of hope and future productivity did exist. As previously mentioned, the Hermetic poets (several of whose work would come to true fruition after World War II) expressed their discontent in cryptic, obscure verse that slipped by the Fascist censors. From exile in Switzerland, Ignazio Silone published the acclaimed novel *PANE E VINO* (1937; *Bread and Wine*, 1937, 1962), which documented the abuses and despair of the Fascist period. And the earliest works of the important NEOREALIST movement appeared.

Like the Verists, the Italian Neorealist writers were committed to drawing accurate, straightforward portraits of everyday life and ordinary people. But they had also been deeply affected by their experiences during the Fascist period and World War II, when they had been forced to confront such issues as the nature of political power and their own role in society. Some of the earliest manifestations of Neorealism were Alberto Moravia's novel *GLI INDIFFERENTI* (1929; *The Time of Indifference*, 1953), which blended realism and allegory in its portrayal of middle-class life; and Cesare Pavese's *Paesi tuoi* (1941; *The Harvesters*, 1961), which chronicles the return of two ex-convicts to the Piedmont home of one of them.

As the war drew to a close, hope for an easing of Italy's social and political difficulties increased, and newly inspired, socially committed writers turned their attention to documenting those difficulties. Some of the best works of this period include Pavese's masterpiece, *LA LUNA E I FALÒ* (1950; *The Moon and the Bonfire*, 1952), the lyrical yet authentically detailed chronicle of an Italian resistance movement member's return to his rural home town after the war; and Elio VITTORINI's *CONVERSAZIONE IN SICILIA* (1941; *In Sicily*, 1947), an allegorical novel about a young man who encounters miserable poverty and despair during a visit to his ancestral village.

An important source of inspiration for Italy's Neorealist writers came from a parallel, and internationally recognized, movement in Italian film (*see* NEOREALIST FILM). From the end of World War II until about 1950, such filmmakers as Roberto Rossellini (1906-1977) and Vittorio De Sica (1901-1974) recreated with documentary-like fidelity the struggles of ordinary urban and rural people at a difficult period in Italy's history.

❖•❖

Croce, Benedetto (1866-1952)
Italian philosopher, literary critic, and historian.

One of the most important of twentieth-century European philosophers, Croce also excelled in the fields of statesmanship, literary criticism, and history. He exerted a strong influence on Italian and other cultures through both his written works and his position as editor of the bimonthly periodical *LA CRITICA* (1903-44). A follower of the eighteenth-century Italian philosopher Giovanni Battista, Croce was an idealistic advocate of civic freedom as well as civic responsibility, asserting that intellectuals should take active roles in public life. Croce served as an important symbol of integrity during the Fascist period through his outspoken opposition to Mussolini's regime. Earlier in the century, Croce had conducted an exhaustive study of Marxism that ultimately led him to condemn not only this but any political system that relies on propaganda and falsehoods to maintain its power.

Croce's theory of art emphasized intuition over reason, and he identified the critic's task as that of identifying and characterizing the unique qualities of an individual work or artist so as to distinguish true or pure art from the false. Croce's most acclaimed writings are collected in the volumes known as the *Filosofia come scienza dello spirito*, comprised of *Estetica* (1902; Aesthetics) and *Filosofia della practica: Economica ed edica* (1913; *Philosophy of the Practical: Economics and Ethics*, 1923), in which he divides all human activity into four realms — theoretical, practical, individual, and universal — each of which is then divided into cognition (involving intuition and logic) and volition (involving economics and ethics).

❖•❖

Montale, Eugenio (1896-1981), Italian poet, critic, and translator.

Considered one of the most important figures in twentieth-century Italian literature, Montale was awarded the Nobel Prize in 1975. His early admiration for the French Symbolist poets, especially Paul Valéry (1871-1945), inspired him to attempt similar innovations with his own poetry. Thus Montale created a compressed, cryptic style and focused on the concrete rather than the sensual — both qualities that made his work a radical departure from the Italian lyric tradition. Much of his writing is dominated by despair and the sense that poetry is a means to analyze and explore — but not resolve or provide consolation for — the mysteries of existence.

416

Montale is often categorized as a member of the Hermeticism movement, whose adherents also strove for innovation and freedom through stripped-down, often obscure verse. Although Montale denied belonging to any particular group or movement, his poetry does resemble that of the Hermeticists in its complexity and its dedication to a decidedly personal mythology.

In addition to his association (at least in the minds of critics) with the Hermeticists, Montale is often linked to the English Modernist poet T. S. ELIOT. Both poets sought through a reevaluation of literary tradition ways to express the existential concerns and anxiety of the twentieth century, and the work of both is filled with desolation. More specifically, Montale is considered an expert practitioner of Eliot's theory of the "objective correlative": the projection of ideas and emotions onto material objects or things that become symbols for humanity's condition.

The poems in Montale's first volume, *Ossi di seppia* (1916; *The Bones of Cuttlefish*, 1983), are centered in the dry, rocky coastal region of Liguria, where Montale grew up. The language in which they are written is groundbreaking due to its sedate tone and conversational diction. Interestingly, despite his desire to "come closer" to his own experience than traditional verse would have allowed him, Montale provides no poetic account of or reference to his years as a soldier in World War I (a significant difference from, for instance, the Hermetic poet Giuseppe Ungaretti).

Montale created a moving chronicle of the years leading up to the beginning of World War II in *Le occasioni* (1939; *The Occasions*, 1987), which is permeated with the pessimism and sense of looming disaster that dominated Italian society during that anxious period. Evident here is Montale's belief that all individuals can do in the face of such disillusioning and chaotic circumstances is to hold on to private values, even if truth is elusive.

✤•✦

Pirandello, Luigi (1867-1936)
Italian novelist, short-story writer, and dramatist.

One of the most acclaimed literary figures of the early twentieth century, Pirandello deftly incorporated philosophical concerns and psychological insights as well as subtle comedy into his works. He is particularly renowned for his dramatic innovations, which were designed to bring actors and audience closer together, and for infusing both his plays and his fiction with a very modern sense of reality's many and changing faces.

Born in Girgenti, Sicily, Pirandello was educated in Rome and Bonn, Germany. His subsequent life was marred by a number of personal and financial troubles, especially the long mental illness of his wife and his son's sojourn as a prisoner of war during World War I. An early supporter of Mussolini, Pirandello ultimately broke with the Fascist

Party. Many commentators detect in Pirandello's work a deep disillusionment and pessimism concerning his nation's future; others, however, attest to the presence of an underlying compassion and desire to portray life in all of its complexity.

Pirandello began his theatrical career writing plays for the *teatro grottesco* (THEATER OF THE GROTESQUE), a forerunner to the later THEATER OF THE ABSURD, which emphasized the illogical, pointless nature of existence. He achieved his first dramatic success with *Così è (se vi pare)* (1917; *Right You Are! [If You Think So]*, 1922), which centers on the concept that all truth is relative. Before that, Pirandello had published two well-received novels: *Il fu Mattia Pascal* (1904; *The Late Mattia Pascal*, 1964), a serio-comic narrative about a bungling, henpecked librarian; and *I vecchi e i giovani* (1908; *The Old and the Young*, 1928), which focuses on the ways in which people need masks and illusions in order to deceive themselves and others and thus maintain relationships.

Pirandello's most famous work is his drama *SEI PERSONAGGI IN CERCA D'AUTURE* (1921; *Six Characters in Search of an Author*, 1922, 1954). *Sei personaggi* takes place in the interior of a playwright's mind and involves a confrontation between some actors and a group of as yet unrealized characters who demand to be given existence. The bare set and frank acknowledgment of the theatre as providing a simulation of life, not life itself, both contributed to the play's uniqueness and innovation. The first time the play was staged, an audience unprepared for such radical innovations actually rioted in protest. Later audiences, however, were more appreciative, and *Sei personaggi* was critically lauded for successfully challenging the conventional relationship between actor and playgoer.

Also acclaimed is *Enrico IV* (1922; *Henry IV*, 1923), in which the protagonist believes he is King Henry IV. When he unexpectedly regains his sanity, he kills the enemy who caused his madness, but then must decide whether to feign insanity in order to avoid retribution or admit that he is now sane. The play provides an eloquent, sympathetic portrait of madness, suggesting that insanity or illusion may sometimes be a logical response to life. In *L'umorismo* (1908; *On Humor*, 1974), a long essay on humor and comedy, Pirandello uses examples from the entire European literary tradition to illustrate his theory that comedy emerges from the conflict between appearance and reality, an opposition that an audience realizes when it becomes aware of the suffering beneath the surface of comedy. This awareness, asserts Pirandello, allows the audience not only to empathize with a character's situation but to better understand him- or herself and other people.

Pirandello was awarded the Nobel Prize in 1934. Modern and contemporary authors influenced by his work are too numerous to mention but include such important playwrights and novelists as Albert CAMUS (*see* EXISTENTIALISM), Eugene IONESCO and Samuel BECKETT (*see* Theater of the Absurd), Eugene O'NEILL (*see* EXPRESSIONISM, United States, and PROVINCETOWN PLAYERS), Harold PINTER (*see* COMEDY OF MENACE), and Edward Albee (1928-).

Sei personaggi in cerca d'auture (1921; *Six Characters in Search of an Author*, 1922, 1954).

One of the most influential plays in twentieth-century drama, *Sei personaggi* takes place entirely in the mind of the playwright, where artistic creation begins. The set is simply a bare stage upon which a company of mediocre actors has assembled for a rehearsal. They are confronted by a group of six figures who explain that they are unrealized characters from the playwright's imagination. They demand that they be granted existence through a play that the playwright has not yet written.

The play was revolutionary in its self-conscious approach to the art and artifice of the theater, which would eventually become a hallmark of the modern drama. In bringing both characters and actors onto the stage and treating them both as real entities, Pirandello was challenging his audience's expectations and concept of reality. His first audience did not appreciate this challenge and rioted, but the play later became an international success.

✦•✦

Silone, Ignazio (1900-1978), Italian novelist, essayist, and playwright.

Silone is best known as the author of *Pane e vino* (1937; *Bread and Wine,* 1937, 1962), one of the most acclaimed novels produced during the dark period in Italy's history when Benito Mussolini's Fascist Party held power.

Silone's childhood was marred by tragedy, for the village in which he was born was destroyed in an earthquake that took the lives of his mother and several brothers. During World War I he became a Socialist, and he joined the Communist Party in 1921. After his brother was killed by the Fascists, Silone fled into the countryside and was sheltered for some time by peasants. He finally escaped to Switzerland, where he remained in exile until after World War II. Although an ideological crisis caused Silone to part ways with the Communist Party in 1931, he retained to the end of his life his own brand of idealism blending socialism and Christianity.

Pane e vino (1937; *Bread and Wine,* 1937, 1962).

The protagonist of *Pane e vino* is Pietro Spina, an antifascist activist who returns to Italy after fifteen years in exile abroad. Disguised as a priest, he travels around the country and witnesses the damage to society wrought by Fascism as well as the disinte-

419

gration of the resistance movement. Threatened by arrest, Spina again flees Italy. Written in a spare, understated, subtly sophisticated style, the novel provides an effective blend of both political and human elements. Silone's compassion and sense of injustice are evident in his portrayal of the Italian peasantry, whose resilience despite their status as powerless *cafoni* (underdogs) is admirable. Silone has been praised for delving beneath the surface of antifascism to expose an underside of doubt, as Spina wonders whether his grandiose ideals have separated him from the humble people for whose freedom he fights.

✦●✦

Svevo, Italo (1861-1928), Italian novelist, essayist, and dramatist.

Many of the most important concerns of Modernism are found in the work of Svevo, who was a leading force in Italian and other European literature during the first quarter of the twentieth century. Influenced by the psychoanalytic theories of Sigmund FREUD, Svevo incorporated psychological insights and motivations into his essentially naturalistic, plainly written works, also using irony and humor to highlight the foibles of the human psyche and the weakness of human morality.

Svevo is most famous for three novels: *Una vita* (1893; *A Life*, 1963), *Senilità* (1898; *As a Man Grows Older*, 1932), and *La coscienza di Zeno* (1923; *The Confessions of Zeno*, 1930). Each is at least partially autobiographical, and each features an introspective, rather ineffectual protagonist who engages in a struggle—whether it is for freedom from his parents, love, or the key to his own identity. Based on Svevo's own humiliating experience of being forced to abandon his studies at age nineteen to become a bank clerk, *Una Vita* features the kind of alienated anti-hero that would come to dominate modern fiction.

This introspective focus is continued in *Senilità* and reaches its most effective expression in *Confessions of Zeno*, which is widely recognized as Svevo's best novel and an important work in the development of the modern Italian novel. *Confessions* was particularly praised by Svevo's friend Irish Modernist James JOYCE, who helped to bring him to the forefront of the European literary scene.

Confessions chronicles the attempt of its anxious, insecure title character to cure his smoking habit and his many psychosomatic ailments through psychoanalysis. The novel retraces fifty-seven-year-old Zeno's entire life, showing how Zeno is able to reorganize his experiences through language and thus triumph over circumstance despite his essential inaction. Zeno concludes that life itself is his problem and—since there is no cure for life but death and he does not wish to die—he may simply declare that he is cured. *Confessions* is markedly modern in its inward focus and its portrayal of existence as a reflection of the narrator's psyche rather than as objective reality.

⇒•⇐
Further Reading

Armes, Roy. *Patterns of Realism: A Study of Italian Neo-Realist Cinema*. New York: A. S. Barnes, 1971.

Calvino, Italo. "Main Currents in Italian Fiction Today." *Italian Quarterly* 4, 13-14 (spring-summer 1960): 3-14.

Cecchetti, Giovanni. *Giovanni Verga*. Boston: Twayne, 1987.

Heiney, Donald. *Three Italian Novelists: Moravia, Pavese, Vittorini*. Ann Arbor, Mich.: University of Michigan Press, 1968.

Jones, Frederic J. *Giuseppe Ungaretti*. Edinburgh, Scotland: Edinburgh University Press, 1977.

Marcus, Millicent. *Italian Cinema in the Light of Neorealism*. Princeton, N.J.: Princeton University Press, 1987.

Molinaro, Julius A., ed. *Petrarch to Pirandello: Studies in Italian Literature in Honour of Beatrice Corrigan*. Toronto: University of Toronto Press, 1973.

Pacifici, Sergio. *A Guide to Contemporary Italian Literature: From Futurism to Neorealism*. Carbondale, Ill.: Southern Illinois University Press, 1962.

———. *The Modern Italian Novel from Capuana to Tozzi*. Carbondale, Ill.: Southern Illinois University Press, 1973.

———. *The Modern Italian Novel from Pea to Moravia*. Carbondale, Ill.: Southern Illinois University Press, 1979.

Pacifici, Sergio, ed. *From Verismo to Experimentalism: Essays on the Modern Italian Novel*. Bloomington, Ind.: Indiana University Press, 1969.

Potter, Joy Hambuechen. *Elio Vittorini*. Boston: Twayne, 1979.

Singh, G. *Eugenio Montale: A Critical Study of His Poetry, Prose, and Criticism*. New Haven, Conn.: Yale University Press, 1973.

Weiss, Beno. *Italo Svevo*. Boston: Twayne, 1987.

Woolf, David. *The Art of Verga: A Study in Objectivity*. Sydney, Australia: Sydney University Press, 1977.

MODERNISM, Poland. *See* YOUNG POLAND

MODERNISM
Russia, 1900s-1930s

The story of Modernism in Russia is best told through the numerous movements that emerged primarily as reactions to REALISM over a span of nearly thirty years, from approximately 1907 to 1934. The most prominent of the Modernist movements, after SYMBOLISM, were ACMEISM, CUBO-FUTURISM, CONSTRUCTIVISM, RUSSIAN FORMALISM, SERAPION BROTHERS, OBERIU, MOSCOW ART THEATER, and IMAGINISM. Major Modernists in Russia affiliated with these movements included Dmitry S.

Merezhkovsky (1865-1941), Andrey BELY, and Alexandr BLOK (*see* SYMBOLISM, Russia), Anna AKHMATOVA, Nikolay GUMILYOV, and Osip MANDELSTAM (*see* Acmeism), Sergey ESENIN (*see* Imaginists), Roman JAKOBSON and Viktor Shklovsky (1893-1984; *see* Russian Formalism), Velemir KHLEBNIKOV and Vladimir MAYAKOV-SKY (*see* Cubo-Futurism), Konstantin STANISLAVSKY (*see* Moscow Art Theater). In addition, Stanisław Przybyszewski of the YOUNG POLAND movement lectured widely in Russia, where he became a chief prophet of Modernism.

Writers following in the wake of the Russian Modernist vanguard included Boris Pasternak (1890-1960; *see* CENTRIFUGE, Cubo-Futurism), Mikhail Zoschenko (1895-1958), and Leonid Leonov (1899-1994; *see* Serapion Brothers, SOCIALIST REALISM); Mikail Sholokov (1905-1984; *see* Socialist Realism), Isaak Babel (1894-1941?), Konstantin Fedin (1892-1977), Fyodor Gladkov (1883-1958), Vsevolod Ivanov (1895-1963), Boris Andreyevich Lavrenyov (1894-1959), Yury Olesha (1899-1960), Boris Pilnyak (pseud. of Boris Andreevich Vogau, 1894-1937?), Evgeny Zamyatin (1884-1937), and Andrey Platonov (1899-1951).

Stylistic innovation in Russia was at this time equated with revolution (of 1905 and of 1917), dissatisfaction with the tsarist regime, and the desire for change in the minds of many, who eagerly sought to create a new literature and art for a new society—as the painter Vladimir Tatlin (1885-1953) said of the Constructivists: "We created the art before we had the society"—but most writers were easier with Modernism's room for ambiguity than with the Revolution's single-mindedness and certainty. Merezhkovsky's famous lecture, "O prichinakh upadka i o novykh techeniyakh sovremennoy russkoy literatury" (1893; "On the Causes of the Decline and on the New Currents in Russian Literature," 1975) was an early Modernist manifesto, calling for Russian poets to attend to the work of the French Symbolists. Russian Modernist literature was characterized by rejection of convention, aesthetic innovation, nihilistic or utopian mood, and urban, technological themes. The journals *Mir Iskusstva* (World of Art) and *Zolotoe runo* (Golden Fleece) were important Modernist vehicles in Russia. The mandates of Socialist Realism in 1934 put a stop to further Modernist development in Russia, and several avant-gardists fell in with the government's program. Others went into exile, were imprisoned, or were killed.

❖•❖

Further Reading

Barron, Stephanie, and Maurice Tuchman, eds. *The Avant-Garde in Russia, 1910-1930: New Perspectives*. Los Angeles: Los Angeles County Museum of Art, 1980; distributed by MIT Press. *Boris Pilnjak*. Amsterdam: North-Holland, 1984. Browning, Gary. *Boris Pilniak: Scythian at a Typewriter*. Ann Arbor, Mich.: Ardis, 1985.

Carden, Patricia. *The Art of Isaac Babel*. Ithaca, N.Y.: Cornell University Press, 1972.

Ehre, Milton. *Isaac Babel*. Boston: Twayne Publishers, 1986.

Erlich, Victor. *Modernism and Revolution: Russian Literature in Transition*. Cambridge, Mass.: Harvard University Press, 1994.

Erlich, Victor, ed. *Twentieth-Century Russian Literary Criticism*. New Haven, Conn.: Yale University Press, 1975.

Gasparov, Boris, Robert P. Hughes, and Irina Paperno, eds. *Cultural Mythologies of Russian Modernism: From the Golden Age to the Silver Age*. Berkeley, Calif.: University of California Press, 1992.

Gibian, George, and H. W. Tjalsma, eds. *Russian Modernism: Culture and the Avant-Garde, 1900-1930*. Ithaca, N.Y.: Cornell University Press, 1976.

Gillespie, David C. *The Twentieth-Century Russian Novel: An Introduction*. Oxford, England; Washington, D.C.: Berg, 1996.

Holthusen, Johannes. *Twentieth Century Russian Literature: A Critical Study*. New York: F. Ungar Publishing Company, 1972.

Lavrin, Janko. *A Panorama of Russian Literature*. London: University of London Press, 1973.

Moore, Harry Thornton. *Twentieth-Century Russian Literature*. Carbondale, Ill.: Southern Illinois University Press, 1974.

Paperno, Irina, and Joan Delancy Grossman, eds. *Creating Life: The Aesthetic Utopia of Russian Modernism*. Stanford, Calif.: Stanford University Press, 1994.

Richardson, William. *Zolotoe Runo and Russian Modernism, 1905-1910*. Ann Arbor, Mich.: Ardis, 1986.

Rühle, Jürgen. *Literature and Revolution: A Critical Study of the Writer and Communism in the Twentieth Century*. Translated and edited by Jean Steinberg. New York: Frederick A. Praeger, Publishers, 1969.

Simmons, Ernest Joseph. *Russian Fiction and Soviet Ideology: Introduction to Fedin, Leonov, and Sholokhov*. New York: Columbia University Press, 1958.

Struve, Gleb. *Russian Literature under Lenin and Stalin, 1917-1953*. Norman, Okla.: University of Oklahoma Press, 1971.

Williams, Robert C. *Artists in Revolution: Portraits of the Russian Avant-Garde, 1905-1925*. Bloomington, Ind.: Indiana University Press, 1977.

Wright, A. Colin. *Mikhail Bulgakov: Life and Interpretations*. Toronto: University of Toronto Press, 1978.

MODERNISM
Sweden, 1940s

The dominant period of Swedish Modernism was the 1940s, though indications of Modernist trends appeared as early as the 1910s. During the intervening decades, the literati was extremely conservative; in addition, Sweden's neutral stance during World War I resulted in the Swedish being more exempt, at least temporarily, from much of the direct trauma other Europeans experienced which fostered Modernist impulses in those places (especially France and England). It was the onset of World War II in the late 1930s that had a more immediate impact on Sweden. Contemporaneous with the PROLETARIAN WRITERS movement, Swedish Modernists had close ties with many of them as well as the FIVE YOUNG MEN. Pär Lagerkvist (1891-1974) early on announced a radical Modernist breakthrough with his poetry collection *Ångest* (1916; Anguish). His theoretical work *Ordkonst och bildkonst* (1913; Verbal and Pictorial Art) can be considered an early Modernist manifesto. Another early Modernist was Birger Sjöberg (1885-1929), influenced in part by the German EXPRESSIONISTS; his collections of lyrics and poems include *Fridas bok* (1922; Frida's Book) and *Kriser och kransar* (1926; Crises and Laurels). Later Modernists were poet and essayist Gunnar Ekelöf (1907-1968), who lived in Paris in 1929-30 and there became acquainted with Modernist aesthetics in France, admiring the SYMBOLISTS and SURREALISTS and bringing them to the attention of those in the Swedish literary scene. His first volume of poetry, *sent på jorden* (1932; *Late Arrival on Earth*, 1967), was greatly indebted to the Surrealists, FREUD, and Igor Stravinsky's (1882-1971) *Le Sacre du Printemps* (1913). Poet Erik Lindegren's (1910-1968) masterpiece was a collection of broken sonnets, *Mannen utan väg* (1942). Newspapers and journals serving as forums for Modernists in Sweden included *Prisma* (1948-50), *40-tal* (1944-47), *Utsikt* (1948-50), and *Poesi* (1948-50).

✤•❧

Further Reading

Warme, Lars G., ed. *A History of Swedish Literature*. Lincoln, Nebr.: University of Nebraska Press, 1996.

MODERNISM
Swedish writers in Finland, 1920s

Like the TORCHBEARERS with whom they were affined, the Swedish-Finnish Modernists did not form a cohesive group but were friends bound for a time by common aesthetic interests; by the 1930s they went their separate ways. The group emerged after Finland became an independent republic in 1919. Comprised of Finland's Swedish-speaking community, Edith Södergran (1892-1923), who had the greatest influence on later Swedish poets than anyone with the possible exception of Johann Runeberg (1804-1877), led the group. Her first volume of poems was *Dikter* (1916; Poems); she was influenced by NIETZSCHE and German literature, and her verse, though romantic in content and imagery, took experimental form for which many attacked her. The group also included poet Elmer Diktonius (1896-1961), poet Gunnar Björling (1887-

1960), poet and theorist Rabbe Enckell (1903-1974), and poet and critic Hagar Olsson (1893-1978), who through the pages of *Ultra* (1922), brought European Modernist literature to Finland. Influenced by DADA and SURREALISM, the Swedish-Finnish Modernists generally rejected regular rhyme, rhythm, and simple imagery. In addition to *Ultra* they also published the magazine *Quosego* (1928-29). They inspired the FIVE YOUNG MEN, as well as the POETS OF THE FORTIES.

❖•❖

Further Reading

Ahokas, Jaakko. "Swedish Literature in Finland at the End of the Nineteenth and the Beginning of the Twentieth Centuries." In his *A History of Finnish Literature*. Bloomington, Ind.: Indiana University, 1973.

Warme, Lars G., ed. *A History of Swedish Literature*. Lincoln, Nebr.: University of Nebraska Press, 1996.

MODERNISM
Ukraine, 1905-1920

In the Ukraine, such Western literary trends as SYMBOLISM cleared the ground for Modernist developments, particularly when Russia again legalized the Ukrainian language for publication in 1905 (printing in Ukrainian had been outlawed since 1876). Modernist poets and fiction writers tended to continue the tradition of writing about village life, but now felt freer to experiment with new aesthetic innovations. Some Modernists were aligned with such groups as YOUNG MUSE and the UKRAINIAN HOME GROUP. The latter's journal, *Ukrayinska khata*, began to regularly publish Modernist literature and criticism, as did the literary magazine *Literaturno-naukovy visnyk* (1898-1932; Literary and Scientific Herald), which, in 1901, published what is considered a manifesto, advocating the writer's right to aesthetic freedom.

Mykhaylo Kotsyubynsky (1864-1913) was perhaps the most representative Modernist in the Ukraine. Influenced by Maurice MAETERLINCK (*see* SYMBOLISM, Belgium), August STRINDBERG (*see* EXPRESSIONISM, Germany), and Norwegian writer Knut Hamsun (1859-1952), Kotsyubynsky's novels include *Fata Morgana* (1910; *Fata Morgana*, 1976) and his major work, *Tini zabutykh predkiv* (1913; *Shadows of Forgotten Ancestors*, 1981), which is fed by Husul-area folk legends and traditions. He is also known for his short stories — "Intermezzo" (1909), for instance, is notable for its psychological representation and impressionistic narrative technique. Stepan Vasylchenko (pseud. of Stepan Panasenko, 1878-1932) wrote short stories inspired by folk tradition and led a romanticist revival, which in turn inspired Yury Yanovsky (1902-1954). Yanovsky began his career as a poet — his collected poems were published belatedly in *Prekrasna Ut* (1929; The Most Beautiful Ut). He later moved into

425

short stories, for which he first gained renown, collected in *Mamutovi byvni* (1925; Mammoth's Tusks) and *Krov zemlyi* (1927; The Blood of the Soil). One of his best novels was *Chotyry shablyi* (1930; Four Sabres). Eventually, Yanovsky joined the FREE ACADEMY OF PROLETARIAN LITERATURE. Other Ukrainian Modernists included Marko Cheremshyna (pseud. of Ivan Semanyuk, 1874-1927), who composed short stories of village life; poet Mykola Chernyavsky (1867-1937), novelist Katrya Hrynevych (1875-1947); prose writer Hnat Khotkevych (1877-1942), and novelist and short-story writer Les (Olexandr) Martovych (1871-1916).

❖•❖

Further Reading

Andrusyshen, C. H., and Watson Kirkconnell, eds. *The Ukrainian Poets 1189-1962*. Toronto: University of Toronto Press, 1963.
Čyževs'kyj, Dmytro. *A History of Ukrainian Literature*. 2nd ed. New York; Englewood, Colo.: The Ukrainian Academy of Arts and Sciences and Ukrainian Academic Press, 1997.
"Literature: The Age of Modernism." In *Ukraine: A Concise Encyclopedia*. Edited by Volodymyr Kubijovyč. Vol. 1. Toronto: University of Toronto Press, 1963.

MODERNISM
United States, 1910s-1930s

If REALISM was the movement through which American writers gained international recognition by following European example, Modernism was the one by which a younger, less idealistic generation often outshined their foreign competitors in innovation and depth. Consonant with the final flowerings — in Henry JAMES, Stephen CRANE, Theodore DREISER, Edith WHARTON, and others — of Realism and NATURALISM, American Modernism possessed neither the cogent theories nor resolute ethical stance of its national predecessors. Rather, it subordinated both theory and ethics to the early twentieth-century concerns of literary experimentation and the exploration of the human mind. Often the two complemented each other and led to significant advancements in technique. For example, the psychological novel, a form first explored by James, was radically modified through STREAM-OF-CONSCIOUSNESS narration and the use of interior monologue (*see* MODERNISM, England and Ireland). Along with this came a heightened interest in the intellectual currents of the time, which were infused with the writings of Sigmund FREUD, Carl JUNG, Henri BERGSON, and Havelock Ellis (1859-1939).

Many American writers intrigued with the new trends they saw coming out of Europe went there, not only to be closer to the centers of innovation, but also to find venues and publishers for their work, since American publishers and literary magazines were resistant to the new literature. F. Scott FITZGERALD (*see* JAZZ AGE) spent much of his time in Europe until the 1930s. T. S. ELIOT, Ezra POUND, and Robert Frost (1874-1963), for example, went to London, the latter to find a publisher for his poetry, while Gertrude STEIN, Edith Wharton, and Ernest HEMINGWAY and other writers of the LOST GENERATION migrated to Paris. Lost Generation writers, in Europe during World War I, responded to its impact — John DOS PASSOS with *Three Soldiers* (1921), Hemingway with *A Farewell to Arms* (1929).

As on the Continent, Modernist activity in the United States was concentrated in large urban centers, in this case, Chicago and New York. One commonly cited date for the genesis of Modernism in the United States is 1912, on the heels of the heyday of the GENTEEL TRADITION, the reevaluation of which helped further the questioning of American cultural assumptions. During this year a number of important events in poetry, drama, and art took place. Many of these events centered around Chicago, the citadel of Midwestern culture, and thus augured a return to the regionalist literature of previous decades (*see* CHICAGO LITERARY RENAISSANCE). Harriet Monroe (1860-1936) founded *Poetry,* which with Pound as its foreign editor brought the likes of English and Irish Modernists T. S. Eliot, William Butler YEATS, James JOYCE, H. D., and other writers on the Continent to the attention of Americans. Pound founded IMAGISM, Vachel LINDSAY published "GENERAL BOOTH ENTERS INTO HEAVEN," and Edna St. Vincent Millay (1892-1950) published "Renascence."

Meanwhile in New York, the Armory show of the following year showcased works by Pablo Picasso (1881-1973), Odilon Redon (1840-1916), and Georges Braque (1882-1963), and DADA arrived in 1916, bringing a taste of the Paris art scene to Americans. Modernist writers centered in New York included William Carlos Williams (1883-1963), e. e. CUMMINGS (*see* Lost Generation), Hart Crane (1899-1932), Marianne Moore (1887-1972), and Jazz Age writer Sinclair LEWIS, whose novel *Main Street* (1920) was the bestseller for 1921. New York's growing diversity was evidenced by such Modernist groups as the YOUNG ONES and the INTROSPECTIVISTS, both comprised of Yiddish-speaking immigrants, and the HARLEM RENAISSANCE. The theater groups PROVINCE-TOWN PLAYERS and WASHINGTON SQUARE PLAYERS rounded out the genres infused with the Modernist spirit.

Other important writers not affiliated with either of the geographical centers but whose contributions nonetheless significantly added to American Modernism were William FAULKNER and his stylistically stunning representations of the deep American South, Kate Chopin (1851-1904), writing about Creole and Cajun life in Louisiana, and Wallace STEVENS, whose sedate home base in Hartford, Connecticut, did not hinder his innovative talent.

Several periodicals nurtured Modernism in the United States. In 1918 sections of James Joyce's *ULYSSES* began running in Margaret Anderson's *Little Review* (1914-29), based in New York; other important magazines there included the *Dial* (1880-1929; founded in Chicago, moved to New York in 1918), which Marianne Moore edited after 1926, the *Masses* (1911-53), the *New Republic* (1914-), and the *Nation* (1865-). The list of representative American Modernist works would include, among others, Crane's homage to the Brooklyn Bridge, "The Bridge" (1926), William Carlos Williams's *In the American Grain* (1925) and *Paterson* (5 vols., 1946-58), Sherwood Anderson's (1876-1941) *Winesburg, Ohio* (1919), Edmund Wilson's (1895-1972) *Axel's Castle* (1931) and *The Shores of Light* (1952), Katherine Anne Porter's (1890-1980) "Flowering Judas" (1930), Willa Cather's (1873-1947) *Death Comes for the Archbishop* (1927), and James Agee's (1909-1955) *Let Us Now Praise Famous Men* (1941) and *A Death in the Family* (1957). However important these and other comparable works were to the spread of Modernism, it was the principal works of the Lost Generation and the Jazz Age— Hemingway's *THE SUN ALSO RISES* (1926), Cummings's *THE ENORMOUS ROOM* (1922), Dos Passos's *U.S.A.* (collected 1938), and Fitzgerald's *THE GREAT GATSBY* (1925) which remain as landmark Modernist novels.

NEW CRITICISM was a late wing of the Modernist vanguard; questions of literary value and inclusion in the canon are still largely decided according to the Modernist touchstones of disinterestedness, hermeticism, and structural unity. In addition to inspiring a mock movement, SPECTRA, in 1916, American Modernists also influenced, among others, the BLACK MOUNTAIN POETS, the BEAT GENERATION and the SAN FRANCISCO SCHOOL, and the CONFESSIONAL POETS.

✦•✦

Faulkner, William (1897-1962), American novelist and short-story writer.

Faulkner was born into a prominent family in Mississippi, where he spent most of his life and set much of his work in the fictional Yoknapatawpha County. While working as a journalist in New Orleans for a brief period, Faulkner met and was encouraged by Sherwood Anderson. Faulkner is renowned for his stories and novels set in the South, but his art far transcends mere regionalism, and he is recognized as a master of evocative language and narrative innovation, including the stream-of-consciousness technique. His first novel was *Soldier's Pay* (1926), inspired by the Lost Generation, but the series of novels dealing with the Old South turning into the New upon which his reputation is built, begins with *Sartoris* (1929), which introduces the old Compson and Sartoris families and the rising Snopes family, and continues with *THE SOUND AND THE FURY* (1929), *The Hamlet* (1940), *The Town* (1957), and *The Mansion* (1960). Other notable works include *As I Lay Dying* (1930), *Sanctuary* (1931), *Light in August* (1932), *Absalom, Absalom!* (1936), *The Wild Palms* (1939), *Intruder in the Dust*

(1948), *A Fable* (1954), *The Reivers* (1962), and the short story "The Bear" in the collection *Go Down, Moses* (1942). Faulkner spent his later years writing scripts in Hollywood. He was awarded the Nobel Prize for literature in 1949.

The Sound and the Fury (1929).

Set in Yoknapatawpha County, Mississippi, *The Sound and the Fury* follows the decline of the Compson family over the first decades of the twentieth century. The novel employs a stream-of-consciousness narrative technique from four different points of view, each one ostensibly more lucid than the last: that of the sons—first, Benjy, who is mentally retarded, then Quentin, a sensitive, depressed young student at Harvard, followed by the oldest brother Jason, a crude, mean-spirited clerk in a store—and finally an omniscient narrator, who many believe represents the perspective of Dilsey, the family's maid. Each brother's narrative is preoccupied with their sister, Caddy, who has recently married, and each narrative shows, in strikingly different ways, how the past remains present for the characters.

➯•➻

Stein, Gertrude (1874-1946)
American novelist, short-story writer, autobiographer, and dramatist.

An early leader of expatriate writers in France, Stein is often regarded as the matriarch of Modernist literature. Upon settling in Paris in 1903, she and her brother Leo began exchanging artistic theories with and financially supporting some of the most controversial painters of the day, including Henri Matisse (1869-1954), Pablo Picasso (1881-1973), Georges Braque (1882-1963), and Juan Gris (1887-1927). Stein's career as a fiction writer, which began at about this time, stemmed directly from her appreciation of CUBIST art, whose characteristics of vivisection, diffusion, and symbolic repetition neatly complemented the atemporal understanding of human consciousness espoused by her chief mentor, William James (1842-1910). More daring than any of her Modernist contemporaries, Stein increasingly defied semantic, grammatic, and compositional laws in her fiction. The result was a conspicuously original style that at its worst has been likened to tedious gibberish and at its best, the rich pulsations of human thought and emotion. Stein's subjects were typically those of commonplace life; however, pioneering treatment of lesbianism and sexual roles, and her intuitive DECONSTRUCTION of language, have contributed to a continually expanding interest in her literary theories and experiments.

Her best works include *Three Lives* (1909), *Tender Buttons* (1914), THE MAKING OF AMERICANS (1925), *The Autobiography of Alice B. Toklas* (1933)—a nonfiction work in which she compared her position in Modernist literature with those of the Lost Generation—and *Q.E.D.* (1971; also published as *Things as They Are*, 1950), an uncharacteristically lucid, semi-autobiographical novel that recounts her road to sexual and psychological self-discovery while a student at Radcliffe. Although it is still difficult to accurately assess Stein's individual importance as a modern writer, it can be safely said that her influence on the modern generation of Hemingway, Fitzgerald, Anderson, Thornton Wilder (1897-1975), the Beats, and numerous others, was immense.

The Making of Americans: Being a History of a Family's Progress (1925).

Stein completed this voluminous work, viewed by herself and many others as her masterpiece, between 1903 and 1911. The novel is a study of the circularity of existence, the everlasting sameness of talk, thought, and endeavor. While concerned with the generation-by-generation development of two German-American families, *The Making of Americans* is, more importantly, an ambitious attempt to depict all personality types in much the same manner that her artistic forebear, Paul Cézanne (1839-1906), assayed to capture all basic forms in his paintings. However, Stein's exceedingly abstract approach, her delimiting of the relative importance of words, and, even, dramatic congruity, have prevented the work from ever reaching a large readership. Even so, Stein has received high praise for the two literary achievements that underlie the novel, namely: the shattering of all technical restrictions and the construction of a thoroughly modern and reflexive prose style.

✦•✦

Stevens, Wallace (1879-1955), American poet and essayist.

After attending Harvard University, Stevens briefly held a job he found unsatisfying at the *New York Herald Tribune*. He returned to school, earned a degree at the New York University Law School, and eventually made a career at an insurance company in Hartford, Connecticut, where he remained employed until his death. Though he was acquainted with William Carlos Williams and Harriet Monroe—who published some of his early verse in *Poetry* (*see* CHICAGO LITERARY RENAISSANCE)—he tended to steer clear of literary society, even as he was writing and publishing some of the most exciting and original verse of all the Modernists. Some of the poems for which Stevens is most renowned include "Sunday Morning" (1915), "The Idea of Order at Key West" (1934), "The Man with the Blue Guitar" (1937), "The Emperor of Ice Cream" (1922), "Anecdote of the Jar" (1919), and "Thirteen Ways of Looking at a Blackbird" (1917). In much of his poetry, Stevens struggled with the problem of the subjectivity of human perception and imagination, with a unique style characterized by the juxtaposition of unusual, vivid, and surprising images. *Harmonium* (1923), Stevens's first volume of poems, was followed by *Ideas of Order* (1935), *Owl's Clover* (1936), *The Man with the Blue Guitar* (1937), *Parts of a World* (1942), *Transport to*

Summer (1947), and *The Auroras of Autumn* (1950). *Collected Poems* appeared in 1954. His essays on the art of the poet, including the well-known "Notes for a Supreme Fiction," were published in *The Necessary Angel* (1951).

❦•❦

Further Reading

Appel, Paul P., ed. *Homage to Sherwood Anderson, 1876-1941*. Mamaroneck, N.Y.: P. P. Appel, 1970.

Baker, Carlos. *The Echoing Green: Romanticism, Modernism, and Phenomena of Transference in Poetry*. Princeton, N.J.: Princeton University Press, 1984.

Bloom, Harold. *Wallace Stevens: The Poems of Our Climate*. Ithaca, N.Y.: Cornell University Press, 1977.

Chabot, C. Barry. *Writers for the Nation: American Literary Modernism*. Tuscaloosa, Ala.: University of Alabama Press, 1997.

Chiari, Joseph. *The Aesthetics of Modernism*. London: Vision, 1970.

Crunden, Robert M. *American Salons: Encounters with European Modernism, 1885-1917*. New York: Oxford University Press, 1993.

Davies, Alistair. *An Annotated Critical Bibliography of Modernism*. Sussex, England: Harvester Press; Totowa, N.J.: Barnes & Noble, 1982.

Ellmann, Richard, and Charles Feidelson, Jr., eds. *The Modern Tradition: Backgrounds of Modern Literature*. New York: Oxford University Press, 1965.

Garvin, Harry, ed. *Romanticism, Modernism, Postmodernism*. Lewisburg, Pa.: Bucknell University Press, 1980.

Hanscombe, Gillian, and Virginia L. Smyers. *Writing for Their Lives: The Modernist Women 1910-1940*. Boston: Northeastern University Press, 1987.

Hayman, David. *Re-forming the Narrative: Toward a Mechanics of Modernist Fiction*. Ithaca, N.Y.: Cornell University Press, 1987.

Hoffman, Michael J. *The Development of Abstractionism in the Writings of Gertrude Stein*. Philadelphia: University of Pennsylvania Press, 1966.

Hoffman, Michael J., and Patrick D. Murphy, eds. *Critical Essays on American Modernism*. New York: G. K. Hall and Company, 1992.

Kenner, Hugh. *A Homemade World: The American Modernist Writers*. New York: Morrow, 1975.

Knapp, James F. *Literary Modernism and the Transformation of Work*. Evanston, Ill.: Northwestern University Press, 1988.

Moreland, Richard C. *Faulkner and Modernism: Rereading and Rewriting*. Madison, Wis.: University of Wisconsin Press, 1990.

Quinones, Ricardo J. *Mapping Literary Modernism: Time and Development*. Princeton, N.J.: Princeton University Press, 1985.

Rosenberg, Harold. *The Tradition of the New*. New York: Horizon Press, 1959.

Ross, Andrew. *The Failure of Modernism: Symptoms of American Poetry*. New York: Columbia University Press, 1986.

431

Singal, Daniel J. *William Faulkner: The Making of a Modernist.* Chapel Hill, N.C.: University of North Carolina Press, 1997.

Symons, Julian. *Makers of the New: The Revolution in Literature, 1914-1939.* New York: Random House, 1987.

Weinstein, Norman. *Gertrude Stein and the Literature of the Modern Consciousness.* New York: Ungar, 1970.

MODERNISMO

Argentina, Colombia, Cuba, Mexico, Nicaragua, Peru, Spain, and Uruguay, c. 1888-1910s

A revolution in linguistic technique, Modernismo, and its ideological companion movement, the GENERATION OF 1898, were the two forces behind the transition from nineteenth-century to twentieth-century writing and aesthetics in Latin-American and Spanish literature. Although Modernismo spanned several genres, poetry, inspired both by a waning native Romanticism and the new experiments of the French SYMBOLISTS, was the prevailing form. The Modernists stressed individuality of expression and tended toward lush, metaphorical language, highly mannered sentiment, and a nostalgic worldview. In addition, they promulgated radical changes in the use of rhyme and meter. The most prominent precursors of the movement were Spanish lyricists Salvador Rueda Santos (1857-1933) and Gustavo Adolfo Bécquer (1836-1870). The former contributed to the development of Nicaraguan Rubén Darío and the latter to that of Andalusian Spaniard Juan Ramón Jiménez, the two great fountainheads of Modernismo.

Darío himself is most often regarded as the founder of the movement for his Parnassian-influenced collection of stories and poems entitled *Azul* (1888); however, several critics have noted the important pioneering work of a number of his Latin American colleagues, including Julián del Casal (1863-1893) and José Martí (1853-1895) of Cuba; Manuel Gutiérrez Nájera (1859-1895) of Mexico; and José Asunción Silva (1865-1896) of Colombia. Other notable Modernistas were José Rodó (1871-1917) of Uruguay; Amado Nervo (1870-1919) and Enrique González Martínez (1871-1952) of Mexico; José Santos Chocano (1875-1934) of Peru; Leopoldo Lugones (1873-1938) of Argentina; Ramón Valle-Inclán (1866-1936) and the Machado brothers (Antonio, 1875-1939, and Manuel, 1874-1947) of Spain. The efforts of these and a host of other writers were supported by such journals as *La revista azul* (1894-96) and *La revista moderna* (1891-1911). The phases of Modernismo, the first ruled by Darío until about 1905, the second by Jiménez through the 1910s, served as a monumental period of artistic transition that effectively ushered in a truly native Spanish and Spanish-American poetry that has continued to bear the imprint of the early Modernistas.

❖•❖

Darío, Rubén (1867-1916)
Nicaraguan poet, short-story writer, and essayist.

Generally considered the founder of Modernismo, a term which he coined, Darío was for much of his career a traveling journalist and diplomat. Consequently, a cultured, cosmopolitan perspective came quite naturally to his poetry. Extremely important to his mature work were his personal associations during the 1890s with French Symbolists Jean Moréas (1856-1910), Paul VERLAINE, and Rémy de Gourmont (1858-1915). One direct outcome was his collection *Proas profanas, y otros poems* (1896; *Proasa Profanas and Other Poems,* 1922), in which he explored the possibilities of internal rhymes, dissonance, asymmetry, and other Symbolist techniques. In what is generally viewed as his best work, *Cantos de vida y esperanza* (1905), Darío gathered together elements from European and American literature, classical mythology, and Christianity to forge a style wholly his own, which, attached to native social and political issues, became progressively more contemplative in his final years. An English translation of his work, *The Selected Poems of Rubén Darío,* was published in 1965.

❖•❖

Jiménez, Juan Ramón (1881-1958), Spanish poet.

Although brief, Jiménez's connection to Modernismo was of central importance to later developments in twentieth-century Spanish literature. From his early collections *Almas de violeta* (1900; Violet Souls) and *Ninfeas* (1900; Waterlilies), which won the admiration of such established figures as Darío and Francisco Villaespesa (1877-1935) and brought Jiménez into direct contact with the Madrid Modernists, Jiménez was regarded as a brilliant and revolutionary young poet. During this period Jiménez especially emulated the poetry of Darío but graudally shed this impressionistic influence for a simpler yet more substantive style, much in the manner of Gustavo Adolfo Bécquer (1836-1870). Jiménez's break with Modernism, probably begun as early as 1905, became complete with the publications of the prose poem *Platero y yo* (1914; *Platero and I,* 1956) and the prose and poetry collection *Diario de un poeta recién casado* (1916; Diary of a Recently Married Poet); in both of these works he fused extended symbolic structure with revealing statements of personal and spiritual growth while refraining from the overwrought, occasionally vacuous, poetic expression of his contemporaries. Jiménez complemented his creative work with a farsighted editorial instinct, publishing in a series of small literary reviews the early work of his artistic heirs, the GENERATION OF 1927. In addition to the works mentioned, Jiménez is also remembered for *Animal de Fondo* (1949), a collection of poems published late in his career that, along with his prodigious and lifelong output, helped gain him the Nobel Prize in 1956.

◆•◆
Further Reading

Aching, Gerard. *The Politics of Spanish American Modernismo*. Cambridge, England: Cambridge University Press, 1997.

Bell, Aubrey F. G. *Contemporary Spanish Literature*. New York: Knopf, 1925.

Brotherston, Gordon. "Modernism and Rubén Darío." In his *Latin American Poetry: Origins and Presence*. Cambridge, England: Cambridge University Press, 1975.

Cardwell, Richard A. *Juan R. Jiménez: The Modernist Apprenticeship 1895-1900*. Berlin: Colloquium Verlag, 1977.

Chandler, Richard E., and Kessel Schwartz. "The Contemporary Age, 1888 to the Present: Modernism." In their *A New History of Spanish Literature*. Baton Rouge, La.: Louisiana State University Press, 1961.

Coester, Alfred L., ed. *Anthology of the Modernista Movement in Spanish America*. Boston: Ginn & Co., 1924.

Coke-Enguidanos, Mervyn. *Word and Work in the Poetry of Juan Ramón Jiménez*. London: Tamesis, 1982.

Craig, George D. *Modernist Trend in Spanish American Poetry*. Berkeley, Calif.: University of California Press, 1934.

Ellis, Keith. *Critical Approaches to Rubén Darío*. Toronto: University of Toronto Press, 1974.

Fiore, Dolores Ackel. *Rubén Darío in Search of Inspiration: Greco-Roman Mythology in His Stories and Poetry*. New York: Las Americas Pub. Co., 1963.

Fogelquist, Donald F. *Juan Ramón Jiménez*. Boston: Twayne, 1976.

Gonzalez-Gerth, Miguel, and George D. Schade, eds. *Rubén Darío Centennial Studies*. Austin, Tex.: Dept. of Spanish and Portuguese, Institute of Latin American Studies, University of Texas at Austin, 1970.

Jrade, Cathy L. *Rubén Darío and the Romantic Search for Unity: The Modernist Recourse to Esoteric Tradition*. Austin, Tex.: University of Texas Press, 1983.

Watland, Charles D. *Poet Errant: A Biography of Rubén Darío*. New York: Philosophical Library, 1965.

Wilcox, John C. *Self and Image in Juan Ramón Jiménez: Modern and Postmodern Readings*. Urbana, Ill.: University of Illinois Press, 1987.

Young, Howard T. *Juan Ramón Jiménez*. New York: Columbia University Press, 1967.

MODERNIST SCHOOL
Taiwan, 1950s

The Modernist School, strongly influenced by contemporary Western poetry, was important to the development of modern vernacular poetry in Taiwan during the 1950s. The School's leader was Chi Hsien (1913-).

⇒•⇐

Further Reading

Hegel, Robert E. "The Search for Identity in Fiction from Taiwan." In *Expressions of Self in Chinese Literature*. Edited by Robert E. Hegel and Richard C. Hessney. New York: Columbia University Press, 1985.

MODERN NŌ
England, Japan, and United States, c. 1900s-1990s

Nō, a form of Japanese drama that originated in the fourteenth century and is predicated upon the poetic depiction of emotional states through masks, music, and dance, has enjoyed a resurgence of interest in the twentieth century due to English translations of numerous classic works. Among the Western writers who have been influenced by Nō are W. B. YEATS (*see* ABBEY THEATER and MODERNISM, England and Ireland), Ezra POUND (*see* MODERNISM, England and Ireland), Paul Claudel (1868-1955), Bertolt BRECHT (*see* EPIC THEATER), and Maurice MAETERLINCK (*see* SYMBOLISM, Belgium). In Japan, the figure most responsible for the revitalization of Nō was Mishima Yukio (1925-1970); his *Kindai Nōgaku Shū* (1956; *Five Modern Nō Plays,* 1980) were among the first examples of the form to be exported to an international audience.

⇒•⇐

Further Reading

Beck, L. Adams. *The Ghost Plays of Japan*. New York: Japan Society, 1933.

Fenollosa, Ernest F., and Ezra Pound. *Noh*. New York: New Directions, 1916. 2nd ed. published as: *The Classic Noh Theatre of Japan*. Westport, Conn.: Greenwood Press, 1977.

Ishibashi, Hiro. *Yeats and the Noh: Types of Japanese Beauty and Their Reflection in Yeats's Plays*. Dublin: Dolmen Press, 1966.

Keene, Donald. *Nō: The Classical Theatre of Japan*. Rev. ed. Tokyo; Palo Alto, Calif.: Kodansha International, 1973.

————. Introduction to *Five Modern No Plays* by Mishima Yukio. Tokyo: C .E. Tuttle, 1980.

Kenny, Don. *On Stage in Japan: Kabuki, Bunraku, Noh, Gagaku*. Tokyo: Shufunotomo, 1974.

Kim, Myung Whan. *Mythopoetic Elements in the Later Plays of W. B. Yeats and the Noh*. Doctoral thesis, Indiana University, 1969.

Konparu, Kunio. *The Noh Theater: Principles and Perspectives*. New York: Weatherhill/Tankosha, 1983.

Londraville, Richard John. *To Asia for a Stage Convention: W. B. Yeats and the Noh*. Albany, N.Y.: Londraville, 1970.

Mishima Yukio. *Five Modern Nō Plays*. Translated by Donald Keene. Tokyo: C. E. Tuttle, 1967.

Mitchell, John D., and Miyoko Watanabe. *Staging Japanese Theatre: Noh & Kabuki: Ikkaku Sennin (The Holy Hermit Unicorn) and Narukami (The Thunder God)*. Key West, Fla.: Institute for Advanced Studies in the Theatre Arts Press, 1994.

Miyakem, Akiko, Sanehide Kodama, and Nicholas Teele, eds. *A Guide to Ezra Pound and Ernest Fenollosa's Classic Noh Theatre of Japan.* Orono, Maine: National Poetry Foundation, University of Maine, 1994.

Nakamura, Yasuo. *Noh: The Classical Theater.* Translated by Don Kenny. New York: Walker/Weatherhill, 1971.

Nathan, John. *Mishima: A Biography.* Boston: Little, Brown, 1974.

O'Neill, P. G. *A Guide to Nō.* Tokyo: Hinoki Shoten, 1972.

Qamber, Akhtar. *Yeats and the Noh, with Two Plays for Dancers by Yeats and Two Noh Plays.* New York: Weatherhill, 1974.

Scott-Stokes, Henry. *The Life and Death of Yukio Mishima.* New York: Farrar, Straus and Giroux, 1974.

Sekine, Masaru, and Christopher Murray. *Yeats and the Noh: A Comparative Study.* Savage, Md.: Barnes & Noble, 1990.

Shimazaki, Chifumi. *The Noh.* Tokyo: Hinoki Shoten, 1972.

Special Noh Committee, Japanese Classics Translation Committee, Nippon Gakujutsu Shinkōkai. *The Noh Drama: Ten Plays from the Japanese.* Rutland, Vt.: C. E. Tuttle, 1955.

Starrs, Roy. *Deadly Dialectics: Sex, Violence, and Nihilism in the World of Yukio Mishima.* Honolulu: University of Hawaii Press, 1994.

Stopes, Marie. *Plays of Old Japan: The Nō.* 2nd ed. London: Eclipse, 1927.

Suzuki, Beatrice Lane. *Nōgaku; Japanese Nō Plays.* London: J. Murray, 1932.

Taylor, Richard. *The Drama of W. B. Yeats: Irish Myth and the Japanese Nō.* New Haven, Conn.: Yale University Press, 1976.

Toki, Zenmaro. *Japanese Nō Plays.* Tokyo: Japan Travel Bureau, 1954.

Tsukui, Nobuko. *Ezra Pound and Japanese Noh Plays.* Washington, D.C.: University Press of America, 1983.

Waley, Arthur. *The Nō Plays of Japan.* London: Allen & Unwin, 1921.

Wolfe, Peter. *Yukio Mishima.* New York: Continuum, 1989.

Yasuda, Kenneth. *Masterworks of the Nō Theater.* Bloomington, Ind.: Indiana University Press, 1989.

Yourcenar, Marguerite. *Mishima: A Vision of the Void.* Translated by Alberto Manguel. New York: Farrar Straus Giroux, 1986.

MOLLA NASREDDIN
Azerbaijan, 1906-1920

It would be difficult to overstate the literary, political, and social impact the militantly liberal journal *Molla Nasreddin* (1906-1930) made not only in Azerbaijan, but in Turkey, Iran — indeed the regions of the Islamic Middle East and Central Asia — during the first decades of the twentieth century. Its founding editor was dramatist and short-story writer Djalil Mamedkulizade (also rendered Jalil Memed Qulizadeh, 1866-1932), best known for his dramatic "comedies" — *Ölüler* (1909; The Victims) and *Deli yighinjagy* (1922; The Assembly of the Mad). His ironic sketches and narratives, popularized in *Molla Nasreddin*, addressed the daily problems and hopes of the peasantry while employing the vernacular language (which is akin to Anatolian Turkish).

Mamedkulizade, like his star contributor, satirist Mirza Alekper Sabir (or Mirza 'Ali Akbar Sabir Tahirzadeh, 1862-1911), believed the poet had an important social rule to fulfill, and if totalitarian shahs, mullahs (Islamic religious leaders), and feudal lords blocked the freedom and prosperity of the people and, in place, encouraged superstitious traditions, they became targets of the journal's venomous aim. Such radicality prompted some, such as Muhammad 'Ali Shah of Iran's Qajar dynasty, to ban *Molla Nasreddin*, but it continued to filter in from across the border. According to critic Hasan Javadi, one contemporary remarked that Sabir's poems "helped the cause of the Iranian constitution [of 1906] more than an army." Azerbaijani peasants received Sabir's traditional verse well, but had little taste for his realistic poetry, his satirically expressed democratic ideals, and the short pieces he called "Taziyanalar" (The Whips).

Javadi describes the period during which *Molla Nasreddin* flourished as "the golden age of Azerbaijani journalism," sparked by the failed Russian revolution of 1905. Other contributors included novelist Muhammad Sa'id Ordubadi (1872-1950) and playwright 'Abulrahim Hagverdiov (1870-1933). Mamedkulizade moved to northern Iran after the 1917 revolution ushered in a political climate hostile to his literary ideals. He returned in 1922 and attempted to reissue *Molla Nasreddin*, but the newly established Soviet republic favored its own organization of proletarian writers.

❖•❖

Further Reading

Ibrahimov, Mirza, ed. *Azerbaijanian Poetry, Classic, Modern, Traditional*. Moscow: Progress Publishers, 1969.

Javadi, Hasan. "'Ali Akbar Sabir, the Poet-Satirist of Azerbaijan." *Turkic Culture: Continuity and Change*. Edited by Sabri M. Akural. Bloomington, Ind.: Turkish Studies, Indiana University, 1987.

MOLODA MUZA. *See* YOUNG MUSE GROUP

MONTREAL MOVEMENT
Canada, 1920s

The work of the Montreal Movement epitomizes a new poetic sensibility which had begun to develop shortly before and between the two world wars, and one which was based in the techniques formulated by the modern British poets. The MODERNIST movement in Canada is said to have begun with a generally accepted emphasis in poetry on the use of simpler diction, a strongly realistic view of the universe, and the inclusion of the elements of metaphysical abstraction. These ideas put Canadian poets in step with much contemporary American, British, and French poetry. The group was started at McGill University in Toronto, and by 1925 the journal, *The McGill Fortnightly Revue*, was introduced by undergraduates F. R. SCOTT, A. J. M. Smith (1902-1980), and Leon Edel (1907-1997). It provided a forum for Modernist poetry and its criticism, and contained recurrent admonition against the "mediocrity" of most of the Canadian poetry then extant; Smith opined that modern poetry must speak to its time with intelligence and the use of other than simple versification. Robert Finch (1900-), Leo Kennedy (1907-), and A. M. KLEIN were other coterie members, along with Edwin J. Pratt (1883-1964). Pratt has been called the primary transitional figure in the group, since his work is made up of his early reliance on romanticism and a stolid nationalism, but whose later interests in the relationships between twentieth-century technology and humane letters gives him Modernist credibility.

A second and similar journal appeared in 1928, begun by Scott and Kennedy, and provided opportunity for publication of both the poetry and the criticism of the writers considered to be the most important, and whose works would later find critical acclaim in the anthology *New Provinces: Poems of Several Authors* (1936; reprint 1976). These writers were highly concerned with the strategies of the British Modernists, and the voices of W. B. YEATS (*see* ABBEY THEATER and MODERNISM, England and Ireland), T. S. ELIOT, James JOYCE (*see* MODERNISM, England and Ireland), and others resound in their work; here there is clear reiteration of a manifesto of a firm rejection, on the part of Canadian poets, of the romanticism and provincialism which had only begun to diminish in their country a decade or two earlier. The new mode demanded the use of free versification, a relinquishing of outmoded prosody and meter, and the often abstruse, metaphoric presentation of the incongruities of existential reality. The poetry of the Montreal group speaks to the skepticism and the mounting uncertainty of a rapidly changing universe, and at the same time demonstrates a diversification of creative energy which is "unmistakably Canadian" and intellectually rewarding.

➤•⬅

Klein, A[braham] M[oses] (1909-1972)
Canadian poet, critic, publisher, and lawyer.

As a student at McGill University, Klein was strongly influenced by the thinking of early members of the Montreal Movement, as well as the work and the critical views of Eliot, W. H. Auden (1907-1973), Dylan Thomas (1914-1953), and Karl Shapiro (1913-) — and especially Joyce's abstruse use of language. His work contains a proliferation of diverse linguistic, stylistic, and metric qualities, all of which demonstrate a vision which strives for unity through variety. His major work, *The Second Scroll* (1951), expresses his total commitment to Zionism and his conviction that there is a strong, human capacity for survival, despite the evils of subjugation, discrimination — even holocaust — and that it remains constant and is renewed through the use of language and its creative dissemination of knowledge; one critic details the striking parallels between Klein's work and Joyce's *ULYSSES* in terms of language and structure and the various, religious creation myths which stress the relationships between good and evil and exile and redemption. His work *The Rocking Chair and Other Poems* (1948) won Canada's Governor General's Award. It does not deal specifically with Jewish themes, but *Hath Not a Jew* (1940) presents a strong affinity for Klein's Jewish background and both works show his concern for the problem of isolation from community and the ability to overcome it through self-realization. Despite his interest in the technical strategies of other Modernists, he is known for the development of an unmistakable voice which is characterized by diverse and subtle rhythmic patterns and a striking stylistic flexibility.

➔•◄

Scott, Frank R. (1899-1985)
Canadian poet, lawyer, and social and political philosopher.

The son of poet F. G. Scott (1861-1944), Frank Scott was educated in Quebec, at Oxford, England, and at McGill University in Toronto. He is especially noted for his diversified service to his country in legal and political fields, and as a poet he is called "the most important catalyst of modern Canadian poetry." An early endeavor was to revitalize Canadian poetry which he felt to be stultified by romanticism, and he found company at McGill in A. J. M. Smith and Leon Edel, who introduced him to the Modernist poets of England and Canada. His early poetry is often satiric and directed toward the established literary tradition; it appeared with work by other members of the group in the *McGill Fortnightly Review*, of which he was a founder. His poetic manifesto of 1931 is a consummate indictment against the old orders of politics, religion, and economics; his argument was then that an outmoded tradition was ripe for change. He was a strong nationalist and a political advocate for social justice; much of his work depicts humankind as individuals who are part of a larger continuum which can only gain coherence through the shared experience brought about by language and poetry. Though his poems are sometimes playful, even satiric, his concern for his country, the universe, his fellow man, and the human spirit are strongly evident. His many publications include the early *Overture* (1945), *Events and Signals* (1954), *The Eye of the Needle* (1957), and *Selected Poems* (1966). Later works are *Trouvailles: Poems from Prose* (1967), *The Dance Is One* (1973), and *Collected Poems* (1984). His *Poems of French Canada* (1977) reflect his interest in the work of French Canadian writers and his translations of their work, particularly of St. Denys Garneau (1912-1943) and Anne Hébert (1916-), have been called a "creative achievement in communications" by the renowned critic Northrop Frye (1912-1991).

✦●✦
Further Reading

Brown, E[dward] K[illoran]. *On Canadian Poetry*. Toronto: Ryerson Press, 1943.

Caplan, Usher. *Like One That Dreamed: A Portrait of A. M. Klein*. Toronto: McGraw-Hill Ryerson, 1982.

Collins, Robert G. *E. J. Pratt*. Boston: Twayne, 1988.

Dudek, Louis. "F. R. Scott and the Modern Poets." *Northern Review* 4, 2 (December-January 1950-51): 4-15.

Garvin, John W., ed. *Canadian Poets*. Toronto: McClelland & Stewart, 1926.

Gustafson, R., ed. *The Penguin Book of Canadian Verse*. Harmondsworth, England: Penguin Books, 1958.

Klein, A. M. *Beyond Sambation: Selected Essays and Editorials, 1928-1955*. Toronto: University of Toronto Press, 1982.

Klinck, Carl F., and Reginald E. Watters, eds. *Canadian Anthology*. Toronto: W. J. Gage, 1955; rev. ed., 1966.

Pitt, David G. *E. J. Pratt, the Master Years, 1927-1964*. Toronto: University of Toronto Press, 1987.

————. *E. J. Pratt, the Truant Years, 1882-1927*. Toronto: University of Toronto Press, 1984.

Rhodenizer, V. B. *A Handbook of Canadian Literature*. Ottawa, Canada: Graphic Pub., 1930.

Scott, F. R., and A. J. M. Smith, eds. *The Blasted Pine: An Anthology of Satire, Invective and Disrespectful Verse: Chiefly by Canadian Writers*. Toronto: Macmillan, 1957; rev. 1967.

Smith, A. J. M. *The Book of Canadian Poetry: A Critical and Historical Anthology*. Chicago: University of Chicago Press; Toronto: W. J. Gage, 1943; rev. ed., Toronto: W. J. Gage, 1957.

Stevens, Peter, ed. *The McGill Movement: A. J. M. Smith, F. R. Scott and Leo Kennedy*. Toronto: Ryerson Press, 1969.

Waddington, Miriam, ed. *The Collected Poems of A. M. Klein*. Toronto: McGraw-Hill Ryerson, 1974.

Wells, Henry, and Karl Klinck. *Edwin J. Pratt: The Man and His Poetry*. Toronto: Ryerson Press, 1947.

Wilson, Milton. *E. J. Pratt*. Toronto: McClelland & Stewart, 1969.

Wilson, Milton, ed. *Poets Between the Wars: E. J. Pratt, F. R. Scott, A. J. M. Smith, Dorothy Livesay, A. M. Klein*. Toronto: McClelland Stewart, 1969.

MOSCOW ART THEATER (Moskovskiy khudozhestvennyy teatr) Russia, 1898-1990s

Called the Moscow Art Open-Accessible Theater until 1902, the Moscow Art Theater was founded by Konstantin Sergeivich STANISLAVSKY, also one of the Theater's best actors and directors, and Vladimir Nemirovich-Danchenko (1858-1943), a playwright and instructor at the Music and Drama School of the Moscow Philharmonic, in 1898. Also known as the "theater of mood," the Moscow Art Theater was the most outstanding theater in Russia and trained most of Russia's most important directors and actors.

Like Andre Antoine's (1858-1943) THÉÂTRE LIBRE and Otto Brahm's (1856-1912) FREIE BÜHNE, the Moscow Art Theater rejected the conventional heavily stylized theater and sought to modernize dramatic performances through employment of the METHOD acting technique (*see* GROUP THEATER, United States), research into the social and historical context of the characters and plays, and attention to educating the public. The first play to be staged there was Alexei K. Tolstoy's (1817-1875) *Tsar Fyodor Ioannovich* (1868). Some of the Theater's outstanding successes were the plays of Anton CHEKHOV (*see* REALISM, Russia): *Chayka* (1896; *The Seagull*, 1912), *Dyadya Vanya* (1899; *Uncle Vanya*, 1912), *Tri sestry* (1901, *The Three Sisters*, 1916), and *Vishnevy sad* (1904; *The Cherry Orchard*, 1908). He became the house playwright and the seagull the official symbol for the Theater. Maxim GORKY (*see* SOCIALIST REALISM, Russia) became affiliated with the Moscow Art Theater in 1902 (the theater was renamed in his honor in 1932); his play *Na dne* (1901; *The Lower Depths*, 1912), with its lower-class protagonists, was staged that year.

Stanislavsky's Method was first used in the 1909 production of *Mesyats v derevne* (1855; A Month in the Country) by Ivan TURGENEV (*see* REALISM, Russia), his best drama and a forerunner of Chekhov's dramatic psychological realism. Other notable productions were Mikhail Afanascyev Bulgakov's (1891-1940) play *Days of the Turbins* (staged at the Theater in 1926; this was Stalin's favorite play), and Vsevolod Ivanov's (1895-1963) *Bronepoezd 14-69* (1922; *Armoured Train 14-69*, 1933), staged in 1927. Actors at the Theater included Vasili Ivanovich Kachalov (1875-1948), Ivan Mikhailovich Moskvin (1874-1946), and Olga Leonardovna Knipper (1870-1959), Chekhov's wife. Vsevolod Emilyevich Meyerhold (1874-1940?) was its renowned stage director.

Chekhov and Gorky influenced Western and Soviet playwrights alike, Aleksandr Nikolayevich Afinogenov (1904-1941) being a notable Soviet example, while Stanislavsky influenced theater elsewhere. He encouraged, for example, the Habima (Yiddish for "stage") when it moved from Poland to Moscow and opened there in 1918; by the 1920s it was a studio of the Moscow Art Theater, but in 1931 moved permanently to Tel Aviv, Israel.

After the 1917 Revolution, Commissar of Education Anatoly Lunacharsky (1875-1933) allowed the Theater to remain active. It toured Europe and the United States in 1922-24, during its heyday, then toured London in later decades. Oleg Nikolayevich Yefremov (1927-), formerly with the Sovremennik Theatre, was hired as artistic director in 1972. The next year the company moved to new quarters for performances on Tversky Boulevard with seating for 1,400.

❖•❖

Stanislavsky, Konstantin Sergeivich (1863-1938)
Russian director and actor.

Previously with the Moscow Society of Art and Literature, Stanislavsky was influenced by the innovative Meininger Company, led by George II, Duke of Saxe-Meiningen (1826-1914), and especially his wife, Ellen Franz (1839-1923). He was the originator of Method acting—which remained a popular practice late in the twentieth century—in which actors are trained to approach a role by doing an introspective personal analysis of the character in relation to him or herself in order to present a more realistic portrayal. Stanislavsky developed Method acting in response to the artificiality of speeches and emotional conveyance of conventional acting at the time. Members of the American Group Theater picked up the Method in the 1930s, as later did Lee Strasberg, as well as Elia Kazan and his Actor's Studio. Stanislavsky described the Method in the book *Rabota aktera nad soboi* (1926; *An Actor Prepares*, 1936).

❖•❖

Further Reading

Benedetti, Jean. *Stanislavski: A Biography*. 2nd ed. New York: Routledge, 1988.
————. *Stanislavski, an Introduction*. New York: Theatre Arts Books, 1982.
Benedetti, Jean, ed. *The Moscow Art Theatre Letters*. New York: Routledge, 1991.
Edwards, Christine. *The Stanislavski Heritage, Its Contribution to the Russian and American Theatre*. New York: New York University Press, 1965.
Golub, Spencer. *The Recurrence of Fate: Theatre and Memory in Twentieth-Century Russia*. Iowa City, Iowa: University of Iowa Press, 1994.
Gorchakov, N. A. *The Theater in Soviet Russia*. New York: Columbia University Press, 1957.
Houghton, Norris. *Moscow Rehearsals: An Account of Methods of Production in the Soviet Theatre*. New York: Octagon Books, 1975.
Leach, Robert, and Victor Borovsky, eds. *A History of Russian Theatre*. Cambridge, England: Cambridge University Press, 1998.
Londré, Felicia Hardison. "The Moscow Art Theatre." In her *The History of World Theater: From the English Restoration to the Present*. New York: Continuum, 1991.
Magarshack, David. *Stanislavsky: A Life*. Boston: Faber and Faber, 1986.
Morgan, Joyce Vining. *Stanislavski's Encounter with Shakespeare: The Evolution of a Method*. Ann Arbor, Mich.: UMI Research Press, 1984.
Munk, Erika, ed. *Stanislavski and America: An Anthology from the Tulane Drama Review*. New York: Hill and Wang, 1966.
Nemirovich-Danchenko, Vladimir. *My Life in the Russian Theatre*. London: Bles, 1968.
Pitcher, Harvey. *Chekhov's Leading Lady: A Portrait of the Actress Olga Knipper*. New York: F. Watts, 1980.
Roose-Evans, James. *Experimental Theatre from Stanislavsky to Peter Brook*. London: Routledge & Kegan Paul, 1984.

Saylor, Oliver M. *Inside the Moscow Art Theatre*. Westport, Conn.: Greenwood Press, 1970.

Stanislavski, Constantin. *My Life in Art*. New York: Theatre Arts Books, 1952.

————. *Stanislavsky's Legacy: A Collection of Comments on a Variety of Aspects of an Actor's Art and Life*. Edited by Elizabeth Reynolds Hapgood. New York: Theatre Arts Books, 1968.

Stenberg, Douglas Graham. *From Stanislavsky to Gorbachev: The Theater-Studios of Leningrad*. New York: P. Lang, 1995.

Strasberg, Lee. *A Dream of Passion: The Development of the Method*. Boston: Little, Brown, 1987.

Worrall, Nick. *The Moscow Art Theatre*. New York: Routledge, 1996.

MOSCOW LINGUISTIC CIRCLE. *See* RUSSIAN FORMALISM

MOUNTAIN PASS. *See* PEREVAL

THE MOVEMENT
England, 1950s

This name described a group of young writers who were making new demands of contemporary poetry, and setting older and more traditional guidelines for it. Their conservatism was in reaction to the poetry of English MODERNISTS T. S. ELIOT and Ezra POUND, and others like them who had changed the shape, form, and linguistic patterns of the poetry which had preceded their own era; they had also developed new critical ways in which to view the literary arts. The writers of The Movement wanted a conscious and intellectually coherent poetry which would clearly depict the times. Their rules included "a reverence for real person or event," stricter adherence to recognizable verse form (notably iambic pentameter or tetrameter), and a commonsense view of both audience and message. Hysteria, incoherence, oblique reference to classical language without explication, and overstated rhetoric must give way to more prescriptive visions of the bleak and unrewarding reality in which they found themselves. An example of their revised stylistic attitudes was in the negative response to the work of Dylan Thomas (1914-1953) and his linguistic and imagistic excess. Philip LARKIN, Kingsley AMIS (1922-1995), and John WAIN (1925-) (*see* ANGRY YOUNG MEN) were innovators of the group; others included Robert Conquest (1917-), Donald Davie (1922-), D. J. Enright (1920-), Thom Gunn (1929-), John Holloway (1920-), and Elizabeth Jennings (1926-).

To publicize their antipathy towards the Modernist poets whose tenets they rejected, the manifesto of the group was introduced by Robert Conquest, editor of *New Lines* (1956), the anthology of the poets of The Movement. In it, Conquest's caveats are about the poetry of the obscure, ambiguous literary elucidation, and mysterious references known only to the poet. He asks for poetry with a vigorous, straightforward style which is told plain. At this time, Amis and Wain were also associated with the group known as the Angry Young Men, whose ideas about creative prose were somewhat in agreement with those of the writers of The Movement; this meld of ideas provided interesting juncture for more than one group who wanted a return to more conventional creative work which would be "polite, knowledgeable, efficient, polished and . . . even intelligent."

It does not surprise that some reaction to the poets of The Movement took place in the observations of poet and critic Alfred Alvarez (1929-). Himself a devotee of the witty and often obscure poetry of William EMPSON (*see* CAMBRIDGE GROUP), Alvarez did find some justification of the methodology of The Movement poets but cautioned that poetry must not fit into the realm of the "ordinary." His criterion was that inspired poets are obliged to "reveal the terrifying aspect of recent history" and the chaos of society; his fear was that the poet as "the man next door" might well lack the power for the task at hand.

But the writers of The Movement found both audience and approbation. Writers such as Larkin, Amis, Davie, and Gunn have continued to develop as poets and have remained in favor with critics, other poets, and the reading public. Their pithy, witty, and slant view of the passing of the old order and value systems of not only England but of Western civilization as we know it has provided some of the most tender and poignant poetic truths of our day.

⋙•⋘

Larkin, Philip (1922-1985), English poet, critic, and essayist.

Most critics today generally agree that Larkin's work is among the best to have come out of the many and frequent movements in modern poetry. His creative work has shown a steady and resounding progress in the polishing of stylistic skills, his careful attention to technique, a perfect ability to convey the dialect and tone of his middle-class speaker, and his technical mastery of what has become known, put by one critic, as the "[Larkin] poetic line — the innovational articulation of tone best found in the music of jazz" — a subject which interested him greatly and about which he wrote some critical material of value.

Larkin admitted to the early influence of Thomas Hardy (1840-1928), which caused him to concentrate more on style, and to revaluate his poetic view of life in examination of the past, which depicts a more carefully ordered existence. His themes are about ordinary people who live mundane lives — clerks, librarians, the "chaps in business suits," university dons — and their terrible, tender, and tenuous ruminations about the world in which they find themselves, one in which tedium is interrupted sporadically by dread, and rarely by the notion that some events provide a measure of the positive.

An example is given in his poem "Church Going" (1955), in which a cyclist explores a country church, having removed his "cycle clips in awkward reverence." As he carefully examines every aspect of the country building—choir stall, pews, altar, pence box— he wonders about the church falling into disuse and concludes: "But superstition, like belief must die/And what remains when disbelief is gone?" And yet, the speaker continues, there is worth in this place, a kind of value needing expression and something of which we should at least be reminded: "It pleases me to stand in silence here,/A serious house and serious earth it is . . ./If only that so many dead lie round." These lines present an acceptance of what is and give a gentle dignity to what was without resorting to a sentimentality which would lower the power of Larkin's message.

His argument with much modern poetry was that its obscurity often divorced it from its public audience, and that the separation of artist from audience defeats the purpose and reduces the importance of poetic message. Thus poetry must be vivid yet unsparing, give pleasure and sadden, if necessary, to be honest, he felt. Critic and admirer Derek Wolcott has responded that this poet's sadness has now become our delight.

»•«

Further Reading

Alvarez, Alfred. *The New Poetry: An Anthology*. Harmondsworth, England: Penguin Books, 1962.

Austin, Allan E. *Roy Fuller*. Boston: Twayne, 1979.

Bedient, Calvin. *Eight Contemporary Poets*. London: Oxford University Press, 1974.

Daiches, David. *The Present Age in British Literature*. Bloomington, Ind.: Indiana University Press, 1958.

Davie, Donald. *These the Companions: Recollections*. Cambridge, England; New York: Cambridge University Press, 1982.

Enright, D. J. *Poets of the 1950's*. Tokyo: Kenkyusha, 1955.

Fussell, Paul. *The Anti-Egoist: Kingsley Amis, Man of Letters*. New York: Oxford University Press, 1994.

Gardner, Philip. *Kingsley Amis*. Boston: Twayne, 1981.

Larkin, Philip. *Required Writing: Miscellaneous Pieces, 1958-1982*. New York: Farrar Straus Giroux, 1983.

McDermott, John. *Kingsley Amis, an English Moralist*. New York: St. Martin's Press, 1989.

Morrison, Blake. *The Movement*. Oxford, England: Oxford University Press, 1980.

Motion, Andrew. *Philip Larkin: A Writer's Life*. New York: Farrar Straus Giroux, 1982.

Salwak, Dale. *John Wain*. Boston: Twayne, 1980.

———. *Kingsley Amis, in Life and Letters*. New York: St. Martin's Press, 1991.

Simms, Jacqueline, ed. *Life by Other Means: Essays on D. J. Enright*. Oxford, England: Oxford University Press, 1990.

Swarbrick, Andrew. *Out of Reach: The Poetry of Philip Larkin*. New York: St. Martin's Press, 1995.

Thwaite, Anthony. *Larkin at Sixty*. London: Faber and Faber, 1982.

Wolcott, Derek. "The Master of the Ordinary." *The New York Review* 36 (June 1, 1989): 37-40.

THE MOVEMENT (De Beweging)
Netherlands, 1905-1920s

A Dutch phenomenon of the first decades of the twentieth century, The Movement arose under the guidance of Albert Verwey (1865-1937) as a reaction to the "art for art's sake" philosophy that ruled the MOVEMENT OF THE EIGHTIES, of which Verwey had been a member. With Aart van der Leeuw (1876-1931), Pietor Hendrik van Moerkerken (1839-1901), and others, Verwey espoused a form of Neoclassical literature in which idea and meaning superceded style and structure.

✦•✦

Further Reading

Bulhof, Francis, ed. *Nijhoff, Van Ostaijen, De stijl: Modernism in the Netherlands and Belgium in the First Quarter of the 20th Century: Six Essays.* The Hague, Netherlands: Nijhoff, 1976.

Weevers, Theodoor. *Vision and Form in the Poetry of Albert Verwey: Poems from the Oorspronkelijk Dichtwerk with Renderings in English Verse.* London: Athlone Press, 1986.

Wolf, Manfred. *Albert Verwey and English Romanticism: A Comparative and Critical Study.* The Hague: H.L. Smits, 1978.

MOVEMENT OF THE EIGHTIES (Beweging van Tachtig)
Netherlands, c. 1885-1900s

Although philosophically divided in its support of both Romanticism and NATURAL-ISM, the Movement of the Eighties was the preeminent force behind the modernization of Dutch literature. From about 1885 until 1894, the Eightiers expressed their distaste for confining traditions and their preoccupation with the life of the individual through numerous works in a variety of genres. The Movement's chief literary outlet was the journal *De Nieuwe Gids* (The New Guide), so named for its expressly stated difference from *De Gids*, the periodical which had until then dominated literary activity in the Netherlands. Among the most prominent Eightiers were Lodewijk van Deyssel (1864-1952), whose works are examples of the group's synthesis of impressionism and REAL-IST representation; Frederik Willem van Eeden (1860-1932), a founder and editor of the journal; Willem Kloos (1859-1938), founder, editor and contributing poet whose introduction to *Mathilde* (1882) by Jacques Perk (1859-1881) is known as the group's manifesto; and Willem Paap (1856-1923). Herman Gorter's (1864-1927) poem "Mei" (May), published in *De Nieuwe Gids* in 1889, reflects the influence of John Keats and is considered an exemplary example of the Movement's tenets. Another member, Albert Verwey (1865-1937), helped to silence the lingering influence of the Eightiers after the turn of the century with his formation of the far more cohesive THE MOVEMENT.

Further Reading

Block, Susan Taylor. *Van Eeden*. Wilmington, N.C.: Lower Cape Fear Historical Society, 1995.

Grierson, Herbert. *Two Dutch Poets*. Oxford, England: Clarendon Press, 1936.

Meijer, Reinder P. "Moralists and Anti-Moralists" and "The Modern Period." In his *Literature of the Low Countries: A Short History of Dutch Literature in the Netherlands and Belgium*. New York: Twayne, 1971.

Smart, D. A. *Pannekoek and Gorter's Marxism*. London: Pluto Press, 1978.

Wolf, Manfred. *Willem Kloos: A Study in the Leadership of Dutch Romanticism*. Thesis, Brandeis University, 1955.

MUCKRAKING
United States, 1900s

The Muckraking movement refers to exposé journalism and fiction that thrived in the United States during the first decade of the twentieth century. Targeting unethical practices in government and business and perilous social and labor conditions, Muckrakers exposed corruption and seaminess in American life and helped further a period of legal reform. Muckraking investigative crusades became popular in magazines, which grew substantially in popularity among middle class readers during this time. The most widely known of the socially committed, collaborating journalists—Lincoln Steffens (1866-1936), Ida Tarbell (1857-1944), and Ray Stannard Baker (1870-1946)—eventually purchased the *American* magazine in 1906 to serve as a forum for Muckraking articles. Additionally, bleak fictional works, such as *The Octopus* (1901) by Frank NORRIS (*see* NATURALISM, United States) and *The Jungle* (1906) by Upton Sinclair (1878-1968), a prominent member of the circle of Muckraking journalists, were based on actual incidents and conditions, dramatising the plight of ordinary people.

Muckrakers shared common goals for improving social conditions in the United States through exhaustive research and documentation of social ills and evils of capitalism. However, more sensationalistic writers of "yellow journalism"—the practice of making accusations based on unsubstantiated rumors, inflicting damage before the facts are known—led to a backlash against investigative journalism as early as 1906, and "muckraking" was used by some as a pejorative term. The term "muckraking" was first applied to exposé journalists by U.S. President Theodore Roosevelt in a speech on April 4, 1906, where he quoted from John Bunyan's *Pilgrim's Progress*: "the Man with the Muckrake, the man who could look no way but downward . . . who was offered a celestial crown for his muckrake . . . but continued to rake to himself the filth of the floor." Roosevelt chastised journalists for focusing attention on the seamier side of American life at the expense of more wholesome elements. Roosevelt lumped all investigative journalists into the muckraker category, whether their stories were sensationalistic or verifiable; the epithet stuck (in fact, Muckrakers enthusiastically adopted the name), but the speech contributed to growing disfavor toward exposé journalism. However, Muckrakers are commonly identified by literary historians as writers from this period who presented conclusive evidence about dishonest public officials, hazardous working conditions, social problems, worthless medicines, and dangerous foods. They generally date the Muckraking movement from 1900 to 1912, when *Hampton's* magazine, the final journal devoted to muckraking, ceased publication.

McClure's magazine was the first muckraking journal. Editor Samuel Sidney McClure (1857-1949) assigned reporters to uncover corruption in business, labor, finance, and city government. Most admired of the many investigative reports that were published in *McClure's* were Tarbell's exposé of unscrupulous practices by the Standard Oil Company (collected and published in 1904 as *The History of the Standard Oil Company)* and Steffens's series on corruption in the city governments of New York, Chicago, Philadelphia, St. Louis, Minneapolis, and Pittsburgh (collected and published in 1904 and 1906, respectively, as *The Shame of the Cities* and *The Struggle for Self-Government)*. Many other magazines began printing investigative reports: those associated with the unimpeachable practices of Muckraking include *Collier's, Everybody's, Harper's,* the *American,* the *Cosmopolitan,* and the *Forum.* The most significant reports were later collected and published: in addition to Tarbell's and Steffens's reports, they include *The Great American Fraud* (1906) by Samuel Hopkins Adams (1871-1958), which exposed ineffectual and dangerous patent medicines and helped promote passage of The Pure Food and Drug Act; Baker's *Following the Color Line: An Account of Negro Citizenship in the American Democracy* (1903); *Frenzied Finance: The Crime of Amalgamated, Inc.* (1905) by Thomas W. Lawson (1857-1925); and *The Treason of the Senate* (1906) by David Graham Phillips (1867-1911). Similar exposés were presented in well-crafted, fictional narratives by Norris and Sinclair. Sinclair's *The Jungle,* based on his observations of unsanitary and dangerous working conditions in Chicago's meat preparation plants and the miserable lives of its workers, is the most celebrated work of the Muckraking movement.

❧•❦

Further Reading

Chalmers, David Mark. *The Muckrake Years.* New York: Van Nostrand, 1974.

Chamberlain, John. "The Muck-Rake Pack." In his *Farewell to Reform: The Rise, Life, and Decay of the Progressive Mind in America.* 2nd ed. New York: John Day, 1933.

Colburn, David R., and George E. Pozzetta, eds. *Reform and Reformers in the Progressive Era.* Westport, Conn.: Greenwood Press, 1983.

Cook, Fred. *The Muckrakers: Crusading Journalists Who Changed America.* Garden City, N.Y.: Doubleday, 1972.

Dawson, Hugh J. "Winston Churchill and Upton Sinclair: An Early Review of *The Jungle*." *American Literary Realism* 24, 1 (fall 1991): 72-78.

Filler, Louis. *Appointment at Armageddon: Muckraking and Progressivism in the American Tradition*. Westport, Conn.: Greenwood Press, 1976.

————. *The Muckrakers*. Chicago: H. Regnery, 1968. New enl. ed.: University Park, Pa.: Pennsylvania State University Press, 1976.

Parry, Sally E. "Upton-Sinclair-Lewis: The Crossed Paths of Two American Reformer Novelists." *Connecticut Review* 16, 1 (spring 1994): 81-92.

Pattee, Fred Lewis. "The Muck-Rake School." In his *The New American Literature: 1890-1930*. New York; London: Century, 1930.

Regier, C. C. *The Era of the Muckrakers*. Chapel Hill, N.C.: University of North Carolina Press, 1932.

Sinclair, Upton. *The Autobiography of Upton Sinclair*. New York: Harcourt, Brace & World, 1962.

Steffens, Lincoln. *The Autobiography of Lincoln Steffens*. New York: Harcourt, Brace, 1931.

Stein, Harry H., and John M. Harrison, eds. *Muckraking: Past, Present and Future*. University Park, Pa.: Pennsylvania State University Press, 1973.

Swados, Harvey. *Years of Conscience: The Muckrakers*. Cleveland: World Pub. Co., 1962.

Tarbell, Ida M. *All in the Day's Work: An Autobiography*. New York: Macmillan, 1939.

Weinberg, Arthur, and Lila Weinberg. *The Muckrakers: The Era in Journalism that Moved America to Reform*. New York: Simon & Schuster, 1961.

MY GROUP
Ukrainian emigrés in Poland, 1930s

One of many groups of Ukrainians living in Warsaw, Poland, during the 1930s, *My* was a nationalist movement and journal inspired by Symon Petlyura (1879-1926) and led by Borys Olkhivsky (1908-1944).

Further Reading

Desroches, Alain. *The Ukrainian Problem and Symon Petlura (The Fire and the Ashes)*. Chicago: Ukrainian Research and Information Institute, 1970.

Luckyj, George S. N. "Ukrainian Literature." In *Columbia Dictionary of Modern European Literature*. 2nd ed. Edited by Jean-Albert Bédé and William B. Edgerton. New York: Columbia University Press, 1980.

MYŌJŌ POETS. *See* NEW POETRY SOCIETY

N

NADREALISTI MOVEMENT
Czechoslovakia, 1930s-1940s

A Slovakian movement that began around 1935 and reached its height during the 1940s, Nadrealisti combined SURREALISTIC expression with opposition to the wartime fragmentation and outside control of Czechoslovakian provinces. Vladimír Reisel (1919-) was the group's leading theoretician.

❦•❦

Further Reading

Petro, Peter. "Slovak Literature: Loyal, Dissident, and Émigre." In *Czechoslovakia 1918-88: Seventy Years from Independence*. Edited by H. Gordon Skilling. New York: St. Martin's Press, 1991.

NAN-SHÊ GROUP. *See* SOUTHERN SOCIETY

NAŠA NIVA GROUP
Byelorussia, 1906-1914

The *Naša Niva* group (most frequently translated as the Our Soil group; also rendered *Našaniŭstva*) took its name from the popular and influential Byelorussian newspaper to which its members contributed, *Naša Niva*. The weekly, founded by Ivan (1881-1919) and Anton (1884-1946) Luckievič and Alaksiej Ulasau (1874-1941), was the second legitimate periodical published in the Byelorussian language after the ban on Byelorussian printing, effected in the 1860s during the rule of the Russian Empire, was lifted in the aftermath of the 1905 revolution. The most renowned of those literary artists whose work supported and helped define *Naša Niva* were the poets Janka Kupala (pseud. of Ivan Łucevič, 1882-1942), Jakub Kołas (pseud. of Kanstantyn

Mickievič, 1882-1956), Maksim Bahdanovich (1891-1917), Maksim Harecki (1893-1939), Aleś Harun (pseud. of Alaksandar Prušynski, 1887-1920), and poet and prose writer Zmitrok Biadula (pseud. of Samuil Plaunik, 1886-1941). Together, through the forum of *Naša Niva*, these writers constituted what has become known as a nationalist literary renaissance of Byelorussia, celebrating its people, its land, and its cultural history. *Naša Niva*, it should be noted, was not strictly a literary journal, but a publication also encompassing articles on agriculture, religion, education—topics addressing national interests. Its first editorial announced, in part: "We shall strive to make all Byelorussians—who do not know who they are,—understand that they are Byelorussians and human beings, that they should learn their rights and help us in their work." But literature became the driving mode and force of the nationalist movement in Byelorussia. Despite the nationalist tone of the literature published in *Nasa Niva,* the periodical was moderate enough, and the Soviet regime still tolerant enough, to endure until Germany invaded Byelorussia in 1915. Bahdanovich was a major force in developing a more cosmopolitan doctrine, Adradženstva (Renaissance), from the nationalist tenets of Našaniŭstva, which some of the *Naša Niva* writers explored: a deliberate study of European trends, such as SYMBOLISM and Impressionism. The sec ondary movement fell apart around 1921 with the rise of Communist revolutionaries in the Byelorussian literary scene.

✦•✦

Further Reading

McMillan, Arnold. *A History of Byelorussian Literature: From Its Origins to the Present Day.*
Giessen, Germany: Wilhelm Schmitz Verlag, 1977.
———. "Tradition and Innovation in the Poetry of Bahdanovič." *Slavonic and East European Review* 56, 2 (April 1978): 261-74.
Rich, Vera, ed. *Like Water, Like Fire: An Anthology of Byelorussian Poetry from 1828 to the Present Day.* London: George Allen & Unwin Ltd., 1971.
Stankievič, St. "Kupala in Fact and Fiction." *Belorussian Review* 3 (1956): 31-58.
———. "Jakub Kolas." *Belorussian Review* 4 (1957): 5-22.

NATIONAL LITERATURE MOVEMENT (Millî Edebiyat)
Turkey, 1910s

The major proponents of the National Literature Movement were Ahmet Hikmet Müftüoglu (1870-1927) and Mehmet Emin Yurdakul (1869-1944). These poets called for patriotism and attention to the plight of the impoverished, especially in rural Turkey, with poetry in simple language that often drew on folk tradition and verse. Like the YOUNG PENS and the DAWN OF THE FUTURE writers, these poets formed their group in the wake of the increasingly liberal conditions that followed the Young Turk revolution in 1908. The National Literature writers renounced the Arabic and Persian aspects of the Turkish linguistic and poetic heritage, writing instead vernacular verse in simple syllabic meter. Some critics consider Müftüoglu and Yurdakul to have been more politically than artistically oriented and motivated in their work, which often consisted of caustic social commentary. A nationalist literary tendency continued, following the establishment of the Republic of Turkey, through the SYLLABISTS movement of the 1920s-1940s.

✦•✦

Further Reading

Stone, Frank A. *The Rub of Cultures in Modern Turkey: Literary Views of Education.* Bloomington, Ind.: Indiana University, 1973.

NATIONAL NEOROMANTICISM
Finland, 1890s-1930

When Finnish writers began to reject the tradition of REALISM which had dominated their literary scene for a decade, they were influenced most by the SYMBOLIST movement which had had almost universal influence, and out of this had developed their own version of it—National Neoromanticism. Juhani Aho (1861-1921), Volter Kilpi (1874-1939), Joel Lehtonen (1881-1934), and Eino Leino (1878-1926) were intrigued by Symbolist concepts which incorporated the creation of new form in both art and letters, variance of familiar linguistic mechanisms, and more emphasis on techniques for the depiction of poetic inner vision of fragmented experience—all in response to the Finnish national and social scene of their time. Aho and Leino were the most prominent of the group—Aho for his impressionistic short stories and his novel, *Juha* (1911), and Leino for the poetic genius which reflected a "profound philosophical inner vision" from which he was able to depict both the conflict and the regeneration of his time. He is also known for his dramas, novels, criticism, and for his translation of most major European, classical writers.

✦•✦

Further Reading

Sarajas, Annamari. "Eino Leino: 1878-1926." Translated by Mary Lomas. *Books from Finland* 12 (1978): 40-46.
Tarkka, Pekka. "Joel Lehtonen and Putkinotko." Translated by David Barrett. *Books from Finland* 11 (1977): 239-45.
———. "The Death of a Poet." Translated by Hildi Hawkins. *Books from Finland* 17, 4 (1983): 129-32.

NATURALISM (For multinational overview, *see* **REALISM**.)

NATURALISM
Denmark, 1870s-1900s

Coeval with REALISM and SYMBOLISM, Naturalism in Denmark was led by Georg Brandes (1842-1927) with his renouncing of Romanticism and modernizing of Danish literature through an emphasis on a NIETZSCHEAN, individualistic approach to the human condition. In his eloquent lectures at the University of Copenhagen from 1871 to 1887, he held that literature should spur public debate on social and moral issues. The Danish Naturalists were fascinated with and influenced by the plays of their contemporary Henrik IBSEN (*see* Realism, Norway), which provided plenty of material for debate. Brandes inspired many younger Danish writers including poet and novelist Herman Bang (1857-1912), Georg's brother dramatist Edvard Brandes (1847-1931), painter and poet Holger Drachmann (1846-1908), novelist Karl Gjellerup (1857-1919), biologist and prose writer Jens Peter Jacobsen (1847-1885), who translated Darwin's *On the Origin of Species* and *Descent of Man* into Danish, and prose writer and dramatist Gustav Wied (1858-1914).

Principal representative works of Danish Naturalism include Jacobsen's novel *Niels Lyhne* (1881; *Niels Lyhne*, 1919) and story "Mogens" (1872; *Mogens and Other Stories*, 1921), Edvard Brandes's dramas, and Drachmann's *Digte* (1872; Poems). Georg Brandes's *Det moderne Gjennembruds Mænd* (1883; The Men of the Modern Breakthrough) provided a survey of the Danish Naturalists.

⋙•⋘

Further Reading

Borum, Poul. *Danish Literature: A Short Critical Survey*. Copenhagen: Det Danske Selskab, 1979.

Bredsdorff, Elias, Brita Mortensen, and Ronald Popperwell. *An Introduction to Scandinavian Literature from the Earliest Times to Our Day*. 1951. Reprint, Westport, Conn.: Greenwood Press, 1970.

Gustafson, Alrik. "Toward Decadence: Jens Peter Jacobsen." In his *Six Scandinavian Novelists*. Minneapolis: University of Minnesota Press for the American-Scandinavian Foundation, 1940.

Halmundsson, Hallberg. *An Anthology of Scandinavian Literature, from the Viking Period to the Twentieth Century*. New York: Collier Books, 1965.

Mitchell, P. M. "The Breakthrough." In his *A History of Danish Literature*. 2nd ed. New York: Kraus-Thomson Organization Ltd., 1971.

Moritzen, Julius. *Georg Brandes in Life and Letters*. Newark, N.J.: D. S. Colyer, Publisher, 1922.

Rossel, Sven H. "The Modern Breakthrough in Denmark." In his *A History of Scandinavian Literature, 1870-1980*. Minneapolis: University of Minnesota Press, 1982.

NATURALISM
England, 1880s-1900s

Not a strong movement in England, the Naturalist extension of Realism — as well as the advent of a scientific, mechanistic age — nonetheless influenced such English writers as Samuel Butler (1835-1902), George ELIOT (*see* REALISM, England), Thomas Hardy (1840-1928); dramatist N. C. Hunter (1908-1971),W. Somerset Maugham (1874-1965), George Moore (1852-1933), and, especially, George Gissing (1857-1903) and John Galsworthy (1867-1933).

Some of the best-known works associated with English Naturalism include Galsworthy's dramas *Strife* (1909), which deals with a labor strike and made his reputation as a playwright, and *Justice* (1910; produced 1916 in New York), which so powerfully portrayed solitary confinement in prisons it was instrumental in eliminating the practice. Gissing's novel *New Grub Street* (1891) critiques the rise of sensationalism and commercialism in journalism.

➤●◄
Further Reading

Barker, Dudley. *A Man of Principle: A View of John Galsworthy*. London: Heinemann, 1963.

Bowlby, Rachel. *Just Looking: Consumer Culture in Dreiser, Gissing, and Zola*. New York: Methuen, 1985.

Brandes, Georg Morris Cohen. *Naturalism in Nineteenth-Century English Literature*. New York: Russell & Russell, 1957.

Collie, Michael. *The Alien Art: A Critical Study of George Gissing's Novels*. Folkestone, England: Dawson; Hamden, Conn.: Archon Books, 1979.

Fréchet, Alec. *John Galsworthy, a Reassessment*. London: Macmillan, 1982.

Gissing, George. *George Gissing on Fiction*. Edited and with an introduction by Jacob and Cynthia Korg. London: Enitharmon Press, 1978.

Marrot, Harold V. *The Life and Letters of John Galsworthy*. London; Toronto: W. Heinemann, 1935.

Poole, Adrian. *Gissing in Context*. Totowa, N.J.: Rowman and Littlefield, 1975.

NATURALISM
France, 1860s-1900s

An extreme branch of the Realistic movement generally associated with Gustave FLAUBERT, French Naturalism, which spanned the last three decades of the nineteenth century, exploded existing barriers of subject matter, language, and characterization while constructing a theoretical base that other national groups adopted as part of their own literary reactions to the lingering influences of REALISM and Romanticism.

Unlike their predecessors, the Naturalists perceived the novel almost exclusively in scientific terms, as the writer's laboratory in which sociological experiments could be undertaken to trace the effects of biological determinism on human actions and aspirations. Numerous controversies—many sparked by the Naturalists' frank explorations of sexual behavior and lower-class life—colored the movement and, especially, the career of its leader, Émile ZOLA. Nonetheless, under Zola's direction, Naturalism became one of the most powerful and sustained forces in all of world literature.

Edmond and Jules de GONCOURT (*see* REALISM, France) are generally credited with anticipating, if not launching, Naturalism in France. Their novel *GERMINIE LACERTEUX (Germinie Lacerteux,* 1887), published in 1864, documented an authentic story of a working-class woman's moral fall. Her lowly death could be seen as the direct result not of free choices but of the determining factors of social position and a frequently hostile environment. The Goncourts' later work, however, strayed far from the Naturalism of Zola. This was due to the brothers' primary interest in individual and unique psychological cases and their painterly, often agrammatical, style. Although the Goncourts and Zola remained members of the informal literary coterie led by Flaubert, artistic and personal disputes erupted regularly. Edmond de Goncourt, especially, sustained an ill-hidden envy of Zola's enormous financial success and this, too, contributed to the marked differences between the Goncourts' writing and that of the true Naturalists.

A more convincing birthdate for Naturalism is 1867, the year in which Zola published *Thérèse Raquin (The Devil's Compact,* 1892). Indebted to *Germinie Lacerteux,* the novel signaled the genesis of Zola's own brand of Realism, which diminished the role of the mind in human behavior and accentuated instead the overpowering effects of hereditary and societal factors. In contrast to the Realists, Zola understood the role of the novelist in the same sociopolitically connected manner as Honoré de Balzac (1799-1850), whom he greatly admired. Balzac's monumental series *La comédie humaine* (1830-50; *Comédie humaine,* 1895-98), concerned with the comprehensive evocation of middle-class life during the first half of the nineteenth century, was of singular importance to Zola's conception and execution of the twenty-volume "Rougon-Macquart" series, begun in 1871 and completed in 1893. Subtitled "The Natural and Social History of a Family under the Second Empire," Zola's masterwork analyzed all the major classes and subclasses against the political backdrop of Napoleon III's regime.

In addition to Balzac's taxonomic representations of the human species, Zola drew upon several extraliterary theories to shape his work. Among the most prominent were those of Auguste Comte (1798-1857). From 1830 to 1842, in his six-volume *Cours de philosophie positive,* Comte outlined a philosophical system for the industrial era, an anti-metaphysical positivism which denied absolute causes and focused on the betterment of humans through the application of sociological science. Comte's successor, Hippolyte Taine (1828-1893), further influenced Zola with his Darwinistic formulations of the literary enterprise in his *Histoire de la littérature anglaise* (1863). From his readings in natural science, Zola absorbed in particular the conclusions on heredity set forth by Prosper Lucas, a now-forgotten French researcher and theoretician. Finally, physiologist Claude Bernard's (1813-1878) treatise *Introduction à l'étude de la médicine expérimentale* (1865) contributed significantly to Zola's method of character dissection and socio-literary experimentation, delineated in LE ROMAN EXPÉRIMENTAL (1880; *The Experimental Novel,* 1880) and *Les romanciers naturalistes* (1881).

From the publication of his novel *L'assommoir* (1877; *Gervaise,* 1879; also published as *Drunkard,* 1958), a study of alcoholism and despair, until his death in 1903, Zola dominated French letters with record-breaking sales and a string of controversies that kept him continually in the public eye. This, coupled with his astonishing productivity and stylistic superiority, served to eclipse the lives and work of virtually all his protégés. Two of his closest followers were Paul Alexis (1847-1901) and Henry Céard (1851-1924) who, together with J. K. Huysmans (1848-1907), Léon Hennique (1851-1935), and Guy de MAUPASSANT (*see* Realism, France), formed the set which gathered at Zola's villa in Médan. Their weekly discussions inspired the publication of *Les soirées de Médan* (1880), a collection of six wartime stories, each from a member of the group. Of Zola's younger set, only Maupassant received enthusiastic acclaim from the public for his contribution. Although Huysmans did distinguish himself with the novels *Marthe* (1876; *Marthe,* 1927) and *En Ménage* (1881; *Living Together,* 1969), he severed all ties with Naturalism in 1884, the year he published *À rebours* (*Against the Grain,* 1922) and fathered the Decadent movement in French literature. This left Alexis and Céard, for Maupassant never considered himself an adherent of any theoretical school and Hennique, critics agree, never seriously applied himself to his trade. Céard and Alexis so regularly subordinated themselves to Zola, aiding him, for example, in the immense research his detailed novels required, that neither ever rose to more than minor status as an independent writer. Following long, stable friendships with Zola, both men eventually shunned their master due to the marital disarray caused by Zola's maintenance of a second family.

These last two ruptures represented not the end of Naturalism but the fulfillment of Maupassant's conviction that every so-called "movement" has at its core the unique personality and intellect of a literary giant. When critics opposed Naturalism they unavoidably confronted the man Zola. Of the numerous attacks his works provoked, the two most notable centered on *La Terre* (1886; *The Soil,* 1886; also published as

Earth, 1954), in which Zola graphically and humorlessly depicted the travail and sordidness of French peasant life. The first, "Manifeste des cinq contre *La Terre*" (1887), published in *Le Figaro* by five associates of Edmond de Goncourt and Alphonse Daudet (1840-1897), consisted of a vituperative rejection of what they perceived to be Zola's immoral, purposeless, invidious literary path. The second, published at the same time by the influential critic Anatole France (1844-1922) in the Parisian journal *Gil Blas,* stated: "Never has a man made such an effort to vilify humanity, to insult every aspect of beauty and love, to deny all that is good and decent." Public blasts such as these, which generally stemmed either from jealousy of Zola's burgeoning wealth or misunderstandings of his literary motives, prevented Zola from professional acceptance beyond his own circles and, in particular, an admission to the French Academy, an honor he continually sought.

The most legitimate criticism of Zola's talents was that of his adaptations and original works for the theater, an inhospitable venue given his blunt disregard for the uses of dramatic conventions. Yet Zola, through his intense and repeated castigations of the contemporary stage's complacency and moderation, helped to liberate French dramatists during the 1880s and 1890s. First and most important among this generation was Henri BECQUE. While not a follower of Zola, Becque believed strongly in the truthful presentation of material and carefully avoided overt commentary, gratuitous sensationalism, or pat conclusions. The combined influence of Zola, Becque, and the later emergence of André Antoine's (1858-1943) THÉÂTRE LIBRE yielded drastic changes in drama in and outside France. Norwegian dramatist Henrik IBSEN (*see* REALISM, Norway), especially, furthered the Naturalist dramatic movement and established severe social criticism as a prominent feature of the rapidly evolving genre.

Like Ibsen, the writers affected by French Naturalistic fiction exerted, in turn, an enormous impact on their own national literatures. The Englishmen George Moore (1852-1933) and Thomas Hardy (1840-1928), and the American Naturalists Jack London (1876-1916), Frank NORRIS, and Theodore DREISER, are but a few of the many late nineteenth-century writers who borrowed extensively from Zola in order to express the pessimistic currents and social concerns of their day. With such a large, multicultural base, Naturalism remained a considerable force well into the first decades of the twentieth century. In France, however, by the fin de siècle, the new surges of SYMBOLISM, Decadence, and the psychological novel had revealed the practical and aesthetic limitations of Naturalism and irreversibly impaired its stronghold on the reading public.

After decades of fluctuating critical analyses, the literary merits of Naturalism, at least in the cases of Zola and his closest rivals, the Goncourts and Maupassant, is incontestable. In his best novels, Zola's "black poetry," his unsettling combination of lowly subject matter, social criticism, lyrical description, and subtle pathos, represents a high point of achievement in the sphere of major world movements.

❧•❧

Becque, Henri (1837-1899), French dramatist, critic, and journalist.

An immensely important figure in the development of French drama, Becque is remembered for his masterful introduction of Naturalistic elements which directly contravened the sentimental and superfluous plays of his mainstream contemporaries. His two most noted works are *LES CORBEAUX* (1882; *The Crows,* 1912; also published as *The Vultures,* 1913) and *La Parisienne* (1885; *The Woman of Paris,* 1913), the latter a prototype of the comédie rosse popularized by Antoine and the Théâtre Libre. Although Becque composed several new plays including the unfinished *Les polichinelles* (1910), during his final years, he ceased offering his works for stage production. Nonetheless, his reputation as an innovative dramatist remains secure. Becque also distinguished himself as an acute, occasionally acerbic, critic. His work *Querelles littéraires* (1890), a collection of reviews and lectures on contemporary and classic French drama, is esteemed for its many fervent and telling assessments.

Les Corbeaux (1882; *The Crows,* 1912; also published as *The Vultures,* 1913).

The first of Becque's two masterpieces, *Les Corbeaux* centers on the life of the Vigneron family who, following the death of Monsieur Vigneron, face all but suffocating financial worries. The people who, with predatory instinct, surround the family and in one sense or another devour its members are depicted matter-of-factly. In this aspect, as well as the subordination of technical contrivances to the development of theme and character, Becque provided a close parallel to the work of Zola. Like the most successful Naturalistic fiction, *Les Corbeaux* presents a dark, but accurate, slice of life, relieved only by the mixture of compassion and outrage provoked in the conscience of the reader or listener.

❧•❧

Zola, Émile (1840-1902)
French novelist, short-story writer, essayist, and dramatist.

The author most synonymous with Naturalism, Zola early during his career abandoned an affection for Romantic writers and adopted as his literary models the Realistic works of Balzac and Flaubert. As he came to equate scientific documentation and experimentation with the novelist's foremost tasks, he conceived the "Rougon-Macquart" series of novels, which, typically, provide close, frank examinations of city and village life while revealing the mechanistic and materialistic forces governing the individual. The last decade of his life Zola shed the impersonal voice of the Naturalist and launched two fiction cycles that incorporated his views on labor problems and other social injustices.

Despite Zola's humanitarian goals, critics have noted an anti-Semitic strain in his work. Zola, however, transcended this prejudice when he championed the cause of a falsely accused Jewish army officer in one of the most notorious trials in modern history. Politically endangered by the reverberations caused by his public essay "J'accuse" (1898; *The Dreyfus Case,* 1898), he was forced into seclusion in England until he received amnesty the following year. None of the novels written during his final years compare with those for which he is best known: *L'assommoir, Nana* (1880; *Nana,* 1880), and *GERMINAL* (1885; *Germinal; or, Master and Man,* 1885). Nonetheless, at the time of Zola's tragic death by asphyxiation, Anatole France, a former antagonist, was able to declare: "He fought social illness wherever he encountered it. Such were the things he hated. In his later books he completely revealed his fervent love for humanity. He tried to divine and foretell a better society."

Le Roman Expérimental (1880; *The Experimental Novel,* 1880).

Zola's most significant manifesto of Naturalism is *Le Roman Expérimental.* In this essay he promulgated his conception of a clinical approach to the observation of daily life, and hence, to the fictional recapitulation and laboratory-like experimentation engendered by the author's conscientiously assembled field notes. Zola's ruling scientific theory was that of genetic inheritance, a biological law whose socioeconomic impact Zola exploited in several of his "Rougon-Macquart" novels.

Germinal (1885; *Germinal; or, Master and Man,* 1885).

One of the finest novels in Zola's "Rougon-Macquart" series, *Germinal* — the outcome of exhaustive eyewitness research by Zola, who accumulated some 900 pages of notes before commencing his narrative — is an epic study of labor exploitation in the coal-mining industry. The workers of Montsou, largely uneducated and accustomed only to the simple pleasures afforded by eating, drinking, ribald humor, and sexual release, are the victims of an increasingly profit-hungry group of owners. Stirred by the socialist views of newcomer Etienne Lantier and plagued by debt, abominable living conditions, and hunger, the workers organize themselves, establish an emergency fund, and, eventually, strike. After a torturous two months, during which time a vicious riot breaks out, Belgian strikebreakers transplanted by the owners force the struggle to a bloody, miserable conclusion.

Despite an ending underscoring the strike's failure and the continued degradation of the workers, *Germinal* was hailed by socialist intellectuals and other sympathizers of the working classes as an immensely important document which graphically detailed the potential evils of capitalism as well as the innate bestiality of all humans. The theme of purposeful germination, of humanity's procreative and imaginative power to effect rebirth and change, which emerges on the final page, meliorates an otherwise dreary narrative of dissipated potential and mindless toil. Zola's highly moral stance in this work has contributed greatly to *Germinal*'s elevated status within the "Rougon-Macquart" cycle. Along with *L'assommoir* and *Nana*, *Germinal* forms the pinnacle of French Naturalism through its representative concern for the working classes and its stunning blend of repellent subject matter and rich, lyrical narration.

➹•➷

Further Reading

Bâcourt, Pierre de, and Cunliffe, J. W. "Émile Zola (1840-1902)." In their *French Literature During the Last Half Century.* New York: Macmillan, 1923.

Barbusse, Henri. *Zola*. New York: Dutton, 1933.

Becker, George J. *Documents of Modern Literary Realism*. Princeton, N.J.: Princeton University Press, 1963.

————. "Émile Zola." In his *Master European Realists of the Nineteenth Century*. New York: F. Ungar Publishing Company, 1982.

Carter, Lawson A. *Zola and the Theater*. New Haven, Conn.: Yale University Press, 1963.

Clark, Barrett H. "Henry Becque: *The Vultures.*" In his *A Study of the Modern Drama: A Handbook for the Study and Appreciation of Typical Plays, European, English, and American, of the Last Three-Quarters of a Century*. Rev. ed. New York: D. Appleton-Century, 1938.

Gassner, John. "Realism and Naturalism: Henry Becque." In his *A Treasury of the Theatre*. Vol. II, *Modern European Drama from Henrik Ibsen to Jean-Paul Sartre*. New York: Simon & Schuster, 1960.

Grant, Elliott M. *Zola's "Germinal": A Critical and Historical Study*. Leicester, England: Leicester University Press, 1962; corrected ed., 1970.

Hemmings, F. W. *The Life and Times of Émile Zola*. New York: Scribner, 1977.

Josephson, Matthew. *Zola and His Time*. New York: Macaulay, 1928.

Knapp, Bettina L. *Émile Zola*. New York: Ungar, 1980.

Lamm, Martin. "The Rise of Naturalism in France." In his *Modern Drama*. New York: Philosophical Library, 1953.

Levin, Harry. *The Gates of Horn: A Study of Five French Realists*. New York: Oxford University Press, 1963.

Nelson, Brian. *Zola and the Bourgeoisie: A Study of Themes and Techniques in "Les Rougon Macquart."* Totowa, N.J.: Barnes & Noble, 1983.

Richardson, Joanna. *Zola*. New York: St. Martin's Press, 1978.

Schom, Alan. *Émile Zola: A Biography*. New York: Holt, 1988.

Schor, Naomi. *Zola's Crowds*. Baltimore: Johns Hopkins University Press, 1978.

Sherard, Robert. *Émile Zola: A Biographical and Critical Study*. London: Chatto & Windus, 1893.

Smethurst, Colin. *Émile Zola: "Germinal."* London: Edward Arnold, 1974.

Smith, Hugh Allison. "Henri Becque and the Théâtre Libre." In his *Main Currents of Modern French Drama*. New York: Holt, 1925.

Turnell, Martin. "Zola." In his *The Art of French Fiction: Prévost, Stendhal, Zola, Maupassant, Gide, Mauriac, Proust*. New York: New Directions, 1959.

Vizetelly, E. A. *Émile Zola, Novelist and Reformer*. London: J. Lane, 1904.

Walker, Philip D. *Émile Zola*. New York: Humanities Press; London: Routledge & Kegan Paul, 1969.

———. *"Germinal" and Zola's Philosophical and Religious Thought*. Amsterdam: J. Benjamins, 1984.

Zakarian, R. H. *Zola's "Germinal": A Critical Study of Its Primary Sources*. Geneva: Librairie Droz, 1972.

Zola, Émile. *The Experimental Novel*. New York: Cassell, 1894.

NATURALISM (Naturalismus)
Germany, 1880s-1890s

Naturalism stirred in Germany during the 1880s with the appearance of *Kritische Waffengänge*, a series of six theoretical pamphlets published from 1882 to 1884 by brothers Heinrich (1855-1944) and Julius (1859-1930) Hart in Berlin, and *Die Gesellschaft*, a Munich journal edited by Michael Georg Conrad (1846-1927) from 1885 to 1902. The latter was a prominent vehicle for Naturalist writing until about 1890. Karl Bleibtreu's (1859-1928) *Revolution der Literatur* (1886) called for a "Neue Poesie," literature that combined REALISM and Romanticism, while Wilhelm Bölsche (1861-1939) vaguely advocated the incorporation of positivism and Darwinism into literature and art in his *Die naturwissenschaftlichen Grundlagen der Poesie* (1887). It was Arno Holz (1863-1929), however, who was the movement's premier theorist, laying out a Naturalist formula in *Die Kunst. Ihr Wesen und ihre Gesetze* (1890-92) — "art = nature - x," where x is the artist's subjectivity. In 1890 Bölsche and the Hart brothers formed the Friedrichshagener Kreis in Friedrichshagen, Germany.

The drama was an important genre in the Naturalist movement in Germany. The THÉÂTRE LIBRE had a strong impact when it visited Berlin in 1887, spurring drama critic Otto Brahm (1856-1912) to found the FREIE BÜHNE, which made Henrik IBSEN's *Gengangere* (1881; *Ghosts,* 1889), with its theme of heredity, its first production upon its opening in 1889 and Gerhart HAUPTMANN's first major Naturalist work, *VOR SONNENAUFGANG* (1889; *Before Dawn*, 1909), its second. Other representative dramatic Naturalist works are *Die Familie Selicke* (1890) by Holz and Johannes Schlaf (1862-1941); Franz Adamus's (1867-1948) trilogy *Jahrhundertwende* (1900); Max Halbe's (1865-1944) *Jugend* (1893; *When Love Is Young*, 1904); the more commercial plays by Hermann Sudermann (1857-1928), *Die Ehre* (1890) and *Heimat* (1893); Hauptmann's *Der Biberpelz* (1893; *The Beaver Coat*, 1912), and the masterpiece of the period, his *Die Weber* (1892; *The Weavers*, 1899). Set in Hauptmann's native Silesia, Poland, the play depicts the 1844 weavers' revolt against a business leader's attempt to introduce mechanical looms, which would effectively destroy their livelihoods.

The major German Naturalist novelist was Max Kretzer (1854-1941), whose early novels *Die beiden Genossen* (1880), *Die Betrogenen* (1881), and *Die Verkommenen* (1883) dealt with working-class life, though others' prose works are notable: Helene Böhlau (1859-1940) and her novels *Im frischen Wasser* (1891), *Der Rangierbahnhof* (1895), and *Halbtier* (1899) and short stories collected in *Ratsmädelgeschichten* (1888) and *Altweimarische Geschichten* (1897); Wilhelm von Polenz (1861-1903) and his novel *Der Büttnerbauer* (1895); and Clara Viebig's (1860-1952) early novels, such as *Rheinlandstöchter* (1897) and *Dilettanten des Lebens* (1898). (*See also* HEIMAT-KUNST.)

The work of poet and prose writer Hermann Conradi (1862-1890), friend of the Hart brothers, foreshadowed the movement. Other writers associated with the movement include friends of the Hart brothers, Holz; August STRINDBERG (*see* EXPRESSION-ISM, Germany); poet, prose writer, and dramatist Richard Dehmel (1863-1920); playwright and short-story writer Otto Erich Hartleben (1864-1905); poet, dramatist, and prose writer Detlev von Liliencron (pseud. of Friedrich, Freiherr von Liliencron, 1844-1909); and Gerhart's brother, playwright and prose writer Carl Hauptmann (1858-1921).

The decline of the movement was anticipated by Hermann Bahr's 1891 essay *Die Überwindung des Naturalismus* — that year he formed the YOUNG VIENNA group with other writers advocating a symbolist neoromanticism — though Naturalism was the dominent aesthetic mode in Germany until about 1898.

❖•❖

Further Reading

Bohm, Erwin Herbert. *The Development of Naturalism in German Poetry from the Hainbund to Liliencron*. Ph.D. thesis, Ohio State University, 1917.

Garten, Hugh F. *Gerhart Hauptmann*. New Haven, Conn.: Yale University Press, 1954.

Holl, Karl. *Gerhart Hauptmann: His Life and His Work, 1862-1912*. Chicago: A. C. McClurg & Company, 1914. Reprint, Freeport, N.Y.: Books for Libraries Press, 1972.

Keil, Günther. *Max Kretzer, a Study in German Naturalism*. New York: Columbia University Press, 1928.

Marshall, Alan. *The German Naturalists and Gerhart Hauptmann: Reception and Influence.* Frankfurt am Main: Lang, 1982.

Maurer, Warren R. *Gerhart Hauptmann.* Boston: Twayne Publishers, 1982.

————. *The Naturalist Image of German Literature: A Study of the German Naturalists' Appraisal of Their Literary Heritage.* Munich: W. Fink, 1972.

Osborne, John. *The Naturalist Drama in Germany.* Manchester, England: Manchester University Press; Totowa, N.J.: Rowman and Littlefield, 1971.

Sinden, Margaret. *Gerhart Hauptmann: The Prose Plays.* Toronto: University of Toronto Press, 1957.

Thomas, Basil Edward. *Growth of the Naturalistic Drama in Germany with Special Reference to Gerhart Hauptmann.* M.A. Thesis, University of Wales, 1931.

NATURALISM (Shizenshugi)
Japan, 1900s-1910s

Immediately following the conclusion of the Russo-Japanese War in 1905, Japanese Naturalism emerged as a revolt against the Ken'yūsha (SOCIETY OF FRIENDS OF THE INKSTONE), the most powerful literary movement of the day. Despite the trend toward Realism in Japanese fiction, a trend first generated by Tsubouchi Shōyō's (1859-1935) theoretical essay *Shōsetsu Shinzui* (1885; The Essence of the Novel) and partially fulfilled by the less Romantically inclined Ken'yusha writers, the Naturalists determined to fashion a literature that explored the fundamental motivations of humanity, that looked beyond the surface at the "ugly truth" of existence with indiscriminate objectivity.

Kosugi Tengai (1865-1952) is often mentioned as the father of Japanese Naturalism. Like other prominent writers at the turn of the century, he read the translated works of French Naturalist Émile ZOLA and then attempted to apply Zola's theory of scientific observation to his own work. In both *Hatsusugata* (1900; New Year's Finery) and *Hayari-uta* (1902; Popular Song) the Naturalist concerns of hereditary and environmental effects on the individual predominate. However, Tengai is remembered less for the two works themselves than for his accompanying prefaces. In them he propounded the Zolaist views that fiction should stimulate the reader in the same manner as natural phenomena and that the writer should unstintingly document the observable world without prettification or flourish. The European who exercised the greatest influence in shaping Japanese Naturalism, though, was not Zola but his contemporary Guy de MAUPASSANT (see REALISM, France). Maupassant, whose works were more readily available in translation, inspired numerous imitations of his stories and of his trademark style — austere, precise, and frequently erotic.

The first major work of Japanese Naturalism, *Hakai* (*The Broken Commandment*, 1974), appeared in 1906. Author Shimazaki TŌSON's (*see* ROMANTIC MOVEMENT,

Japan) vivid portrayal of a young schoolmaster's struggle against caste discrimination represented a significant advance for the nation's modern novel, for it broke barriers in both subject matter and narrative style. A year later, TAYAMA KATAI published *FUTON* (1907; *The Quilt and Other Stories*, 1981). Now considered inferior to *Hakai, Futon* nonetheless established the course for later Naturalists and is regarded as the movement's most representative work.

From 1907 until the movement's demise around 1920, the Japanese Naturalists developed a unique, markedly confessional narrative form. The term Neo-Naturalism was occasionally employed to distinguish their nonscientific method from the Zolaism of Tengai. Highly controversial for its preoccupation with the sordid aspects of human sexuality, the movement never gained a large public audience; however, acceptance among literary circles, the *bundan*, was widespread.

In addition to Tōson and Katai, other adherents of Naturalism included novelists Iwano Hōmei (1873-1920), Masamune Hakuchō (1879-1962), Tokuda Shūsei (1871-1943), Mayama Seika (1878-1948), and critic Shimamura Hōgetsu (1871-1918). The I-NOVEL that these writers helped spawn is often mentioned as their sole legacy, for the two dominant figures of the era, Mori Ōgai (1862-1922) and Natsume Sōseki (1867-1916), brilliantly opposed the Naturalists and the reigning bundan with their finer attention to language, structure, characterization, and philosophical import. However, the Naturalists hold a unique, pivotal position in modern Japanese letters. In addition to elevating fiction to the status of the traditionally esteemed genres of poetry and nonfiction, they catalyzed virtually all the major forms of the modern novel, however different from their original.

❧•❦

Tayama Katai (1871-1930)
Japanese novelist and short-story writer.

Considered one of the pioneers of modern Japanese fiction, Katai began his career as a writer of romantic stories in the Ken'yūsha style. His exposure to Western literature and to such early Japanese Realists as Kunikida Doppo (1871-1908), led him to fashion a distinctively unornamented and objective style. The first modern work of his to attract attention was *Jūemon no Saigo* (1902; The End of Jūemon), an exploration of the innate savagery of humanity. Following this Katai published *Futon* (1907; *The Quilt and Other Stories*, 1981), a novel commonly regarded as the fountainhead of Naturalism and the prototype for the first I-Novels. Refining his method through lessened subjectivity, he produced *Sei* (1908; Life), *Tsume* (1908; The Wife), *Inaka Kyōshi* (1909; The Country Teacher), *En* (1910; The Bond), and *Toki wa sugiyuku* (1916; Time Goes

By). Although for many years an ardent proponent of Japanese Naturalism, Katai in his later career produced novels with a mystical bent as well as historical fictions.

Futon (1907; *The Quilt and Other Stories*, 1981).

Considered the seminal novel of the Naturalist movement, *Futon* represents Katai's first full-scale attempt to implement the precepts of French Naturalism. Although written in an approximation of the colloquial, yet objective, style that typifies Shimazaki Tōson's *Hakai* (1906; *The Broken Commandment*, 1974), Katai's work further distinguishes itself through its unabashed concern with the individual. Had it appeared before the Russo-Japanese War, *Futon* would have incited the furor of a population whose culture deplored exhibitionism and the promotion of personal before social interest. However, following the war and the rapid inculcation of Western culture, native traditions were gradually questioned and an age of confession and disillusionment—fueled by Naturalist writings—ensued. Katai's story, drawn from his own life, focuses on Takenaka Tokio, a world-weary novelist whose love for his wife has long since dissipated. When an attractive young woman named Yokoyama Yoshiko seeks his literary tutelage, Tokio readily accepts. His attraction to Yoshiko forms the basis of his inner conflict: he wishes to act upon his newly discovered love but is inhibited by conventional mores. Before he is able to, Yoshiko divulges her relationship with a university student; Tokio vengefully apprises her parents and Yoshiko is called home. The novel closes with Tokio burying his tear-stained face in the quilt Yoshiko has used. Rarely read in contemporary Japan, the novel still holds an important position in the nation's literary history.

➯•➱

Further Reading

Keene, Donald. "Naturalism." In his *Dawn to the West: Japanese Literature of the Modern Era*. Vol. 1. New York: Holt, Rinehart, & Winston, 1984.

Okazaki Yoshie, ed. "The Establishment of Naturalism." In his *Japanese Literature in the Meiji Era*. Translated by V. H. Viglielmo. Tokyo: Ōbunsha, 1955.

Powell, Irena. "The Naturalist Avant-garde and the Formation of the Modern Bundan." In her *Writers and Society in Modern Japan*. Tokyo: Kodansha, 1983.

Rubin, Jay. "The Rise of Naturalism." In his *Injurious to Public Morals: Writers and the Meiji State*. Seattle: University of Washington Press, 1984.

Walker, Janet A. *The Japanese Novel of the Meiji Period and the Ideal of Individualism*. Princeton, N.J.: Princeton University Press, 1979.

Yamanouchi Hisaaki. "From Romanticism to Naturalism: Kitamura Tokoku and Shimazaki Toson." In his *The Search for Authenticity in Modern Japanese Literature*. Cambridge, England: Cambridge University Press, 1978.

NATURALISM
Korea, 1920s

Korean Naturalism, a movement which displayed characteristics of both European and Japanese Naturalistic literature, did not emerge until around 1920. The goal of the Koreans, like that of Émile ZOLA and others, was to expose the squalid aspects of contemporary life and simultaneously attack traditional codes of social and personal behavior. Much of their fiction was written in the form of first-person narratives, a technique, first popularized by the Japanese I-NOVELists, which helped to underscore the intellectual isolation of the Naturalists. Yom Sang-sop (1897-1963) and Hyon Chin-gon (1900-1943) were among the most outstanding writers of the movement.

❖•❖

Further Reading

Kim, Soonsik Baek. "Colonial and Postcolonial Discourse in the Novels of Yom Sang-sop, Chinua Achebe and Salman Rushdie." *Dissertation Abstracts International* 53, 1 (July 1992): 143A.

O'Rourke, Kevin. "The Korean Short Story of the 1920s and Naturalism." *Korea Journal* 17, 3 (1977): 48-63.

Yoon, Hwan Hee. "A Rhetoric of the Short Story: A Study of the Realistic Narratives of Flaubert, Maupassant, Joyce, and Hyon Chin'gon." *Dissertation Abstracts International* 52, 8 (February 1992): 2918A.

NATURALISM
Norway, 1880s

Largely overshadowed by the dominance of Henrik IBSEN's REALIST social dramas and the controversial writings of Bjørnstjerne Bjørnson (1832-1910), the Norwegian Naturalist writers wielded influence briefly, during the decade of the 1880s. The chief distinction between the Realists and Naturalists in Norway was that the latter—significantly influenced by the polemicism of Danish Naturalist Georg Brandes (1842-1927)—adopted a far more pessimistic, doctrinaire, and contentious attitude towards literary debate of the human condition and was more apt to accentuate the deterministic aspects of existence in their creative works. In particular, the painful reality of women's social and psychological subservience became one of the foremost subjects of the Norwegian Naturalists. Novelists Jonas Lie (1833-1908) and Amalie Skram (1846-1905), with exacting detail, excelled in this vein of problem literature. Other writers affined, to varying degrees, with Naturalism included Arne Garborg (1851-1924); Hans Jœger (1854-1910), leader of the radical group Kristiania-Bohême; and Alexander Kielland (1849-1906). Virtually all of the Naturalist writers may be regarded as important, but transitional, figures, who extended the power of Realistic literature to disturb and motivate the public. Like Realism, Naturalism subsided in the 1890s as Neoromanticism ushered in the twentieth century.

➯•➱

Further Reading

Rossel, Sven H. "Nordic Literature in the 1880s." In his *A History of Scandinavian Literature, 1870-1980*. Minneapolis: University of Minnesota Press, 1982.

NATURALISM (Naturalismo)
Spain, 1880s-1890s

A minor movement in late-nineteenth-century Spanish literature, Naturalism was an extension of REALISM and Costumbrismo fiction that won a small group of adherents during the 1880s and 1890s. Among this group were Jacinto Benavente (1866-1954), Vicente Blasco Ibáñez (1867-1928), Clarín (1852-1901), Emilia Pardo Bazán (1852-1921), Felipe Trigo (1864-1916), and Eduardo Zamcois (1873-1971).

➯•➱

Further Reading

Brown, Donald Fowler. *The Catholic Naturalism of Pardo Bazan*. Chapel Hill, N.C.: University of North Carolina Press, 1958.

NATURALISM
United States, 1880s-1910s

A contemporaneous extension of late-nineteenth-century American REALISM, the American Naturalists sought to go beyond the accurate representation of life and describe and analyze social ills in an effort to stimulate readers toward ameliorative social thought and action. Contemporaries of the American Naturalists, the MUCKRAKERS had some of the same social concerns; through investigative reporting, they exposed corruption in business and government and promoted social reform. During the 1880s and 1890s William Dean HOWELLS and Hamlin Garland (1860-1940) in particular did much to expose Americans to European Realists and NATURALISTS whom they admired—Henrik IBSEN, Bjørnstjerne Bjørnson (1832-1910), and other Norwegian REALISTS; Russian Realists Leo TOLSTOY and Fyodor DOSTOEVSKY; French Naturalist Émile ZOLA and Realist Gustave FLAUBERT, and such Spanish NATURALISTS and Realists as Benito PÉREZ GALDÓS and Emilia Pardo Bazán (1852-1921)—thus stimulating the Naturalist mode among such American writers as Stephen CRANE, Theodore DREISER, Frank NORRIS, Maxwell Anderson (1888-1959), John DOS PASSOS (*see* LOST GENERATION), Harold Frederic (1856-1898), Robert Welch

Herrick (1868-1938), Jack London (1876-1916), John O'Hara (1905-1970), Eugene O'NEILL (1888-1953; *see* EXPRESSIONISM, United States, and PROVINCETOWN PLAYERS), and PROLETARIAN writers James T. FARRELL and John STEINBECK.

Inspired by Charles Darwin's (1809-1882) theories, the American Naturalists found heredity and evolution to be potent fields to explore through literature. They perceived heredity as a natural law in a world where humans are part of nature and subject to its forces. Philosopher Herbert Spencer's (1820-1903) belief in the survival of the fittest was influential as well. But always there was tension between the Naturalists' idealism — that society can be improved and progress is possible — and fatalistic determinism: biological, psychological, social, economic. Socially, the Naturalists were also responding to the pre-industrial American Dream juxtaposed with the reality of widespread poverty and the devastating social effects of the Industrial Revolution. The most singularly damning appraisal of the evils of American society came from Dreiser, an aging Naturalist writer whose career had long suffered from censorship; unfortunately, Dreiser's *AN AMERICAN TRAGEDY* (1925) was the most overlooked work of the decade. Materialistic progress was, however, inevitable, as evidenced by the newly industrialized United States. As residents of the country that led the world in industrialization, the Naturalists were given to describing humanity in terms of the technology it had surrounded itself with, finding the mechanistic in the human, and using idioms inspired by such new inventions of the day as steam engines and typewriters. Later, American EXPRESSIONISTS would produce an even more extreme articulation of the Naturalists' exploration of man's relationship to technology.

The novel was the primary genre Naturalists used to address these concerns, often employing allegory and symbolism. Characters were often lower-middle- and lower-class Americans and stood for "typical" members of a given social group, be it businessmen, prostitutes, or factory workers; more emphasis was placed on social role and position than on individual identity or interior consciousness. Protagonists in Naturalist novels are often tragic in the sense that the author shows us their potential, but environmental circumstances surrounding them do not allow its development. They were often antiheroes, because the beast, driven by the life force, dwells within each individual. Underneath the polish of civility, characters were drawn as "pawns on a chessboard," subject to conditions more powerful than any imagined individual character, spirit, or other transcendent, romantic notion. Some of the more representative Naturalist novels include Crane's *MAGGIE* (1893), Dreiser's *An American Tragedy* (1925), Norris's *McTEAGUE* (1899), Dos Passos's *Manhattan Transfer* (1925) and *U.S.A.* (1930-36), Farrell's *Studs Lonigan* (1932-35), Frederic's *The Damnation of Theron Ware* (1896), and London's *The Call of the Wild* (1903), *The Sea Wolf* (1904), and *Martin Eden* (1909).

Garland, a principal theorist, put forth his theory of "veritism" in *Crumbling Idols* (1894); where Howells thought the novelist's focus should be on striving to accurately portray reality, though without breaking contemporary boundaries of good taste, Garland believed literature should not shy away from depicting poverty and other harsh realities, even if it meant stretching, or breaking, those boundaries. Writers he supported included Frederic and Crane. But it was Norris who, as a prolific writer of essays and reviews and the longest-living and most vocal (because of Dreiser's relative silence) American Naturalist, did the most to popularize the movement. Naturalism, he wrote, should go beyond the Howellsian "teacup tragedies" and delve into "the unplumbed depths of the human heart, and the mystery of sex, and the problems of life, and the black, unsearched penetralia of the soul of man."

Critic Donald Pizer writes about Naturalist remnants in the novels of the American Proletarian writers as well as such later novelists as Saul Bellow (1915-), Norman Mailer (1923-), William Styron (1925-), Richard Wright (1908-1960), John O'Hara (1905-1970), Erskine Caldwell (1903-1987), James Jones (1921-1977), Nelson Algren (1909-1981), and Ernest HEMINGWAY (*see* LOST GENERATION).

Naturalist fiction has been criticized as being reductionist in its determinism as well as for its sensationalism in its treatment of such taboo subjects as sex, disease, and depravity, though it is in Naturalist literature that the seeds of the MODERNIST treatment of sex were largely sown. Modernism gradually gained prominence, with the impulse to steer away from the empiricism of Naturalism and revisit such narrative themes as individual subjectivity and cultural mythos.

➤●◄

Crane, Stephen (1871-1900)
American novelist, short-story writer, journalist, and poet.

Born into a well-off family, Crane lived a life of poverty by his own choice, working as a war correspondent, and died young of tuberculosis. Many of his stories, vignettes, and sketches are descriptions of events he observed or participated in during his travels around the southern and western United States, Mexico, and Cuba. He moved to England in 1897, and though he continued travelling, he kept his residence in England until he died.

Leo Tolstoy was a great influence on Crane, especially *Sebastopol* (1855-56; translated 1887) and *VOINA I MIR* (1869; *War and Peace,* 1886), as were Flaubert, Zola, and other French writers, but meetings with artists at New York's Art Student League in the early 1890s made a deep impression on him as well. Eventually, the IMAGISTS would claim Crane as a precursor for his metaphorical use of imagery to convey psychological states.

Garland much admired Crane's work in which he saw the fulfillment of his theory of impressionistic veritism and helped him get published. Crane's first book was his only published collection of poetry, *The Black Riders* (1895).

His best-known short stories include "The Blue Hotel" (1896), "The Bride Comes to Yellow Sky" (1898), "An Experiment in Misery" (1894), and "The Open Boat" (1897). More popular, though, was his second novel, *The Red Badge of Courage* (1895), which made him internationally famous.

Maggie: A Girl of the Streets (1893).

Owing to the novel's sordid subject matter, Crane couldn't find a publisher until 1896; he paid to have it privately published under the pseudonym of Johnston Smith in 1893. Crane's intention in writing the novel was to demonstrate "that environment is a tremendous thing and often shapes lives regardlessly."

Young Maggie Johnson lives in New York's Bowery slum with an alcoholic and abusive mother, ineffective father, and brother who introduces her to the man who will eventually desert her. She becomes a prostitute to survive and finally commits suicide out of despair and shame. Crane represents the Bowery as a world in which natural laws reign supreme but whose inhabitants nonetheless tether themselves to middle-class notions of morality and respectability, holding false, romantic illusions about their own physical reality. People live combatively, led by their animal natures, amoral except in relation to perceived social expectations of presenting the appearance of virtue.

❧•❦

Dreiser, Theodore (1871-1945), American novelist.

His father lost his mill to fire soon after Dreiser's birth and the family never regained economic comfort. Dreiser found work as a journalist and magazine editor. He has been cited as the best Naturalist after ZOLA; he was the first American writer to seriously follow Zola's formula, in *Sister Carrie* (1900), whose publication Frank Norris, editor at Doubleday, urged. Doubleday had second thoughts about publishing the novel because of its portrayal of immorality, but finally did release it.

Not an accomplished stylist, and often critiqued for clumsy prose, Dreiser's characters had what he termed "chemical compulsions." He called for literature to tell the truth. No matter how ugly or sordid, the writer's aim should be "to express what we see honestly and without subterfuge: this is morality as well as art." He was an activist against censorship, something he had experienced firsthand with several of his works. Other novels include *Jennie Gerhardt* (1911), *The "Genuis"* (1915), and a three-part study of a corrupt American business tycoon, known as the Trilogy of Desire: *The Financier* (1912), *The Titan* (1914), and *The Stoic* (1947). Though best known for novels and poetry, Dreiser also wrote plays and short stories. Critic H. L. Mencken (1880-1956) compared Dreiser's impact on American literature to Darwin's on biology.

An American Tragedy (1925).

Based on a 1906 murder case in New York, *An American Tragedy*, according to one critic, was "the worst-written great novel in the world," referring to the novel's potency in spite of Dreiser's awkward style. Antihero protagonist Clyde Griffiths is a factory worker bitter about his social and economic position. After he impregnates a working girl, he meets and falls in love with a girl from a wealthy family. The way he chooses to deal with his obligation to the first woman is to kill her by drowning her in the lake. As it turns out, she drowns accidentally before he can put his plan in motion and he is eventually condemned to death row. As one critic puts it, the novel "seeks to deflate the American dream. . .by showing how directly that dream is related to socially destructive acts." Two years after its publication, the novel was banned in Boston. The popular 1951 film *A Place in the Sun* was based on the novel.

❧•❦

Norris, Frank (1870-1902)
American novelist, short-story writer, and journalist.

Norris grew up in San Francisco, where his father, a prosperous jeweler, moved the family. He studied painting in Paris and fought with the British in the Boer War. He wrote articles for the *San Francisco Chronicle* as well as the small San Francisco weekly newspaper, *Wave*. In *The Responsibilities of the Novelist* (1903), a kind of Naturalist manifesto, Norris proclaimed Realism, more than Romanticism, to be antithetical to what the novelist's purpose should be. "Realism stultifies itself. It notes only the surface of things." He read ZOLA's Naturalism as "a form of romanticism. . . . Everything is extraordinary, imaginative, grotesque even, with a vague note of terror quivering throughout like the vibrations of an ominous and low-pitched diapason." Also known for his "A Plea for Romantic Fiction," in which he describes a Naturalism as a synthesis of the conflict between Realism's concern with surface details and Romanticism's with mysteries. Norris's other Naturalist works include *Blix* (1899), *Vandover and the Brute* (1914), and his study of American capitalism and its moral weaknesses in the "Wheat Trilogy": *The Octopus* (1901), *The Pit* (1903), and the unwritten but planned finale, The Wolf—in which wheat signifies the life force, the railroad signifies the machine, and their interactions are determined by greed.

McTeague: A Story of San Francisco (1899).

Considered a masterpiece of American Naturalism, from the novel's first pages Norris shows McTeague experiencing lust for the first time as a struggle between his brutish nature and a better self which only vaguely realizes that he should behave in a civilized manner. Selfish instinct presents an almost insurmountable challenge to social morality: "Below the fine fabric of all that was good in him ran the foul stream of hereditary evil, like a sewer. The vices and sins of his father and of his father's father, to the third and fourth and five hundredth generation, tainted him. The evil of an entire race flowed in his veins. Why should it be? He did not desire it. Was he to blame?" Greed in particular motivates much of the action: how McTeague loses his dental practice, his wife, and his life.

❦•❦

Further Reading

Ahnebrink, Lars. *The Beginnings of Naturalism in American Fiction: A Study of the Works of Hamlin Garland, Stephen Crane, and Frank Norris with Special Reference to Some European Influences, 1891-1903*. Cambridge, Mass.: Harvard University Press, 1950.

Auerbach, Erich. *Mimesis: The Representation of Reality in Western Literature*. Translated by Willard R. Trask. Princeton, N.J.: Princeton University Press, 1953.

Baguley, David. *Naturalist Fiction: The Entropic Vision*. Cambridge, England: Cambridge University Press, 1990.

Block, Haskell M. *Naturalistic Triptych: The Fictive and the Real in Zola, Mann, and Dreiser*. New York: Random House, 1970.

Boller, Paul F., Jr. *American Thought in Transition: The Impact of Evolutionary Naturalism, 1865-1900*. Chicago: Rand McNally, 1969.

Borus, Daniel H. *Writing Realism: Howells, James, and Norris in the Mass Market*. Chapel Hill, N.C.: University of North Carolina Press, 1989.

Bowlby, Rachel. *Just Looking: Consumer Culture in Dreiser, Gissing, and Zola*. New York: Methuen, 1985.

Campbell, Donna M. *Resisting Regionalism: Gender and Naturalism in American Fiction, 1885-1915*. Athens, Ohio: Ohio University Press, 1997.

Chase, Richard. *The American Novel and Its Tradition*. Garden City, N.Y.: Doubleday Anchor, 1957.

Civello, Paul. *American Literary Naturalism and Its Twentieth-Century Transformations: Frank Norris, Ernest Hemingway, Don DeLillo*. Athens, Ga.: University of Georgia Press, 1994.

Conder, John J. *Naturalism in American Fiction: The Classic Phase*. Lexington, Ky.: University Press of Kentucky, 1984.

Conn, Peter. *The Divided Mind: Ideology and Imagination in America, 1898-1917*. Cambridge, England: Cambridge University Press, 1983.

Cowley, Malcolm. "A Natural History of American Naturalism." In *Documents of Modern Literary Realism*. Edited by George J. Becker. Princeton, N.J.: Princeton University Press, 1963. Originally published in *Kenyon Review* (summer 1947).

Fiedler, Leslie A. *Love and Death in the American Novel*. New York: Criterion, 1960.

Furst, Lilian R., and Peter N. Skrine. *Naturalism*. London: Methuen, 1971.

Geismar, Maxwell. *Rebels and Ancestors: The American Novel, 1890-1915*. Boston: Houghton Mifflin, 1953.

Gogol, Miriam, ed. *Theodore Dreiser: Beyond Naturalism*. New York: New York University Press, 1995.

Graham, Don. *The Fiction of Frank Norris: The Aesthetic Context*. Columbia, Mo.: University of Missouri Press, 1978.

———. "Naturalism in American Fiction: A Status Report." *Studies in American Fiction* 10 (1982): 1-16.

Hakutani, Yoshinobu, and Lewis Fried, eds. *American Literary Naturalism: A Reassessment*. Heidelberg: Carl Winter, 1975.

Halliburton, David. *The Color of the Sky: A Study of Stephen Crane*. Cambridge, England; New York: Cambridge University Press, 1989.

Hedrick, Joan D. *Solitary Comrade: Jack London and His Work*. Chapel Hill, N.C.: University of North Carolina Press, 1982.

Hicks, Granville. *The Great Tradition: An Interpretation of American Literature Since the Civil War*. New York: Macmillan, 1993.

Hochmann, Barbara. *The Art of Frank Norris, Storyteller*. Columbia, Mo.: University of Missouri Press, 1988.

Howard, June. *Form and History in American Literary Naturalism*. Chapel Hill, N.C.: University of North Carolina Press, 1985.

Jordan, David, ed. *Regionalism Reconsidered: New Approaches to the Field*. New York: Garland Publishing, 1994.

Kaplan, Harold. *Power and Order: Henry Adams and the Naturalist Tradition in American Fiction*. Chicago: University of Chicago Press, 1981.

Kazin, Alfred. *On Native Grounds: An Interpretation of Modern American Prose Literature*. New York: Reynal and Hitchcock, 1942.

Labor, Earle. *Jack London*. New York: Twayne Publishers, 1974.

Lamprecht, Sterling P. *The Metaphysics of Naturalism*. New York: Appleton-Century-Crofts, 1967.

Lundquist, James. *Jack London: Adventures, Ideas, and Fiction*. New York: Ungar, 1987.

———. *Theodore Dreiser*. New York: Ungar, 1974.

Martin, Ronald E. *American Literature and the Universe of Force*. Durham, N.C.: Duke University Press, 1981.

Matthiessen, F. O. *Theodore Dreiser*. Westport, Conn.: Greenwood Press, 1973 [1951].

Michaels, Walter Benn. *The Gold Standard and the Logic of Naturalism: American Literature at the Turn of the Century*. Berkeley, Calif.: University of California Press, 1987.

Mitchell, Lee Clark. *Determined Fictions: American Literary Naturalism*. New York: Columbia University Press, 1989.

Nagel, James. *Stephen Crane and Literary Impressionism*. University Park, Pa.: Pennsylvania State University Press, 1980.

Newlin, Keith. *Melodramatic Naturalism: London, Garland, Dreiser, and the Campaign to Reform the American Theater*. Ph.D. diss., Indiana University, 1991.

Pizer, Donald. *Critical Essays on Theodore Dreiser*. Boston: G. K. Hall, 1981.

————. *The Novels of Frank Norris*. New York: Haskell House Publishers, 1973 [1966].

————. *The Novels of Theodore Dreiser: A Critical Study*. Minneapolis: University of Minnesota Press, 1976.

————. *Realism and Naturalism in Nineteenth-Century American Literature*. Carbondale, Ill.: Southern Illinois University Press, 1966. Rev. ed., 1984.

————. *The Theory and Practice of American Literary Naturalism: Selected Essays and Reviews*. Carbondale, Ill.: Southern Illinois University Press, 1993.

————. *Twentieth-Century American Literary Naturalism: An Interpretation*. Carbondale, Ill.: Southern Illinois University Press, 1982.

Pizer, Donald, ed. *The Cambridge Companion to American Realism and Naturalism: Howells to London*. Cambridge, England: Cambridge University Press, 1995.

Pizer, Donald, and Earl N. Harbert, eds. *Dictionary of Literary Biography*. Vol. 12, *American Realists and Naturalists*. Detroit: Gale Research Co., 1982.

Powers, Lyall Harris. *Henry James and the Naturalist Movement*. East Lansing, Mich.: Michigan State University Press, 1971.

Seltzer, Mark. *Bodies and Machines*. New York: Routledge, 1992.

Stromberg, Roland N., ed. *Realism, Naturalism, and Symbolism: Modes of Thought and Expression in Europe*. New York: Walker, 1968.

Taylor, Gordon O. *The Passages of Thought: Psychological Representations in the American Novel, 1870-1900*. New York: Oxford University Press, 1969.

Theodore Dreiser's An American Tragedy. Edited and with an introduction by Harold Bloom. New York: Chelsea House, 1988.

Walcutt, Charles C. *American Literary Naturalism: A Divided Stream*. Minneapolis: University of Minnesota Press, 1956.

Walcutt, Charles C., ed. *Seven Novelists in the American Naturalist Tradition: An Introduction*. Minneapolis: University of Minnesota Press, 1974.

Westbrook, Perry D. *Free Will and Determinism in American Literature*. Rutherford, N.J.: Fairleigh Dickinson University Press, 1979.

Wilson, Christopher P. *The Labor of Words: Literary Professionalism in the Progressive Era*. Athens, Ga.: University of Georgia Press, 1985.

NATURALISMO. *See* NATURALISM, Spain

NATURISM (Naturisme)
France, 1890s-1900

Naturism was a short-lived movement in France reacting against SYMBOLISM's intricate aestheticism and melancholy and ÉCOLE ROMANE's classicism. Poet Saint-Georges de Bouhélier (pseud. for Stéphane Georges de Bouhélier-Lepelletier, 1876-1947) led the way, founding the magazine *L'Académie française* in 1892 and calling for a return to simplicity and nature in poetry, hence "Naturism." Maurice Le Blond's *Essai sur le naturisme* (1896) published by *Mercure de France*, one of the French Symbolists' main organs, was the first manifesto, charging that Stéphane MALLARMÉ and his group had created a gulf between the poet and the natural world.

The journal *La Plume* devoted an issue to the movement in 1897; Le Blond became its primary literary critic the next year. Another manifesto, by Bouhélier, was published in the journal *Revue naturiste* (1897-), while critic Jean Viollis's "Observations sur le naturisme" (1897) appeared in *Mercure de France*.

Saint-Georges de Bouhélier wrote a volume of poetry, *Eglé ou les concerts champêtres* (1897), in which he attempted to embody his aesthetic stance but which was panned by contemporary critics. Francis Jammes (1868-1938) was another poet associated with the movement. His first volume of poetry was a notable example of the naturisme mode: *De l'Angélus de l'aube à l'Angélus du soir* (1898; From the Morning Prayer to the Evening Prayer). Other poets named in connection with the movement include Comtesse Mathieu du Noailles (Anna de Noailles, 1876-1933) and her volume *Le cœur innombrable* (1901; The Numberless Heart), Maurice Magre (1877-1941), Albert Fleury (n.d.), Eugène Montfort (1877-1936), and Joachim Gasquet (1873-1921).

By 1900 the movement had lost its momentum, producing little lasting literary accomplishments to bolster its theoretical leaning.

❖•❖

Further Reading

Cornell, Kenneth. *The Symbolist Movement*. New Haven, Conn.: Yale University Press, 1951.
Day, Patrick L. *Saint-Georges de Bouhélier's Naturisme: An Anti-Symbolist Movement in Late Nineteenth-Century French Poetry*. New York: P. Lang, 1996.

NAYĪ KAHĀNI. *See* NEW STORY MOVEMENT

NAYĪ KAVITĀ. *See* NEW POETRY MOVEMENT

NAZUSTRICH
Ukraine, 1934-1939

Active from 1934 until 1939, *Nazustrich* (Toward) was a minor western Ukrainian movement and journal whose members included poet Svyatoslav Hordynsky (1906-1993), short-story writer Yuriy Kosach (1909-1990), and critic, poet, and fiction writer Mykhaylo Rudnytsky (1889-1975).

❦•❦
Further Reading

Luckyj, George S. N. "Western Ukraine and Emigration, 1919-39." In his *Ukrainian Literature in the Twentieth Century: A Reader's Guide*. Toronto: University of Toronto for the Shevchenko Scientific Society, 1992.

NEGISHI TANKA SOCIETY
Japan, 1899-1900s

The Negishi Tanka Society was formed by Masaoka Shiki (1867-1902) in 1899, a year before Shiki's primary rival, Yosano Tekkan (1873-1935), formed the *Myōjō* Poets (*see* NEW POETRY SOCIETY). Shiki, a pioneering haiku poet, was interested in revitalizing the closely related classical tanka verse form. Unlike Tekkan, however, he adopted a largely conservative approach, insisting that each poem be founded upon some traditionally accepted element of beauty in the manner of the eighth-century *Manyōshū* poems. His most significant concept was that of *shasei*, the direct, objective depiction of the outer world. After his death in 1902, this concept was variously interpreted by his chief followers, Itō Sachio (1864-1913) and Nagatsuka Takashi (1879-1915). Shiki's influence best sustained itself through Sachio, who founded the tanka journal *Araragi*. Sachio is remembered for his advocacy of *rensaku*, the careful conception and arrangement of several thematically related tankas. The succeeding *Araragi* editors Shimagi Akahiko (1876-1926) and Saitō Mokichi (1882-1953), despite swerving from some of Shiki's original ideals, firmly established tanka as a quintessential form of modern Japanese poetry.

❦•❦
Further Reading

Beichman, Janine. *Masaoka Shiki*. Boston: Twayne, 1982.

Clough, S. D. P. *Tanka, Haiku, Sijo: Versions of Japanese and Korean Poetry*. Oxford, England: S. D. P. Clough, 1973.

Corman, Cid, ed. and trans. *Peerless Mirror: Twenty Tanka from the Manyōshū*. Cambridge, Mass.: Firefly Press, 1981.

Keene, Donald. "The Modern Tanka." In his *Dawn to the West: Japanese Literature in the Modern Era*. Vol. 2. New York: Holt, Rinehart, & Winston, 1984.

Lowitz, Leza, Miyuki Aoyama, and Akemi Tomioka, eds. and trans. *A Long Rainy Season: Haiku & Tanka*. Berkeley, Calif.: Stone Bridge Press, 1994.

Nagakawa, Atsuo. *Tanka in English: In Pursuit of World Tanka*. Tokyo: New Currents International, 1987.

Nakao, Takeo. *The Japanese Mind: Wartime Japanese Feelings as Expressed in Tanka Poems*. Tokyo: Booklink International, 1992.

Saitō, Mokichi. *Red Lights: Selected Tanka Sequences from Shakkō*. Edited and translated by
Seishi Shinoda and Sanford Goldstein. West Lafayette, Ind.: Purdue Research Foundation, 1989.
Ueda, Makoto. *Modern Japanese Tanka, an Anthology*. New York: Columbia University Press,
1996.

NEGRISMO. *See* AFRO-CUBANISM

NÉGRITUDE
African and West Indian emigrés in France, 1930s-1960s

Négritude as a movement began in Paris during the early 1930s as a handful of black
African and West Indian students joined forces to combat white discrimination and attitudes of cultural superiority. The founders of the group—poet Aimé Césaire (1913-),
poet Léon-Gontran Damas (1912-1978), and poet and former president of Senegal
(1960-80) Léopold Sédar Senghor (1906-)—envisioned Négritude as a way to assert
an essence of black identity and begin to reclaim control from European, particularly
French, hegemony. They gained inspiration from the HARLEM RENAISSANCE writers
in the United States, such as W. E. B. DuBois (1868-1963) and Langston HUGHES
(1902-1967), as well as from West Indian thinkers and poets, such as Jacques Roumain
(1907-1944) and his important *Bois d'ébène* (1945; *Ebony Wood*, 1972), René Maran
(1887-1960), Jean Price-Mars (1876-1969), and others associated with *LA REVUE
INDIGÈNE*. Price-Mars's *Ainsi parla l'oncle,* wrote Senghor, "gave legitimacy to the
reasons for my search, confirmed what I had felt. For by showing me the treasures of
Negritude that he had discovered in and on the land of Haiti, he taught me to find the
same values, but surer and stronger, on and in the land of Africa." The manifesto *Légi-
time Défense* (1932) appeared in Paris signed by a group of young students from
Martinique and called for the recovery of the original black personality and rejection of
European cultural and political institutions; it also had a radical impact on Césaire and
Senghor. The term became popular after it appeared in the celebrated long poem by
Aimé Césaire, *Cahier d'un retour au pays natal* (1939; *Return to My Native Land*,
1969).

Damas, Césaire, and Senghor published the journal *L'Étudiant noir* (c.1932/34-
c.1939/40; Black Student) and attracted young black writers in Paris, such as Birago
Diop (1906-1989), a practicing veterinarian and poet who was later appointed ambas-
sador to Tunisia by Senghor. After World War II, they founded *Présence Africaine*
(1947-), edited by Alioune Diop (1910-1980). In 1948 Senghor's anthology appeared.
From the founding of *Présence Africaine* the group gradually grew to include Jacques
Rabémananjara (1913-), a poet from Madagascar who met Senghor and Césaire in
Paris in the 1950s after his release from a French prison in Madagascar for allegedly

leading a political coup attempt; Guy Tirolien (1917-), a West Indian poet who had met Senghor earlier in a German prison camp during the war; West Indian poet Paul Niger (1917-1962); poet and student of Senghor David Diop (1927-1960; brother-in-law of Alioune; no relation to Birago); Cameroonian poet Elolongué Epanya Yondo (1930-); and Mauritian poet Edouard Maunick (1931-), who met the founders in Paris during the late 1950s.

Senghor produced what is considered the most systematic statement on Négritude in his essays in *Libertié I: Négritude et Humanisme* (1964). During the intervening two decades, however, the idea of Négritude flourished among black students and writers in France, parts of Africa, and the Caribbean. Négritude may be broadly defined as anti-assimilationist; it called for the inversion of the values of stereotypical characteristics which white Europeans often attached to black people in order to recoup a culturally strong and healthy sense of identity and celebrate blackness. For example, where Gobineau, in his *Essai sur l'inégalité des races humaines* (1853; Essay on the Inequality of the Human Races) claimed that Africans are overly emotional and inca-pable of rationalism, Senghor asserted that European reason is "hellenic" and that "emotion is Negro," and is a great strength. Senghor challenged Descartes's assertion ("I think, therefore I am") with "I feel, therefore I am." Césaire did not formulate a doctrine of Négritude. He became disenchanted with the mysticism in Senghor's theory, and began to espouse a more revolutionary approach. In his *Discours sur le colonial-isme* (1950; *Discourse on Colonialism*, 1972), Césaire's discussions of the role of the artist in societies fighting for political and cultural independence reveals his adherence to MARXIST alternatives.

Senghor appealed to an educated Parisian audience — white and black — whose sus-picion of excessive rationality and an increasingly mechanized society was evidenced in the popularity of such movements as CUBISM, EXISTENTIALISM, and SURREALISM. Surrealist André BRETON wrote the preface to Césaire's *Cahier d'un retour au pays natal*, and proponent of existentialist philosophy Jean-Paul SARTRE's famous essay "Orphée noir" (Black Orpheus) appeared in Senghor's *Anthologie de la nouvelle poésie négre et malgache* (1948), describing Négritude from a Marxist perspective. French-Algerian poet and writer Frantz Fanon (1925-1961) challenged Sarte's reading (that Négritude was "dedicated to its own destruction") in his *Peau noire, masques blancs* (1952; *Black Skin, White Masks*, 1967), calling instead for an emphasis on political action.

These early debates reflect the controversy that continues to surround the doctrine of Négritude. More recently, writers such as Abiola Irele (n.d.), Biodun Jeyifu (n.d.), Omafume Onoge (n.d.), and Sembene Ousmane (1923-) have been reevaluating

Négritude. Among its shortcomings, some assert, are its reliance on nativism and ahistoricism, its ability to be read as a confirmation of the worst white stereotypes, and its failure to affect concrete political, social, and economic change. Still, it is recognized by many as an important cultural strategy grounded in its historical situation. At a conference on African literature in Dakar during the 1960s, Ousmane said, "There was a time when négritude meant something positive. It was our breastplate against a culture that wanted at all costs to dominate us. But that is past history."

✦•✦

Further Reading

Adotevi, S. "Negritude Is Dead: The Burial." In *New African Literature and the Arts*. Edited by J. Okpaku. Vol. 3. New York: T. Crowell, 1973.

Ba, Sylvia Washington. *The Concept of Negritude in the Poetry of Leopold Sédar Senghor*. Princeton, N.J.: Princeton University Press, 1973.

Beier, Ulli, ed. *Introduction to African Literature: An Anthology of Critical Writings from "Black Orpheus."* London: Longman; Evanston, Ill.: Northwestern University Press, 1967.

Berrian, A., and R. Long, eds. *Negritude: Essays and Studies*. Hampton, Va.: Hampton Institute Press, 1967.

Blair, Dorothy S. *African Literature in French*. Cambridge, England: Cambridge University Press, 1976.

Césaire, Aimé. *Discourse on Colonialism*. New York: MR, 1972.

———. *Return to My Native Land*. Translated by J. Berger and A. Bostock. Paris: Présence Africaine, 1969.

Cook, Mercer. "The Poetry of Léon Damas." *African Forum* 2, 4 (spring 1967): 129-32.

———. "African Voices of Protest." In *The Militant Black Writer in Africa and the United States*. Edited by Mercer Cook and Stephen E. Henderson. Madison, Wis.: University of Wisconsin Press, 1969.

Damas, Léon-Gontran. "Price-Mars, the Father of Haitianism." *Présence Africaine* 4-5, 32-33 (January 1968): 204-18.

———. "Poems from *Pigments*." *Black World* 21, 3 (January 1972): 13-28.

Dash, J. Michael. "Before and Beyond Negritude." In *A History of Literature in the Caribbean, I: Hispanic and Francophone Regions*. Edited by James A. Arnold, Julio Rodriques-Luis, et al. Amsterdam: Benjamins, 1994.

———. "Marvellous Realism: The Way Out of Negritude." In *The Post-Colonial Studies Reader*. Edited by Bill Ashcroft, Gareth Griffiths, and Helen Tiffin. London: Routledge, 1995.

Davis, Gregson. *Aime Cesaire*. Cambridge, England: Cambridge University Press, 1997.

Diakhaté, Lamine. "The Myth in Senegalese Folk Poetry." *Présence Africaine* 11, 39 (1961): 13-31.

Egejuru, Phanuel Akubueze. *Towards African Literary Independence: A Dialogue with Contemporary African Writers*. Westport, Conn.: Greenwood Press, 1980.

Fanon, Frantz. *Black Skin, White Masks*. New York: Grove Press, 1967.

————. *The Wretched of the Earth*. New York: Grove Press, 1965.

Finn, Julio. *Voices of Negritude*. London: Quartet, 1987.

Frutkin, Susan. *Aimé Césaire: Black between Worlds*. Coral Gables, Fla.: Center for Advanced International Studies, University of Miami, 1973.

Gérard, Albert S. "Historical Origins and Literary Destiny of Negritude." *Diogenes* 48 (1964): 14-37.

Gérard, Albert S., ed. *European-Language Writing in Sub-Saharan Africa*. Budapest: Akadémiai Kiadó, 1986.

Hymans, Jacques Louis. *Leopold Sédar Senghor: An Intellectual Biography*. Edinburgh, Scotland: Edinburgh University Press, 1971.

Irele, Abiola. *The African Experience in Literature and Ideology*. London: Heinemann, 1981. Reprint, Bloomington, Ind.: Indiana University Press, 1990.

Irele, Abiola, ed. *Selected Poems of Léopold Sédar Senghor*. Cambridge, England: Cambridge University Press, 1977.

Jahn, Jahnheinz. *"Aimé Césaire." Black Orpheus* 2 (1958): 32-36.

————. *Neo-African Literature: A History of Black Writing*. Translated by Oliver Coburn and Ursula Lehrburger. New York: Grove Press, 1968.

Jeyifo, Biodun. "The Nature of Things: Arrested Decolonization and Critical Theory." *Research in African Literatures* 21 (spring 1990): 33-48.

Jones, Edward A. *Voices of Negritude: The Expression of Black Experience in the Poetry of Senghor, Césaire and Damas*. Valley Forge, Pa.: Judson Press, 1971.

Jules-Rosette, Bennetta. *Black Paris: The African Writer's Landscape*. Urbana, Ill.: University of Illinois Press, 1998.

Kennedy, Ellen Conroy, ed. *The Negritude Poets: An Anthology of Translations from the French*. Foreword by Maya Angelou. New York: Thunder's Mouth Press, 1989.

Kesteloot, Lilyan. *Black Writers in French: A Literary History of Negritude*. Philadelphia: Temple University Press, 1974.

King, Bruce, and Kolawole Ogungbesan, eds. *A Celebration of Black and African Writing*. Zaria, Nigeria: Ahmadu Bello University Press, 1975.

Kubayanda, Josaphat B. *The Poet's Africa: Africanness in the Poetry of Nicolas Guillen and Aime Cesaire*. New York: Greenwood Press, 1990.

Markovitz, Irving Leonard. *Leopold Sédar Senghor and the Politics of Negritude*. New York: Atheneum, 1969.

Mezu, Sebastan Okechukwu. *The Poetry of Léopold Sédar Senghor*. London: Heinemann; Rutherford, N.J.: Fairleigh Dickinson University Press, 1973.

Moore, G. "The Politics of Negritude." In *Protest & Conflict in African Literature*. Edited by Cosmo Pieterse and Donald Munro. New York: Africana Pub. Corp., 1969.

Nkosi, Lewis. *Tasks and Masks: Themes and Styles of African Literature*. Harlow, England: Longman, 1981.

Onoge, O. F. "The Crisis of Consciousness in Modern African Literature: A Survey." In *Marxism and African Literature*. Edited by Georg M. Gugelberger. London: Longman, 1985.

Owomoyela, Oyekan. "European Language Poetry." In his *African Literatures: An Introduction*. Waltham, Mass.: Brandeis University, African Studies Association, 1979.

Racine, Daniel L., ed. *Léon-Gontran Damas, 1912-1978: Founder of Negritude: A Memorial Casebook*. Washington, D.C.: University Press of America, 1979.

Sartre, Jean-Paul. "Orphée noir." In *Anthologie de la nouvelle poésie nègre et malgache de langue française*. Edited by Leopold Sédar Senghor. Paris: Presses Universitaires de France, 1977. Translated by J. MacCombie in "Black Orpheus." *Massachusetts Review* 6, 1 (1964-65).

Senghor, Leopold Sédar. *Liberté I: Négritude et Humanisme*. Paris: Editions du Seuil, 1964.

————. *Nocturnes*. Translated by John Reed and Olive Wake. New York: Third Press, 1971.

————. "On Negrohood: Psychology of the African-Negro." *Diogenes* 37 (1962): 2.

Shapiro, Norman R., ed and trans. *Negritude: Black Poetry from Africa and the Caribbean*. New York: October House, 1970.

Spleth, Janice S. *Léopold Sédar Senghor*. Boston: Twayne, 1985.

Vaillant, Janet G. *Black, French, and African: A Life of Léopold Sédar Senghor*. Cambridge, Mass.: Harvard University Press, 1990.

Wise, Christopher. "The Dialectics of Negritude: Or, The (Post)Colonial Subject in Contemporary African-American Literature." In *Postcolonial Discourse and Changing Cultural Contexts: Theory and Criticism*. Westport, Conn.. Greenwood, 1995.

NEOARISTOTELIANS. *See* CHICAGO CRITICS

NEOCLASSIC GROUP
Ukraine, 1920s

The Ukrainian Neoclassic Group, aptly named for its advocacy of traditional forms and rules of composition, consisted of a small number of poets and critics centered in Kiev. During the 1920s the group's members, the most important of which were Maxym Rylsky (1895-1964) and Mykola Zerov (1890-1941), actively countered the work of various proletarian movements and, consequently, significantly affected later Ukrainian writers. Other members were Mykhaylo Dray-Khmara (1889-1938) and Osvald Burghardt (1891-1947).

❖•❖
Further Reading

Asher, Oksana. *Letters from the Gulag: The Life, Letters, and Poetry of Michael Dray-Khmara*. New York: R. Speller, 1983.

Luckyj, George S. N. "The Failed Revolution, 1917-32." In his *Ukrainian Literature in the Twentieth Century: A Reader's Guide*. Toronto: University of Toronto for the Shevchenko Scientific Society, 1992.

NEOCLASSICISM
Sudan, 1930s

The Neoclassicist trend in the Sudan was prominent during the 1930s. Among the poets associated with Neoclassicism åre Muhammad Sa'id al-'Abbassi (1881-1963), whose poetry reflects Sufi influences; 'Abdallah al-Banna (1890-?); and 'Abdallah al-Rahman (1891-1964). The Neoclassicists in the Sudan were influenced by contemporary neo-classical trends in Egypt, as seen, for example, in the work of Ahmad Shawqī (1869-1932). They tended, however, to continue writing in classical Arabic poetic style using traditional form, diction, and subject matter while resisting influences from the West.

❖•❖
Further Reading

Jayyusi, Salma Khadra. *Trends and Movements in Modern Arabic Poetry*. Vol. 2. Leiden, Netherlands: E. J. Brill, 1977.

NEOREALISM
Italy, 1930s-1950s

The Italian Neorealist writers shared with the members of the earlier VERISMO movement a commitment to accurate, straightforward portrayals of everyday life and ordinary people. But the Neorealist movement emerged from the cauldron of Fascism and World War II, and its practitioners had been deeply affected by their experiences during this difficult period in their country's history. In fact, some of the first examples of Neorealist literature — including works by Alberto MORAVIA, Cesare PAVESE, and Elio VITTORINI — were actually written before the end of the Fascist regime. The brutalities and repression of Fascism led intellectuals to question the nature of both political power and their own role in society. With the end of the war came flickers of hope that Italy's social and political difficulties would ease, and writers opposed to corruption and tyranny and fired with the spirit of renewal increasingly turned their attention to documenting those difficulties.

An important source of inspiration for Italy's Neorealist writers came from a parallel, and internationally recognized, movement in Italian film (*see* NEOREALIST FILM) that centered on many of the same concerns, especially the postwar struggles of ordinary urban and rural people. Socially committed and psychologically insightful American literature also exerted a significant influence, as translations of works by such authors as John STEINBECK (*see* PROLETARIAN LITERATURE, United States) and John DOS PASSOS (*see* LOST GENERATION) became readily available to Italian readers.

Perhaps the earliest manifestation of a movement that would reach its peak after World War II was Alberto Moravia's novel *GLI INDIFFERENTI* (1929; *The Time of Indifference*, 1953), which featured an economical, realistic narrative style and an effective use of allegory in its portrayal of middle-class life. Cesare Pavese achieved a skillful blend of symbolism and accurate detail in *Paesi tuoi* (1941; *The Harvesters*, 1961), which chronicles the return of two ex-convicts to the Piedmont home of one of them. Generally acknowledged as Pavese's masterpiece, however, is *LA LUNA E I FALÒ* (1950; *The Moon and the Bonfire*, 1952), in which a former member of the Italian resistance movement travels back to his rural home after the war. Written in an unacademic but lyrical style, this novel explores the contrast between urban and rural life and the question of whether one can ever return to the world of one's childhood.

Along with Pavese, Elio Vittorini is credited with introducing Italian readers to American literature through his many translations. After an early liaison with the Fascists, Vittorini turned to the left and took part in the resistance movement. His awareness of the suffering of the Italian peasantry is evident in his acclaimed work *CONVERSAZIONE IN SICILIA* (1941; *In Sicily*, 1947), an allegorical novel about a young man who encounters miserable poverty and despair during a visit to his ancestral village. Despite its simple prose and realistic focus, the novel features abstract characters and archetypal symbols that deepen its effect.

Other notable members of the Neorealist movement include Carlo Levi (1902-1975), whose experiences while exiled by the Fascist regime to Sicily are chronicled in *Cristo si è fermato a Eboli* (1945; *Christ Stopped at Eboli*, 1947), a compassionate portrait of the grueling lives of southern farmers; Vasco Pratolini (1913-1991), whose novel *Cronache di poveri amanti* (1947; *A Tale of Poor Lovers*, 1949) takes place in an urban setting; and Vitaliano Brancati (1907-1954), who criticized Italian society under Fascism in *Il bell'Antonio* (1949; *Bell'Antonio*, 1978). Carlo Bernari's (1909-) work focuses on the plight of the working class, while Carlo Cassola (1917-1987) wrote about the resistance movement and Giorgio Bassani (1916-) about the lives of middle-class Italian Jews. Curzio Malaparte (1898-1957) was an early sympathizer of the Fascists whose later contempt for the regime is evident in his novel *Kaputt* (1944). Carlo Gadda (1893-1973) is lauded for his inventive experimental fiction, into which he incorporated a variety of local dialects.

By the end of the 1950s, Italy had entered a period of economic expansion that led to the rise of the "industrial novel," which focused on the lives of factory workers and the psychological fallout of the clash between industrial and agricultural societies. Younger writers also became increasingly interested in exploring the psychological underpinnings of existence rather than in providing realistic portraits of social conditions. Nevertheless, some of Italy's most important contemporary writers may be said to have begun as Neorealists. Examples include Italo Calvino (1923-1985), whose first novel *Il sentiero dei nidi di ragno* (1947; *The Path to the Nest of Spiders*, 1959) is both a straightforward, realistic account of the wartime resistance movement and a foreshadowing of his later work blending the real and the fantastic; and Leonardo Sciascia (1921-), author of *Le parrochie di regalpetra* (1956; *Salt in the Wound*, 1969), which documents the harsh conditions endured by Sicilian peasants. Elsa Morante's (1918-1985) first major work, *Menzogna e sortilegio* (1948; *House of Liars*, 1951), the saga of three generations of a southern Italian family told through the perspective of a troubled adolescent girl, combines realistic description with modern psychological concerns. The works of Pier Paolo Pasolini (1922-1975) reveal his interest in local dialects and folklore; his first novel, *Ragazzi di vita* (1955; *The Ragazzi*, 1968) revolves around the residents of Rome's slums in the period just after the end of World War II.

❧•❦

Moravia, Alberto (1907-)
Italian novelist, short-story writer, essayist, and playwright.

A major twentieth-century author as well as one of the most important in his own country, Moravia has incorporated such complex concerns as politics, sexuality, psychology, philosophy, and art into his diverse works. Moravia views the world as essentially decadent and corrupt, and humanity as subservient to lust, which — along with the pursuit of money — people use as a substitute for love and personal integrity.

Moravia established himself as a Neorealist with *Gli indifferenti* (1929; *The Time of Indifference*, 1953), which is considered one of the earliest Neorealist novels. In the years following the end of World War II, Moravia's writing became more socially conscious, even exhibiting a MARXIST orientation, as he focused with increased sympathy on the concerns of ordinary people. Particularly acclaimed is the novel *La ciociara* (1957; *Two Women*, 1958), which chronicles the experiences of a shopkeeper and her daughter in wartime Rome, and the short story collection *Racconti romani* (1954; *Roman Tales*, 1957), which features an effective use of colloquial language in its portrayal of working-class characters. By contrast, the protagonists of Moravia's later works tend to be artists involved in creative or sexual dilemmas.

Gli indifferenti (1929; *The Time of Indifference*, 1953).

In this novel Moravia provides an authentically detailed portrait of a middle class dominated by the drive for sex and material gain. The novel's characters are isolated, apathetic, and disillusioned, and their pursuit of happiness through sex and money is ultimately unsatisfying. Moravia managed to evade the censors of the Fascist regime, with its tendency to squash anything critical of society, through skillfully employed allegory and satire.

❖•❖

Pavese, Cesare (1908-1950), Italian poet, novelist, editor, and translator.

Pavese is renowned both for his own writings and for his influential translations of American literature and criticism into Italian. In fact, Pavese's fiction was heavily influenced by his admiration of several American authors, particularly Herman Melville (1819-1891) and Sherwood Anderson (1876-1941). Among the dominant concerns in Pavese's writings are the contrast between urban and rural (or cultured and unsophisticated), the need to reconnect with one's heritage, and the conflicting desires for solitude and for connection with others. Pavese employed a style that maintained its poetic quality despite its essentially unliterary, unacademic nature; he incorporated phrases from the Piedmontese vernacular in his effort to convey a sense of real life while also lending his writing mythical significance.

Pavese's first literary publication was a volume of poetry, *Lavorare stanca* (1936; *Hard Labor*, 1976), in which are evident many of the same themes found in his later fiction. Perhaps the strongest of these themes is the question of whether the exile can truly find redemption through a return to his native region; Pavese concludes here that he can only feel himself more alienated in the end. These poems are written in a direct, unpretentious style and feature working-class settings and characters. Recognized as one of the earliest Neorealist novels, *Paesi tuoi* (1941; *The Harvesters*, 1961) is both a sociological portrait of the rural residents of Italy's Piedmont region and an exploration of psychological concerns that are symbolically conveyed. Composed in a notably ungrammatical narrative style, the novel relates how the return of two ex-convicts to the village home of one of them leads not to the expected resumption of a peaceful life but to violent murder. Pavese's most acclaimed work is *La luna e i falò* (1950; *The Moon and the Bonfire*, 1952), which was published only a few months before the author's suicide.

***La luna e i falò* (1950; *The Moon and the Bonfire*, 1952).**

Like Pavese's previous publications, this novel centers on the conflicting need to reconnect with one's past and the impossibility of recapturing what one has lost. The novel portrays both the experiences of the protagonist, Anguilla, during his involvement with the Italian resistance movement (thus providing a detailed portrait of that important period in the country's history) and his later return to the region in which he grew up. One particularly interesting aspect of the novel is its perspective on America, the promised land that attracted so many impoverished Italians during the first half of the twentieth century: whereas Pavese had once viewed America as full of promise, he now casts it as sterile and disillusioning to those who lose their roots by fleeing there.

❖•❖

Vittorini, Elio (1908-1966), Italian novelist, critic, and translator.

Along with Cesare Pavese, Vittorini is famous both for his own writings and for his pioneering translations of the works of American literature that so influenced the Neorealist movement. Written in a deceptively simple prose, Vittorini's fiction features an adept blend of realism, lyricism, and allegory and evidences his awareness of complex social and political issues. Vittorini joined the Fascist party in 1925 but became disillusioned and split with the regime in 1936; he later became a Communist but eventually left that party as well. During World War II, Vittorini was active in the Italian resistance movement.

Conversazione in Sicilia (1941; *In Sicily*, 1947).

This, Vittorini's most acclaimed work, relates allegorically the story of Silvestro, a young printer drawn back to his rural birthplace by the news that his parents have separated and by his own quest for identity. As the novel begins, Silvestro is mired in a state of extreme indifference and lethargy, but his apathy begins to crack as he travels by train toward Sicily and finally reaches his mother's village. Accompanying his mother on her nursing rounds, Silvestro witnesses miserable poverty and suffering. Next Silvestro travels around the countryside with a knife-grinder, who introduces him to a variety of people with whom he discusses "the sorrows of the injured world." The book's concluding section is highly meditative, and includes such episodes as Silvestro's encounter with his dead brother. He finally returns to the city. Lauded for both its authentic details and its psychological depth, *Conversazione in Sicilia* is a complex, cryptic work that calls for societal renewal, chronicling a quest that begins in despair but moves through a gradual return of vitality toward the ideal of collective action to save humanity.

❖•❖

Further Reading

Armes, Roy. *Patterns of Realism: A Study of Italian Neo-Realist Cinema*. New York: A.S. Barnes, 1971.

Calvino, Italo. "Main Currents in Italian Fiction Today." *Italian Quarterly* 4, 13-14 (spring-summer 1960): 3-14.

Heiney, Donald. *Three Italian Novelists: Moravia, Pavese, Vittorini*. Ann Arbor, Mich.: University of Michigan Press, 1968.

Marcus, Millicent. *Italian Cinema in the Light of Neorealism*. Princeton, N.J.: Princeton University Press, 1987.

Molinaro, Julius A., ed. *Petrarch to Pirandello: Studies in Italian Literature in Honour of Beatrice Corrigan*. Toronto: University of Toronto Press, 1973.

Pacifici, Sergio. *A Guide to Contemporary Italian Literature: From Futurism to Neorealism.* Carbondale, Ill.: Southern Illinois University Press, 1962.

————. *The Modern Italian Novel.* Vol. 3. *From Pea to Moravia.* Carbondale, Ill.: Southern Illinois University Press, 1979.

Pacifici, Sergio, ed. *From Verismo to Experimentalism: Essays on the Modern Italian Novel.* Bloomington, Ind.: Indiana University Press, 1969.

Potter, Joy Hambuechen. *Elio Vittorini.* Boston: Twayne, 1979.

NEOREALISM
Portugal, 1920s-1990s

Observers of Portuguese society invariably mention the strong current of pessimism that runs through all aspects of the nation's culture. In twentieth-century Portuguese literature, however, this strain has been countered by — or at least interwoven with — a desire for social reform that is evidenced in the Neorealistic fiction and poetry written as early as the 1920s but especially thriving after World War II.

Several centuries of economic decline, followed by the rise to power of a military dictatorship determined to keep its citizenry in a near-feudal status, resulted in the widespread impoverishment of Portugal's urban and rural populations. In addition, those who sought a better life through labor in Portuguese colonies — especially Brazil — were often subjected to harsh working conditions and isolation. Writers grew increasingly aware of and incensed about the nineteenth-century-style hardships endured by the Portuguese people, even as much of the rest of the world seemed to move smoothly into the twentieth century. The result was that the philosophy of art for art's sake that had been promulgated by the *presencistas* (*see PRESENCA*), the influential group of MODERNISTS who produced the journal *Presenca* from 1927 to 1940, gave way to a trend toward plain, journalistic portrayals of ordinary life and exposés of human suffering.

In a manner typical of the continuous cultural exchange between Portugal and its largest colony, Portugal's Neorealists were influenced by such Brazilian writers as Jorge Amado (1912-), José Lins de Rêgo (1901-1957), and Graciliano Ramos (1892-1953). Also significant in the development of Portuguese Neorealism were two Marxist-oriented journals, *Diabo* (1934-40) and *Nascente* (1937-40), which published the work of artists whose strong sense of social responsibility attracted the unfavorable attention and censorship of Antonio Salazar's (1889-1970) regime (1932-68).

Perhaps the earliest practitioner of Neorealism in Portugal was José Ferreira de CASTRO, whose autobiographical novels about the Portuguese emigrant experience were extremely popular in the late 1920s and early 1930s. Another writer who could be considered an early Neorealist was Raúl Brandão (1867-1930), who blended NATURALISM with philosophical concerns in novels written during the first two decades of the century.

487

Other important figures in the Neorealist movement were physician, poet, and novelist Fernando NAMORA and (António) Alves REDOL, whose novel *Gaibeus* (1939; Weed Picker) is sometimes called Portugal's first truly Neorealistic work. Joaquim Soeiro Pereira Gomes (1910-1949) used Naturalistic description in *Esteiras* (1941; Inlets), a novel about the exploitation of child workers. Aquilino Ribeiro's (1885-1963) unconventional work features a deft use of the vernacular and a dedication to exposing corruption and greed; Ribeiro openly opposed Salazar and was jailed in 1958.

Critics have used the term "ethical realism"—a technique that combines a subjective point of view with a Neorealist approach—to describe the works of several Portuguese authors. Perhaps the best-known proponents of ethical realism are José Rodrigues Miguéis (1901-1980) and Irene Lisboa (1892-1958). The latter (who also published under the name Joao Falco, thus highlighting the obstacles facing female writers in societies as conservative as Portugal's; *see also* THREE MARIAS) chronicled the daily lives and struggles of city dwellers in *Solidao* (1939; Solitude) and of rural people in *Cronicas da serra* (1961; Hill Tales).

A strain of Neorealism was also introduced into Portuguese poetry, which had traditionally been dominated by lyrical Romanticism, in the middle of the twentieth century. Its most prominent expression was the publication of the *Novo cancionero* (1941-42; New Songbook), a somewhat incohesive series of volumes by ten socially committed poets, several of whom—most notably Fernando Namora—later became novelists. Namora was still a medical student when he produced *Terra* (1941; Earth). Another significant Neorealist poet was José Gomes Ferreira (1900-), whose collection *Poeta militante* (1977-78; Militant Poet) features stark poems focused on oppression and injustice.

❖•❖

Castro, José Ferreira de (1898-1974), Portuguese novelist.

Considered one of the first Portuguese Neorealists, Castro dominated the movement throughout his career, which coincided with the oppressive regime of military dictator Antonio Salazar. A proponent of literature that directly confronted the tangible realities of history, society, and nature as well as individual identity, Castro repeatedly attempted to focus attention on the despair of his country's rural poor. In such novels as *EMI-GRANTES* (1928; *Emigrants*, 1962) and *A SELVA* (1930; *The Jungle*, 1934), his two most famous works, he expresses both the deep pessimism of Portuguese culture—particularly of its middle class—and a sincere desire for social change.

Emigrantes (1928; *Emigrants*, 1962).

This autobiographical novel chronicles the bleak, lonely, physically grueling lives of Portuguese workers in Brazil, where Castro went to work as a young man. It also conveys the disillusionment experienced by such emigrés on their return to Portugal, which in their homesickness they had remembered as a pleasanter place than the impoverished nation that confronts them. Characterized by a loose narrative structure and impassioned but journalistically detailed language, *Emigrantes* was a major best-seller in both Portugal and Brazil.

A selva (1930; *The Jungle*, 1934).

This novel paints a harrowing portrait of the harsh conditions endured by the Portuguese laborers on a Brazilian rubber plant modeled after the one on which Castro worked as a young man. Translated into a number of other languages, *A selva* was named in a 1973 UNESCO survey as one of the ten most popular books in the world.

Namora, Fernando (1919-1989), Portuguese novelist and poet.

Renowned as both a poet and novelist, Namora was one of the most prominent members of the Portuguese Neorealist movement. His work reflects his experiences as a physician working among both the urban and the rural poor. Namora's first significant novel, *Fogo na noite escura* (1943; Fire in the Dark Night) incorporates psychological analysis into its portrayal of social problems. Also acclaimed are *Minas da Sao Francisco* (1946; Mines of Sao Francisco) and the subtle, introspective *Domingo à tarde* (1961; Sunday Afternoon).

Redol, (António) Alves (1911-1969), Portuguese novelist.

Redol's novel *Gaibeus* (1939; Weed Picker), considered by some commentators the first true Portuguese Neorealist novel, chronicles the hardships endured by three Portuguese farmhands. In his foreword to the novel, Redol stated that *Gaibeus* was a work of social protest and a document of human suffering rather than an expression of artistic intent.

Further Reading

Brasil, Jaime. "Ferreira de Castro." *Books Abroad* 31 (1957): 117-21.

Campbell, Roy. *Portugal*. London: Max Reinhardt, 1957.

Ellison, Fred P. "The Myth of the Destruction and Re-creation of the World in Ferreira de Castro's *A selva*." *Luzo-Brazilian Review* 15 (supplementary volume, 1978): 101-9.

Faria, Almeida, Alberto de Lacerda, Vianna Moog, Jorge de Sena, and Robert D. Pring-Mill. *Studies in Modern Portuguese Literature*. Tulane Studies in Romance Languages and Literature, No. 4. New Orleans, La.: Tulane University, 1971.

Megenny, William. "Descriptive Sensationalism in Ferreira de Castro." *Romance Notes* 13 (1971): 61-66.

Moser, G. "Portuguese Literature in Recent Years." *Modern Language Journal* 44 (1960): 245-54.

————. "Portuguese Writers of This Century." *Hispania* 50 (1966): 947-54.

Schneider, Marshall J., and Irwin Stern, eds. *Modern Spanish and Portuguese Literatures.* New York: Continuum, 1988.

NEOREALIST FILM
Italy, 1945-1950

Although it flourished for only a short period, Italian Neorealist film exerted a strong influence not only on the concurrent Neorealist movement in Italian literature but on filmmakers and other artists worldwide. The Italian Neorealist filmmakers responded to the aftermath of a turbulent, troubling period in their country's history—including two decades of rule by the repressive Fascist regime and the devastations of World War II—by faithfully documenting the postwar problems and conditions of Italy's ordinary people.

Rejecting the shallow, escapist bent of contemporary movies, they sought to create a highly authentic art form that directly presented physical, social, and psychological realities. To achieve this end they merged the methods of documentary filmmaking with standard studio techniques, incorporating authentic settings, natural lighting, both scripted and unscripted dialogue, and minimal direction. The Neorealist films tend to center on working-class characters (often portrayed by non-actors) and feature a leftist orientation. Although they tended to be quickly and crudely made, the bold approach and compassionate orientation of the Neorealist films lent them universal appeal.

The most acclaimed of the Italian Neorealist films include *Roma, città aperta* (1945; Rome, Open City), an anti-Fascist chronicle of life during the Nazi occupation, and *Paisan* (1946), a set of six wartime vignettes, both directed by Roberto Rossellini (1906-1977); and Vittorio De Sica's (1901-1974) *Sciuscià* (1946; Shoeshine) and *Ladri di biciclette* (1948; The Bicycle Thief). Also notable is Luchino Visconti's (1906-1976) *La terra tre ma* (1948; The Earth Shook), based on Ignazio SILONE's (*see* MODERNISM, Italy) acclaimed novel *Pane e vino* (1937; *Bread and Wine*, 1962).

✦•✦

Further Reading

Armes, Roy. *Patterns of Realism: A Study of Italian Neo-Realist Cinema.* New York: A. S. Barnes, 1971.

Marcus, Millicent. *Italian Cinema in the Light of Neorealism.* Princeton, N.J.: Princeton University Press, 1987.

NEOROMANTICISM, FINLAND. *See* **NATIONAL NEOROMANTICISM**

NEOROMANTICISM, ICELAND. *See* PROGRESSIVE ROMANTICISM

NEOROMANTICISM
Latvia, 1890s-1900s

Along with the NEW CURRENT MOVEMENT, Neoromanticism dominated Latvian literature during the 1890s and early 1900s. Two key writers of the movement, which owed much to its German counterpart, were Jānis Poruks (1871-1911) and Fricis Bārda (1880-1919).

❖•❖
Further Reading

Rubulis, Aleksis. "Latvian Literature." In his *Baltic Literature: A Survey of Finnish, Estonian, Latvian, and Lithuanian Literatures*. Notre Dame, Ind.: University of Notre Dame Press, 1970.

NEOROMANTICISM
Ukraine, 1920s-1930s

One of the latest flourishings of Neoromanticism was that in the Ukraine, which was confined to the years between the two world wars. The greatest champions of the movement were poets Volodymyr Sosyura (1898-1965) and Olexa Vlysko (1908-1934).

❖•❖
Further Reading

"Literature." In *Ukraine: A Concise Encyclopaedia*. Edited by Volodymyr Kubijovyc. Vol. I. Toronto: University of Toronto Press, 1963.
Luckyj, George S. N. *Ukrainian Literature in the Twentieth Century: A Reader's Guide*. Toronto: University of Toronto Press for the Shevchenko Scientific Society, 1992.

NÉPI WRITERS. *See* POPULIST MOVEMENT

NEUEN REALISMUS. See COLOGNE SCHOOL OF NEW REALISM

NEUE SACHLICHKEIT. *See* NEW OBJECTIVITY

NEW APOCALYPSE POETS
England, 1938-1940s

The main leaders of the New Apocalypse group were Henry Treece (1911-1966), G. S. Fraser (1915-1980), and J. F. Hendry (1911-), and its poetic manifesto appeared in

Hendry's introduction to the anthology *The New Apocalypse* (1940); other members included George BARKER, Dorian Cooke (n.d.), Norman McCAIG, Robert Melville (n.d.), Nicholas Moore (1918-), Philip O'Connor (1916-1966) and Dylan Thomas (1914-1953), who is now remembered less as an Apocalyptic poet than as the writer whose early prose style inspired the group with its surreal and often bizarre linguistic flamboyancy and vision. Unlike Hendry and the others, Thomas's celebration of procreation and life overrode his despair of it.

Hendry describes Apocalyptic writing as concerned with "the study of living, the collapse of social norms and the emergence of new and more 'organic ones'." Its main thrust is to depict the fragmentation of humankind and the decay of political, philosophic, and scientific systems. It is only when the writer breaks through the structure of language and social convention that the work can speak to a way to relate to the environment and deal with the problem of living in a machine, or object-oriented society. Myth, he notes, as a projection of self (which is not object) can be visualized as the "field of presentation" which becomes the literary vehicle for self expression. The poet's use of symbolic/prophetic myth allows for individual opposition to those objects (machines, automobiles, bombers, etc.) which are antipathetic to intellectual and spiritual survival. Hendry saw humankind as in constant danger of becoming "object," depersonalized and equated with machines — expendable, replaceable, and finally worthless.

Specifically, Apocalyptic writing depicts the universal horror of the twentieth century. Its incoherence is metaphor for the disjunction of life brought about by the agony of war and the threat of annihilation. In Hendry's poem "Picasso for Guernica" (1940), the speaker becomes "the arm thrust candle through the wall/ . . . /the axis of anger!" The critic G. S. Fraser has defined Apocalyptic poetry as a dialectical development of SURREALISM, in which brutal excess describes the disintegration of a society in which the poet is reduced to inarticulate protest; thus, if such poetry is called inferior, the blame lies with an inferior society which has inspired it. Francis Scarfe, in his critical work *Auden and After* (1969), notes that the Apocalyptic movement means "liberation from . . . the parochial world of observation which was evolved by the followers of Auden," but cautions that, while the poet must express his concern for the state of life, he must express that concern in a valuable, meaningful language which can be clearly conceptualized and understood. While Scarfe sees a need for revolt, he demands that poetry must provide some synthesis out of "a dissipation of energy into occasional good lines, wrapped in the brown paper bag of mediocrity."

Of the poets mentioned, the critical consensus is that only Barker and McCaig developed their early Apocalyptic poetry into the more substantial creative activity found in their later works. Other anthologies issued by the group were *The White Horseman* (1941) and *The Crown and the Sickle* (1945).

Barker, George (1913-1991), English poet.

He continued to write poetry of social criticism for two decades after the Apocalyptic manifesto was published and is said by the critic and poet George Tomlinson to be one of the two best poets to come out of the movement. He was inspired to write verses on the death of W. B. YEATS (*see* ABBEY THEATRE and MODERNISM, England and Ireland), and his *The True Confession of George Barker* (1950, 1964) is said to be an example of the importance of the dissenting poetry of the century. There is in his work evil and violence, but it is often combined with a morbid tenderness and pity. In "To My Son" (1950), he describes the birth of a child as "laid/ . . . cold upon the doorstep of a house/Where few are happy and times get worse . . ." In his prose work, *The Dead Seagull* (1913), Barker notes that violent death, because of war, had surrounded him since birth, and his poetry reflects the statement. Other works include *Poems* (1935), *Lament and Triumph* (1940), and *A Vision of Beasts and Gods* (1954).

McCaig [also MacCaig], Norman (1910-), Scottish poet.

His verse is pithy, intense, and contains "philosophic comedy and a craggy integrity." His mature work concentrates upon themes of Scotland, and are often sensuously descriptive and delicately impressionistic. They include *Far Cry* (1943), *Riding Lights* (1955), *A Common Grace* (1957), *The White Bird* (1973), and *Collected Poems* (1985). One critic defends his talent in showing a continuous attempt to successfully polish and synthesize his ideas, while another admires his simple, resolute style.

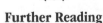

Further Reading

Cooke, Dorian, J. F. Hendry, and Norman McCaig, et al. *The New Apocalypse: An Anthology of Criticism, Poems and Stories*. London: Fortune, 1940.

Fraser, G. S. *Vision and Rhetoric: Studies in Modern Poetry*. London: Faber and Faber, 1959; New York: Barnes & Noble, 1960.

Rosenthal, M. L. *The New Poets: American and British Poetry Since World War II*. London: Oxford University Press, 1967.

Scarfe, Francis. *Auden and After: The Liberation of Poetry, 1930-1941*. London: Routledge, 1942.

Treece, Henry. *How I See Apocalypse*. London: L. Drummond, 1946.

NEW CRITICISM
United States, 1930s-1950s

Before the development of a modern formal literary criticism in England and the United States, literary scholars tended to be guided by personal taste and concerned themselves with describing a work of literature's aesthetic, moral, or social value. In contrast, the New Critics gave their attention to textual analysis rather than to romanticist, impressionistic description laudatory or disparaging, the author's biography, or concern with evaluating a work's social or aesthetic merits. The New Critics were also rebelling against MARXIST CRITICISM and NEW HUMANISM. Though others would be counted among the New Critics, a cohesive critical group whose efforts epitomized the new critical trend did exist in the so-called Southern critics, Cleanth Brooks (1906-1994), John Crowe RANSOM, Allen Tate (1899-1979), and Robert Penn Warren (1905-1989) — FUGITIVES all in younger days. The term "New Criticism" was first used by Joel Spingarn (1875-1939) in his 1910 essay delivered at Columbia University, *The New Criticism* (1911), but Ransom popularized it in his book *The New Criticism* (1941).

Profoundly influenced by T. S. ELIOT's essay "Tradition and the Individual Talent" (1919), notably his emphasis on irony in poetry, the American New Critics had also taken note of the work of other English scholars: I. A. Richards (1893-1979) and his *Principles of Literary Criticism* (1924) and *Science and Poetry* (1926, 1935) and F. R. Leavis's (1895-1978) *The Great Tradition* (1948).

Though New Critics differed on many points, they generally agreed on the primacy of close reading — predicated on the view that the literary critic should concentrate on giving attention to the text and its language. They saw a work of literature as an organic whole, ahistorical, complete unto itself. Regard for the author's intention or its historical or cultural context is not necessary for "unpacking" or "opening up" the text. The literary work was considered an "object" important only in and of itself, having a language of its own outside the author's intentions or the culture in which it was produced. Key concepts in close reading were irony, paradox, the text as a verbal icon, reconciliation of opposites, balance of tensions, ambiguity, fallacies (of authorial intent, of affect, etc.) and heresies, most famously, the heresy of paraphrase. It is Brooks to whom students are indebted for the phrase "the heresy of paraphrase" — almost certain to have been heard at least once in college poetry classes across the United States during the latter decades of the twentieth century — referring to his adament opposition to any analytical attempt to reduce poetry to prosaic meaning, which does "violence" to the poem. As Brooks put it in his famous *The Well Wrought Urn* (1947), "Indeed, whatever statement we may seize upon as incorporating the 'meaning' of the poem, immediately the imagery and the rhythm seem to set up tensions with it, warping and twisting it, qualifying and revising it."

The methodology for close reading was provided by Brooks and Warren in their influential college textbook collaborations *Understanding Poetry* (1938) and *Understanding Fiction* (1943). Other important texts produced by the New Critics include Tate's *Reason in Madness: Critical Essays* (1941), Ransom's *The World's Body* (1938), William EMPSON's *THE SEVEN TYPES OF AMBIGUITY* (1930; rev. ed., 1953; *see* CAMBRIDGE GROUP), and *The Verbal Icon: Studies in the Meaning of Poetry* (1954) by William K. Wimsatt, Jr. (1907-1975). Murray Krieger (1923-) wrote about the critical movement in *The New Apologists for Poetry* (1956).

The journal *Scrutiny* (1932-53), published in England, served as a forum for Leavis and his followers, while Ransom started the *Kenyon Review* (1939-70, 1979-) in the United States, which he edited until 1958.

René Wellek (1903-1995), with Austin Warren (1899-1986), wrote the important *Theory of Literature* (1949; rev. ed., 1956), which pointed out New Criticism's shortcomings, notably, its neglect of literary history. R. P. Blackmur (1904-1965) later wrote against the technique of close reading and argued against New Criticism's neglect to consider moral value of works of literature to society. Likewise, Yvor Winters (1900-1968) also didn't want to completely dispense with evaluation of human values in literature; Brooks criticized his contention that a kind of moral content paraphrase is desirable.

New Criticism had run its course by the 1960s, by which time it had infiltrated English literature departments and journals all over the United States, infusing a new sophistication into English and American literary criticism which was still strong into the 1980s. The READER-RESPONSE CRITICISM AND RECEPTION THEORY school owes its emergence in part to the dominance of the New Critics over the first half of the twentieth century. R. S. Crane and the other CHICAGO CRITICS reacted against the New Critics, as did the JUNGIAN mythological critics.

❖•❖

Further Reading

Berman, Art. *From the New Criticism to Deconstruction: The Reception of Structuralism and Post-Structuralism*. Urbana, Ill.: University of Chicago Press, 1988.

Burgum, Edwin Berry, ed. *The New Criticism: An Anthology of Modern Æsthetics and Literary Criticism*. New York: Prentice-Hall, 1930.

Fekete, John. *The Critical Twilight: Explorations in the Ideology of Anglo-American Literary Theory from Eliot to McLuhan*. London: Routledge & K. Paul, 1977.

Frye, Northrop. *Anatomy of Criticism*. Princeton, N.J.: Princeton University Press, 1957.

Graf, Gerald. *Literature Against Itself*. Chicago: University of Chicago Press, 1979.

Jancovich, Mark. *The Cultural Politics of the New Criticism*. Cambridge; New York: Cambridge University Press, 1993.

Rice, Philip, and Patricia Waugh, eds. *Modern Literary Theory: A Reader*. 2nd ed. London; New York: E. Arnold, 1992; distributed in the USA by Routledge, Chapman, and Hall.

Robey, David. "Anglo-American New Criticism." In *Modern Literary Theory: A Comparative Introduction*. Edited by Ann Jefferson and David Robey. London: Batsford, 1982.

Thompson, E. M. *Russian Formalism and Anglo-American New Criticism; A Comparative Study*. The Hague: Mouton, 1971.

Winchell, Mark R. *Cleanth Brooks and the Rise of Modern Criticism*. Charlottesville, Va.: University Press of Virginia, 1996.

Young, Thomas Daniel, ed. *The New Criticism and After*. Charlottesville, Va.: University Press of Virginia, 1976.

NEW CULTURE MOVEMENT. *See* MAY FOURTH MOVEMENT

NEW CURRENT MOVEMENT
Latvia, 1890s-1900s

A Latvian socialist movement of the 1890s, New Current was led by Jānis Rainis (1865-1929) and his wife, Aspazija (1868-1943). Their poetry and dramas, in particular, addressed Russian expansionism and social injustices within Latvia.

✤•✦

Further Reading

Biemelte, L., and S. Viese. *Where Rainis Lived and Worked*. Riga, Latvia: Liesma Pub. House, 1965.

Rubulis, Aleksis. "Latvian Literature." In his *Baltic Literature: A Survey of Finnish, Estonian, Latvian, and Lithuanian Literatures*. Notre Dame, Ind.: University of Notre Dame Press, 1970.

Sudrubkalns, J. *Janis Rainis, 1865-1965*. Riga, Latvia: Zinatne, 1965.

Ziedonis, Arvids. *The Religious Philosophy of Janis Rainis*. Waverly, Iowa: Latvju Gramata, 1969.

NEW HISTORICISM. *See* MARXIST CRITICISM

NEW HUMANISM
United States, 1910s-1930s

A modern critical movement that had its roots in ancient classical tradition, New Humanism had both beneficial and interesting influence in its time, but was also criticized for an "aristocratic" idealism which ran against the current of many of the philosophical, political, and social mores of the early twentieth century. The concept was engendered by Harvard professor of English Irving S. Babbitt (1865-1933), Paul Elmer More (1865-1933), and Norman Foerster (1887-1972), editor of *Humanism in America,* the journal which contains exemplary essays and implicit manifesto. These writers were adamant in their denial of the creative freedom of expression as found in the tenets of REALISM, Romanticism, and NATURALISM, since they felt such freedom exposed the human condition at its animalistic worst and did not invoke, as a rule, the orderly, ethical artistic restraint necessary for the enlightenment of democratic progress and well-being. Freedom of will, however, was extolled as "subjection to [that] inner law" which can only be arrived at through order, reason, and a universal code of values to be found in Greek, classical philosophy. Scientific method was "transcended" along with religious dogma, since both were seen to oppose free will, but Christian moral doctrine was recognized, as were the intellectual aspects of the religions of Oriental and East Indian culture. T. S. ELIOT (*see* MODERNISM, England and Ireland) was a student of Babbitt, and an early follower; he later found New Humanism to be "an insufficient substitute for religion" but remained, in his later work, influenced by much of Babbitt's thinking. The conservative, humanistic ideology of the movement has been viewed by some as restrictive and applicable only to an elitist intelligentsia which remains detached from political and historical criteria. Conversely, Babbitt has been defended for his efforts to perpetrate the most significant aspects of the classical literary heritage and its application as mechanism for the assessment of human values.

As an educator, Babbitt was primarily concerned with what he considered to be an American educational discrepancy caused by "the excesses of the elective system of undergraduate education." He argued that this permitted students too much freedom for self-expression which, in turn, deprived them of the exercise of a mental discipline which can be found only in the imposition of a curriculum which is informed by the classical tradition. Babbitt was most disturbed by his view of a diminishing, in the educational system, of the teaching of reasoned discipline which would rise above the influence of social and political influence. The reestablishment of what Edmund Burke (1729-1797) had called a "natural [educated] aristocracy" and what Matthew Arnold (1822-1888) named a "saving remnant" was important to Babbitt for maintaining a democracy in which the highest of ethical and moral standards would remain intact. His initial volume of essays, *Literature and the American Culture: Essays in Defense of the Humanities* (1908), contains his manifesto for change and his attack of the educational system which he found insufficient. In *The New Laokoon: An Essay on the Confusion of the Arts* (1910), he assesses the literature of the Romantic era to be "the greatest debauch of descriptive writing the world has ever known," because of its excessive, dramatic representation of sense and feeling. Moreover, he considered free verse to be "lawless" and to have little to do with universal values. He remained firmly fixed in his attitude that environment, history, and politics were subordinate to a writer's creative activity and in his rejection of any religious dogma which does not allow for freedom of the individual for ethical and moral choice. The moral tenets of Christianity were accepted, but not the supernatural ones. He praised certain elements of Confucianism, and translated the Buddhist tract *The Dhammapada* in 1936. He accompanied this with his essay "Buddha and the Occident," in which he explains his admiration for the Eastern religious philosophy of self-determination.

During the twenties, Babbitt's conservative ideas for educational and philosophical reform were enthusiastically received by a following of former students, writers, and academic colleagues, and the New Humanist movement was at its peak. But by the thirties, there were dissenting voices. Some of these argued that to divorce literature and its criticism from the general audience of a democratic culture was to make it socially irrelevant, and that to inhibit access to all modern literature, poetry, and art was to also inhibit awareness of a world which must be recognized and dealt with on realistic terms. With the advent of NEW CRITICISM and the theory of objective explication of the work of art for its own sake, interest in New Humanism declined, but would be remembered, not so much as a battle between ancient and modern critical tradition, but for the retention of a legacy of classical values combined with whatever is necessary for the formulation of a literature which best informs the human condition.

New Humanism formally ended as a movement in about 1930, but it is noted that it has influenced other important movements, such as the FUGITIVES/AGRARIANS, to develop the conservative, moral, and aesthetic standards which form a basis for specific ideologies.

✦•✦

Further Reading

Aaron, Daniel. *Writers on the Left*. Oxford, England: Oxford University Press, 1961.

Blackmur, R. P. "Humanism and Symbolic Imagination: Notes on Rereading Irving Babbitt." In *The Lion and the Honeycomb: Essays in Solicitude and Critique*. New York: Harcourt Brace, 1959.

Brennan, Stephen C. *Irving Babbitt*. Boston: Twayne, 1987.

Brown, Clarence Arthur. *The Achievement of American Criticism*. New York: Ronald Press, 1954.

Bullock, A. *The Humanist Tradition in the West*. New York: Norton, 1985.

Chang, Hsin-Hai. "Irving Babbitt and Oriental Thought." *Michigan Quarterly Review* 4 (fall 1965): 234-44.

Dakin, Arthur H. *Paul Elmer More*. Princeton, N.J.: Princeton University Press, 1960.

Duggan, Francis X. *Paul Elmer More*. New York: Twayne, 1966.

Eliot, T. S. "The Humanism of Irving Babbitt." In *Selected Essays, 1911-1932*. New York: Harcourt, Brace, 1950.

———. "Second Thoughts About Humanism." In *Selected Essays, 1911-1932*. New York: Harcourt, Brace, 1950.

Fausset, Hugh I'Anson. "The New Humanism Disputed." In his *The Proving of Psyche*. New York: Harcourt, Brace, 1929.

Goldsmith, Arnold L. "The Case for Ethical Criticism." In his *American Literary Criticism: 1905-1965*. Vol. III. Boston: G. K. Hall, Twayne, 1979.

Gratton, C. Hartley, ed. *The Critique of Humanism: A Symposium*. New York: Brewer & Warren, 1930.

Hindus, Milton. *Irving Babbitt, Literature, and the Democratic Culture*. New Brunswick, N.J.: Transaction Publishers, 1994.

Hoeveler, J. David, Jr. *The New Humanism: A Critique of Modern America, 1900-1940*. Charlottesville, Va.: University Press of Virginia, 1977.

Kariel, Henry S. "Democracy Limited: Irving Babbitt's Classicism." *Review of Politics* 13 (October 1951): 430-40.

Kazin, Alfred. *On Native Grounds*. New York: Reynal & Hitchcock, 1942.

Leander, Folke. *Humanism and Naturalism: A Comparative Study of Ernest Seillière, Irving Babbitt, and Paul Elmer More*. Göteborg, Sweden: Elanders Boktryckeri Aktiebolag, 1937.

Levin, Harry. *Refractions: Essays in Comparative Literature*. New York: Oxford University Press, 1966.

Lewisohn, Ludwig. *Expression in America*. New York: Harper & Brothers, 1932.

Lora, Ronald. *Conservative Minds in America*. Chicago: Rand McNally, 1971.

McKean, Keith F. *The Moral Measure of Literature*. Denver: A. Swallow, 1961.

Manchester, Frederick, and Odell Shepard, eds. *Irving Babbitt: Man and Teacher*. New York: Putnam's Sons, 1941.

Mercier, Louis J. A. *The Challenge of Humanism*. New York: Oxford University Press, 1933.

Nevin, Thomas R. *Irving Babbitt: An Intellectual Study*. Chapel Hill, N.C.: University of North Carolina Press, 1984.

O'Connor, William Van. *An Age of Criticism: 1900-1950*. Chicago: H. Regnery, 1952.

Panichas, George, ed. *Irving Babbitt: Representative Writings*. Lincoln, Nebr.: University of Nebraska Press, 1981.

Panichas, George A., and Claes G. Ryn, eds. *Irving Babbitt in Our Time*. Washington, D.C.: Catholic University of America Press, 1986.

Pritchard, John Paul. *Criticism in America*. Norman, Okla.: University of Oklahoma Press, 1956.

———. *Return to the Fountains*. Durham, N.C.: Duke University Press, 1942.

Seaton, James. "Irving Babbitt: Midwestern Intellectual." *Midamerica* 18 (1991): 22-30.

Shafer, Robert. *Paul Elmer More and American Criticism*. New Haven, Conn.: Yale University Press, 1935.

Spiller, Robert E., et al., eds. *A Literary History of the United States*. New York: Macmillan, 1948.

Stovall, Floyd, ed. *The Development of American Literary Criticism*. Chapel Hill, N.C.: University of North Carolina Press, 1955.

Tanner, Stephen L. *Paul Elmer More: Literary Criticism as the History of Ideas*. Provo, Utah: Brigham Young University, 1987.

Wilson, Edmund. *The Triple Thinkers*. New York: Harcourt, Brace, 1938.

Winters, Yvor. *In Defense of Reason*. New York: Swallow Press; Morrow, 1947.

Zabel, Morton Dauwen, ed. *Literary Opinion in America*. New York: Harper & Brothers, 1937.

NEW JAPANESE LITERATURE ASSOCIATION
Japan, 1945-1990s

The phoenix of the left-wing New Japanese Literature Association (Shin-Nihon Bungakkai) grew directly from the ashes of the Japanese proletarian literary movement that had been destroyed in the early 1930s by the rising tide of right-wing nationalism. In fact, lip service to democratic ideals aside, the Association's first years were fundamentally a continuation of the work of the earlier proletarian school carried out primarily by many of the same authors along with members of the Communist Party and its sympathizers. The Association sponsored local literary groups that often coincided with labor unions and had a goal of producing worker-written literature. Inevitable disputes within the Association over the proper relation between politics and literature led to the creation of numerous rival groups, some of which, including the supporters of the magazines *Kindai Bungaku* (Modern Literature) and *Jimmin Bungaku* (People's Literature), exerted a significant influence on Japanese left-wing literature in their own right.

The years immediately following World War II saw the Association exhort its members to create what it termed "democratic literature." That is, literature that would combine artistic integrity with revolutionary subject matter, as written by worker/writers. Counterintuitively, "democracy" in this sense referred to a recognition that all classes of people would have to work together to achieve standard Communist ideals. Three general types of story emerged: writers such as Miyamoto Yuriko (1899-1951), Tokunaga Sunao (1899-1958) and Sata Ineko (1904-1998) produced autobiographical works of self-analysis dealing with the authors' lives during the war; Noma Hiroshi (1915-1991), Tezuka Hidetaka (1906-), Shikibe Haruo (n.d.), and others wrote representative stories of everyday citizens dealing with the war and Fascism; and stories that focused on the lives of farmers and workers were written by authors including Inaba Shingo (1909-), Hamada Kyōtarō (n.d.), Ozawa Kiyoshi (1922-), Watanabe Katsuo (n.d.), and Shōda Chūji (n.d.).

However, the expected synthesis of literature and politics was never fully realized. Stories from the more accomplished writers were often out of touch with the lives of the workers they portrayed, while the writings of the workers themselves were lacking in creative essentials. Partially in recognition of this problem, the Association promulgated a five-point plan for the future in 1950 that would move beyond the creation of literature to its dissemination as a tool for raising class consciousness. The main points of the plan were to create a cohesive ideology for the Association, to seek out and encourage worker/critics to complement their coterie of worker/writers, a rededication to the goal of cooperating with a range of other organizations to achieve their aims and, amidst rising concern over the effect of the U.S. occupation of Japan, a more explicit consideration of both international and domestic circumstances in the Association's battle against capitalism. Among the Association's most influential authors in its post-1950 existence was Nakano Shigeharu (1902-1979), who was one of the Association's founding members in addition to being a poet, critic, and author of the prize-winning novels *Muragimo* (1954; The Mind), *Nashi no Hana* (1957; Pear Blossoms) and *Kō, Otsu, Hei, Tei* (1965; ABCD).

As the political tenor of Japan became more conservative and an increasing number of writers became disenchanted with the Communist Party, the Association's influence on the general literary scene began to wane. However, a commendable legacy can be read in the nonpolitical aspects of the Association's attempts to expose a wide range of Japanese citizenry to literature.

✦•✦

Further Reading

Keene, Donald. *Dawn to the West: Japanese Literature of the Modern Era.* Vol. 1. New York: Holt, Rinehart & Winston, 1984.
Shea, George Tyson. *Leftwing Literature in Japan: A Brief History of the Proletarian Literary Movement.* Tokyo: Hosei University Press, 1964.

NEW JOURNALISM
United States, 1960s-1990s

The most popular of several terms (others include the nonfiction novel and literary nonfiction) used to describe an innovative approach to nonfiction prose that became prominent in the 1960s, New Journalism refers to writing that combines conventional journalistic methods with such fictional techniques as STREAM-OF-CONSCIOUSNESS narrative (*see* MODERNISM, England and Ireland), extensive dialogue, shifting viewpoints, and minutely detailed scene-setting and character-sketching. In an essay published in a 1973 anthology of representative pieces, New Journalism's most prominent practitioner, Tom WOLFE, identified some of the most important elements of this genre. According to Wolfe, its characteristics include the presentation of people in dramatic scenes, with dialogue delivered verbatim rather than in selected quotes; the use of a variety of points of view; and detailed descriptions of scenes and milieus as well as people's distinguishing behaviors and mannerisms.

Although the first writing labeled "New Journalism" appeared in the early 1960s, critics have identified precedents for this unconventional style in earlier decades and even centuries. For instance, the highly descriptive journalistic pieces produced by Mark

TWAIN (*see* REALISM, United States) and Stephen CRANE (*see* NATURALISM, United States) in the late nineteenth century, as well as those by John Hersey (1914-1993) and George Orwell (1903-1950) in the first half of the twentieth, resemble New Journalism in their departure from the standard presentation of unadorned facts. Several commentators have identified the work of Wolfe and others as simply the next logical stage in the evolution of journalism, following directly in the footsteps of reporters and prose writers active in the 1930s, 1940s, and 1950s, such as Lincoln Steffens (1866-1936), Hutchins Hapgood (1869-1944), James Agee (1909-1955), Ben Hecht (1894-1964), and A. J. Liebling (1904-1963).

In any case, New Journalism as a self-conscious movement grew out of a dissatisfaction with the "inverted pyramid" of standard reporting, the structure by which facts are ranked according to their conventionally perceived importance and presented in a voice and from a perspective that is assumed to be completely objective. The appearance of the New Journalism has been seen as a response to the multiplying contradictions and incomprehensibility of modern life; from this perspective, practitioners of this highly subjective writing style may be classified either as Realists who want to make sense of things or Modernists who assert the impossibility of making any such sense. The profound societal change, fragmentation, and disillusionment of the 1960s have often been cited as critical factors in the development of New Journalism, as writers sought new, more flexible modes to convey their impressions of the upheaval occurring around them. Some of the broad themes these writers attempted, in their different ways, to illuminate include the impact of science and technology on contemporary culture and the ongoing struggle to define and achieve the American dream.

Although commentators differ in their interpretations of the New Journalists' motives or goals (some, for example, contend that their purpose is cultural insight, while others claim that their intentions are primarily rhetorical), it may safely be said that the movement's practitioners try to go beyond the mere presentation of information to explore and convey particular people, places, and events as they exist or occur at a specific moment in time. Like writers of fiction, New Journalists select and arrange details and images in order to dramatize and interpret their subject matter. They seek to portray people and events in all their true complexity, to help their readers experience as fully as possible the look and feel of what they are describing. Thus another important element of New Journalism is the exhaustive research it entails.

Perhaps the best known practitioner of the New Journalism — and certainly an instrumental force in its development— is the essayist Tom Wolfe, who has written about a wide variety of aspects of American culture in a verbally inventive, energetic style that reveals his sharp ear for vernacular speech. Many commentators trace the origin of the New Journalism to a 1963 article Wolfe wrote for *Esquire* magazine, which comprised his random notes on a custom car and hot rod show he'd been assigned to cover. Entitled "Varoom! Varoom! There Goes That Kandy-Kolored Tangerine-Flake Baby," this article is widely considered the American public's introduction to the unusual style — replete with colorful stream-of-consciousness descriptions and dialogue presented verbatim — that would become known as the New Journalism. In essays collected in a series of critically acclaimed volumes published over the next several decades, Wolfe has explored such topics as Hugh Hefner, the drug culture of the 1960s, wealthy liberals, contemporary art and architecture, and the American space program.

The second most notable New Journalist is probably Hunter S. Thompson (1939-). Like Wolfe, Thompson became a New Journalist in the early 1960s when, writing an account of the Hell's Angels motorcycle gang for *The Nation,* he found conventional journalism inadequate to his purposes. Thompson's best-known works are *Fear and Loathing in Las Vegas: A Savage Journey to the Heart of the American Dream* (1971) and *Fear and Loathing: On the Campaign Trail '72* (1973). The former volume chronicles Thompson's drug-drenched adventures in the company of his Samoan lawyer sidekick, Dr. Gonzo, and paints a lurid portrait of Las Vegas and of American society in general; the latter presents a vituperative view of the 1972 presidential campaign. Thompson's characteristic style, which features a morally indignant tone and frequent use of parody, satire, or outright insult, is known as "gonzo journalism" (a tribute to the companion of his nightmarish sojourn in Las Vegas).

Also frequently mentioned as an important New Journalist is the often controversial, prolific writer Norman Mailer (1923-), whose "nonfiction narratives" blend facts with fictional techniques, especially the use of metaphor. In *The Armies of the Night: History as a Novel, the Novel as History* (1968), for which Mailer received both a Pulitzer Prize and the National Book Award, he relates his involvement in the 1967 antiwar march on the Pentagon. *The Executioner's Song* (1979) is a lengthy book on the convicted murderer Gary Gilmore, who requested and received the death sentence in 1977. Mailer shifts between the viewpoints of doctors, lawyers, police, and journalists, as well as Gilmore's friends and relatives, to create a complex portrait of his life and death. Like other practitioners of New Journalism, Mailer explicitly acknowledges his own involvement with the material presented.

Another prominent figure in the New Journalism movement is Gay Talese (1932-), whose exhaustively researched, critically acclaimed books have examined the power structure of the *New York Times* (*The Kingdom and the Power,* 1969), organized crime (*Honor Thy Father,* 1971), and the sexual revolution (*Thy Neighbor's Wife,* 1980). Truman Capote (1924-1984) also exerted a seminal influence on the development of New Journalism, particularly with the publication of *In Cold Blood* (1965), which Capote claimed was the first work in a new literary genre he termed the nonfiction novel. In this book Capote employs irony, suspenseful scene-setting, and novelistic character-sketching to recount the 1959 murder of a Kansas farm family. Joan Didion (1934-) chronicles the moral dissolution and cultural chaos of America in such works as *Slouching Towards Bethlehem* (1968) and *The White Album* (1979); *Salvador* (1983) relates the political turbulence, violence, and fear Didion experienced during a two-week stay in El Salvador. Other writers who could be classified as New Journalists include George Plimpton (1927-), Terry Southern (1926-), and Michael Herr (1940-)—pieces by each of whom appeared in the 1973 anthology *The New Journalism*—as well as John McPhee (1931-), Annie Dillard (1945-), Lewis Thomas (1913-1993), and Tracy Kidder (1945-).

Wolfe, Tom (1931-), American essayist, journalist, critic, and novelist.

An important figure in the development of New Journalism, Wolfe was among the first not only to practice this innovative technique but to articulate its characteristics. Through his imaginatively written, lively essays on a wide variety of topics, Wolfe has proven himself an astute commentator on contemporary society.

After earning a Ph.D. in American Studies at Yale University, Wolfe began working as a newspaper reporter. His first experiments with language more creative than that normally used by journalists were made in pieces he wrote for the *New York Herald Tribune*'s Sunday magazine. In 1963, Wolfe was assigned to cover a customized car and hot rod show for *Esquire* magazine. Frustrated by the inadequacy of standard reporting methods to convey the garishness of his topic, Wolfe sent his editor the notes he'd made, which comprised a collection of random thoughts and observations as well as sequences of overheard dialogue. The resulting article, "Varoom! Varoom! There Goes That Kandy-Kolored Tangerine Flake Baby," published intact, helped to propel Wolfe to celebrity. It was later published in a 1965 volume that was influential in establishing New Journalism as a movement: *The Kandy-Kolored Tangerine-Flake Streamlined Baby* contains twenty-two essays on such topics as rich New York divorcees, disc jockeys, Las Vegas, and Cassius Clay. Although a few critics faulted Wolfe's style as shallow (most notably Dwight McDonald, who labeled it "parajournalism"), many others called it an exciting and insightful new form of nonfiction prose.

Wolfe continued his examination of American life and culture in subsequent volumes, including *The Pump House Gang* (1968)—in which he focused on the "alternative lifestyles" he'd observed in California, New York, and London—and *The Electric Kool-Aid Acid Test* (1968), which vividly portrays the early 1960s drug culture dominated by such LSD-celebrating figures as Ken Kesey (1935-) and his followers, the Merry Pranksters. The controversial *Radical Chic and Mau-Mauing the Flak Catchers* (1970) contains two essays, the first satirizing wealthy liberals at a fundraising party for the Black Panthers, the second describing the process by which urban blacks posed as political militants in order to intimidate the government bureaucrats assigned to their communities. Wolfe articulated the tenets of the genre he had helped to create in his lengthy introduction to *The New Journalism* (1973), an anthology of representative pieces.

In *The Painted Word* (1975), Wolfe indicts the New York art world as shallow and dictatorial, and *From Bauhaus to Our House* (1981) similarly impugns contemporary architecture. Wolfe's most consistently praised work, THE RIGHT STUFF (1979), an exhaustively researched examination of the early years of the manned space program, won several major awards, and a film version of the book appeared in 1983. Wolfe has written a novel, *The Bonfire of the Vanities* (1987), in which he focuses on the chaotic nature of modern life from the perspective of a wealthy New Yorker whose involvement in a hit-and-run accident whose victim is a poor black teenager, leads to his downfall. His next novel, *A Man in Full* (1998), also revolves around an interracial crime in Atlanta in the 1990s.

The Right Stuff (1979).

Wolfe won the National Book Award and the National Book Critics Circle Award for *The Right Stuff*, a study of the manned space program that focuses on the seven Project Mercury astronauts—Scott Carpenter, Gordon Cooper, John Glenn, Gus Grissom, Wally Schirra, Alan Shepard, and Deke Slayton—as well as test pilot Chuck Yeager. Six years in the making (and loaded with meticulous detail and behind-the-scenes information), the book was praised for its extensive research and success in portraying the astronauts as fallible human beings rather than one-dimensional mythical figures.

Referring to the courage and technical skill demanded of the men he studied, Wolfe defines "the right stuff" as a combination of "stamina, guts, fast neural synapses and old-fashioned hell-raising." Wolfe shows how these astronauts—who were the first in the world to make orbital space flights—were used for propagandistic purposes in the competition between the United States and the Soviet Union to dominate not just terra firma but the reaches of space. They were presented to the public as super-straight, All-American role models, when in reality only John Glenn lived up that image. While exposing their weaknesses, Wolfe portrays the astronauts as possessing exceptional talent and bravado.

❧•❧

Further Reading

Anderson, Chris. *Style as Argument: Contemporary American Nonfiction.* Carbondale, Ill.: Southern Illinois University Press, 1987.

Connery, Thomas B., ed. *A Sourcebook of American Literary Journalism: Representative Writers in an Emerging Genre.* New York: Greenwood Press, 1992.

505

Hellmann, John. *Fables of Fact: The New Journalism as New Fiction.* Urbana, Ill.: University of Illinois Press, 1981.

Hollowell, John. *Fact and Fiction: The New Journalism and the Nonfiction Novel.* Chapel Hill, N.C.: University of North Carolina Press, 1977.

Johnson, Michael. *The New Journalism.* Lawrence, Kans.: University of Kansas Press, 1971.

Lounsberry, Barbara. *The Art of Fact: Contemporary Artists of Nonfiction.* New York: Greenwood Press, 1990.

Shomette, Doug, ed. *The Critical Response to Tom Wolfe.* Westport, Conn.: Greenwood Press, 1992.

Weber, Ronald, ed. *The Reporter as Artist: A Look at the New Journalism Controversy.* New York: Hastings House, 1974.

Wolfe, Tom, and Johnson, E. W., eds. *The New Journalism.* New York: Harper and Row, 1973.

Zavarzadeh, Mas'ud. *The Mythopoeic Reality: The Postwar American Nonfiction Novel.* Urbana, Ill.: University of Illinois Press, 1976.

NEW LEF. *See* LEFT FRONT OF THE ARTS

NEW LITERATURE GROUP (Edebeyat-i Cedide)
Turkey, 1896-1901

The publication of *Servet-i Fünun* (The Wealth of Science), a newspaper supplement in Istanbul under the editorship of the poet Tevfik Fikret (1867-1915), attracted many young Turkish writers from 1896 until Sultan Abdulhamid II (1842-1918) closed it down in 1901, because of work by Fikret and others written against the sultan in favor of Western social and aesthetic ideas. Writers who contributed to the journal and followed Fikret, such as poet Cenap Sehabettin (1870-1934), and novelists Halit Ziya Uşakligil (1866-1945) and Mehmed Rauf (1875-1931), were very interested in the work of Émile ZOLA and the AESTHETICISTS—which made up a notable avant-garde movement in England in the 1890s—and the French SYMBOLISTS of the nineteenth century. French literature in general was extremely popular in Turkey, which had been building a remarkable national library of translations of foreign work in all fields since the Tanzimat reforms, which began in 1839. Contemporaries, such as Ahmet Mithat (1844-1912), whose novels have been termed "didacticist," criticized what he considered their elitist "art for art's sake" approach. The New Literature Group experimented with verse and narrative forms, stretching and often breaking literary conventions which, at that time, still followed Arabic and Persian tradition (*see also DIWAN SCHOOL OF POETS*). They employed, however, Arabic and Persian vocabulary and rejected the use of colloquial language, a practice which came into serious conflict with the later rise of SOCIALIST REALISM in Turkey. Scholars consider Fikret a forerunner of Europeanized, Modernist Turkish literature, a trend which would be continued by the DAWN OF THE FUTURE group a decade later.

❖•❖
Further Reading

Halman, Talat Sait, ed. *Contemporary Turkish Literature: Fiction and Poetry*. Rutherford, N.J.:
Fairleigh Dickinson University Press, 1982.

Karpat, Kemal H. "Social Themes in Contemporary Turkish Literature." *The Middle East
Journal* 14, 1 (winter 1960): 29-44.

Menemencioğlu, Nermin. "Modern Turkish Poetry." *The Western Review* 23 (spring 1959):
199-223.

Stone, Frank A. *The Rub of Cultures in Modern Turkey: Literary Views of Education*.
Bloomington, Ind.: Indiana University, 1973.

NEW LITERATURE MOVEMENT
China, 1917-1937

The call for language reform in China generally dates from an essay written by HU SHIH (*see* MAY FOURTH MOVEMENT) that appeared in 1917, "WEN-HSÜEH KAI-LIAN CH'U-I." Although the movement would become more radical under the influence of others, Hu Shih believed that China's literary history had a long tradition of subsuming popular forms, which would make it both inevitable and logical that the then-current classical wen-yen style of written Chinese, which was notoriously difficult to learn and long the province of the country's elite, would eventually give way to use of the vernacular pai-hai (plain language) as a means of accepted literary expression. Further, he was among the first to explicitly recognize the dignity of pai-hai as a form of expression onto itself. Before this, use of vernacular Chinese had been limited to the semi-pornographic "Butterfly" fiction, which was somewhat akin to American Pulp Fiction.

Hu Shih's essay, which nowhere uses the terms "literary revolution," was published in *Hsin ch'ing-nien*, at the time edited by Ch'en Tu-hsiu (1879-1942), a dean of National Peking University where Hu Shih also was a professor. Ch'en Tu-hsiu , who would found the Chinese Communist Party in 1920, seized on the potential radical aspects of the essay and, along with other professors at National Peking University, began openly casting the movement in terms of a revolution, believing only a total transformation of Chinese society, effected in part by the literary revolution, would allow China to be able to deal adequately with growing foreign intervention in its affairs.

China at the time was suffering from a national crisis brought on by a series of international and domestic incidents. The Republican Revolution of 1912 had overthrown China's last emperor but had neither unified the country nor put an end to Western and Japanese exploitation that had intensified since China's humiliation during the Sino-Japanese War of 1895. Tensions came to a head when, in 1919, the Treaty of

Versailles ceded rights to what had been German-occupied territory in China's Shantung province to the Japanese. Student demonstrations against this broke out at the National Peking University on May 4, 1919, and quickly spread to other parts of the country. Numerous politically active pai-hai periodicals and literary societies sprung up soon after, validating the continued use of the vernacular as a movement. (Interestingly, many of those responsible for the literary revolution had studied in Japan and looked to that country as a model for the Westernization of their own.)

Played out against continued war between the Chinese Nationalists (Kuomintang), based in China's south, and the warlord governments of the north, the rift between liberal supporters of pai-hai, who believed the use of vernacular offered more opportunity for freedom of expression and the ability to express one's individuality, and the radicals, who viewed pai-hai as a revolutionary tool, continued to widen. Nationwide demonstrations in 1925 following a memorial for a Chinese worker shot by his Japanese foreman, during which police killed 12 demonstrators, was a watershed for the left. The continued inability of the Nationalists to resist Japanese aggression along with a violent anti-Communist purge of the Nationalists in 1927 pushed even more writers in this direction; however, the decade prior to the beginning of war with Japan in 1937 saw a number of literary figures begin producing mature work that did not put political ends above art.

Fiction, poetry, and drama were all influenced by the New Literature Movement. Important fiction included stories by LU HSÜN as well as *TZU-YEH* (1933; *Midnight*, 1957) by Mao Tun (1896-1981), *Chia* (1931; *The Family*, 1958) by Pa Chin (1904-), popular fiction by Shen Cong-wen (1903-), and *Water* (1933) by Shen's wife Ting Ling (1904-1986), an important writer of the Communist era (until she was denounced for her right-wing leanings in 1957) whose early work had a surprisingly FEMINIST tone. Also important to the movement was LAO SHÊ (*see* ALL-CHINA ANTI-AGGRESSION FEDERATION OF WRITERS AND ARTISTS), who spent 11 years in London and whose writing was influenced by Charles DICKENS (*see* REALISM, England). Although Lao Shê is known for the use of humor in many of his novels, a style usually wanting in writings of the New Literature Movement, his best-known book, *LO-TO HSIANG-TZU* (1938; *Rickshaw*, 1979; originally translated with an unapproved happy ending as *Rickshaw Boy*, 1945), is a tragedy that explores how an unsympathetic society can erase one's individuality. After the Sino-Japanese War (1937-45), the formerly apolitical writer turned to propagandist themes in his writings.

Significant poets included KUO MO-JO, who cofounded the influential CREATION SOCIETY literary association; Ai Ching (1910-), whose poems tend to Communist propaganda yet display the poet's interest in the French SYMBOLISTS; and the founders of the CRESCENT SOCIETY of Chinese poetry, Hsu Chih-mo (1896-1931) and Wen I-to

(1889-1946), both of whom sought to meld traditional Chinese themes with romantic Western ones, albeit in vastly different styles. Drama saw important works by T'ien Han (1898-1968), another founder of the Creation Society; Tsao Yu (1910-1996), who was perhaps the first to successfully bring Western methods to the Chinese theater in works such as *Lei-yü* (1934; *Thunder and Rain*, 1936); and Hung Shen (1894-1955), whose plays centered on rural life.

The Sino-Japanese war of 1937-45 and the Chinese civil war of 1945-49 effectively destroyed the New Literature Movement. After the Communists gained control of the country in 1949, a repudiation of many of the movement's writers began and publication of significant modern Chinese literature essentially ceased.

→•←

Lu Hsün (pseud. of Chou Shu-jên, 1881-1936)
Chinese short-story writer and critic.

Lu Hsün is universally acclaimed as the greatest modern Chinese writer. He explicitly chose to write, although trained in medicine, as a way to combat what he viewed as China's social ills. He was educated in Japan, where he absorbed that country's embrace of progressive Western ideas. Although best known for his fiction, he was an important essayist who, with his brother Chou Tso-jên (1885-1966?), founded the YÜ SSU literary society and magazine as a vehicle for the New Literature Movement. A believer in the movement's more liberal views, he was caustically criticized by the Communists until disillusionment with the Nationalist government led him to sympathize with the Communist movement in 1929. However, he never actually joined the party and actively sought to keep his fiction from degenerating into mere ideological ranting while continuing to criticize Chinese society in general. After his death, the Communists effectively coopted him as a literary figure while ignoring the aspects of his writing that might work to their detriment. He also produced poetry and, often with his brother, notable translations of Western writers.

"K'uang-jen jih-chi" (1918; "The Diary of a Madman," 1941).

Originally published in *Hsin ch'ing-nien*, "K'uang-jen jih-chi" is notable for being the first work written entirely in Chinese to use the Western short story form. Looking to Nikolai Gogol's (1809-1852) story, "Notes of a Madman" (1835), as his inspiration, Lu Hsün uses the title character's belief that everyone wants to kill and eat him to represent traditional Chinese society as inherently "cannibalistic" to one's spirit.

Ah Q cheng-chuan (1921; *The True Story of Ah Q*, 1926).

This is Lu Hsün's most famous story. It tells of the tribulations of Ah Q during the fall of China's last dynasty in 1912. Ah Q is a lower-class village bully of the weak in a town where most inhabitants are stronger, physically and economically. This results in a series of embarrassments that Ah Q faces by claiming spiritual victory despite his humiliations, a tendency which many readers believed to exist in China as a country.

⇛•⇚

Further Reading

Goldman, M., ed. *Modern Chinese Literature in the May Fourth Era*. Cambridge, Mass.: Harvard University Press, 1977.

Hsia, C.T. *A History of Modern Chinese Fiction*. New Haven, Conn.: Yale University Press, 1971.

Hsu, Kai-yu. *The Chinese Literary Scene: A Writer's Visit to the People's Republic*. New York: Vintage Books, 1975.

Liu, Wu-chi. "The Modern Period, 1900-1950." In *A History of Chinese Literature. With a Supplement on the Modern Period* by Herbert Allen Giles. New York: F. Ungar Publishing Company, 1967.

Průšek, Jaroslav, ed. *Studies in Modern Chinese Literature*. Berlin: Akademie-Verlag, 1964.

Shou-yi, Ch'en. *Chinese Literature: A Historical Introduction*. New York: Ronald Press Co., 1961.

Vohra, Ranbir. *Lao She and the Chinese Revolution*. Cambridge, Mass.: East Asian Research Center, Harvard University, 1974; distributed by Harvard University Press.

Widmer, Ellen, and David Der-wei Wang, eds. *From May Fourth to June Fourth: Fiction and Film in Twentieth-Century China*. Cambridge, Mass.: Harvard University Press, 1993.

NEW NOVEL (Nouveau Roman)
France, 1950s-1960s

The French New Novelists experimented with innovative narrative techniques in fiction, not as a cohesive group, but as individual stylists undertaking the common project of pushing fiction to new extremes. The New Novel movement is considered to have emerged with the 1953 publication of Alain ROBBE-GRILLET's *Les gommes* (*The Erasers*, 1954); then in 1956 came Michel BUTOR's *L'EMPLOI DU TEMPS* (*Passing Time*, 1960). The third major writer of the movement, Nathalie SARRAUTE, wrote a novel *TROPISMES* (*Tropisms*, 1963) published in 1939 and considered a prototype New Novel; it was reissued in 1957. Les Éditions de Minuit, a publishing company founded during World War II, published many of the New Novelists' novels. The magazine *Esprit* featured the New Novelists in its July-August 1958 issue.

No group manifesto or treatise was written but individual ones abounded: Robbe-Grillet's *Pour en nouveau roman* (1963; *For a New Novel,* 1966) contained essays which first began appearing in French periodicals around the mid-1950s. In "From Realism to Reality," he advocates the construction of, rather than the transcription of, reality. Sarraute's *L'Ère du soupçon* (1956; *The Age of Suspicion*, 1963) described the new focus of the New Novel of exploring the role of the first person pronoun. (By the

510

1960s most French New Novels were written in the first person.) Jean Ricardou (1932-), one of the movement's principal theorists, wrote *Problèmes du nouveau roman* (1967; Problems of the New Novel), *Pour une théorie du nouveau roman* (1971; For a Theory of the New Novel), and *Le nouveau roman* (1973; The New Novel). In the essay *Le Livre à venir* (1959) Maurice Blanchot (1907-) expresses his skepticism that literature can be defined and opposes attempts to categorize it.

The New Novelists each employed his or her own innovative techniques, but generally they experimented with plot and characterization to the point of diminishing them in favor of description. For this reason, the New Novel has also been referred to as the *anti-roman* (as Jean-Paul SARTRE [*see* EXISTENTIALISM] put it in the preface to Sarraute's *Portrait d'un inconnu* [1948; *Portrait of a Man Unknown*, 1958]), or the antinovel. Some have also called the movement the *école du regard,* "the school of sight," because the New Novelists' fiction is often a very visual literature, with a heavy focus on representing perception of physical objects, especially in Robbe-Grillet's novels.

Other characteristics and techniques of New Novels include: endeavors to represent the full range of human experience of time, such as the expansion and compression of time (in Claude Mauriac's [1914-] *L'agrandissement* [1963; The Enlargement], for example, the novel covers two minutes in time); skepticism regarding causal relations, occasioning deviations from traditional chronology; use of CUBIST and collage techniques; and peopling the novels with antihero protagonists, the authors themselves as characters, and characters who are not named or who are otherwise difficult to distinguish or recognize — as, for instance, in Sarraute's *Les fruits d'or* (1963; *The Golden Fruits*, 1964) and *Entre la vie et la mort* (1968; *Between Life and Death*, 1969). Such elements combine to create a narrative that is as much a puzzle as it is a novel, for which reason critics frequently compare New Novels to mystery or detective novels.

Like Jorge Luis BORGES (*see* MAGIC REALISM), the New Novelists proclaim through their work the "fictionality of fiction." The novels invite the reader to collaborate in the unfolding of the narrative, and conclusions are hard to come by. As one critic put it, the New Novelists' work "stressed the realities of representation instead of the representation of realities; or, as Jean Ricardou once argued, it focused on the adventures of writing rather than on the writing of adventures."

Robbe-Grillet eschews the idea that the novelist has a responsibility to society: "For us, literature is not a means of expression, but a search. And it does not even know for what it searches. . . . [But] we prefer our searches, our doubts, our contradictions, our joy of having yet invented something."

Often singled out as precursors are James JOYCE (*see* MODERNISM, England and Ireland), Franz KAFKA (*see* MODERNISM, Austria and Germany), and Marcel PROUST (*see* MODERNISM, France), Existentialists André Malraux (1901-1976) and Sartre, OULIPO member Raymond Queneau (1903-1976) with his *Exercices de style* (1947; *Exercises in Style*, 1958) and his novel *Le chiendent* (1933; *The Bark-Tree*, 1968), which can be considered the first circular/self-destructive New Novel, Raymond Roussel (1877-1933), and Georges Bernanos's (1888-1948) novel *Sous le soleil de Satan* (1926).

The New Novelists follow phenomenology, and Existentialism, though without Sartre's tenet of commitment. Sartre, however, approved of Sarraute's and Butor's fiction, and a little less strongly, Robbe-Grillet's.

Other writers and works associated with the New Novel movement include Samuel BECKETT (*see* THEATER OF THE ABSURD), whose novel *Molloy* (1951; *Molloy*, 1955) critics often cite as an early New Novel; Maurice Blanchot's novels *Aminabad* (1942), *Le dernier mot* (1947), *Les Très-Haut* (1948; *The Most High*, 1996), *Le ressassement éternal* (1951), and *Celui qui ne m'accompagnait pas* (1953; *The One Who Was Standing Apart from Me*, 1993); Marguerite Duras (1914-1996), who associated with the group but did not consider herself a member; Rayner Heppenstall (1911-1981); Claude Mauriac's novels *Le dîner en ville* (1959; The Dinner Party) and *La marquise sortit à cinq heures* (1961; The Marquise Went Out at Five); Claude Ollier's (1922-) novel *La mise en scène* (1959; The Staging); Robert Pinget's (1919-1997) novels *Graal flibuste* (1956; Filibustering Grail), *Baga* (1958; *Baga*, 1967), *Le fiston* (1959; Sonny), and *L'inquisitoire* (1962; The Inquisitor); Claude Simon's (1913-) novels *Le tricheur* (1946; The Trickster), *L'herbe* (1958; *The Grass*, 1960), *Le route des Flandres* (1960; *The Flanders Road*, 1961), *Histoire* (1967; *Histoire*, 1968), and *La bataille de Pharsale* (1969; *The Battle of Pharsalus*, 1971); Philippe Sollers (1936-), a founder in 1960 of *TEL QUEL*, a journal also associated with the New Novelists in the early 1960s; and Jean-Marie Le Clézio (1940-) and the novels *Le Procès-verbal* (1963; *The Interrogation*, 1964) and *Le Déluge* (1966), and short stories in *La Fièvre* (1965; *Fever*, 1966); and Jean Cayrol (1911-).

Conflict between some of the New Novelists regarding what fiction should do and be reached a turning point at the 1971 conference at Cerisy organized by Ricardou. By the 1980s the New Novelists had effectively departed from the work they had been doing in earlier decades. As early as the mid-1960s Robbe-Grillet was propounding the Nouveau Nouveau Roman, New New Novel, which further stretched narrative's relationship to reality. The *Tel Quel* writers also extended the New Novelists' experiments.

Some contend that the New Novel movement was to a significant degree a media creation, citing the publisher Minuet's interest in promoting its New Novelists. During the 1960s, Robbe-Grillet, Butor, and Sarraute enjoyed immense publicity and success. All three were invited to represent French writers at the 1964 conference of the European Community of Writers. Very generally speaking, French critics have not been as taken with the New Novelists as were American ones; Simone de BEAUVOIR (*see* EXISTEN-TIALISM and FEMINIST CRITICISM), for example, wrote that "one of the constants of that literature is boredom: it takes away from life its salt, its fire, its *élan* toward the future." To the extent that any of the above obtains, however, it remains difficult to argue that the New Novelists have not had a large impact on the art of Western fiction in the latter half of the twentieth century.

➽●❧

Butor, Michel (1926-), French novelist, critic, dramatist, and poet.

Born in northern France, Butor has lived and taught at universities in Egypt, Germany, Greece, the United States, England, and Switzerland. Representative New Novels include *Passage de Milan* (1954; Milan Passage), *L'emploi du temps* (1956; *Passing Time*, 1960), *La modification* (1957; *A Change of Heart*, 1959), and *Degrés* (1960; *Degrees*, 1966), but Butor went on to produce a remarkable variety of texts that are difficult to categorize: part theory, part criticism, part travel writing, part autobiographical prose — all seeking ways to, as he put it in an essay in *Répertoire I* (1960), "forc[e] the real to reveal itself."

L'emploi du temps (1956; *Passing Time*, 1960).

This novel, Butor's second, takes the form of a diary the protagonist Jacques Revel keeps as he endeavors to cope with life in a gloomy, industrial northern English city. The narrative employs labyrinths, a detective story, and biblical and mythological figures and tales as symbols, while the presentation of events in Revel's recent past are juxtaposed with the present he largely sacrifices in order to spend his time writing.

➽●❧

Robbe-Grillet, Alain (1922-)
Breton-born French novelist, critic, and screenplay writer.

Until 1955 Robbe-Grillet worked as an agronomist, researching fruits in Morocco, Martinique, Guinea, and Guadeloupe. That year he became an editor for the publisher Éditions de Minuit and fostered the publication of New Novels. Robbe-Grillet's works say little about the actual material environment and everything about the perceiver, forcing the reader's attention, for example, on the geometric linear surface of objects — in order to communicate their neutrality. His minute descriptions of inanimate objects owe something to Raymond Roussel's (1877-1933) novel *Locus Solus* (1914; *Locus Solus*, 1970). He rejects analysis as an authorial intrusion — his protagonists' inner states of mind are not analyzed but "objectified" in terms of what they see. These cinematic and photographic techniques appeared not only in his narratives, but led easily to his work writing such screenplays as *L'année dernière à Marienbad* (1961; *Last Year at Marienbad*, 1962) and directing such films as *L'immortelle* (1963; *The Immortal One*, 1971), *Trans-Europ-Express* (1966), and *Glissements progressifs du plaisir* (1974; Slow Slide into Pleasure). His New Novels include *Les gommes* (1953; *The Erasers*, 1964), *Le voyeur* (1955; *The Voyeur*, 1958), *LA JALOUSIE* (1957; *Jealousy*, 1959), and *Dans le Labyrinthe* (1959; *In the Labyrinth*, 1960).

A few years after the New Novel movement was underway, Robbe-Grillet propounded the Nouveau Nouveau Roman, New New Novel, represented by his novel *La maison de rendez-vous* (1965; *La Maison de Rendez-vous*, 1966). In a 1959 article, critic Bruce Morrissette describes a cartoon which apparently appeared in an unnamed magazine in order to "illustrate the uneasiness caused in certain literary quarters" by Robbe-Grillet's experiments. It "show[s] the Tree of Literature with numerous well-known Novelists and Critics clinging to its branches, while below, sawing away at the trunk, stands a smiling Robbe-Grillet."

La jalousie (1957; *Jealousy*, 1959).

Playing on the fact that the French word *jalousie* can mean both jealousy and window blind, Robbe-Grillet in this novel explores subjective and objective reality through the observations and perceptions of the narrator-husband, suspicious that his wife is unfaithful.

✦•✦

Sarraute, Nathalie (1900-)
Russian-born French novelist, critic, and dramatist.

Sarraute was born in Russia of Russian Jewish parents, but had been raised in Paris since the age of eight. There she escaped from German police during the Nazis' occupation of France. A practicing lawyer until 1940, Sarraute nonetheless had a lifelong interest in literature, writing her first book *Tropismes* in 1939 (*Tropisms*, 1963). Other novels include *Portrait d'un inconnu* (1948; *Portrait of a Man Unknown*, 1958), *Le Planétarium* (1959; *The Planetarium*, 1960), *Les fruits d'or* (1963; *The Golden Fruits*, 1964), *Entre la vie et la mort* (1968; *Between Life and Death*, 1969), and *Vous les entendez* (1972; *Do You Hear Them?*, 1973).

Tropismes (1939, 1957; *Tropisms*, 1963).

A collection of twenty-four brief sketches she termed "micro-dramas," *Tropismes* presents a series of interconnected characters and situations. Borrowing the term from biology where "tropism" is an organism's involuntary movement in response to external stimuli, in this work it signifies individual responses to and interactions with others. Sarraute's psychological focus is on a group of women living in a Paris apartment building. For its narrative innovations, particularly its representation of conversations, it was so admired as a model for the New Novel that Éditions de Minuit reissued it in 1957.

⤖•⤖

Further Reading

Babcock, Arthur E. *The New Novel in France: Theory and Practice of the* Nouveau Roman. New York: Twayne; London: Prentice Hall International, 1997.

Besser, Gretchen R. *Nathalie Sarraute*. Boston: Twayne Publishers, 1979.

Brewer, Maria Minich. *Claude Simon: Narrativities without Narrative*. Lincoln, Nebr.: University of Nebraska Press, 1995.

Britton, Celia. *Claude Simon*. London; New York: Longman, 1993.

————. *Claude Simon: Writing the Visible*. New York: Cambridge University Press, 1987.

————. *The Nouveau Roman: Fiction, Theory, and Politics*. New York: St. Martin's Press, 1992.

Cruickshank, John, ed. *The Novelist as Philosopher*. Oxford, England: Oxford University Press, 1962.

Duncan, Alastair. *Claude Simon: Adventures in Words*. Manchester, England: Manchester University Press, 1994; distributed by St. Martin's Press.

Duncan, Alastair, ed. *Claude Simon: New Directions: Collected Papers*. Edinburgh, Scotland: Scottish Academic Press, 1985.

Fletcher, John. *Alain Robbe-Grillet*. London: Methuen, 1983.

————. *Claude Simon and Fiction Now*. London: Calder and Boyars, 1975.

Heath, Stephen. *The Nouveau Roman: A Study in the Practice of Writing*. Philadelphia: Temple University Press, 1972.

Jefferson, Ann. *The Nouveau Roman and the Poetics of Fiction*. Cambridge, England: Cambridge University Press, 1980.

Jiménez-Fajardo, Salvador. *Claude Simon*. Boston: Twayne Publishers, 1975.

Kadish, Doris Y. *Practices of the New Novel in Claude Simon's* L'herbe *and* La route des Flandres. Fredericton, Canada: York Press, 1979.

Leki, Ilona. *Alain Robbe-Grillet*. Boston: Twayne Publishers, 1983.

Le Sage, Laurent. *The French New Novel*. University Park, Pa.: Pennsylvania State University Press, 1962.

Lindsay, Cecile. *Reflexivity and Revolution in the New Novel: Claude Ollier's Fictional Cycle*. Columbus, Ohio: Ohio State University Press, 1990.

Mauriac, Claude. *The New Literature*. New York: Braziller, 1959.

Mercier, V. *The New Novel from Queneau to Pinget*. New York: Farrar, Straus and Giroux, 1971.

Minogue, Valerie. *Nathalie Sarraute and the War of Words: A Study of Five Novels*. Edinburgh, Scotland: Edinburgh University Press, 1981.

Moore, Henry T. *French Literature Since World War II*. Carbondale, Ill.: Southern Illinois University Press, 1966.

Morrissette, Bruce. *The Novels of Robbe-Grillet*. Ithaca, N.Y.: Cornell University Press, 1975.

————. "The New Novel in France." *Chicago Review* 15, 3 (winter-spring 1962): 1.

Peyre, Henri. *French Novelists of Today*. New York: Oxford University Press, 1967.

Rahv, Betty T. *From Sartre to the New Novel*. Port Washington, N.Y.: Kennikat Press, 1974.

Ramsay, Raylene L. *The French New Autobiographies: Sarraute, Duras, and Robbe-Grillet*. Gainesville, Fla.: University Press of Florida, 1996.

Rosmarin, Léonard A. *Robert Pinget*. New York: Twayne Publishers, 1995.

Roudiez, Leon Samuel. *French Fiction Today: A New Direction*. New Brunswick, N.J.: Rutgers University Press, 1972.

Spencer, M. C. *Michel Butor*. New York: Twayne Publishers, 1974.

Stoltzfus, Ben Frank. *Alain Robbe-Grillet and the New French Novel*. Carbondale, Ill.: Southern Illinois University Press, 1961.

Sturrock, John. *The French New Novel: Claude Simon, Michel Butor, Alan Robbe-Grillet*. London: Oxford University Press, 1969.

Thompson, William, ed. *The Contemporary Novel in France*. Gainesville, Fla.: University Press of Florida, 1995.

Troiano, Maureen DiLonardo. *New Physics and the Modern French Novel: An Investigation of Interdisciplinary Discourse*. New York: P. Lang, 1995.

Watson-Williams, Helen. *The Novels of Nathalie Sarraute: Towards an Aesthetic*. Amsterdam: Rodopi, 1981.

Yale French Studies 24 (summer 1959).

NEW OBJECTIVITY (Neue Sachlichkeit)
Germany, 1920s

Neue Sachlichkeit was a critical term popular in Germany, particularly Berlin, during the 1920s, but did not refer to an organized movement or group of closely aligned writers. Art critic Gustav F. Hartlaub (1884-1963) used the phrase to describe the almost neonaturalistic art of such painters as Otto Dix (1891-1961) and Max Beckmann (1884-1950) and illustrator George Grosz (1893-1959), whose work was displayed at the 1925 exhibit at the Mannheim gallery, of which Hartlaub was then director. A popular 1928 song about die neue Sachlichkeit, "Es Liegt in der Luft" (There's Something in the Air), attests to the phrase's currency.

The term gained usage also to describe literature reacting against the excesses of EXPRESSIONISM, characterized by REALISM, earthiness, sobriety — some say a reversion to NATURALISM. Fiction, plays, even poetry were often attempts at precise reportage, eyewitness accounts with attention to functionalism, social commentary, and an almost surgical exactitude of representation. Such writers as Hans Carossa (1878-1956) and Ludwig Renn (pseud. of Arnold Friedrich Vieth von Golssenau, 1889-1979) employed the diary form, the former in his novel *Rumänisches Tagebuch*

(1924) dealing with his experiences as a doctor in World War I, the latter most notably in the successful novel *Krieg* (1928) in which a soldier reports on the war.

Other works representative of New Objectivity include the play *Die Verbrecher* (The Criminals; produced in 1928 by the DEUTSCHES THEATER) by Ferdinand Bruckner (Theodore Tagger, 1891-1958); the novel *Berlin Alexanderplatz* (1929) by Alfred Döblin (1878-1957), who later rejected New Objectivity in an essay "Der Bau des epischen Werks" (1928; The Structure of the Epic Work); the poem "Berlin in Figures" by Erich Kästner (1899-1974); and the novel *Der Streit um den Sergeanten Grischa* (1927) by Arnold Zweig (1887-1968).

Critics often cite Bertolt BRECHT (*see* EPIC THEATER) in connection with the movement, who, when his contract with the Deutsches Theater expired in 1925, began writing short prose pieces to earn a living, choosing to do so in New Objectivity style. Other artists whose work demonstrates New Objectivity tenets include poet and novelist Walter Bauer (1904-1976); novelist Hans Fallada (pseud. of Rudolf Ditzen, 1893-1947); fiction writer Anna Seghers (pseud. of Netty Radvanyi, 1900-1983); poet and prose writer Kurt Tucholsky (1890-1935); playwrights Marieluise Fleisser (Marieluise Hairdl, 1901-1974), Ödön von Horváth (1901-1938), and Carl Zuckmayer (1896-1977); reporter Egon Erwin Kisch (1885-1974); and Brecht colleagues composer Kurt Weill (1900-1950) and stage designer Erich Engel (1891-1966).

Many of the writers contributed to *Die Weltbühne* (1918-), a progressive cultural and political journal which was banned in Germany in 1933 when Hitler mandated that all literature serve the regime's purposes, but survived in, at various points, Paris, Zurich, and Prague, and the influence of New Objectivity remained evident in theater through the 1940s, though in exile.

❧•❦

Further Reading

Barton, Brigid S. *Otto Dix and Die neue Sachlichkeit, 1918-1925.* Ann Arbor, Mich.: UMI Research Press, 1981.

Lange, Victor. "Recollection and Recovery." In his *Modern German Literature, 1870-1940.* Port Washington, N.Y.: Kennikat Press, 1945.

Loffler, Fritz. *Otto Dix, Life and Works.* New York: Holmes & Meier, 1982.

McGreevy, Linda F. *The Life and Works of Otto Dix: German Critical Realist.* Ann Arbor, Mich.: UMI Research Press, 1981.

Taylor, Ronald. *Literature and Society in Germany 1918-1945.* Totowa, N.J.: Barnes & Noble Books, 1980.

Willett, John. *Art and Politics in the Weimar Period: The New Sobriety, 1917-1933.* New York: Pantheon Books, 1978.

517

NEW POETRY MOVEMENT (Nayī Kavitā)
India, 1930s-1960s

Poet, novelist, critic, and leading proponent of Nayī Kavitā, Saccidanada Ajñeya (pseud. S. H. Vatsyayana Agyeya, 1911-) was influenced by psychoanalytic theory (*see* FREUDIAN and JUNGIAN CRITICISM). He edited three anthologies: *Tār saptak* (1933), representing both poetry and aesthetic statements by the New Poets; *Dūsrā saptak* (1951); and *Tīsrā saptak* (1959). In a symposium paper published in 1959 Ajñeya described the prayogavādī, or experimentalist, trend as "a profound ethical concern, the quest for new values and searching examination of the basic sanctions or sources of value." This questioning—of aesthetic as well as social standards, of linguistic thought and issues relating to SEMIOTICS—was more the common denominator among the Nayī Kavitā writers, rather than adherence to any particular stylistic modes or advocacy of specific techniques or ideologies, though many were influenced by the PROGRESSIVE WRITERS' MOVEMENT. Writers associated with Nayī Kavitā include poet Bhārat Bhūṣaṇ Agravāl (1919-1975), poet and dramatist Dharmavīr Bhāratī (1926-), Nemichandra Jain (1917-), critic Prabhākar Mācwe (n.d.), Girijā Kumār Māthur (1919-), Naresh Mehtā (1922-), Bhavani Prasad Mishra (1913-), Gajānan Mādhav Muktibodh (1917-1964), Raghuvīr Sahāy (1929-), Sarveśvar Dayāl Saksenā (1927-), MARXIST critic Rām Bilās Sharmā (1912-), Kedārnāth Singh (1934-), and Samsher Bahādur Singh (1911-). Critic Namawar Singh (1927-) discusses tenets of experimentalism in prose (*see* NEW STORY MOVEMENT) and poetry in, respectively, *Kahānī: Naī Kahānī* (1966; Story: The New Story) and *Kavitāke Naye Pratimāna* (1968; The New Standards of Poetry), accounting for the Nayī Kavitā movement as being a calculated literary reaction against Chāyāvāda (*see* ROMANTICIST MOVEMENT).

❧•❦

Further Reading

Agarwal, Bhratbhooshan. *Dissections*. Translated by Vishnu Khare. Calcutta: P. Lal, 1983.

Ajñeya [Sachchidananda H. Vatsyayan]. "Hindi Literature." In *Contemporary Indian Literature: A Symposium*. New Delhi: Sahitya Akademi, 1959.

George, K. M., ed. *Comparative Indian Literature*. 2 vols. Trichur, India: Kerala Sahitya Akademi; Madras: Macmillan India, 1984-85.

Kulshreshtha, C.M. *T. S. Eliot and Modern Hindi Poetry: A Study of Four Major Poets*. New Delhi: Allied Publishers Private, 1982.

Misra, Vidyaniwas, ed. *Modern Hindi Poetry: An Anthology*. Bloomington, Ind.: Indiana University Press, 1965.

Nagendra, ed. *Literary Criticism in India*. Meerut, India: Sarita Prakashan, 1976.

Singh, Namwar. "Hindi [literature]." In *Indian Literature since Independence: A Symposium*. Edited by K. R. Srinivasa Iyengar. New Delhi: Sahitya Akademi, 1973.

NEW POETRY MOVEMENT
Korea, 1900s-1910s

The New Poetry Movement in Korea coincided with the birth of modern literature in that country. The seminal work of the movement was Ch'oe Nam-son's (1890-1957) "Hae esŏ pada ege" (1908; "From the Sea to the Children," 1964), a poem influenced by George Gordon, Lord Byron (1788-1824) which exemplifies the movement's dedication to importing Western literature and culture. Ch'oe edited *Sonyŏn* (1908-11; Children), Korea's first modern literary magazine.

❖•❖

Further Reading

Lee, Peter H. "Twentieth-Century Literature: Verse." In his *Korean Literature: Topics and Themes*. Tucson, Ariz.: University of Arizona Press for the Association for Asian Studies, 1965.

NEW POETRY SOCIETY (*Myōjō* Poets)
Japan, 1900s

The *Myōjō* (Morning Star) Poets, and their eponymous journal, were led by Yosano Tekkan (1873-1935), generally regarded as the founder of the modern tanka verse form. Yosano, and his second wife, Yosano Akiko (1876-1942), were among the most influential Japanese poets writing during the first decade of the twentieth century. Their verse typically combined a nostalgic yearning for the classical past with vigorous affirmations of their individuality, passion, and nationalism. Followers of the Yosanos included Kubota Utsubo (1877-1967), Takamura Kōtarō (1883-1956), and Mizuno Yōshū (1883-1947). However, the movement lacked cohesiveness and these and other writers soon departed. In addition, the accomplishments of the Yosanos were overshadowed by those of their chief rival, the NEGISHI TANKA SOCIETY, as well as by the independent experimentations of the best-known tanka poet of the era, Ishikawa Takuboku (1886-1912).

❖•❖

Further Reading

Keene, Donald. "Tekkan, Akiko, and the *Myōjō* Poets." In his *Dawn to the West: Japanese Literature in the Modern Era*. Vol. 2. New York: Holt, Rinehart & Winston, 1984.

NEW PSYCHOLOGIST SCHOOL (Shinshinrigaku-ha)
Japan, 1930s

Of the several small Japanese movements that European MODERNISM spawned during the 1920s and 1930s, one of the most significant—after the NEW SENSATIONALIST SCHOOL—was the New Psychologist School. Like most such movements, New Psychology preoccupied itself with fiction and how best to incorporate the stylistic techniques of a select group of Europeans into original Japanese works of art. New Psychology originated in Sigmund FREUD's theories of the unconscious mind and James JOYCE's (*see* MODERNISM, England and Ireland) similar reconstructions of human thought in his experimental masterpiece, *ULYSSES* (1922). In 1927, Itō Sei (1905-1970) began reading *Ulysses* in the original English. By 1930, he and two colleagues, Tsujino Hisanori (1909-1937) and Nagamatsu Sadamu (1904-), had undertaken the monumental task of translating Joyce's work. The serialized publication of Itō's version, as well as the concurrent appearance of Marcel PROUST's (*see* MODERNISM, France) works in translation, significantly shaped much of the new Japanese writing during the 1930s. However, Itō alone emerged as the most vigorous champion of New Psychology, proclaiming Joyce his master and adopting the STREAM-OF-CONSCIOUSNESS method and the interior monologue as essential elements of his art (*see* MODERNISM, England and Ireland).

In addition to his editorship of several small avant-garde magazines and his work as a literary critic, Itō published numerous fictional works evincing his struggles to perfect a style equal in beauty and import to that of his avowed master. While never matching in his stories or novels the creativity or depth found in Joyce's work, Itō is nonetheless remembered — apart from his distinction as a historian — as a major practitioner of Modernism, whose pioneering translation of *Ulysses,* one of the most important novels of the twentieth century, radically altered the way in which Japanese writers could begin to probe the psychology of their characters.

❖•❖

Further Reading

Keene, Donald. "Modernism and Foreign Influences." In his *Dawn to the West: Japanese Literature in the Modern Era.* New York: Holt, Rinehart & Winston, 1984.

Putzar, Edward. "Modernism and Tradition." In his *Japanese Literature: A Historical Outline.* Tucson, Ariz.: University of Arizona Press, 1973.

NEW SCHOOL OF ATHENS
Greece, 1880s-1900s

Influenced in part by SYMBOLIST and free verse techniques of the French Parnassians, the New School of Athens writers sought to reinvigorate Greek literature by turning away from romanticist and classicist impulses and striving to produce objective, descriptive poetry. Some involved themselves, through their works, in a linguistic revolt against the purist *katharevousa* Greek in favor of the demotic, or vernacular, Greek. Nikolaos Politis (1852-1921) was an important advocate of the latter. He collected folk

520

tales and songs in, for example, *Meletai peri tou viou kaites glosses Hellenikou laou* (1904; Traditions of the Greek People). Ioannis Psykharis (1854-1929) published what was described as a travel journal — *To taxidhi mou* (1888; My Journey) — which also had a great impact on furthering demotic usage.

Kostes Palamas (1859-1943) is widely considered the central poet of the school. His epic poems, *O dhodhekaloghos tou ghiftou* (1907; *The Twelve Words of the Gypsy*, 1964) and *I floghera toy vasilya* (1910; *The King's Flute*, 1967), display his knowledge in fields such as mythology, history, philosophy, and European literatures while espousing the importance of the use and richness of the demotic for a nationalistic poetic expression.

Other poets involved include Costas Crystallis (1868-1894), Yorghos Dhrossinis (1859-1949), Nikolaos Kambas (1857-1932), Miltiadis Malakasis (1869-1943), John (Ioannis) Polemis (1862-1925), and Yorghos Straittigis (1860-1938). Palamas and, to varying extents, other New School of Athens writers served as significant models for such younger writers as Ioannis Gryparis (1872-1942), Constantine Hatzopoulos (1871-1920), and Lambros Porfyras (1879-1932).

❧•❦

Further Reading

Doulis, T. "Ideological, Historical, and Cultural Background." In *Disaster and Fiction: Modern Greek Fiction and the Asia Minor Disaster of 1922*. Berkeley, Calif.: University of California Press, 1977.

Friar, Kimon. *Modern Greek Poetry*. New York: Simon & Schuster, 1973.

Lorentzatos, Zissimos. "The Lost Center." In *The Lost Center and Other Essays on Greek Poetry*. Edited by Kay Cicellis. Princeton, N.J.: Princeton University Press, 1980.

Maskaleris, Thanasis. "Palamas and World Literature." In *Modern Greek Writers*. Edited by Edmund Keeley and Peter Bien. Princeton, N.J.: Princeton University Press, 1972.

Robinson, C. "Greece in the Poetry of Costis Palamas." *Review of National Literatures* (fall 1974): 42-45.

Sherrard, Philip. "Costis Palamas." In *The Marble Threshing Floor: Studies in Modern Greek Poetry*. London: Valentine, Mitchell, 1956.

Trypanis, C. A. *Medieval and Modern Greek Poetry: An Anthology*. Oxford, England: Clarendon Press, 1951.

NEW SENSATIONALIST SCHOOL (Shinkankaku-ha)
Japan, 1920s

A transitory literary movement of the 1920s, the New Sensationalist School is remembered chiefly for its pioneering use of MODERNIST techniques in the short, prose poem-like fiction which it published during its five-year existence. The movement remains interesting to historians for its defiant counteraction of Japanese NATURALISM and its resistance to Proletarian Literature, another major branch of Japanese writing that became the predominant form by the end of the decade. The group consisted of Yokomitsu Riichi (1898-1947), Kawabata Yasunari (1899-1972), Kataoka Teppei (1894-1944), Nakagawa Yoichi (1897-?), and a few others. There was, however, little unity of intent among the members and the movement became largely associated with Yokomitsu alone. Through the journal *Bungei Jidai*, Yokomitsu popularized such causes as EXPRESSIONISM and DADA—European movements that had surfaced following World War I and exerted a sizeable influence on the New Sensationalists. His growing reputation as a sensual, occasionally decadent, writer was the result of his exposure to the French writers of the 1920s, among them Paul Morand (1888-1976), whose works, in their attention to an esoteric style at the expense of overt theme, seemed devoid of ethical substance.

Despite leaving no lasting works from this formative period in his career, and being overshadowed in later years by his friend Kawabata, Yokomitsu sustains recognition as an important stylist, whose movement, founded upon new techniques rather than political ideologies or self-conscious artistic exposure, greatly advanced literary experimentation in Japan.

Further Reading

Keene, Dennis. Introduction to *Love, and Other Stories* by Yokomitsu Riichi. Tokyo: Japan Foundation, 1974.

———. *Yokomitsu Riichi, Modernist*. New York: Columbia University Press, 1980.

Keene, Donald. "Modernism and Foreign Influences." In his *Dawn to the West: Japanese Literature in the Modern Era*. New York: Holt, Rinehart, & Winston, 1984.

Nakamura Mitsuo. "New Sense School." In his *Contemporary Japanese Fiction, 1926-1968.* Tokyo: Kokusai Bunka Shinkokai, 1969.

NEW SENSIBILITY MOVEMENT
Germany, 1970s-1980s

Also known as New Subjectivism, New Sensibility was a German movement that was most prominent during the 1970s and 1980s. Gabriele Wohmann (1932-), who was also an adherent of GROUP 47, typified the movement with short stories and novels devoid of social and political messages yet highly attuned to the psychological crises of the postmodern individual.

❖•❖
Further Reading

Copenhaver, Jane Louise. *Death as Background in the Novels of Gabriele Wohmann*. Master's thesis, University of Texas at Austin, 1977.

Demetz, Peter. *After the Fires: Recent Writing in the Germanies, Austria, and Switzerland*. San Diego: Harcourt Brace Jovanovich, 1986.

Morris-Farber, Nina. *Critical Reception of the Works of Gabriele Wohmann in West Germany, Switzerland, and Austria*. Thesis, New York University, 1979.

NEW STORY MOVEMENT (Nayī Kahāni)
India, 1950s-1960s

Television and short-story writer Kamaleshvar (1932-) and dramatist and prose writer Mohan Rakesh (1925-1972) edited the journal *Naī Kahāniān* which, in 1954, began highlighting essays on new short fiction and publishing short stories by writers dealing with lower middle and middle-class urban life in the newly independent Indian state. Straddling the ideological concerns of SOCIALIST REALISM and subjective experiential expression, novelists and short-story writers such as Mennū Bhandārī (1931-), Uṣā Priyamvada (1931-), Nirmal Varmā (1929-), and Rajendra Yādav (1929-) are the most prominent associated with the movement.

Critic Namawar Singh (1927-) discusses experimentalism in prose and poetry (*see also* NEW POETRY MOVEMENT, India) in, respectively, *Kahānī: Naī Kahānī* (1966; Story: The New Story) and *Kavitāke Naye Pratimāna* (1968; The New Standards of Poetry).

❖•❖
Further Reading

Enact 73-74 (1973) [special issue devoted to Rakesh].

George, K. M., ed. *Comparative Indian Literature*. 2 vols. Trichur, India: Kerala Sahitya Akademi; Madras: Macmillan India, 1984-85.

Journal of South Asian Literature 9, 2-3 (1973) and 14, 3-4 (1979) [special issues devoted to Rakesh].

Ratan, Jai, ed. *Contemporary Hindi Short Stories*. Calcutta: Writers Workshop, 1962.

Roadarmel, Gordon C. *The Theme of Alienation in the Modern Hindi Short Story*. Thesis, University of California at Berkeley, 1969.

Sinha, R. "Mohan Rakesh: A Visionary Short-Story Writer." *Indian Literature* 20, 1 (1978): 93-114.

Taneja, G. "Mohan Rakesh: The Story Teller." *Indian Literature* 17, 1-2 (1974): 104-11.

Williams, R. "*Jivan* and *Zindagi*: An Analysis of Mohan Rakesh's Short Story 'Savorless Sin'." *Journal of South Asian Literature* 13, 1-4 (1977-78): 39-43.

NEW TENDENCY SCHOOL
Japan, c. 1906-1910s

The New Tendency School was launched around 1906 by Kawahigashi Hekigotō (1873-1937), a disciple of Masaoka Shiki (1867-1902), as a response to the HOTOTOGISU SCHOOL of Takahama KYOSHI, with whom Hekigotō had developed severe theoretical differences regarding the future of the haiku form. Aligned with Japanese NATURALISM, the New Tendency School stressed bold experimentation, independence from topical and formal constraints, and, especially, the honest expression of individual experience. Ogiwara Seisensui (1884-1976), a chief follower of Hekigotō, eventually found even the New Tendency School's relatively modern approach to short-form poetry too restrictive and founded his own magazine, *Sōun*, in 1911. As Hekigotō's influence began to wane, Seisensui attracted a number of key disciples, including Ozaki Hōsai (1885-1926) and Taneda Santōka (1882-1940). By approximately 1915, the original movement had so divided itself as to become unrecognizable.

➜•◄

Further Reading

Taneda, Santōka. *Mountain Tasting: Zen Haiku*. Translated and introduced by John Stevens. New York: Weatherhill, 1980.

NEW TIDE. *See* MAY FOURTH MOVEMENT

NEW WAVE (Nouvelle Vague)
France, 1950s-1960s

A movement in French cinema that paralleled as well as helped inspire such avant-garde literary movements as the NEW NOVEL and DECONSTRUCTION, the New Wave began—according to one of its most successful directors, François Truffaut (1932-1984)—with Alain Resnais's (1922-) film *Nuit et Brouillard/Night and Fog, Toute la Mémoire du Monde* (1956). The directors of the New Wave, many of them former critics for *Cahiers du Cinéma*, were united primarily in their conviction that each cinematic work they produced should be completely controlled by the director alone. This concept, known as the auteur theory, revolutionized filmmaking both in and outside of France and launched the careers of several important directors, in addition to Resnais and Truffaut, including Claude Chabrol (1930-), Jean-Luc Godard (1930-), Louis Malle (1932-), and Roger Vadim (1928-). New Novelists Michel BUTOR, Alain ROBBE-GRILLET, and Nathalie SARRAUTE are among the writers of the literary counterestablishment who contributed to the New Wave movement, which flourished during the early 1960s.

❧•❦
Further Reading

Turk, Edward Baron. *Child of Paradise: Marcel Carné and the Golden Age of French Cinema*. Cambridge, Mass.: Harvard University Press, 1989.

NEW WAVE MOVEMENT
Iran, 1960s-1970s

The New Wave movement in Iran signifies a period during which a number of Iranian poets produced innovative writing, marked by experiments in form, subject matter, and style as well as the influence of the work of Nima Yushij (1895-1959), who was criticized by conservative, pro-monarchy writers and scholars for being political and even substandard. The poets associated with New Wave writing include Ahmad-Reza Ahmadi (1940-), Ahmad Shamlu (1925-), Forugh Farrokhzad (1935-1967), Nader Naderpour (1929-), Mehdi Akhavan Sales (1928-), Yadollah Ro'ya'i (1932-), and Siyavush Kasrai (1926-). The literary journal *Ferdowsi* was a prominent site for debates over the issue of poetry as a vehicle for social and political commitment. Of the New Wave poets, many critics consider the poetry of Farrokhzad important, in particular for its frank explorations of sexuality and its forceful depictions of the experience of being a woman in a conservative, patriarchal society. Shamlu is perhaps the leading figure in contemporary Iranian poetry, admired for his poetry's blend of lyricism and social concerns.

During the oppressive regime of Mohammad Reza Pahlavi (1919-1980), the socially informed poetry of New Wave poets was popular and influential among professionals, white-collar workers, and students but failed to reach many of Iran's poor, who ultimately backed the religious leadership of Ayatollah Khomeini (1900?-1989) and the Islamic Republican Party's coup of 1978-79. As a result, the influence of the literary contributions made by the New Wave poets—many of whom exiled themselves or went into hiding in response to the ascendancy of the new government—was likely to be stronger outside Iran.

❧•❦
Further Reading

The Literary Review: An International Journal of Contemporary Writing 18, 1 (fall 1974) [special issue on contemporary Persian literature].

Ricks, Thomas M., ed. *Critical Perspectives on Modern Persian Literature*. Washington, D.C.: Three Continents Press, 1984.

Yar-Shater, Ehsan. "The Modern Literary Idiom." In *Iran Faces the Seventies*. Edited by Ehsan Yar-Shater. New York: Praeger, 1971.

NEW WRITERS' CIRCLE (Pujangga Baru)
Indonesia, 1930s

Of crucial importance to the development of modern Indonesian literature, the New Writers' Circle, under the direction of Amir Hamzah (1911-1946) and Sutan Takdir Alisjahbana (1908-1994), replaced native traditions with those inherent in European literature. The movement also included Armijn Pané (1908-1970).

❖•❖
Further Reading

Nababan, Sri Utari S. *A Linguistic Analysis of the Poetry of Amir Hamzah and Chairil Anwar.* Doctoral thesis, Cornell University, 1966.
Noer, Deliar, ed. *Culture, Philosophy, and the Future: Essays in Honor of Sutan Takdir Alisjahbana on His 80th Birthday.* Jakarta, Indonesia: Dian Rakyat, 1988.
Udin, S. *Spectrum: Essays Presented to Sutan Takdir Alisjahbana on His Seventieth Birthday.* Jakarta, Indonesia: Dian Rakyat, 1978.
Yaapar, Md-Salleh Bin. *Mysticism and Poetry: A Hermeneutical Reading of the Poems of Amir Hamzah.* Doctoral thesis, Temple University, 1994.

NEW YORK GROUP
Latvian emigrés in the United States, 1950s-1960s

The Latvian New York Group, active during the 1950s and 1960s, consisted of several emigré writers who number among the most outstanding in modern Latvian literature. The two who have enjoyed the greatest reputations are Gunars Salins (1924-) and Linards Tauns (1922-1963).

❖•❖
Further Reading

Ezergailis, Inta. "The Intervention of Art in the Poetry of Gunars Salins." *Lituanus: Baltic States Quarterly of Arts & Sciences* 26, 3 (1980): 50-62.
Ivask, Astrid. "Gunars Salins: Poet of the Two Suns." *Books Abroad* 43 (1969): 55-58.
Johansons, A. "Latvian Literature in Exile." *Slavonic and East European Review* 30 (1952): 466-75.
Silbajoris, Rimvydas. "Poetic Text and Human Feeling in Gunars Salins and Henrikas Radauskas." *Journal of Baltic Studies* 13, 2 (1982): 91-97.

NEW YORK GROUP
Ukrainian emigrés in the United States, 1960s

The Ukrainian New York Group consisted of a young generation of emigré writers active during the 1960s. Members included Emma Andiyevska (1931-), Bohdan Boychuk (1927-), Bohdan Rubchak (1935-), and Yuriy Tarnawsky (1934-).

➤•➤
Further Reading

Boychuk, Bohdan. *Memories of Love: The Selected Poems of Bohdan Boychuk*. Edited by Mark
    Rudman. Translated by David Ignatow and Mark Rudman in collaboration with the author.
    Riverdale-on-Hudson, N.Y.: Sheep Meadow Press, 1989.

NEW YORK SCHOOL
United States, 1950s-1960s

Influenced by MODERNIST poets such as T. S. ELIOT, Gertrude STEIN, and Ezra
POUND, as well as by such French SURREALISTS as Jacques Prévert (1900-1977), the
New York School of poetry had its origin in the friendship between three Harvard
University students in the early 1950s. Leaving Cambridge for New York City, John
Ashbery (1927-), Kenneth Koch (1925-), and Frank O'Hara (1926-1966) were united
by their skeptical worldview and their conviction that verse should be open-ended,
without concrete definition. Influenced as much by the urban setting in which they
worked as by the city's avant-garde art scene—O'Hara was curator of the Museum of
Modern Art until his death in the mid-1960s, and all experimented with playwriting—
Ashbery, Koch, and O'Hara were joined by poets Barbara Guest (1920-), Ted Berrigan
(1934-1983), and James Schuyler (1923-1991) in their poetic assault on the brittle academic verse of the mid twentieth century.

Speaking of the loosely aligned "New York School," Koch once characterized its work
as "anti-traditional, opposed to certain heavy uses of irony and symbolism." Rather, a
formal experimentation with the timbre of words defined the movement's oeuvre, as
well as the lack of any overt "meaning." The abstraction that characterized contemporary New York City artists such as composer John Cage (1912-1992) and painters
Willem de Kooning (1904-1997) and Jackson Pollack (1912-1956) also colored the
works of Ashbery and Guest in particular. Self-revelation—the goal of Romanticism—no longer applied in their neo-Nietzschean view: rather, their verse celebrated
and reflected non-sense, uncertainty, and the discontinuity of modern life.

➤•➤
Further Reading

Bloom, Harold, ed. *John Ashbery*. New York: Chelsea House, 1985.
Gooch, Brad. *City Poet: The Life and Times of Frank O'Hara*. New York: Knopf, 1993; distrib-
    uted by Random House.
Lehman, David. *The Last Avant-Garde: The Making of the New York School of Poets*. New York:
    Doubleday, 1998.
Perloff, Marjorie. *Frank O'Hara: Poet among Painters*. New York: G. Braziller, 1977.

Schultz, Susan M., ed. *The Tribe of John Ashbery and Contemporary Poetry*. Tuscaloosa, Ala.: University of Alabama Press, 1995.

Shapiro, David. *John Ashbery: An Introduction to the Poetry*. New York: Columbia University Press, 1979.

NIETOS DEL '98. *See* GENERATION OF 1927

NIETZSCHE, Friedrich Wilhelm (1844-1900)
German philosopher and writer

A consummate prose stylist whose vast body of work almost resists classification, Friedrich Wilhelm Nietzsche was one of the most influential intellectuals of the past two centuries. Bringing a totally new viewpoint to the study of Western religion, morality, and social structures, Nietzsche's ideas regarding the origin and purpose of human values have since pervaded most intellectual arenas, including those of theology, philosophy, psychology, and literature. His influence has been paramount in the development of Existentialism and psychoanalysis: Sigmund FREUD was indebted to Nietzsche for the derivation of sublimation and repression, while the philosophers Martin Heidegger (1889-1976) and Jean-Paul SARTRE (*see* EXISTENTIALISM) acknowledge Nietzsche's influence in their formation of the Existentialist tenet that people act of their own volition in a world that has no ultimate purpose. In addition, literary deconstructionist Jacques DERRIDA (*see* DECONSTRUCTION) and French Marxist Michel Foucault (1926-1984) have both claimed Nietzsche as a significant influence. Thomas MANN (*see* MODERNISM, Austria and Germany), Ayn Rand (1905-1982), George Bernard SHAW (*see* EDWARDIAN LITERATURE), André Gide (*see NOUVELLE REVUE FRANÇAISE*), Hermann Hesse (1877-1962), William Butler YEATS (*see* ABBEY THEATER and MODERNISM, England and Ireland), and John Gardner (1933-1982) are but a few of his literary descendants; even the BEAT poets of the 1950s recognized a debt to Nietzsche in the formation of their apocalyptic vision.

Nietzsche was born in Röcken, in Prussian Saxony, the son of a Lutheran pastor who died when Friedrich was only four. At school he quickly demonstrated his brilliance — as well as his skepticism — graduating from private Protestant schools in 1864 and excelling in the study of both classical philology and theology at the Universities of Bonn and, later, Leipzig. He would graduate from Leipzig in 1869, without fulfilling the requirements for a degree in classical literature, but on the strength of his published writing alone.

Appointed professor of classical philology at the University of Basel on the strong recommendation of his professors — and despite the fact that he had completed neither his thesis nor required dissertation at Leipzig — then twenty-four-year-old Nietzsche became a Swiss citizen. He served as a medical orderly in the Franco-Prussian war of 1870, returning to his post at Basel a few months later in ill health. Two years later, he published his first book, *Die Geburt der Tragödie* (1872; *The Birth of Tragedy*, 1910, 1968). In this highly controversial work, he contrasted what he termed "Dionysian" and "Apollonian" aesthetical values — harmonious restraint versus passionate self-abandonment — and dedicated the volume to his good friend, composer Richard Wagner (1813-1883), whom Nietzsche considered to be the only valid successor to the pre-Socratic Greek tragedians. In this early period, during which Nietzsche also published four "meditations," he exhibited a Romantic attitude that acknowledged a debt to Arthur Schopenhauer (1788-1860), whose vision of heroic vitalism — the "will to power" — was, with the music of Wagner, a major influence on the young philosopher's early efforts to create new values for his age. He would repudiate *Die Geburt der Tragödie* in later years as "offensively Hegelian."

In 1878, after Wagner had completed the text of his opera *Parsifal,* Nietzsche withdrew both his praise and his friendship; he felt that *Parsifal*'s moralistic undertones were merely politically expedient; he found the composer's overt anti-Semitism objectionable; and he believed that Wagner's integrity had been subverted by "Christian influences" rooted, Nietzsche felt, in the corruption of an ennobling "aristocratic" morality. This rejection would also extend to the works of Schopenhauer; Nietzsche soon realigned his philosophical foundations with those of Voltaire (1694-1778), Goethe (1749-1832), and Socrates (470-399 B.C.). Works of this period, such as *Menschliches, Allzumenschliches* (2 vols., 1878; *Human, All Too Human*, 1909-11) and *Die fröhliche Wissenschaft* (1882; *The Gay Science*, 1974), embrace the reasoned, scientific perspective of enlightened French *philosophes,* continue to experiment with diverse literary genres, and begin to occupy themselves with the origins of conceptual "good" and "evil," a meditation that would increasingly become the philosopher's central focus.

By 1879 Nietzsche, now partially blind and in almost constant pain, was forced to resign from teaching; he received a small pension from the University of Basel and spent the next ten years at various health spas and resorts throughout Switzerland, France, and Italy, isolating himself from all but limited social contact and producing a stream of brilliant works. *Also Sprach Zarathustra* (*Thus Spake Zarathustra*, 1909, 1954), a narrative modeled on the Lutheran Bible and published in four parts in 1883 and 1885; *Zur Geneaologie der Moral* (1887; *On the Genealogy of Morals*, 1968), which outlines the way power figures in ideologies; and *Jenseits von Gut und Böse* (1886; *Beyond Good and Evil*, 1967) each reflect the philosopher's mature outlook. Ultimately three of his most influential texts, they were little read in their day. While it is difficult to pinpoint actual theories in these highly literary works, full of irony, metaphor, and illusion as they are, characteristic themes include a repudiation of any actual basis for democratic, Christian, or liberal ethics; the assertion that "God is dead"; the celebration of the *Übermensch* (Overman or Superman); and an extension of nihilism that Nietzsche termed "perspectivism."

Nietzsche grappled with the origin and purpose of moral values within human societies. Concluding that, despite the attempts of organized religion and philosophy, life has no idealized higher purpose, he maintained that the act of judging or evaluating actions, character, or events cannot be objective; such attempts at evaluation reflect subjectively on the judge rather than on the object under scrutiny. The outcome of such "perspectivism," as he termed it, is that no ideological perspective regarding existence can ever result in absolute, concrete knowledge of reality. Hence, all moral ideologies and religious codes are rendered invalid and obsolete due to the subjective basis of their foundation of knowledge. Rather, they exist as representations of what Nietzsche terms an "ascetic ideal." In Judeo-Christian theology, for example, the sufferings of mankind—especially the lower classes and the slave class—are made endurable by their portrayal as trials wrought by God; human life and death are therefore presumed to have greater cosmic significance than for any other earthly creature. Suffering becomes a basis for atonement, furthering the individual believer's sense of his or her ultimate importance in the cosmos. Along with Christianity's promise of a better afterlife, secular philosophies also attempted to transcend reality by promoting such concepts as the soul, duty, the importance of the intellectual sphere, and the search for "truth." All such concepts offer alternative realities, ways of escaping a life that is experientially unpleasant.

Nietzsche's mystical "eternal return of the same" or "eternal recurrence," which he outlines at length in *Also Sprach Zarathustra,* is an antithesis to such alternative realities embodied in Western notions of both time and history. Rather than adopting the Christian conceit that man has importance within the cosmos because of his unique relationship with God, Nietzsche stresses the importance of accepting and affirming, without resentment, the reality of one's existence as purposeless—that what has been is and will be, in an endless cycle. Central to this philosophy is the anti-Kantian concept of "nihilism"—that no objective basis for moral truth exists, and that existence is meaningless above and beyond itself. Believing his own age to be in a state of flux because of Western society's inability to accept what the Positivism of the nineteenth century had proven—that the basis of the code of moral absolutes had, in fact, collapsed and that "God is dead"—Nietzsche viewed the continued promotion of the Judeo-Christian ethic, as well as the rising nationalism endemic to late nineteenth-century Europe, as a desperate attempt to adopt surrogate idols.

The Nietzschean concept of the "Superman" derives from these nihilistic beliefs. Refusing to resort to intellectual self-deception, but instead fearlessly accepting a reality composed of the ceaseless repetition of the horrors of physical existence, the Superman would be unshackled by either nationalism or the concepts of "good" and "evil" promoted by moral and religious codes based in cruelty and self-denial. Guided instead by his acceptance of eternal recurrence and judging each action as independent of any moral or religious censure other than its direct effect, such a person could create and impose his own law, take full responsibility for controlling his own reality, and thus embody the life-affirming "will to power." Such a Superman, Nietzsche argues, would be as unlike modern man as modern man is from the primates.

Along with the concepts of "eternal recurrence," the "Superman," and the "will to power," Nietzsche's formulation of "perspectivism" has influenced many of his intellectual successors. Deconstructionism, in particular, owes a debt to Nietzsche's nihilistic viewpoint in its own efforts to cast doubt upon the Western metaphysical tradition. Through deconstructionist assertions that interpreting literary texts cannot be done because, at base, no single, objective meaning or "truth" exists, philosophers such as Jacques Derrida, Paul DE MAN (*see* YALE SCHOOL), and J. Hillis Miller (1928-) have built arguments on the foundations laid by Karl MARX, Freud, Heidegger, and Nietzsche. Parallels have been drawn between Nietzsche and Jacques LACAN (*see* FREUDIAN CRITICISM) on dream theory; with José Ortega y Gasset (1883-1955) on culture; with Ludwig Wittgenstein (1889-1951) on language. Foucault has cited Nietzsche's *Zur Geneaologie der Moral* as establishing a new historiography. Marxist theorists such as Georg LUKÁCS (*see* MARXIST CRITICISM) and Jürgen Habermas (1929-), while remarking against Nietzsche's condemnation of socialism, have, not surprisingly, employed his philosophy as a basis for their own philosophical rejection of organized religion.

The year 1888 would be the last year of Nietzsche's productivity as an intellectual: it witnessed the completion of *Der Fall Wagner* (1888; *The Case of Wagner*, 1968), a summary of his philosophy entitled *Die Götzen-Dammerung* (1889; *The Twilight of the Idols*, 1954), and the autobiography *Ecce Homo,* which would be withheld from publication by Nietzsche's sister, Elizabeth, until 1908. By 1889 Nietzsche had undergone a total mental and physical paralysis, later concluded to be the result of dormant tertiary syphilis. Collapsing in the middle of a street in Turin, Italy, in January of that year, he was put under the care of first his mother and then, after 1897, his sister in Weimar. He never fully recovered his sanity and died at Weimar in 1900.

Tragically, Nietzsche's philosophy fell into undeservedly ill-repute shortly after his death, and decades would pass before scholars would be able to reconstruct much of his work. His sister Elizabeth, married to a staunch anti-Semite and motivated by personal greed and her own Fascist beliefs, actively altered and even forged portions of her brother's texts in an effort to subvert his stance against nationalism and anti-Semitism. Her editorial handiwork resulted in 1901's *Der Wille zur Macht* (*The Will to Power*, 1967), a distorted interpretation of the philosopher's ideas that resurfaced in the 1930s as a propaganda tool of Germany's National Socialist Party. An additional perversion of the Nietzschean concept of the "will to power," *Also Sprach Zarathustra* was distributed to German combat troops during World War I.

❧•❧

Further Reading

de Man, Paul. *Allegories of Reading: Figural Language in Rousseau, Nietzsche, Rilke, and Proust*. New Haven, Conn.: Yale University Press, 1979.

Gillespie, Michael Allen, and Tracy B. Strong, eds. *Nietzsche's New Seas: Explorations in Philosophy, Aesthetics, and Politics*. Chicago: University of Chicago Press, 1988.

Hayman, Ronald. *Nietzsche: A Critical Life*. New York: Oxford University Press, 1980.

Heller, Eric. *The Importance of Nietzsche: Ten Essays*. Chicago: University of Chicago Press, 1988.

Hollingdale, R. J. *Nietzsche: The Man and His Philosophy*. London: Routledge & K. Paul, 1965.

Jacobs, Carol. *The Dissimulating Harmony: The Image of Interpretation in Nietzsche, Rilke, Artaud, and Benjamin*. Baltimore, Md.: Johns Hopkins University Press, 1978.

Jaspers, Karl. *Nietzsche: An Introduction to the Understanding of His Philosophical Activity*. Tucson, Ariz.: University of Arizona Press, 1965.

Kaufmann, Walter. *Nietzsche: Philosopher, Psychologist, Antichrist*. Princeton, N.J.: Princeton University Press, 1974.

Nehamas, Alexander. *Nietzsche, Life as Literature*. Cambridge, Mass.: Harvard University Press, 1985.

Reichert, H. W. *Friedrich Nietzsche's Impact on Modern German Literature: Five Essays*. Chapel Hill, N.C.: University of North Carolina Press, 1975.

Rickels, Laurence A., ed. *Looking after Nietzsche*. Albany, N.Y.: State University of New York Press, 1990.

Shapiro, Gary. *Nietzschean Narratives*. Bloomington, Ind.: Indiana University Press, 1989.

NINE POWERS GROUP (Devĕtsil)
Czechoslovakia, 1920s

A Czechoslovakian movement of the early 1920s, Devĕtsil was formed by Vítězslav Nezval (1900-1958) and Karel Teige (1900-1951), and attracted, among others, Jiří Wolker (1900-1924), whose ballad poetry displayed his desire for proletarian revolution as well as his youthful idealism and celebration of life. Devĕtsil grew out of a concern for producing proletarian literature, akin to SOCIALIST REALISM, in the wake of the Russian Revolution of 1917 and the founding of the Czech Communist Party in 1921. The informal assembly of writers, intellectuals, and revolutionaries that resulted helped form the basis of POETISM, a "pure poetry" (poetry for poetry's sake) movement with which Nezval and Teige were intimately involved.

❖•❖

Further Reading

French, A. *The Poets of Prague: Czech Poetry between the Wars*. London: Oxford University Press, 1969.

Novák, Arne. "Modern Literature." In his *Czech Literature*. Ann Arbor, Mich.: Michigan Slavic Publications, 1976.

Otruba, Mjomír, and Zdeněk Pešat, eds. *The Linden Tree: An Anthology of Czech and Slovak Literature, 1890-1960*. Prague: Artia, 1962.

Three Czech Poets: Vítězslav Nezval, Antonín Bartušek, Josef Hanzlík. Harmondsworth, England: Penguin Books, 1971.

Wellek, René. "Twenty Years of Czech Literature: 1918-1938." In his *Essays on Czech Literature*. The Hague: Mouton, 1963.

NITTIOTALISTER
Sweden, 1890s-1900s

A Swedish Neoromantic movement that was launched in the late 1880s and that flourished throughout the 1890s, Nittiotalister is perhaps best remembered for its revitalization of lyric poetry and its counteraction of pessimistic literary trends in European writing. Some of the most prominent Nineties writers were Gustaf Fröding (1860-1911), Carl Heidenstam (1859-1940), Erik Karlfeldt (1864-1931), and Selma Lagerlöf (1858-1940).

❖•❖

Further Reading

Austin, Paul Britten. *Gustaf Fröding (1860-1911): His Life and Poetry, a Short Biography*. Karlstad, Sweden: Föreningen Alsters herrgård, 1986.

Berendsohn, Walter A. *Selma Lagerlöf, Her Life and Work*. Adapted from the German by George F. Timpson. London: Ivor Nicholson & Watson, 1931; Garden City, N.Y.: Doubleday, Doran, 1932.

Borland, Harold Howie. *Nietzsche's Influence on Swedish Literature, With Special Reference to Strindberg, Ola Hansson, Heidenstam and Fröding*. Göteborg, Sweden: Elanders, 1956.

Delblanc, Sven. *Selma Lagerlöf*. Stockholm: Swedish Institute, 1986.

Edström, Vivi Blom. *Selma Lagerlöf*. Translated by Barbara Lide. Boston: Twayne, 1984.

Green, Brita. *Selma Lagerlöf: Herr Arnes Penningar*. Hull, England: Dept. of Scandinavian Studies, University of Hull, 1977.

Larsen, Hanna Astrup. *Selma Lagerlöf*. Garden City, N.Y.: Doubleday, Doran, 1936.

Maule, Harry E. *Selma Lagerlöf: The Woman, Her Work, Her Message, Including Liberal Quotation from Dr. Lagerlöf's Own Autobiographical Writings and from Some of Her Critics*. Garden City, N.Y.: Doubleday, Page, 1926.

533

Olson-Buckner, Elsa. *The Epic Tradition in Gösta Berlings Saga*. Brooklyn, N.Y.: T. Gaus, 1978.

Petré, Maja. *Selma Lagerlöf and Her Home at Mårbacka: A Chronicle in Pictures*. Stockholm: Bonnier, 1958.

St. Andrews, Bonnie. *Forbidden Fruit: On the Relationship Between Women and Knowledge in Doris Lessing, Selma Lagerlöf, Kate Chopin, Margaret Atwood*. Troy, N.Y.: Whitston, 1986.

Schoultz, Gösta von. *Mårbacka, Home of Selma Lagerlöf*. Sunne, Sweden: Mårbacka Foundation, 1958.

Vrieze, F. S. de. *Fact and Fiction in the Autobiographical Works of Selma Lagerlöf*. Stockholm: Almqvist & Wiksell, 1958.

Wivel, Henrik. *Selma Lagerlöf: Her Works of Life*. Minneapolis: Center for Nordic Studies, University of Minnesota, 1991.

NŌ or NOH DRAMA. *See* MODERN NŌ

NOIGANDRES. *See* CONCRETE POETRY

NONFICTION NOVEL. *See* NEW JOURNALISM

NOOR-EESTI. *See* YOUNG ESTONIA GROUP

NORTH AFRICA GROUP OF WRITERS
France, 1950s

The North Africa Group of Writers was a French movement of the 1950s. Led by the Algerian-born novelist, dramatist, and editor Emmanuel Roblès (1914-1995), the North Africa Group found its inspiration in the ideals of the French Resistance, of which Roblès and close friend Albert CAMUS (*see* EXISTENTIALISM) were a part. Specifically, Roblès applauded all literature and social action that promoted harmonious, egalitarian living.

❖•❖

Further Reading

Kilker, Marie J. Petrone. *The Theatre of Emmanuel Roblès, an American Introduction with a Checklist on Criticism and Production*. Thesis, Southern Illinois University, 1972.

O'Nan, Martha. *Emmanuel Roblès*. Brockport, N.Y.: Dept. of Foreign Languages, State University of New York, 1983.

Roblès, Emmanuel. *Three Plays*. Translated with an introduction by James A. Kilker; with a bibliography of the theater of Roblès by Marie J. Kilker. Carbondale, Ill.: Southern Illinois University Press, 1977.

NOUCENTISMO/NOVECENTISMO
Spain, 1900s-1930s

These two movements can be considered together, since they were both made up of Catalan writers, had similar creative aims, and were generally active at about the same time. Their manifesto, *La nacionalitat catalana,* was presented at the First Congress of the Catalan Language in 1906 by Carles Riva (1893-1959) and gave a name to the Noucentismos. The group that followed, Novecentismos, titled themselves after a work which had appeared in the journal *900,* which had been started to propagate FUTURIST trends; both names translate as "the spirit of the new century."

The Noucentismes aimed to revive the Catalan tongue and to promote a kind of MODERNIST humanism in work which would show attention to precision of form and meter in new poetic structure. Major participants were Jaime Agelet (1888-1981), Juan Arbó Sebastià (1902-), Josep Carner (1884-1971), who was noted for his grace, "lightness and style," Ventura Gassal (1893-1942), Gueran de Liost (1878-1933), Josep Sebastià Pons (1886-1942), Eugenio d'Ors y Rovira (1882-1954), Enric Prat de la Riba (1870-1917), and Joachim Ruyra (1858-1939), who was also a member of the REALIST movement.

Members of Novecentismo showed considerable Modernist inclination, specifically in the influences of EXPRESSIONISM, Futurism, and SURREALISM. Their tendency was to incorporate elements of these other groups in their work in order to remain open to any new concepts which would revitalize their own linguistic and literary traditions. Group members were Manuel Lenores Rivas (1878-1938), Gregorio Martínez Sierra (1881-1948), José Ortega y Gasset (1883-1955), Ramón Pérez de Ayala (1881-1962), Carles Riba Bracóns (1897-1959), Pedro Salinas (1892-1951), and Ramon Valle-Inclán (1866-1936). Some of these writers who were connected to other movements were Ortega y Gasset to EXISTENTIALISM and the GENERATIONS OF 1898 and 1927, de Ayala to Generation of 1898, Salinas to Generation of 1927 and to ULTRAISM, and Valle-Inclan to MODERNISMO and the Generation of 1898.

❧•❦

Further Reading

Ortega y Gasset, José. *The Dehumanization of Art, and, Notes on the Novel.* Princeton, N.J.: Princeton University Press, 1948.
Triadu, Joan, and Joan Gili, eds. *Anthology of Catalan Lyric Poetry.* Berkeley, Calif.: University of California Press, 1953.

NOUVEAU ROMAN. *See* NEW NOVEL

NOUVELLE REVUE FRANÇAISE
France, 1908-1943

As a journal which would enjoy lengthy repute, *La Nouvelle Revue Française* began as a monthly literary publication in 1909 at the instigation of the actor and director Jacques Copeau (1879-1949), the writer André GIDE (1869-1951), and the novelist and critic Jean Schlumberger (1877-1968). It was to give both name and focus to a group of young writers who were agreed that the influence of SYMBOLISM could no longer serve for artistic reflection of the MODERNIST impulse. The goal was twofold: these writers would retain what was best of the former French literary tradition (Gustave FLAU-BERT's [*see* REALISM, France] notion of "the absolute value of art" is one example), but would demand the absolute freedom for the artist from political or moral encumbrance and the adhering to what had come to be known as "fashionable" writing. Further, they would encourage modes of experimentation of all valid methods for creative expression which were then extant, as well as to seek out any new theories which showed promise.

The journal occasioned a renewal of interest in the work of Paul Claudel (1868-1955) and Paul Valéry (1871-1945). Claudel's mature work shows Modernist tendencies in his rejection of traditional form for a new one of his own, i.e., his experimentation which inculcated a belief that "the rhythm of the poem should follow that of the poet's breathing." Moreover, Valéry was now encouraged to continue his work again in 1912 by André Gide, after a long hiatus. The work of several as yet unknown writers was brought to public attention through publication, among whom were Roger Martin du Gard (1881-1958), François Mauriac (1885-1970), who would receive the Nobel Prize in 1952, Jean Girandoux (1882-1944), and Saint-John Perse (1887-1975). In addition to sponsoring the work of poetry and fiction writers, *Nouvelle Revue Française* encouraged interest in the dramatic efforts of promising writers whose plays were being presented and acclaimed at the new THÉÂTRE DU VIEUX-COLOMBIER, which opened at the instigation of Copeau and others in 1913 and which is said to have presided over "the renovation of French theater." Martin du Gard's *Jean Baron* (1913) and a number of Gide's dramas were presented there in the years following World War I.

Nouvelle Revue Française continued to maintain its influence as Modernism made itself forcefully felt among the French literati, until the German occupation of France during World War II. It was then taken over by the eccentric writer Pierre-Eugene Drieu La Rochelle (1893-1945), whose attempt to turn it into a pro-Nazi organ failed, after which it ceased publication until 1951 when a special edition to honor Gide was presented. In 1953, *Nouvelle Revue Française* resumed full publication and remained an active participant in French literary journalistic circles; at century's end it continued to appear monthly as one of the most prestigious influences on the Paris intellectual scene.

⇥•⇤

Gide, André (1869-1951), French critic, dramatist, essayist, and novelist.

Known for his prolific output in all primary genres of literature, Gide is also remembered as a controversial figure for his dichotomous vision. It combined, on the one hand, his violent reaction to his strict and prohibitive Protestant upbringing, and, on the other, an avid search for self-expression of personal spirituality, which gave him reputation in some circles as a moralist; his atheism, sensuality, and passion for complete freedom of all the senses were never completely reconciled with a religious ethic he was unable to negate. His "luminous intelligence" made him a leading figure in the Paris of the 1920s and was based in his demand for experimentation with literary form and his strong conviction that literature must be transformed, and freed from outworn traditions which hampered it. It has been generally agreed that his spirit was one of essential French Modernism.

Gide's early work shows a strong Symbolist influence and rather an adolescent search for self. As he matured, his attempts to free himself became apparent in *Paludes* (1896), and in his use of the ironic mode in *La Retour de l'enfant prodigue* (1907; *The Return of the Prodigal*, 1953). His novel, *La Porte étroite* (1909; *Strait Is the Gate*, 1924), his connection with *Nouvelle Revue Française*, and his association with the Paris avant-garde brought some public notice, but it was not until World War I and immediately afterward that his full reputation as "the foremost representative of the modern literature of introspection" was achieved. Themes of social and political disenchantment, revelation of the painful process of coming to terms with existence which foreshadowed the concepts of French EXISTENTIALISM, and a passionate desire for a literary credo which combined moral discipline with the unrestrained freedom of expression caused one critic to acclaim him a "literary giant who dominated his time." Some of his most convincing work is found in his *Journals 1899-1949* (1939, 1946, 1950; trans. 1953). Notable fiction includes *L'immoraliste* (1902; *The Immoralist*, 1930), *Les Caves du Vatican* (1914; *The Vatican Cellars,*1952), and *La Symphonie Pastorale* (1919; *The Pastoral Symphony*, 1931), this last considered important for psychological insight. His essay *Corydon* (1924; *Corydon*, 1950) is the defense and affirmation of his homosexuality and a novel published a year later, *Les Fauz Monnayeurs* (*The Counterfeiters,* 1927) describes the hypocrisy of adherence to convention; similar admonition is revealed in his prose drama, *Oedipe* (1931). He also translated works by Shakespeare and Joseph CONRAD (*see* MODERNISM, England and Ireland) and is noted for his essays which criticize the colonization of French Africa and which both admire and decry Communism in the Soviet Union. He was awarded the Nobel Prize in 1947.

Further Reading

Claudel, Paul. *Correspondance Paul Claudel—Jacques Rivière, 1907-1924*. Paris: Gallimard, 1984.

———. *Poetic Art*. Translated by Renee Spodheim. New York: Philosophical Library, 1948.

Cornick, Martyn. *Intellectuals in History: The Nouvelle Revue Française Under Jean Paulhan, 1925-1940*. Amsterdam; Atlanta, Ga.: Rodopi, 1995.

Gide, André. *André Gide—Paul Valéry Correspondence, 1898-1942*. Edited by Robert Mallet. Paris: Gallimard, 1955.

———. *The André Gide Reader*. Edited by David Littlejohn. New York: Knopf, 1971.

———. *Conversations with Andre Gide*. Translated by Michael Lebeck. New York: G. Braziller, 1965.

O'Brien, Justin, ed. *From the N.R.F.: An Image of the Twentieth Century from the Pages of the Nouvelle Revue Française*. New York: Farrar, Straus and Cudahy, 1958.

Vagianos, Sylvia Caides. *Paul Claudel and La Nouvelle Revue Française (1909-1918)*. Geneva: Droz, 1979.

NOUVELLE VAGUE. *See* NEW WAVE, France

NOVECENTISMO. *See* NOUCENTISMO/NOVECENTISMO

NOVÍSÍMOS
Spain, 1960s-1970s

Also known as "culturalismo," the Novísímos was a group of poets in Spain reacting against the SOCIALIST REALISM dominant since the 1940s, who were young adults during the counterculture movement and social unrest of the 1960s. The Ley de Prensa opened Spanish borders to Western popular culture and until the early 1970s, these poets attained prominence, basking in American camp, jazz, and Hollywood movies, and producing a metapoetry marked by intertextuality, allusions to marginal or little-known figures, and attempts to question and subvert the traditional culture. In much Novísímos poetry, one can find references to ads for consumer products, collages of pop images, comics, and dedications to the likes of the Rolling Stones, as in the collection of Leopoldo María Panero (1948- ; son of poet Leopoldo Panero [1909-1962]), *Así se fundó Carnaby Street* (1970). Some proponents, such as José María Álvarez (1942-) in, for example, his collection *Museo de cera* (1974; Wax Museum) and Guillermo Carnero (1947-), felt the poet's voice had value only in how it manipulates, thereby commenting on, what has been written before. They influenced a younger generation of poets and were the subject of a parodic poem, "Oda a los nuevos bardos" (Ode to the New Bards), by Angel González (1925-) in his collection *Palabra sobre palabra* (1986).

Other writers associated with the Novísímos trend include Manuel Vázquez Montalbán (1939-), Antonio Martínez Sarrión (1939-), Félix de Azúa (1944-), Pedro Gimferrer (1945-) and his volume *La muerte en Beverly Hills* (1967), Vicente Molina Foix (1946-), and Ana María Moix (1947-) in *Balades del dulce Jim* (c1969). José María Castellet edited an anthology, *Nueve novísimos poetas españoles* (1970), which was dedicated to Aretha Franklin and Julie Driscoll along with a nod to Mae West.

❖•❖

Further Reading

Cobb, Carl W. "Spanish Poetry since 1939." In his *Contemporary Spanish Poetry (1898-1963)*. Boston: Twayne Publishers, 1976.

Marson, Ellen Engelson. "Mae West, Superman and the Spanish Poets of the Seventies." In *Literature and Popular Culture in the Hispanic World: A Symposium*. Edited by Rose S. Minc. Gaithersburg, Md.: Hispamêerica, 1981.

Mayhew, Jonathan. "Postmodernism, Culturalism, Kitsch." In his *The Poetics of Self-Consciousness: Twentieth-Century Spanish Poetry*. Cranbury, N.J.: Associated University Presses, 1994.

NOVYI LEF. *See* LEFT FRONT OF THE ARTS

NUEVOS, LOS
Peru, 1960s

Los Nuevos consisted of an alliance of poets, including Julio Ortega (1942-), Antonio Cisneros (1942-), Rodolfo Hinostroza (1941-), and Mirko Lauer (1947-), who made their mark in Peruvian literature during the early and mid-1960s. Influenced in particular by the works of Ezra POUND (*see* MODERNISM, England and Ireland), the Los Nuevos group frequently addressed the Peruvian social climate in their poetry, which was first anthologized in *Los Nuevos* (1967). Los Nuevos was immediately succeeded by *ESTOS 13*.

❖•❖

Further Reading

Adler, Heidrun. "Julio Ortega's Peruvian Inferno." *Latin American Theatre Review* 15, 1 (fall 1981): 53-58.

Morris, Robert J. "The Theatre of Julio Ortega." *Latin American Theatre Review* 6, 1 (1972): 41-51.

NYUGAT GROUP
Hungary, 1908-1920s

The appearance of the first issue of the hugely influential literary magazine *Nyugat* (West) on January 1, 1908, ushered in the MODERNIST era in Hungarian literature.

539

The writers affiliated with *Nyugat* sought to foster the flow of western European aesthetic and cultural ideas to Hungary, such as SYMBOLISM, NATURALISM, impressionism, and the work of Friedrich NIETZSCHE and Henri BERGSON. Sometimes compared to the contemporary French periodical *NOUVELLE REVUE FRANÇAISE, Nyugat*'s key era of dominance was before the Communist uprising of 1918-19.

Nyugat's founders were Paul Ignotus (pseud. of Hugo Veigelsberg, 1869-1949), its first editor-in-chief, and Erno Osvát (1877-1929), an editor who rarely wrote, but made his mark by detecting talented writers to publish in the journal for about twenty years. He first published short-story writer, novelist, and dramatist Zsigmond Móricz (1879-1942), who in turn influenced the POPULIST writers prominent in the 1930s, fiction writer and humorist Frigyes Karinthy (1887-1938), and poet Arpád Tóth (1886-1928), among others. Some members' poems were published in *Holnap* (1908, 1909; Tomorrow), a two-volume anthology.

Among the most important literary figures who contributed to the journal was poet Endre Ady (1877-1919), who was greatly influenced by French Symbolism. Though he lived in Paris after 1903, he is considered the figurehead of the movement. Many critics consider Ady's third book of poetry, *Új versek* (1906; New Poems), to have inaugurated Modernism in Hungarian poetry. Poet Mihály Babits (1883-1941) became editor of the journal after Ignotus left and remained editor until his death. Poet and prose writer Deszo Kosztolányi (1885-1936), first chairman of Hungarian PEN (Poets, Playwrights, Editors, Essayists, and Novelists), helped invigorate Hungarian literature via his friendships with Thomas MANN (*see* MODERNISM, Austria and Germany) and Maxim GORKY (*see* SOCIALIST REALISM, Russia). Poet and novelist Margit Kaffka (1880-1918) was involved with *Nyugat* from its beginnings and wrote a novel based on the group—*Állomások* (1917; Stations). Initially she wrote poetry, but her prose, often dealing with the emancipation of women, has ensured her literary reputation. Kaffka's most highly regarded novel is *Színek és évek* (1912; Colors and Years). Short-story writer and novelist Sándor Bródy (1863-1924) was influenced by French Naturalism, in particular, by Émile ZOLA; he in turn influenced many *Nyugat* writers. Fiction writer Viktor Cholnoky (1868-1912) wrote stories on bizarre themes, blending the real and the supernatural. His brother László (1879-1929) wrote stories in a similar vein. Critic Aladár Schöpflin (1872-1950), on staff at Nyugat, wrote a renowned monograph on Ady: *Ady* (1934).

Ady and Móricz were the most important literary figures of the magazine's heyday and also used it as a forum for their radical leftist social ideology. Karinthy was influenced by H. G. Wells (1866-1946) and utopian literature, though his humorous parodic writings were very popular. Some members of the group, such as Babits, Kosztolányi, and

Tóth, translated W. B. YEATS (*see* ABBEY THEATER and MODERNISM, England and Ireland), Symbolists Émile Verhaeren (1855-1916), Paul VERLAINE, and Stefan George (1868-1933), as well as Oscar Wilde (1854-1900), Rainer Maria Rilke (1875-1926), George Gordon, Lord Byron (1788-1824), Edgar Allan Poe (1809-1849), Walt Whitman (1819-1892), and other Western writers.

Other writers who gathered around *Nyugat* were prose writer Géza Csáth (1887-1919), Kosztolányi's cousin; economist and literary critic Miksa Fenyo (1877-1972), coeditor of *Nyugat* with Osvát; poet and novelist Milán Füst (1888-1967); poet Oszkár Gellért (1882-1967), who later edited *Nyugat*; critic Albert Gyergyai (1893-1981), whose interest in French literature led him to translate French REALIST Gustave FLAUBERT and Marcel PROUST (*see* MODERNISM, France); financial sponsor and critic Lajos Hatvany (1880-1961); poet Gyula Juhász (1883-1937); poet Simon Kemény (1883-1945); poet Anna Lesznai (1885-1966); poet Erno Szép (1884-1953); fiction writer and dramatist Dezso Szomory (1869-1944); novelist Jeno J. Tersánszky (1888-1969); and novelist Gyula Török (1888-1918).

The fiction of Gyula Krúdy (1878-1933) was a forerunner of the Modernist STREAM-OF-CONSCIOUSNESS technique; another innovation of his was to break up linear narrative and traditional time structure. Though he was friends with Ady and contributed to the journal, however, Krúdy eschewed identification with any literary group or movement.

Critics have identified subsequent "generations" of writers associated with the journal or its traditions. The "second generation" of *Nyugat* writers were generally said to be more Populist-oriented; some of these included poet József Fodor (1898-1973), prose writer Sándor Márai (1900-1989), folk poet György Sárközi (1899-1945), and poet Lorinc Szabó (1900-1957). The "third generation" of *Nyugat* writers are sometimes referred to as "the essayists' generation." Though some were roughly the same age as the "second generation" writers, their work did not come to the fore until after the poets' dominance had run its course, while "third generation" poets tended to eschew the avant-garde for a return to classical rationalism. Some writers associated with this third generation include Transylvanian poet Jeno Dsida (1907-1938); critic Gábor Halász (1901-1945); poet Zoltán Jékely (1913-1982); poet László Kálnoky (1912-); poet Miklós Radnóti (1909-1944), who earlier in his career had opposed the tenets of *Nyugat*; poet György Rónay (1913-1978); essayist László Szabó (1905-); literary historian and novelist Antal Szerb (1901-1945), who wrote the influential *Magyar irodalomtörténet* (1934; The History of Hungarian Literature); poet István Vas (1910-); poet Sándor Weöres (1913-); and poet Gyozo Csorba (1916-).

During World War I, literary competition emerged via the avant-garde and antiwar literary journal *Ma* (*see* TODAY GROUP), edited by Lajos Kassák (1887-1967). After World

War I growing Populist concerns began to overshadow those of the more cosmopolitan focus of *Nyugat*. *Nyugat* died with Babits when in 1941 the government denied its license renewal application, though its legacy continued in the journal *Magyar csillag* (1941-44) led by Babits's protégé, Populist writer Gyula Illyés (1902-1983).

❖•❖

Further Reading

Czigány, Lorant. *The Oxford History of Hungarian Literature: From the Earliest Times to the Present*. Oxford, England: Clarendon Press, 1984.

Fenyo, Mario D. *Literature and Political Change: Budapest, 1908-1918*. Philadelphia: American Philosophical Society, 1987.

Karátson, André. "The Translation and Refraction of Symbolism: A Survey of the Hungarian Example." In *The Symbolist Movement in the Literature of European Languages*. Edited by Anna Balakian. Budapest: Akadémiai Kiadó, 1982.

Klaniczay, Tibor, ed. *A History of Hungarian Literature*. Budapest: Corvina, 1982.

Reményi, Joseph. *Hungarian Writers and Literature: Modern Novelists, Critics, and Poets*. New Brunswick, N.J.: Rutgers University Press, 1964.

O

OBERIU (Obedinenie Real'nogo Iskusstva/Association for Real Art) Russia, c. 1927-1930

The OBERIU, active from approximately 1927 to 1930, represented one of the latest manifestations of reactionary MODERNIST writing in Soviet Russia. Centered in Leningrad, the OBERIU actively repudiated SOCIALIST REALISM as well as art for art's sake and instead sought a middle ground in which critical and philosophical expression could be united with literary experimentation. Although they reflected many of the traits of DADA, EXPRESSIONISM, IMAGISM, FUTURISM, and SURREALISM, the OBERIU was nonetheless one of the most unique European literary groups of the postwar era. Vital to the life of OBERIU were the numerous gatherings it conducted, in which a mixture of skits, choral readings, poem recitations, lectures, music, and painted props comprised an evening's experimental performance. Underlying such activities was the presumption that new and startling associations of words, ideas, and objects were at the heart of intellectual and emotional growth. Konstantin Vaginov (1899-1934), Nikolay Zabolotsky (1903-1958), and a number of other writers and painters were among the OBERIU avant-garde. However, it was Daniil Kharms (1905-1942) and Alexandr Vvedensky (1904-1941) who not only orchestrated the group's events but also produced its most brilliant work. Both writers excelled at the fusion of black humor, social commentary, absurdist narrative, and a modified version of *zaum* — a special Futurist language of neologism and nonsense. Unfortunately, both writers suffered from severe censorship with the rise of Socialist Realism and the police state, so much so that much of their controversial writing remained unpublished and undiscovered until the 1960s. Since then, there has been a generally increasing interest in Kharms and Vvedensky's bold experiments, which immediately bring to mind those of such universally esteemed THEATER OF THE ABSURD innovators as Samuel BECKETT and Eugene IONESCO.

❖•❖
Further Reading

Anemone, Anthony Alfred. *Konstantin Vaginov and the Leningrad Avant-Garde, 1921-1934.* Doctoral thesis, University of California at Berkeley, 1985.

Björling, Fiona. Stolbcy *by Nikolaj Zabolockij: Analyses.* Stockholm: Almqvist & Wiksell, 1973.

Cornwell, Neil, ed. *Daniil Kharms and the Poetics of the Absurd: Essays and Materials.* New York: St. Martin's Press; London: Macmillan, 1991.

Demes, Georgette Helene. *Classical Structures and Themes in Nikolaj Zabolockij's* Triumph of Agriculture. Doctoral thesis, University of Pittsburgh, 1984.

Gibian, George, ed. *Russia's Lost Literature of the Absurd: Selected Works of Daniil Kharms and Alexander Vvedensky, a Literary Discovery.* Ithaca, N.Y.: Cornell University Press, 1971.

Goldstein, Darra. *Nikolai Zabolotsky: Play for Mortal Stakes.* Cambridge, England: Cambridge University Press, 1993.

————. *Nikolai Zabolotsky's Utopian Vision.* Washington, D.C.: Kennan Institute for Advanced Russian Studies, 1987.

Levin, Ilya Davidovich. *The Collision of Meanings: The Poetic Language of Daniil Kharms and Aleksandr Vvedenskii.* Doctoral thesis, University of Texas at Austin, 1986.

Milner-Gulland, R. R. "'Left Art' in Leningrad: The OBERIU Declaration." *Oxford Slavonic Papers* 3 (1970).

Nakhimovsky, Alice Stone. *Laughter in the Void: An Introduction to the Writings of Daniil Kharms and Alexander Vvedenskii.* Wien: Wiener Slawistischer Almanach, 1982.

Peters, James Franklin. *A Study of the Early Poetry of Nikolaj Zabolockij.* Doctoral thesis, University of Washington, 1974.

Roberts, Graham. *The Last Soviet Avant-Garde: OBERIU — Fact, Fiction, Metafiction.* Cambridge, England: Cambridge University Press, 1997.

Zabolotsky, Nikolay. *The Life of Zabolotsky.* Edited by R. R. Milner-Gulland. Translated by R. R. Milner-Gulland and C. G. Bearne. Cardiff, Wales: University of Wales Press, 1994.

OBJECTIVISM
Spain, 1950s

Informed by both Italian NEOREALISM and the French NEW NOVEL, writers who employed Objectivism as a narrative strategy sought to depict social ills in Spain without incurring the censorship of the Franco dictatorship. The most successful Objectivist fiction and drama presented ostensibly nonpolitical themes presented with a passive, cinematic distance. The major practitioners included novelists Ignacio Aldecoa (1925-1969), Rafael Sánchez Ferlosio (1927-), and Camilio José CELA (*see* TREMENDISMO), and the two most prominent dramatists in post-Civil War Spain — Antonio Buero Vallejo (1916-) and Alfonso Sastre (1926-), founder of the "Theater of Social Agitation." One critic remarks on the influence of Antoine's THÉÂTRE LIBRE in the latter.

Aldecoa's *Gran Sol* (1959; Grand Banks), Cela's *La colmena* (1951; *The Hive,* 1953), and Sánchez Ferlosio's *El Jarama* (1956; *The One Day of the Week,* 1962) are good examples of Objectivist novels, while Buero Vallejo's *Historia de una escalera* (1949; Story of a Staircase) and Sastre's *Escuadra hacia la muerte* (1953; *Condemned Squad,* 1961) represent the apex of Objectivist theater. The appearance of Luis Martín-Santos's (1924-1964) novel *Tiempo de silencio* (*Time of Silence,* 1964) in 1962, which played to the movement's most simplistic and dualistic tendencies, had the effect of jarring the Objectivists into seeking other modes of expression.

✦●✦

Further Reading

Schneider, Marshall J., and Irwin Stern, eds. *Modern Spanish and Portuguese Literatures.* New York: Continuum, 1988.

OBJECTIVISM
United States, 1930s

Although some commentators question whether Objectivism ever really existed as a distinct, cohesive literary movement, the term "objectivists" denotes a small group of American poets who shared some of the same convictions about poetry and who—perhaps more importantly—supported and promoted each other's work. The movement's mentors were the renowned MODERNIST poets Ezra POUND and William Carlos Williams (1883-1963), neither of whose achievements may be neatly classified under the category of Objectivism but each of whom influenced and contributed to it.

Objectivism refers not to the neutral viewpoint suggested in the word "objective" but to the idea of considering a poem an object—a distinct entity that may be appreciated for its own structural, aural, visual, and intellectual qualities rather than as a symbol of some other thing or emotion.

Objectivism was a direct descendent of IMAGISM, an artistic movement that arose around 1910 as a reaction against the pastoral sentimentality of the Georgian period. Led by English and American poets T. E. Hulme and Ezra Pound, Imagism called for the extremely precise presentation of individual images, as opposed to description loaded with adjectives. The movement was popularized by poet Amy LOWELL, which led Pound to turn away in scorn at what he termed the unmusical, sentimental "Amygists."

During the late 1920s, Pound was thrilled to discover a young poet named Louis Zukofsky, whose work exhibited the stylistic spareness and intellectual daring and rigor Pound valued and whom he recognized as a major talent. Pound published Zukofsky's first major work, "Poem Beginning 'The'" in *Exile*, the journal he edited. He also introduced Zukofsky to Williams, his friend and literary soulmate, and convinced Harriet Monroe, the influential editor of *Poetry* magazine, to publish Zukofsky's work. Pound even succeeded in convincing Monroe to invite Zukofsky to edit a special "Objectivist" issue of *Poetry*. The issue appeared in February of 1931 and featured the work of such writers as Robert McAlmon (1896-1956), George Oppen (1908-1984), Williams, Carl Rakosi (1903-), Basil Bunting (1900-1985), and Kenneth Rexroth (1905-1982). Just as Pound and Zukofsky had hoped, the issue stirred up a great deal of controversy, and many critics now feel that it signalled the presence of a true avant-garde in American literature.

Describing the Objectivist ethos in a 1961 letter to Mary Ellen Solt (1920-), George Oppen claimed that the group was "very much concerned with poetic form, and form not merely as texture, but as the shape that makes a poem possible to grasp . . . . 'Objectivist' meant, not an objective viewpoint, but to objectify the poem, to make the poem an object. Meant form." Inspired by Williams's credo of "No ideas but in things" and faithful to the Imagist reverence for clarity of detail, the Objectivists concentrated on the process of making the poem an object and on the visual and aural aspects of verse. At the same time, they managed to incorporate philosophical and political concerns as well as personal references into their work.

Shortly after the publication of the "Objectivist" issue of *Poetry*, Zukofsky and Williams began to discuss the idea of publishing an anthology of Objectivist poetry in homage to Pound. Following some false starts, *An "Objectivist" Anthology* was published in 1932 by the shortlived TO Publishers, under the direction of George Oppen and his wife Mary. This led to the founding of the Objectivist Press, established by Zukofsky and his friends (with financial contributions from Pound, Williams, and a number of other backers). This collaborative effort came about not so much because of a strong artistic alignment between the writers involved but because Depression-era editors, distrustful of anything avant-garde in such financially precarious times, almost always rejected their work, and they were beginning to despair of ever seeing it published.

The group's statement of purpose, written by Charles Reznikoff (1894-1976), is deliberately noncommittal about its artistic aims: "The Objectivist Press is an organization of writers who are publishing their own work and that of other writers whose work they think ought to be read." The Objectivist Press published only a few books, including Williams's *Collected Poems, 1921-1931* (which sold out), Oppen's *Discrete Series*, and Reznikoff's *Jerusalem the Golden* (all in 1934) before finally folding.

The leading Objectivist poet is undoubtedly Zukofsky, who never achieved widespread recognition during his lifetime but whose often difficult, sometimes controversial, but highly influential work some commentators rank on the same level as that of Pound and James JOYCE (*see* Modernism, England and Ireland). Zukofsky's crowning achievement is his long poem "A," which he began in 1928 and worked on for the next forty-eight years. The poem (segments of which appeared in print at various intervals before the finished work was published in 1978) is structured in 24 movements like a musical composition, and in fact reveals at every turn Zukofsky's deep love for and interest in music.

Another acclaimed poet classified as an Objectivist is George Oppen, whose work manifests his reverence for nature, his interest in relationships between individuals as well as between people and the world around them, and his constant self-questioning. In such volumes as *Discrete Series* (1934), *The Materials* (1962), and *Of Being Numerous* (1968), Oppen achieved an effective melding of philosophical concerns and the "intensity of vision" he had admired in the work of the Imagists. Charles Reznikoff's poems are rooted in the life of the city streets, reflecting his urban Jewish background. They tend to be short but full of sharply drawn, highly suggestive images and are characterized by an irregular but still musical meter. Reznikoff's publications include *By the Waters of the Manhattan* (1962), *By the Well of Living and Seeing* (1974), and *The Complete Poems* (1976 and 1978).

✤●✤

Zukofsky, Louis (1904-1978), American poet, translator, and editor.

Underappreciated for most of his career, Zukofsky is considered by many critics a major figure in twentieth-century American poetry. A leader of the shortlived, loosely aligned Objectivist movement during the 1930s, Zukofsky created a distinguished, innovative body of work that influenced such younger poets as Robert Creeley (1926-) and Robert Duncan (1919-1988).

Born to Russian immigrants in New York City, Zukofsky spoke only Yiddish at home and learned English from his playmates on the city streets. He was a precocious child whose early interest in poetry led him to begin writing it himself in his late teens, when he came under the influence of the Imagist poets, especially HILDA DOOLITTLE and Ezra Pound. In his own verse, Zukofsky applied Pound's concept of poetry as composed of sight, sound, intellection, and rhythm. He pared down his writing to draw attention to its individual elements — such as prepositions, conjunctions, and articles — and thus heighten the impact of each word.

Zukofsky's first important poem was "Poem Beginning 'The'" (1926), which featured a masterful use of irony, satire, and comedy as well as poignant passages about such topics as the lives of Zukofsky's parents in Russia. The poem was rejected by twenty-four editors before the acclaimed Modernist poet Ezra Pound accepted it for publication in his journal *Exile*. Pound immediately recognized Zukofsky's talent and established with him what would be a lifelong friendship and mentorship. Pound considered Zukofsky his successor and the natural leader of the group of like-minded poets who were starting to be known as "Objectivists" due to their predilection for making the poem itself an object rather than a symbolic representation of something else. Pound introduced Zukofsky to the important and innovative poet William Carlos Williams, whose work was an important influence on the Objectivist ethos.

In 1928, Zukofsky began writing a poem entitled "A" that he would work on over the next forty-eight years—publishing segments of it at various intervals—and that is now viewed as his greatest achievement. Structured like a musical composition in twenty-four movements, the poem manifests Zukofsky's deep interest and involvement in music (his wife was a composer and his son a concert pianist) as well as his desire to create fresh, immediate, and intellectually rigorous verse. "A" comprises a kind of journal recording both the poet's free-verse musings and his experiments with such formal devices as the sonnet. It interweaves personal, political, artistic, and even scientific themes and concerns, linking them through the recurring guiding presences of Bach and Shakespeare (who represent music and poetry) and pitting different disciplines (such as physics and philosophy) and languages (such as Hebrew and Latin) against each other. The poem was considered extremely avant-garde in format and subject matter at the time of its first appearance, although contemporary readers find it quite accessible.

To his own disappointment and that of his many admirers—comprised mainly of other poets—Zukofsky did not during his lifetime achieve the recognition that most literary commentators now believe he deserves. His published works include *"A"* (1978), *All: The Collected Poems* (1965 and 1966), and two volumes of literary criticism, *Bottom: On Shakespeare* (1963) and *Prepositions* (1967).

❧•❦

Further Reading

Breslin, James E. *William Carlos Williams, an American Artist*. New York: Oxford University Press, 1970.

Brinnin, John Malcolm. *William Carlos Williams*. Minneapolis: University of Minnesota Press, 1963.

Crozier, Andrew. "Inaugural and Valedictory: The Early Poetry of George Oppen." In *Modern American Poetry*. Edited by R.W. Butterfield. London: Vision Press, 1984.

Freeman, John, ed. *Not Comforts/But Vision: Essays on the Poetry of George Oppen*. Devon, England: Interim Press, 1985.

Heller, Michael. "The Objectivists: Some Discrete Speculations." *Ohio Review* 26 (1981): 85-95.

Heller, Michael, ed. *Carl Rakosi: Man and Poet*. Orono, Maine: National Poetry Foundation, University of Maine, 1993.

Perelman, Bob. *The Trouble with Genius: Reading Pound, Joyce, Stein, and Zukofsky*. Berkeley, Calif.: University of California Press, 1994.

Rieke, Alison. *The Senses of Nonsense*. Iowa City, Iowa: University of Iowa Press, 1992.

Sharp, Tom. "The 'Objectivists' Publications." *Sagetrieb* 3, 3 (winter 1984): 41-47.

Terrell, Carroll F., ed. *Louis Zukofsky, Man and Poet*. Orono, Maine: National Poetry Foundation, University of Maine, 1979.

Weaver, Mike. *William Carlos Williams: The American Background*. Cambridge, England: Cambridge University Press, 1971.

Zukofsky, Louis. "Comment." *Poetry* 37 (February 1931): 268-85.

OCTOBER GROUP (Oktyabr)
Russia, 1922-1928

The October group was founded in Russia in 1922, shortly after PROLETKULT was absorbed by the Soviet Ministry of Education. The Octobrists, affiliated with the SMITHY writers, published the literary journal *Na postu* (On-Guard), and later *Oktyabr*, in which they espoused nineteenth-century REALISM and neglected avant-garde attempts, a stance the government found very agreeable. Art was a vehicle for "social command" — according to Octobrist critic Georgy Lelevich (pseud. of Labory Kalmanson, 1901-1945), an "instrument for emotional infection, a means of organizing the reader's psyche in conformity with the interests of a given class." Representative literary works include Alexander Fadeyev's (1901-1956) *Razgrom* (1927; *The Rout*, 1955) and Yury Libedinsky's (1898-1959) *Rozhdeniye geroya* (1930; Birth of a Hero). October, in effect an instrument of the Party, mandated that literature reflect the interests of the proletariat. The group was often known as the Napostovtsky or Onguardists.

Members included Leopold Averbakh (1903-), Semyon Rodov (1893-1968), Alexander Bezymensky (1898-1973), Dmitry Furmanov (1891-1926), Illarion Vardin (n.d.), and Boris Volin (1886-1957). The Octobrists especially deplored the tenets of the PEREVAL group, though some members — Artym Vesyoly (1899-1939), Mikhail Golodnyi (1903-1948), Mikhail Svetlov (1903-1964), A. Yasnyi (n.d.) — left October to join Pereval.

October actively supported the development of proletarian literary groups all over the Soviet Union — VAPP (All-Union Association of Proletarian Writers), MAPP (Moscow Association of Proletarian Writers), LAPP (Leningrad Association of Proletarian Writers), etc., and, eventually, the incorporation of all the Russian groups into RAPP (Russian Association of Proletarian Writers) in 1928.

As VAPP's most dominant faction, October sought to impose party ideology on all writers in the Union; it so stridently asserted its dictates, and so alienated large numbers of

Russian writers, that the government subsumed all literary groups under a single Union of Writers which became the center of the production of Russian SOCIALIST REALISM. Averbakh, among others, was arrested in 1937 as an enemy of the Party.

❖●❖

Further Reading

Ermolaev, Herman. *Soviet Literary Theories 1917-1934: The Genesis of Socialist Realism*. Berkeley, Calif.: University of California Press, 1963.

Hingley, Ronald. "The Literary Profession: Movements and Theories." In his *Russian Writers and Soviet Society, 1917-1978*. New York: Random House, 1979.

Struve, Gleb. *Russian Literature under Lenin and Stalin, 1917-1953*. Norman, Okla.: University of Oklahoma Press, 1971.

Terras, Victor, ed. *Handbook of Russian Literature*. New Haven, Conn.: Yale University Press, 1985.

Weeks, Walter J. *Jurij Nikolaevic Libedinskij: A Preliminary Analysis of His Prose and Drama, 1920-1930*. Doctoral thesis, Brown University, 1971.

ODIN TEATRET. *See* THIRD THEATER

OFFICINA GROUP. *See* GROUP 63

ONDA. *See* WAVE

ONEIRIC MOVEMENT
Romania, 1960s

Launched by Leonid Dimov (1926-) during the 1960s, the Oneiric Movement renewed interest in SURREALISM through a combination of musicality, dream imagery, and irrationality in its creative work. Virgil Tanase (1940-) and Dumitru Tsepeneag (1936-) were other members of the movement.

❖●❖

Further Reading

Calinescu, Matei. "Romanian Literature: Dealing with the Totalitarian Legacy." *World Literature Today* 65, 2 (spring 1991): 244-48.

ONITSHA CHAPBOOKS
Nigeria, 1950s

Onitsha chapbooks, broken-English novellas of Nigerian city life, were a popular form of entertainment among the lower middle classes in southeastern Nigeria. The majority of these chapbooks were printed in the town of Onitsha. Cyprian Ekwenski (1921-) was the preeminent writer in the chapbook genre, which during the 1950s helped form the foundation of modern Nigerian literature.

❖•❖

Further Reading

Emenyonu, Ernest N. *Cyprian Ekwensi*. London: Evans Brothers, 1974.

Emenyonu, Ernest N., ed. *The Essential Ekwensi: A Literary Celebration of Cyprian Ekwensi's Sixty-Fifth Birthday*. Ibadan, Nigeria: Heineman Educational Books (Nigeria), 1987.

"Feature on Cyprian Ekwensi." *West Africa* 3844 (May 6-12, 1991): 697.

Greene, Michael Thomas. *Sons of the Fathers: Four Nigerian Writers*. Doctoral thesis, State University of New York at Buffalo, 1979.

Greenstein, Susan M. "Cyprian Ekwensi and Onitsha Market Literature." In *Essays on African Literature*. Edited by W. L. Ballard. Atlanta, Ga.: School of Arts and Sciences, Georgia State University, 1973.

OPOYAZ. *See* RUSSIAN FORMALISM

ORIENTE GROUP
Cuba, 1910s

This group of poets was influenced by MODERNISMO and experimented with free verse in Cuba during the 1910s. Regino Eladio Boti y Barreiro (1878-1958) published volumes of poetry, biography, and criticism. Sócrates Nolasco (1884-1980), born in the Dominican Republic, is known for his stories of rural life, oral narrative traditions and folklore, as in, for example, *Cuentos del sur* (1939; Stories of the South) and *Cuentos cimarrones* (1958; Wild Stories). And José Manuel Poveda (1888-1926) wrote poems, stories, and essays, as well as edited the journals *El Figaro, Heraldo de Cuba*, and *La Nación*. Poveda, especially, was interested in European trends, new and surprising word choices, and idiosyncratic expression (such as "our I above our selves").

❖•❖

Further Reading

"Boti, Regino." In *Dictionary of Twentieth-Century Cuban Literature*. Edited by Julio A. Martínez. New York: Greenwood Press, 1990.

ORIGENES GROUP
Cuba, 1944-1956

This was a group of poets who clustered around the journal *Origenes*, among others, and José Lezama Lima (1910-1976), the major figure involved in the journal. José Rodríguez Feo (1920-); Gastón Baquero Diego (1916-), who also founded the journal *Clavileño* in

1944; Cintio Vitier (1921-), who published an anthology of the *Origenes* members' poetry, *Lo cubano en la poesía* (1958); and Fina García Marruz (1923-) were poets and critics who contributed to the journal and, to some degree or another, agreed with its aim: to search for origins through language and poetry. Though each poet is unique, Lezama Lima's hermeticism seems to have set the tone for much of the poetry appearing in the journal: metaphysical, exploratory, reflective, TRANSCENDENTALIST.

⇒•⇐

Further Reading

Anderson Imbert, Enrique. *Spanish-American Literature: A History*. Detroit: Wayne State
    University Press, 1963.

ORPHEU GROUP
Portugal, 1910-1915

The *Orpheu* group took its name from the title of a short-lived journal, *Orpheu* (1915), whose founders sought to revitalize Portuguese literature by rejecting its traditional romanticism in favor of a more innovative, self-consciously esoteric approach. Although the group's members—who included the celebrated poet Fernando PESSOA (*see PRESENCA*); the versatile painter, playwright, and poet Jose de ALMADA-NEGREIROS; and poet Mario de SA-CARNEIRO—were viewed by many as lunatics at the time of *Orpheu's* publication, it is now generally acknowledged that their activities signalled the advent of MODERNISM in Portuguese literature.

Portugal's political and social atmosphere at the beginning of the twentieth century exerted an important influence on the formation of the *Orpheu* group. Three centuries had passed since the relatively short period of Portugal's glory as a leading force in the European exploration and conquest of various regions of the world, particularly Brazil and parts of Africa. Portugal's standing as a world power and its economic stability had declined drastically, and a decisive blow had been delivered in 1890 when England, Portugal's old ally, seized Portuguese territory in Africa to block construction of a strategic railroad that would have run the length of the continent. In 1910, Portugal's weak monarchy was replaced with an equally ineffective republic that sustained several dozen revolutions before, in 1926, a military dictatorship took over the reins of government.

For several centuries, the literature of this gloomy realm had been overlooked, if not repressed, and Antonio Salazar's (1889-1970) dictatorship (1932-68) ushered in a particularly bleak period of oppression and censorship. Nevertheless, in the earliest years of the Portuguese republic, a few writers' hopes for change and revitalization were rekindled. Their immediate antecedents were the intellectuals of the "Coimbra Group," also called the "Portuguese Generation of 1870." That date refers to the year in which writers Jose Maria Eca de Queiroz (1845-1900) and Antero de Quental (1842-1891) delivered a series of lectures criticizing the chauvinism and fatalistic bent of the Portuguese literary tradition and advocating the introduction of European influences. Considered one of Portugal's most accomplished nineteenth-century authors, Eca de Queiroz wrote novels of social analysis intended to jar his readers from lethargy and expose the failing of both the Portuguese government and the nation's complacent middle class.

Like these predecessors, the founders of the *Orpheu* group were impatient with their country's stodgy literary conventions. In addition, they were inspired by the desire for change and renewal that the 1910 revolution had sparked. Fernando Pessoa, for example, who had been born to Portuguese parents but raised in South Africa, had recently returned to Portugal and had begun writing for the first time in Portuguese rather than English. In his enthusiasm for his native language he foresaw a major expansion of literature in Portuguese, with himself as a driving force.

Despite these noble intentions, only two issues of *Orpheu* appeared before the journal — perhaps succumbing to the ridicule with which it was met — ceased publication. Its importance lies primarily in its crucial influence on the founders of another journal, *Presenca*, which would, a little over a decade later, further establish Modernism in Portuguese literature.

→•←

Almada-Negreiros, Jose de (1893-1970)
Portuguese playwright, poet, and novelist.

A talented painter, dramatist, poet, and novelist, Almada-Negreiros was a cofounder of the influential journal *Orpheu* and perhaps the most outspoken member of the *Orpheu* group, expressing his disdain for the Portuguese bourgeouisie in highly vituperative language. The poems published in *A invencao do dia claro* (1921; The Invention of Clear Day) and the novel *Nome de guerra* (written 1925, published 1938; Psuedonym) manifest a rich, visually intense writing style that blends irony with sentimentalism and realism with intellectual abstraction and expressionism.

→•←

Sa-Carneiro, Mario de (1890-1916), Portuguese poet.

A leading figure among Portugal's early Modernists, a cofounder of the influential journal *Orpheu*, and a close friend of the renowned poet Fernando PESSOA, Sa-Carneiro wrote poetry marked by its affinity with the nineteenth-century French SYMBOLIST poet Arthur RIMBAUD. Although Sa-Carneiro employed essentially traditional poetic forms, his language was startlingly lush and inventive, and his work is said to mark a shift toward experimentation. The poems in his best-known volume, *Dispercao* (1914; Dispersion), evidence Sa-Carneiro's interest in the perennial struggle between coarse human nature and the yearning for spiritual transcendence. Infused with a strong sense of doom, desperation, and self-pity, this work chronicles the break-up of personality that culminated in Sa-Carneiro's suicide in Paris during World War I.

✦•✦

Further Reading

Campbell, Roy. *Portugal*. London: Max Reinhardt, 1957.

Faria, Almeida, Alberto de Lacerda, Vianna Moog, Jorge de Sena, and Robert D.Pring-Mill. *Studies in Modern Portuguese Literature*. Tulane Studies in Romance Languages and Literature, No. 4. New Orleans, La.: Tulane University, 1971.

Moser, G. "Portuguese Literature in Recent Years." *Modern Language Journal* 44 (1960): 245-54.

―――. "Portuguese Writers of This Century." *Hispania* 50 (1966): 947-54.

Schneider, Marshall J., and Irwin Stern, eds. *Modern Spanish and Portuguese Literatures*. New York: Continuum, 1988.

ORPHISM. *See* SIMULTANÉISME

OULIPO (Ouvroir de littérature potentielle/Workshop for Potential Literature)
France, 1960s-1990s

A group of ten writers and mathematicians founded the Ouvroir de Littérature Potentielle, or Oulipo, on November 24, 1960, at Cerisy-la-Salle, to be "a secret laboratory of literary structures," as founding member Albert-Marie Schmidt (1901-1966) put it. The Oulipo initially was a subcommittee of the Collège de Pataphysique, an organization devoted to the work of Alfred Jarry (1873-1907). Founded in 1948, the Collège de Pataphysique—which also counted among its members THEATER OF THE ABSURD proponents Eugène IONESCO and Boris Vian (1920-1959)—was named after Jarry's word for the "science des solutions imaginaires," the science of imaginary solutions.

Since its inception the Oulipo has dedicated itself to the discovery of new structures and forms for literary works as well as the rediscovery of old forms, such as the lipogram, for example, a text composed without using a given letter or letters of the alphabet. The Oulipian project is not to be confused, however, with STRUCTURALISM, which is built upon linguistic theories on the structure of language. In a 1986 forward to Warren F. Motte, Jr.'s *Oulipo: A Primer of Potential Literature*, critic and founding member Noël Arnaud (1919-) remarked that "Aside from personal friendships . . . there were no relations between the Oulipo and the structuralists; the latter, moreover, enveloped themselves in a ponderous sobriety that rendered them impervious to

Oulipian facetiae." (Arnaud, however, exempted his acquaintance Claude Lévi-Strauss [1908-] from this characterization.)

Schmidt wrote in 1963 that Oulipo "likes to think that it is preparing, with fear, laughter, gluttony, intoxication, and trembling, a future for French literature, a future brightened by substantific and medullary discoveries." One of the original Oulipian definitions of its enterprise was: "Oulipians: rats qui ont à construire le labyrinthe dont ils se proposent de sortir" (rats who must build the labyrinth from which they propose to escape).

The Oulipo adamantly holds that writing should be guided by craft and formal limitations, not inspiration. François Le Lionnais (1901-1984), another original member, wrote that "Oulipo's goal is to discover new structures and to furnish for each structure a small number of examples." And to do so in order to help future writers avoid dependence on inspiration. The group is particularly fascinated with mathematics and harvests a great number of its structural ideas from that discipline. The notion of a fundamental relationship between math and literature is an idea that goes back to Pythagoras and his contention that all music and poetics ultimately could be rendered in mathematical terms. According to Le Lionnais, mathematics "proposes thousands of possibilities for exploration, both algebraically (recourse to new laws of composition) and topologically (considerations of textual contiguity, openness and closure)." The mathematical specialty of combinatorics also serves as a fertile field for Oulipian discoveries. Of particularly strong influence has been Nicolas Bourbaki's *Eléments d'histoire de Mathématique* (1960; Bourbaki is the pseudonym for a group of French mathematicians who specialize in set theory).

Integral to their experimental project is the Oulipians' strong sense of being part of a tradition which they continue to evolve. Oulipians consider the "Grands Rhétoriqueurs" of the fifteenth and sixteenth centuries, such as François Villon (c.1431-c.1463), their literary ancestors, whose work Le Lionnais called "plagiarism by anticipation." The Oulipo is also interested in obscure writers (some of whom they dub "literary madmen") and literary curiosities as well as canonical literature. Some of the latter include François Rabelais (c.1490-1553), Laurence Sterne (1713-1768), and Raymond Roussel (1877-1933).

Oulipo Secretary, poet Jacques Bens (n.d.), published the minutes of Oulipo meetings from 1960 to 1963 in *Oulipo 1960-1963* (1980). At a 1961 meeting:

> Jean Queval intervened to ask if we are in favor of literary madmen. To this delicate question, F. Le Lionnais replied very subtly:
> —We are not against them, but the literary vocation interests us above all else.
> And R. Queneau stated precisely:
> —The only literature is voluntary literature.

While Oulipians consider it crucial that the writing of literature be voluntary — conscious and constrained by formal limitations — the driving force behind Oulipo is the pursuit of potential literature. Raymond Queneau (1903-1976), regarded by many as the most influential member, defines it thus: "The word 'potential' concerns the very nature of literature, that is, fundamentally it's less a question of literature strictly speaking than of supplying forms for the good use one can make of literature. We call potential literature the search for new forms and structures which may be used by writers in any way they see fit." He adds that "potential literature is that which doesn't yet exist."

According to Le Lionnais, the quest for potential literature falls into two categories—the analytic and the synthetic: "Analytic lipo seeks possibilities existing in the work of certain authors unbeknownst to them. Synthetic lipo constitutes the principal mission of the Oulipo; it's a question of opening new possibilities previously unknown to authors." In the "First Manifesto," Le Lionnais wrote, "The analytic tendency investigates works from the past in order to find possibilities that often exceed those their authors had anticipated. . . . The synthetic tendency . . . is a question of developing new possibilities unknown to our predecessors [such as Boolian haikus, which apply the theories of nineteenth-century mathematician George Boole]. . . . Anoulipism is devoted to discovery, Synthoulipism to invention. From one to the other there exist many subtle channels."

Jacques Bens compared the idea of potential literature with the *commedia dell-arte*, which did not achieve its potential until it was performed on stage. He also wrote that "a potential work is a work which is not limited to its appearances, which contains secret riches, which willingly lends itself to exploration." Along these lines, Queneau has remarked that "Mallarmé's sonnets are very high-grade material, like the fruit fly in genetics."

Queneau's book of poetry *Cent mille milliards de poèmes* (1961; One Hundred Thousand Billion Poems) is an outstanding example of potential literature. The collection contains only ten sonnets, but Queneau composed them so that the first line of each could replace the first line of the other nine sonnets, the second line of each could replace the second line of any of the rest, and so on. Thus the book literally contains 10^{14}, or 100,000 billion poems. What makes the work *potential* is that no one person could ever read every possible sonnet. Queneau calculated that it would take at least a million centuries to read all the possible combinations of sonnets even if one read a sonnet per minute, eight hours a day, two hundred days a year.

Jacques Roubaud (1932-) maintains that "a text written according to a constraint must speak of this constraint" and "a text written according to a mathematizable constraint must contain the consequences of the mathematical theory it illustrates." His autobiographical work *Le Grand Incendie de Londres* (1989) is constructed according to a model of mathematical branches; as a result, the text proceeds associatively rather than linearly.

Other notable examples of potential literature include *La Disparition* (1969; *A Void*, 1995) by Georges Perec (1936-1982), a lipogram taking the form of a novel written without using the letter "e"; *Se una notte d'inverno un viaggiatore* (1979; *If on a winter's night a traveler*, 1981) by Italo Calvino (1923-1985); *41 Sonnets irrationnels* (1965) by Jacques Bens; *ε* (1967) by Jacques Roubaud; *Zinga 8* (1967) by Jacques Duchateau (1929-); and *Poèmes Algol* (1968) by Noël Arnaud.

Initially, Oulipians wanted to limit their membership to ten, but then expanded to thirteen. By the mid-1980s, there were twenty-five. Members are still counted to be members after they die, thus the list of twenty-five includes, for example, Le Lionnais and Perec, who are deceased. Founding members were poet, novelist, and critic Raymond Queneau, chemical engineer and mathematician François Le Lionnais, literature professor Albert-Marie Schmidt, philosopher Latis (?-1973), Noël Arnaud (1919-), writer Jean Lescure (1912-), mathematician Claude Berge (n.d.), critic Jacques Duchateau, and poet, novelist, and critic Jean Queval (1913-). The newer members are historian Marcel Bénabou (n.d.), librarian, bibliographer, and publisher André Blavier (n.d.), computer scientist Paul Braffort (n.d.), fiction writer Italo Calvino, critic François Caradec (n.d.), French professor Ross Chambers (1932-), architect and writer Stanley Chapman (n.d.), painter Marcel Duchamp (1887-1968; *see also* DADA), mathematician and writer Luc Etienne (?-1984), critic Paul Fournel (1947-), poet and fiction writer Jacques Jouet (1947-), fiction writer Harry Mathews (1930-), poet Michèle Métail (n.d.), novelist Georges Perec, and poet and mathematician Jacques Roubaud.

A 1964 issue of *Temps Mêlés* focused on the Oulipo. That same year a Belgian radio station broadcast one of their meetings. The group published a collection of members' works in 1973, *La Littérature potentielle*; in 1981 another collection was published as *Atlas de littérature potentielle*. François Le Lionnais wrote two manifestos: *La Lipo* and *Le Second Manifeste,* both of which appear in *La Littérature potentielle*. A collection of Oulipian "applications" of discovered structures, or literary texts, was published in 1981, *La Bibliothèque Oulipienne.*

Some Oulipians have been pioneers in combining computer science and literary production. Paul Braffort heads the Atelier de Recherches et Techniques Avancées (A.R.T.A.; Workshop of Advanced Studies and Techniques) at the Centre Pompidou, a group seeking to employ computers in the Oulipian project.

The group held influence into the 1990s and inspired a number of web sites devoted to Oulipian and Oulipian-related literary activity. In addition, before his death in 1984, Le Lionnais organized the Oumupo for music, the Oulipopo for detective fiction, the Oupeinpo for painting, the Oucuipo for cooking, and the Oucinépo for film.

❧•❧

Further Reading

Birkerts, Sven. "House of Games" [review of Perec's *Life: A User's Manual*]. *The New Republic* (February 8, 1988): 38-40.
Ireland, Susan. "Jacques Roubaud." In *The Contemporary Novel in France.* Edited by William Thompson. Gainesville, Fla.: University Press of Florida, 1995.
Mathews, Harry. "That Ephemeral Thing" [review of Perec's *Life: A User's Manual*]. *New York Review of Books* 35, 10 (June 16, 1988): 34-37.
Motte, Warren F., trans. and ed. *Oulipo: A Primer of Potential Literature.* Lincoln, Nebr.: University of Nebraska Press, 1986.
Queneau, Raymond, ed. *Oulipo Laboratory: Texts from the Bibliothèque Oulipienne.* London: Atlas Press, 1995.
Roubaud, Jacques. "'What Have They Done to Us?' The Theory Monster and the Writer." In *Ideas from France: The Legacy of French Theory.* Edited by Lisa Appignanesi. London: Free Association Books, 1989.
Simon, Linda. "The Unspeakable Life of a Child" [review of Perec's *W or the Memory of Childhood*]. *New York Times Book Review* (January 8, 1989): 16.

OUR OWN THINGS. *See* WIE EEGIE SANIE

OUR SOIL GROUP. *See NAŠA NIVA* GROUP

OXFORD GROUP
Norway, 1930s

The relationship of Norwegian literature to the Oxford Group has no connection to the Church of England movement of the same name which began in the late nineteenth century, but rather from Norwegian writer Ronald FANGAN's interest in a movement begun by the American evangelist Frank Buchman (1878-1961), who later dropped the word "Oxford" and titled his organization Moral Rearmament. Buchman's claim was that he and his adherents would reestablish the biblical morality which could lead the universe out of chaos and into new enlightenment.

Fangan had been, in the Norway of the twenties, a major intellectual force in humane letters; he was known as a staunch Christian humanist in his fight against the evils of radicalism and the pessimistic, nihilistic attitudes which had been precipitated by the

Communistic sympathies in Norway between the two world wars. He founded the journal *Vor Verden* in about 1925, and it was based in a liberal-conservative manifesto with strong religious overtones. His ideas and his journal attracted many young writers of the time whose work reflects a concern with problems of ecclesiastic faith and a "deep commitment to self-knowledge and self-accusation." Generally speaking, Norwegian writers were traditionally slow to recognize modern literary forms and resistant to change from archaic modes. Most writers remained isolated and deeply conscious of the refuge of self-examination as a retreat from universal social problems. However, Fangan's brilliant and insightful talent placed him at the forefront of some of the MODERNIST, experimental writing of the time, since he was able to incorporate the ideas of such major modern thinkers as Alfred Adler (1870-1937), Sigmund FREUD, and Aldous Huxley (1894-1963) in his work.

Fangan, Ronald (1895-1946), Norwegian novelist, dramatist, and essayist.
Early plays written by Fangan were *Syndefald* (1920; The Fall), *Fienden* (1922; The Enemy), and *Den forjoettede* (1926; The Promised Day), in which the influence of August STRINDBERG (*see* EXPRESSIONISM, Germany) and Henrik IBSEN (*see* REALISM, Norway) can be seen and which gave him credibility as a rising young writer. Later explorations of Norwegian culture and mores led to the novels *Duel* (1932; *Duel*, 1934) and *En Kvinnes vei* (1933; A Woman's Way). After his conversion to Buchman's tenets, his writing became less introspective and more concerned with social morality; while his enthusiasm for the new moral strategy caused him to proselytize seriously enough to draw other writers into his circle, his early and vigorous intellectuality diminished noticeably. Later works include *På bar bunn* (1936; On Rock Bottom), *Allerede ne* (1937; Already Now), *Borgerfesten* (1939; Civic Festival), and his final novel, *En lysets engel* (1945; *Both Are My Cousins*, 1949), which is an indictment of the Nazi occupation and its effects in Norway.

Further Reading

Austin, H[enry] W[ilfred] "Bunny." *Frank Buchman as I Knew Him*. London: Grosvenor Books, 1975.

Bach, Giovanni. *The History of Scandinavian Literature*. Edited and translated by Frederika Blankner. New York: Dial Press, 1938.

Beyer, Harald. *A History of Norwegian Literature*. New York: New York University Press for the American-Scandinavian Foundation, 1956.

Buchman, Frank. *Remaking the World*. New York: R. M. McBride, 1949. New rev. ed., London: Blandford Press, 1961.

Ekman, Nils Gösta. *Experiment with God: Frank Buchman Reconsidered*. Translated by John Morrison. London: Hodder and Stoughton, 1972.

Frank Buchman, Eighty. By his friends. London: Blandford, 1958.

Govig, Stewart D. *Ronald Fangen and the Oxford Group Movement in Norway*. Doctoral thesis, New York University, 1966.

————. "Ronald Fangen: A Christian Humanist." *American Scandinavian Review* 49 (summer 1961): 152-59.

Howard, Peter. *Frank Buchman's Secret*. Garden City, N.Y.: Doubleday, 1961.

————. *That Man Frank Buchman*. London: Blandford Press, 1946.

————. *The World Rebuilt: The True Story of Frank Buchman and the Men and Women of Moral Re-Armament*. London: Blandford Press, 1951.

Jorgenson, Theodore. *History of Norwegian Literature*. New York: Macmillan, 1933.

Koht, Halvdan, and Sigmund Skard. *The Voice of Norway*. New York: AMS Press, 1967 [1944].

Lean, Garth. *On the Tail of a Comet: The Life of Frank Buchman*. Colorado Springs, Colo.: Helmers & Howard, 1988.

Marcel, Gabriel. *Fresh Hope for the World: Moral Re-Armament in Action*. Translated by Helen Hardinge. London: Longmans, 1960.

Mowat, R[obert] C[ase]. *The Message of Frank Buchman: A Study of Remaking the World*. Rev. ed. London: Blandford Press, 1953.

————. *Modern Prophetic Voices: From Kierkegaard to Buchman*. 2nd ed. Oxford, England: New Cherwell Press, 1994.

The Oxford Group Movement: A Careful Examination of Its Aims and Methods, Together with some Constructive Proposals. Reprint of four editorial articles from *The Life of Faith* (October 4, 11, 18, and 25, 1933). London: Marshall, Morgan, & Scott, 1933.

Spoerri, Theophil. *Dynamic out of Silence: Frank Buchman's Relevance Today*. Translated by John Morrison and Peter Thwaites. London: Grosvenor Books, 1976.

Veldt, Donald James. *Content Analysis Study of Frank Buchman's Published Speeches, with Emphasis on Criticism of Major Themes and Persuasive Tactics*. Thesis, Purdue University, 1969.

What Is the Oxford Group? New York: Oxford University Press, 1933.

Williamson, Geoffrey. *Inside Buchmanism: An Independent Inquiry into the Oxford Group Movement and Moral Re-Armament*. London: Watts, 1954.

P

PAI-HUA. *See* **MAY FOURTH MOVEMENT**

PARNASSIANISM. *See* **AESTHETICISM/DECADENCE; SYMBOLISM**

PAU BRASIL GROUP. *See* **MODERNISM, Brazil**

PEREVAL
Russia, 1920s

Pereval ("mountain pass" or "divide") was formed in Moscow in 1923 when some members of the OCTOBER and other literary groups—Mikhail Golodnyi (1903-1948), Mikhail Svetlov (1903-1964), Artym Vesyoly (1899-1939), and A. Yasnyi (n.d.)—broke away and gathered with other young writers from diverse backgrounds who had no previous group affiliation. The Pereval writers neither strongly adhered to Communist Party ideology nor denounced it—their emphasis was on cooperation and unity among the classes. Pereval identified itself as a peasant-worker group and consisted of many Party members who believed art should serve the people, but that writers should be free to write what and how they wanted.

Other members included poet Eduard Bagritsky (1895-1934), Andrey Platonov (1899-1951), Boris Guber (1903-1937), Valentina Dynnik (1898-?), S. Pakentreiger (n.d.). They met in the offices of the Circle publishing company, held readings of their work, published their work in *miscellanies*—eight in all—between 1924 and 1932, and engaged in public polemics with their rivals, LEFT FRONT OF THE ARTS and the October Group or the affiliated RAPP (Russian Association of Proletarian Writers). In 1929, some Pereval members left to join RAPP.

Alexandr Voronsky (1884-1943) edited the journal *Krasnaya Nov'* (Red Virgin Soil), which printed their manifesto in 1927; it was signed by 56 writers, including Dmitri

Gorbov (1894-?), Anna Karavaeva (1893-1979), Ivan Kataev (1902-1939), A. Lezhnev (pseud. of Abram Zelikovich Gorelik, 1893-1938), and Mikhail Prishvin (1873-1954). *Krasnaya Nov'* also published the works of Fellow Travelers, writers who neither belonged to the proletarian class nor subscribed to or propagated Party ideology. Voronsky didn't like the exclusivity and insularity of literary organizations and felt they impeded the development of individual talent. Without becoming a member himself, Voronsky finally sanctioned Pereval, however, because the fight against literary groups was a losing battle, and the members affiliated themselves closely with the aims of his journal.

Voronsky, Lezhnev, and Gorbov were the main theoreticians, and discussed their aesthetics in, respectively, *Iskusstvo kak poznanie zhizni I sovremennost* (1924; Art as Cognition of Life and the Contemporary Scene); *Sovremenniki* (1927; Contemporaries) and *Literaturnye budni* (1929; Literary Working Days); and *Poiski Galatei* (1929; In Search of Galatea) . They favored "organic realism." Inspired by the ideas of critic and journalist Vissarion Belinsky (1811-1848) and early MARXIST Georgy Plekhanov (1856-1918), organic realism conceived an artistic work as having an organic uniqueness "where elements of thought and feeling are recast esthetically." The artist's role is to use intuition and Realist techniques to present the "new truth of life." By the late 1920s, Pereval literature could be recognized for its lyricism, expression of universal emotional experiences, and peasant themes. Pereval criticism tended to privilege craftsmanship and exhuberence over ideological content.

By 1927, Pereval had an estimated membership of 250 writers, both in Moscow and in outlying areas. Pereval died out at the end of the 1920s. Along with all the other non-RAPP groups, the Party subsumed all literary groups under one Union of Socialist Writers in 1932, which would allow only literature that adhered to the tenets of SOCIALIST REALISM.

❖•❖

Further Reading

Brown, Edward J. *Russian Literature Since the Revolution*. New York: Collier, 1963. Rev. enl. ed., Cambridge, Mass.: Harvard University Press, 1982.

Glinka, Gleb. *Pereval: The Withering of Literary Spontaneity in the U.S.S.R.* New York: Research Program on the U.S.S.R., 1953.

Jordan, Marion. *Andrei Platonov*. Letchworth, England: Bradda Books, 1973.

Hingley, Ronald. "Movements and Theories." In his *Russian Writers and Soviet Society 1917-1978*. New York: Random House, 1979.

Maguire, Robert A. *Red Virgin Soil: Soviet Literature in the 1920s*. Princeton, N.J.: Princeton University Press, 1968.

Seifrid, Thomas. *Andrei Platonov: Uncertainties of Spirit*. Cambridge, England: Cambridge University Press, 1992.

Terras, Victor, ed. *Handbook of Russian Literature*. New Haven, Conn.: Yale University Press, 1985.

Teskey, Ayleen. *Platonov and Fyodorov: The Influence of Christian Philosophy on a Soviet Writer*. Amersham, England: Avebury, 1982.

PHENOMENOLOGY. *See* DECONSTRUCTION, EXISTENTIALISM, GENEVA SCHOOL, READER-RESPONSE CRITICISM, SEMIOTICS, STRUCTURALISM

PLÉIADE DU CONGO GROUP
Democratic Republic of Congo, 1964-1966

The independence from Belgian rule in the Democratic Republic of Congo led to an environment in which literary societies formed among the new Western educated class of Congolese people. French-speaking poet, linguist, and folklorist Clémentine Faik-Nzuji (1944-) led the Pléiade du Congo poetry group. From 1964 to 1966 she edited its journal, *Le Cahier de la Pléiade du Congo,* which provided a forum for many intellectuals. She has published volumes of poetry as well as folklore research such as her work on Luba proverbs, *Enigmes Luba, Nshinga* (1970).

⤙•⤚

Further Reading

Gérard, Albert S., and Lokangaka Losambe. "Congolese Literature: Democratic Republic of Congo." In *Encyclopedia of World Literature in the Twentieth Century*. 3rd ed. Edited by Steven R. Serafin. Farmington Hills, Mich.: St. James Press, 1999.

PLOUGH (Pluh)
Ukraine, 1920s

A Ukrainian movement of the 1920s, Plough was led by Serhiy Pylypenko (1891-1943), whose focus was to unite writers of the peasant class.

⤙•⤚

Further Reading

"Literature." In *Ukraine: A Concise Encyclopaedia*. Edited by Volodymyr Kubijovyc. Toronto: University of Toronto Press, 1963.

Luckyj, George S. N. "The Failed Revolution, 1917-32." In his *Ukrainian Literature in the Twentieth Century: A Reader's Guide*. Toronto: University of Toronto Press for the Shevchenko Scientific Society, 1992.

PLURALIST MOVEMENT
Dominican Republic, 1960s-1970s

Manuel Rueda (1921-) was a major proponent of literary pluralism in the Dominican Republic during the 1960s and 1970s. He advocated an eclectic approach to avant-garde expression, with attention to musicality and orthography. Rueda's poems in *Con el tambor de las islas* (1975) reflect his aesthetics as do essays such as Margarita Luna de Espaillat's (n.d.) "Conexiones de la música de vanguardia con el pluralism," contained in the same volume.

❧•❧

Further Reading

Alvarez-Altman, Grace. "Literary Onomastics Typology of Relevance to Ontology in 'The Miracle of Aunt Beatriz' by the Dominican Dramatist Manuel Rueda." *Literary Onomastics Studies* 9 (1982): 209-16.

POESIA 61. See POETRY 61 MOVEMENT

POESIA SORPRENDIDA, LA. See SURPRISED POETRY MOVEMENT

POETIC REALISM
Turkey, 1941-1950

Orhan Veli Kanik (1915-1950) was the leader of this small group of poets who published their work in a joint collection entitled *Garip* (Bizarre) in 1941, after their work had been appearing in *Varlik* (*see* SEVEN TORCHES) during the 1930s. Along with Melih Cevdet Anday (1915-) and Oktay Rifat (1914-), Kanik in the introduction to *Garip* declared the poetic manifesto of the group: "In order to be saved from the boring and suffocating influence of the literature which for long years had ruled our tastes and wills, shaping and molding them, we have to rid ourselves of everything which that literature has taught us." Their poetry, while not very popular when first published among the common man about and for whom it was written, excited the educated community and consummated the trend toward MODERNISM and away from tradition in Turkish literature.

During the 1940s Kanik, Anday, and Rifat wrote often ironic militant poetry directed toward both the urban and rural masses, employing slang and conversational syntax while focusing on themes of impoverishment, powerlessness, and political corruption. Thus, critics frequently refer to their work as Poetic Realism. They also published several issues of a literary periodical called *Yaprak* (The Leaf). The group lost its cohesiveness and impact after Kanik's premature death, but its influence on later poets remains substantial. After Kanik's death Anday continued to a large extent the group's tenets of SOCIALIST REALISM in his verse as well as incorporating mythological elements, while Rifat experimented with the SURREALIST and abstract poetic techniques associated with the SECOND NEW. While many followed the example set by the group — Bedri Rahmi Eyuboğlu (1908-1973), Orhon Murat Ariburnu (1918-), Nevzat Üstün (1924-1979), and Ceyhun Atuf Kansu (1919-1978)—others, such as the Second New, found in the *Garip*'s work something to strongly defy: REALISM.

❖•❖

Further Reading

Halman, Talat Sait, ed. *Contemporary Turkish Literature: Fiction and Poetry*. Rutherford, N.J.: Fairleigh Dickinson University Press, 1982.

Menemencioğlu, Nermin. "Modern Turkish Poetry." *The Western Review* 23 (spring 1959): 199-223.

Stone, Frank A. *The Rub of Cultures in Modern Turkey: Literary Views of Education*. Bloomington, Ind.: Indiana University, 1973.

POETISCHER REALISMUS. *See* REALISM, Austria, Germany, and Switzerland

POETISM
Czechoslovakia, 1920s-1930s

Poetism was formed around 1924 from writers associated with NINE POWERS GROUP (Devětsil) who felt that a more "pure poetry" should be developed in Czech literature. Poetism was characterized by poetry which aspired to be playful, non-cognitive, and dissociated from social purposes. Its focus was on sensuality and eroticism, fantasy and the fantastic — especially evident in the work of founder Vítězslaw Nezval (1900-1958). His friendship with Louis ARAGON, Paul ÉLUARD, and Philippe Soupault (1897-1990) fed the development of French SURREALISM, as well as Poetism; during these earlier years of his production, his work showed similarities to FUTURISM. Just as important as Nezval to Poetism was Karel Teige (1900-1951), who articulated its theoretical underpinnings and was also influenced by French literature.

As did several other writers, poet Konstantín Biebl (1898-1951) joined Poetism from Devětsil in the mid-1920s. Jaroslav Seifert (1901-1986) had begun his career with writing proletarian poetry but eventually saw Poetism as a positive movement for Czech literature and culture. Another proponent of Poetism was Josef Hora (1891-1945), a poet and novelist, who also had previously written proletarian novels and poetry characteristic of the Devětsil writers.

Other poets influenced by Poetism included František Halas (1901-1949), who strove in his poetry to overcome his own morbid, nihilist tendencies by creating a vision in which death and life are conflated and Vladimir Holan (1905-1980), who wrote subjective poetry exploring dreams, memory, and fairy tales. Novelist Vladislaw Vančura (1891-1942) produced novels in poetic prose exploring the nihilist, grotesque, and animalistic in contemporary Czechoslovakia, such as *Pekař Jan Marhoul* (1924; The Baker Marhoul) and *Pole orná a valečná* (1925; Fields of Work and War).

While Poetism as a movement was relatively shortlived—its members had struck out in various individual directions by 1930—its influence on future Czech literature and culture was substantial.

✥•✥

Further Reading

French, A. *The Poets of Prague: Czech Poetry between the Wars*. London: Oxford University Press, 1969.

Novák, Arne. "Modern Literature." In his *Czech Literature*. Ann Arbor, Mich.: Michigan Slavic Publications, 1976.

Otruba, Mjomír, and Zdeněk Pešat, eds. *The Linden Tree: An Anthology of Czech and Slovak Literature, 1890-1960*. Prague: Artia, 1962.

Three Czech Poets: Vítězslav Nezval, Antonín Bartušek, Josef Hanzlík. Harmondsworth, England: Penguin Books, 1971.

Wellek, René. "Twenty Years of Czech Literature: 1918-1938." In his *Essays on Czech Literature*. The Hague: Mouton, 1963.

POETRY 61 MOVEMENT (*Poesia 61*)
Portugal, 1961

Developing in reaction to CONCRETE POETRY, such as that of E. M. de Melo e Castro (1932-), *Poesia 61* was a journal that appeared five times in 1961; its contributors included poets Gastão Cruz (1941-), Luiza Neto Jorge (1939-), and Fiama Hasse Pais Brandão (1938-). Their aim, according to Cruz, was to explore "the issue of poetic realism and, essentially, the issue of the relationship between realism and the avant-garde." João Miguel Fernandes Jorge (1949-) is among the younger Portuguese poets influenced by the short-lived movement.

✥•✥

Further Reading

Martinho, Fernando J. B. "From Revolution to Apocalypse: Two Decades of Portuguese Poetry." In *After the Revolution: Twenty Years of Portuguese Literature, 1974-1994*. Edited by Helena Kaufman and Anna Klobucka. Lewisburg, Pa.: Bucknell University Press; London: Associated University Presses, 1998.

POETS' CLOISTER (Skit poetov)
Russian emigrés in Czechoslovakia, 1920s-1930s

A group of Russian emigré writers situated in Prague, the Poets' Cloister served as an important vehicle for traditional and MODERNIST Russian literature during the 1920s and 1930s. The driving force of the Cloister was Alfred Bem (1886-1945), a prominent scholar and editor whose literary reviews, and book-length studies of such figures as Russian SYMBOLIST Alexandr BLOK and Russian REALISTS Ivan TURGENEV, Leo TOLSTOY, and Fyodor DOSTOEVSKY, significantly enhanced the intellectual climate in Russia, Czechoslovakia, and other eastern European countries.

❖•❖

Further Reading

Bubenikova, Milusa, and Lenka Vachalovska. "The Unknown Heritage of a Russian Emigré in Czechoslovakia: A. Bem." *Litteraria Pragensia: Studies in Literature and Culture* 2, 4 (1992): 70-76.

POETS OF THE FORTIES (Fyrtiotalister)
Sweden, 1940s

A Swedish movement, the Poets of the Forties were marked by EXISTENTIAL pessimism and an aesthetics that valued erudition and stylistic depth. Primary influences for the Forties Poets included T. S. ELIOT (*see* MODERNISM, England and Ireland), Franz KAFKA (*see* Modernism, Austria and Germany), and the sociopolitical aftermath of World War II. Karl Vennberg (1910-) is generally considered the leader of the movement; others were Karl Werner Aspenström (1918-1997), Erik Lindegren (1910-1968), Stig Dagerman (1923-1954), Ragnar Thoursie (1919-), Sven Alfons (1918-), and Elsa Grave (1918-).

❖•❖

Further Reading

Algulin, Ingemar. *A History of Swedish Literature*. Stockholm: The Swedish Institute, 1989.
Aspenström, Werner. *The Blue Whale and Other Pieces*. Selected, introduced, and translated by Robin Fulton. London: Oasis Books, 1981.
———. *Thirty Seven Poems from Four Books*. Translated and introduced by Robin Fulton. London: Oasis Books, 1977.
Lundell, Torborg. *Lars Ahlin*. Boston: Twayne, 1977.
Steene, Birgitta. "Erik Lindegren: An Assessment." *Books Abroad* 49, 1 (winter 1975): 29-32.
Stig Dagerman. Lampeter, Wales: Swedish English Literary Translators' Association, 1984.
Thompson, Laurie. *Stig Dagerman*. Boston: Twayne, 1983.
Warme, Lars G. *A History of Swedish Literature*. Lincoln, Nebr.: University of Nebraska Press, Lincoln & London, in cooperation with the American-Scandinavian Foundation, 1996.

POPORANISM
Romania, 1910s

Like SĂMĂNĂTORISM, Poporanism was a late-nineteenth-, early twentieth-century Romanian movement devoted to literature about the peasants and common people. However, Poporanism was much more closely aligned with REALISM and NATURAL-ISM in its objective approach to narration and portraiture. Novelist and short-story writer Ion Agârbiceanu (1882-1963), Marxist critic Garabet Ibrăileanu (1871-1936), and poet George Topîrceanu (1886-1937) were among those associated with the movement.

❖•❖

Further Reading

Zaciu, Mircea. *Ion Agârbiceanu, 1882-1982*. Bucharest: Cartea Românească, 1982.

POPULAR NATIONAL SCHOOL
Hungary, 1890s-1900s

A turn-of-the-century Hungarian movement that coincided with Hungary's one-thou-sand-year anniversary of its nationhood in 1896, the Popular National School was bound to the traditions of Romanticism and REALISM. Influenced in part by national-ist writer Sándor Petofi (1823-1849?), Pál Gyulai (1826-1909) and Mór Jókai (1825-1904) were the primary practitioners of the School.

❖•❖

Further Reading

Czigány, Lóránt. *The Oxford History of Hungarian Literature: From the Earliest Times to the Present*. Oxford, England: Clarendon Press, 1984.
Fenyo, Mario D. *Literature and Political Change: Budapest, 1908-1918*. Philadelphia: American Philosophical Society, 1987.
Klaniczay, Tibor, ed. *A History of Hungarian Literature*. Budapest: Corvina, 1982.

POPULISME
France, 1929-1930

The Populisme group is one of a confluence of literary movements both large and small, some of which would outlast others in influence, but all of which would change the way writers and readers would look at the poetry, the fiction, and the drama of MODERNISM. Populisme was given its impetus by manifestos written in 1929 and 1930 which demanded that fiction exemplify both the joys and the sorrows of the working class and be best written by writers who understood the milieu. Major proponents of the thesis have been Eugene Dabit (1898-1936), Louis Guilloux (1899-1980), Leon Lemonnier (1892-1953), Henri Poulaille (1896-1980), and André Thérive (1891-1967). Dabit, originally a skilled tradesman, is best known for his novel, *L'Hôtel du Nord* (1929; trans. 1931), and his journal, *Journal intime 1928-1936* (1936); Guilloux for *Le Pain des Rêves* (1942; The Bread of Dreams); and Thérive for *Sans âme* (1928; Without Soul) and *Le Charbon ardent* (1929; Charbon the Lover). Populist novels continued to be written and well received in France at the end of the twentieth century, and an annual prize, *Prix populiste,* is awarded.

❖•❖
Further Reading

Chapman, Rosemary. *Henry Poulaille and Proletarian Literature 1920-1939.* Amsterdam; Atlanta: Rodopi, 1992.

Green, Mary Jean Matthews. *Louis Guilloux, an Artisan of Language.* York, S.C.: French Literature Publications, 1980.

Maricourt, Thierry. *Henry Poulaille, 1896-1980.* Lavallolis-Perret, France: Manya, 1992.

O'Connell, David. "Eugène Dabit: A French Working-Class Novelist." *Research Studies* 41, 4 (December 1973).

Orlando, David Anthony. *The Novels of Eugene Dabit and French Literary Populisme of the 1930s.* Doctoral thesis, Dept. of French and Italian, Stanford University, 1972.

Rahhal, George M. *The Social Ideas in the Novels of André Thérive.* Master's thesis, University of Oklahoma, 1941.

POPULIST MOVEMENT (Népi Writers)
Hungary, 1930s

The Populist Movement emerged in Hungary during the economically depressed early 1930s, when the country, still organized under a feudalist system, was known as "the land of three million beggars." *NYUGAT* editor Mihály Babits first referred to the *népi* ("of the people" or populist) poets in his preface to *Új anthológia* in 1932. Formed sometime after the uprising of 1918-19, the Populist writers advocated the preservation of Hungarian village life and values and sought a third socioeconomic alternative to capitalism and Soviet socialism. One concrete proposal was to redistribute ownership of the land, the greater portion of which was held by large, powerful estates (which was accomplished in 1945 after the Soviets ousted the Germans from Hungary).

The Populist trend encompassed several literary and narrative genres: poetry, novels, short stories, and, perhaps most notably, sociological writing. This last was composed by writers known as *falukutatók*, or village explorers. Zsigmond Móricz (1879-1942), a member of *Nyugat* earlier in his career, was a practitioner of village research and writing during the 1930s and influenced the Populist writers. Many Populist writers had been born into the peasantry and returned to their village origins physically, or at least narratively, holding the conviction that if they did not compile records of and speak for "the people," no one would. In addition, the idea of Hungarianness was an important Populist tenet; since the origins of Hungarian ethnicity had not been fully explicated, some considered the peasantry to hold racial clues.

Other forerunners who inspired the Populist writers include lyric folk poet József Erdélyi (1896-1978) and his collection *Ibolyalevél* (1922; Violet Leaf); short-story writer and novelist János Kodolányi (1899-1969), especially his short story "Sötétség" (1922; Darkness); and most importantly, Dezso Szabó (1879-1945), whose novel *Az elsodort falu* (1919; The Village That Was Swept Away) made a huge impact.

One of the Populist movements' major proponents was one of the few to come from a middle-class background, novelist and essayist László Németh (1901-1975), who aimed to reinvigorate social thought through the innovative use of metaphor. Many of Németh's Populist essays are collected in *Kisebbségben* (1939; In Minority) and *A minoség forradalma* (1940; The Revolt of Quality). His novels *Emberi színjáték* (1928, 1944; Human Comedy) and *Gyász* (1935; Mourning) are good examples of Populist fiction.

Another major literary figure associated with the Populist movement was poet, essayist, and novelist of rural Hungary Gyula Illyés (1902-1983), who as a young man lived in Paris where he fell under the spell of such SURREALISTS as André BRETON, Paul ÉLUARD, and Louis ARAGON. Some critics consider Illyés's *Pusztáp népe* (1936; People of the Puszta*, 1967) the most important Populist work. In it, Illyes recounts his experiences and hardships growing up in a feudal village.

Populist sociological writing can be found in Zoltán Szabó's *A tardi helyzet* (1936; The Situation at Tard), which led to a series called *Magyarország Felfedezése* (The Discovery of Hungary), edited by György Sárközi (1899-1945), including such volumes as *Néma forradalom* (1937; Silent Revolution) by Imre Kovács, *Viharsarok* (1937; Stormy Corner) by Géza Féja (1900-1978) — who as a result was prosecuted for slandering the nation — and *Futóhomok* (1937; Drifting Sand) by Ferenc Erdei (1910-1970). Documentary realist József Darvas (1912-1973) described growing up in a village in *Alegnagyobb magyar falu* (1937; The Greatest Hungarian Village). His *Egy paraszt-család története* (1939; *A History of a Peasant Family*, 1939) is notable as well. Péter Veres's (1897-1970) best works are the autobiographical *Számadás* (1937; Accounting) and *Falusi krónika* (1941; A Village Chronicle). Poet Gyula Takáts (1911-) joined the movement in 1937 and wrote a sociological survey of the Transdanubia from which he came.

Fiction writers working in the Populist mode included Pál Szabó (1893-1970), whose short stories about peasant life are collected in *Emberek* (1930; *The People of the Plains*, 1932); his trilogy of village novels—*Lakodalom* (1942; Wedding), *Keresztelo* (1942; Baptism), and *Bölcso* (1943; Cradle)—was published together in 1949 as *Talpalatnyi föld* (The Soil Under Your Feet). Áron Tamási (1897-1966), a Transylvanian, wrote plays, short stories, and novels dealing with the Hungarian peasantry, most notably, the Abel trilogy (1932-34): *Ábel Amerikában* (Abel in America), *Ábel a rengetegben* (Abel in the Wilderness), and *Ábel az országban* (Abel in the Country). Dénes Barsi (1905-1968) edited the journal *Kelet Népe*. His novel *Jehova tanúja* (1957; Jehovah's Witness), though published after the movement had subsided, is a good representative work, a well-written novel that captures the psychological reality of agricultural workers.

Poetry was not a prominent genre among the Populists, but folk poet István Sinka (1897-1969) deserves mention. A herdsman until he was nearly forty years old, Sinka was influenced by Hungarian ballad traditions. His first collection of poetry was *Himnuszok Kelet kapujában* (1934; Hymns at the Gates of the East). In addition, Sinka wrote short stories and an autobiography, *Fekete bojtár vallomásai* (1942-44; Confessions of a Black Herdsman).

The journal *Válasz* (The Answer), which the poet Pál Gulyás (1899-1944) helped found in 1934, was the main forum for the Populists. It was discontinued in 1938 and revived in the mid-1940s. Other important magazines of the Populists were Németh's *Tanú* (1932-36; Witness) and *Kelet Népe* (1935-42; People of the East).

The apex of the Populist movement came in 1937 when many of the writers issued a manifesto titled "Márciusi Front" (March Front), in reference to the March 1848 revolution, and formed an anti-Fascist group under the same name. By the mid-1940s, however, the movement had subsided as the German presence in Hungary silenced many. After the Soviets ousted the Nazis, Communism grew in prominence in the Hungarian government and most Populist writers were imprisoned, silenced, or exiled.

⇾•⇽

Further Reading

Czigány, Lorant. *The Oxford History of Hungarian Literature: From the Earliest Times to the Present*. Oxford, England: Clarendon Press, 1984.

Klaniczay, Tibor, ed. *A History of Hungarian Literature*. Budapest: Corvina, 1982.

Reményi, Joseph. *Hungarian Writers and Literature: Modern Novelists, Critics, and Poets*. New Brunswick, N.J.: Rutgers University Press, 1964.

PORCH GROUP (*De Stoep*)
Dutch Antilles, 1940s

The *De Stoep* group consisted of a number of Dutch writers who exiled themselves to the Dutch Antilles from Nazi-occupied Holland. Writing in both Dutch and Papiamento during the 1940s, *De Stoep* writers published their work — often experimenting in a SURREALIST vein — in the journal of the same name as well as in a collection, *Doffe Orewoed* (1948; Ecstacy in Undertone). Christiaan J. H. Engels (pseud. Luc Tournier; 1907-) modelled *De Stoep* after a late nineteenth-century journal in the Antilles, *Notras y Letras*. Other writers included poet, editor, and novelist Silvio A. (Tip) Marugg (1923-); poet Yolanda Corsen (pseud. Oda Blinder; 1918-1969); her brother, poet and short-story writer Charles S. Corsen (1927-); poet, short-story writer, and priest Michael Mohlmann (pseud. Wim van Nuland; 1920-); and critic and essayist Henrik de Wit (n.d.).

✦•✦

Further Reading

Debrot, Cola. *Literature of the Netherlands Antilles*. Netherlands Antilles: Departement van Cultuur en Opvoeding van de Nederlandse Antillen, 1964.

PORTUGUESE RENASCENCE
Portugal, 1910s-1920s

The beginning of the twentieth century found Portuguese literature in a state of dormancy; many of its finest writers had died, some prematurely, and some had withdrawn for political reasons. The events which had disrupted the monarchy and the ominous portents which signalled the upheaval of World War I were causing political and social instability; for the most part, creativity in the arts was at low ebb. But in 1912, under the political aegis of the *Renascenta Portuguesa,* which had been designed to renew public consciousness and a new spirit of Portuguese spirit and national purpose, a group of idealists combined their efforts to revive intellectual purpose, as well. Their manifesto appeared in the journal *A Aguia* (1910-32; The Eagle) of which the major poet, Joaquim Teixeira de Pascoaes (1877-1952), was the coeditor. Collaborators were Teofilo Braga (1834-1924), Leonardo Coimbra (1884-1960), Jaime Cortesao (1884-1960), Bernardine Machado (1851-1944), Fernando PESSOA (*see PRESENCA*), António Sérgio de Sousa (1883-1969), Manuel Teixiera-Gomes (1860-1941), and Afonso Lopes Vieira (1878-1946). Primarily of a traditionalist persuasion, these writers were singularly influenced by a political nationalism which was manifest in their work, and also by a technique which Pascoaes called "saudosismo," which epitomized a desire for a "pantheistic solidarity with all things." Portuguese Renascence poets connected to other groups included Cortesao and Sousa to *SEARA NOVA,* and Pessoa to *ORPHEU* and to *Presenca*. The Portuguese Renascence disbanded after a short time, but many recent writers continue to present lyric poetry of the traditional mode and to ignore, in the main, literary critical movements of a strictly MODERNIST bent.

☙•❧

Further Reading

Bell, Aubrey F. G. *Poems from the Portuguese*. Oxford, England: Blackwell, 1913.
———. *Portuguese Literature*. Oxford, England: Clarendon Press, 1922.
———. *Studies in Portuguese Literature*. Oxford, England: Blackwell, 1914.
Camoes, Luis de. *The Lusiads*. Translated by William C. Atkinson. Harmondsworth, England: Penguin Books, 1952.
———. *The Lusiads*. Translated by Leonard Bacon. New York: Hispanic Society of America, 1950.
Castro, Eugenio de. *Dona Briolanja and Other Poems*. Translated by Leonard S. Downes. Lisbon: Tipografia de Liga dos Combatentes da Grande General, 1944.
Livermore, H. V., et al. *Portugal and Brazil: An Introduction*. Oxford, England: Clarendon Press, 1953.
Quental, Antero de. *Sonnets and Poems of Anthero de Quental*. [sic] Translated by S. Griswold Morley Berkeley, Calif.: University of California Press, 1922.
Trend, J. B., ed. *Portuguese Poems with Translations*. Cambridge, England: R. I. Severs, 1954.

POSTCOLONIAL AND CULTURAL THEORY. *See* MARXIST CRITICISM

POSTHUMANISMO
Dominican Republic, 1920s-1930s

The Posthumanists were active as a group in the Dominican Republic during the 1920s. Poet and philosopher Andrés Avelino Garcia (1900-1974) composed the group's statement, "Manifesto Postumista," which appeared in his collection *Fantaseos* in 1921. The other major figures in the group were poet Domingo Moreno Jimenes (1894-?) and poet and critic Rafael Augusto Zorrilla (1892-1937). In 1922 they published *Del movimento postumista* (The Posthumous Movement), a pamphlet containing some of their poetry. They experimented with free verse—most notably, Moreno Jimenez—and creole forms, and declined to explore European trends. They preferred instead to work within a regional, folk-oriented literary aesthetics against which some later writers, such as those of the SURPRISED POETRY MOVEMENT, reacted.

☙•❧

Further Reading

Anderson, Imbert Enrique. *Spanish-American Literature*. Translated by John V. Falconieri. Detroit: Wayne State University Press, 1963.

POSTMODERNISM. *See* **BEAT GENERATION, BLACK MOUNTAIN POETS, CONFESSIONAL POETS, CYBERPUNK, DECONSTRUCTION, MODERNISM, NEW NOVEL, NEW YORK SCHOOL, READER-RESPONSE CRITICISM, SAN FRANCISCO SCHOOL,** *TEL QUEL* **GROUP**

POST-SHINGEKI MOVEMENT
Japan, 1960-1990s

In the years from the turn of the century to 1960, the Shingeki (New Theater) movement in Japan, which had popularized modern Western theater in the country through its reliance on producing translated European and American dramas, had increasingly become identified with traditional left-wing political ideology. Supporters of the Shingeki movement were among the millions of Japanese strenuously opposing renewal of the U.S.-Japan Mutual Security Treaty, whose terms include the right of the United States to station its forces in Japan. Ratification of the treaty in 1960 despite this opposition led many younger Shingeki supporters to doubt the ability of the movement to reflect either modern, postwar Japanese life or the realities of the war itself. The post-Shingeki movement that emerged in response to this believed the solution was to create a theater whose unifying principle had less to do with ideology than with the very nature of theater itself.

Three major companies and their respective director/playwrights were responsible for the birth of post-Shingeki: Jōkyō Gekijo (Situation Theater) founded by Kara Jurō (1940-), Kuro Tento 68/71 (Black Tent Theater 68/71) founded by Satoh Makoto (1943-), and Waseda Shōgekiō (Waseda Little Theater) founded by Suzuki Tadashi (1939-). Structurally, the work of each, and of post-Shingeki in general, is characterized by the use of alternative venues for production as a way of protesting the artificial barriers between the audience and the actors. Also of note is an emphasis on the importance of the director and, especially, the actor. The rising creative importance of the latter is one example of post-Shingeki's embrace of practices adapted from traditional Noh and Kabuki theater, both of which were spurned by Shingeki proponents. Of critical importance to post-Shingeki (as it is to avant-garde theater, post-Shingeki's Western analogue) is a disregard for the linear trappings of earlier Western theater. This is exemplified in post-Shingeki's dialogue and its use of meta-theatrical constructs, especially in works such as Jurō's *The Virgin's Mask* (1969) and *Futari no onna* (1979; Two Women).

The key to post-Shingeki thematically is the explicit synthesis of motifs drawn specifically from current Japanese life (as opposed to those imported from other Western countries via Shingeki translations) with the older traditional forms. For example, plays such as Makoto's trilogy *Harō Hōro! Owaranai owari ni tsuite no sanshō* (1966; *Hello Hero! Three Episodes in the Unending Ending*, 1972) and *Nezumi Kozō Jirokichi* (1970; *Nezumi Kozō: The Rat*, 1986) explore the use of apotheosis to transform mortal characters battling a sense of helplessness over their lives into mythical beings empowered to transform their existences.

Other important playwrights of the movement, including Betsuyaku Minoru (1937-), Terayama Shuji (1936-) and Shimizu Kunio (1890-1954), have also contributed to post-Shingeki, whose legacy may properly be termed the emergence of the first truly Japanese modern theater.

✥•✥

Further Reading

Arnott, Peter D. *The Theatres of Japan*. London: Macmillan; New York: St. Martin's Press, 1969.

Brandon, James R. "Training at the Waseda Little Theatre: The Suzuki Method." *Drama Review* 22 (December 1978): 29-42.

Goodman, David G. *Satoh Makoto and the Post-Shingeki Movement in Japanese Contemporary Theatre*. Ph.D. diss., Cornell University, 1982; Ann Arbor, Mich.: UMI, 1984.

Goodman, David G., ed. *After Apocalypse: Four Japanese Plays of Hiroshima and Nagasaki*. New York: Columbia University Press, 1986.

Ortolani, Benito. *The Japanese Theatre. From Shamanistic Ritual to Contemporary Pluralism*. Leiden, Netherlands; New York: E. J. Brill, 1995.

Pronko, Leonard Cabell. *Guide to Japanese Drama*. Boston: G. K. Hall, 1984.

Rolf, Robert T. "Tokyo Theatre 1990." *Asian Theatre Journal* 9, 1 (1992).

Rolf, Robert T., and John K. Gillespie. *Alternative Japanese Drama: Ten Plays*. Honolulu: University of Hawaii Press, 1992.

Tadashi, Suzuki. *The Way of Acting: The Theatre Writings of Tadashi Suzuki*. New York: Theatre Communications Group, 1986.

Takaya, Ted T., ed. *Modern Japanese Drama: An Anthology*. New York: Columbia University Press, 1979.

POSTSTRUCTURALISM. *See* DECONSTRUCTION, FEMINIST CRITICISM, GENEVA SCHOOL, PRAGUE LINGUISTIC CIRCLE, READER-RESPONSE CRITICISM, RUSSIAN FORMALISM, STRUCTURALISM

PRAGUE LINGUISTIC CIRCLE
Czechoslovakia, 1920s-1930s

An important offshoot of RUSSIAN FORMALISM, the Prague Linguistic Circle was founded in 1926 by an assortment of Russian and Czech scholars, including seminal Formalist Roman JAKOBSON, Jan Mukařovský (1891-1975), Vilém Mathesius (1882-

575

1945), Pyotr Bogatyre (1893-1971), and Nikolai Trubetzkoy (1890-1938). During the period from 1920 to 1937, Jakobson worked in Czechoslovakia first as a translator and cultural attaché and later as a doctoral student and eventual chair of Russian Philology and Old Czech Literature. Before inaugurating the Linguistic Circle, he developed close ties with members of the NINE POWERS GROUP and POETISM movements. However, it was through his friendship with Mukařovský that Jakobson consciously refined his most important linguistic theories, which came to serve as the foundation for the two chief descendants of Formalism: STRUCTURALISM and SEMIOTICS. Consequently, Prague has been recognized, along with Moscow and Paris, as one of the primary centers of modern interpretive theory.

⋙•⋘

Further Reading

Matejka, Ladislav, ed. *Sound, Sign and Meaning: Quinquagenary of the Prague Linguistic Circle.* Ann Arbor, Mich.: Dept. of Slavic Languages and Literatures, University of Michigan, 1976.
Steiner, Peter, ed. *The Prague School: Selected Writings 1929-1946.* Austin, Tex.: University of Texas Press, 1982.

PRAYOGAVADA (Experimentalism). *See* NEW POETRY MOVEMENT (Nayī Kavitā)

PRESENÇA
Portugal, 1927-1940

Presença was a journal of literary criticism that played a central role in the establishment of MODERNISM in Portugal. Like that of its predecessor *ORPHEU*, *Presença*'s genesis was sparked by a dissatisfaction with the staid romanticism of the Portuguese literary tradition. Indeed, *Presença*'s founders drew inspiration from the example set by the *Orpheu* writers and shared the earlier group's commitment to innovation and to art for its own sake.

Referred to as *presencistas*, the journal's supporters sought to introduce Portuguese readers to the tenets of Modernism as they were already being practiced by European writers in bold, exciting ways. Such authors as the French CUBIST and SYMBOLIST poets, respectively, Guillaume APOLLINAIRE and Paul Valéry (1871-1945), novelists Marcel PROUST (*see* MODERNISM, France) and André GIDE (*see NOUVELLE REVUE FRANÇAISE*), and the Italian dramatist Luigi PIRANDELLO (*see* MODERNISM, Italy) were at the forefront of a movement that called for a reevaluation of the purpose of art and the artist's role. They were intentionally rejecting convention and embracing stylistic and thematic experimentation.

576

Portugal's *presencistas* assumed a daunting role when they set out to revitalize their national culture, for they faced not only a long tradition of resistance to change and the peculiarly Portuguese penchant for *saudosismo* (a melancholy form of nostalgia blended with resignation to suffering; *see* PORTUGUESE RENASCENCE) but an oppressive government hostile to their aims. In fact, one of the *Presenca* group's central tenets was its opposition to the use of art as a tool of political propaganda—a favorite practice of the regime of Portugal's military dictator Antonio Salazar (1889-1970). The *presencistas* resisted all nonartistic limitations on art, insisting on the artist's autonomy and advocating an essentially unacademic literature in which emotion is favored over intellect.

Presenca was founded by poet Jose REGIO, who remained the journal's editor throughout its existence, and Joao Gaspar Simoes (1903-). Simoes is the author of *Eloi* (1932), a psychological novel that evidences the influence of Modernist novelists James JOYCE (*see* MODERNISM, England and Ireland) and Proust as well as the psychological theories of Sigmund FREUD. Other members of the *Presenca* group included the renowned poet Fernando PESSOA and the novelists Branquinho da Fonseca (1905-1974) — who led a small revolt against the journal's editors, claiming their philosophy tended to stifle individual experimentation — Miguel Torga (1907-1995), and Edmundo Bettancourt (1899-1973).

That *Presenca* ceased publication in 1940 might be attributed to Portuguese readers' growing appetite for NEOREALISTIC literature, which emphasized the need for social reforms rather than aesthetic concerns.

⇒•⇐

Pessoa, Fernando (1888-1935), Portuguese poet.

Recognized not only as Portugal's greatest modern poet but as an important figure in twentieth-century literature in general, Pessoa published only one book during his lifetime (*Mensagem* [1934; Message]) and was not widely appreciated until after his death. Despite his idiosyncracies, Pessoa is a quintessentially modern writer in his innovative techniques and concern with individual identity.

Pessoa grew up in South Africa and was still living in that country when he gained recognition for Shakespearian-style sonnets written in English. It was not until about 1912, after Pessoa's return to Portugal, that he began to write in his native language. At this time Pessoa became associated with the Portuguese Renascence, which urged a return to cultural stature through a renewed emphasis on *saudosismo*. Several years later, Pessoa was also a member of the short-lived but influential *Orpheu* Group and an active participant in the Modernist journal *Presenca*.

Pessoa's response to the classic twentieth-century question of identity was unique: he developed a set of separate poetic voices he called "heteronyms" to reflect and express different aspects of himself. Although he wrote some poems in his own voice (which he termed an "orthonym"), Pessoa is best known for work attributed to three major heteronyms, each with his own biography, philosophical approach, and literary style. Through these autonymous personae, Pessoa could escape the limitations of a single poetic viewpoint and explore the shifting, often conflicting realities of personal identity.

Pessoa channeled the impulsive, innovative side of his nature into the heteronymn Alvaro de Campos, a Scottish-educated naval engineer, futurist, and modernist whose poems are written in an experimental, rhapsodic, free-verse style. By contrast, Ricardo Reis was a neoclassicist who produced well-wrought poems in such traditional forms as the Horatian ode. A world-weary sophisticate, Reis projected a fatalistic philosophy of resignation. Alberto Caeiro was an intellectual with a strongly paganistic bent and an inspirational focus; his poems are focused on the material, sensual world and disdain of the supernatural. Under his own name, Pessoa wrote poems that reveal a preoccupation with the occult (although he does not seem to align himself with any particular doctrine) and with esthetic concerns.

✦•✦

Regio, Jose (1901-1969), Portuguese poet.

Editor of the innovative critical review *Presenca* for all thirteen years of its existence, Regio was the moving spirit behind the journal's attempt to introduce Portuguese readers to modern literary theory and technique. Regio stressed the importance of artistic originality and authenticity, and viewed art as a means to explore both the conscious and unconscious depths of the individual personality. In his own poetry, which is fairly traditional in form but features vivid imagery and sonorous language, Regio often treated the myth of man's fallen nature and the conflict between body and soul, reason and faith, good and evil.

✦•✦

Further Reading

Campbell, Roy. *Portugal*. London: Max Reinhardt, 1957.

Faria, Almeida, Alberto de Lacerda, Vianna Moog, Jorge de Sena, and Robert D. Pring-Mill. *Studies in Modern Portuguese Literature*. Tulane Studies in Romance Languages and Literature, No. 4. New Orleans, La.: Tulane University, 1971.

Moser, G. "Portuguese Literature in Recent Years." *Modern Language Journal* 44 (1960): 245-54.

———. "Portuguese Writers of This Century." *Hispania* 50 (1966): 947-54.

Parker, John W. *Three Twentieth-Century Portuguese Poets*. Johannesburg, South Africa: Witwatersrand University Press, 1960.

Ramalho, Americo da Costa. "Fernando Pessoa: Portugal's Greatest Modern Poet." In his *Portuguese Essays*. Lisbon: National Secretariat for Information, 1968.

Schneider, Marshall J., and Irwin Stern, eds. *Modern Spanish and Portuguese Literatures*. New York: Continuum, 1988.

Severino, Alex. "Fernando Pessoa's Legacy: The *Presenca* and After." *World Literature Today* (winter 1979): 5-7.

PROFIL
Norway, 1960s

Published at the University of Oslo, *Profil* was the literary journal ascribed to by a group of young writers during the 1960s who were in controversy with the SYMBOLIC MODERNISTS of the 1950s, and whose experimental, symbolic work they considered to be irrelevant to the needs of Norwegian society and its readers. They insisted, rather, upon literary focus on the realistic, political, and social needs of their country. Primarily MARXIST in their orientation, these writers remained dedicated to political, socioeconomic revision, write with "extreme simplicity of style and expression," and are thought to be among the most talented and energetic of modern Norwegian writers. Group members included Espen Haavardsholm (1945-), Paal Helge Haugen (1945-), Tor Obrestad (1938-), Einar Okland (1940-), Dag Solstad (1943-), and Jan Erik Vold (1939-).

✦•✦

Further Reading

Grogaard, John Fredrik. *Jan Erik Vold, 50*. Oslo: Gyldendal Norsk Forlag, 1989.

Haugen, Paal-Helge. *Stone Fences: A Book from the Inner Townships from Childhood in the Fifties*. Translated by William Mishler and Roger Greenwald. Columbia, Mo.: University of Missouri Press, 1986.

Kittang, Atle. *History and Modernity in the Contemporary Norwegian Novel: Dag Solstad, Liv Koltzow, Kjartan Flogstad, Oystein Lonn; and, Allegory, Intertextuality and Irony in Dag Solstad*. Minneapolis: Center for Nordic Studies, 1989.

PROGRESSIVE ROMANTICISM
Iceland, 1910s

This movement grew out of the traditional Romanticism which had led Iceland into MODERNISM in the mid-nineteenth century, had influenced its literature for a half a century and which, by the turn of the century, had transformed into the NEOROMANTICISM which had had a major impact in Germany, Latvia, Norway, and the Ukraine. The term Progressive Romanticism is specifically Icelandic in origin; its two most important advocates, Einar Benediktsson (1864-1940) and Jóhann Sigurjónsson (1880-

579

1919), argued that the word "progressive" defined more clearly their creative desire to depict the limitless progress which could be made in Iceland, after having gained independence from Denmark in 1918 and the opportunity to participate with the European community in a new and rapid-paced century. Benediktsson's enthusiasm for his country's revised socioeconomic situation gave his work new impetus and him reputation as one of Iceland's most important and widely read poets. Sigurjónsson, a dramatist as well as a popular poet, not only influenced all of Iceland's modern poetry but gained a wider continental audience when he moved to Denmark, wrote about Iceland in the Danish language, and became an important literary force in middle Europe as well.

❧•❦

Further Reading

Beck, Richard. *History of Icelandic Poets: 1800-1940*. Ithaca, N.Y.: Cornell University Press, 1950.

Carleton, P. *Tradition and Innovation in Twentieth Century Icelandic Poetry*. Doctoral thesis, University of California, 1967.

Einarsson, Stefan. *A History of Icelandic Literature*. Baltimore, Md.: Johns Hopkins University Press, 1950.

————. *History of Icelandic Prose Writers: 1800-1940*. Ithaca, N.Y.: Cornell University Press, 1948.

Ivask, Ivar, and Gero von Wilpert, eds. *World Literature Since 1945*. New York: Ungar, 1973.

PROGRESSIVE WRITERS' MOVEMENT
India/Pakistan, 1930s-1940s

Contemporary with the struggle for independence from England, the MARXIST-influenced Progressive Writers' Movement was founded in 1936 in Lucknow by Sajjad Zaheer (1905-1973), Faiz Ahmad Faiz (1911-1984), Ali Sardar Jafri (1912-), and others. Novelist and short-story writer Premchand (pseud. of Dhanpat Rai Srivastav, 1880-1936) sat as president at that first assembly. Zaheer, along with André GIDE (*see NOU-VELLE REVUE FRANÇAISE*), Maxim GORKY (*see* SOCIALIST REALISM, Russia), E. M. Forster (1879-1970), and others, had participated in the International Association of Writers for Defence of Culture Against Fascism, which was organized in Paris in 1935. A collaborative volume of short stories, *Angare* (1931-32; Embers), written by Zaheer, Ahmed Ali (1910-1994) and Mahmuduzzafar (1908-1955), also is considered precursory to the Progressive Writers' Movement.

The movement sought to contribute to social justice for the Indian and later, Pakistani, underclasses. The social and literary goals of the Progressive Writers' Movement, as described by critic I. Husain, were "promotion of scientific mentality" and "condemna-

580

tion of tendencies of backward looking and racial prejudice, group worship, and exploitation of the poor by the rich." Literature "should be rescued from backward looking writers and brought into line with the aspirations of common people," should preserve "the healthy traditions" of culture, and discuss the basic problems of Indian life. The manifesto was written and signed in London by Zaheer, Mulk Raj Anand (1905-), and other writers and students.

Progressive, or pragativāda, writers struggled with the problems of Socialist Realism: how to portray life realistically, that is, whose life to portray, and how? Some attempted to depict life from a detached viewpoint; others turned to a subjective, inward-looking style. The movement was controversial, socialist in outlook, dangerous to successive regimes. Some of the more vocal and popular members, such as Faiz and Zaheer, were imprisoned during the early 1950s for alleged attempts to overthrow the government. By that time the movement, perhaps the most significant literary/cultural group in the Indian subcontinent during the first half of the twentieth century, began to lose the intensity of previous years.

Many important and popular Urdu writers belonged, including Faiz, widely recognized as the leading Urdu poet of the twentieth century, a Lenin Peace Prize-winning writer, who also edited the literary magazine, *Adh-i-Latif*, as well as the newspaper *Pakistan Times*, and worked with labor unions; journalist, short-story writer, and poet Ahmad Nadim Qasmi (1916-); Ali Sardar Jafri, who edited several journals, including *Naya Adab* (New Literature) and an Indian socialist periodical, *Indian Literature*, from Bombay; poet N. M. Rashid (1910-1975), poet, lyricist, and editor of *Naya Adab* (New Literature); poet, songwriter, and film director Akhtar-ul-Iman (1915-); poet and lyricist Sahir Ludhianvi (pseud. of Abd-al-Haye, 1921-1980); Kaifi Azmi (pseud. of Athar Husain Rizvi, 1924-); prose writer, journalist, and film director Khvāja Ahmad 'Abbās (1914-); editor and prose writer Krishan Chandar (1914-); short-story writer Saadat Hasan Manto (1912-1955); short-story writer Ismat Chugtai (1915-); Josh (pseud. of Shabbir Hasan Khan, 1896-?); Majaz (pseud. of Asrarul Haq, 1911-1955); education administrator Muhammud Din Tasir (1902-1950); Sindhi poet and short-story writer Shaikh Ayaz (1923-); and prose writer Qurratulain Hyder (or Haidar, 1927-).

Though the movement was strongest among Urdu writers, some working in other Indian languages were active as well: Bengali editor, novelist, and president of the Bengali Progressive Writers' Association Mānik Bandyopādhyāy (or Banerji, 1908-1956); Bengali novelist and essayist Tārāshankar Bandyopādhyāy (or Banerji, 1898-1971), and Bengali poets Sudhindranath Datta (1901-1960) and Buddhadeva Bose (1908-); Hindi poets Nagarjun (1911-1998) and Shiv Mangal Singh "Suman" (1916-); Tamil poet and Communist leader Jeeva (P. Jivanandam, 1907-1963), Tamil critic and activist Thiru Vi. Ka. (1883-1954), Tamil poets C. Raghunathan (1923-) and K. C. S. Arunachalam (1921-); Kannada writers A. N. Krishnarao (1908-1971), Niranjana (pseud. for Kulakunda Shivarāya, 1923-), Basavaraj Kattimani (1919-), and Ta.Rā.Su. (pseud. of T. R. Subbarao, 1920-); and some of the earlier Chāyāvāda writers (*see* ROMANTICIST MOVEMENT) as well as later writers associated with the NEW POETRY MOVEMENT/NAYĪ KAVITĀ.

✥•✥

Further Reading

Ali, Ahmed. "The Progressive Writers' Movement and Creative Writers in Urdu." In *Marxist Influences and South Asian Literature*. Edited by Carlo Coppola. Vol. 1. East Lansing, Mich.: Asian Studies Center, Michigan State University, 1974.

Ali, M. "The Poetry of Faiz." *Pakistan Review* 12 (1964): 5-8.

Bandopadhyay, Manohar. *Life and Works of Premchand*. New Delhi: Publications Division, Ministry of Information and Broadcasting, Government of India, 1981.

Contemporary Urdu Verse. Translated by Rajinder Singh Verma. Delhi: Atma Ram, 1989.

Coppola, Carlo, ed. "The All-India Progressive Writers' Association." In his *Marxist Influences and South Asian Literature*. Vol. 1. East Lansing, Mich.: Asian Studies Center, Michigan State University, 1974.

Dryland, Estelle. *Faiz Ahmed Faiz, 1911-1984: Urdu Poet of Social Realism*. Lahore, Pakistan: Vanguard, 1993.

Faiz, Alys. "Faiz: A Personality Sketch." *Journal of South Asian Literature* 10, 1 (1974): 123-39.

Faiz, Faiz Ahmad. *Eleven Poems, and Introduction*. Translated by C. M. Naim and Carlo Coppola. Calcutta: R. Nandy, 1971.

———. "The Legacy of Literature." *Lotus: Afro-Asian Writings* 30, 4 (October-December 1976): 18-20.

Faiz A. Faiz, the Living Word. Tunis, Tunisia: Lotus, 1987.

George, K. M., ed. *Comparative Indian Literature*. 2 vols. Trichur, India: Kerala Sahitya Akademi; Madras: Macmillan India, 1984-85.

Gopal, Madan. *Munshi Premchand. A Literary Biography*. New York: Asia Pub. House, 1964.

Govindan, M., ed. *Poetry and Renaissance: Kumaran Asan Birth Centenary Volume*. Rev. ed. Madras: Sameeksha, 1974.

Gupta, Prakash Chandra. *Prem Chand*. New Delhi: Sahitya Akademi, 1968.

Hasan, Khalid, and Faruq Hassan, eds. *Versions of Truth: Urdu Short Stories from Pakistan*. New Delhi: Vikas, 1983.

Husain, Imdad. *An Introduction to the Poetry of Faiz Ahmed Faiz*. Lahore, Pakistan: Vanguard, 1989.

Jamal, Mahmood, trans. *The Penguin Book of Modern Urdu Poetry*. Harmondsworth, England: Penguin Books, 1986.

Jones, A., and Carlo Coppola. "Interview with Faiz." *Journal of South Asian Literature* 10, 1 (1974): 141-44.

Kumar, Jainendra. *Premchand: A Life in Letters*. Translated by Sunita Jain. Agra, India: Y. K. Publishers, 1993.

Lall, I. J. "Faiz: Poet with Vitality." *Indian Literature* 18, 4 (1975): 58-62.

Machwe, Prabhakar. "A Personal View of the Progressive Writers' Movement." In *Marxist Influences and South Asian Literature*. Edited by Carlo Coppola. Vol. 1. East Lansing, Mich.: Asian Studies Center, Michigan State University, 1974.

Madan, Indar Nath. *Premchand, an Interpretation*. Lahore, Pakistan: Minerva Book Shop, 1946.

Malik, M. "The Pakistan Poet: Faiz." *Lotus: Afro-Asian Writings* 22 (1974): 36-41.

Misra, Shiv Kumar, ed. *Premchand, Our Contemporary*. New Delhi: National Pub. House, 1986.

Narain, Govind. *Munshi Prem Chand*. Boston: Twayne, 1978.

Narang, G. C. "Tradition and Innovation in Urdu Poetry." In *Poetry and Renaissance: Kumaran Asan Birth Centenary Volume*. Edited by M. Govindan. Rev. ed. Madras: Sameeksha, 1974.

Naravane, Vishwanath S. *Premchand, His Life and Work*. New Delhi: Vikas, 1980.

Pandey, Geetanjali. *Between Two Worlds: An Intellectual Biography of Premchand*. New Delhi: Manohar, 1989.

"The Poet Faiz Ahmed Faiz." *Lotus: Afro-Asian Writings* 30, 4 (October-December 1976): 120-22.

Rahabara, Hamsarāja. *Prem Chand: His Life and Work*. Delhi: Atma Ram, 1957.

Rai, Amrit. *Premchand, a Life*. New Delhi: People's Pub. House, 1982.

————. *Premchand, His Life and Times*. Translated by Harish Trivedi. Delhi; Oxford: Oxford University Press, 1991.

Ray, G. L., and A. K. Ghosh, eds. *Premchand: A Bibliography*. Calcutta: National Library, 1980.

Sadiq, Mohammed. *A History of Urdu Literature*. London: Oxford University Press, 1964. 2nd rev. ed., Delhi: Oxford University Press, 1984.

Sahni, Bhisham, and C. P. Paliwal, eds. *Prem Chand: A Tribute*. New Delhi: Prem Chand Centenary Celebrations Committee, 1980.

Schulz, Siegfried A. *Premchand, a Western Appraisal*. New Delhi: Indian Council for Cultural Relations, 1981.

Swan, Robert O. *Munshi Premchand of Lamhi Village*. Durham, N.C.: Duke University Press, 1969.

PROJECTIVE VERSE. *See* BLACK MOUNTAIN POETS

PROLETARIAN LITERATURE
Czechoslovkia, 1920s-1930s

In Czechoslovakia, Proletarian Literature surfaced during the 1920s and 1930s as a minor movement. Two of the most important Proletarian writers were Jiří Wolker (1900-1924) and Jaroslav Seifert (1901-1986), both of whom helped launch POETISM in an attempt to combine revolutionary sentiment with a general appreciation of life's wonders. Other writers affiliated with the movement included Jindřich Hořejší (1886-1941) and Josef Hora (1891-1945).

⇒•⇐

Further Reading

Horálek, Rudolf, ed. *In Memoriam Josefa Hory*. Konín, Poland: Kruh Prátel Dobré Knihy, 1945.
Jagasich, Paul. *All the Beauty of the World*. Hampden-Sydney, Va.: Hampden-Sydney College, 1991.
Jaroslav Seifert: A Literary Retrospective. Hampden-Sydney, Va.: Hampden-Sydney Poetry
    Review, 1985.
Seifert, Jaroslav. *The Selected Poetry of Jaroslav Seifert*. Translated by Ewald Osers. Edited and
    with additional translations by George Givian. New York: Macmillan, 1986.

PROLETARIAN LITERATURE
England, 1930s

Proletarian Literature was the name given to a literary school of thought which denied
the concept of "art for art's sake" and contended that literature should reflect the experiences of its readers and address itself to the resolution of social, economic, and political problems wherever they exist. The rise of the Marxist-socialist political agenda
between the two world wars gave impetus to the British Proletarian Literature movement. Ralph Bates (1899-?) and Walter Greenwood (1903-1974) devoted their creative
impulse to the cause of the working class; there were similar movements taking place
in middle Europe, Scandinavia, and the United States. Since MARXIST theory serves to
explain the interaction between social class and economic structure, some writers of
the group saw Communism as the exemplary way to reduce the social injustice and
bias which exists where there is an imposed class system. In the previous century,
REALIST writers such as George ELIOT and Charles DICKENS had concerned themselves with social problems; other movements such as ANGRY YOUNG MEN, KITCHEN
SINK DRAMA, and THE MOVEMENT — all of which appeared in the 1950s — represent
similar desires on the part of the writers to speak to socio-political issues. World War II
and the Nazi and Fascist regimes caused writers like Bates to continue to maintain the
Proletarian cause, but to discredit the war regimes as antihumanist and counterpro-
ductive to a stable society.

⇒•⇐

Further Reading

Garbett, Cyril. *In an Age of Revolution*. New York: Oxford University Press, 1952.
Maxwell, D. E. S. *Poets of the Thirties*. New York: Barnes & Noble; London: Routledge & Kegan
    Paul, 1969.
Symons, Julian. *The Thirties: A Dream Revolved*. London: Cresset Press, 1960.
Tindall, William York. *Forces in Modern British Literature: 1885-1946*. New York: Knopf, 1947.
Warren, Austin. *A Rage for Order*. Chicago: University of Chicago Press, 1948.
Wilson, Robert N. *Man Made Plain: The Poet in Contemporary Society*. Cleveland: H. Allen, 1958.

PROLETARIAN LITERATURE
United States, 1930s

The Proletarian Literature movement in the United States flourished simultaneously with other like organizations in England, Czechoslovakia, Sweden, and Russia (*see also* PROLETARIAN WRITERS). Early in the century the work of American writers William Dean HOWELLS (*see* REALISM, United States), Upton Sinclair (1878-1968), David Levinsky (n.d.), and Max Eastman (1883-1969) exposed the social and economic pressures of the working class, but it was not until the thirties that Proletarian Literature became its own literary movement, and thus an active literary and critical force in its own right. The Great Depression then extant had caused some writers to examine more closely than before the tenets of MARXIST philosophy as manifesto for literary agenda; marked emphasis in creative work was placed on the exploitation of the working class which was engendered by the American capitalist, socio-political construct. Examples are such novels as John DOS PASSOS's *U.S.A.* (1938; *see* LOST GENERATION), James T. FARRELL's trilogy *Studs Lonigan* (1935), John STEINBECK's *The Grapes of Wrath* (1939), Richard Wright's *Native Son* (1940), and Clifford ODETS's drama *WAITING FOR LEFTY* (1935; *see* GROUP THEATER).

The Marxist purpose of Proletarian Literature is that writers must use art exclusively as a medium for the exposure of bourgeois culture in their efforts to free workers from their "economic chains," and that any other artistic motive is politically inexcusable. But World War II brought an end to the depressed American economy, a lessening of interest in Marxist theory during the Soviet-Nazi collaboration, and the end of Proletarian Literature as a formally organized movement. Recent critics have observed that the best of such fiction and drama has been presented in works where more than just political belief is expressed, and that they remain most valuable for their insightful expression and exposure of certain dilemmas of the modern situation and their impact upon the whole of the human condition. Journals which were available for expression and manifestos of Proletarian Literature were *The Masses*, *New Masses*, *The Anvil*, and early issues of *The Partisan Review*. Early participants in the movement were Victor Francis Calverton (1900-1940), Robert Cantwell (1908-1978), Jack Conroy (1899-1980), Edward Dahlberg (1900-1977), John Dos Passos, James T. Farrell, Waldo Frank (1899-1967), Joseph Freeman (1897-1965), Michael Gold (1894-1967), Albert Halper (1904-1984), Josephine Herbst (1897-1969), Granville Hicks (1901-1982), John Howard Lawson (1894-1977), Grace Lumpkin (1892?-1980), Clifford Odets, Irwin Shaw (1913-1984), John Steinbeck, and Richard Wright (1908-1960).

→•←

Farrell, James T. (1904-1979), American novelist.

Farrell's *Note on Literary Criticism* (1936) embodies the Proletarian literary view and is noted as the movement's most important statement. His best-known work is the trilogy *Studs Lonigan* (1935), which delineates the experiences of a young Catholic boy who grows up on Chicago's South Side, of the moral insensibility which affects him as a result of his connections to the underworld, and of the frustration which leads to defeat and death. Farrell's naturalistic, STREAM-OF-CONSCIOUSNESS (*see* MODERNISM, England and Ireland) techniques show the influence of Theodore DREISER (*see* NATURALISM, United States), Marcel PROUST (*see* MODERNISM, France), and James JOYCE (*see* MODERNISM, England and Ireland), but also reveal his avid interest in the social injustices which perpetuate the tragic circumstances of his characters. A later series of novels, *A World I Never Made* (1936), *No Star Is Lost* (1938), *Father and Son* (1940), *My Days of Anger* (1943), and *The Face of Time* (1953) are about the character Danny O'Neill, based on the earlier prototype, Studs Lonigan. These are similar tales of the difficulties of growing up in an indifferent society. Farrell also published many short stories; collections include *Calico Show* (1934), *$1000 a Week* (1942), *To Whom It May Concern* (1944), and *American Dream Girl* (1950). Critical works include *The League of Frightened Philistines* (1945) and *Literature and Morality* (1947). Other novels are *Ellen Rogers* (1941), *Bernard Clare* (1946), and *This Man and This Woman* (1951). Farrell has been criticized for his pessimistic point of view on the one hand and lauded for his objective, sociological insight on the other.

❖•❖

Steinbeck, John (1902-1968), American novelist, short story and nonfiction writer, and war-correspondent.

Steinbeck's initial novel, *Cup of Gold* (1929), is about the pirate Henry Morgan. In the thirties Steinbeck became interested in the problems of the working class and wrote much about the farming communities in California. His short stories, *Pastures of Heaven* (1932), contain characters who are strongly connected to the land—simple folk who depend on nature for life, and who are often itinerant, poor, displaced—and with whom Steinbeck felt deeply sympathetic. *To a God Unknown* (1933), *Tortilla Flat* (1935), and *In Dubious Battle* (1936) demonstrate his feelings even more and established his reputation as a writer dealing with serious social issues. His novel/drama, *Of Mice and Men* (1937), depicts two migrant workers who dream of owning a farm but are incapable of dealing with the reality of a world beyond their understanding and thus become victims of a system over which they have no control. This work was followed by *The Grapes of Wrath* (1939), which established him as one of the best of the Proletarian writers of his time and won him a Pulitzer Prize. Other works which present his deep compassion for simple working people, and his strong belief that life is holy, fragile, and can be easily destroyed by circumstance are *Cannery Row* (1954) and *The Wayward Bus* (1941). His long novel, *East of Eden* (1952), is based on the biblical tale of Cain and Abel, as metaphor for both the psychological and environmental situations. Nonfiction works *Bombs Away: The Story of a Bomber Team* (1942), *Russian Journal* (1948), and *Once There Was a War* (1958) depict his experiences during World War II and contain excerpts of his war correspondences. Final works are philosophical reminiscences such as *Winter of Our Discontent* (1961) and *Travels with Charlie* (1962), this last about journeys with his dog. He was awarded the Nobel Prize for literature in 1962.

➻•❦

Further Reading

Aaron, Daniel. *Writers on the Left: Episodes in American Literary Communism*. New York: Harcourt, Brace & World, 1961.

Baldwin, James. "Everybody's Protest Novel." In his *Notes of a Native Son*. Boston: Beacon Press, 1955.

Beach, Joseph Warren. *American Fiction, 1920-1940*. New York: Macmillan, 1941.

Becker, George J. *John Dos Passos*. New York: Ungar, 1974.

Bevilacqua, Winifred Farrant. *Josephine Herbst*. Boston: Twayne, 1985.

Bittner, William. *The Novels of Waldo Frank*. Phildelphia: University of Philadelphia Press, 1958.

Blake, Casey Nelson. *Beloved Community: The Cultural Criticism of Randolph Bourne, Van Wyck Brooks, Waldo Frank & Lewis Mumford*. Chapel Hill, N.C.: University of North Carolina Press, 1990.

Bloom, Harold, ed. *Richard Wright*. New York: Chelsea House, 1987.

Bloom, James D. *Left Letters: The Culture Wars of Mike Gold and Joseph Freeman*. New York: Columbia University Press, 1992.

Browder, Laura. *Rousing the Nation: Radical Culture in Depression America*. Amherst, Mass.: University of Massachusetts Press, 1998.

Carr, Gary L. *The Left Side of Paradise: The Screenwriting of John Howard Lawson*. Ann Arbor, Mich.: UMI Research Press, 1984.

Colley, Iain. *Dos Passos and the Fiction of Despair*. London: Macmillan; Totowa, N.J.: Rowman & Littlefield, 1974.

Davis, Robert Gorham. *John Dos Passos*. Minneapolis: University of Minnesota Press, 1962.

Davis, Robert Murray, ed. *Steinbeck: A Collection of Critical Essays*. Englewood Cliffs, N.J.: Prentice-Hall, 1972.

Douglas, Ann. "Studs Lonigan and the Failure of History in Mass Society." *American Quarterly* 29, 5 (winter 1977): 487-505.

Fabre, Michel. *The World of Richard Wright*. Jackson, Miss.: University Press of Mississippi, 1985.

Foley, Barbara. *Radical Representations: Politics and Form in U.S. Proletarian Fiction, 1919-1941*. Durham, N.C.: Duke University Press, 1993.

Fontenrose, Joseph Eddy. *John Steinbeck, an Introduction and Interpretation*. New York: Barnes & Noble, 1963.

French, Warren G. *John Steinbeck*. New York: Twayne, 1961. 2nd ed., rev., Boston: Twayne, 1975.

———. *John Steinbeck's Fiction Revisited*. New York: Twayne; Toronto: Maxwell Macmillan Canada, 1994.

———. *John Steinbeck's Nonfiction Revisited*. New York: Twayne; London: Prentice Hall International, 1996.

Fried, Lewis. *Makers of the City*. Amherst, Mass.: University of Massachusetts Press, 1990.

Gates, Henry Louis, and K. A. Appiah, eds. *Richard Wright: Critical Perspectives Past and Present*. New York: Amistad, 1993.

Giles, James R. *Irwin Shaw*. Boston: Twayne, 1983.

Hayashi, Tetsumaro. *Steinbeck's Literary Dimension: A Guide to Comparative Studies*. Series II. Metuchen, N.J.: Scarecrow Press, 1991.

Herbst, Josephine. "Studs Lonigan in Conclusion: *Judgement Day* by James T. Farrell, Vanguard Press." *New Masses* 15 (May 21, 1935): 25-26.

Hicks, Granville. *Proletarian Literature in the United States: An Anthology*. New York: International Publishers, 1935.

Hoffman, Frederick. *The Modern Novel in America, 1900-1950*. Chicago: H. Regnery, 1951.

Hook, Andrew, ed. *Dos Passos: A Collection of Critical Essays*. Englewood Cliffs, N.J.: Prentice-Hall, 1974.

Howe, Irving. "Black Boys and Native Sons." In his *A World More Attractive; a View of Modern Literature and Politics*. 1963. Reprint, Freeport, N.Y.: Books for Libraries Press, 1970.

Levenson, Leah. *Granville Hicks, the Intellectual in Mass Society*. Philadelphia: Temple University Press, 1993.

McCarthy, Paul. *John Steinbeck*. New York: F. Ungar, 1980.

Miller, Eugene E. *Voice of a Native Son: The Poetics of Richard Wright*. Jackson, Miss.: University Press of Mississippi, 1990.

Mishra, Kshamanidhi. *American Leftist Playwrights of the 1930s: A Study of Ideology and Technique in the Plays of Odets, Lawson, and Sherwood*. New Delhi: Classical Pub. Co., 1991.

Modern Fiction Studies 26, 3 (autumn 1980). Special issue on John Dos Passos.

Noble, Donald R., ed. *The Steinbeck Question: New Essays in Criticism*. Troy, N.Y.: Whitston, 1993.

Owens, Louis. *John Steinbeck's Re-Vision of America*. Athens, Ga.: University of Georgia Press, 1985.

Pizer, Donald. "The 1930s." In his *Twentieth-Century American Literary Naturalism: An Interpretation*. Carbondale, Ill.: Southern Illinois University Press, 1982.

Rampersad, Arnold, ed. *Richard Wright: A Collection of Critical Essays*. Englewood Cliffs, N.J.: Prentice-Hall, 1995.

Roberts, Nora Ruth. *Three Radical Women Writers: Class and Gender in Meridel Le Sueur, Tillie Olsen, and Josephine Herbst*. New York: Garland, 1996.

Rosen, Robert C. *John Dos Passos: Politics and the Writer*. Lincoln, Nebr.: University of Nebraska Press, 1981.

Timmerman, John H. *The Dramatic Landscape of Steinbeck's Short Stories*. Norman, Okla.: University of Oklahoma Press, 1990.
————. *John Steinbeck's Fiction: The Aesthetics of the Road Taken*. Norman, Okla.: University of Oklahoma Press, 1986.
Wagner-Martin, Linda. *Dos Passos: Artist as American*. Austin, Tex.: University of Texas Press, 1979.
Wald, Alan M. *James T. Farrell: The Revolutionary Socialist Years*. New York: New York University Press, 1978.
Wilcox, Leonard. *V. F. Calverton: Radical in the American Grain*. Philadelphia: Temple University Press, 1992.
Williams, Jonathan. *Edward Dahlberg, a Tribute: Essays, Reminiscences, Correspondence, Tributes*. New York: D. Lewis, 1970.
Wixson, Douglas C. *Worker-Writer in America: Jack Conroy and the Tradition of Midwestern Literary Radicalism, 1898-1990*. Urbana, Ill.: University of Illinois Press, 1994.

PROLETARIAN WRITERS (Arbetardiktare)
Sweden, 1930s

Considered one of the most important Swedish literary groups of the interwar years, the Proletarian Writers were unique among European proletarian groups for their lack of dogmatism and their unaffected identification with working-class life. Vilhelm Moberg (1898-1973), one of Sweden's most outstanding novelists, has often been linked with the Proletarians. Other notable figures include Gustav Hedenvind-Eriksson (1880-1967), Moa Martinson (1890-1964), Eyvind Johnson (1900-1976), Jan Fridegård (1897-1968), Martin Koch (1882-1940), and Ivar Lo-Johansson (1901-1990).

Further Reading

Algulin, Ingemar. *A History of Swedish Literature*. Stockholm: The Swedish Institute, 1989.
Eidevall, Gunnar. *Vilhelm Moberg*. Stockholm: The Swedish Institute, 1988.
Graves, Peter. *Jan Fridegård: Lars Hård*. Hull, England: Orton and Holmes, 1977. 2nd rev. ed., Hull, England: Dept. of Scandinavian Studies, University of Hull, 1994.
Holmes, Philip. *Vilhelm Moberg*. Boston: Twayne, 1980.
Lång, Helmer. "Moberg, the Emigrant Saga and Reality." *Swedish Pioneer Historical Quarterly* 23, 1 (January 1972): 3-24.
McKnight, Roger. *Moberg's Emigrant Novels and the Journals of Andrew Peterson: A Study of Influences and Parallels*. New York: Arno Press, 1979.
Moberg, Vilhelm. "Why I Wrote The Emigrants." *Industria International* 11E (1964): 60-64, 140, 142, 144, 146.
————. "Hooch and Hymnals: Vilhelm Moberg Looks Twice at American Society." Translated and edited by Roger McKnight. *Swedish-American Historical Quarterly* 39, 4 (October 1988): 101-21.
Orton, Gavin. *Eyvind Johnson*. New York: Twayne, 1972.

————. *Eyvind Johnson: Nu Var Det 1914*. 3rd ed. Hull, England: Dept. of Scandinavian Studies, University of Hull, 1980.

Warme, Lars G. *A History of Swedish Literature*. Lincoln, Nebr.: University of Nebraska Press, Lincoln & London, in cooperation with The American Scandinavian Foundation, 1996.

PROLETKULT
Russia, 1910s-1920s

Founded before the October 1917 Revolution by Alexander Bogdanov (pseud. of Alexander Alexandrovich Malinovsky, 1873-1928), this cultural movement included the earliest PROLETARIAN LITERATURE movement in Russia. Proletkult stood for Proletarskie kul'turno-prosvetitel'skie organizatsii (Proletarian Cultural and Educational Organization) and aimed to develop a new culture for the rising proletariat and train new writers who came from the proletarian class. Bogdanov thought, further, that proletarian art must function to help the proletariat "organize its forces in social labor, struggle, and construction." Proletkult was formed with the assistance of Anatoly Lunacharsky (1875-1933), who, in his later position as Minister of Education, oversaw funding to literary and other cultural groups. Other members included future SMITHY poets Vladimir Kirillov (1890-1943), Alexei Gastev (1882-1941), Vasili Kazin (1898-1981), and Mikhail Gerasimov (1889-1939).

Members disagreed on what to do with the culture of the past; some, such as Bogdanov and Lunacharsky, felt that by "critically reworking it from the collective labor point of view," earlier masterpieces could be incorporated into the new culture, while others, such as Kirillov, agreed with the FUTURISTS that the art of the past needs to be shucked out the window. Kirillov proposed burning the artwork of Raphael and demolishing the museums. Many of the new writers were former factory workers, sailors, soldiers, and others from the working classes. A popular theme was the exaltation of factory and other manual work, sometime using religious language.

The period of Proletkult's greatest activity ranges from 1917 to 1920: the group published a journal, *Proletarskaya Kultura* (Proletarian Culture) and other periodicals, held a conference, and set up literary studios to teach and nurture new writers. Valery Bryusov (1873-1924), Andrey BELY (*see* SYMBOLISM, Russia), Evgeny Zamyatin (1884-1937), and others taught in the literary studios. Proletkult also engaged in public attacks on writers who did not suppport the Soviet program. Proletkult tried to form a coalition with other groups but only succeeded with LEFT FRONT OF THE ARTS (LEF) in 1923. Both groups agreed that the artist had to put art (and society) above him or herself, because art had to express a common will, i.e., the will to construct and inspire a proletariat-run society. But LEF could not long abide Proletkult's aversion to Modernist artistic experimentation, so the alliance was short-lived.

By 1920 there are said to have been 400,000 Proletkult members, 80,000 of whom were enrolled in the literary studios. Also in 1920, the group was subsumed under the Ministry of Education, because Lenin and Trotsky disliked Proletkult's independent attempt to define the new Soviet culture; Bogdanov was not subservient to the Party. Many members had scattered — some to form such groups as the Smithy (and its Petrograd branch, Kosmist) in 1919 and, later, the OCTOBER GROUP. In 1932 it was dissolved into the Union of Soviet Writers, along with every other literary group in the country.

❖•❖

Further Reading

Brown, Edward J. *The Proletarian Episode in Russian Literature, 1928-1932*. New York: Columbia University Press, 1953.

Ermolaev, Herman. *Soviet Literary Theories 1917-1934*. Berkeley, Calif.: University of California Press, 1963.

Hingley, Ronald. "Movements and Theories." In his *Russian Writers and Soviet Society 1917-1978*. New York: Random House, 1979.

Patrick, George Z. *Popular Poetry in Soviet Russia*. Berkeley, Calif.: University of California Press, 1929.

Struve, Gleb. *Russian Literature under Lenin and Stalin 1917-1953*. Norman, Okla.: University of Oklahoma Press, 1971.

Terras, Victor. *Handbook of Russian Literature*. New Haven, Conn.: Yale University Press, 1985.

PROTEST LITERATURE, South Africa. *See* BLACK CONSCIOUSNESS MOVEMENT

PROVINCETOWN PLAYERS
United States, 1915-1929

One of the most notable acting companies spawned by the LITTLE THEATER MOVEMENT in America, the Players originated in Provincetown, Massachusetts, in 1915, a few short years after the arrival of the Irish Players in New York and Maurice Browne's (1881-1955) formation of the Little Theater in Chicago. Unlike their closest competitors, the WASHINGTON SQUARE PLAYERS, the Provincetown group devoted themselves exclusively in their initial years to the production and encouragement of new and innovative American drama. In addition, they emphasized the importance of the writer and director to a successful staging before that of the actor, who until this time had been the dominant figure in the theatrical equation. The Provincetown Players, whose principal members included George Cram Cook, Susan Glaspell, and Eugene O'Neill, shared the same sense of loss — social, moral, spiritual, and psychological — that pervaded many early twentieth-century literary circles. Each of them had digested and largely accepted Friedrich NIETZSCHE's anti-idealism and doctrine of human power and each of them, more importantly, had founded their conception of art on the tragic plight of the modern, isolated individual.

The husband-wife team of Cook and Glaspell represented the guiding spirit of the Provincetown Players. After acquiring valuable literary experience and a strong Socialist outlook through their association with such avant-garde luminaries as Floyd Dell (1887-1969) during the early years of the CHICAGO LITERARY RENAISSANCE, Cook and Glaspell abandoned their Midwestern surroundings in 1913, married in New Jersey, and joined a New York group of bohemian intellectuals and artists named the Liberal Club. The Club's excoriation, among other targets, of American commercial theater, and its practice of spending winters in New York's Greenwich Village and summers in the Cape Cod village of Provincetown, fueled the couple's resolve to launch a communal, self-sustaining theater with artistic integrity and innovation as the theoretical foundation. Following a few private readings of their first joint effort, a FREUDIAN one-act entitled *Suppressed Desires* (1915) which had been rejected by the Washington Square Players, Glaspell and Cook secured a fish house near their summer retreat, christened it the Wharf Theatre, and produced their own and three other plays during the first season with the aid of then-aspiring set designer Robert Edmond Jones (1887-1954). The following summer the company doubled its playbill with the help of O'Neill, whom Cook and Glaspell had recently befriended and whose dramatic talents they quickly championed. Beginning with the winter season of 1916-17 and extending to that of 1921-22, the Players competed directly with the New York establishment through their playhouse in Greenwich Village. The long list of dramatists whose works were featured, although heavily favoring Glaspell and O'Neill, included Dell, John Reed (1887-1920), Edna St. Vincent Millay (1892-1950), Djuna BARNES (*see* LOST GENERATION), Edna Ferber (1887-1968), Alfred Kreymborg (1883-1966), Wallace STEVENS (*see* MODERNISM, United States), Theodore DREISER (*see* NATURALISM, United States), Paul Green (1894-1981), and Maxwell Bodenheim (1892-1954).

Eventually disgusted by the Players' growing affinity with Broadway—largely due to O'Neill's mounting genius — Cook declared a sabbatical for the group in 1922, travelled with Glaspell to Greece, and from there issued a letter declaring the termination of the Provincetown experiment. A season later, O'Neill joined with Jones and Kenneth MacGowan (1888-1962) to revive the Players as the Experimental Theater. The group weathered another reorganization in 1925, and O'Neill's departure in 1926, before ceasing production altogether in 1929.

Despite the dependence of the movement on the singular artistry of O'Neill, the Provincetown Players were the first of the little theaters to gain national attention for the drama form as a vehicle of both literary and cultural importance. In addition, Cook's willingness to produce plays unacceptable to mainstream theaters, especially the early efforts of O'Neill, hastened the modernization of American drama and made possible the later, equally revolutionary works of such writers as Tennessee Williams (1911-1983), Arthur Miller (1915-), and Edward Albee (1928-).

❖•❖

Cook, George Cram (1873-1924)
American director, novelist, and dramatist.

Cook is remembered as the highly individual, visionary manager of the Provincetown Players. His predominant interests were classic Greek theater, the interrelationship of the arts, and the search for meaning and value in modern society. Initially, O'Neill's dramas lent themselves perfectly to the pursuit of these interests. However, Cook's extreme idealism, his belief that a close-knit theatrical group with a pure artistic mission could singlehandedly renew and unite national culture and consciousness, predisposed the association to failure. Ironically, his greatest creative achievement, aside from the founding of the Provincetown Players, may have been his courageous marshalling of financial and human resources for the set construction and staging of O'Neill's *THE EMPEROR JONES* (1920), one of the first of Cook's productions to ascend to the venues of Broadway he so loathed.

❖•❖

Glaspell, Susan (1882-1948)
American dramatist and novelist.

Although Glaspell was greatly overshadowed during her lifetime by O'Neill, her posthumous reputation as a serious and inventive playwright — one of the first to capably and originally address women's issues and problems — continues to grow. Glaspell's first play, a one-act entitled *TRIFLES* (1916), is often considered her best, even when compared to her last-performed work, *Alison's House* (1930), a less than commercially successful full-length drama, based loosely on Emily Dickinson's (1830-1886) life, which won a Pulitzer Prize in 1931. In *Trifles* she initiated one of her most revolutionary techniques, that of never allowing her story's main character to appear onstage. Following this work, her dramas acquired an increasingly literary and ambiguous, as opposed to dramatic and telling, structure and consequently suffered. From approximately 1931 until her death, Glaspell resided in Provincetown, abandoning her career as dramatist for that of minor novelist.

593

Trifles (1916).

One of the most widely anthologized American one-acts written during the early twentieth century, *Trifles* is a study in contrasting sexual roles. The play takes place in a rustic setting and concerns a woman imprisoned on suspicion of murdering her husband. An attorney, a sheriff and his wife, and a farmer and his wife visit the homestead where the murder allegedly occurred to collect clues. The men divide from the two women, who, sensitive to the minutiae and overlooked significances of commonplace signs, gradually discover that the woman committed the crime after enduring unspeakable cruelty at the hands of her husband. They conspire to hide the evidence, for they realize they share in the cycle of their neighbor's tragedy. More than a simple feminist indictment of sexual domination, *Trifles* exposes as well the universal problem of omitted acts of selfless assistance; in this play the omission of the two women who have not visited until now is as great a crime as the commission of the imprisoned woman.

❖•❖

O'Neill, Eugene (1888-1953), American dramatist.

O'Neill, the member most responsible for the Provincetown Players special position in literary history, was a writer steeped in the traditions of nineteenth-century melodrama, for his father, classically trained actor James O'Neill (1847-1920), had reigned for some twenty-five years as Edmond Dantes in Alexandre Dumas's (1802-1870) *The Count of Monte Cristo*. In spite or because of this background, O'Neill demonstrated from his earliest plays onward a gift for dramatic realism which resembled first NATURALISM and then EXPRESSIONISM before maturing into the distinctively barren, personal, and psychologically haunting MODERNISM of his final period. O'Neill began writing his apprentice plays — many of them one-acts focusing on the people and places he had encountered as a seaman and waterfront vagabond — in 1913, the year of his discharge from a tuberculosis sanatorium. After having spent less than a year at Princeton the previous decade, he resumed academic studies at Harvard, enrolling in George Pierce Baker's 47 WORKSHOP. He soon departed, however, due partially to Baker's heavy-handed, though not entirely unfavorable, criticisms.

In 1916 he submitted one of his workshop efforts, *Bound East for Cardiff*, to Cook and Glaspell, who enthusiastically accepted it to launch their second summer season. O'Neill immediately became involved with directing and acting as well as writing for the Players. When the company relocated to New York, O'Neill suggested that they be renamed the Playwrights' Theatre. His first major artistic success came in 1920 with the production of *Beyond the Horizon*, a full-length work which also became the first of the Players' repertoire to advance to Broadway. The following year the play garnered a

594

Pulitzer Prize and brought O'Neill widespread recognition. However, another of his plays produced that same year, *The Emperor Jones* (1920), more fully anticipated the symbolical and experimental nature of his mature work and thus stands as a revolutionary turning point in American drama. Throughout the 1920s O'Neill continued to challenge established rules of dramaturgy in such well-known works as *Anna Christie* (1921), *THE HAIRY APE* (1922), *Desire Under the Elms* (1924), and *Strange Interlude* (1928). By this time he had entered his final, greatest period of creativity and surpassed nearly all other Western playwrights as the driving force of Modernist drama. (*See also* Expressionism, United States.)

The Emperor Jones (1920).

Considered the first example of Expressionistic drama in America, *The Emperor Jones* marks a departure from the REALISM of O'Neill's closest American predecessor: playwright, producer, and director David Belasco (1859-1931). The story is that of a black American named Brutus Jones who has escaped prison and become dictator over the natives of a West Indies island. The action is primarily psychological and intensifies as Jones is forced to flee through the dense, ghost-ridden jungle from a revolting band of islanders. Consonant with Expressionistic drama, the doubt and guilt within, and the deterioration of, Jones's psyche is directly conveyed to the audience by the stark, foreboding setting, by Jones's terrifyingly introspective monologues, and by the unsettling recurrence of a drumbeat, which continues through the night and into the dawn until Jones is finally caught and executed.

Although generally less esteemed than the later Expressionist play *THE HAIRY APE*, *The Emperor Jones* has remained a popular choice for small company performance and its theme of the moral and psychological corruption and decay of the modern individual has remained a powerful reminder of the shortcomings of capitalistic society.

➤•◄

Further Reading

Bach, Gerhard. "Susan Glaspell: Provincetown Playwright." *Great Lakes Review: A Journal of Midwest Culture* 4, 2 (1978): 31-43.

Bigsby, C. W. E. "Provincetown: The Birth of Twentieth-Century American Drama." In his *A Critical Introduction to Twentieth-Century American Drama*. Vol. 1, *1900-1940*. Cambridge, England: Cambridge University Press, 1982-85.

Deutsch, Helen, and Stella Hanau. *The Provincetown: A Story of the Theatre*. New York: Farrar & Rinehart, 1931.

France, Rachel. "Susan Glaspell." In *Dictionary of Literary Biography*. Vol. 7, pt. 1, *Twentieth-Century American Dramatists*. Edited by John MacNicholas. Detroit: Gale Research Co., 1981.

Frenz, Horst. *Eugene O'Neill*. New York: Ungar, 1971.

Geddes, Virgil. *The Melodramadness of Eugene O'Neill*. Brookfield, Conn.: Brookfield Players, 1934.

Glaspell, Susan. *The Road to the Temple*. London: E. Benn, 1926.

Goldman, Arnold. "The Culture of the Provincetown Players." *Journal of American Studies* 12, 3 (December 1978): 291-310.

Longman, Stanley Vincent. "New Forces at Work in the American Theatre: 1915-1925." In *Dictionary of Literary Biography*. Vol. 7, pt. 2, *Twentieth-Century American Dramatists*. Edited by John MacNicholas. Detroit: Gale Research Co., 1981.

O'Neill, Eugene. *The Theatre We Worked For: The Letters of Eugene O'Neill to Kenneth MacGowan*. Edited by Jackson R. Bryer. New Haven, Conn.: Yale University Press, 1982.

The Provincetown Plays. 6 vols. New York: F. Shay, 1916-18.

Radel, Nicholas F. "Provincetown Plays: Women Writers and O'Neill's American Intertext." *Essays in Theatre* 9, 1 (November 1990): 31-43.

Roy, Emil. "Eugene O'Neill's *The Emperor Jones* and *The Hairy Ape* as Mirror Plays." *Comparative Drama* II (spring 1968): 21-31.

Sarlós, Robert Károly. *Jig Cook and the Provincetown Players: Theatre in Ferment*. Amherst, Mass.: University of Massachusetts Press, 1982.

———. "Eugene O'Neill and the Provincetown Players: Watershed in American Theatre." In *Eugene O'Neill in China: An International Centenary Celebration*. Edited by Liu Haiping and Lowell Swortzell. New York: Greenwood, 1992.

Sayler, Oliver. *Our American Theatre*. New York: Brentano's, 1923.

Tiusanen, Timo. *O'Neill's Scenic Images*. Princeton, N.J.: Princeton University Press, 1968.

Waterman, Arthur E. *Susan Glaspell*. New York: Twayne, 1966.

PRZEDMIEŚCIE GROUP (City Outskirts)
Poland, 1930s

The Przedmieście Group, founded in Warsaw in 1933, was a cooperative effort between Helena Boguszewska (1886-1978) and Jerzy Kornacki (1908-) to publish novels grounded in the social facts and issues of the time. In particular, Boguszewska and Kornacki attempted to document the lives of workers in various trades or professions along with the milieus they inhabited. Ironically, Bruno Schulz (1892-1942), one of the modern masters of the macabre and surreal, was an early associate of the group.

✦•✦

Further Reading

Miłosz, Czesław. "Independent Poland: 1918-1939—The Novel and the Short Story." In his *The History of Polish Literature*. London: Macmillan, 1969. Rev. ed., Berkeley, Calif.: University of California Press, 1983.

PUJANGGA BARU. *See* NEW WRITERS' CIRCLE

PYLON SCHOOL
England, 1930s

The name was taken from the title of an early poem by Stephen Spender (1909-1995), "The Pylons," one of a number of his initial works which depict the effects of a burgeoning industrial and technological society. Other members of the group were W. H. Auden (1907-1973), C. Day-Lewis (1904-1972), and Louis MacNeice (1907-1963). The work of the young Pylons has been called deliberately self-conscious, in their attempts to keynote airplanes, buildings, super-highways, trains, and power stations. Other works reflected their shared left-wing views which were precipitated by Auden's term "the public chaos" of their time. Auden was to develop into a poet of great stature and his mature work is said to have influenced the generation of poets who followed him with an impact comparable to that of William Butler YEATS (*see* ABBEY THEATER and MODERNISM, England and Ireland); by the fifties Auden was known as a major poet of distinction and his work continues to maintain the reputation. Spender was early concerned with the responsibility of the writer to treat socio-political issues and remained so. He divided his many literary talents among the genres of poetry, critical works, and translations of works by Federico García Lorca (1898-1936), Rainer Maria Rilke (1875-1926), Freidrich von Schiller (1759-1805), and other writers of note.

✦•✦

Further Reading

Carter, Ronald, ed. *Thirties Poets: "The Auden Group": A Casebook*. London: Macmillan, 1984.
O'Neill, Michael. *Auden, MacNeice, Spender: The Thirties Poetry*. New York: St. Martin's Press, 1992.
Sternlicht, Sanford V. *Stephen Spender*. New York: Twayne; Toronto: Maxwell Macmillan Canada; New York: Maxwell Macmillan International, 1992.
Weatherhead, A. Kingsley. *Stephen Spender and the Thirties*. Lewisburg, Pa.: Bucknell University Press, 1975.
Whitehead, John. *A Commentary on the Poetry of W. H. Auden, C. Day Lewis, Louis MacNeice, and Stephen Spender*. Lewiston, N.Y.: E. Mellen Press, 1992.

Q

QUADRIGA
Poland, 1920s-1930s

Quadriga, also transliterated as Kwadryga, was a Polish poetry movement of the 1920s and 1930s that opposed the detached aestheticism of the *SKAMANDER* GROUP. Although only a loose affiliate, Konstanty Gałczyński (1905-1953) is generally regarded as Quadriga's finest poet and social critic. Like Czesław MIŁOSZ and the *ŻAGARY* GROUP, Gałczyński ominously foreshadowed World War II through his Catastrophist outlook.

❖•❖

Further Reading

Koźniewski, Kazimierz. "The Legend of Janusz Korczak, Gałczyński, and Tuwim on the 25th Anniversary of Their Deaths." *New Polish Publications, a Monthly Review of Polish Books* 26, 8-9 (August-September 1978): 1-2, 6-9.

Miłosz, Czesław. "Independent Poland: 1918-1939 — Poetry." In his *The History of Polish Literature*. London: Macmillan, 1969. Rev. ed., Berkeley, Calif.: University of California Press, 1983.

R

RAB'E GROUP
Iran, 1930s

The writers of the Rab'e Group furthered the MODERNIST trend in Persian literature in Iran during the 1930s. Resemblances to European modes, such as REALISM and SUR-REALISM, are found in the stories and novels of Sadeq Hedayat (or Sadiq Hidayat, 1903-1951), who studied in Belgium and France and spent much of his life in Paris, where he committed suicide; the poetry of Mas'ud Farzad (1906-), who spent many years in England as a translator and scholar of English literature; and the fiction and prose of Buzurg 'Alavi (1904-), who went to university in Berlin. The group collaborated on a number of collections of their works which emphasized non-monarchical ideology, cosmopolitanism, and the modernization of Persian literature. Hedayat and 'Alavi, along with Shin Partaw (n.d.), published a collection of short stories entitled *Aniran* (Non-Iranian) in 1931. Mujtaba Minuvi (n.d.), another figure associated with the group, wrote the preface to Hedayat's historical play, *Maziyar,* in 1933. Hedayat and Farzad together produced *Vagh Vagh Sahab* (1933; Mister Bow-wow), a collection of 34 narratives criticizing contemporary Iranian culture. Written in a mock verse parodying traditional Persian poetic techniques, *Vagh Vagh Sahab* presents "cases" of cultural corruption existing in theater, literary production and scholarship, film, and the intelligentsia at large. The group had some impact on the Iranian literary scene until Reza Shah Pahlavi's government ordered its dissolution in 1936. The following year, 'Alavi — active in a Marxist group — was imprisoned with other members for violating Pahlavi's 1931 ban on Communist organizations and was not released until 1941. Of the group, Hedayat is considered most prominent, especially for his novel, *Buf-i Kur* (1937; *The Blind Owl*, 1957, 1974), though he is known as well for dramas, translations of Franz KAFKA's (*see* MODERNISM, Austria and Germany) work, and Persian folklore studies.

599

✤•✦

Further Reading

Hidayat, Sadiq. *The Blind Owl and Other Hedayat Stories.* Edited by Russell P. Christiansen. Compiled by Carol L. Sayers. Minneapolis: Sorayya, 1984.

Hillman, M. C. "Major Voices in Contemporary Persian Literature." *Literature East and West* 20, 1-4 (January-December 1976).

————. "Revolution, Islam, and Contemporary Persian Literature." In *Iran: Essays on a Revolution in the Making.* Edited by Ahmad Jabbari and Robert Olson. Lexington, Ky.: Mazda Publishers, 1981.

Kamshad, Hassan. *Modern Persian Prose Literature.* Bethesda, Md.: Iranbooks, 1996.

AL-RĀBITA AL-QALAMIYYA. See **SOCIETY OF THE PEN**

RAPP (Russian Association of Proletarian Writers). *See* OCTOBER GROUP and SOCIALIST REALISM, Russia

READER-RESPONSE CRITICISM AND RECEPTION THEORY
Germany and United States, c. 1938-1990s

Like DECONSTRUCTION, the GENEVA SCHOOL, SEMIOTICS, STRUCTURALISM, and a number of other twentieth-century movements in literary criticism, Reader-Response Criticism and Reception Theory, as the two names suggest, place an almost paramount importance on the hermeneutical, or interpretive, aspect of the author-text-reader relationship. Several leading theorists of the movement have noted that Response Criticism is in fact a longstanding tradition, reaching back as far as Aristotle's *Poetics* (4th c. B.C.) and the writings of Longinus (c. 213-273 A.D.). However, not until seminal theorist Louise Rosenblatt's (1904-) 1938 study *Literature as Exploration* (3rd ed., 1976) was the reader accorded the position of prominence, above both that of author and text, in hermeneutical explorations. The dominance of NEW CRITICISM in the first half of the century certainly aided this cause, but the school's extreme restriction of the reader's emotive reactions to the literary work precluded the type of creative, personal criticism promoted by the Response and Reception schools.

Following Rosenblatt's impetus, a group of German scholars at the University of Konstanz developed what they termed Rezeptionsästhetik, a theory of historical relativism in interpretation founded on the principles of Phenomenology and Hermeneutics first outlined by Hans-Georg Gadamer (1900-?), Edmund Husserl (1859-1938), and Roman Ingarden (1893-1970). The chief proponent of this German school was Hans Robert Jauss (1921-), whose pioneering lecture "Literaturgeschichte als

600

Provokation der Literaturwissenschaft" (1969; "Literary History as a Challenge to Literary Theory," in *New Literary History,* 1970-71) paved the way for such later works as Rainer Warning's (n.d.) *Rezeptionsasthetik: Theorie und Praxis* (1975) and Wolfgang Iser's (1926-) *Der implizite Leser* (1972; *The Implied Reader,* 1974) and *Der Akt des Lesens: Theorie Asthetischer Wirkung* (1976; *The Act of Reading: A Theory of Aesthetic Response,* 1978). Iser's work, in particular, has been of fundamental importance in the United States for a burgeoning school of Reader-Response critics, of whom Stanley Fish (1938-), David Bleich (1940-), and Buffalo School leader Norman Holland (1927-) — also connected with FREUDIAN CRITICISM — are the most prominent figures. Bleich's special focus on transactive criticism, in which the text is said not to exist until the reader transacts with it, and Fish's interest in communities of readers, have engendered much of the critical discussion in America during the 1970s and 1980s. An additional aspect of the movement in recent years is its relationship to FEMINIST CRITICISM. Among the Reader-Response Feminist theorists, Elizabeth A. Flynn (1944-) is perhaps the most notable. The most promising feature of the movement as a whole is its warm reception among educational circles due to its democratic point-of-view and uniquely metacritical process: students are taught both that no response is without value and that a conscious attention to the *construction* of meaning, especially within the dynamics of the classroom, is far more instructive than a mere review of standard interpretations.

⇒•⇐

Further Reading

Amacher, Richard E., and Victor Lange, eds. *New Perspectives in German Literary Criticism*. Princeton, N.J.: Princeton University Press, 1979.

Bleich, David. *Readings and Feelings: An Introduction to Subjective Criticism*. Urbana, Ill.: National Council of Teachers of English, 1975.

Clifford, John, ed. *The Experience of Reading: Louise Rosenblatt and Reader-Response Theory*. Portsmouth, N.H.: Boynton/Cook Publishers, 1991.

Everman, Welsh D. *Who Says This? The Authority of the Author, the Discourse, and the Reader*. Carbondale, Ill.: Southern Illinois University Press, 1988.

Farrell, Edmund J., and James R. Squire, eds. *Transactions with Literature: A Fifty-Year Perspective: For Louise M. Rosenblatt*. Urbana, Ill.: National Council of Teachers of English, 1990.

Fish, Stanley. *Is There a Text in This Class?* Cambridge, Mass.: Harvard University Press, 1980.

Freund, Elizabeth. *The Return of the Reader: Reader-Response Criticism*. London: Methuen, 1987.

Holland, Norman N. *The Dynamics of Literary Response*. New York: Oxford University Press, 1968.

———. *5 Readers Reading*. New Haven, Conn.: Yale University Press, 1975.

Holub, Robert C. *Reception Theory: A Critical Introduction*. London: Methuen, 1984.

Iser, Wolfgang. *The Act of Reading: A Theory of Aesthetic Response*. Baltimore, Md.: Johns Hopkins University Press, 1978.

————. *The Implied Reader: Patterns of Communication in Prose Fiction from Bunyan to Beckett*. Baltimore, Md.: Johns Hopkins University Press, 1974.

————. *Prospecting: From Reader Response to Literary Anthropology*. Baltimore, Md.: Johns Hopkins University Press, 1989.

Jauss, Hans Robert. *Toward an Aesthetic of Reception*. Translated by Timothy Bahti. Minneapolis: University of Minnesota Press, 1982.

Koelb, Clayton. *The Incredulous Reader: Literature and the Function of Disbelief*. Ithaca, N.Y.: Cornell University Press, 1984.

Mileur, Jean-Pierre. *The Critical Romance: The Critic as Reader, Writer, Hero*. Madison, Wis.: University of Wisconsin Press, 1990.

Rosenblatt, Louise M. *Literature as Exploration*. New York: D. Appleton-Century, 1938. 5th ed., New York: Modern Language Association, 1995.

————. *The Reader, the Text, the Poem: The Transactional Theory of the Literary Work*. Carbondale, Ill.: Southern Illinois University Press, 1978.

————. *Writing and Reading: The Transactional Theory*. Champaign, Ill.: University of Illinois at Urbana-Champaign, 1988.

Spolsky, Ellen, ed. *The Uses of Adversity: Failure and Accommodation in Reader Response*. Lewisburg, Pa.: Bucknell University Press, 1990.

Suleiman, Susan, and Inge Crosman, eds. *The Reader in the Text*. Princeton, N.J.: Princeton University Press, 1980.

Tompkins, Jane P., ed. *Reader-Response Criticism: From Formalism to Post-Structuralism*. Baltimore, Md.: Johns Hopkins University Press, 1981.

REALISM and NATURALISM: An Overview

One of the most problematic terms in literary criticism is Realism. The word, which derives from *Poetischer Realismus*, a German phrase coined in 1802, has been ever since variously employed to describe an ontological philosophy, a theory of painting, a narrative style, a concerted cultural revolt against Romanticism and idealism, a distinct literary period, and a ubiquitous quality of modern writing. When understood as a broad-based and persistent aesthetic movement, a concept which tends to subsume each of these definitions, Realism becomes considerably clarified in meaning. The first stirrings of Realism as a purposive, self-conscious movement occurred in Europe around 1830 and the last significant rumblings around 1914, near the outbreak of World War I, the end of the EDWARDIAN Age, and the meteoric rise of MODERNISM. Although the distinct literary and social heritages of the dozen or so countries in which Realism flourished led to marked differences in the literature produced, each national movement championed several essentially identical principles. These—the belief in verisimilitude of setting, character, language, and event—served to unify and inspire the efforts of numerous original writers interested, above all, in the advancement of the novel, the form which came to dominate the era.

Although it may well be argued that the traditions of poetic and dramatic Realism —
as evidenced by the works of Homer (9th-8th? c. B.C.), Euripedes (c. 484-406 B.C.),
Aeschylus (525-456 B.C.), Christopher Marlowe (1564-1593), Shakespeare, and Ben
Jonson (1572-1637) — have enjoyed longer and richer traditions than novelistic
Realism, it was the novel almost exclusively that excited the minds of those nineteenth-
century writers intent on revolutionizing the role of the creative artist. Novelistic
Realism has its roots in a work often termed the first modern European novel, Miguel
de Cervantes's (1547-1616) *Don Quixote* (1605, 1615). The publication of *Don Quixote* marked one of the most important watersheds in literary history. Its satirization of
imaginative literature and corresponding concern with the various levels of human
perception hastened the demise of the chivalric romance and inaugurated the gradual
ascendancy of true-to-life narration. In the eighteeenth century, Cervantes's innovations were furthered, particularly in England, by such writers as Daniel Defoe (1660-
1731), Henry Fielding (1707-1754), Tobias Smollett (1721-1771), and Samuel
Richardson (1689-1761). However, Neoclassicism, with its emphasis on lofty sentiment
and the emulation of Greek and Latin models of poetry and drama, tended to dominate
serious literature. In the early nineteenth century, the precursors of Realistic literature
became more widespread. Accurate portraiture of society, particularly bourgeois or
middle-class life, became commonplace following the pioneering work of Jane Austen
(1775-1817) in England; Stendhal (1783-1842) and Honoré de Balzac (1799-1850) in
France; and Nikolai Gogol (1809-1852) and Nikolai Nekrasov (1821-1877) in Russia.
In Germany, however, the advancement towards Realism was slowed by the enormous
influence of Romanticist Johann Wolfgang von Goethe (1749-1832) and the tradition
of the early nineteenth-century Bildungsroman (novel of formation), though this form,
and such important subtypes as the Künstlerroman (artist-novel), gradually became
well-suited to both Realistic and Modernistic novel-writing. Notwithstanding the special
situation in Germany, Romanticism, with its emphasis upon lyric poetry, nature, the
imagination, and the sublimity of the individual, began to be systematically replaced
by Realism throughout Europe from about the mid-nineteenth century onwards.

As a recognized school of thought, however, Realism first emerged in France through
the painting techniques of Gustave Courbet. Champfleury (pseud. of Jules Husson,
1821-1889), a minor novelist and critic, outlined the artistic principles of Courbet in *Le
réalisme* (1857; Realism) while urging writers to mimic Courbet's style of close,
detailed observance. Gustave FLAUBERT, probably the single most influential writer in
the Realistic vein, preceded this work with a prolonged narrative experimentation —
the completely unidealized, objective presentation of a story of adultery. The novel that
emerged was *MADAME BOVARY* (1857; *Madame Bovary*, 1881). Flaubert's talent for
subtle satire and his keen understanding of moral tragedy elevated both his novel and

the genre as a whole to a station of unprecedented importance. With Flaubert's example of unobtrusive narration to guide the experiments of an international circle of admirers—namely, Edmond and Jules de GONCOURT, Émile ZOLA, Guy de MAUPASSANT, Henry JAMES, Ivan TURGENEV, and Giovanni VERGA—the novel became the vehicle par excellence for documenting nineteenth-century society. Turgenev in Russia, the Brothers Goncourt in France, and James in America were among those novelists who most notably emulated and expanded upon Flaubert's method. Greatly adding to the movement's force was Flaubert's chief disciple, Guy de Maupassant, who became responsible for resurrecting and refining the short story form, a powerful vehicle for Realistic expression which was significantly futhered through the stylistic developments of such writers as Anton CHEKHOV and Realist-Modernist Ernest HEMINGWAY (*see* LOST GENERATION).

Surprisingly, Flaubert eventually rejected his demanding method, almost as if to say that complete documentary objectivity was more an ideal than an attainable reality, more a hollow artistic invention than an ultimate creative end. Although such text-oriented disillusionment was atypical of the movement's writers, a broader psychological and social disillusionment was not. Increasingly, the Industrial Age held sway over their minds, as did advancements in scientific knowledge. One of the most influential extra-literary works was Charles Darwin's *On the Origin of Species* (1859), which propounded the theory of evolution and, indirectly, shattered longstanding religious assumptions. The writings of Friedrich NIETZSCHE, Karl MARX, and Søren Kierkegaard (1813-1855) all added to the Darwinian assumptions that humanity must rely on itself, rather than transcendent aid, for the betterment of the human condition. Positivism and Pragmatism became the watchwords of the Western intelligentsia, Populism and Socialism those of the working classes. Realism, despite its austere Flaubertian roots, largely became, during the 1880s and 1890s, a venue for social criticism and satiric commentary. Zola's manifesto *LE ROMAN EXPÉRIMENTAL* (1880; *The Experimental Novel*, 1880) and his novel *GERMINAL* (1885; *Germinal; or, Master and Man*, 1885) played central roles in this development, in which the initial tenets of Realism were carried to such an extreme that a new movement, NATURALISM, was born. Writers in the United States, a country then plagued by rapid growth through immigration and widespread problems of poor living conditions and injustice in the workplace, were particularly receptive to the clear-eyed humanitarian, if deterministic, message of Zola's Naturalism. Foremost among this group were Stephen CRANE, Frank NORRIS, Theodore DREISER, and Jack London (1876-1916). Interestingly, their decidedly reactionary stance and techniques helped to legitimize as mainstream the work of their Realistic counterparts (i.e., James, Mark TWAIN, and William Dean HOWELLS, who were once regarded as equally reactionary by the Romantic mainstream.

Beyond the roots, highlights, and turning points of the two closely related movements, what is important to remember is that Realism and Naturalism, no less or more so than Modernism, or a number of diverse twentieth-century movements, including PROLETARIAN LITERATURE, MAGIC REALISM, and the NEW NOVEL, stood for the development of literary forms and techniques capable of supporting one particular generation's view of reality; the UNRELIABLE NARRATOR (*see* REALISM, United States), the LOCAL COLOR sketch, structural irony, vernacular dialogue, the anti-hero—these were the tools used by a host of writers including George ELIOT, Charles DICKENS, James, Flaubert, Fyodor DOSTOEVSKY, Leo TOLSTOY, Henrik IBSEN, August STRINDBERG, Gerhart HAUPTMANN, Benito PÉREZ GALDÓS, George Gissing (1857-1903), Arno Holz (1863-1929), Emilia Pardo Bazán (1851-1921), Amalie Skram (1846-1905), and Premchand (1880-1936) as they embarked on their investigations of the unconscious mind, the rise of religious skepticism, and changing class structures and cultural mores. Undoubtedly, the Realists were the first to so deliberately schematize and popularize true-to-life narration, in such indisputable classics as *Madame Bovary, VOINA I MIR* (1869; *War and Peace,* 1886), *THE PORTRAIT OF A LADY* (1881), *OUR MUTUAL FRIEND* (1864-65), *BRAT'YA KARAMAZOVY* (1879-80; *The Brothers Karamazov,* 1912), *MIDDLEMARCH* (1871-72), *Die Weber* (1892), and *AN AMERICAN TRAGEDY* (1925). Yet they were by no means the last; Modernists Thomas MANN, Marcel PROUST, and James JOYCE, the three preeminent novelists of the twentieth century, each drew upon the traditions of Realism in order to create something at once artistically new and independent, yet inescapably rooted in the literary past. As New Novelist Alain ROBBE-GRILLET has written, "Realism is the ideology which each brandishes against his neighbor, the quality which each believes he possesses for himself alone. And it has always been the same: out of a concern for [R]ealism each new literary school has sought to destroy the one which preceded it." Still what remains unique of the Realistic movement as a whole is the sheer enormity in terms of works, names, and nations it encompassed. The epoch of Realism, one unprecedented in daring, scope, and achievement, ushered in the twentieth century and the beginnings of modern literature as no other could.

✦•✦

Realism: A Timeline

1780   Approximate beginning of the Industrial Revolution.

1830   Stendhal publishes *Le rouge et le noir* (*The Red and the Black,* 1898); Balzac publishes the first novel of his multivolume series, *La comédie humaine* (*Comédie humaine,* 1895-98).

1833   Pushkin publishes *Eugene Onegin* (*Eugene Onegin,* 1937).

1842   Gogol publishes *Myortvye dushi* (*Dead Souls,* 1887).

605

1848   Marx and Engels publish *Das kommunistische Manifest* (*Communist Manifesto*, 1850, 1872); Second French Republic formed.

1852   Turgenev publishes *Zapiski okhotnika* (*A Sportsman's Sketches*, 1895).

1854   Beginning of the Crimean War, which lasts until 1856.

1857   Flaubert publishes *MADAME BOVARY (Madame Bovary,* 1881); Champfleury publishes *Le réalisme.*

1859   Darwin publishes *On the Origin of Species.*

1861   Ten states secede from the union and the American Civil War begins; emancipation of Russian serfs declared.

1862   Turgenev publishes *OTTSY I DETI* (*Fathers and Sons*, 1867).

1864   The Brothers Goncourt publish *GERMINIE LACERTEUX* (*Germinie Lacerteux*, 1887).

1867   DeForest publishes *MISS RAVENEL'S CONVERSION FROM SECESSION TO LOYALTY*; Marx publishes first volume of *Das Kapital* (*Capital*, 1886, 1907-9).

1869   Tolstoy publishes *VOINA I MIR* (*War and Peace,* 1886); U.S. transcontinental railroad completed.

1872   Nietzsche publishes *Die Geburt der Tragödie* (*The Birth of Tragedy*, 1910, 1968).

1876   Alexander Graham Bell invents the telephone.

1879   Thomas Edison invents the incandescent light bulb; Dostoevsky publishes *BRAT'YA KARAMAZOVY* (*The Brothers Karamazov*, 1912).

1881   James publishes *THE PORTRAIT OF A LADY.*

1883   Nietzsche begins publishing *Also Sprach Zarathustra* (*Thus Spake Zarathustra,* 1909, 1954).

1884   Twain publishes *THE ADVENTURES OF HUCKLEBERRY FINN.*

1885   Howells publishes *THE RISE OF SILAS LAPHAM.*

1887   Pérez Galdós publishes *FORTUNATA Y JACINTA* (*Fortunata and Jacinta: Two Stories of Married Women*, 1973).

1889   Verga publishes *Mastro-Don Gesualdo.*

1894   Dreyfus affair brought to trial in France.

1903   Wright brothers make first airplane flight.

1904   Russo-Japanese War.

1905   Russian Revolution.

1925   Dreiser publishes *AN AMERICAN TRAGEDY*; FITZGERALD publishes *THE GREAT GATSBY* at the height of the JAZZ AGE.

REALISM (Poetischer Realismus)
Present-day Austria, Germany, and Switzerland, c. 1848-1880s

Originating with the emergence of a united, though disordered, Germany in 1848, German (Poetic) Realism was, for the most part, unconnected with the other strains of Realism present throughout Europe. More artful, or poetic, in form, the new German Realistic novella and lyric poem (the movement's two primary genres) represented a reaction to both the idealism of Friedrich von Schiller (1759-1805) and the proto-NAT-URALISTIC, political activist writing characteristic of the 1830s. Consequently, criticism of social institutions and a concern for the individual's place in society is virtually absent in the works of this period; instead, such writers as Theodor Fontane (1819-1898), Gottfried Keller (1819-1890), Conrad Ferdinand Meyer (1825-1898), Theodor Storm (1817-1888), Wilhelm Raabe (1831-1910), and Adalbert Stifter (1805-1868) generally focused on specific regions, character types, and crises, providing detailed geographical and psychological studies tinged with a Romantic appreciation of nature and a longing for the past. Their best works remained inescapably linked to the Bildungsroman tradition launched by Johann Wolfgang von Goethe (1749-1832). Stifter's *Der Nachsommer* (1857; *Indian Summer*, 1985), is often cited as the movement's most exemplary and influential novel. Among its twentieth-century champions was Realist-MODERNIST Thomas MANN.

❖•❖

Further Reading

Alt, A. Tilo. *Theodor Storm*. New York: Twayne, 1973.

Artiss, David. *Theodor Storm: Studies in Ambivalence*. Amsterdam: Benjamins, 1978.

Bance, Alan. *Theodor Fontane: The Major Novels*. Cambridge, England: Cambridge University Press, 1982.

Beddow, Michael. *The Fiction of Humanity: Studies in the "Bildungsroman" from Wieland to Thomas Mann*. Cambridge, England: Cambridge University Press, 1982.

Bennett, Edwin K. *A History of the German Novelle from Goethe to Thomas Mann*. Cambridge, England: Cambridge University Press, 1934. 2nd ed., 1961.

Berman, Russell A. "The Authority of Address: Adalbert Stifter" and "The Dissolution of Meaning: Theodor Fontane." In his *The Rise of the Modern German Novel: Crisis and Charisma*. Cambridge, Mass.: Harvard University Press, 1986.

Bernd, Clifford A. *German Poetic Realism*. Boston: Twayne, 1981.

———. *Theodor Storm's Craft of Fiction: The Torment of a Narrator*. Chapel Hill, N.C.: University of North Carolina Press, 1963. 2nd ed., 1966.

Davis, Gabriele A. Wittig. *Novel Associations: Theodor Fontane and George Eliot within the Context of Nineteenth-Century Realism*. New York: P. Lang, 1983.

Hart, Gail. *Readers and Their Fictions in the Novels and Novellas of Gottfried Keller*. Chapel Hill, N.C.: University of North Carolina Press, 1989.

Laane, Tiiu V. *Imagery in Conrad Ferdinand Meyer's Prose Works: Form, Motifs, and Functions*. Berne, Switzerland: P. Lang, 1983.

McCormick, E. Allen. *Theodor Storm's Novellen: Essays on Literary Technique*. Chapel Hill, N.C.: University of North Carolina, 1964.

Michielsen, Gertrude. *The Preparation of the Future: Techniques of Anticipation in the Novels of Theodor Fontane and Thomas Mann*. Berne, Switzerland: P. Lang, 1978.

Pascal, Roy. "Adalbert Stifter: Indian Summer." In his *The German Novel*. Manchester, England: Manchester University Press, 1956.

Paulin, Roger. *The Brief Compass: The Nineteenth Century German Novelle*. Oxford, England: Clarendon Press, 1985.

Ruppel, Richard R. *Gottfried Keller: Poet, Pedagogue, and Humanist*. New York: P. Lang, 1988.

Sammons, Jeffrey L. ed. *German Novellas of Realism*. New York: Continuum, 1989.

Silz, Walter. *Realism and Reality: Studies in the German Novelle of Poetic Realism*. Chapel Hill, N.C.: University of North Carolina Press, 1954.

Stocksieker Di Maio, Irene. *The Multiple Perspective: Wilhelm Raabe's Third-Person Narratives of the Braunschweig Period*. Amsterdam: Benjamins, 1981.

Swales, Martin. *The German "Bildungsroman" from Wieland to Hesse*. Princeton, N.J.: Princeton University Press, 1978.

————. *The German Novelle*. Princeton, N.J.: Princeton University Press, 1977.

Swales, Martin, and Erika Swales. *Adalbert Stifter: A Critical Study*. Cambridge, England: Cambridge University Press, 1984.

REALISM
Catalonia, Spain, 1900s

A product of the Catalonia region of Spain, Catalan Realism was important to the development of the modern novel in that country. Two of the most widely known writers associated with the movement, which flourished around the turn of the century, were Narcis Oller i Moragues (1846-1930) and Victor Català (1873-1966).

❖•❖

Further Reading

Canepari, Sandra Joan. "Benito Perez Galdos and Narcis Oller: Vision of a Real and a Novelistic Society." *Dissertation Abstracts International* 38 (1977): 2158A.

Yates, Alan. "'Artistic Thinking' in Narcis Oller's *La bogeria*." In *Hispanic Studies in Honour of Geoffrey Ribbans*. Edited by Ann L. Mackenzie and Dorothy S. Severin. Liverpool, England: Liverpool University Press, 1992.

————. "Economic Change and Economic Attitudes in Nineteenth-Century Catalonia: Narcis Oller's Study of the Miser in *L'Escanyapobres* (1884)." *Romance Studies* 23 (spring 1994): 73-83.

REALISM
Denmark, 1880s-1900s

Unlike the majority of its European namesakes, Danish Realism surfaced following the rise of NATURALISM, which, under the guidance in Denmark of Georg Brandes (1842-1927), adopted a particularly individualistic, NIETZSCHEAN approach to the human condition. It was against this strong aesthetic current as well as a lesser element of Neoromanticism in Danish literature that Karl Larsen (1860-1927), the chief Danish Realist, battled. Larsen, known for his ideologically neutral stories about the Copenhagen slums, is credited with reinvigorating Danish prose during the latter years of the nineteenth century.

⇸•⇷

Further Reading

Mitchell, P. M. *A History of Danish Literature*. 2nd ed. New York: Kraus-Thomson Organization Ltd., 1971.

REALISM
England, 1850s-1890s

Realism is a literary term fraught with ambiguity, in part, because of its ability to refer to that diverse phenomenon known as "real life." Its meaning in terms of the literary movement may be better understood when set in its historical context. During the nineteenth century, Realism was a concept set up in opposition to Romanticism, previously the dominant literary mode. Realism referred to works of art which attempted to present objective portrayals of everyday life, rather than the idealized heroic quests characteristic of romanticist literature, often expressed in poetry. In the literary arena, the rise of the novel form itself was linked to the then-growing aesthetic fashionability of Realistic over Romanticist representations.

In England, Realism emerged as a literary tendency during the middle and late decades of the nineteenth century. It was closely connected with developments in the contemporary cultural milieu and was the dominant technique in English literature until shortly after the turn of the century (by which time changes in stylistic texture and content required a new descriptive critical term — MODERNISM). Fed by French REALISM as well as the flowering of the biological, mechanical, and social sciences which increasingly engaged popular imagination and thought, many works produced at the time reflected these interests by implicitly or explicitly drawing on such examinations of life as the evolutionary theories articulated by Charles Darwin (1809-1882) in *On the Origin of Species by Means of Natural Selection* (1859) and the well-known social journalism conducted by Henry Mayhew (1812-1887), collected in *London Labour and the London Poor* (1851). In addition, England experienced general upheaval caused by the Industrial Revolution, the subsequent population shift from the countryside to cities, and political waves felt from the revolution in France some decades earlier. René Wellek, in "The Concept of Realism in Literary Scholarship," notes "the far greater consciousness that man is a being living in society rather than a moral being facing God." Which is not to say that moral concerns were absent from the works of Realist writers.

Social reform was a prominent theme in such Realist literary works as George ELIOT's *MIDDLEMARCH* (1871-72), Elizabeth Gaskell's *Mary Barton* (1848), and the vast array of Charles DICKENS's novels. Foremost among earlier and contemporary influences on the English Realists were Matthew Arnold (1822-1888) and John Stuart Mill (1806-1873). Arnold, in *Culture and Anarchy* (1869), asserted that the spread of culture and education from the higher to the lower classes would help to ensure social harmony and stability. Mill's writings on utilitarian doctrine urged that public morality be founded on achieving the greatest happiness for the greatest number of people in society. Amid outbreaks of lower-class revolt against discriminatory governmental institutions and economic practices, some strove to attain social stability by such means as Parliamentary reform.

The English Realists built upon literary precedents set memorably by Daniel Defoe (1660-1731), with his Realistic focus on a lower-class heroine's social condition in *Moll Flanders* (1722), and Henry Fielding (1707-1754), who in *Tom Jones* (1749) presented a Naturalist if satirically stretched portrayal of English society. A historically more immediate precursor of English Realist novelists was, of course, Jane Austen (1775-1817). Her rejection of sentimentality and Romanticism depicted in such novels as *Sense and Sensibility* (1811) foreshadows later Realists as do her attempts at psychologically detailed characterizations in *Emma* (1816) and *Mansfield Park* (1814).

Realism influenced several important later movements. Its attention to science and determinism became more pronounced in the NATURALISM of, for example, Émile ZOLA. Realism can also be counted among the forerunners to Modernism with its beginnings of antiheroism in character formation and, as Wellek noted, the development of a turn toward attempting to portray subjective reality through STREAM-OF-CONSCIOUSNESS narrative (*see* MODERNISM, England and Ireland), which was posited as being more real than external reality and that ultimately excludes the ordinary concrete reality associated with Realism. Realist techniques also paved the way for the SOCIALIST REALISM that emerged around the world during the twentieth century.

Despite a surfeit of English Realists, only Dickens and Eliot are regarded to be among the world's greatest novelists. Thomas Hardy (1840-1928), a writer of the first rank, is generally considered separately due not only to his belatedness, but to the nature of his achievement which can be seen more as an early contribution to Modernist technique and mood, with its dark plots and its characters, such as Jude Fawley in *Jude the Obscure* (1896), who find themselves in uncertain worlds and are not so confident of what constitutes healthy social and individual morality.

Since receiving serious academic attention during the twentieth century, Dickens has been described as part of the English Realist trend though, as many critics contend, most of his characters read better as exaggerated types than as such psychologically realistic people as Eliot brilliantly drew. It is rather his panoramic vision and bitingly imaginative portrayal of multiple and interdependent social worlds hinging on the political-economic realities of mid-nineteenth-century England that warrants his status as a Realist.

George Eliot combined immense philosophical learning with acute powers of insight into human nature to create novels, one of which has come to be considered by many the representative Realist novel of the nineteenth century, *Middlemarch*. Her early career ranged from translating German theological-philosophical works to contributing to and assisting in editing the *Westminster Review* (1823-), one of the most prominent journals of the time, which covered scientific, philosophical, and aesthetic topics during her service (1851-54). Her longtime companion, philosopher George Henry Lewes (1817-1878), encouraged her to write fiction, and the intense emotional and intellectual partnership between the two undoubtedly nourished both their careers. Along with her own monumental achievements, she completed Lewes's *The Biographical History of Philosophy*, upon his death.

Other important nineteenth-century English writers whom critics consider Realists include Robert Browning (1812-1889) and Elizabeth Gaskell (1810-1865). Browning's use of idiomatic speech in his dramatic monologues, along with his psychologically discerning characterizations, shine in such poems as "My Last Duchess" (1845) and "Andrea del Sarto" (1855). Gaskell lived most of her adult life in Manchester, the hub of the new industrialization in England. One of her novels, *North and South* (published in serial form in 1854-55 in Dickens's *Household Words*), focused on the increasing gulf between the recently urbanized north and rural south of England, where a social infrastructure based on aristocracy was increasingly threatened. Another, *Mary Barton* (1848), explored relations between workers and employers and examined workers' living conditions. One factor making her novels so powerful was her close proximity to the people she drew on for her characters.

611

Later generations of writers sometimes included under the rubric of English Realists are novelist Arnold Bennett (1867-1931), known especially for his Clayhanger trilogy (1910-16), with its regionalist and Naturalist qualities; dramatist and novelist John Galsworthy (1867-1933), whose plays tended to explore social ethics; critic and novelist George Gissing (1857-1903), whose posthumously collected *Critical Studies of the Works of Charles Dickens* (1924), in addition to novels such as *Demos* (1886) and *The Nether World* (1889), evince his concern with themes of poverty and capitalism; novelist, short-story writer and poet Rudyard Kipling (1865-1936), known for his use of popular speech and his enthusiastic attention to technology and England's imperial role in the world; novelist, short-story writer and dramatist W. Somerset Maugham (1874-1965), whose first novel, *Liza of Lambeth* (1897), was influenced by Zola's Naturalism; novelist Arthur Morrison (1863-1945); Irish dramatist Sean O'CASEY (1880-1964), known for his Naturalistic plays dealing with Irish working-class political and economic concerns (*see* ABBEY THEATER); poet and autobiographer Siegfried Sassoon (1886-1967), whose most famous poems drew upon his experiences as a soldier during World War I and explored in riveting, audacious detail the ugly realities of war; and novelist and journalist H(erbert) G(eorge) Wells (1866-1946) who, while perhaps best remembered as a creator of science fiction, also marked the world of letters with his sociological and scientific writings.   •

✥•✥

Dickens, Charles (1812-1870), English novelist and essayist.

Enormously popular in his own time, Dickens remains a towering figure in English literature. He began his career by contributing short satiric pieces—*Sketches by 'Boz'* (collectively published, 1836-37)—to such periodicals as the *Monthly Magazine* and *The Evening Chronicle* in 1833. His novels, beginning with *The Pickwick Papers* (1836), appeared in serial form and were followed by a hungry reading public. His arduous childhood struggle against poverty—during which his father was imprisoned for indebtedness and he at twelve years of age went to work at a factory—finds thematic expression in the total of his work, which can be described as an exploration of money in society: of those who have and those who have not, and their attitudes toward, aspirations or renunciations of financial prosperity and social prestige. From *David Copperfield* (1849-50), in which he draws heavily on his own early experiences, to *OUR MUTUAL FRIEND* (1864-65), his last completed novel, the possession of money and social standing are shown to be determinants of character, even if they are determinants that are resisted. The melodramatic dialogues and turns of plot which pepper Dickens's fictional constructions can be seen in the light of his lifelong love of drama and his own theatrical activities, which included his well-attended public readings. His genius for weaving detail and metaphor into plot indicates a precursor of SYMBOLISM, his unabashed portrayals of meanness and virtue among representatives from all segments of society express his social consciousness, but his lively humor and sheer storytelling ability reveal the rare gift of a master entertainer who also inspires his audience to think.

Our Mutual Friend (1864-65).

While not Dickens's most popular or well-known novel, *Our Mutual Friend* warrants special attention not only as his last completed work but as a novel in which his continuing growth as an artist in a Realist vein gleams, and his art seems on the verge of further enriching the mine of Victorian-era Realist fiction. As did all of Dickens's novels, *Our Mutual Friend* appeared in monthly installments, a common publishing practice in London at the time. The novel keeps the reader abreast of developments both within and between various social circles. One of the main plots concerns the story of Bella Wilfer, a young middle-class woman, and John Harmon, a.k.a. John Rokesmith, a young heir whose inheritance depends on his marriage to Bella, who had been unacquainted with him. The plot employs numerous situational charades and masquerades which finally culminate in not only their marriage but Bella's eventual discovery of John's real identity, which he had kept hidden from her with the help of his elderly former caretakers, the Boffins. Meanwhile, Eugene Wrayburn, an upper-class barrister, and Bradley Headstone, a schoolmaster from a working-class background, compete for the affection of Lizzie Hexam, daughter of a corpse-finding boatman of the Thames. It is particularly within this latter plot — in Dickens's characterizations of Headstone and Wrayburn — that an increased depth can be detected, a departure from his usual caricaturistic style. Woven into these main plots are various minor players and their worlds, which intersect with the others in interesting ways. Dickens gives us the adventures of Silas Wegg, a grotesque who contrives to steal what he believes is Mr. Boffin's, not John Harmon/Rokesmith's, inheritance, the ascent and plunge of the Veneerings, whose name wittily alludes to their social position, and several other colorful characters whose paths cross and crisscross the plots and subplots.

✦•✦

Eliot, George (pseud. of Marian Evans, 1819-1880)
English novelist, translator, editor, and essayist.

Daughter of an estate manager with strong Anglican beliefs, George Eliot incurred some familial stress when she adopted a more secular humanistic form of religion as a young woman. Her family's comfortable status allowed her to attain educational opportunities which expanded well beyond the limits of most women at the time. She read German, French, and Italian as well as the classical languages, and her continued interest in and study of scientific developments, philosophical debates, and social movements eventually earned her the reputation of being the most intellectual English novelist up to her time. Her work with the *Westminster Review*, as well as her home life—both with her family and with George Henry Lewes, with whom she lived from 1854 until his death in 1878—kept her in contact with some of the nineteenth century's most distinguished thinkers. In addition to her novels, she is noted for her translation of the German work of unorthodoxy, *Das Leben Jesu* (1835-36; *The Life of Jesus*, 1846) by David Friedrich Strauss (1808-1874) and Ludwig Feuerbach's *Das Wesen des Christenthums* (1841; *The Essense of Christianity*, 1854). Most of her novels examined provincial English life—*Adam Bede* (1859), *The Mill on the Floss* (1860), *Silas Marner* (1861), and *Middlemarch* (1871-72). This proved to be her most fruitful focus. By dealing with a seemingly narrow environment, with which she personally was very familiar, she created to great effect intricately rich characters who were involved with personal and public issues, the implications and potential consequences of which extended beyond "mere" village life. Three departures from this mode were *Felix Holt* (1866), in which the main character was a politically radical working man in Loamshire; *Romola* (1862-63), a more scholarly than aesthetic treatment of fifteenth-century Florence; and *Daniel Deronda* (1876), her last completed novel, which caused some stir because of its examination of relations between Jewish and Anglo-English citizens. Cited as one of the premier English Realists, she articulates the impossibility of truly realistic depictions in Chapter XVII of *Adam Bede* (1859): "My strongest effort is . . . to give no more than a faithful account of men and things as they have mirrored themselves in my mind. The mirror is doubtless defective, the reflection faint or confused; but I feel as much bound to tell you as precisely as I can what that reflection is." Eliot's now undisputed importance as a nineteenth-century thinker and novelist and the legacy of her work are invaluable not only to the FEMINIST scholars who have embraced her, but to anyone at all appreciative of English literature to the enrichment of which she contributed so much.

Middlemarch, A Study of Provincial Life (1871-72).

Considered by many the most important English novel of the nineteenth century, *Middlemarch* marks a high point in Eliot's career as well as a brilliant example of English Realism. Set in the early 1830s, just before the passing of the 1832 Reform Bill, the novel develops the stories of several marriages—Dorothea Brooke-Casaubon to Casaubon's cousin, Will Ladislaw; Fred Vincy to Mary Garth; and Tertius Lydgate to Rosamond Vincy—along with the family members and others involved, constructing their personal and relational histories in intricate psychological and social detail. In addition to sensitive character analysis, their stories broaden to engulf important contemporary developments, such as questions of public and personal morality, social and biological evolution, political and economic restructuring and reform, and England's tumultuous transformation from agrarianism to industrialization. Despite the occasionally didactic tone of the omniscient narrator, the novel is esteemed for its ironic yet empathetic portrayals, the sheer subtle wit of the language, and its provocative blending of social, moral, and personal dilemmas, implications and consequences; or, as the often-quoted finale puts it: "the effect of her being on those around her was incalculably diffusive; for the growing good of the world is partly dependent on unhistoric acts; and that things are not so ill with you and me as they might have been, is half owing to the number who lived faithfully a hidden life, and rest in unvisited tombs."

⤙•⤚

Further Reading

Alden, Patricia. *Social Mobility in the English Bildungsroman: Gissing, Hardy, Bennet, and Lawrence*. Ann Arbor, Mich.: UMI Research Press, 1986.

Auerbach, Erich. *Mimesis: The Representation of Reality in Western Literature*. Translated by Willard Trask. Garden City, N.Y.: Doubleday, 1957.

Auster, Henry. *Local Habitations: Regionalism in the Early Novels of George Eliot*. Cambridge, Mass.: Harvard University Press, 1970.

Beaty, Jerome. *"Middlemarch" from Notebook to Novel: A Study of George Eliot's Creative Method*. Urbana, Ill.: University of Illinois Press, 1960.

Becker, George J., ed. *Documents of Modern Literary Realism*. Princeton, N.J.: Princeton University Press, 1963.

Bloom, Harold, ed. *Charles Dickens*. New York: Chelsea House, 1987.

Brooks, Christopher L. *Signs for the Times: Symbolic Realism in the Mid-Victorian World*. London: Allen & Unwin, 1984.

Carlisle, Janice. *The Sense of an Audience: Dickens, Thackeray, and Eliot at Mid-Century*. Athens, Ga.: University of Georgia Press, 1981.

Casagrande, Peter J. *Hardy's Influence on the Modern Novel*. Totowa, N.J.: Barnes & Noble, 1987.

Chase, Karen. *Eros and Psyche: The Representation of Personality in Charlotte Bronte, Charles Dickens, and George Eliot*. New York: Methuen, 1984.

Chesterton, G. K. *Appreciations and Criticism of the Works of Charles Dickens*. London: J. M. Dent; New York: Dutton, 1911.

Davis, Gabriele A. Wittig. *Novel Associations: Theodor Fontane and George Eliot Within the Context of Nineteenth Century Realism*. New York: P. Lang, 1983.

Ermarth, Elizabeth D. *Realism and Consensus in the English Novel*. Princeton, N.J.: Princeton University Press, 1983.

Gissing, George. "The Place of Realism in Fiction." In *Selections Autobiographical and Imaginative from the Works of George Gissing*. London: J. Cape, 1929.

Karl, Frederick. *George Eliot: A Biography*. London: HarperCollins Publishers, 1995.

Levine, George. *Darwin and the Novelists: Patterns of Science in Victorian Fiction*. Cambridge, Mass.: Harvard University Press, 1988.

———. *The Realistic Imagination: English Fiction from Frankenstein to Lady Chatterley*. Chicago: University of Chicago Press, 1981.

Lukács, Georg. *Studies in European Realism*. New York: Grosset & Dunlap, 1964.

Meckier, Jerome. *Hidden Rivalries in Victorian Fiction: Dickens, Realism, and Revaluation*. Lexington, Ky.: University Press of Kentucky, 1987.

Shaw, George Bernard. *Shaw on Dickens*. Edited by Dan Laurence and Martin Quinn. New York: Ungar, 1985.

Watkins, Gwen. *Dickens in Search of Himself: Recurrent Themes and Characters in the Works of Charles Dickens*. Totowa, N.J.: Barnes & Noble, 1986.

Wellek, René. "The Concept of Realism in Literary Scholarship." In his *Concepts of Criticism*. New Haven, Conn.: Yale University Press, 1963.

REALISM
France, 1850s-1870s

Realism, the most sweeping movement of twentieth-century world literature, began in France during the middle of the nineteenth century. One of the chief accomplishments of the early Realists was the conscious elevation of the novel form to the highest literary art, above even poetry, which had, through the determined efforts of the Neoclassicists and Romantics, enjoyed a prolonged position as the preeminent European form for human expression. In contrast to Romanticism, a movement of immense popularity in French literature due to such enduring luminaries as Victor Hugo (1802-1885) and George Sand (1804-1876), Realism was predicated upon the concrete, objective representation of ordinary people and events; accordingly, the only true work of art was one which mirrored actual, everyday life. The long form of the novel, then, became the perfect choice for the Realists, whose approach to their subject matter paralleled the patient and thorough research of empirical scientists.

Stendhal (1783-1842) and Honoré de Balzac (1799-1850) are the writers most commonly mentioned as forerunners of the movement, which gained full force only after 1850, when both men had died. Stendhal's characteristically self-revealing fiction and Balzac's array of exotic and one-dimensional characters aside, the two novelists significantly expanded the boundaries of the French novel. The former, through such works as *Le rouge et le noir* (1830) and *La chartreuse de Parme* (1839), demonstrated a vast capacity for convincingly exploring his characters' passions, motives, and other psychological tendencies; the latter, through his prodigious series of some ninety interrelated stories and novels known as *La comédie humaine* (1830-50; *Comédie humaine*, 1895-98), exemplified a form of literary portraiture minutely concerned with specific locales, social classes, and the impact of the industrial age. In an 1842 preface he announced his intent to record and interpret his era, much in the manner of a historian or biographer. During the decades that followed, similar statements became the banner cry of the Realists. The Romantic slogan "la liberté dans l'art" would now, under the Realists, become "la sincerité dans l'art."

Often described as a Romantic by nature, Gustave FLAUBERT emerged during the 1850s as the leading Realist in France. His ascendancy came after attempts — early versions of his philosophical fable *La tentation de Saint Antoine* (1874) — to create a French equivalent of Johan Wolfgang von Goethe's (1749-1832) *Faust* (1790-1831). Heeding the advice of such close literary friends as Louis Bouilhet (1822-1869) and Maxime du Camp (1822-1894), who considered the project too lyrical and remote from everyday reality, Flaubert began fashioning a new style, method of selection, and concern for the commonplace similar to that of Balzac yet completely divested of subjective tone, authorial intrusion, or picturesqueness. His goals, documented in his numerous letters, were in fact to remove all traces of authorship in his work, to avoid geographically distinct settings and exceptional or unusual characters, and to construct a narrative language at once poetically sonorous and emotionally, even spiritually, barren. "The artist," he wrote, "ought to be in his work like God in creation, invisible and omnipotent."

After more than five years of assiduous apprenticeship to his revolutionary ideals, he produced *MADAME BOVARY* (1857; *Madame Bovary*, 1881). The work, which first appeared in installments in du Camp's *Revue de Paris*, was met with immediate approbation by younger French writers and vehement censure by government officials and members of the bourgeoisie. Flaubert was forced to exonerate himself and his work at a widely publicized immorality trial and did so brilliantly, defending the moral necessity of detailing his heroine's dissolute, and ultimately fatal, life.

The literary significance of Flaubert's *Madame Bovary* resided not simply in the volatile subject matter nor the self-effacing narration but in the unswerving attention to the semantics and rhythm of language, the relentless search for the *seul mot juste* or "unique right word" which preserved the aesthetic beauty and philosophical austerity of his artistic vision. Ironically, though Flaubert was hailed as the consummate Realist, the master for such followers as Ernest Feydeau (1821-1873) and Edmond Duranty (1833-1880), he came to despise the notion of a literary school or movement founded upon a particular concept or preamble. His very satirization of the illusory world of the bourgeois in *Madame Bovary*, and later in *L'Éducation sentimentale* (1870) and *Bouvard et Pécuchet* (1881), stemmed from his acute understanding that every author's representations of life were, necessarily, individual, subjective, and incomplete. Perfection therefore arose not when the author shackled his art to an impossible doctrine but when he strove with infinite precision and impersonality to depict, from shifting points of view, his carefully chosen subject matter. It is notable that Champfleury (1821-1889), a minor novelist, critic, and proponent of the Realist painter Gustave Courbet (1819-1877), rather than Flaubert, formulated a theoretical platform for the movement in his *Le réalisme* (1857).

During the 1860s, Edmond and Jules de GONCOURT surfaced as the most devoted and accomplished practitioners of Flaubertian Realism. As early as 1856 the Goncourts employed the term Realism to define a form of stylistically pure documentary writing they hoped to sustain in their work. Nine years later they published *GERMINIE LACERTEUX* (1864; *Germinie Lacerteux*, 1887), a novel which for its pioneering portrayal of the working classes foreshadowed the advent of NATURALISM. In their notorious preface the Goncourts lambasted the undiscriminating reader of confessional romances and escapist fiction and heralded the novel, in their hands, as "the great, serious, impassioned, living form of literary study and social examination." They conceived and carried out, before Émile ZOLA popularized the method, a form of narrative experimentation similar to the psychological case study, in which a subject was drawn, set in motion, and followed to a logical conclusion.

Like Flaubert, the Goncourts eschewed the tenets of Zola's Naturalistic school, which from approximately 1875 onward came increasingly to portray the most loathsome and reprehensible qualities of humanity at the expense of all others and with little regard for the redeeming merits or careful style and organization. More Naturalistic, at least in terms of subject matter, was Flaubert's foremost literary disciple, Guy de MAUPASSANT. During the 1880s, following Flaubert's sudden death, Maupassant created numerous stories which exemplified the form and beauty of his master's work yet focused as much on the life of prostitutes and peasants as on the middle and upper classes. Although enormously successful during his lifetime, Maupassant was continually afflicted with physical and emotional tragedies, experiences which lent an unrelenting pessimistic determinism to his fiction. Violent, erotic, and perverse elements appeared regularly in his work and caused many reviewers to label him a Naturalist. However, in the long preface to his novel *Pierre et Jean* (1888; *Pierre and Jean*, 1962), Maupassant echoed Flaubert's conception of the serious writer's inviolate individuality and made clear his own autonomy from the confining labels of both Realism and Naturalism. "Each of us," he asseverated, "makes, individually, a personal illusion of the world. It may be a poetic, sentimental, joyful, melancholy, sordid, or dismal one, according to our nature. The writer's goal is to reproduce this illusion of life faithfully, using all the literary techniques at his disposal." The writer's function, additionally, "is not to tell us a story, to entertain or to move us, but to make us think and to make us understand the deep and hidden meaning of events."

The major Realists—Flaubert, the Goncourts, and Maupassant—achieved these goals in works that greatly influenced the development of modern fiction, not only in Europe but around the world. Despite their differing methods of execution, these writers were united in their skeptical, often critical, portrayal of dehumanizing bourgeois values and their outright satirization of Romantic idealism. If their fiction, according to

C. A. Sainte-Beuve (1804-1869) and other scholars of their period, lacks moral meaning, feeling, or hope, their ascetic devotion to the craft of Realistic narration more than compensates for such severe selectivity.

✦•✦

Flaubert, Gustave (1821-1880)
French novelist, short-story writer, and dramatist.

Regarded as one of the most painstaking writers in literary history, Flaubert earned lasting fame as the author of *Madame Bovary* (1857; *Madame Bovary*, 1881), one of the most influential novels in nineteenth-century literature. In this work, as in his later efforts, he sought to develop a prose "as rhythmical as verse and as precise as the language of science." He hoped, by so doing, to prove that any facet of reality, no matter how insipid or ephemeral, could be transformed into an art of timeless grandeur. Such works as *Salammbô* (1863; *Salammbô*, 1886), a novel of ancient Carthage, and *La tentation du Saint Antoine* (1874; *The Temptation of Saint Antony*, 1895) attest to his independence from what is commonly understood as Realism, yet his thorough documentation and narrative objectivity even in his highly imaginative fiction place him firmly within the literary tradition he inaugurated. In addition to *L'Éducation sentimentale* (1870; *Sentimental Education*, 1898), *Trois Contes* (1877; *Three Tales*, 1903), and the unfinished *Bouvard et Pécuchet* (1881; *Bouvard and Pécuchet*, 1896), Flaubert is esteemed for his *Correspondence* (1894-99; *The Selected Letters of Gustave Flaubert*, 1954) in which he recorded his monumental literary and personal struggles and the many insights on his craft which emerged from them.

Madame Bovary (1857; *Madame Bovary*, 1881).

Flaubert's masterpiece, *Madame Bovary*, is widely considered the most important work of nineteenth-century French literature. The story centers on Emma Bovary, the romantic but disenchanted wife of a mediocre Normandy village doctor. Her life increasingly becomes one long hopeless attempt to transcend the ennui of her marriage and the bovine complacency that her husband, Charles, represents. The two lovers she takes are, like all the major characters of the novel, similarly imprisoned by their own shortcomings and limited perceptions of their psychological and social milieus. Emma's flights and deceptions, from which she gleans only temporal love and enjoyment, result in severe indebtedness and a pervasive disillusionment which leads her to suicide. Flaubert's utilization of shifting points of view, meticulous ordering of scenes, and stylistically heightened rendering of an embarrassingly real tapestry of life firmly established the novel as the preeminent literary form by the mid-nineteenth century and signalled, above all else, a new artistic consciousness, one interested in the intimate and authentic documentation of ordinary life.

619

❖•❖

Goncourt, Edmond (1822-1896) and Jules (1830-1870) de
French diarists, novelists, biographers, and critics.

The Goncourt brothers, who wrote collaboratively until Jules's death, distinguished themselves not only as early French Realists but as experts of eighteenth-century French manners, history, and painting as well as Japanese art of the same period. From their first publications in the 1850s their name was at the fore of an influential literary circle composed, at one time or another, of Flaubert, Zola, Ivan TURGENEV (*see* REALISM, Russia), Alphonse Daudet (1840-1897), Maupassant, Hippolyte Taine (1828-1893), and Ernest Renan (1823-1892). Their best-known work, the twenty-two volume *Journal: Mémoires de la vie littéraire* (1887-96, 1956-59; partial translations include *The Goncourt Journals: 1851-70*, 1937, and *Paris and the Arts, 1851-1896: From the Goncourt Journal*, 1971), contains intimate portraits of these and other major writers and thinkers from the latter half of the nineteenth century. Aside from their *Journal,* their greatest success came in the novel *Germinie Lacerteux* (1864; *Germinie Lacerteux,* 1887). There they presented an intensive and exacting case study of a single character, a method which formed one of their chief contributions to literary Realism. Although their novels have long since faded into obscurity, the Goncourts themselves rank prominently in literary histories for their pioneering formulations of both Realism and Naturalism.

Germinie Lacerteux (1864; *Germinie Lacerteux,* 1887).

Germinie Lacerteux, next to *Madame Bovary* the most influential work of French Realism, is the story of the titular heroine's dual lives as a respected housekeeper and desolate debauchee. Germinie's sordid second life, the existence of which she conceals from her employer until her death, is ironically precipitated by her two greatest qualities: a capacity for devoted love and a generous, self-sacrificing spirit. Despite the seeming insignificance of her life as well as the detached narration of her moral decline from churchgoer to drunkard, thief, and prostitute, the elevated style in which her story is told conveys upon her a sense of poignant heroism. While little read now, *Germinie Lacerteux* is assured of being remembered as the first Realistic novel of working-class life in European literature.

❖•❖

Maupassant, Guy de (1850-1893)
French short-story writer, novelist, journalist, and poet.

Universally acclaimed as one of the finest short-story writers of all time, Maupassant began his career as a journalist and author of licentious verse. His close relationship with Flaubert, whom he regarded as his mentor, influenced him greatly and led him to focus his talents on fiction. "BOULE DE SUIF" (1880), his first major published story, appeared in *Les soirées de Médan* alongside the work of several French Naturalists, with whom he regularly exchanged literary views. Due to the immense success of this story, which many critics consider his greatest, and to his ensuing industriousness, Maupassant became the most saleable author in France next to Zola. His legacy of over three hundred stories and six novels represents for many an astonishing achievement, given his relatively short career and years of unrelieved suffering from the debilitating effects of syphillis. Like Flaubert, Maupassant considered a finely honed, concise, evocative style to be the essence of all great fiction. His development of such an enduring style, coupled with his resurrection of the short story form to encompass his heavily ironic, iconoclastic worldview, have earned him generations of admirers and emulators.

"Boule de Suif" (1880; "Boule de Suif" in *The Complete Short Stories of Guy de Maupassant,* 1955).

Set around 1870 during the Franco-Prussian War, the story depicts a group of French travelers en route to the port city of Havre. The heroine, nicknamed Boule de Suif ("ball of fat"), is a good-natured prostitute who is looked upon by her coachmates with a mixture of superiority and disdain. She wins their momentary gratitude, however, when she thoughtfully offers them food from her basket. Later, the passengers are detained at an inn behind Prussian lines. A Prussian officer demands that Boule de Suif succumb to his desires before anyone may leave. Acting against her private morality, but in consideration of the platitudes her companions have burdened her with, she bends to the Prussian's will. The story closes when the passengers, hypocritical in their disregard for the weeping Boule de Suif, resume their journey. The power of "Boule de Suif," a masterpiece of its genre, arises from Maupassant's subtle fusion of Realistic narration and a wistful irony which suggests the reform-minded fiction of his Naturalistic contemporaries.

❖•❖

Further Reading

Auerbach, Erich. "Germinie Lacerteux." In his *Mimesis: The Representation of Reality in Western Literature.* Translated by Willard Trask. Princeton, N.J.: Princeton University Press, 1953.

Baldick, Robert. *The Goncourts.* New York: Hillary House; London: Bowes & Bowes, 1960.

Becker, George J. *Master European Realists of the Nineteenth Century.* New York: Ungar, 1982.

Billy, Andre. *The Goncourt Brothers.* Translated by Margaret Shaw. London: A. Deutsch, 1960.

Bloom, Harold, ed. *Gustave Flaubert's "Madame Bovary."* New York: Chelsea House, 1988.

Brombert, Victor. *The Novels of Flaubert: A Study of Themes and Techniques.* Princeton, N.J.: Princeton University Press, 1966.

621

Cazamian, Louis. "Realism." In his *A History of French Literature*. Oxford, England: Clarendon Press, 1955.

de Man, Paul, ed. *"Madame Bovary," by Gustave Flaubert: Backgrounds and Sources, Essays in Criticism*. Translated by Paul de Man. New York: Norton, 1965.

Dugan, John R. *Illusion and Reality: A Study of Descriptive Techniques in the Works of Guy de Maupassant*. The Hague: Mouton, 1973.

Galantiere, Lewis, ed. and trans. *The Goncourt Journals: 1851-1870* by Edmond and Jules de Goncourt. Garden City, N.Y.: Doubleday, 1937.

Gans, Eric. *Madame Bovary: The End of Romance*. Boston: Twayne, 1989.

Grant, Richard B. *The Goncourt Brothers*. New York: Twayne, 1972.

James, Henry. "Guy de Maupassant." In his *Partial Portraits*. London: Macmillan, 1888.

Jarman, Laura M. *The Goncourt Brothers: Modernists in Abnormal Psychology*. Albuquerque, N.Mex.: University of New Mexico Press, 1939.

LaCapra, Dominick. *"Madame Bovary" on Trial*. Ithaca, N.Y.: Cornell University Press, 1982.

Levin, Harry. *The Gates of Horn: A Study of Five French Realists*. New York: Oxford University Press, 1986.

Lowe, Margaret. *Towards the Real Flaubert: A Study of Madame Bovary*. Oxford, England: Clarendon Press, 1984.

Lukács, Georg. *Studies in European Realism*. New York: Grosset & Dunlap, 1964.

Ramazani, Vaheed K. *The Free Indirect Mode: Flaubert and the Poetics of Irony*. Charlottesville, Va.: University Press of Virginia, 1988.

Starkie, Enid. *Flaubert: The Making of the Master*. New York: Atheneum, 1967.

————. *Flaubert the Master*. New York: Atheneum, 1971.

Steegmuller, Francis, ed. *The Letters of Gustave Flaubert* by Gustave Flaubert. Cambridge, Mass.: Harvard University Press, 1980-82.

Sullivan, Edward Daniel. *Maupassant: The Short Stories*. Great Neck, N.Y.: Barron's Educational Series, 1962.

Thibaudet, Albert. "Realism." In his *French Literature from 1795 to Our Era*. Translated by Charles Lam Markmann. New York: Funk & Wagnalls, 1968.

Thorlby, Anthony. *Gustave Flaubert and the Art of Realism*. London: Bowes & Bowes, 1956.

Tolstoy, Leo. *Guy de Maupassant*. London: Brotherhood Pub. Co., 1898.

Weinberg, Bernard. *French Realism: The Critical Reaction, 1830-1870*. New York: Modern Language Association of America, 1937.

Wellek, René. "The Concept of Realism in Literary Scholarship." In his *Concepts of Criticism*. New Haven, Conn.: Yale University Press, 1963.

Williams, D. A., ed. *The Monster in the Mirror: Studies in Nineteenth-Century Realism*. Oxford, England: Oxford University Press, 1978.

Williams, Roger L. *The Horror of Life: Charles Baudelaire, Jules de Goncourt, Gustave Flaubert, Guy de Maupassant, Alphonse Daudet*. Chicago: University of Chicago Press, 1980.

Zola, Émile. *Experimental Novel and Other Essays*. New York: Cassell, 1893.

REALISM
Iceland, 1880s-1890s

Realism emerged in Iceland in 1882 with the formation of the *VERĐANDI* GROUP. One *Verðandi* writer, Gestur Pálsson (1852-1891), is often mentioned as the model Icelandic Realist due to his sympathetic portrayals of the lower classes. Other Realists outside *Verðandi* include novelist Jón Trausti (1873-1918) and poets Thorsteinn Erlingsson (1858-1914) and Stephan Stephansson (1853-1927).

✦•✦

Further Reading

Finnbogi, Gudmundsson. *Stephan G. Stephansson in Retrospect: Seven Essays*. Reyjavik, Iceland: Icelandic Cultural Fund, 1982.

McCracken, Jane W. *Stephan G. Stephansson, the Poet of the Rocky Mountains*. Edmonton, Canada: Alberta Culture, Historical Resources Division, 1982.

Stephansson, Stephan G. *Stephan G. Stephansson, Selected Prose & Poetry*. Translated by Kristjana Gunnars. Red Deer, Canada: Red Deer College Press, 1988.

Wood, Kerry. *The Icelandic-Canadian Poet, Stephen Gudmundsson Stephansson, 1853-1927*. Red Deer, Canada: K. Wood, 1974.

REALISM, India. *See* PROGRESSIVE WRITERS' MOVEMENT

REALISM
Latin America, 1910s-1930s

Realism in Latin America emerged following the Mexican Revolution and the decolonization effected after World War I. Contemporaneous with the PROLETARIAN LITERATURE movements in Europe and the United States, Realism almost shaded into a form of SOCIALIST REALISM which was not subservient to the Communist program but did examine unjust economic systems and oppression. Though many of its practitioners were influenced by European Realists, Realism in Latin America metamorphosed into a largely regionalist literary trend that further developed traditional Costumbrismo, a Spanish literary style characterized by detailed rendering of a region's language, customs, and scenery, as well as indigenous peoples, as did the CRIOLLISTS.

Precursors included Alberto Blest Gana (1830-1920) — building on the Costumbrismo tradition, he led the advance of the social novel in Chile with *La aritmética en el amor* (1860; The Arithmetic of Love) — and in Argentina, Eugenio Cambaceres's (1843-1888) acclaimed novel, *Sin rumbo* (1885; Aimless), was influenced by French NATURALIST Émile ZOLA, as was *En la sangre* (published in serial form in *Sud América* in 1887; In the Blood).

623

In reaction against the Romanticism of the nineteenth century, many Latin American Realist novelists held that literature could foster unification and nationalism among the diverse peoples of the region in order to create a new kind of culture and civilization. In Peru, practitioners included Ciro Alegría (1909-1967), who wrote regionalist fiction of the Peruvian Indians, such as the novels *La serpiente de oro* (1935; *The Golden Serpent*, 1963) and *El mundo es ancho u ajeno* (1941; *Broad and Alien Is the World*, 1941) — the latter is also representative of APRISMO literature — and José María Arguedas's (1911-1969) novels *Yawar Fiesta* (1940; *Yawar Fiesta*, 1985) and *Los ríos profundos* (1958; *Deep Rivers*, 1978). In Mexico, proponents were known for their Revolutionary novels: Mariano Azuela (1873-1952), whose French Naturalist-influenced work began appearing in the late 1900s, is best known for *Los de abajo* (1916; *The Underdogs*, 1929), while Martín Luis Guzmán (1887-1976), also affiliated with the ATHENEUM OF YOUTH, provided another example with his autobiographical *El águila y la serpiente* (1928; *The Eagle and the Serpent*, 1930). Mexican novelist and short-story writer José Rubén Romero (1890-1952) produced notable Costumbrismo writing in *Apuntes de un lugareño* (1932; Notes of a Provincial) and *Desbandada* (1934; At Random). In Argentina, major Realist writers were Manuel Gálvez (1882-1962), whose novels, such as *La maestra normal* (1914; The High School Teacher), deal with social issues; Ricardo Güiraldes (1886-1927; *see also* Criollismo, GAUCHO LITERATURE, and ULTRAISM) and his renowned regionalist novel *Don Segundo Sombra* (1926; *Don Segundo Sombra: Shadows on the Pampas*, 1935); and Argentine-born Chilean novelist and short-story writer Manuel Rojas Sepúlveda (1896-1973), who blended MODERNISM and Socialist Realism in early stories collected in *Hombres del sur* (1926; Men of the South) and *El delincuente* (1929; The Delinquint) and his major novel, *Hijo de ladrón* (1951; *Born Guilty*, 1955). Venezuelan Rómulo Gallegos (1884-1968) wrote novels with realistic portrayals of lower-class protagonists, such as the regionalist novel *Doña Bárbara* (1929; *Doña Bárbara*, 1931). Colombian poet and novelist José Eustasio Rivera (1889-1928) penned a novel which is considered the most important Colombian novel until Gabriel GARCÍA MARQUEZ's *CIEN AÑOS DE SOLEDAD* (1967; *One Hundred Years of Solitude*, 1970; *see* MAGIC REALISM) — *La vorágine* (1924; *The Vortex*, 1935), regarded as having served as a model for the Latin American regionalist novel. Ecuadorian playwright and fiction writer Jorge Icaza (1906-) wrote the highly influential Indianist novel *Huasipungo* (1934; *Huasipungo: The Villagers*, 1964). Uruguayan short-story writer and poet Horacio Quiroga's (1878-1937; *see also* COUNCIL OF BRILLIANT KNOWLEDGE and GENERATION OF 1900) early Modernist poems appear in *Los arrecifes de coral* (1901; The Coral Reefs), while the best collections of his regionalist stories are *Cuentes de amor, de locura, y de muerte* (1917; Stories of Love, Madness, and Death) and *Los desterrados* (1926; The Exiled). Cubans associated with Realism are poet Mariano Brull (1891-1956); fiction writer Jésus Castellanos (1879-1912); fiction writer and playwright Alfonso Hernández Catá (1885-1940), whose notable Costumbrismo novel is *El bebedor de lágrimas* (1926); novelist Carlos Loveira (1882-1928) and his novels *Juan Criollo* (1928; Creole Juan), *Los inmorales* (1919), *Generales y doctores* (1920), and *Los ciegos* (1922); and playwright and essayist José Antonio Ramos (1885-1946), whose socialist dramas—such as *Tembladera* (1918), *Libertá* (1911), *Satanás* (1913), *Calíban Rex* (1914), and *El hombre fuerte* (1915)—are indebted to Henrik IBSEN (*see* REALISM, Norway).

✦•✦

Further Reading

Franco, Jean. *An Introduction to Spanish-American Literature*. Cambridge, England: Cambridge University Press, 1969.

———. *The Modern Culture of Latin America: Society and the Artist*. London: Pall Mall, 1967.

Robe, Stanley L. *Azuela and the Mexican Underdogs*. Berkeley, Calif.: University of California Press, 1979.

Sommers, J. "The Indian-Oriented Novel in Latin America: New Spirit, New Forms, New Scope." *Journal of Inter-American Studies* 6 (1964): 249-65.

REALISM
Latvia, 1880s-1900s; 1920s-1930s

Indebted to the epic nineteenth-century novel *Mernieku laiki* (1879; The Times of Land-Surveyors) written by brothers Reinis (1839-1920) and Matīss Kaudzītes (1848-1926), Latvian Realism resurfaced during the 1920s and 1930s in works by Augusts Deglavs (1862-1922), Jēkabs Janševskis (1865-1931), Jānis Jaunsudrabinš (1877-1962), Aīda Niedra (1898-1972), and others. The Latvian Realists were known for a prose style that closely mimicked the indigenous dialects of the Latvian people.

✦•✦

Further Reading

Herbermann, Clemens, et al. *Jānis Jaunsudrabinš in Westfalen*. Münster, Germany: Jaunsudrabinš Museum, 1982.

Rubulis, Aleksis. "Latvian Literature." In his *Baltic Literature: A Survey of Finnish, Estonian, Latvian, and Lithuanian Literatures*. Notre Dame, Ind.: University of Notre Dame Press, 1970.

REALISM
Norway, 1870s

With his 1871 lectures at the University of Copenhagen, published as *Hovedstrøm-ninger i det nittende Aarhundredes Litteratur* (1872-90; *Main Currents in Nine-teenth Century Literature*, 1901-5), Danish critic Georg Brandes (1842-1927) was a significant figure in the lives of the major Norwegian Realists, as well as writers in other parts of Scandinavia (*see also* NATURALISM, Denmark) — dramatist Henrik IBSEN, and novelists Bjørnstjerne Bjørnson (1832-1910), Kristian Elster (1841-1881), Alexander Kielland (1849-1906), and Jonas Lie (1833-1908). Bjørnson led a reaction against Romanticism, denouncing it as inhibiting genuine social progress and sparking an era of literary concern with accurately portraying contemporary social issues and injustices such as labor, the position of women, education of children: "A literature of our day shows that it is alive by taking up problems for discussion." Thus, the Norwegian Realists paid close attention to social philosophers. Kielland adhered to English utilitarian doctrine, Bjørnson was strongly influenced by the empiricism of Herbert Spencer (1820-1903), and although Ibsen claimed to disagree with John Stuart Mill's (1806-1873) philosophy, his later plays showed its influence.

The Norwegian Realists' writing was characterized by individualistic styles and anti-conservativism. During the early 1870s Bjørnson wrote his important and acclaimed Realist plays — *En fallit* (1875; *The Bankrupt*, 1914) and *Redaktøren* (1875; *The Editor*, 1914) — while living in Rome. Elster's novels, influenced by Ivan TURGENEV (*see* REALISM, Russia) and Søren Kierkegaard (1813-1855), include *Solskyer* (1887; Sunny Clouds) and *Tora Trondal* (1879). Other representative Realist works include Lie's novels *Den Fremsynte eller Billeder fra Nordland* (1870; *The Visionary*, 1894), *Tremasteren 'Fremtiden'* (1872; *The Barque Future; or, Life in the Far North*, 1879), and *Lodsen og hans Hustru* (1874; *The Pilot and His Wife*, 1876), Keilland's short story collection *Novelletter* (1879; *Tales of Two Countries*, 1891), and, of course, Ibsen's masterful plays.

The Realist trend in Norwegian writing developed in the next decade into the more extreme and deterministic form of Realism known as Naturalism.

✦•✦

Ibsen, Henrik (1828-1906), Norwegian dramatist and poet.

A playwright whose influence on twentieth-century drama has been monumental, Ibsen was born in a small southern Norwegian town, began but did not complete a university education, and left Norway to live in Italy and Germany for most of his adult ife. His plays *Brand* (1866; *Brand*, 1891) and *Peer Gynt* (1867; *Peer Gynt*, 1892), ritten in Italy, brought him renown throughout Scandinavia. His important Realist plays, notable in part for his drawings of complex and rounded female characters, include *Samfundets støtter* (1877; *Pillars of Society*, 1888), *Et dukkehjem* (1879; *Nora, or a Doll's House*, 1880), *Gengangere* (1881; *Ghosts*, 1889), *En folkefiende* (1882; *An Enemy of the People*, 1890), and *Vildanden* (1884; *The Wild Duck*, 1891).

Et dukkehjem (1879; *Nora, or a Doll's House*, 1880).

In this play Ibsen broke new artistic ground by seriously examining the unequal ethical standards that apply respectively to women and men in society. In his notes for the play he wrote: "A woman cannot be herself in the society of the present day, which is an exclusively masculine society, with laws framed by man and with a judicial system that judges feminine conduct from a masculine point of view." Nora, a quintessentially Ibsenian woman character, is a conventionally compliant married woman who, unbeknownst to her husband, commits forgery for his sake. This action brings the two into an honest confrontation for the first time in their married life, while Nora, also for the first time, rebels against the role society has dictated to her.

✦•✦

Further Reading

Andreas-Salomé, Lou. *Ibsen's Heroines*. Translated with an introduction by Siegfried Mandel. Redding Ridge, Conn.: Black Swan Books, 1985.

Beyer, Harald. *A History of Norwegian Literature*. New York: New York University Press for the American-Scandinavian Foundation, 1956.

Brandes, Georg. *Henrik Ibsen. Björnstjerne Björnson. Critical Studies*. New York: Macmillan, 1899.

Downs, Brian W. *Modern Norwegian Literature, 1860-1918*. Cambridge, England: Cambridge University Press, 1966.

McFarlane, James, ed. *The Cambridge Companion to Ibsen*. Cambridge, England: Cambridge University Press, 1997.

————. *Henrik Ibsen: A Critical Anthology*. Harmondsworth, England: Penguin, 1970.

Meyer, Hans Georg. *Henrik Ibsen*. Translated by Helen Sebba. New York: Ungar, 1972.

Northam, John. *Ibsen: A Critical Study*. Cambridge, England: Cambridge University Press, 1973.

Rossel, Sven H. *A History of Scandinavian Literature, 1870-1980*. Translated by Anne C. Ulmer. Minneapolis: University of Minnesota Press, 1982.

Shepherd-Barr, Kirsten. *Ibsen and Early Modernist Theatre, 1890-1900*. Westport, Conn.: Greenwood Press, 1997.

REALISM
Poland, 1870s-1880s

Also known as Positivism, in reference to Auguste Comte's (1798-1857) philosophical influence, Polish Realism was centered in Warsaw around three major writers in particular: Henryk Sienkiewicz (1846-1916), Eliza Orzeszkowa (1841-1910), and Bolesław Prus (pseud. of Aleksandr Głowacki, 1845-1912). Departing from the Romanticist tradition common throughout Europe in the earlier part of the century, they championed Realistic and, early on, rather didactic representations on such themes as social injustice, political corruption, poverty, village life, equal rights for Jews, and the emancipation of women in short stories and novels, most notably such novels as *Marta* (1873) and *Nad Niemnem* (1888; On the Banks of Niemen) by Orzeszkowa and *Lalka* (1890; *The Doll*, 1972) by Prus and his earlier short stories. Sienkiewicz, who was awarded the Nobel Prize in 1905, achieved international popularity with his novel *Quo Vadis?* (1896; *Quo Vadis?*, 1896) and is most renowned for the historical novels he wrote from the 1880s on, but in the 1870s he was writing short stories dealing with social injustice, for example, "Szkice weglem" (1877; "Charcoal Sketches," 1897) and "Za chlebem" (1880; "For Daily Bread," 1897).

Orzeszkowa and Prus are considered forerunners of the YOUNG POLAND movement which by the 1890s was in force reacting against Realism and gaining prominence with its attention to SYMBOLISM and other MODERNIST tendencies.

✥•✥

Further Reading

Dyboski, Roman. *Modern Polish Literature*. London; New York: H. Milford, Oxford University Press, 1924.

Gardner, Monica Mary. *The Patriot Novelist of Poland, Henryk Sienkiewicz*. London: J. M. Dent, 1926.

Giergielewicz, Mieczyslaw. *Henryk Sienkiewicz*. New York: Twayne Publishers, 1968.

Kridl, Manfred. *A Survey of Polish Literature and Culture*. New York: Columbia University Press, 1956.

Krzyzanowski, Julian. *A History of Polish Literature*. Warsaw: Polish Scientific Publishers, 1978.

————. "Boleslaw Prus' *The Doll*: An Ironic Novel." In *Russian and Slavic Literature*. Edited by Richard Freeborn et al. Cambridge, Mass.: Slavica Publishers, 1976.

Miłosz, Czesław. "Positivism." In his *The History of Polish Literature*. New York: Macmillan, 1969. Rev. ed., Berkeley, Calif.: University of California Press, 1983.

REALISM
Russia, 1852-1900s

The Realistic literary movement—a nearly universal phenomenon behind the development of nineteenth- and twentieth-century fiction—is generally thought to have first arisen in France. Yet by 1857, the time at which a small group of French writers, most particularly Gustave FLAUBERT, had successfully begun to adapt the techniques of Realistic painting and scientific inquiry to prose narration, Russian Realism was qualitatively underway. More so in Russia than within any other nation, Realism dominated the literary scene during the last half of the nineteenth century, not only through the numbers of writers it attracted and the several masterpieces it fostered, but by its unparalleled longevity and paramount influence on later writing around the world. Although like their French contemporaries in their search for the social and physiologi- cal truths of their time, the Russians placed an equally great emphasis on the moral and political impact of their works. Consequently, the invisible narrator of Flaubertian Realism, generally omniscient and nonintrusive, is rarely found among the works of Leo TOLSTOY and Fyodor DOSTOEVSKY, arguably the two greatest practitioners of Russian Realism.

Naturalism, as practiced by Nikolai Gogol (1809-1852) and formulated into theory by Vissarion Belinsky (1811-1848), was the direct forerunner of Realism in Russia. Gogol's greatest achievement, the novel *Myortvye dushi* (*Dead Souls*, 1887), appeared in 1842 as the first volume of an unfinished epic of provincial Russia. The work's strikingly rich characterizations, profusion of narrative voices, and lyrical portrayals of the drab and the grotesque heavily influenced a generation of writers, among them Nikolai Nekrasov (1821-1877), whose "physiologies" of the downtrodden and the impoverished heralded a new, taboo-shattering emphasis upon truth and reality in literature. To these ideals of the Naturalists Belinsky dedicated his "View of Russian Literature in 1846," an essay generally considered the manifesto of the movement. The effect of the short-lived Naturalist School on the early Realists was inescapable; younger writers such as Ivan TURGENEV, Ivan GONCHAROV, and Dostoevsky recognized and welcomed in the new liter- ature a satirization, or repudiation, of Romantic characters, plots, and themes, and an attendant regard for the numerous social problems Russian citizens then faced.

Realism, also termed Critical Realism, probably emerged by the late 1840s but did not fully emancipate itself from Naturalism until 1852, when Turgenev published *Zapiski okhotnika* (1847-52; *A Sportsman's Sketches*, 1895). A collection of rural short stories and slice-of-life portraits, Turgenev's work received national attention both for its preci- sion of detail and for its tacitly persuasive condemnation of the serfdom tradition. Of immediate importance to Turgenev during this initial stage of his career was critic and friend Pavel Annenkov (1813-1887), who in 1849 became the first Russian to definitive- ly employ the term Realism. In an 1852 letter to Turgenev, Annenkov urged his contem- porary to further diminish the authorial presence in his work and to proceed to the long novel as the genre best able to contain the vast sociological tableaus that would, inevi- tably, be the hallmark of the movement. Turgenev's *OTTSY I DETI* (1862; *Fathers and Sons*, 1867), a sweeping portrayal of the conflict between Russian revolutionary and conservative ideologies, fulfilled Annenkov's exhortations, gained renown throughout Europe, and helped overcome the cultural and artistic anonymity which had hitherto plagued Russian writers.

Although Turgenev remained for much of his life a politically oriented author, controversies surrounding the publication of *Ottsy i deti* provoked his voluntary exile and progressive literary disassociation from specifically national concerns. Tolstoy, widely considered the archetypal Russian Realist, was befriended by Turgenev during the 1850s. Tolstoy enhanced his reputation as the author of *Detstvo* (1852; *Childhood*, 1862) through his ties to Turgenev and other St. Petersburg writers who contributed to the radical journal *Sovremmenik* (Commentary). His role as both correspondent of and participant in the Crimean War resulted in his sketch collection *Sevastopolskiye rasskazy* (1855-56; *Sebastopol*, 1887), a work commissioned by *Sovremmenik*'s director, Nekrasov, and for which Tolstoy earned high praise. Yet Tolstoy, despite his immense talents, quickly alienated himself from this group with his brash behavior, vacillating artistic motives, and aristocratic leanings. With the publication of VOINA I MIR (1869; *War and Peace*, 1886), however, he reaffirmed his moral commitment to literature and to the tenets of pictorial exactitude espoused by the Realists. A deeply moving work, *Voina i mir* sparked a nationwide concern for the spiritual regeneration of Czarist Russia, a concern memorably recapitulated a decade later in Dostoevsky's greatest novel, BRAT'YA KARAMAZOVY (1879-80; *The Brothers Karamazov*, 1912).

Like Turgenev, Dostoevsky was an early admirer of the younger writer Tolstoy's narrative abilities, particularly his skill at depicting the various mental states of his characters. Of all the Realists, however, Dostoevsky was the most strikingly original in his approach to psychological reality. While close to Gogol and the Naturalists in his love of lyrical language, he greatly differed from them in his interest in the dark truths of both external and internal states. Two of his initial literary successes, *Bednye lyudi* (1846; *Poor Folk*, 1894) and *Dvoynik* (1846; *The Double*, 1917) have often been claimed as prominent Naturalistic works, but by the 1850s Dostoevsky had largely transcended pure Naturalism. Fusing Gothic and Romantic as well as Naturalistic elements, he aspired not to create detached or one-sided representations of reality but to develop hauntingly vital and comprehensive works that plumbed the depths of the human psyche and explored the emotional and spiritual climate of an entire society. In his *Dvevnik pisatelya* (1876-80; *Diary of a Writer*, 1949) he explained his conception of a higher Realism: "I have a completely different view of reality and 'realism' than our realists and critics. My idealism is more real than theirs. With their realism you could not explain a hundredth part of real facts that actually took place."

What each of the great triumvirate of nineteenth-century Russian novelists did share was an adulation of past European classics of verisimilitude. At the crown of this hierarchy was Miguel de Cervantes's (1547-1616) *Don Quixote* (1605, 1615). Other works included Daniel Defoe's (1660-1731) *Robinson Crusoe* (1719), Samuel Richardson's (1689-1761) *Pamela* (1740-41), and Henry Fielding's (1707-1754) *Tom Jones* (1749).

In addition, early nineteenth-century French novels, especially those of George Sand (1804-1876), Stendhal (1783-1842), and Honoré de Balzac (1799-1850), exerted a notable influence on the Russians. Yet, the single greatest work which provided the Realists their impetus and inspiration was one written by the Russian poet Alexander Pushkin (1799-1837). Now regarded as the father of modern Russian literature, Pushkin spanned the eras of Neoclassicism, Romanticism, and Realism. In 1823 he announced he was undertaking a novel in verse, in the manner of Lord Byron's *Don Juan* (1819-24). Completed and published a decade later as *Eugene Onegin* (1833), the long narrative poem explored Russia's most important contemporary class, the landed gentry, through the eyes of the unfortunate lovers Tatyana Larin and Eugene Onegin. Both characters — antithetical but equally revealing in outlook — served as brilliant prototypes for nineteenth-century novelists, as did the poem's architechtonics, which afforded both a convincing mirror and a poignant indictment of Russian society.

Despite Turgenev's similarity to Flaubert in his musical approach to style, Tolstoy's emulation of Stendhal's philosophic method, and Dostoevsky's assimilation of Balzac's sensationalism, the Russian Realistic movement remained, in fundamental ways, palpably different from that of the French. Pushkin's influence in this respect is unmistakable. Most significant for the Russian Realists was their preoccupation with the actions, motivations, and beliefs of their characters. This dominant interest led, particularly in the work of Dostoevsky, to point-of-view experimentations and psychological insights which anticipated many later developments in the modern novel. Perhaps of equal importance was Tolstoy's, Dostoevsky's, and, to a limited extent, Turgenev's native belief in the ultimate goodness of humanity. The majority of people these authors observed were frequently unhappy or directionless; they deserved, in the authors' view, sympathy and moral guidance. The world these Realists depicted in their fiction was not so much deterministic — like that of the French — as it was confused, impersonal, and in need of radical restructuring. The primary exponent of this belief was Tolstoy who, from the publication of *Voina i mir* until his death, increasingly refuted the power of science, rationalism, and social institutions to effect humanitarian changes in Russia. Instead, he glorified simple, natural, cooperative living, living infused with a sense of spiritual harmony, as the means by which the health of the nation could be ensured.

The deaths of Turgenev and Dostoevsky in the early 1880s left a sizeable vacuum in the movement. Tolstoy, however, though far removed from the St. Petersburg literary scene, remained an omnipresent force. His humanitarian code of brotherly love and nonresistance to evil, emphasized in his fiction and in his daily living, had a profound effect during this decade on short-story writer Anton CHEKHOV, who would eventually earn the title of the last great Russian Realist. By 1890, following his medical and socioeconomic study of the penal settlement on Sakhalin Island, Chekhov had rejected Tolstoy's beliefs, though still retained ties with the elderly writer. Consequently, the didactic element in his fiction virtually disappeared. The most important stories Chekhov produced appeared during the final decade of his life. Considered excellent examples of purely objective Realism, Chekhov's narratives were startlingly mimetic pictures of ordinary Russian life. "DAMA S SOBACHKOI" (1899; "The Lady with the Dog," 1917), one of his last and best stories, sparked a letter from Maxim GORKY, in which he wrote: "You're killing [R]ealism. And you'll kill it soon for a long time to come. That form has outlived its time. It's a fact! No one after you can go any further on that path; no one can write so simply about simple things as you can." Gorky, the founder of SOCIALIST REALISM, a movement which inherited many techniques and concerns of the Realist tradition, may have been precipitous in his declaration of Realism's demise. Yet, his acknowledgement of Chekhov's virtuosic descriptive powers, partially due to his fellow writer's pioneering modernization of the short story form, was testament to Realism's extraordinary achievements and impact, even some fifty years after the movement had begun.

Russian Realism, admittedly, was never a tightly knit, homogeneous school of a few writers. Rather, it was an informed, literary response to Russia's shifting political, social, and artistic climate which grew to shape the nature and direction of writers and works for over half a century. No other movement in Russian literature had as great an impact on the development of modern fiction. Despite its waning presence following the emergence of such movements as SYMBOLISM and FUTURISM, Realism continues to exert its influence on many of the major writers of the twentieth century.

⇒•⇐

Chekhov, Anton (1860-1904), Russian short-story writer and dramatist.

Chekhov is considered, alongside Tolstoy, as the greatest Realist writer living at the close of the nineteenth century. In 1884 he launched dual careers in medicine and literature, following graduation from Moscow University. His medical background caused him to view reality with a scientist's eye; consequently, he expressed his artistic credo with the affirmation: "For chemists there is nothing unclean on the earth. The writer must be as objective as the chemist." The author of numerous ephemeral humorous pieces prefatory to this initial stage, Chekhov became by the late 1880s a predominantly serious writer. The first major recognition of his talent came in 1887 when his collection *V sumerkakh* (1887; At Twilight) received the Pushkin prize. As Chekhov sought outlets other than lowbrow reviews for his work, his narrative method quickly matured into the emotionally detached examinations of ordinary, often unhappy, people which sustain his best fiction. "Step" (1888; "The Steppe," 1915), "Palata No. 6" (1892; "Ward

No. 6," 1903), and "Dama s sobachkoi" (1899; "The Lady with the Dog," 1917) are prominent among the many stories he composed which helped earn him a reputation as one of the greatest short-story writers of all time.

Chekhov is equally well regarded for his development of the Russian drama, a genre to which he devoted considerable energy from approximately 1896 until his death. Critics place four of his plays—*Chayka* (1896; *The Sea Gull*, 1912), *Dyadya Vanya* (1899; *Uncle Vanya*, 1912), *Tri sestry* (1901; *Three Sisters*, 1916), and *Vishnevy sad* (1903; *The Cherry Orchard*, 1912)—among the most important works in the history of modern drama. Chekhov's stage characters, like his fictional characters, underscore the shortcomings of humanity through their repeated miscommunications, deceits, and egocentric lives. The assiduity with which Chekhov transposed the fundamental truths of daily existence to the drama and to the short-story forms justifies his position as a Realist of the first rank, who carried the art of Tolstoy, Dostoevsky, and others of the previous generation firmly into the twentieth century.

"Dama s sobachkoi" (1899; "The Lady with the Dog," 1917).

Suggested in part by Tolstoy's *Anna Karenina* (1875-77; *Anna Karenina*, 1886), "Dama s sobachkoi" is a coolly told, occasionally impressionistic narrative of marital infidelity, love, and longing. In Yalta a banker named Dmitrii Gurov makes the acquaintance of Anna Sergeevna von Dierderitz. Both are married but vacationing alone. After a week of informal, though meaningful, encounters, the two make love. Although Anna is overcome by guilt as well as the realization that her married life is vacuous, Dmitrii is not, for he is a cynic who believes in brief and uncomplicated affairs. Yet, to his surprise, he becomes steadfast in his love for Anna and the secret relationship blossoms. The two lovers suffer continuously, however. When apart, they think of each other; when together, they think of the dual lives they have been forced to lead. The story closes without a clear resolution of their predicament. Chekhov's final hint of future hope for the couple accords with his conviction that although humans are frequently subject to grief and helplessness, patience and the exercise of individual will can bring about change.

❖•❖

Dostoevsky, Fyodor Mikhailovich (1821-1881)
Russian novelist, short-story writer, and journalist.

Dostoevsky began his writing career in 1833 with a translation of Balzac's *Eugenie Grandet* (1833). In later years, he drew upon Balzac's work and that of other Western writers, including Sand, Victor Hugo (1802-1885), Charles DICKENS (*see* REALISM, England), and Edgar Allan Poe (1809-1849), to furnish characters, themes, and incidents for some of his best fiction. The greatest literary influence on Dostoevsky, how ever, was Gogol, whose elaborate style and documentation of harsh realities Dostoevsky successfully fused with his highly individual method of psychological Realism. The theme of suffering and salvation which dominates his work is the outgrowth of the barbaric treatment he received, from 1850 to 1854, during his imprisonment in a Siberian labor camp. His only crime was to have been linked to a utopian political group which discussed and published banned literature. An early masterpiece, *Zapiski iz myortvogo doma* (1862; *The House of the Dead*, 1911), arose from his torturous experiences, as did a firm belief in Christian redemption. In the years that followed, despite considerable personal and financial difficulties, Dostoevsky published a prodigious body of writing. Some of his most significant works include *Prestupleniye i nakazaniye* (1866; *Crime and Punishment*, 1886), *Idiot* (1869, *The Idiot*, 1887), *Besy* (1872; *The Possessed*, 1913), and *Brat'ya Karamazovy* (1879-80; *The Brothers Karamazov*, 1912).

In each of them Dostoevsky explored the dual nature of the human spirit, humanity's potential for good and evil. Perhaps more than any other writer in world literature, Dostoevsky was able to write, with equal authority and conviction, of the sublime and the sordid. It is this achievement, coupled with his stunning powers of observation, that has earned him a place among the great writers of all time.

Brat'ya Karamazovy (1879-80; *The Brothers Karamazov*, 1912).

Widely acclaimed as Dostoevsky's greatest novel, *Brat'ya Karamazovy* is also one of the most complex and significant masterpieces of modern world literature. The central story—variously interpreted as a sensational murder tale, theophilosophical inquiry, collection of psychological case studies, and moral examination of the entire Russian nation—concerns the lives of three brothers, Dmitri, Ivan, and Alyosha. In the provincial town of Skotoprigonyevski their lives become dangerously entwined with that of their father, Fyodor. An incurable egoist, drunkard, and lecher, Fyodor exerts an enormous influence on each of his sons, who despite having vastly differing personalities recognize in themselves the genetic evil (Karamazov is the Russian word for "dirt") that unites them. When Dmitri is accused of murdering Fyodor, a trial ensues. Eventually, the servant Smerdyakov, who may in fact be the bastard son of Fyodor, confesses to the crime and shortly after hangs himself. Despite receiving a sound defense, Dmitri is judged guilty. Suffering abounds in the closing chapters of the novel, but Alyosha, who has pledged to follow Dmitri to Siberia, helps expiate the pain and guilt through his innate goodness and his vision of a better future.

The work was so well received in Russia that an illustrious banquet was held in Dostoevsky's honor and Turgenev, an often bitter rival of Dostoevsky, hailed the novel for its divine wisdom, veracity, and relevancy to the times. Although its placement within the Realistic tradition is occasionally disputed, *Brat'ya Karamazovy* is an undisputed literary classic, one of the great novels in the history of world literature.

⤞•⤝

Goncharov, Ivan Aleksandrovich (1812-1891)
Russian novelist, travel writer, and short-story writer.

Although not as well known today as the major Russian Realists, Goncharov was an immensely popular writer during his time and one of the central shapers of the Realist tradition. Like Dostoevsky, Goncharov achieved his first success writing in the Naturalistic vein. His *Obyknovennaya istoriya* (1847; *A Common Story*, 1894) systematically attacked Romanticism through its ironic portrayal of a naive provincial. The work, sometimes considered the first Realistic novel in Russian literature, was followed much later by *Fregat Pallada* (1858; *The Voyage of the Frigate Pallada*, 1965), a clear-eyed, wryly humorous collection of essays and stories describing Goncharov's travel experiences in Japan. In 1859 Goncharov published his greatest work, OBLOMOV (*Oblomov*, 1915), The product of over a decade of labor, the novel won instantaneous acclaim for the comical portrait of its title character, who became an archetype for all that was slothful and superfluous in Russian society. Goncharov's final novel, *Obryv* (1869; *The Precipice*, 1915) was far less esteemed due to its digressiveness and overtly anti-nihilistic moralizing.

Oblomov (1859; *Oblomov*, 1915).

Oblomov is a largely plotless novel that records the idealism and decay of its hero, an indolent member of the Russian gentry. Born to a life of leisure, Oblomov is incapable of apprehending, let alone participating in, the active world around him. His love for Olga Ilyinskaya arouses him for a time from his torpor and isolation, but the relationship fails as a result of his social limitations. The novel ends with Oblomov passing from dreamy remembrances of his childhood to a peaceful acceptance of death. More comic than tragic in outlook, the novel nonetheless was received as a serious death toll for Romanticism and a forceful proclamation of a new era in Russian literature and social history.

⤞•⤝

Tolstoy, Leo (1828-1910)
Russian novelist, short-story writer, essayist, and dramatist.

Tolstoy is considered the supreme Realistic writer and one of the greatest novelists in world literature. His high reputation is due to his comprehensive portraits of Russian society in *Voina i mir* (1869; *War and Peace*, 1886) and *Anna Karenina* (1875-77; *Anna Karenina*, 1886) and to such later, moral fictions as *Smert Ivana Ilyicha* (1886; *The Death of Ivan Iliitch*, 1888). Before he began his career, Tolstoy studied moral philosophy and read the works of Dickens, Laurence Sterne (1713-1768), Pushkin, and Lermontov, all of which deeply affected his approach to fiction. After achieving some

635

success as the author of two autobiographical novels and a series of military sketches, he announced in 1859 his abandonment of literary life and instead concentrated on the management of his country estate and the establishment of a school for his serfs' children. From his teaching experience he derived and published a complete, practicable theory of elementary education. By this time Tolstoy had returned to literature, completed *Voina i mir*, and begun work on *Anna Karenina*.

In 1878 Tolstoy experienced a profound religious conversion which delivered him from a major intellectual crisis concerning the possibility of life's meaninglessness. He expressed his dualistic, pacifist Christianity that arose from this crisis in several polemical, exegetical, and devotional works. Although soon considered subversive by Czarist authorities and the Orthodox Church, Tolstoy was, during these last decades of his life, one of the most admired and influential figures on the European continent. Although Tolstoy's post-conversion works are generally less esteemed than those written earlier, his narrative style and his enduring examination of the problem of free will has often mitigated unfavorable assessments. In the final analysis, Tolstoy's exalted position in world literature remains a product of his powers of Realistic description, his acute understanding of human behavior, and his prophetlike awareness of the good and evil of individuals, social institutions, nations.

Voina i mir (1869; *War and Peace*, 1886).

Like *Brat'ya Karamazovy* (1879-80; *The Brothers Karamazov*, 1912), Tolstoy's most celebrated work resists simple classification. Set in early nineteenth-century Russia during the Napoleonic era, the novel simultaneously functions as historical romance, study of family life, bildungsroman, epic war narrative, and subtle exposé on the passage of time and inevitability of change. A vast array of both historical and fictional characters and a seemingly plotless, multifarious story further complicates a straightforward reading or understanding. Yet, Tolstoy's artistic command of this immense Realistic novel — its very scope and length analogous to the breadth and continuity of human experience — is considered incontrovertible. The story essentially revolves around four main characters: Princess Natasha Rostova, Pierre Bezuhov, Prince Andrey Bolkonsky, and General Michael Kutuzov, commander of the Russian army. Both Kutuzov and Natasha embody Tolstoy's ideal of the natural Russian, attuned to the flux of historical and psychological time, empowered with the virtues of patience, spiritual strength, and *joie de vivre*. In quest of the natural, of an acceptance of reality that provides meaning for their lives, are Andrey and Pierre, who both love Natasha. Andrey achieves an inner peace shortly before his death from battle wounds; Pierre, after suffering imprisonment under the French, awakens to an appreciation of the essential events and cycles of life and finds in Natasha, with whom he eventually unites and raises a family, a perfect complement to share the joys and sorrows of life.

Although occasionally viewed as a novel solely of the privileged classes, *Voina i mir* is sympathetic to all classes of humanity, particularly the poor who, in the guise of such figures as the peasant Karataev, exemplify the purest and noblest heights of the human soul. Like few others novelists in world literature, Tolstoy evoked in *Voina i mir* the overwhelming grandeur and tragedy inherent in earthly existence and the unending flow of historical progress that unites everything, that makes change and improvement possible.

➣•➢

Turgenev, Ivan (1818-1883)
Russian novelist, short-story writer, and dramatist.

Turgenev is generally credited with launching Realism in Russia. Following a brief foray into Romantic poetry, he turned to fiction and began publishing a series of stories on the erroneousness of serfdom, a conviction he had held since witnessing numerous atrocities as a child on his parents' estate. Collected in 1852 as *Zapiski okhotnika* (*A Sportsman's Sketches*, 1895), Turgenev's close, unemotional studies of rural life won the admiration of numerous writers eager to renounce the Romantic and Naturalistic tendencies of the time. He reached the height of his art — a blend of penetrating social examination, tempered lyricism, and revealing irony — in 1862 with *Ottsy i deti* (*Fathers and Sons*, 1867). To Turgenev's dismay, the work was denounced by both radicals and conservatives. His main character, whom he intended to be received sympathetically, was viewed by the left as a poor caricature of their ideals and by the right as a too favorable portrait of a dangerous subversive. The controversy became so embroiled that Turgenev, in effect, exiled himself to Germany, Italy, and France for long periods of time throughout the remainder of his life. In France, especially, Turgenev enjoyed the popularity that had eluded him in Russia. His stature was greatly enhanced there through his close ties with Flaubert, the Brothers GONCOURT, Émile ZOLA, and other writers of the Realist and Naturalist schools. However, Turgenev's last full-length novels, *Dym* (1867; *Smoke*, 1868) and *Nov'* (1877; *Virgin Soil*, 1877), as well as his late experimentations in prose poetry, did little to increase his contemporary reputation. Today Turgenev is ranked, largely upon the enduring interest of *Ottsy i deti*, second only to Tolstoy and Dostoevsky among all nineteenth-century Russian novelists.

Ottsy i deti (1862; *Fathers and Sons*, 1867).

Turgenev's most famous novel, *Ottsy i deti*, covers the period in Russian history directly preceding the emancipation of the serfs in 1861. The central character is Yevgeny Bazarov, a nihilist recently graduated from medical school. A man of volatile temperament, Yevgeny cannot abide the aristocratic aloofness and bourgeois complacency that pervade his country; he seeks sweeping revolution and the advancement of intelligence and science to solve Russia's social evils. Arkady Kirsanov functions for a time as Yevgeny's naive disciple. Gradually, however, Yevgeny's ineffectuality, his failure to persuade others of his views, becomes painfully apparent. Following Yevgeny's death from infection, Arkady happily settles down to marriage and a life of convention that is no different than that of his father.

Although Turgenev imbued Yevgeny with nearly all his political leanings and personal characteristics and thus risked creating a fundamentally didactic narrative, his novel is considered a triumph of Realistic artistry as well as an invaluable record of nineteenth-century sociopolitical history in Russia.

⤗•⤛

Further Reading

Bayley, John. *Tolstoy and the Novel*. London: Chatto & Windus, 1966.

Becker, George J. "Leo Tolstoy," "Fyodor Dostoevsky," "Anton Chekhov." In his *Master European Realists of the Nineteenth Century*. New York: Ungar, 1982.

Borras, F. M. *Maxim Gorky and Lev Tolstoy*. Leeds, England: Leeds University Press, 1968.

Cizevskij, Dmitrij. *History of Nineteenth-Century Russian Literature*. Vol. II, *The Age of Realism*. Nashville, Tenn.: Vanderbilt University Press, 1974.

Crankshaw, Edward. *Tolstoy: The Making of a Novelist*. New York: Viking, 1974.

Debreczeny, Paul, and Thomas Eekman, eds. *Chekhov's Art of Writing: A Collection of Critical Essays*. Columbus, Ohio: Slavica Publishers, 1977.

Ehre, Milton. *Oblomov and His Creator: The Life and Art of Ivan Goncharov*. Princeton, N.J.: Princeton University Press, 1973.

Fanger, Donald. *Dostoevsky and Romantic Realism, a Study of Dostoevsky in Relation to Balzac, Dickens and Gogol*. Cambridge, Mass.: Harvard University Press, 1965.

Fennell, John, ed. *Nineteenth-Century Russian Literature: Studies of Ten Russian Writers*. Berkeley, Calif.: University of California Press, 1973.

Freeborn, Richard. "The Novels of Goncharov." In his *The Rise of the Russian Novel from "Eugene Onegin" to "War and Peace": Studies in the Russian Novel*. Cambridge, England: Cambridge University Press, 1973.

Gorky, Maxim. *Reminiscences of Leo Nikolaevich Tolstoy*. New York: Huebsch, 1920.

Greenwood, E. B. *Tolstoy: The Comprehensive Vision*. New York: St. Martin's Press, 1975.

Gunn, Elizabeth. *A Daring Coiffeur: Reflections on "War and Peace" and "Anna Karenina."* London: Chatto & Windus; Totowa, N.J.: Rowman & Littlefield, 1971.

Holquist, Michael. *Dostoevsky and the Novel*. Evanston, Ill.: Northwestern University Press, 1986.

Jackson, Robert L. *The Art of Dostoevsky: Deliriums and Nocturnes*. Princeton, N.J.: Princeton University Press, 1981.

Knowles, A. V. *Ivan Turgenev*. Boston: Twayne, 1988.

Kramer, Karl D. *The Chameleon and the Dream: The Image of Reality in Cexov's Stories*. The Hague: Mouton, 1970.

Lukács, Georg. "Tolstoy and the Development of Realism." In his *Studies in European Realism*. New York: Grosset & Dunlap, 1964.

McLean, H. *Nikolai Leskov: The Man and His Art*. Cambridge, Mass.: Harvard University Press, 1977.

Magarshack, David. *Dostoevsky*. New York: Harcourt, Brace & World, 1962.

—————. *Turgenev: A Life*. New York: Grove Press; London: Faber and Faber, 1954.

Mirsky, D. S. "The Age of Realism: The Novelists." In his *A History of Russian Literature*. Edited by Francis J. Whitfield. New York: Knopf, 1927; New York: Vintage Books, 1958.

Mooney, Harry J., Jr. *Tolstoy's Epic Vision: A Study of "War and Peace" and "Anna Karenina."* Tulsa, Okla.: University of Tulsa Press, 1968.

Muckle, James Y. *Nikolai Leskov and the "Spirit of Protestantism."* Birmingham, England: Dept. of Russian Language & Literature, University of Birmingham, 1978.

Nabokov, Vladimir. *Lectures on Russian Literature*. Edited by Fredson Bowers. New York: Harcourt Brace Jovanovich, 1981.

Pritchett, V. S. *The Gentle Barbarian: The Life and Work of Turgenev*. New York: Random House, 1977.

Proffer, Carl R., and Ronald Meyer. *Nineteenth-Century Russian Literature in English: A Bibliography of Criticism and Translations*. Ann Arbor, Mich · Ardis, 1990.

Schapiro, Leonard. *Turgenev: His Life and Times*. New York: Random House, 1978.

Simmons, Ernest J. *Chekhov: A Biography*. Boston: Little, Brown, 1962.

—————. *Introduction to Russian Realism*. Bloomington, Ind.: Indiana University Press, 1965.

Slonim, Marc. "Turgenev," "Goncharov and Ostrovsky," "Dostoevsky," "Tolstoy," "Chekhov." In his *An Outline of Russian Literature*. New York: Oxford University Press, 1958.

Terras, Victor. *A Karamazov Companion: Commentary on the Genesis, Language and Style of Dostoevsky's Novel*. Madison, Wis.: University of Wisconsin Press, 1981.

Troyat, Henri. *Tolstoy*. Garden City, N.Y.: Doubleday, 1967.

Wasiolek, Edward. *Dostoevsky, the Major Fiction*. Cambridge, Mass.: MIT Press, 1964.

Winner, Thomas. *Chekhov and His Prose*. New York: Holt, Rinehart & Winston, 1966.

REALISM (Realismo)
Spain, 1870s-1890s

The Realist movement in Spain was directly related to Costumbrismo, a highly special-ized, region-by-region local color fiction important in the eighteenth and nineteenth centuries. Modeled after Costumbrismo, Realism in the Spanish novel was like its pre-decessor opposed to Romanticism, particularly the use of flat character types, narrow descriptions of native life, and unlikely plot developments and resolution. Most scholars agree that the first, albeit transitional, examples of the Realist regional novel were pub-lished by Fernán Caballero (pseud. of Cecilia Böhl von Faber, 1796-1877) from 1849 onward. Other Costumbristas included Larra (1809-1837), Mesonero Romanos (1803-1882), and Estébanez Calderón (1799-1867).

A more stylistically sophisticated and psychologically complex form of Realism emerged after 1870, in the work of Pedro Antonio Alarcón (1833-1891), Clarín (pseud. of Leopoldo Alas y Ureña, 1852-1901), Luis Coloma (1851-1915), Emilia Pardo Bazán (1851-1921), José María Pereda (1833-1906), Benito PÉREZ GALDÓS, and critic Juan Valera (1824-1905). Although some of these authors were more rigid in their reproductions of landscape, customs, and speech than others, they all shared an interest in revivifying the Spanish novel, a once-towering genre in European literature, while examining individual and social characteristics in the context of their nation's past and future. Representative works include Alarcón's novel *Cosas que fueron* (1871), Clarín's novel *La regenta* (1884), Coloma's novel *Pequeñeces* (2 vols., 1890), and María Pereda's sketches in *Escenas montañesas* (1864). Pardo Bazán was notorious for her NATURALIST novels, beginning with *La tribuna* (1883), about life and work in a tobacco factory; she conducted research in person for two months, following the influence of French author Émile ZOLA. Her essays in *La cuestión palpitante* (1883), however, examined Zola's Naturalism and cited its focus on determinism as a weakness and supported the advantages of Realism's more embracing, open approach. Valera's *Apuntes sobre el arte nuevo de escribir novelas* (1886-87) took up issues Pardo Bazán brought into literary debate.

➤●◄

Pérez Galdós, Benito (1843-1920), Spanish novelist and dramatist.
Widely considered the most influential Spanish novelist after Cervantes, Pérez Galdós grew up in the Canary Islands where his work as a journalist prepared him to write Realist fictional portrayals. In his novels he rebelled against the Romanticist style and depicted characters and situations with the natural language of ordinary dialogue and with attention to contemporary moral and social issues. He admired Russian, English, and French Realists, and in fact is often compared to TOLSTOY, DOSTOEVSKY, DICKENS, and Balzac. His novels include *La Desheredada* (1881; *The Disinherited Lady*, 1957), *Tormento* (1884; *Torment*, 1952), *La de Bringas* (1884; *The Spendthrifts*, 1952), *FORTUNATA Y JACINTA* (4 vols., 1886-87; *Fortunata and Jacinta: Two Stories of Married Women*, 1973), *Realidad* (1889), and *Misericordia* (1897).

Fortunata y Jacinta (4 vols., 1886-87; *Fortunata and Jacinta: Two Stories of Married Women*, 1973).
Considered his masterpiece, *Fortunata y Jacinta* tells the story of two women in love with the same man, Juanito Santa Cruz. Pérez Galdós's penchant for Hegelian dialecticism plays out in his portrayals of the women. Jacinta, the wife, is depicted as representing "social forces or civilization," she is "barren"; Fortunata is the beautiful mistress and is drawn to evoke "natural forces or barbarism." Fortunata, dying after giving birth

to Juanito's child, gives it to Jacinta, who has been unable to have children, thus creating a synthesis from opposition toward the progression of life.

❖•❖

Further Reading

Berkowitz, Hyman Chonon. *Perez Galdos, Spanish Liberal Crusader*. Madison, Wis.: University of Wisconsin Press, 1948.

Bull, William E. *Clarín, the Critic in Action*. Stillwater, Okla.: Oklahoma State University, 1963.

Chandler, Richard E., and Kessel Schwartz. "The Regional Novel." In their *A New History of Spanish Literature*. Baton Rouge, La.: Louisiana State University Press, 1961.

Charnon-Deutsch, Louis. *The Nineteenth-Century Spanish Story: Textual Strategies of a Genre in Transition*. London: Tamesis Books, 1985.

DeCoster, Cyrus Cole. *Juan Valera*. New York: Twayne, 1974.

Engler, Kay. *The Structure of Realism: The "Novelas contemporáneas" of Benito Pérez Galdós*. Chapel Hill, N.C.: University of North Carolina, Department of Romance Languages, 1977.

Eoff, Sherman H. *The Novels of Pérez Galdós: The Concept of Life as Dynamic Process*. St. Louis, Mo.: [s.n.], 1954.

————. "Pereda's Realism, His Style." In *Studies in Honor of Frederick W. Shipley*, Freeport, N.Y.: Books for Libraries Press, 1968.

Flynn, Gerard C. *Luis Coloma*. Boston: Twayne, 1987.

Gilman, Stephen. *Galdós and the Art of the European Novel, 1867-1887*. Princeton, N.J.: Princeton University Press, 1981.

Goldman, Peter B., ed. *Conflicting Realities: Four Readings of a Chapter by Pérez Galdós (Fortunata y Jacinta, Part III, Chapter IV)*. London: Tamesis, 1984.

González-Arias, Francisca. *Portrait of a Woman as Artist: Emilia Pardo Bázan and the Modern Novel in France and Spain*. New York: Garland, 1992.

Pattison, Walter T. *Benito Pérez Galdós*. Boston: Twayne, 1975.

Ribbans, G. "Contemporary History in the Structure and Characterization of "Fortunata y Jacinta." In *Galdós Studies*. Edited by J. E. Varey. London: Tamesis, 1970.

Walton, Leslie B. *Perez Galdos and the Spanish Novel of the Nineteenth Century*. London; Toronto: J. M. Dent & Sons; New York: E. P. Dutton, 1927.

REALISM
Sudan, 1950s-1960s

Following upon a Romantic movement which lasted until the middle of the twentieth century in Sudan, Realism became the dominant literary force and occasionally merged with an indigenous form of SOCIALIST REALISM. Chief writers in fiction included al-Tayyib Zarūq (1935-), Salāh Ahmad Ibrāhīm (1933-), and Alī al-Mak (1937-). In poetry, the most notable writers were al-Mahdī al-Majdhūb (1919-) and Ismāīl Hasan (?-1982).

⇥•⇤
Further Reading

Osman, Ahmed I. "Folklore as a Mode of Expression in the Poetic Experience of the Sudanese
Poet Muhammad al-Mahdi al-Majdhub." *Georgetown Journal of Languages and
Linguistics* 3, 2-4 (1995): 204-17.

REALISM
United States, 1880s-1910s

In the lexicon of modern literary movements, Realism is probably the term most frequently employed yet most ambiguously described. Two factors, in particular, seem to
account for this. Firstly, a vast number of writers since the Civil War have, consciously
or not, employed the salient attributes of so-called Realistic narration in their works,
which nonetheless naturally diverge in style, structure, and mood. Secondly, an oft-
repeated and presumably accurate axiom—that all modern fiction is either fundamentally Romantic or Realistic—has presaged a wealth of scholarship which, regardless of philosophical orientation or ostensible purpose, tends to categorize and discuss
works distant in time and technique with regular reference to these labels. Regardless
of these and other obstacles, Realism may perhaps best be understood as a broad-based
literary movement which had its beginnings in the latter decades of the nineteenth
century and continued through the twentieth, as the predominant form of fictional
expression throughout the literary world. Briefly stated, Realism is, in contrast to
Romanticism, a theory predicated upon the concrete, objective representation of ordinary people and events. Accordingly, the only true work of art for the early Realists was
one which mirrored actual, everyday life.

In 1867, John William DEFOREST, an ethnologist, novelist, and Civil War captain, published *MISS RAVENEL'S CONVERSION FROM SECESSION TO LOYALTY*. The novel, an unstinting
reproduction of the war and its impact on the individual, marked the advent of Realism
in America. William Dean HOWELLS, who shortly became the chief exponent of the
movement, was at that time assistant editor for the *Atlantic Monthly*. Recognizing
immediately the value of DeForest's vibrant, detailed scenes of the South, he solicited
the writer for short regional pieces written in a similar vein. DeForest responded instead
with additional novels, including *Kate Beaumont* (1872), a study of South Carolina's
people and customs which Howells esteemed as that author's finest work.

Although DeForest's career floundered, for various reasons, Howells's catapulted;
throughout the remainder of the century he rose to prominence as editor-in-chief first
for the *Atlantic* and, later, for *Harper's Magazine*, during which time he not only pub-

lished a prodigious body of work but also relentlessly championed the cause of Realism through his essays and review. An ardent admirer of LOCAL COLOR writing, Howells satisfied the post-Civil War fascination readers had for the sectional differences in their burgeoning nation through picturesque, often humorous short fiction that authentically detailed the peculiarities of a given region. Some of Howells's major contributors included Bret HARTE, who gained wide popularity as a chronicler of the Far West; Hamlin GARLAND, who depicted the Midwest; George Washington Cable (1844-1925) and Joel Chandler Harris (1848-1908), who portrayed the South; and Mary E. Wilkins Freeman (1852-1930) and Sarah Orne Jewett (1849-1909), who documented the New England region. Consequently, the *Atlantic Monthly*, and the careers of the Local Colorists, flourished during the 1870s, the formative decade of American Realism.

Howells's literary acquaintances were numerous and of considerable significance to his artistic development. His two most important and lasting friendships were with Mark TWAIN, an association which began shortly after Howells wrote a highly favorable review of *The Innocents Abroad* (1869), and Henry JAMES, whom he had met even earlier and who published at the beginning of his career a glowing account of *Italian Journeys* (1867), a detailed nonfiction study of Howells's experiences while serving as American consul in Venice. Each man explored in his early work the clash between Old and New World traditions, a theme which became the hallmark of James's mature, international novels. Each, also, was fundamentally a moralist who believed the highest purpose of fiction was to demonstrate the innate potential of the human spirit to overcome the trappings of egoism, deceit, and depravity. Through their lengthy correspondence and conversations, their conception of Realism and the physical world clarified itself and found expression in Howells's two most famous statements, that "Morality penetrates all things, it is the soul of all things" and that "Realism is nothing more and nothing less than the truthful treatment of material."

Although their narrative methods differed—Howells, for instance, preferred an omniscient narrator while Twain and James experimented with other points of view, especially limited third- and first-person—the three writers agreed on several philosophical and technical points which distanced them from the Romantics as well as the NATURALISTS, the latter a group who by the 1890s seriously threatened the future of Realism. These points included: a repudiation of determinism, an acceptance of human reason as superior to human passion, an understanding of fiction as living social history, a conscious abstention from authorial commentary, an unwillingness to subordinate content to form, a conviction that no subject was unworthy of narrative treatment, a resistance to tragedy, and a guiding determination to present life as it typically appeared, not as one wished it, nor as it was only under unusual circumstances.

During the 1880s each of the writers attained artistic maturity with such classics as *THE PORTRAIT OF A LADY* (1881), *THE ADVENTURES OF HUCKLEBERRY FINN* (1884), and *THE RISE OF SILAS LAPHAM* (1885). Although Local Color writing continued as a subdivision of Realism, it now increasingly focused on universal themes, if not locales, while shedding its sentimentality, frequently stereotypical characters, and simple moralizing; Jewett's *The Country of the Pointed Firs* (1896) signalled the apex of the form during the nineteenth century. Virtually all the Realists, in turn, came to regard their position in society with increasing seriousness as they recognized the not always welcome impact of economic expansion and scientific advances on the ethical course of their nation. True, their methods of gathering and analyzing the data of experience were closely allied with those of Charles Darwin, William James, and others; yet, they could not pursue their task of documentation without the accompanying compulsion to somehow indicate the means for society's improvement.

The literary models the Realists chose spanned several centuries as well as several nations. Spanish picaresque narratives of the sixteenth century and their later English counterparts, Daniel Defoe's *Robinson Crusoe* (1719) and *Moll Flanders* (1722), served as edifying examples of effective characterization and skillful presentation of detail. More significant, though, were the works of the Realists' immediate European predecessors, notably Stendhal, Gustave FLAUBERT, Honoré de Balzac; Fyodor DOSTOEVSKY, Ivan TURGENEV, Leo TOLSTOY, Jane Austen, and George ELIOT. At the same time Howells was assimilating the styles and concerns of these writers, particularly the Russians, he was actively promoting them through his periodicals. The principal technical advances of American Realism, interestingly, stemmed not from Howells but his friends Twain and James. Twain's contribution to the direction of American literature proved immense. In addition to his emergence as the nation's foremost humorist, his elevation of spoken idiom to that of colorful literary language opened a pathway for countless later masters of natural dialogue, including William FAULKNER (*see* MODERNISM, United States) and Ernest HEMINGWAY (*see* LOST GENERATION). James's innovations were of a subtler nature and, probably, of more resounding influence to twentieth-century writing. Through continual experimentation with point of view, an outgrowth of his acute interest in his characters' states of mind, James perfected the use of UNRELIABLE NARRATORS who, in their psychological complexities and realistically limited perceptions, presaged later literary innovations, such as the interior monologue and STREAM-OF-CONSCIOUSNESS narration, techniques commonly associated with Modernism.

To his credit, Howells acknowledged the superiority of both novelists. His own best role, that of apologist and polemicist, perfectly complemented their work. The resistance to Realism throughout the nineteenth century was, despite the movement's success, both sizeable and vociferous. Howells himself sparked much of the furor from idealists and Romantics, steadfast admirers of Nathaniel Hawthorne (1804-1864) and Herman Melville (1819-1891), with his pronouncement in 1882 that fiction had, through the efforts of Realism's "chief luminary," James, surpassed that of Charles DICKENS (*see* Realism, England) and William Makepeace Thackeray (1811-1863) and, by insinuation, that of all previous American writers. The primary charge Howells fought to deny was that Realism had, in fact, plunged the craft of literary expression to unforgivable depths with its detached portrayal of the commonplace and its complete lack of conventional heroes and heroines, whose nobility supposedly elevated a creative work to high art. What it had done, instead, was to greatly expand the purview, and thus the responsibility and distinction, of the novelist. As James confidently wrote in his essay "The Art of Fiction" (1885): "There is no impression of life, no manner of seeing it and feeling it, to which the novelist may not offer a place."

Ironically, just as Realism effectively triumphed over Romanticism by the early 1890s, Naturalism surfaced and began attacking the movement for not having advanced far enough, for refraining from treating the more vulgar aspects of existence, despite a supposedly egalitarian approach to subject matter. Unfortunately, Howells's early support of such Naturalist writers as Stephen CRANE, Frank NORRIS, and Garland, was largely diminished by the denigrating assessments of Ambrose Bierce (1842-1914?), H. L. Mencken (1880-1956), and Sinclair LEWIS (*see* JAZZ AGE), to name but a few of the iconoclastic writers of the next generation who wished to publicly repudiate Realism's monumental influence. Nonetheless, Realism carried its impact well into the twentieth century, particularly through the later novels of James and his close colleague Edith WHARTON. However, of special importance at this late juncture was Howells's friend Henry ADAMS, considered one of the last great defenders of Realism and of nineteenth-century society in general. With his ironic autobiographical novel *THE EDUCATION OF HENRY ADAMS* (privately printed, 1907; published, 1918), Adams grappled with the weighty problem of the social and moral devolution of humanity. His contemplative, skeptical, and sweeping approach, artfully reinforced with the changing symbols of Western civilization, showed Realism at its inventive and critical best and in so doing provided a formal example that many later Modernist writers adopted.

With Howells's death in 1920 came, finally, the certain demise of Realism as a cohesive movement. Yet, its repercussions have been felt throughout the twentieth century. The Modernist, PROLETARIAN, and regional fiction of John DOS PASSOS (*see* LOST GENERATION), Thomas Wolfe (1900-1938), James Gould Cozzens (1903-1978), James T. FARRELL (*see* PROLETARIAN LITERATURE, United States), Erskine Caldwell (1903-1987), Hemingway, Cather (1873-1947), Faulkner, Lewis, John STEINBECK (*see* Proletarian Literature, United States), and countless others owes an incalculable debt to the pioneering work of the Realists and Local Colorists. The final accomplishment of these writers was to sharpen narrative observation to a fine art while greatly expanding the scope of fiction through incisive studies of virtually all settings and segments of American society.

❖•❖

Adams, Henry (1838-1918)
American autobiographer, historian, biographer, and novelist.

Renowned as the most perceptive and eloquent social critic of his time, Adams came from a distinguished family of Bostonian statesmen; his great-grandfather John was the second president of the United States, his grandfather John Quincy was the sixth president, and his father, Charles Francis, was a respected congressman who during his career served under Abraham Lincoln as foreign minister to Great Britain. Instead of choosing politics as a career, Adams satisfied his love for art, history, and scholarship first as an instructor at Harvard and editor of *The North American Review* and, soon after, as an author of several exceptional literary works. Already by the 1880s, in his early novels and biographies, Adams was exploring his most important theme: the disintegration of historical institutions and human morality in the wake of scientific progress. This was even more true of his landmark nine-volume study, *History of the United States During the Administrations of Jefferson and Madison* (1889-91). Adams followed this work with a singularly brilliant account of life and ideology in thirteenth-century Europe. Entitled *Mont St. Michel and Chartres* (1904), this work, which underscores the importance of the Virgin Mary symbol in the Middle Ages, is often read as a companion piece to Adams's masterpiece, *The Education of Henry Adams*. After public appearance in 1918, *The Education* won a Pulitzer prize for autobiography; however, the work has since been regarded as transcending individual genres and representing, instead, a creative-philosophical watershed, an archetypal work teetering on the brink of modern and pre-modern history, literature, and life.

The Education of Henry Adams (1907).

The Education of Henry Adams is a work which may be read on several levels. It is, firstly, a third-person account of Adams's own maturation and education, of the purposes of education, and of its own specific impact on his adult life. Secondly, it is an ambitious attempt to educate the reader, not only about Adams, but about the grand passage of culture and history of which Adams had been a part. Thirdly, and most importantly, it is an ironic disquisition on the *failure* of Adams's education in light of the demands of present and future society, powerfully represented by the imposing presence of the dynamo, the Western mechanical replacement for the Virgin of the

Middle Ages. As the narrative progresses, through a large, mysteriously unexplained gap in chronology, toward the twentieth century, *The Education* becomes more and more prophetic and pessimistic in tone. The central message obtains during Adams's visit to the 1900 Chicago Exhibition. It is here, when he observes the dynamo, that he realizes the diminishing power of humans and the increasing power of external forces to affect the course of history. In the penultimate chapter, entitled "A Law of Acceleration," Adams summarizes his thesis: "The movement from unity into multiplicity, between 1200 and 1900, was unbroken in sequence, and rapid in acceleration. Prolonged one generation longer, it would require a new social mind. As though thought were common salt in indefinite solution it must enter a new phase subject to new laws. Thus far, since five or ten thousand years, the mind had successfully reacted, and nothing yet proved that it would fail to react—but it would need to jump."

⇒•⇐

DeForest, John William (1826-1906)
American novelist, historian, and short-story writer.

DeForest first earned his distinction as a remarkably objective writer with *History of the Indians of Connecticut from the Earliest Known Period to 1850* (1851), a seminal study of the Connecticut tribes. However, exposure to European culture and the works of the French Realists gradually steered him away from a career as historian and biographer. Before the Civil War, DeForest published two travel books as well as his first novels, which, though melodramatic, displayed his talent for accurate depiction. In 1867 he rose to fame as the forerunner of the Realist movement led by Howells with his *Miss Ravenel's Conversion from Secession to Loyalty* (1867). The work, perhaps in part due to its shocking scenes and language, never gained a wide readership. Although DeForest continued writing for three more decades, his works were generally met with public indifference. Although an inferior stylist, DeForest is considered crucially important to the development of Realism, and Naturalism, in America.

Miss Ravenel's Conversion from Secession to Loyalty (1867).

The heroine of DeForest's best-known novel is Lillie Ravenel, a New Orleans belle who marries Lieutenant Colonel John Carter, a handsome, dissolute officer on leave from the war because of an injury. Lillie's conversion is a gradual one, made possible by her father's persevering moral foresight, her ill-fated union to Carter, and her postwar rejuvenation and commitment to Captain Edward Colburne, a Northerner whose deep love she had previously spurned. DeForest's novel is unique in nineteenth-century fiction for its pioneering, Realistic depiction of war's devastation and its indelible mark on the nature of society and the individual.

647

❦•❦

Howells, William Dean (1837-1920)
American novelist, critic, and essayist.

The chief theoretician and practitioner of American Realism, Howells was both a prolific novelist and highly influential literary critic. During his long career as an editor,
first for the *Atlantic Monthly* and later for *Harper's Magazine,* he encouraged the
writers of his day to compose stories with a high degree of verisimilitude, capturing
the people and places of their own realm of experience without concern for the contrivances of plot and structure. The best of his monthly columns for *Harper's* were
assembled as *Criticism and Fiction* (1891) and form the most extensive nonfiction
record of his literary theories. For Howells, though, his fiction became his most forceful and sustained summation of his artistic concepts. His best novels, essentially close
studies of characters who face ethical dilemmas, include *A Modern Instance* (1882),
The Rise of Silas Lapham (1885), and *A Hazard of New Fortunes* (1890), the last of
which documents his increasing tendency in later years to address social and economic problems in his work. Since the advent of American Naturalism, Howells's literary
reputation has suffered. However, despite his alleged prudery and consciously limited
view of the observable world, his work has in recent years benefited from favorable
reappraisals. Critics generally agree that Howells's contribution to modern American
literature is immense. Through his encouragement of James, Twain, Jewett, Harte,
Garland, and others, and through his relentless defense of objective, reportorial narration, he established a model of writing that has proven the predominant form in twentieth-century American fiction.

The Rise of Silas Lapham (1885).

Howells's most popular work, *The Rise of Silas Lapham,* takes place in nineteenth-century Boston amid the post-Civil War industrial boon. Lapham, the protagonist, is a
savvy though socially inept entrepreneur whose ethical judgment has deteriorated as
his financial success has grown. The construction of Lapham's palatial new home
functions as the novel's central metaphor, for through it Howells repudiates the shallow
materialism which at that time prevailed. When Lapham's meteoric rise reverses itself
he faces a difficult moral dilemma; his decision to accept a huge financial loss rather
than sacrifice his remaining integrity effectively signals his true rise, his steady
improvement in moral character. A masterpiece within Howells's canon, the novel has
also been considered the near quintessential formulation of the positivistic theory of
Realism he espoused, for in it he depicted the lives of his characters with exacting
detail and, avoiding didacticism, upheld the fundamentally moral aspect of human
existence, the delicate interdependence of each member of modern society.

❧•❧

James, Henry (1843-1916)
American novelist, short-story writer, critic, and essayist.

James ranks, above all the Realists, as the preeminent theorist-novelist and one of the most complex, innovative, and influential writers in the English language. Unlike Howells and Twain, James was primarily concerned not with the external but with the internal reality of experience. That is, he chose in his fiction to focus on the psychological peculiarities of his characters, their perceptions of the outer world, their handling of various crises, the subtle nuances of their behavior, and their emotional and social growth. His governing theme, the impact of European civilization on the naive American, afforded him a particularly telling lens through which to examine his characters' minds and develop his pioneering use of self-conscious narrators. From 1875 until his death, James resided in Europe, where he established an enviable literary reputation, first through the novels *Roderick Hudson* (1876), *The American* (1877), and *The Europeans* (1878); later through *Daisy Miller* (1879) and *The Portrait of a Lady* (1881), and finally through *The Wings of the Dove* (1902), *The Ambassadors* (1903), and *The Golden Bowl* (1904).

Distinguished not only for his technical achievements in style, theme, and characterization, but for his numerous essays on his craft — notably "The Art of Fiction" — James is recognized as a powerful force in modern literature whose importance to the Realistic movement, both in America and abroad, cannot be overestimated.

The Portrait of a Lady (1881).

Considered the most balanced and carefully wrought of James's novels, *The Portrait of a Lady* centers around the maturation of Isabel Archer, a young American heiress who has come to Europe at the invitation of her aunt, Mrs. Touchett, to absorb the rich culture and social niceties that England, France, and Italy have to offer. Two suitors seek to win Isabel's promise of marriage but she firmly refuses both. While in Italy, however, she is inescapably charmed by Gilbert Osmond, a worldly American expatriate intent on controlling her inheritance. Following her marriage to Osmond, Isabel becomes increasingly aware of her husband's decadence and his indifference toward her. Yet, she forms a strong bond with Pansy, purportedly Osmond's daughter from his first marriage. Near the end of the novel, Isabel uncovers the truth underlying Osmond's greatest deceit: that Pansy is in fact his illicit daughter by Madame Merle, a calculating woman who has been in Isabel's confidence for years, since secretly promoting to her former lover the idea of a convenient marriage to Isabel.

Once innocent and provincial, Isabel now penetrates with resolute clarity the reality of her unfortunate marriage. Her heroism emerges as neither self-pitying nor spiteful, for she has embraced her fate of honestly caring for the daughter of a man whom she despises while avoiding the moral corruption of those around her.

James's novel marks a high point in the Realist movement—and indeed all of literature—for its trenchant, inexorable development of character without the benefit of authorial intrusion.

✥•✥

Twain, Mark (pseud. of Samuel Langhorne Clemens, 1835-1910)
American novelist, short-story writer, journalist, essayist, and memoirist.

The most popular of the Realists, Twain began his career as a humorous writer of Local Color sketches and travel essays. He gained wide fame in 1865 with the publication of "JIM SMILEY AND HIS JUMPING FROG," an amusing tale which cleverly contrasted the sober conservatism of the educated Easterner with the unrefined vigor and amiability of the New Frontiersman. The story, later reprinted in *The Celebrated Jumping Frog of Calaveras County, and Other Sketches* (1867), was particularly important to the early development of American Realism for its use of vernacular discourse and optimistic, rather than idealistic, view of humanity. In later decades, Twain solidified his reputation as one of America's foremost men of letters with such works as *The Adventures of Tom Sawyer* (1876), *Life on the Mississippi* (1883), and *The Adventures of Huckleberry Finn* (1884). Although he continued in his later years to publish notable works of fiction, including *A Connecticut Yankee in King Arthur's Court* (1889) and *The Tragedy of Pudd'nhead Wilson, and the Comedy Those Extraordinary Twins* (1894), a growing pessimism clouded his comic genius and culminated in the unfinished novel *The Mysterious Stranger* (1916). Nonetheless, Twain is commonly regarded as the father of modern American literature, the first of the Realists to successfully countervail Romanticism and New England literary traditions while creating lasting works of art.

The Adventures of Huckleberry Finn (1884).

Set in the 1850s along the banks of the Mississippi River, *Huckleberry Finn* is a rambling picaresque narrative of two runaways: Jim, a black slave who fears an impending sale to a new owner, and Huck, an adolescent outcast who fakes his own death in order to escape his drunkard father. Their voyage downriver, filled with comic escapades and misadventures, is a source of both immense worry and valuable moral growth for Huck. Although he has befriended Jim, he can only with great difficulty overcome the guilt endemic to his ingrained Southern belief in the rightness of slavery and the wrongness of abetting a slave to freedom. Despite the novel's pervasive humor—largely the fruit of Huck's vivid, colloquial narration—its message, then, is essentially one of moral seriousness. Twain's intent was not simply to readdress the politically settled issue of slavery but to call into question all forms of subjugation and social injustice.

The Adventures of Huckleberry Finn continues to be the most widely studied and commended of Twain's works; for its sustained use of spoken idiom as a literary language it is often called the first of modern American novels and, therefore, the capstone of nineteenth-century Realism.

❖•❖

Unreliable Narrator.

A character who functions as the reader's imperfect guide to the events and other characters in a work of fiction is known as an unreliable narrator. James is considered an early master of unreliable narration, which he employed with maximum effect in *The Turn of the Screw* (1897) and *The Ambassadors* (1903). A technical breakthrough in modern literature, unreliable narration was one of several devices the Realists, and Modernists beginning with Joseph CONRAD, used to provide plots with their own momentum and to preclude the necessity for authorial intrusion.

❖•❖

Wharton, Edith (1862-1937), American novelist and short-story writer.

Although Wharton began her writing career in the 1890s, it was not until the publication of *The House of Mirth* in 1905 that she was recognized as a major American writer. Indicative of much of her work, the novel critically portrays the trivialities and machinations of upper-class New York society. Following some less distinguished works, Wharton published her best-known and most atypical work, *ETHAN FROME* (1911). Shrouded in Naturalistic determinism and concerning the dismal marriage of an aging couple, the work is partially a reflection of Wharton's own troubled marriage, which she severed in 1912. From about this time, Wharton assumed permanent residence in France and maintained social ties with many expatriate writers, including close friend Henry James, with whom she is often compared. Although Wharton continued writing until her death, her last significant work, *The Age of Innocence*, was published in 1920. For this novel she received the Pulitzer Prize a year later. In recent years, Wharton's canon has received favorable reevaluations, particularly by FEMINIST writers who perceive in much of her fiction a cutting assessment of the unequal roles assigned to women and men in the pre-modern era.

Ethan Frome (1911).

A novella set in the rural New England town of Starkfield, *Ethan Frome* is the story of an unstable triangle formed by a poor farmer, Ethan; his sickly wife, Zeena; and their live-in maid, Zeena's cousin, Mattie Silver. Ethan is the symbol of unfulfilled longing and talent, for he once entertained the ambition of becoming an engineer or chemist. Zeena, by contrast, is the symbol of a repressive, Puritanical society: her marriage to Ethan was one of convenience and, rather than publicly dismantle it now, she contents herself with nagging and hypochondria. The recent arrival of the young and innocent Mattie brings new life and hope to Ethan. However, Zeena soon becomes conscious of this nascent romance and insists that Mattie be replaced. In a stunningly climactic scene, Ethan and Mattie resolve to commit suicide together, rather than endure life apart. However, they succeed only in crippling themselves permanently and must return to the stifling environment of the farm to be cared heartlessly for by Zeena. Because of its harsh depictions of the New England landscape, ironic treatment of character, implicit criticism of conventional society, and careful ordering of events, *Ethan Frome* is widely recognized as one of the most masterfully wrought and memorable novels of the Realistic-Naturalistic tradition.

❧•❧

Further Reading

Auchincloss, Louis. *Henry Adams*. Minneapolis: University of Minnesota Press, 1971.

Auerbach, Erich. *Mimesis: The Representation of Reality in Western Literature*. Translated by W. R. Trask. Garden City, N.Y.: Doubleday, 1953.

Bennett, George N. *The Realism of William Dean Howells, 1889-1920*. Nashville, Tenn.: Vanderbilt University Press, 1973.

————. *William Dean Howells: The Development of a Novelist*. Norman, Okla.: University of Oklahoma Press, 1959.

Berthoff, Warner. *The Ferment of Realism: American Literature 1884-1919*. New York: Free Press, 1965.

Borus, Daniel H. *Writing Realism: Howells, James, and Norris in the Mass Market*. Chapel Hill, N.C.: University of North Carolina Press, 1989.

Cady, Edwin H. *The Realist at War: The Mature Years, 1885-1920, of William Dean Howells*. Syracuse, N.Y.: Syracuse University Press, 1958.

————. *The Road to Realism: The Early Years, 1837-1885*. Syracuse, N.Y.: Syracuse University Press, 1956.

Canby, Henry Seidel. *Turn West, Turn East: Mark Twain and Henry James*. Boston: Houghton Mifflin, 1951.

Carrington, George C. *The Dramatic Unity of "Huckleberry Finn."* Columbus, Ohio: Ohio State University Press, 1976.

DeVoto, Bernard. *Mark Twain's America*. Boston: Little, Brown, 1932.

Duckett, Margaret. *Mark Twain and Bret Harte*. Norman, Okla.: University of Oklahoma Press, 1964.

Dusinberre, William. *Henry Adams: The Myth of Failure*. Charlottesville, Va.: University Press of Virginia, 1980.

Eble, Kenneth E., ed. *Howells: A Century of Criticism*. Dallas: Southern Methodist University Press, 1962.

Edel, Leon. *Henry James: A Life*. Rev. ed. New York: Harper & Row, 1985.

Goodman, Susan. *Edith Wharton's Women: Friends and Rivals*. Hanover, N.H.: University Press of New England, 1990.

Haight, Gordon S., ed. Introduction to *Miss Ravenel's Conversion from Secession to Loyalty* by John William DeForest. New York: Harper & Row, 1939.

Howells, William Dean. *Criticism and Fiction*. New York: Harper & Brothers, 1891.

James, Henry. *The Art of the Novel*. New York: Scribner's Sons, 1934.

Jordy, W. H. *Henry Adams: Scientific Historian*. New Haven, Conn.: Yale University Press, 1952.

Krook, Dorothea. *The Ordeal of Consciousness in Henry James*. Cambridge, England: Cambridge University Press, 1962.

Larkin, Maurice. *Man and Society in Nineteenth-Century Realism: Determinism and Literature*. Totowa, N.J.: Rowman & Littlefield, 1977.

Light, James F. *John William DeForest*. New York: Twayne, 1965.

McKay, Janet H. *Narration and Discourse in American Realistic Fiction*. Philadelphia: University of Pennsylvania Press, 1982.

McMurray, William. *The Literary Realism of William Dean Howells*. Carbondale, Ill.: Southern Illinois University Press, 1967.

Miller, James E., Jr. *Theory of Fiction: Henry James*. Lincoln, Nebr.: University of Nebraska Press, 1972.

O'Brien, Edward J. "Bret Harte and Mark Twain." In his *The Advance of the American Short Story*. New York: Dodd, Mead, 1923.

Pizer, Donald. *Realism and Naturalism in Nineteenth-Century American Literature*. Carbondale, Ill.: Southern Illinois University Press, 1966.

Pizer, Donald, and Earl N. Harbert, eds. *American Realists and Naturalists*. Detroit: Gale Research Co., 1982.

Powers, Lyall. *Henry James and Edith Wharton: Letters, 1900-1915*. New York: Scribner's, 1990.

Rowe, John C. *Henry Adams and Henry James: The Emergence of a Modern Consciousness*. Ithaca, N.Y.: Cornell University Press, 1976.

Sayre, Robert F. *The Examined Self: Benjamin Franklin, Henry Adams, Henry James*. Princeton, N.J.: Princeton University Press, 1964.

Wagenknecht, Edward. *Mark Twain: The Man and His Work*. New Haven, Conn.: Yale University Press, 1935. 3rd ed., Norman, Okla.: University of Oklahoma Press, 1961.

———. *The Novels of Henry James*. New York: Ungar, 1983.

Walton, Geoffrey. *Edith Wharton: A Critical Interpretation*. Rev. ed., Rutherford, N.J.: Fairleigh Dickinson University Press, 1982.

Wasserstrom, William. *The Ironies of Progress: Henry Adams and the American Dream*. Carbondale, Ill.: Southern Illinois University Press, 1984.

Wellek, René. "The Concept of Realism in Literary Scholarship." In his *Concepts of Criticism*. New Haven, Conn.: Yale University Press, 1963.

Williams, D. A. *The Monster in the Mirror: Studies in Nineteenth-Century Realism*. New York: Oxford University Press, 1978.

REALISMO. *See* **REALISM, Spain**

RECEPTION THEORY. *See* **READER-RESPONSE CRITICISM AND RECEPTION THEORY**

REGION-TRADITION MOVEMENT
Brazil, 1920s-1930s

This movement flourished in Brazil during the 1920s and 1930s and was based on the continuation of a literary concept which had begun early in the century with the work of Euclides de Cunha (1866-1909) (*see* VERDE-AMARELISMO). It was reinvigorated by Gilberto Freyre (1900-1987) and José Lins de Rêgo (1901-1957). Freyre was a novelist, anthropologist, and social historian. These combined talents provided the background for a consuming interest in the use of his creative ability to examine Brazilian culture in terms of its marked ethnocentricity and the variability of its traditions. His work is noted to have given impetus to an awakening of a strong nationalism in Brazil and the recognition that a mixed racial heritage will biologically enrich a nation rather than diminish it. His massive output of work included fiction as well as philosophical and sociological studies which spoke to his fervent desire to resolve the many-faceted problems extant in his country. *Casa grande e senzala* (1933; *The Master and the Slaves,* 1945) and *Sobrados e mucombos* (1933; *The Mansions and the Shanties,* 1945) show application of his ability to provide a two-volume tour de force which remain national classics.

❧•❦

Further Reading

Bandiera, M. *Brief History of Brazilian Literature.* Washington, D.C.: Pan American Union, 1958.
Ellison, F. P. *Brazil's New Novel: Four Northeastern Masters: José Lins do Rego, Jorge Amado, Graciliano Ramos, Rachel de Quieroz.* Berkeley, Calif.: University of California Press, 1954.
Loos, Dorothy Scott. "Gilberto Freyre as a Literary Figure." *Revista hispánica moderna* 34 (July-October 1968): 714-72.
Martins, H. *The Brazilian Novel.* Bloomington, Ind.: Indiana University, 1976.
Rose, Theodore E. *An Historical Survey of the Development of the Regional Novel of Northeastern Brazil and More Especially of the Works of José Lins do Rêgo.* Doctoral thesis, New York University, 1959.
Skidmon, T. "Gilberto Freyre and the Early Brazilian Republic: Some Notes on Methodology." *Comparative Studies in Society and History* 6 (July 1964): 490-505.
Tannenbaum, F. Introduction to *The Mansions and the Shanties* by Gilberto Freyre. New York: Knopf, 1963.

RENAISSANCE GROUP. *See NAŠA NIVA* **GROUP**

REVIVAL MOVEMENT/UJAULENNIE. *See UZVYŠŠA* **GROUP**

REVUE INDIGÈNE GROUP, *LA*
Haiti, 1927-1928

La Revue Indigène was a journal headed by poet, novelist, and anthropologist Jacques Roumain (1907-1944) and ethnographer and physician Jean Price-Mars (1876-1969). Normil Sylvain (1901-1929) composed a manifesto appearing in the first issue (1927), which called for writers to work for Haiti's solidarity and independence from United States occupation by emphasizing folklore, traditional rural life, and African heritage. Jacques Roumain's collection of poems, *Bois d'ébène* (1945; *Ebony Wood,* 1972), and Price-Mars's cultural study of Haiti, *Ainsi parla l'oncle* (1928; Thus Spoke the Uncle), were profoundly influential; the founders of NÉGRITUDE found inspiration in its lyrical affirmations of Africanness. Roumain's most acclaimed novel is *Gouverneurs de la rosée* (1944; *Masters of the Dew,* 1947). Price-Mars and Roumain founded l'Institut d'Ethnologie in Haiti. Poet, novelist, and critic Philippe Thoby-Marcelin (1904-1975), poet Antonio Vieux (1904-1964), and poet Emile Roumer (1903-) were also among the prominent members of the group.

❖•❖

Further Reading

Antoine, Jacques Carmeleau. *Jean Price-Mars and Haiti.* Washington, D.C.: Three Continents Press, 1981.

Finn, Julio. *Voices of Negritude.* London: Quartet, 1987.

Fowler, Carolyn. *A Knot in the Thread: The Life and Work of Jacques Roumain.* Washington, D.C.: Howard University Press, 1980.

Garret, Naomi Mills. *The Renaissance of Haitian Poetry.* Paris: Présence Africaine, 1963.

Kennedy, E. C. "Jacques Roumain." In her *The Negritude Poets.* New York: Viking, 1975.

Knight, Vere W. "Haiti and Martinique." In *A Celebration of Black and African Writing.* Edited by Bruce King and Kolawole Ogungbesan. Zaria, Nigeria: Ahmadu Bello University Press, 1975.

REZEPTIONSÄSTHETIK. *See* **READER-RESPONSE CRITICISM AND RECEPTION THEORY**

ROMANTICIST MOVEMENT (CHĀYĀVĀDA)
India, 1920s-1930s

The Chāyāvāda, or Romanticist, movement in Indian literature was constituted of some prominent poets whose compositions may be said, as a group, to represent aesthetic responses to social and cultural conditions facing Indians during the early decades of the twentieth century, such as nationalist movements fighting for independence from England, increased technological development, World War I and, to some extent, the popularity of the English Romantic poets. In addition, though he wrote mainly in Bengali, critics credit Nobel Prize winner Rabindranath Tagore (1861-1941) for inspiring and popularizing Romanticism in Hindi, and other Indian-language, poetry.

Leading writers associated with Chāyāvāda, a largely Hindi movement, were dramatist, novelist and poet Jayashankar Prasad (1889-1937), poet Sumitrandan Pant (1900-), and poet Nirālā (Suryakant Tripathi, 1896-1961); Pant and Nirālā later associated with the PROGRESSIVE WRITERS. Generally speaking, poetic themes associated with Chāyāvāda involve humanism, nature, mortality, spontaneity, and the value of emotional and subjective experience and expression. Critics mention numerous other writers working in the Romanticist vein during the 1920s and 1930s—among them: poet Mahadevi Varma (1907-1987) and dramatist Ramkumar Varma (1905-), also writing in Hindi; Bhaskar Ramchandra Tambe (1874-1941) writing in Marāthī; dramatist Umā Shankar Joshī (1911-) writing in Gujarātī; Rāyaprolu Subbārāo (n.d.) writing in Telugu; poet Dattatreya Ramachandra Bendre (1896-?) writing in Kannada; and poet Kumāran Āshān (1873-1924) writing in Malayalam.

Works representative of the Chāyāvāda trend include Pant's *Pallava* (1926; The New Leaves), *Vīnā* (1927), and *Guñjan* (1932; Humming); Prasad's volumes of poetry, *Āsū* (1925; Tears), *Lahar* (1933; Ripples) and, especially, the epic poem *Kāmāyani* (1936); and Nirālā's formal poetic innovations in *Rām kī Śakti Pūjā* (1936), *Anāmikā* (1923; Nameless), *Parimal* (1930; Fragrance), *Gītikā* (1936; Songbook), and *Tulasī-dāsa* (1938). During the 1930s, tenets of REALISM and MARXISM had begun making a strong impact on these and other Indian writers and, while Romanticist influences continued to appear in later works, Chāyāvāda had lost its dominance.

✦•✦

Further Reading

Ajñeya [S. H. Vatsyayan]. "Hindi Literature." In *Contemporary Indian Literature: A Symposium*. 2nd ed. New Delhi: Sahitya Akademi, 1959.

George, K. M., ed. *Comparative Indian Literature*. 2 vols. Trichur, India: Kerala Sahitya Akademi; Madras: Macmillan India, 1984-85.

Nagendra, ed. *Literary Criticism in India*. Meerut, India: Sarita Prakashan, 1973.

Singh, Namwar. "Hindi [literature]." In *Indian Literature since Independence: A Symposium*. Edited by K. R. Srinivasa Iyengar. New Delhi: Sahitya Akademi, 1973.

ROMANTIC MOVEMENT
Japan, 1890s-1900s

The Japanese Romantic Movement consisted of a small group of middle Meiji period writers who shared not so much a strong philosophic bond with European Romanticists as a deep admiration for nineteenth-century English love poetry and its inherent focus on individual perception and emotion. Despite lacking the breadth, insight, or influence of their Western counterparts, the Japanese Romantics helped revolutionize their nation's literature during the 1890s by concentrating, in their poetry, criticism, and translations, on the inner life, by championing the struggle of the emotional, alienated, suffering human soul in conflict with a state-oriented society.

One of Japan's most distinguished writers, Mori Ōgai (1862-1922), was the first to introduce Romanticism to Eastern readers. Following several years of direct exposure to European culture and literature, Ōgai returned to Japan in 1888 and shortly thereafter founded the New Voices Society. Ōgai's profound admiration for the German Romantics resulted in the publication of *Omokage* (1889; Vestiges) the following year. A vastly influential anthology, *Omokage* presented Japanese readers for the first time with translations of works by Heinrich Heine (1797-1856), Joseph Viktor Von Scheffel (1826-1886), and Karl Theodor Körner (1791-1813), as well as selections from Lord Byron (1788-1824) and William Shakespeare. Through this collection and the various original writings which appeared in the Society's journal, the possibilities for the latent Japanese Romantic Movement were born.

Although Romanticism in Japan directly coincided with the life of the journal *Bungakkai* (1893-98), scholars generally discern its beginnings in leader Kitamura Tōkoku's first published work, *Soshū no Shi* (1889; The Prisoner's Tale), a long poem modeled after Byron's *The Prisoner of Chillon* (1816). In addition to Byron, the poetry of Percy Bysshe Shelley (1792-1822), John Keats (1795-1821), and William Wordsworth (1770-1850), and the essays of Thomas Carlyle (1795-1881), John Ruskin (1819-1900), and, particularly, Ralph Waldo Emerson (1803-1882) exerted a sizeable influence on the movement, which, though dominated by Tōkoku, included such writers as Togawa Shūkotsu (1870-1939), Hoshino Tenchi (1862-1950), Hirata Tokuboku (1873-1943), and Shimazaki Tōson. Tōson's major contribution, that of crafting in *Wakana Shū* (1897) a model for all modern Japanese poetry, is often regarded as a singular achievement. Yet, his literary maturation proceeded directly from his association with *Bungakkai* and Tōkoku.

Japanese Romanticism, otherwise deficient in literary output and regularly overshadowed by the Ken'yūsha (SOCIETY OF FRIENDS OF THE INKSTONE) writers, dwindled into obscurity by the first decade of the twentieth century. Although Tōson, after shifting to prose writing and the tenets of NATURALISM proclaimed Tōkoku a true genius whose influence on him, and hence a major branch of Japanese literature, was immense, the fundamental significance of the movement was in truth less sizeable, though yet of unmistakable impact on the future of the nation's literature. Indeed, for its absorption in the emotional and spiritual life of the individual, the Japanese Romantic Movement anticipated to a considerable degree the focus of much, if not most, modern Japanese writing.

❖•❖

Tōkoku, Kitamura (1868-1894), Japanese poet and essayist.

The heart of the Japanese Romantic Movement, Tōkoku was a member of the samurai class intensely concerned with individual rights and freedoms. He resolved during his brief, five-year career to influence political and social currents in the same manner that French Romanticist Victor Hugo (1802-1885) had. In 1887 he embraced Christianity as a source of knowledge and insight for both his spiritual and intellectual life. Throughout his poems and essays on literary aesthetics, Tōkoku propounded the sovereignty of art and the human imagination over governmental authority or reigning morality. The essay "Ensei shika to Josei" (1892; The Pessimist-Poet and Womanhood), one of his most representative works, begins: "Love is the secret key to life." With this resounding message, Tōkoku singlehandedly altered the way in which Japanese authors treated love, a subject that had long been either cheapened or trivialized. His slight literary output—rarely read today—and his suicide at the age of twenty-six have prevented him from fully earning the distinction one critic accorded him as ranking among the first few completely modern Japanese writers.

❖•❖

Tōson, Shimazaki (1872-1943)
Japanese poet, novelist, short-story writer, and essayist.

Although more often remembered for his affiliation with Japanese Naturalism, Tōson was one of the founding members of *Bungakkai* and the only Romantic to gain lasting fame as an important modern Japanese poet. In 1897, three years after Tōkoku's death, he published the first collection of his verse, *Wakana Shū* (1897; Seedlings). The enormous success of this work prompted further collections, which included *Hitotsubashu* (1898), *Natsugusa* (1898), and *Rakubai Shū* (1901). After turning to fiction—a move spurred by his friendship with Tayama KATAI—Tōson quickly gained an even greater reputation for his realistic portrayal of individuals grappling with the momentous effects of modernization in Japan. *Hakai* (1906; *The Broken Commandment,* 1974) and *Yoake Mae* (1929-35; Before the Dawn) are generally considered his two finest achievements. *Haru* (1908; Spring) remains of interest to historians for its autobiographical account of Tōson's early years as a poet and his friendship with Tōkoku.

Wakana Shū (1897).

The undisputed fountainhead of modern Japanese poetry, *Wakana Shū* consists of poems that combine traditional Japanese forms and meter with a bold new style and an intense awareness of the many changes within Japan at the turn of the century. Although earlier examples of *shintaishi* (poetry in the modern style) exist, Tōson's collection was the first that was uniformly successful in both form and content. With such poems as "Akikaze no Uta" (Song of the Autumn Wind) and "Hatsukoi" (First Love), Tōson revealed his essentially Romantic outlook and emulation of Western poets, such as Shelley, as well as many traditional Japanese love poets. The matchless lyricism of his first collection has inspired several generations of readers; yet critics have faulted Tōson for the vague sense of his lines. Nevertheless, when regarded as the outpourings of an acutely sensitive, youthful writer, *Wakana Shū* is one of the most significant works that appeared near the close of the nineteenth century, when the course toward modern Japanese literature was being fervently sought.

⤞•⤝

Further Reading

Keene, Donald. "Kitamura Tōkoku and Romanticism." In his *Dawn to the West. Japanese Literature in the Modern Era.* New York: Holt, Rinehart, & Winston, 1984.

Kunitomo Tadao. "Literature of Idealism and Romanticism." In his *Japanese Literature Since 1868.* Tokyo: Hokuseido Press, 1938.

McClellan, Edwin. *Two Japanese Novelists: Sōseki and Tōson.* Chicago: University of Chicago Press, 1969.

Mathy, Francis. "Kitamura Tōkoku: Essays on the Inner Life." *Monumenta Nipponica* 24, 1 (1969).

Morita, James R. "Shimazaki Tōson's Four Collections of Poems." *Monumenta Nipponica* 25, 3-4 (1970): 325-69.

Okazaki Yoshie. "The Flowering of Romantic Poetry and Its Development" and "The Literary Theory of Romanticism and Idealism." In his *Japanese Literature in the Meiji Era.* Tokyo: Ōbunsha, 1955.

ROMANTIC POETS
Sudan, 1930s-1940s

During the 1930s and 1940s a number of Sudanese writers began gaining attention for breaking with classical Arabic literary conventions, in part, as a reaction against the stringent traditionalism of NEOCLASSICISM which had been dominant in the Sudan. Poet and essayist Hamza Tambal (1893-1960) was a major force in reaching out to other Sudanese poets. In 1927 he had published a group of essays in the journal *al-Hadāra* calling for Sudanese poets to create a specifically Sudanese, rather than

Arabic, poetry; to emphasize Sudanese experience, language, and culture rather than to conform to classical styles. The leading poet affiliated with Romanticism in the Sudan was al-Tījānī Yūsuf Bashīr (1912-1937). His Sufi background informs his poetry, focusing as it does on the mystical, beauty, spirituality, and God. Tījānī's poetry appears in one collection, published posthumously, *Ishrāqa* (1942; Illuminations). Like poet and essayist Muhammad Ahmad Mahjūb (1910-1976), Tījānī contributed literary articles to the prominent Sudanese journal, *al-Fajr*. Tījānī and others, such as poet Idrīs Jammā' (1922-1980), experimented with the sort of Romantic themes and language seen in the work of writers such as the APOLLO poets and Kahlīl Gibrān (1883-1931) and the SOCIETY OF THE PEN. Mahjūb, for example, worked with free verse and indigenous language and subject matter, while Tījānī read poetry and criticism by the Apollo and *DIWAN* writers of Egypt, as well as by Gibrān and other Arabic writers who emigrated to the United States.

❖•❖

Further Reading

Badawi, M. M. "Tijani." In *A Critical Introduction to Modern Arabic Poetry*. Cambridge, England; New York: Cambridge University Press, 1975.

Jayyusi, Salma Khadra. "The Romantic Current in Modern Arabic Poetry." In *Trends and Movements in Modern Arabic Poetry*. Vol. 2. Leiden, Netherlands: Brill, 1977.

Jayyusi, Salma Khadra, ed. *Modern Arabic Poetry: An Anthology*. New York: Columbia University Press, 1987.

RONDISMO
Italy, 1920s

Rondismo, a movement in Italian prose that arose through the post-World War I periodical *La ronda* (1919-23), sought to detach literature from social and political concerns, despite the concurrent rise of Fascism. *La ronda* editor Vincenzo Cardarelli (1887-1959) and writers Riccardo Bacchelli (1891-1985) and Emilio Cecchi (1884-1966) were key members of the movement. Although short-lived, Rondismo helped elevate Italian literature to a new level of artistry and seriousness.

❖•❖

Further Reading

Pacifici, Sergio. *A Guide to Contemporary Italian Literature, from Futurism to Neorealism*. Cleveland: World Publishing Company, 1962.

Pesaresi, Massimo Mandolini. "Vicenzo Cardarelli." In *Twentieth-Century Italian Poets*. First series. *Dictionary of Literary Biography*. Vol. 114. Detroit: Gale Research, 1992.

RUCH MŁODOKASZUBSKI. *See* **YOUNG KASHUBIAN MOVEMENT**

RUIMTE GROUP
Belgium, 1917-1921

A Belgian movement and journal which ran from 1917 until 1921, *Ruimte* (or Space) embraced the various tendencies of CUBISM, DADA, and EXPRESSIONISM while demonstrating a vital concern with the wartime and postwar social and political milieu. The most celebrated member of *Ruimte* was Paul van Ostaijen (1896-1928), who is considered one of the finest poets in twentieth-century Belgian literature.

⋙•⋘

Further Reading

Beekman, E. M. *Homeopathy of the Absurd: The Grotesque in Paul van Ostaijen's Creative Prose*. The Hague: Nijhoff, 1970.
Bulhoff, Francis, ed. *Nijhoff, Van Ostaijen, De Stijl: Modernism in the Netherlands and Belgium in the First Quarter of the 20th Century: Six Essays*. The Hague: Nijhoff, 1976.
Mallinson, Vernon. *Modern Belgian Literature, 1830-1960*. London: Heinemann, 1966.

RUSSIAN FORMALISM
Russia, 1910s-c. 1930

Predating NEW CRITICISM in its primary focus on the literary text, as opposed to the author, Russian Formalism was aligned with CUBO-FUTURISM in that two of its foremost scholars, Viktor Shklovsky (1893-1984) and Roman JAKOBSON, were members of the poetic movement and benefited from the pioneering language theories and morphological experimentations of Velemir KHLEBNIKOV (*see* Cubo-Futurism).

Both Shklovsky and Jakobson were scholars of philology: Shklovsky at the University of Petrograd (St. Petersburg) and Jakobson at the University of Moscow. Through his founding of Opoyaz (Society of the Study of Poetic Language) in 1916, Shklovsky became the first Russian to regularly promote the literary work and a corresponding scientific attention to its rhetorical strategies, traditional literary structures, and hidden systems of organization. Such formalist phrases as "making it [the world of objects] strange" and "laying bare the device," which were later borrowed by American critics, underscore Shklovsky's aesthetic idealism, his valuation of the work of art as a complexly ordered and intrinsically meaningful entity. Jakobson, founder of the Moscow Linguistic Circle, which included students as well as poets (notably Cubo-Futurist Vladimir MAYAKOVSKY), worked closely with Shklovsky and the Opoyaz theorists until the eventual merger of the two groups. Unfortunately, Formalism, given its conscious avoidance of the writer's thematic concerns, or, more importantly, of the state's post-revolution preferences for a social-based literature, found itself in great disfavor during the 1920s, by which time Jakobson, and numerous other writers, had left the country. When the Moscow-St. Petersburg Opoyaz was dissolved in 1923, many of its members continued their theoretical work within the LEF organization. Yet persistent harrassment by Anatoly Lunacharsky (1875-1933), Leon Trotsky (1879-1940), and other upholders of SOCIALIST REALISM caused Shklovsky to recant the essential tenets of Formalism in 1930.

The movement continued, however, in Czechoslovakia with the work of Jakobson and other members of the PRAGUE LINGUISTIC CIRCLE. Eventually, theorists throughout Europe and the United States came to adopt Formalism in one sense or another. Jakobson's statement, voiced in 1921, that "the object of study in literary science is not literature but 'literariness,' that is, what makes a given work a literary work," became the guiding principle not only of the New Formalists but of several other related movements, including STRUCTURALISM, DECONSTRUCTION, and SEMIOTICS. In addition, this textual-based focus, which led to repeated study of such metafictional or self-consciously literary works as Laurence Sterne's (1713-1768) *Tristram Shandy* (1759-67), helped influence the direction of experimental writing for the next several decades. Among the numerous writers in Russia associated with the movement were Boris Eikhenbaum (1886-1959), Jakobson, Shklovsky, Boris Tomashevsky (1890-1957), Yury Tynyanov (1894-1943), Evgeny Zamyatin (1884-1937), Viktor Zhirmunsky (1891-1971), Osip Brik (1888-1945), and Vladimir Propp (1895-1970), whose *Morfologiia skazki* (1928; *Morphology of the Folktale*, 1958, 1968), though initially underappreciated, later became a minor classic among Structuralist circles for its compelling conclusions about the constancy of generic elements.

→•←

Jakobson, Roman (1896-1982)
Russian-born philologist, essayist, and theoretician.

A Formalist during the earliest stages of the movement, Jakobson is the most distinctive and celebrated of its numerous figures. Beginning with his emigration to Czechoslovakia in 1920, Jakobson embarked upon one of the most illustrious and influential careers in twentieth-century literary theory. Among his most important achievements are his cofounding of the Prague Linguistic Circle in 1926, his lifelong philological study of the medieval Russian epic poem *The Tale of Igor* (c. 1187), and his numerous monographs on Slavic grammar, neurolinguistics, and the history of human communication. Following his emigration in 1941 to the United States, where he became a naturalized citizen and taught at Harvard, the Massachusetts Institute of

Technology, and a number of other universities, he gained international prominence, as much for his lectures and organization of various congresses as for his immense body of published work. Among the many modern theorists who have acknowledged their debt to him, two of the foremost are French anthropologist Claude Lévi-Strauss (1908-) and American linguist Noam Chomsky (1928-).

❖•❖

Further Reading

Armstrong, Daniel, and C. H. van Schooneveld, eds. *Roman Jakobson: Echoes of His Scholarship*. Lisse, Netherlands: Peter de Ridder Press, 1977.

Bann, Stephen, and John E. Bowlt, eds. *Russian Formalism: A Collection of Articles and Texts in Translation*. Edinburgh, Scotland: Scottish Academic Press, 1973.

Bennett, Tony. *Formalism and Marxism*. London: Methuen, 1979.

Erlich, Victor. *Russian Formalism: History, Doctrine*. The Hague: Mouton, 1955. 3rd ed., New Haven, Conn.: Yale University Press, 1981.

Erlich, Victor, ed. *Twentieth-Century Russian Literary Criticism*. New Haven, Conn.: Yale University Press, 1975.

Field, Andrew, comp. "Viktor Shklovsky on the Development of Literary Criticism and Poetry." *The Complection of Russian Literature: A Cento*. New York: Atheneum, 1971.

Holenstein, Elmar. *Roman Jakobson's Approach to Language*. Bloomington, Ind.: Indiana University Press, 1976.

Jackson, Robert Louis, and Stephen Rudy, eds. *Russian Formalism: A Retrospective Glance: A Festschrift in Honor of Victor Erlich*. New Haven, Conn.: Yale Center for International and Area Studies, 1985.

Jakobson, Roman. *The Framework of Language*. Ann Arbor, Mich.: University of Michigan, 1980.
———. *Poetry of Grammar and Grammar of Poetry*. Vol. 3, *Selected Writings*. The Hague: Mouton, 1981.

Jameson, Fredric. "The Formalist Projection." In his *The Prison-House of Language: A Critical Account of Structuralism and Russian Formalism*. Princeton, N.J.: Princeton University Press, 1972.

Lemon, Lee T., and Marion J. Reis. *Russian Formalist Criticism: Four Essays*. Lincoln, Nebr.: University of Nebraska Press, 1965.

Maguire, Robert A. *Red Virgin Soil: Soviet Literature in the 1920s*. Princeton, N.J.: Princeton University Press, 1968.

Matejka, Ladislav, and Krystyna Pomorska, eds. *Readings in Russian Poetics: Formalist and Structuralist Views*. Cambridge, Mass.: MIT Press, 1971.

Medvedev, P. N., and M. M. Bakhtin. *The Formal Method in Literary Scholarship: A Critical Introduction to Sociological Poetics*. Baltimore, Md.: Johns Hopkins University Press, 1978.

Mirsky, D. S. *Contemporary Russian Literature 1881-1925*. New York: Kraus Reprint, 1972.

O'Toole, L. M., and Ann Shukman, eds. *Formalism: History, Comparison, Genre*. Oxford, England: Holdan Books, 1977.

663

Pomorska, Krystyna. *Russian Formalist Theory and Its Poetic Ambiance*. The Hague: Mouton, 1968.

Sheldon, R. "The Formalist Poetics of Viktor Shklovsky." *Russian Literature Triquarterly* 2 (winter 1972): 351-71.

Stacy, R. H. "The Formalists." In *Russian Literary Criticism: A Short History*. Syracuse, N.Y.: Syracuse University Press, 1974.

Struve, Gleb. "Literary Criticism and Controversies." In *Russian Literature under Lenin and Stalin 1917-1953*. Norman, Okla.: University of Oklahoma Press, 1971.

Thompson, Ewa. *Russian Formalism and Anglo-American New Criticism: A Comparative Study*. The Hague: Mouton, 1971.

Wellek, René. *Concepts of Criticism*. New Haven, Conn.: Yale University Press, 1963.

———. "Russian Formalism." In his *A History of Modern Criticism: 1750-1950*. Vol. 7. New Haven, Conn.: Yale University Press, 1991.

Wellek, René, and Austin Warren. *Theory of Literature*. New York: Harcourt, Brace & Co., 1949.

S

SĂMĂNĂTORISM
Romania, 1900s

Based upon the Romanian word *semăna*, meaning "to sow," Sămănătorism emerged as a reaction to the elitism of the nineteenth-century movement Junimea. The Sămănătorists, even more so than the POPORANISTS, were rural, idealistic, and traditional in outlook. Their chief members were editor Alexandru Vlahuţa (1858-1919), poet George Coşbuc (1866-1918), and historian-statesman Nicolae Iorga (1871-1940).

❖•❖

Further Reading

Alexandrescu-Dersca Bulgaru, Maria Matilda. *Nicolae Iorga, a Romanian Historian of the Ottoman Empire*. Bucharest: Publishing House of the Academy of the Socialist Republic of Romania, 1972.

Oldson, William O. *The Historical and Nationalistic Thought of Nicolae Iorga*. Boulder, Colo.: East European Quarterly, 1974; distributed by Columbia University Press.

SAN FRANCISCO SCHOOL
United States, 1960s

In 1956 Allen GINSBERG's "HOWL" (*see* BEAT GENERATION) signaled the poetic renaissance of the San Francisco Bay area. Rooting itself in the drug-induced and spiritually inspired poetics of such Beat poets as Robert Duncan (1919-1988) and Gregory Corso (1930-), the San Francisco School embraced a growing politicism and a vision of poetry as a vehicle for social change. Liberated by MODERNIST poets Gertrude STEIN and Ezra POUND — and overtly proclaiming the rights of homosexuals first championed in Duncan's "The Homosexual in Society" (1944) — a reaction to the cultural stasis of suburbia reverberated in the works of Ginsberg, Kenneth Rexroth (1905-1982), and Lawrence Ferlinghetti (1919-), whose widely read *A Coney Island of the*

Mind (1958) had smashed the stale conformity of the Eisenhower years. By the 1960s the antisocial verse of the Beats had given way to an overt poetic attack on American values and politics. This Vietnam-Era outcry gained a national figurehead in Ginsberg, whose extemporaneous readings popularized U.S. poetry for new generations.

Ferlinghetti, believing it a poet's duty to agitate, added his surreal, leftist voice to the chorus. Other writers, including Denise Levertov (1923-), William Everson (1912-1994), and Philip Lamantia (1927-), spoke to the moment: U.S. involvement in the war in southeast Asia, sexual freedom, the civil rights movement. But it was Ginsberg— fueled by personal circumstances and the artistic visions of William Blake and the CUBIST painters—whose enjambed, fragmentary, spontaneous "reality sandwiches" best embodied the timely, rather than eternal, predicaments of mankind addressed by the San Francisco poets.

➸•➹

Further Reading

Di Prima, Diane. *Memoirs of a Beatnik*. New York: Traveller's Companion, 1969.

Ferlinghetti, Lawrence, and Nancy J. Peters. *Literary San Francisco: A Pictorial History from Its Beginnings to the Present*. San Francisco: City Lights Books, 1980.

French, Warren G. *The San Francisco Poetry Renaissance, 1955-1960*. Boston: Twayne, 1991.

Meltzer, David, comp. *The San Francisco Poets*. New York: Ballantine, 1971.

Silesky, Barry. *Ferlinghetti, the Artist in His Time*. New York: Warner Books, 1990.

SAPLINGS (*Maladniak*)
Byelorussia, 1923-1932

The journal *Maladniak* (Saplings), edited by Michas Carot (pseud. of Michas Kudzielka, 1896-1938), began to appear in Byelorussia in 1923 as a forum for revolutionary Communist literature. The following year, *Maladniak* officially became the journal for the "all-Byelorussian union of poets and writers"; membership was reportedly up to 500. But within a few short years, disenchanted members would break off and form their own groups. The most prominent of these were the FLAME GROUP, which lured Carot away, and *UZVYŠŠA*. Satirist Kandrat Krapiva (1896-?), who left to join *Uzvyšša*, referred to the Party line propaganda clothed in the stilted, slipshod literary discourse of the more impassioned, and perhaps less talented, *Maladniak* members as "Sturm und Drang."

The journal was discontinued by 1932, when the Byelorussian Writers' Union mandated the existence of only one literary journal, *Polymia revalucyi*, an instrument of the Soviet Writers' Union instituted the same year.

See also SOCIALIST REALISM, Byelorussia.

❖•❖
Further Reading

Adamovich, A. "The Sovietization of Belorussian Literature." *Belorussian Review* 1 (1955): 98-106.

————. "UZVYŠŠA—The Belorussian Literary Club." *Belorussian Review* 4 (1957): 23-55.

McMillan, Arnold A. *A History of Byelorussian Literature*. Giessen, Germany: Wilhelm Schmitz Verlag, 1977.

SARDIO GROUP
Venezuela, 1950s

Formed in 1955 in Venezuela, the Sardio Group was part of the Spanish-American MODERNIST movement. Sharing many of the same techniques and attitudes of English and American writers prominent during the post-World War I era, the Sardio Group helped universalize the content of Venezuelan fiction. The central figure of the group was novelist Salvador Garmendia (1928-).

❖•❖
Further Reading

Bell, Keith R. *The Novels of Salvador Garmendia, a Critical Study*. Doctoral thesis, University of Oklahoma, 1980.

Williams, Jennifer Patrice. *A Critical Analysis of the Short Stories of Salvador Garmendia*. Thesis, University of the West Indies, Mona, Jamaica, 1989.

SBURĂTORUL GROUP
Romania, 1920s

Centered around Romanian editor-critic Eugen Lovinescu (1881-1943), *Sburătorul* (The Goblin) was a MODERNIST movement and journal which refuted the rural pre-occupations and Romantic outlook of SĂMĂNĂTORISM. Lovinescu is especially remembered for his championing of Liviu Rebreanu's (1885-1944) *Ion* (1920; *Ion*, 1967), one of the most distinguished NATURALISTIC novels in Romanian fiction.

❖•❖
Further Reading

Balan, Ion Dodu. *A Concise History of Romanian Literature*. Bucharest: Editura Stiintifica si enciclopedica, 1981.

Ciopraga, Constantin. "Rebrean, or The Afirmation of the Novel." In his *The Personality of Romanian Literature: A Synthesis*. Translated by Stefan Avadanei. Iasi, Romania: Junimea Publishing House, 1981.

Piru, Al. *Liviu Rebreanu*. Bucharest: Meridiane Publishing House, 1965.

SCOTTISH RENAISSANCE
Scotland, c. 1920-1950

The leading exponent of this movement was C. M. Grieve, whose pseudonym, Hugh MacDiarmid, is synonymous with a strong revitalization of Scottish poetry because of his effort to place Scotland within an international literary movement of both change and the exchange of artistic creativity in the twentieth century. A modern poet, MacDiarmid's work shows the influence of writers T. S. ELIOT and W. B. YEATS (*see* MODERNISM, England and Ireland) in its complexity, but is expressed in MacDiarmid's language of Scots and Gaelic, a language known as "Lallans" — a synthetic Scots mode of linguistic expression; MacDiarmid is said to have remarked that "the Scottish soul . . . cannot be expressed in English." His early lyrics abound with borrowed Gaelic and a revival of old Scots words which often have no English translation, and require note guides of explanation.

MacDiarmid was at his peak in the thirties, and had early adjusted his thinking and his work to the proletariat vision. He became a Marxist socialist, at the same time remaining a fierce Scottish nationalist. His poem "First Hymn to Lenin" (1931) presents the passion and clarity of intent that would lead him to found a liberal quarterly with which to air his views about dialectical materialism. But his nationalistic fervor was as intense, in his desire to enlarge upon the tradition set by Robert Burns (1759-1796), "the plough-boy poet," and to create a new intellectual atmosphere in which Scotland's modern poets would seek to examine problems of the human condition in terms of their own, singular culture in its contemporary development.

Another member of the movement was William Soutar (1898-1943), a mystic poet whose brilliant imagery in his English-language poems combines ancient Scots balladry with abstraction which is generally absent from the older form, in his attempt to convey a contemporary view. His Scots-language poetry is more traditional in style and adheres to the old conventions. His talent lay in the ability to separate his two visions, and to provide the excellence of both.

In the work of Sydney Goodsir Smith (1915-) there can be found an intense lyricism, beautiful in its simplicity. Written in Scots, the poetry contains traditional and national directness of statement, but is contemporary in its depictions of the harshness of modern life. Smith is best known for his modern love poem "Under the Eildon Tree" (1948) in which he draws upon the ancient lovers, Orpheus and Eurydice, Dido and Aeneas, and their love experiences combined with the more contemporary Bobby Burns and lover Highland Mary to present a cycle of twenty-four elegies which relate to the universal theme of love and its underlying complexity.

Finally, critic and poet Edwin Muir (1887-1959) is mentioned for recognizing the validity of the new Scottish movement, yet feeling that the English language would best serve his participation in it as a poet. Muir's poetry contains a combination of an inherently Scots view of subjective reality in relation to the external world; this provides creative work of "high intellectual and spiritual quality" which becomes more universal than nationalistic in scope and expresses the Scottish world around the poet as a working part of all nations in a resolution of contemporary problems. A modern thinker in every way, Muir felt answers could be found in modern philosophy, with concentration on the psychoanalytic, the archetypal world, and investigation of the "mind within the mind." His poetic aim was to present the truth with integrity; his sincerity was indisputable.

The above-mentioned do not account for all members of what continues to be a strong movement that presents, in poetry, that unique quality of Scottish temperament and creative ability which adds dimension to the contemporary literary milieu.

⋙•⋘

MacDiarmid, Hugh (pseud. of Christopher Murray Grieve, 1892-1978) Scottish poet and journalist.

MacDiarmid's early career as an editor and journalist inspired him to attempt to revitalize his Scottish culture in a renaissance of its poetry, as written in its own language (Gaelic-Celtic-Scots), and to demonstrate to the literary world that Scottish poetry had a rightful place in the Modernist movement. His earliest work, "Sangschaw" (1925), is made up of short lyrics, written in a synthesis (his own) of the medieval Scots language used by the poet William Dunbar (1465-1530?) and the patois of the Lowlands Scots known as "Lallans." His later epic "A Drunk Man Looks at the Thistle" (1936) is made up of a series of related lyrics and is one of his finest poems. It has been called a dream poem, patterned after that medieval form and style in which sleep releases the narrator's most acute perception and allows for a visionary worldview; MacDiarmid's speaker is drunken, and simulates the "sleepy" mode of expression—but the language is lyrical, ironic, philosophical, and repentant at different levels of the narration—and the technique demonstrates MacDiarmid's careful mastery of the message. The speaker serves to bring "man, and Scotland face to face with the universe and all that lies within it." The poetic language is Lallans; the message is strong, clear, and intellectually introspective. The invention—to make Everyman of a Scottish peasant—and to make it work is a tour de force.

In later work, MacDiarmid tended more and more towards the use of the English language, and to relate his work to the contemporary world and an attempt to understand it. Another late and remarkable work is the unique and lengthy (over 6000 lines) "In

Memoriam James Joyce: From a Vision of World Language" (1955). It contains numerous free-metered, unrhymed verse paragraphs which are at times conversational, for example, "Come. Climb with me . . . Even the sheep are different/ . . . some white-faced, some black/ some with horns and some without . . ." These lines, when compared to two of his shorter, bitter antiwar poems, "Another Epitaph on the Army of Mercenaries" and "In the Children's Hospital," show the diversification of both style and creativity.

Critics now see MacDiarmid as the greatest Scottish poet since Burns, and one who stands with Eliot, Yeats, and James JOYCE (*see* MODERNISM, England and Ireland), all of whom were admirers, as a contributor to the Modernist movement in literature.

⤖•⬸

Further Reading

Alldritt, Keith. *Modernism in the Second World War: The Later Poetry of Ezra Pound, T. S. Eliot, Basil Bunting, and Hugh MacDiarmid*. New York: P. Lang, 1989.

Baglow, John. *Hugh MacDiarmid: The Poetry of Self*. Kingston, Canada: McGill-Queen's University Press, 1987.

Bold, Alan Norman. *MacDiarmid: Christopher Murray Grieve, a Critical Biography*. Amherst, Mass.: University of Massachusetts Press, 1988.

Boutelle, Ann Edwards. *Thistle and Rose: A Study of Hugh MacDiarmid's Poetry*. Lewisburg, Pa.: Bucknell University Press, 1980.

Campbell, Ian. *Lewis Grassic Gibbon*. Edinburgh, Scotland: Scottish Academic Press, 1985.

Duval, Kulgin Dalby, ed. *Hugh MacDiarmid, a Festschrift*. Edinburgh, Scotland: [s.n.], 1962.

Herbert, W. N. *To Circumjack MacDiarmid: The Poetry and Prose of Hugh MacDiarmid*. Oxford, England: Clarendon Press; New York: Oxford University Press, 1992.

MacDiarmid, Hugh (C. M. Grieve). *Lucky Poet: A Self-Study in Literature and Political Ideas, Being the Autobiography of Hugh MacDiarmid*. London: Methuen, 1943.

Morgan, Edwin. *Hugh MacDiarmid*. Edited by Ian Scott-Kilvert. Harlow, England: Longman, 1976.

Muir, Edwin. *Collected Poems*. 2nd ed. New York: Oxford University Press, 1965.

———. *Essays on Literature and Society*. London: Hogarth, 1949.

Reid, John Macnair. *Modern Scottish Literature*. Edinburgh, Scotland: Oliver and Reed, 1945.

Young, Douglas, ed. *Scottish Verse, 1881-1951*. London: Nelson, 1952.

Wittig, Kurt. *The Scottish Tradition in Literature*. Edinburgh, Scotland: Oliver and Boyd, 1958.

SEARA NOVA GROUP
Portugal, 1921-1974

Formed after the break-up of the PORTUGUESE RENASCENCE movement, the *Seara Nova* group and its review were launched in 1921 by António Sérgio de Sousa (1883-1969). The movement, devoted to democratic-socialist ideals, lasted until the demise of the review in 1974 and attracted such figures as Raúl Brandão (1867-1930), José Rodrigues Miguéis (1901-1980), and Aquilino Ribeiro (1885-1963).

❖•❖

Further Reading

Almeida, Onésimo T., ed. *José Rodrigues Miguéis: Lisbon in Manhattan*. Providence, R.I.: Gávea-Brown, 1984.

Duarte, Maria Angelina. *Socio-Political Undercurrents in Four Works by José Rodrigues Miguéis*. Doctoral thesis, University of Minnesota, 1980.

Kerr, John Austin. *Aspects of Time, Place and Thematic Content in the Prose Fiction of José Rodrigues Miguéis as Indications of the Artist's Weltansicht*. Thesis, University of Wisconsin, 1970.

————. *Miguéis to the Seventh Decade*. University, Miss.: Romance Monographs, 1977.

SECOND NEW (Ikinci Yeni)
Turkey, 1950s-c. 1960

In reaction to the poetic realism of the *Garip* movement of the 1950s (*see* POETIC REALISM), a younger group of poets banded together to deploy an abstract mode of verse that aimed beyond SURREALISM, sometimes referred to as "meaningless" or "obscurantist" poetry. The proponents of this group were Ilhan Berk (1916-), Cemal Süreya (1931-), Attilâ Ilhan (1925-), Edip Cansever (1928-), and Turgut Uyar (1926-). Berk, generally considered the Second New's spokesman, indicated the group's general inclination with the statement that "art is for innovation's sake." They were greatly influenced by the Surrealist verse of Asaf Halet Çelebi (1907-1958) and Ercument Behzat Lav (1903-). Critics, such as Memet Fuat (1926-), bemoaned the nihilist and aesthetically narcissistic qualities of this poetry, citing its reflection of a society in which poets are "shoved into nothingness." Such judgment may have stemmed from the tendency of these poets to use abstruse language and disjointed images which proceed so opaquely that the reader is required, as with much MODERNIST poetry, to make large creative and intellectual leaps in order to approximate some understanding of the poems. In their own diverse ways Berk, Ilhan, and Uyar strive to blend what they perceive to be strengths of the Ottoman poetic tradition with what they consider valuable in Western Modernist literature, rather than to completely renounce the elitist literary past. They continued to be quite prominent literary figures in Turkey at the end of the century; Cansever's verse has moved through much experimentation into a deeper obscurantism, while Süreya, in addition to writing poetry, has branched out into criticism and editing a journal (*Papirus*, 1960-61 and 1966-70) and two anthologies. As a group they made a startling impact on Turkish literature, although a vigorous countertrend—the SOCIALIST REALISM of the *Garip* and the VILLAGE FICTION writers—has also had powerful influence.

671

❖•❖
Further Reading

Halman, Talat Sait, ed. *Contemporary Turkish Literature: Fiction and Poetry*. Rutherford, N.J.: Fairleigh Dickinson University Press, 1982.

Menemencioğlu, Nermin. "Modern Turkish Poetry." *The Western Review* 23 (spring 1959): 199-223.

SELF-RELIANCE GROUP
Vietnam, 1930s

Founded during the 1930s, the Self-Reliance Group was part of a trend in Vietnamese poetry devoted to modernizing both style and subject matter. Hàn Mac Tu (1913-1940), The-Lu (1907-), Xuân Diêu (1917-), and Nhat-Linh (1906-1963) numbered among the group's members.

❖•❖
Further Reading

O'Harrow, Stephen. "Some Background Notes on Nhat Linh (Nguyen tuong Tam, 1906-1963)." *France-Asie/Asia* 22, 193 (1968): 205-20.

SEMIOTICS
Czechoslovakia, France, Italy, Russia, and United States, c. 1957-1990s

The study of signs and sign systems, Semiotics is often discussed in conjunction with STRUCTURALISM. Both movements descended from the theories of the RUSSIAN FORMALISTS and the PRAGUE LINGUISTIC CIRCLE; all four, in turn, were anticipated by the independently proposed linguistic philosophies of American Charles Sanders Peirce (1839-1914) — a founder of Pragmatism — and Swiss-born Ferdinand de Saussure (1857-1913). Saussure's *Cours de linguistique générale* (1916; *Course in General Linguistics,* 1959) is generally considered to be the seminal document of Semiotics. In this work, he distinguished between the "signifier" (the sign, word, or phrase employed as a symbol) and the "signified" (the object, concept, or action represented by the symbol), underscoring his view that all language systems are based on arbitrary assignments (i.e., there is no intrinsic reason why the word "horse" should represent the species *equus caballus,* itself an equally arbitrary name). What is of utmost interest to the semiotician is the way in which these arbitrary signs assume meaning through their interrelationships and their existence within grammatical, generic, rhetorical, and cultural systems.

Semiotic study has so melded with the work of the Structuralists that the list of practitioners within each movement is nearly identical. Roland Barthes (1915-1980), for example, is commonly mentioned as a seminal thinker of both groups. Other prominent writers who have been associated with Semiotics include A. J. Greimas (1917-1992), Julia Kristeva (1941-), Yury Lotman (1922-), and Severo Sarduy (1937-). However, a specifically Italian and distinctive trend has emerged during the 1970s and 1980s through the philosophical essays, criticism, and novels of Italo Calvino (1923-1985) and Umberto Eco (1932-). Like Structuralism, Semiotics continues to attract a large number of adherents, often critical, under the rubric of Poststructuralist theory.

See also DECONSTRUCTION.

✦•✦

Further Reading

Baran, Henryk, ed. *Semiotics and Structuralism: Readings from the Soviet Union.* White Plains, N.Y.: International Arts and Sciences Press, 1976.

Barthes, Roland. *Mythologies.* Edited and translated by Annette Lavers. New York: Hill and Wang, 1972.

————. *Roland Barthes by Roland Barthes.* Translated by Richard Howard. New York: Hill and Wang, 1977.

————. *S/Z.* Translated by Richard Miller. New York: Hill and Wang, 1974.

————. *Writing Degree Zero and Elements of Semiology.* Boston: Beacon Press, 1968.

Berger, Arthur A. *Signs in Contemporary Culture: An Introduction to Semiotics.* Salem, Wis.: Sheffield Pub. Co., 1989.

Champagne, Roland A. "Resurrecting RB: Roland Barthes, Literature, and the Stakes of Literary Semiotics." *Semiotica* 107, 3-4 (1995): 339-48.

Copeland, James E., ed. *New Directions in Linguistics and Semiotics.* Houston, Tex.: Rice University Studies, 1984.

Coward, Rosalind, and John Ellis. *Language and Materialism: Developments in Semiology and the Theory of the Subject.* London: Routledge & Kegan Paul, 1977.

Culler, Jonathan. *Saussure.* Hassocks, England: Harvester Press, 1976. 2nd ed., *Ferdinand de Saussure.* Ithaca, N.Y.: Cornell University Press, 1986.

Garvin, Harry R., and Patrick Brady, eds. *Phenomenology, Structuralism, and Semiology.* Lewisburg, Pa.: Bucknell University Press, 1976.

Gorlee, Dinda L. *Semiotics and the Problem of Translation: With Special Reference to the Semiotics of Charles S. Peirce.* Amsterdam: Rodopi, 1994.

Hawkes, Terence. *Structuralism and Semiotics.* Berkeley, Calif.: University of California Press, 1977.

Lucid, Daniel P., ed. and trans. *Soviet Semiotics: An Anthology.* Baltimore, Md.: Johns Hopkins University Press, 1977.

Matejka, Ladislav, and Irwin R. Titunik, eds. *Semiotics of Art: Prague School Contributions.* Cambridge, Mass.: MIT Press, 1976.

Noth, Winfried. *Handbook of Semiotics.* Bloomington, Ind.: Indiana University Press, 1995.

Oller, John W., Jr. "Adding Abstract to Formal and Content Schemata: Results of Recent Work in Peircean Semiotics." *Applied Linguistics* 16, 3 (September 1995): 273-306.

673

Propp, Vladimir. *Morphology of the Folktale*. Translated by Laurence Scott. Bloomington, Ind.:
   Research Center, Indiana University, 1958. 2nd rev. ed., Austin: University of Texas Press, 1968.
Rauch, Irmengard. "Deconstruction, Prototype Theory, and Semiotics." *American Journal of
   Semiotics* 9, 4 (1992): 131-40.
Sebeok, Thomas A. *American Signatures: Semiotic Inquiry and Method*. Edited by Iris Smith.
   Norman, Okla.: University of Oklahoma Press, 1991.
Sebeok, Thomas A., Alfred S. Hayes, and Mary Catherine Bateson, eds. *Approaches to Semiotics*.
   The Hague: Mouton, 1964.
Todorov, Tzvetan. *The Poetics of Prose*. Ithaca, N.Y.: Cornell University Press, 1977.

SERAPION BROTHERS
Russia, 1920s

Intimately tied to the MODERNIST, postrevolutionary era of Russian literature, the Serapion Brothers were a group of a dozen or so male writers, augmented by a group of four Serapion Maidens, who formed in 1921 and dedicated themselves to promoting open literary discourse and honoring the individual creative act. They derived their name and ideologically liberal platform from German Romantic E. T. A. Hoffmann (1776-1822) and his collection *Die Serapionsbrüder* (1819-21). Established writer Evgeny Zamyatin (1884-1937), author of the banned dystopian novel *My* (1920-21; *We*, 1924), lent direction and distinction to the group. His lectures on craftsmanship, delivered at the Petrograd House of Arts where meetings were usually held, were of invaluable use to the Serapions. Although strict rules governing composition and political outlook were judiciously avoided by both Zamyatin and the Serapions, the writers were generally united in their rejection of nineteenth-century REALISM (though not that of Fyodor DOSTOEVSKY) and their opposition to the state-affiliated PROLETKULT.

The best-known prose writers were Modernists Konstantin Fedin (1892-1977) and Vsevolod Ivanov (1895-1963), Veniamen Kaverin (1902-), unofficial leader Lev Lunts (1901-1924), RUSSIAN FORMALIST Viktor Shklovsky (1893-1984), Mikhail Slonimsky (1897-1972), and humorist/satirist Mikhail Zoshchenko (1895-1958). Some readily assimilated the techniques and concerns of Western authors while others chose to develop instead, through the example of Maxim GORKY, SOCIALIST REALISM, and Skaz narration, a method of evaluating the impact of the Revolution. The foremost poets were Elizaveta Polonskaya (1890-1969) and Nikolai Tikhonov (1896-1979); the former became known for her temporal lyric poetry, the latter, for his adherence to ACMEISM. By approximately 1929 the Serapions had largely disintegrated, having published only one collective volume of work, *Serapionovy Brat'ya: Al'manakh pervyi* (1922). However, even those members who had not achieved distinction during the life of the group went on to do so in the coming decades. Consequently, the Serapion Brothers, who formed the cornerstone of Russian Modernism, are remembered as one of the most influential Russian literary groups of the twentieth century.

✜•✜

Further Reading

Kern, Gary. Introduction to *The Serapion Brothers: A Critical Anthology*. Edited by Gary Kern and Christopher Collins. Ann Arbor, Mich.: Ardis, 1975.

Oulanoff, Hongor. *The Serapion Brothers*. The Hague: Mouton, 1966.

SERVET-I FÜNUN. See NEW LITERATURE GROUP (Edebeyat-i Cedide)

SESTIGERS
South Africa, 1960s

A large Afrikaner group formed during the 1960s, the Sestigers — many of whom had studied and traveled extensively in Europe — were writers of fiction, poetry, and drama who were united in their protests against apartheid and other forms of discrimination in South Africa. Breyten Breytenbach (1939-), Étienne Leroux (1922-), André P. Brink (1935-), Chris Barnard (1939-), Abraham H. De Vries (1937-), and Ingrid Jonker (1933-1965) are some of the more notable writers associated with the movement.

✜•✜

Further Reading

Aucamp, Hennie. *House Visits: A Collection of Short Stories*. Selected and translated by Ian Ferguson. Cape Town, South Africa: Tafelberg, 1983.

Breytenbach, Breyten. *And Death White as Words: An Anthology of the Poetry of Breyten Breytenbach (A Bilingual Text With English Translations)*. Selected, edited, and introduced by A. J. Coetzee. London: Collings, 1978.

————. *End Papers: Essays, Letters, Articles of Faith, Workbook Notes*. New York: Farrar, Straus, & Giroux, 1986.

Brink, André P. *Mapmakers: Writing in a State of Siege*. London: Faber and Faber, 1983.

Golz, Hans-Georg. *Staring at Variations: The Concept of "Self" in Breyten Breytenbach's Mouroir, Mirrornotes of a Novel*. Frankfurt am Main; New York: P. Lang, 1995.

In Memoriam Ingrid Jonker. Cape Town, South Africa: Human & Rosseau, 1966.

Jolly, Rosemary Jane. *Colonization, Violence, and Narration in White South African Writing: André Brink, Breyten Breytenbach, and J. M. Coetzee*. Athens, Ohio: Ohio University Press, 1996.

Rich, Paul B. *Tradition and Revolt in South African Fiction: The Novels of André Brink, Nadine Gordimer and J. M. Coetzee*. York, England: University of York, Centre for Southern African Studies, 1981.

SEVEN TORCHES (*Yedi Meş'ale*)
Turkey, 1920s

The Seven Torches consisted of a group of seven young friends in Ankara, Turkey, who in 1928 frequently met to discuss their discontent with current literature, and eventually published the journal *Meşale* (Torch, discontinued after eight issues). In an effort to spread poetry that was free from cliches and unnecessary artistic and formal strictures, they pledged "liveliness, sincerity and always the new." Members of the group were Sabri Esat Siyavuşgil (1907-1968), Yasar Nabi Nayir (1908-), Muammer Lutfi (n.d.), Kenan Hulusi Koray (1906-1943), Ziya Osman Saba (1910-1957), Vasfi Mahir Kocatürk (n.d.), and Cevdet Kudert Solok (n.d.). All were writers, poets, or publishers producing work influenced by French SURREALISM, an aesthetic mode the Seven Torches seemed to find particularly effective in avoiding official censorship or condemnation while expressing controversial views. Nayir went on to publish what would become the most influential literary journal in Turkey, *Varlik* (Existence, 1933-), while Siyavuşgil in 1942 brought forth a renowned translation of *Cyrano de Bergerac*. Faruk Nafiz Çamlibel (1898-1973) also produced poetry some critics would associate with the movement.

Further Reading

Karpat, Kemal H. "Social Themes in Contemporary Turkish Literature — Part I." *The Middle East Journal* 14,1-2 (winter, spring 1960): 29-44.
Stone, Frank A. *The Rub of Cultures in Modern Turkey: Literary Views of Education*. Bloomington, Ind.: Indiana University, 1973.

SHESTYDESYATNYKY. *See* GENERATION OF THE 1960s

AL-SHIHAB
Algeria, 1920s

An Algerian movement and journal, *Al-Shihab* emerged in 1925 as the leading force behind a national renaissance of Arabic writing. A key figure of the movement was poet Muhammed al-Īd Khalifa (1904-1979), who combined classical training and Koran-style phrasing with a modern understanding of contemporary affairs.

Further Reading

Bamya, Aida A. "Algerian Literature." In *Encyclopedia of World Literature in the Twentieth Century*. 3rd ed. Edited by Steven R. Serafin. Farmington Hills, Mich.: St. James Press, 1999.

SHINKANKAKU-HA. *See* NEW SENSATIONALIST SCHOOL

SHINSHINRIGAKU-HA. *See* **NEW PSYCHOLOGIST SCHOOL**

SHIRAKABA-HA. *See* **WHITE BIRCH SCHOOL**

SHISHŌSETSU. *See* **I-NOVEL**

SHIZENSHUGI. *See* **NATURALISM, Japan**

SIBIU GROUP
Romania, 1940s

The Sibiu Group was formed in Romania after World War II by poets, dramatists, and critics who advocated a humanist aestheticism based on the related philosophies of German Johan Christoph Friedrich von Schiller (1759-1805) and Romanian Lucian Blaga (1895-1961). The foremost members of Sibiu were Ştefan Augustin Doinaş (1922-), Ion Negoiţescu (1921-), Cornel Regman (1919-), and Radu Stanca (1920-1962).

⋙•⋘

Further Reading

Doinaş, Ştefan Augustin. *Alibi, and Other Poems*. Translated by Peter Jay and Virgil Nemoianu. London: Anvil Press Poetry, 1975; distributed by Collings.

SIMULTANÉISME (Simultanism)
France, 1910s

A loose mixture of CUBISM, FUTURISM, and UNANIMISME, Simultanéisme was a French MODERNIST movement in art and poetry. Guillaume APOLLINAIRE used the term "Orphism" to refer to the visual arts branch of the movement. Although some credit Henri-Martin Barzun (1881-?) — an associate of the ABBAYE GROUP and creator of Dramatism, an aesthetic program which incorporated Simultanist characteristics — as the founder of Simultanism, the archetypal literary Simultanist was Blaise Cendrars (pseud. of Frederic Sauser-Hall, 1887-1961), who is also occasionally linked with the contemporaneous FANTAISISTES GROUP.

Poet Cendrars transmuted his travelling adventures into lyric poetry and picaresque novels and tried to adapt the techniques of musical composition to poetry. His most representative Simultanist poem is *La Prose du Transsibérien et de la petite Jehanne de France* (1913; *The Prose of the Transsiberian and of Little Jeanne of France*, 1966), which he considered a poem-object, "un livre simultané." Marked by freedom of structure, image association, and vocabulary, it was printed on one long sheet of paper accompanied by paintings by Sonia Delauney (1885-1979, who, with her husband, Robert (1885-1941), also were practitioners.

❧•❦

Further Reading

Albert, Walter, ed. *Selected Writings of Blaise Cendrars*. New York: New Directions, 1966.

Bochner, Jay. *Blaise Cendrars: Discovery and Re-Creation*. Toronto: University of Toronto Press, 1978.

Caws, Mary Ann. "Spectacle and Outward Movement: Blaise Cendrars: A Cinema of Poetry." In her *The Inner Theatre of Recent French Poetry: Cendrars, Tzara, Péret, Artaud, Bonnefoy*. Princeton, N.J.: Princeton University Press, 1972.

Chefdor, Monique. *Blaise Cendrars*. Boston: Twayne, 1980.

Chefdor, Monique, and Jay Bochner, eds. "Special Issue on Blaise Cendrars." *Studies in 20th Century Literature* 3, 2 (1979): 113-207.

Cohen, Arthur A. *The Delaunays, Apollinaire and Cendrars*. New York: Cooper Union School of Art and Architecture, 1972.

Miller, Henry. "Blaise Cendrars." *World Review of Reviews* new series 24 (February 1951): 38-44.

Yack, Dan. *Blaise Cendrars: An Essay*. Cambridge, Mass.: Simba, 1981.

SIURU GROUP
Estonia, 1917-1920s

Influenced by EXPRESSIONISM and FUTURISM, the Siuru Group erupted just after Estonia was granted independence in 1917. Headed by poets Marie Under (1883-1980) and Henrik Visnapuu (1889-1951) — the former generally considered the national poet of Estonia — the Siuru Group covered a diverse range of forms and concerns. Other key members of the group were novelist August Gailit (1891-1960) and poet-critic Johannes Semper (1892-1970).

❧•❦

Further Reading

Kõressaar, Viktor, and Aleksis Rannit. *Estonian Poetry and Language: Studies in Honor of Ants Oras*. Stockholm: Kirjastus Vaba Eesti for Estonian Learned Society in America, 1965.

Mägi, Arvo. "Neo-Romanticism and Expressionism." In his *Estonian Literature: An Outline*. Stockholm: The Baltic Humanitarian Association, 1968.

Nirk, Endel. "From the Revolutions of 1917 to 1940." In his *Estonian Literature*. Translated by Arthur Robert Hone and Oleg Mutt. 2nd ed. Tallinn, Estonia: Perioodika, 1987.

Oras, Ants. *Marie Under and Estonian Poetry*. New York: Foundation for Estonian Arts and Letters, 1977.

SKAMANDER GROUP
Poland, 1920s-1930s

The *Skamander* Group, or Skamandrites, were the dominant MODERNIST poetry circle among those which formed in Poland near the end of World War I. However, save for their occasional assimilation of elements from Russian and Italian FUTURISM, both politically and aesthetically they advanced little beyond the traditions established by the YOUNG POLAND movement during the late nineteenth and early twentieth century. Numerous writers were affiliated with the movement and its journal. Those most closely allied with its central tendency to combine antibourgeois, eclectic expression with traditional verse forms were Jarosław Iwaszkiewicz (1894-1980), Jan Lechoń (1899-1956), Antoni Słonimski (1895-1976), Julian Tuwim (1894-1954), and Kazimierz Wierzyński (1894-1969). Virtually from its inception until its demise in 1939, the *Skamander* Group was assailed by smaller, more progressive circles of poets, particularly the Polish Futurists and the CRACOW AVANT-GARDE.

⇥•⇤

Further Reading

Allen Shore, Lena. *Julian Tuwim as Poet and Jew: In the Ideological Context of His Time*. Doctoral thesis, Dropsie University, Philadelphia, 1980.
Dudek, Jolanta. *The Poetics of W.B. Yeats and K. Wierzyński, a Parallel*. Krakow, Poland: Nakł. Uniwersytetu Jagiellońskiego, 1993.
Koźniewski, Kazimierz. "The Legend of Janusz Korczak; Gałczyński and Tuwim on the 25th Anniversary of Their Deaths." *New Polish Publications, a Monthly Review of Polish Books* 26, 8-9 (August-September 1978): 1-2, 6-9.
Kryński, Magnus J. *Julian Tuwim, a Story Continued*. New York: Czas Pub., 1974.
———. *Politics and Poetry, the Case of Julian Tuwim*. New York: Czas Pub., 1973.
Leśmian, Bolesław. *Mythematics and Extropy*. 2 vols. Stevens Point, Wis.: A. R. Poray, 1984-92.
Matuszewski, Ryszard. *Iwaszkiewicz*. Translated by Marsha Brochwicz. Warsaw: Author's Agency, 1972.
Miłosz, Czesław. "Independent Poland: 1918-1939 — Poetry: 'Skamander'." In his *The History of Polish Literature*. London: Macmillan, 1969. Rev. ed., Berkeley, Calif.: University of California Press, 1983.
Staff, Leopold. *An Empty Room*. Translated by Adam Czerniawski. Newcastle Upon Tyne, England: Bloodaxe Books, 1983.
Stone, Rochelle Heller. *Bolesław Leśmian: The Poet and His Poetry*. Berkeley, Calif.: University of California Press, 1976.
Terlecki, Tymon. "The Dionysian and Apollonian Antimony in Kazimierz Wierzyński's Early Poetry." In *For Wiktor Weintraub*. The Hague: Mouton, 1975.
Yurieff, Zoya. *Joseph Wittlin*. New York: Twayne, 1973.

SKIT POETOV. *See* POETS' CLOISTER

SMITHY (Kuznitsa)
Russia, 1920s

The Smithy was formed in 1920 by a few members of PROLETKULT, primarily lyric poets, who wished to expand their choices of forms and styles yet still adhere to the theory that literature exists for the purposes of propaganda. Romantic metaphors and idealistic expressions of the future of Communism characterized the poetry of the group, which was comprised of Vasily Aleksandrovsky (1897-1934), Alexei Kapitonovich Gastev (1882-1941), Mikhail Gerasimov (1889-1939), Vasili Kazin (1898-1981), Vladimir Kirillov (1890-1943), and Semyon Rodov (1893-1968). As the character of the Party grew more severe, many of the Smithy poets disassociated themselves from it. The Smithy continued, however, until the eradication of all autonomous literary organizations in 1932.

❖•❖

Further Reading

Shearer, David Randall. *Aleksey Gastev, Russian Modernism and the Proletarian Cultural Tradition: A Study in the Development of Social Thought in Twentieth Century Russia.* Master's thesis, Ohio State University, 1979.

SOCIALIST REALISM
Azerbaijan, 1930s-1950s

Socialist Realism became a strong literary force in Azerbaijan following the establishment of the Union of Writers in 1932. Dramatist Djafar Djabarly (1899-1934), novelist Muhammad Sa'id Ordubady (1872-1950), and poet Samed Vurgun (1906-1956) typified the movement's emphasis on patriotism and sympathy for the proletariat.

❖•❖

Further Reading

Hitchins, Keith. "Azerbaijani Literature." In *Encyclopedia of World Literature in the Twentieth Century.* 3rd ed. Edited by Steven R. Serafin. Farmington Hills, Mich.: St. James Press, 1999.

SOCIALIST REALISM
Bulgaria, 1930s-1950s

Socialist Realism gained prominence in Bulgaria particularly after World War II under the vigilant eye of Soviet party officials. Although numerous writers were forced to uphold Socialist Realist methods, some, such as Georgi Karaslavov (1904-1980), readily embraced the ideological and aesthetic program of Communism.

680

❖•❖

Further Reading

Karaslavov, Georgi. *Tango and Other Stories*. Edited by M. Alexieva. Translated by M. Todorov. Sofia, Bulgaria: Sofia Press, 1972.

Pondev, Todor, Hristo K. Radev, and Géorgi Bojkov, eds. *Forever Living in the Memory of the People*. Translated by Boris Bossilokov. Sofia, Bulgaria: Printing House of the BZNS Publishers, 1982.

SOCIALIST REALISM
Byelorussia, 1930s-1950s

From the 1930s through the 1950s, Socialist Realism controlled virtually all facets of literary expression in Byelorussia. Consequently, the high literary standards established by the *NAŠA NIVA* GROUP early in the century generally suffered. A few notable exceptions were the writings of Kuzma Chorny (1900-1944), Uladzimier Dubowka (1900-1975), and Kandrat Krapiva (1896-?), all former, rehabilitated members of the *UZVYŠŠA* GROUP.

See also SAPLINGS *(Maladniak)*.

❖•❖

Further Reading

Adamovich, A. "The Sovietization of Belorussian Literature." *Belorussian Review* 1 (1955): 98-106.
———. "UZVYŠŠA — The Belorussian Literary Club." *Belorussian Review* 4 (1957): 23-55.
McMillan, Arnold A. *A History of Byelorussian Literature*. Giessen, Germany: Wilhelm Schmitz Verlag, 1977.

SOCIALIST REALISM, China. *See* LEAGUE OF LEFT-WING WRITERS

SOCIALIST REALISM
Chuvashia, 1930s-1950s

Socialist Realism in the Soviet republic of Chuvashia emerged as early as 1923, when the Union of Chuvashian Authors and Journalists was formed. During the 1930s and 1940s such writers as Semyon Elger (1894-1966), Ivan Ivnik (1914-1942), Petr Khusangay (1907-1970), Petr Osipov (1900-), and Ilya Tuktash (1907-) upheld nationalist themes in a variety of genres.

❖•❖

Further Reading

Krueger, John R. "Part One: Literature." In his *Chuvash Manual: Introduction, Grammar, Reader, and Vocabulary*. Bloomington, Ind.: Indiana University Publications, 1961.

SOCIALIST REALISM
Czechoslovakia, 1940s-1950s

Socialist Realism dominated Czechoslovakian writing during the 1940s and 1950s. Peter Karvaš (1922-), Marie Majerová (1882-1967), and Marie Pujmanová (1893-1958) were among those who most readily sympathized with the movement and with the plight of the working classes. However, opposition to party control and censorship was considerable and led to the forced emigration of several writers, including Milan Kundera (1929-), a sometime practitioner of MAGIC REALISM and one of the foremost philosophical novelists in modern literature.

❧•❦

Further Reading

Ptáčník, Karel. *Born in 1921*. Translated by Alice Denešová. Prague: Artia, 1965.
Rudinsky, Norma. *The Context of the Marxist-Leninist View of Slovak Literature, 1945-1969*.
   Pittsburgh, Pa.: Center for Russian and East European Studies, University of Pittsburgh, 1986.

SOCIALIST REALISM
England, 1930s-1950s

In England Socialist Realism was a minor movement, though MARXIST theory itself attracted and continues to attract a number of adherents among a broad spectrum of writers. The foremost proponent of Socialist Realism was essayist and critic Ralph Fox (1900-1937), who in such works as *A Winter in Arms* (1937) and *The Novel and the People* (1937), proposed to remodel English fiction via protagonists who embodied the ideals of Marxism.

❧•❦

Further Reading

Essays on Socialist Realism and the British Cultural Tradition. London: Arena, 1952?.
Tempska, Urszula. *"Beauty That Must End": English Avant-Garde Aesthetics in the 1930s*.
   Doctoral thesis, University of Texas at Austin, 1993.

SOCIALIST REALISM
France, 1930s-1950s

In the late 1920s and 1930s there had been a tradition of populist literature, POPULISME, in France, but by the mid-1930s the Communist influence had gained dominance. The major proponent of Socialist Realism in France was Louis Aragon (1897-1982), who in 1932 helped form the leftist Association des Escrivains et Artistes

Révolutionnares (AEAR). A poem of his demonstrating a revolutionary function for literature, "La prise du pouvoir," was published in the first issue of *Commune* (July 1933), the organization's journal, which Aragon also served editorially. Formerly a SURREALIST, Aragon had reached a moment of crisis in which he saw Surrealism and Communism as incompatible, leading to his change of allegiance from the Surrealists (some of whom did join the Party in 1927, such as Paul ÉLUARD, though Aragon was the only one to stay a member through the 1930s) to the Socialist Realists. In 1928 Aragon met Russian novelist, short-story writer, and future Resistance activist Elsa Triollet (1896-1970), who acquainted him with Soviet ideology and literature and later became his wife. In 1930 Aragon attended the second Soviet Writers' Conference in Kharkov. He went to the Soviet Union again in 1934, along with Jean-Richard Bloch (1884-1947), Paul Nizan (1905-1940), and André Malraux (1901-1976), to the First All-Union Congress of Soviet Writers in Moscow, out of which came the dictates of Socialist Realism.

Members of the adamantly anti-Fascist French Communist Party, formed in 1920, and the French Socialist Realists were profoundly affected by the Soviet Union's pact with the Nazis during World War II. *Commune* was banned, many Communists were rounded up by the Nazis, tortured, and killed, and others formed the Resistance, which had much to do with the Party's favorable reputation after the war. Nizan, for example, was active in the Resistance and killed as a result of his activities.

As with other Socialist Realists in other countries, the novel was the French writers' preferred genre to put forth the socialist ideology and program mandated by Andrey Zhdanov (1896-1948). André Stil (1921-) was an adherent who won the Stalin Prize for his novel *Le premier choc* (2 vols., 1951-53; *The First Clash*, 1954). Other representative Socialist Realist novels were Aragon's "real world" series — *Les cloches de Bâle* (1934; *Bells of Basel*, 1936), *Les beaux quartiers* (1936; *Residential Quarter*, 1938), *Les voyageurs de l'impériale* (1942; *The Century Was Young*, 1947), *Aurélien* (1944; *Aurélien*, 1946) — and the massive *Les Communistes* (6 vols., 1949-51; The Communists). Other members were novelist and Resistance activist Roger Vailland (1907-1965) and novelist Pierre Courtade (1915-1963). Significant theoretical formulations include Aragon's *Pour un réalisme socialiste* (1935; For Socialist Realism), in which he endorses Socialist Realism as a way by which the writer can attempt to influence change in his or her society. Stil's *Vers le réalisme socialiste* (1952), like Aragon's *Pour un réalisme socialiste*, presents the standard Soviet literary values of optimism, accurate language and historical context, and didacticism.

By the late 1940s, debate was growing prevalent, with Albert CAMUS and Jean-Paul SARTRE (*see* EXISTENTIALISM), among others, arguing against Socialist Realism's privileging of function over aesthetics. By the 1950s, a New Left was emerging; with the invasion of Hungary and more revelation of other horrors, Vailland and some others left the Party. A leading Socialist Realist journal was *La Nouvelle Critique*, and French Socialist Realists set up Battailes du Livre, meetings to attract working-class people to Socialist Realist literature. By the mid-1960s, however, essays by such writers as André Gisselbrecht (n.d.) and Claude Prévost (1927-) in the pages of *La Nouvelle Critique* signalled the beginning of the end of Socialist Realist dominance in France, many writers realizing the ineffectiveness of classic Socialist Realism. In his late novels, even Aragon's disaffection with Socialist Realism is apparent.

❧•❦

Further Reading

Adereth, Maxwell. *Commitment in Modern French Literature: Politics and Society in Péguy, Aragon, and Sartre*. New York: Schocken Books, 1967.

Becker, Lucille Frackman. *Louis Aragon*. New York: Twayne, 1971.

Brosman, Catharine Savage. *Malraux, Sartre and Aragon as Political Novelists*. Gainesville, Fla.: University of Florida Press, 1964.

Caute, David. *Communism and the French Intellectuals, 1914-1960*. London: André Deutsch, 1964.

Clark, David L. *Louis Aragon and Paul Eluard: From Surrealism to the Resistance*. Thesis, Northern Illinois University, 1975.

Flower, J. E. *Literature and the Left in France: Society, Politics and the Novel since the Late Nineteenth Century*. Totowa, N.J.: Barnes & Noble Books, 1983.

Geohegan, C. G. "Surrealism and Communism: The Hesitations of Aragon from Kharkov to the 'Affaire Front Rouge'." *Journal of European Studies* 8, 1 (March 1978): 12-33.

Josephson, Hannah, and Malcolm Cowley, eds. *Aragon, Poet of Resurgent France*. London: Pilot Press, 1946.

Kimyongür, Angela. *Socialist Realism in Louis Aragon's Le Monde Réel*. Hull, England: University of Hull Press, 1995.

Mackinnon, Lachlan. *The Lives of Elsa Triolet*. London: Chatto & Windus, 1992.

Rühle, Jürgen. *Literature and Revolution: A Critical Study of the Writer and Communism in the Twentieth Century*. New York: Frederick A. Praeger, Publishers, 1969.

SOCIALIST REALISM
Germany, 1950s-1960s

The first meeting of the Central Committee of the Socialist Unity Party in 1951 brought the mandates of Soviet-style artistic Socialist Realism to East Germany. Major practitioners were eventual head of the Ministry of Culture Johannes R. Becher (1891-1958), Erwin Strittmatter (1912-), and Danish-born immigrant Martin Andersen Nexø (1869-1954). Bertolt BRECHT (*see* EPIC THEATER), though enamored of MARXIST ideals,

684

was considered too influenced by Western modes of experimentation, and thus not a worthy model.

During the 1960s the BITTERFELD MOVEMENT, led by Strittmatter and Christa Wolf (1929-), was a socialist literary experiment intended to encourage workers to become writers and turned out, in fact, to be instrumental in undoing the primacy of Socialist Realist tenets in East German fiction.

✦•✦

Further Reading

Chung, Hilary, ed., with Michael Falchikov, et al. *In the Party Spirit: Socialist Realism and Literary Practice in the Soviet Union, East Germany and China*. Amsterdam; Atlanta, Ga.: Rodopi, 1996.

Durzak, Manfred, "German Literature." In *World Literature Since 1945: Critical Surveys of the Contemporary Literatures of Europe and the Americas*. Edited by Ivar Ivask and Gero von Wilpert. New York: Ungar, 1973.

Rühle, Jürgen. *Literature and Revolution: A Critical Study of the Writer and Communism in the Twentieth Century*. Translated and edited by Jean Steinberg. New York: Frederick A. Praeger, Publishers, 1969.

SOCIALIST REALISM
Hungary, 1940s-1950s

The Communist Party was legalized in Hungary after 1945; a socialist government took power by 1949. Many writers had moved to Russia before World War II, including MARXIST critic Georg LUKÁCS, József Révai (1898-1959), formerly an adherent of the TODAY GROUP who left to join the Communist movement and dictated literary policy in Hungary between 1949 and 1953, playwright Gyula Háy (1900-), novelist Béla Illés (1895-1974), film theorist Béla Balázs (1884-1949), and poets Lajos Kónya (1914-1972), László Benjámin (1915-), and Zoltán Zelk (1906-1981).

✦•✦

Further Reading

Czigány, Lorant. *The Oxford History of Hungarian Literature: From the Earliest Times to the Present*. Oxford, England: Clarendon Press, 1984.

Gömöri, George. "Hungarian Literature." In *World Literature Since 1945: Critical Surveys of the Contemporary Literatures of Europe and the Americas*. Edited by Ivar Ivask and Gero von Wilpert. New York: Ungar, 1973.

Klaniczay, Tibor, ed. *A History of Hungarian Literature*. Budapest: Corvina, 1982.

SOCIALIST REALISM
Kazakhstan, 1930s-1950s

In Kazakhstan Socialist Realism served as the literary standard from the 1930s through the 1950s. The chief practitioner of the movement was dramatist Ghabit Makhmud-ŭlï Müsrepov (1902-).

❖•❖

Further Reading

Allworth, Edward. "Kazakh Literature." In *Encyclopedia of World Literature in the Twentieth Century.* 3rd ed. Edited by Steven R. Serafin. Farmington Hills, Mich.: St. James Press, 1999.

SOCIALIST REALISM
Kirgizia, 1930s-1950s

Kirgizia was a relatively hospitable Soviet republic for the spread of Socialist Realism. Some of the foremost Socialist Realists in Kirgizia were Joomart Bokombaev (1910-1944), Tügelbay Sïdïbekov (1912-), Aalï Tokombaev (1904-), and Joomart Turusbekov (1910-1943).

❖•❖

Further Reading

Allworth, Edward. "The Focus of Literature." In his *Central Asia: A Century of Russian Rule.* New York: Columbia University Press, 1967.

SOCIALIST REALISM
Latvia, 1940s-1950s

Socialist Realism in Latvia obtained following World War II, effectively silencing free literary expression. However, at least two contemporary novelists, Visvaldis Lāms-Eglons (1923-1992) and Zigmunds Skujiņš (1926-), have succeeded in combining Socialist Realist thought with original and socially conscientious literary expression.

❖•❖

Further Reading

Ivask, Astrid. "Latvian Literature." In *Encyclopedia of World Literature in the Twentieth Century.* 3rd ed. Edited by Steven R. Serafin. Farmington Hills, Mich.: St. James Press, 1999.

SOCIALIST REALISM
Lithuania, 1940s-1950s

In Lithuania Socialist Realism emerged during World War II. Four members of the leftist group THIRD FRONT—Petras Cvirka (1909-1947), Kostas Korsakas (1909-), Salomėja Neris (1904-1945), and Antanas Venclova (1906-)—joined FOUR WINDS figure Teofilis Tilvytis (1904-1969) to form the core of party-sanctioned writing during the postwar era. A well-known former SYMBOLIST, Vincas Mykolaitis (1893-1967), was among those who attempted to adapt to the confining trend with limited success.

❖•❖

Further Reading

Silbajoris, Rimvydas. "Lithuanian Literature." In *World Literature since 1945: Critical Surveys of the Contemporary Literatures of Europe and the Americas.* Edited by Ivar Ivask and Gero von Wilpert. New York: Ungar, 1973.

Silbajoris, Rimvydas, ed. *Mind against the Wall: Essays on Lithuanian Culture under Soviet Occupation.* Chicago: Institute of Lithuanian Studies Press, 1983.

SOCIALIST REALISM
Poland, 1940s-1950s

Polish Socialist Realism may be said to have begun with FUTURIST Bruno Jasieński's (1901-1939) relocation to Moscow and publication in 1932 of *Chelovek menyaet kozhu* (Man Changes Skin), one of the first Russian Socialist Realist novels. However, it was not until 1949 that the movement was sanctioned as the sole medium for literary expression in Poland. Among the more prominent followers of Socialist Realism were novelists Leon Kruczkowski (1900-1962), Roman Bratny (1921-), and Jerzy Putrament (1910-1986). Czcsław MIŁOSZ (*see ŻAGARY* GROUP), a member of the Resistance who emigrated from Poland in 1951, was the most important of the numerous writers who objected to the totalitarian control of government and art in Poland.

❖•❖

Further Reading

Kolesnikoff, Nina. *Bruno Jasienski: His Evolution from Futurism to Socialist Realism.* Waterloo, Canada: Wilfrid Laurier University Press, 1982.

SOCIALIST REALISM
Russia 1930s-1950s

Arguably the most nefarious and widespread of all twentieth-century literary movements, Socialist Realism began to emerge in Russia and around the world following the October Revolution of 1917. Two powerful Soviet organizations, the All-Union Association of Proletarian Writers (VAPP) and the Russian Association of Proletarian Writers (RAPP), dominated literary activity in the following decades through censorious tactics founded on state authority. RAPP especially discouraged the fence-sitting of uncommitted writers, known as the fellow travelers, and urged them to embrace Communist ideology. In 1932 these bodies were dissolved and replaced by the Union of Soviet Writers. In 1934 at the First All-Union Congress of Soviet Writers in Moscow, Maxim GORKY led the movement toward a Soviet revolutionary approach to literature, which would spread throughout the Soviet empire and beyond. Attendees assumed that Karl MARX's theory of history had come to pass, with a new socialist society born via the Revolution. Out of this assumption, Socialist Realist writers and theorists developed a doctrinaire program for writing literature and producing other art in the service of the nurturance of the Soviet socialist society. Socialist Realism also was a reaction against Alexander Voronsky's (1884-1943) advocacy of literary and artistic REALISM as a way of understanding reality.

At the first congress, Andrey Zhdanov (1896-1948), the senior government official in attendance, put forth his definition of Socialist Realism, which was approved and remained the officially sanctioned doctrine until the advent of *glasnost* (openness) in the 1980s under Mikhail Gorbachev (1931-). Zhdanov proscribed Socialist Realist tenets and condemned any other literary efforts as "formalist," effectively stifling the individual imagination to a monumental extent. Socialist Realism would involve an extreme determinism in which an individual was a direct product of his or her class, and plot was a manifestation of history as class struggle. Writers were to be "engineers of human minds." Characteristics a work of literature must have included: a "positive hero," who is an idealized representative of a good Soviet citizen, along with typical characters and situations (during World War II Stalin banned many of Shakespeare's plays, among them *Hamlet*, because its hero hesitates and thinks too much); the story should be set in a specific historical context; *ideinost* — ideological content and commitment (due to this mandate, Socialist Realist literature embarked upon an unusually false idealization of Soviet life, unprecedented glorification of Stalin, and crude vilification of the West); *narodnost*, attention to the needs and aspirations of the common people; and, most importantly, *partinost* — party-mindedness or spirit.

Also presented at the conference was a report on contemporary world literature and proletarian art, which favorably mentioned André Malraux (1901-1976), Jean-Richard Bloch (1884-1947), German EXPRESSIONIST Johannes Becher (1891-1958), Ludwig Renn (1889-1979), André GIDE (*see NOUVELLE REVUE FRANÇAISE*), Theodore DREISER (*see* NATURALISM, United States), and John DOS PASSOS (*see* LOST GENERATION) — considered an especially great revolutionary writer — as well as such proven friends as Romain Rolland (1866-1944), George Bernard SHAW (*see* EDWAR-DIAN LITERATURE), and Upton Sinclair (1878-1968). But the most discussed literary figure was James JOYCE (*see* MODERNISM, England and Ireland), whose work, in spite of its radical aesthetic innovations and the fact that little of his work was known to attendees or even available in translation, was held up as the apex of criticism of decadent bourgeois literature. Critic and playwright Vsevolod Vishnevsky (n.d.), for instance, saw in *ULYSSES* a strong critique of capitalist Britain.

Several proletarian groups and organizations of the 1920s preceded Socialist Realism: the OCTOBER GROUP, PEREVAL, PROLETKULT, the SMITHY, LEFT FRONT OF THE ARTS, CONSTRUCTIVISM. In addition, a short-lived tolerance and lack of organized cultural program immediately after the Revolution allowed many small avant-garde movements to flourish until the late 1920s: ACMEISM, CUBO-FUTURISM, EGO-FUTURISM, MEZZANINE OF POETRY, the IMAGINISTS, OBERIU, and the SERAPION BROTHERS. Fellow travelers included Leonid Leonov (1899-1994); Isaak Babel (1894-1941?), Boris Pilnyak (pseud. of B. Vogau; 1894-1937?), Mikhail Prishvin (1873-1954), and Alexei Tolstoy (1882-1945).

Eventually, however, the state alienated, or worse, numerous MODERNIST writers. Ivan Dunin (1870-1953), Alexey Remizov (1877-1957), and Dmitry Merezhkovsky (1865-1941) are among the many who emigrated to Western Europe and the United States. Nikolay GUMILYOV, leader of the Acmeists, was shot as a counterrevolutionary. Fellow Acmeist Osip MANDELSTAM died in a camp. Aleksandr Solzhenitsyn (1918-), Babel, Pilnyak, and many other dissenting writers were arrested, imprisoned, and often killed. In 1938 Boris Pasternak (1890-1960) was persecuted for the non-Marxist philosophy depicted in *Doktor Zhivago* (1957; *Doctor Zhivago*, 1958). Politicians Nicolai Bukharin (1888-1938) and Karl Radek (1885-1939), who also spoke at the first congress, were both later killed in the purges. Only a small minority of writers wholeheartedly accepted the Revolution and Socialist Realism's tenets; the rest realized that without belonging to the Union of Soviet Writers, a writer could not hope to be regularly published.

Georgy Valentinovich Plekhanov (1856-1918) emerged as one of the earliest Marxist aesthetic theorists. Plekhanov's *Unaddressed Letters: Art and Social Life* (1899-1918; collected and published in 1957) asserts the necessity of utilizing a materialist view of history as he attempts to analyze the cultural and aesthetic production in both European and non-European cultures. Other critics who contributed to formulating Socialist Realist tenets were Isak Nusinov (1889-1950) and P. Rozhkov (n.d.).

Gorky's *MAT* (1907; *Mother*, 1907) was considered a model for the Socialist Realist novel. Socialist critics strongly approved of Mikhail Aleksandrovich Sholokov's (1905-1984)

Tikhy Don (4 vols., 1928-40; *The Silent Don*, 1942; *And Quiet Flows the Don*, 1934; and *The Don Flows Home to the Sea*, 1941) as well, though its tone was a bit more impartial than the best Socialist Realist novel should have. Other representative Socialist Realist writers and works include Mikhail Zoshchenko's (1895-1958) novel *Istoriya odnoy zhizni* (1935; The Story of Our Life); Sholokov's (1905-1984) *Podnyataya tselina* (1931-32; Virgin Soil Upturned); Bruno Jasieński's (1901-1938) *Chelovek menyaet kozhu* (1932; Man Changes Skin); Nikolay Alexeyevich Ostrovsky's (1904-1936) *Kak zakalyalas' stal'* (1935; *The Making of a Hero*, 1937); Alexei Tolstoy's *Khleb* (1937; *Bread*, 1937); Alexander Fadeyev's (1901-1956) *Razgrom* (1927; *The Rout*, 1955); Boris Polevoy (1908-1981); Pyotr Pavlenko's (1899-1951) novel *Na vostoke* (1937; In the East); Dmitry Furmanov's *Chapayav* (1923; *Chapayav*, 1935); Aleksandr Serafimovich's (1863-1949) *Zhelezny potok* (1924; *The Iron Flood*, 1935); Valentin Kataev's (1897-1986) *Vremya, vperyod!* (1932; *Time, Forward!*, 1933); Leonov's *Sot'* (1931) and *Doroga na Okean* (1935; The Road to the Ocean); novelist Alexey Chapygin (1870-1937); and novelist Vera Fyodorovna Panova (1905-1973). Socialist Realist plays by Nikolay Fyodorovich Pogodin (1900-1962) include *Moy drug* (1932; My Friend), produced in 1934 by the Theater of the Revolution, *Aristokraty* (1934; Aristocrats), and *Chelovek s ruzhyom* (1937; The Man with the Rifle). Konstantin Simonov (1915-) was one of the rare Socialist poets. Notable practitioners elsewhere were Henri Barbusse (1873-1935), Louis ARAGON (*see* SURREALISM), Bertolt BRECHT (*see* EPIC THEATER), Anna Seghers (1900-1983), and, in Germany, Martin Anderson Nexø (1869-1954).

Though the Union of Soviet Writers had a membership of up to 8,700 by 1981, Socialist Realism had been losing significance since the Thaw of the 1950s, during which Absurdist literature (*see* THEATER OF THE ABSURD), FREUDIANISM, and Decadent literature were still banned, but a variety of new artistic devices were allowed in post-Stalin Russia. Because they were not as relentlessly monitored as writers in the Soviet Union, writers in Poland, Romania, Hungary, Czechoslovakia, and the former Yugoslavia were able to be more critical of Socialist Realism, and contributed to its lessening power.

See also BITTERFELD MOVEMENT, MINSK GROUP, VILLAGE PROSE.

❧•❧

Gorky, Maxim (pseud. of Aleksei Peshkov, 1868-1936) · Russian novelist, critic, and dramatist.

Gorky was born into a lower-middle-class family, and both parents were deceased by the time he was ten. Gorky, whose self-chosen name means "Maxim the Bitter," thus soon began traveling and working at various odd jobs at a very early age. As a young man, Gorky became involved in revolutionary movements, moving to Capri, Italy, as a political missionary from 1906 to 1913. Despite his long personal association with Lenin and with the Bolshevik party in general, and his uncompromising pacifism during World War I—which made him sympathize with the Bolshevik attitude on the question of the war and its further conduct—Gorky was hostile toward the Bolsheviks between the two revolutions and in the early days of the regime. He denounced Lenin in his newspaper *Novaya Zhizn* during 1917-18, after which Lenin persuaded him to go abroad. Gorky lived in Germany, then settled in Italy for several years. In 1928 Gorky made a brief triumphant reentry into the Soviet Union and was feted there on the occasion of his sixtieth birthday. A year later he went to Russia again, this time remaining until his death, believed to have been ordered by Stalin.

It was Gorky who discovered Vsevolod Ivanov (1895-1963) and helped Konstantin Fedin (1892-1977) to his feet, and in general, the Serapion Brothers as a group owed much to Gorky's sympathetic interest and help. His influential force in all matters of literary policy, facilitated by his newfound friendship with Stalin, was particularly great during the last four years of his life. Some of his most noted literary works include *Ocherki i rasskazy* (1898; Sketches and Stories); the play *Na dne* (1901; *The Lower Depths*, 1912), which was performed at the MOSCOW ART THEATER; his highly acclaimed autobiographical trilogy, *Detstvo* (1913; *My Childhood*, 1914), *V lyudyakh* (1914; *In the World*, 1917), and *Moi universitety* (1922; *My University Days*, 1923); the novels *Ispoved* (1908; *A Confession*, 1909) and *Delo Artamonovykh* (1925; *Decadence*, 1927; *The Artamonov Business*, 1948); and his biographical works on Tolstoy and Lenin—*Vospominania o Lev Nikolaeviche Tolstom* (1919; *Reminiscences of Leo Nikolaevich Tolstoy*, 1920) and *V. I. Lenin* (1924; *Days with Lenin*, 1932).

Mat (1907; *Mother*, 1907).

Considered the first Socialist Realist novel and a model for others, Gorky wrote *Mat* while staying in the Adirondack Mountains in New York State. The novel tells the story of a woman's self-actualization through her activities in support of the revolutionary effort in which her son is also involved. Though never lauded for aesthetic reasons, the novel was widely read, and easily so among the less educated, and thus was extremely successful as Communist propaganda. The Soviet state hailed it as a masterpiece of Socialist Realism.

→•←

Further Reading

Banks, Miranda, ed. *The Aesthetic Arsenal: Socialist Realism under Stalin*. Long Island City, N.Y.: Institute for Contemporary Art, P.S. 1 Museum, 1993.

Bullitt, Margaret M. "Toward a Marxist Theory of Aesthetics: The Development of Socialist Realism in the Soviet Union." *Russian Review* 35 (1976).

Clark, Barrett Harper. *Intimate Portraits, Being Recollections of Maxim Gorky. . .* New York: Dramatists Play Service, 1951.

Clark, Katerina. *The Soviet Novel: History as Ritual.* Chicago: University of Chicago Press, 1981.

Erlich, Victor, ed. *Twentieth-Century Russian Literary Criticism.* New Haven, Conn.: Yale University Press, 1975.

Ermolaev, Herman. *Mikhail Sholokhov and His Art.* Princeton, N.J.: Princeton University Press, 1982.

―――. *Soviet Literary Theories, 1917-1934: The Genesis of Socialist Realism.* Berkeley, Calif.: University of California Press, 1963.

Fitzpatrick, Sheila. *The Commissariat of Enlightenment: Soviet Organization of Education and the Arts under Lunacharsky, October 1917-1921.* Cambridge, England: Cambridge University Press, 1970.

Hare, Richard. *Maxim Gorky, Romantic Realist and Conservative Revolutionary.* London: Oxford University Press, 1962.

Hayward, M., and L. Labedz, eds. *Literature and Revolution in Soviet Russia, 1917-1962: A Symposium.* London; New York: Oxford University Press, 1963.

Hingley, Ronald. *Russian Writers and Soviet Society, 1917-1978.* New York: Random House, 1979.

Holthusen, Johannes. *Twentieth-Century Russian Literature: A Critical Study.* New York: F. Ungar Publishing Company, 1972.

Iakimenko, Lev Gregorevich. *Sholokhov: A Critical Appreciation.* Moscow: Progress Publishers, 1973.

Ingwersen, Faith. *Quests for a Promised Land: The Works of Martin Andersen Nexo.* Westport, Conn: Greenwood Press, 1984.

James, Caradog Vaughan. *Soviet Socialist Realism: Origins and Theory.* New York: St. Martin's Press, 1973.

Khrushchev, Nikita. *The Great Mission of Literature and Art.* Moscow: Progress Publishers, 1964.

Lahusen, Thomas. *How Life Writes the Book: Real Socialism and Socialist Realism in Stalin's Russia.* Ithaca, N.Y.: Cornell University Press, 1997.

LeRoy, Gaylord C., comp. *Preserve and Create: Essays in Marxist Literary Criticism.* New York: Humanities Press, 1973.

Londré, Felicia Hardison. "The Soviet Golden Age." In her *The History of World Theater: From the English Restoration to the Present.* New York: Continuum, 1991.

Moore, Harry Thornton. *Twentieth-Century Russian Literature.* Carbondale, Ill.: Southern Illinois University Press, 1974.

Nabokov, Vladimir. "Russian Writers, Censors, Readers" and "Maxim Gorki." In his *Lectures on Russian Literature.* New York: Harcourt Brace Jovanovich; Bruccoli Clark, 1981.

O'Connor, Timothy Edward. *The Politics of Soviet Culture: Anatolii Lunacharskii.* Ann Arbor, Mich.: UMI Research Press, 1983.

Ovcharenko, A. *Socialist Realism and the Modern Literary Process.* Moscow: Progress Publishers, 1978.

Robin, Régine. *Socialist Realism: An Impossible Aesthetic*. Translated by Catherine Porter. Stanford, Calif.: Stanford University Press, 1992.

Scherr, Barry P. *Maxim Gorky*. Boston: Twayne, 1988.

Scott, H. G., ed. *Problems of Soviet Literature: Reports and Speeches at the First Writers' Congress*. Moscow: Leningrad, Co-operative Publishing Society of Foreign Writers in the U.S.S.R., 1935.

Shneidman, N. N. *Soviet Literature in the 1970s: Artistic Diversity and Ideological Conformity*. Toronto: University of Toronto Press, 1979.

Simmons, Ernest Joseph. *Russian Fiction and Soviet Ideology: Introduction to Fedin, Leonov, and Sholokhov*. New York: Columbia University Press, 1958.

Simonov, Konstantin M. *Always a Journalist*. Moscow: Progress Publishers, 1989.

Struve, Gleb. "Socialist Realism: Theory," "Socialist Realism: Practice," and "Socialist Realism in Drama and Poetry." In his *Russian Literature under Lenin and Stalin, 1917-1953*. Norman, Okla.: University of Oklahoma Press, 1971.

Swayze, Harold. *Political Control of Literature in the USSR: 1946-1959*. Cambridge, Mass.: Harvard University Press, 1962.

Tertz, Abram [A. Sinyavsky]. *On Socialist Realism*. New York: Pantheon Books, 1960.

Weil, Irwin. *Gorky: His Literary Development and Influence on Soviet Intellectual Life*. New York: Random House, 1966.

White, John J. *Literary Futurism: Aspects of the First Avant Garde*. Oxford, England: Clarendon Press; New York: Oxford University Press, 1990.

Wolfe, Bertram D. *The Bridge and the Abyss: The Troubled Friendship of Maxim Gorky and V. I. Lenin*. New York: F. A. Praeger for the Hoover Institution on War, Revolution and Peace, Stanford University, 1967.

Yarmolinsky, Avrahm. *Literature under Communism: The Literary Policy of the Communist Party of the Soviet Union from the End of World War II to the Death of Stalin*. Bloomington, Ind.: Indiana University, 1960.

SOCIALIST REALISM
Slovenia, 1930s-1950s

In Slovenia the height of Socialist Realism was reached in the 1940s. Ciril Kosmač (1910-1980), Miško Kranjec (1908-1983), and Voranc Prežihov (1893-1950) were all instrumental figures of the movement.

❖•❖

Further Reading

Barac, Anton. "Between the Two Wars." In his *A History of Yugoslav Literature*. Ann Arbor, Mich.: Michigan Slavic Publications, Department of Slavic Languages and Literatures, University of Michigan, 1976.

693

SOCIALIST REALISM
Turkey, 1930s-1950s

In Turkey writers of Socialist Realism came to closely identify with the plight of the rural worker, leading to a unique genre of national literature, the village novel. Following the early example of Sabahattin Ali (1906-1948), such later writers as Fakir Baykurt (1929-), Orhan Kemal (1914-1970), and Yaşar Kemal (1922-) developed VILLAGE FICTION as a major Turkish literary form, one that has persisted since the mid-1950s.

❖•❖

Further Reading

Burke, Edward Walter. *The Social Criticism of Sabahattin Ali*. Master's thesis, University of Utah, 1976.

SOCIALIST REALISM
Ukraine, 1930s-1950s

Socialist Realism in the Ukraine received its impetus through several figures, including poet Pavlo Tychyna (1891-1967), dramatist Olexandr Kornychuk (1902-), and novelist Iryna Vilde (1907-1982). However, the writer most significant to the movement throughout the Soviet Union was Nikolay Ostrovsky (1904-1936), whose novel *Kak zakalyalas' stal'* (1935; *The Making of a Hero*, 1937) became a minor classic of Communist literature.

❖•❖

Further Reading

Parkhomenko, Mikhail Nikitich. *Renovation of Traditions*. Translated by Olga Shartse. Moscow: Progress Publishers, 1976.

SOCIALIST REALISM
United States, 1930s-1950s

Although PROLETARIAN LITERATURE was a significant force in American writing of the 1930s, Socialist Realism itself was a far less prominent or lasting phenomenon. Social, rather than Socialist, Realism found mouthpieces particularly among leftist dramatists, including Clifford ODETS, who launched his career with the GROUP THEATER, and Lillian Hellman (1905-1984). However, the clearest spokesperson for authentic Socialist Realism was novelist Howard Fast (1914-), who joined the Communist Party in 1943 but eventually denounced it and its artistic policies in 1956.

☙•❧
Further Reading

Fast, Howard. *Being Red*. Boston: Houghton Mifflin, 1990.

Macdonald, Andrew. *Howard Fast, a Critical Companion*. Westport, Conn.: Greenwood Press, 1996.

Meyer, Hershel D. *History and Conscience: The Case of Howard Fast*. New York: Anvil-Atlas Publishers, 1958.

Traister, Daniel. *Being Read: The Career of Howard Fast*. Philadelphia: University of Pennsylvania Libraries, 1994.

SOCIALIST REALISM
Yakut, 1930s-1950s

In the eastern Siberian region of Yakut, Socialist Realism manifested itself in several genres. The central figure of the movement was poet, dramatist, and short-story writer Bylatan Ölöksüöyebis Oyunsky (1893-1939). Other key writers were Erilik Eristin (1892-1943), Künde (pseud. of Alexey Andreevich Ivanov, 1898-1934), and Kün Jiribine (pseud. of S. Savin, 1903-1970).

☙•❧
Further Reading

Krueger, John R. "Yakut Literature." In *Encyclopedia of World Literature in the Twentieth Century*. 3rd ed. Edited by Steven R. Serafin. Farmington Hills, Mich.: St. James Press, 1999.

SOCIETY OF FRIENDS OF THE INKSTONE (Ken'yūsha)
Japan, 1885-1903

Ken'yūsha began in 1885 as the lighthearted concept of a group of young Tokyo students whose sole premise for writing was literature for literature's sake. This same year, Tsubouchi Shōyō (1859-1935) published his landmark essay, *Shōsetsu Shinzui* (1885; The Essence of the Novel), which proclaimed European REALISM and its accompanying fictional techniques as the desired model for future Japanese fiction. However, the Ken'yūsha writers, composed of Ozaki Kōyō, Maruoka Kyūka (1865-1927), Ishibashi Shian (1867-1927), and others, were largely unaffected by Shōyō's principles during their initial years of publication. Indeed, the magazine they launched, *Garakuta Bunko* (Rubbishheap Library) featured primarily trivial pieces written in the style of *gesaku* (Edo) fiction, a form which flourished during the first decades of the nineteenth century and was characterized by hackneyed, sensational plots.

Despite its less than serious stance, *Garakuta Bunko*, the first literary journal ever published in Japan, anticipated the predilections of a continually growing readership.

Led by Kōyō, Ken'yūsha capitalized on the public's temporarily waning interest in European culture and increasing nationalism with the regular production of highly melodramatic tales composed in the recognizable styles of previous eras. The figure whose works exerted the greatest influence on Kōyō and his followers was Ihara Saikaku (1642-1693), a seventeenth-century writer of popular fiction. Saikaku's method relied heavily on the compressed style and rhetorical devices of haikai poetry to present a frequently irreverent view of humanity's most common foibles and vices. Nearly all the Ken'yūsha writers attempted to emulate Saikaku and, like him, produced stylistically dazzling works with stereotypical characters and unsophisticated plots.

A notable exception was the work of Yamada BIMYŌ, whose repudiation of gesaku fiction and conviction that literature ought to be serious quickly alienated him from Ken'yūsha. Shortly before the appearance of what is commonly considered the first modern Japanese novel, Futabatei Shimei's (1864-1909) *Ukigumo* (1887-89; *Japan's First Modern Novel: Ukigumo*, 1967), Bimyō published in *Garakuta Bunko* a story entitled "Chokai Shōsetsu Tengu" (1886; Mockery and Reproof for a Braggart Novelist). Of slight literary interest, "Mockery" is historically important for its utilization of *GEMBUN ITCHI* style, the same style which would appear in Futabatei's work and lay the foundation for modern Japanese prose. By the time Bimyō had published his most famous story, "Kocho" (1889; The Butterfly), Kōyō had effectively ousted him from the Society, purportedly as much for his scandalous private life as for his divergent literary views.

Eventually, the Ken'yūsha writers began more closely adhering to the precepts of Shōyō while incorporating *gembun itchi* prose in their works. Kōyō's first example of this trend toward realistic expression was *Futari Nyōbō* (1891-92; Two Wives). Nevertheless, the movement ascended as the nation's most popular and powerful literary school until Kōyō's death in 1903 not because of *gembun itchi* writing but, instead, for the skillfully wrought scenes of melodrama that had become the society's trademark. The most successful of all such works was Kōyō's *KONJIKI YASHA* (1897-1903; *The Golden Demon*, 1905), a serialized, elegantly written novel which restricted the gembun itchi style to passages of dialogue.

Kōyō's Saikakuesque style, supervision of Japan's first literary periodical, and mentorship of a number of young disciples who launched independent paths in fiction, including Tokuda Shūsei (1871-1943), Oguri Fūyō (1875-1926), and Izumi Kyōka (1873-1939), are perhaps Ken'yūsha's most salient and noteworthy attributes. Yet the contributions of several minor writers of the society, particularly Hirotsu Ryūrō's development of the "tragic" novel and Kawakami Bizan's of the "problem" novel, deserve mention. Finally, Yamada Bimyō's pioneering innovations in style, though largely completed after his separation from the movement, serve to characterize Ken'yūsha as a group of writers who became increasingly concerned with crafting the most suitable mode of narration to satisfy the shifting tastes of the time in which they lived.

✤•✦

Gembun Itchi.

A term used to describe the early stylistic experimentations of Futabatei Shimei and Yamada Bimyō which led directly to modern Japanese literary prose, *gembun itchi* translates as "unity of speech and writing." *Gembun itchi* reflected the Japanese writers' exposure to nineteenth-century European literature and their emerging need to express more accurately, incisively, and naturally the routine, realistic experiences of the individual. Defenders of *gembun itchi* argued that the most versatile and exacting form of expression was colloquial speech and that the written imitation of this spoken language represented a significant advance for writers too long accustomed and confined to ornate, classical language.

✤•✦

Ozaki Kōyō (1867-1903), Japanese novelist and short-story writer.

Considered the guiding force of the Ken'yūsha, Kōyō led a career that represented an artistic compromise between the stylistic richness but intellectual vacuity of Edo fiction and the perfectly contrasting style and subject matter of Realism, which gained considerably in popularity near the turn of the century. The first work that brought him national recognition was *Ninin Bikuni Iro Zange* (1889; Two Nuns' Confessions of Love), an imitative medieval tale. The style — terse in the manner of Ihara Saikaku, yet graceful with its classical flourishes — fascinated readers and critics alike, so much so that the recent colloquial experiments of Futabatei Shimei and Yamada Bimyō were greatly overshadowed. This same year, Kōyō accepted an appointment as literary editor for *Yomiuri Shimbun*, a leading Tokyo daily. The majority of his later work, including his most successful novels, appeared in installments there, alongside the works of other Ken'yūsha writers, whose careers he sought to further. Gradually, Kōyō began employing the *gembun itchi* style, first in passages of dialogue and eventually throughout his stories. Despite his belief that the new style, however suited to the evocation of modern experience, could never convey lofty sentiments or produce lasting works of art, his use of it in such novels as *Ao Budō* (1895; Green Grapes), *Tajō Takon* (1896; Passions and Griefs), and, at least partially, *Konjiki Yasha* (1897-1903; *The Golden Demon*, 1905) has assured him continued acknowledgment as an important transitional writer, whose devotion to the problem of style contributed significantly to the development of modern Japanese literature.

697

Konjiki Yasha (**1897-1903;** *The Golden Demon*, **1905).**

Kōyō's last and most ambitious work, *Konjiki Yasha* is an unfinished novel about usury and thwarted love. Written in a style indebted to Saikaku and Takizawa Bakin (1767-1848), the story follows the moral degeneration of Hazama Kan'ichi, who becomes a misanthropic moneylender after being jilted, for reasons of social advantage, by the woman he loves. Once immensely popular for both its poetic style and forceful theatrics, *Konjiki Yasha* is among the most dated of Kōyō's works, its critical history forming an exact parallel to the movement that fostered it.

Yamada Bimyō (1868-1910), Japanese novelist and essayist.

Unlike other early members of Ken'yūsha, Bimyō readily conceded the superiority of European fiction and endeavored to create a revolutionary new style capable of conveying the truths of human existence. By 1886 he had completely abandoned his initial admiration for the moralistic fantasies of Bakin, explaining that despite Bakin's serious outlook in comparison to other gesaku writers, his lavish romances were far removed from the realities of modern life. Two years later Ken'yūsha severed relations with him, ostensibly because he had published a story in a rival magazine. Although Bimyō was the first of the Ken'yūsha writers to gain stature among literary circles, he rapidly lost his position due to family difficulties. His fiction is little regarded today, yet his development of and theoretical reflections upon *gembun itchi* have earned him a unique place in the history of modern Japanese letters.

Further Reading

Keene, Donald. "Kōyō and the Ken'yūsha." In his *Dawn to the West: Japanese Literature in the Modern Era*. New York: Holt, Rinehart, & Winston, 1984.

Morita, James R. "*Garakuta Bunko*." *Monumenta Nipponica* XXIV, 3 (1969): 219-33.

Taeusch, Carl F. "Realism in the Novels of Ozaki Kōyō." *Journal of the Association of Teachers of Japanese* 10, 2-3 (1975): 159-78.

Twine, Nanette. "The *Gembunitchi* Movement: Its Origin, Development, and Conclusion." *Monumenta Nipponica* XXXIII, 3 (1978): 333-56.

SOCIETY OF THE PEN (al-Rābita al-Qalamiyya)
Lebanese emigrés in the United States, c. 1920-c. 1930s

The writers of the Society of the Pen and the ANDALUSIAN LEAGUE are often referred to collectively as *al-Mahjar* (also rendered *Mahgar*; emigré) *al-Amriki* poets, because many members of both groups emigrated from Lebanon to the Americas during the wave of emigration from the Middle East from the 1890s to the 1920s. But most contemporary critics agree that their poetry reflects widely varying tendencies, though work from both groups is inundated with themes of alienation and nostalgia for their homeland. While the Andalusian League was founded in Brazil, where Ilyas Farhāt (1893-?) and others had settled, the Society of the Pen writers lived in New York and gathered under the leadership of Khalīl Gibrān (1883-1931).

The Society of the Pen writers were generally less nationalistic and less bonded to Arabic tradition than were the Andalusian League poets, and more inclined toward philosophical abstraction and universalization of human, rather than solely Arab, experience. Gibrān, the spiritual and intellectual guiding force, wrote prose poetry, essays, short stories—much of it in English—that belied the influence of English Romanticism and American Transcendentalism, and exuded a subjectivity, metaphysics, and idealized appreciation of the natural world. According to Badawi, Mīkhā'īl Nu'aima's (1889-?) *al-Ghirbāl* (1923; The Sieve) contains something of an unofficial manifesto of the group, espousing as it does "the repudiation of traditional excessive verbiage and conventionalism, and the attempt to rise above provincialism by making literature primarily the expression of universal human thought and feeling." Yet, Nu'aima, the Society's secretary, would also write that the goal of the Society was "to lift Arabic literature from the quagmire of stagnation and imitation, and to infuse a new life into its veins so as to make of it an active force in the building up of the Arab nations."

Notable members of the Society included Nasīb 'Arida (1887-1946), a one-time president of the group, who published one of their main journals, *al-Funūn* (1912-18; The Arts); Amīn Rahānī (1876-1940); and Ilyā Abū Mādī (1889-1957), considered by many scholars one of the most gifted poets in the Society. Other members included Rashīd Ayyūh (1872-1941) and Abdul Masīh Haddād (n.d.), editor of another of the group's periodicals, *al-Sā'ih* (1918-31). The work of most of these writers appeared frequently in Egyptian journals and newspapers during the 1920s and 1930s. A contemporary, and equally influential, group in Egypt, the *DIWAN* SCHOOL OF POETS, acknowledged the *mahjar* poets by including 'Abbās Mahmūd al-'Aqqād's (1889-1964) attack on Gibrān in their critical work, *al-Diwan* (1921); Ibrāhīm al-Māzinī (1890-1949), however, was kinder in his appraisal of Gibrān. Later, Ahmad Zakī Abū Shādī (1892-1955) of the APOLLO SCHOOL admired the Society of the Pen poets in his book *al-Shafaq al-bākī* (1927).

✦•✦

Further Reading

Badawi, Muhammad M. *A Critical Introduction to Modern Arabic Poetry.* Cambridge, England: Cambridge University Press, 1975.

Boullata, Issa J., ed. *Critical Perspectives on Modern Arabic Literature.* Washington, D.C.: Three Continents Press, 1980.

Hawi, Khalil S. *Khalil Gibran, His Background, Character, and Works*. Beirut: American
    University of Beirut, 1972.
Jayyusi, Salma Khadra. *Trends and Movements in Modern Arabic Poetry*. Vol. I. Leiden,
    Netherlands: E. J. Brill, 1977.
Naimy, Nadeem N. *The Lebanese Prophets of New York*. Beirut: American University of Beirut,
    1985.
————. *Mikhail Naimy, an Introduction*. Beirut: American University of Beirut, 1967.
Ostle, R. C., ed. *Studies in Modern Arabic Literature*. Wilts, England: Aris & Phillips Ltd., 1975.

SOLARIA GROUP
Italy, 1926-1934

Although lacking the longevity and theoretical depth of *LA CRITICA*, *Solaria* (1926-34)
was one of the most important Italian literary periodicals of the Fascist era. The tradition of RONDISMO—the strict separation of politics and literature—guided the
diverse group of *Solaria* writers and critics, many of whom were interested in fashioning and encouraging works based upon those of such MODERNIST luminaries as
Marcel PROUST and James JOYCE. The most important contributors to *Solaria* included poets Eugenio MONTALE (*see* HERMETICISM) and Umberto Saba (1883-1957),
Hermeticist Salvatore QUASIMODO, and novelists Cesar PAVESE (*see* NEOREALISM),
Italo SVEVO (*see* MODERNISM, Italy), and Carlo Emilio Gadda (1893-1973).

❧•❦

Further Reading

Almansi, Guido, and Bruce Merry. *Eugenio Montale, the Private Language of Poetry*.
    Edinburgh, Scotland: Edinburgh University Press, 1977.
Becker, Jared. *Eugenio Montale*. Boston: Twayne, 1986.
Biasin, Gian-Paolo. *Montale, Debussy, and Modernism*. Princeton, N.J.: Princeton University
    Press, 1989.
————. *The Smile of the Gods: A Thematic Study of Cesare Pavese's Works*. Translated by
    Yvonne Freccero. Ithaca, N.Y.: Cornell University Press, 1968.
Cambon, Glauco. *Eugenio Montale's Poetry: A Dream in Reason's Presence*. Princeton, N.J.:
    Princeton University Press, 1982.
Cary, Joseph. *A Ghost in Trieste*. Chicago: University of Chicago Press, 1993.
————. *Three Modern Italian Poets: Saba, Ungaretti, Montale*. New York: New York
    University Press, 1969. 2nd ed., Chicago: University of Chicago Press, 1993.
Furbank, Philip Nicholas. *Italo Svevo: The Man and the Writer*. Berkeley, Calif.: University of
    California Press, 1966.
Gatt-Rutter, John. *Italo Svevo: A Double Life*. Oxford, England: Oxford University Press, 1988.
Huffman, Claire. *Montale and the Occasions of Poetry*. Princeton, N.J.: Princeton University
    Press, 1983.
O'Healy, Áine. *Cesare Pavese*. Boston: Twayne, 1988.

Quasimodo, Salvatore. *Complete Poems*. Introduced and translated by Jack Bevan. New York: Schocken Books, 1984.

————. *Selected Writings*. Edited and translated by Allen Mandelbaum. New York: Farrar, Straus, & Cudahy, 1960.

Saba, Umberto. *The Dark of the Sun: Selected Poems*. Translated by Christopher Millis. Lanham, Md.: University Press of America, 1994.

————. *The Stories and Recollections of Umberto Saba*. Translated by Estelle Gilson. Riverdale-on-Hudson, N.Y.: Sheep Meadow Press, 1993.

Sbragia, Albert. *Carlo Emilio Gadda and the Modern Macaronic*. Gainesville, Fla.: University Press of Florida, 1996.

Singh, G. *The Achievement of Eugenio Montale*. Belfast, Northern Ireland: Queen's University, 1972.

————. *Eugenio Montale: A Critical Study of His Poetry, Prose, and Criticism*. New Haven, Conn.: Yale University Press, 1973.

Staley, Thomas F. *Essays on Italo Svevo*. Tulsa, Okla.: University of Tulsa, 1969.

Thompson, Doug. *Cesare Pavese, a Study of the Major Novels and Poems*. Cambridge, England: Cambridge University Press, 1982.

Veneziani Svevo, Livia. *Memoir of Italo Svevo*. Translated by Isabel Quigley. Marlboro, Vt.: Marlboro Press, 1990.

Weiss, Beno. *Italo Svevo*. Boston: Twayne, 1987.

West, Rebecca J. *Eugenio Montale, Poet on the Edge*. Cambridge, Mass.: Harvard University Press, 1981.

SOOTHSAYERS MOVEMENT (Arbujad)
Estonia, 1930s

Active during the tenuous Estonian independence of the 1930s, the Soothsayers Movement reacted to the threats of Nazism and Soviet expansionism with a coolly ordered, nonidealistic form of poetry which owed much to the work of Alexandr BLOK (*see* SYMBOLISM, Russia), Vsevolod Ivanov (1895-1963), and Paul Claudel (1868-1955). Leading members of the Soothsayers included Betti Alver (1906-) and husband Heiti Talvik (1904-1947). Other members included Ain Kaalep (1926-), Bernard Kangro (1910-), Jaan Kaplinski (1941-), Ilmar Laaban (1921-), Uku Masing (1909-), Ants Oras (1900-), and August Sand (1914-1969).

✤•✦

Further Reading

Aspel, Alexander. "The Hour of Destiny: The Poetry of Betti Alver." *Books Abroad* 43 (1969): 46-50.

————. "Ice, Stars, Stones, Birds, Trees: Three Major Postwar Estonian Poets Abroad." *Books Abroad* 47 (1973): 642-52.

"Estonian Emigration." *Baltic Forum* 1 (1989): 98-102.

Grabbi, Hellar. "For a New Heaven and a New Earth: Comments on the Poetry of Jaan Kaplinski." *Books Abroad* 47 (1973): 658-63.

Gross, Philip. "Independent Europe: Estonia: A Grain of the Here and Now." *Poetry Review* 80, 2 (summer 1990): 54-55.

"Heiti Talvik, From Decadent Dream to Martyrdom." *Journal of Baltic Studies* 8 (1977): 142-49.

Ivask, Ivar. "Uku Masing: A Poet Between East and West." *Journal of Baltic Studies* 8 (1977): 16-21.

————. "Reflections of Estonia's Fate in the Poetry of Betti Alver and Jaan Kaplinski." *Journal of Baltic Studies* 10 (1979): 352-60.

Lehiste, Ilse. "Three Estonian Writers and the Experience of Exile." *Lituanus: Baltic States Quarterly of Arts & Sciences* 18, 1 (1972): 15-31.

————. "Language Barriers and the Poetry of Ilmar Laaban." *Journal of Baltic Studies* 9 (1978): 305-11.

Leitch, Vincent B. "Religious Vision in Modern Poetry: Uku Masing Compared with Hopkins and Eliot." *Journal of Baltic Studies* 5 (1974): 281-94.

Mägi, Arvo. "Neo-Realism of the Independence Period." In his *Estonian Literature: An Outline*. Stockholm: The Baltic Humanitarian Association, 1968.

Puhvel, Jaan. "Four Arbiters of Literature in the 20th-Century Estonia: Tuglas, Semper, Oras and Aspel." *Books Abroad* 47 (1973): 636-42.

Silbajoris, Rimvydas. "Some Recent Baltic Poets: The Civic Duty to Be Yourself." *Journal of Baltic Studies* 20, 3 (fall 1989): 243-56.

SOUTH CHINA SOCIETY
China, 1920s

Led by T'ien Han (1898-1968), the South China Society attempted the staging of vernacular plays, an undertaking which met with little success until the advent of leftist and Realistic drama in the 1930s.

❖•❖

Further Reading

Kaplan, Randy Barbara. "The Pre-Leftist One-Act Dramas of Tian Han (1898-1968)." *Dissertation Abstracts International* 47, 5 (November 1986): 1532A.

————. "Planting the Seeds of Theatrical Realism in China: Tian Han's Contributions to Modern Chinese Drama, 1920-1929." *World Literature Today* 62, 1 (winter 1988): 55-61.

————. "Images of Subjugation and Defiance: Female Characters in the Early Dramas of Tian Han." *Modern Chinese Literature* 4, 1-2 (spring-fall 1988): 87-98.

————. Introduction to "The Night a Tiger Was Captured." Translated by Randy Barbara Kaplan. *Asian Theatre Journal* 11, 1 (spring 1994): 1-34.

Tung, Constantine. "T'ien Han and the Romantic Ibsen." *Modern Drama 9* (1967): 389-95.

SOUTHERN SOCIETY (Nan-shê)
China, 1909-1924

The Southern Society was one of the early literary societies that sprung up as part of China's NEW LITERATURE MOVEMENT, which sought to discard traditional Chinese language and forms of expression and replace them with Western models. The Society was founded in Shanghai in 1909 and its writings were at first primarily geared toward the overthrow of the Manchu regime. When this was accomplished in 1912 following the abdication of China's last emperor and the creation of a republican form of government, Nan-shê continued as an organ of support for Chinese Nationalists (Kuomintang) led by Sun Yat-sen, who was China's nominal president at the time. The Society numbered over 1,000 members at its peak.

The major figures of the Southern Society were the poet and historian Liu Ya-tzu (1887-1958), who was the Society's founder, and the novelist and poet Su Man-shu (1884-1918), who was also known as Su Yuan-ying or Su Hsuan-ying. Liu Ya-tzu was a member of the Kuomintang (although he broke with the party and gave his support to the Communists in the 1940s) and his early writings were volatile poems and essays encouraging the anti-Manchu revolution. His *Nan-shê chi-lüeb* (1940) is the authoritative chronicle of the Society's activities. In addition to his numerous critically praised poems, his other important published works include *Man-shu ch'üan-chi* (1928-31), a five-volume biographical work on Su Man-shu that collected Man-shu's literary output, and *Huai-chiu chi* (1947), a collection of biographical essays. Su Man-Shu, who was at various times a Buddhist monk, newspaper reporter, and teacher, wrote widely on an eclectic range of subjects. He is best known for his autobiographical *Tuan-hung ling-yen chi* (1912; *The Lone Swan*, 1924) and the collection *Yen-tzu-han sui-pi* (1913; Random Notes from a Swallow's Mausoleum), but also translated Victor Hugo, George Gordon (Lord) Byron, and Mary Shelley, in addition to writing works on Sanskrit grammar and a Chinese-English dictionary.

⇒●⇐

Further Reading

Boorman, Howard L., ed. *Biographical Dictionary of Republican China*. New York: Columbia University Press, 1967-79.

Lee, Leo Ou-fan. *The Romantic Generation of Modern Chinese Writers*. Cambridge, Mass.: Harvard University Press, 1973.

McAleavy, Henry. *Su Man-Shu: A Sino-Japanese Genius*. London: China Society, 1960.

SOZIALISTICHER REALISMUS. *See* **SOCIALIST REALISM, Germany**

SPECTRA
United States, 1916-1918

The Spectra group has the distinction of having been not a bona fide literary group or movement, but a hoax perpetrated by three American poets — Witter Bynner (1881-1968), a.k.a. Emanuel Morgan; Arthur Davison Ficke (1883-1945), a.k.a. Anne Knish; and, later, Marjorie Allen Seiffert (1885-?), a.k.a. Elijah Hay. The hoax began when Bynner and Ficke, inspired by, but growing slightly annoyed with, the proliferation of literary movements such as IMAGISM and VORTICISM, decided to pen some purposely bizarre verse, create a theory and manifesto to go with it, invent eccentric and mysterious personas as the authors, and foist it all upon the American literati to see what would happen. The result was *Spectra: A Book of Poetic Experiments*, published in 1916 by Mitchell Kennerley, who had previously published poems by both Ficke and Bynner. He accepted the manuscript as genuine but, when informed of the project, agreed to secrecy.

The Spectrists received attention from such prestigious quarters as Harriet Monroe's (1860-1936) *Poetry* (*see also* CHICAGO LITERARY RENAISSANCE). William Carlos Williams's (1883-1963) review, *Others,* edited by Alfred Kreymborg, devoted a special issue to the new movement. And Bynner himself did much to publicize the fabrication, reviewing the book for *New Republic.* Under their pseudonyms Bynner and Ficke wrote an essay entitled "The Spectric School of Poetry" for *Forum* in 1916 as well.

Ficke and Bynner attempted to draw others into the hoax; they approached E. A. Robinson (1869-1935), Edna St. Vincent Millay (1892-1950), and George Sterling (1869-1926) to join them. The first did not produce Spectric specimens, Millay declined to participate, and the latter's poetic contributions were considered too Spectric even for the Spectrists. Eventually they enlisted Seiffert, who went so far as to enter, under her alias, what would become a prolonged correspondence with an apparently unsuspecting William Carlos Williams.

The hoax was not exposed until April 26, 1918, when Bynner lectured at the Twentieth Century Club in Detroit and was asked by a young man whether he was Emanuel Morgan and whether Arthur Davison Ficke was Anne Knish; Bynner answered truthfully. The revelation, as might be expected, spread around and caused embarrassment and enmity among some of those taken in, such as Amy LOWELL (*see* Imagism) and Harriet Monroe. But others took it all in good humor. A few, Alfred Kreymborg for example, suggested that Ficke and Bynner wrote better poetry as Knish and Morgan — an opinion Ficke, to some extent, shared.

The exposé also provoked counter-hoaxes, the most notable of which was directed at Bynner. Malcolm Cowley (1898-1989) and his friend S. Foster Damon (1893-1971) created a young poet-farmer who was drafted into the service and used the New York address of literary critic Kenneth Burke (1897-1993) for correspondence. Conrad Aiken (1889-1973) and Amy Lowell were also taken in by this counter-hoax.

The importance of humor in the Spectric project may be expressed in the following lines from Morgan and Knish's poetic collaboration, "Prism on the Present State of Poetry":

> Laughter, dear friends, will do for kindling;
> And we shall wear ridiculous beads of flame
> To tinkle toward the corners of the world,
> Slapping with light the faces of old fools.

✦•✦

Further Reading

Bynner, Witter. "The Spectric Poets." *New Republic* [Fall Literary Review] (November 18, 1916): 13.

Morgan, Emanuel, and Anne Knish. *Spectra: A Book of Poetic Experiments*. 1916. Reprinted in *The Spectra Hoax* by William Jay Smith. Middletown, Conn.: Wesleyan University Press, 1961.

Morris, L., ed. *The Young Idea, An Anthology of Opinion concerning the Spirit and Aims of Contemporary Literature*. New York: Duffield, 1917.

Others [special Spectra issue] (January 1917).

Smith, William Jay. *The Spectra Hoax*. Middletown, Conn.: Wesleyan University Press, 1961.

STIJL, DE
Holland, 1917-1928

Primarily an artistic movement, *De Stijl* nonetheless had a literary impact on western Europe. Like CONCRETE POETRY, which aesthetic project has affinities with *De Stijl*, the members were from diverse professional backgrounds. Founder Theo van Doesburg (pseud. I. K. Bonset, 1883-1931; given name Christian Emil Marie Küpper) was a painter and architect. Other members included painter Piet Mondriaan (1872-1944), artist Bart van der Leck (1876-1958), and painter Antony Kok (n.d.). Artist Vilmos Huszár (1884-1960) designed a logo for the journal's cover and was also instrumental in founding the group. In 1920, *De Stijl*'s expansion into literary concerns, propelled mainly by van Doesburg, was dramatized by the appearance of a manifesto in the journal's pages which called for a new poetry to supersede rationality and subjectivity, and engender "the spiritual renovation of the word," through the employment of:

> syntax
> prosody
> typography
> arithmetic
> orthography

Though some, most notably Kurt Schwitters in a piece in Robert Motherwell's *The Dada Painters and Poets* (1989), associate van Doesburg with DADA, van Doesburg himself claims *De Stijl*'s literary and artistic formulations to be counter to those of Dada; however, van Doesburg recognized Dada's contributions to literature and occasionally included Dada poets in issues of *De Stijl*.

The group lost momentum by the late 1920s and the journal stopped publication in 1928, save for a 1932 commemorative issue in honor of van Doesburg on the occasion of his death.

✥•✥

Further Reading

Baljeu, Joost. *Theo van Doesburg*. New York: Macmillan, 1974.

Bann, Stephen, ed. *The Tradition of Constructivism*. New York: The Viking Press, 1974.

Blotkamp, Carel, et al. *De Stijl: The Formative Years*. Translated by Charlotte I. Loeb and Arthur L. Loeb. Cambridge, Mass.: MIT Press, 1986.

Bock, Manfred, et al. *De Stijl, 1917-1931: Visions of Utopia*. Edited by Mildred Friedman. Minneapolis: Walker Art Center; New York: Abbeville Press, 1982.

Doig, Allan. *Theo van Doesburg: Painting into Architecture, Theory into Practice*. Cambridge, England: Cambridge University Press, 1986.

Farrell, Edmund J., and James R. Squire, eds. *Transactions with Literature: A Fifty-Year Perspective for Louise M. Rosenblatt*. Urbana, Ill.: National Council of Teachers of English, 1990.

Gadamer, Hans Georg. *Hans-Georg Gadamer on Education, Poetry, and History: Applied Hermeneutics*. Edited by Dieter Misgeld and Graeme Nicholson. Translated by Lawrence Schmidt and Monica Reuss. Albany, N.Y.: State University of New York Press, 1992.

Hedrick, Hannah Lucille. *Theo van Doesburg, Propagandist and Practitioner of the Avant-Garde, 1909-1923*. Ann Arbor, Mich.: UMI Research Press, 1980.

Jaffé, Hans L. *De Stijl*. New York: H. N. Abrams, 1971.

———. *De Stijl, 1917-1931*. Cambridge, Mass.: Belknap Press of Harvard University Press, 1986.

Joosten, J., and R. P. Welsh. "The Birth of *De Stijl*, Part I: Piet Mondrian." *Artforum* XI (April 1973): 50-59.

Krispyn, E. "Literature and *De Stijl*." In *Nijhoff, Van Ostaijen, "De Stijl"* by F. Bulhoff. The Hague: Nijhoff, 1976.

Lemoine, Serge. *Mondrian and De Stijl*. Translated by Charles Lynn Clark. New York: Universe Books, 1987.

Mansbach, Steven A. *Visions of Totality: Laszlo Moholy-Nagy, Theo Van Doesburg, and El Lissitzky*. Ann Arbor, Mich.: UMI Research Press, 1980.

Overy, Paul. *De Stijl*. London: Thames and Hudson, 1991.

Oxenaar, R. W. "The Birth of *De Stijl*, Part II: Bart van der Leck." *Artforum* XI (June 1973): 10, 36-43.

Straaten, Evert van. *Theo van Doesburg: Constructor of the New Life*. Translated by Ruth
   Koenig. Otterlo, Netherlands: Kröller-Müller Museum, 1994.
————. *Theo van Doesburg: Painter and Architect*. The Hague: SDU, 1988.
Weaver, Mike. "Concrete Poetry [includes Manifesto II of De Stijl]." *The Lugano Review* 1 (sum-
   mer 1966): 124-25 and in *The Journal of Typographic Research* 1, 3 (July 1967): 325-26.

STOEP, DE. See PORCH GROUP

STONE AND SKY MOVEMENT
Colombia, 1930s

Founded in the late 1930s in Colombia, the Stone and Sky Movement emphasized a
lucid connection between ideas and imagery and the construction of verse that was at
once simple and elegant. The Stone and Sky poets, of whom Jorge Rojas (1911-) and
Eduardo Carranza (1913-) were the most representative, held aesthetic ideals similar
to those of MODERNISTS Juan Ramón JIMÉNEZ and Paul Valéry (1871-1945).

✦●✦

Further Reading

"Eduardo Carranza." In *Spanish American Authors: The Twentieth Century*. New York: Wilson,
   1992.
Foster, David William, comp. "Colombia." In *Handbook of Latin American Literature*. New
   York: Garland, 1987.
Quessep, Giovanni. *Eduardo Carranza*. Bogotá: Produltura, 1990.

STORM CIRCLE (*Der Sturm*)
Germany, 1910s

The name was given to a small group of artists and writers who adopted the concept of
EXPRESSIONISM as their basis for creativity and was also the name of a journal begun
by Herwath Walden (1878-1941) which, along with its companion, *Die Aktion,* published the work and contained the manifesto of the group. Expressionism, given its
name in France, can best be described as a violent reaction to the REALISM which had
begun in the mid-nineteenth century and had become a universal literary criterion.
Emotional, visionary, and prophetic, the Expressionist wished to distort reality and to
find new language with which to express it. In poetry, new word formations, often incoherent, combined with the dissonant and assonant rhythms found in jazz music, and
what one critic observes as "convulsive, lyrical outbursts," depicted the disorientation of
the participants of a disintegrating universe. In painting, abstraction and the rejection
of traditional representation, bizarre, often grotesque configurations in an attempt to

distort nature became honest elements for the presentation of human suffering and alienation, war, and violence. Examples of the mode are the works of the painter Oskar Kokoschka (1886-1980), whose written works include *Mörder Hoffnung der Frauen* (1907; *Murderer, the Women's Hope*, 1963) and *Der brennende Dornbusch* (1911). The most radical form of Expressionist drama to come out of the group was that of August Stramm (1874-1915); his work was featured in *Der Sturm* and includes such pieces as *Erwachen* (1915) and *Geschehen* (1915). Alfred Döblin (1878-1957) was a Social Democrat, an early and ardent resister of political tyranny, and cofounder of *Der Sturm*; his novels depict the frustration of the individual caught up in the social pressure of the Germany of the time. Like other small movements of its kind, Der Sturm was short-lived, but remains important as a forerunner of CUBISM and DADA and other like movements, all of which have come under criticism for a distortion of nature which seems to lead away from beauty. However, the artists who formulated the works of art argued that self-expression of the truth — though painful — contains its own and terrible beauty. Other members of Der Sturm were Else Lasker-Schüler (1869-1945) and Franz Marc (1880-1916).

❧•❦

Further Reading

Benton, Tim, et al., eds. *Expressionism*. Milton Keynes, England: Open University Press, 1975.

Brustein, Robert Sanford. *The Theatre of Revolt: An Approach to the Modern Drama*. Boston: Little, Brown, 1964.

Bulhoff, Francis. *Nijhoff, Van Ostaijen, "De Stijl."* The Hague: Nijhoff, 1976.

Carey, Frances, and Antony Griffiths. *The Print in Germany, 1880-1933: The Age of Expressionism*. London: British Museum Press, 1984.

Flores, Ángel, ed. *Anthology of German Poetry from Hölderlin to Rilke in English Translation*. Garden City, N.Y.: Anchor Books, 1960.

Gombrich, E. H. "Experimental Art." In his *The Story of Art*. New York: Phaidon, 1950. 16th ed., London: Phaidon, 1995.

Hamburger, Michael, and Christopher Middleton, eds. *Modern German Poetry, 1910-1960*. New York: Grove Press, 1962.

Höllerer, Walter, ed. *Transit*. Frankfurt am Main: Surhkamp, 1956.

Palmer, L. U. "The Language of German Expressionism." Ph.D. diss., University of Illinois, 1938.

Rose, William. "The Spirit of Revolt in German Literature." In his *Men, Myths and Movements*. London: Allen & Unwin, 1931.

Salinger, H. *Twentieth Century German Verse*. Princeton, N.J.: Princeton University Press, 1952.

Spender, Stephen. "Poetry and Expressionism." *New Statesman* 15 (March 12, 1938): 407-9.

STREAM OF CONSCIOUSNESS. *See* MODERNISM, England and Ireland

STRUCTURALISM
France, 1950s-1970s

Indebted to RUSSIAN FORMALISM, and to the theories of Swiss-born linguist Ferdinand de Saussure (1857-1913), Structuralism was launched in France by Belgian-born anthropologist Claude Lévi-Strauss's (1908-) *Les structures élémentaires de la parenté* (1949; *The Elementary Structures of Kinship,* 1969), a study of primitive marital and familial rites. In this and succeeding works, Lévi-Strauss propounded the view that virtually all cultural phenomena are founded upon communication and can best be understood through the application of modern linguistic theory; in short, for him, the science of humans equals the science of language and its component structures.

During the late 1950s and throughout the 1960s, beginning with Roland Barthes's (1915-1980) *Mythologies* (1957; *Mythologies,* 1973), a number of French critics, including Tzvetan Todorov (1940-) and Gérard Genette (1930-), began consciously applying the theories of Saussure and Lévi-Strauss to the scientific study of literature, specifically, of the way in which the morphological and phonological aspects of language acquire significance within a complex system of literary motifs, techniques, and conventions. A wide variety of writers, many with ties to MARXIST CRITICISM, FREUDIAN CRITICISM, or DECONSTRUCTION, have been grouped under the heading of Structuralism; these include Louis Althusser (1918-1990), Gaston Bachelard (1884-1962), Maurice Blanchot (1907-), Noam Chomsky (1928-), Jonathan Culler (1944-), Paul DE MAN (*see* YALE SCHOOL), Michel Foucault (1926-1984), René Girard (1923-), Lucien Goldmann (1913-1970), A. J. Greimas (1917-1992), Roman JAKOBSON (*see* Russian Formalism), Julia Kristeva (1941-), Jacques LACAN (*see* Freudian Criticism), David Lodge (1935-), Jean Ricardou (1932-), and Philippe Sollers (1936-). Perhaps the most important writer to be associated with Structuralism, at least as a reactionary thinker, is Jacques DERRIDA, founder of Deconstruction and one of the leaders of the Poststructuralist avant-garde. The importance of his work, and that of the Structuralists, Semioticians (*see* SEMIOTICS), and Formalists, is that it has elevated the critic, or reader, to an interpretive-creative status even beyond that afforded by NEW CRITICISM, and has led to a variety of interdisciplinary advancements and related movements, most notably the READER-RESPONSE theory popular within the education field.

❧•❧

Further Reading

Badcock, C. R. *Lévi-Strauss: Structuralism and Sociological Theory.* New York: Holmes & Meier, 1976.

Boon, James A. *From Symbolism to Structuralism: Lévi-Strauss in a Literary Tradition.* Oxford, England: Blackwell, 1972.

709

Clarke, Simon. *The Foundations of Structuralism: A Critique of Lévi-Strauss and the Structuralist Movement*. Brighton, England: Harvester Press; Totowa, N.J.: Barnes & Noble, 1981.

Culler, Jonathan. *Structuralist Poetics*. Ithaca, N.Y.: Cornell University Press, 1975.

Dews, Peter. *Logics of Disintegration: Post-Structuralist Thought and the Claims of Critical Theory*. London: Verso, 1987.

Gardner, Howard. *The Quest for Mind: Piaget, Lévi-Strauss, and the Structuralist Movement*. New York: Knopf, 1973.

Gras, Vernon W., ed. *European Literary Theory and Practice: From Existential Phenomenology to Structuralism*. New York: Dell, 1973.

Harland, Richard. *Superstructuralism: The Philosophy of Structuralism and Post-Structuralism*. London: Methuen, 1987.

Hawkes, Terence. *Structuralism and Semiotics*. Berkeley, Calif.: University of California Press, 1977.

Holenstein, Elmar. *Roman Jakobson's Approach to Language: Phenomenological Structuralism*. Translated by Catherine and Tarcisius Schelbert. Bloomington, Ind.: Indiana University Press, 1976.

Kurzweil, Edith. *The Age of Structuralism*. New York: Columbia University Press, 1980.

Lavers, Annette. *Roland Barthes: Structuralism and After*. Cambridge, Mass.: Harvard University Press, 1982.

Leach, Edmund. *Claude Lévi-Strauss*. New York: Viking, 1970.

Macksey, Richard, and Eugenio Donato, eds. *The Languages of Criticism and the Sciences of Man: The Structuralist Controversy*. Baltimore, Md.: Johns Hopkins University Press, 1970.

Merquior, J. G. *From Prague to Paris: A Critique of Structuralist and Post-Structuralist Thought*. London: Verso, 1986.

Milner, Andrew, and Chris Worth, eds. *Discourse and Difference: Post-Structuralism, Feminism, and the Moment of History*. Clayton, Australia: Centre for General and Comparative Literature, Monash University, 1990.

Pavel, Thomas. *The Feud of Language: A History of Structuralist Thought*. Oxford, England: Blackwell, 1989.

Poster, Mark. *Critical Theory and Poststructuralism: In Search of a Content*. Ithaca, N.Y.: Cornell University Press, 1989.

————. *The Mode of Information: Poststructuralism and Social Context*. Chicago: University of Chicago Press, 1990.

Rossi, Ino. *The Logic of Culture: Advances in Structural Theory and Methods*. South Hadley, Mass.: J. F. Bergin, 1982.

Sarup, Madan. *An Introductory Guide to Post-Structuralism and Post-Modernism*. Athens, Ga.: University of Georgia Press, 1989.

Seung, T. K. *Structuralism and Hermeneutics*. New York: Columbia University Press, 1982.

Sheriff, John K. *The Fate of Meaning: Charles Peirce, Structuralism and Literature*. Princeton, N.J.: Princeton University Press, 1989.

Sturrock, John, ed. *Structuralism and Since: From Lévi-Strauss to Derrida*. Oxford, England: Oxford University Press, 1979.

710

Tavor-Bannet, Eve. *Structuralism and the Logic of Dissent: Barthes, Derrida, Foucault, Lacan*. Urbana, Ill.: University of Illinois Press, 1989.

Thody, Philip. *Roland Barthes: A Conservative Estimate*. Atlantic Highlands, N.J.: Humanities Press, 1983.

Todorov, Tzvetan. *The Poetics of Prose*. Ithaca, N.Y.: Cornell University Press, 1977.

———. *Theories of the Symbol*. Oxford, England.: Blackwell; Ithaca, N.Y.: Cornell University Press, 1982.

Ungar, Steven, and Betty R. McGraw, eds. *Signs in Culture: Roland Barthes Today*. Iowa City, Iowa: University of Iowa Press, 1989.

Wasserman, George R. *Roland Barthes*. Boston: Twayne, 1981.

Weedon, Chris. *Feminist Practice and Poststructuralist Theory*. Oxford, England: Blackwell, 1987.

Wiseman, Mary. *The Ecstasies of Roland Barthes*. London: Routledge, 1988.

STURM, DER. See STORM CIRCLE

SURPRISED POETRY MOVEMENT (La Poesia Sorprendida)
Dominican Republic, 1940s

The Surprised Poetry Movement was launched in 1943 in the Dominican Republic in an effort to counteract *costumbrismo*, or regional, writing with innovative poetry that supported more cosmopolitan themes and sophisticated effects. The three writers most commonly associated with the movement are Franklin Mieses Burgos (1907-), Lupo Hernández Rueda (1930-), and Manuel Rueda (1921-).

Further Reading

Borrel Garrido, Sandra. *Pluralismo: Manuel Rueda*. Santo Domingo, Dominican Republic: Taller, 1988.

Foster, David William. "Dominican Republic." In his *Handbook of Latin American Literature*. New York: Garland, 1987.

SURREALISM
Belgium, 1920s-1930s

Though the most prominent proponent of Surrealism in Belgium, painter and writer René Magritte (1898-1967), became acquainted with the French Surrealists during an extended stay in Paris, proponents in Belgium created a more provincial, local brand of Surrealist work. Most were influenced more by Jean Paulhan (1884-1968) than by André BRETON. Poet Achille Chavée (1906-1969) led some Belgian Surrealists from his home base in Hainaut. His collections include the early *Pour cause déterminée* (1935;

For a Determined Reason) and *Le Cendrier de chair* (1936; The Ashtray of Flesh), both lauded by Breton, and *Une foi pour toutes* (1938; Once and for All) and *D'ombre et de sang* (1946; Of Shadow and Blood). Camille Goëmans (1900-1960), prose poet Marcel Lecomte (1900-1966), and theorist Paul Nougé (1895-1967) founded the journal *Correspondance* in 1924. Other writers associated with the group were Paul Colinet (1898-1957), E. L. T. Mesens (1903-1970), Paul Neuhuys (1897-?), Louis Scutenaire (1905-1987), and musician André Souris (1899-1970). A collection of Belgian Surrealist works appears in *Anthologie du Surréalisme en Belgique* (1972).

❖•❖

Further Reading

Mallinson, Vernon. *Modern Belgian Literature 1830-1960*. New York: Barnes & Noble, 1966.

SURREALISM
Czechoslovakia, 1930s

Vítězslav Nezval (1900-1958), an adherent of POETISM, was influenced by André BRETON and initiated Surrealism in Czechoslovakia in 1934. His Surrealist works include *Edison* (1928; Edison), *Žena v množnémčísle* (1936; Woman in the Plural), *Praha s prsty deště* (1936; Prague with the Fingers of Rain), *Absolutní hrobař* (1937; The Absolute Gravedigger), and *Pět minut za městem* (1939; Five Minutes behind the Town). Another significant Czech practitioner was poet Konstantín Biebl (1898-1951).

❖•❖

Further Reading

French, Alfred. *The Poets of Prague*. London; New York: Oxford University Press, 1969.
Novák, Arne. *Czech Literature*. Translated by Peter Kussi. Ann Arbor, Mich.: Published under the auspices of the Joint Committee on Eastern Europe, American Council of Learned Societies by Michigan Slavic Publications, 1976.
Pynsent, Robert. *Czech Prose and Verse*. London: University of London, Athlone Press, 1979.

SURREALISM
England, 1920s-1930s

The 1936 International Surrealist Exhibition in London sparked interest among several English writers to form their own Surrealist group. They included Hugh Sykes Davies (1909-1984?), David Gascoyne (1916-), Roland Penrose (1900-1984), Herbert Read (1893-1968), Dylan Thomas (1914-1953), and Ruthven Todd (1914-). Representative collections of English Surrealist poetry include Gascoyne's *Man's Life Is This Meat* (1936). In addition, Gascoyne and Read published books on the Surrealists: the former translated poetry of the French Surrealists and wrote *A Short Survey of Surrealism* (1935), while the latter edited a collection of essays by the French Surrealists in *Surrealism* (1936).

⇥•⇤

Further Reading

Jackaman, Rob. *The Course of English Surrealist Poetry since the 1930s.* Lewiston, Pa.: E. Mellen Press, 1989.

Ray, Paul C. *The Surrealist Movement in England.* Ithaca, N.Y.: Cornell University Press, 1971.

SURREALISM
France, 1920s-1930s

Surrealism, a movement that embraced philosophy and politics as well as literature and art, was founded in Paris in the 1920s and flourished between the two world wars. André BRETON, a French poet, essayist, and critic and the primary force behind the movement, announced its tenets in his *Surrealist Manifesto* of 1924. As an outgrowth of the earlier DADA movement, it was a revolt against logical, rational, and systemized thought and signalled a direct indebtedness to the theories of Sigmund FREUD in its emphasis on the importance of dreams and the realm of the unconscious. Yet unlike the Dadaists, the Surrealists were less committed to destruction and nihilistic exhibition than to the pursuit and presentation of innovative modes of expression. Declaring the current state of French letters to be in decay, the Surrealists set out to release literature and the arts from the constraints of moral purpose and aesthetic strictures and to "create an evocation freed from time and space and movement."

The creative process outlined in Breton's manifesto called for "psychic automatism": the linking, through AUTOMATIC WRITING or painting, of unrelated objects and ideas, as evidenced in the first Surrealist work, *LES CHAMPS MAGNÉTIQUES* (1920; The Magnetic Fields), a collaborative effort of Breton and Philippe Soupault (1897-1990). These images are drawn from the unconscious and presented in a format in which the irrational, disconnected images of dreams are revealed without concern for logical, moral, or aesthetic order. The writers of the movement thus abandoned the established rules of poetry and prose in pursuit of a new method through which the newly created image, the product of the juxtaposition of unlike elements, attains an independent meaning and life. Thematically, the Surrealists explored the realms of love, especially erotic love, the revolt against social and moral restraints, and the primacy of the imagination as revealed in the unconscious. For Breton, Surrealism offered a fusion of inner and outer reality: "there exists a certain point in the mind from which life and death, the real and the imaginary, the past and the future, what is communicable and what is incommunicable, the high and the low, cease to be contradictory." According to its practitioners, Surrealist art thus projected a superior manifestation of the human psyche.

The Surrealists were as deliberately provocative in their behavior as in their art. Intending to shock a complacent world, they staged brash public displays that gained the movement a reputation for notoriety and scandal. They aimed these demonstrations at the postwar malaise of Europe, particularly the bourgeois urbanity of France in the 1920s. Revolutionary in intent, the Surrealists wished to change the world: to liberate the imagination, to pursue and replicate the spirit of exaltation and ecstasy, and to free the French language from the stagnation of the past.

With fellow poet Louis ARAGON, Breton founded the journal *La Révolution surréaliste* in the early 1920s, which served as a platform for their artistic ideals. Later in the decade many of the movement's adherents were drawn to the Communist Party, and in 1930 the journal's title became *Surréalisme au service de la révolution* to reflect this change. Breton wrote two succeeding Surrealist Manifestos, one in 1930 and another in 1942, in which he expanded on his original conception of Surrealism and attempted, in part, to integrate his artistic and political theories. He had hoped that the Communists would accept and espouse Surrealism, but when he was disappointed in this endeavor, he broke with the Party in 1935, after which the periodical ceased publication. *Minotaure*, first published in 1934, soon became the primary publishing source for the Surrealists, and Breton served on its staff.

The London International Surrealist Exhibition in 1936 provided further evidence of the growth and influence of the movement, which was carried on in England by such writers as Herbert Read (1893-1968), David Gascoyne (1916-), and Hugh Sykes Davies (1909-1984?). As the movement spread throughout Europe, the Spanish poets Rafael Alberti (1902-), Vicente Aleixandre (1898-1984), and Luis Cernuda (1902-1963) experimented with the new forms offered by Surrealism, and the German poet and painter Jean (Hans) Arp (1887-1966) was also a noted early exponent. American writers contemporary with the movement whose works reflect its direct influence include Henry MILLER (*see* LOST GENERATION) and Anaïs Nin (1903-1977). Notable literary works produced by the early Surrealists include Breton's *NADJA* (1928; *Nadja*, 1960), Aragon's *LE PAYSAN DE PARIS* (1926; Paris Peasant), and Paul ÉLUARD's *CAPITALE DE LA DOULEUR* (1926; *Capital of Pain*, 1973).

The movement as a whole began to disintegrate toward the outbreak of World War II as some of its more important proponents, notably Éluard and Aragon, broke with the Surrealists. Yet the continuing vitality of the concept of Surrealism and its effect on the arts can be seen in the successful Surrealist Exhibitions held in Paris in 1947, 1959, and 1965.

Artists associated with the early Surrealist movement in France include the poets Éluard, Aragon, Antonin Artaud (1896-1948), Benjamin Péret (1899-1959), René Char (1907-1988), and Soupault, and the artists Pablo Picasso (1881-1973), Joan Miró (1893-1983), Giorgio de Chirico (1888-1978), Max Ernst (1891-1976), Salvador Dalí (1904-1989), and the artist and photographer Man Ray (1890-1976). The poets and artists of the movement deliberately ignored the aesthetic distinctions that traditionally separated creative fields and took their inspiration and direction from the same set of principles. This unity of purpose produced collaborative works of distinction, such as Éluard's and Ernst's *Les Malheurs des immortels* (1922; *The Misfortunes of the Immortals*, 1943), as well as the cross-fertilization of ideas, such as Dalí's paranoiac-critical method, which influenced Surrealists in a variety of genres and forms.

The movement's adherents acknowledged the influence of the English and German Romantics and the Marquis de Sade, who symbolized the life of revolt. Of primary importance to the foundations of Surrealism were the works of the nineteenth-century French poets Charles BAUDELAIRE, Gérard de Nerval (1808-1855) and Comte de Lautréamont (1846-1870), the SYMBOLIST movement in French literature, particularly the poetry of Stéphane MALLARMÉ, and Arthur RIMBAUD, as well as the work of the early twentieth-century poet Guillaume APOLLINAIRE (*see* CUBISM). These poets share a similar concern with the representation of sensation, the importance of the hallucinatory or irrational, the juxtaposition of unlike images, and the belief that art must be liberated from a moral context. Apollinaire is in fact credited with the first use of the term "surrealist" to describe one of his own works, *Les mamelles de Tirésias* (1917; *The Breasts of Tiresias*, 1961).

The effect of the Surrealist movement has been felt throughout the artistic world, and it is one of the most important and influential movements of the twentieth century. It has affected a number of aesthetic fields and movements, including Artaud's concept of the THEATER OF CRUELTY in France and the works of Spanish filmmaker Luis Buñuel. While few writers would claim to be Surrealists today, the movement's focus on the importance of dreams and its understanding of the unconscious as a source of art and creative impulse has made a profound and lasting contribution to modern literature.

Aragon, Louis (1897-1982), French poet, novelist, and essayist.

With André Breton, Aragon was one of the founders of Surrealism, and like Breton, was first attracted to the Dadaist movement in art. With Breton he founded the periodical *Littérature* and later the first organ of the Surrealists, *La Révolution surréaliste*. He joined the Communist Party in the late 1920s and his experiences at the Congress of Revolutionary Writers in 1930 caused him to break with the Surrealists to pursue literature that was more politically oriented. During the Second World War he became one of the preeminent poets of the Resistance. The publications that most strongly reflect his Surrealistic tendencies include *Le Mouvement perpétuel* (1925) and *Le Paysan de Paris* (1926; Paris Peasant).

Le Paysan de Paris (1926; Paris Peasant).

This novel, often called a prose poem, is considered one of the primary works of Surrealism and a masterpiece of early twentieth-century French literature. Aragon revelled in the little-known aspects of Paris, and in the work he chronicles life in the streets of the city in the 1920s, transforming reality through the lens of the Surrealist imagination. He is witness to the random events that govern life, focussing especially on the disorder and the effect of chance, which confirm "the face of the infinite in the concrete forms" displayed everywhere about him. The imagery evokes the fantastic in the mundane, illuminating the realm where dream and reality converge, a concept that is central to the Surrealist vision. Thematically, *Le Paysan de Paris* is concerned with the primacy of love and the idea that poetry is not a rarefied practice, but a function of everyday life.

❖•❖

Automatic Writing.

The writers of the Surrealist school used the term "automatic writing" to denote their efforts to penetrate and replicate the flow of images generated by the unconscious, without regard for logic, coherence, or aesthetic correctness. The method was created to subvert ordinary moral or literary principles and to allow for the spontaneous succession of unlike images. Often the result of self-induced states of hallucination or hypnosis, the technique provided a means of capturing the essence of dreams, a central aim of the Surrealists. An example is *Les Champs Magnétiques* (1920), a collaborative effort of Breton and Soupault.

❖•❖

Breton, André (1896-1966), French poet, essayist, and novelist.

The founder of Surrealism, Breton was first influenced by Dadaism, whose affinity for the illogical and irrational is reflected in Surrealism. As a young man Breton served in the medical corps of the French Army, and the movement's indebtedness to the theories of Freud had their origin in Breton's experiences dealing with psychiatric patients during World War I. He collaborated with a number of his fellow Surrealists, most notably Éluard, with whom he published *L'Immaculée conception* (1930; The Immaculate Conception), and Soupault, with whom he published a volume entitled *Les Champs Magnétiques* (1920), reflecting their early experiments in automatic writing.

716

Soupault was banished from the movement in 1926 when he rejected its growing left-ist political tendencies.

Breton's own disaffection with the Communists led to his break with the Party in 1935, and in 1941, out of favor with the Vichy government, he left France to live in the United States. Here he became involved with other expatriate artists, and with Dadaist Marcel Duchamp presented an exhibition of modern art in New York. In 1942 he delivered a speech at Yale University that is considered his third manifesto of Surrealism. Returning to France after the war, Breton once again became the center of Surrealism, now fostering a new, younger group of artists, and he remained committed to the movement he founded until his death.

Les Champs Magnétiques (1920; The Magnetic Fields).

A collaborative effort of Breton and Soupault, *Les Champs Magnétiques* is considered to be the first Surrealist document. The novel was published before Breton announced the principles of the movement in his 1924 manifesto, but it reflects the experiments in automatic writing that proved to be an important method for the early proponents of Surrealism. The work is written at different "speeds," all noted in the text, that reveal the individual speaker's visions, assembled as they were given and evoking the states of dream and hypnosis that were central to the Surrealist's concept of capturing images without regard for their logical coherence or aesthetic precision.

Nadja (1928; *Nadja*, 1960).

Breton's novel *Nadja* is one of the most important works associated with Surrealism. He is the protagonist in this autobiographical novel in which he chronicles, in the form of a diary, his relationship with a seriously disturbed young woman named Nadja. The novel reflects the linking of insanity and eroticism that so often characterizes Surrealist works, for Breton saw Nadja as a source of revelation, an oracular being who embodied the essence of Surrealism. The narrative begins with the question "Who am I?" and proceeds, in a style where thoughts, dreams, and meditations are randomly ordered, to chart the effect of Nadja's growing madness on Breton. He is at once attracted and repelled by her descent into insanity, for it is a source of her "divinity" as a Surrealistic medium, but also proves to be the root of his horror. The novel ends with Nadja's confinement in an asylum.

❖•❖

Éluard, Paul (1895-1952), French poet.

Éluard was an early and passionate member of the Surrealist movement and, like his fellow writers in the movement, experimented with automatic writing and dream transcription. He also collaborated with other Surrealist artists on a number of works, including *Les Malheurs des immortels* (1922; *Misfortunes of the Immortals*, 1943) with Max Ernst, and *Donner à voir* (1940) with Picasso. Although Surrealism was a great influence on his early poetry, Éluard remained a traditionalist in many aspects, and he broke with the movement in 1938. Like Aragon, he became a Communist and one of the most famous poets of the Resistance. He is noted as one of the major French poets of the modern era and is best remembered for his politically inspired verse as well as his love poetry. Among his collections that most profoundly reflect the Surrealists' influence are *Capitale de la douleur* (1926; *Capital of Pain*, 1973), *Les Dessous d'une vie ou la pyramide humaine* (1926), and *La Rose publique* (1934).

Capitale de la douleur (1926; *Capital of Pain*, 1973).

An early work of Éluard's Surrealist period, *Capitale de la douleur* reflects his recurrent themes of the liberating force of love and of woman as the eternal feminine and source of personal and poetic nurturance, a concept he shared with such fellow Surrealists as Breton and Aragon. In lyrical, economic language, he describes the "city of sorrow" where the lover's dejection is paralleled to the hope and ecstasy of love. It is a work that celebrates the couple and the duality of love, and it vividly displays Éluard's gift for the imagery of paradox. He explores love as the ultimate experience, offering the fusion of sorrow and ecstasy, and the reconciliation of the temporal and the infinite.

✦•✦

Further Reading

Balakian, Anna. *Andre Breton: Magus of Surrealism*. New York: Oxford University Press, 1971.

————. *Surrealism: The Road to the Absolute*. New York: Noonday Press, 1959.

Bigsby, C. W. E. *Dada and Surrealism*. London: Methuen, 1972.

Bree, Germaine. *Twentieth-Century French Literature*. Chicago: University of Chicago Press, 1983.

Breton, André. *What Is Surrealism?* London: Faber and Faber, 1936.

Carrouges, Michel. *Andre Breton and the Basic Concepts of Surrealism*. University, Ala.: University of Alabama Press, 1974.

Caws, Mary Ann. *The Poetry of Dada and Sur-realism*. Princeton, N.J.: Princeton University Press, 1970.

Fowlie, Wallace. *Age of Surrealism*. New York: Swallow Press, 1950.

Gersham, Herbert S. *The Surrealist Revolution in France*. Ann Arbor, Mich.: University of Michigan Press, 1969.

Matthews, J. H. *An Introduction to Surrealism*. University Park, Pa.: Pennsylvania State University Press, 1961.

Nadeau, Maurice. *The History of Surrealism*. Translated by Richard Howard. London: Cape, 1968.

Rubin, William S. *Dada, Surrealism, and Their Heritage*. New York: Museum of Modern Art, 1968.

SURREALISM
Germany, 1920s-1930s

Surrealism was not a cohesive movement in Germany, but its influence was felt. Noted writers who practiced Surrealist techniques were EXPRESSIONISTS Gottfried Benn (1886-1956), Alfred Döblin (1878-1957), and August Stramm (1874-1915), as well as poet and novelist Hermann Kasack (1896-1966) and playwright and novelist Hans Erich Nossack (1901-1977).

❖•❖

Further Reading

Bithell, Jethro. "Existentialism and Surrealism, Political and Religious Phases." In his *Modern German Literature, 1880-1950*. London: Methuen, 1959.

SURREALISM
Latin America, 1920s-1930s

André BRETON's notion of the liberating effects of Surrealism and its techniques, such as AUTOMATIC WRITING, had particular salience in Latin America, whose artists and intellectuals were coming to terms with the cultural effects of the colonial experience. The French Surrealists made an impact on the *CONTEMPORÁNEOS* in Mexico as well as such Latin American poets as Chilean poet Pablo Neruda (1904-1973) in his volume of Surrealist poetry *Residencia en la tierra* (1935; Residence on Earth), Mexican poet Octavio Paz (1914-1998), and Peruvian poets César Moro (1903-1956) and Emilio Adolfo Westphalen (1911-). The journal *Negro sobre blanco*, published in Argentina, was a forum for Surrealist-inspired literature.

❖•❖

Further Reading

Franco, Jean. "The Avant-Garde in Poetry." In his *An Introduction to Spanish-American Literature*. Cambridge, England: Cambridge University Press, 1969.
Vallejo, César. *Autopsy on Surrealism*. Translated by Richard Schaaf. Willimantic, Conn.: Curbstone Press, 1982.

SURREALISM
Portugal, 1947-1965

Although the Surrealist Movement flourished in France during the period between the two world wars, few Surrealist writers surfaced in Portugal until the late 1940s. While the dominant trend in the Portuguese literature of that period was toward the

719

social commitment of the NEOREALIST movement, a small group of poets and novelists chose to practice the tenets espoused in André BRETON's Surrealist Manifesto of 1924.

The most prominent of the Portuguese Surrealists was Mário Cesariny de VASCONCELOS, whose work reflects the rebellion against logic and attempt to free the imagination promulgated by the French Surrealists. Another important Portuguese Surrealist was Alexandre O'Neill (1924-), whose poetry portrays daily life through close observation and strings of associated words. The poems in O'Neill's best-known volume, *Na reina da Dinamarca* (1958; In the Kingdom of Denmark) blend sarcasm and sentimentality to reveal the weakness and hypocrisy of the middle class.

Also significant in Portuguese Surrealism are António Maria Lisboa (1925-1953), whose poetry identifies eroticism as the key to self-discovery and stability, and Ruben A. Leitao (1920-1975), author of the notable Surrealist novel *A torre de Barbela* (1964; The Tower of Barbela).

❖•❖

Vasconcelos, Mário Cesariny de (1924-), Portuguese poet.

The most renowned of the Portuguese Surrealists, Vasconcelos joined his French counterparts in rebelling against tradition and literary constraints and attempting to unharness the power of the imagination and of dreams. Vasconcelos's poety is intense, vigorous, and suggestive, with flashes of both lyrically expressed eroticism and the social realism that dominates his earlier writings. His best-known volume is *Corpo visivel* (1950; Visible Body), which evidences the influence of the French Surrealists in its thematic focus on love, ironic tone, experimental language, and celebration of nonsense. A nonsensical world is also portrayed in *Pena capital* (1957; Capital Punishment).

❖•❖

Further Reading

Campbell, Roy. *Portugal*. London: Max Reinhardt, 1957.

Faria, Almeida, Alberto de Lacerda, Vianna Moog, Jorge de Sena, and Robert D. Pring-Mill. *Studies in Modern Portuguese Literature*. Tulane Studies in Romance Languages and Literature, No. 4. New Orleans, La.: Tulane University, 1971.

Moser, G. "Portuguese Literature in Recent Years." *Modern Language Journal* 44 (1960): 245-54.

————. "Portuguese Writers of This Century." *Hispania* 50 (1966): 947-54.

Schneider, Marshall J., and Irwin Stern, eds. *Modern Spanish and Portuguese Literatures*. New York: Continuum, 1988.

SURREALISM
Spain, 1920s-1930s

No organized Surrealist movement of writers existed, nor were any manifestos issued; nonetheless, Spanish writers took note of the French group's activities. Many of the GENERATION OF 1927 writers experimented with Surrealist techniques, including Rafael Alberti (1902-), Vicente Aleixandre (1898-1984), Luis Cernuda (1902-1963), Federico García Lorca (1898-1936), and Emilio Prados (1899-1962), though perhaps the most internationally famous Spanish Surrealist was artist Salvadore Dalí (1904-1989). Dalí and Luis Buñuel (1900-1983) collaborated on the Surrealist films *Un chien andalou* (1929) and *L'âge d'or* (1930). Others who employed Surrealist techniques were Azorín (1873-1969), Antonio Espina García (1894-1972), Vicenç Josep Foix (1893-1993), Ramón Gómez de la Serna (1888-1963), Benjamín Jarnés (1888-1949), Juan Larrea (1895-1982), and José Moreno Villa (1887-1955). Much Spanish Surrealist writing appeared in *Gaceta de arte* (1932-36), a literary journal published in the Canary Islands.

❖•❖
Further Reading

Havard, Robert. *From Romanticism to Surrealism: Seven Spanish Poets*. Totowa, N.J.: Barnes & Noble, 1988

Ilie, Paul. *The Surrealist Mode in Spanish Literature: An Interpretation of Basic Trends from Post-Romanticism to the Spanish Vanguard*. Ann Arbor, Mich.: University of Michigan Press, 1968.

Morris, C. B. *Surrealism and Spain, 1920-1936*. Cambridge, England: Cambridge University Press, 1972.

SURREALISM
Sweden, 1930s

Inspired in part by a visit to Paris in 1929-30, poet Gunnar Ekelöf (1907-1968) became the most prominent populizer of Surrealism in Sweden, particularly to writers associated with the journal *Spektrum*, which published his work. His collection *sent på jorden* (1932; *Late Arrival on the Earth*, 1967) employed Surrealist techniques. Artur Lundkvist (1906-1991), associated with a contemporary group of poets, FIVE YOUNG MEN, was also considered a Swedish Surrealist.

❖•❖
Further Reading

Rossel, Sven H. *A History of Scandinavian Literature 1870-1980*. Minneapolis: University of Minnesota Press, 1982.

Warme, Lars G., ed. *A History of Swedish Literature*. Lincoln, Nebr.: University of Nebraska Press, 1996.

SYLLABISTS (Hececiler)
Turkey, 1920s-1940s

The Syllabists, sometimes known as the Five Syllabists (Bes Hececiler), advocated a nationalist poetry to reflect the ideals of the new Republic of Turkey, established by Kemal Atatürk (1881-1934) in 1923. Among these ideals was the cultivation of a purely Turkish culture; the Syllabists — Orhan Seyfi Orhon (1890-1972), Faruk Nafiz Çamlibel (1898-1973), Enis Behiç Koryürek (1891-1949), Halit Fahri Ozansoy (1891-1971), and Yusuf Ziya Ortaç (1895-1967) — supported this by reviving folk poetry and lore, and adhering to the simple meter, Turkish vocabulary, and vernacular style employed by traditional Turkish folk poets. Adhering to some of the traditional subject matter, they wrote love poetry and poetry inspired by the natural world as well as patriotic verse. Like the NATIONAL LITERATURE and YOUNG PENS writers before them, they aided the linguistic and cultural reforms of the 1920s and 1930s by keeping Arabic and Persian vocabulary and syntax out of their work. The work of the Syllabist poets continued to influence the Turkish literary milieu into the 1940s.

❖•❖

Further Reading

Karpat, Kemal H. "Social Themes in Contemporary Turkish Literature." *The Middle East Journal* 14, 1-2 (winter, spring 1960).

SYMBOLIC MODERNISM
Norway, 1950s

A Norwegian poetry movement of the 1950s, Symbolic Modernism emphasized freedom from traditional rules governing meter, syntax, and association of imagery and ideas. Central figures included Peter R. Holm (1931-), Stein Mehren (1935-), and Tarjei Vesaas (1897-1970). During the 1960s the CONCRETE POETRY of Jan Erik Vold (1939-) and others largely deflated the movement's power and influence.

❖•❖

Further Reading

Chapman, Kenneth Garnier. *Tarjei Vesaas*. New York: Twayne, 1970.
Hermundsgård, Frode. *Child of the Earth: Tarjei Vesaas and Scandinavian Primitivism*. New York: Greenwood Press, 1989.
Thoe, J. Scott. *Vesaas' Imagery as a Key to the Interpretation of His Novels*. Doctoral thesis, University of Washington, 1975.
Vesaas, Tarjei. *30 Poems*. Selected and translated by Kenneth G. Chapman. Oslo: Universitetsforlaget, 1971.

SYMBOLISM: An Overview

Symbolism, a hugely influential international movement integral to the development of MODERNISM, began in the 1870s among a group of Parisian poets inspired by the earlier poet Charles BAUDELAIRE and led by Stéphane MALLARMÉ. The movement opened new floodgates to literary experimentation; its theories and fruits were a stepping stone to others in a time of growing complexity and uncertainty throughout Europe. The Symbolists searched for a literature that would reflect a deeper experience of existence than did REALIST or NATURALIST literature. In part, they were responding to limitations imposed by a materialistic reality governed by positivistic science. Their refusal to accept that science completely explained reality led to a renewed search for God and for the world hidden by the material world. Emanuel Swedenborg's (1688-1772) notion — "that everything, form, movement, number, color, perfume, in the spiritual as well as in the *natural*, is significant, reciprocal, converse, *correspondent*" — cast a long shadow over the Symbolists.

The use of symbols in literature is nothing new, of course. In the Western tradition, one can begin with Plato (c. 428-348 or 347 B.C.), who postulated the existence of a realm of true objects, of which objects in this world were only inadequate imitations, to the Neoplatonist philosopher Plotinus (205-270 A.D.), who reasoned that everything, being part of the divine, reveals imperfect traces of the divine, to Dante's (1265-1321) and medieval European mystics' religious and theological and, above all, allegorical usage, to the German Romanticists Friedrich Schelling (1775-1854), August Wilhelm Schlegel (1767-1845), and Goethe (1749-1832), to English Romantic poets Samuel Coleridge (1772-1834) and William Blake (1757-1827), to one of the French Symbolists' chief sources of inspiration, American writer Edgar Allan Poe (1809-1849). Broadly tracing the latter end of the tradition, critic Anna Balakian writes that the "romanticist aspired to the infinite, the symbolist thought he could discover it, the SURREALIST believed he could create it."

What was new about the Symbolists was that they used symbols to evoke and suggest, rather than stand for, realities. A symbol before the latter nineteenth century was, according to critic Henri Peyre (1901-1988), "a sign that as such demands deciphering, an interpretation by whoever is exposed to it or is struck by it and who wishes to understand it and savor its mystery. This sign represents or evokes in a concrete manner what is innate within it, the thing signified and more or less hidden. The two meanings, one concrete and the other ulterior and perhaps profound, are fused into a single entity in the symbol." To the French Symbolists, the possible meanings are multiple, depending upon who is interpreting the symbol.

As the initial wave of Modernism, particularly in such countries as France, Russia, and Germany, Symbolism spread to other countries, as writers from throughout the West—

Maurice MAETERLINCK and Émile Verhaeren (1855-1916) from Belgium, Stefan George (1868-1933) and Hugo von Hofmannsthal (1874-1929) from Germany, Jean Moréas (1856-1910) from Greece, Arthur Symons (1865-1945), W. B. YEATS (*see* MODERNISM, England and Ireland), and George Moore (1852-1933) from the British Isles, Azorín (pseud. of José Martínez Ruiz, 1873-1969) and Antonio (1875-1939) and Manuel (1874-1947) Machado from Spain, and Stuart Merrill (1863-1915) and Francis Viélé-Griffin (1864-1937) from the United States—found their way to Paris at some point or other during the turn of the century to personally acquaint themselves with the French Symbolists, but these foreign writers would interpret Symbolism according to their own aesthetic inclinations and heritage and transmute it into something distinct in their own literatures.

SYMBOLISM
Belgium, 1880s-1900s

While Parnassianism still held strong sway in Belgium's literary milieu, Symbolism got underway after some sputtering attempts largely through the efforts of poet and theorist Albert Mockel (1866-1945), a friend of French Symbolist Stéphane MALLARMÉ. During the early 1880s such literary magazines as *La Jeune Belgique* and *La Basoche* published works by Georges Rodenbach (1855-1898), Émile Verhaeren (1855-1916), and Maurice MAETERLINCK as well as French Symbolists such as René Ghil (1862-1925) and Stuart Merrill (1863-1915), but it wasn't until Mockel founded the literary review *La Wallonie* in 1886 that the new aesthetic had its own forum. Initially intending to publish regionalist literature popular at the time, in particular that of Wallonie, Mockel revised the magazine's focus to also "welcome the Symbolists not as a *governing* and pontificating school [alluding to the Parnassians and NATURALISTS] . . . [but as] a group of sincere and delicate artists who bring us what is New," thus feeding the polemical fires and ensuring several years of sometimes biting, sometimes amusing debate between the opposing literary camps.

A considerably less antagonistic dialogue ensued through the late 1880s and early 1890s between the Belgian *La Wallonie* and the French *La Revue Indépendente*, with both magazines publishing and critiquing both French and Belgian Symbolists. A like literary reciprocity began in 1892 between the Belgian review *Floréal* and German Symbolist Stefan George's (1868-1933) new magazine *Die Blätter für die Kunst*.

The principal theoretical work on Symbolism in Belgium was Mockel's *Propos de littérature* (1894). The Belgian Symbolists favored the landscape of Belgium as a source from which to reap symbols to evoke the inner world and endeavored to write poetry that was affined as much with the visual arts as with music, with Charles Van Leberghe

(1861-1907), for example, citing English pre-Raphaelite painters Dante Rossetti (1828-1882) and Edward Burne-Jones (1833-1898) as providing inspiration for one of the most representative Symbolist poems, his *La Chanson d'Eve* (1904).

✥•✦

Maeterlinck, Maurice (1862-1949), Belgian dramatist, poet, and essayist.

Maeterlinck became acquainted with the work of Mallarmé, Paul VERLAINE, Arthur RIMBAUD, and Philippe de Villiers de l'Isle-Adam (1838-1889) when he spent time in Paris in the mid-1880s. He was a strong proponent of the position that Symbolism, more than an aesthetic, is constitutive of a worldview conducive to fostering the soul. He was largely responsible for creating Symbolist theater, in which characterization is subordinated to the suggestion of impressions; plot is subordinated to scene, light, and sound; and dialogue to repetitious, incantational sounds, and phrases resembling music — all of it more the enactment and presentation of Symbolist poetry than dramatization of a conventional plot with conflict and action.

Maeterlinck was inspired by Villiers de l'Isle-Adam and his play *Axël* (1890; *Axel*, 1925) as well as by the mystics Emanuel Swedenborg (1688-1772) and Jan van Ruysbroeck (1293-1381). His Symbolist plays include *La princesse Maleine* (1889; *Princess Maleine*, 1894), *L'Intruse* (1890; *The Intruder*, 1894), *Les aveugles* (1890; *The Blind*, 1894), and *PELLÉAS ET MÉLISANDE* (1892; *Pelléas and Mélisande*, 1894). These are considered precursory to such later theater as that of Samuel BECKETT (*see* THEATER OF THE ABSURD). Though best known as a dramatist, Maeterlinck also wrote a volume of poetry, *Serres chaudes* (1889; Hothouses), and metaphysical, philosophical prose in *Le trésor des humbles* (1896; *The Treasure of the Humble*, 1897), *La vie des abeilles* (1901; *The Life of the Bee*, 1901), and *La vie des termites* (1926; *The Life of the White Ant*, 1927). He influenced German Symbolist dramatists Gerhart Hauptmann (1862-1946) and Hugo von Hofmannsthal (1874-1929) and attracted the admiration of Mallarmé. Maeterlinck won the Nobel Prize for literature in 1911.

Pelléas et Mélisande (1892; *Pelléas and Mélisande*, 1894).

Maeterlinck's best-known play was first produced in 1893 and is widely considered a masterpiece of Symbolist theater. In 1902 Claude Debussy wrote an opera based on it. Goulad, the prince of a fictional kingdom, meets Mélisande, a young woman with no knowledge of her past and no sense of her identity, in the forest and marries her. She soon meets and falls in love with Pelléas, Goulad's brother, after which Goulad kills Pelléas. Mélisande dies giving birth to Goulad's child. True to his Symbolist vision, Maeterlinck depicts the characters as having no control over these events, their lives and deaths determined by fate.

725

❖•❖

Further Reading

Balakian, Anna. *The Symbolist Movement: A Critical Appraisal*. New York: New York University Press, 1977.

Cornell, Kenneth. *The Symbolist Movement*. New Haven, Conn.: Yale University Press, 1951.

Hess, Elizabeth. "The Symbolist Movement in Belgium." In *The Symbolist Movement in the Literature of European Languages*. Edited by Anna Balakian. Budapest: Akadémiai Kiadó, 1982.

Legrand, Francine-Claire. *Symbolism in Belgium*. Brussels: Laconti, 1972.

Mallinson, Vernon. *Modern Belgian Literature, 1830-1960*. New York: Barnes & Noble, 1966.

Mathews, Andrew Jackson. *'La Wallonie' 1886-1892: The Symbolist Movement in Belgium*. New York: King's Crown Press, 1947.

Sondrup, Steven P. *Hofmannsthal and the French Symbolist Tradition*. Bern: H. Lang, 1976.

SYMBOLISM
Bulgaria, 1905-1920s

Symbolism in Bulgaria grew dominant after the first Symbolist poems were published in the literary magazine *MISUL* (Thought) in 1905, a journal which fostered the spread of Western art and literature to Bulgaria. Principle practitioners included lyric poet Dimcho Debelyanov (1887-1916), killed in World War I; poet Nikolay Liliev (pseud. of Nikolay Mikhaylov, 1885-1960); and poet Geo Milev (pseud. of Georgi Kasabov, 1895-1925), who turned to EXPRESSIONISM after the war, and eventually Communism. Milev translated Russian and German Symbolists into Bulgarian. Other Bulgarian Symbolists were Lyudmil Stoyanov (n.d.), Emanuil Papdimitrov (n.d.), Christo Yassenov (1889-1925), and Peyo K. Yavorov (1878-1914), who was associated with *Misul*. A main theorist of the movement was Teodor Trayanov (1882-1945), also a major poet. His journal *Khiperion* (1922- ; Hyperion) sustained Symbolism past its heyday, into the 1920s. These poets read the works of the French, German, and Russian Symbolists, corresponded with them, and read their journals. Milev founded the magazine *Vezni* (1919- ; The Scales) as a forum for Symbolist poetry. But the Bulgarians' emphasis overall was more socially oriented than the French Symbolists' primacy of the individual, and not as influenced by such philosophers as Arthur Schopenhauer (1788-1860). With the rise of class conflicts they were more concretely concerned with social ethics. The Second Balkan War of 1913 coaxed several out of the Symbolist ivory tower toward nationalist sentiments; by the end of World War I and the Bolshevik revolution, remaining stragglers abandoned it as well.

An anthology appeared in 1907. Representative works include Trayanov's poetry collection *Regina mortua* (1908; The Dead Queen) and *Himni i baladi* (1911; Hymns and

726

Ballads), Milev's narrative poem *Septemvri* (1924; *September*, 1961), and Yavorov's *Bezsunitsi* (1907; Insomnias) and *Podir senkite na oblatsite* (1910; Chasing the Clouds' Shadows).

✤●✦

Further Reading

Dimov, Georgi. "Symbolism in Bulgarian Literature." In *The Symbolist Movement in the Literature of European Languages*. Edited by Anna Balakian. Budapest: Akadémiai Kiadó, 1982.

Moser, Charles A. *A History of Bulgarian Literature, 865-1944*. The Hague: Mouton, 1972.

Pinto, Vivian. *Bulgarian Prose and Verse*. London: The Athlone Press, 1957.

SYMBOLISM
Czechoslovakia, 1890s

Influenced by both French and Belgian Symbolists and by Czechoslovakia's own Romanticist tradition, many new trends in poetry flowered during the 1890s in Czechoslovakia including the Symbolist trend and free verse imported from Paris. Otokar Březina (pseud. of Václav Ignác Jebavy, 1868-1929), is the most representative Symbolist poet in Czechoslovakia, most of whose works were published between 1895 and 1901. He read the French Symbolists and their philosophical mentors Arthur Schopenhauer (1788-1860), Henri BERGSON, and Friedrich NIETZSCHE. Březina's volumes of poetry include *Tajemné dálky* (1895; Mysterious Expanses), with its fin de siècle mood, and *Svítání na západe* (1896; Dawn in the West), marking his mysticism and his shift to a more spiritually optimistic Symbolist outlook in *Vetry od pólu* (1897; Polar Winds). Karel Hlavácek (1874-1898) wrote in a more decadent, melancholy vein. His notable Symbolist collections are *Pozde k ránu* (1896; Shortly Before Dawn) and *Mstivá kantiléna* (1898; Vengeful Cantilena). Antonín Sova (1864-1928) was an exponent of free verse and other Symbolist techniques, especially in the section *Údolí nového království* (The Valley of a New Kingdom) in the volume *Jeste jednou se vrátíme* (1900; We Shall Return Once More). Another poet who experimented with the Symbolist mode was Otakar Theer (1880-1917). Symbolist fiction was not as remarkable, though some major novelists who were influenced by Symbolism were Ruzena Svobodová (1868-1920) and Frána Srámek (1877-1952).

✤●✦

Further Reading

Hájková, Alena. "Czech Symbolist Poetry." In *The Symbolist Movement in the Literature of European Languages*. Edited by Anna Balakian. Budapest: Akadémiai Kiadó, 1982.

727

SYMBOLISM
Denmark, 1890s

Symbolism in Denmark arose in the late 1880s as followers of Georg Brandes (1842-1927) — influenced also by Holger Drachmann (1846-1908; *see* NATURALISM, Denmark), the mysticism of NIETZSCHE, and contemporary French literature — favored intuition over scientific models and reacted against the REALISM and Naturalism that had been dominant in literary trends in Scandinavia since the 1870s. French Symbolist writing appeared in the journal *Ny Jord* (1888-89; New Soil) which also published the new generation of Danish writers inspired by them: Sophus Claussen (1865-1931), Viggo Stuckenberg (1863-1905), and Johannes Jørgensen (1866-1956). Helge Rode (1870-1937) is also often identified with the Danish Symbolists, especially his mystical religious poetry in *Hvide Blomster* (1892; White Flowers).

Claussen, whose poetry is closest to the French Symbolists', writes about his association with Paul VERLAINE and other French Symbolists while visiting Paris in *Antonius i Paris* (1896). Stuckenberg's Symbolist writing is best seen in his play *Den vilde Jæger* (1894; The Wild Hunter), in which the influence of Maurice MAETERLINCK can be detected (*see* SYMBOLISM, Belgium). Jørgensen was the movement's leading proponent and theorist in Denmark. His journal *Taarnet* (1893-94; The Tower) was a prominent vehicle for Symbolists in Denmark. (*Taarnet* was named after French Symbolist Joris Karl Huysmans's [1848-1907] protagonist Durtal's refuge in the novel *Là-Bas* [1891]). Jørgensen's works include the poetry volume *Stemringer* (1892; Moods) and translations of Charles BAUDELAIRE, Stéphane MALLARMÉ, and Stuart Merrill. He wrote the manifesto "Symbolism" that appeared in the journal *Tilskueren* (1892; The Spectator) and fed debate with the Naturalists who were critical of Symbolism. In 1896 Jørgensen converted to Catholicism and broke away from the Symbolist movement and from his friends Claussen and Stuckenberg. His most important Symbolist work was *Bekendelse* (1894; Confession), which shows his poetic development; the first part employs the Symbolist techniques of synesthesia and musicality, then the volume moves into nature and religious poetry.

✥•✥

Further Reading

Jones, W. Glyn. *Johannes Jørgensen*. New York: Twayne Publishers, 1969.

Sjoberg, Leif, and Niels Lyhne Jensen. "Symbolism in Denmark." In *The Symbolist Movement in the Literature of European Languages*. Edited by Anna Balakian. Budapest: Akadémiai Kiadó, 1982.

SYMBOLISM
England and Ireland, 1890s-1900s

English precursors of Symbolist writing include William Blake (1757-1827), Percy Bysshe Shelley (1792-1822), and, later, such AESTHETICS as Walter Pater (1839-1894) and Oscar Wilde (1854-1900) who added humor to the decadant style in such works as *The Picture of Dorian Gray* (1890). The French Symbolists had been influenced by English-language literature: leader Stéphane MALLARMÉ taught English literature, and many of their theoretical underpinnings derive from the work of an English-language poet—Edgar Allan Poe (1809-1849). Walt Whitman (1819-1892) was also admired.

But the French Symbolist movement reached the British Isles largely through poet and literary critic Arthur Symons (1865-1945). Symons visited Paris in 1890 and was befriended by Paul VERLAINE and other French Symbolists. George Moore (1852-1933) also had visited Mallarmé's salon in Paris and wrote about it in *Confessions of a Young Man* (1888), but it was Symons's account of the French movement in *The Symbolist Movement in Literature* (1899) that popularized it in England. In his account he wrote that Symbolism is "an attempt to spiritualise literature," "a literature in which the visible world is no longer a reality, and the unseen world no longer a dream."

On Symons's urging, Verlaine did a lecture tour in England in 1893. He and Symons also translated each other's poems. Symons relayed his experience to William Butler YEATS (*see* MODERNISM, England and Ireland). The latter, now considered a principal English practitioner of Symbolism, was already primed for the movement's mystical aspects when Symons brought the French to his attention while they were housemates in London in 1895-96. Yeats had joined Madame Helena Blavatsky's Theosophical Society in 1887, studied such mystical philosophers as Emanuel Swedenborg (1688-1772) and Jakob Boehme (1575-1624), and wrote about William Blake's Symbolist poetry.

Yeats later also visited Paris. He described his Symbolist verse system in *A Vision* (1925), based in part on channellings from his wife through automatic writing. Yeats's Symbolism informed his project to foster an IRISH RENAISSANCE, "an Irish literature which, though made by many minds, would seem the work of a single mind, and turn our places of beauty or legendary association into holy symbols." As part of the Renaissance, Sean O'CASEY (1880-1964), John Millington SYNGE (1871-1909), and, less successfully, Yeats brought Symbolist dramatic techniques to the theater at Dublin's ABBEY THEATER.

Representative Symbolist works by Yeats include the volumes *The Wind among the Reeds* (1899), informed by Charles BAUDELAIRE's poem "Correspondances," and *The*

Shadowy Waters (1900). In the essay "The Symbolism of Poetry" (1900), he writes: "all sounds, all colours, all forms, either because of their preordained energies or because of long association, evoke indefinable and yet precise emotions, or, as I prefer to think, call down among us certain disembodied powers, whose footsteps over our hearts we call emotions." The Great Memory holds humankind's most profound symbols and images— "whatever the passions of men have gathered about becomes a symbol in the Great Memory, and in the hands of him who has the secret it is a worker of wonders, a caller-up of angels or of devils." Further, "I believe in three doctrines: (1) That the borders of our mind are ever shifting, and that many minds can flow into one another, as it were, and create or reveal a single mind, a single energy. (2) That the borders of our memories are as shifting, and that our memories are part of one great memory, the memory of Nature herself. (3) That this great mind and great memory can be evoked by symbols."

Critics occasionally cite T. S. ELIOT as a Symbolist. He did not consider himself such, though he was inspired by the French, via Symons's book, and introduced some of their techniques—for example, the use of persona and symbolic use of images from the ordinary world—into the modern English poem, most notably in *THE WASTE LAND,* which made a huge impact after its publication in 1922 (*see* MODERNISM, England and Ireland). Eliot was introduced to the work of the French Symbolists through Symon's *The Symbolist Movement in Literature* (1899). As a result he read Jules Laforgue (1860-1887), Arthur RIMBAUD, then Paul Verlaine and Tristan Corbière (1845-1875). Eliot's objective correlative— "The only way of expressing emotion in the form of art is by finding an 'objective correlative'; in other words, a set of objects, a situation, a chain of events which shall be the formula of that *particular* emotion; such that when the external facts which must terminate in sensory experience, are given, the emotion is immediately evoked" — is a Symbolist tenet, echoing Mallarmé's definition of Symbolism as "evoking an object so as to reveal a mood or, conversely, the art of choosing an object and extracting from it an 'état d'âme'."

Others in England, such as Ezra POUND and D. H. LAWRENCE, had other ideas of what literature should do and be. Pound, for example, criticized the Symbolists in his *CANTOS,* in particular Yeats and Baudelaire, for Symbolism's subjectivity and privileging of dream over fact (*see* MODERNISM, England and Ireland).

✥•✥

Further Reading

Balakian, Anna. *The Symbolist Movement: A Critical Appraisal.* New York: New York University Press, 1977.

Balakian, Anna, ed. *The Symbolist Movement in the Literature of European Languages.* Budapest: Akadémiai Kiadó, 1982.

Bowra, C. M. *The Heritage of Symbolism*. London: Macmillan, 1967.

Donoghue, Denis. "Yeats: The Question of Symbolism." In *The Symbolist Movement in the Literature of European Languages*. Edited by Anna Balakian. Budapest: Akadémiai Kiadó, 1982.

Engelberg, Edward. *The Symbolist Poem: The Development of the English Tradition*. New York: Dutton, 1967.

Hamilton, Scott. *Ezra Pound and the Symbolist Inheritance*. Princeton, N.J.: Princeton University Press, 1992.

Temple, Ruth Z. "Eliot: An English Symbolist?" In *The Symbolist Movement in the Literature of European Languages*. Edited by Anna Balakian. Budapest: Akadémiai Kiadó, 1982.

Wilson, Edmund. *Axel's Castle: A Study in the Imaginative Literature of 1870-1930*. New York: Charles Scribner's Sons, 1931.

SYMBOLISM
France, 1870s-1890s

The Symbolist movement began in France during the 1870s and by late in the next decade had brought about not only a renewal of French poetry, which had been in decline since the rise of the prose-oriented REALIST and NATURALIST trends of the 1850s 60s, but also played a major role in the birth of MODERNISM. The principal Symbolists—Stéphane MALLARMÉ, Paul VERLAINE, and Arthur RIMBAUD—were profoundly indebted to Charles BAUDELAIRE and especially his volume of poetry *LES FLEURS DU MAL* (*Les Fleurs du Mal*, 1926), published in 1857. Therein they discovered aesthetic ideas upon which they built to counteract their dissatisfaction with Parnassianism, Realism, and Naturalism. Three other works, all published in 1873, had an important impact on the Symbolists: Rimbaud's *UNE SAISON EN ENFER* (*A Season in Hell*, 1932), *Les amours jaunes* by Tristan Corbière (Edouard Joachim, 1845-1875), and *Le Coffret de santal* by Charles Cros (n.d.), containing suggestive, musical poems concerned with sensation and emotion. The Symbolists also rebelled against the strong classical tradition in French literature, with its strict metrical rules, and brought subjectivity back to a poetry that had been ruled by the precise, realist, and scientifically oriented verse of the Parnassians, with whom Rimbaud and Verlaine had earlier in their careers been affiliated. The time was ripe for the Symbolists' aesthetic sensibility, with the end of the nineteenth century bringing with it in France a world-weary cultural mood known as fin de siècle and the popularity of mysticism during the latter half of the century in the form of Swedenborgism, after philosopher Emanuel Swedenborg (1688-1772).

Also referred to as Decadent poetry (*see* AESTHETICISM/DECADENCE), the Symbolists were rebelling against the Romantic tradition, though they also represented a return to Romanticism, with its emphasis on the subjective and the intuitive, as opposed to Realism. What was new about the Symbolists was their insistence that symbols should suggest emotions and ideas rather than describe or directly represent them. Mallarmé used the word *suggérer*— to awaken or propose the idea of a meaning. His definition of Symbolism is that which "evok[es] an object little by little so as to reveal a mood or, conversely, the art of choosing an object and extracting from it an 'état d'âme'." As in Romanticism, Symbolists and, later, SURREALISTS, searched for the mystical, the infinite, and the dreamworld that exists between this world and the next.

Paul Fort's (1872-1960) Théâtre d'art (1890-92) produced Symbolist plays by Maurice MAETERLINCK (*see* SYMBOLISM, Belgium), Jules Laforgue (1860-1887), Stuart Merrill (1863-1915), and others, and sometimes used musical accompaniment and atomizers to disperse perfume during performances. Composer Richard Wagner (1813-1883) was another large influence on the French Symbolists who attempted to convey through words what he did through music. Paul Valéry (1871-1945) saw Symbolism's goal as reclaiming from music what also belonged in poetry and described the effect as "this constant hovering between sound and sense." Edgar Allan Poe (1809-1849) was another theoretical source for the Symbolists' endeavors to write a musical poetry; he wrote "that indefiniteness is an element of the true musical expression [of poetry] . . . a suggestive indefiniteness of vague and therefore of spiritual *effect*." In fact, English literature in general played a role in several of the Symbolists' personal development. Mallarmé taught English literature, Verlaine had spent time in England, Merrill and Francis Viélé-Griffin (1864-1937) were Americans living in Paris. They also admired Walt Whitman's (1819-1892) free verse.

The Symbolists enlisted several techniques to prod open the veil separating the artist from the unseen, in particular, *vers libre* (free verse), prose poems, alliteration, assonance, synesthesia, and musicality—all in the service of portraying the subjective world of the poet and the attempt to reveal the infinite, the ineffable. They used symbols to suggest the Platonic ideal reality (often referred to by the Symbolists as the "essential Idea") of which the world is only an approximation, rather than to describe or define, and write a poetry that is evocative rather than comparative. Some symbols were used more often than others, for example: rain to suggest boredom; swans and lilies to suggest the quest for the ideal; the sea and bells to suggest spiritual misery; liturgical words for mystical ambiance.

René Ghil (1862-1925) wrote an early proto-manifesto, *Traité du Verbe* (1886), for which Mallarmé wrote a preface; later, Ghil propounded his theory of "école instrumentiste," which pushed to extremes the notion of musicality in poetry. But it was Jean Moréas (pseud. of Iannis Papadiamantopoulos, 1856-1910) who published the first manifesto of the French Symbolists on September 18, 1886, in the magazine *Le figaro*, in which he criticized "realist theater, naturalistic novels, and Parnassian poetry." The publication of Moréas's manifesto was met with denunciatory articles from many reviews. The new literature was attacked for obscurity and self-isolation of its practitioners, who were thought to be denying the "real world." A year earlier, responding to an article that accused the new poets of being decadents who were associated with morphine use, satanic ritual, and "perverted mysticism" — as the parodic Adore Floupette had described them — Moréas had referred to the new movement's practitioners as *symboliste*, and asserted their artistic quest for beauty and for the attempt to provide literary form for the Ideal. (Henri Beauclair [1860-1919] and Gabriel Vicaire [1848-1900] pulled off a literary hoax in 1885 which was a parody of decadence *Les Déliquescences d'Adoré Floupette, poète décadent*). Moréas cited as prose precursors Stendhal (1783-1842), Honoré de Balzac (1799-1850), Gustave FLAUBERT, and Edmond de GONCOURT (*see* REALISM, France) in *Les Premières Armes du symbolisme* (1899). In 1891 he broke away from the Symbolists and started the neoclassicist ÉCOLE ROMANE.

The French Symbolist movement peaked in influence between 1885 and 1895. Verlaine was instrumental in popularizing it, while Mallarmé was the acknowledged leader and driving force behind it since around 1884. He hosted gatherings on Tuesdays at his place on the rue de Rome, visited by numerous other European artists, such as Albert Mockel (*see* Symbolism, Belgium), future Surrealist André GIDE, the Portuguese poet Eugénio de Castro (1869-1944), British and Irish writers Oscar Wilde (1854-1900), Arthur Symons (1865-1945), W. B. YEATS (*see* MODERNISM, England and Ireland), and George Moore (1852-1933), Stefan George (1868-1933; *see* Symbolism, Germany), and such artists as Edgar Degas (1834-1917) and James Whistler (1834-1903). Other gatherings took place at banquets hosted by the magazine *La Plume* during the early 1890s.

Until the late 1880s, collaboration with Belgian Symbolists was important because of the lack of French journals publishing the Symbolists; Mockel's *La Wallonie* provided one of the few periodical outlets for the French Symbolists' work. Soon the gap was filled with *La Revue wagnérienne* (founded by Téodor de Wyzewa [1863-1917] and Édouard Dujardin [1861-1949]), *La Vogue* (1886; managed by Gustave Kahn [1859-1936]), *La Revue indépendante* (headed by Dujardin; after 1888 Kahn was literary criticism editor), *La Décadence* (1886), *L'Ermitage* (1890-), and *Le Mercure de France* (1890-1965).

While most French Symbolist output took the form of poetry, prose poetry, or drama, a few novels are worth mentioning. Joris Karl Huysmans's (1848-1907) novel *À rebours* (1884; *Against the Grain*, 1922) contributed to the public's impression of both the notion of the decadence of the Symbolists and Mallarmé's position as head of an important salon; the protagonist, modelled on Mallarmé, wishes to withdraw from material reality and live in his imaginative perception of experience. Wyzewa made a

Symbolist novelistic attempt with *Valbert* (1881), and Remy de Gourmont (1858-1915), better known as the editor of *Le Livre des masques* (1896, 1898; Book of Masks), published the novel *Sixtine* in 1890.

Other writers associated with the French Symbolist movement include the poets Paul Bourget (1852-1935) and Henri de Régnier (1864-1936), Marcel Schwob (1867-1905), dramatists Paul Claudel (1868-1955) and Philippe Auguste Mathias de Villiers de l'Isle-Adam (1838-1889), whose play *Axël* (1890; *Axel*, 1925) was highly influential. Tristan Corbiére and Jules Laforgue were not really members of the group, but T. S. ELIOT (*see* Symbolism, England and Ireland, and Modernism, England and Ireland) considered them Symbolists. Valéry came a bit later and revived Symbolist poetry toward the end of World War I.

Symbolism left an indelible mark on later writers, in France and around the world. By the mid to late 1890s, however, critical rumblings against Symbolism's obscurity and pessimism grew louder and the call to seek new directions gave rise to NATURISM, HUMANISME, and the beginnings of Surrealism.

Baudelaire, Charles (1821-1867), French poet and essayist.

Considered to have produced the first major modern Symbolist work, the poetry collection *Les fleurs du mal* (1857; *Les Fleurs du Mal*, 1926), Baudelaire attended the salon of Parnassian Théophile Gautier (1811-1872) from about 1849 and dedicated *Les fleurs du mal* to him. Later Symbolists all followed him in some measure. Edgar Allan Poe (1809-1849) was an enormous influence on Baudelaire who, upon first reading Poe in 1847, felt "a strange commotion." Poe's work did not so much inspire Baudelaire as reinforce his own aesthetic direction; Poe's *The Poetic Principle* (1850), for example, pointed to a kind of "pure poetry," in which poetry can aspire to being like music, an aspiration Baudelaire shared. About his aesthetic philosophy, Baudelaire wrote: "It is that admirable, that immortal instinct for Beauty which causes us to consider the Earth and its spectacles as a glimpse, as a *Correspondence* of Heaven. The insatiable thirst for what is beyond, and which life reveals, is the most living proof of our immortality. It is simultaneously by means of poetry and *across and beyond* poetry, by means of music and *across and beyond* music, that the soul glimpses the splendors situated beyond the tomb; and when an exquisite poem brings tears to the eyes, these tears are not the proof of an excess of enjoyment but they are much rather the witness of an irritated melancholy, of a postulation of the nerves, of a nature exiled in the imperfect and which would like to take immediate possession, on this earth of ours, of the paradise revealed. Thus the principle of poetry is, strictly and simply, the human aspiration towards a superior Beauty, and the manifestation of this principle is in an enthusiasm, a rapture of the soul; an enthusiasm quote independent of passion, which is the intoxication of the heart, and of truth, which is the nourishment of reason" (quoted from "Théophile Gautier" in *Oeuvres*; originally in "Notes Nouvelles sur Edgar Poe" in *Nouvelles Histoires Extraordinaires* [1857]). During his lifetime, Baudelaire also attracted attention for the novella *La Fanfarlo* (1847) and his critical writings of contemporary literature and art in reviews, in addition to his poetry.

Les fleurs du mal (1857; *Les Fleurs du Mal*, 1926).

This volume contains Baudelaire's most important poem, "Correspondances," considered a manifesto which holds that poetry should create bridges between the exterior, natural world and the inner world of the artist. Baudelaire was the first to integrate the Romanticist ideas of Swedenborg, particularly that of correspondences between the present world and the next, between the human and the divine — enormously influential to Symbolist proponents everywhere — into the writing of Symbolist poetry. The poem does betray, however, ambivalence about Swedenborgian doctrine and Baudelaire's seeming preference for earthly, sensual means, rather than spiritual ones, for bridging the outer world and the inner world of the individual. Shortly after the collection was published, authorities took Baudelaire to trial, charging that some of the content was morally offensive, and six of the poems were censored from the second edition, published in 1861.

✦•✦

Mallarmé, Stéphane (1842-1898), French poet and theorist.

Born in Paris, Mallarmé earned a living most of his life as an English teacher in various French towns. Eventually he settled in Paris where he would preside over the most significant literary meetingplace of the time. Mallarmé laid out the Symbolist movement's aesthetic principles in his important *Divagations* (1897), which was influenced partly by Poe, and which articulated Symbolism's main goal as to suggest rather than tell, and to create an atmosphere in which metaphysical truths can be realized rather than to reproduce material reality: "To name an object is to banish the major part of the enjoyment derived from a poem, since this enjoyment consists in a process of gradual revelation."

He also wrote about Symbolist theater in a series of articles titled "Sur le Théâtre" (1886-87). Other works include *Vers et Prose* (1887), though the dramatic poems *L'Aprés-midi d'un faune* (1876; The Afternoon of a Faun) and *Hérodiade* (1876-87) are considered his best. Artist Édouard Manet (1832-1883) illustrated the long poem *L'Aprés-midi d'un faune*, Mallarmé's most famous work. The poem follows the efforts of the faun Pan to escape material, worldly sensuality through the more powerful world of artistic imagination, memory, and dreams, in which the faun finds himself confused about whether he dreamed or remembered something. In *Hérodiade*, written at about the same time, Mallarmé carries out this escapist strategy to the point where the escaper is shown to tire of the escape. Mallarmé wrote progressively obscure poetry; he believed that the most meaningful symbols were those most meaningful to the person writing. His well-known swan sonnet, "Le vierge, le vivace et le bel aujourd'hui" (1885), presents the image of the beautiful bird silenced at the moment of its revelatory song. His last collection of verse, *Un Coup de dés* (1897; A Cast of the Dice) employed typographical oddities, and the poetry broke so many syntactical and punctuational rules some critics refer to it as anti-poetry.

❖•❖

Rimbaud, Arthur (1854-1891), French poet.

Rimbaud grew up in the Ardennes region of France and began his literary career very early on, in his teens running away from home to go to Paris. There he affiliated himself with the Parnassians, requesting publication in their journals. Verlaine, too, was early on a Parnassian. Rimbaud and Verlaine left Paris together in 1872, by then both having turned away from Parnassianism, only to return and get involved in the Symbolist movement. Their homosexual relationship and violent fights caused them to be outcasts in Paris literary society during the 1870s. Rimbaud then stopped writing by the time he was 22 and spent the rest of his life travelling, working as a trader in Ethiopia, only to return home ill and die at the age of 37. Rimbaud cultivated the idea of the poet-seer (le poète-voyant) or prophet who, through poetry, presented a vision of the higher reality beyond ordinary reality. His major works are the prose poems he mastered in *Une saison en enfer* (1873; *A Season in Hell*, 1932) and *Les Illuminations* (1886; *Rimbaud's Illuminations*, 1953), containing Rimbaud's major writings, which Verlaine published unbeknownst to Rimbaud while the latter was in Africa.

Une saison en enfer (1873; A Season in Hell, 1932).

Profoundly influential to later Symbolists, this collection of autobiographical prose and poetry has been compared to Dante's (c.1265-1321) *Divine Comedy* (1310-14), suggesting as it does a period of moral and spiritual crisis in Rimbaud's life, and describing tormenting visions of a descent into hell so that there can be a rising up, a spiritual regeneration via the "alchemy of the Word."

❖•❖

Verlaine, Paul (1844-1896), French poet.

As did Rimbaud, with whom he eventually had a tumultuous intimate relationship, Verlaine associated with the Parnassians early in his career, having been inspired to become a poet after reading Baudelaire's *Les Fleurs du Mal*. His *Les Poètes maudits*

736

(1883; The Cursed Poets) popularized the poets who would be associated with French Symbolism, with its biographical and critical articles on Rimbaud, Mallarmé, Villiers de l'Isle-Adam, and Corbiere. His manifesto is contained in the poem "L'Art poétique" (1874). Verlaine's most representative Symbolist work is *ROMANCES SANS PAROLES* (1874; *Romances without Words*, 1921); another notable collection is *Sagesse* (1881; Wisdom), composed while he was serving a two-year sentence for wounding Rimbaud with a gun when the latter tried to end their relationship.

Romances sans paroles (1874; *Romances without Words*, 1921).

This volume, widely considered his masterpiece, represents a poetic reinvigoration in Verlaine, in part, as a result of his relationship to Rimbaud and study of his poetry. In this collection Verlaine emphasizes the musicality of words over meaning and draws scenes evocative of various moods.

❖•❖

Further Reading

Austin, Lloyd. *Poetic Principles and Practice: Occasional Papers on Baudelaire, Mallarmé, and Valéry*. Cambridge, England: Cambridge University Press, 1987.

Babuts, Nicolae. *Baudelaire: At the Limits and Beyond*. Newark, Del.: University of Delaware Press; London: Associated University Presses, 1997.

Balakian, Anna. *The Symbolist Movement: A Critical Appraisal*. New York: New York University Press, 1977.

Balakian, Anna, ed. *The Symbolist Movement in the Literature of European Languages*. Budapest: Akadémiai Kiadó, 1982.

Bertocci, Angelo P. *From Symbolism to Baudelaire*. Carbondale, Ill.: Southern Illinois University Press, 1964.

Block, Haskell M. *Mallarmé and the Symbolist Drama*. Detroit: Wayne State University Press, 1977.

Bloom, Harold. *Stéphane Mallarmé*. New York: Chelsea House Publishers, 1987.

Bowie, Malcolm, Alison Fairlie, and Alison Finch, eds. *Baudelaire, Mallarmé, Valéry: New Essays in Honour of Lloyd Austin*. Cambridge, England: Cambridge University Press, 1982.

Bowra, C. M. *The Heritage of Symbolism*. London: Macmillan, 1967.

Chadwick, Charles. *Rimbaud*. London: The Athlone Press, 1979.

————. *Symbolism*. London: Methuen & Company Ltd., 1971.

Chiari, Joseph. *The Poetic Drama of Paul Claudel*. New York: Gordian Press, 1969.

————. *Symbolisme from Poe to Mallarmé: The Growth of a Myth*. Foreword by T. S. Eliot. London: Rockliffe, 1956.

Cornell, Kenneth. *The Symbolist Movement*. New Haven, Conn.: Yale University Press, 1951.

Fowlie, Wallace. *Poem & Symbol: A Brief History of French Symbolism*. University Park, Pa.: Pennsylvania State University Press, 1990.

Frey, John A. *Motif Symbolism in the Disciples of Mallarmé*. New York: AMS Press, 1957, 1969.

Hertz, David M. *The Tuning of the Word: The Musico-Literary Poetics of the Symbolist Movement*. Carbondale, Ill.: Southern Illinois University Press, 1987.

Houston, John P. *French Symbolism and the Modernist Movement: A Study of Poetic Structures*. Baton Rouge, La.: Louisiana State University Press, 1980.

————. *Patterns of Thought in Rimbaud and Mallarmé*. Lexington, Ky.: French Forum, 1986.

Houston, John P., and Mona Tobin Houston, eds. *French Symbolist Poetry: An Anthology*. Bloomington, Ind.: Indiana University Press, 1980.

Kugel, James L. *The Techniques of Strangeness in Symbolist Poetry*. New Haven, Conn.: Yale University Press, 1971.

La Sage, Laurent. *The Rhumb Line of Symbolism: French Poets from Sainte-Beuve to Valéry*. University Park, Pa.: Pennsylvania State University Press, 1978.

Lawler, James R. *The Language of French Symbolism*. Princeton, N.J.: Princeton University Press, 1969.

Lehmann, A. G. *The Symbolist Aesthetic in France, 1885-1895*. Oxford, England: Basil Blackwell, 1968.

MacIntyre, Carlyle F., trans. *French Symbolist Poetry*. Berkeley, Calif.: University of California Press, 1958.

Mangravite, Andrew, trans. *An Anthology of French Symbolist & Decadent Writing Based Upon "The Book of Masks" by Remy de Gourmont*. London: Atlas Press, 1994.

Millan, Gordan. *A Throw of the Dice: The Life of Stéphane Mallarmé*. New York: Farrar, Straus, Giroux, 1994.

Nicholls, Peter. *Modernisms: A Literary Guide*. Berkeley, Calif.: University of California Press, 1995.

Peyre, Henri, ed. *Baudelaire, a Collection of Critical Essays*. Englewood Cliffs, N.J.: Prentice-Hall, 1962.

————. *What Is Symbolism?* University, Ala.: University of Alabama Press, 1980.

Porter, Laurence M. *The Crisis of French Symbolism*. Ithaca, N.Y.: Cornell University Press, 1990.

Quennell, Peter. *Baudelaire and the Symbolists*. Freeport, N.Y.: Books for Libraries Press, 1971.

Raymond, Marcel. *From Baudelaire to Surrealism*. London: Methuen & Company Ltd., 1970.

St. Aubyn, Frederic C. *Stéphane Mallarmé*. Updated ed. Boston: Twayne Publishers, 1989.

Starkie, Enid. *Baudelaire*. London: Faber and Faber, 1957.

Symons, Arthur. *The Symbolist Movement in Literature*. London: W. Heinemann, 1899. Reprint, New York: AMS Press, 1980.

Thompson, William J., ed. *Understanding* Les fleur du mal: *Critical Readings*. Nashville, Tenn.: Vanderbilt University Press, 1997.

Turquet-Milnes, Gladys R. *The Influence of Baudelaire in France and England*. Folcroft, Pa.: Folcroft Library Editions, 1977.

West, T. G., ed. *Symbolism: An Anthology*. London: Methuen, 1980.

Wilson, Edmund. *Axel's Castle: A Study in the Imaginative Literature of 1870-1930*. New York: Charles Scribner's Sons, 1931.

Wing, Nathaniel. *The Limits of Narrative: Essays on Baudelaire, Flaubert, Rimbaud, and Mallarmé*. Cambridge, England: Cambridge University Press, 1986.

SYMBOLISM
Germany, 1880s-1900s

More commonly known in Germany as Neuromantik (New Romanticism), Moderne (Modernism), or der Kreis um Stefan George (Stefan George's Circle), notable characteristics of German Symbolism were the practitioners' anti-NATURALISM coupled with the use of classical illusions and the idealization of ancient Greek culture. Their chief representative was Stefan George (1868-1933), who attended Stéphane MALLARMÉ's salon when he spent time in Paris in the late 1880s and early 1890s, becoming acquainted with Paul VERLAINE and other French poets, and visited Belgium where he befriended Belgian Symbolists Charles Van Leberghe (1861-1907) and Émile Verhaeren (1855-1916). Upon his return to Germany George attracted such writers as his most prominent protégé, poet and dramatist Hugo von Hofmannsthal (1874-1929); critic Hermann Bahr (1863-1934), who, along with George, attended Mallarme's gatherings in Paris and referred to the movement as Impressionism; and literary historian Friedrich Gundolf (1880-1931), among others.

The group published a journal, *Blätter für die Kunst* (1892-1919; Pages on Art), through which they preached a free and intellectual art, aesthetics over reportage, attention to form, and the focus on creating beauty The first issue stated their intention to find "Spiritual Art according to the new emotional trends and formal goals — an art for art's sake." Working under the shadow of Goethe's definition — "True symbolism is present when the particular represents the universal, not as a dream or shadow, but as a vivid and instantaeous revelation of the inscrutable," where the inscrutable is God, nature, or Idea — German Symbolists tried to give the particular new meaning.

Representative German Symbolist works include George's poetry collections *Hymnen* (1890), *Pilgerfahrten* (1891), *Algabal* (1892), *Die Bücher der Hirten- und Preisgedichte, der Sagen und Sänge und der hängenden Gärten* (1895), and *Das Jahre der Seele* (1897); and Hofmannsthal's poems "Mein Garten," "Die Töchter der Gärtnerin," "Leben," and "Vorfühling," and the play *Das kleine Welttheater* (1897; *The Little Theater of the World*, 1961). Also counted among the German Symbolists are Gerhart HAUPTMANN (*see* FREIE BÜHNE), whose plays show the influence of Maurice MAETERLINCK's Symbolist theater (*see* SYMBOLISM, Belgium), and Rainer Maria Rilke (1875-1926), who, though he knew George, was never a member of the circle. Rilke picked up on Charles BAUDELAIRE's *LES FLEURS DU MAL*'s (1857; *Les Fleurs du Mal*, 1926) darker elements. His *Dinggedichte* (object poems) in the two-volume collection *Neue Gedichte* (1907-8; *New Poems*, 1964), are Symbolist in style, the most famous being "Der Panther" ("The Panther," 1940).

The German Symbolists influenced Willem Kloos (1859-1938) and Albert Verwey (1865-1937) who, after their visit to Germany, returned to Holland and started the MOVEMENT OF THE EIGHTIES. George inspired Gottfried Benn (1886-1956) tremendously (*see* EXPRESSIONISM, Germany). After 1900, though, George had abandoned his Symbolist tenets, though it was only then that his Symbolist verse had an effect on the German literary scene — in part, because of his disciples in the Circle. By the early years of the twentieth century other European trends were having an impact in Germany, FUTURISM and Filippo MARINETTI's anti-Symbolism, for instance, and other writers were seeking new directions for German literature. Preeminent among them were the STORM CIRCLE (*Der Sturm*) and the rise of Expressionism.

❖•❖

Further Reading

Balakian, Anna. *The Symbolist Movement: A Critical Appraisal.* New York: New York University Press, 1977.

Bithell, Jethro. *Modern German Literature, 1880-1950.* London: Methuen, 1959.

Broch, Hermann. *Hugo von Hofmannsthal and His Time: The European Imagination, 1860-1920.* Translated, edited, and with an introduction by Michael P. Steinberg. Chicago: University of Chicago Press, 1984.

Durzak, Manfred. "Models for Symbolism and Expressionism: Stefan George and Herwath Walden." In *The Symbolist Movement in the Literature of European Languages.* Edited by Anna Balakian. Budapest: Akadémiai Kiadó, 1982.

Gsteiger, Manfred. "Expectation and Resignation: Stefan George's Place in German and in European Symbolist Literature." In *The Symbolist Movement in the Literature of European Languages.* Edited by Anna Balakian. Budapest: Akadémiai Kiadó, 1982.

Kovach, Thomas A. *Hofmannsthal and Symbolism: Art and Life in the Work of a Modern Poet.* New York: P. Lang, 1985.

Wais, Kurt. "German Poets in the Proximity of Baudelaire and the Symbolists." In *The Symbolist Movement in the Literature of European Languages.* Edited by Anna Balakian. Budapest: Akadémiai Kiadó, 1982.

SYMBOLISM
Lithuania, 1900s-1920s

The Russian Symbolists inspired several Lithuanian poets who made an impact on Lithuanian literature between the Russian revolutions of 1905 and 1917. These poets worked in a social environment largely hostile to the non-nationalist impulses Symbolist poetry presented. Considered decadent by many of their peers, such poets as Jurgis Baltrusaitis (1873-1944), Balys Sruoga (1896-1947), Vincas Mykolaitis Putinas (1893-1967), and Faustas Kirsa (1891-1964) held that poetry should express the transcendent in human existence through the use of symbols, in which a symbol of the exterior world becomes a symbol for interior experience. Putinas wrote that the artist "created a higher synthesis" by using art to unite the material world with the "immortal idea of deity into perfect harmony."

Baltrusaitis held a literary salon in Moscow, attended by Sruoga as well as the Russian Symbolists Andrey BELY, Valery Yakovlevich Bryusov (1873-1924), Konstantin Bal'mont (1867-1943), and Vyacheslav Ivanovich Ivanov (1866-1949). Sruoga, influenced by Baltrusaitis, Bal'mont, and Paul VERLAINE (*see* SYMBOLISM, France), spearheaded the move in Lithuanian poetry away from nationalism and toward literary freedom and experimentation.

Representative works of the Lithuanian Symbolists include Putinas's poetry volumes *Pastai* (1921; Works) and *Tarp dvieju ausfa* (1927; Between Two Dawns), and Sruoga's collections of poems, *Saule ir smiltys* (1920; Sun and Sand) and *The Dievu takais* (1923; The Tropes of the Gods).

❖•❖

Further Reading

Kubilis, Vitautas. "Symbolism in Baltic Literatures." In *The Symbolist Movement in the Literature of European Languages*. Edited by Anna Balakian. Budapest: Akadémiai Kiadó, 1982.

Rubulis, Aleksis. "Lithuanian Literature." In his *Baltic Literature: A Survey of Finnish, Estonian, Latvian, and Lithuanian Literatures*. Notre Dame, Ind.: University of Notre Dame Press, 1970.

SYMBOLISM
Portugal, 1890s-1920s

Portuguese writers were active in the Symbolist Movement — which originated in France in the late nineteenth century with the innovative work of such poets as Charles BAUDELAIRE, Paul VERLAINE, Stéphane MALLARMÉ, and Arthur RIMBAUD — during the first two decades of the twentieth century. Like their French models, the Portuguese Symbolists used bold imagery, unconventional rhyme schemes or "free verse," and highly metaphorical language, focusing on the emotions and attempting to liberate art from moral constraints. In addition to the most famous of their group, Eugénio de Castro (1869-1944), the Portuguese Symbolists included Antonio Nobre (1867-1903) and Camilo Pessanha (1867-1926), a native of the Portuguese colony of Macau. The preface to Castro's volume *Oaristos* (1890; Intimacies) became a treatise for the Portuguese Symbolists. Challenging what he viewed as the empty, commonplace rhetoric of his poetic predecessors, Castro called for a poetry that celebrated art for art's sake and elevated word play over meaning. The poems in Nobre's *So* (1892; Alone) contain traces of the mysterious, quintessentially Portuguese blend of anguish and nostalgia known as *saudosismo* (*see* PORTUGUESE RENASCENCE). Pessanha's poetry is marked by an ethereal lyricism and brooding sense of alienation; in his best-known volume, *Clepsidra* (1920; Water Clock), he employs natural images of movement and change to reflect emotional turbulence.

✦●✦

Further Reading

Campbell, Roy. *Portugal*. London: Max Reinhardt, 1957.

Faria, Almeida, Alberto de Lacerda, Vianna Moog, Jorge de Sena, and Robert D. Pring-Mill. *Studies in Modern Portuguese Literature*. Tulane Studies in Romance Languages and Literature, No. 4. New Orleans, La.: Tulane University, 1971.

Moser, G. "Portuguese Literature in Recent Years." *Modern Language Journal* 44 (1960): 245-54.

————. "Portuguese Writers of This Century." *Hispania* 50 (1966): 947-54.

Sayers, Raymond S. "The Impact of Symbolism in Portugal and Brazil." In *Waiting for Pegasus: Studies of the Presence of Symbolism and Decadence in Hispanic Letters*. Edited by Roland Grass and William R. Risley. Macomb, Ill.: Western Illinois University, 1979.

Schneider, Marshall J., and Irwin Stern, eds. *Modern Spanish and Portuguese Literatures*. New York: Continuum, 1988.

SYMBOLISM
Romania, 1900s-1910s

The Symbolist literary trend played a role in revitalizing Romanian literature early in the twentieth century. Alexandru Macedonski (1854-1920) headed the aesthetic rebellion against the earlier nineteenth-century Junimea (Youth) group, which shunned the merging of politics and literature as well as sponsored high standards, some argued elitist, for literary production.

As the leader of the Symbolist movement in Romania, Macedonski, who had lived in France for several years and wrote some volumes of poetry in French, started a journal, *Literatorul* (The Literary Man), to be a forum for Symbolist and other MODERNIST writing as well as socially and politically engaged literature in reaction against Junimea. Macedonski inspired other Romanian poets to experiment with innovations in poetic styles and themes, among them, Dimitrie Anghel (1872-1914), Ion Minulescu (1881-1944), and Ovid Densusianu (1873-1937), who founded another journal for the Romanian Symbolists, *Viata nova* (New Life). George Bacovia (1884-1957) had a notable influence on later poets. His first volume was *Plumb* (1916; Lead), which exhibited the Symbolist tendency in its poems' musicality and pessimism.

Adherents of the roughly contemporary movements in Romania, POPORANISM and SĂMĂNĂTORISM — both of which advocated poetry for and about the peasantry — opposed Symbolism's internationalism and decadence.

⇒•⇐

Further Reading

Angelescu, Victor. "Romanian Literature." In *Columbia Dictionary of Modern European Literature*. 2nd ed. Jean-Albert Bédé and William B. Edgerton, gen. eds. New York: Columbia University Press, 1980.

Demaitre, Ann. "Romanian Literature." In *Encyclopedia of World Literature in the Twentieth Century*. 3rd ed. Edited by Steven R. Serafin. Farmington Hills, Mich.: St. James Press, 1999.

SYMBOLISM
Russia, 1890s-1917

Called the Silver Age of Russian culture, Symbolism in Russia ushered in an era of cultural rebirth until it became a casualty of the Bolshevik Revolution of 1917. The Russian Symbolists were in part reacting against literary REALISM — by the 1880s the great Russian Realists' heyday had passed — as well as materialism, Darwinism, and industrialization. Literary historians usually consider 1892 to be the year of Symbolism's birth in Russia, seeing the publication of Dmitry Merezhkovsky's (1865-1941) collection of poems *Simvoly* (Symbols) as well as his famous lecture, "O prichinakh upadka i o novykh techeniyakh sovremennoy russkoy literatury" (1893; "On the Causes of the Decline and on the New Currents in Russian Literature," 1975), which was considered a manifesto. Merezhkovsky proposed that Russian poets reinvigorate the lyric tradition by paying attention to French Symbolist poetry. The transcript of his lecture appeared in print in the September 1892 issue of *Vestnik Evropy* (The European Herald), which also published a long article on the French Symbolists.

The Russian Symbolists — Alexandr BLOK, Andrey BELY, Valery Yakovlevich Bryusov (1873-1924), Vyacheslav Ivanovich Ivanov (1866-1949), Konstantin Bal'mont (1867-1943), and others—were not a single cohesive group, but a conglomerate of associations between writers. No single manifesto spoke for them all, but one of Bal'mont's essays, "An Elementary Statement about Symbolist Poetry," was prominent.

Far more so than the French, the Russian Symbolists expressed feelings of end-of-the-century apocalypticism and malaise; Bely, in fact, thought the color of the sunset seemed to change around the year 1900. There was also a mood of foreboding, of some impending newness; the feeling among many was that time had stopped and progress had halted. Literature had been largely socially didactic and utilitarian. Symbolism to the Russians had potential as a renewing philosophical and spiritual system, a world

743

view, a way of life. Ivanov and Blok, for example, tended to be even more religiously and mystically oriented than the French and the Belgians and viewed Symbolism as leading to a higher reality.

The Russian Symbolists were informed by the influence of lyric poets Fyodor Tyutchev (1803-1873) and Afanasy Fet (1820-1892) and by the French Symbolists after their works found their way into Russia in the 1890s, especially Charles BAUDELAIRE's poem "Correspondances." But philosopher and poet Vladimir Solovyov (1853-1900) is considered the most important forerunner of the Russian Symbolist poets. Open to Western thought, as opposed to the contemporary slavophilic trend, Solovyov wrote lyric mystical poetry and held that symbols express the metaphysical. He penned some lines that became a slogan: "Dear friend, you do not see / That everything visible / Is only a reflection, only a shadow / Of that which is invisible to our eyes."

The journal *Vesy* (1904-9; The Scales), edited by Bryusov, was the Russian Symbolists' primary forum. Its first issue contained another manifesto by Bryusov — "Keys to the Mysteries"; the following year he published "A Holy Sacrifice," in which he discusses a Symbolist's aesthetic role. Other journals that published the Symbolists' work included *Mir Iskusstva* (1899-1904; World of Art), *Apollon* (1909-17; Apollo), *Zolotoe runo* (1906-9; The Golden Fleece), and later, *Trudy i dní* (1912-16; Works and Days).

When Bryusov published his anthology of the Russian Symbolists, *Russkiye simvolisty* (1894-95; Russian Symbolists), it attracted much critical attention. Other important Russian Symbolist works were Blok's poem "Dvenadtsat" (1918; "The Twelve," 1920); Bal'mont's collection *Pod severnym nebom* (1894; Under the Northern Sky), which contains original poems as well as translations of such English-language poets as Edgar Allan Poe (1809-1849), Walt Whitman (1819-1892), and Percy Bysshe Shelley (1792-1822); and Bely's poems in *Zoloto v lazuri* (1904; Gold in the Azure) and *Pepel* (1909; Ashes) and theoretical writings in *Simvolizm* (1910; Symbolism) and *Lug zelyony* (1910; The Green Meadow). Other Russian Symbolists were Fyodor Sologub (1863-1927), whose poems and novels reveal a dualistic view of the world; poet, novelist, and essayist Zinaida Hippius (or, Gippius; 1869-1945) who married Merezhkovsky and later wrote political poetry; and poet Innokenty Fedorovich Annensky (1856-1909) who also wrote tragic plays along classical lines with modern psychological analysis.

Though the Bolshevik Revolution put an effective end to Russian Symbolism and other such manifestations of "bourgeois decadence," it had suffered from some splintering as early as 1910, when Blok, Bely, and Ivanov argued against Bryusov, who held Symbolism to be only an aesthetic method. By the beginning of World War I ACMEISM and FUTURISM had risen up prominently in opposition to the Symbolists' mysticism.

❖•❖

Bely, Andrey (pseud. for Boris Nikolaevich Bugayev, 1880-1934)
Russian poet, novelist, and theorist.

His interest in the ideas of occultist philosopher Rudolph Steiner (1861-1925), founder of anthroposophy, a division of theosophy, led Bely to adopt his pseudonym in an effort to avoid embarrassing his well-known mathematician father. Bely's important theoretical writings appear in *Simvolizm* (1910; Symbolism) and *Lug zelyony* (1910; The Green Meadow), which discuss the use of the sounds of words to provoke certain emotional responses: "Music . . . is the very soul of all the arts. Every true symbol is necessarily musical." The drive to make poetry musical is evident in his major poetry collections *Zoloto v lazuri* (1904; Gold in the Azure), *Pepel* (1909; Ashes), and *Urna* (1909; The Urn). Throughout his poetry, his apocalypticism is evident in the use of the images of the leopard, the sun, and Sophia, the feminine ideal of religious spirituality.

Bely's stylistically innovative novels have been compared to James JOYCE's *ULYSSES* (*see* MODERNISM, England and Ireland). *Peterburg* (1916; *Petersburg*, 1978) depicts a world on the verge of a time bomb explosion, and *Kotik Letayev* (1916; *Kotik Letaev*, 1971) employs STREAM OF CONSCIOUSNESS to convey the perceptual development of a child. Later, from 1918 to 1920, Bely affiliated himself with PROLETKULT.

❖•❖

Blok, Alexandr (1880-1921), Russian poet and dramatist.

Often considered the greatest Russian poet of the twentieth century, Blok is known for his mysticism, inspired by Vladimir Solovyev's (1853-1900), innovations in lyric drama, and use of inexact rhyme and meter. His collections of poetry include the idealistic *Stikhi o prekrasnoy dame* (1904; Poems about the Beautiful Lady), inspired by his wife, Lyubov Mendeleeva, and the later, darker volumes *Gorod* (1904-6; The City), *Snezhnaya maska* (1906-7; The Snow Mask), *Strashni mir* (1909-16; Horrible World), the Revolution-inspired "Dvenadtsat" (1918; "The Twelve," 1920), and *Skify* (1919; The Scythians). His plays include *Blalaganchik* (1906; *The Puppet Show*, 1963), *Neznakomka* (1907; The Stranger), *Pesnya sudby* (1909; *The Song of Fate*, 1938), and *Roza i krest* (1913; *The Rose and the Cross*, 1936).

"Dvenadtsat" (1918; "The Twelve," 1920).

Divided into twelve sections and providing a good example of Blok's metrical innovations, the poem envisions Christ's return during the violent 1917 revolution in St. Petersburg, leading twelve Red Army soldiers, who turn out to be, implicitly, the twelve apostles.

❦•❦

Further Reading

Auty, Robert, and Dimitri Obolensky, eds. *An Introduction to Russian Language and Literature*. Cambridge, England: Cambridge University Press, 1977.

Barnes, Christopher J., ed. *Studies in Twentieth-Century Russian Literature: Five Essays*. New York: Barnes & Noble, 1976.

Bristol, Evelyn. "Idealism and Decadence in Russian Symbolist Poetry." *Slavic Review* 39 (1980): 269-80.

Christa, Boris. "Andrey Bely and the Symbolist ." In *The Symbolist Movement in the Literature of European Languages*. Edited by Anna Balakian. Budapest: Akadémiai Kiadó, 1982.

Donchin, Georgette. *The Influence of French Symbolism on Russian Poetry*. The Hague: Mouton, 1958.

Elsworth, John, ed. *The Silver Age in Russian Literature: Selected Papers from the Fourth World Congress for Soviet and East European Studies, Harrogate, 1990*. New York: St. Martin's Press, 1992.

Erlich, Victor, ed. *Twentieth-Century Russian Literary Criticism*. New Haven, Conn.: Yale University Press, 1975.

Green, Michael, ed. *The Russian Symbolist Theatre: An Anthology of Plays and Critical Texts*. Ann Arbor, Mich.: Ardis Publishers, 1986.

Holthusen, Johannes. *Twentieth-Century Russian Literature: A Critical Study*. New York: Frederick Ungar Publishing Company, 1972.

Kalbouss, George. *The Plays of the Russian Symbolists*. East Lansing, Mich.: Russian Language Journal, 1982.

Kobilinski-Ellis, Leo. *Russian Symbolists*. Letchworth, England: Bradda Books, 1972.

Malmstad, John E., ed. *Andrey Bely: Spirit of Symbolism*. Ithaca, N.Y.: Cornell University Press, 1987.

Maslenikov, Oleg A. *The Frenzied Poets: Andrey Biely and the Russian Symbolists*. Berkeley, Calif.: University of California Press, 1952.

Paperno, Irina, and Joan Delaney Grossman, eds. *Creating Life: The Aesthetic Utopia of Russian Modernism*. Stanford, Calif.: Stanford University Press, 1994.

Peterson, Ronald E. *A History of Russian Symbolism*. Amsterdam: John Benjamins Publishing Company, 1993.

Peterson, Ronald E., ed. *The Russian Symbolists: An Anthology of Critical and Theoretical Writings*. Ann Arbor, Mich.: Ardis, 1986.

Pyman, Avril. *A History of Russian Symbolism*. Cambridge, England; New York: Cambridge University Press, 1994.

―――. *The Life of Aleksandr Blok*. 2 vols. Oxford, England; New York: Oxford University Press, 1979-80.

Rice, Martin P. *Valery Briusov and the Rise of Russian Symbolism*. Ann Arbor, Mich.: Ardis, 1975.

Richardson, William. *Zolotoe Runo and Russian Modernism, 1905-1910*. Ann Arbor, Mich.: Ardis, 1986.

Russian Literature Triquarterly 4 (1972). Symbolism issue.

Wachtel, Michael. *Russian Symbolism and Literary Tradition: Goethe, Novalis, and the Poetics of Vyacheslav Ivanov*. Madison, Wis.: University of Wisconsin Press, 1994.

West, James. *Russian Symbolism: A Study of Vyacheslav Ivanov and the Russian Symbolist Aesthetic*. London: Methuen, 1970.

SYMBOLISM
Ukraine, 1910s-1920s

Symbolism reached the Ukraine later than other countries on the Eurasian continent. Prior to its nationhood, reached in 1918, Ukrainian literature had been dominated by folk traditions until literature in the Ukrainian language was outlawed by the Russian Empire in 1876. Mykola Filyansky (1873-1937) was an early practitioner of Symbolist verse. Pavlo Tychyna (1891-1967) was one of Ukraine's greatest and most popular MODERNIST poets. His most notable collection was *Sonyashni Klyarnety* (1918; The Clarinets of the Sun); later he continued to write under the strictures of SOCIALIST REALISM. Other poets who experimented with Symbolist writing were Volodymyr Kobylyansky (1895-1919), whose sole volume of poetry was *My dar* (1920; My Gift), inspired by German Romanticists; Yakiv Savchencko (1890-1937), whose work was marked by a mystical pessimism; Volodymyr Svidzinsky (1885-1941); and Dmytro Zahul (1890-1938).

❖•❖

Further Reading

Andrusyshen, C. H., and Watson Kirkconnell, eds. *The Ukrainian Poets 1189-1962*. Toronto: University of Toronto Press, 1963.

Cyzevs'kyj, Dmytro. *A History of Ukrainian Literature*. 2nd ed. New York; Englewood, Col.: The Ukrainian Academy of Arts and Sciences and Ukrainian Academic Press, 1997.

T

TAHT AL-SUR. *See* UNDER THE RAMPARTS

TALLER GROUP
Mexico, 1939-1941

A short-lived, but influential Mexican movement of the late 1930s and early 1940s, the Taller Group owed its socially conscientious, EXISTENTIALIST tenor to poet Octavio Paz (1914-1998), also known for his association with SURREALISM.

Further Reading

Ivask, Ivar, comp. *The Perpetual Present: The Poetry and Prose of Octavio Paz*. Norman, Okla.: University of Oklahoma Press, 1973.

Kushigian, Julia Alexis. *Orientalism in the Hispanic Literary Tradition: In Dialogue with Borges, Paz, and Sarduy*. Albuquerque, N.Mex.: University of New Mexico Press, 1991.

Paz, Octavio. *One Word to the Other: Octavio Paz*. Translated by Amelia Simpson. Mansfield, Tex.: Latitudes, 1992.

Underwood, Leticia Iliana. *Octavio Paz and the Language of Poetry: A Psycholinguistic Approach*. New York: P. Lang, 1992.

Wilson, Jason. *Octavio Paz*. Boston: Twayne, 1986.

———. *Octavio Paz, A Study of His Poetics*. Cambridge, England: Cambridge University Press, 1979.

TANK GROUP
Ukrainian emigrés in Poland, 1930s

Founded during the 1930s in Warsaw, the Tank Group was an important center of literary activity for Ukrainian emigrés. Two such writers were poet and novelist Natalia Livytska-Kholodna (1902-) and poet Yury Lypa (1900-1944).

❧•❧
Further Reading

Kindratovych, Petro. "Yuriy Lypa: On the 50th Anniversary of His Tragic Death." *Ukrainian Review* 41, 3 (1994): 64-66.

Luckyj, George S. N. "Western Ukraine and Emigration, 1919-39." In his *Ukrainian Literature in the Twentieth Century.* Toronto: University of Toronto for the Shevchenko Scientific Society, 1992.

TEATRO DEL GROTTESCO. *See* THEATER OF THE GROTESQUE

TEL QUEL GROUP
France, 1960s-1980s

Launched during the 1960s in France by theorist and novelist Philippe Sollers (pseud. of Philippe Joyaux, 1936-), later a proponent of the Nouveau Nouveau Roman (New New Novel; *see* NEW NOVEL), *Tel Quel* was a leftist-oriented, avant-garde journal which supported the idea of a broad cultural revolution within the country. The group of writers and intellectuals associated with or hailed by *Tel Quel*—among them Sollers's wife, FEMINIST CRITIC Julia Kristeva (1941-); DECONSTRUCTIONIST Jacques DERRIDA, STRUCTURALISTS Roland Barthes (1915-1980) and Michel Foucault (1926-1984); and New Novelist Alain ROBBE-GRILLET—were united in their sharply analytical approaches to language, particularly their skeptical view of the mimetic and semantic properties of words, particularly when founded upon outdated philosophies and value systems. Like much of the French counter-orthodoxy, *Tel Quel* dwindled in influence by the late 1970s but continued to be regarded as an important force in Postmodernist thought.

❧•❧
Further Reading

Barthes, Roland. *Writer Sollers.* Translated and introduced by Philip Thody. Minneapolis: University of Minnesota Press, 1987.

Burke, Seán. *The Death and Return of the Author: Criticism and Subjectivity in Barthes, Foucault and Derrida.* Edinburgh, Scotland: Edinburgh University Press, 1992.

Caws, Mary Ann, ed. *About French Poetry from Dada to "Tel Quel": Text and Theory.* Detroit: Wayne State University Press, 1974.

Champagne, Roland A. *Literary History in the Wake of Roland Barthes: Re-Defining the Myths of Reading.* Birmingham, Ala.: Summa Publications, 1984.

———. *Philippe Sollers.* Amsterdam; Atlanta, Ga.: Rodopi, 1996.

Crownfield, David R. *Body/Text in Julia Kristeva: Religion, Women, and Psychoanalysis.* Albany, N.Y.: State University of New York Press, 1992.

Culler, Jonathan. *Roland Barthes*. New York: Oxford University Press, 1983.

Dillon, M. C. *Semiological Reductionism: A Critique of the Deconstructionist Movement in Postmodern Thought*. Albany, N.Y.: State University of New York Press, 1995.

Doane, Janice, and Devon Hodges. *From Klein to Kristeva: Psychoanalytic Feminism and the Search for the "Good Enough" Mother*. Ann Arbor, Mich.: University of Michigan Press, 1992.

Ffrench, Patrick. *The Time of Theory: A History of* Tel Quel *(1960-1983)*. Oxford: Clarendon Press; New York: Oxford University Press, 1995.

Hayman, David. *Re-Forming the Narrative: Toward a Mechanics of Modernist Fiction*. Ithaca, N.Y.: Cornell University Press, 1987.

Kritzman, Lawrence. "The Changing Political Ideology of Tel Quel." *Contemporary French Civilization* 2 (1978): 405-21.

Lechte, John. *Julia Kristeva*. London: Routledge, 1990.

Marx-Scouras, Danielle. *The Cultural Politics of* Tel Quel*: Literature and the Left in the Wake of Engagement*. University Park, Pa.: Pennsylvania State University Press, 1997.

————. "Requiem for the Postwar Years: The Rise of Tel Quel." *French Review: Journal of the American Association of Teachers of French* 64, 3 (February 1991): 407-16.

Mowitt, John. *Text: The Genealogy of an Antidisciplinary Object*. Durham, N.C.: Duke University Press, 1992.

Payne, Michael. *Reading Theory: An Introduction to Lacan, Derrida, and Kristeva*. Oxford, England: Blackwell, 1993.

Ryan, Michael. *Marxism and Deconstruction: A Critical Articulation*. Baltimore, Md.: Johns Hopkins University Press, 1982.

Rylance, Rick. *Roland Barthes*. New York: Harvester Wheatsheaf, 1994.

Sim, Stuart. *Beyond Aesthetics: Confrontations with Poststructuralism and Postmodernism*. Toronto: University of Toronto Press, 1992.

Tel Quel. Paris: Editions du Seuil, 1960-1982.

Thompson, William, ed. *The Contemporary Novel in France*. Gainesville, Fla.: University Press of Florida, 1995.

TERAZ GROUP
Poland, 1960s-1970s

One of several innovative Polish poetry groups of the 1960s and 1970s, the Teraz Group is noted for its association with "naked poetry" and uncensored, underground publications. Two of its chief members were Julian Kornhauser (1946-) and Adam Zagajewski (1945-). Ryszard Krynicki (1943-), Edward Balcerzan (1937-), and Stanisław Barańczak (1946-) were also associated with Teraz.

✦•✦

Further Reading

Barańczak, Stanisław, and Clare Cavanagh, eds. *Polish Poetry of the Last Two Decades of Communist Rule: Spoiling Cannibals' Fun*. Evanston, Ill.: Northwestern University Press, 1991.

Davies, Robert A., and John M. Gogol, eds. *Citizen R. K. Does Not Live: Poems of Ryszard Krynicki*. Selected and introduced by Stanisław Barańczak. Forest Grove, Ore.: Mr. Cogito Press, 1985.

Zagajewski, Adam. *Canvas*. Translated by Renata Gorczynski, Benjamin Ivry, and C. K. Williams. New York: Farrar Straus Giroux, 1991.

———. *Solidarity, Solitude: Essays*. Translated by Lillian Vallee. New York: Ecco Press, 1990.

TERROIR SCHOOL
Canada, 1900-1930s

A French-Canadian movement begun in 1902, the Terroir School encouraged poetry founded upon native language, tradition, and ancestry. The most prolific member of Terroir was Blanche Lamontagne (1889-1958), who incorporated religion and folk songs in her work.

Further Reading

"Blanche Lamontagne-Beauregard." In *History of French-Canadian Literature*. Edited by Gerard Tougas. 2nd ed. Westport, Conn.: Greenwood Press, 1976.

"Lamontagne-Beauregard, Blanche." In *The Oxford Companion to Canadian History and Literature*. Edited by Norah Story. Toronto: Oxford University Press, 1967.

TESTING OF THE AGE (Khitsam or Khitsan)
Burma, 1930s

A Burmese movement, the Testing of the Age is thought to have begun in 1928 with the publication of poet and short-story writer Zodji's (also rendered Zawgyi; pseud. for U Thein Han, 1907-) *Pitauk Pan* (1928; The Padauk Flower); it flourished through the 1930s. The prose work of earlier writers U Hpo Kya (n.d.) and Pi Mounin (Pi Monin, 1883-1940) is said to foreshadow the development of the Khitsan style. Testing of the Age writers eschewed ornamental language and classical rules of composition for literature that embodied modern ideals and experiences, drawing on knowledge of Western literature and often depicting Burmese village life. They expressed a humanistic and nationalist spirit during the years that led up to the independence of Burma from Britain in 1947. Many of the members were influenced by their professor of Burmese literature at Rangoon University, Pe Maung Tin (1888-?). Short-story writer Theippam Maung Wa (Sein Tin, 1899-1942) is considered one of the foremost representatives of the movement. Other writers associated with the movement are poet Min Thuwum (1909-) and novelist, dramatist, and short-story writer Maun Htin (Htin Phat, 1909-). Several collections of Khitsan literature were published, including *Khitsam Kabja mja*

(1934 and 1941; Khitsan Poems), *Khitsam Poumpyin mja 1* (1934; Khitsan Stories I), and *Toumpwinhsain Khitsam Sapei* (1955; Trefoil of Khitsan Literature).

⤙•⤚
Further Reading

Aung San Suu Kyi. "Literature and Nationalism in Burma." In *Freedom from Fear and Other Writings*. Edited by Michael Aris. London: Viking, 1991. Originally published as "Socio-Political Currents in Burmese Literature, 1910-1940." In *Burma and Japan: Basic Studies on Their Cultural and Social Structure*. Tokyo: Burma Research Group, Tokyo University of Foreign Studies, 1987.

Min Latt. "Mainstreams in Burmese Literature: A Dawn That Went Astray." *New Orient: Journal for the Modern and Ancient Cultures of Asia and Africa* 3, 6 (1962): 172-76.

"Zawgyi's Patriotic Poems." *Oway Magazine* 5, 1 (January 1936).

THEATER GUILD
United States, 1919-1950

A branch of the Little Theater Movement in the United States that catered to an upscale, subscription audience, the Theater Guild was organized in 1919 by several members of the recently defunct WASHINGTON SQUARE PLAYERS. The Guild, based in New York City, quickly gained prestige for its presentation of the best literary dramas of the MODERNIST era. Founders Lawrence Langner (1890-1962) and Lee Simonson (1888-1967), among others, played crucial roles in selecting and directing dramas recognized for their brilliance and innovation. Works by George Bernard SHAW and Eugene O'NEILL dominated the Guild's playlist, but several other dramatists were also featured, including Leonid Andreyev (1871-1919), Maxwell Anderson (1888-1959), Philip Barry (1896-1949), Henrik IBSEN (*see* REALISM, Norway), Elmer RICE (*see* EXPRESSIONISM, United States), and August STRINDBERG and Ernst TOLLER (*see* Expressionism, Germany). The Guild also distinguished itself with successful revivals of classic plays by Ben Jonson (c. 1572-1637), Christopher Marlowe (1564-1593), and others.

By 1925 the Theater Guild, though still affiliated with Expressionism and other dramatic currents, had merged with mainstream commercial theater and it was left to such nascent movements as the GROUP THEATER, whose experimental beginnings the Guild reluctantly supported, to carry on the traditions of little theater. During the 1930s the Guild occasionally followed trends in leftist theater but tended generally towards noncontroversial works. In 1943 the Guild attained the height of its popularity with the Richard Rodgers (1902-1979) and Oscar Hammerstein (1895-1960) production of *Oklahoma!* In 1950 the Guild was taken over by the American National Theatre and Academy.

❖•❖
Further Reading

Eaton, Walter Prichard. *The Theatre Guild, the First Ten Years*. New York: Brentano's, 1929.
Langner, Lawrence. *G. B. S. and the Lunatic: Reminiscences of the Long, Lively and Affectionate Friendship between George Bernard Shaw and the Author*. New York: Atheneum, 1963.
———. *The Magic Curtain: The Story of a Life in Two Fields, Theatre and Invention, by the Founder of the Theatre Guild*. New York: Dutton, 1951.
Nadel, Norman. *A Pictorial History of the Theatre Guild*. New York: Crown Publishers, 1969.
Theatre Guild. *The Theatre Guild Anthology, with an Introduction by the Board of Directors of the Theatre Guild*. New York: Random House, 1945.
Waldau, Roy S. *Vintage Years of the Theatre Guild, 1928-1939*. Cleveland: Press of Case Western Reserve University, 1972.

THEATER LABORATORY
Poland, 1959-1969

Founded in 1959 and directed by Polish-born Jerzy Grotowski (1933-), the Theater Laboratory was a nomadic company that downplayed the use of props and design and assigned central importance to the technique and instincts of the actor. Grotowski, intensively concerned with dramatic training and the preservation of a noncommercial theater, eventually devoted himself entirely to research, teaching, and theory on these subjects. His impact on contemporary world theater is considerable; his influence has been noticed especially in the work of Royal Shakespeare Company director Peter Brook (1925-), choreographer Jerome Robbins (1918-1998), and Italian director Eugenio Barba (1936-), whose Odin Teatret (*see* THIRD THEATER) stemmed directly from his three year association with Grotowski.

❖•❖
Further Reading

Burzyński, Tadeusz, and Zbigniew Osiński. *Grotowski's Laboratory*. Translated by Bolesław Taborski. Warsaw: Interpress, 1979.
Grotowski, Jerzy. *Towards a Poor Theatre*. New York: Simon & Schuster, 1968.
Kolankiewicz, Leszek, ed. *On the Road to Active Culture: The Activities of Grotowski's Theatre Laboratory Institute in the Years 1970-1977*. Translated by Bolesław Taborski. Wrocław, Poland: Instytut Aktora-Teatr Laboratorium PrasZG, 1978.
Kumiega, Jennifer. *Laboratory Theatre/Grotowski/The Mountain Project*. Dartington, England: Dept. of Theatre, Dartington College of Arts, 1978.
———. *The Theatre of Grotowski*. London: Methuen, 1985.
Littlewood, Joan. *Joan's Book: Joan Littlewood's Peculiar History as She Tells It*. London: Methuen, 1994.

Osiński, Zbigniew. *Grotowski and His Laboratory*. Translated and abridged by Lillian Vallee and Robert Findlay. New York: PAJ Publications, 1986.

Richards, Thomas. *At Work with Grotowski on Physical Actions*. London: Routledge, 1995.

Temkine, Raymonde. *Grotowski*. Translated by Alex Szogyi. New York: Avon, 1972.

THEATER OF ALIENATION. *See* **BERLIN ENSEMBLE; EPIC THEATER**

THEATER OF CRUELTY
France, 1930s-1960s; also Germany, Poland, Spain, United States

Although short-lived and unsuccessful, the Theater of Cruelty was an important link in French drama between the early modern work of Alfred Jarry (1873-1907) and the post-World War II flowering of the THEATER OF THE ABSURD. Antonin Artaud (1896-1948), a follower of SURREALISM, began implementing his revolutionary conceptions of drama as early as 1927, when he opened his Théâtre Alfred Jarry with Roger Vitrac (1899-1952) in Paris. However, the Surrealist movement, under André BRETON's direction, proved if not hostile then at least indifferent to Artaud's goals and a true Surrealist theater never developed. Yet, convinced that the commercial theater of the future was one that powerfully affected the audience through all of the senses, that more resembled mystical ritual than simplistic romance, and that graphically exposed the heights and depths of human behavior, Artaud composed his first manifesto in 1932, "Le Théâtre de la Cruauté." As he outlined in this and following manifestos, collected as *Le Théâtre et son double* (1938; *The Theatre and Its Double*, 1958), the Theater of Cruelty's purpose was not to enact physical violence but instead to violently reveal — through mime, gesture, lighting, music, and scenery as well as language — the fundamental poetry of existence, the fundamental power and magic of human communication and thought.

Jarry's *Ubu Roi* (1896; *Ubu Roi*, 1951) and Guillaume APOLLINAIRE's (*see* CUBISM) *Les mamelles de Tirésias* (1917; *The Breasts of Tiresias*, 1961) were contemporary inspirations for Artaud's theater. However, like the dramatists of the Absurd, his influences also extended to classical and Elizabethan drama, the psychological theories of Sigmund FREUD, and ritualistic oriental theater. In 1935 Artaud received financial backing to attempt his own experimental production of *Les Cenci*, a tragic story adapted from the earlier versions of Percy Bysshe Shelley (1792-1822) and Stendhal (1783-1842). The work ran for only a few performances, but remains an important landmark for two reasons. First, it launched the career of Roger Blin (1907-1984), who would later gain fame as perhaps the most important director within the Theater of the Absurd; second, through its emphasis on a total theatrical experience, a strong communion of production, player, and audience, it came to represent one of the earliest examples of TOTAL THEATER, a form later championed by one of Artaud's greatest admirers, Jean-Louis Barrault (1910-1994). Yet, it was Artaud's theories rather than his creative work that directly affected most of the younger dramatists and directors of the decades that immediately followed. Beginning with EXISTENTIALIST Albert CAMUS, Artaud may be said to have anticipated the work of a long list of dramatic figures and movements, including Absurdists Jean GENET and Arthur Adamov (1908-1970); Fernando Arrabal (1932-) and his THEATER OF PANIC; Jacques Audiberti (1900-1965); Jerzy Grotowski (1933-) and his THEATER LABORATORY; Peter Brook (1925-); and Peter WEISS (*see* THEATER OF FACT). Both Genet's *Les Paravents* (1961; *The Screens*, 1962) and Weiss's *Marat/Sade* (1964) remain outstanding models of Cruelty Theater. Even in recent years, Artaud's influence has continued to emerge in a host of new experimental groups throughout Europe and America.

✤•✦

Further Reading

Ahrends, Gunter. "The Nature and Function of Cruelty in the Theatre of Artaud and Foreman." *Forum Modernes Theater* 9, 1 (1994): 3-12.

Artaud, Antonin. *The Theatre and Its Double*. New York: Grove Press, 1958.

Brown, Erella. "Cruelty and Affirmation in the Postmodern Theater: Antonin Artaud and Hanoch Levin." *Modern Drama* 35, 4 (December 1992): 585-606.

Guicharnaud, Jacques. "The Gaping Mask." In his *Modern French Theatre: From Giraudoux to Genet*. New Haven, Conn.: Yale University Press, 1967. Rev. ed., 1974.

Knapp, Bettina L. "Antonin Artaud and the Theatre of Cruelty." In *Twentieth-Century European Drama*. Edited by Brian Docherty. New York: St. Martin's, 1994.

Plunka, Gene A., ed. *Antonin Artaud and the Modern Theater*. Rutherford, N.J.: Fairleigh Dickinson University Press, 1994.

Sellin, Eric. *The Dramatic Concepts of Antonin Artaud*. Chicago: University of Chicago Press, 1968.

Sloniowski, Jeanette Marie. "The Cinema of Cruelty: Affective Rhetoric in the Cinema." *Dissertation Abstracts International* 54, 5 (November 1993): 1575A.

Sontag, Susan. "Marat/Sade/Artaud." *Partisan Review* 32 (1965): 210-19.

THEATER OF FACT
Germany, 1960s

In its purest form, the Theater of Fact, or modern documentary drama, would present an entirely objective retelling of historical events based on equally objective sources. It would seem to be a part of man's continued attempt to create fiction that exactly mirrored "real life," a desire that earlier led to the emergence of REALISM and NATURAL-

ISM. In practice, the documentary drama has often been used to present quite subjective interpretations of history, often for sociopolitical ends, due to both the strictures inherent in the genre and the intentions of its playwrights. Its origins are found in the work of the German theater director Erwin Friedrich Max Piscator (1893-1966), who created a form of AGITPROP theater in the 1920s to provide his audience with tangible demonstrations of complex social issues. The incorporation of multimedia effects, such as photographs and film segments, with standard theatrical elements created an appearance of objectivity that would inform Piscator's development of the documentary drama after he became director of the new Freie Volksbühne (Free Folk Theater) in 1962. (Thus, the influence of the apparent ability of film to objectively capture daily life, a concept still being struggled with today, cannot be denied its place in the movement.)

Pioneers of the Freie Volksbühne include Rolf HOCHHUTH and Heinar KIPPHARDT, both of whom attempted to approach objectivity through their use of existing documentary sources as the basis of their work, even appending supporting materials into the text of the plays. However, neither playwright is entirely able to escape the inevitable subjectivity involved in choosing which source materials to use and Hochhuth's drama especially is marred in this sense by his inability to avoid incorporating standard theatrical structures to make his play more "literary." Kipphardt is able to avoid many of Hochhuth's obstacles by discovering what may be the most suitable form for documentary theater, the courtroom drama based on trial transcripts. Paring theatricality down to the bare minimum, *DIE ERMITTLUNG* (1965; *The Investigation*, 1965) by Peter WEISS does away with even trying to recreate a courtroom or make the characters anything more than ciphers for the text, and Weiss relies on the choice of sources and the order in which they are presented to provide his desired effect. A hallmark of most of these early Theater of Fact productions was a focus on the events and aftermath of World War II, especially to show how an "objective" view of history can easily blur the moral culpability of individuals, and the use of the free-verse form for dialogue.

The progenitors of the Theater of Fact saw their movement extended with the plays of fellow Germans Dieter Forte (1935-) and Hans Enzensberger (1929-), and the use of the documentary drama quickly spread to other countries, establishing an ongoing tradition of political drama with the production of such plays as Kenneth Brown's (1936-) *The Brig* (1963), about life in a U.S. Marine Corps prison; the THEATER WORKSHOP's *Oh What a Lovely War* (1965), dealing with World War I; Donald Freed's (1932-) *Inquest* (1970), dealing with the Rosenberg trial and executions; Eric Bentley's (1916-) *Are You Now or Have You Ever Been* (1972), about the McCarthy hearings; and Jon Blair and Norman Fenton's *The Biko Inquest* (1983), dealing with the South African inquest into Steven Biko's death.

❖•❖

Hochhuth, Rolf (1931-), German dramatist.

Influenced by Friedrich von Schiller's (1759-1805) concepts of free will, Hochhuth's explorations of historical episodes and use of factual characters and source materials mark his place within the Theater of Fact. However, even in his most "documentary" work he was unwilling to divorce himself from what he believed to be the author's responsibility to provide one's plays with overtly stylistic elements such as the creation of fictive characters and use of soliloquies. His later plays, especially after the death of Piscator, continued to deal with topical issues and, occasionally, "real" people, but shied away from pretensions to strict objectivity.

Der Stellvertreter (1963; *The Deputy*, 1964).

Der Stellvertreter is a scathing, explosively controversial drama denouncing Pope Pius XII's actions during World War II and specifically holding him accountable for not intervening on the Jews' behalf despite his knowledge of the Nazi program for their extermination. Although many source documents are included in the play's dialogue and stage directions, the play is essentially a symbolic treatment of individual responsibility during a time of crisis.

Die Soldaten (1967; *The Soldiers*, 1968).

Hochhuth again explores the theme of personal responsibility in another highly controversial, quasi-documentary context with this play. In it, he equates the fire-bombing of the German city of Dresden by the Allies with the actions of the Germans during the Holocaust to further his explicit goal of convincing countries to outlaw the bombing of civilians in any future war. The play expressly holds Winston Churchill responsible for Dresden, though it also seems to place importance on the surrounding circumstances under which Churchill was operating, to some extent mitigating his ability to exercise free will. Nonetheless, the play was at first banned in England, a situation that eventually led to the elimination of theater censorship in that country in 1968.

❖•❖

Kipphardt, Heinar (1922-), German dramatist.

Kipphardt was initially a practicing doctor and dramaturge. He started writing conventional plays in the 1950s in which he hoped to inspire others to create dramas to deal with current social issues. His Theater of Fact work was more fully "documentary" than Hochhuth's, though no less controversial. Interestingly, many of his plays were first written for television, a medium that has today enthusiastically embraced a bastardization of the documentary drama in many forms. After retiring from the stage entirely in the 1970s, he began a revival of the German documentary drama in the early 1980s.

757

In der Sache J. Robert Oppenheimer (1964; *In the Matter of J. Robert Oppenheimer*, 1967).

Kipphardt uses the actual transcripts from Oppenheimer's 1954 hearing before the U.S. Atomic Energy Commission, during which he was denied continued security clearance to continue military work, as the sole text of his play. In addition, other Piscatorian multimedia effects (film, tape recordings, headlines) are used to heighten the appearance of objectivity. The play uses Oppenheimer's realization of scientists' responsibility for their work as a metaphor for the responsibility all mankind should hold for human survival.

❖•❖

Weiss, Peter (1916-1982), German dramatist.

Originally recognized for his play *Marat/Sade* (1964), a work that combined aspects of the THEATER OF THE ABSURD and the THEATER OF CRUELTY, standing somewhere between Franz KAFKA-influenced SURREALISM and the Theater of Fact, Weiss's best documentary dramas offered a further refinement of the form. His most significant examples offered an increased effort to exactly echo duplicate source materials without regard to plot or characterization while becoming increasingly biased in their selection as a reflection of Weiss's own Marxist beliefs. A tendency to further abstraction and the introduction of standard theatrical modes marked his later plays, although he returned to his earlier themes by the time of his final play.

Die Ermittlung (1965; *The Investigation*, 1965).

Weiss's presentation of the Auschwitz trials held in Frankfurt in 1964, like Kipphardt's Oppenheimer, relies on the original participants' words for its text. However, it is presented in an austere manner devoid of standard theatrical attempts to impart anything beyond the words themselves. *Die Emermittlung* explores how political circumstances ascertain culpability of individuals while proposing that the then-current world view maintained the same values as that responsible for the Holocaust, which, the play goes on to imply, like all genocide, is the inevitable extension of capitalist society.

❖•❖

Further Reading

Paget, Derek. *True Stories? Documentary Drama on Radio, Screen, and Stage.* Manchester, England: Manchester University Press, 1990; distributed in USA and Canada by St. Martin's Press.

Patterson, Michael. *German Theatre Today: Post-War Theatre in West and East Germany, Austria and Northern Switzerland.* London: Pitman, 1976.

Thomas, R. Hinton, and Keith Bullivant. *Literature in Upheaval: West German Writers and the Challenge of the 1960s.* Manchester, England: Manchester University Press, 1974.

THEATER OF IRELAND. *See* ABBEY THEATER

THEATER OF PANIC (Théâtre Panique)
France, 1960s

A descendant of SURREALISM, the THEATER OF CRUELTY, and the THEATER OF THE ABSURD, the Theater of Panic was conceived by Spanish-born French dramatist Fernando Arrabal (1932-) in 1962. Especially from this time onward, Arrabal has attempted to emulate the fearsome and occasionally paradoxical qualities of the Greek god Pan in his dramas, intending thereby to jolt his audiences into a heightened awareness of themselves and their world, much in the manner of Antonin Artaud (1896-1948) and Absurdist Jean GENET. Arrabal's dramas, of which the most representative is *L'Architecte et l'empereur d'Assyrie* (1967; *The Architect and the Emperor of Assyria*, 1969), typically contain provocative language, chaotic plots, role-shifting among bizarre characters, and violent and confounding resolutions. All of these elements serve to support Arrabal's conception of reality as governed by chance and the delightful interplay of antitheses.

✦•✦
Further Reading

Donahue, Francis. "Arrabal: Organic Playwright." *Midwest Quarterly* XXV (winter 1984): 187-200.
Donahue, Thomas John. *The Theater of Fernando Arrabal: A Garden of Earthly Delights*. New York: New York University Press, 1980.
Gautier, Marie-Lise Gazarian. "Fernando Arrabal." In *Interviews with Spanish Writers*. Edited by Marie-Lise Gazarian Gautier and Manuel Alvar. Elmwood Park, Ill.: Dalkey Archive Press, 1991.
Podol, Peter L. *Fernando Arrabal*. Boston: Twayne, 1978.
Schumacher, Claude. "Arrabal's Theatre of Liberation." In *Twentieth-Century European Drama*. Edited by Brian Docherty. New York: St. Martin's, 1994.

THEATER OF SILENCE (Théâtre de L'Inexprimé)
France, 1920s

The Theater of Silence was essentially the movement of one man, Frenchman Jean-Jacques Bernard (1888-1972). During the 1920s and 1930s Bernard promulgated a form of drama in which the unspoken and the inexpressible were emphasized by means of long pauses and broken and trailing dialogue. The form owed much to the work of Belgian SYMBOLIST Maurice MAETERLINCK, who during the 1890s originated the similarly psychological and suggestive static drama. Although Bernard's Theater was only marginally successful, his theories helped later dramatists to concentrate less on the action and more on the emotions of their characters. Certain elements of the Theater of Silence resurfaced during the rise of the THEATER OF THE ABSURD, especially in the work of Englishman Harold PINTER (*see* COMEDY OF MENACE).

✦•✦

Further Reading

Branford, K. A. *A Study of Jean-Jacques Bernard's Théâtre de l'Inexprimé.* University, Miss.: Romance Monographs, 1977.

THEATER OF THE ABSURD
France, 1950s-1960s; also Czechoslovakia, England, Germany, Poland, Switzerland, United States

Following Albert CAMUS (*see* EXISTENTIALISM) and other philosophers who used the term "absurd" to describe the agonizing situation of the self-aware, purposeful human being trapped in a hostile, meaningless universe, drama critic Martin Esslin (1918-) aptly applied the term in his 1961 book, *The Theater of the Absurd*, to characterize the themes and techniques of several playwrights who, chiefly during the 1950s and 1960s, dramatized this philosophical plight.

The Absurdists were influenced by DADA and SURREALISM, particularly by the works of Alfred Jarry (1873-1907), Antonin Artaud (1896-1948), and Roger Vitrac (1899-1952), and they rejected Naturalistic theater of the sort written by Henrik IBSEN (*see* REALISM, Norway) and Anton CHEKHOV (*see* REALISM, Russia) as artificial and untrue to real human experience. In a number of books and essays, Esslin has shown how the Absurdist dramatists rebelled against the conventional rules that a play must contain a plot with a beginning, middle, and solution, or must feature characters who develop consistently. Absurdism holds that the world is essentially mysterious and unintelligible, and these playwrights attempted to remake theater in order to dramatize this state of affairs. In a universe devoid of rational purpose, and therefore lacking an immanent moral code and universal rules of conduct, there is little point in presenting a contrivedly rational narrative, or in exploring character, or in solving problems.

The techniques of Absurdism include "pure" theater, that is, non-narrative kinetics such as are demonstrated by jugglers, mimes, or acrobats, who can be seen as *dramatis personae* in such works as the play *Jumpers* by Tom Stoppard (1937-). Similarly, the audience can expect silly irrationality, clowning, and mad-scenes from the characters. Allied to this presentation of man as Fool or butt of jokes comes a devaluation of language itself. Just as the characters are unpredictable and psychologically unstable, their dialogue is usually incoherent. Particularly in the works of Eugène IONESCO and

Samuel BECKETT, the two major exemplars of this mode of drama, conversations usually go nowhere, dialogues become monologues or peter out into silence. The characters seek logical explanations for their reality, which the events of the drama then belie, or they may cheerfully utter streams of contradictory statements and congratulate themselves on their agreement. Absurdist dialogue relies heavily on questions that remain unanswered and on repetition of phrases, especially meaningless phrases and clichés. In the plays of Ionesco and Harold PINTER (*see* COMEDY OF MENACE), the dialogue may feature frenzied, wild talk that contributes a sense of despair and menace to the proceedings.

These techniques create a production which partakes heavily of dreamlike states and fantasy, which symbolize the tragicomic absurdity and mystery of human existence. Its message being that our world is just as ridiculous as what unfolds on stage, the Theater of the Absurd is ultimately Existentialist, focusing above all on a rather incredulous attitude toward and stunned perception of "reality," as well as of human experience.

The Theater of the Absurd began in France around 1950, the year Ionesco's first play, *La Cantatrice chauve* (*The Bald Soprano*, 1958), opened. Jean GENET is also considered a founder of the movement, and although he cited Artaud and Luigi PIRANDELLO (*see* MODERNISM, Italy) as influences, his works are so unabashedly filled with sex and violence that they almost literally exploded onto the Parisian theater scene. Other French writers associated with Absurdism are Arthur Adamov (1908-1970), Robert Pinget (1919-1997), Boris Vian (1920-1959), and Alain ROBBE-GRILLET (*see* NEW NOVEL). Adamov's plays depict characters whose efforts to make sense of life — as in *La Parodie* (1947) — or its trappings — such as the mysterious manuscript of *L'Invasion* (1950) — are farcical failures; they also show the crazy proliferation of regulations and inhumanity of industrial society, as in *Le Ping-Pong* (1955). The early plays of Fernando Arrabal (1932-), a Moroccan-born Spanish playwright whose works were published in French, partake of Absurdism and Surrealism to present a grotesque vision of the oppressive nature of existence. For instance, his *Le Cimetière des Voitures* (1959; *The Automobile Graveyard,* 1960) uses illogical speech and action to dramatize the loss of human value and morality in a too-technological world.

The movement spread rapidly throughout the West. The plays of Swiss writer Max Frisch (1911-1991) exemplify a typical theme of Absurdist plays, a contempt for bourgeois complacency and its suffocation of the individual spirit. Frisch's drama is clearly Existentialist, concerned with the problems of identity and being true to oneself. His characters develop a variety of poignant and even grotesque ways to escape the deadly routine of a pointless existence.

The works of Wolfgang Hildesheimer (1916-1991), considered Germany's foremost representative of the Theater of the Absurd, and Günter Grass (1927-) share these themes. Hildesheimer's ironic, witty plays, including *Der Drachenthron* (1955; The Dragon Throne) and *Die Verspätung* (1961; The Delay), rage against the various forms of dishonesty and neurosis arising from the different roles we play in the modern world. Known primarily for his novels, Grass wrote a few dramas that satirize the complacency of a postwar Germany devoted to consumption and the modern conveniences. His play *Die Plebejer proben den Aufstand* (1966; The Plebeians Rehearse the Uprising) features Bertolt BRECHT (*see* EPIC THEATER) as a character who, ironically, is too involved in theater to support a workers' uprising.

American dramatists soon saw the possibilities offered by the new theater. Multiple-award-winning playwright Edward Albee (1928-) frequently depicts the cruelty and tensions underlying domestic relationships, as is the case in the August STRINDBERG (*see* EXPRESSIONISM, Germany)-influenced *Who's Afraid of Virginia Woolf?* (1962). *The Sandbox* (1960) and *The American Dream* (1961), savage critiques of the emptiness of family relations, are one-act plays influenced by the works of Beckett and Ionesco. *The Zoo Story* (1960), about a confrontation between two strangers, dramatizes the modern inability to communicate. *Tiny Alice* (1965) is a bizarre investigation into the nature of religious faith and self-deception. Other American Absurdists include Jack Gelber (1932-), Arthur Kopit (1937-), and Jean-Claude Van Itallie (1936-).

It should be emphasized that Absurdism is frequently very funny, and Czech-born Tom Stoppard, one of England's major playwrights, exemplifies the Theater of the Absurd at its wittiest. *Rosencrantz and Guildenstern Are Dead* (1967) uses two minor characters from William Shakespeare's *Hamlet* to dramatize the senselessness of human existence. *Jumpers* (1972) gestures toward a murder-mystery structure, though it satirizes the tools of philosophy by using acrobats to represent professors of that discipline. *Hapgood* (1988), likewise, has a thriller plot, but undermines the moral and epistemological confidence of that genre by employing as its major metaphor the quantum theory of physics, with its irreconcilable ambiguities and insistence that knowledge cannot reach closure. His other plays include *The Real Inspector Hound* (1968), *After Magritte* (1970), *Travesties* (1974), *Dirty Linen* (1976), *Every Good Boy Deserves Favor* (1977), *Night and Day* (1978), and *The Real Thing* (1982). Harold Pinter is another major English playwright. His early works have been called "comedies of menace," because they often show ordinary people menaced by mysterious agencies and forces. *The Dumb Waiter* (1960) and *THE BIRTHDAY PARTY* (1958), for example, deal with assassins and frighteners, though the reasons for the characters' actions are never explained. Other English Absurdists include N. F. Simpson (1919-) and David Campton (1924-).

Eastern European dramatists used Absurdism to characterize the dehumanizing regimes of their societies. In Poland, where native drama already revealed Absurdist traits, Sławomir Mrożek (1930-) wrote about social and political programs, frequently using a single family or social unit as a microcosm in which to demonstrate the logical results of illogical principles and ideologies. His characters are usually either victims or oppressors. His most famous play, *Tango* (1965), a psychological drama of sorts, sees a son rebel against his bohemian parents and try to establish purposeful order within the family, but he is killed and domestic power seized by their butler, a boor but a pragmatist. The works of Tadeusz Różewicz (1921-) likewise satirize contemporary society. In *Kartoteka* (1961; *The Card Index*, 1969), the identity of the main character keeps changing, while a variety of characters represent the humdrum banality of modern life. *Świadkowie albo Nasza mała stabilizacja* (1962; *The Witnesses*, 1970) returns to the Absurdist suspicion of communication, as characters use meaningless dialogue which is inadequate to express their true feelings and selves. Adam Tarn (1902-1972), Jaroslav Marek Rymkiewicz (1934-), Tymoteusz Karpowicz (1921-), Miron Bialoszewski (1922-), Zbigniew Herbert (1924-), and Stanisław Grochowiak (1934-1976) are other well-known Polish dramatists.

Václav Havel (1936-), who became president of Czechoslovakia in 1989 and then of the Czech Republic in 1993, is frequently compared with Franz KAFKA (*see* MODERNISM, Austria and Germany). His dissident works show characters trying to retain their individuality and dignity while being metaphorically imprisoned and suffocated by a totalitarian bureaucracy. His blackly humorous plays *Vyrozumění* (1966; *The Memorandum*, 1967) and *Ztížená možnost soustředění* (1968; *The Increased Difficulty of Concentration*, 1972) attack the emptiness of clichés and meaningless banalities, symptoms of a repressive society.

Absurdism has had an extremely wide-reaching influence upon succeeding drama; its themes and techniques may be spied within countless otherwise realistic plays.

Beckett, Samuel (1906-1989), Irish dramatist, novelist, and poet.
Born in Dublin, Beckett moved to France in the late 1920s, where his experiences teaching English to French students provided him the same sort of revelation about language as Ionesco describes. Like the other Absurdists, Beckett rejected the Cartesian notion that the world may be diagrammed into simplistic oppositions and understood in a rational, totalizing way. He achieved worldwide fame with the publication of *En Attendant Godot* (1952; *Waiting for Godot*, 1954), a drama about two passive, hopeless tramps who wait for somebody who never appears. Their hilariously banal dialogue reveals their terrified paralysis and despair in the face of the total meaningless-

ness of the universe. The audience must sympathize when Vladimir moans, "I can't take much more of this," but Estragon replies, almost ominously, "That's what you think." Beckett's other plays include *Fin de Partie* (1957; *Endgame*, 1958), *La Dernière Bande* (1959; *Krapp's Last Tape*, 1958), and *Oh les Beaux Jours* (1963; *Happy Days*, 1961).

✥•✥

Genet, Jean (1910-1986), French novelist, dramatist, and poet.

Genet's notorious early careers as male prostitute, thief, pornographer, and convict provided color and content to his prose and drama, which frequently deal with confining spaces and investigations into the psychology of power, especially with issues of domination and submission. *Les Bonnes* (1954; *The Maids*, 1954) is concerned with the relationship between masters and servants. *Le Balcon* (1956; *The Balcony*, 1957) shows clients at a brothel who dress up as Bishop, Judge, General, and so on to act out their erotic fantasies. An uprising in the streets outside allows these men a chance to perform these roles in actuality. Among the props are numerous mirrors and peepholes, the latter allowing voyeurism and surveillance, which help to demolish the theater's "fourth wall." The theme of costuming calls into question the nature of identity and social roles and shows that moral evil may be committed by those who society believes are supposed to prevent and punish it. *Les Paravents* (1961; *The Screens*, 1962) is another play that collapses preconceptions of identity and blurs the lines between illusion and reality.

✥•✥

Ionesco, Eugène (1912-1994), Romanian-born French dramatist.

His plays, deeply metaphysical and highly amusing classics of Absurdism, flout all conventions and audience expectations. They include *La Cantatrice chauve* (1953; *The Bald Soprano*, 1958), *La Leçon* (1953; *The Lesson*, 1958), *Jacques, ou, La Soumission* (1953; *Jack, or, The Submission*, 1958), *Les Chaises* (1954; *The Chairs*, 1958), and *Le Rhinocéros* (1959; *Rhinoceros*, 1960). In *Notes and Counter-Notes* (1962), Ionesco described the vision that imbues his plays, a vision born when he was studying English: "For me what happened was a kind of collapse of reality. The words turned into sounding shells devoid of meaning . . . and the world appeared to me in an unearthly, perhaps its true, light, beyond understanding and governed by arbitrary laws. . . . At certain moments the world appeared to me emptied of meaning, reality seems unreal. It is this feeling of unreality, the search for some essential reality, nameless and forgotten — and outside it I do not feel I exist — that I have tried to express through my characters, who drift incoherently, having nothing of their own apart from their anguish, their remorse, their failures, the vacuity of their lives." Critics frequently call his outrageous plays a form of shock therapy designed to provoke the audience into understanding their own complicity in the modern breakdown in communication.

✦●✦

Further Reading

Abbott, Anthony S. *The Vital Lie: Reality and Illusion in Modern Drama*. Tuscaloosa, Ala.: University of Alabama Press, 1989.

Acheson, James, and Kateryna Arthur, eds. *Beckett's Later Fiction and Drama: Texts for Company*. New York: St. Martin's Press, 1987.

Alvarez, A. *Samuel Beckett*. New York: Viking, 1973.

Astro, Alan. *Understanding Samuel Beckett*. Columbia, S.C.: University of South Carolina Press, 1990.

Baldwin, Helene L. *Samuel Beckett's Real Silence*. University Park, Pa.: Pennsylvania State University Press, 1981.

Beja, Morris, S. E. Gontarski, and Pierre Astier, eds. *Samuel Becket, Humanistic Perspectives*. Columbus, Ohio: Ohio State University Press, 1983.

Ben-Zvi, Linda. *Samuel Beckett*. Boston: Twayne, 1986.

Blau, Herbert. *The Impossible Theater: A Manifesto*. New York: Macmillan, 1964.

Blocker, H. Gene. *The Metaphysics of Absurdity*. Washington, D.C.: University Press of America, 1979.

Brater, Enoch. *Beyond Minimalism: Beckett's Late Style in the Theater*. New York: Oxford University Press, 1987.

Brater, Enoch, and Ruby Cohn, eds. *Around the Absurd: Essays on Modern and Postmodern Drama*. Ann Arbor, Mich.: University of Michigan Press, 1990.

Chaudhuri, Una. *No Man's Stage: A Semiotic Study of Jean Genet's Major Plays*. Ann Arbor, Mich.: UMI Research Press, 1986.

Coe, Richard N. *The Vision of Jean Genet*. New York: Grove Press, 1968.

Cohn, Ruby. *Just Play: Beckett's Theater*. Princeton, N.J.: Princeton University Press, 1980.

Connor, Steven. *Samuel Beckett: Repetition, Theory, and Text*. Oxford, England: Blackwell, 1988.

Davis, Robin J., and Lance St. J. Butler, eds. *Make Sense Who May: Essays on Samuel Beckett's Later Works*. Totowa, N.J.: Barnes and Noble Books, 1989.

Docherty, Brian, ed. *Twentieth-Century European Drama*. New York: St. Martin's Press, 1994.

Duckworth, Colin. *Angels of Darkness: Dramatic Effect in Samuel Beckett with Special Reference to Eugène Ionesco*. London: Allen and Unwin, 1972.

Esslin, Martin. *Reflections: Essays on Modern Theatre*. Garden City, N.Y.: Doubleday, 1969.

————. *The Theatre of the Absurd*. Garden City, N.Y.: Doubleday, 1961. Rev., updated ed., Garden City, N.Y.: Anchor Books, 1969.

Esslin, Martin, ed. *Samuel Beckett: A Collection of Critical Essays*. Englewood Cliffs, N.J.: Prentice-Hall, 1965.

Fletcher, Beryl S. *A Student's Guide to the Plays of Samuel Beckett*. 2nd ed., rev. and expanded. London: Faber and Faber, 1985.

765

Fletcher, John. *Beckett, a Study of His Plays*. 2nd ed., rev. and enl. London: Methuen, 1978.

Gaensbauer, Deborah B. *The French Theater of the Absurd*. Boston: Twayne, 1991.

Gidal, Peter. *Understanding Beckett: A Study of Monologue and Gesture in the Works of Samuel Beckett*. New York: St. Martin's Press, 1986.

Giles, Jane. *The Cinema of Jean Genet: Un Chant D'Amour*. London: BFI Publishing, 1981.

Gontarski, S. E. *The Beckett Studies Reader*. Gainesville, Fla.: University Press of Florida, 1993.

————. *The Intent of Undoing in Samuel Beckett's Dramatic Texts*. Bloomington, Ind.: Indiana University Press, 1985.

————. *On Beckett: Essays and Criticism*. New York: Grove Press, 1986.

Hinchliffe, Arnold P. *The Absurd*. London: Methuen, 1974.

Homan, Sidney. *Beckett's Theaters: Interpretations for Performance*. Lewisburg, Pa.: Bucknell University Press, 1984.

Kennedy, Andrew K. *Samuel Beckett*. Cambridge, England: Cambridge University Press, 1989.

Kernan, Alvin B., ed. *The Modern American Theater: A Collection of Critical Essays*. Englewood Cliffs, N.J.: Prentice-Hall, 1967.

Knapp, Bettina L. *Jean Genet*. Rev. ed. Boston: Twayne, 1989.

Lyons, Charles R. *Samuel Beckett*. New York: Grove Press, 1983.

McCarthy, Patrick A. *Critical Essays on Samuel Beckett*. Boston: G. K. Hall, 1986.

McMahon, Joseph H. *The Imagination of Jean Genet*. Westport, Conn.: Greenwood Press, 1980.

Mayberry, Bob. *Theatre of Discord: Dissonance in Beckett, Albee, and Pinter*. Rutherford, N.J.: Fairleigh Dickinson University Press, 1989.

Murphy, P. J. *Reconstructing Beckett: Language for Being in Samuel Beckett's Fiction*. Toronto: University of Toronto Press, 1990.

Oswald, Laura. *Jean Genet and the Semiotics of Performance*. Bloomington, Ind.: Indiana University Press, 1989.

Pilling, John. *Samuel Beckett*. London: Routledge and Kegan Paul, 1976.

Plunka, Gene A. *Antonin Artaud and the Modern Theater*. Rutherford, N.J.: Associated University Presses, 1994.

————. *The Rites of Passage of Jean Genet: The Art and Aesthetics of Risk Taking*. Rutherford, N.J.: Fairleigh Dickinson University Press, 1992.

Ricks, Christopher B. *Beckett's Dying Words: The Clarendon Lectures, 1990*. Oxford, England: Clarendon Press; New York: Oxford University Press, 1993.

Sartre, Jean Paul. *Saint Genet, Actor and Martyr*. Translated by Bernard Frechtman. New York: New American Library, 1964.

Styan, J. L. *Modern Drama in Theory and Practice*. Cambridge, England: Cambridge University Press, 1981.

Webb, Eugene. *The Plays of Samuel Beckett*. Seattle: University of Washington Press, 1974.

Zyla, Wolodymyr T., ed. *From Surrealism to the Absurd: Proceedings of the Comparative Literature Symposium, January 29 and 30, 1970*. Lubbock, Tex.: Interdepartmental Committee on Comparative Literature, Texas Tech University, 1970.

THEATER OF THE GROTESQUE (Teatro del Grottesco)
Italy, 1910s

A short-lived Italian movement that surfaced during World War I with Luigi Chiarelli's (1884-1947) tragedy *La maschera e il volto* (1916; *The Mask and the Face*, 1924), the Theater of the Grotesque emphasized through the interplay of irony, symbol, dream, and character the cloudy and ultimately shocking distinction between appearance and reality. Among Chiarelli's followers were Luigi Antonelli (1882-1942), Massimo Bontempelli (1878-1960), and Pier Maria Rosso di San Secondo (1887-1956). However, it was MODERNIST luminary Luigi PIRANDELLO, in his prewar novels and postwar dramas, who most thoroughly inspired and directed the course of the group. Among more prominent dramatic movements, the Theater of the Grotesque is perhaps most closely affined with the THEATER OF THE ABSURD.

Further Reading

Bassnett, Susan. *Luigi Pirandello*. New York: Grove Press, 1983.
Bentley, Eric. *The Pirandello Commentaries*. Evanston, Ill.: Northwestern University Press, 1986.
Bishop, Thomas. *Pirandello and the French Theater*. New York: New York University Press, 1960.
Büdel, Oscar. *Pirandello*. New York: Hillary House, 1966.
Cambon, Glauco. *Pirandello: A Collection of Critical Essays*. Englewood Cliffs, N.J.: Prentice-Hall, 1967.
DiGaetani, John Louis, ed. *A Companion to Pirandello Studies*. New York: Greenwood Press, 1991.
Günsberg, Maggie. *Patriarchal Representations: Gender and Discourse in Pirandello's Theatre*. Oxford, England; Providence, R.I.: Berg, 1994.
Matthaei, Renate. *Luigi Pirandello*. Translated by Simon and Erika Young. New York: Ungar, 1973.
Paolucci, Anne. *Pirandello's Theater: The Recovery of the Modern Stage for Dramatic Art*. Carbondale, Ill.: Southern Illinois University Press, 1974.
Ragusa, Olga. *Luigi Pirandello: An Approach to His Theatre*. Edinburgh, Scotland: Edinburgh University Press, 1980.
Starkie, Walter. *Luigi Pirandello, 1867-1936*. 3rd ed., rev. and enl. Berkeley, Calif.: University of California Press, 1965.
Vittorini, Domenico. *The Drama of Luigi Pirandello*. Foreword by Luigi Pirandello. New York: Russell & Russell, 1969.

THEATER WORKSHOP
England, 1940s-1970s

Founded in 1945 by British director Joan Littlewood (1914-) and her husband, Ewan McColl (1915-?), the Theater Workshop was the successor to Littlewood's Theater of Action and Theater Union. Left-wing, working-class, and improvisational, her Workshop concentrated on rewriting classic dramas as well as producing the work of new

Irish and English playwrights. Two of the Workshop's most notable productions were Brendan Behan's (1923-1964) *The Hostage* (1958) and the company's own *Oh, What a Lovely War!* (1965). From 1961 until 1973, Littlewood's direct connection with Workshop productions was sporadic. However, her pioneering emphases on the malleability of text and the compositional and ad-lib roles of actor and director greatly influenced the development of contemporary British drama. More specifically, her innovative use of song, slang, black humor, montage, documentary, and social criticism have established the Theater Workshop as an important precursor of 1960s FRINGE THEATER.

Further Reading

Goorney, Howard, and Ewan MacColl, eds. *Agit-prop to Theatre Workshop: Political Playscripts, 1930-50*. Manchester, England: Manchester University Press, 1986.
————. *The Theatre Workshop Story*. London: Methuen, 1981.
Kearney, Colbert. *The Writings of Brendan Behan*. New York: St. Martin's Press, 1977.
MacColl, Ewan. "The Grass Roots of Theatre Workshop." *Theatre Quarterly* 3 (January-March 1973): 58-68.

THÉÂTRE ALFRED JARRY. *See* **THEATER OF CRUELTY**

THÉÂTRE DE LA CRUAUTÉ. *See* **THEATER OF CRUELTY**

THÉÂTRE DE L'INEXPRIMÉ. *See* **THEATER OF SILENCE**

THÉÂTRE DU VIEUX-COLOMBIER
France, 1910s-1920s

A highly influential experimental company, the Théâtre du Vieux-Colombier was launched by Jacques COPEAU in 1913 in Paris. Copeau, convinced that existing French theater promoted superfluous entertainment and neglected the classics, launched a revolution in staging, direction, and the training of actors. His concept of the "bare stage" and his respect for the literary significance of the text led to a renewal of integrity in French dramatic productions.

Although Copeau relied heavily on the works of Shakespeare and Molière (1622-1673), he also introduced his audiences to contemporary works by Paul Claudel (1868-1955), André GIDE (*see NOUVELLE REVUE FRANÇAISE*), and Jules ROMAINS (*see* UNANIMISME) Despite financial difficulties—and the departures of actor Charles Dullin (1885-1949) in 1921 and stage manager Louis Jouvet (1887-1951) in 1922 to form their own theaters (*see* CARTEL)—the Théâtre du Vieux-Colombier enjoyed great artistic success, particularly from 1920 until 1924. At the end of this period, however,

Copeau retreated to his native Burgundy to work full-time with his École du Vieux Colombier, a close-knit group of actors which he and others had been training through a variety of mediums and methods since 1921. Copeau's legacy as a principal catalyst of the LITTLE THEATER MOVEMENT, with which he had considerable contact outside France, especially in New York under the auspices of the THEATER GUILD, has ensured the fame of his small theatrical company, from which serious modern French theater may be said to have sprung.

❧•❧

Copeau, Jacques (1879-1949), French dramatist, director, and critic.

Copeau helped found the *NOUVELLE REVUE FRANÇAISE* in 1909, serving first as its literary director and later as its chief editor. With the sponsorship of the *Nouvelle Revue*, Copeau assumed management of the Théâtre du Vieux-Colombier in 1913. In his manifesto published that same year, "Un Essai de rénovation dramatique: Le Théâtre du Vieux Colombier," he wrote: "The tyranny of the stage and its gross artificiality will act on us like a discipline in forcing us to concentrate all of truth in the feelings and actions of our characters. May the other marvels vanish and, for the new works, leave us with a bare stage." Although some considered Copeau's approach to drama needlessly austere, others applauded his radical concepts and innovations, particularly his intensive retraining of actors to be pure conduits of dramatic language rather than artificial and ostentatious spectacles on the stage. Copeau, who aided in the development of Jouvet's Théâtre de l'Athénée, Dullin's Théâtre de l'Atelier, and Michel Saint-Denis's (1897-1971) Compagnie des Quinze, eventually drew acclaim from the French establishment late in his career and was awarded the directorship of the Comédie Française in 1940.

❧•❧

Further Reading

Blessing, Juliette Breffort. "Washington, Action Dramatique: Jacques Copeau's Tribute to Franco-American Friendship." *Theatre Survey: The Journal of the American Society for Theatre Research* 30, 1-2 (May-November 1989): 147-53.

Guicharnaud, Jacques. "Directors and Productions: Jacques Copeau." In his *Modern French Theatre: From Giraudoux to Genet*. New Haven, Conn.: Yale University Press, 1967.

Pocknell, Brian. "The Theatre du Vieux Colombier and the Renewal of the Commedia dell'Arte in France." In *The Science of Buffoonery: Theory and History of the Commedia dell'Arte*. Edited by Domenico Pietropaolo. Ottawa, Canada: Dovehouse, 1989.

Rudlin, John. *Jacques Copeau*. Cambridge, England: Cambridge University Press, 1986.

Whitmore, Richard Alan. "The Emerging Ensemble: The Vieux-Colombier and the Group Theatre." *Theatre Survey: The Journal of the American Society for Theatre Research* 34, 1 (May 1993): 60-70.

THÉÂTRE LIBRE
France, 1887-1896

Inspired by the Realistic and Naturalistic works of Paul Alexis (1847-1901), Henri BECQUE (*see* NATURALISM, France), Émile ZOLA (*see* Naturalism, France), and, especially, Henrik IBSEN (*see* REALISM, Norway), the Théâtre Libre represented a pivotal development in modern dramatic production. The guiding spirit of the movement was actor and producer André Antoine (1858-1943). In 1887 Antoine founded the Libre — so named for its Zolaesque intent to defy censorship — as a private club and proceeded to direct works of a new generation of French dramatists as well as those by important authors outside France, including Ibsen, Bjørnstjerne Bjørnson (1832-1910), Gerhart HAUPTMANN (*see* FREIE BÜHNE), August STRINDBERG (*see* EXPRESSIONISM, Germany), Leo TOLSTOY (*see* Realism, Russia), and Giovanni VERGA (*see* VERISMO). In so doing, Antoine pioneered the multinational LITTLE THEATER MOVEMENT, which spawned such companies as Otto Brahm's (1856-1912) Freie Bühne, Konstantin STANISLAVSKY's MOSCOW ART THEATER, and Jacques COPEAU's THÉÂTRE DU VIEUX-COLOMBIER.

Antoine's rejection of romantic boulevard drama and the heavily stylized theater of the Comédie Française led to an emphasis on the *comédie rosse* (bitter comedy) form. Authentic dialogue, natural delivery, drab settings, and generally pessimistic conclusions became primary elements of the Théâtre Libre productions. Despite several critical successes and a brief European tour, Antoine's experimental venture failed financially. With Antoine's departure in 1894 the original company may be said to have disintegrated. However, Antoine's later work with the Théâtre Antoine and the Théâtre Royal de L'Odéon served to broaden his vision of a modern theater based upon literary and realistic integrity.

❖•❖

Further Reading

Gerould, Daniel. "Oscar Metenier and Comedie Rosse: From the Theatre Libre to the Grand Guignol." *The Drama Review* 28, 1 (spring 1984): 15-28.

Knapp, Bettina L. "The Reign of the Theatrical Director: Antoine and Lugne-Poe." *The French Review: Journal of the American Association of Teachers of French* 61, 6 (May 1988): 866-77.

Waxman, Samuel M. *Antoine and the Theatre Libre*. Cambridge, Mass.: Harvard University Press, 1926.

Whitmore, Richard Alan. "The Emerging Ensemble: The Vieux-Colombier and the Group Theatre." *Theatre Survey: The Journal of the American Society for Theatre Research* 34, 1 (May 1993): 60-70.

THÉÂTRE PANIQUE. *See* THEATER OF PANIC

THÉÂTRE TOTAL. *See* TOTAL THEATER

THEATRICAL ARTS RESEARCH SOCIETY (Kŭk Yesel Yŏn'guhoe) Korea, 1931-1938

Part of the modern movement in Korean drama, the Theatrical Arts Research Society was noted for its experimental stance and interest in staging both native drama and contemporary Western works. The most notable writer associated with the Society was dramatist Yu Ch'i-jin (1905-).

✤●❖

Further Reading

Cho, Oh Kon. *Chi-Jin Yoo: A Patriotic Playwright of Korea.* Thesis, Michigan State University, 1972.
Paik, Eui Hyun. *An English Translation of Chi Jin Yoo's So with Its Costume and Scenic Design.* Thesis, University of Georgia, 1970.

THIRD FRONT MOVEMENT (Trečias Frontas) Lithuania, 1930s

A leftist Lithuanian movement, the Third Front was active during the 1930s. Important members included novelist Petras Cvirka (1909-1947) and poets Salomėja Neris (1904-1945), Kostas Korsakas (1909-), and Antanas Venclova (1906-).

✤●❖

Further Reading

Lehiste, Ilse. "An Acoustic Analysis of the Metrical Structure of Orally Produced Lithuanian Poetry." *Journal of Baltic Studies* 21, 2 (summer 1990): 145-55.
Rannit, Aleksis. "Two Venclovas." *Lituanus: Baltic States Quarterly of Arts & Sciences* 25, 3 (1979): 22-23.

THIRD THEATER (Odin Teatret) Italy, 1960s

An itinerant dramatic movement founded in 1964 by Italian director Eugenio Barba (1936-), the Third Theater derived its name from its identification with third world culture, history, and economics. Prior to his creation of the Third Theater, Barba served as apprentice to Jerzy Grotowski (1933-) and his THEATER LABORATORY. The two directors shared an intensive interest in the dramatic company as a close-knit community and in the individual actor as an instrument of performance to be carefully trained and nourished.

771

❖•❖
Further Reading

Barba, Eugenio. *Beyond the Floating Islands*. Translations by Judy Barba, et al. New York: PAJ
Publications, 1986.

——. *The Floating Islands: Reflections with Odin Teatret*. Edited by Ferdinando Taviani.
Translations by Judy Barba, et al. Gråsten, Denmark: Drama, 1979.

——. "The Steps on the River Bank." *Drama Review* 38, 4, T144 (winter 1994): 107-19.

Brook, Peter. *On the Borderline of Theatre, Art and Life: Interviews with P. Brook, R. Cieslak
and E. Barba*. Edited by V. Hagnell. Lund, Sweden: Institute for Research in the Dramatic
Arts, University of Lund, 1977.

Christoffersen, Erik Exe. *The Actor's Way*. Translated by Richard Fowler. London and New York:
Routledge, 1993.

Klein, Stacy A. *Eugenio Barba, Master Craftsman and the Odin Teatret's Oxyrhyncus
Evangeliet*. [sic] Doctoral thesis, Tufts University, 1988.

Watson, Ian. *Towards a Third Theatre: Eugenio Barba and the Odin Teatret*. London and New
York: Routledge, 1993.

THREE MARIAS
Portugal, 1970s

During the years before the 1974 military overthrow of the repressive regime of António
Salazar (1889-1970), women in Portugal continued in a decades-long struggle against
economic, political, and social oppression; the right to vote, for example, was not
extended to all Portuguese women until 1969. When three young women writers in
Portugal wrote a book in 1971 dealing with the historical oppression of women and
gained worldwide attention, as well as the appellation the "Three Marias," they cast a
spotlight on the unequal status of women in Portugal and set a model for future
Portuguese women writers.

Novelist Maria Isabel Barreno (1939-) initiated the formation of the group after a volume of poetry by Maria Teresa Horta (1937-) — *Minha Senhora de Mim* (1971;
Milady of Me) — was banned for its erotic content, though similar works by male writers were not ordinarily subject to the same fate. Barreno enlisted Horta and fiction
writer Maria Velho da Costa (1938-) to collaborate on a book about the condition of
women. They met twice a week to discuss their memories as children and adolescents,
and current experiences as married women who worked outside the home as well as
inside, maintaining households and raising children, and wrote letters to each other
regularly on these subjects.

The result was *Novas cartas portuguesas* (1972; *The New Portuguese Letters*, 1975), a
collection of poems, essays, sketches, and letters. Their model for the letters was *Lettres*

Portugaises (Letters of a Portuguese Nun), a classic seventeenth-century text containing letters allegedly written by Mariana Alcoforado, a young Portuguese woman who became a nun after her French lover deserted her. Using the epistolary narrative form and bringing Mariana into the text, they drew a discursive line through history, connecting past with current oppression, and disrupted the norms of that narrative tradition. As they assert in the book's First Letter, "all of literature is a long letter to an invisible other, a present, a possible, or a future passion that we rid ourselves of, feed, or seek."

In the spring of 1972, under a recent law that made writers morally responsible for their work, they were arrested for the book's sexually explicit content—the charges being "abuse of the freedom of the press" and "outrage to public decency"—and the book was banned. Their trial began in July of 1973 and was the center of much public attention. All charges against the women were dropped in May of 1974, when, after the military overthrew Salazar, the presiding, and sympathetic, judge felt free to dismiss the case and praised the book's literary value. Afterward, Costa, who approached the feminist movement much more cautiously than her coauthors and advocated speaking out against all forms of oppression—racial and economic as well as sexual—publicly estranged herself from the ardent feminist views of Barreno and Horta.

➜•❖

Further Reading

Fonseca, Mary Lyndon. "The Case of the Three Marias." *Ms. Magazine* 3 (January 1975): 84-85, 108.

Sadlier, Darlene J. "Radical Form in *Novas Cartas Portuguesas*." In her *The Question of How: Women Writers and New Portuguese Literature*. New York: Greenwood Press, 1989.

TIDE (Het Getij)
Netherlands, 1920s-1930s

A Dutch movement of the 1920s and 1930s, the Tide served as an important source of MODERNIST and EXPRESSIONIST poetry. Led by Herman van den Bergh (1897-1967), the movement also included Martinus Nijhoff (1894-1953) and Jan Jacob Slauerhoff (1898-1936).

➜•❖

Further Reading

Akker, Wiljan van den. "Two Poets and a Nightingale: Nature, Romanticism and Roland Holst Versus Urbanization, Modernism and Nijhoff." *Dutch Crossing: A Journal of Low Countries Studies* 40 (spring 1990): 109-24.

Bakker, Martin. "'Fatherland' and 'Mother Tongue' in Nijhoff's Poetry." *Canadian Journal of Netherlandic Studes* 8, 1 (spring 1988): 15-20.

————. "Notes on Nijhoff's War Poems." *Canadian Journal of Netherlandic Studies* 11, 1
     (spring 1990): 23-29.
Dunkelberg, Kendall. "The Structure of the Double Volta in Nijhoff's Experimental Sonnets."
     Dutch Crossing: A Journal of Low Countries Studies 41 (summer 1990): 23-34.
Fokkema, D. W. "Nijhoff's Modernist Poetics in European Perspective." In *Comparative
     Poetics/Poetique Comparative/Vergleichende Poetik: In Honour of Jan Kamerbeek Jr.*
     Edited by D. W. Fokkema, Elrud Kunne-Ibsch, and A. J. A. Zoest. Amsterdam: Rodopi, 1976.
Lefevere, Andre. "Slauerhoff and 'Po Tsju I': Three Paradigms for the Study of Influence."
     Tamkang Review 10 (1979): 67-77.
Lulofs, Frank. "A Closer Look at M. Nijhoff's Poem 'Langs een wereld' (Passing Worlds)."
     Translated by Cora Weir and Alastair Wein. In *Modern Dutch Studies: Essays in Honour of
     Peter King.* Edited by Michael Wintle and Paul Vincent. London: Athlone, 1988.
Meyer, Herman. "On the Spirit of Verse." In *The Disciplines of Criticism: Essays in Literary
     Theory, Interpretation, and History.* New Haven, Conn.: Yale University Press, 1968.

TIOTALISTER
Sweden, 1910s

Tiotalister, or writers of the 1910s, was a Swedish group devoted to Realistic, socially conscientious fiction. Each member specialized in documenting a particular urban region of Sweden and its characteristic problems, according special attention to the developing middle class. Hjalmar Bergman (1883-1931), Gustaf Hellström (1882-1953), and Ludvig Nordström (1882-1942) were representative writers of the period. Of the three, only Bergman may be labeled predominantly pessimistic in outlook.

⤞•⤝

Further Reading

Bock, Sigge. *Lowly Who Prevail: Vistas to the Work of Hjalmar Bergman.* Stockholm: S.
     Bokke, 1990.
Jenner, Lars. *The Literary Author as Ethnographer: Ludvig Nordström and His Stories from
     the Archipelago.* Master's thesis, University of Washington, 1992.
Linder, Erik Hjalmar. *Hjalmar Bergman.* Translated by Catherine Djurklou. [sic] Boston:
     Twayne, 1975.
Petherick, Karin. *Hj. Berman:* Markurells I Wadköping. 2nd ed. Studies in Swedish Literature 4.
     Hull, England: Orton & Holmes, 1975.

TISH GROUP
Canada, 1960s

The *Tish* Group of poets formed in Vancouver in 1961. Intimately linked to the Canadian counterculture movement, the *Tish* Group sought the same aesthetic freedoms and concerned themselves with many of the same issues as the SAN FRANCISCO SCHOOL. A key influence on the *Tish* poets was American Robert Duncan (1919-1988), whose penchant for poem sequences and the emulation of spoken idioms was, in turn, indebted to the work of Walt Whitman (1819-1892). George Bowering (1935-) and Frank Davey (1940-) were among the original editor-poets of *Tish*, an inexpensively produced literary magazine that eventually sparked an entire industry of West Coast Canadian periodicals.

⤖•⬅

Further Reading

Banting, Pamela. *Body, Inc.: A Theory of Translation Poetics.* Winnipeg, Canada: Turnstone Press, 1995.

Bowering, George. *Autobiology.* Vancouver, Canada: New Star Books, 1972.

———. *Condensed: By One Inside & Fifty-Odd Outside H & Z.* Toronto: Letters, 1988.

Fenton, William. *Re-Writing the Past: History and Origin in Howard O'Hagan, Jack Hodgins, George Bowering and Chris Scott.* Rome: Bulzoni, 1988.

Harris, John. *George Bowering and His Works.* Toronto: ECW Press, 1992.

Kröller, Eva-Marie. *George Bowering: Bright Circles of Colour.* Vancouver, Canada: Talonbooks, 1992.

TODAY AND TOMORROW. *See* VAN NU EN STRAKS

TODAY GROUP (*Ma* Group)
Hungary, 1920s

A response to the Hungarian movement *NYUGAT*, Today owed much of its vitality to avant-garde luminary Lajos Kassák (1887-1967), the leading figure of the nation's MODERNISTS since 1915. Today thrived during the late 1910s and early 1920s due to its politically committed, FUTURISTIC style. Other writers associated with the journal, *Ma* (Today), and movement were Tibor Déry (1894-1977), Aladár Komját (1891-1937), Zsigmond Remenyik (1902-1962), József Lengye (1896-1975), and Gyula Illyés (1902-1983; *see also* POPULIST MOVEMENT).

⤖•⬅

Further Reading

Fenyo, Mario D. *Literature and Political Change: Budapest, 1908-1918.* Philadelphia: American Philosophical Society, 1987.

Kassák, Lajos. *Lajos Kassák: Retrospective Exhibition, April-May 1984.* Essays by Paul Kovesdy, John E. Bowlt, and Eva Körner. New York: Matignon Gallery, 1984.

TORCHBEARERS GROUP (Tulenkantakjat)
Finland, 1920s-1930s

Closely affiliated with the Swedish-Finnish MODERNISTS, the Finnish Torchbearers Group was comprised largely of poets who wrote between the two world wars. Led by Uuno Kailas (1901-1933), Katri Vala (1901-1944), and Olavi Paavolainen (1903-1964), the Torchbearers exhibited the influences of EXPRESSIONISM, SURREALISM, and FUTURISM in their often intensely emotional, occasionally violent, and typically intro-spective responses to developments in the modern world. Other writers associated with the movement — whose avowed purpose was to internationalize Finnish literature — include Yrjö Jylhä (1903-1956), Arvi Kivimaa (1904-?), Unto Seppänen (1904-1955), Elina Vaara (1903-), Lauri Viljanen (1900-), and Mika Waltari (1908-1979).

✦•✦

Further Reading

Hinshaw, David. *Heroic Finland*. New York: Putnam's Sons, 1952.
"Kivimaa, (Kaarlo) Arvi." In *Dictionary of Scandinavian Biography*. Edited by Ernest Kay. London: Melrose Press, 1972.
Laitinen, Kai. "Post-War Literature — A Finnish View." In *Finland: Creation and Construction*. Edited by Hillar Kallas and Sylvie Nickels. London: Allen & Unwin, 1968.
Ravila, Paavao Ilmari, ed. *Finnish Literary Reader*. Bloomington, Ind.: Indiana University Press, 1965.
"Waltari, Mika." In *Dictionary of Scandinavian Biography*. Edited by Ernest Kay. London: Melrose Press, 1972.

TOTAL THEATER (also Totaltheater and Théâtre Total)
England, France, Germany, Italy, 1940s-1970s

First conceived in Germany in 1926 by Walter Gropius (1883-1969) for EPIC THEATER director Erwin Piscator (1893-1966), Total Theater may be said to have made its first successful debut in 1947 with Frenchman Jean-Louis Barrault's production of Franz KAFKA's *DER PROZESS* (begun 1914, published 1925; *The Trial*, 1937; *see* MOD-ERNISM, Austria and Germany). Both a theory of direction and a blueprint for staging, Total Theater accentuates the director's own personal vision over the text and enables the audience to experience a panoramic, multimedia interpretation of that text. Versatile, oval theaters featuring several stages were preferred by directors of Total Theater, whose productions typically relied as much on lighting, music, costume, and supplementary props as on acting itself. In addition to Barrault's work, the experiments of Joan Littlewood (1914-) and her THEATER WORKSHOP, as well as that of other English and European directors, have played an important role in the development of modern theater.

✦•✦

Further Reading

Kirby, E. T., ed. *Total Theater: A Critical Anthology*. New York: Dutton, 1969.

TRANSACTIVE CRITICISM. *See* READER-RESPONSE CRITICISM AND RECEPTION THEORY

TRANSCENDENTALIST GROUP
Cuba, 1937-1940s

The Transcendentalist group was founded in Cuba in 1937 by José Lezama Lima (1910-1976), who began their journal, *Verbum*. It sought to take Cuban and Caribbean literature beyond the traditional costumbrista, or regionalist, literary mode of expression and focus on poetic language itself or, as Lezama Lima put it, the "union of the stellar and the verbal." Lezama Lima was strongly influenced by European SYMBOLIST and MODERNIST poets, such as T. S. ELIOT and Paul Valéry (1871-1945). His first volume of poetry, *Muerte de Narciso* (Death of Narcissus), also appeared in 1937. His influence spread to Puerto Rican poets and critics Félix Franco Oppenheimer (1912-) and Eugenio Rentas Lucas (1910-), both of whom later also participated in the ENSUE-ÑISMO GROUP, Francisco Lluch Mora (1924-), and Francisco Matos Paoli (1915-). Lezama Lima continued gathering groups of writers around him during his career; into the 1940s, he was the center of the *ORIGENES* journal and group.

✦•✦

Further Reading

Souza, Raymond D. *Major Cuban Novelists: Innovation and Tradition*. Columbia, Mo.: University of Missouri Press, 1976.

TRANSYLVANIAN HELICON GROUP
Romania, 1920s

Formed in 1926 in the Hungarian enclave of Transylvania, the Transylvanian Helicon Group consisted of some twenty-seven writers devoted to a geographically and culturally distinct literature, termed Transylvanism. Numerous independent writers were influenced by the Helicon Group, whose members displayed traces of SYMBOLISM, EXPRESSIONISM, and, especially, *NYUGAT* literature in their works. Four key members of the group were Lajos Áprily (1887-1967), János Bartalis (1893-1976), Jeno Dsida (1907-1938), and Sándor Reményik (1890-1941).

❖•❖
Further Reading

Gomori, George. "The Myth of Youthful Love in E. A. Poe's 'Annabel Lee' and Jeno Dsida's 'Serenade for Ilonka.'" *New Comparison* 9 (spring 1990): 117-27.

TREČIAS FRONTAS. *See* THIRD FRONT MOVEMENT

TREMENDISMO
Spain, 1940s

A post-Spanish Civil War movement, Tremendismo owed its origins to Camilo José CELA's NATURALISTIC novel *LA FAMILIA DE PASCUAL DUARTE* (1942; *The Family of Pascual Duarte*, 1947, 1964). The tremendously shocking and violent scenes in the novel are emblematic of the movement's emphasis on the absurdities and injustices of contemporary life. The movement, though it dwindled in force after less than a decade, remained strongly influential on social protest writers of newer generations. Other practitioners of Tremendismo included Carmen Laforet (1921-) and Luis Romero (1916-).

❖•❖

Cela, Camilo José (1916-)
Spanish novelist, short-story writer, and travel writer.

One of the most revered Spanish writers of the twentieth century, Cela launched his career with *La Familia de Pascual Duarte* (1942; *The Family of Pascual Duarte*, 1947, 1964). Between 1944 and 1955, he published five additional novels, each differing from the previous in structure, subject matter, and technical experimentation. After devoting himself to a number of other literary forms, especially the travel genre, Cela returned to writing long fiction in 1969 with *San Camilo, 1936* (Saint Camilo's Day, 1936). Like the majority of his writing, this work broke new ground in Spanish writing—in this case for its boldly erotic, occasionally pornographic language. Part MODERNIST, part EXISTENTIALIST, part NEOREALIST, Cela is considered one of the most gifted and unpredictable writers in modern Spanish literature.

La Familia de Pascual Duarte (1942; *The Family of Pascual Duarte*, 1947, 1964).

Frequently compared to Albert CAMUS's *L'ÉTRANGER* (1942; *The Outsider*, 1946; also published as *The Stranger*, 1946; *see* Existentialism, France), Cela's most famous novel explores the dark violence and tragedy of Spanish peasant Pascual Duarte's life, as revealed through his memoirs and the interpretations of an undisclosed "Transcriber."

After growing up in an atmosphere of poverty, hatred, and neglect, Pascual is condemned to a primitive moral existence, in which he defends himself and his dignity by spilling the blood of his enemies. One of his enemies is his mother, whom he kills in a particularly nightmarish episode. Another is a wealthy landowner, for whose murder Pascual now awaits execution. Cela's thematic intent, other than to shock, is obfuscated by the doubt he places on the veracity of Pascual's contrite state of mind, for his memoirs have apparently been written in order to stay his execution. The protagonist's cloudy morality, the excessive violence, the disturbing note of despair, the overtones of Franco's dictatorial regime — all contribute to the multi-layered meanings of the novel, which is regarded as among the most important works of twentieth-century Spanish fiction.

✦•✦

Further Reading

Andrews, Jean. "Jane Austen's Little 'Inch of Ivory' and Carmen Laforet's *Nada,* What Else Could a Woman Write About?" In *Women Writers in Twentieth-Century Spain and Spanish America.* Edited by Catherine Davies. Lewiston, N.Y.: Mellen, 1993.

Donahue, Francis. "Cela and Spanish 'Tremendismo'." *Western Humanities Review* 20 (1966): 301-6.

Foster, David William. *Forms of the Novel in the Work of Camilo José Cela.* Columbia, Mo.: University of Missouri Press, 1967.

Johnson, Roberta. *Carmen Laforet.* Boston: Twayne, 1981.

Jordan, Barry. *Laforet:* Nada. London: Grant and Cutler in association with Tamesis, 1993.

Kirsner, Robert. *The Novels and Travels of Camilo José Cela.* Chapel Hill, N.C.: University of North Carolina Press, 1966.

McGiboney, Donna Janine. "Language, Sexuality and Subjectivity in Selected Works by Ana Maria Matute, Carmen Laforet, and Merce Rodoreda." Ph.D. diss., State University of New York at Stony Brook, 1993.

McPheeters, D. W. *Camilo José Cela.* New York: Twayne, 1969.

Thompson, Currie K. "Perception and Art: Water Imagery in *Nada.*" *Romance Quarterly* 32, 3 (1985): 291-300.

Ullman, Pierre. "The Moral Structure of Carmen Laforet's Novels." In *The Vision Obscured: Perceptions of Some Twentieth-Century Catholic Novelists.* Edited by Melvin J. Friedman. New York: Fordham University Press, 1970.

TSO-I TSO-CHIA LIEN-MENG. *See* LEAGUE OF LEFT-WING WRITERS

TSO-I WEN-HUA TSUNG T'UNG-MENG. *See* LEAGUE OF LEFT-WING WRITERS

TSENTRIFUGA. *See* CENTRIFUGE

TULENKANTAKJAT. *See* **TORCHBEARERS GROUP**

TURIA GROUP
Spain, 1950s

Founded in the early 1950s by two leading Spanish novelists, Juan Goytisolo (1931-)
and Ana María Matute (1925-), the Turia Group initially shared several traits with
OBJECTIVISM but eventually assumed the highly individual concerns and experimental techniques of its various members.

✦•✦

Further Reading

Díaz, Janet. *Ana María Matute*. New York: Twayne, 1971.

Gazarian, Marie-Lise. *The Literary World of Ana María Matute*. Coral Gables, Fla.: University
of Miami, Iberian Studies Institute, 1993.

Goytisolo, Juan. *Forbidden Territory: The Memoirs of Juan Goytisolo, 1931-1956*. Translated
by Peter Bush. San Francisco: North Point Press, 1989.

————. *Space in Motion*. Translated by Helen R. Lane. New York: Lumen Books, 1987.

Pérez, Genaro J. *Formalist Elements in the Novels of Juan Goytisolo*. Potomac, Md.: J. Porráa
Turanzas, North American Division, 1979.

Pope, Randolph D. *Understanding Juan Goytisolo*. Columbia, S.C.: University of South
Carolina Press, 1995.

Schwartz, Kessel. *Juan Goytisolo*. New York: Twayne, 1970.

Six, Abigail Lee. *Juan Goytisolo: The Case for Chaos*. New Haven, Conn.: Yale University Press,
1990.

Ugarte, Michael. *Trilogy of Treason: An Intertextual Study of Juan Goytisolo*. Columbia, Mo.:
University of Missouri Press, 1982.

U

UJHOLD GROUP
Hungary, 1950s-1960s

One of several Hungarian magazines founded following World War II, *Ujhold* (New Moon) was the ideological successor to Mihály Babits's (1883-1941) humanist periodical *NYUGAT*. In both poetry and prose, the *Ujhold* Group expressed the EXISTENTIALIST plight of modern society; important writers of the movement included Iván Mándy (1918-), Ágnes Nemes Nagy (1921-), Géza Ottlik (1912-1990), János Pilinszky (1921-), and Magda Szábo (1917-).

❖•❖

Further Reading

Klaniczay, Tibor, ed. *A History of Hungarian Literature*. Budapest: Corvina, 1982.
Pilinszky, János. *Conversations with Sheryl Sutton: The Novel of a Dialogue*. Translated by Peter Jay and Eva Major. Manchester, England: Carcanet in cooperation with Corvina Books, 1992.
———. *The Desert of Love: Selected Poems*. Translated by János Csokits and Ted Hughes. With a memoir by Ágnes Nemes Nagy. Rev. and enl. ed. London: Anvil Press Poetry, 1989.

UKRAINIAN HOME GROUP (Ukrayinska Khata)
Ukraine, 1920s

A coterie of MODERNIST writers centered in the eastern Ukraine, the Home Group specialized in lyric verse and literary criticism. Hryhoriy Chuprynka (1879-1929), Oleksander Oles (1878-1944), and Mykola Vorony (1871-1942) numbered among the group's members.

❖•❖

Further Reading

Čyževs'kyj, Dmytro. *A History of Ukrainian Literature*. New York: The Ukrainian Academy of Arts and Sciences and Ukrainian Academic Press, 1997.

Rahojsa, Usievalad. "Two Little-Known Belarusian-Ukrainian Cultural Contacts." *Ukrainian Review* 41, 3 (1994): 67-68.

ULTRAISM
Latin America and Spain, 1920s

Ultraism, the poetic movement that inaugurated avant-garde writing in Spain during the 1920s, shared many principles with CREATIONISM and the earlier movement's founder, Vicente Huidobro (1893-1948). These principles — that modern Spanish poetry should be purged of sentimental language and symbols, that formal structures should be abandoned, and that pure expressions of experience should be sought — appeared in a number of manifestos, the first such being leader Guillermo de Torre's (1900-1976) *Manifiesto vertical ultraíste* (1920). This work, signed by six followers of Torre, as well as the new MODERNIST poems being published by the group, soon captured the attention of more notable literary figures, particularly Jorge Luis BORGES, who exported the movement to Argentina in 1921. Borges, however, soon abandoned the more peculiar tendencies of Ultraism and became better known in later years for his pioneering stories of MAGIC REALISM. By 1924 Ultraism had expired in Spain, though its experimentalist fervor was later channeled effectively by the GENERATION OF 1927.

❖•❖

Further Reading

Agheana, Ion Tudro. *The Meaning of Experience in the Prose of Jorge Luis Borges*. New York: P. Lang, 1988.

Costa, René de. *Vicente Huidobro: The Careers of a Poet*. Oxford, England: Oxford University Press, 1984.

Engelbert, Jo Anne. *Macedonio Fernández and the Spanish American New Novel*. New York: New York University Press, 1978.

Faris, Wendy B. *Labyrinths of Language: Symbolic Landscape and Narrative Design in Modern Fiction*. Baltimore, Md.: Johns Hopkins University Press, 1988.

Wood, Cecil G. *The Creacionismo of Vicente Huidobro*. Fredericton, Canada: York Press, 1978.

Zuleta, Emilia de. *Guillermo de Torre*. Buenos Aires: Ediciones Culturales Argentinas, 1962.

UNANIMISME
France, c. 1908-1920

In some ways, Unanimisme was a reaction by new French poets of the day — including Georges DUHAMEL, Jules ROMAINS, and Charles VILDRAC — against the isolation of the self-intuitively centered poets and their work, and it embodied the notion that only the shared emotions and activity of the artist, "in the cult of life, of teeming nature and the fertile city" would provide the new poetry of actuality, as it included the socio-cultural and philosophic elements of a contemporary world. Such poetry would appeal to the masses, since its message would report how they lived and thought. The grouping of individuals was of prime importance, and the poet must be an active participant in the agglomeration in order to produce poetry of any significance. The operative word was "unity" — between the people and their environment, the city, and in their responses to the burgeoning society of technology; emphasis on the collective participation of humanity, and the merging of individual psyche with the universe provided the basis for all activity — particularly the creative.

Between about 1910 and 1913, Unanimisme was only one of the many literary forces in France to precipitate a new thrust in artistic and intellectual enterprise. Innovative ideas about the sciences and new insight into the theories of Sigmund FREUD and Carl JUNG had all combined for a rekindling of interest in contemporary art and its philosophy, the drama and poetry. New and exciting works were being presented by Marcel PROUST (*see* MODERNISM, France), André GIDE (*see NOUVELLE REVUE FRAN-ÇAISE*), and Jean Cocteau (1889-1963). After World War I, those writers who had survived it would continue to make statements about the state of art and to develop new journals of critical inquiry. As one critic has noted, the closing years of the nineteenth century and the phrase "fin de siècle" had caused perhaps a stagnation in both the graphic arts and the literature. Now, however, France was ready to move into the Modernist movement.

❖•❖

Duhamel, Georges (1884-1966)
French poet, dramatist, novelist, and critic.

A chemist's son, Duhamel became a physician and served as a surgeon in World War I. His early poetry, published at L'ABBAYE, was made up of light verse, and in 1911 he turned to the writing of drama for creative satisfaction. Notable works were *La Luminiere* (1911) and *Dans l'ombre des statues* (1912). *Vie des martyrs: 1914-1916* and *Civilisation: 1914-1917* were tales about his war experiences, and contain his indictment of war, its inhumanity, and the irresponsibility of a society which had engendered it. His fictional output, between the wars and published in the twenties and thirties, depict the "anxieties and maladjustments" of a period which was in shock after a war and concerned about the prospect of another. *Vie et aventure of Saladin*, a five-volume novel published between 1920 and 1932, presents the protagonist of the LOST GENERATION, restless and a stranger to his environment. Saladin is a victim — of his circumstances and his surroundings. In his inability to cope with a society in which he finds neither substance nor succor, he finally succumbs to misery and frustration in the care of a loving wife and his mother. His regeneration comes on his death bed. He has been fatally injured while saving the life of a child and determines, just before death, that his own life had not been in vain. He has become the pathetic hero. Duhamel's other lengthy saga, *Le Chronique des Pasquiers* (1933-44), chronicles the lives of members of a middle-class family from the 1880s through World War II. One criticism of the work is that his fictional family and Duhamel's actual family are too closely related "to allow for proper play of the imagination." More favorable remarks are that the writer's sensitivity, his compassion, and his insights into the complexities of familial transition from one century to another are ably drawn and provide interesting reference to French life as lived in preparation for the second great war of the twentieth century.

During World War II, Duhamel once again cared for civilian casualties in the service of country. Afterwards, he published essays, criticism, and his memoirs. Out of favor with critics in the 1950s, Duhamel's character, Saladin, has recently been revived as exemplary of the alienated hero in an outrageous and unsympathetic society. In 1935, Duhamel was elected to the Academie Francaise, France's most prestigious intellectual consortium.

❖•❖

Romains, Jules (pseud. of Louis Farigoule, 1885-1972)
French poet, novelist, and dramatist.

Romains taught philosophy upon receiving his degrees from the École Normale Superiéure, in 1909, but early poems, *La Vie Unanime* (1908), were published while he was at l'Abbaye. An enthusiastic "unanimiste," Romains worked vigorously for the movement, along with Duhamel, Charles Vildrac, and René Arcos (1881-1948). In 1910, Romains presented the group's manifesto, *Manuel de Deification,* as a key to the understanding of the modern world. He saw the community as an organism and the individual as its most integral part; one could not exist without the other. The city should make up the "music" of life, and human beings must be conscious of that fact. To not recognize the importance of the larger unit of society blinds us to reality.

Optimistic and certain of his views, Romains's first novel, *Mort de Quelqu'un* (1911), inculcates them. Godard, the main character, serves to benefit his community after his death — more so than when alive. A mediocre day worker, at his death the community around him comes alive in its preparation for his funeral. The procession is viewed by all, traffic stops, and unknown witnesses take active part in the mourning. Godard affects the community, without conscious participation. In death he has become a source of energy and of life force. In *Les Hommes de Bonne Volanti* (1932-46), Romains describes Paris as a collective unit, between 1908 and 1933, and presents the lives of the proletariat, in that unit, at the turn of the century. Their destinies are played out against the excitement, fear and the uncertainty, though faith in the future was still extant. But World War I, its inhumanity and the anxiety that followed it caused "a world that [had] lost its direction." However, despite the anguish which preceded World War II, the novel reiterates the premise that the relationships between individuals and their interaction within the dynamics of the unified group provided them with optimal ways in which human beings can survive. What Romains wanted to present was that hope for survival lies within the aggregate of society in a novel "about the times." One critic suggests that it is rather a "document of the times," no more and no less.

For his verse, for his dramas and his prose works, Romains was elected to the French Academy in 1946. His influence on later writers and his excellent standing among his peers places him among the gifted writers of the first and exciting postwar generation of modern French writers.

✦•✦

Vildrac, Charles (pseud. of Charles Messager, 1882-1971)
French critic, dramatist, and poet.

Brother-in-law of Duhamel, Vildrac was very much influenced by him and others at l'Abbaye. In 1901, his article about free verse, "Le Vers Librisme," indicated his strong and early interest in Modernist poetry. He later collaborated with Duhamel to write a treatise, *Notes sur le technique poetique* (1910), and followed it with demonstration of his idea in *Livres d'Amour*, in the same year An English translation appeared in 1923 as *The Book of Love*. From then until the 1950s, Vildrac's work was concerned with presentation of the bonding between the artist, his environment and everything in it. His poetry and his plays were popular for the insight and perception which Vildrac had in depiction of the human condition in ordinary times and in time of crisis. His best-known drama, *La Paquebot Tenacity* (1919), which appeared in English in 1921 in translation, *The Steamship Tenacity*, depicts the strong dependency of working-class men upon each other in work, in life, and in nature. All of Vildrac's work speaks to the importance of the Unanimist credo and was carefully and thoughtfully presented.

✦•✦

Further Reading

Alden, D. W., and R. A. Brooks, eds. *A Critical Bibliography of French Literature*. Vol. 6. Syracuse, N.Y.: Syracuse University Press, 1980.

Bree, Germaine, and Margaret Guiton. *The French Novel from Gide to Camus*. New York: Harcourt, Brace & World, 1962.

Cruickshank, John. "French Literature since 1870." *French Literature from 1660 to the Present* by W. D. Howarth, Henri M. Peyre, and John Cruikshank. London: Methuen, 1974.

Keating, L. Clark. *Critic of Civilization: Georges Duhamel and His Writings*. Lexington, Ky.: University of Kentucky Press, 1965.

Norrish, Peter J. *Drama of the Group: A Study of Unanimism in the Plays of Jules Romains*. Cambridge, England: Cambridge University Press, 1958.

UNDER THE RAMPARTS (Taht al-Sūr)
Tunisia, 1940s

After World War II and before the liberation of Tunisia from French and other European powers, a nationalist trend manifested in Tunisian literature, notably via the Taht al-Sur group, which took its name from the cafe in which its members gathered. Dramatist and short-story writer 'Ali Du'ājī (1909-1949) was the most prominent literary figure in the group of artists and writers.

✤•✦

Further Reading

Abdel Jaouad, Hédi. "Tunisian Literature." In *Encyclopedia of World Literature in the Twentieth Century*. 3rd ed. Edited by Steven R. Serafin. Farmington Hills, Mich.: St. James Press, 1999.

UNION OF WRITERS OF THE U.S.S.R. *See* SOCIALIST REALISM, Russia

UNITY THEATER
England, 1930s-1940s

An outgrowth of the left-wing Workers' Theater Movement, the Unity Theater opened in London in 1936 with the English premiere of Clifford ODETS's *WAITING FOR LEFTY*, which had been a prominent success at the American GROUP THEATER the previous year. In 1937 the Unity Theater solidified its place in dramatic history with the first London production of a Bertolt BRECHT (*see* EPIC THEATER) work, *Señora Carrar's Rifles*, as well as the first British example of Living Newspaper. Producing important dramas on contemporary issues by an international list of writers who included Stephen Spender (1909-1995), Jean-Paul SARTRE (*see* EXISTENTIALISM), Sean O'CASEY (*see* ABBEY THEATER), and Arthur Adamov (1908-1970), the Unity continued until its facilities burned down in 1975. Directors of the Theater included André van Gyseghem (1906-) and Herbert Marshall (1906-1991).

✤•✦

Further Reading

Chambers, Colin. *The Story of Unity Theatre*. London: Lawrence and Wishart, 1989.

UNRELIABLE NARRATOR. *See* REALISM, United States

AL-'USBA AL-ANDALUSIYYA. *See* ANDALUSIAN LEAGUE

UZVYŠŠA GROUP
Byelorussia, 1920s

The *Uzvyšša* (or Excelsior) group was formed by discontented SAPLING members who felt that the revolutionary ideology of the Bolsheviks, which included ignoring past cultural heritage, stifled genuine literary creativity, not to mention nationalist feeling. They banded together in 1926, after painstakingly petitioning the Byelorussian Central Committee to sanction their formation, and began publishing their journal, *Uzvyšša*, in 1927. Some of the founding members — poet Uladzimier Dubowka (1900-1975), poet Jazep Pušča (pseud. of Jazep Płaščynski, 1902-1964), and critic Adam Babareka (1899-1937) — had collaborated together earlier when, in 1923, they formed the "Vitaism" (later renamed the *Ujaulennie* [Revival]) movement, which celebrated vitality and life, and apparently coexisted with their involvement in the Sapling group; a favorite refrain was "whatever is without motion dies." They chose the name excelsorism, or *uzvyšenstva*, to herald their independence from the Saplings. In their "Theses on the Formation of *Uzvyšša*," published in its first issue, they laid out a manifesto declaring their intention to culturally enrich the Byelorussian language and employ in their literature: "symbolism of social value," "concentration of imagery," "dynamism of composition," "cultivation of typically Byelorussian genres," "unity of the creative literary idea," "variety of formal realities," and "*akvityzm*" (acquitism). Other members included prose writer Kuzma Chorny (1900-1944), prose writer Michas Zarecki (1901-1941), and the satirist Kandrat Krapiva (pseud. of Kandrat Arrachovic, 1896-?).

The *Uzvyšša* group embodied in Byelorussia an anti-sovietization literary phenomenon taking place throughout the Soviet Union at the time; there was also, for example, the FREE ACADEMY OF PROLETARIAN LITERATURE (*Vaplite*) in the Ukraine and the PEREVAL group in Russia.

In 1929, the Byelorussian Association of Proletarian Writers was supported by the Byelorussian Central Committee in demanding "confessions of errors" from *Uzvyšša*'s members (which many produced in February 1930). Pušča's volume of poetry, *Listy da sabaki* (1927; Letters to a Dog) and Dubouka's *I purpurovych vietraziau uzvivy* (1927; And the Purple Sails Unfurled) attracted much negative attention from Communist Party critics for their "bourgeois ideology" and "blatant nationalism." Dubowka, Pušča, and Babareka resisted and were arrested that year, tried, and exiled. In 1931, splintered and dispirited, *Uzvyšša* announced its termination. Subsequent official Soviet historical accounts barely acknowledged the existence of the *Uzvyšša* group.

❖•❖

Further Reading

Adamovich, A. "The Sovietization of Byelorussian Literature." *Byelorussian Review* 1 (1955): 98-106.

————. "UZVYŠŠA — The Byelorussian Literary Club." *Byelorussian Review* 4 (1957): 23-55.

McMillan, Arnold B. *A History of Byelorussian Literature: From Its Origins to the Present Day.* Giessen, Germany: Wilhelm Schmitz Verlag, 1977.

V

VAN NU EN STRAKS (Today and Tomorrow)
Belgium, 1890s-1900s

Led by essayist and novelist August Vermeylen (1872-1945), *Van nu en straks* and its eponymous monthly were driving forces behind the literary and cultural revival of Flemish in Belgium during the 1890s and early 1900s. Other key figures of the movement—which embraced Impressionism, NATURALISM, and a liberal, art for art's sake philosophy—were novelists Cyriel Buysse (1859-1932), Stijn Streuvels (1871-1969), and Herman Teirlinck (1879-1967); theorist Prosper van Langendonck (1862-1920); and poet Karel van de Woestijne (1878-1929).

⋙•⋘

Further Reading

Gezelle, Guido. *Guido Gezelle, Karel Van de Woestijne in English Translation*. New York: Belgian Government Information Center, 1950.
Mallinson, Vernon. *Modern Belgian Literature, 1830-1960*. London: Heinemann, 1966.
Meijer, Reinder P. "Moralists and Anti-Moralists." In his *Literature of the Low Countries: A Short History of Dutch Literature in the Netherlands and Belgium*. New York: Twayne, 1971.

VAPLITE. *See* FREE ACADEMY OF PROLETARIAN LITERATURE

VERDE-AMARELISMO
Brazil, 1920s

By the second decade of the century, Brazilian writers had become increasingly aware of MODERNISM and were willing to embrace it. They had learned of its impact in Europe; São Paulo writers gave it enthusiastic reception and its influence had spread to other parts of the country, as well. Verde-Amarelismo, or "green-yellowness," was one of many movements begun in São Paulo for the purpose of creative exposition of many of the elements of the primitive, Amerindian tradition. The manifesto was strongly nationalistic and had for its intellectual basis the work of the earlier writer, Euclides de Cunha (1866-1909; *see* REGION-TRADITION MOVEMENT), who had deplored the degradation of the peasants and called for a more deeply compassionate examination of Brazilian culture and its ancient traditions. He was joined in this point of view by Alberto Torres (1865-1977). Their journal, *Anta*, was named for the tapir, a beast which was symbolic of the savage cruelty which existed in much of the region. The poetry of these writers conceptualized the reality of Brazilian nationality as the microcosm of universal reality in its animalistic aspects. The group was founded by Paulo Menotti Picchia (1892-?), Richardo Cassiano (1895-1974), and Plinio Salgado (1901-1975).

❖•❖

Further Reading

Muricy, José Cândedo de Andrade, ed. *A Nova Letteraria Brazileira: Critica e Antologia (The New Brazilian Literature: Criticism and Anthology)*. Porto Alegre, Brazil: Livraria do Globo, Barcellos, Bertaso & Cia., 1936.

VERNACULAR MOVEMENT. *See* MAY FOURTH MOVEMENT

VERISMO
Italy, 1860s-1910s

Verismo emerged in Italy as part of a worldwide trend toward REALISM, which during the late nineteenth and early twentieth centuries was being advocated elsewhere by such notable European and American authors as Emile ZOLA, Honoré de Balzac (1799-1850), and Stephen CRANE. The Realist and NATURALIST writers sought to create objective works that described human experience in accurate, impersonal, and simplified language. In Italy, Verismo was also a reaction against the extreme romanticism and overblown rhetoric of traditional Italian literature. It was additionally influenced by the interest in regionalism spurred by Italy's belated entrance into the industrialization of the modern age.

A moving force in the emergence and development of Verismo was Francesco De Sanctis (1817-1883), who is considered the founder of modern Italian literary criticism. Influenced by the Italian philosopher and historian Giambattista Vico (1668-1744) and the German philosopher Georg Hegel (1770-1831), both of whom viewed existence as a dynamic, ever-evolving process, De Sanctis employed a sociological and psychological approach in his evaluations of literary works. He believed that truth could be attained through a unification of the ideal and the real.

Giovanni VERGA is widely recognized as the leading novelist of the Verismo movement, as well as an important figure in twentieth-century literature in general. Like other Verists, Verga was influenced by the French Realist authors, particularly Gustave FLAUBERT and his concept of the impersonal narrator. He also took inspiration from the great nineteenth-century Italian novelist Alessandro Manzoni (1785-1873), whose sympathetic portrayal of Sicilian peasants in his acclaimed work *I promessi spozi* (1827; *The Betrothed*, 1898) was a bold departure from the aristocratic pretensions of the Italian literature of the period.

Verga's best-known work, *I MALAVOGLIA* (1881; *The House by the Medlar Tree*, 1890, 1964), depicts the struggles and resilience of a family of fishermen living in a small coastal village. Evident in the novel is Verga's highly effective merging of literary Italian with dialect speech and syntax, the achievement of which many critics consider a turning point in Italian literature. This new language came close to actual, ordinary local speech without crossing the line into pure dialect, thus retaining its literary quality. Verga also incorporated into this and other works — notable examples of which include the novel *Mastro-don Gesualdo* (1889; *Mastro-Don Gesualdo*, 1893, 1923, 1979) and the short stories collected in *Cavalleria Rusticana and Other Stories* (1928) — a form of indirect discourse that anticipated the method employed by the Italian novelists Cesare PAVESE and Elio VITTORINI as well as the great Irish Modernist author James JOYCE.

Another acclaimed member of the Verismo movement is Luigi CAPUANA, a native of Sicily who became a friend of Verga (and critical champion of his work) after moving to Milan in 1875. Both Capuana's early interest in the folklore of his native region and his later exposure to the work of the French Naturalists are evident in his best-known novels, *Giacinta* (1879) and *Profumo* (1890), which feature realistic, even scientifically clinical depictions of their protagonists' tragic lives.

Other notable practitioners of Verismo include Salvatore Di Giacomo (1860-1934), Matilde Serao (1850-1927), and Federico De Roberto (1861-1927).

❧•❦

Capuana, Luigi (1839-1915), Italian novelist, critic, and journalist.

Capuana is recognized as an important and influential member of the Verismo movement that emerged in Italy in the late nineteenth century. Born in Sicily, Capuana developed an early interest in the folklore of his native region, particularly folk ballads, which he collected. Capuana's career as an intellectual and literary critic blossomed after he moved to Florence in 1864. There he discovered the work of such French authors as Gustave Flaubert and Honoré de Balzac as well as the philosophical theories of Georg Hegel and Francesco De Sanctis. After returning for some years to Sicily, Capuana moved to Milan in 1875, where he befriended Giovanni Verga, who was to become (partly through the enthusiastic support of Capuana) the most renowned novelist of the Verismo movement.

In his two most famous novels, *Giacinta* (1879) and *Profuma* (1890), Capuana incorporated the objective, clinical approach he had learned from the Naturalists, employing an impersonal narrative voice to convey both accurate description and psychological insights. The story of a young woman who is traumatized and permanently damaged by her rape at fourteen, *Giacinta* features a nonchronological structure and the use of flashbacks. Also psychological in focus is *Profuma*, which centers on a woman whose anxiety is manifested in a strange body odor. Capuana explores the themes of guilt and individual responsibility in *Il Marchese di Roccaverdina* (1901; The Marquis of Roccaverdina), which chronicles a nobleman's murder of his humble mistress' husband.

Verga, Giovanni (1840-1922), Italian novelist.

Verga is recognized as the leading novelist of the Verismo movement as well as a major figure in Italian and twentieth-century literature. Among his greatest achievements was the creation of a new language that replaced the grandiosity of traditional literary Italian with a vital narrative form that incorporated elements of local dialect while retaining its artistic quality.

Born into a wealthy Sicilian family, Verga spent many of his early years on his father's estate, where he developed a knowledge of and sympathy for his country's rural people and way of life. He later moved to Florence, and then to Milan, where he became part of that city's lively literary scene. In Milan he met the critic and novelist Luigi Capuana, who would become a lifelong friend and stalwart supporter, and read the works of such French writers as Honoré de Balzac, Guy de MAUPASSANT, Gustave Flaubert, and Emile Zola. In forming his own approach to fiction, Verga was also influenced by the great nineteenth-century author Alessandro Manzoni, whose novel *I promessi spozi* (1827; *The Betrothed*, 1898) comprised a sympathetic portrait of rural Sicilians irrevocably bound by tradition.

Verga's earliest novels were historical romances peopled primarily with upper-class characters. The breakthrough in his career occurred in 1874 when he wrote the short story "Nedda," which chronicles the tragic life of an olive picker whose lover and child both fall prey to poverty and illness. This "Sicilian sketch" is notable for its unusual perspective, restrained, economical language, and fatalistic tone.

Acknowledged as Verga's greatest work is the novel *Il Malavoglia* (1881; *The House by the Medlar Tree*, 1890, 1964), in which the rural milieu and pessimistic mood evident in "Nedda" are brilliantly presented. Originally projected as the first in a series of five novels (to be entitled *I vinti*—the vanquished) that would depict various levels of society in a developing nation, *Il Malavoglia* focuses on a family of fishermen, the Malavoglia, who live in the coastal village of Aci Trezza. The novel chronicles the family's difficulties after their boat is wrecked and their home lost, showing how each generation struggles with traditional values and the demands of modern life. The novel's central theme is that people need the religion or myth of family and home to sustain them. Verga has been widely praised for his innovation not only in language but in character development, which is achieved indirectly rather than through description.

Verga finished only one more novel of *I vinti*: *Mastro-don Gesualdo* (1889), which takes place in a social milieu one level above that of *Il Malavoglia*. This novel concerns a bricklayer, Don Mazzaró, who marries into an impoverished aristocratic family but never achieves his goal of rising to a new social stratum. His greed for money and possessions, which he has equated with happiness, ultimately leave him alienated and lonely. Like all of Verga's work, *Mastro-don Gesualdo* is dominated by pessimism, depicting characters who are driven by their various hungers, frustrated in their yearning for happiness, but—despite their sometimes reprehensible qualities or behavior—somehow admirable in their ability to survive.

Il Malavoglia (1881; *The House by the Medlar Tree*, 1890, 1964).

Recognized as the greatest novel of Verismo, Italy's contribution to the late-nineteenth-century worldwide trend toward Realism, *Il Malavoglia* was originally presented as the first in a planned series of five novels that would depict the struggle for existence at successively higher levels of society. In the preface to *Il Malavoglia*, Verga stated that the series, to be entitled *I vinti* (the vanquished) would show its characters progressing in their desires from simple material needs to wealth to aristocratic vanity and social and political ambition, concluding with the story of a man who has achieved all these things but is destroyed by them. As it happened, Verga completed only the first two of these projected works.

Il Malavoglia concerns a family of impoverished fishermen who encounter death, defeat, and misery but retain their love for one another and also ultimately manage to reassert their traditional values. The family is headed by the old patriarch 'Ntoni; his son Bastianazzo, and grandchildren, 'Ntoni, Luca, Alessi, Lia, and Mena, live with him in the village of Aci Trezza. While transferring a large cargo, the family's boat is wrecked and Bastianazzo killed, and their subsequent inability to pay the mortgage on their house results in its loss. 'Ntoni is drafted into the navy and subsequently rejects the way of life his grandfather represents. He kills a customs guard and is sent to jail, and when he eventually returns to the village he finds that he is now out of place there. Meanwhile, Alessi has managed to buy back the family's house and is doggedly rebuilding their position.

In several important ways *Il Malavoglia* manifests the influence of the writers whose works Verga had studied and admired: it features a Flaubertian impersonal narrator, for instance, as well as Manzoni's basic respect for ordinary people. But the novel is notably innovative—particularly in the Italian context—in its narrative blend of literary language with everyday speech and its indirect delineation of character.

➤•◄

Further Reading

Cecchetti, Giovanni. *Giovanni Verga*. Boston: Twayne, 1987.
Molinaro, Julius A., ed. *Petrarch to Pirandello: Studies in Italian Literature in Honour of Beatrice Corrigan*. Toronto: University of Toronto Press, 1973.
Pacifici, Sergio. *The Modern Italian Novel from Capuana to Tozzi*. Carbondale, Ill.: Southern Illinois University Press, 1973.
Pacifici, Sergio, ed. *From Verismo to Experimentalism: Essays on the Modern Italian Novel*. Bloomington, Ind.: Indiana University Press, 1969.
Woolf, David. *The Art of Verga: A Study in Objectivity*. Sydney: Sydney University Press, 1977.

VERÐANDI GROUP
Iceland, 1880s-1900s

Central to the development of REALISM in Icelandic literature, the *Verðandi* Group consisted of four writers heavily influenced by Danish critic Georg Brandes (1842-1927). The most important member of the group was novelist and short-story writer Einar H. Kvaran (1859-1938). From the journal's inception in 1882 until approximately 1900, Kvaran helped redirect the course of Icelandic literature through works brimming with social criticism, regional detail, and psychological insight. The movement waned, however, when Kvaran's personal aesthetic evolved into a form of spiritual romanticism in the latter decades of his career. The other members included Holger Drachmann (1846-1908), Hannes Hafstein (1861-1922), and Gestur Pálsson (1852-1891).

➤•◄

Further Reading

Eddy, Beverley Driver. "The Use of Myth in Holger Drachmann's Forskrevet." *Scandinavian Studies* 61, 1 (winter 1989): 41-54.
Koefoed, H. A. "The Viking Stone: A Philological Essay." *NOWELE: North-Western European Language Evolution* 21-22 (April 1993): 447-53.

Liet, Henk van der. "A Fleeting Glimpse of Former Times: Holger Drachmann's Melodramas *Volund Smed* and *Renaessance*." *Scandinavica* 33, 2 (November 1994): 183-99.

VIENNA GROUP (Wiener Gruppe)
Austria, 1950s-1960s

The influential Wiener Gruppe consisted of a group of friends who studied and collaborated on various avant-garde poetic and theatrical projects in Vienna, Austria. Architect and writer Friedrich Achleitner (1930-); poet Hans Carl Artmann (1924-); poet and music and composition scholar Gerhard Rühm (1930-); poet and actor Konrad Bayer (1932-1964); and novelist, jazz musician, and theoretician Oswald Wiener (1935-) came together between 1950 and 1955.

They read the SURREALISTS, German EXPRESSIONISTS, and Gertrude STEIN (*see* MODERNISM, United States); studied DADA, linguistic theory, cybernetics, and music; created and collaborated on montages, dialect, sound, and visual, or CONCRETE POETRY; and held cabarets and experimental theater. After 1954, these events were held in a nightclub, Exil.

Artmann wrote the first manifesto for the group in 1953, "Eight Point proclamation of the Poetic Act"; Achleitner's poem "The good soup," however, is considered to be so representative of the group's aesthetic tenets it has been called an unofficial manifesto as well. By 1957 they were joined by poet, playwright, and prose writer Friedrike Mayröcker (1924-) and poet, translator, and radio playwright Ernst Jandl (1925-). Rühm associated with Concrete Poets elsewhere, such as Eugen GOMRINGER, Haroldo and Augusto de CAMPOS, and Decio PIGNATARI, and edited a volume about the group, *Die Wiener Gruppe*, in 1967. Achleitner, Artmann, and Rühm collaborated on a collection of dialect poems, *hosn rosn baa* (1959). Their work often appeared in the periodical *Manuskripte* until 1962 when they formed their own journal, *edition 62* (two issues). But by then, the group had begun to lose cohesiveness, and the members moved off into other interests and projects. Wiener's work from this period is difficult, if not impossible, to obtain, since he has preferred to detach himself from it.

✵•✵

Further Reading

Artmann, Hans. *The Best of H. C. Artmann*. Frankfurt am Main: Suhrkamp, 1970.
Bann, Stephen. *Concrete Poetry: An International Anthology*. London: London Magazine, 1967.
Solt, Mary Ellen, comp. *Concrete Poetry: A World View*. Bloomington, Ind.: Indiana University Press, 1968.
Waldrop, Rosmarie, and Harriett Watts, trans. and eds. *The Vienna Group: Six Major Austrian Poets*. Barrytown, N.Y.: Station Hill Press, 1985.

VIERNES GROUP
Venezuela, 1940s

Founded following the death of Venezuelan dictator Juan Vicente Gómez in 1936, the *Viernes* Group published a journal of the same name and stressed increased sophistication in Venezuelan poetry, drawing upon SURREALISM and other trends of the MODERNIST era. The most important poets of *Viernes* were Otto D'Sola (1912-), Vicente Gerbasi (1912-), Rafael Olivares Figueroa (1893-1972), and Pascual Venegas Filardo (1911-).

❖•❖

Further Reading

Dunham, Lowell. "Venezuelan Literature." In *Encyclopedia of World Literature in the Twentieth Century*. 3rd ed. Edited by Steven R. Serafin. Farmington Hills, Mich.: St. James Press, 1999.

VIJFTIGERS. *See* FIFTIES POETS

VILLAGE FICTION
Turkey, 1950s

Literary SOCIALIST REALISM in Turkey took popular hold during the 1950s and was expressed largely in the form of the "village novel." Earlier works by Sabahattin Âli (1906-1948) and the DAWN OF THE FUTURE writer Yakup Kadri Karaosmanoğlu (1889-1974), especially his *Yaban* (1932; The Outlander), gave precedent to realistic, often incriminating, portrayals of village life in simple vernacular language. During the first half of the twentieth century, rural Turkey began experiencing the painful transition from feudalism to capitalism. In 1940, the Republic began sponsoring Village Institutes, which were to educate the Turkish peasantry without advocating a taste for urban life. By 1945 the Institutes had established a literary journal, *Köy Enstitüleri Dergisi* (Review of the Village Institutes), in which many of the village writers' early works appeared.

Most of the writers associated with Village Fiction were educated in the Institutes and went on to teach in them. One, Mahmut Makal (1930-), holds the distinction of producing the novel many literary historians consider the first village novel proper, *Bizim Köy* (1950; *A Village in Anatolia*, 1954). Others include Fakir Baykurt (1929-), Talip Apaydin (1926-), and Mehmet Başaran (1926-). In their advocacy of social change and their unrelenting pursuit of publicizing the living conditions and political situation in the villages — largely in Anatolia — some of these writers faced harsh repercussions from the Turkish Republic, which imprisoned those with especially strong voices, such as Âli, Makal, and the internationally renowned Yaşar Kemal (Kemal Sadik Gökçali, 1922-). The Turkish Democratic Party also took Baykurt to court for the first book of his trilogy, *Yilanlarin Öcü* (1958; The Vengeance of the Serpents), but the case was dismissed. Kemal, with his *Ince Memed* (1955; *Memed, My Hawk*, 1961), quickly assumed a position of national prominence and has been considered by the Nobel Committee. Critics have noted the influence of William FAULKNER (*see* MODERNISM, United States) in Kemal's lyrical, Modernist narrative style and his construction of myth-infused village-scapes.

Contemporary to the rise of Village Fiction was the rise of an urban lower- and lower-middle class literature, sometimes referred to as *lumpenproletariotism*. Such writers as Sait Faik Abasiyanik (1906-1954), Kemal Bilbaşar (1910-), Samim Kocagöz (1916-), Aziz Nesin (1915-1995), Orhan Kemal (1914-1970), and Oktay Akbal (1923-) exemplified this trend while often writing of the challenges faced by the peasant who goes to the city, usually to find employment. As well as lending vitality to the ongoing language purification movement, Village Fiction has remained popular in Turkey through the 1980s.

✦●✦

Further Reading

Evin, Ahmet Ö., ed. Special issue on Yaşar Kemal. *Edebiyat* 5 (1980).

Halman, Talat Sait, ed. *Contemporary Turkish Literature: Fiction and Poetry*. Rutherford, N.J.: Fairleigh Dickinson University Press, 1982.

Karpat, Kemal H. "Social Themes in Contemporary Turkish Literature." *The Middle East Journal* 14, 1-2 (winter, spring 1960).

Rathbun, Carole. *The Village in the Turkish Novel and Short Story, 1920 to 1955*. The Hague: Mouton, 1972.

Stone, Frank A. *The Rub of Cultures in Modern Turkey; Literary Views of Education*. Bloomington, Ind.: Indiana University, 1973.

VILLAGE PROSE
Russia, 1950s-1960s

A prominent literary development within post-Stalin Russia, Village Prose was a fiction genre that focused, with conscious objectivity, on the social, economic, moral, and spiritual life of the peasant population. Removed from the deleterious effects of Communism and condemned to a crude life of subservience, this class of Soviet society represented for many of the village writers the simple, untarnished, archetypically Russian element of pre-Revolutionary times. Predecessors of the movement include Russian REALISTS Leo TOLSTOY and Anton CHEKHOV, and a number of ruralists from the 1920s. Some of the more notable writers of Village Prose, which flourished through the 1960s, were, Fyodor Abramov (1920-1983), Vasily Belov (1932-), Valentin Rasputin (1937-), Vladimir Soloukhin (1924-), Alexandr Yashin (1913-1968), Sergey Zalygin (1913-), and, occasionally, Aleksandr Solzhenitsyn (1918-).

❖•❖

Further Reading

Amalrik, Andreî. *Involuntary Journey to Siberia*. Translated by Manya Harari and Max Hayward. New York: Harcourt Brace Jovanovich, 1970.

————. *Nose! Nose? No-se! and Other Plays*. Translated and with an introduction by Daniel Weissbort. New York: Harcourt Brace Jovanovich, 1973.

————. *Notes of a Revolutionary*. Translated by Guy Daniels. New York: Knopf, 1982.

Gillespie, David C. *Valentin Rasputin and Soviet Russian Village Prose*. London: Modern Humanities Research Association, 1986.

Kotenko, N[ikolai]. N. *Valentin Rasputin*. Translated by Holly Smith. Soviet Writers of Today. Moscow: Raduga Publishers, 1988.

Polowy, Teresa. *The Novellas of Valentin Rasputin: Genre, Language, and Style*. New York: P. Lang, 1989.

Porter, Robert C. *Four Contemporary Russian Writers*. Oxford, England: Berg, 1989.

Rasputin, Valentin. *Siberia on Fire: Stories and Essays*. Selected, translated, and with an introduction by Gerald Mikkelson and Margaret Winchell. DeKalb, Ill.: Northern Illinois University Press, 1989.

Soloukhin, Vladimir. *Scenes from Russian Life*. Translated and with an introduction by David Martin. London: P. Owen, 1988.

VISNYK
Ukraine, 1933-1939

Formed in the Polish-ruled section of the Ukraine during the 1930s, an era of extreme, state-enforced repression for Soviet writers, *Visnyk* represented a haven for numerous emigrés, many of them poets. The journal and movement lasted until the outbreak of World War II and was an important source of literature stressing heroism and national destiny. Dmytro Dontsov (1883-1973), Bohdan Kravtsiv (1904-1975), Oksana Lyaturynska (1902-1970), Yury Lypa (1900-1944), Yevhen Malanyuk (1897-1968), Leonid Mosendz (1897-1948), Oleh Olzhych (1909-1944), Oleksa Stefanovych (1900-1970), and Olena Teliha (1907-1942) all numbered among the members of *Visnyk*.

❖•❖

Further Reading

Kindratovych, Petro. "Yuriy Lypa: On the 50th Anniversary of His Tragic Death." *Ukrainian Review* 41, 3 (1994): 64-66.

Luckyj, George S. N. "Western Ukraine and Emigration, 1919-39." In his *Ukrainian Literature in the Twentieth Century: A Reader's Guide*. Toronto: University of Toronto Press for the Shevchenko Scientific Society, 1992.

"Oleh Olzhych." *Ukrainian Review* 41, 3 (1994): 61-63.

VITAISM. *See UZVYŠŠA* GROUP

VORTICISM
England, 1914-1915

A collective of painters, sculptors, and writers living in and around London, Vorticism was a short-lived movement with tenets inspired by Italian FUTURISM and later evidenced in works of MODERNISM. The movement is dated from 1914 to 1915, concurrent with the two issues of *Blast*, the movement's forum. *Blast* featured work by Ezra POUND (*see* Modernism, England and Ireland), Ford Madox Ford (1873-1939), Wyndham LEWIS (1882-1957), and T. E. Hulme (1883-1917), among others. Characterized by aggressive, vituperative and abstract expression, Vorticism offered a more experimental approach than works of the IMAGISM movement that Pound was also championing at the time. The highly individual forms of expression in Vorticism and the outbreak of World War I, when Lewis, Hulme, and Vorticist sculptor Henri Gaudier-Brzeska (1891-1915) were inducted into military service, contributed to the movement's short life. Some critics argue that Vorticism's tenets were realized chiefly in visual arts and that no writings exist as paradigms of the group's explicit goals. However, many Vorticist values are evident in later works by Pound, Lewis, and T. S. ELIOT (*see* Modernism, England and Ireland), all commonly characterized as Modernists.

Pound originally applied the term "Vorticism" to a group of painters led by Lewis, but he adapted the term to describe an erasure of distinctions between visual and literary art. The first contextual appearance of "Vorticism" occurred in Pound's 1908 poem, "Plotinus": "As one that would draw through the node of things, / Back-sweeping to the vortex of the cone." According to Pound, Vorticism aimed to filter sculpture, painting, philosophy, and poetry through "a VORTEX, from which, through which, and into which, ideas are constantly rushing"; he later added, "Vorticism is art before it has spread itself into flaccidity, into elaboration and secondary applications."

The tenets are evident in the abstract drawings and paintings of Lewis and the primitive, yet gently rounded shapes of Gaudier-Brzeska's sculptures. These stylistic features were inspired by a 1912 exhibit of Italian Futurism in London. Vorticism was originally intended by Lewis and Pound as a renaissance combining revolutions in technology, science, and art, but the group's energy was dissipated by World War I and the subsequent deaths in battle of Gaudier-Brzeska and Hulme. Following the war, Lewis briefly resurrected the movement and called it Group X. Pound applied the group's didacticism in his later poem, *Hugh Selwyn Mauberly,* and in many of his *CANTOS.*

❖•❖

Lewis, (Percy) Wyndham (1882-1957)
English essayist, novelist, and painter.

Said to belong to the "most robust ethos of the twenties," Lewis is noted for a satiric view of life which is evident in his novels *Tarr* (1918), *The Apes of God* (1930), and *The Human Age* (1955). Of his many works, these are representative, timewise, of the direction in which his fiction moved, i.e., each one is more pronounced than the last in its representation of life in the modern age as fragmented by elements of mass civilization, mechanization, and "every kind of whirlwind of force and emotion." His anger about the futility of war is evident in some of his work, one example being *Blasting and Bombardiering* (1937), which describes his wartime experiences. Political and literary tracts include *The Art of Being Ruled* (1927), *Hitler* (1931), *Men Without Art* (1934), and *The Demon of Progress in the Arts* (1954). He was extolled by Ezra Pound for his vitality, his enormous energy, and his encompassing view of life ". . . the whole of it, beauty, heaven . . . every kind of whirlwind force and emotion." His Fascist sympathies and his disillusion with the British political situation between the two wars caused him to emigrate to Canada at the outbreak of the second. In 1949, his work ended with his blindness.

❖•❖

Further Reading

Cork, Richard, *Vorticism and Its Allies,* London: Arts Council of Great Britain, 1974.

Dasenbrock, Reed Way, *The Literary Vorticism of Ezra Pound and Wyndham Lewis: Towards the Condition of Painting.* Baltimore, Md.: Johns Hopkins University Press, 1985.

Foshay, Toby Avard. "Wyndham Lewis's Vorticist Metaphysic." *Ariel* 24, 2 (April 1993): 45-63.

Holloway, John. "Wyndham Lewis: The Massacre and the Innocents." *Hudson Review* (summer 1957): 171-88.

————. "Tank in the Stalls: Notes on the 'School of Anger'." *Hudson Review* (summer 1957): 424-29.

Krieger, Murray. *The New Apologists for Poetry.* Minneapolis: University of Minnesota Press, 1956.

Materer, Timothy. *Vortex: Pound, Eliot and Lewis.* Ithaca, N.Y.: Cornell University Press, 1979.

Perkins, David. *A History of Modern Poetry.* Cambridge, Mass.: Belknap Press of Harvard University, 1976.

Pound, Ezra. "Vorticism." *Fortnightly Review* 90 (1914): 461-71.

Pound, Ezra, and Wyndham Lewis. *Pound/Lewis: The Letters of Ezra Pound and Wyndham Lewis.* Edited by Timothy Materer. New York: New Directions, 1985.

800

Riding, Laura. *A Survey of Modernist Poetry*. London: Heinemann, 1927.

Shattuck, Roger. *The Banquet Years: The Arts in France, 1885-1918: Alfred Jarry, Henri Rousseau, Erik Satie, Guillaume Apollinaire*. New York: Harcourt Brace, 1959.

Wagner, Geoffrey Atheling. *Wyndham Lewis: A Portrait of the Artist as the Enemy*. New Haven, Conn.: Yale University Press, 1957.

Wees, William C. *Vorticism and the English Avant-Garde*. Toronto: University of Toronto Press, 1972.

WASHINGTON SQUARE PLAYERS
United States, 1910s

Part of the LITTLE THEATER MOVEMENT in the United States, the Washington Square Players formed in Greenwich Village in 1914 and devoted themselves to the production of works of high literary merit. Dramatists whose plays were featured included Anton CHEKHOV (*see* REALISM, Russia), Henrik IBSEN (*see* REALISM, Norway), Eugene O'NEILL (*see* EXPRESSIONISM, United States, and PROVINCETOWN PLAYERS), and George Bernard SHAW (*see* EDWARDIAN LITERATURE). Principals of the company included Lawrence Langner (1890-1962) and Lee Simonson (1888-1967). With several of their associates, including Robert Edmond Jones (1887-1954), they banded together in 1919 to reform the Washington Square Players as the THEATER GUILD, which came to rival traditional theater companies with its many commercial successes.

➩•◄

Further Reading

Fogg Art Museum. *Three Designers for the Contemporary Theatre: Robert Edmond Jones, Donald Oenslager, Lee Simonson*. Cambridge, Mass.: Fogg Art Museum, 1950.
Langner, Lawrence. *The Magic Curtain: The Story of a Life in Two Fields, Theatre and Invention*. London: G. G. Harrap, 1952.
Pendleton, Ralph, ed. *The Theatre of Robert Edmond Jones*. Middletown, Conn.: Wesleyan University Press, 1958.
Silvestri, Vito N. "The Washington Square Players: Those Early Off-Broadway Years." *Quarterly Journal of Speech* 51 (1965): 35-44.
Washington Square Plays: 1. The Clod, by Lewis Beach. *2. Eugenically Speaking*, by Edward Goodman. *3. Overtones*, by Alice Gerstenberg. *4. Helena's Husband*, by Philip Moeller. Drama League Series of Plays 20. Garden City, N.Y.: Doubleday, Page, 1916.

WAVE (Onda)
Mexico, 1960s

A Mexican movement of the 1960s resembling the BEAT GENERATION, The Wave promoted both aesthetic and cultural rebellion. Its two most important voices were fiction writers José Agustín (1944-) and Gustavo Sainz (1940-).

❧•❧

Further Reading

Counts, Roberta Weaver. *Alienation of Youth in the Novels of Gustavo Sainz and José Agustín.* Thesis, University of Tennessee, Knoxville, 1975.

WEDGE GROUP (Kiila)
Finland, 1930s

Founded in 1936, the Wedge Group was a MARXIST-Leninist Finnish organization of writers and artists. The primary literary purpose of this group was to foster lyric poetry championing the working classes. Members included Viljo Kajava (1909-), Jarno Pennanen (1906-1969), Elvi Sinervo (1912-), and Arvo Turtiainen (1904 1980).

❧•❧

Further Reading

Ahokas, Jaakko. *A History of Finnish Literature.* Bloomington, Ind.: Indiana University, 1973.

WEN-HSÜEH YEN-CHIU HUI. *See* LITERARY RESEARCH ASSOCIATION

WHITE BIRCH SCHOOL (Shirakaba-ha)
Japan, 1910-1923

Formed by graduates of the Peers' School, an exclusive Tokyo academy, the White Birch School was one of the leading anti-NATURALIST groups of the early twentieth century. The members of the movement took their name from the arts journal they launched in 1910. Espousing optimistic humanism, a philosophy far more prevalent among the Japanese public than the pessimistic determinism of the Naturalists, the White Birch writers quickly gained national favor.

The key figures of the group included Shiga Naoya, Mushakōji Saneatsu, Arishima Takeo (1877-1923), and Satomi Ton (1888-1983). Each enjoyed an enviable ancestry, aristocratic upbringing, and accompanying freedom from financial concerns which allowed them to write entirely from personal conviction and experience. Although divergent in narrative styles and degrees of idealism, these writers shared a strong interest in Western literature and art. Through *Shirakaba* they exposed and promoted such writers and artists as Leo TOLSTOY (*see* REALISM, Russia), Maurice MAETERLINCK (*see* SYMBOLISM, Belgium), Henrik IBSEN (*see* REALISM, Norway), Walt Whitman (1819-1892), Vincent Van Gogh (1853-1890), Auguste Rodin (1840-1917), and Paul Cézanne (1839-1906). They saw in the various creations of these Americans and Europeans a robust affirmation of individual potential, a humanistic belief to which they wholeheartedly committed themselves. Thus occupied with the self and the auto-biographical evocation of experience, their stories and novels occasionally resemble those of the Japanese Naturalists. However, the White Birch writers generally bestowed a native nobility in their main characters which they linked to their dominant theme of the eventual, if not immediately attainable, happiness of humanity.

Shiga Naoya, given his reclusive, spiritual lifestyle, mastery of the I-NOVEL, and development of a subtle, highly emotive style, became a virtual deity among many younger writers. Yet he departed the movement within the first few years and, despite his overwhelming influence, is therefore not considered its main force. Instead, Mushakōji was the movement's chief theoretician and its most fully realized example of what the modern individual should be. Profoundly affected by the writings and social ideals of Tolstoy, Mushakōji passionately defended the movement in its early years against accusations of technical simplicity, social irrelevance, political ignorance, and intellectual naiveté on the grounds that White Birch writers stood for the fundamental purity of humanity. If their style and subject matter appeared simple, this was due to their correspondingly simple, yet incomparably powerful, message.

In 1918, at the height of the movement, Mushakōji founded a cooperative community, which he termed New Village, in southeastern Kyushu. Neither capitalistic nor socialistic in nature, the community represented Mushakōji's greatest ideal, that people, working together, could indeed form a "world brotherhood." Mushakōji continued to formulate his humanistic vision in fiction as this community and others thrived. However, by 1923, the same year as the great Tokyo earthquake, *Shirakaba* ceased publication and the movement effectively dissolved. With the exception of Shiga, the Shirakaba writers are little regarded today. Their importance as a movement resides more in their popularization of Western literature and art and their advancement of humanitarian ideals than in the typically predictable characters and stories they produced.

Mushakōji Saneatsu (1885-1976), Japanese novelist and dramatist.

Considered the most representative writer of the White Birch School, Mushakōji was greatly influenced in his early career by his exposure to Christianity and to the works of Leo Tolstoy. During the first of the five periods his professional life is generally divided into, he helped found and edit the journal *Shirakaba* and published works championing the sanctity and supremacy of the human spirit in modern society. During the second period, from the founding of his experimental village in 1918 until the end of *Shirakaba* in 1923, he reached artistic maturity, shedding the puritanism of Tolstoy and embracing the less structured optimism of Maurice Maeterlinck. Several of his best works, including *Kōfukumono* (1919; The Happy Man) and *Yūjō* (1919; *Friendship*, 1958), appeared at this time. From 1923 until 1936 Mushakōji's philosophy became increasingly Communistic; during this third period he launched a second career as a painter and also wrote numerous biographical novels, including a fictional life of Gautama Buddha. His interest in painting and other fine arts, particularly Oriental, continued during his fourth period; many full-length novels, such as *Ai to Shi* (1939; *Love and Death*, 1958) and *Akatsuki* (1942; Dawn) date from this time. In the final, postwar stage of his career, Mushakōji enjoyed renewed popularity with the publication of his long novel *Shinri Sensei* (1949-50; The Teacher of Truth). His works in general are characterized by a simple style, irrepressible humor, and panoramic presentation of the ultimate triumph of the human ego.

Yūjō (1919; *Friendship*, 1958).

Yūjō, conceived at the height of the White Birch movement, is Mushakōji's most popular work. The story details a downtrodden writer's unrequited love for the sister of a friend. Nojima reveals his love for Sugiko to another friend, a successful writer named Ōmiya. Out of allegiance to Nojima, Ōmiya sails for Europe upon discovering his attraction for Sugiko, an attraction that Sugiko shares with him. The novel concludes with Sugiko joining Ōmiya in Europe. When Nojima discovers his fate, he resolves to endure it stoically. The novel has maintained its appeal to readers due to its anti-Naturalist grandeur and, ironically, the character of Ōmiya, rather than Mushakōji's presumed alter ego, Nojima.

⤖•⬺

Shiga Naoya (1883-1971), Japanese short-story writer and novelist.

Although he published relatively few works during his long life, Shiga is nonetheless considered one of the most influential Japanese writers of the twentieth century. Central to his artistic sensibility was his seven-year apprenticeship, beginning in 1900, to Christian leader Uchimura Kanzō (1861-1930). More immediately important to the content of his fiction, though, was his antagonistic relationship with his father. During the years 1912-14, considered to be crucial to his formation as a writer, Shiga confronted his innermost feelings and unabashedly exposed his troubled family life in some of his finest stories, including the novella *Otsu Junkichi* (1912; Otsu Junkichi), a retelling of his wish, never realized, to marry the family maid despite his father's abhorrence of the idea. Later works, particularly *Wakai* (1917; Reconciliation) and "Kinosaki ni te" (1917; At Kinosaki), demonstrate Shiga's increasing passivity toward the self-actualization tenets of the White Birch writers and concomitant interest in a quiet, contemplative life in harmony with nature. Yet, he drew heavily on his stormy relationship with his father for his best-known work and only novel, *An'ya Koro* (1937; *A Dark Night's Passing*, 1976); originally begun as *Tokito Kensaku* in 1912, the first half of Shiga's masterwork was not published until 1922. After completing the novel, Shiga produced little else, and nothing of lasting literary significance. His immense stature in modern Japanese fiction is attributed to his perfection of the short-story form and significant influence on the I-Novel, his nuanced style, and the unqualified praise he received from such eminent writers as Akutagawa Ryūnosuke (1892-1927), Tanizaki Jun'ichirō (1886-1965), and Kawabata Yasunari (1889-1972).

An'ya Koro (1937; *A Dark Night's Passing*, 1976).

Written over a twenty-five-year span, *An'ya Koro* traces the protagonist Kensaku's life through a turbulent five-year period. At the beginning, Kensaku is haunted by memories of his father's indifference toward him. His closest family relationship is with his brother, but his life is generally unhappy and characterized by ennui. Turning to sexual dissipation to fill the void within him, he seeks the company of prostitutes, but also fantasizes about relations with his grandfather's mistress, O-Ei. He eventually succeeds in repressing his carnal desires and finds purpose and meaning as a writer attuned to the natural surroundings of Onomichi, where he has retreated. As monotony and poor health return to plague him, Kensaku again thinks of O-Ei and proposes marriage. O-Ei refuses, informing him that his real father is in fact his grandfather, who had carried on an illicit affair with his mother. In the second half of the novel, Kensaku marries Naoku but an unhappiness settles over him when their first child dies in infancy. The discord between the couple increases when Naoko is seduced by a cousin. After a six-month retreat to a Buddhist temple, during which time Kensaku experiences the regenerative powers of scriptures and nature, he returns to his wife, filled with a deep, enduring peace. Despite Shiga's anomalous membership with the White Birch School, his novel remains an important outgrowth of the movement for its uncompromising attention to the positive realization of the self.

✥•✥

Further Reading

Keene, Donald. "The Shirakaba School." In his *Dawn to the West: Japanese Literature of the Modern Era*. New York: Holt, Rinehart, & Winston, 1984.

Kohl, Stephen W., et al. *The White Birch School (Shirakabaha) of Japanese Literature: Some Sketches and Commentary*. Eugene, Ore.: Asian Studies Committee, University of Oregon, 1975.

Mathy, Francis. *Shiga Naoya*. New York: Twayne, 1974.

Sibley, William F. *The Shiga Hero*. Chicago: University of Chicago Press, 1979.

Ueda, Makoto. "Shiga Naoya." In his *Modern Japanese Writers and the Nature of Literature*. Stanford, Calif.: Stanford University Press, 1976.

WIE EEGIE SANIE (Our Own Things)
Surinam and the Netherlands, 1950s

During the 1950s a group of Surinamese students and workers in Amsterdam founded the Wie Eegie Sanie group in response to the new, often racist, culture in which they were living. The literary branch of the group, led by Eddy Bruma (1925-), sought to produce creole literature and a sense of cultural independence. Bruma, known for his poetry, is perhaps most noted for his political, historical plays — some of which he composed yearly for Surinam's Emancipation Day celebrations. After arriving in Holland in 1953, poet Trefossa (Henri Frans de Ziel, 1916-) joined the group. Upon his return to Surinam, he published a volume of creole poetry, *Trotji* (1957), which would diminish resistance to the use of creole languages in Surinamese schools. Trefossa also helped to legitimatize creole as a literary medium for Surinamese writers.

✦•✦

Further Reading

Voorhoeve, J., and Ursy Lichtweldt, eds. *Creole Drum. An Anthology of Creole Literature in Surinam*. New Haven, Conn.: Yale University Press, 1975.

WIENER GRUPPE. *See* VIENNA GROUP

WORKSHOP FOR POTENTIAL LITERATURE. *See* OULIPO

WSPÓŁCZESNOŚĆ GENERATION
Poland, 1956-1971

A Polish movement begun in 1956 and lasting until 1971, the Współczesność Generation emphasized freedom from poetic restrictions. Among earlier multinational movements that exerted an influence on the Generation were EXISTENTIALISM and SURREALISM. Perhaps the most visible figure of the Generation was Stanisław Grochowiak (1934-1976), who engendered a new style of poetry termed "turpism," which eschewed light, idyllic subject matter in favor of the ugly and shocking.

807

⇉●⇇
Further Reading

Białoszewski, Miron. *A Memoir of the Warsaw Uprising*. Edited and translated by Madeline Levine. Evanston, Ill.: Northwestern University Press, 1991.

Kuncewicz, Piotr. *Grochowiak*. Warsaw: Author's Agency, 1976.

Miłosz, Czesław. "World War II; First Twenty Years of Peoples' Poland — Poetry." In his *The History of Polish Literature*. London: Macmillan, 1969. Rev. ed., Berkeley, Calif.: University of California Press, 1983.

Morgan, Edwin. *East European Poets*. With: *Poetry in Public*, by Alasdaire Clayre. Milton Keynes, England: Open University Press, 1976.

WU-SSU YÜN-TUNG. *See* MAY FOURTH MOVEMENT

Y

YALE SCHOOL (American Deconstruction)
United States, 1970s

Deconstruction was the dominant critical trend in the United States during the 1970s. Indebted to the work of French scholar Jacques DERRIDA, founder of DECONSTRUC- TION, American Deconstruction is known for its highly skeptical view of knowledge founded upon metaphysical principles. Consequently, the Yale School writers, though they place a fundamental emphasis on linguistic structure, nevertheless regard litera- ture, indeed all writing, as inherently reflexive, referring to nothing beyond its own, self-differentiating verbal signs. What perhaps best distinguishes the Yale critics from Derrida is the conviction that literary language, despite its inevitable heterogeneity, subtly affirms itself as perhaps the most accessible, verifiable reality in the modern age of doubt. Although American literary theory has in recent years attempted to overcome the seeming intellectual impasse left by Deconstructive readings, the Yale School has continued to shape PostSTRUCTURALIST thought in several innovative ways.

The four critics most often associated with American Deconstruction are Paul DE MAN, J. Hillis Miller (1928-), Geoffrey Hartman (1929-), and Harold Bloom (1930-). By 1970 all were members of the English department at Yale University except Miller, who transferred from Johns Hopkins two years later. An academic atmosphere open to new European thought, Yale provided a receptive ground for the scholars' shared repudia- tion of NEW CRITICISM, a widely accepted native tradition which affirmed the organic unity of a literary work. Adopting the unconventional approach of Derrida, who first introduced his Deconstruction strategy to American scholars in 1966, the Yale critics focused almost exclusively on the rhetorical elements of writing, as had the New Critics, but did so with the assumption that each possible interpretation could be counterbal- anced with another. For the Yale critics, ambiguity was the one discernible feature of all discourse.

Each of the Yale critics, admittedly, developed their Deconstructive thought in distinctive ways. Both Bloom and Hartman have, in fact, demonstrated a sympathetic but far from subservient attitude toward Derridean Deconstruction. Beginning with his study *The Anxiety of Influence* (1973), Bloom introduced into his readings a heavily FREUDIAN component. The crux of his highly influential theory is that within all serious literature there dwells the undercurrents of the individual author's rebellion against looming artistic and ideological ancestors. Similarly humanistic as opposed to grammatical in orientation is the work of Hartman. In true Deconstructionist manner Hartman affirms the creative and autonomous status of criticism, elevating the role of the reader while decanonizing the original text. However, in such works as *Criticism in the Wilderness* (1980), he uncovers the dangers of non-hermeneutical interpretation that overlooks or avoids sociopolitical, theological, and historical issues.

Next to Derrida, de Man is considered the most faithful and profound theoretician of Deconstruction. Yet, the most conspicuous apologist for the movement during its years of maturation was Miller. A former adherent of the GENEVA SCHOOL, whose members focused on the acquisition of meaning through perception of an author's consciousness, Miller eventually arrived, through contact with Derrida and de Man's theories, at an unequivocal denial of language as a referential medium. Vincent Leitch notes that Miller's volte-face occurred with a 1971 review of M. H. Abrams's *Natural Supernaturalism*. In this essay, Miller states: "Language is from the start fictive, illusory, displaced from any direct reference to things as they are. The human condition is to be caught in a web of words which weaves and reweaves for man through the centuries the same tapestry of myths, concepts, metaphorical analogies, in short, the whole system of Occidental metaphysics." It is this pervasive tradition that Deconstruction in its purest sense attempts to render meaningless. Consequently, more orthodox critics have heatedly questioned the purposes of such interpretation. Abrams labelled the movement "suicidal." William Pritchard described the Yale critics as the "hermeneutical mafia." Despite such critical resistance, a topic de Man himself addresses in the posthumously published *The Resistance to Theory* (1986), the Deconstructive methodology of the Yale School has won numerous admirers. Although the Yale School may be said to have dissolved with the passing of de Man in 1983, the issues addressed by its foremost members continue to occupy leading theorists throughout the world.

❧•❦

De Man, Paul (1919-1983)
Belgian-born American essayist, critic, and scholar.

De Man, who served as Sterling Professor of Comparative Literature at Yale, is regarded as the first writer outside France to seriously apply the theories of Derrida to the investigation of literature. Beginning with *Blindness and Insight: Essays in the Rhetoric of*

810

Contemporary Criticism (1971; 2nd ed., 1983), de Man displayed a remarkable understanding not only of the rhetorical operations of language but of the variegated nature of critical discovery itself. Like several of his Yale School colleagues, de Man was instrumental in renewing critical debate of the Romantic tradition, especially concerning the question of the philosophical and aesthetic orientation of such writers as Jean-Jacques Rousseau (1712-1778) and William Wordsworth (1770-1850). Some of his most important conclusions on this subject are contained in *Allegories of Reading* (1979) and the posthumously published *The Rhetoric of Romanticism* (1984).

Blindness and Insight (1971).

Informed by the EXISTENTIALIST positions of Jean-Paul SARTRE and Martin Heidegger (1889-1976) as well as the theories of Derrida, *Blindness and Insight* is nonetheless one of the most original and influential collections of Poststructuralist literary criticism. One of the central points de Man makes in this difficult work is that blindness is "the necessary correlative of the rhetorical nature of literary language," whether it be the blindness of the text, the reader, or the critic. In perhaps his most famous essay, "The Rhetoric of Blindness: Jacques Derrida's Reading of Rousseau," de Man questions the conclusions of a study by Derrida on the writings of Rousseau, generally thought to be an adherent of the logocentric, or oral, tradition of communication. Countering Derrida's assumption that Rousseau was unaware of the subversive qualities of his text, de Man asserts that Rousseau had, in fact, employed a highly self-conscious, even flawless, rhetorical strategy which denied Derrida's subversive approach. The original text, then, receives a greater degree of distinction under de Man than under Derrida. Both theorists, however, remain firm in their commitment to delimiting meaning in the realm of literary discourse.

✦•✦

Further Reading

Arac, Jonathan, et al, eds. *The Yale Critics: Deconstruction in America*. Minneapolis: University of Minnesota Press, 1983.

Atkins, G. Douglas. "J. Hillis Miller, Deconstruction, and the Recovery of Transcendence." In *Reading Deconstruction — Deconstructive Reading*. Lexington, Ky.: University Press of Kentucky, 1983.

Cain, William E. "Deconstruction in America: The Literary Criticism of J. Hillis Miller." In *The Crisis in Criticism: Theory, Literature, and Reform in English Studies*. Baltimore, Md.: Johns Hopkins University Press, 1984.

————. "Robert Penn Warren, Paul de Man, and the Fate of Criticism." In *The New Criticism and Contemporary Literary Theory: Connections and Continuities*. Edited by William J. Spurlin and Michael Fischer. New York: Garland, 1995.

Culler, Jonathan. *On Deconstruction: Theory and Criticism after Structuralism*. Ithaca, N.Y.: Cornell University Press, 1982.

Currie, Mark. "The Voices of Paul de Man." *Language and Literature: Journal of the Poetics and Linguistics Association* 2, 3 (1993): 183-96.

Deconstruction and Criticism: Harold Bloom, Paul de Man, Jacques Derrida, Geoffrey H. Hartman, J. Hillis Miller. New York: Seabury Press, 1979.

Derrida, Jacques, ed. *Memoires for Paul de Man.* New York: Columbia University Press, 1986.

Graef, Ortwin de. *Serenity in Crisis: A Preface to Paul de Man 1939-1960.* Lincoln, Nebr.: University of Nebraska Press, 1993.

Harari, Josué V. *Textual Strategies: Perspectives in Post-Structuralist Criticism.* Ithaca, N.Y.: Cornell University Press, 1979.

Hartman, Geoffrey. *Saving the Text: Literature, Derrida, Philosophy.* Baltimore, Md.: Johns Hopkins University Press, 1981.

Leitch, Vincent B. "The Lateral Dance: The Deconstructive Criticism of J. Hillis Miller." *Critical Inquiry* 6 (1980): 593-607.

Lentricchia, Frank. "Paul de Man: The Rhetoric of Authority." In his *After the New Criticism.* Chicago: University of Chicago Press, 1980.

Miller, J. Hillis. *The Ethics of Reading: Kant, de Man, Eliot, Trollope, James, and Benjamin.* New York: Columbia University Press, 1987.

Moynihan, Robert. *A Recent Imagining: Interviews with Harold Bloom, Geoffrey Hartman, J. Hillis Miller, Paul de Man.* Hamden, Conn.: Archon Books, 1986.

Norris, Christopher. *Deconstruction: Theory and Practice.* London: Methuen, 1982.

Pritchard, William H. "The Hermeneutical Mafia; or, After Strange Gods at Yale." *Hudson Review* 28 (1975): 601-10.

Schultz, William R. *Genetic Codes of Culture? The Deconstruction of Tradition by Kuhn, Bloom, and Derrida.* New York: Garland, 1994.

Schwarz, Daniel R. "The Fictional Theories of J. Hillis Miller: Humanism, Phenomenology, and Deconstruction in *The Form of Victorian Fiction* and *Fiction and Repetition*." In his *The Humanistic Heritage: Critical Theories of the English Novel from James to Hillis Miller.* Philadelphia: University of Pennsylvania Press, 1986.

Sturrock, John, ed. *Structuralism and Since: From Levi-Strauss to Derrida.* Oxford, England: Oxford University Press, 1979.

Waters, Lindsay, and Wlad Godzich, eds. *Reading de Man Reading.* Minneapolis: University of Minnesota Press, 1989.

YEDI MEŞ'ALE. See **SEVEN TORCHES**

YORUBA OPERA
Nigeria, 1940s

An important movement in Nigerian drama, the Yoruba Opera arose in the 1940s via Hubert Ogunde's (1916-1990) Concert Company. Combining elements of dance and music with myths, moralizing, and satire, Ogunde and fellow dramatists E. Kola Ogunmola (1925-1973) and Duro Ladipo (1931-1978) helped popularize this uniquely Nigerian genre throughout West Africa and in various parts of Europe.

❧•❦

Further Reading

Anyanwu, Mike, and Adavi Abraham, eds. *A Journey Fulfilled: Impressions and Expressions on Hubert Ogunde*. Ibadan, Nigeria: Caltop Publications, 1994.

Clark, Ebun. *Hubert Ogunde, the Making of Nigerian Theatre*. Oxford, England: Oxford University Press, 1979.

Ladipó, Duro. *Three Yoruba Plays*. Translated by Ulli Beier. Ibadan, Nigeria: Mbari Publications, 1964.

Obafemi, Olu. *Committed Theatre and Nationalist Struggle in Colonial Nigeria: Hubert Ogunde's* Strike and Hunger. Ibadan, Nigeria: Bookman Educational and Communications Services, 1990.

Ogbodo, Abraham. "Aiming High." In *African Guardian* 6, 2 (January 21, 1991): 47.

YOUNG ESTONIA GROUP (Noor-eesti)
Estonia, 1905-1910s

Led by poet and critic Gustav Suits (1883-1957), the Young Estonians were closely allied with the SYMBOLISTS, particularly German poet Stefan George (1868-1933), who served as Suits's mentor. Other members included Johannes Aavik (1880-1973), August Alle (1890-1952), Ernst Enno (1875-1934), Aino Kallas (1878-1956), Jaan Oks (1884-1918), Villem Ridala (1885-1942), and Friedebert Tuglas (1886-1971). Together they helped reform and internationalize Estonian writing during the first decades of the twentieth century.

❧•❦

Further Reading

Kallas, Aino Krohn. *The White Ship: Estonian Tales*. Translated by Alex Matson. Freeport, N.Y.: Books for Libraries Press, 1971.

Mägi, Arvo. "Neo-Romanticism and Expressionism." In his *Estonian Literature: An Outline*. Stockholm: The Baltic Humanitarian Association, 1968.

Nirk, Endel. "Noor-Eesti." In his *Estonian Literature*. Translated by Arthur Robert Hone and Oleg Mutt. 2nd ed. Tallinn, Estonia: Perioodika, 1987.

YOUNG FRISIAN MOVEMENT
Netherlands, 1915-1935

Devoted to the resurrection and modernization of Frisian literature in the Netherlands, the Young Frisian Movement emerged in 1915 under the leadership of critic, poet, and

813

dramatist Douwe Kalma (1896-1953). An elaborate and archaic poetic style precluded complete success for the movement, which lasted until about 1935.

⋙•⋘

Further Reading

Krol, Jelle. "Douwe Kalma (1896-1953) and Great Britain: A Literary Relationship." *Dutch Crossing: A Journal of Low Countries Studies* 18, 2 (winter 1994): 84-99.

YOUNG ISRAEL
Israel, 1950s

Centered in Haifa and active during the first decade of Israeli independence, Young Israel was comprised of young Yiddish writers, such as Moyshe Yungman (1922-1983), led by veteran author David Pinski (1872-1959). Like many twentieth-century Yiddish groups, Young Israel was significantly influenced by the pioneering works of Y. L. Peretz (1852-1915).

⋙•⋘

Further Reading

Liptzin, Solomon. *A History of Yiddish Literature.* Middle Village, N.Y.: Jonathan David Publishers, 1972.

YOUNG KASHUBIAN MOVEMENT (Ruch Młodokaszubski)
Poland, 1910s

The Young Kashubian Movement was the product of Slavic Kashubs centered near Gdansk, Poland. Beginning with Alexander Majkowski's (1876-1938) founding of the journal *Gryf* in 1908, the Kashubian writers upheld a literature based on early oral traditions and attempted to preserve their native culture in the face of both German and Soviet expansionism. The Young Kashubians, whose members also included Leon Heyke (1885-1939), Jan Karnowski (1886-1939), Jan Patock (1886-1940), and Franciszek Sędzicki (1882-1957), wrote in a variety of genres, though poetry was the most prominent. Kashubian literature remains active today as a highly localized literary phenomenon.

⋙•⋘

Further Reading

Stone, Gerald. "The Language of Cassubian Literature and the Question of a Literary Standard." *The Slavonic and East European Review* 50, 121 (October 1972): 521-29.

YOUNG MUSE GROUP (Moloda Muza)
Ukraine, 1920s

Prominent during the 1920s, the Young Muse Group was, along with the UKRAINIAN HOME GROUP, a leading force in MODERNIST poetry in the Ukraine. Some of the chief members of the group were Stepan Charnetsky (1881-1945), Ostap Lutsky (1883-1941), and Vasyl Pachovsky (1878-1942).

❖•❖

Further Reading

Čyževs'kyj, Dmytra. *A History of Ukrainian Literature*. New York: The Ukrainian Academy of
  Arts and Sciences and Ukrainian Academic Press, 1997.
"Literature." In *Ukraine: A Concise Encyclopaedia*. Edited by Volodymyr Kubijovyč. Vol. 1.
  Toronto: University of Toronto Press, 1963.

YOUNG ONES (Die Yunge)
United States, 1920s

A New York-based group of immigrant Jewish writers, the Young Ones emerged in 1907 as a response to then-prevalent sociopolitical writing in Yiddish literature. In place of this, the Young Ones offered highly personal poetry whose themes included the negative psychological effects of urbanization. By 1919 the influence of the Young Ones, comprised of some dozen writers, including Moyshe Leib Halpern (1886-1932) and Mani Leib (1883-1953), receded due to the even more modern and psychologically based writing of the INTROSPECTIVISTS.

❖•❖

Further Reading

Gittleman, Sol. *From Shtetl to Suburbia: The Family in Jewish Literary Imagination*. Boston:
  Beacon Press, 1978.
Wisse, Ruth R. *A Little Love in Big Manhattan: Two Yiddish Poets*. Cambridge, Mass.: Harvard
  University Press, 1988.

YOUNG PENS (*Genç Kalemler*)
Turkey, 1910s

The Young Pen movement was one of various literary groups that sprang up after the 1908 Young Turk revolution paved the way for more artistic freedom in Turkey. Short-story writer and essayist Ömer Seyfeddin (1884-1920) and poet, sociologist, and education theorist Ziya Gökalp (1876-1924) were among the most prominent members in the apparently short-lived group. Their journal, *Genç Kalemler* (1910), stressed the use of the Turkish vernacular, as opposed to the ideologies of groups such as the NEW LITERATURE GROUP and DAWN OF THE FUTURE. The Young Pens were concerned with creating a national Turkish literature and identity for the common man. In order to achieve this, they advocated dropping Arabic and Persian elements from Turkish literature and renounced imitation of non-Turkish literature—both European and Eastern. Seyfeddin's views on establishing this new Turkish literature, expressed in his essay, "Yeni Lisan" (1911; The New Language), were greatly influential in the institution of language reforms in 1928 during the administration of Kemal Atatürk (1881-1934). His stories are marked by realistic, often bitter, portrayals of ordinary life in simple language. Gökalp contributed poetry to the journal calling for the strengthening of the Turkish heritage. The language debate, seen in the early decades of the twentieth century in the contradictory aims of these movements, remained unresolved at the century's end.

⇻•⇺

Further Reading

Karpat, Kemal H. "Social Themes in Contemporary Turkish Literature." *The Middle East Journal* 14, 1 (winter 1960): 29-44.

Stone, Frank A. *The Rub of Cultures in Modern Turkey; Literary Views of Education.* Bloomington, Ind.: Indiana University, 1973.

YOUNG POLAND (Młoda Polska)
Poland, 1890s-1910s

A massive, heterogeneous movement in Polish literature that is sometimes, though inaccurately, referred to as Neoromanticism, Young Poland began in the 1890s and extended until the end of World War I. Paralleling aesthetic currents in other European countries, Young Poland reacted against REALISM and Positivism while embracing SYMBOLISM and various strains of MODERNISM; in effect, it constituted, through its linguistic and structural experimentation and its close attention to the theories of Friedrich NIETZSCHE and other late-nineteenth-century iconoclasts, the birth and early development of modern Polish literature. The leading Young Poland writers, primarily poets, dramatists, and critics, were Jan Kasprowicz (1860-1926), Stanisław Brzozowski (1878-1911), Stanisław Przybyszewski (1868-1927), Zenon Przesmycki (1861-1944), Kazimierz Tetmajer (1865-1940), and Stanisław Wyspiański (1869-1907). Despite various individual emphases, these writers were united by a belief that in a world of diminishing universal values new values could best be sustained through art, literature, and music. This art for art's sake aesthetic was adopted by several successor movements of Young Poland, the most notable of which were the *SKAMANDER*

816

GROUP and *ZDROJ* GROUP. Although the influence of Young Poland was formidable during the first decades of the twentieth century, eventually, through such reactionary movements as the CRACOW AVANT-GARDE and FUTURISM, new definitions of and values for Modernist writing prevailed.

➜•◄

Further Reading

Carpenter, Bogdana. *The Poetic Avant-Garde in Poland, 1918-1939*. Seattle: University of Washington Press, 1983.
Miłosz, Czesław. "Young Poland." In his *The History of Polish Literature*. New York: Macmillan, 1969. Rev. ed., Berkeley, Calif.: University of California Press, 1983.

YOUNG VIENNA GROUP (Jungwien)
Austria, 1890s-1900

Founded in 1891 by Hermann Bahr (1863-1934), Young Vienna was a group of poets and dramatists who championed Decadence (*see* AESTHETICISM/DECADENCE), Impressionism, and SYMBOLISM as the most suitable aesthetic platforms for depicting fin de siècle unrest, which in vanishing imperial Vienna took on additional historical and psychological significance. Among Bahr's coterie, dramatist Arthur Schnitzler (1862-1931), best remembered as the author of *Anatol* (1893) and *Reigen* (1900, produced 1912; *Dance of Love,* 1965), was the figure who most closely identified with the sensuality and despair that characterized the period. Schnitzler's appreciation of the theories of his countryman Sigmund FREUD lent to his works an additional component of psychological intensity that allied Young Vienna with later MODERNIST writers. Other writers associated with the movement included Symbolist Hugo von Hofmannsthal (1874-1929), Richard Beer-Hofmann (1866-1945), and Peter Altenberg (1859-1919).

➜•◄

Further Reading

Liptzin, Sol. *Arthur Schnitzler*. New York: Prentice-Hall, 1932.
Schnitzler, Arthur, and Donald Daviau, eds. *The Letters of Arthur Schnitzler to Hermann Bahr*. Chapel Hill, N.C.: University of North Carolina Press, 1978.

YOUNG VILNA
Lithuania, 1930s

Named for the Lithuanian city in which it was centered, Young Vilna was a short-lived, nontraditional Yiddish movement whose members included Hirsh Glik (1922-1944),

Chaim Grade (1910-1982), and Abraham Sutzkever (1914-). With the onslaught of World War II one of the movement's dominant themes became the chaos and bloodshed of the Holocaust.

✦●✦

Further Reading

Grade, Chaim. *My Mother's Sabbath Days: A Memoir*. New York: Knopf, 1986.
Leftwich, Joseph. *Abraham Sutzkever: Partisan Poet*. New York: T. Yoseloff, 1971.
Liptzin, Sol. "Young Vilna." In his *A History of Yiddish Literature*. Middle Village, N.Y.: Jonathan David Publishers, 1972.
Sutzkever, Abraham. *A. Sutzkever: Selected Poetry and Prose*. Translated by Barbara and Benjamin Harshav. Berkeley, Calif.: University of California Press, 1991.
————. *Burnt Pearls: Ghetto Poems of Abraham Sutzkever*. Translated by Seymour Mayne. Oakville, Canada: Mosaic Press/Valley Editions, 1981.

YOUNG YIDDISH GROUP
Poland, 1920s

Formed in 1919 and based in Poland, the Young Yiddish Group drew upon EXPRESSIONISTIC and MODERNIST techniques to create a literature that focused on both Jewish tradition and the plight of the modern individual. Yankev Adler (1895-1949) and Moyshe Broderzon (1890-1956) were both associated with the movement.

✦●✦

Further Reading

Adler, Jankel. *Jankel Adler*. New York: Galerie Chalette, 1959.
————. *Jankel Adler, 1895-1949*. London: The Arts Council, 1951.
Hayter, Stanley William. *Jankel Adler*. London: Nicholson & Watson, 1948.
Themerson, Stefan. *Jankel Adler, an Artist Seen from One of Many Possible Angles*. London: Gaberbocchus Press, 1948.

YUNGE, DIE. *See* YOUNG ONES

YÜ SSU GROUP
China, 1924-1930

The literary society Yü Ssu (Brief Discourses, or Random Talks) and its eponymous magazine, both founded in Peking in 1924, were significant vehicles of expression for the ideas of China's NEW LITERATURE MOVEMENT, a literary outgrowth of the revolution of 1912 that had culminated with the abdication of the last Chinese emperor and creation of a republican government. Important aspects of this movement included use of a vernacular Chinese language and an increasing interest in Western forms of expression, both of which were explored by *Yü Ssu*. The magazine was theoretically devoted to publishing essays on any topic that might interest its readers, save politics. It was hoped this stance would prevent *Yü Ssu* from becoming embroiled in the civil wars rampant during this time. Nonetheless, *Yü Ssu*'s support of individualism, especially as represented by the essays of LU Hsün (*see* MAY FOURTH MOVEMENT), led to persecution of its contributors by the local right-wing government, which forced *Yü Ssu* to move from Peking to Shanghai in 1928, and the magazine had to cease publication in 1930. Ironically, as Communist power began to coalesce during this time, Lu Hsün and *Yü Ssu* also came under attack from the left for their views, although Lu Hsün would eventually become reconciled to the Communist cause in his later years and his entire literary legacy would be coopted by them after his death.

The major figures involved with founding both the magazine and the literary society surrounding its publication included Lu Hsün (the pen name for Chou Shu-jên) and his brother, Chou Tso-jên (1885-1966?). Both brothers had studied Japanese, classical Greek, and English literature extensively, and, although Lu Hsün is better known for his fiction, both brothers were masters of the essay form, a style that was long popular in China throughout its history and one to which *Yü Ssu* was devoted. Lu Hsün's essays were a glaring exception to the generally nonconfrontational writings often found in *Yü Ssu*. They tended to be sharply polemical, as he believed it was important for an author to write about society's ills, and he did not refrain from attacking those he thought responsible for them. Chou Tso-jên's work was more in the liberal, humanitarian mode that was standard for the magazine, and he too was highly regarded during this time. Other significant contributors to the *Yü Ssu* society and magazine were brothers Sun Fu-yuan and Sun Fu-hsi as well as Liu Fu (1891-1934), Li Hsiao-feng, and Lin Yutang (1895-1976).

❖•❖

Further Reading

Giles, Herbert A. *A History of Chinese Literature. With a Supplement on the Modern Period by Liu Wu-chi.* New York: F. Ungar Publishing Company, 1967.

Hsia, Chih-tsing. *A History of Modern Chinese Fiction.* New Haven, Conn.: Yale University Press, 1971.

Scott, Dorothea Hayward. *Chinese Popular Literature and the Child.* Chicago: American Library Association, 1980.

Z

ŻAGARY GROUP
Poland, 1930s

Żagary was among the most prominent movements and journals of the second Polish avant-garde, which took place during the 1930s. Czesław Miłosz was among the founders of *Żagary*, a group of politically active university students which also included Teodor Bujnicki (1907-1944), Jerzy Zagórski (1907-), Jerzy Putrament (1910-1986), and Aleksander Rymkiewicz (1913-?). In their poetry these writers prophesied, through a new form of dark SYMBOLISM, the cataclysmic events of World War II, and quickly gained for their group a new label, the Catastrophists. Miłosz's *Poemat o czasie zastygłym* (1933; "Poem of the Frozen Time") and *Trzy zimy* (1936; "Three Winters") (see *Collected Poems*) are considered the two outstanding works of the movement.

❧•❧

Miłosz, Czesław (1911-)
Lithuanian-born Polish poet, essayist, historian, and novelist.

In addition to his association with *Żagary*, Miłosz was an active member of the Polish underground in Warsaw during World War II. Following the war he served in a diplomatic capacity but his profound opposition to totalitarianism and the strictures of SOCIALIST REALISM led him to immigrate first to France in 1951 and eventually to the United States a decade later. The first of many works in English translation in which he explores themes of cruelty, freedom, and exile in a personal, historical context was the essay collection *Zniewolony umysł* (1953; *The Captive Mind,* 1953). Other important works by Miłosz include the moral autobiography *Rodzinna Europa* (1959; *Native Realm: A Search for Self-Definition,* 1968); the novels *Zdobycie władzy* (1955; *The Seizure of Power,* 1955, also translated as *The Usurpers,* 1955) and *Dolina Issy* (1955; *The Issa Valley,* 1981); the essay collection *Widzenie nad zatoką San Francisco*

820

(1969; *Visions from San Francisco Bay,* 1982); his *History of Polish Literature* (rev. ed., 1983); and an impressive body of poems, most recently reprinted in *The Collected Poems 1931-1987* (1988), that has earned him the title of greatest living Polish poet. Miłosz was awarded the Nobel Prize in literature in 1980.

❖•❖

Further Reading

Carpenter, Bogdana. *The Poetic Avant-Garde in Poland, 1918-1939.* Seattle: University of Washington Press, 1983.

Czarnecka, Ewa, and Aleksander Fiut. *Conversations with Czesław Miłosz.* Translated by Richard Lourie. San Diego: Harcourt Brace Jovanovich, 1987.

Fiut, Aleksander. *The Eternal Moment: The Poetry of Czesław Miłosz.* Berkeley, Calif.: University of California Press, 1990.

Miłosz, Czesław. *The Captive Mind.* Translated by Jane Zielono. New York: Vintage Books, 1953.

————. *The Witness of Poetry.* Cambridge, Mass.: Harvard University Press, 1983.

————. "Independent Poland: 1918-1939 — Poetry — Toward the Second Vanguard: 'Żagary'." In his *The History of Polish Literature.* London: Macmillan, 1969. Rev. ed., Berkeley, Calif.: University of California Press, 1983.

ZAUMNYI YAZYK. *See* CUBO-FUTURISM

ZAVETY (Behests) SCHOOL
Russia, 1910s

A Russian movement of the prerevolutionary era, Zavety concerned itself primarily with fiction on rural themes. Mikhail Prishvin (1873-1954), Alexey Remizov (1877-1957), and Evgeny Zamyatin (1884-1937) were the most prominent members of Zavety.

❖•❖

Further Reading

Collins, Christopher. *Evgenij Zamjatin, an Interpretive Study.* The Hague: Mouton, 1973.

Edwards, T. R. N. *Three Russian Writers and the Irrational: Zamyatin, Pilnyak, and Bulgakov.* Cambridge, England: Cambridge University Press, 1982.

Images of Aleksei Remizov: Drawings and Handwritten and Illustrated Albums from the Thomas P. Whitney Collection. Essay and catalog of the exhibition by Greta Nachtailer Slobin. Checklist of the exhibition by Jane Sharp. Exhibition organized by Judith Barter. Amherst, Mass.: Mead Art Museum, 1985.

Kern, Gary, ed. *Zamyatin's* We: *A Collection of Critical Essays.* Ann Arbor, Mich.: Ardis, 1988.

New Views on Zoshchenko, Zamiatin, Bulgakov, and Pasternak. Russian Studies in Literature 32, 1. New York: M. E. Sharpe, 1996.

Richards, David. *Zamyatin, a Soviet Heretic*. New York: Hillary House, 1932.

Shane, Alex M. *The Life and Works of Evgenij Zamjatin*. Russian and East European Studies. Berkeley, Calif.: University of California Press, 1968.

Slobin, Greta N., ed. *Aleksej Remizov: Approaches to a Protean Writer*. Columbus, Ohio: Slavica Publishers, 1986.

————. *Remizov's Fictions, 1900-1921*. DeKalb, Ill.: Northern Illinois University Press, 1991.

Zamyatin, Evgeny. *A Soviet Heretic: Essays*. Translated and edited by Mirra Ginsberg. Evanston, Ill.: Northwestern University Press, 1992.

Zirin, Mary Fleming. *Prišvin and the "Chain of Kaščej."* Doctoral thesis, University of California at Los Angeles, 1972.

ZDROJ GROUP
Poland, 1917-1922

A Polish EXPRESSIONIST movement and journal, *Zdroj* was active from 1917 until 1922. The guiding lights of *Zdroj* were Jerzy Hulewicz (1886-1941) and Stanisław Przybyszewski (1868-1927); another important though loosely associated member was Emil Zegadłowicz (1888-1941), who transferred elements of *Zdroj* to his *CZARTAK* GROUP. Others included Wacław Berent (1873-1940) and Józef Wittlin (1896-1976).

❧•❦

Further Reading

Baer, Joachim T. "Wacław Berent: His Life and Work." In *Antemurale* 18 (1974).

Szwede, Irena. *The Works of Stanisław Przybyszewski and Their Reception in Russia at the Beginning of the XX Century*. Doctoral thesis, Dept. of Slavic Languages and Literatures, Stanford University, 1970.

Weichsel, John. *Stanisław Przybyszewski, His Life and Writings*. New York: Knopf, 1915.

Yurieff, Zoya. *Joseph Wittlin*. New York: Twayne, 1973.

Zolman, Hanna Ann. *Stanisław Przybyszewski and His Lyrical Universe*. Doctoral thesis, UCLA, 1980.

ZLATOROG GROUP. *See* GOLDEN HORN

ZNANIE GROUP
Russia, 1890s-1900s

A St. Petersburg publishing group formed in 1898, *Znanie* ("knowledge") was joined in 1900 by Maxim GORKY. From this time until about 1911, *Znanie*, under the direction of Gorky and K. P. Pyatnitsky (n.d.), became the foremost source for works of Critical Realism—the antecedent of SOCIALIST REALISM—in Russia. The *Znanie*

Group was known especially for its series of literary almanacs, which began appearing in 1903. The list of both Russian and foreign authors whose writings were featured in the *Znanie* almanacs is extensive and includes Leonid Andreyev (1871-1919), Ivan Bunin (1870-1953), Aleksandr Serafimovich (1863-1949), Ivan Shmelyov (1873-1950), Vikenty Veresayev (1867-1945), Gustave FLAUBERT (*see* REALISM, France), Gerhart HAUPTMANN (*see* FREIE BÜHNE), Knut Hamsun (1859-1952), and Walt Whitman (1819-1892). Following the first Russian Revolution of 1905, political and artistic dissension within *Znanie*, caused by Gorky's radical views, led to several writers' abandonment of the movement. Within a few years, the circulation of *Znanie* began a steady decline, culminating in the publication of a final issue in 1913, long after Gorky himself had severed his editorial ties with the company.

➻•➻

Further Reading

Luker, Nicholas, ed. *An Anthology of Russian Neo-Realism: The "Znanie" School of Maxim Gorky*. Ann Arbor, Mich.: Ardis, 1982.

Mirsky, D. S. "The Znanie School of Fiction." In *Contemporary Russian Literature, 1881-1925*. London: G. Routledge; New York: Knopf, 1926.

APPENDIX 1

A Timeline of
Literary Movements

1840s

Austria, Germany, and Switzerland	Realism (c. 1848-1880s)

1850s

France	Realism (1850s-1870s)
England	Realism (1850s-1890s)
Russia	Realism (1852-1900s)
France	Félibrige Movement (1854-1920s)

1860s

France	Naturalism (1860s-1900s)
Italy	Verismo (1860s-1910s)

1870s

Norway	Realism (1870s)
Poland	Realism (1870s-1880s)
France	Symbolism (1870s-1890s)
Spain	Realism (1870s-1890s)
Denmark	Naturalism (1870s-1900s)
United States	Local Color School (1870s-1900s)
Argentina and Uruguay	Gaucho Literature (1870s-1920s)

1880s

Norway	Naturalism (1880s)
Germany	Naturalism (1880s-1890s)
Iceland	Realism (1880s-1890s)

1880s *(Continued)*

Spain	Naturalism (1880s-1890s)
England	Aestheticism/Decadence (1880s-1900)
Belgium	Symbolism (1880s-1900s)
Denmark	Realism (1880s-1900s)
England	Naturalism (1880s-1900s)
Germany	Symbolism (1880s-1900s)
Greece	New School of Athens (1880s-1900s)
Iceland	*Verðandi* Group (1880s-1900s)
Latvia	Realism (1880s-1900s)
United States	Genteel Tradition (1880s-1900s)
	Naturalism and Realism (1880s-1910s)
Canada	Confederation Poets (1880s-1920s)
Germany	Deutsches Theater (1880s-1960s)
Netherlands	Movement of the Eighties (c. 1885-1900s)
Japan	Society of Friends of the Inkstone (1885-1903)
France	Théâtre Libre (1887-1896)
Argentina, Colombia, Cuba, Mexico, Nicaragua, Peru, Spain, and Uruguay	Modernismo (c. 1888-1910s)
Germany	Freie Bühne (1889-1894)

1890s

Czechoslovakia	Symbolism (1890s)
Denmark	Symbolism (1890s)
Austria	Young Vienna Group (1890s-1900)
France	Naturism (1890s-1900)
Argentina, Chile, and Venezuela	Criollismo (1890s-1900s)
Belgium	*Van nu en straks* (1890s-1900s)
England and Ireland	Symbolism (1890s-1900s)
Germany	Jugendstil (1890s-1900s)
Hungary	Popular National School (1890s-1900s)
Japan	Romantic Movement (1890s-1900s)
Latvia	Neoromanticism (1890s-1900s)
	New Current Movement (1890s-1900s)
Russia	*Znanie* Group (1890s-1900s)
Sweden	Nittiotalister (1890s-1900s)

Uruguay	Generation of 1900 (1890s-1900s)
France	École Romane (1890s-1910s)
Poland	Young Poland (1890s-1910s)
Ireland	Irish Renaissance (1890s-1920s)
Portugal	Symbolism (1890s-1920s)
Russia	Symbolism (1890s-1917)
Finland	National Neoromanticism (1890s-1930)
France	Breton Movement (1890-1950)
Bulgaria	*Misul* Group (1892-1907)
Croatia, Serbia, and Slovenia	Modernism (1895-1918)
Canada	Literary School of Montreal (1895-1925)
Turkey	New Literature Group (1896-1901)
Spain	Generation of 1898 (c. 1898-1910s)
Russia	Moscow Art Theater (1898-1990s)
Japan	Negishi Tanka Society (1899-1900s)

1900s

England and Ireland	Edwardian Literature (c. 1900-1911)
Canada	Terroir School (1900-1930s)
Italy	Modernism (1900-1950s)
Cuba	Arpas Cubana Group (1900s)
Finland	Loafers (1900s)
France	Humanisme (1900s)
Italy	Intimismo (1900s)
Japan	New Poetry Society (1900s)
Romania	Sămănătorism (1900s)
Spain (Catalonia)	Realism (1900s)
United States	Muckraking (1900s)
Uruguay	Council of Brilliant Knowledge (1900s)
Italy	Crepuscolarismo (1900s-1910s)
Japan	Naturalism (1900s-1910s)
Korea	New Poetry Movement (1900s-1910s)
Paraguay	Generation of 1900 (1900s-1910s)
Romania	Symbolism (1900s-1910s)
Canada	Local Color School (1900s-1920s)
Japan	Hototogisu School (1900s-1920s)
Lithuania	Symbolism (1900s-1920s)

1900s *(Continued)*

Spain	Noucentismo/Novecentismo (1900s-1930s)
France	Modernism (1900s-1930s)
Germany	Heimatkunst (1900s-1930s)
Russia	Modernism (1900s-1930s)
England, Japan, and United States	Modern Nō (1900s-1990s)
Italy	*La Critica* (1903-1944)
Ireland	Abbey Theater (1904-1930s)
Czechoslovakia	Modernism (1905-1910s)
Estonia	Young Estonia Group (1905-1910s)
Norway	Generation of 1905 (1905-1920)
Ukraine	Modernism (1905-1920)
Bulgaria	Symbolism (1905-1920s)
Netherlands	The Movement (1905-1920s)
United States	47 Workshop (1905-1933)
Azerbaijan	*Füyüzat* Movement (1906-1907)
France	Abbaye Group (1906-1908)
Japan	New Tendency School (c. 1906-1910s)
Byelorussia	*Naša Niva* Group (1906-1914)
Azerbaijan	*Molla Nasreddin* (1906-1920)
France	Unanimisme (c. 1908-1920)
Hungary	*Nyugat* Group (1908-1920s)
France	*Nouvelle Revue Française* (1908-1943)
Turkey	Dawn of the Future (1909-1912)
China	Southern Society (1909-1924)

1910s

Cuba	Oriente Group (1910s)
France	Cubism (1910s)
	Fantaisistes Group (1910s)
	Futurism (1910s)
	Little Theater Movement (1910s)
	Simultanéisme (1910s)
Georgia	Blue Horns Group (1910s)
Germany	Little Theater Movement (1910s)
	Storm Circle (1910s)
Iceland	Progressive Romanticism (1910s)

828

Italy	Theater of the Grotesque (1910s)
Poland	Young Kashubian Movement (1910s)
Romania	Poporanism (1910s)
Russia	Centrifuge (1910s)
	Ego-Futurism (1910s)
	Little Theater Movement (1910s)
	Mezzanine of Poetry (1910s)
	Zavety (Behests) School (1910s)
Sweden	Tiotalister (1910s)
Turkey ·	*Mehian* Group (Armenians) (1910s)
	National Literature Movement (1910s)
	Young Pens (1910s)
United States	Little Theater Movement (1910s)
	Washington Square Players (1910s)
Portugal	*Orpheu* Group (1910-1915)
Russia	Acmeism (1910-1917)
England	Georgian Poets (1910-1922)
Japan	White Birch School (1910-1923)
Czechoslovakia	Expressionism (1910s-1920s)
France	Théâtre du Vieux-Colombier (1910s-1920s)
Germany	Expressionism (1910s-1920s)
Italy	Futurism (1910s-1920s)
Japan	I-Novel (1910s-1920s)
Portugal	Portuguese Renascence (1910s-1920s)
Russia	Proletkult (1910s-1920s)
Ukraine	Futurism (1910s-1920s)
	Symbolism (1910s-1920s)
United States	Chicago Literary Renaissance (1910s-1920s)
Austria and Germany	Modernism (1910s-c. 1930)
Russia	Russian Formalism (1910s-c. 1930)
England and Ireland	Modernism (1910s-1930)
Latin America	Realism (1910s-1930)
Mexico	Atheneum of Youth (1910s-1930s)
United States	Modernism (1910s-1930s)
	New Humanism (1910s-1930s)
England	Bloomsbury Group (1910s-1940s)
England, France, and United States	Freudian Criticism (1910s-1990s)

1910s *(Continued)*

Cuba	Cenáculo Group (1911-1913)
England and United States	Imagism (1912-1917)
Egypt	*Diwan* School of Poets (c. 1912-1919)
Russia	Cubo-Futurism (1912-1930)
England	Vorticism (1914-1915)
United States	Provincetown Players (1915-1929)
Netherlands	Young Frisian Movement (1915-1935)
Italy	Hermeticism (1915-1940s)
Peru	*Colónida* Movement (1916)
Chile and Spain	Creationism (1916-1918)
United States	Spectra (1916-1918)
China	May Fourth Movement (1916-1921)
France, Germany, Switzerland, and United States	Dada (1916-1923)
Belgium	*Ruimte* Group (1917-1921)
Poland	*Zdroj* Group (1917-1922)
Holland	*De Stijl* (1917-1928)
Estonia	Siuru Group (1917-1920s)
China	New Literature Movement (1917-1937)
United States	Carolina Playmakers (1918-1970s)
Sweden	*Clarté* (1919-1930s)
United States	Theater Guild (1919-1950)

1920s

Algeria	*Al-Shihab* (1920s)
Argentina	Boedo Group (1920s)
	Florida Group (1920s)
Brazil	*Festa* Group (1920s)
	Verde-Amarelismo (1920s)
Byelorussia	Flame Group (1920s)
	Uzvyšša Group (1920s)
Canada	Montreal Movement (1920s)
China	Creation Society (1920s)
	Literary Research Association (1920s)
	South China Society (1920s)

Cuba	Manzanillo Group (1920s)
Czechoslovakia	Nine Powers Group (1920s)
Finland	Modernism (Swedish writers) (1920s)
France	Lost Generation (American writers) (1920s)
	Theater of Silence (1920s)
Georgia	Futurism (1920s)
Germany	*Merz* (1920s)
	New Objectivity (1920s)
Hungary	Today Group (1920s)
Italy	Rondismo (1920s)
Japan	New Sensationalist School (1920s)
Korea	Naturalism (1920s)
Latin America	Ultraism (1920s)
Lithuania	Four Winds Movement (1920s)
Poland	Futurism (1920s)
	Young Yiddish Group (1920s)
Romania	Gîndirea (1920s)
	Sburătorul Group (1920s)
	Transylvanian Helicon Group (1920s)
Russia	Constructivism (1920s)
	Imaginists (1920s)
	Left Front of the Arts (1920s)
	Pereval (1920s)
	Serapion Brothers (1920s)
	Smithy (1920s)
Spain	Ultraism (1920s)
Turkey	Seven Torches (1920s)
Ukraine	Kiev Group (1920s)
	Link (1920s)
	Neoclassic Group (1920s)
	Plough (1920s)
	Ukrainian Home Group (1920s)
	Young Muse Group (1920s)
United States	Expressionism (1920s)
	Harlem Renaissance (1920s)
	Jazz Age (1920s)
	Young Ones (1920s)
Venezuela	Generation of 1918 (1920s)

1920s *(Continued)*

Belgium	*Het Fonteintje* (1920s-1930s)
	Surrealism (1920s-1930s)
Brazil	Region-Tradition Movement (1920s-1930s)
Cuba	Afro-Cubanism (1920s-1930s)
Czechoslovakia	Poetism (1920s-1930s)
	Poets' Cloister (Russians) (1920s-1930s)
	Prague Linguistic Circle (1920s-1930s)
	Proletarian Literature (1920s-1930s)
Dominican Republic	Posthumanismo (1920s-1930s)
England	Surrealism (1920s-1930s)
Finland	Torchbearers Group (1920s-1930s)
France	Cartel (1920s-1930s)
	Surrealism (1920s-1930s)
Germany	Surrealism (1920s-1930s)
India	Romanticist Movement (1920s-1930s)
Latin America	Surrealism (1920s-1930s)
Latvia	Realism (1920s-1930s)
Netherlands	Tide (1920s-1930s)
Poland	Cracow Avant-Garde (1920s-1930s)
	Quadriga (1920s-1930s)
	Skamander Group (1920s-1930s)
Spain	Generation of 1927 (1920s-1930s)
	Surrealism (1920s-1930s)
Sweden	Five Young Men (1920s-1930s)
Ukraine	Neoromanticism (1920s-1930s)
United States	Fugitives (1920s-1930s)
	Introspectivists Movement (1920s-1930s)
Bulgaria	Golden Horn (1920s-1944)
Belgium	*Journal de Poètes* (1920s-1940s)
Turkey	Syllabists (1920s-1940s)
United States	Hard-Boiled School (1920s-1940s)
Germany	Epic Theater (1920s-1950s)
England, Europe, and United States	Marxist Criticism (1920s-1970s)
Portugal	Neorealism (1920s-1990s)
United States	Society of the Pen (Lebanese writers) (c. 1920-1930s)
Scotland	Scottish Renaissance (c. 1920-1950)

Puerto Rico	Diepalismo (1921)
Portugal	*Seara Nova* Group (1921-1974)
Poland	Gang Group (1922-1925)
Mexico	Estridentismo (1922-1927)
Poland	*Czartak* Group (1922-1928)
Russia	October Group (1922-1928)
Brazil	Modernism (c. 1922-1940s)
Byelorussia	Saplings (1923-1932)
China	*Yü Ssu* Group (1924-1930)
Czechoslovakia	*DAV* Group (1924-1937)
Byelorussia	Minsk Group (c. 1925-1937)
Ukraine	Free Academy of Proletarian Literature (1925-1929)
England	Gate Theater (1925-1940)
Italy	*Solaria* Group (1926-1934)
Haiti	*La Revue Indigène* Group (1927-1928)
Russia	OBERIU (c. 1927-1930)
Portugal	*Presenca* (1927-1940)
China	Crescent Society (1928-1930s)
Mexico	*Contemporáneos* (1928-1931)
France	Populisme (1929-1930)

1930s

Brazil	Antropofagia Group (1930s)
Burma	Testing of the Age (1930s)
Chile	Generation of 1938 (1930s)
China	League of Left-Wing Writers (1930s)
Colombia	Stone and Sky Movement (1930s)
Czechoslovakia	Surrealism (1930s)
Ecuador	Group of Guayaquil (1930s)
	Grupo Elan (1930s)
Egypt	Apollo School of Poets (1930s)
England	Cambridge Group (1930s)
	Proletarian Literature (1930s)
	Pylon School (1930s)
Estonia	Soothsayers Movement (1930s)
Finland	Wedge Group (1930s)
France	*Le Grand Jeu* (1930s)
Greece	Generation of 1930 (1930s)

1930s *(Continued)*

Hungary	Populist Movement (1930s)
Indonesia	New Writers' Circle (1930s)
Iran	Rab'e Group (1930s)
Japan	New Psychologist School (1930s)
Latin America	Aprismo (1930s)
Lithuania	Third Front Movement (1930s)
	Young Vilna (1930s)
Netherlands	*Forum* Group (1930s)
Norway	Oxford Group (1930s)
Peru	Aprismo (1930s)
Poland	Authenticism (1930s)
	My Group (Ukrainians) (1930s)
	Przedmieście Group (1930s)
	Tank Group (Ukrainians) (1930s)
	Żagary Group (1930s)
South Africa	Dertigers (1930s)
Spain	Generation of 1936 (1930s)
Sudan	Neoclassicism (1930s)
Sweden	Proletarian Writers (1930s)
	Surrealism (1930s)
Ukraine	Logos Group (1930s)
United States	Agitprop Theater (1930s)
	Objectivism (1930s)
	Proletarian Literature (1930s)
Vietnam	Self-Reliance Group (1930s)
Yugoslavia	*Hid* Group (1930s)
	Kalangya Group (1930s)
Czechoslovakia	Nadrealisti Movement (1930s-1940s)
England	Unity Theater (1930s-1940s)
India	Progressive Writers' Movement (1930s-1940s)
Pakistan	Progressive Writers' Movement (1930s-1940s)
Sudan	Romantic Poets (1930s-1940s)
Azerbaijan	Socialist Realism (1930s-1950s)
Bulgaria	Socialist Realism (1930s-1950s)
Byelorussia	Socialist Realism (1930s-1950s)
Chuvashia	Socialist Realism (1930s-1950s)

England	Socialist Realism (1930s-1950s)
France	Socialist Realism (1930s-1950s)
Italy	Neorealism (1930s-1950s)
Kazakhstan	Socialist Realism (1930s-1950s)
Kirgizia	Socialist Realism (1930s-1950s)
Russia	Socialist Realism (1930s-1950s)
Slovenia	Socialist Realism (1930s-1950s)
Turkey	Socialist Realism (1930s-1950s)
Ukraine	Socialist Realism (1930s-1950s)
United States	New Criticism (1930s-1950s)
	Socialist Realism (1930s-1950s)
Yakut	Socialist Realism (1930s-1950s)
France	Négritude (1930s-1960s)
	Theater of Cruelty (1930s-1960s)
Germany	Theater of Cruelty (1930s-1960s)
India	New Poetry Movement (1930s-1960s)
Poland	Theater of Cruelty (1930s-1960s)
Spain	Theater of Cruelty (1930s-1960s)
United States	Theater of Cruelty (1930s-1960s)
Canada, England, and United States	Jungian Criticism (1930s-1990s)
Ukraine	*Dzvony* (1930-1939)
Korea	Theatrical Arts Research Society (1931-1938)
United States	Group Theater (1931-1941)
Brazil	Andalusian League (1932-1940s)
Ukraine	*Visnyk* (1933-1939)
England	Group Theater (1933-1953)
Ukraine	*Nazustrich* (1934-1939)
Cape Verde	*Claridade* Movement (1936-1960)
Cuba	Transcendentalist Group (1937-1940s)
England	New Apocalypse Poets (1938-1940s)
China	All-China Anti-Aggression Federation of Writers and Artists (1938-1945)
Australia	Jindyworobak Movement (1938-1950s)
Germany and United States	Reader-Response Criticism and Reception Theory (c. 1938-1990s)
Mexico	Taller Group (1939-1941)
Pakistan	Assembly of Men of Good Taste (1939-1940s)

1940s

Brazil	Generation of 1945 (1940s)
Dominican Republic	Surprised Poetry Movement (1940s)
Dutch Antilles	Porch Group (1940s)
England	The Inklings (1940s)
France	Lettrism (1940s)
Guatemala	Dawn Group (1940s)
	Grupo *Acento* (1940s)
Iceland	Form Revolution (1940s)
Japan	Decadents (1940s)
Nigeria	Yoruba Opera (1940s)
Poland	Condemned Generation Poets (1940s)
Puerto Rico	Generation of 1940 (1940s)
Romania	Bucharest Group (1940s)
	Sibiu Group (1940s)
Spain	Grupo *Espadaña* (1940s)
	Tremendismo (1940s)
Sweden	Modernism (1940s)
	Poets of the Forties (1940s)
Tunisia	Under the Ramparts (1940s)
Uruguay	Generation of 1945 (1940s)
Venezuela	*Viernes* Group (1940s)
China	Hu Feng Clique (1940s-1950s)
Czechoslovakia	Socialist Realism (1940s-1950s)
Finland	Modernism (1940s-1950s)
Hungary	Socialist Realism (1940s-1950s)
Iceland	Modernism (1940s-1950s)
Latvia	Socialist Realism (1940s-1950s)
Lithuania	Socialist Realism (1940s-1950s)
Poland	Socialist Realism (1940s-1950s)
France	Existentialism (1940s-1960s)
Germany	Existentialism (1940s-1960s)
Spain	Existentialism (1940s-1960s)
England	Theater Workshop (1940s-1970s)
	Total Theater (1940s-1970s)
France	Total Theater (1940s-1970s)
Germany	Total Theater (1940s-1970s)
Italy	Total Theater (1940s-1970s)

Japan	Matinée Poétique (1940s-1970s)
Turkey	Poetic Realism (1941-1950)
Canada	*First Statement* Group (1942-1945)
Czechoslovakia	Group 42 (1942-c. 1948)
Australia	Ern Malley Hoax (1943-1955)
Cuba	*Origenes* Group (1944-1956)
Italy	Neorealist Film (1945-1950)
Indonesia	Generation of 1945 (1945-1960s)
Japan	New Japanese Literature Association (1945-1990s)
Portugal	Surrealism (1947-1965)
Germany	Group 47 (1947-1967)
Denmark	*Heretika* Poets (1948-1953)
Germany	Berlin Ensemble (1949-1950s)

1950s

Algeria	Generation of 1954 (1950s)
Angola	Association of Angola's Native Sons (1950s)
Belgium	COBRA (1950s)
	Fifties Poets (1950s)
Chile	Generation of 1950 (1950s)
Denmark	COBRA (1950s)
England	Comedy of Menace (1950s)
	Jazz Poetry (1950s)
	Kitchen Sink Drama (1950s)
	The Movement (1950s)
France	North Africa Group of Writers (1950s)
Holland	COBRA (1950s)
Hungary	Generation of 1955 (1950s)
Indonesia	Generation of 1950 (1950s)
Israel	Young Israel (1950s)
Lithuania	Earth Movement (1950s)
Malaysia	Generation of the 1950s (1950s)
Netherlands	Experimentalists (1950s)
	Fifties Poets (1950s)
	Wie Eegie Sanie (1950s)
Nigeria	Onitsha Chapbooks (1950s)
Norway	Symbolic Modernism (1950s)
Puerto Rico	Ensueñismo Group (1950s)

1950s *(Continued)*

Spain	Objectivism (1950s)
	Turia Group (1950s)
Surinam	Wie Eegie Sanie (1950s)
Taiwan	Blue Stars Society (1950s)
	Modernist School (1950s)
Turkey	Second New (1950s)
	Village Fiction (1950s)
United States	Chicago Critics (1950s)
Venezuela	Sardio Group (1950s)
England	Angry Young Men (1950-1960)
Austria	Concrete Poetry (1950s-1960s)
	Vienna Group (1950s-1960s)
Belgium	Concrete Poetry (1950s-1960s)
Brazil	Concrete Poetry (1950s-1960s)
Czechoslovakia	May Group (1950s-1960s)
	Theater of the Absurd (1950s-1960s)
Denmark	Modernism (1950s-1960s)
England	Concrete Poetry (1950s-1960s)
	Theater of the Absurd (1950s-1960s)
France	New Novel (1950s-1960s)
	New Wave (1950s-1960s)
	Theater of the Absurd (1950s-1960s)
Germany	Concrete Poetry (1950s-1960s)
	Socialist Realism (1950s-1960s)
	Theater of the Absurd (1950s-1960s)
Hungary	*Ujhold* Group (1950s-1960s)
India	New Story Movement (1950s-1960s)
Italy	Group 63 and *Officina* Group (1950s-1960s)
Nicaragua	Exteriorismo (1950s-1960s)
Norway	Concrete Poetry (1950s-1960s)
Paraguay	Generation of 1940 (1950s-1960s)
Poland	Theater of the Absurd (1950s-1960s)
Russia	Village Prose (1950s-1960s)
Sudan	Realism (1950s-1960s)
Sweden	Concrete Poetry (1950s-1960s)
Switzerland	Concrete Poetry (1950s-1960s)
	Theater of the Absurd (1950s-1960s)

United States	Beat Generation (1950s-1960s)
	Black Mountain Poets (1950s-1960s)
	Concrete Poetry (1950s-1960s)
	Confessional Poets (1950s-1960s)
	Living Theater (1950s-1960s)
	New York Group (Latvians) (1950s-1960s)
	New York School (1950s-1960s)
	Theater of the Absurd (1950s-1960s)
France	Structuralism (1950s-1970s)
Switzerland	Geneva School (1950s-1970s)
Latin America	Magic Realism (1950s-1990s)
Canada	Hexagone Group (1953-1963)
England	The Group (1955-1965)
Poland	Wspøłczesność Group (1956-1971)
Czechoslovakia, France, Italy, Russia, and United States	Semiotics (c. 1957-1990s)
Poland	Theater Laboratory (1959-1969)

1960s

Canada	*Tish* Group (1960s)
East Germany	Bitterfeld Movement (1960s)
Ecuador	Grupo Tzántzico (1960s)
England	Fringe Theater (1960s)
	Kontynenty Group (1960s)
France	Deconstruction (1960s)
	Theater of Panic (1960s)
Germany	Cologne School of New Realism (1960s)
	Group 61 (1960s)
	Theater of Fact (1960s)
Israel	Metarealism (1960s)
Italy	Literature and Industry (1960s)
	Third Theater (1960s)
Mexico	Wave (1960s)
Nigeria	Mbari Club (1960s)
Norway	*Profil* (1960s)
Peru	Los Nuevos (1960s)
Romania	Oneiric Movement (1960s)

1960s *(Continued)*

Scotland	Fringe Theater (1960s)
South Africa	Sestigers (1960s)
Ukraine	Generation of the 1960s (1960s)
United States	Deconstruction (1960s)
	Fringe Theater (1960s)
	New York Group (Ukrainians) (1960s)
	San Francisco School (1960s)
Dominican Republic	Pluralist Movement (1960s-1970s)
Iran	New Wave Movement (1960s-1970s)
Poland	Teraz Group (1960s-1970s)
Spain	Novísimos (1960s-1970s)
Cape Verde	Antievasion Group (1960s-c. 1975)
France	*Tel Quel* Group (1960s-1980s)
England	Feminist Criticism (1960s-1990s)
	Gay Theater (1960s-1990s)
France	Feminist Criticism (1960s-1990s)
	OuLiPo (1960s-1990s)
United States	Feminist Criticism (1960s-1990s)
	Gay Theater (1960s-1990s)
	New Journalism (1960s-1990s)
Japan	Post-Shingeki Movement (1960-1990s)
Portugal	Poetry 61 Movement (1961)
Zaire	Pléiade du Congo Group (1964-1966)
Belgium	*Komma* Group (1965-1969)

1970s

Canada	Four Horsemen (1970s)
Peru	Estos 13 (1970s)
Portugal	Three Marias (1970s)
South Africa	Black Consciousness Movement (1970s)
United States	Yale School (1970s)
Germany	New Sensibility Movement (1970s-1980s)

1980s

United States	Cyberpunk (1980s-1990s)

Chronology by Country

A

Algeria
Al-Shihab (1920s)
Generation of 1954 (1950s)

Angola
Association of Angola's Native Sons (1950s)

Argentina
Gaucho Literature (1870s-1920s)
Modernismo (c. 1888-1910s)
Criollismo (1890s-1900s)
Boedo Group (1920s)
Florida Group (1920s)

Australia
Jindyworobak Movement (1938-1950s)
Ern Malley Hoax (1943-55)

Austria
Realism (c. 1848-1880s)
Young Vienna Group (1890s-1900)
Modernism (1910s-30s)
Concrete Poetry (1950s-60s)
Vienna Group (1950s-60s)

Azerbaijan
Füyüzat Movement (1906-7)
Molla Nasreddin (1906-20)
Socialist Realism (1930s-50s)

B

Belgium
Symbolism (1880s-1900s)
Van nu en straks (1890s-1900s)
Ruimte Group (1917-1921)
Het Fonteintje (1920s-30s)
Surrealism (1920s-30s)
Journal de Poètes (1920s-40s)
COBRA (1950s)
Fifties Poets (1950s)
Concrete Poetry (1950s-60s)
Komma Group (1965-69)

Brazil
Festa Group (1920s)
Verde-Amarelismo (1920s)
Region-Tradition Movement (1920s-30s)
Modernism (c. 1922-40s)
Antropofagia Group (1930s)
Andalusian League (1932-1940s)
Generation of 1945 (1940s)
Concrete Poetry (1950s-60s)

Bulgaria
Misul Group (1892-1907)
Symbolism (1905-1920s)
Golden Horn (1920s-1944)
Socialist Realism (1930s-50s)

Burma
Testing of the Age (1930s)

Byelorussia
Naša Niva Group (1906-14)
Flame Group (1920s)
Uzvyšša Group (1920s)
Saplings (1923-32)
Minsk Group (c. 1925-37)
Socialist Realism (1930s-50s)

C

Canada
Confederation Poets (1880s-1920s)
Literary School of Montreal (1895-1925)
Local Color School (1900s-20s)
Terroir School (1900-1930s)
Montreal Movement (1920s)
Jungian Criticism (1930s-90s)
First Statement Group (1942-45)
Hexagone Group (1953-63)
Tish Group (1960s)
Four Horsemen (1970s)

Cape Verde
Claridade Movement (1936-60)
Antievasion Group (1960s-c. 1975)

Catalonia (Spain)
Realism (1900s)
Noucentismo/Novecentismo (1900s-30s)

Chile
Criollismo (1890s-1900s)
Creationism (1916-18)
Generation of 1938 (1930s)
Generation of 1950 (1950s)

China
Southern Society (1909-24)
May Fourth Movement (1916-21)

New Literature Movement (1917-37)
Creation Society (1920s)
Literary Research Association (1920s)
South China Society (1920s)
Yü Ssu Group (1924-30)
Crescent Society (1928-1930s)
League of Left-Wing Writers (1930s)
All-China Anti-Aggression Federation of
    Writers and Artists (1938-45)
Hu Feng Clique (1940s-50s)

Chuvasia
Socialist Realism (1930s-50s)

Colombia
Modernismo (c. 1888-1910s)
Stone and Sky Movement (1930s)

Croatia
Modernism (1895-1918)

Cuba
Modernismo (c. 1888-1910s)
Arpas Cubana Group (1900s)
Oriente Group (1910s)
Cenáculo Group (1911-13)
Manzanillo Group (1920s)
Afro-Cubanism (1920s-1930s)
Transcendentalist Group (1937-1940s)
Origenes Group (1944-56)

Czechoslovakia
Symbolism (1890s)
Modernism (1905-10s)
Expressionism (1910s-20s)
Nine Powers Group (1920s)
Poetism (1920s-30s)
Poets' Cloister (1920s-30s)
Prague Linguistic Circle (1920s-30s)
Proletarian Literature (1920s-30s)
DAV Group (1924-37)
Surrealism (1930s)

Nadrealisti Movement (1930s-40s)
Socialist Realism (1940s-50s)
Group 42 (1942-c. 1948)
May Group (1950s-60s)
Theater of the Absurd (1950s-60s)
Semiotics (c. 1957-90s)

D

Democratic Republic of Congo
Pléiade du Congo Group (1964-66)

Denmark
Naturalism (1870s-1900s)
Realism (1880s-1900s)
Symbolism (1890s)
Heretika Poets (1948-53)
COBRA (1950s)
Modernism (1950s-60s)

Dominican Republic
Posthumanismo (1920s-30s)
Surprised Poetry Movement (1940s)
Pluralist Movement (1960s-70s)

Dutch Antilles
Porch Group (1940s)

E

East Germany
Bitterfeld Movement (1960s)

Ecuador
Group of Guayaquil (1930s)
Grupo Elan (1930s)
Grupo Tzántzico (1960s)

Egypt
Diwan School of Poets (c. 1912-19)
Apollo School of Poets (1930s)

England
Realism (1850s-90s)
Aestheticism/Decadence (1880s-1900)
Naturalism (1880s-1900s)
Symbolism (1890s-1900s)
Modern Nō (c. 1900s-90s)
Edwardian Literature (c. 1900-11)
Georgian Poets (1910-22)
Modernism (1910s-30s)
Bloomsbury Group (1910s-40s)
Freudian Criticism (1910s-90s)
Imagism (1912-17)
Vorticism (1914-15)
Surrealism (1920s-30s)
Marxist Criticism (1920s-70s)
Gate Theater (1925-40)
Cambridge Group (1930s)
Proletarian Literature (1930s)
Pylon School (1930s)
Unity Theater (1930s-40s)
Socialist Realism (1930s-50s)
Jungian Criticism (1930s-90s)
Group Theater (1933-53)
New Apocalypse Poets (1938-1940s)
The Inklings (1940s)
Theater Workshop (1940s-70s)
Total Theater (1940s-70s)
Comedy of Menace (1950s)
Jazz Poetry (1950s)
Kitchen Sink Drama (1950s)
The Movement (1950s)
Angry Young Men (1950-60)
Concrete Poetry (1950s-60s)
Theater of the Absurd (1950s-60s)
The Group (1955-65)
Fringe Theater (1960s)
Kontynenty Group (1960s)
Feminist Criticism (1960s-90s)
Gay Theater (1960s-90s)

Estonia
Young Estonia Group (1905-1910s)

Siuru Group (1917-1920s)
Soothsayers Movement (1930s)

F

Finland
National Neoromanticism (1890s-1930)
Loafers (1900s)
Modernism, Swedish (1920s)
Torchbearers Group (1920s-30s)
Wedge Group (1930s)
Modernism (1940s-50s)

France
Realism (1850s-70s)
Félibrige Movement (1854-1920s)
Naturalism (1860s-1900s)
Symbolism (1870s-90s)
Théâtre Libre (1887-96)
Naturism (1890s-1900)
École Romane (1890s-1910s)
Breton Movement (1890-1950)
Humanisme (1900s)
Modernism (1900s-30s)
Abbaye Group (1906-1908)
Unanimisme (c. 1908-20)
Nouvelle Revue Française Group (1908-43)
Cubism (1910s)
Fantaisistes Group (1910s)
Futurism (1910s)
Little Theater Movement (1910s)
Simultanéisme (1910s)
Théâtre du Vieux-Colombier (1910s-20s)
Freudian Criticism (1910s-90s)
Dada (1916-23)
Lost Generation (1920s)
Theater of Silence (1920s)
Cartel (1920s-30s)
Surrealism (1920s-30s)
Populisme (1929-30)
Le Grand Jeu (1930s)
Socialist Realism (1930s-50s)

Négritude (1930s-60s)
Theater of Cruelty (1930s-60s)
Lettrism (1940s)
Existentialism (1940s-60s)
Total Theater (1940s-70s)
North Africa Group of Writers (1950s)
New Novel (1950s-60s)
New Wave (1950s-60s)
Theater of the Absurd (1950s-60s)
Structuralism (1950s-70s)
Semiotics (c. 1957-90s)
Deconstruction (1960s)
Theater of Panic (1960s)
Tel Quel Group (1960s-80s)
Feminist Criticism (1960s-90s)
Oulipo (1960s-90s)

G

Georgia
Blue Horns Group (1910s)
Futurism (1920s)

Germany
Realism (c. 1848-1880s)
Naturalism (1880s-90s)
Symbolism (1880s-1900s)
Deutsches Theater (1880s-1960s)
Freie Bühne (1889-94)
Jugendstil (1890s-1900s)
Heimatkunst (1900s-30s)
Little Theater Movement (1910s)
Storm Circle (1910s)
Expressionism (1910s-20s)
Modernism (1910s-30s)
Dada (1916-23)
Merz (1920s)
New Objectivity (1920s)
Surrealism (1920s-30s)
Epic Theater (1920s-50s)
Theater of Cruelty (1930s-60s)
Reader-Response Criticism & Reception
   Theory (c. 1938-1990s)

Existentialism (1940s-60s)
Total Theater (1940s-70s)
Group 47 (1947-67)
Berlin Ensemble (1949-1950s)
Concrete Poetry (1950s-60s)
Socialist Realism (1950s-60s)
Theater of the Absurd (1950s-60s)
Cologne School of New Realism (1960s)
Group 61 (1960s)
Theater of Fact (1960s)
New Sensibility Movement (1970s-80s)

Greece
New School of Athens (1880s-1900s)
Generation of 1930 (1930s)

Guatemala
Dawn Group (1940s)
Grupo *Acento* (1940s)

H

Haiti
La Revue Indigène Group (1927-28)

Holland
De Stijl (1917-28)
COBRA (1950s)

Hungary
Popular National School (1890s-1900s)
Nyugat Group (1908-1920s)
Today Group (1920s)
Populist Movement (1930s)
Socialist Realism (1940s-50s)
Generation of 1955 (1950s)
Ujhold Group (1950s-60s)

I

Iceland
Realism (1880s-90s)

Verðandi Group (1880s-1900s)
Progressive Romanticism (1910s)
Form Revolution (1940s)
Modernism (1940s-50s)

India
Romanticist Movement (1920s-30s)
Progressive Writers' Movement (1930s-40s)
New Poetry Movement (1930s-60s)
New Story Movement (1950s-60s)

Indonesia
New Writers' Circle (1930s)
Generation of 1945 (1945-60s)
Generation of 1950 (1950s)

Iran
Rab'e Group (1930s)
New Wave Movement (1960s-70s)

Ireland
Symbolism (1890s-1900s)
Irish Renaissance (1890s-1920s)
Edwardian Literature (c. 1900-11)
Abbey Theater (1904-1930s)
Modernism (1910s-30s)

Israel
Young Israel (1950s)
Metarealism (1960s)

Italy
Verismo (1860s-1910s)
Intimismo (1900s)
Crepuscolarismo (1900s-10s)
Modernism (1900-1950s)
La Critica (1903-44)
Theater of the Grotesque (1910s)
Futurism (1910s-20s)
Hermeticism (1915-40s)
Rondismo (1920s)
Solaria Group (1926-34)

Neorealism (1930s-50s)
Total Theater (1940s-70s)
Neorealist Film (1945-50)
Group 63 and *Officina* Group (1950s-60s)
Semiotics (c. 1957-90s)
Literature and Industry (1960s)
Third Theater (1960s)

J

Japan
Society of Friends of the Inkstone (1885-
    1903)
Romantic Movement (1890s-1900s)
Negishi Tanka Society (1899-1900s)
New Poetry Society (1900s)
Naturalism (1900s-10s)
Hototogisu School (1900s-20s)
Modern Nō (c. 1900s-90s)
New Tendency School (c. 1906-1910s)
White Birch School (1910-23)
I-Novel (1910s-20s)
New Sensationalist School (1920s)
New Psychological School (1930s)
Decadents (1940s)
Matinée Poétique (1940s-70s)
New Japanese Literature Association
    (1945-90s)
Post-Shingeki Movement (1960-90s)

K

Kazakhstan
Socialist Realism (1930s-50s)

Kirgizia
Socialist Realism (1930s-50s)

Korea
New Poetry Movement (1900s-10s)
Naturalism (1920s)
Theatrical Arts Research Society (1931-38)

L

Latin America
Realism (1910s-30s)
Ultraism (1920s)
Surrealism (1920s-30s)
Aprismo (1930s)
Magic Realism (1950s-90s)

Latvia
Realism (1880s-1900s; 1920s-30s)
Neoromanticism (1890s-1900s)
New Current Movement (1890s-1900s)
Socialist Realism (1940s-50s)

Lithuania
Symbolism (1900s-20s)
Four Winds Movement (1920s)
Third Front Movement (1930s)
Young Vilna (1930s)
Socialist Realism (1940s-50s)
Earth Movement (1950s)

M

Malaysia
Generation of the 1950s (1950s)

Mexico
Modernismo (c. 1888-1910s)
Atheneum of Youth (1910s-30s)
Estridentismo (1922-27)
Contemporáneos (1928-1931)
Taller Group (1939-41)
Wave (1960s)

N

Netherlands
Movement of the Eighties (c. 1885-1900s)
The Movement (1905-1920s)
Young Frisian Movement (1915-35)

Tide (1920s-30s)
Forum Group (1930s)
Experimentalists (1950s)
Fifties Poets (1950s)
Wie Eegie Sanie (1950s)

Nicaragua
Modernismo (c. 1888-1910s)
Exteriorismo (1950-1960s)

Nigeria
Yoruba Opera (1940s)
Onitsha Chapbooks (1950s)
Mbari Club (1960s)

Norway
Realism (1870s)
Naturalism (1880s)
Generation of 1905 (1905-20)
Oxford Group (1930s)
Symbolic Modernism (1950s)
Concrete Poetry (1950s-60s)
Profil (1960s)

P

Pakistan
Progressive Writers' Movement (1930s-40s)
Assembly of the Men of Good Taste (1939-
    1940s)

Paraguay
Generation of 1900 (1900s-10s)
Generation of 1940 (1950s-60s)

Peru
Modernismo (c. 1888-1910s)
Colónida Movement (1916)
Aprismo (1930s)
Los Nuevos (1960s)
Estos 13 (1970s)

Poland
Realism (1870s-80s)
Young Poland (1890s-1910s)
Young Kashubian Movement (1910s)
Zdroj Group (1917-22)
Futurism (1920s)
Young Yiddish Group (1920s)
Gang Group (1922-25)
Czartak Group (1922-28)
Cracow Avant-Garde (1920s-30s)
Quadriga (1920s-30s)
Skamander Group (1920s-30s)
Authenticism (1930s)
My Group (1930s)
Przedmieście Group (1930s)
Tank Group (1930s)
Żagary Group (1930s)
Theater of Cruelty (1930s-60s)
Condemned Generation Poets (1940s)
Socialist Realism (1940s-50s)
Theater of the Absurd (1950s-60s)
Współczesność Generation (1956-71)
Theater Laboratory (1959-69)
Teraz Group (1960s-70s)

Portugal
Symbolism (1890-1920)
Orpheu Group (1910-15)
Portuguese Renascence (1910s-20s)
Neorealism (1920s-90s)
Seara Nova Group (1921-74)
Presença (1927-40)
Surrealism (1947-65)
Poetry 61 Movement (1961)
Three Marias (1970s)

Puerto Rico
Diepalismo (1921)
Generation of 1940 (1940s)
Ensueñismo Group (1950s)

847

R

Romania
Sămănătorism (1900s)
Symbolism (1900s-10s)
Poporanism (1910s)
Gîndirea (1920s)
Sburătorul Group (1920s)
Transylvanian Helicon Group (1920s)
Bucharest Group (1940s)
Sibiu Group (1940s)
Oneiric Movement (1960s)

Russia
Realism (1852-1900s)
Znanie Group (1890s-1900s)
Symbolism (1890s-1917)
Moscow Art Theater (1898-1990s)
Modernism (1900s-30s)
Centrifuge (1910s)
Ego-Futurism (1910s)
Little Theater Movement (1910s)
Mezzanine of Poetry (1910s)
Zavety (Behests) School (1910s)
Proletkult (1910s-20s)
Russian Formalism (1910s-c. 1930)
Acmeism (1910-17)
Cubo-Futurism (1912-30)
Constructivism (1920s)
Imaginists (1920s)
Left Front of the Arts (1920s)
Pereval (1920s)
Serapion Brothers (1920s)
Smithy (1920s)
October Group (1922-28)
OBERIU (c. 1927-30)
Socialist Realism (1930s-50s)
Village Prose (1950s-60s)
Semiotics (c. 1957-90s)

S

Scotland
Scottish Renaissance (c. 1920-50)
Fringe Theater (1960s)

Serbia
Modernism (1895-1918)

Slovenia
Modernism (1895-1918)
Socialist Realism (1930s-50s)

South Africa
Dertigers (1930s)
Sestigers (1960s)
Black Consciousness Movement (1970s)

Spain
Realism (1870s-90s)
Naturalism (1880s-90s)
Modernismo (c. 1888-1910s)
Generation of 1898 (c. 1898-1910s)
Realism, Catalonia (1900s)
Noucentismo/Novecentismo (1900s-30s)
Creationism (1916-18)
Ultraism (1920s)
Generation of 1927 (1920s-30s)
Surrealism (1920s-30s)
Generation of 1936 (1930s)
Theater of Cruelty (1930s-60s)
Grupo *Espadaña* (1940s)
Tremendismo (1940s)
Existentialism (1940s-60s)
Objectivism (1950s)
Turia Group (1950s)
Novísimos (1960s-70s)

Sudan
Neoclassicism (1930s)
Romantic Poets (1930s-40s)
Realism (1950s-60s)

848

Sweden
Nittiotalister (1890s-1900s)
Tiotalister (1910s)
Clarté (1919-1930s)
Five Young Men (1920s-30s)
Proletarian Writers (1930s)
Surrealism (1930s)
Modernism (1940s)
Poets of the Forties (1940s)
Concrete Poetry (1950s-60s)

Switzerland
Realism (c. 1848-1880s)
Dada (1916 23)
Concrete Poetry (1950s-60s)
Theater of the Absurd (1950s-60s)
Geneva School (1950s-70s)

T

Taiwan
Blue Stars Society (1950s)
Modernist School (1950s)

Tunisia
Under the Ramparts (1940s)

Turkey
New Literature Group (1896-1901)
Dawn of the Future (1909-12)
Mehian Group (1910s)
National Literature Movement (1910s)
Young Pens (1910s)
Seven Torches (1920s)
Syllabists (1920s-40s)
Socialist Realism (1930s-50s)
Poetic Realism (1941-50)
Village Fiction (1950s)
Second New (1950s-c. 1960)

U

Ukraine
Modernism (1905-20)
Futurism (1910s-20s)
Symbolism (1910s-20s)
Kiev Group (1920s)
Link (1920s)
Neoclassic Group (1920s)
Plough (1920s)
Ukrainian Home Group (1920s)
Young Muse Group (1920s)
Neoromanticism (1920s-30s)
Free Academy of Proletarian Literature
  (1925-29)
Logos Group (1930s)
Socialist Realism (1930s-50s)
Dzvony (1930-39)
Visnyk (1933-39)
Nazustrich (1934-39)
Generation of the 1960s (1960s)

United States
Local Color School (1860s-1900s)
Genteel Tradition (1880s-1900s)
Realism (1880s-1910s)
Naturalism (1880s-1910s)
Muckraking (1900s)
Modern Nō (c. 1900s-90s)
47 Workshop (1905-33)
Little Theater Movement (1910s)
Washington Square Players (1910s)
Chicago Literary Renaissance (1910s-20s)
Modernism (1910s-30s)
New Humanism (1910s-30s)
Freudian Criticism (1910s-90s)
Imagism (1912-17)
Provincetown Players (1915-29)
Spectra (1916-18)
Dada (1916-23)
Carolina Playmakers (1918-1970s)
Theater Guild (1919-50)

849

Expressionism (1920s)
Harlem Renaissance (1920s)
Jazz Age (1920s)
Young Ones (1920s)
Fugitives/Agrarians (1920s-30s)
Introspectivists Movement (1920s-30s)
Society of the Pen (c. 1920-1930s)
Hard-Boiled School (1920s-40s)
Marxist Criticism (1920s-70s)
Agitprop Theater (1930s)
Objectivism (1930s)
Proletarian Literature (1930s)
New Criticism (1930s-50s)
Socialist Realism (1930s-50s)
Theater of Cruelty (1930s-60s)
Jungian Criticism (1930s-90s)
Group Theater (1931-41)
Reader-Response Criticism & Reception
    Theory (c. 1938-1990s)
Chicago Critics (1950s)
Beat Generation (1950s-60s)
Black Mountain Poets (1950s-60s)
Concrete Poetry (1950s-60s)
Confessional Poets (1950s-60s)
Living Theater (1950s-60s)
New York Group (1950s-60s)
New York School (1950s-60s)
Theater of the Absurd (1950s-60s)
Structuralism (1950s-70s)
Semiotics (c. 1957-90s)
Deconstruction (1960s)
Fringe Theater (1960s)
New York Group (1960s)

San Francisco School (1960s)
Feminist Criticism (1960s-90s)
Gay Theater (1960s-90s)
New Journalism (1960s-90s)
Yale School (1970s)
Cyberpunk (1980s-90s)

Uruguay
Gaucho Literature (1870s-1920s)
Modernismo (c. 1888-1910s)
Generation of 1900 (1890s-1900s)
Council of Brilliant Knowledge (1900s)
Generation of 1945 (1940s)

V

Venezuela
Criollismo (1890s-1900s)
Generation of 1918 (1920s)
Viernes Group (1940s)
Sardio Group (1950s)

Vietnam
Self-Reliance Group (1930s)

Y

Yakut
Socialist Realism (1930s-50s)

Yugoslavia
Hid Group (1930s)
Kalangya Group (1930s)

Journals Cited

Advocate (Los Angeles, Calif.)
African Forum (New York, N.Y.)
African Guardian (Oshodi, Lagos, Nigeria)
African Literature Today (London, England)
Africa Report (New York, N.Y.)
American Journal of Semiotics (Bloomington, Ind.)
American Literature (Durham, N.C.)
American Literary Realism (Jefferson, N.C.)
American Quarterly (Baltimore, Md.)
American Scandinavian Review (New York, N.Y.)
Americas (Washington, D.C.)
Americas Review (Houston, Tex.)
Anales de la Literatura Espanola Contemporanea (Boulder, Colo.)
Annali Istituto Universitario Orientale (Rome, Italy)
Antemurale (Rome, Italy)
Applied Linguistics (Oxford, England)
Ararat (New York, N.Y.)
Ariel (Calgary, Alberta, Canada)
Artes Liberales (Nacogdoches, Tex.)
Artforum (New York, N.Y.)
Asemka: A Literary Journal of the University of Cape Coast, Ghana (Cape Coast, Ghana)
Asia Major (Seattle, Wash.)
Asian Theatre Journal (Honolulu, Hawaii)
Asiatic Review (London, England)
Athanor (Bari, Italy)
Baltic Forum (Gothenburg, Sweden)
Belorussian Review (Munich, Germany)
Black Orpheus (Lagos, Nigeria)

Black World (Chicago, Ill.)

Bloody Horse (Johannesburg, South Africa)

Books Abroad (Norman, Okla.)

Books from Finland (Helsinki, Finland)

Boundary 2 (Durham, N.C.)

Callaloo (Baltimore, Md.)

Canadian Journal of Italian Studies (Hamilton, Ontario, Canada)

Canadian Journal of Netherlandic Studies (Windsor, Ontario, Canada)

Canadian Modern Language Review (North York, Ontario, Canada)

Canadian Poetry (London, Ontario, Canada)

Canadian Review of Comparative Literature (Edmonton, Alberta, Canada)

Canadian Slavic Studies (Montreal, Quebec, Canada)

Canadian Slavonic Papers (Edmonton, Alberta, Canada)

Charioteer (New York, N.Y.)

Chasqui (Tempe, Ariz.)

Chicago Review (Chicago, Ill.)

China Quarterly (Oxford, England)

Chinese Literature (Peking, China)

Christopher Street (New York, N.Y.)

College Language Association Journal (Baltimore, Md.)

Commonwealth Essays and Studies (Dijon, France)

Comparative Literature (Eugene, Oreg.)

Comparative Literature Studies (University Park, Pa.)

Comparative Studies in Society and History (Cambridge, England)

Confluencia: Revista Hispanica de Cultura y Literatura (Greeley, Colo.)

Connecticut Review (New Britain, Conn.)

Contemporary French Civilization (Bozeman, Mo.)

Contemporary Literature (Madison, Wis.)

Critic (Cape Town, South Africa)

Critical Inquiry (Chicago, Ill.)

Critical Quarterly (Oxford, England)

Critique: Studies in Modern Fiction (Washington, D.C.)

Dance International (Vancouver, British Columbia, Canada)

Delphian Quarterly (Chicago, Ill.)

De Vlaamse Gids (Antwerp, Belgium)

Diacritics (Baltimore, Md.)

Diogenes (Oxford, England)

Dissertation Abstracts International (Ann Arbor, Mich.)

Drama Review (Cambridge, Mass.)

Drum (Johannesburg, South Africa; Accra, Ghana; et al.)

Dutch Crossing: A Journal of Low Countries Studies (London, England)

Dutch Studies (The Hague, Netherlands)

Edebiyat: Journal of Middle Eastern Literatures (Chur, Switzerland)

Enact (New Delhi, India)

English Journal (Urbana, Ill.)

Essays in Criticism (Oxford, England)

Essays in Theater (Guelph, Ontario, Canada)

Essays on Canadian Writing (Toronto, Ontario, Canada)

Ethnic and Racial Studies (London, England; New York, N.Y.)

Fortnightly Review (London, England)

Forum for Modern Language Studies (Oxford, England)

Forum Italicum (Buffalo, N.Y.)

Forum Modernes Theater (Tuebingen, Germany)

Foundation: The Review of Science Fiction (Reading, England)

France-Asie/Asia (Tokyo, Japan)

French Review: Journal of the American Association of Teachers of French
    (Champaign, Ill.)

Genders (New York, N.Y.)

Georgetown Journal of Languages and Linguistics (Baltimore, Md.)

Georgia Review (Athens, Ga.)

German Quarterly (Cherry Hill, N.J.)

Great Lakes Review: A Journal of Midwest Culture (Chicago, Ill.)

Harvard Library Bulletin (Cambridge, Mass.)

Hispania (Greeley, Colo.)

Hispanic Journal (Indiana, Pa.)

Hudson Review (New York, N.Y.)

Hungarian P.E.N. (Budapest, Hungary)

Hypotheses: Neo-Aristotelian Analysis (Port Washington, N.Y.)

Illinois Quarterly (Normal, Ill.)

Index on Censorship (London, England)

Indiana Journal of Hispanic Literatures (Bloomington, Ind.)

Indian Literature (New Delhi, India)

Industria International (Stockholm, Sweden)

Irish Times (newspaper; Dublin, Ireland)

Ironwood (Tucson, Ariz.)

Italian Culture (Pittsburgh, Pa.)

Italian Quarterly (New Brunswick, N.J.)

Joliso: East African Journal of Literature and Society (Nairobi, Kenya)

Journal of American Culture (Bowling Green, Ohio)

Journal of American Studies (Cambridge, England)

Journal of Arabic Literature (Leiden, Netherlands)

Journal of Baltic Studies (Madison, Wis.; Hackettstown, N.J.)

Journal of Byelorussian Studies (London, England)

Journal of European Studies (Bucks, England)

Journal of Inter-American Studies (Gainesville, Fla.)

Journal of South Asian Literature (East Lansing, Mich.)

Journal of Spanish Studies: Twentieth Century (Manhattan, Kans.)

Journal of the Association of Teachers of Japanese (Portland, Oreg.)

Journal of the New African Literature and the Arts (New York, N.Y.)

Journal of Ukrainian Studies (Edmonton, Alberta, Canada)

Kentucky Romance Quarterly (Lexington, Ky.)

Kenyon Review (Gambier, Ohio)

Language and Literature: Journal of the Poetics and Linguistics Association
    (Harlow, Essex, England)

Language Quarterly (Tampa, Fla.)

Latin American Literary Review (Pittsburgh, Pa.)

Latin American Research Review (Albuquerque, N.M.)

Latin American Theatre Review (Lawrence, Kans.)

Literary Onomastics Studies (Brockport, N.Y.)

Literary Review: An International Journal of Contemporary Writing (Madison, N.J.)

Literature and Psychology (Providence, R.I.)

Literature East and West (Austin, Tex.)

Litteraria Pragensia: Studies in Literature and Culture (Amsterdam, Netherlands)

Lituanus: Baltic States Quarterly of Arts & Sciences (Chicago, Ill.)

Lotus: Afro-Asian Writings (Cairo, Egypt)

Lugano Review (Lugano, Switzerland)

Luzo-Brazilian Review (Madison, Wis.)

Malay Mail (newspaper; Kuala Lumpur, Malaysia)

Maske und Kothurn (Vienna, Austria)

Massachusetts Review (Amherst, Mass.)

Matatu: Journal for African Culture and Society (Amsterdam, Netherlands)

Melus (Los Angeles, Calif.)

Michigan Quarterly Review (Ann Arbor, Mich.)

Midamerica (East Lansing, Mich.)

Midcontinent American Studies Journal (Lawrence, Kans.)
Middle East Journal (Washington, D.C.)
Midwest Quarterly: A Journal of Contemporary Thought (Pittsburg, Kans.)
Modern Chinese Literature (Boulder, Colo.)
Modern Drama (Toronto, Ontario, Canada; Downsview, Ontario, Canada)
Modern Fiction Studies (Baltimore, Md.)
Modern Hebrew Literature (Ramat Gan, Israel)
Modern Language Journal (Malden, Mass.)
Modern Language Review (Leeds, England)
Monumenta Nipponica (Tokyo, Japan)
Mosaic: Journal for the Interdisciplinary Study of Literature (Winnipeg, Manitoba, Canada)
Ms. Magazine (New York, N.Y.)
Narrative (Columbus, Ohio)
National Review (New York, N.Y.)
New Classic (Johannesburg, South Africa)
New Comparison (Colchester, England)
New Hungarian Quarterly (Budapest, Hungary)
New Literary History (Baltimore, Md.)
New Masses (New York, N.Y.)
New Polish Publications, a Monthly Review of Polish Books (Warsaw, Poland)
New Republic (Washington, D.C.)
News from the Ukraine (Kiev, Ukraine)
New Statesman (London, England)
Newsweek (New York, N.Y.)
New Theatre Quarterly (Cambridge, England)
New Yorker (New York, N.Y.)
New York Review of Books (New York, N.Y.)
New York Times Book Review (New York, N.Y.)
Nieuw Vlaams Tijdschrift (Antwerp, Belgium)
North American Review (Cedar Falls, Iowa)
North Carolina Historical Review (Raleigh, N.C.)
North Carolina Literary Review (Greenville, N.C.)
North Dakota Quarterly (Grand Forks, N.D.)
Northern Review (Whitehorse, Yukon, Canada)
Northwest Missouri State College Studies (Maryville, Mo.)
Nouvelle Revue Française (Paris, France)
NOWELE: North-Western European Language Evolution (Odense, Denmark)

Ohio Review (Athens, Ohio)
Okike: An African Journal of New Writing (Nsukka, Enugu State, Nigeria)
Others (New York, N.Y.)
Oway Magazine (Rangoon, Burma)
Oxford Slavonic Papers (Oxford, England)
Pacific Quarterly (Hamilton, New Zealand)
Pakistan Review (Lahore, Pakistan)
Panjab University Research Bulletin (Candigarh, India)
Papers on China (Cambridge, Mass.)
Partisan Review (Boston, Mass.)
Pinter Review (Frankfort, Ky.)
Poetics of the Avant-Garde (Durham, N.C.)
Poetics Today (Durham, N.C.)
Poetry (Chicago, Ill.)
Poetry Review (London, England)
Point of Contact (Syracuse, N.Y.)
Polish Review (New York, N.Y.)
Présence Africaine (Paris, France)
Prooftexts: A Journal of Jewish Literary History (Baltimore, Md.)
Publications of the Modern Language Association (New York, N.Y.)
Publishers Weekly (New York, N.Y.)
Quadrant (Sydney, Australia)
Quarterly Journal of Speech (Los Angeles, Calif.)
Research in African Literatures (Bloomington, Ind.)
Research Studies (Pullman, Wash.)
Review (New York, N.Y.)
Review of Contemporary Fiction (Normal, Ill.)
Review of National Literatures (Whitestone, N.Y.)
Review of Politics (Notre Dame, Ind.)
Revista hispanica moderna (New York, N.Y.)
Revista-Review Interamericana (San German, Puerto Rico)
Romance Notes (Chapel Hill, N.C.)
Romance Quarterly (Washington, D.C.)
Romance Studies (Swansea, Wales)
Romanic Review (New York, N.Y.)
Russian Literature Triquarterly (Ann Arbor, Mich.)
Russian Review (Columbus, Ohio; Stanford, Calif.)
Sagetrieb (Orono, Maine)

Journals Cited

Salmagundi (Saratoga Springs, N.Y.)
Saturday Review (New York, N.Y.)
Scandinavian Studies (Provo, Utah)
Scandinavica (Norwich, England)
Science-Fiction Studies (Greencastle, Ind.)
Semiotica (Hawthorne, N.Y.)
Signs (Chicago, Ill.)
Slavic and East European Journal (Tucson, Ariz.)
Slavic Review (Cambridge, Mass.)
Slavonic and East European Review (Leeds, England)
Southern Folklore Quarterly (Gainesville, Fla.)
Southern Review (Baton Rouge, La.)
Southwestern Review (Lafayette, La.)
Soviet Literature (Moscow, former U.S.S.R.)
SPAN: Journal of the South Pacific Association for Commonwealth Literature and Language Studies (Hamilton, New Zealand)
Spirit: A Magazine of Poetry (South Orange, N.Y.)
Staffrider (Fordsburg, South Africa)
Stages (New York, N.Y.)
Studies in American Fiction (Boston, Mass.)
Studies in Short Fiction (Newberry, S.C.)
Studies in 20th Century Literature (Manhattan, Kans.)
Swedish-American Historical Quarterly (Chicago, Ill.)
Swedish Pioneer Historical Quarterly (Chicago, Ill.)
Symposium (Syracuse, N.Y.)
Tamkang Review (Tamsui, Taipei, Taiwan)
Tel Quel (Paris, France)
Texas Quarterly (Austin, Tex.)
Texas Studies in Language and Literature (Austin, Tex.)
Theater (New Haven, Conn.)
Theatre Arts (New York, N.Y.)
Theatre Journal (Baltimore, Md.)
Theatre Quarterly (London, England; Cambridge, England)
Theatre Survey: The Journal of the American Society for Theatre Research (Washington, D.C.)
Theoria: A Journal of Studies in the Arts, Humanities and Social Sciences (Pietermaritzburg, South Africa)
Third Rail: A Review of International Arts & Literature (Los Angeles, Calif.)

Thomas Wolfe Review (Akron, Ohio)
Time (New York, N.Y.)
Torre de Papel (Iowa City, Iowa)
Transition: An International Review (Paris, France; The Hague, Netherlands; New York, N.Y.)
Translation and Literature (Edinburgh, Scotland)
Twentieth Century Literature (Hempstead, N.Y.)
Ukrainian Review (London, England)
Unisa English Studies: Journal of the Department of English (Pretoria, South Africa)
University of Denver Quarterly (Denver, Colo.)
Visible Language (Chicago, Ill.)
West Africa (London, England)
Western Humanities Review (Salt Lake City, Utah)
Western Review (Iowa City, Iowa)
West Virginia University Philological Papers (Morgantown, W.V.)
Women's Studies (New York, N.Y.)
World Literature Today (Norman, Okla.)
World Review of Reviews (London, England)
Yale French Studies (New Haven, Conn.)

Appendix 4

Web Sites

This listing of web sites is organized under four headings: General Literary Sites, Regional and National Literature-Related Sites, Movement and Author-Related Sites, and Electronic Text (e-text) Databases. It is not an exhaustive listing of all literary web sites, but is limited mainly to academic sites. The editors took every care to determine that sites listed here were operating at the time of publication; because of the dynamic nature of the Internet, however, we cannot guarantee their continued availability.

✦•✦

General Literary Sites

The Academy of American Poets
http://www.poets.org/

The Association of Literary Scholars and Critics
http://www.rci.rutgers.edu/~wcd/alsc!.htm

ÉCLAT! The "Essential" Comparative Literature And Theory Site, Comparative Literature and Literary Theory Department, University of Pennsylvania, Philadelphia
http://ccat.sas.upenn.edu/CompLit/Eclat/

Electronic Poetry Center, State University of New York at Buffalo
http://wings.buffalo.edu/epc/

The English Server, English Department, Carnegie Mellon University, Pittsburgh, Pennsylvania
http://eserver.org/

Guide to Philosophy on the Internet, Peter Suber, Professor, Philosophy Department, Earlham College, Richmond, Indiana
http://www.earlham.edu/~peters/philinks.htm

The Internet Public Library Online Literary Criticism Guide
http://www.ipl.org/ref/litcrit/guide.html

Literary Resource on the Web, by Jack Lynch, Assistant Professor, English Department, Rutgers University, Newark, New Jersey
http://andromeda.rutgers.edu/~jlynch/Lit/

Modern Language Association
http://www.mla.org

Philosophy Resources, Rhodes College, Memphis, Tennessee
http://www.rhodes.edu/Philhtmls/philnet.html

Valdosta Home Page of Philosophy Resources, Ron Barnette, Professor, Philosophy Department, Valdosta State University, Valdosta, Georgia
http://www.valdosta.peachnet.edu/~rbarnett/phi/resource.html

Voice of the Shuttle: Web Page for Humanities Research, by Alan Liu, English Department, University of California at Santa Barbara
http://humanitas.ucsb.edu/

The Window: Philosophy on the Internet, Philosophy Department, Trinity College, Hartford, Connecticut
http://www.trincoll.edu/~phil/philo

❖•❖

Regional and National
Literature-Related Web Sites

African Literature Resources, Karen Fung, Deputy Curator, Africa Collection, Hoover Library, Stanford University, California
http://www-sul.stanford.edu/depts/ssrg/africa/lit.html

American Literature on the Web, Akihito Ishikawa, Professor, Department of English, Nagasaki College of Foreign Languages, Japan
http://www.nagasaki-gaigo.ac.jp/ishikawa/amlit/index.htm

Asian Studies WWW Virtual Library, T. Matthew Ciolek, Research School of Asian and Pacific Studies, Australian National University, Canberra, Australian Capital Territory, Australia
http://coombs.anu.edu.au/WWWVL-AsianStudies.html

The Canadian Literature Archive, St. John's College, the English Department, and the Dafoe Library, University of Manitoba, Winnipeg, Canada
http://canlit.st-john.umanitoba.ca/Canlitx/Canlit_homepage.html

German Authors on the WWW, German Language Program in the Department of Modern Languages, Department of German Studies, and the Germanic Linguistics Program in the Department of Linguistics, Cornell University, Ithaca, New York
http://www.arts.cornell.edu/german/links/authors.html

Internet Resources for French Language and Literature Studies, University of Arizona Library, Tucson
http://www.ccp.arizona.edu/users/jennalyn/french.html

An Introduction to the Francophone Literature of the Maghreb, Rachid Aadnani, Debbie Folaron, and Michael Tolev, Maghrebi Studies Group, Binghamton University, Binghamton, New York
http://maghreb.net/writers

Irish Literary Sources and Resources, Michael Sundermeier, Professor of Communications, Creighton University, Omaha, Nebraska
http://mockingbird.creighton.edu/english/micsun/IrishResources/irishres.htm

Japanese Literature links page, Mitsuharu Mitsuoka, Associate Professor of Language and Culture, Nagoya University, Japan
http://lang.nagoya-u.ac.jp/~matsuoka/Japan.html

Literature in Australia and New Zealand, George P. Landow, Professor, English Department, Brown University, Providence, Rhode Island
http://www.stg.brown.edu/projects/hypertext/landow/post/misc/australov.html

Literature in Latin America links, Latin American Network Information Center (LAN-IC), Latin American Studies, University of Texas at Austin
http://www.lanic.utexas.edu/la/region/literature/

Literature of the Indian Subcontinent in English, George P. Landow, Professor, English Department, Brown University, Providence, Rhode Island
http://www.stg.brown.edu/projects/hypertext/landow/post/misc/indiaov.html

Literatures of the Middle East resources, Middle East Studies, Columbia University, New York
http://www.columbia.edu/cu/libraries/indiv/area/MiddleEast/literatures.html

Luso-Brazilian Literature and Culture links, Niedja Fedrigo, Lecturer, Department of Romance Languages and Literatures, University of Michigan, Ann Arbor
http://www-personal.umich.edu/~niedja/bookmark.htm

Web Sites

REESWeb: Russian and East European Studies Internet Resources on Language and Literature, Center for Russian and East European Studies, University of Pittsburgh, Pennsylvania
http://www.ucis.pitt.edu/reesweb/Lang/langind.html

Tennessee Bob's Famous French Links, Bob Peckham, Professor, French Department, University of Tennessee-Martin
http://www.utm.edu/departments/french/french.html

Turkish Poetry Homepage, Sibel Adali, Professor, Department of Computer Science, Rensselaer Polytechnic Institute, Troy, New York
http://www.cs.rpi.edu/~sibel/poetry/

Twentieth-Century Literature (Italian), Cultural Tidbits on Italy, Italian Embassy in Ottawa, Canada
http://www.mi.cnr.it/WOI/tidbits/lit5.html

✥•✥

Movement and Author-Related Sites

ACMEISM

"Three Russian Poets: A Posthumous Publication," by the late Dr. Kenneth Humphreys, Librarian, University of Birmingham, United Kingdom, in *Research Library Bulletin* (summer 1995)
http://lib10.bham.ac.uk/isgPublications/rlbulletin/summer95/russian.htm

Akhmatova, Anna
Anna Akhmatova page, Academy of American Poets
http://www.poets.org/LIT/poet/aakhmfst.htm

Mandelstam, Osip Emilievich
Tristia by Osip Mandelstam, posted by University of Virginia Library, Charlottesville
http://etext.virginia.edu/cyrillic/mandelstam/

AESTHETICISM/DECADENCE
Wilde, Oscar
University of Minnesota Oscar Wilde Page, Department of English, Minneapolis
http://english.cla.umn.edu/Courseweb/1017/OscarWilde/HOME

Ballad of Reading Gaol, Charmides and Other Poems, The Duchess of Padua, De Profundis, being the first complete and accurate version of 'Epistola in carcere et vinculis,' the last prose work in English of Oscar Wilde, Essays and Lectures, A Florentine

862

Tragedy, The Happy Prince & Other Tales, A House of Pomegranates, An Ideal Husband, The Importance of Being Earnest, Intentions, La Sainte Courtisane, Lady Windermere's Fan, Lord Arthur Savile's Crime, The Picture of Dorian Gray, Oscar Wilde Miscellaneous, Poems, Salome, Selected Poems of Oscar Wilde, The Soul of Man under Socialism, A Woman of No Importance by Oscar Wilde, Project Gutenberg
http://www.promo.net/pg/_authors/i-_wilde_oscar_.html

THE BEAT GENERATION
"Beat Culture and the New America," DeYoung Museum Exhibition, Fine Arts Museums of San Francisco, California
http://www.thinker.org/deyoung/exhibitions/beat/index.html

Burroughs, William S.
The William S. Burroughs Files: *InterWebZone*
http://www.hyperreal.org/wsb/

Ginsberg, Allen
Allen Ginsberg Memorial, The Naropa Institute, Boulder, Colorado
http://www.naropa.edu/ginsberg.html

"America" by Allen Ginsberg, posted by Al Filreis, Professor, English Department, University of Pennsylvania, Philadelphia
http://www.english.upenn.edu/~afilreis/88/america.html

Holmes, John Clellon
"Gone In October" by John Clellon Holmes in *Representative Men*, 1988
http://www.systime.dk/fagbank/engelsk/Beatgen/goneinoc.htm

Kerouac, Jack
"Essentials of Spontaneous Prose" by Jack Kerouac, posted by Al Filreis, Professor, English Department, University of Pennsylvania, Philadelphia
http://www.english.upenn.edu/~afilreis/88/kerouac-spontaneous.html

McClure, Michael
Michael McClure Home Page, curated by John Jacob, assisted by Michael McClure and Karl Young
http://www.thing.net/~grist/l&d/mcclure/mcclure.htm

Michael McClure Online Works, Electronic Poetry Center, State University of New York at Buffalo
http://wings.buffalo.edu/epc/authors/mcclure/

Web Sites

Snyder, Gary
From "The Language of Life with Bill Moyers," PBS, Wnetstation (Kravis Multimedia Education Center)
http://www.wnet.org/archive/lol/snyder.html

Gary Snyder Homepage at University of California, Davis
http://wwwenglish.ucdavis.edu/faculty/snyder/snyder.htm

Gary Snyder page, Academy of American Poets
http://www.poets.org/LIT/poet/gsnydfst.htm

BLACK MOUNTAIN POETS

Olson, Charles
Charles Olson page, Electronic Poetry Center, State University of New York at Buffalo
http://wings.buffalo.edu/epc/authors/olson/

CHICAGO LITERARY RENAISSANCE

Sandburg, Carl
Carl Sandburg page, Academy of American Poets
http://www.poets.org/LIT/poet/csandfst.htm

CONCRETE POETRY

"Concrete Poetry" by Larry Wendt in *Switch*, on-line magazine of the CADRE Institute of the School of Art and Design, San Jose State University, California
http://cadre.sjsu.edu/switch/sound/articles/wendt/ng1.htm

Campos, Augusto de
Using a web search engine, many sites for Augusto de Campos can be found in the Portuguese and Spanish languages.

Finlay, Ian Hamilton
"*The Dancers Inherit the Party* and *Glasgow Beasts* by Ian Hamiltan Finlay: A Clean Achievement" by John Aberdein in *Oarkney Arts Review* (journal)
http://www.orknet.co.uk/oar/oar10/finlay.htm

Excerpt from interview in *Transcript* (journal)
http://www.dundee.ac.uk/transcript/volume2/issue2_1/finlay.htm

Pignatari, Décio
Using a web search engine, many sites for Décio Pignatari can be found in the Portuguese and Spanish languages.

Web Sites

CONFESSIONAL POETS

Berrymore, John
John Berrymore page, Academy of American Poets
http://www.poets.org/LIT/poet/jberrfst.htm

Lowell, Robert
Robert Lowell page, Academy of American Poets
http://www.poets.org/LIT/poet/rlowefst.htm

Plath, Sylvia
Sylvia Plath page, Academy of American Poets
http://www.poets.org/LIT/poet/splatfst.htm

Sexton, Anne
Anne Sexton page, Academy of American Poets
http://www.poets.org/LIT/poet/asextfst.htm

Anne Sexton reading some of her poems (audio), Harper Audio (HarperCollins)
http://town.hall.org/radio/HarperAudio/053094_harp_ITH.html

Snodgrass, W. D.
W. D. Snodgrass page, Academy of American Poets
http://www.poets.org/LIT/poet/wdsnofst.htm

DADA
Dada and Surrealism: Texts and Extracts, by Gerry Carlin, Department of English,
University of Wolverhampton, United Kingdom
http://www.wlv.ac.uk/~fa1871/surrext.html

Dada Defined, by Al Filreis, Professor, English Department, University of Pennsylvania,
Philadelphia
http://www.english.upenn.edu/~afilreis/88/dada-def.html

Dadaism (music-related), The Computer-Assisted Music Instruction Lab, School of
Music, University of Illinois, Urbana-Champaign
http://camil40.music.uiuc.edu/Projects/EAM/Dadaism.html

International Dada Archive, University of Iowa Libraries, Iowa City
http://www.lib.uiowa.edu/dada/index.html

Arp, Jean (Hans)
Jean Arp, International Dada Archive, University of Iowa Libraries, Iowa City
http://www.lib.uiowa.edu/dada/arp.html

Web Sites

Ball, Hugo
Hugo Ball, International Dada Archive, University of Iowa Libraries, Iowa City
http://www.lib.uiowa.edu/dada/ball.html

Duchamp, Marcel
"Dada Perfume: A Duchamp Interview" by John Perreault in *Review* (journal)
http://plexus.org/review/perreault/dada.html

"Dada Without Duchamp/Duchamp Without Dada; Avant-Garde Tradition and the Individual Talent" by Marjorie Perloff, Electronic Poetry Center, State University of New York at Buffalo
http://wings.buffalo.edu/epc/authors/perloff/dada.html

Hausmann, Raoul
Raoul Hausmann, International Dada Archive, University of Iowa Libraries, Iowa City
http://www.lib.uiowa.edu/dada/hausmann.html

DECONSTRUCTION
"Structuralism/Poststructuralism" by Mary Klages, Professor, English Department, University of Colorado at Boulder
http://www.colorado.edu/English/ENGL2012Klages/1derrida.html

"Deconstruction: Some Assumptions" by John Lye, Professor, English Department, Brock University, St. Catharines, Ontario, Canada
http://www.brocku.ca/english/courses/4F70/deconstruction.html

"The Natural Beauty of Deconstruction" by Vadim Linetski in *Perforations* 10 (journal of Public Domain, Inc., Atlanta, Georgia)
http://www.pd.org/topos/perforations/perf10/natbeauty.html

"The Promise of Expression to the 'Inexpressible Child': Deleuze, Derrida and the Impossibility of Adult's Literature" by Vadim Linetski in *Perforations* 11 (journal of Public Domain, Inc., Atlanta, Georgia)
http://www.pd.org/topos/perforations/perf11/unspkable_chld.html

Derrida, Jacques
"Jacques Derrida 'Structure, Sign, and Play in the Discourse of the Human Sciences': A Reading Guide" by Mary Klages, Professor, English Department, University of Colorado at Boulder
http://www.colorado.edu/English/ENGL2012Klages/2derrida.html

Jacques Derrida page by Warren Hedges, English Department, Southern Oregon University, Ashland
http://www.sou.edu/English/IDTC/People/derrida.HTM

Web Sites

Derridean Links by Timothy Leuers, Kurume University, Japan
http://www.mii.kurume-u.ac.jp/~leuers/Derrida.htm

Différance (excerpt), commentary by John Lye, Professor, English Department, Brock
University, St. Catharines, Ontario, Canada
http://www.brocku.ca/english/courses/4F70/diffr.html

EPIC THEATER

Brecht, Bertolt

International Brecht Society Homepage, Mark Silberman, Department of German,
University of Wisconsin, Madison
http://polyglot.lss.wisc.edu/german/brecht/

"Bertolt Brecht Turns 100: A Web Exhibit" by Marje Schuetze-Coburn, Feuchtwanger
Librarian, University of Southern California, Los Angeles
http://www.usc.edu/dept/Info/FML/Brecht/

EXISTENTIALISM

Existentialism page, Center for the Advancement of Applied Ethics, Carnegie Mellon
University, Pittsburgh, Pennsylvania
http://www.lcl.cmu.edu/CAAE/80254/Sartre/Sartre.html

Philosophy Quick Guide: Existentialism, Information Services Division, University of
Southern California, Los Angeles
http://www-lib.usc.edu/Info/Phil/Guides/ps-106.html

Beauvoir, Simone de

Simone de Beauvoir page, The Window: Philosophy on the Internet, Philosophy
Department, Trinity College, Hartford, Connecticut
http://www.trincoll.edu/~phil/philo/phils/beauvoir.html

Camus, Albert

"The Absurd Hero" by Robert D. Lane, Classics, Philosophy, and Religious Studies,
Institute of Practical Philosophy, Malaspina University-College, Nanaimo, British
Columbia, Canada
http://www.mala.bc.ca/www/ipp/absurd.htm

Husserl, Edmund

The Husserl Page, Bob Sandmeyer, Graduate Student, Department of Philosophy,
University of Kentucky, Lexington
http://sac.uky.edu/~rsand1/husserl.html

Web Sites

Malraux, André
"Towards a Philosophy of Culture East West: Transcendent Images in Andre Malraux'
The Temptation of the West" by Paul M. Belbutowski in *ASVI* [American Society for
Value Inquiry] *Newsletter* (April 1995)
http://daniel.drew.edu/~tmagnell/ASVI/april95.html#15

Sartre, Jean-Paul
A selection from *Existentialism and Human Emotions* by Jean-Paul Sartre, posted by
David Banach, Department of Philosophy, St. Anselm College, Manchester, New
Hampshire
http://www.anselm.edu/homepage/dbanach/exist.htm

"Summary of Some Main Points from Sartre's Existentialism and Human Emotions"
by David Banach, Department of Philosophy, St. Anselm College, Manchester, New
Hampshire
http://www.anselm.edu/homepage/dbanach/sartreol.htm

EXPRESSIONISM

Döblin, Alfred
Alfred Döblin page, Kuusankoski Public Library, Finland
http://www.kirjasto.sci.fi/adoblin.htm

Alfred Döblin page, Feuchtwanger Memorial Library, University of Southern California,
Los Angeles
http://www.usc.edu/dept/Info/FML/Doblin.html

Kaiser, Georg
Bibliography of the Georg Kaiser Collection edited by Marianne Henn, compiled by
Erika Radenovich-Banski, University of Alberta, Edmonton, Alberta, Canada
http://www.ualberta.ca/~german/kaiser/kaiser.htm

Mann, Heinrich
Heinrich Mann (1871-1950), *German Exiles in Southern California*, Feuchtwanger
Memorial Library, University of Southern California, Los Angeles
http://www.usc.edu/dept/Info/FML/H_Mann.html

O'Neill, Eugene
Beyond The Horizon: A Play in Three Acts by Eugene G. O'Neill, Project Bartleby
Archive, Columbia University, New York
http://www.columbia.edu/acis/bartleby/oneill/

Web Sites

Werfel, Franz

Franz Werfel (1890-1945) & Alma Mahler-Werfel (1879-1964), *German Exiles in Southern California,*
Feuchtwanger Memorial Library, University of Southern California, Los Angeles
http://www.usc.edu/dept/Info/FML/Werfel.html

FEMINIST CRITICISM

Beauvoir, Simone de. *See* **Existentialism**

Cixous, Hélène

Hélène Cixous: A Bibliography, Critical Theory Resource, University of California at Irvine
http://sun3.lib.uci.edu/~scctr/Wellek/cixous/index.html

Stanford Presidential Lectures and Symposia in the Humanities and Arts: Hélène Cixous, Stanford University, California
http://prelectur.stanford.edu/lecturers/cixous/index.html

"Both/Between: Excerpt from *The Newly Born Woman*" by Hélène Cixous in *(Re)Soundings* 2,1 (on-line journal at Millersville University, Pennsylvania)
http://www.millersv.edu/~resound/*vol2iss1/hungerford/newlyborn.html

"Guardian of Language: An Interview with Hélène Cixous" by Kathleen O'Grady in *Women's education des femmes* 12,4 (winter 1996-97): 6-10.
http://humanitas.ucsb.edu/liu/grady-cixous.html

"Helene Cixous: 'The Laugh of the Medusa'" by Mary Klages, Professor, English Department, University of Colorado at Boulder
http://www.colorado.edu/English/ENGL2012Klages/cixous.html

Gilbert, Sandra M.

Sandra M. Gilbert's Web Page, English Department, University of California at Davis
http://wwwenglish.ucdavis.edu/faculty/gilbert/gilbert.htm

Kristeva, Julia

Julia Kristeva: A Bibliography, compiled by Hélène Volat, University Libraries, State University of New York at Stony Brook
http://www.sunysb.edu/library/kristeva.htm

"Julia Kristeva: The Stranger's Stranger" by Anna Smith, Department of English in *UC Research*, University of Canterbury, New Zealand
http://www.canterbury.ac.nz/publish/research/97/A16.htm

FREUD, SIGMUND, AND FREUDIAN CRITICISM

"Psychoanalytic Thought," Southern Oregon University, Ashland
http://www.sou.edu/English/IDTC/Issues/Subject/psycho/ovrview.htm

Sigmund Freud and the Freud Archives, The Abraham A. Brill Library, New York
Psychoanalytic Institute and Society
http://plaza.interport.net/nypsan/freudarc.html

Freudian Links by Timothy Leuers, Lecturer, Institute of Foreign Language Education
and Research, Kurume University, Japan
http://www.mii.kurume-u.ac.jp/~leuers/Freud.htm

Empson, William

Critical Essays on William Empson by John Constable, Faculty of Integrated Human
Studies, Kyoto University, Japan, in *Critical Thought Series* 3 (Scolar Press: Aldershot, 1993)
http://tori.ic.h.kyoto-u.ac.jp/pub/foihs/staffpages/jc/Empson.html

Lacan, Jacques

Jacques Lacan (notes for a lecture course) by Mary Klages, Professor, English
Department, University of Colorado at Boulder
http://www.colorado.edu/English/ENGL2012Klages/lacan.html

Lacanian Links by Timothy Leuers, Lecturer, Institute of Foreign Language Education
and Research, Kurume University, Japan
http://www.mii.kurume-u.ac.jp/~leuers/Lacan.htm

FUGITIVES/AGRARIANS

Ransom, John Crowe

John Crowe Ransom page, Academy of American Poets
http://www.poets.org/LIT/poet/jcranfst.htm

Tate, Allen

Allen Tate page, Academy of American Poets
http://www.poets.org/LIT/poet/atatefst.htm

Warren, Robert Penn

Robert Penn Warren page, Academy of American Poets
http://www.poets.org/LIT/poet/rpwarfst.htm

FUTURISM

Italian Futurism by Larry Wendt in *Switch*, on-line magazine of the CADRE Institute of
the School of Art and Design at San Jose State University, California
http://cadre.sjsu.edu/switch/sound/articles/wendt/folder6/ng63.htm#1

Futurism, WebMuseum, Paris
http://www.fhi-berlin.mpg.de/wm/paint/glo/futurism/

"Information Overload: Futurism, Technology, and the Word" by Michael Heumann in
Perforations 7 (journal of Public Domain, Inc., Atlanta, Georgia)
http://noel.pd.org/topos/perforations/perf7/info-overload/infover.html

Marinetti, Filippo Tommaso
The Joy of Mechanical Force and *Futurist Manifesto* by F. T. Marinetti, posted by
Jim English, Professor, English Department, University of Pennsylvania, Philadelphia
http://dept.english.upenn.edu/~jenglish/English104/marinetti.html

GEORGIAN POETS
Lost Poets of the Great War by Harry Rusche, Department of English, Emory University,
Atlanta, Georgia
http://www.emory.edu/ENGLISH/LostPoets/index.html

HARLEM RENAISSANCE
"Poets of the Harlem Renaissance and After," Exhibit, The Academy of American Poets
http://www.poets.org/lit/EXH/EX006.htm

Collaborative General Bibliography by Jamey Brogan, Center for Electronic Projects in
American Culture Studies, under direction of Randy Bass, Department of English,
Georgetown University, Washington, D.C.
http://www.georgetown.edu/tamlit/collab_bib/harlem_bib.html

Cullen, Countee
Countee Cullen page, Academy of American Poets
http://www.poets.org/LIT/poet/ccullfst.htm

DuBois, W. E. B.
The Souls of Black Folk by W. E. B. DuBois, Project Gutenberg
http://www.promo.net/pg/_authors/i-_du_bois_w_e_b_william_edward_
        burghardt_.html

Hughes, Langston
Langston Hughes page, Academy of American Poets
http://www.poets.org/LIT/poet/lhughfst.htm

Langston Hughes page, The Poetry Archive, Advanced Network & Services, Inc.
http://tqd.advanced.org/3247/cgi-
bin/dispover.cgi?frame=none&poet=hughes.langston

Johnson, James Weldon

James Weldon Johnson page, Academy of American Poets
http://www.poets.org/LIT/poet/jwjohfst.htm

McKay, Claude

Claude McKay page, Academy of American Poets
http://www.poets.org/poets/LIT/poet/cmckafst.htm

Toomer, Jean

The Jean Toomer Page, Roger Blackwell Bailey, English Department, San Antonio
College, San Antonio, Texas
http://www.accd.edu/sac/english/bailey/toomer.htm

Jean Toomer page, Academy of American Poets
http://www.poets.org/LIT/poet/jtoomfst.htm

INKLINGS

C. S. Lewis (and the Inklings) Resources Web Site, Bruce L. Edwards, Professor of
English, Bowling Green State University, Ohio
http://ernie.bgsu.edu/~edwards/lewis.html

JAZZ AGE

Fitzgerald, F. Scott

The F. Scott Fitzgerald Centenary Page, University of South Carolina, Columbia
http://www.sc.edu/fitzgerald/index.html

JUNG, CARL, AND JUNGIAN CRITICISM

The Jung Index
http://jungindex.net

C. G. Jung, Analytical Psychology and Culture, by Donald Williams, M.A., Jungian
analyst, Boulder, Colorado, Dolores E. Brien, Ph.D., editor of *The Round Table Review*,
and Donald Sedgwick, Ph.D., Jungian analyst, Charlottesville, Virginia
http://www.cgjung.com

Campbell, Joseph

The Joseph Campbell Foundation, Hawaii
http://www.jcf.org

LOST GENERATION

cummings, e. e.

e. e. cummings page, Academy of American Poets
http://www.poets.org/LIT/poet/eecumfst.htm

D[oolittle]., H[ilda].

H. D. International Society, contact person: Cassandra Laity, Department of English,
Drew University, Madison, New Jersey
http://www.well.com/user/heddy/hdsoc.html

H.D. (Hilda Doolittle), Academy of American Poets
http://www.poets.org/LIT/poet/hdoolfst.htm

Hemingway, Ernest

The Ernest Hemingway Foundation of Oak Park, Illinois
http://oprf.com/Hemingway/

Ernest Hemingway reading Nobel acceptance speech (audio), Harper Audio
(HarperCollins)
http://town.hall.org/radio/HarperAudio/012494_harp_ITH.html

MAGIC REALISM

"An Archaeology of the Boom: Modern Latin American Prose Fiction" by Harry Vélez
Quiñones, Professor of Spanish, University of Puget Sound, Washington
http://www.ups.edu/faculty/velez/FL380/Intro_2.htm

Borges, Jorge Luis

The Jorge Luis Borges Center for Studies & Documentation, University of Aarhus,
Denmark
http://www.hum.aau.dk/Institut/rom/borges/english.htm

Carpentier, Alejo

Alejo Carpentier page by Harry Vélez Quiñones, Professor of Spanish, University of
Puget Sound, Washington
http://www.ups.edu/faculty/velez/FL380/Carmain.htm

Carter, Angela

"'Black Venus'—Jeanne Duval and Charles Baudelaire Revisited by Angela Carter" by
Susanne Schmidt in *Erfurt Electronic Studies in English* (1997), Institut für Anglistik
und Amerikanistik Erfurt, Pädagogische Hochschule Erfurt, Germany
http://www.ph-erfurt.de/~neumann/eese/artic97/schmid/acbib.html

Web Sites

Fuentes, Carlos
"The Face in the Mirror: Carlos Fuentes on the Novel" by Shea Dean in *Brown Alumni Magazine*, December 1996
http://www.brown.edu/Administration/Brown_Alumni_Magazine/97/12-96/elms/
        feuntes.html

Kundera, Milan
Bibliography by Martin Irvine, Communication, Culture, and Technology Program, Georgetown University, Washington, D.C.
http://www.georgetown.edu/irvinemj/english016/kundera/kundera.html

Llosa, Mario Vargas
Mario Vargas Llosa resources by Harry Vélez Quiñones, Professor of Spanish, University of Puget Sound, Washington
http://www.ups.edu/faculty/velez/FL380/Varmain.htm

Rushdie, Salman
Salman Rushdie page by George P. Landow, Professor, English Department, Brown University, Providence, Rhode Island
http://www.stg.brown.edu/projects/hypertext/landow/post/rushdie/rushdieov.html

MARX, KARL, AND MARXIST CRITICISM
Cultural Logic, on-line journal edited by David Siar, Winston-Salem State University and Gregory Meyerson, North Carolina State University
http://eserver.org/clogic/

Marx and Engels' Writings, The English Server, Carnegie Mellon University, Pittsburgh, Pennsylvania
http://eserver.org/marx/

Marxism page, Rick Kuhn, Senior Lecturer, Department of Political Science, Australian National University, Canberra, Australian Capital Territory, Australia
http://online.anu.edu.au/polsci/marx/marx.html

Marxisms, Campus Community, Southern Oregon University, Ashland
http://www.sou.edu/English/IDTC/Issues/History/marx.HTM

MODERNISM
An Index of Web Sites on Modernism, The Malcom S. Forbes Center for Research in Culture and Media Studies, Brown University, Providence, Rhode Island
http://www.modcult.brown.edu/people/Scholes/modlist/Title.html

Web Sites

Modernism Timeline, 1890-1940 by John Mark Eckman, Instructor, Department of English, University of Washington, Seattle
http://faculty.washington.edu/eckman/timeline.html

The Modernist Revolution, Exhibit, Academy of American Poets
http://www.poets.org/LIT/exh/ex001fst.htm

Conrad, Joseph

Almayer's Folly, Amy Foster, The Arrow of Gold, The End of the Tether, Falk, Heart of Darkness, The Mirror of the Sea, Notes on Life and Letters, An Outcast of the Islands, A Personal Record, The Secret Agent, The Secret Sharer, The Shadow Line, Tales of Unrest, To-morrow, Twixt Land & Sea, Typhoon, Within The Tides, Youth, A Narrative, and others by Joseph Conrad, Project Gutenberg
http://www.promo.net/pg/_authors/i-_conrad_joseph_.html

Eliot, T. S.

Poems (1920), *Prufrock and Other Observations* (1917), *The Sacred Wood: Essays on Poetry and Criticism* (1920), *The Waste Land* (1922) by T. S. Eliot, Bartleby Archive, Columbia University, New York
http://www.columbia.cdu/acis/bartlcby/eliot/

T. S. Eliot reading *The Waste Land* (audio), Harper Audio (HarperCollins)
http://town.hall.org/radio/HarperAudio/011894_harp_ITH.html

T. S. Eliot page, Academy of American Poets
http://www.poets.org/LIT/poet/tselifst.htm

Thomas Stearns Eliot page, The Poetry Archives, Advanced Network & Services, Inc.
http://tqd.advanced.org/3247/cgi-bin/dispover.cgi?frame=none&poet=eliot.t.s

Faulkner, William

William Faulkner on the Web by John B. Padgett, Instructor, English Department, University of Mississippi, University, Mississippi
http://www.mcsr.olemiss.edu/~egjbp/faulkner/faulkner.html

William Faulkner reading from various works (audio), Harper Audio (HarperCollins)
http://town.hall.org/Archives/radio/IMS/HarperAudio/080294_harp_ITH.html

Joyce, James

James Joyce: WWW Resources by Brittney Chenault, Instruction/Reference Librarian, Livingston Lord Library, Moorhead State University, Minnesota
http://www.moorhead.msus.edu/~chenault/joyce.htm

Web Sites

Dubliners, A Portrait of the Artist as a Young Man, Ulysses by James Joyce, Bibliomania, Data Text Publishing Ltd.
http://www.bibliomania.com/Fiction/joyce/index.html

Lawrence, D. H.
D. H. Lawrence page, Academy of American Poets
http://www.poets.org/LIT/poet/dhlawfst.htm

Lady Chatterly's Lover, Sons & Lovers, Women in Love by D. H. Lawrence, Bibliomania, Data Text Publishing Ltd.
http://www.bibliomania.com/Fiction/dhl/index.html

Pound, Ezra
Ezra Pound page, Electronic Poetry Center, State University of New York at Buffalo
http://wings.buffalo.edu/epc/authors/pound/

Ezra Pound page by Eiichi Hishikawa, Professor of Literature, Kobe University, Japan
http://www.lit.kobe-u.ac.jp/~hishika/pound.htm

Ezra Pound page, Academy of American Poets
http://www.poets.org/LIT/poet/epounfst.htm

Stein, Gertrude
Gertrude Stein Online
http://www.tenderbuttons.com/

Time-Sense, on-line journal on Gertrude Stein, edited by Sonja Streuber, Department of English, University of California at Davis
http://www.tenderbuttons.com/timeense/review.html

Tender Buttons by Gertrude Stein, Bartleby Archive, Columbia University, New York
http://www.cc.columbia.edu/acis/bartleby/stein/

Stevens, Wallace
Wallace Stevens page, Academy of American Poets
http://www.poets.org/LIT/poet/wstevfst.htm

Wallace Stevens page by Al Filreis, Professor, English Department, University of Pennsylvania, Philadelphia
http://www.english.upenn.edu/~afilreis/Stevens/homehtml

Wallace Stevens Journal, publication of the Wallace Stevens Society, Clarkson University, Potsdam, New York
http://www.clarkson.edu/~wsj/index.html

Hartford Friends of Wallace Stevens page, Wesleyan University, Middletown, Connecticut
http://www.wesleyan.edu/wstevens/stevens.html

Feigning with the Strange Unlike: A Wallace Stevens WWW Site by David Lavery, Professor, English Department, Middle Tennessee State University, Murfreesboro
http://www.mtsu.edu/~dlavery/wstoc.htm

Wallace Stevens reading some of his poetry (audio), Harper Audio (HarperCollins)
http://town.hall.org/radio/HarperAudio/021594_harp_ITH.html

Williams, William Carlos
William Carlos Williams, Academy of American Poets
http://www.poets.org/LIT/poet/wcwilfst.htm

Woolf, Virginia
Virginia Woolf Web by Hiroko Fukushima with support of John Constable, Faculty of Integrated Human Studies, Kyoto University, Japan
http://www.aianet.or.jp/~orlando/VWW/english.html

Yeats, William Butler
W. B. Yeats page by Eiichi Hishikawa, Professor of Letters, Kobe University, Japan
http://www.lit.kobe-u.ac.jp/~hishika/yeats.htm

W. B. Yeats page, Academy of American Poets
http://www.poets.org/LIT/poet/wbyeafst.htm

The Wind Among the Reeds, *Responsibilities and Other Poems*, and *The Wild Swans at Coole* by William Butler Yeats, Bartleby Archive, Columbia University, New York
http://www.columbia.edu/acis/bartleby/yeats

NATURALISM

Crane, Stephen
Maggie, Girl of the Streets and *The Red Badge of Courage* by Stephen Crane, Project Gutenberg
http://www.promo.net/pg/_authors/i-_crane_stephen_.html

Dreiser, Theodore
Sister Carrie and *The Financier* by Theodore Dreiser, Project Gutenberg
http://www.promo.net/pg/_authors/i-_dreiser_theodore_.html

Frederic, Harold
The Damnation of Theron Ware and *The Market-Place* by Harold Frederic,
Project Gutenberg
http://www.promo.net/pg/_authors/i-_frederic_harold_.html

Herrick, Robert
From *The Lyrical Poems of Robert Herrick* by Robert Herrick, Project Gutenberg
http://www.promo.net/pg/_authors/i-_herrick_robert.html

London, Jack
*Adventure, All Gold Canyon, Amateur Night, Batard, Before Adam, Burning
Daylight, The Call of the Wild, The Dream of Debs, The Enemy of All the World, The
Faith of Men, The Game, The Heathen, The House of Mapuhi, A Hyperborean Brew,
The Inevitable White Man, The Iron Heel, The Jacket (Star-Rover), Jerry of the
Islands, John Barleycorn, The Leopard Man's Story, Local Color, Love of Life and
Other Stories, The Marriage of Lit-lit, Martin Eden, Mauki, The Minions of Midas,
Moon-Face, Moon-Face and Other Stories, The Night-Born, The One Thousand
Dozen Planchette, The Red One, A Relic of the Pliocene, Samuel, The Sea Wolf, The
Sea-Farmer, The Seed of McCoy, The Shadow and the Flash, South Sea Tales, South of
the Slot, The Story of Jees Uck, The Strength of the Strong, Tales of the Fish Patrol, The
Terrible Solomons, Too Much Gold, The Unparalleled Invasion, War of the Classes,
The Whale Tooth, White Fang, Yah! Yah! Yah!* by Jack London, Project Gutenberg
http://www.promo.net/pg/_authors/i-_london_jack_.html

Zola, Emile
Study Questions for Zola's *Germinal* by Paul Brians, Professor, Department of English,
Washington State University, Pullman
http://www.wsu.edu:8080/~brians/hum_303/germinal.html

NEW CRITICISM
The New Criticism, David Arnason, Professor of English, St. John's College,
University of Manitoba, Winnipeg, Canada
http://130.179.92.25/Arnason_DE/New_Criticism.html

Richards, I. A.
I. A. Richards page by John Constable, Faculty of Integrated Human Studies,
Kyoto University, Japan
http://tori.ic.h.kyoto-u.ac.jp/pub/richards/iar.html

NEW YORK SCHOOL

Ashbery, John
John Ashbery page, Academy of American Poets
http://www.poets.org/LIT/poet/jashbfst.htm

NIETZSCHE, FRIEDRICH

The Nietzsche Page, Douglas Thomas, Assistant Professor, Annenberg School for
Communication, University of Southern California, Los Angeles
http://www.usc.edu/~douglast/nietzsche.html

POSTCOLONIAL STUDIES

Contemporary Postcolonial and Postimperial Literature in English, George P. Landow,
Professor, English Department, Brown University, Providence, Rhode Island
http://stg.brown.edu/projects/hypertext/landow/post/misc/postov.html

Postcolonial Studies web site by Deepika Petraglia-Bahri, English Department, Emory
University, Atlanta, Georgia
http://www.emory.edu/ENGLISH/Bahri/

PROLETARIAN LITERATURE, United States

Steinbeck, John
Center for Steinbeck Studies, San Jose State University, California
http://www.sjsu.edu/depts/steinbec/srchrome.html

READER-RESPONSE THEORY

Reader-Response: Various Positions, John Lye, Associate Professor, Department of
English, Brock University, St. Catharines, Ontario, Canada
http://www.brocku.ca/english/courses/4F70/rr.html

REALISM

The Victorian Web by George P. Landow, Professor, English Department, Brown
University, Providence, Rhode Island
http://www.stg.brown.edu/projects/hypertext/landow/victorian/victov.html

Azuela, Mariano
The Underdogs by Mariano Azuela, Project Gutenberg
http://www.promo.net/pg/_authors/i-_azuela_mariano_.html

879

Balzac, Honoré de

The Atheist's Mass, The Ball at Sceaux, The Duchesse de Langeais, The Elixir of Life, Father Goriot, The Firm of Nucingen, The Magic Skin, The Message, The Purse, Unconscious Comedians, Ursula, and others by Honoré de Balzac, Project Gutenberg
http://www.promo.net/pg/_authors/balzac_honore_de_.html#fathergoriot

Browning, Robert

Robert Browning page, The Poetry Archive, Advanced Network & Services, Inc.
http://tqd.advanced.org/3247/cgi-bin/dispover.cgi?frame=none&poet=browning.robert

Cather, Willa

Alexander's Bridge, My Antonia, O Pioneers!, Song of the Lark, The Troll Garden and Selected Stories by Willa Cather, Project Gutenberg
http://www.promo.net/pg/_authors/i-_cather_willa_sibert_.html

Dickens, Charles

The Dickens Page by Mitsuharu Matsuoka, Associate Professor of Language and Culture, Nagoya University, Japan
http://lang.nagoya-u.ac.jp/~matsuoka/Dickens.html

American Notes, Barnaby Rudge: A Tale of the Riots of 'Eighty, The Battle of Life, Bleak House, A Child's History of England, The Chimes, The Cricket on the Hearth, A Christmas Carol, David Copperfield, Dombey and Son, George Silverman's Explanation, Hard Times, The Haunted House, The Haunted Man and the Ghost's Bargain, Holiday Romance, Hunted Down: The Detective Stories of Charles Dickens, The Lamplighter: A Farce in One Act, Lazy Tour of Two Idle Apprentices, Little Dorrit, Martin Chuzzlewit, Master Humphrey's Clock, Mudfog and Other Sketches, The Mystery of Edwin Drood, Nicholas Nickleby, The Old Curiosity Shop, Oliver Twist, Our Mutual Friend, The Pickwick Papers, Pictures from Italy, Reprinted Pieces, The Signal Man, Sketches by Boz, Illustrative of Everyday Life and Every-day People, Sketches of Young Couples, Sketches of Young Gentlemen, Speeches: Literary and Social, Sunday under Three Heads, A Tale of Two Cities, Three Ghost Stories, To Be Read at Dusk, The Trial for Murder, The Uncommercial Traveller, and others by Charles Dickens, Project Gutenberg
http://www.promo.net/pg/_authors/i-_dickens_charles_.html

Dostoyevsky, Fyodor

Notes from the Underground by Fyodor Dostoyevsky, Project Gutenberg
http://www.promo.net/pg/_authors/i-_dostoyevsky_fyodor_.html

Eliot, George
Adam Bede, Middlemarch, Silas Marner by George Eliot, Project Gutenberg
http://www.promo.net/pg/_authors/i-_eliot_george_.html

Flaubert, Gustave
Herodias, Salammbo, A Simple Soul by Gustave Flaubert, Project Gutenberg
http://www.promo.net/pg/_authors/i-_flaubert_gustave.html

Gaskell, Elizabeth Cleghorn
Elizabeth Gaskell Information Page by Mitsuharu Mitsuoka, Associate Professor of
Language and Culture, Nagoya University, Japan
http://lang.nagoya-u.ac.jp/~matsuoka/Gaskell.html

Cranford by Elizabeth Cleghorn Gaskell, Project Gutenberg
http://www.promo.net/pg/_authors/i-_gaskell_elizabeth_cleghorn_.html

Gissing, George
Gissing in Cyberspace by Mitsuharu Mitsuoka, Associate Professor of Language and
Culture, Nagoya University, Japan
http://lang.nagoya-u.ac.jp/~matsuoka/Gissing.html

Howells, William Dean
The William Dean Howells Society home page by Donna Campbell, Professor,
Department of English, Gonzaga University, Spokane, Washington
http://www.gonzaga.edu/faculty/campbell/howells/

*Emile Zola, Henry James, Jr., The Man of Letters as a Man of Business, A
Psychological Counter-Current in Recent Fiction, The Rise of Silas Lapham* by
William Dean Howells, Project Gutenberg
http://www.promo.net/pg/_authors/i-_howells_william_dean_.html

James, Henry
The Henry James Scholar's Guide to Web Sites by Richard Hathaway, Professor, English
Department, State University of New York at New Paltz
http://www.newpaltz.edu/~hathaway/

Kipling, Rudyard
Rudyard Kipling page, The Poetry Archive, Advanced Network & Services, Inc.
http://tqd.advanced.org/3247/cgi-bin/dispover.cgi?frame=none&poet=kipling.rudyard

Lewis, Sinclair
Babbit and *Main Street* by Sinclair Lewis, Project Gutenberg
http://www.promo.net/pg/_authors/i-_lewis_sinclair_.html

Robinson, Edwin Arlington
Children of the Night,The Man against the Sky, The Three Taverns by Edwin Arlington
Robinson, Project Gutenberg
http://www.promo.net/pg/_authors/i-_robinson_edwin_arlington_.html

Tolstoy, Leo
Tolstoy Library
http://www.tolstoy.org/

Twain, Mark
Twain Web, Mark Twain Forum home page, Massachusetts Institute of Technology,
Cambridge
http://web.mit.edu/linguistics/www/forum/twainweb.html

Mark Twain web guide by Jim Zwick, Twain scholar
http://marktwain.about.com/

Wharton, Edith
Edith Wharton Society home page by Donna Campbell, Professor, Department of
English, Gonzaga University, Spokane, Washington
http://www.gonzaga.edu/faculty/campbell/wharton/index.html

*The Age of Innocence, Bunner Sisters, The Early Short Fiction of Edith Wharton,
The Glimpses of the Moon, House of Mirth, The Reef, Summer, The Touchstone*
by Edith Wharton, Project Gutenberg
http://www.promo.net/pg/_authors/i-_wharton_edith_.html

SAN FRANCISCO SCHOOL

DiPrima, Diane
Diane DiPrima Papers at Department of Rare Books and Special Collections, William F.
Ekstrom Library, University of Louisville, Kentucky
http://www.louisville.edu/library/uarc/diprima.html

Ferlinghetti, Lawrence
"Baseball Canto" by Lawrence Ferlinghetti, posted by Al Filreis, Professor, English
Department, University of Pennsylvania, Philadelphia
http://www.english.upenn.edu/~afilreis/88/baseball-canto.html

"[The Wounded Wilderness of Morris Graves]" by Lawrence Ferlinghetti, posted by
Department of English, Emory University, Atlanta, Georgia
http://www.emory.edu/ENGLISH/classes/Paintings&Poems/Ferlinghetti.html

SEMIOTICS

Applied Semiotics/Sémiotique Appliquée, on-line peer-reviewed journal edited by Peter G. Marteinson and Pascal G. Michelucci, Department of French, University of Toronto, Ontario, Canada
http://www.chass.utoronto.ca:8080/french/as-sa/

Semiotics page, Martin Ryder, School of Education, University of Colorado at Denver
http://cudenner.edu/~mryder/itc_data/semiotics.html

Peirce, Charles S.

Charles S. Peirce page, Joseph Ransdell, Associate Professor, Department of Philosophy, Texas Tech University, Lubbock
http://www.peirce.org

STRUCTURALISM

Background Materials: Formalist and Structuralist Ideas by David Arnason, Professor of English, St. John's College, University of Manitoba, Winnipeg, Canada
http://130.179.92.25/Arnason_DE/Backmaterials.html

Some Elements of Structuralism and Its Application to Literary Theory by John Lye, Associate Professor, Department of English, Brock University, St. Catharines, Ontario, Canada
http://www.brocku.ca/english/courses/4F70/struct.html

Barthes, Roland

Barthean Codes by David Arnason, Professor of English, St. John's College, University of Manitoba, Winnipeg, Canada
http://130.179.92.25/Arnason_DE/Barthean_Codes.html

Blanchot, Maurice

Maurice Blanchot Resource page by Reginald Lilly, Associate Professor, Department of Philosophy & Religion, Skidmore College, New York
http://lists.village.virginia.edu/~spoons/blanchot/blanchot_mainpage.htm

Foucault, Michel

Michel Foucault, The Window: Philosophy on the Internet, Philosophy Department, Trinity College, Hartford, Connecticut
http://www.trincoll.edu/~phil/philo/phils/foucault.html

Michel Foucault Page, Campus Community, Southern Oregon University, Ashland
http://www.sou.edu/English/IDTC/People/fouclt2.HTM

Web Sites

Levi-Strauss, Claude

"Claude Levi-Strauss: The Structural Study of Myth" by Mary Klages, Professor, English Department, University of Colorado at Boulder
http://www.colorado.edu/English/ENGL2012Klages/levi-strauss.html

Saussure, Ferdinand

Saussurescape by Warren Hedges, Assistant Professor, English Department, Southern Oregon University, Ashland
http://www.sou.edu/English/IDTC/Projects/Saussure/saussrex.htm

SURREALISM

Dada and Surrealism: Texts and Extracts, Gerry Carlin, Professor, Department of English, University of Wolverhampton, United Kingdom
http://www.wlv.ac.uk/~fa1871/surrext.html

SYMBOLISM

Rimbaud, Arthur

The Rimbaud Pages: An Introduction to Rimbaud by Tony McNeill, French Studies, University of Sunderland, United Kingdom
http://www.sunderland.ac.uk/~os0tmc/rimbaud/rimbmain.htm

THEATER OF THE ABSURD

Albee, Edward

"Listen to Edward Albee" (audio), International Theatre Institute of the United States
http://iti-usa.org/audio.html

Edward Albee, Great Writers Series, Knowledge TV, Public Educational Television Service, British Columbia, Canada
http://www.ola.bc.ca/knowledge/primetime/literature/great/albe.html

Beckett, Samuel

The Samuel Beckett Endpage, including The Official Page of the Samuel Beckett Society by Porter Abbott and Benjamin Strong, English Department, University of California at Santa Barbara
http://humanitas.ucsb.edu/projects/beckett/endpage.html

Genet, Jean

Jean Genet page, Kuusankoski Public Library, Finland
http://www.kirjasto.sci.fi/jgenet.htm

Web Sites

Stoppard, Tom

Tom Stoppard's *Arcadia*, a Study Guide, by Larry Opitz, Associate Professor of Theatre, Skidmore College, New York
http://www.skidmore.edu/academics/lsi/arcadia/index.html

VORTICISM

Lewis, Wyndham

Wyndham Lewis page by John Constable, Faculty of Integrated Human Studies, Kyoto University, Japan
http://tori.ic.h.kyoto-u.ac.jp/pub/Lewis/Lewis.html

YALE SCHOOL

Hartman, Geoffrey

Geoffrey Hartman: A Bibliography, Critical Theory Resource, University of California at Irvine
http://sun3.lib.uci.edu/~scctr/Wellek/hartman/index.html

Miller, J. Hillis

J. Hillis Miller: A Bibliography, Critical Theory Resource, University of California at Irvine
http://sun3.lib.uci.edu/~scctr/Wellek/miller.html

"Synopsis of J. Hillis Miller's *The Critic as Host*" by John Lye, Professor, English Department, Brock University, St. Catharines, Ontario, Canada
http://www.brocku.ca/english/courses/4F70/host.html

ŻAGARY GROUP

Miłosz, Czesław

Czesław Miłosz Page, International Poetry Archive, University of North Carolina Press and the North Carolina Arts Council
http://metalab.unc.edu/ipa/milosz/

❖•❖

Electronic Text (E-Text) Databases

Alex Catalog of Electronic Texts, Eric Lease Morgan, Librarian, North Carolina State University Libraries, Raleigh
http://sunsite.berkeley.edu/alex/

Antologia (frammentaria) della Letteratura Italiana, Center for Advanced Studies,
Research and Development in Sardinia, Italy
http://www.crs4.it/HTML/Literature.html

ARTFL (American and French Research on the Treasury of the French Language)
Project, University of Chicago [accessible through subscription]
http://humanities.uchicago.edu/ARTFL/ARTFL.html

Bartleby Archive, Columbia University, New York
http://www.cc.columbia.edu/acis/bartleby

Bibliomania, Data Text Publications Ltd.
http://www.bibliomania.com

Electronic Text Collections in Western European Literature, WESSWEB, Association of
College and Research Libraries
http://www.lib.virginia.edu/wess/index.html

Project Gutenberg
http://www.promo.net/pg/_authors/_A_index.html

Project Runeberg: Nordic Literature Online, Lysator, Linköping University, Linköping,
Sweden
http://www.lysator.liu.se/runeberg/

The Wiretap Electronic Text Archive
http://wiretap.area.com/

Movements Index

This index lists literary movements discussed in the text, by foreign and alternate names and by English translations. Movement entries are indicated by boldfaced page numbers.

E

F

Movements Index

G

Movements Index

M

Movements Index

N

Movements Index

Movements Index

Movements Index

Movements Index

INDEX 2

Author Index

This index lists novelists, short-story writers, poets, essayists, theorists, and selected other people who appear in this volume. Featured authors are indicated in bold-faced type as are the page numbers on which their entries appear.

B

Author Index

E

Author Index

H

Author Index

Author Index

Author Index

Author Index

Author Index

Author Index

947

Title Index

This index lists journals, books, manifestos, stories, poems, plays, essays, and selected other titles that appear in the entries in this volume. Foreign-language works are indexed under the first word of the foreign title, even when the first word is an article. Foreign-language works that have been translated into English are cross-referenced under the English title. Featured works are indicated in bold-faced type as are the page numbers on which their entries appear.

Λ

B

C

957

Title Index

Title Index

963

Title Index

Title Index

Title Index

F

Title Index

Title Index

973

G

Title Index

H

Title Index

977

I

Title Index

J

Title Index

K

L

Title Index

Title Index

Title Index

Title Index

M

Title Index

Title Index

Title Index

Title Index

N

Title Index

Title Index

Title Index

Title Index

Title Index

Title Index

Title Index

Title Index

Q

R

Title Index

S

Title Index

1011

Title Index

Title Index

Title Index

Title Index

T

Title Index

1019

Title Index

V

Title Index

W

Title Index

Y

Title Index

Z

Country and Nationality Index

Country and Nationality Index

F

G

Country and Nationality Index

Country and Nationality Index

Country and Nationality Index

Ukrainian emigrés in Poland

Ukrainian emigrés in U.S.

United States

Uruguay

Country and Nationality Index